management

SECOND CANADIAN EDITION

Chuck Williams
Texas Christian University

Alex Z. Kondra
Athabasca University

Conor Vibert
Acadia University

NELSON EDUCATION

NELSON EDUCATION

Management, Second Canadian Edition
Chuck Williams, Alex Z. Kondra, Conor Vibert

Associate Vice President, Editorial Director:
Evelyn Veitch

Publisher:
Veronica Visentin

Director of Marketing:
Kelly Smyth

Senior Developmental Editor:
Joanne Sutherland

Photo Researcher/Permissions Coordinator:
Indu Ghuman

Content Production Manager:
Tannys Williams

Production Service:
Graphic World Inc.

Copy Editor:
Valerie Adams

Proofreader:
Graphic World Inc.

Indexer:
Graphic World Inc.

Senior Manufacturing Coordinator:
Joanne McNeil

Design Director:
Ken Phipps

Interior Design:
Kyle Gell Designs

Cover Design:
Wil Bache

Cover Image:
©Ablestock/Images.com

Compositor:
Graphic World Inc.

Printer:
RR Donnelley

Printed and bound in the United States
4 5 13 12

For more information contact Nelson Education Ltd., 1120 Birchmount Road, Toronto, Ontario, M1K 5G4. Or you can visit our Internet site at http://www.nelson.com

Library and Archives Canada Cataloguing in Publication Data

Williams, Chuck, 1959–
Management/Chuck Williams, Alex Kondra, Conor Vibert.—2nd Canadian ed.

ISBN-13: 978-0-17-625260-1
ISBN-10: 0-17-625260-6

1. Management—Textbooks. I. Kondra, Alex II. Vibert, Conor, 1962– III. Title.

HD31.W512007 658
C2006-906219-6

brief contents

contents

Part 3 Meeting the Competition 211

About this Edition

If you walk down the aisle of the business section in your local bookstore (or surf the "Business" page at Amazon.ca), you'll find hundreds of books that explain precisely what companies need to do to be successful. Unfortunately, these books tend to be faddish, changing every few years. Lately, the best-selling business books have emphasized technology, leadership, and dealing with change, whereas ten years ago the hot topics were re-engineering, going global, mergers, and management buyouts.

One thing that hasn't changed, though, and never will, is the importance of good management. Management is getting work done through others. Organizations can't succeed for long without it. Well-managed companies are competitive because their work forces are smarter, better trained, more motivated, and more committed. Furthermore, good management leads to satisfied employees who, in turn, provide better service to customers. Because employees tend to treat customers the same way that their managers treat them, good management can improve customer satisfaction. Finally, companies that practise good management consistently have greater revenues and profits than companies that don't.

In writing the first Canadian edition of *Management*, our goal was to develop a textbook that students would enjoy, that students would refer to for practical, theory-driven advice using Canadian and international examples, and that encouraged students to put theory-driven knowledge into practice for themselves. For the second edition, our goal was to update the content to reflect the changing face of management and to keep the text relevant, fresh, and interesting for students. In short, the ideas and concepts you'll learn about in this book can improve the performance of the organization and department where you work, can help you solve job-related problems, and can improve your own job performance—even if you're not a manager.

So, welcome to *Management*, Second Canadian Edition! Please take a few minutes to read the preface and familiarize yourself with the approach (combining theory with specific stories and examples) in *Management*. This is time well spent. After all, besides your instructor, this book will be your primary learning tool.

Combining Theory with Specific, Up-to-Date Stories and Examples

Say "theory" to college students and they assume that you're talking about complex, arcane ideas and terms that have nothing to do with the "real world," but which need to be memorized for a test and then forgotten (of course, after the final exam). However, students needn't be wary of theoretical ideas and concepts. Theories are simply good ideas. And good theories are simply good ideas that have been tested through rigorous scientific study and analysis.

Where textbooks go wrong is that they stop at theory and read like dictionaries. Or they focus on theoretical issues related to research rather than practice. However, good management theories (i.e., good ideas) needn't be complex and arcane. In fact, the late Rensis Likert, an organizational psychologist, once said that there is nothing as practical as a good theory.

So, to make sure that you're exposed to good ideas (i.e., good theories) that you can refer to for practical, theory-driven advice, and that encourage you to put theory-driven knowledge into practice for yourselves, each chapter in this book contains many stories and examples that illustrate how managers are using management ideas in their organizations.

To be honest, much of the material in the following chapters is fairly standard, research-based information. You'll find it in most textbooks. Is it important for students to know this information? You bet! Is it likely that students will find this and the thousands of other pieces of theory and research-based facts throughout the book particularly compelling or interesting (and thus easier to learn)? Ah, there's the problem. However, what if we combined theory and research with specific "real-world" stories and examples that illustrated good or poor use of those theories? That is our strategy, and we think you will enjoy reading about them.

The stories and examples you'll read in each chapter are relevant and up-to-date. You'll read about the issues facing Pierre Lafontaine as he tried to transform Swimming Canada. You'll read about the challenges facing Hanspeter Stutz as he attempted to build a profitable winery. You'll also learn about Grant Thornton and how it sought to structure itself for success. On average, each chapter has 25 to 30 stories or examples to help you understand how management concepts and theories are being used in the business world.

In short, both research and theory and stories and examples are important for effective learning. Therefore, this book contains hundreds of specific examples and stories to make management theories and ideas more interesting. So, to get more out of this book, read and understand the theories and theoretical ideas. Then read the stories or examples to learn how those ideas should or should not be used in practice. You'll find that both are current and up-to-date.

So, What's New?

If you're already familiar with the first edition's approach of reinforcing research and theory with stories and examples, you may be asking yourself "So, what's new?" The answer is "quite a bit."

To keep pace with the evolution of management, the second edition underwent a rigorous review process that identified where we could strengthen and refine the text. Reviewers indicated that several of the boxed features were not being used in class, so we have streamlined each chapter to focus on the main content, retaining only the most popular box, "What Really Works?"

For this edition, all 16 of the "What Would You Do?" chapter-opening cases are new and feature organizations like the Liberal Party of Canada, Tim Hortons, the Gap, WestJet, Inco, Bell Canada, and MTV International, among others.

What brand new things will you find in this edition of *Management*? To start, you'll find:

DOING THE RIGHT THING

DON'T EMBELLISH YOUR RÉSUMÉ

Your résumé is supposed to help you get the interview that can get you a job. So where do you draw the line between making yourself look attractive to a potential employer and lying? Despite the strong temptation to improve your odds of getting a job, embellishing your résumé is wrong. Moreover, the information on your résumé is legally binding. If you misrepresent information or lie on your résumé, and many do, you're breaking the law and can be fired. But where should you draw the line? In general, if what you put on your résumé feels wrong, don't do it. More specifically, don't embellish job titles, responsibilities, employment dates, college degrees, certifications, general qualifications, or previous experience in any way. Do the right thing: Tell the truth on your résumé.[53]

Doing the Right Thing

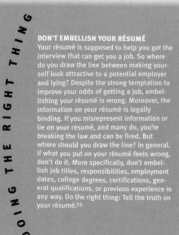

In each chapter you'll find this new boxed feature containing practical, useful advice to help you become a more ethical manager or businessperson. Topics include ethical competitive analysis, avoiding the slippery slope of cheating, dealing with gifts from suppliers, protecting confidential information, worker safety, not cheating on travel expenses, enforcing fair and safe working conditions in foreign factories, giving credit rather than taking it, and many more.

Self-Assessments

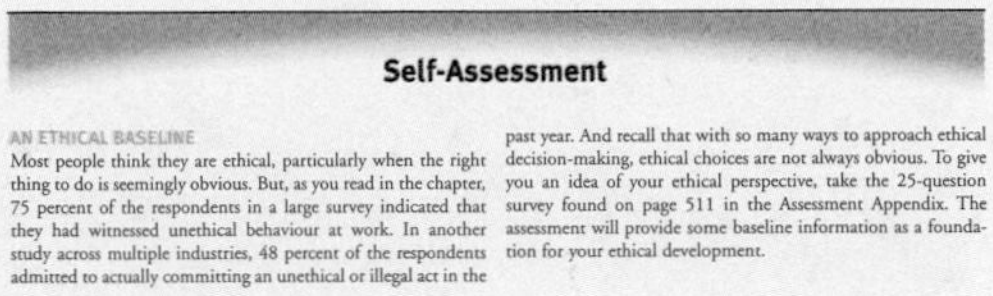

Self-Assessment

AN ETHICAL BASELINE

Most people think they are ethical, particularly when the right thing to do is seemingly obvious. But, as you read in the chapter, 75 percent of the respondents in a large survey indicated that they had witnessed unethical behaviour at work. In another study across multiple industries, 48 percent of the respondents admitted to actually committing an unethical or illegal act in the past year. And recall that with so many ways to approach ethical decision-making, ethical choices are not always obvious. To give you an idea of your ethical perspective, take the 25-question survey found on page 511 in the Assessment Appendix. The assessment will provide some baseline information as a foundation for your ethical development.

Each chapter has a related assessment questionnaire to help students consider how their own perspectives influence their management skills. A brief description of each assessment tool is given at the end of each chapter and directs students to the page in the Self-Assessment Appendix where the particular inventory is located. All of the assessments are placed together in the appendix so students can see patterns in their own perceptions and behaviours. Basic scoring information follows each questionnaire, and the Instructor Manual contains directions for using the assessment tools in class.

Take Two Videos

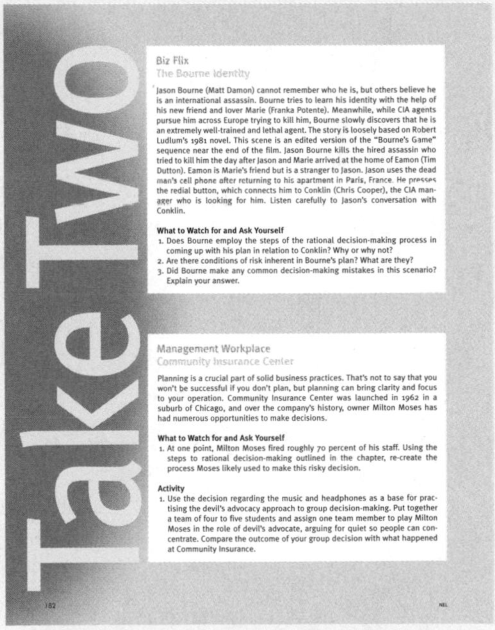

Take Two

Biz Flix
The Bourne Identity

Jason Bourne (Matt Damon) cannot remember who he is, but others believe he is an international assassin. Bourne tries to learn his identity with the help of his new friend and lover Marie (Franka Potente). Meanwhile, while CIA agents pursue him across Europe trying to kill him, Bourne slowly discovers that he is an extremely well-trained and lethal agent. The story is loosely based on Robert Ludlum's 1981 novel. This scene is an edited version of the "Bourne's Game" sequence near the end of the film. Jason Bourne kills the hired assassin who tried to kill him the day after Jason and Marie arrived at the home of Eamon (Tim Dutton). Eamon is Marie's friend but is a stranger to Jason. Jason uses the dead man's cell phone after returning to his apartment in Paris, France. He presses the redial button, which connects him to Conklin (Chris Cooper), the CIA manager who is looking for him. Listen carefully to Jason's conversation with Conklin.

What to Watch for and Ask Yourself

1. Does Bourne employ the steps of the rational decision-making process in coming up with his plan in relation to Conklin? Why or why not?
2. Are there conditions of risk inherent in Bourne's plan? What are they?
3. Did Bourne make any common decision-making mistakes in this scenario? Explain your answer.

Management Workplace
Community Insurance Center

Planning is a crucial part of solid business practices. That's not to say that you won't be successful if you don't plan, but planning can bring clarity and focus to your operation. Community Insurance Center was launched in 1962 in a suburb of Chicago, and over the company's history, owner Milton Moses has had numerous opportunities to make decisions.

What to Watch for and Ask Yourself

1. At one point, Milton Moses fired roughly 70 percent of his staff. Using the steps to rational decision-making outlined in the chapter, re-create the process Moses likely used to make this risky decision.

Activity

1. Use the decision regarding the music and headphones as a base for practising the devil's advocacy approach to group decision-making. Put together a team of four to five students and assign one team member to play Milton Moses in the role of devil's advocate, arguing for quiet so people can concentrate. Compare the outcome of your group decision with what happened at Community Insurance.

NEL

When we asked professors how they used video in the classroom, we discovered two distinct preferences. Some like to use short video examples to reinforce certain points in the chapter; others like longer video cases that looked at various companies in-depth. In response to this feedback, each chapter of *Management*, Second Canadian Edition, contains two video options. The first is a film clip from a popular Hollywood movie that relates to chapter content. For example, students will see a "Biz Flix" clip from *The Bourne Identity* for Chapter 4 on Planning. The second video option is a longer segment based on a single company. We take you inside some very successful privately held companies, including Theatrical Lighting Systems, Auntie Anne's Pretzels, and Wahoo's Fish Taco. These longer segments, called "Management Workplace," last an average of 12 minutes and provide a deeper look at a single company, its operations, and how it addresses various management issues every day. Both the "Biz Flix" and the "Management Workplace" video guide students on what to look for and think about as they watch the video. Detailed teaching notes for both videos are in each chapter of the Instructor Manual.

Acknowledgements

Let's face it; writing a textbook is a long and lonely process. It's surely among the most difficult (and rewarding) projects that we have ever tackled. And, as we sat in front of our computers on opposite sides of the country with a rough outline in front of us, it was easy at times to feel isolated. But, as we found out, a book like this doesn't get done without the help of many other talented people.

First, we'd like to thank the outstanding team from Nelson for the support (and patience) they provided while we developed this book. Pure and simple, everyone at Nelson has been great to work with throughout the entire project. Special thanks go to Joanne Sutherland who was our senior developmental editor and with whom we had the most contact while writing the book. We'd also like to thank our publisher, Veronica Visentin, and our copy editor, Valerie Adams. Thanks to all of you and here's to many more editions.

We'd like to thank an outstanding set of reviewers whose diligent and thoughtful comments helped shape this Second Canadian Edition.

Lewie Callahan, Lethbridge Community College
Laurie Coady, Okanagan University College
Raymond Dart, Trent University
Janice Edwards, College of the Rockies
Diane Jurkowski, York University
Daniel Mah, Medicine Hat College
Michael K. Mauws, Athabasca University
Brian McAteer, Humber College
Thomas McKaig, Ryerson University
Ernie Rainbow, Durham College
Kerry Rempel, Okanagan University College
George Stroppa, Douglas College
Michael Teed, Bishops University
Susan Thompson, Trent University
Richard Yip-Chuck, Humber College

The support package for the text was developed with the help of two outstanding colleagues. Special thanks go to Kerry Rempel of Okanagan University College for her work on the Test Bank and PowerPoint slides, and to Jeffrey Young of Mount Saint Vincent University for his work on the CBC video exercises. Finally, our families deserve the greatest thanks of all for their love, patience, and support. Writing a textbook is an enormous project with incredible stresses and pressures on authors as well as their loved ones. However, throughout this project, our wives, Sonia and Janette, were unwavering in their support of our writing. Colin, Brendan, Jennifer, and Sean also deserve special thanks for their patience and for understanding why Dad was locked away at the computer for all of this time.

Conor Vibert
Acadia University

Alex Z. Kondra
Athabasca University

Text Features

Features of *Management,* Second Canadian Edition

Management, Second Canadian Edition, offers a wide variety of pedagogical features to help you learn and apply the concepts at hand. Take a few minutes to familiarize yourself with these features. Doing so will help you get more out of the book and your management class.

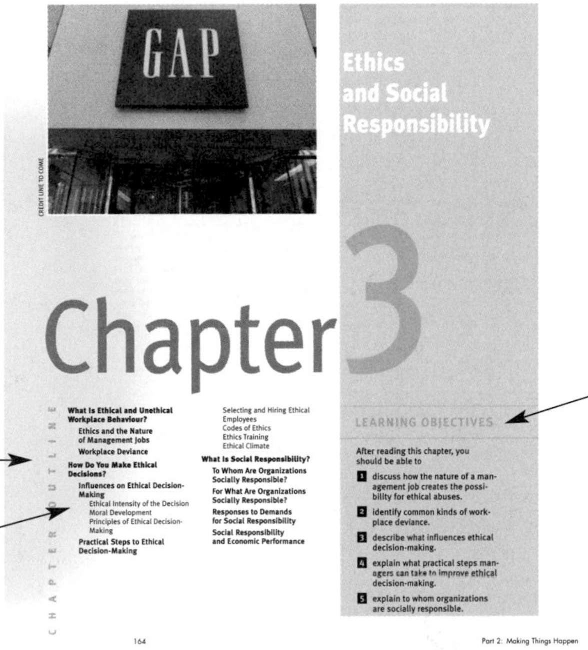

GAP

CREDIT LINE TO COME

Ethics and Social Responsibility

Chapter 3

CHAPTER OUTLINE

What Is Ethical and Unethical Workplace Behaviour?
- **Ethics and the Nature of Management Jobs**
- **Workplace Deviance**

How Do You Make Ethical Decisions?
- **Influences on Ethical Decision-Making**
  - Ethical Intensity of the Decision
  - Moral Development
  - Principles of Ethical Decision-Making
- **Practical Steps to Ethical Decision-Making**
  - Selecting and Hiring Ethical Employees
  - Codes of Ethics
  - Ethics Training
  - Ethical Climate

What Is Social Responsibility?
- **To Whom Are Organizations Socially Responsible?**
- **For What Are Organizations Socially Responsible?**
- **Responses to Demands for Social Responsibility**
- **Social Responsibility and Economic Performance**

LEARNING OBJECTIVES

After reading this chapter, you should be able to

1. discuss how the nature of a management job creates the possibility for ethical abuses.
2. identify common kinds of workplace deviance.
3. describe what influences ethical decision-making.
4. explain what practical steps managers can take to improve ethical decision-making.
5. explain to whom organizations are socially responsible.

164

Part 2: Making Things Happen

At the beginning of each chapter, you'll find a **Chapter Outline.**

The outline is broken out into **sections and subsections** and corresponds with the headings and subheadings within the chapter.

The Chapter Outline corresponds with the numbered **Learning Objectives.** There is one Learning Objective for each of the major sections in the chapter, and these are listed both at the beginning of the chapter and at the beginning of each major section.

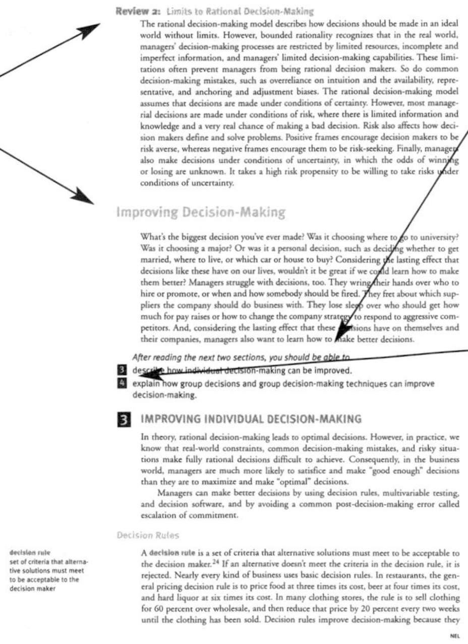

Review 2: Limits to Rational Decision-Making

The rational decision-making model describes how decisions should be made in an ideal world without limits. However, bounded rationality recognizes that in the real world, managers' decision-making processes are restricted by limited resources, incomplete and imperfect information, and managers' limited decision-making capabilities. These limitations often prevent managers from being rational decision makers. So do common decision-making mistakes, such as overreliance on intuition and the availability, representative, and anchoring and adjustment biases. The rational decision-making model assumes that decisions are made under conditions of certainty. However, most managerial decisions are made under conditions of risk, where there is limited information and knowledge and a very real chance of making a bad decision. Risk also affects how decision makers define and solve problems. Positive frames encourage decision makers to be risk averse, whereas negative frames encourage them to be risk-seeking. Finally, managers also make decisions under conditions of uncertainty, in which the odds of winning or losing are unknown. It takes a high risk propensity to be willing to take risks under conditions of uncertainty.

Improving Decision-Making

What's the biggest decision you've ever made? Was it choosing where to go to university? Was it choosing a major? Or was it a personal decision, such as deciding whether to get married, where to live, or which car or house to buy? Considering the lasting effect that decisions like these have on our lives, wouldn't it be great if we could learn how to make them better? Managers struggle with decisions, too. They wring their hands over who to hire or promote, or when and how somebody should be fired. They fret about which suppliers the company should do business with. They lose sleep over who should get how much for pay raises or how to change the company strategy to respond to aggressive competitors. And, considering the lasting effect that these decisions have on themselves and their companies, managers also want to learn how to make better decisions.

After reading the next two sections, you should be able to

3. describe how individual decision-making can be improved.
4. explain how group decisions and group decision-making techniques can improve decision-making.

3 IMPROVING INDIVIDUAL DECISION-MAKING

In theory, rational decision-making leads to optimal decisions. However, in practice, we know that real-world constraints, common decision-making mistakes, and risky situations make fully rational decisions difficult to achieve. Consequently, in the business world, managers are much more likely to satisfice and make "good enough" decisions than they are to maximize and make "optimal" decisions.

Managers can make better decisions by using decision rules, multivariable testing, and decision software, and by avoiding a common post-decision-making error called escalation of commitment.

Decision Rules

decision rule
set of criteria that alternative solutions must meet to be acceptable to the decision maker

A **decision rule** is a set of criteria that alternative solutions must meet to be acceptable to the decision maker.[24] If an alternative doesn't meet the criteria in the decision rule, it is rejected. Nearly every kind of business uses basic decision rules. In restaurants, the general pricing decision rule is to price food at three times its cost, beer at four times its cost, and hard liquor at six times its cost. In many clothing stores, the rule is to sell clothing for 60 percent over wholesale, and then reduce that price by 20 percent every two weeks until the clothing has been sold. Decision rules improve decision-making because they

NEL

Each section ends with a **Review** that effectively summarizes the concepts presented in that section of the chapter.

Learning Objective icons appear in the margin beside the headings of each major section to indicate where content relevant to that objective is contained.

Together, the chapter outline, learning objectives, section headings (which mark the beginning of a section), and section reviews (which mark the end of a section) allow you to break the chapter into smaller, self-contained sections that can be read in their entirety over multiple study sessions.

Nancy Garapick. Victor Davis. Alex Bauman. Mark Tewkesbury. If you followed competitive swimming in Canada over the last two decades, then you would recognize the names. Whether it be the World Aquatic Championships, the Commonwealth Games, or the Olympic Games, the success of these four swimmers and many others helped to create a global swimming powerhouse that for many years challenged Americans, Australians, and other leading swimming nations on medal podiums throughout the world.

The success that characterized the Canadian swimming scene throughout much of the 1980s and 1990s did not carry on into the new millennium. If the 1984 Olympic Games represented the pinnacle of success for Canada in terms of medal performance, the 2004 Athens Games were its low point. Few medals were won and few personal best times attained. Sadly, the entire team's performance was epitomized by a well-publicized squabble between members of the men's relay team. The incident involved one member, Rick Say, being caught on camera venting his frustration. In response, 1992 gold medallist Mark Tewkesbury lashed out publicly at the Olympic coaching staff.

What Would You Do?

The 2004 Olympics represented yet another controversy for Swimming Canada, an organization that increasingly was featured in the news, not for the achievements of swimmers from coast to coast but rather for a seeming unending series of missteps. While the nation celebrated a number of medal successes at the 2000 Sydney Olympics, many were also aware of the legal proceedings initiated by one high-profile swimmer not chosen for the team. While Swimming Canada proclaimed the virtues of its eight National Swim Centres, the media focused its attention on the infighting surrounding the hiring of a young female coach for the national team. While the team prepared for the Athens Olympics, a growing cadre of former national team swimmers began to publicly discuss the failings of the once-proud program and its head coach. Coupled with these problems was a growing concern that the club system in Canada was no longer producing enough swimmers who might excel at the national and international levels. Further, swimming was becoming an expensive sport—too expensive for many families.

The performance of Canadian swimmers at the 2004 Olympics proved to be catalyst for change. Unaccustomed to such negative publicity, reeling from the mediocre outcomes of the national swim team, and pressured by increasingly important stakeholders, Swimming Canada's head coach and CEO was fired within days. The issue now became what should board members of Swimming Canada do? What steps needed to be taken in order to return to the glory years of the '90s and '80s?

If you were on the board of Swimming Canada, what would you do?

NEL

The **What Would You Do?** chapter-opening vignettes set the scene for introducing business problems. In each case a manager faces an interesting problem or situation that is tied to the information presented in the chapter. You are called upon to think like managers and apply what you've learned in order to provide the solutions to unique problems posed by each case.

296 Part 3: Meeting the Competition

achieve successful change. Managers should avoid these errors when leading change: not establishing urgency, not creating a guiding coalition, lacking a vision, undercommunicating the vision, not removing obstacles to the vision, not creating short-term wins, declaring victory too soon, and not anchoring changes in the corporation's culture.

What Really Happened?[48]

In the opening case, you learned about the struggles facing Swimming Canada. Read the answers to the opening case to find out how it is addressing these problems.

What were the main challenges facing Swimming Canada?

In 2004, Swimming Canada was perceived as an organization in decline, bouncing from scandal to scandal. At the 2004 Athens Olympics, it experienced its lowest medal count in 40 years. Its swimming alumni wanted a change in leadership and went to the press demanding it. Its swimmers fought among themselves and its former CEO was accused of being biased against swimmers from one province in particular. The same CEO was also embroiled in controversy surrounding the hiring of

What steps were taken initially to turn the situation around?

Immediately following the 2004 Athens Olympics, Swimming Canada's CEO was fired and the hunt for a new leader began. A number of steps were taken to initiate a turnaround. In November of that year, a new Swimming Canada board was elected. In March of 2005, a strategic plan was then created by a series of working groups. This led to the selection of Quebec-born Pierre Lafontaine as CEO. Lafontaine brought with him almost 30 years of experience in competitive swimming, the most recent being with the Australian Institute of Sport. He also brought with him a philosophy suggesting that success will follow effective organization and planning. So what would be his overarching theme? Rebuild at the grassroots level. To do so, Lafontaine realized that he would need

gram. Underlying the objectives was a belief that the core of swimming in Canada had to return to its rightful home—the local swim club and the youngsters who swim on a daily basis. What would be the specific objectives that would guide the efforts of Lafontaine and his team? Win three Olympic swimming medals in London; double the number of registered swimmers in Canada to deepen the talent pool (that's about 5000 per year for seven years to about 70 000); break every existing provincial and Canadian record, some a quarter-century old; double Swimming Canada's operating budget to roughly $7 million; and provide swimmers, coaches, and officials with a plan to promote progression and development.

What have been the initial results of

The **What Really Happened?** end-of-chapter wrap-ups provide information to understand how things turned out, what the real company did and why, and whether it worked. This is a great way for you to compare your own thinking with that of real managers.

W H A T R E A L L Y W O R K S

Devil's Advocacy and Dialectical Inquiry[56]

Ninety percent of the decisions managers face are well-structured problems that recur frequently under conditions of certainty. For example, showing up at an airline ticket counter without your ticket is a well-structured problem. It happens every day (recurs frequently), and it's easy to determine if you have your ticket or not (conditions of certainty).

Well-structured problems are solved with programmed decisions, in which a policy, procedure, or rule clearly specifies how to solve the problem. Thus, there's no mystery about what to do when someone shows up without a ticket. After you present identification to prove who you are, and after you pay a transaction fee (around $120), the airline gives you another ticket.

In some sense, programmed decisions really aren't decisions, because anyone with any experience knows what to do. There's no thought involved. What keeps managers up at night is the other 10 percent of problems. Ill-structured problems that are novel (no one's seen them before) and exist under conditions of uncertainty are solved with nonprogrammed decisions. Nonprogrammed decisions do not involve standard methods of resolution. Every time managers make a nonprogrammed decision, they have to figure out a new way of handling a new problem. That's what makes them so tough.

Both the devil's advocacy and dialectical inquiry approaches to decision-making can be used to improve nonprogrammed decision-making. Both approaches work because they force decision makers to identify and criticize the assumptions underlying the nonprogrammed decisions that they hope will solve ill-structured problems.

DEVIL'S ADVOCACY

There is a 58 percent chance that decision makers who use the devil's-advocacy approach to criticize and question their solutions will produce better-quality decisions than decisions based on the advice of experts.

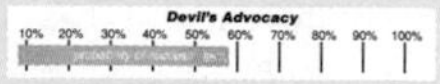

DIALECTICAL INQUIRY

There is a 55 percent chance that decision makers who use the dialectical-inquiry approach to criticize and question their solutions will produce better-quality decisions than decisions based on the advice of experts.

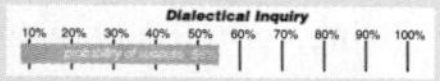

Note that each technique has been compared to decisions obtained by following experts' advice. So, while these probabilities of success, 58 percent and 55 percent, seem small, they very likely understate the effects of both techniques. In other words, the probabilities of success would have been much larger if both techniques had been compared to unstructured decision-making processes.

Each **What Really Works?** section is based on meta-analysis research, which provides the best scientific evidence that management professors and researchers have about what works and what doesn't work in management. An easy-to-understand index known as the "probability of success" is used to indicate how well a management idea or strategy is likely to work in the workplace.

Located in every chapter, **Doing the Right Thing** boxes contain practical, useful advice to help you become a more ethical manager or businessperson.

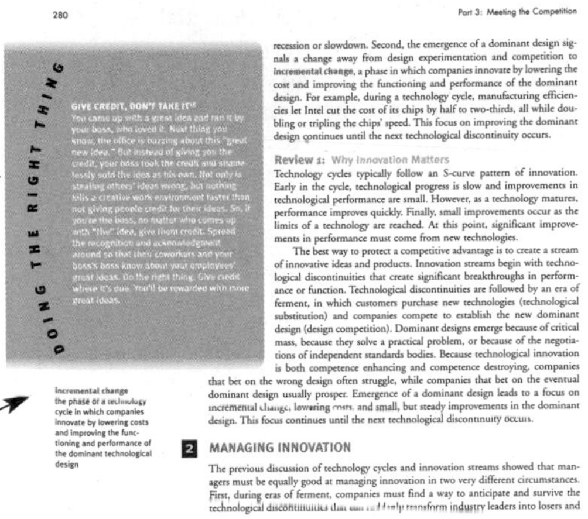

Key terms appear in boldface in the text, with definitions in the margins to make it easy to check your understanding. A complete alphabetical list of key terms appears at the end of each chapter as a study checklist, with page citations for easy reference.

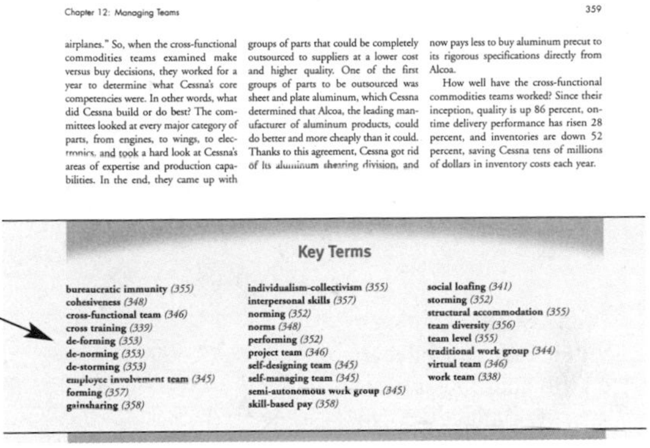

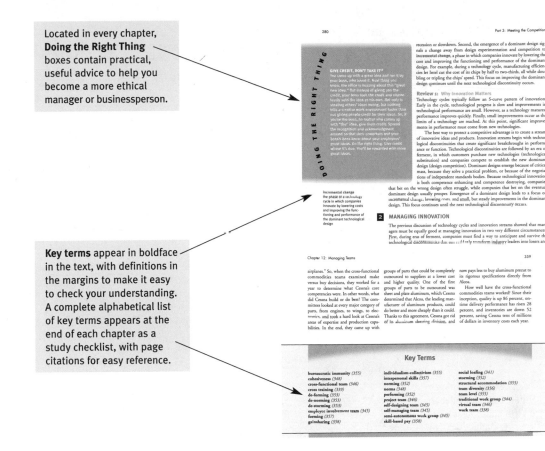

End-of-Chapter Assignments

At the end of each chapter in *Management*, there are a variety of assignments from which to choose. This gives instructors more choice in selecting just the right assignment for their classes. It also gives students a greater variety of activities, making it less likely that you'll repeat the same kind of assignment chapter after chapter.

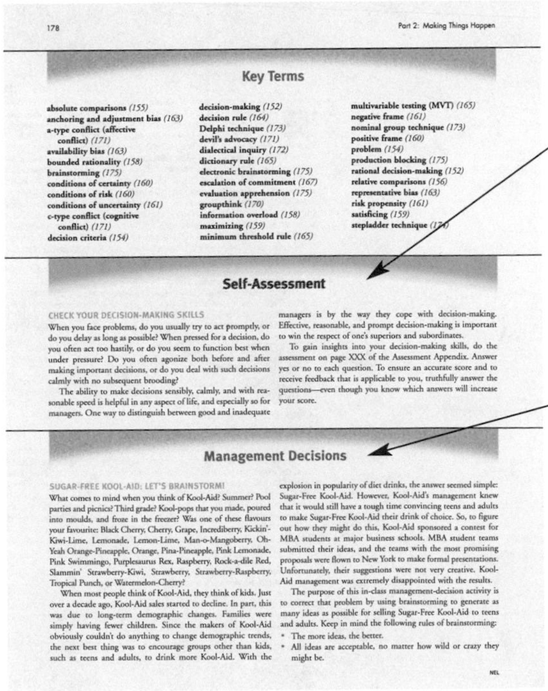

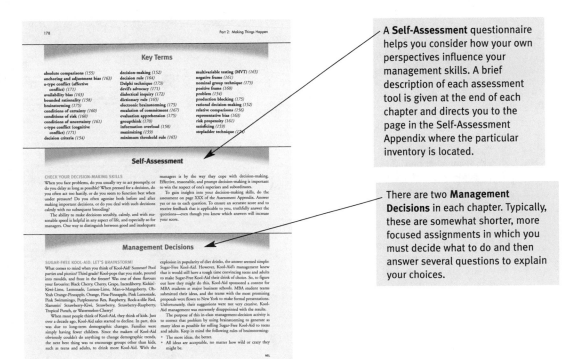

A **Self-Assessment** questionnaire helps you consider how your own perspectives influence your management skills. A brief description of each assessment tool is given at the end of each chapter and directs you to the page in the Self-Assessment Appendix where the particular inventory is located.

There are two **Management Decisions** in each chapter. Typically, these are somewhat shorter, more focused assignments in which you must decide what to do and then answer several questions to explain your choices.

Develop Your Management Potential assignments are self-directed activities that are designed to help you build skills you can use now. These assignments de-emphasize traditional "book-learning" in order to develop the practical knowledge and skills that help managers perform their jobs better.

180 Part 2: Making Things Happen

Develop Your Management Potential

MAKING BETTER DECISIONS[68]

Modern research shows that managers who make the best decisions don't overanalyze things by relying on rational decision-making models, nor do they oversimplify them by relying solely on their intuition. Instead, many managers utilize a concept referred to as "recognitional decision-making." Recognitional decision-making leads to quicker decisions than rational decision-making because it integrates the use of memory in connection with the context of a situation in order to develop an immediate feel of the current situation. Recurrences from previous experiences help provide sample solutions to current problems. Managers then subconsciously combine these recurrences with their intuition and imagination to help develop potential solutions for the current dilemma. Once a manager has a potential solution(s) in mind, he or she then begins to practise a mental game to see how the situation will play out. This approach is often compared to the strategies used by professional chess players when analyzing their next move. Professional chess players calculate each possible move and the subsequent move(s) of their opponents in their heads. By analyzing the opponent's expected move, chess players narrow their options for moves until one results in the best possible option (or least negative consequence), given the current situation. Unfortunately, making good decisions, like becoming a master chess player, requires a lot of experience and practice. Managers and potential managers can improve their decision-making skills by practising the following activities.

First, define your decision criteria for a given situation. For example, if when making decisions under the pressure of a deadline, you often underestimate the length of time it takes to accomplish a task, you should begin by dissecting the situation to see if certain patterns exist. By knowing the components of the decision and by determining which components give you the most trouble, chances are that you can determine the best approach to simplify your choices should this type of decision recur. To reinforce your decision-making ability, intentionally place yourself into situations where these commonalities exist. Doing so will provide further experience and help strengthen your decision-making ability.

Second, obtain feedback regarding current and previous decisions you have made. For example, if part of your job involves scheduling tasks, you can obtain feedback concerning your decisions by logging the expected time to complete a task and comparing that to the actual time taken. Analyzing the factors that contributed to the difference will help you recall them in the future, thus increasing your accuracy. Keep in mind that in most cases, feedback will not occur on its own; it has to be collected.

Third, practise decision-making by reading case studies of actual problems and placing yourself in the shoes of the decision maker. This textbook reinforces this approach by offering a "What Would You Do?" case scenario for each chapter. The scenarios build on information presented in the text and discuss current problems of real-world situations. By comparing your answer to the "What Really Happened" answer, you can determine your decision-making ability and see if you understood and retained the information from the chapter.

Fourth, practise decision-making under conditions of uncertainty. Recall some previous decisions that you have made. Was uncertainty present, and if so, how did you handle it? What steps did you take, or could you have taken, that would have helped reduce the uncertainty or ambiguity involved?

Lastly, improve recognitional decision-making by using the expertise of others. If you respect and admire others for their ability to make quick, competent decisions, approach those people and ask them how they were able to arrive at their decisions. Also, ask what clues directed them to the solution that they chose.

Making decisions is a skill not unlike many other skills you have learned. The more you practise, the better decisions you will make. As your skill progresses, you'll notice that you now quickly and effortlessly make decisions that previously caused you grief. Additionally, you will be able to recognize patterns and recall potential solutions due to your increased decision-making experience.

Exercise

Recall a tough decision involving conditions of uncertainty that you recently made. Some examples include finding a roommate, buying a car, or picking your classes for next semester. The decision you select for this exercise should be one that you felt could have been improved. Analyze that decision using the five activities discussed above. After you analyze the decision, determine what steps you might take in the future to improve your decision-making ability, should this type of situation arise again.

Discussion Questions allow you to further apply chapter concepts to other business situations.

208

Discussion Questions

1. What are the costs and benefits of planning? Give examples of situations when planning has been either advantageous or disadvantageous.
2. If you were buying a new car, what decision criteria would you rely on and why?
3. What is the relationship among bounded rationality, satisficing, and information overload? Give examples where bounded rationality, satisficing and information overload have affected decisions you have made.
4. Define and give examples of common decision-making mistakes (intuition, availability bias, representative bias, or anchoring and adjustment bias).

NEL

or to bad l
success is c
when we fa
What tl
process. Th
formance s
mance sta
deviations. When we put all the blame on external forces rather than our own actions, we stop ourselves from identifying and correcting performance deviations. Furthermore, by not learning from our mistakes, we make it even more likely that we will fail again.

Your task in this Developing Your Management Potential is to begin the process of learning from failure. This is not an easy thing to do. When *Fortune* magazine writer Patricia Sellers wrote an article called "So You Fail," she found most of the people she contacted reluctant to talk about their failures. She wrote,

> Compiling this story required months of pleading and letter writing to dozens of people who failed and came back. "If it weren't for the 'F' word, I'd talk," lamented one senior executive who got fired twice, reformed his know-

between a failure and a mistake is how badly you felt afterwards. Years afterwards, a real failure still makes you cringe when you think about it. What was the situation? What were your goals? And how did it turn out?

2. Describe your initial reaction to the failure. Were you shocked, surprised, angry, or depressed? Initially, who or what did you blame for the failure? Explain.
3. One purpose of control is to identify and correct performance deviations. With that in mind, describe three mistakes that you made that contributed to your failure. Now that you've had time to think about it, what would you have done differently to prevent these mistakes? Finally, summarize what you learned from your mistakes that will increase your chances of success the next time around.

Discussion Questions

1. What sort of strategies could a company use to reduce customer defections? Why do they work?
2. There are five different methods that managers (managerial control) can use to achieve control in their organizations. What are they and when would they be most appropriate to use? Give examples.
3. What kinds of organizations have a great deal of control over their resource flows? Which have little control and why? How can organizations increase control over their resource flows?
4. There are three basic control methods: feedback control, concurrent control, and feedforward control. Define each and give examples of when they might be most appropriate to use.

Each **Critical Thinking Video Case** is available on the book's Web site at www.management2e.nelson.com. You can view the CBC video clip that accompanies the chapter and apply what you've learned to answer the Critical Thinking Questions.

Critical Thinking Video Case

CBC

Visit www.management2e.nelson.com to view this chapter's CBC video case.

Take Two Videos—each chapter contains two video options.

"Biz Flix" is a film clip from a popular Hollywood movie that relates to chapter content.

"Management Workplace" is a longer segment providing a deeper look at a single company, its operations, and how it addresses various management issues every day.

Both the "Biz Flix" and the "Management Workplace" videos guide you on what to look for and think about as you watch the videos.

Take Two

Biz Flix
Lorenzo's Oil

This film tells the true story of young Lorenzo Odone who suffers from adrenoleukodystrophy (ALD), an incurable degenerative brain disorder. (Six actors and actresses play Lorenzo throughout the film.) Physicians and medical scientists offer little help to Lorenzo's desperate parents, Michaela (Susan Sarandon) and Augusto (Nick Nolte). They use their resources to learn about ALD to try to save their son. Director George Miller co-wrote the script, which benefited from his medical training as a physician. Six months after Lorenzo's ALD diagnosis, his condition fails to improve with a restricted diet. Michaela and Augusto continue their research at the National Institutes of Health library in Bethesda, Maryland. Michaela finds a report of a critical Polish experiment that showed positive effects of fatty acid manipulation in rats. Convinced that a panel of experts could systematically focus on their problem, they help organize the First International ALD Symposium. This scene is an edited version of the symposium sequence that appears about midway through the film. The film continues with the Odones' efforts to save their son.

What to Watch for and Ask Yourself

1. Do the scientists present data or information during the symposium?
2. If it is information, who transformed the data into information? Speculate about how such data become information.
3. What do you predict will be the next course of action for the Odones?

Management Workplace
Data Management

Have you ever thought of data as money? Probably not in your personal life, but in business, information has a cost and therefore a related value. Businesses across the world that rely heavily on computer technology understand the value of their data and implement ways to protect their data and data networks from theft, damage, or incompetence. Still, it is easy to be lulled into overconfidence (or sheer laziness) when it comes to computer upgrades or simple virus protection. Nevertheless, data management should be a priority for all companies. In this video, managers from some of the largest names in data protection (Symantec, Trend Micro, McAfee) talk about the threats to data and data networks and the ways you can safeguard your computer against attacks.

What to Watch for and Ask Yourself

1. According to the video, are upgrades really necessary?
2. Describe the nature of data protection.
3. Explain the paradox of ubiquitous computing described in the video. That is, how has the pervasiveness of computer technology made our lives easier and more difficult at the same time?

NEL 149

Student Supplements

CengageNOW™ for *Management*, Second Canadian Edition

CengageNOW Personalized Study is a diagnostic tool (featuring a chapter specific Pre-test, Study Plan, and Post-test) which empowers students to master concepts, prepare for exams, and be more involved in class. This study tool provides immediate and ongoing feedback regarding what students are mastering and why they're not—to both the instructor and the student. It provides links to an integrated eBook so students can easily review topics and also contains animations, links to websites, videos and more as part of their Study Plan. Each copy of the second Canadian Edition of *Management* contains a 4-month single-sign-on access card to *CengageNOW*.

InfoTrac

(http://infotrac-college.com)

Packaged free with every new copy of *Management*, Second Canadian Edition, is a password for the InfoTrac database by Gale Research. InfoTrac enables students to connect with the real world of management through academic journals, business and popular magazines and newspapers, and a vast array of government publications. InfoTrac can also be a valuable tool for working through the "Management Decisions" at the end of each chapter.

Management, Second Canadian Edition, Web Site

(www.management2e.nelson.com)

The *Management* Web site contains a wealth of resources for both instructors and students. Here is what's available for students at the *Management* Web site:

- Learning Objectives from the text
- Lecture notes for each chapter
- Links to the URLs from the book
- Study Tips and Personal Productivity Tips
- Multiple-choice quiz questions for each chapter
- Internet exercises for each chapter
- CBC video clips and cases
- Flashcards of the key terms and definitions from the text

Instructor Supplements

Instructor's Manual

Care has been taken to develop an Instructor's Manual that helps professors create interesting and relevant classes. Each chapter of the Instructor's Manual opens with a pedagogy grid that details all of the pedagogy in the chapter and the companies and teaching points presented. By giving you all the options you have in the chapter and the chapter content addressed by each option, you will be able to decide what you want to emphasize and assign your students. Following the pedagogy grid are lesson plans.

Each type of lesson plan includes pre-class preparation for professor and for students; how to organize the content for the chapter during the class period; a list of possible assignments; and more. A detailed chapter outline (lecture notes) is also provided in the Instructor's Manual. The lecture notes include additional examples, teaching notes for key concepts and for feature boxes, and prompts for where to show the videos. Solutions for chapter features are included, plus ten discussion questions per chapter, five group activities per chapter, additional case studies, and Internet activities for each chapter.

Test Bank

The Test Bank for *Management*, Second Canadian Edition, contains a comprehensive selection of questions from which to choose. Each chapter contains an average of 65 true-false, 70 multiple-choice, 10 short-answer, and five critical-thinking essay questions. Thorough solutions are provided for each question, including difficulty ratings and page references where solutions appear in the text. A correlation table at the beginning of each test bank chapter makes it easy for instructors to select the appropriate mix of questions for their students.

ExamView

A computerized version of the test bank is available on your Instructor Resource CD-ROM. The ExamView testing software is a Windows-based program that is both easy to use and attractive. With this program you create, edit, store, print, and otherwise customize your quizzes, tests, and exams. You won't believe that testing software has come this far!

PowerPoint® Slides

A rich set of PowerPoint slides, with teaching notes, will make class preparations easy and interesting. The approximately 30 to 40 slides per chapter cover all key concepts, terms, features, cases, and even some exhibits from the text. Animations and transitions add movement to many of the slides, allowing instructors to show one point at a time and adding a dynamic feel that will hold student interest throughout the presentation.

Instructor Resource CD-ROM (IRCD)

For your convenience, the Instructor's Manual, Test Bank, ExamView software, and PowerPoint presentations are available on a single CD-ROM, the IRCD.

Video Package

Nothing helps students master management concepts like seeing them put into practice in the real world. This video package will add visual impact and current, real-world examples to your lectures.

CBC

CBC Video segments are available on VHS and on the *Management*, Second Canadian Edition, Web site. These segments are from several different CBC programs and are used as the basis for the Critical Thinking Video Cases. Teaching notes are included for each of the video cases in the Instructor's Manual.

Take Two Videos are available on DVD and VHS. New videos from Small Business School, a program broadcast on PBS, give an extensive look into the workings of interesting and successful companies like Wahoo's Fish Taco, Diversified Chemical, Black Diamond, and Tires Plus. In addition to these longer segments, each chapter has a movie clip that ties into the management concepts presented in the chapter. Clips are short, so you can view and review them easily and quickly. The Instructor's Manual includes detailed notes for both the "Biz Flix" and "Management Workplace" videos so that you can incorporate video into your class in a meaningful way.

JoinIn™ on Turning Point®

Now you can author, deliver, show, assess and grade all in PowerPoint ... with NO toggling back and forth between screens! JoinIn on TurningPoint is the only classroom response software tool that gives you true PowerPoint integration. With JoinIn you are no longer tied to your computer—you can walk about your classroom as you lecture, showing slides and collecting and displaying responses with ease. JoinIn enables your students to respond to multiple-choice questions, short polls, interactive exercises, and peer-review questions—all with a simple click on a hand-held device. You can take attendance, check student comprehension of difficult concepts, collect student demographics to better assess student needs, and even administer quizzes without collecting paper or grading. There is simply no easier or more effective way to turn your lecture hall into a personal, fully interactive experience for your students. If you can use PowerPoint, you can use JoinIn on TurningPoint!

Management, Second Canadian Edition, Web Site (www.management2e.nelson.com)

The *Management* Web site contains a wealth of resources for both instructors and students. Here is what's available for instructors at the *Management* Web site:

- The full PowerPoint presentation slides
- Solutions to the student Internet Exercises
- Files for the full Instructor's Manual are also available online. If you don't have your materials on hand, you can download the chapters you need and customize them to suit your lesson plan.

Meet the Authors

Chuck Williams
Texas Christian University

Chuck Williams is an Associate Professor of Management at the M.J. Neeley School of Business at Texas Christian University, where he has also served as an Associate Dean and the Chair of the Management Department. He received his B.A. in Psychology from Valparaiso University, and specialized in the areas of Organizational Behavior, Human Resources, and Strategic Management while earning his M.B.A and Ph.D. in Business Administration from Michigan State University. Previously, he taught at Michigan State University and was on the Faculty of Oklahoma State University.

His research interests include employee recruitment and turnover, performance appraisal, and employee training and goal-setting. Chuck has published research in the *Journal of Applied Psychology*, the *Academy of Management Journal*, *Human Resource Management Review*, *Personnel Psychology*, and the *Organizational Research Methods Journal*. He was a member of the *Journal of Management*'s Editorial Board, and serves as a reviewer for numerous other academic journals. He was also the Webmaster for the Research Methods Division of the Academy of Management (www.aom.pace.edu/rmd). Chuck is also a co-recipient of the Society for Human Resource Management's Yoder-Heneman Research Award.

Chuck has consulted for a number of organizations, General Motors, IBM, JCPenney, Tandy Corporation, Trism Trucking, Central Bank and Trust, StuartBacon, the City of Fort Worth, the American Cancer Society, and others. He has taught in executive development programs at Oklahoma State University, the University of Oklahoma, and Texas Christian University.

Chuck teaches a number of different courses, but has been privileged to teach his favourite course, Introduction to Management, for nearly 20 years. His teaching philosophy is based on four principles: (1) courses should be engaging and interesting; (2) there's nothing as practical as a good theory; (3) students learn by doing; and (4) students learn when they are challenged. The undergraduate students at TCU's Neeley School of Business have named him instructor of the year. He has also been a recipient of TCU's Dean's Teaching Award.

Alex Z. Kondra
Athabasca University

Alex Z. Kondra is an Associate Professor in the Centre for Organizational Analysis and Marketing, School of Business, Athabasca University in Athabasca, Alberta. He obtained a Ph.D. in Industrial Relations from the University of Alberta in 1995. Previously he was on faculty at the Fred C. Manning School of Business of Acadia University in Wolfville, Nova Scotia. At Athabasca University, he teaches Organization Theory, Managing Change, and Administrative Principles. His current research interests focus on changing organizational and industry structures, organizational ethics, and organizational culture. He has published in the journals *Organization Studies, Journal of Labor Research, Journal of Individual Employment Rights,* and the *Journal of Collective Negotiations in the Public Sector.* He also serves as an academic reviewer for numerous academic journals and conferences and has chaired the Organizational Theory division of the Administrative Sciences Association of Canada Conference.

Conor Vibert
Acadia University

Conor Vibert is an Associate Professor of Business Strategy at the Fred C. Manning School of Business of Acadia University in Wolfville, Nova Scotia. He obtained a Ph.D. in Organizational Analysis from the University of Alberta in 1996. At Acadia University, he teaches Business Strategy and Organization Theory; his current research interests focus on the application of the Internet to contemporary business issues. He is the author of *Theorizing on Macro-organizational Behavior: A Handbook of Ideas and Explanations* and *Competitive Intelligence: A Framework for Web-Based Analysis and Decision-Making.* Conor has published in *Competitive Intelligence Review, Education and Information Technology, Workplace Review,* and the *Journal of Competitive Strategy.* He is a recipient of the 2002 Outstanding Teacher Award for Acadia's Faculty of Professional Studies as well as a recipient of the 2000 Acadia University President's Award for Innovation. He is also the co-developer of the Acadia Management Interview Series Video Database.

Part 1

Introduction to Management

CP PHOTO/DIMITRIOS PAPADOPOULOS

Management

Chapter 1

CHAPTER OUTLINE

LEARNING OBJECTIVES

After reading this chapter, you should be able to

1. describe what management is.
2. explain the four functions of management.
3. describe different kinds of managers.
4. explain the major roles and subroles that managers perform in their jobs.
5. explain what companies look for in managers.
6. discuss the top mistakes that managers make in their jobs.
7. describe the transition that employees go through when they are promoted to management.
8. explain how and why companies can create competitive advantage through people.

What Would You Do?

January of 2006 was a special time in Canadian politics. A federal election late in January altered the political landscape in a manner unforeseen for more than a decade. Confounding the pundits and the critics after eight weeks of hard campaigning, the party with the most elected members turned out to be not the Liberal Party of Canada but their arch-nemesis, the Conservatives. The natural governing party, as some labelled the Liberals, saw its hold on power dissipate in a matter of weeks following a slow holiday start for all the parties. One consequence of the electoral defeat was the resignation of Prime Minister Paul Martin as head of the Liberal Party. So what happened? Media headlines around the time of the election offered important hints for the demise of the Liberals. A *Globe and Mail* headline screamed "Liberal campaign leaves a bitter aftertaste; As Martin exits, grumblings about boss's inner circle feed resentments in fractious party." CBC News had its own interesting ideas captured in two headline banners: "Why the Liberals collapsed in Quebec" and "Whatever became of Paul Martin?"

The Liberals lost power for a number of reasons.[1] Commenting on the performance of Paul Martin as prime minister, a *Toronto Star* editorial suggested the following: "In his internal party feud with former prime minister Jean Chrétien, he divided the Liberals. He was viewed as unfocused, a 'ditherer.' And his election campaign was considered lacklustre. All of these, coupled with the Quebec sponsorship scandal that occurred before he became prime minister, contributed to the defeat of Martin and the Liberals in the end."

The sponsorship scandal referred to the efforts by the federal government in the 1990s and the new millennium to stem the tide of the sovereignty movement in Quebec. Allegations of corruption and kickbacks to senior Liberal operatives in the province led to the creation, by the Paul Martin government, of the Gomery Commission to investigate these alleged activities. The commission was a disaster for the Liberals, and its findings were covered daily in the Quebec media. The findings were numerous and included points such as "clear evidence of political involvement in the administration of the Sponsorship Program," "a veil of secrecy surrounding the administration of the Sponsorship Program," and "an absence of transparency in the contracting process."

As Jeffrey Simpson of the *Globe and Mail* put it, "the Gomery inquiry and what preceded it ruined the Liberals' reputation in Quebec, and tarnished the party's standing in the rest of Canada. Today, the most significant change in Canadian politics has been the Liberals' collapse in Quebec, a collapse due in large measure to Gomery."

Another *Globe and Mail* editorial captured the concerns of Liberals following the election: "Born in the 19th century, on top of the world for much of the 20th, the Liberal Party of Canada is in disarray today. Relegated to second place in Parliament, it finds itself in debt and in shock, scrambling to figure out what went wrong while leadership contenders jostle for advantage. Worst of all, it is a party with an incoherent agenda, merely a hodgepodge of programs cobbled together for electoral expediency."

But if one set of stories and headlines offered a theme of doom and gloom, another set was more balanced, suggesting a smoother road ahead. Take, for example, *The Times of London* story heading "Canada dry; A Conservative victory that should not be overinterpreted" or "Down, yes, but Liberals not destroyed," a heading found in the *Winnipeg Free Press.*

Writing in the *Winnipeg Free Press,* Mark Kennedy captured the sentiments of believers:

> Prime Minister Paul Martin quickly killed any chances of a messy drawn-out internal power struggle by announcing on election night that he will quit as party leader.... The Liberals, who many feared could be reduced to third-party status behind the Bloc Quebecois, elected many more MPs than expected. Instead of the rump of 60 MPs that some pollsters had predicted, the Liberals come into Parliament with a respectable corps of 103 MPs.... With Martin's departure, that feud is history. Liberals can once again become friends with each other.

If you were running the Liberal Party of Canada and you were looking into the future after the election of 2006, what would you do?

The issues facing the Liberal Party of Canada are fundamental to any organization: What is management, and what should managers do? Good management is basic to running an organization, sustaining it into the future, starting a business, growing a business, and maintaining a business once it has achieved some measure of success.

This chapter begins by defining management and discussing the functions of management. Next, we look at what managers do by examining the four kinds of managers and reviewing the various roles that managers play. Third, we investigate what it takes to be a manager by reviewing management skills, what companies look for in their managers, the most serious mistakes managers make, and what it is like to make the tough transition from being a worker to being a manager. We finish this chapter by examining the competitive advantage that companies gain from good management. In other words, we end the chapter by learning how to establish a competitive advantage through people.

What Is Management?

"Over the last decade, almost three quarters of all business and government organizations in Canada used the services of a management consultant."[2] These recipients had many consultants to choose from, as over 25 000 Canadian establishments offered management, scientific, and technical services to businesses and the general public.[3] How large is the market for such services? Well, consider that each year, Canadian federal, provincial, and municipal governments alone spend more than $600 million for similar services. Further, it's estimated that Canadian management consultants were paid well over $6 billion in 2001.[4] What private and public entities are really paying for is management advice. Clearly, companies are looking for help with basic management issues, such as how to make things happen, how to beat the competition, how to manage large-scale projects and processes, and how to effectively lead people. This textbook will help you understand some of the basic issues that management consultants help companies resolve (and, unlike the government and business sectors, this won't cost you millions of dollars).

After reading the next two sections, you should be able to

1. describe what management is.
2. explain the three functions of management.

1 MANAGEMENT IS ...

Many of today's managers got their start welding on the factory floor, clearing dishes off tables, helping customers fit a suit, or wiping up a spill in aisle 3. Lots of you will start at the bottom and work your way up, too. There's no better way to get to know your competition, your customers, and your business. But whether you begin your career at the entry level or as a supervisor, your job is not to do the work, but to help others do their work. **Management** is getting work done through others. Pat Carrigan, a former elementary school principal who became a manager at a General Motors car parts plant, said, "I've never made a part in my life, and I don't really have any plans to make one. That's not my job. My job is to create an environment where people who do make them can make them right, can make them right the first time, can make them at a competitive cost, and can do so with some sense of responsibility and pride in what they're doing. I don't have to know how to make a part to do any of those things."[5]

management
getting work done through others

Pat Carrigan's description of managerial responsibilities indicates that managers also have to be concerned with efficiency and effectiveness in the work process. **Efficiency** is getting work done with a minimum of effort, expense, or waste.

efficiency
getting work done with a minimum of effort, expense, or waste

But, by itself, efficiency is not enough to ensure success. For years, Chrysler Motor Company (now DaimlerChrysler, www.daimlerchrysler.ca) watched its sales, market share, and profits shrink, despite being able to make a car for much less than either Ford or General Motors. It wasn't until Chrysler began producing award-winning car designs such as the Dodge Stratus, Chrysler Concorde, Dodge Ram truck, and its completely redesigned, aerodynamic minivans that it began to regain market share and profitability. So, besides being concerned about efficiency, managers must also strive for **effectiveness**, which is accomplishing tasks that help fulfill organizational objectives.

effectiveness
accomplishing tasks that help fulfill organizational objectives

REVIEW 1: MANAGEMENT IS ...

Good management is working through others to accomplish tasks that help fulfill organizational objectives as efficiently as possible.

2 MANAGEMENT FUNCTIONS

Traditionally, a manager's job has been described according to the classical functions of management: planning, organizing, leading, and controlling. **Planning** is determining organizational goals and a means for achieving them. **Organizing** is deciding where decisions will be made, who will do what jobs and tasks, and who will work for whom in the company. **Controlling** is monitoring progress toward goal achievement and taking corrective action when progress isn't being made. **Leading** is inspiring and motivating workers to work hard to achieve organizational goals.

planning
determining organizational goals and the means for achieving them

organizing
deciding where decisions will be made, who will do what jobs and tasks, and who will work for whom

controlling
monitoring progress toward goal achievement and taking corrective action when needed

leading
inspiring and motivating workers to work hard to achieve organizational goals

Studies indicate that managers who perform these management functions well are better managers. The more time that chief executive officers (CEOs) spend planning, the more profitable their companies are.[6] Over a 25-year period, one telecommunications firm found that employees with better planning and decision-making skills were more likely to be promoted into management jobs, to be successful as managers, and to be promoted into upper levels of management.[7]

The evidence is clear. Managers serve their companies well when they plan, organize, lead, and control. However, companies with familiar names such as the Bank of Montreal, CN, Air Canada, General Motors, and Zellers are facing tremendous changes and are asking—if not demanding—that managers change the way they perform these functions. According to *Fortune* magazine (www.fortune.com), these changes are embodied in the difference between "old" management and "new" management. Old-style managers think of themselves as the "manager" or the "boss." New-style managers think of themselves as sponsors, team leaders, or internal consultants. Old-style managers follow the chain of command (reporting to the boss, who reports to the next boss at a higher managerial level, etc.), while new-style managers work with anyone who can help them accomplish their goals. Old-style managers make decisions by themselves. New-style managers ask others to participate in decisions. Old-style managers keep proprietary company information confidential. New-style managers share that information with others. Old-style managers demand long hours. New-style managers demand results.[8]

Such changes don't make the classical managerial functions obsolete. Indeed, managers are still responsible for performing the functions of management. For example, consider this description of a new-style manager and the people she works with (not the people who work for her, which is "old" management). The managerial functions represented by each action have been inserted in brackets.

> Three years ago Ransom asked her workers at a 100-person manufacturing facility to redesign the plant's operations [planning and organizing]. As she watched, intervening only to answer the occasional question [controlling], a team of hourly workers established training programs, set work rules for absenteeism [controlling], and reorganized the once traditional factory into five customer-focused business units [organizing and leading]. As the workers took over managerial work [decision-making, organizing, and leading], Ransom used her increasing free time to attend to the needs of customers and suppliers [planning and controlling].[10]

WHAT REALLY WORKS

Meta-Analysis

Some studies show that two drinks a day increase life expectancy by decreasing your chances of having a heart attack. Yet other studies show that two drinks a day will shorten your life expectancy. For years, we've "buttered" our morning toast with margarine instead of butter because it was supposed to be better for our health. However, new studies now show that the trans-fatty acids in margarine may be just as bad for our arteries as butter. Confusing scientific results like these frustrate ordinary people who want to "eat right" and "live right." It also makes many people question just how useful most scientific research really is.

Managers also have trouble figuring out what works, based on the scientific research published in different academic journals. It's common for the *Globe and Mail's Report on Business* (www.globeandmail.com) to quote a management research article from one of these journals that says that total quality management is the best thing since sliced bread (without butter or margarine). Then, just six months later the *Report on Business* will quote a different article from the same journal that says that total quality management doesn't work. If management professors and researchers have trouble deciding what works and what doesn't, how can practising managers know?

Thankfully, a research tool called **meta-analysis**, which is a study of studies, is helping management scholars understand how well their research supports management theories. However, meta-analysis is also useful for practising managers, because it shows what works and the conditions under which management techniques may work better or worse in the "real world." Meta-analysis is based on the simple idea that if one study shows that a management technique doesn't work and another study shows that it does, an average of those results is probably the best estimate of how well that management practice works (or doesn't work).

Fortunately, you don't need a Ph.D. to understand the statistics reported in a meta-analysis. In fact, one primary advantage of meta-analysis over traditional significance tests is that you can convert meta-analysis statistics into intuitive numbers that anyone can easily understand. Each meta-analysis reported in the "What Really Works?" section of each chapter is accompanied by an easy-to-understand statistic called the probability of success. As its name suggests, the probability of success shows how often a management technique will work.

For example, meta-analyses suggest that the best predictor of a job applicant's on-the-job performance is a test of general mental ability. In other words, smarter people tend to be better workers. The average correlation (one of those often-misunderstood statistics) between scores on general mental ability tests and job performance is .60. However, very few people understand what a correlation of .60 means. What most managers want to know is how often they will hire the right person if they choose job applicants based on general mental ability test scores.

Well, our user-friendly statistics indicate that it's wise to have job applicants take a general mental ability test. In fact, the probability of success, shown in graphical form below, is 76 percent. This means that an employee hired on the basis of a good score on a general mental ability test stands a 76 percent chance of being a better performer than someone picked at random from the pool of all job applicants. So chances are, you're going to be right much more often than you are wrong if you use a general mental ability test to make hiring decisions.

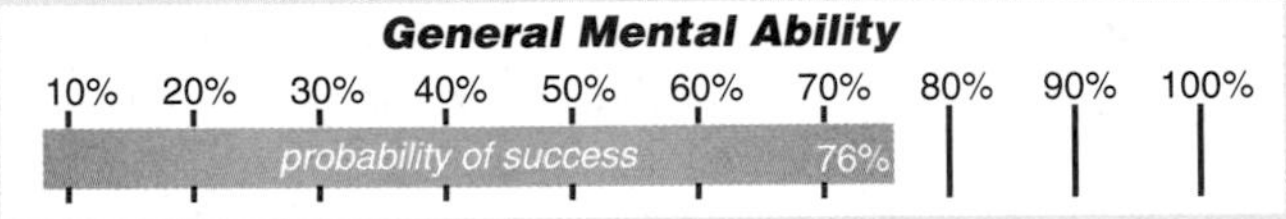

In summary, each "What Really Works?" section in this textbook is based on meta-analysis research, which provides the best scientific evidence that management professors and researchers have about what really works and what really doesn't work in management. An easy-to-understand index known as the "probability of success" will be used to indicate how well a management idea or strategy is likely to work in the workplace. In today's competitive, fast-changing, global marketplace, few managers can afford to overlook proven management strategies like the ones discussed in "What Really Works?"[9]

meta-analysis
a study of studies, a statistical approach that provides the best scientific estimate of how well management theories and practices work

Traditional Management Functions	Table of Contents for This Text		
	Part One	**Introduction to Management**	
		Chapter 1	Management
		Chapter 2	Organizational Environments and Cultures
		Chapter 3	Ethics and Social Responsibility
	Part Two	**Making Things Happen**	
Planning		Chapter 4	Planning
		Chapter 5	Managing Information
Controlling		Chapter 6	Decision-Making
		Chapter 7	Control
	Part Three	**Meeting the Competition**	
		Chapter 8	Global Management
		Chapter 9	Organizational Strategy
		Chapter 10	Innovation and Change
		Chapter 11	Organizational Structures and Processes
	Part Four	**Organizing People, Projects, and Processes**	
Organizing		Chapter 12	Managing Teams
		Chapter 13	Managing Human Resource Systems
		Chapter 14	Managing Service and Manufacturing Operations
	Part Five	**Leading**	
Leading		Chapter 15	Motivation and Leadership
		Chapter 16	Managing Communication

EXHIBIT 1.1
Management Functions and Organization of the Textbook

As indicated within the brackets, Ransom and the members of her work group still perform the classical management functions. They just do them differently than old-style managers used to.

To reconcile the "new" with the "old," this textbook is organized around these four management functions (see Exhibit 1.1), which have evolved out of the traditional functions:

- Making Things Happen
- Meeting the Competition
- Organizing People, Projects, and Processes
- Leading

Note that these functions do not replace the classical functions of management; they build on them. For example, two of the three chapters under "Part 2: Making Things Happen" are classical management functions (planning and controlling). Furthermore, two of the four classical functions of management, organizing and leading, remain as part of the "new" management functions. Finally, a brand new management function, "Meeting the Competition," has been added to reflect the importance of adapting and innovating to remain competitive in today's ever-changing and increasingly global marketplace.

Aside from an emphasis on these new management functions, this book stands out from the crowd for a number of other reasons. The book was written in response to the similarity and dryness of these traditional principles, and its main premise is in keeping management simple, with a focus on what really works for managers, while also presenting management theory through stories and cases rather than lists and lists of topics. It captures the key activities and realities of management (such as risk, decision-making, people, and projects) at all levels without overwhelming the student with theory and research.

Now let's take a close look at each of the management functions, which can be categorized as making things happen; meeting the competition; organizing people, projects, and processes; and leading.

Making Things Happen

Prior to its acquisition by Sears Roebuck, Lands' End (www.landsend.ca) had been, for most of its existence, a small, informally run organization. Exceptional products and the advent of Web-based ordering contributed to the development of a large, loyal base of customers located throughout the United States, Canada, and Europe. Struggling under tremendous growth (pre-acquisition revenues were approximately $3.2 billion a year), the founder of this successful catalogue retailer, Gary Comer, looked outside the company to hire a new CEO to institute modern management methods. Comer hired William End (no relationship to the company name). End quickly introduced the latest management techniques: production teams, performance appraisal systems based on peer reviews (rather than supervisor-based reviews), and over 20 different training courses, such as effective communication. Although some of the techniques worked, others resulted in a large number of lost, late, or undelivered orders. Employees, many of whom had worked at the company since its inception, strongly resisted the changes. Furthermore, confusion resulted because too many changes were made in too little time.

In his zeal to introduce the latest management techniques, End forgot that the most important management function is making things happen. To "make things happen," you must determine what you want to accomplish, plan how to achieve these goals, gather and manage the information needed to make good decisions, and control performance, so that you can take corrective action if performance falls short. In his estimation, company founder Gary Comer took corrective action when he fired William End for his failure to make things happen at Lands' End. In Chapters 4 to 7, you will learn more about how to make things happen. These include planning, managing information, decision-making, and controlling.

Meeting the Competition

Microsoft was not in business 25 years ago. Yet only recently, because of its dominance of the software industry, the *Financial Post* (www.nationalpost.com), *Newsweek*, and the *Report on Business* were abuzz about antitrust action on the part of the U.S. federal government that could have broken Microsoft into several smaller, less dominant companies.[11] Not too long ago, these magazines and newspapers said the same thing about IBM and its dominance of the computer industry. But because of stiff competition from Compaq, Dell, and dozens of other manufacturers of "IBM-compatible" computers, IBM lost billions of dollars and saw its market share in personal computers drop from 80 percent to 8 percent by the early 1990s. Today, no one worries anymore about IBM dominating the computer industry. What made the difference in the fortunes of these two companies?

With free trade agreements that promote international competition, shorter product development cycles, and barriers to entry falling in most industries, market followers will continue to topple market leaders as companies are exposed to more competition than ever in the next decade. Companies that want to remain market leaders must consider the threat from international competitors, have a well-thought-out competitive strategy, be able to embrace change and foster new product and service ideas, and structure their organizations to quickly adapt to changing customers and competitors. Thus, "meeting the competition" is a critical management function in today's business world. In Chapters 8 to 11, you will learn some management skills for meeting the competition. More specifically, you will enhance your understanding of global management and organizational strategy. You will also learn about how organizations innovate, change, and adapt their structures to their competitive environments.

Organizing People, Projects, and Processes

Ford Motor Company purchased Jaguar, a British automaker. Under Ford's guidance, Jaguar's new management laid off one-third of its employees and reorganized its North American operations into three smaller divisions. To emphasize its renewed commitment to customer satisfaction, Jaguar's new vice president of customer care met with Jaguar dealers to talk to them about working harder to please customers. But instead of lecturing the dealers, they lectured him. How could they take care of customers, they said, when Jaguar's management wasn't taking care of them, when all Jaguar's management did was put out recurring fires? The new vice president was surprised and admittedly not prepared for two days of "ranting" from Jaguar dealers.[12]

Like other managers who have tried to "re-engineer" their companies, Jaguar's vice president of customer care found out that large-scale changes won't work without simultaneous consideration of people issues and work processes (how the work gets done).[13] Therefore, our next management function is "organizing people, projects, and processes." You will learn about this management function throughout Chapters 12 to 14. Under this heading, you will enhance your understanding of how to manage teams, human resource systems, service and manufacturing operations, and communications. You will also learn about motivating people.

Leading

In these litigious times, managers are sued for sexual harassment, wrongful discharge, and discrimination. They are shot at, lampooned in the funny pages (*Dilbert* is the fastest-growing syndicated cartoon strip in years), and, in general, not accorded the respect they once had. In this time of corporate layoffs, many would argue that managers are to be feared and disliked.

How is it, then, in this time of corporate distrust, that Mary Ash, founder of Mary Kay cosmetics (www.marykay.ca), and Yves Landry, former CEO of Chrysler Canada, still garnered the respect and admiration of the people they lead or led? Gloria Mayfield, a former IBMer and a graduate of Harvard's MBA program, says, "I didn't see much recognition at IBM. At Mary Kay, if you do well, you know for a fact you'll get recognition. It's not influenced by politics." Not bad for a company that employs 26 000 independent beauty consultants in Canada alone. Mayfield goes on to say that "Mary Kay

CP PHOTO/PAUL CHIASSON

From humble beginnings a quarter century ago as a swim team coach in Pointe Clare, Quebec, Pierre Lafontaine has learned a thing or two about managing. As CEO of Swimming Canada, his task is to return an aquatic program to the glory days of the 1980s and early 1990s, when seeing a Canadian on an Olympic podium was not an exception to the rule.

calls you her daughter and looks you dead in the eye. She makes you feel you can do anything. She's sincerely concerned about your welfare."[14]

At Chrysler Canada, so respected was Landry that Buzz Hargrove, head of the Canadian Auto Workers (www.caw.ca), admitted that Landry "was not offended at all that the union had different ideas about how to do things in the work place. That was unique in dealing with most of the country's business leadership."[15]

No one who has worked for an ordinary manager would ever deny the positive effects that inspirational leaders such as Mary Kay and Yves Landry can bring to their companies. Thus, our last management function is leading. You will find more about this traditional function in Chapters 12 and 15.

Review 2: Management Functions

Managerial jobs have traditionally been described according to the classical functions of management: planning, organizing, controlling, and leading. Although managers still perform these managerial functions, it's also true that companies and the managers who run them have undergone tremendous changes in the last decade. Accordingly, this text incorporates the classical functions of management into broader, updated management functions: making things happen; meeting the competition; organizing people, projects, and processes; and leading.

What Do Managers Do?

Not all managerial jobs are the same. The demands and requirements placed on the chief executive officer of Canadian Tire Corporation are significantly different from those placed on the manager of your local Sobey's or Superstore outlet.

After reading the next two sections, you should be able to

3 describe different kinds of managers.

4 explain the major roles and subroles that managers perform in their jobs.

3 KINDS OF MANAGERS

As shown in Exhibit 1.2, there are four different kinds of managers with different jobs and responsibilities: top managers, middle managers, first-line managers, and team leaders.

Top Managers

top managers
executives responsible for the overall direction of the organization

Top managers hold positions such as chief executive officer (CEO) or chief operating officer (COO) and are responsible for the overall direction of the organization. Top managers have the following responsibilities.[16] First, they are responsible for creating a context for change. In fact, it may be suggested that the CEOs of GEAC Computer Corp., Fisheries Products International, PanCanadian Energy Corp. (now EnCana), and Nortel Networks all left the executive suite within a year's time precisely because they had not moved fast enough to bring about significant changes in their companies.[17] Creating a context for change also includes forming a long-range vision or mission for their companies. As one CEO said, "The CEO has to think about the future more than anyone."

Second, much more than used to be the case, top managers are responsible for helping employees develop a sense of commitment to the business. Stories at DaimlerChrysler Canada (www.daimlerchrysler.ca) abound about Landry's willingness to address the concerns of his employees. One such story has Landry "voluntarily trading in his starched white shirt for a blue collar outfit and [taking] to the shop floor along with Canadian Auto Workers head Buzz Hargrove working on a minivan line and learning from those he regarded as his fellow plant workers."[18] The point of the story is

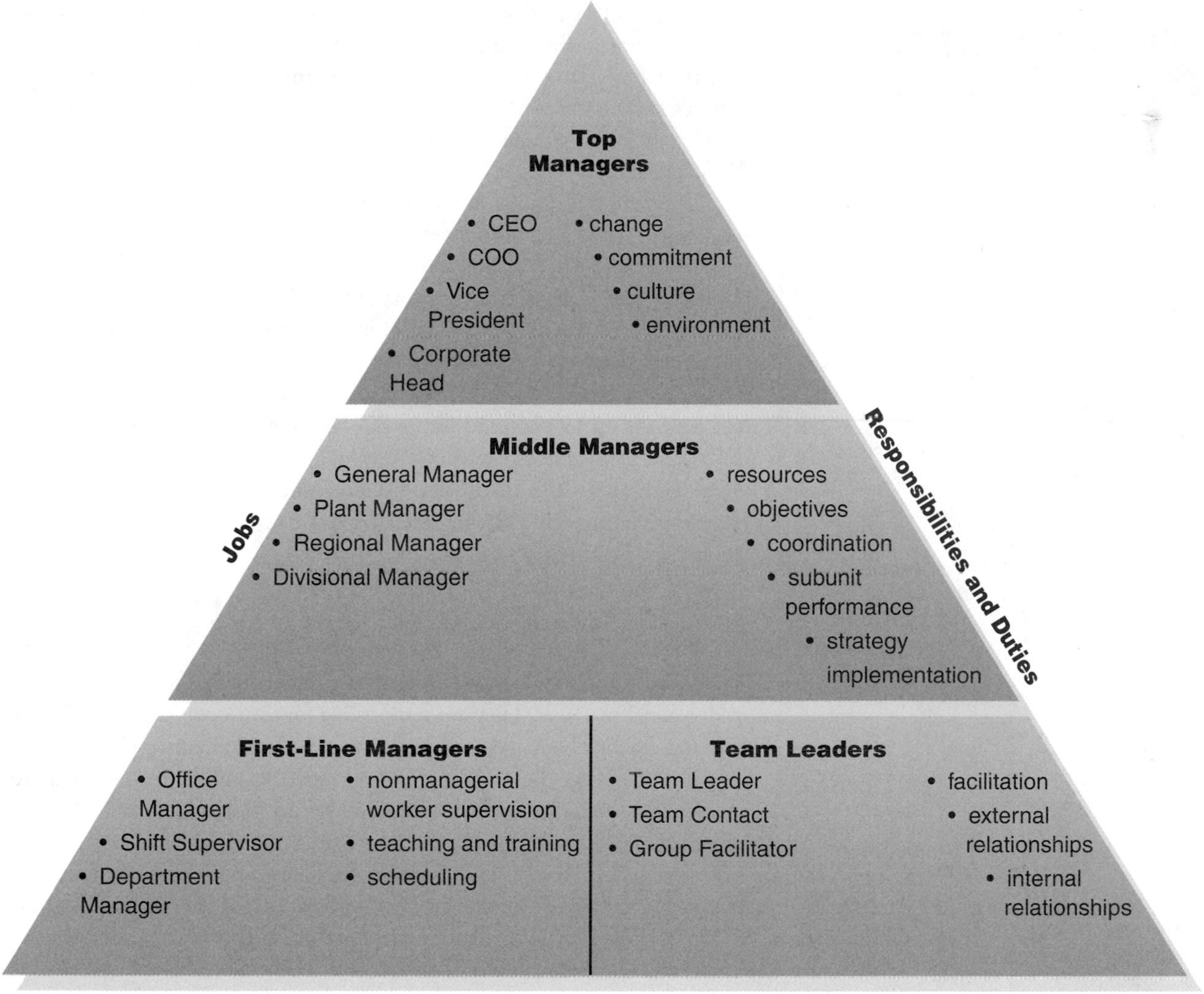

EXHIBIT 1.2
Jobs and Responsibilities of Four Kinds of Managers

that Landry, supposedly the most important person in the company, felt it necessary to understand the problems of assembly-line workers, supposedly some of the least important persons in the company, so he could more effectively deal with their concerns and those of customers.

Third, top managers are responsible for creating a positive organizational culture through language and action. Top managers impart company values, strategies, and lessons through what they do and say to others, both inside and outside the company. One CEO said, "I write memos to the board and our operating committee. I'm sure they get the impression I dash them off, but usually they've been drafted ten or twenty times. The bigger you get, the more your ability to communicate becomes important. So what I write, I write very carefully. I labor over it."[19]

Finally, top managers are responsible for monitoring their business environments. This means that top managers must closely monitor customer needs, competitors' moves, and long-term business, economic, and social trends. How important is this task? Just ask the CEOs of telecommunications companies such as Telus, SaskTel, Bell, or Aliant. Their difficult task has been to try to make sense of chaotic product and service markets that have seen better days.

So how important are top managers? Consider the following example. At age 39, Rajesh Subramaniam, the head of Canadian operations for Federal Express, is a 14-year veteran of FedEx and the youngest senior executive ever at the $30 billion company. In its list of the top 100 companies in Canada, *Marketing* magazine recently ranked FedEx

DOING THE RIGHT THING

TELL AND SHOW PEOPLE THAT ETHICS MATTER

One of the most important things managers can do is to tell people that ethics matter. When Charles Holliday, Jr., CEO of Du Pont, was a young manager, he was told by Du Pont's then-CEO Dick Heckert, "This company lives by the letter of its contracts and the intent of those contracts." Said Holliday, "I still remember the expression on his face when he said those words, and I've lived by that philosophy ever since." In today's business world, however, with one-third of workers reporting that they've seen their bosses lie, steal from the company, or break the law, talk clearly isn't enough. Holliday says, "Just saying you're ethical isn't very useful. You have to earn trust by what you do every day." So, tell the people whom you manage that ethics matter. Then show them by doing the right thing yourself.[20]

Canada 35th. Relaxed and affable, Subramaniam ignores his BlackBerry, which is constantly buzzing with calls, and his computer, chiming the arrival of new e-mails, as he chats about the philosophy underpinning FedEx's success—people, service, profit. "If you take good care of your people, they will go the extra mile to deliver the best service, and then profit takes care of itself," explains Subramaniam, an engineering graduate from the prestigious Indian Institute of Technology in Mumbai. He has vowed to personally meet each one of FedEx's 5000 Canadian employees, and after 18 months on the job, he has shaken hands with about 90 percent of them. Canada's culturally diverse work force gives it a distinct competitive advantage globally, he says. When Subramanian was appointed in 2003 to head Canadian operations, morale was bad and profits were flat. Today, according to in-house surveys, morale is soaring and profit is up 19 percent. Before Subramaniam came along, employees didn't feel appreciated, says Leon Gayle, a FedEx courier. That changed when Subramaniam instituted policies such as an across-the-board Christmas bonus and allowing couriers to be off the road by 1:00 P.M. in the event of bad winter weather.[21]

Middle Managers

middle managers managers responsible for setting objectives consistent with top management's goals, and planning and implementing subunit strategies for achieving these objectives

Middle managers hold positions such as plant manager, regional manager, or divisional manager. They are responsible for setting objectives consistent with top management's goals and planning and implementing subunit strategies for achieving these objectives. One specific middle-management responsibility is to plan and allocate resources to meet objectives. Deans at Canadian universities such as Carleton or Dalhousie spend much of their time allocating resources among competing departments and planning for changes in student enrollments. Another major responsibility is to coordinate and link groups, departments, and divisions within a company. Project managers of flight simulators at CAE Electronics (www.cae.com) in Montreal undertake these responsibilities.

A third responsibility of middle management is to monitor and manage the performance of the subunits and individual managers who report to them. Finally, middle managers are also responsible for implementing the changes or strategies generated by top managers.

First-Line Managers

first-line managers managers who train and supervise performance of nonmanagerial employees and who are directly responsible for producing the company's products or services

First-line managers hold positions such as office manager, shift supervisor, or department manager. The primary responsibility of first-line managers is to manage the performance of entry-level employees, who are directly responsible for producing a company's goods and services. Thus, first-line managers are the only managers who don't supervise other managers. For example, as a result of their large bilingual work forces, Montreal and New Brunswick are home to a number of large telemarketing operations. These are the firms whose sales representatives always seem to call you at home during dinner or your favourite TV show. Working as a telemarketing representative can be a high-stress, thankless job. However, it is the job of each shift supervisor to encourage, monitor, and reward the performance of that shift's telemarketing representatives.

First-line managers also spend time teaching entry-level employees how to do their jobs. Because telemarketing work is so stressful, most workers quit after three or four months on the job. In fact, any stay over three months is considered long-term employment. Because employee turnover is so high, telemarketing supervisors are constantly training new employees. This is one of the reasons that supervisors listen in on telemarketing representatives' phone calls: to observe their performance so that they can teach them how to make sales.

First-line managers also make detailed schedules and operating plans based on middle management's intermediate-range plans. In fact, contrary to the long-term plans of top managers (three to five years out), and the intermediate plans of middle managers (six to eighteen months out), first-line managers engage in plans and actions that typically produce results within two weeks.[22]

Team Leaders

The fourth kind of manager is a team leader. This is a relatively new kind of management job that developed as companies shifted to self-managing teams, which, by definition, have no formal supervisor. In traditional management hierarchies, first-line managers are responsible for the performance of nonmanagerial employees and have the authority to hire and fire workers, make job assignments, and control resources. By contrast, team leaders have a much different role, because nearly all of the functions performed by first-line managers under traditional hierarchies are now performed by teams in this new structure. Instead of directing individuals' work, **team leaders** facilitate team activities toward goal accomplishment. For example, Hewlett-Packard advertises its team leader positions with an ad that says, "Job seeker must enjoy coaching, working with people, and bringing about improvement through hands-off guidance and leadership."[23] Team leaders who fail to understand this key difference often struggle in their roles.

team leaders
managers responsible for facilitating team activities toward goal accomplishment

Team leaders fulfill the following responsibilities.[24] First, team leaders are responsible for facilitating team performance. This doesn't mean team leaders are responsible for team performance. They aren't. The team is. Team leaders help their teams plan and schedule work, learn to solve problems, and work effectively with each other. Eric Doremus, a team leader whose team helped develop the B-2 bomber, said, "My most important task was not trying to figure out everybody's job. It was to help this team feel as if they owned the project by getting them whatever information, financial or otherwise, they needed. I knew that if we could all charge up the hill together, we would be successful."[25]

Second, team leaders are responsible for managing external relationships. Team leaders act as the bridge or liaison between their teams and other teams and other departments and divisions in a company. Third, team leaders are responsible for internal team relationships. Getting along with others is much more important in team structures, because team members can't get work done without the help of their teammates. And when conflicts arise in a six-, seven-, or eight-person team, the entire team suffers. So it is critical for team leaders to know how to help team members resolve conflicts. For example, at XEL Communications Inc., a provider of voice and data transmission equipment for Canadian telecommunications service providers, the standard procedure is for a team leader to take the fighting team members to a conference room. The team leader attempts to mediate the disagreement, hearing each side, and encouraging the team members to agree to a practical solution.[26]

REVIEW 3: KINDS OF MANAGERS

There are four different kinds of managers. Top managers are responsible for creating a context for change, developing attitudes of commitment and ownership, creating a positive organizational culture through words and actions, and monitoring their companies' business environments. Middle managers are responsible for planning and allocating resources, coordinating and linking groups and departments, monitoring and managing the performance of subunits and managers, and implementing the changes or strategies generated by top managers. First-line managers are responsible for managing the performance of nonmanagerial employees, teaching direct reports how to do their jobs, and making detailed schedules and operating plans based on middle management's intermediate-range plans. Team leaders are responsible for facilitating team performance, managing external relationships, and facilitating internal team relationships.

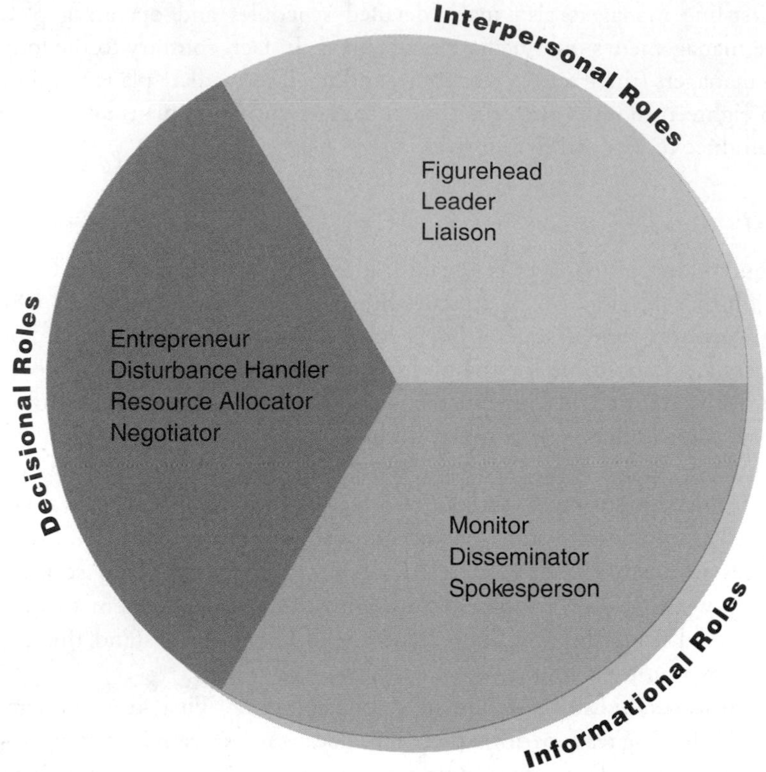

Source: Adapted and reprinted by permission of Harvard Business Review (Exhibit 1) from "The Manager's Job: Folklore and Fact" by Mintzberg H., March–April/1990. Copyright © 1990 by the Harvard Business School Publishing Corporation; all rights reserved.

EXHIBIT 1.3
Mintzberg's Managerial Roles and Subroles

4 MANAGERIAL ROLES

So far, we have described managerial work by focusing on the functions of management (making things happen; meeting the competition; organizing people, projects, and processes; and leading) and by examining the four kinds of managerial jobs (top managers, middle managers, first-line managers, and team leaders). Although these are valid and accurate ways of categorizing managerial work, if you followed managers around as they performed their jobs, you would probably not use the terms planning, organizing, leading, and controlling to describe what they do.

In fact, that's exactly the same conclusion that McGill University business professor Henry Mintzberg came to when he followed five North American CEOs around. Mintzberg spent a week "shadowing" each CEO and analyzing their mail, whom they talked to, and what they did. Mintzberg concluded that managers fulfill three major roles while performing their jobs:[27]

1. interpersonal roles
2. informational roles
3. decisional roles

In other words, managers talk to people, gather and give information, and make decisions. Furthermore, as shown in Exhibit 1.3, these three major roles can be subdivided into ten subroles. Let's examine each major role—interpersonal, informational, and decisional—and their ten subroles.

Interpersonal Roles

More than anything else, management jobs are people-intensive. Estimates vary with the level of management, but most managers spend between two-thirds and four-fifths of their time in face-to-face communication with others.[28] If you're a loner, or if you consider dealing with people to be a "pain," you may not be cut out for management work. In fulfilling the interpersonal role of management, managers perform three interpersonal subroles: figurehead, leader, and liaison.

In the **figurehead role**, managers perform ceremonial duties, like greeting company visitors, making opening remarks when a new facility opens, or representing the company at a community luncheon to support local charities. Each time that Coca-Cola (www.cocacola.com) opens a new bottling plant somewhere around the world, Coke's CEO flies in on the Coke corporate jet for an opening celebration. In the **leader role**, managers motivate and encourage workers to accomplish organizational objectives. Acadia University (www.acadiau.ca) in Wolfville, Nova Scotia, recognizes outstanding innovations from both its faculty and staff members by offering an annual award, called the President's Award for Innovation, the brainchild of former president Kelvin Ogilvie. It is awarded for ideas that increase the use of the laptop computers that are issued to all faculty members and students. Successful innovations to date have included real-time business-case-analysis pedagogy, virtual learning environments, and laptop-based sound-recording studios. Finally, in the **liaison role**, managers deal with people outside their units. Studies consistently indicate that managers spend as much time with "outsiders" as they do with their own subordinates and their own bosses.

figurehead role
the interpersonal role managers play when they perform ceremonial duties

leader role
the interpersonal role managers play when they motivate and encourage workers to accomplish organizational objectives

liaison role
the interpersonal role managers play when they deal with people outside their units

Informational Roles

While managers spend most of their time in face-to-face contact with others, most of that time is spent obtaining and sharing information. Indeed, Mintzberg found that the managers in his study spent 40 percent of their time giving and getting information from others. In this regard, management can be viewed as processing information, gathering information by scanning the business environment and listening to others in face-to-face conversations, and then sharing that information with people inside and outside the company. Mintzberg described three informational subroles: monitor, disseminator, and spokesperson.

In the **monitor role**, managers scan their environment for information, actively contact others for information, and, because of their personal contacts, receive a great deal of unsolicited information. Besides receiving firsthand information, managers monitor their environment by reading local newspapers and papers such as the *Globe and Mail* or *Financial Post* to keep track of customers, competitors, and technological changes that may affect their businesses. However, electronic monitoring and distribution services such as Canada NewsWire (www.canadanewswire.com) and Rocketinfo (www.rocketnews.com) deliver customized electronic newspapers to managers, including only the stories on topics the managers specify.

monitor role
the informational role managers play when they scan their environment for information

Because of their numerous personal contacts, and because of the access they have to subordinates, managers are often hubs for distribution of critical information. In the **disseminator role**, managers share the information they have collected with their subordinates and others in the company. Although there will never be a complete substitute for face-to-face dissemination of information, a primary method of communication in large companies such as Intel, maker of Pentium processors, and BellAliant (www.aliant.ca), an eastern Canadian–based provider of telecommunications services and technologies, is e-mail. David Rathbun, a senior vice president at Aliant, estimates that he regularly spends two hours per day writing and responding to his e-mail—in other words, gathering and disseminating information.[29]

disseminator role
the informational role managers play when they share information with others in their departments or companies

In contrast to the disseminator role, in which managers distribute information to employees inside the company, in the **spokesperson role**, managers share information with people outside their departments and companies. One of the most common ways in which CEOs serve as spokespeople for their companies is at annual meetings with company shareholders or the board of directors. For example, at McDonald's shareholder meeting, Michael Quinlan, who had been CEO for 11 years, announced that Jack Greenberg would replace him as McDonald's new CEO. Quinlan stayed on as chairperson of McDonald's board of directors.[30]

spokesperson role
the informational role managers play when they share information with people outside their departments or companies

Decisional Roles

While managers spend most of their time in face-to-face contact with others, obtaining and sharing information, that time, according to Mintzberg, is not an end in itself. The time spent talking to and obtaining and sharing information with people inside and outside of the company is useful to managers because it helps them make good decisions. According to Mintzberg, managers engage in four decisional subroles: entrepreneur, disturbance handler, resource allocator, and negotiator.

In the **entrepreneur role**, managers adapt themselves, their subordinates, and their units to incremental change. In the **disturbance handler role**, managers respond to pressures and problems so severe that they demand immediate attention and action. Managers often play the role of disturbance handler when the company board hires a new CEO who is charged with turning around a failing company. When Nortel Networks' (www.nortelnetworks.com) CEO John Roth retired in October 2001, he handed the controls over to his chief financial officer, Frank Dunn,[31] whose role would be nothing short of designated saviour in the face of the collapse of the market for many of the firm's telecommunications products. In an effort to turn around the troubled firm, Dunn proceeded to drastically cut Nortel's work force, product lines, and research and development expenditures while closing facilities around the world.

In some instances, entrepreneur-style managers will follow disturbance handlers. When GEAC Computer Corp.'s 1999 acquisition, enterprise resource planning firm JBA Holdings Plc, began losing approximately $1 million a week during 2000, its newly hired CEO, a turnaround expert or disturbance handler, John Caldwell, took drastic action by laying off 30 percent of its work force, altering his top management team, and focusing its product offerings. Once the financial crisis was stabilized, Caldwell was in turn let go by GEAC's board of directors and replaced by its chief operating officer, Paul Birch, who then played an entrepreneur role seeking out new but less risky acquisitions to help the Toronto-based firm grow.[32]

resource allocator role
the decisional role managers play when they decide who gets what resources

negotiator role
the decisional role managers play when they negotiate schedules, projects, goals, outcomes, resources, and employee raises

In the **resource allocator role**, managers decide who will get what resources and how many resources they get.

In the **negotiator role,** managers negotiate schedules, projects, goals, outcomes, resources, and employee raises. For example, every three years the United Auto Workers labour union renegotiates its labour contract with the "Big Three" auto companies—Ford, DaimlerChrysler, and General Motors.

Review 4: Managerial Roles

Managers perform interpersonal, informational, and decisional roles in their jobs. In fulfilling the interpersonal role, managers act as figureheads by performing ceremonial duties, as leaders by motivating and encouraging workers, and as liaisons by dealing with people outside their units. In performing their informational role, managers act as monitors by scanning their environment for information, as disseminators by sharing information with others in the company, and as spokespersons by sharing information with people outside their departments or companies. In fulfilling decisional roles, managers act as entrepreneurs by adapting their units to incremental change, as disturbance handlers by responding to larger problems that demand immediate action, as resource allocators by deciding who will get what resources and how many resources they will get, and as negotiators by bargaining with others about schedules, projects, goals, outcomes, and resources.

What Does It Take to Be a Manager?

> I didn't have the slightest idea what my job was. I walked in giggling and laughing because I had been promoted and had no idea what principles or style to be guided by. After the first day I felt like I had run into a brick wall. (Sales Representative 1).

> Suddenly, I found myself saying, boy, I can't be responsible for getting all that revenue. I don't have the time. Suddenly you've got to go from [taking care of] yourself and say now I'm the manager, and what does a manager do? It takes a while thinking about it for it to really hit you ... a manager gets things done through other people. That's a very, very hard transition to make.[33] (Sales Representative 2).

The above statements were made by two star sales representatives, who, on the basis of their superior performance, were promoted to the position of sales manager. Their comments clearly indicate that at first they did not feel confident about their ability to do their jobs as managers. Like most new managers, these sales managers were suddenly faced with the realization that the knowledge, skills, and abilities that led to success early in their careers (and which were probably responsible for their promotion into the ranks of management) would not necessarily help them succeed as managers. As sales representatives, they were responsible only for managing their own performance. But as sales managers, they were now directly responsible for supervising all the sales representatives in their sales territories. Furthermore, they were now held directly accountable for whether those sales representatives achieved their sales goals.

If performance in nonmanagerial jobs doesn't necessarily prepare you for a managerial job, then what does it take to be a manager?

After reading the next three sections, you should be able to

5 explain what companies look for in managers.
6 discuss the top mistakes that managers make in their jobs.
7 describe the transition that employees go through when they are promoted to management.

5 WHAT COMPANIES LOOK FOR IN MANAGERS

Broadly speaking, when companies look for employees who would be good managers, they look for individuals who have technical skills, human skills, and conceptual skills, and are motivated to manage.[34] Exhibit 1.4 shows the relative importance of these four skills to the jobs of team leaders, first-line managers, middle managers, and top managers.

Technical skills are the ability to apply the specialized procedures, techniques, and knowledge required to get the job done. For the sales managers described above, technical skills are the ability to find new sales prospects, develop accurate sales pitches based on customer needs, and close the sale.

technical skills
the ability to apply the specialized procedures, techniques, and knowledge required to get the job done

Technical skills are most important for lower-level managers, because these managers supervise the workers who produce products or serve customers. Team leaders and first-line managers need technical knowledge and skills to train new employees and help employees solve problems. Technical knowledge and skills are also needed to troubleshoot problems that employees can't handle. Technical skills become less important as managers rise through the managerial ranks, but they are still important. Indeed, Bill Gates, founder and former CEO of Microsoft Corporation, used to spend roughly 40 percent of his time dealing with the technical issues related to development of Microsoft software products.

Human skill is the ability to work well with others. Managers with "people" skills work effectively within groups, encourage others to express their thoughts and feelings, are sensitive to others' needs and viewpoints, and are good listeners and communicators. Human skills are equally important at all levels of management, from first-line supervisors to CEOs. However, because lower-level managers spend much of their time solving technical problems, upper-level managers may actually spend more time dealing directly with people. On average, first-line managers spend 57 percent of their time with people, middle managers spend 63 percent of their time directly with people, and top managers spend as much as 78 percent of their time dealing with people.[35]

human skill
the ability to work well with others

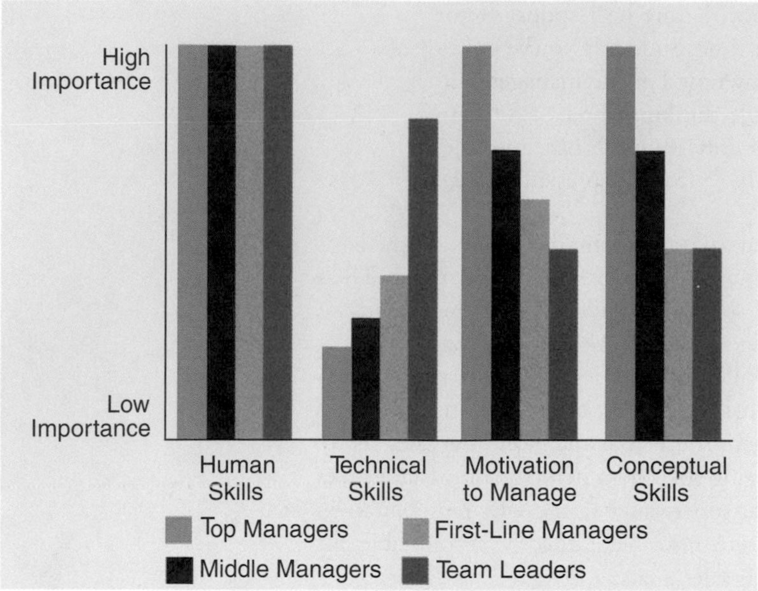

EXHIBIT 1.4
Relative Importance of Managerial Skills to Different Managerial Jobs

conceptual skill
the ability to see the organization as a whole, how the different parts affect each other, and how the company fits into or is affected by its environment

motivation to manage
an assessment of how enthusiastic employees are about managing the work of others

Conceptual skill is the ability to see the organization as whole, how the different parts of the company affect each other, and how the company fits into or is affected by its external environment, such as the local community, social and economic forces, customers, and competition. Good managers have to be able to recognize, understand, and reconcile multiple complex problems and perspectives. In other words, managers have to be smart! In fact, intelligence makes so much difference for managerial performance that managers with above-average intelligence typically outperform managers of average intelligence by approximately 48 percent.[36] Clearly, companies need to be careful to promote smart workers into management. Conceptual skill increases in importance as managers rise through the management hierarchy.

However, there is much more to good management than intelligence. For example, making the department genius a manager can be disastrous if that genius lacks technical skills, human skills, or one other factor known as the motivation to manage. **Motivation to manage** is an assessment of how motivated employees are to interact with superiors, participate in competitive situations, behave assertively toward others, tell others what to do, reward good behaviour and punish poor behaviour, perform actions that are highly visible to others, and handle and organize administrative tasks. Implicit in the research of Dr. Barry Wright of Brock University is the need for managers to be extremely motivated when performing certain tasks. He examined the human toll that managers face when charged with organizational downsizing and found that the personal costs include social and organizational isolation, a decline in personal well-being, and decreased family functioning.

Managers typically have a stronger motivation to manage than their subordinates, and managers at higher levels usually have stronger motivation to manage than managers at lower levels. Furthermore, managers with stronger motivation to manage are promoted faster, are rated by their employees as better managers, and earn more money than managers with a weak motivation to manage.[37]

Review 5: What Companies Look for in Managers

Companies do not want one-dimensional managers. They want managers with a balance of skills. They want managers who know their stuff (technical skills), are equally comfortable working with blue-collar and white-collar employees (human skills), are able to assess the complexities of today's competitive marketplace and position their companies for success (conceptual skills), and want to assume positions of leadership and power (motivation to manage). Technical skills are most important for lower-level managers, human skills are equally important at all levels of management, and conceptual skills and motivation to manage increase in importance as managers rise through the managerial ranks.

6 MISTAKES MANAGERS MAKE

Another way to understand what it takes to be a manager is to look at the mistakes managers make. One mistake is to assume too many personal responsibilities. For example, as mayor of Calgary, Al Duerr, a husband and father of two children, typically worked 60 to 80 hours a week. On top of this, in 1995 Duerr enrolled in an MBA program at the University of Calgary; he completed it in 2001. Not surprisingly, he decided not to run for re-election that year, following more than a decade as mayor. During one hectic 60-day period, Duerr found himself arriving at the office at 8:00 A.M., undertaking mayoral functions until he left for evening classes, and then meeting late in the evening with union officials to resolve a transit strike.[38] Duerr's example suggests that we can learn just as much from what managers shouldn't do as we can from what they should do. Exhibit 1.5 lists the top ten mistakes managers make.

1.	Insensitive to others: abrasive, intimidating, bullying style.
2.	Cold, aloof, arrogant.
3.	Betrayal of trust.
4.	Overly ambitious: thinking of next job, playing politics.
5.	Specific performance problems with the business.
6.	Overmanaging: unable to delegate or build a team.
7.	Unable to staff effectively.
8.	Unable to think strategically.
9.	Unable to adapt to boss with different style.
10.	Overdependent on advocate or mentor.

Source: M.W. McCall, Jr. & M.M. Lombardo, "What Makes a Top Executive?" *Psychology Today*, February 1983, 26–31.

EXHIBIT 1.5
Top Ten Mistakes That Managers Make

Several studies of North American and British managers have compared "arrivers," managers who made it all the way to the top of their companies, to "derailers," managers who were successful early in their careers but were knocked off the "fast track" by the time they reached middle to upper levels of management.[39] The first result they found was that there were few differences between arrivers and derailers. For the most part, both groups were talented and both groups had weaknesses. But what distinguished derailers from arrivers was that derailers possessed two or more "fatal flaws" with respect to the way that they managed people! By contrast, arrivers, who were by no means perfect, usually had no more than one fatal flaw, or they had found ways to minimize the effects of their flaws on the people with whom they work.

The number one mistake made by derailers was that they were insensitive to others by virtue of their abrasive, intimidating, and bullying management style. The authors of one study cited the manager who walked into his subordinate's office and interrupted a meeting by saying, "I need to see you." When the subordinate tried to explain that he wasn't available because he was in the middle of a meeting, the manager barked, "I don't give a damn. I said I wanted to see you now."[40] Not surprisingly, only 25 percent of derailers were rated by others as being good with people, compared to 75 percent of arrivers.

The second mistake was that derailers were often cold, aloof, or arrogant. While this sounds like insensitivity to others, this has more to do with derailed managers being so smart, so expert in their areas of knowledge, that they treated others with contempt because they weren't experts, too.

The third and fourth mistakes made by derailers, betraying a trust and being overly ambitious, indicate a lack of concern for co-workers and subordinates. Betraying a trust doesn't mean being dishonest. Instead, it means making others look bad by not doing what you said you would do when you said you would do it. That mistake, in itself, is not fatal, because managers and their workers aren't machines. Tasks go undone in every company every single business day. There's always too much to do and not enough time, people, money, or resources to do it. The fatal betrayal of trust is failing to inform others when things would not be done on time. This failure to admit mistakes, to quickly inform others of the mistakes, to take responsibility for the mistakes, and then to fix the mistakes without blaming others clearly distinguished the behaviour of derailers from arrivers.

The fourth mistake, mentioned above, was being overly political and ambitious. Managers who always have their eye on their next job rarely do more than establish superficial relationships with peers and co-workers. In their haste to gain credit for successes that would be noticed by upper management, they make the fatal mistake of treating people like they don't matter.

The fatal mistakes of being unable to delegate, to build a team, and to staff effectively indicate that many derailed managers were unable to make the most basic transition to managerial work: to quit being hands-on "doers" and get work done through others. Two things go wrong when managers make these mistakes. First, when managers meddle in decisions that their subordinates should be making, when they can't quit being doers, they alienate the people who work for them. Second, because they are trying to do their subordinates' jobs in addition to their own, managers who fail to delegate to their workers will not have enough time to do much of anything well.

Not being able to build a team is a fatal management mistake. Managers on the diversity council, pictured here, work as a team to ensure that their company has a diverse employee base. Effective diversity managers take care to build strong teams and avoid making a fatal management mistake.

WWW.COMSTOCK.COM

For example, before becoming president of Harvard University, Neil Rudenstine's management style had always been to take on more and more work himself. So when he became a university president, and the demands placed on him increased, he responded by working even longer hours, usually 12 to 14 hours a day. While it is the norm for university presidents to put in long hours, Dr. Rudenstine made it even tougher on himself by failing to delegate work to his associates. Figuring out how to solve the shortage of parking spaces on campus or arranging to have contractors fix leaky roofs are not good uses of a university president's time. Indeed, the combination of long hours and his inability to delegate led to mental and physical exhaustion and a physician-mandated leave of absence from his job as Harvard University president.[41]

Review 6: Mistakes Managers Make

Another way to understand what it takes to be a manager is to look at the top mistakes managers make. Five of the most important mistakes made by managers are being abrasive and intimidating; being cold, aloof, or arrogant; betraying trust; being overly ambitious; and failing to build a team and then delegate to that team.

7 THE TRANSITION TO MANAGEMENT: THE FIRST YEAR

In her book *Becoming a Manager: Master of a New Identity*, Harvard Business School professor Linda Hill followed the development of 19 people in their first year as managers. Two overall themes emerged from Dr. Hill's study. First, becoming a manager produced a profound psychological transition that changed the way these managers viewed themselves and others. Second, the only way to really learn how to manage was to be a manager. As shown in Exhibit 1.6, a good way to appreciate the magnitude of the changes these managers experienced is to describe their thoughts, expectations, and realities as they evolved over the course of their first year in management.

Initially, the managers in Hill's study believed that their job was to exercise formal authority and to manage tasks—basically being the boss, telling others what to do, making decisions, and getting things done. One manager said, "Being the manager means running my own office, using my ideas and thoughts." In fact, most of the new managers were attracted to management positions because they wanted to be "in charge." Surprisingly, the new managers did not believe that their job was to manage people. The only two aspects of people management mentioned by the new managers were hiring and firing.

MANAGER'S INITIAL EXPECTATIONS	AFTER SIX MONTHS AS A MANAGER	AFTER A YEAR AS A MANAGER
• Be the boss	• Initial expectations were wrong	• No longer "doers"
• Formal authority	• Fast pace	• Communication, listening, and positive reinforcement
• Manage tasks	• Heavy workload	
• Job is not managing people	• Job is to be problem-solver and trouble-shooter for subordinates	• Job is people development

Source: L.A. Hill, *Becoming a Manager: Mastery of a New Identity* (Boston, MA: Harvard Business School Press, 1992).

EXHIBIT 1.6
The Transition to Management: Initial Expectations, after Six Months, and after a Year

After six months, most of the new managers had come to the conclusion that their initial expectations about managerial work were wrong. Management wasn't being "the boss." It wasn't just about making decisions and telling others what to do. The first surprise to the new managers was the fast pace and heavy workload involved in being a manager. One manager stated, "This job is much harder than you think. It is 40 to 50 percent more work than being a producer! Who would have ever guessed?" The pace of managerial work was startling, too. Another manager said, "You have eight or nine people looking for your time ... coming into and out of your office all day long."

Informal descriptions like this are consistent with studies that indicate that the average first-line manager spends no more than two minutes on a task before being interrupted by a request from a subordinate, a phone call, or an e-mail. The pace is somewhat less hurried for top managers, who spend an average of approximately nine minutes on a task before having to switch to another. In practice, this means that supervisors may perform 30 different tasks per hour, while top managers perform seven different tasks per hour, with each task typically different from the one that preceded it. A manager described this frenetic level of activity by saying, "The only time you are in control is when you shut your door, and then I feel I am not doing the job I'm supposed to be doing, which is being with the people."

The other major surprise after six months on the job was that the managers' expectations about what they should do as managers were very different from their subordinates' expectations. Initially, the managers defined their jobs as helping their subordinates perform their jobs well. For the managers, who still defined themselves as doers rather than managers, assisting their subordinates meant going out on sales calls or handling customer complaints. One manager said, "I like going out with the rep, who may need me to lend him my credibility as manager. I like the challenge, the joy in closing. I go out with the reps and we make the call and talk about the customer; it's fun." But when the managers "assisted" in this way, their subordinates were resentful and viewed their help as interference. What the subordinates wanted in the way of assistance was for their managers to solve problems that they couldn't solve. Once the managers realized this contradiction, they embraced their role as problem-solver and troubleshooter. Thus, they could help without interfering with their subordinates' jobs.

After a year on the job, most of the managers no longer thought of themselves as doers, but managers. In making the transition, they finally realized that people management was the most important part of their jobs. Most of the managers now regretted the rather heavy-handed approach they had used in their early attempts to manage their subordinates: "I wasn't good at managing ..., so I was bossy like a first-grade teacher." "Now I see that I started out as a drill sergeant. I was inflexible, just a lot of how-to's." By the end of the year, most of the managers had abandoned their authoritarian approach for one based on communication, listening, and positive reinforcement. One manager explained, "Last night at five I handed out an award in the boardroom to an individual. It was the first time in his career that he had done [earned] $100 000, and

I gave him a piece of glass [a small award] and said I'd heard a rumour that somebody here just crossed over $100 000 and I said congratulations, shook his hand, and walked away. It was not public in the sense that I gathered everybody around. But I knew and he did too."

Finally, after beginning their year as managers in frustration, the managers came to feel comfortable with their subordinates, with the demands of their jobs, and with their emerging managerial styles. While being managers had made them acutely aware of their limitations and their need to develop as people, it also provided them with an unexpected reward of the "thrill" of coaching and developing the people who worked for them. One manager said, "It gives me the best feeling to see somebody do something well after I have helped them. I get excited."

Review 7: The Transition to Management: The First Year

Managers often begin their jobs by using more formal authority and less people management. However, most managers find that being a manager has little to do with "bossing" their subordinates. After six months on the job, the managers were surprised at the fast pace, the heavy workload, and that "helping" their subordinates was viewed as interference. After a year on the job, most of the managers no longer thought of themselves as doers, but managers who get things done through others. And, because they finally realized that people management was the most important part of their job, most of them had abandoned their authoritarian approach for one based on communication, listening, and positive reinforcement.

Why Management Matters

If you walk down the aisle of the "business" section in your local bookstore, you will find hundreds of books that explain precisely what companies need to do to be successful. Unfortunately, business books tend to be faddish, changing every few years. Lately, the best-selling business books have emphasized technology, re-engineering, and going global, whereas ten years ago the hot topics were joint ventures, mergers, and management buyouts. One thing that hasn't changed, though, is the importance of good people and good management: Companies can't succeed for long without them.

After reading the next section, you should be able to

8 explain how and why companies can create competitive advantage through people.

8 COMPETITIVE ADVANTAGE THROUGH PEOPLE

In his book *Competitive Advantage Through People*, Stanford University business professor Jeffrey Pfeffer contends that what separates top companies from their competitors is the way they treat their work forces; in other words, management. Managers in top-performing companies use ideas like employee ownership, incentive pay, employee participation and empowerment, and the other techniques explained in Exhibit 1.7 to develop work forces that are smarter, better trained, more motivated, and more committed than their competitors' work forces. And, as indicated by the phenomenal growth and return on investment earned by the companies in his study, smarter, better trained, and more committed work forces provide superior products and service to customers, who keep buying and who, by telling others about their positive experiences, bring in new customers.

Pfeffer also argues that companies that invest in their people will create long-lasting competitive advantages that are difficult for other companies to duplicate. Indeed, studies clearly demonstrate that sound management practices can produce substantial advantages in three critical areas of organizational performance: sales revenues, profits,

1. **Employment Security**—Employment security is the ultimate form of commitment that companies can make to their workers. Employees can innovate and increase company productivity without fearing the loss of their jobs.
2. **Selective Hiring**—If employees are the basis for a company's competitive advantage, and those employees have employment security, then the company needs to aggressively recruit and selectively screen applicants in order to hire the most talented employees available.
3. **Self-Managed Teams and Decentralization**—Self-managed teams are responsible for their own hiring, purchasing, job assignments, and production. Self-managed teams can often produce enormous increases in productivity through increased employee commitment and creativity. Decentralization allows employees who are closest to (and most knowledgeable about) problems, production, and customers to make timely decisions. Decentralization increases employee satisfaction and commitment.
4. **High Wages Contingent on Organizational Performance**—High wages are needed to attract and retain talented workers and to indicate that the organization values its workers. Employees, like company founders, shareholders, and managers, need to share in the financial rewards when the company is successful. Why? Because employees who have a financial stake in their companies are more likely to take a long-run view of the business and think like business owners.
5. **Training and Skill Development**—Like a high-tech company that spends millions of dollars to upgrade computers or research and development labs, a company whose competitive advantage is based on its people must invest in the training and skill development of its people.
6. **Reduction of Status Differences**—These are fancy words that indicate that the company treats everyone, no matter what their job, as equals. There are no reserved parking spaces. Everyone eats in the same cafeteria and has similar benefits. The result: much improved communication as employees focus on problems and solutions rather than how they are less valued than managers.
7. **Sharing Information**—If employees are to make decisions that are good for the long-run health and success of the company, they need to be given information about costs, finances, productivity, development times, and strategies that were previously known only by company managers.

Source: J. Pfeffer, *The Human Equation: Building Profits by Putting People First* (Boston, MA: Harvard Business School Press, 1996).

EXHIBIT 1.7
Competitive Advantage Through People: Management Practices

and customer satisfaction. For example, a study of nearly 1000 North American firms indicated that companies that use just some of the ideas shown in Exhibit 1.7 had approximately $43 000 more sales per employee and approximately $6000 more profit per employee than companies that didn't.[42] For a 100-person company, these differences amount to $4.3 million more in sales and more than $600 000 extra in annual profit! For a 1000-person company, the difference grows to an additional $43 million in sales and at least $6 million more in annual profit!

Another study found that poorly performing companies that adopted management techniques as simple as setting expectations (setting goals, results, and schedules), coaching (informal, ongoing discussions between managers and subordinates about what is being done well and what could be done better), reviewing (annual, formal discussion about results), and rewarding (adjusting salaries and bonuses based on employee performance and results) were able to improve average return on investment from 5.1 percent to 19.7 percent and increase sales by $150 000 per employee![43] So, in addition to significantly improving the profitability of healthy companies, sound management practices can turn around failing companies.

Research also indicates that managers have an important effect on customer satisfaction. However, many people find this surprising. They don't understand how managers, who are largely responsible for what goes on inside the company, can affect what

DOING THE RIGHT THING

At the U.S. Military Academy, there is a strict code of conduct: "A cadet will not lie, cheat or steal, nor tolerate those who do." The code is concise and unmistakable. Regrettably, there is no equivalent code for managers although there's no doubt they need one. Numerous studies and well-known corporate scandals have revealed the distressing state of managerial ethics in today's business world. Lying to shareholders about profits, cheating to win business, and stealing from companies have become all too common. And, because managers set the standard for others in the workplace, unethical behaviour and practices quickly spread when they don't do the right thing. Therefore, twice in each chapter, you'll find practical, useful advice to help you become a more ethical manager by "Doing the Right Thing."

goes on outside the company. They wonder how managers, who often interact with customers under negative conditions (when customers are angry or dissatisfied), can actually improve customer satisfaction. It turns out that the way managers influence customer satisfaction is through employee satisfaction. When employees are satisfied with their jobs, their bosses, and the companies they work for, they provide much better service to customers.[44] In turn, customers are more satisfied, too.

Review 8: Competitive Advantage Through People

Why does management matter? Well-managed companies are competitive because their work forces are smarter, better trained, more motivated, and more committed. Furthermore, companies that practise good management consistently have greater revenues and profits than companies that don't. Finally, good management matters because good management leads to satisfied employees who, in turn, provide better service to customers. Because employees tend to treat customers the same way that their managers treat them, good management can improve customer satisfaction.

What Really Happened?[45]

At the beginning of this chapter, you read about the challenges facing the Liberal Party of Canada. How might the party respond to its election defeat? Only time will tell. One thing is clear: The electoral defeat was not as bad as everyone had feared. One reason for this is a perception that Paul Martin did achieve a number of important successes during his tenure as prime minister. A *Toronto Star* editorial suggested the following:

> Martin did bring in new rules ... to ensure such bureaucratic and political wrongdoing could not happen again ... he also set up the Gomery commission.... On the policy front too, ... [h]e started by giving new impetus to the renewal of Canada's public health-care system with the $41 billion, 10-year agreement he achieved with the provincial premiers.... Further Martin did commit Canada to do its part by agreeing to abide by the Kyoto accord. And ... he gave new hope to Canada's forgotten aboriginal people with a $5.1 billion package of health-care, housing and education initiatives.

Despite these successes, the party did lose the election. With that said, how might it turn itself around?

Making Things Happen

To start, it should make things happen. But what exactly is it that should happen. One important response is to develop concrete policies on important issues. For instance, a *Globe and Mail* editorial argues that a number of questions need to be answered: "How should Liberals realistically deal with the threat and promise of globalization? How do they juggle the need for security at the border and the vetting of immigrants with the outlook of a trading nation? How should social policy be restructured? The Liberals have a tradition of re-imagining themselves in defeat. After the Tories' massive win in 1984, the Liberals held a policy convention in 1986 followed by expert gatherings on such themes as the economy. They revived that approach in the early 1990s, producing many ideas that wound up in their winning platform in 1993."

Meeting the Competition

The next task would be to meet the competition. Former Liberal policy advisor Tom Axworthy argues that

> Parties sometimes lose because their agenda is not supported by most voters. But the Liberals have a strong policy record. Most Canadians were for daycare, against ballistic missile defence and in favour of balanced budgets and social investments.... But if the Conservatives now have the levers of power, what can Liberals do to change the context? ... The way to do this is ... to look at strengthening assets—the Liberals are still the party of urban Canada, with not one Conservative elected in Montreal, Toronto or Vancouver—and diminishing the negatives by bringing in fresh faces and new voices.

Leading

The third task to be accomplished involves leading the party. Before this can occur, a leader must be chosen. Among those mentioned as strong candidates are Bob Rae (former NDP premier of Ontario), Michael Ignatieff (a newly elected MP, former Harvard professor, and an academic currently employed at the University of Toronto), and Ken Dryden (a former Cabinet Minister in the Martin government and a former goaltender for the Montreal Canadiens).

Organizing People, Projects, and Processes

Finally, aside from leading, meeting the competition, and making things happen, people, projects and processes need to be organized. Former federal cabinet minister John Manley offers some suggestions:

> First, Liberals must, with humility, acknowledge the breach of trust that occurred with the Canadian people. Like it or not ... Canadians had their fill of a governing party that was seemingly always under investigation.... Second, ... [t]he Liberal Party should be a political home for those who are socially progressive [and] economically responsible.... Third, the party must ... focus on the big challenges of the day and prepare a program that appeals to moderate and progressive voters.... Finally, ... the first task of the new leader will be to unite and heal the party.

Key Terms

conceptual skill *(17)*
controlling *(5)*
disseminator role *(15)*
disturbance handler role *(15)*
effectiveness *(5)*
efficiency *(4)*
entrepreneur role *(15)*
figurehead role *(14)*
first-line managers *(12)*
human skill *(17)*
leader role *(14)*
leading *(5)*
liaison role *(14)*
management *(4)*
meta-analysis *(6)*
middle managers *(12)*
monitor role *(15)*
motivation to manage *(17)*
negotiator role *(16)*
organizing *(5)*
planning *(5)*
resource allocator role *(16)*
spokesperson role *(15)*
team leaders *(13)*
technical skills *(17)*
top managers *(10)*

Self-Assessment

IS MANAGEMENT FOR YOU?

As you learned earlier, many managers begin their careers in management with specific notions about what it means to be the boss. Although you may want to manage because of the excitement, status, power, or rewards, knowing how to manage is not automatic; it requires specific skills and competencies as well as a desire to manage. On page 510, in the Assessment Appendix, you will find a 20-question assessment designed to provide insight into your aptitude for management. You will be asked to rate each question according to the following scale:

ML = Most like me
SL = Somewhat like me
NS = Not sure
SU = Somewhat unlike me
MU = Most unlike me

The assessment is meant to establish your baseline ability in the skills covered in this chapter. It will not tell you whether you have "what it takes" to be a manager. It will, however, give you feedback on general skills that influence your overall managerial style. So, turn to page 510 to get started!

Management Decisions

WHO DESERVES THE PROMOTION?

This week was destined to be a difficult one. After eight years, I had finally achieved a long sought-after goal—managing director of a medium-sized public relations firm based in Ottawa. Our firm had experienced steady growth over the last decade due in part to a decision made years ago to focus our resources on helping Canada's provincial and territorial governments promote their positions nationwide. Also tied to this success was a strong sense of teamwork and collegiality among a loyal, committed group of employees. Unfortunately, growth had forced on me an important decision.

Celine, my first boss and long-time mentor, laughed when I asked her what she thought I should do. "You're the one who wanted to be an executive, hotshot. What do *you* think you should do?" she asked with a laugh. "Seriously, I can't make this decision for you. Trust your instincts. But remember, you're going to have to live with the consequences of your decision for a long time."

Celine was right. Whomever I promoted was going to be working with me and supervising one of my units for at least three years. And whomever I didn't promote was going to be disappointed for a long time, too. But who deserved the promotion? Should it go to Mathieu? When I asked him why he wanted the promotion, he said he had earned it by turning in three solid years of performance. Or should it go to Valerie? Valerie's teams had been top producers. When I asked her why she wanted the promotion, she said it was because she was getting burned out in her current job and needed a change. However, she also mentioned that management had been a long-time goal.

Questions

1. Who would you promote, Mathieu or Valerie? Why?
2. In order of importance, name three criteria that companies should use when deciding whom to promote. Explain why each is important and why they can help companies make good promotion decisions.

Management Decisions

EENY MEENY MINY MO ...

You are the regional director of research and development for a mid-sized chemical company. This morning, two project directors called to schedule appointments to see you concerning a memo your office released yesterday informing all staff members of budget cuts for the new fiscal year. Because of factors beyond the company's control—a slowing economy, declining sales, lowered earnings projections, and so forth—company officials have mandated an across-the-board cost reduction of 15 percent in all departments. Unfortunately, this reduction will affect your department the most since research and development costs have averaged 23 percent of the company's total expenditures over the last five years. Despite the fact that every dollar invested in chemical research today will yield two dollars of operating income over six years, only one of the two lead projects your department is working on will be fully funded under the new budget. Both project directors will be campaigning for their specific project, and it will be your decision to choose which one receives full funding and which one does not. As you check your daily calendar for possible meeting times, you recall that both projects are equally viable and are expected to require approximately the same amount of money and resources. In meeting with each project director individually, however, you will need to gather specific information in order to make an unbiased, informed decision.[46]

Questions

1. Assuming the role of decision maker, write the script for the part of the meeting in which you tell your project directors you can fund only one project.
2. Assuming the role of resource allocator, what questions will you likely ask to help you make your decision?

Develop Your Management Potential

INTERVIEW TWO MANAGERS[47]

Welcome to the first "Develop Your Management Potential" activity! These assignments have one purpose: to help you develop your present and future capabilities as a manager. What you will be learning through these assignments is not traditional "book-learning" based on memorization and regurgitation, but practical knowledge and skills that help managers perform their jobs better. Lessons from some of the assignments—for example, goal setting—can be used for immediate benefit. Other lessons will obviously take time to accomplish, but you can still benefit now by making specific plans for future improvement.

Step 1: Interview Two Practising Managers

In her book *Becoming a Manager: Master of a New Identity*, Harvard Business School professor Linda Hill conducted extensive interviews with 19 people in their first year as managers. To learn firsthand what it's like to be a manager, interview two managers you know, asking them some of the same questions, shown below, that Professor Hill asked her managers. Be sure to interview managers with different levels of experience. Interview one person with at least five years' experience as a manager and then interview another person with no more than two years' experience as a manager. Ask the managers these questions:

1. Briefly describe your current position and responsibilities.
2. What do your subordinates expect from you on the job?
3. What are the major stresses and challenges you face on the job?
4. What, if anything, do you dislike about the job?
5. What do you like best about your job?
6. What are the critical differences between average managers and top-performing managers?
7. Think about the skills and knowledge that you need to be effective in your job. What are they and how did you acquire them?
8. What have been your biggest mistakes thus far? Could you have avoided them? If so, how?

Step 2: Prepare to Discuss Your Findings

Prepare to discuss your findings in class or write a report (if assigned by your instructor). What conclusions can you draw from your interview data?

Discussion Questions

1. Junior hockey is an important part of the social fabric of many smaller Canadian cities and towns. Many of these teams are run as businesses. What is the difference between an efficiently run hockey team and an effectively run team?
2. Four management functions are used to organize this text. Describe each briefly and indicate which of the four would clearly be considered different from the traditional management functions.
3. Take a quick look at the career section of your local newspaper. Find one ad that seeks to attract a solid candidate for a middle manager position. With regard to that company and that particular position, what four major responsibilities might a successful candidate be assigned?
4. Go to the Monster.ca Web site. Browse the available jobs by company. Identify one job that looks particularly appealing to you. If you were given the task of hiring an individual for this position, which four sets of characteristics would you look for in such a manager?
5. Despite changes over the last decade, most bank branches still have managers. Think of the manager at the branch nearest you. A few tellers and administrators probably report to this individual. From time to time he or she may make mistakes while performing his or her duties. Describe at least three of the five most important mistakes that he or she might make.

Critical Thinking Video Case

CBC

Visit www.management2e.nelson.com to view this chapter's CBC video case.

Take Two

Biz Flix
8 Mile

Jimmy "B-Rabbit" Smith, Jr. (Eminem) wants to be a successful rapper and to prove that a white man can create moving sounds. He works days at a plant run by the North Detroit Stamping Company and pursues his music at night, sometimes on the plant's grounds. The film's title refers to Detroit's northern boundary, which divides the city's white and African-American populations. This film gives a gritty look at Detroit's hip-hop culture in 1995 and Jimmy's desire to be accepted by it. Eminem's original songs "Lose Yourself" and "8 Mile" received Golden Globe and Academy Award nominations. This scene is an edited composite of two brief sequences involving the stamping plant. The first half of the scene appears early in the film as part of "The Franchise" sequence. The second half appears in the last 25 minutes of the film as part of the "Papa Doc Payback" sequence. In the first part of the scene, Jimmy's car won't start so he rides the city bus to work and arrives late. The second part occurs after Jimmy is beaten by Papa Doc (Anthony Mackie) and Papa Doc's gang. Jimmy's mother (Kim Basinger) returns to their trailer and tells him she won $3200 at bingo. The film continues to its end with Jimmy's last battle (a rapper competition).

What to Watch for and Ask Yourself

1. What is your perception of the quality of Jimmy's job and his work environment?
2. What is the quality of Jimmy's relationship with Manny, his foreman (Paul Bates)? Does the relationship change? If it does, why?
3. How would you react to this type of work experience?

Management Workplace
Theatrical Lighting Systems

When David Milly started Theatrical Lighting Systems in 1981, entertainment lighting was minimal at most. Often, the managers of an entertainment venue would simply leave the house lights on; if they were really sophisticated, they might highlight the performer with a single spotlight. Over the next two decades, however, sophisticated, computer-controlled lighting systems became the norm, and Milly's company grew into a full-service provider of lighting equipment, design, and service. To keep up with his company's growth, Milly had to shift from being the guy in the trusses rigging the lights to being a full-time manager.

What to Watch for and Ask Yourself

1. Which of the four management functions are addressed in the video?
2. Describe David Milly's transition to management.
3. List the different kinds of managers referenced in the video.
4. Does David Milly have what it takes to be a manager? Support your answer with concepts from the chapter.

PHOTO: INDU GHUMAN

Organizational Environments and Cultures

Chapter 2

CHAPTER OUTLINE

LEARNING OBJECTIVES

After reading this chapter, you should be able to

1. discuss how changing environments affect organizations.
2. describe the four components of the general environment.
3. explain the five components of the specific environment.
4. describe the process that companies use to make sense of their changing environments.
5. explain how organizational cultures are created and how they can help companies be successful.

What Would You Do?

It's the summer of 2000 and Tim Hortons seems to be on top of the world as it surveys its empire. A little donut shop set up 36 years earlier by a former hockey player and police officer, it is now one of the strongest franchises in Canada, with annual sales of $1.6 billion, 1700 outlets, and an aggressive expansion plan into the United States. In Canada, it is even predicted that in the next year or two that Tim Hortons will overtake McDonald's in total annual sales. One in three cups of coffee sold in Canada comes from Tim Hortons, and Canada—a country with more donut shops per capita than any other country—seems to be a country in love with coffee and donuts. Canadian soldiers even take tins of Tim Hortons coffee with them on overseas deployment, and one of your competitors, Country Style Donuts, recognizes your dominance and sets its sights on becoming number two in the market—they are not even considering challenging your dominant position. Even the purchase of the company by U.S.–based Wendy's International doesn't seem to have slowed the company down or tainted its image as a Canadian icon. Even though you appear to be the undisputed coffee-and-donuts champion, and may even soon be the biggest fast-food franchise in Canada, you can see the storm clouds gathering on the horizon.[1]

Obesity levels are reaching unprecedented levels and the rates of diabetes are skyrocketing. Canadians, and North Americans in general, are becoming increasingly health conscious. Popular culture is even reflecting the changing landscape of the fast-food industry. In *Super Size Me*, filmmaker Morgan Spurlock decided to only eat McDonald's food for a month, during which time he ate every item on the menu at least once and only super-sized items when asked. The results? Eating 5000 calories per day, Spurlock gained 25 pounds, increased his cholesterol from a healthy 160 to an unhealthy 230, and developed liver problems that later subsided after he lost weight.

With almost a quarter of Canadians obese, obesity is—no pun intended—at epic proportions, and that could affect Tim Hortons in terms of lawsuits, regulation, and complaints from public interest groups. For example, a group of obese U.S. teenagers sued McDonalds', claiming its food had made them fat. While a judge threw the case out, any fast-food restaurant could be a target and the cost of defending the company could easily exceed several million dollars per case, and that's only if you win. Other competitors have responded to the growing public health concerns. At Subway, a 6-inch roast beef sandwich with lettuce, tomatoes, onions, green peppers, pickles, olives, and fat-free honey mustard sauce is just 320 calories and 5 grams of fat. Also, Subway's spokesperson, Jared Fogle, is famous for having lost 250 pounds (about 114 kg) by eating at Subway twice a day.

If the general interest in health-consciousness isn't enough, along comes the Atkins diet. It's so popular that food manufacturers are attempting to have their products "Atkins certified" in order to take advantage of the growing interest in the diet. A central feature of the Atkins diet is to significantly reduce a person's intake of carbohydrates—and some fast-food restaurants have been experimenting with low-carbohydrate foods in response to the craze. The concern about fat and carbohydrates pretty much focuses on what a donut is—fat and carbohydrates. You know it's only a matter of time before more of your competitors will respond to these trends, just as Subway has.

If the growing interest in eating health food wasn't worrying enough, an aggressive new U.S. competitor is entering your market—Krispy Kreme. Although Krispy Kreme has only about a third of the sales (all U.S.) of Tim Hortons, its growth rate has been phenomenal. It has doubled its sales and stores over the last five years, including an incredible 40 percent increase in sales in the last year alone. Even Hollywood has jumped on the Krispy Kreme bandwagon, with Nicole Kidman declaring them "God's gift to donut lovers," and the product has been seen on over 80 TV shows. It now has plans to aggressively enter the Canadian market and take Tim Hortons head on. In the meantime, Tim Hortons's U.S. expansion plans haven't gone well, with the company losing millions of dollars. And now even McDonald's seems to be entering the fray with a plan to open ten McCafés in Ontario.

Should Tim Hortons pay attention to what its customers traditionally want—donuts and coffee—and not healthy food? After all, the list of "healthy" fast-food items that have not sold well is very long: McDonald's Lite Mac, McLean Deluxe, and McSalad Shakers; Wendy's Light Menu; Burger King's low-sodium pickles and veggie burger; and Taco Bell's Border Lights. If you focus on your traditional line of food, how do you respond to the threat of Krispy Kreme?

If you were in charge of Tim Hortons, what would you do?

Even when you are a successful company, remaining successful is a very difficult task. Wherever you look, you see changes and forces beyond your control that threaten your ability to make your new business a success. This chapter examines the internal and external forces that affect companies.

External Environments

external environments all events outside a company that have the potential to influence or affect it

External environments are all the events outside a company that have the potential to influence or affect it. For example, Canada exported more than $10 billion worth of lumber to the United States in 2000. In mid-2002, after many years of threatening to place tariffs on Canadian exports, the United States imposed a 27 percent tariff on softwood lumber. This significantly affected producers in British Columbia, Quebec, Ontario, and Alberta, with exports from Quebec and Ontario falling by more than half. Canadian trade officials and industry groups appealed to the World Trade Organization (WTO) and under the North American Free Trade Agreement (NAFTA). In August 2005 Canada won a major NAFTA judgment, but the U.S. government ignored the ruling and appealed an unfavourable WTO ruling.[2] In the meantime, the effect on some companies and communities has been devastating. Thousands of jobs have been lost, mills have closed, and the economies of entire towns have been ruined.[3] In mid-2006, it appeared that the U.S. and Canadian governments had come to a resolution, but until the final agreement is signed, the industry will continue to struggle.

After reading the next four sections, you should be able to

1. discuss how changing environments affect organizations.
2. describe the four components of the general environment.
3. explain the five components of the specific environment.
4. describe the process that companies use to make sense of their changing environments.

1 CHANGING ENVIRONMENTS

Let's examine the three basic characteristics of changing external environments: environmental change, environmental complexity and munificence, and uncertainty.

Environmental Change

environmental change the rate at which a company's general and specific environments change

stable environment environment in which the rate of change is slow

dynamic environment environment in which the rate of change is fast

punctuated equilibrium theory theory that holds that companies go through long, simple periods of stability (equilibrium), followed by short periods of dynamic, fundamental change (revolution), and ending with a return to stability (new equilibrium)

Environmental change is the rate at which a company's general and specific environments change. In **stable environments**, the rate of environmental change is slow. In **dynamic environments**, the rate of environmental change is fast. While it would seem that companies would either be in stable external environments or dynamic external environments, recent research suggests that companies often experience both stable and dynamic external environments. According to **punctuated equilibrium theory**, companies go through long, simple periods of stability (equilibrium), followed by short, complex periods of dynamic, fundamental change (revolutionary periods), finishing with a return to stability (new equilibrium).[4]

One example of punctuated equilibrium theory is the Canadian airline industry. Twice in the last 30 years, the Canadian airline industry has experienced revolutionary periods. The first occurred with the advent of airline deregulation that began in 1978 in response to U.S. deregulation. Prior to deregulation, the industry was dominated by the "friendly duopoly" of CP Air and Air Canada that shared over 95 percent of the market, but the federal government controlled where airlines could fly, when they could fly, prices they could charge, and the number of flights they could have on a particular route. Although full deregulation was not seen in Canada until 1988, airlines had more choices to make and many competitors such as Wardair, which was primarily a charter airline,

CP PHOTO/LARRY MACDOUGAL

Air Canada and WestJet now exist in a relatively stable two-company environment.

and Pacific Western Airlines, a regional carrier, expanded and new air carriers were started. Competition among the airlines was fierce, and Pacific Western Airlines purchased several smaller airlines, including Wardair. In 1987 it purchased the much larger CP Air to form Canadian Airlines. Canadian Airlines was a truly national carrier, and although somewhat smaller than Air Canada, it was in a position to compete with Air Canada on an even basis. After experiencing substantially increased levels of competition, two companies again dominated the skies, Canadian Airlines and Air Canada, and a period of relative stability was seen. The dominance of these two carriers was first seriously challenged in 1996 with the emergence of WestJet Airlines, which started as a western-based airline. Canadian, too, was a western-based airline. Competition once again increased and a faltering Canadian Airlines was purchased by Air Canada in 2000, leaving only two national carriers, Air Canada and WestJet. Several smaller carriers tried to take advantage of the failure of Canadian Airlines, some of which have since gone bankrupt. Now Air Canada and WestJet dominate the Canadian skies and there appears to be no serious challengers on the horizon. These two periods of stability followed by revolution and regained stability illustrate punctuated equilibrium theory well.[5]

Environmental Complexity and Munificence

Environmental complexity is the number of external factors in the environment that affect organizations. **Simple environments** have few environmental factors, whereas **complex environments** have many environmental factors. For example, the baking industry exists within a relatively simple external environment. Except for more efficient ovens (i.e., technology), bread is baked, wrapped, and delivered fresh to stores each day much as it always has been. Baking bread is a highly competitive, but simple business environment that has experienced few changes.

environmental complexity the number of external factors in the environment that affect organizations

simple environment an environment with few environmental factors

complex environment an environment with many environmental factors

By contrast, in recent years, cereal companies such as Kellogg's, maker of Kellogg's Corn Flakes, Frosted Flakes, Sugar Pops, and other popular cereals, find themselves in a more complex environment in which three significant changes have occurred. The first significant change has been more competition. Twenty-five years ago, Kellogg's competed against just a few cereal companies, such as General Mills and Post. Today, Kellogg's competes against those companies, as well as private-label store brands (IGA, President's Choice, Safeway, etc.).

The second important change in the cereal industry has been significant price cuts. For years, Kellogg's made gross profits of 50 percent on a box of cereal. Yet, with profits that high, private-label store brands could still make a profit of $1 per box by slashing the price that consumers paid.

The third significant change has been the entrance of Wal-Mart into the grocery business. Wal-Mart often relies on cheaper private-label store brands, such as its own soft drinks, produced by Canada's Cott Corporation, and Old Roy dog food. Consumers like these products because they cost substantially less than brand-name products. However, Wal-Mart prefers private-label store brands because, even with their lower prices, the store makes a higher profit on these brands. So when Wal-Mart aggressively expanded into the grocery business in the last few years, Kellogg's saw its market share drop even more as Wal-Mart pushed cheaper private-label cereals. Together, these three changes have made Kellogg's external environment much more complex than it used to be.[6]

environmental munificence
degree to which an organization's external environment has an abundance or scarcity of critical organizational resources

Environmental munificence is the degree to which an organization's external environment has an abundance or scarcity of critical organizational resources. For example, the primary reason that flat-screen, LCD (liquid crystal display) TVs with lifelike pictures are six times more expensive per inch than regular TVs, two times more expensive than rear projection TVs, and 25 percent more expensive than plasma TVs is that there aren't enough LCD screen factories to meet demand. At $2 billion to $3 billion each, LCD factories are the scarce resource in this industry. Without more of them, LCD TV prices will remain high. LCD factories are complex and difficult to build because, like computer chips, LCD flat screens must be made in expensive, super-clean environments. Furthermore, the manufacturing process is complex and difficult to manage because the liquid crystal, which can be ruined by just one speck of dust, must be poured onto glass in a layer thinner than a piece of paper. Finally, even in current LCD factories, production is further restricted because most produce LCD glass panels that are only 43 inches by 49 inches (109 cm by 125 cm). These can be cut into one dozen 17-inch (43 cm) LCD screens for computer monitors, but just two 30-inch (76 cm) LCD screens for TVs. By contrast, only Sharp has a factory that can produce LCD glass panels that are 59 inches by 71 inches (150 cm by 180 cm). In comparison, these larger panels can be cut into as many as eight 32-inch (81 cm) LCD screens for TVs or six 37-inch (94 cm) screens for TVs.[7] To address these shortages, LCD manufacturers plan to build 12 new factories in the next few years at a total cost of between $15 billion and $20 billion.

Uncertainty

uncertainty
extent to which managers can understand or predict which environmental changes and trends will affect their businesses

Exhibit 2.1 shows that environmental change, complexity, and resources (i.e., munificence) affect environmental **uncertainty**, which is how well managers can understand or predict the external changes and trends affecting their businesses. Starting at the left side of the figure, environmental uncertainty is lowest when there is little complexity and change, and resources are plentiful. In these environments, managers feel confident that they can understand and predict the external forces that affect their business. By contrast, the right side of the figure indicates that environmental uncertainty is highest when there is much complexity and change, and resources are scarce. In these environments, managers may not be at all confident that they can understand and predict the external forces affecting their businesses.

Review 1: Changing Environments

Environmental change, complexity, and munificence are the basic components of external environments. Environmental change is the rate at which conditions or events affecting a business change. Environmental complexity is the number of external factors in an external environment. Environmental munificence is the scarcity or abundance of resources available in the external environment. The greater the rate of environmental change and environmental complexity and the lower the environmental munificence, the less confident managers are that they can understand and predict the trends affecting

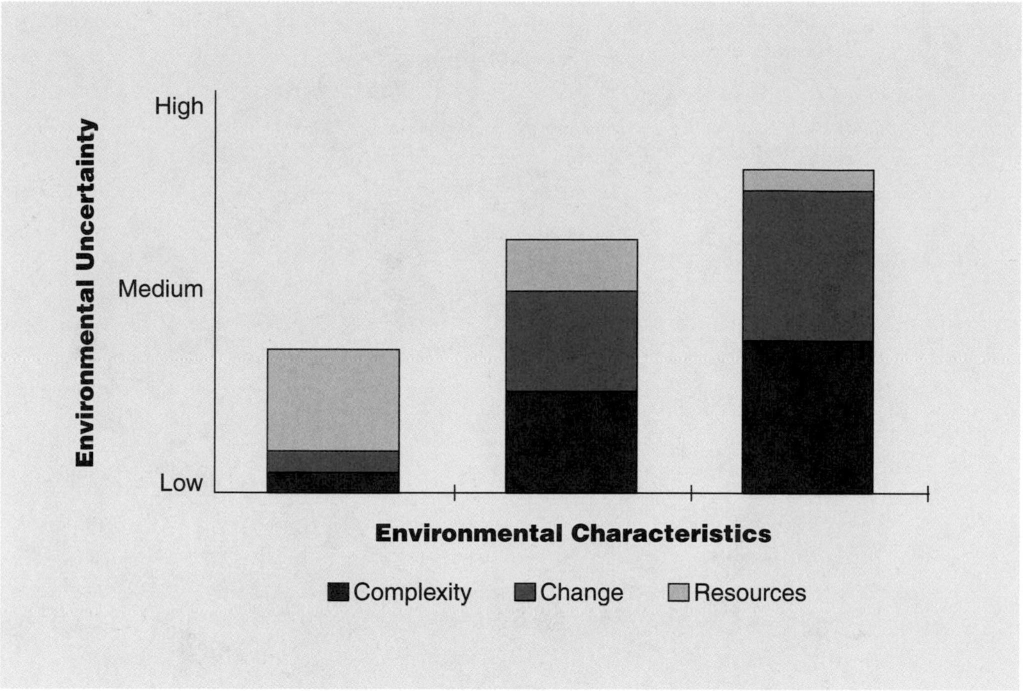

EXHIBIT 2.1
Environmental Change, Complexity, and Munificence

their businesses. According to punctuated equilibrium theory, companies experience periods of stability followed by short periods of dynamic, fundamental change, followed by a return to periods of stability.

2 GENERAL ENVIRONMENT

Exhibit 2.2 shows the two kinds of external environments that influence organizations: the general environment and the specific environment. The **general environment** consists of the economy and the technological, sociocultural, and political/legal trends that indirectly affect all organizations. Changes in any sector of the general environment eventually affect most organizations. By contrast, each organization has a **specific environment** that is unique to that firm's industry and directly affects the way it conducts day-to-day business. The specific environment, which will be discussed in detail in the next section of this chapter, includes customers, competitors, suppliers, industry regulation, and advocacy groups.

general environment
the economic, technological, sociocultural, and political trends that indirectly affect all organizations

specific environment
the customer, competitor, supplier, industry regulation, and public pressure group trends that are unique to an industry and that directly affect how a company does business

Let's take a closer look at the four components of the general environment that indirectly affect all organizations: economy, technological component, sociocultural component, and political/legal component.

Economy

The current state of a country's economy affects most organizations operating in it. A growing economy means that, in general, more people are working and therefore have relatively more money to spend. More products are being bought and sold than in a static or shrinking economy. While a growing economy doesn't mean that sales of an individual firm are necessarily growing, it does provide an environment favourable to business growth.

For example, in 2005 Canada was in its 14th straight year of economic expansion.[8] So, according to economic statistics, Canadian businesses exist in a relatively healthy, growing economy. In contrast, Japan, after having suffered from a decade of recession, could be finally turning an economic corner. Japanese companies such as Mazda Motors had been reporting regular, if not record, losses. Unemployment, while still low by Canadian standards, had been growing. Now there are signs of an economic turnaround

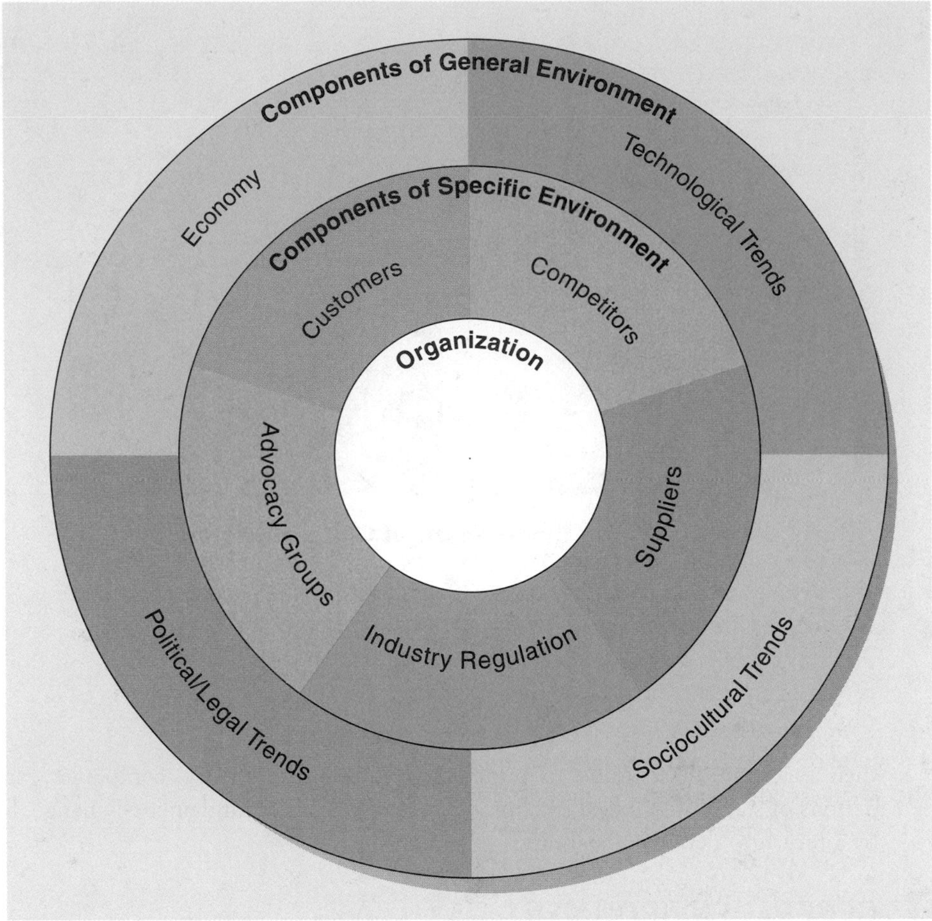

EXHIBIT 2.2
General and Specific Environments

but economists are still unsure as to whether the upturn is sustainable, especially given that the Japanese economy contracted in the last quarter of 2004.[9]

Of course, by the time you read this, the Japanese economy could be enjoying healthy growth rather than struggling to recover, and the Canadian economy could be shrinking as the U.S. economy slows in the wake of Hurricane Katrina and takes its toll on the Canadian economy. Because the economy influences basic business decisions, such as whether to hire more employees, expand production, or take out loans to purchase equipment, managers scan their economic environments for signs of change. Unfortunately, the economic statistics that managers rely on when making these decisions are notoriously poor predictors of *future* economic activity. A manager who decides to hire ten more employees because economic data suggest future growth could very well have to lay those newly hired workers off when the economic growth does not occur. In fact, a famous economic study found that at the beginning of a business quarter (a period of only three months), even the most accurate economic forecasters could not accurately predict whether economic activity would grow or shrink in that same quarter![10]

business confidence indices
indices that show managers' level of confidence about future business growth

Because economic statistics are such poor predictors, some managers try to predict future economic activity by keeping track of business and consumer confidence. **Business confidence indices** show how confident managers are about future business growth. For example, the Conference Board of Canada (www.conferenceboard.ca) quarterly asks CEOs of approximately 1000 Canadian businesses to express their optimism (or pessimism) about future business sales and prospects. They also survey Canadian consumers about their optimism about the Canadian economy. Managers often prefer business and consumer confidence indices to economic statistics, because they know that the level of confidence reported by real managers and consumers affects their purchasing decisions. In other words, it's reasonable to expect managers and consumers to make decisions today that are in line with their expectations concerning the economy's future. So if the Conference Board of Canada's Index of Business Confidence or Index of Consumer Confidence suddenly drops, managers would think hard about hiring new employees or might stop plans to increase production for fear of being stuck with unsold inventory should the economy slow dramatically in the future.

Technological Component

Technology is the knowledge, tools, and techniques used to transform inputs (raw materials, information, etc.) into outputs (products and services). For example, the knowledge of authors, editors, and artists (technology) and the use of equipment such as computers and printing presses (also technology) transformed paper, ink, and glue (raw material inputs) into this book (the finished product).

technology
knowledge, tools, and techniques used to transform inputs (raw material) into outputs (finished products or services)

Changes in technology can help companies provide better products or produce their products more efficiently. For example, advances in surgical techniques and imaging equipment have made open-heart surgery much faster and safer in recent years. While technological changes can benefit a business, they can also threaten it. For example, over the last few years, with sales of blank CDs up 40 percent, and more than 400 million songs downloaded *for free* at Kazaa.com alone (the largest music file swapping Web site), it's no surprise that sales of music CDs have dropped 26 percent between 1999 and 2002.[11] British college student Dave Watson says, "You'd be hard-pressed to find a group of students who've never downloaded music. You can't stop them, as long as it's free."[12] How extensive is this technological threat to the music industry? When a *Wired* magazine reporter logged on to Kazaa on a quiet Monday morning, he found at least a hundred copies of each song on the Billboard 100 and 13 of the 15 songs on Mariah Carey's new CD, which hadn't even been released to the public.[13] Companies must embrace new technology and find effective ways to use it to improve products and services or decrease costs. If they don't, they will lose out to those that do. Chapter 10, "Innovation and Change," provides a more in-depth discussion of how technology affects a company's competitive advantage.

Sociocultural Component

The sociocultural component of the general environment refers to the demographic characteristics and general behaviour, attitudes, and beliefs of people in a particular society. Sociocultural changes and trends influence organizations in two important ways.

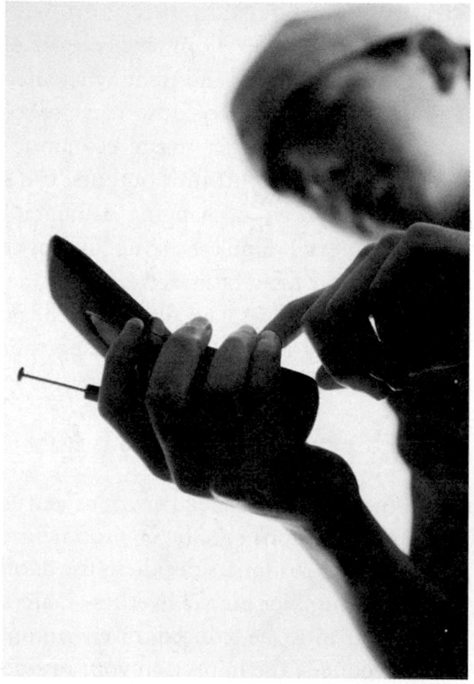
PHOTODISC GREEN/GETTY IMAGES

Many parents have provided teenagers with cell phones to help keep them in touch with their children, partly as a result of an increasing number of women in the work force.

First, changing demographic characteristics, such as the number of people with particular skills, or the growth or decline in particular population segments (single or married; old or young; men or women; or visible minorities, Aboriginals, or the disabled, etc.) affect how companies run their businesses. For example, women with children are much more likely to work outside the home today than 30 years ago. In 1976, only 39 percent of women with children under 16 years old and 28 percent of women with children under three years old worked outside the home. In 2003, those percentages had risen to 72 percent and 63 percent, respectively.[14] Because of these changes, many more companies now offer child-care as a benefit to attract and retain scarce, talented workers of both genders. One example is Hydro One, formerly known as Ontario Hydro, which provides space and pays the occupancy costs for Hydro Kids, its on-site daycare.[15]

Second, sociocultural changes in behaviour, attitudes, and beliefs also affect the demand for a business's products and services. Today's harried worker/parent can hire baby-proofing agencies (to baby-proof their homes), emergency babysitting services, bill payers, birthday party planners, kiddie taxi services, personal assistants, and personal chefs.[16] All of these services are a direct result of the need for free time, which is a result of the sociocultural changes associated with a much higher percentage of women in the workplace.

Political/Legal Component

The political/legal component of the general environment includes the legislation, regulation, and court decisions that govern and regulate business behaviour. Throughout the last decade, new legislation and regulations have placed additional responsibilities on companies. Unfortunately, many managers are unaware of these new responsibilities. For example, the Canadian Human Rights Act prohibits discrimination against those who are infected with HIV/AIDS. Discrimination against anyone with HIV/AIDS could result in the company having to pay damages and back pay.

Many managers are also unaware of the potential legal risks associated with traditional managerial decisions such as recruiting, hiring, and firing employees. Indeed, it is increasingly common for businesses and managers to be sued for negligent hiring and supervision, defamation, invasion of privacy, emotional distress, fraud, and misrepresentation during employee recruitment.[17] Likewise, there were few wrongful dismissal cases (i.e., unfairly firing employees) in the past but, for example, it is estimated that about 10 percent of all trials scheduled in Calgary's Court of Queen's Bench involve allegations of wrongful dismissal, and court awards can exceed $100 000 and are increasing in size.[18]

Not everyone agrees that companies face severe legal risks. Indeed, many believe that government should do more to regulate and restrict business behaviour, and that it should be easier for average citizens to sue dishonest or negligent corporations. From a managerial perspective, the best medicine against legal risk is prevention. As a manager, it is your responsibility to educate yourself about the laws and regulations and potential lawsuits that could affect your business. Failure to do so may put you and your company at risk of sizable penalties, fines, or legal charges.

Review 2: General Environment

The general environment consists of economic, technological, sociocultural, and political/legal events and trends that affect all organizations. Because the economy influences basic business decisions, managers often use economic statistics and business confidence indices to predict future economic activity. Changes in technology, which is used to transform inputs into outputs, can be a benefit or a threat to a business. Sociocultural trends, such as changing demographic characteristics, affect how companies run their businesses. Similarly, sociocultural changes in behaviour, attitudes, and beliefs affect the demand for a business's products and services. Court decisions and revised federal and provincial laws have placed much larger political/legal responsibilities on companies. The best way to manage legal responsibilities is to educate managers and employees about laws and regulations and potential lawsuits that could affect a business.

3 SPECIFIC ENVIRONMENT

In contrast to general environments that indirectly influence organizations, changes in an organization's specific environment directly affect the way a company conducts its business. If customers decide to use another product, or a competitor cuts prices 10 percent, or a supplier can't deliver raw materials, or federal regulators specify that industry pollutants must be reduced, or environmental groups accuse your company of selling unsafe products, the impact on your business is immediate.

Let's examine how the different aspects of the specific environment affect businesses. These can be broken down into the customer component, competitor component, supplier component, industry regulation component, and advocacy groups.

Customer Component

Customers purchase products and services. Companies cannot exist without customer support. Therefore, monitoring customers' changing wants and needs is critical to business success.

There are two basic strategies for monitoring customers: reactive and proactive. *Reactive customer monitoring* is identifying and addressing customer trends and problems after they occur. One reactive strategy is to identify customer concerns by listening closely to customer complaints. Not only does listening to complaints help identify problems, but the way in which companies respond to complaints indicates how closely they are attending to customer concerns. For example, companies that respond quickly to customers' letters of complaint are viewed much more favourably than companies that are slow to respond or never respond. In particular, studies have shown that when a company's follow-up letter thanks customers for writing, offers a sincere, specific response to the customer's complaint (i.e., not a form letter, but an explanation of how the problem will be handled), and contains a small gift, coupons, or a refund to make up for the problem, customers will be much more likely to purchase products or services again from that company.[19] For example, when Tim Hortons head office receives a customer complaint, a district manager immediately visits the franchise in question in order to respond to the customer by the end of the day.[20] By contrast, companies that don't respond promptly to customer complaints are likely to find customer rants and tirades posted publicly on places like www.planetfeedback.com (a Google search will reveal many more of these types of sites, some specifically targeting a single company). Customers hope that posting complaints on these sites will force someone to address their problems. It worked for Lena West. The day after she posted a complaint against Budget Rent-a-Car, she received an e-mail containing an apology and a promise to solve her problem.[21]

Proactive monitoring of customers means trying to sense events, trends, and problems before they occur (or before customers complain). For example, over the next few years, more stores that sell toys will offer electronic gift cards—not gift certificates, but gift cards—that are preprogrammed with a dollar amount and are "swiped" like credit cards. With kids' bedrooms stuffed full of every toy you can think of, savvy retailers have already noticed that parents and grandparents would rather give gift cards because they don't have to worry about getting the wrong toy or a toy that the kids already have.[22] Likewise, an example of proactive monitoring in the fast-food industry is multi-branding, where two or more food chains share space under the same roof. Multi-branding brings in more customers by giving them more choice. For example, Wendy's and Tim Hortons are often located together in order to increase sales.

Competitor Component

Competitors are companies in the same industry that sell similar products or services to customers. GM, Ford, and DaimlerChrysler all compete for automobile customers. CBC, CTV, and Global compete for TV viewers' attention. And Tim Hortons, Subway, and McDonald's compete for fast-food customers' dollars. Often, the difference between business success and failure comes down to whether your company is doing a better job of satisfying customer wants and needs than your competitors. Consequently, companies need to keep close track of what their competitors are doing. To do this, managers perform what's called a **competitive analysis**, which is deciding who your competitors are, anticipating competitors' moves, and determining competitors' strengths and weaknesses. Surprisingly, because they tend to focus on only two or three well-known competitors with similar goals and resources, managers often do a poor job of identifying potential competitors.[23]

competitors
companies in the same industry that sell similar products or services to customers

competitive analysis
a process for monitoring competitors that involves identifying competitors, anticipating their moves, and determining their strengths and weaknesses

DOING THE RIGHT THING

THE TEN COMMANDMENTS FOR ETHICAL COMPETITIVE ANALYSIS

Sometimes, in their zeal to dig up information about competitors, managers and employees commit unethical or illegal acts such as digging through trash dumpsters on a competitor's property or paying a competitor's employees for information about secret designs or components. Fuld & Company, a major consulting firm in competitive intelligence, offers these "ten commandments" for ethical competitive analysis:

- Thou shalt not lie when representing thyself.
- Thou shalt observe thy company's legal guidelines as set forth by the legal department.
- Thou shalt not tape-record a conversation.
- Thou shalt not bribe.
- Thou shalt not plant eavesdropping devices.
- Thou shalt not deliberately mislead anyone in an interview.
- Thou shalt neither obtain from nor give price information to thy competitor.
- Thou shalt not swap misinformation.
- Thou shalt not steal a trade secret (or steal employees away in hopes of learning a trade secret).
- Thou shalt not knowingly press someone for information if it may jeopardize that person's job or reputation.[26]

The second mistake managers make when analyzing the competition is to underestimate potential competitors' capabilities. When this happens, managers don't take the steps they should to continue to improve their products or services. The result can be significant decreases in both market share and profits.

For nearly a decade, traditional phone companies have ignored the threat to their business from VOIP (voice over Internet protocol)—that is, the ability to make telephone calls over the Internet. Early on, software products made it possible to make inexpensive long-distance phone calls on the Internet. All you needed was an Internet service provider; a computer with a sound card, speakers, and a microphone; and Internet phone software. The sound quality was only as good as AM radio, but since the calls were so much cheaper and people were used to poor-quality sound on their cell phones, it didn't matter.[24]

Today, though, because phone companies were slow to adopt VOIP capabilities themselves, they're facing a rash of new, unexpected VOIP competitors, all of whom plan to slash prices and take their market share using the high-speed Internet services connect to peoples' homes. Vonage (www.vonage.ca), an Internet phone company, charges just $19.99 per month (maybe less by the time you read this) for unlimited calling in Canada, the United States, and Puerto Rico. Its international long-distance charges are generally cheaper than your local long-distance provider. How much of a threat is Internet phone service to traditional phone companies today? Jeff Pulver, CEO of Pulver.com, which owns Free World Dialup, an Internet phone company, said that within the next few years, "it's quite possible that 50% or more of voice traffic will take place off the traditional public telephone network and run on the Internet wireless or other systems."[25]

Supplier Component

Suppliers are companies that provide material, human, financial, and informational resources to other companies. Stelco, Canada's largest steel producer, buys iron ore from suppliers to make steel products. When IBM sells a mainframe computer, it also provides support staff, engineers, and other technical consultants to the company that bought the computer. If you're shopping for desks, chairs, and office supplies, chances are Office Depot will be glad to help your business open a revolving charge account to pay for your purchases.

suppliers
companies that provide material, human, financial, and informational resources to other companies

supplier dependence
degree to which a company relies on a supplier because of the importance of the supplier's product to the company and the difficulty of finding other sources of that product

A key factor influencing the relationship between companies and their suppliers is how dependent they are on each other.[27] **Supplier dependence** is the degree to which a company relies on a supplier because of the importance of the supplier's product to the company and the difficulty of finding other sources of that product. Supplier dependence is very strong in the diamond business, given that De Beers Consolidated Mines provides 65 percent of the wholesale diamonds in the world. Because De Beers typically offers better diamonds at cheaper prices, it has dominated the diamond industry for more than a century, controlling the supply, price, and quality of the best diamonds on the market. An example of the degree of this control is that De Beers' 125 customers, or "sightholders," as they're known in the industry, are summoned to De Beers' London office ten times a year and given a shoebox of diamonds that they have to buy. If they refuse, they lose the opportunity to purchase any more diamonds. Today, De Beers is considering selling diamonds under the De Beers brand name, putting it in direct competition with each of its 125 sightholders, but there is little the sightholders can do. Said one, "Imagine if the Ford car company said, 'I'm going to make a bad car this year, and you have to buy it or I'll never sell you a car again.'"[28]

Buyer dependence is the degree to which a supplier relies on a buyer because of the importance of that buyer to the supplier and the difficulty of selling its products to other buyers. For example, because it believed that the clothes sold in its stores were too expensive, Wal-Mart's Canadian division sent letters to its clothing suppliers, demanding a "retroactive, nonnegotiable price rollback of between 4 and 10 percent." So if Wal-Mart had purchased $100 000 of goods from a supplier in the last six months, it expected to receive a refund from the supplier totalling between $4000 and $10 000. The suppliers were furious, but had little choice since Wal-Mart was one of their largest customers.[29]

As Wal-Mart's demand indicates, greater buyer or seller dependence can lead to **opportunistic behaviour**, in which one party benefits at the expense of the other. Opportunistic behaviour between buyers and suppliers will never be completely eliminated. However, many companies believe that both buyers and suppliers can benefit by improving the buyer–supplier relationship. General Motors, for example, which has a long history of adversarial relationships with its suppliers, has an "Ambassador Program." The Ambassador Program is designed to improve communication between GM and its suppliers by assigning a GM executive (but not the GM executive who makes purchases from the company) to meet regularly with the supplier to discuss problems or new ideas. In contrast to opportunistic behaviour, buyer–supplier transactions such as GM's Ambassador Program emphasize **relationship behaviour**, which focuses on establishing a mutually beneficial, long-term relationship between buyers and suppliers. Like General Motors, the trend in the last decade is for companies to reduce the number of suppliers they deal with and to improve the relationships they have with remaining suppliers.[30]

buyer dependence
degree to which a supplier relies on a buyer because of the importance of that buyer to the supplier and the difficulty of selling its products to other buyers

opportunistic behaviour
transaction in which one party in the relationship benefits at the expense of the other

relationship behaviour
mutually beneficial, long-term exchanges between buyers and suppliers

industry regulation
regulations and rules that govern the business practices and procedures of specific industries, businesses, and professions

Industry Regulation Component

In contrast to the political/legal component of the general environment that affects all businesses, the **industry regulation** component consists of regulations and rules that govern the business practices and procedures of specific industries, businesses, and professions. Regulatory agencies and government departments affect businesses by creating and enforcing rules and regulations to protect consumers, workers, or society as a whole. For example, after many years of debate, the federal government passed the Employment Equity Act, which is enforced by the Canadian Human Rights Commission (www.chrc-ccdp.ca). This act places a responsibility on federally regulated employers to increase the representation of four historically disadvantaged groups (women, Aboriginals, visible minorities, and persons with disabilities). In addition, it also enforces the Canadian Human Rights Act, which places further responsibilities on federally regulated employers. Failure to comply with the Employment Equity Act or the Human Rights Act can lead to fines of as much as $50 000. Not only must one be aware of the acts themselves, employers must constantly monitor regulations under the act and new policies developed by the Canadian Human Rights Commission.

There are almost 100 federal government agencies, departments, and regulatory commissions that can affect nearly any kind of business (see http://canada.gc.ca/depts/major/depind_e.html). Exhibit 2.3 lists some of the most influential federal agencies and commissions.

However, businesses are not just subject to federal regulations. They must also meet provincial, county, and city regulations, too. Surveys indicate that managers rank keeping up to date with and implementing government regulations as one of the most demanding and frustrating parts of their jobs.

DOING THE RIGHT THING

DEALING WITH GIFTS AND SUPPLIERS

In hopes of getting a buyer's business or getting more business, suppliers sometimes offer buyers trips to exotic locations, dinners at expensive restaurants, or expensive gifts. Excessive gift giving and receiving creates a conflict of interest between what's best for the company (purchasing items of the best quality and cost) and what's personally best for the buyer who receives the gifts. Follow these general guidelines to avoid conflicts of interest:

- Remember that there is no such thing as a free lunch.
- Make sure that business meals and entertainment (parties, outings, sporting events) have a valid business purpose and that the buyer and the supplier take turns paying for or hosting them.
- Don't accept gifts worth more than $25 in value. If an offered gift is worth $25, report it to your manager who can decide whether it is appropriate to keep the gift.
- Never accept cash or cash equivalents, such as gift certificates.
- Don't accept discounts on goods and services, unless they are generally available to others.
- Don't accept offers to own stock in suppliers' companies.
- Don't allow personal friendships with suppliers to influence buying decisions.[31]

FEDERAL AGENCY	REGULATORY RESPONSIBILITIES
Environmental Assessment Agency www.ceaa-acee.gc.ca	Reduces and controls pollution through research, monitoring, standard setting, and enforcement activities
Canadian Human Rights Commission www.chrc-ccdp.ca	Promotes fair hiring and promotion practices
Canadian Radio-television and Telecommunications Commission (CRTC) www.crtc.gc.ca	Regulates communications by radio, television, wire, satellite, and cable
Bank of Canada www.bank-banque-canada.ca	As the nation's central bank, controls interest rates and money supply, and monitors the Canadian banking system to produce a growing economy with stable prices
Competition Tribunal www.ct-tc.gc.ca	Restricts unfair methods of business competition and misleading advertising
Health Canada www.hc-sc.gc.ca	Protects nation's health by making sure food, drugs, and cosmetics are safe
Canadian Industrial Relations Board www.cirb-ccri.gc.ca	Monitors union elections and stops companies from engaging in unfair labour practices
Canadian Centre for Occupational Health and Safety www.ccohs.ca	Saves lives, prevents injuries, and protects the health of workers

EXHIBIT 2.3
Federal Regulatory Agencies and Commissions

Advocacy Groups

Advocacy groups are groups of concerned citizens who band together to try to influence the business practices of specific industries, businesses, and professions. The members of a group generally share the same point of view on a particular issue. For example, environmental advocacy groups might try to get manufacturers to reduce smokestack pollution emissions. Unlike the industry regulation component of the specific environment, advocacy groups cannot force organizations to change their practices. However, they can use a number of techniques to try to influence companies: public communications, media advocacy, and product boycotts.

advocacy groups
groups of concerned citizens who band together to try to influence the business practices of specific industries, businesses, and professions

The **public communications** approach relies on *voluntary* participation by the news media and the advertising industry to get an advocacy group's message out. For example, the Canadian Cancer Society (www.cancer.ca) undertakes public information campaigns on a variety of issues, including tobacco use and diets, that aims to reduce the rate of cancer in Canada by reducing smoking rates and improving people's eating habits. To accomplish its goals, the Canadian Cancer Society makes heavy use of public service announcements on TV and radio (as part of their community service, TV and radio stations donate this time). It also maintains an extensive Web site, provides a toll-free number to disseminate cancer information, provides a community services directory, issues news releases, and works in conjunction with other groups to make Canadians more aware of cancer-related issues.

public communications
an advocacy group tactic that relies on voluntary participation by the news media and the advertising industry to get an advocacy group's message out

In contrast to the public communications approach, media advocacy is a much more aggressive form of advocacy. A **media advocacy** approach typically involves framing issues as public issues (i.e., affecting everyone); exposing questionable, exploitative, or unethical practices; and forcing media coverage by buying media time or creating controversy that is likely to receive extensive news coverage. People for the Ethical Treatment of Animals (PETA), which has offices around the world, uses controversial publicity stunts and advertisements to try to change the behaviour of large organizations, fashion designers, medical researchers, and anyone else it believes is hurting or mistreating animals. PETA's co-founder and president Ingrid Newkirk says, "People now know that if they do something ghastly to an animal, they can't necessarily get away with it. When we

media advocacy
an advocacy group tactic of framing issues as public issues, exposing questionable, exploitative, or unethical practices, and forcing media coverage by buying media time or creating controversy that is likely to receive extensive news coverage

started, nobody knew what animal rights meant.... Now, it's an issue." PETA protesters have skated in only bikini briefs on the Rideau Canal in Ottawa in –25°C weather while wearing banners saying, "We'd Rather Bare Skin Than Wear Skin." From PETA's perspective, any animal-based product is bad. One of PETA's latest protests is the distribution of 2000 blood-covered, knife-holding, "evil Colonel Sanders" bobble-head dolls to news organizations and KFC restaurants. PETA spokesman Joe Hinkle said, "We'd like them to stop breeding and drugging chickens so that they grow so big that they actually cripple under their own bulk." KFC issued this response, saying, "PETA has disparaged our brand and misrepresented the truth about our responsible industry-leading animal welfare standards. KFC is committed to the humane treatment of chickens."[32]

A **product boycott** is a tactic in which an advocacy group actively tries to convince consumers to not purchase a company's product or service. For example, Pamela Anderson narrated a five-minute video that called for a boycott of KFC because she felt that chickens used for their products were being mistreated. It was produced by PETA and distributed on the organization's Web site.[33]

product boycott
an advocacy group tactic of protesting a company's actions by convincing consumers not to purchase its product or service

Review 3: Specific Environment

The specific environment is made up of five components: customers, competitors, suppliers, industry regulators, and advocacy groups. Companies can monitor customers' needs by identifying customer problems after they occur or by anticipating problems before they occur. However, because they tend to focus on well-known competitors, managers often underestimate their competition or do a poor job of identifying future competitors. Since suppliers and buyers are very dependent on each other, that dependence sometimes leads to opportunistic behaviour, in which one benefits at the expense of the other. Regulatory agencies affect businesses by creating rules and then enforcing them, and the number of rules and regulations continues to increase. Advocacy groups cannot regulate organization practices. However, through public communications, media advocacy, and product boycotts, they try to convince companies to change their practices.

4 MAKING SENSE OF CHANGING ENVIRONMENTS

In Chapter 1, you learned that managers are responsible for making sense of their business environments. However, our just-completed discussions of the general and specific environments indicate that making sense of business environments is not an easy task. Because external environments can be dynamic, confusing, and complex, managers use a three-step process to make sense of the changes in their external environments. The steps are environmental scanning, interpreting environmental factors, and acting on threats and opportunities.

Environmental Scanning

Environmental scanning is searching the environment for important events or issues that might affect an organization. Managers scan the environment to stay up to date on important factors in their industry. Managers also scan their environments to reduce uncertainty. For example, with one out of every four new car buyers purchasing highly profitable sports utility vehicles (SUVs), auto executives haven't paid much attention to environmental groups' complaints about SUVs' extremely poor gas mileage. Now, however, with market research showing that current SUV owners are unhappy with their vehicles' poor gas mileage and that potential car buyers in their teens and 20s are beginning to express strong disapproval of SUVs as well, auto executives are beginning to pay attention—because their sales and profits could be affected. James Schroer, DaimlerChrysler's executive vice president for sales and marketing, says that the increasingly negative view of SUVs is "a big deal, and it's real."[34]

environmental scanning
searching the environment for important events or issues that might affect an organization

Organizational strategies also affect environmental scanning. In other words, managers pay close attention to trends and events that are directly related to their companies' abilities to compete in the marketplace.[35] A major trend that is affecting television advertising is the increasing use of digital video recorders (DVRs). DVRs allow people to record TV shows and watch them at a later time. Of course, this allows people to easily skip the commercials, a trend that affects both TV stations, who derive revenue from the ads, and the companies who advertise on TV. In response to this matter, Montreal-based etc.tv Inc. has launched a pilot program that offers viewers interactive ads. An icon appearing in the corner of the TV during ads allows viewers to access video on demand. These videos will be ads that run from 2 to 20 minutes. Many hope that this flexibility in advertising will create new advertising strategies that will allow companies to reach their target market. Large organizations such as Procter & Gamble and the National Bank of Canada have already signed up for the service. This practice may be an interesting strategy to deal with environmental changes.[36]

Environmental scanning is important because it contributes to organizational performance. Environmental scanning helps managers detect environmental changes and problems before they become organizational crises.[37] Furthermore, companies whose CEOs do more environmental scanning have higher profits.[38] CEOs in better-performing firms scan their firms' environments more frequently and scan more key factors in their environments in more depth and detail than do CEOs in poorer-performing firms.[39]

Interpreting Environmental Factors

After scanning, managers determine what environmental events and issues mean to the organization. Typically, managers view environmental events and issues as either threats or opportunities. When managers interpret environmental events as threats, they take steps to protect the company from further harm. For example, in France, the neighbourhood boulangerie, boucherie, fromagerie, patisserie, and poissonnerie (bakery, butcher, cheese, pastry, and fish shops) have begun to go out of business in large numbers. Their existence is now threatened by the Carrefour, huge hypermarkets that are sometimes as large as three football fields. French shoppers load up on cartloads of groceries once a week at the Carrefour to save scarce time and money. One of the best buys is France's traditional loaf of bread, the baguette, which sells for about $1.50 at small bakeries but goes for 60 cents at the hypermarket. So with their businesses in decline, the

AP/WIDE WORLD PHOTOS

Environmental factors such as the rise of the Carrefour in France have forced many smaller, specialized food retailers out of business.

neighbourhood boulangerie, boucherie, fromagerie, patisserie, and poissonnerie have turned to the French government for help, asking it to enact laws limiting construction of new hypermarkets. They're also asking the French government to prevent hypermarkets from selling products below cost, a practice that hypermarkets say they don't use.[40]

By contrast, when managers interpret environmental events as opportunities, they will consider strategic alternatives for taking advantage of the event to improve company performance. In the snack business, Hostess Frito-Lay saw opportunities in the increasing demand for healthier snacks. By being quick to market with Baked Frito-Lay Potato Crisps, Baked Tostitos, and Rold Gold Fat Free Pretzels, Hostess Frito-Lay captured a large share of the Canadian low-fat snack market.[41]

Acting on Threats and Opportunities

After scanning for information on environmental events and issues, and interpreting them as threats or opportunities, managers have to decide how to respond to these environmental factors. However, deciding what to do under conditions of uncertainty is difficult. Managers are never completely confident that they have all the information they need, or that they correctly understand the information they have.

Because it is impossible to comprehend all the factors and changes, managers rely on simplified models of external environments called cognitive maps. **Cognitive maps** summarize the perceived relationships between environmental factors and possible organizational actions. For example, the cognitive map shown in Exhibit 2.4 represents a small clothing store owner's interpretation of her business environment. The map shows three kinds of variables. The first, shown as rectangles, are environmental factors such as Wal-Mart or a large mall 20 minutes away. The second, shown in ovals, are potential actions that the store owner might take, such as a low-cost strategy; a good value, good service strategy; or a large selection of the latest fashions strategy. The third, shown as trapezoids, are company strengths, such as low employee turnover, and weaknesses, such as small size.

cognitive maps
graphic depictions of how managers believe environmental factors relate to possible organizational actions

EXHIBIT 2.4
Cognitive Maps

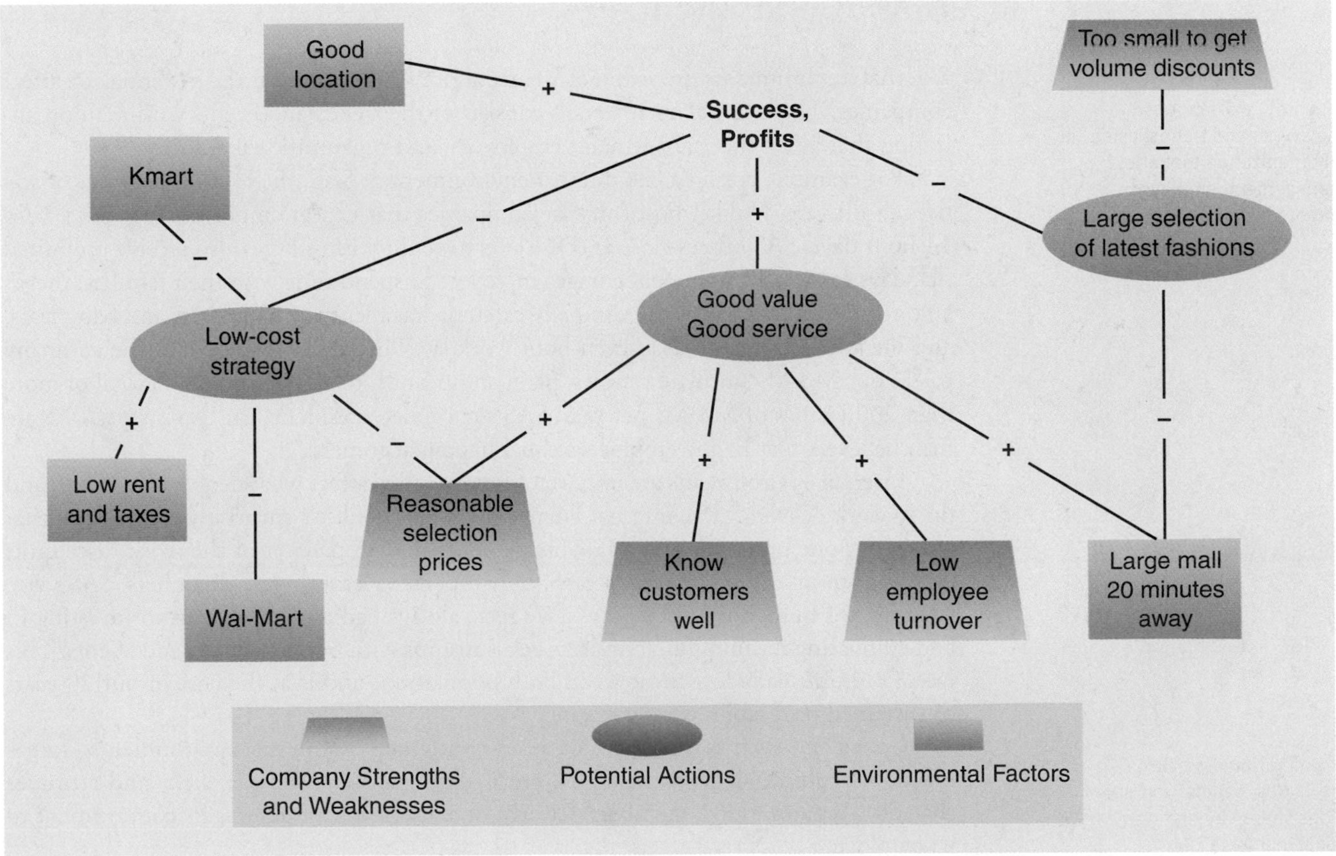

The arrows on the map indicate whether the manager believes there is a positive or negative relationship between variables. For example, the manager believes that a low-cost strategy wouldn't work, because Wal-Mart and Zellers are nearby. Offering a large selection of the latest fashions would not work either—not with the small size of the store and that large nearby mall. However, this manager believes that a good value, good service strategy would lead to success and profits, because of low employee turnover, knowing customers well, a reasonable selection of clothes at reasonable prices, and a good location.

In the end, managers must complete all three steps—environmental scanning, interpreting environmental factors, and acting on threats and opportunities—to make sense of changing external environments. Environmental scanning helps managers more accurately interpret their environments and take actions that improve company performance. Through scanning, managers keep tabs on what competitors are doing, identify market trends, and stay alert to current events that affect their companies' operations. Armed with the environmental information they have gathered, managers can then take action to minimize the impact of threats and turn opportunities into increased profits.

Review 4: Making Sense of Changing Environments

Managers use a three-step process to make sense of external environments: environmental scanning, interpreting information, and action. Managers scan their environments based on their organizational strategies, their need for up-to-date information, and their need to reduce uncertainty. When managers identify environmental events as threats, they take steps to protect the company from harm. When managers identify environmental events as opportunities, they formulate alternatives for taking advantage of them to improve company performance. Using cognitive maps can help managers visually summarize the relationships between environmental factors and the actions they might take to deal with them.

Internal Environments

internal environment
the events and trends inside an organization that affect management, employees, and organizational culture

External environments are external trends and events that have the potential to affect companies. The **internal environment** consists of the trends and events within an organization that affect the management, employees, and organizational culture.

For example, consider the internal environment at SAS, the leading provider of statistical software. Unlike most software companies that expect employees to work 12- to 14-hour days, SAS offices close at 6 P.M. every evening. Employees also receive unlimited sick days each year. And to encourage employees to spend time with their families, there's an on-site daycare facility, the company cafeteria has plenty of highchairs and baby seats, and the company even has a seven-hour workday. Plus, every Wednesday, the company passes out M&M chocolate candies, plain and peanut, to all employees—a total of more than 200 tonnes of M&Ms per year. SAS senior vice president Jim Davis says, "We are firm believers that happy employees equal happy customers."[42]

Internal environments are important because they affect what people think, feel, and do at work. Given SAS's internal environment, it shouldn't surprise you to know that almost no one quits. In a typical software company, 25 percent of the work force quits each year to take another job. At SAS, only 4 percent leave.[43] Jeff Chambers, SAS's vice president of human resources, says "We have always had a commitment to investing in and cultivating meaningful, long-term relationships with our employees and clients. This has led to unusually low turnover in both populations and is at the core of our 28 years of sustained profitability and success."[44]

organizational culture
the values, beliefs, and attitudes shared by organizational members

Comments such as these reflect the key component in internal environments—organizational culture. **Organizational culture** is the set of key values, beliefs, and attitudes shared by organizational members. Clearly, one of SAS's key values is its commitment to its employees.

After reading the next section, you should be able to

5 explain how organizational cultures are created and how they can help companies be successful.

5 ORGANIZATIONAL CULTURES: CREATION, SUCCESS, AND CHANGE

Let's take a closer look at the creation and maintenance of organizational cultures, successful organizational cultures, and changing organizational cultures.

Creation and Maintenance of Organizational Cultures

Organizational culture, often referred to as corporate culture, can be strong and enduring. Shared values, beliefs, attitudes, and assumptions drive organizational culture. Organizations also have subcultures, or cultures within cultures. For example, different divisions within an organization that are located in different parts of the country or the world will often share some similar elements of culture, but there may also be things that make them a little different. Within the same company, managers in Toronto and Hawaii may have different beliefs about how managers should dress or communicate with each other.

Visible elements of corporate culture are called **visible artifacts**. The way people dress, company rituals and ceremonies, and corporate offices are all visible artifacts. IBM was once referred to as "the men in the blue suits" because most of their employees dressed in dark blue suits and employees' dress reflected the uniformity and strength of IBM's organizational culture. In addition to dress, language and forms of communication can indicate the level of formality expected within a workplace. The way language is used in the workplace can also tell you a lot about an organization. How do co-workers address each other? How do you address your boss? Is it by first name or is it Ms. Smith? Is communication formal and usually written or is it informal and usually in person? What sort of job titles are used? The answers to these questions can speak loudly about organizational culture. For example, Wal-Mart calls employees "associates" to indicate their importance in the success of the organization, while at AdFarm, a small Calgary advertising firm that was named one of Canada's best employers, there are no job titles, increasing the feeling of belonging.[45] Each of these patterns of behaviour forms part of the corporate culture and tells us something about the organization.

visible artifacts
visible signs of an organization's culture, such as the office design and layout, company dress codes, and company benefits and perks such as stock options, personal parking spaces, or the private company dining room

A primary source of organizational culture is the company founder. Founders such as Thomas J. Watson (IBM), Frank Stronach (Magna), Bill Gates (Microsoft), or John Forzani (Forzani) create organizations in their own images that they imprint with their beliefs, attitudes, and values. Microsoft employees share founder Bill Gates's intensity for staying ahead of software competitors. Says a Microsoft vice president, "No matter how good your product, you are only 18 months away from failure."[46]

While company founders are instrumental in the creation of organizational cultures, founders retire, die, or choose to leave their companies. For example, neither Michael Cowpland, founder of Corel Corporation, nor Mitch Kapor, founder of Lotus software, which created Lotus 1-2-3, one of the first and most successful spreadsheet programs, is still with the company he created. Yet they both still work in the computer industry. So when the founders are gone, how are the founders' values, attitudes, and beliefs sustained in the organizational culture? Answer: stories and heroes.

Organizational members tell **stories** to make sense of organizational events and changes, and to emphasize culturally consistent assumptions, decisions, and actions.[47] At Wal-Mart, stories abound about founder Sam Walton's thriftiness as he strove to make Wal-Mart the low-cost retailer that it is today:

organizational stories
stories told by organizational members to make sense of organizational events and changes, and to emphasize culturally consistent assumptions, decisions, and actions

> In those days, we would go on buying trips with Sam, and we'd all stay, as much as we could, in one room or two. I remember one time in Chicago when we stayed eight of us to a room. And the room

> wasn't very big to begin with. You might say we were on a pretty restricted budget. (Gary Reinboth, one of Wal-Mart's first store managers)[48]

Today, Sam Walton's thriftiness still permeates Wal-Mart. Everyone, including top executives and the CEO, flies coach rather than business or first class. When travelling on business, it's still the norm to share rooms (though two to a room, not eight!) at inexpensive hotels like Motel 6 and Super 8 instead of more expensive Holiday Inns. Likewise, on business travel, Wal-Mart will reimburse only up to US$15 per meal, which is half to one-third the reimbursement rate at similar-sized companies (remember, Wal-Mart is the largest company in the world). And, at one of its annual meetings, CEO Lee Scott reinforced Sam Walton's beliefs by exhorting Wal-Mart employees to bring back and use the free pencils and pens from their travels. Most people in the audience didn't think he was kidding.[49]

organizational heroes people celebrated for their qualities and achievements within an organization

A second way in which organizational culture is sustained is by creating and celebrating heroes. By definition, **organizational heroes** are organizational people admired for their qualities and achievements within the organization. Consider the case of Bowa Builders, a full-service construction company. When it was renovating a large auto dealership, its carpet subcontractor mistakenly ordered the new carpet to be delivered two weeks *after* it was scheduled to be installed. Rather than allow construction to be delayed, a Bowa employee kept the project on schedule by immediately reordering the carpet, flying to the carpet manufacturer's factory, renting a truck, and then driving the carpet back to the auto dealership, all within 48 hours of learning about the problem. CEO and company co-founder Larry Weinberg says this story is told and retold within Bowa Builders as an example of heroic customer service. Moreover, the car dealership was so delighted with this extraordinary service it has referred $12 million to $15 million in new business to Bowa Builders.[50]

organizational rituals routine activities that emphasize the organization's culture

organizational ceremonies planned activities or events that emphasize culturally consistent assumptions, decisions, and actions

organizational symbols something that represents another thing

A third way in which organizational culture is sustained is through **rituals**, **ceremonies**, and **symbols**. Wal-Mart is famous for having all its employees gather before the store opens and sing the national anthem and perform the company cheer.[51] Annual employee awards ceremonies can reinforce company values, and company picnics are examples of **organizational ceremonies** that provide opportunities for organizations to transmit and maintain its culture. One can consider physical artifacts such as buildings, logos, stories, slogans, rituals, and ceremonies to be organizational symbols that represent organizational values.[52]

Successful Organizational Cultures

Preliminary research shows that organizational culture is related to organizational success. As shown in Exhibit 2.5, cultures based on adaptability, involvement, a clear mission, and consistency can help companies achieve higher sales growth, return on assets, profits, quality, and employee satisfaction.[53] Weak corporate cultures can leave companies without vision leading to unfocused strategies and unmotivated employees. On the other hand, a strong corporate culture can stifle change or create conflict when organizations merge.

Adaptability is the ability to notice and respond to changes in the organization's environment. Previously, we discussed the difficulty that CEO Louis Gerstner was having trying to turn around IBM. Frustrated with his inability to change IBM culture, Gerstner eventually decreed that the core IBM beliefs set forth by founder Thomas J. Watson, Sr. (excellence, customer satisfaction, and respect for the individual) were to be replaced with the eight new goals shown in Exhibit 2.6. Instead of responding to his attempts to improve the company, many IBMers were shocked because Thomas J. Watson, Jr., who succeeded his father as IBM's CEO, once stated that IBM's success was dependent on its ability to change everything "except those basic beliefs."[54]

In cultures that promote higher levels of employee involvement in decision-making, employees feel a greater sense of ownership and responsibility. For example, at Hewlett-Packard, each "business," such as laser printers, calculators, or personal computers, makes its own decisions. So when the video products division was deciding which computer

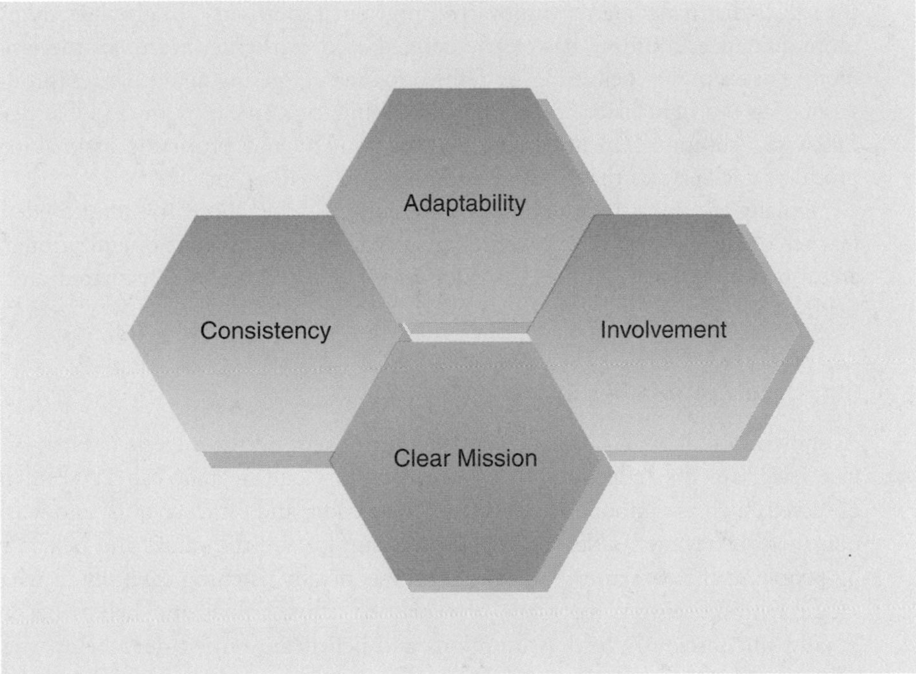

EXHIBIT 2.5
Successful Organizational Cultures

Source: D.R. Denison & A.K. Mishra, "Toward a Theory of Organizational Culture and Effectiveness," *Organization Science* 6 (1995): 204–223.

chips to use in its products, it chose not to use H-P's own computer chips because they were too expensive. Instead, they purchased integrated circuits for half the price from one of the H-P computer chip division's competitors. Because involvement and participation are so central to H-P's culture, no one (even in the H-P computer chip division) questioned this decision.[55]

A company's **vision** is its purpose or reason for existing. In organizational cultures in which there is a clear organizational vision, the organization's strategic purpose and direction are apparent to everyone in the company. And, when managers are uncertain about their business environments, the vision helps guide the discussions, decisions, and behaviour of the people in the company. At F.H. Faulding & Company, an Australian-based provider of health-care products and services that does business in 70 countries, the vision is "delivering innovative and valued solutions in healthcare."[56] This vision lets employees know why the company is in business (to deliver health-care solutions) and

company vision
a company's purpose or reason for existence

EXHIBIT 2.6
IBM's New Cultural Principles

1.	The marketplace is the driving force behind everything we do.
2.	At our core, we are a technology company with an overriding commitment to quality.
3.	Our primary measures of success are customer satisfaction and shareholder value.
4.	We operate as an entrepreneurial organization with a minimum of bureaucracy and a never-ending focus on productivity.
5.	We never lose sight of our strategic vision.
6.	We think and act with a sense of urgency.
7.	Outstanding, dedicated people make it all happen, particularly when they work together as a team.
8.	We are sensitive to the needs of all employees and to the communities in which we operate.

Source: L. Hays, "Gerstner Is Struggling as He Tries to Change Ingrained IBM Culture," *The Wall Street Journal*, 13 May 1994, A1.

the values that really matter (innovative and valued solutions). To give its employees even more guidance, Faulding has clearly defined each of the key words in the vision statement. For example, "delivering" is defined to mean targeting quality drugs, products, and services to the right place at the right time while concentrating on a global perspective. Likewise, "solutions" means being focused, timely, and profitable by making quality products and services that satisfy customers' and partners' needs.

Finally, in consistent organizational cultures, the company actively defines and teaches organizational values, beliefs, and attitudes. Consistent organizational cultures are also called strong cultures, because the core beliefs are widely shared and strongly held.

Changing Organizational Cultures

As shown in Exhibit 2.7, organizational cultures exist on three levels.[57] First, on the surface level, are the reflections of an organization's culture that can be seen, heard, or observed, such as symbolic artifacts (e.g., dress codes and office layouts, and workers' and managers' behaviours). Next, just below the surface, are the values and beliefs expressed by people in the company. You can't see these, but by listening carefully to what people say and how decisions are made or explained, those values and beliefs become clear. Finally, unconsciously held assumptions and beliefs are buried deep below the surface. These are the unwritten views and rules that are so strongly held and so widely shared that they are rarely discussed or even thought about unless someone attempts to change them or unknowingly violates them. When it comes to changing cultures, it can be very difficult to change unconscious assumptions and beliefs held deep below the surface. Instead, managers should focus on the parts of the organizational culture they can control; these include observable surface-level items, such as workers' behaviours and symbolic artifacts, and expressed values and beliefs, which can be influenced through employee selection. Let's see how these can be used to change organizational cultures.

behavioural addition
the process of having managers and employees perform new behaviours that are central to and symbolic of the new organizational culture that a company wants to create

behavioural substitution
the process of having managers and employees perform new behaviours central to the "new" organizational culture in place of behaviours that were central to the "old" organizational culture

One way of changing a corporate culture is to use behavioural addition or behavioural substitution to establish new patterns of behaviour among managers and employees.[58] **Behavioural addition** is the process of having managers and employees perform a new behaviour, while **behavioural substitution** is having managers and employees perform a new behaviour in place of another behaviour. The key in both instances is to choose behaviours that are central to and symbolic of the "old" culture you're changing and the "new" culture that you want to create. For example, Claudette MacKay-Lassonde, CEO of Enghouse Systems Ltd. (a small software company located in Markham, Ontario), wanted to transform Enghouse's culture. Despite having a good product line, Enghouse suffered a $3.2 million loss in 1994 and the threat of bankruptcy became a reality. MacKay-Lassonde implemented a strategic planning process, restructured the company, and tightened financial controls. Three years later, Enghouse turned a profit. She says, "The reality is that a turnaround means a culture change."[59] Sometimes organizations change their name and/or logo to help reinforce cultural change.

The second way in which managers can begin to change corporate culture is to change visible artifacts of their old culture, such as the office design and layout, company dress codes, and who benefits (or doesn't) from company benefits and perks such as stock options, personal parking spaces, or the private company dining room. At Petro-Canada, once a Crown corporation, corporate jets were eliminated and senior executives had to purchase their own golf-club memberships. Even their Calgary headquarters, dubbed "Red Square" and a symbol of federal government intrusion in the private sector, was sold and only half of it was leased back. Change was in the air, and the company eventually sold its large Canadian art collection, gave up its most expensive office space, and closed the executive dining room.[60]

Corporate cultures are very difficult to change. Consequently, there is no guarantee that behavioural substitution, behavioural addition, or changing visible cultural artifacts will change a company's organizational culture. However, these methods are some of the best tools that managers have for changing culture, because they send the clear message to managers and employees that "the accepted way of doing things" has changed.

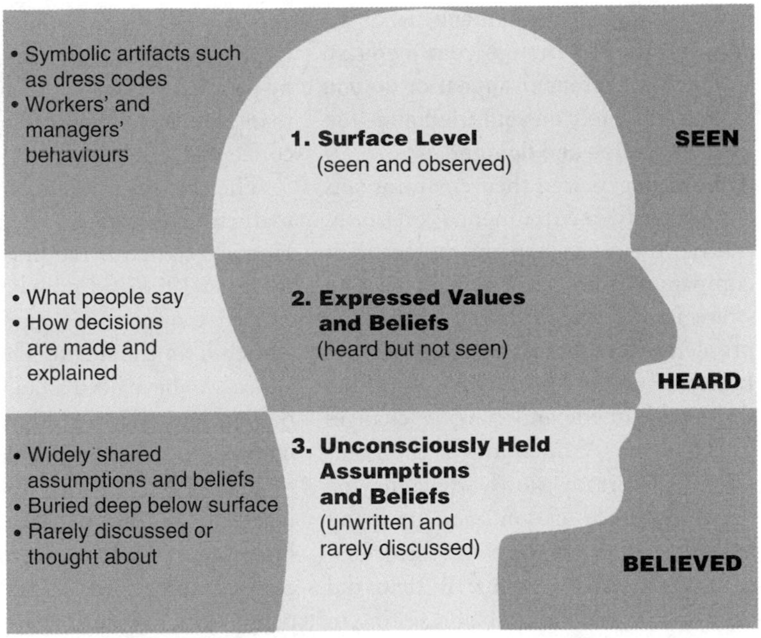

EXHIBIT 2.7
Three Levels of Organizational Culture

Review 5: Organizational Cultures: Creation, Success, and Change

Organizational culture is the set of key values, beliefs, and attitudes shared by organizational members. Organizational cultures are often created by company founders and then sustained through the telling of organizational stories and the celebration of organizational heroes. Adaptable cultures that promote employee involvement, that make clear the organization's strategic purpose and direction, and that actively define and teach organizational values and beliefs can help companies achieve higher sales growth, return on assets, profits, quality, and employee satisfaction. Behavioural substitution, behavioural addition, and changing visible artifacts are ways in which managers can begin to change their organizational cultures.

What Really Happened?[61]

Managers use a three-step process to make sense of external environments. First, they scan their environments based on their organizational strategies, their need for up-to-date information, or their need to reduce uncertainty. Second, when they identify environmental events such as threats, they take steps to protect their companies from harm. And third, when they identify environmental events as opportunities, they formulate strategies to improve company performance. As mentioned earlier in the chapter, managers need to pay close attention to trends and events that are directly related to their companies' abilities to compete in the marketplace. Environmental scanning is important because it contributes to organizational performance. Companies can succeed by scanning their business environments for events and trends, interpreting what those changes mean, and then acting to adapt to those changes.

So the question is "Are the threats serious, and if so how will you respond?" Just because you are a Canadian icon and dominate your market niche does not mean that you can survive anything. Many great companies have gone out of business because they were unable to adapt to changing times.

Many managers become complacent. Because a company is on top it can become beholden to the formula that brought it such great success. While having a successful strategy is clearly important, you can't answer this question without taking a look at external environments, meaning the forces and events outside a company that have the potential to influence or affect it. Organizations are influenced by two kinds of external environments: the general environment, which consists of economic, technological, sociocultural, and political/legal events and trends, and the specific environment, which consists of customers, competitors, suppliers, industry regulators, and advocacy groups. There are two basic strategies for monitoring customers: reactive and proactive. *Reactive customer monitoring* is identifying and addressing customer trends and problems after they occur. *Proactive monitoring* of customers means trying to sense events, trends, and problems before they occur (or before customers complain).

Even though Tim Hortons is on top, it must be aware of any developments in its highly competitive environment. Tim Hortons has been very successful in evolving with a changing environment. The changes have come over a long period of time. Some of the changes have been symbolic (a change in organizational symbols) but reflective of a changing marketplace. In 1988 the process of reshaping the company's image began when it began phasing out the word "Donuts" in all of its signage. Tim Hortons attempted to broaden its menu's appeal in the early 1990s with sandwiches; however, it didn't market the new products much, and the new menu items didn't catch on with customers.

Given that you recognize that the marketplace is changing, competition is increasing, and you failed with the first

major change in your menu, what do you do? Do you change your menu so that it has a broader appeal or do you retrench and rely on your tried-and-true formula: coffee and donuts?

After managers scan their environments and identify environmental events as threats, they take steps to protect their companies from harm by formulating strategies to deal with the impending problems. The top management at Tim Hortons was very proactive in scanning the environment and making changes to its menu. As mentioned, the company was already slowly downplaying the importance of donuts in its menu and had removed the word "Donuts" from its restaurant signs. It then did extensive market research and testing to see what customers would like and began changing the menu. It started to add drive-through windows to all its locations to tap into a market populated by people wanting to run and go, rather than stop and linger, to enjoy a cup of coffee and a donut.

The changes in the menu and a slick marketing campaign have paid off. Tim Hortons started by adding bagels to its menu in 1996 and now has items such as iced cappuccino, soup, sandwiches, and chili on the menu. The Atkins diet appears to have been a fad that is slowly fizzling out. Tim Hortons essentially ignored the threat without any detrimental effect. Nonetheless, customer interest in healthier choices has increased, and Tim Hortons has successfully responded. In 2002, the company's sales in Canada exceeded that of McDonald's, and Krispy Kreme appears to be in full retreat. Krispy Kreme had planned to open 32 stores in Canada, but before it had done so, it was already closing stores for lack of business. It had hung on to its coffee and donuts product line with little product diversification or innovation, unlike Tim Hortons. On the other hand, Tim Hortons plans on doubling the number of U.S. locations to 500 by 2007, and as of 2006 has over 2400 locations in Canada. Clearly, the research and development the company undertook, coupled with the environmental scanning, has paid off. Wendy's has now spun Tim Hortons off from the parent chain, offering shares to the public, and Tim's remains the king of the fast food industry in Canada, even though donuts now account for a small portion of total sales.

Key Terms

advocacy groups *(42)*
behavioural addition *(50)*
behavioural substitution *(50)*
business confidence indices *(36)*
buyer dependence *(41)*
cognitive maps *(45)*
company vision *(49)*
competitive analysis *(39)*
competitors *(39)*
complex environment *(33)*
dynamic environment *(32)*
environmental change *(32)*
environmental complexity *(33)*
environmental munificence *(34)*
environmental scanning *(43)*
external environments *(32)*
general environment *(35)*
industry regulation *(41)*
internal environment *(46)*
media advocacy *(42)*
opportunistic behaviour *(41)*
organizational ceremonies *(48)*
organizational culture *(46)*
organizational heroes *(48)*
organizational rituals *(48)*
organizational stories *(47)*
organizational symbols *(48)*
product boycott *(43)*
public communications *(42)*
punctuated equilibrium theory *(32)*
relationship behaviour *(41)*
simple environment *(33)*
specific environment *(35)*
stable environment *(32)*
supplier dependence *(40)*
suppliers *(40)*
technology *(37)*
uncertainty *(34)*
visible artifacts *(47)*

Self-Assessment

CHECK YOUR TOLERANCE FOR AMBIGUITY

Think of the difference between playing chess (where you can see all the pieces and anticipate attacks and plan counterattacks) and playing poker (where no one knows anyone else's hand, and you have to make guesses based on your interpretation of opponents' betting patterns). In chess, there is little ambiguity, whereas in poker there is tremendous ambiguity. Although many people liken business to a game of chess, probably because of the strategic aspects of the game, business is actually more like poker. The business environment is complex and uncertain, and managers never really know all the cards the opposition is holding. Managers must learn to adapt to environmental shifts and new developments—sometimes on a daily basis. For some managers, however, this can be a challenging task because everyone has a different comfort level when it comes to ambiguity. For some, not knowing all the details can be a source of significant stress, whereas for others uncertainty can be energizing.

As a manager, you will need to develop an appropriate tolerance for ambiguity. For example, being stressed out every time interest rates change can be counterproductive, but completely ignoring the economic environment can be detrimental to your company's performance. On page 511 of the Assessment Appendix, you will find a 22-question survey designed to help you get a sense of your tolerance for ambiguity.

Management Decisions

CULTURE SHOCK

As a vice president of a medium-sized software technology company located in Ottawa, you have been involved in several acquisitions of smaller firms over the last few years, each having resulted in increased growth and profitability for your firm. Recently, your company has been discussing plans to acquire a small, relatively new, computer-networking services company located in California's Silicon Valley. Your firm is interested in this acquisition because it has the skills, equipment, and knowledge desperately needed but currently lacking in your firm. Additionally, some of your current clients are located in and around Silicon Valley.

The firm being considered has a solid reputation and a growing number of customers located in Canada. If this acquisition occurs, it will serve to broaden the services currently provided by your firm, increase your firm's presence nationwide, and strengthen your firm's core competencies by alleviating the need to outsource certain activities. Investment capital has already been garnered to facilitate the acquisition.

Tomorrow morning, you and several other top executives will decide whether to go ahead with the proposed acquisition. Unfortunately, one item makes you uncomfortable with this plan. In comparing the two companies, you have found that your firm's corporate culture differs dramatically from that of the firm being considered. Although some of your colleagues denounce this as being an insignificant problem and one that can be easily solved, you consider it to be one of high importance.

Your firm is larger and more bureaucratic, is formal in structure, and utilizes centralized decision-making techniques. Typically before key decisions are made, an extensive amount of time is spent involving group discussions and developing consensus before any action is taken. Additionally, there is a clear chain of command within your firm, and individuals have distinct job descriptions and duties. On the other hand, the proposed company's structure and culture appear to be very informal. The organizational hierarchy is relatively flat, with key decisions being made at all levels. Employees have no clear responsibilities or duties and are empowered to "take the ball and run with it." The firm's founder claims that it is their unique culture that has resulted in the firm's rapid growth in market share, profitability, and innovativeness.

Your main fear regarding the proposed acquisition is that the new company's culture will be too different to effectively mesh the two companies together. Further, it is your belief that the employees of the new company will feel trapped and constrained by your firm's formalized structure. As you look over the acquisition proposal, the projections and possibilities are certainly appealing. If the acquisition becomes a success, your firm could stand to become the largest, most powerful communications firm in the industry. Tomorrow morning, you and four others will vote to move ahead or abandon the proposed acquisition.[62]

Questions

1. How will you vote and why?
2. If you vote to pursue the acquisition, what changes might you recommend to ensure that the acquisition and subsequent transition succeed?
3. If you vote to abandon the acquisition, what changes might you propose that (if accepted by the group) would change your mind regarding pursuing the acquisition?

Management Decisions

CULTURAL CHANGE: EVOLUTION OR REVOLUTION?

Tandem Computer makes "fault tolerant" computers guaranteed to keep working during power outages, natural disasters, and catastrophic computer glitches that would easily shut down standard computers. Since 1974, Tandem has sold its computers at high prices and high profit margins to stock exchanges, phone companies, banks, airlines, and other companies whose businesses are dependent on uninterrupted computer service. Tandem computers are used in 75 percent of all ATM transactions, 66 percent of all credit card transactions, and 70 percent of electronic interchange networks (data sharing between companies).

Jimmy Treybig, Tandem's CEO, founded the company with $1.5 million in venture capital money from Thomas Perkins, who chairs Tandem's board of directors. That $1.5 million investment grew into a company with $3.1 billion in annual revenues. During its 20-year run of success, Treybig developed a patriarchal culture at Tandem. Once a week, at every Tandem facility, there was a "beer bust." Attendance wasn't mandatory, but most people wanted to attend. The point: not to promote drinking, but to get to know each other better and encourage informal communication, which is often lacking in corporate environments. Treybig's stated management philosophy was that

(1) all people are good;
(2) workers, management, and company are all the same thing;
(3) every single person in the company must understand the essence of the business;
(4) every employee must benefit from the company's success;
(5) you must create an environment where all the above can happen. (Ward, 1995)

One symbol of this philosophy was that Tandem's sales representatives had one of the most generous compensation plans in the industry, earning $150 000 to $600 000 a year. In all, CEO Treybig was well liked and ran the company like an extended family.

Unfortunately, the party ended a few years ago. Customers began refusing to pay premium prices for Tandem's computers, especially since they used Tandem's proprietary software, Guardian, which was not compatible with other kinds of computers. In just three years, profits, which had been running between $150 million and $300 million annually, dropped to a loss of more than $750 million. Customers wanted Tandem to produce computers that run UNIX, an "open" operating system that runs on different kinds of computers, unlike Guardian, which runs only on Tandem computers.

The company's struggles have not only affected profits, but have also begun to affect Tandem's organizational culture. Said CEO Treybig, "Nothing is as fun as it used to be. My wife says I never use the word 'fun' anymore. In the 1980s you could just do a good job and make money. But nowadays, you have to be the best. I mean, every day you have to really worry about being successful. The bar for success is higher. It takes fun out of it" (Ward, 1995).[63]

Questions

1. At critical times like this, CEOs have two basic choices: evolutionary change or revolutionary change. Explain which would be the best choice for returning Tandem to profitability. Why?
2. Either approach will affect Tandem's family-like culture. Depending on which you chose, explain three ways in which a company like Tandem could incrementally change its culture or change its culture in a revolutionary way.

Develop Your Management Potential

DEALING WITH THE PRESS

In this age of 24-hour cable news channels, tabloid news shows, and aggressive local and national news reporters intent on exposing corporate wrong-doing, one of the most important skills for a manager to learn is how to deal effectively with the press. Test your ability to deal effectively with the press by putting yourself in the following situation. To make the situation more realistic, read each scenario and then give yourself two minutes to write a response to each question.

Fatty Restaurant Food Contributes to Heart Attacks

Today, in the nation's capital, a public-interest group held a press conference to release the results of a study that found that the food sold in most Chinese restaurants is high in fat. The group claims that the most popular Chinese dishes, such as orange chicken, pork fried rice, and Hunan beef, contain nearly as much fat as the food you get from fast-food chains such as McDonald's, Wendy's, and Burger King. (Much of it is fried or is covered with heavy sauces.) Furthermore, the group says that customers who hope to keep their cholesterol and blood pressure low by eating Chinese food are just fooling themselves.

A TV reporter from Channel 5 called your Szechuan-style Chinese restaurant, Szechuan, to get your response to this study. When she and the camera crew arrived, she asked you the following questions. (To simulate these conditions, give yourself only two minutes to write a response to each question.)

1. "A new study released today claims that food sold in Chinese restaurants is on average nearly as fattening as that sold at fast-food restaurants. How healthy is the food that you serve at Szechuan's?"
2. "Get the camera in close here [camera closes in to get the shot] because I want the audience at home to see that you don't provide any information on your menu about calories, calories from fat, or cholesterol. Without this information [camera pulls back to get a picture of you and the reporter], how can your customers know that the food that you serve is healthy for them?"
3. "These new studies were based on lunches and dinners sampled from Chinese restaurants across the country. A local company, Huntington Labs, has agreed to test foods from local restaurants so that we can provide accurate information to our viewers. Would you agree to let us sample the main dishes in your restaurant to test the level of calories, calories from fat, and cholesterol? Furthermore, can we take the cameras into your restaurant, so that we can get your customers' reactions to these studies?"

Discussion Questions

1. Universities and colleges have elements of culture that are shared and some elements that are unique to each university or college. Thinking of your university or college, what elements of its culture are shared with other universities or colleges and which are unique?
2. Punctuated equilibrium theory states that industries go through alternating periods of stability and change. Identify an industry that has been relatively stable which is now being transformed by a change in the external environment. What caused the change and what are the likely consequences of the change?
3. Uncertainty refers to how well managers can understand or predict the external changes and trends affecting their businesses. Name an organization that faces a low level of uncertainty and explain why it has a low level of uncertainty. Name an organization that faces a high level of uncertainty and explain why it has a high level of uncertainty. What could it do to reduce the level of uncertainty it faces?
4. Advocacy groups are groups of concerned citizens who band together to try to influence the business practices of specific industries, businesses, and professions. Identify an advocacy group and provide examples of activities they undertake to communicate their position. Do you think their activities are effective? Why or why not?
5. Give an example of an attempted product boycott. Which group(s) initiated the boycott and why? Was the boycott effective? Why or why not? How did the company that was boycotted respond and was the response effective?

Critical Thinking Video Case

Visit www.management2e.nelson.com to view this chapter's CBC video case.

CBC

Take Two

Biz Flix
Brazil

Set somewhere in the twentieth century, the retro-futuristic world of *Brazil* is a gritty, urban cesspool patched over with cosmetic surgery and "designer ducts for your discriminating taste." Automation pervades every facet of life from the toaster and coffee machine to doorways, but paperwork, inefficiency, and mechanical failures are the rule. Brazil stars Jonathan Pryce in the role of Sam, a low-level bureaucrat whose primary interests in life are his vivid dream fantasies to the tune of "Brazil," a 1940s big-band hit. In this scene, Sam is starting a new job and is being assigned an office and employee identification number.

What to Watch for and Ask Yourself

1. Describe the culture at Sam's new employer.
2. How easy would it be to change the culture at Sam's new company?
3. In which kind of business environment do you think the culture at Sam's employer is able to operate most successfully?

Management Workplace
Boston Duck Tours

After a bus tour of the United States that passed through Memphis, Andy Wilson was inspired to create a unique tourism company in Boston. Even though he had a great idea, enlisted the aid of a consultant to prepare a solid business plan, and cultivated a source for the technology he needed, Andy still faced challenges in the external environment. Nonetheless, he preserved and created Boston Duck Tours, the number one tourist attraction in the state of Massachusetts.

What to Watch for and Ask Yourself

1. What components of the external business environment does Andy Wilson mention in the video?
2. How would you characterize Andy's relationship with Bob McDowell?
3. Outline the external environment of Boston Duck Tours.
4. How would you describe the culture of Boston Duck Tours?

© JAMES LEYNSE/CORBIS

Chapter 3

Ethics and Social Responsibility

CHAPTER OUTLINE

LEARNING OBJECTIVES

After reading this chapter, you should be able to

1. discuss how management creates the possibility for ethical abuses.
2. identify common kinds of workplace deviance.
3. describe what influences ethical decision-making.
4. explain what practical steps managers can take to improve ethical decision-making.
5. explain to whom organizations are socially responsible.
6. explain for what organizations are socially responsible.
7. explain how organizations can become socially responsible.
8. explain whether social responsibility hurts economic performance.

When you decided to join the Gap and become its new CEO (Gap Inc. runs Gap, Banana Republic, and Old Navy clothing stores), your teenage daughter's response was "Doesn't Gap use sweatshops?" You weren't surprised by her question, as the company had received intense negative new coverage regarding the treatment of workers in the overseas factories from which Gap buys its clothes.[1]

For example, a worker for a Gap supplier in Lesotho, Africa, complained, "The factory is dusty. We can't escape breathing in the fibers. When we cough, if the t-shirt we were working on was made of blue fabric, then our mucus would be full of blue fibers." A worker in another Gap supplier factory in Bangladesh said, "If we make simple mistakes, they beat us up. I made some small mistakes one time, so the supervisor came and slapped my head and pulled my ears. And if we make mistakes, they don't pay us for our work." In El Salvador, where workers complained about abuse and terrible working conditions, worker Maria Luz Panameno said, "I'm very proud to sew pants for Gap, but the board of directors should not be proud of what is happening to us. Gap has abandoned us." Some workers even complained that wages were so low that they couldn't buy enough food for themselves and their families. Steve Weingarten, a union organizer who tries to unionize and represent factory workers, said, "We want Gap to stop exploiting sweatshop labor around the world. We want them to pay a wage that allows a decent standard of living and allows workers to organize unions to improve their conditions in factories."

What Would You Do?

Is Gap the only company facing these problems? No. Kirk Douglass of Pivot International, a manufacturing company that owns factories in the Philippines and does work with Chinese companies, said, "If you go into almost any plant in the non-developed countries of the Far East, you're going to see things that OSHA [the U.S. Occupational Safety and Health Administration] or EPA [the U.S. Environmental Protection Agency] would shut down tomorrow." For years, because of strong competition and finicky consumers, retailers like Gap have quickly switched orders from one factory or country to another searching for the lowest prices they could get. And, according to protest groups, that intense pressure to keep prices low has encouraged factory owners and managers to do everything they could to cut their costs, including mistreating workers. And with 4000 factories in 50 countries supplying clothes for Gap, Banana Republic, and Old Navy stores, protest groups see Gap as a big part of the problem.

With intense negative publicity, protest groups calling for worldwide boycotts of Gap products and stores, and the company losing money, you couldn't find a much tougher situation as a new CEO. Since Gap is a publicly traded company, one of your most important responsibilities is to keep shareholders happy by making sure the company is profitable. And that means that your overseas suppliers have to keep their prices low. On the other hand, negative publicity and boycotts may lower sales and reduce profits. So how do you decide whose interests—stakeholders, suppliers, overseas workers, or protesters—take precedence? Furthermore, is Gap really responsible for the terrible treatment of overseas workers? In other words, is this your problem or is this a problem that the managers and owners of overseas factories need to address? Finally, how should Gap respond? Should you do nothing, make minimal changes, or aggressively tackle these issues no matter the effect on the company's bottom line?

If you were the new CEO of Gap Inc., what would you do?

The Gap's dilemma is one managers face regarding ethics and social responsibility. Unfortunately, one of the "real world" aspects of these decisions is that no matter what you decide, someone or some group will be unhappy with the decision. Managers don't have the luxury of choosing theoretically optimal, win-win solutions that are obviously correct to everyone involved. In practice, solutions to ethics and social responsibility problems aren't optimal. Often, they are "make-do" or "do the least harm" kinds of solutions. Clear rights and wrongs rarely reveal themselves to managers charged with "doing the right thing." The business world is much messier than that.

What Is Ethical and Unethical Workplace Behaviour?

ethics
the set of moral principles or values that defines right and wrong for a person or group

Ethics is the set of moral principles or values that defines right and wrong for a person or group. In light of highly publicized cases such as Enron, Worldcom, Tyco, and Adelphia, it is not surprising that several studies have produced distressing results about the state of ethics in today's business world. In a broad survey of 2300 workers, 75 percent indicated that they had seen unethical behaviour at work, such as deceptive sales practices, unsafe working conditions, environmental breaches, and mishandling of confidential or proprietary information within the last year.[2] A similar survey of 2293 workers found that less than half (47 percent) felt that the senior leaders in their companies were ethical.[3] Furthermore, 60 percent of workers felt substantially pressured to commit unethical or illegal acts at work. Only 6 percent reported feeling little pressure to commit such acts.[4] Finally, in a study of 1324 randomly selected workers, managers, and executives across many industries, 48 percent of respondents admitted to committing an unethical or illegal act in the past year! These acts included cheating on an expense account, discriminating against co-workers, forging signatures, paying or accepting kickbacks, and "looking the other way" when environmental laws were broken.[5] Interestingly, this somewhat depressing picture may be having a positive impact.

However, these studies also contained good news. When people are convinced that they work in an ethical work environment, they are six times more likely to stay with that company than if they believe that they work in an unethical environment.[6] In short, a lot of work needs to be done to make workplaces more ethical, but, and this is very important, managers and employees want this to happen. A recent article in the *National Post* is telling: "Ethical Business Practices Come into Fashion" screamed the headline highlighting Nike's decision to list the identities and locations of the 700 companies that manufacture its products, a move that was well received.[7]

After reading the next two sections, you should be able to

1 discuss how the nature of a management job creates the possibility for ethical abuses.

2 identify common kinds of workplace deviance.

1 ETHICS AND THE NATURE OF MANAGEMENT JOBS

ethical behaviour
behaviour that conforms to a society's accepted principles of right and wrong

Ethical behaviour follows accepted principles of right and wrong. Probably the most famous recent example of unethical corporate behaviour involves the American energy trading company Enron. By using a complex web of "off-balance-sheet" partnerships and active efforts to avoid paying corporate taxes, its senior executives managed to overstate its earnings by over US$600 million. These actions led to the eventual bankruptcy of the company as well as the loss of billions of dollars in future pension income for employees and in shareholders' investments. On the other hand, Wal-Mart (www.walmart.com) has very strict guidelines concerning its employees' ethical behaviour. Any employee who accepts anything of value (dinner, free tickets to a sports event, a round of golf, etc.) from a company that Wal-Mart does business with will immediately be dismissed. Wal-Mart employees aren't even permitted to allow representatives from other companies to buy them a cup of coffee. Furthermore, to encourage employees to behave ethically, all of

Wal-Mart's suppliers and vendors are required to do business with Wal-Mart employees in "glass rooms," visible to anyone who walks through the lobby at company headquarters. Finally, the walls in each of these glass rooms are covered with posters that say, "Any item received [from a supplier or vendor] will be returned to sender at their expense."[8]

© CHIP EAST/REUTERS/CORBIS

Former Worldcom CEO Bernard Ebbers is pictured here arriving at court where he was eventually found guilty of fraud, conspiracy, and filing false documents, which led to the massive US$11 billion accounting fraud at the telecommunication carrier.

Unethical management behaviour occurs when managers personally violate accepted principles of right and wrong. The authority and power inherent in some management positions can tempt managers to engage in unethical practices. In the case of Tyco, its CEO Dennis Kozlowski was accused of failing to pay over US$1 million in sales taxes on sales of artwork after his efforts to hide the transactions were discovered. Since managers often control company resources, there is a risk that some managers will cross over the line from legitimate use of company resources to personal use of those resources. For example, treating a client to dinner is a common and legitimate business practice in many companies. But what about treating a client to a ski trip? Taking the company jet to attend a business meeting in Winnipeg is legitimate. But how about using the jet to come home to Toronto by way of Calgary and the skiing wonders of Lake Louise? Human resources can be misused as well. For example, using employees to do personal chores, such as picking up the manager's dry cleaning, is unethical behaviour.

Handling information is another area in which managers must be careful to behave ethically. Information is a key part of management work. Managers collect it, analyze it, act on it, and disseminate it. However, they are also expected to deal in truthful information and, when necessary, to keep confidential information confidential. Leaking company secrets to competitors, "doctoring" the numbers, wrongfully withholding information, or lying are some possible misuses of the information entrusted to managers. For example, in Hong Kong, "Ba dan" literally means white sheet. At Bausch & Lomb's (www.bauschandlomb.com) Hong Kong division, managers used the term "Ba dan" to refer to the fake sales numbers they sent to company headquarters each month. To maintain its status as Bausch & Lomb's top international division, Hong Kong managers would fake the sales numbers for its Southeast Asian customers. Then, to make the fake numbers look like real sales, it would ship its product (glasses and contact lenses) to a phony customer warehouse.[9] Bausch & Lomb used company auditors plus its internal security department, which was run by ex-Secret Service agents and police officers, to set up "sting" operations to catch the employees who were running the "Ba dan" scam in Hong Kong.

A third area in which managers must be careful to engage in ethical behaviour is the way in which they influence the behaviour of others, especially those they supervise. Managerial work gives managers significant power to influence others. If managers tell employees to perform unethical acts (or face punishment), such as "faking the numbers to get results," they are abusing their managerial power. This is sometimes called the "move it or lose it" syndrome. "Move it or lose it" managers tell employees, "Do it. You're paid to do it. If you can't do it, we'll find somebody who can."[10]

Not all unethical managerial influence is intentional, however. Sometimes managers unintentionally influence employees to act unethically by creating policies that inadvertently reward employees for unethical acts. For example, in an attempt to make its automotive repair shops more profitable, Sears restructured its incentive system. It paid mechanics and shop managers a commission depending on the number of batteries, shock absorbers, oil changes, or tune-ups they sold per work shift. However, this pay system put the workers' best interests (higher pay) directly in conflict with the interests of customers (honest repair work). What management was trying to accomplish was greater productivity, but instead, employees started selling unneeded parts and repair work. This practice became so widespread that many customers and government regulators accused Sears of cheating customers by selling unnecessary parts and repairs. Sears management has since ended the incentive program.[11]

Setting goals is another way that managers influence the behaviour of their employees. If managers set unrealistic goals, the pressure to perform and to achieve these goals can influence employees to engage in unethical business behaviours. For example, at Bausch & Lomb, there was tremendous pressure to achieve double-digit increases in revenues each year. Said a former company president, "Once you signed up for your target number, you were expected to reach it," no excuses accepted. As a result, Bausch & Lomb has changed its compensation and reward systems to reward managers and employees for long-term rather than short-term performance.

Review 1: Ethics and the Nature of Management Jobs

Ethics is the set of moral principles or values that define right and wrong. Ethical behaviour occurs when managers follow those principles and values. Because they set the standard for others in the workplace, managers can model ethical behaviour by using resources for company and not personal business. Furthermore, managers can encourage ethical behaviour by handling information in a confidential and honest fashion, by not using their authority to influence others to engage in unethical behaviour, by not creating policies that unintentionally reward employees for unethical behaviour, and by setting reasonable rather than unreasonable goals.

Unfortunately, as will become apparent throughout this chapter, the issue of appropriate behaviour is not a simple one. Managers are often responsible for addressing behaviours or potential behaviours that are ethical or unethical. These unfortunately need to be distinguished from legal and illegal behaviours. In the following paragraphs you will read about employee theft or "shrinkage," which is not only a criminal offence in Canada but is also unethical. But also keep in mind the situation of an employee lying to a customer about a boss being out of town when that individual is actually in the office. Although dishonest, morally wrong, and from the point of view of the recipient of the message, unethical, this act is not a criminal act and hence not illegal. These examples illustrate the dilemma that many managers face when seeking to respond to controversial behaviour and the need for organizations to develop solid codes of conduct to help decision makers. Before addressing this issue, let us first discuss the concern of workplace deviance.

2 WORKPLACE DEVIANCE

Depending on which study you look at, one-third to three-quarters of all employees admit that they have stolen from their employers or committed computer fraud, embezzled funds, vandalized company property, sabotaged company projects, or been "sick" from work when they really weren't sick. Experts estimate that unethical behaviours like these, which researchers call "workplace deviance," may cost companies as much as US$400 billion a year.[12] Further, one survey estimates that 20 percent of Canadian workers know when deviant behaviour is occurring in their workplace. Indeed, in Canada alone, the same survey places the cost at $23 000 per company per year.[13]

workplace deviance unethical behaviour that violates organizational norms about right and wrong

production deviance unethical behaviour that hurts the quality of work produced

property deviance unethical behaviour aimed at the organization's property

More specifically, **workplace deviance** is unethical behaviour that violates organizational norms about right and wrong. Exhibit 3.1 shows that workplace deviance can be categorized by how deviant the behaviour is, from minor to serious, and by the target of the deviant behaviour, either the organization or particular people in the workplace.[14] One kind of workplace deviance, called **production deviance**, hurts the quality and quantity of work produced. Examples include leaving early, taking excessively long work breaks, purposely working slower, or intentionally wasting resources.

Property deviance is unethical behaviour aimed at company property. Examples include sabotaging, stealing, or damaging equipment or products, or overcharging for

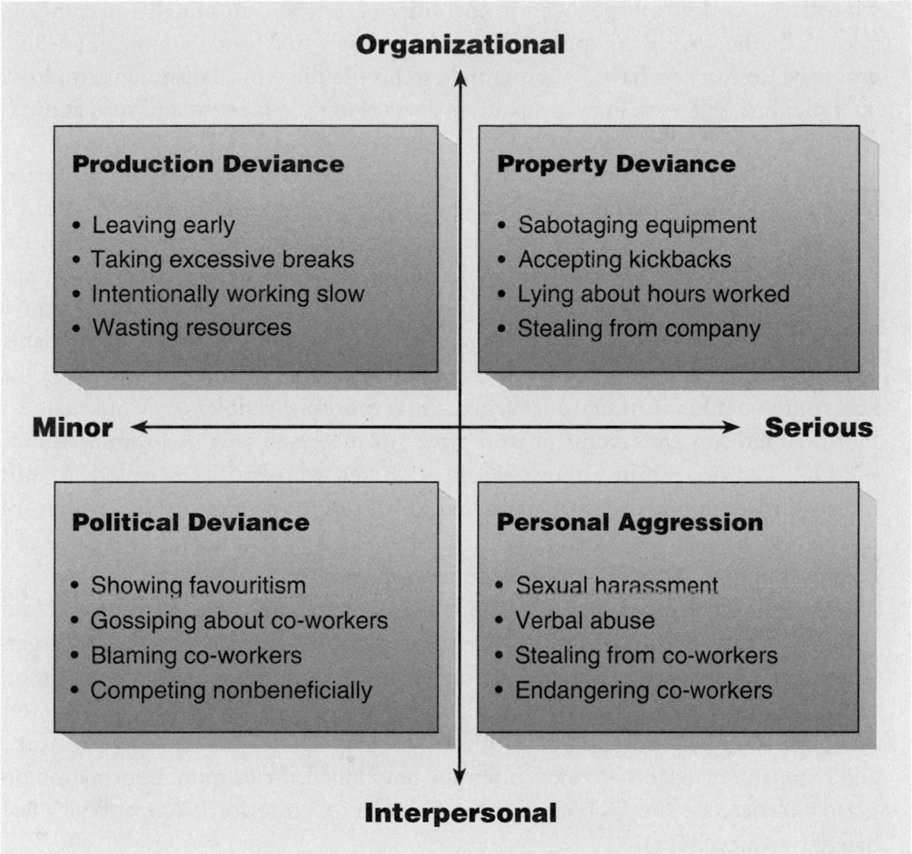

EXHIBIT 3.1 Types of Workplace Deviance

Source: Academy of Management, PO Box 3020, Briar Cliff Manor, NY 10510-8020. "A Typology of Deviant Workplace Behaviors," (Figure), S.L. Robinson & R.J. Bennett. *Academy of Management Journal*, 1995, Vol. 38. Reproduced by permission of the publisher via Copyright Clearance Center.

services and then pocketing the difference. While it's certainly scary to think about, Boeing, the passenger jet manufacturer, has had instances of product sabotage. In a number of instances during routine product testing, the manufacturer has found wires cut in its 737 jets. Each 737 has 57 600 km of wiring. No one has ever been caught for cutting the wires. A spokesperson for EasyJet (www.easyjet.com), a London-based airline, recently said, "This incident is very disturbing, and we are demanding a full investigation into how it could have happened. We need a guarantee from Boeing that these planes are 100 percent free of any further problems. Like all airlines, we rely on the manufacturer delivering a safe product."[15] Sometimes, however, property deviance occurs with company property, rather than company products. An employee planted a software bomb in the centralized file server that contained one company's key programs and data. The code destroyed the programs and data that ran the machines in the company's manufacturing plant. The company lost $10 million as a result, including $2 million in reprogramming costs. Eighty employees had to be laid off because of lost business resulting from the incident.[16]

shrinkage employee theft of company merchandise

Another common form of property deviance, called **shrinkage,** is the theft of company merchandise by employees. One industry in particular, retail, tracks losses of this nature fairly intensely. One estimate places shrinkage costs for traditional Canadian retailers at more than $3 million a day and more than $3 billion for the entire industry or 1.8 percent of annual sales.[17] These shrinkage costs represent 33 percent of all corporate losses in the retail sector attributed to criminal activity of one type or another. Further, the Retail Council of Canada (www.retailcouncil.org) estimates the average loss for an employee theft at over $600. Not surprisingly, some firms have been hit harder than others. Recent figures suggest companies such as Chapters Inc. and Shoppers Drug

Mart have faced shrinkage losses in the order of 2.1 percent and 1.5 percent of annual sales.[18] In the case of Shoppers Drug Mart, that works out to more than $6 million annually. Researchers have also attempted to profile the typical dishonest employee. Such an individual will work for a company an average of nine months and steal approximately $1500 worth of goods or services.[19]

political deviance
using one's influence to harm others in the company

personal aggression
hostile or aggressive behaviour toward others

While workplace and production deviance harm companies, political deviance and personal aggression are unethical behaviours that hurt particular people within companies. **Political deviance** is using one's influence to harm others in the company. Examples include making decisions based on favouritism rather than performance, spreading rumours about co-workers, or falsely blaming others for mistakes. **Personal aggression** is hostile or aggressive behaviour toward others. Examples include sexual harassment, verbal abuse, stealing from co-workers, or personally threatening co-workers. One of the fastest-growing kinds of personal aggression is workplace violence. More than 2 million North Americans are victims of workplace violence each year. A prominent example is the OC Transpo case in Ottawa, where a worker, who had been teased for stuttering, returned to the work site with a gun and killed four co-workers.[20] In another infamous case, Concordia University engineering professor Valery Fabrikant killed three of his academic colleagues at the institution's downtown campus.[21]

If recent evidence is any indication, approximately 60 Canadians are killed at work annually.[22] Perhaps more disturbing are the results of an International Labor Organization study that suggests women employed in Canadian workplaces are four times more likely to be on the receiving end of workplace violence than their American counterparts.[23] Although many victims are police officers, security guards, or taxi drivers, store owners and company managers are most often the ones killed.[24] For more information on workplace violence, see the Web site for the Canadian Centre for Occupational Health and Safety (www.ccohs.ca).

Review 2: Workplace Deviance

Workplace deviance is behaviour that violates important organizational norms about right and wrong and harms the organization or its workers. Production deviance and property deviance harm the company, whereas political deviance and personal aggression harm individuals within the company.

How Do You Make Ethical Decisions?

On a cold morning in the midst of a winter storm, schools were closed and most people had decided to stay home from work. However, Richard Addessi had already showered, shaved, and dressed for the office. Addessi, whose father worked at IBM for 36 years, was just four months short of his 30-year anniversary with the company. Addessi kissed his wife Joan goodbye, but before he could get to his car he fell dead on the garage floor of a sudden heart attack. Having begun work at IBM at the age of 18, he was just 48 years old.[25]

You're the vice president in charge of benefits at IBM (www.ibm.com). Yes or no, given that he was four months short of full retirement, do you award full retirement benefits to Mr. Addessi's wife and daughters? If the answer is yes, they will receive his full retirement benefits of $1800 a month and free lifetime medical coverage. If you say no, Mrs. Addessi and her daughters will receive only $340 a month. They will also have to pay $473 a month just to continue their current medical coverage. As the VP in charge of benefits at IBM, what would be the ethical thing to do?

After reading the next two sections, you should be able to

3 describe what influences ethical decision-making.

4 explain what practical steps managers can take to improve ethical decision-making.

3 INFLUENCES ON ETHICAL DECISION-MAKING

So what did IBM decide to do? Since Richard Addessi was four months short of 30 years with the company, IBM officials felt they had no choice but to give Joan Addessi and her two daughters the smaller, partial retirement benefits. Do you think that IBM's decision was ethical? Probably many of you don't. You wonder how the company could be so heartless as to not give Richard Addessi's family the full benefits to which you believe they were entitled. Yet others might argue that IBM did the ethical thing by strictly following the rules laid out in its pension benefit plan. After all, being fair means applying the rules to everyone.

Let's examine why, while some ethical issues are easily solved, for many there are no clearly right or wrong answers. The ethical answers that managers choose depend on the ethical intensity of the decision, the moral development of the manager, and the ethical principles used to solve the problem.

Ethical Intensity of the Decision

Managers don't treat all ethical decisions the same. The manager who has to decide whether to deny or extend full benefits to Joan Addessi and her family is going to treat that decision much more seriously than the manager who has to deal with an assistant who has been taking computer disks home for personal use. The difference between these decisions is one of **ethical intensity**, which is how concerned people are about an ethical issue. When addressing issues of high ethical intensity, managers are more aware of the impact their decisions have on others. They are more likely to view the decision as an ethical or moral decision rather than an economic decision. They are also more likely to worry about doing the "right thing."

ethical intensity
the degree of concern people have about an ethical issue

Ethical intensity depends on six factors:[26]

- magnitude of consequences
- social consensus
- probability of effect
- temporal immediacy
- proximity of effect
- concentration of effect

magnitude of consequences
the total harm or benefit derived from an ethical decision

social consensus
agreement on whether behaviour is bad or good

Magnitude of consequences is the total harm or benefit derived from an ethical decision. The more people who are harmed, or the greater the harm to those people, the larger the consequences. **Social consensus** is agreement on whether behaviour is bad or good. For example, other than the act of self-defence, most people agree that killing is wrong. However, people strongly disagree about whether abortions or the death penalty are wrong. **Probability of effect** is the chance that something will happen and then result in harm to others.

probability of effect
the chance that something will happen and then result in harm to others

Temporal immediacy is the time between an act and the consequences the act produces. Temporal immediacy is stronger if a manager has to lay off workers next week as opposed to three months from now. **Proximity of effect** is the social, psychological, cultural, or physical distance of a decision maker to those affected by his or her decisions. In the previous example, proximity of effect would be greater for the manager who works with employees who are to be laid off than it would be for a staff person who works where no layoffs are occurring. Finally, whereas the magnitude of consequences is the total effect across all people, **concentration of effect** is how much an act affects the average person. Cheating 10 investors out of \$10 000 apiece is a greater concentration of effect than cheating 100 investors out of \$1000 apiece.

temporal immediacy
the time between an act and the consequences the act produces

proximity of effect
the social, psychological, cultural, or physical distance between a decision maker and those affected by his or her decisions

Many people will likely feel IBM was wrong to deny full benefits to Joan Addessi. Why? Because IBM's decision met five of the six characteristics of ethical intensity. The difference in benefits (\$23 000 per year) is likely to have serious consequences on the family.

concentration of effect
the total harm or benefit that an act produces on the average person

The decision is certain to affect them. It will affect them immediately. We can closely identify with Joan Addessi and her daughters (as opposed to IBM's faceless, nameless corporate identity). And the decision will have a concentrated effect on the family with regard to their monthly benefits ($1800 and free medical coverage if you award full benefits versus $340 a month and medical care coverage that costs $473 per month if you don't).

The exception, as we will discuss below, is social consensus. Not everyone will agree that IBM's decision was unethical. The judgment also depends on your level of moral development and which ethical principles you use.

Moral Development

A friend has given you the latest version of Microsoft Word. She stuffed the computer disks in your backpack with a note saying that you should install it on your computer and get it back to her in a couple of days. You're tempted. You have papers to write, notes to take, presentations to plan. Besides, all of your friends have the same version of Microsoft Word. They didn't pay for it either. Copying the software to your hard drive without buying your own copy clearly violates copyright laws. But no one would find out. Even if they do, Microsoft isn't going to come after you. Microsoft goes after the big fish, companies that illegally copy and distribute software to their workers. Your computer has booted up, and you've got your mouse in one hand and the installation disk in the other. What are you going to do?[27]

preconventional level of moral development
first level of moral development in which people make decisions based on selfish reasons

conventional level of moral development
second level of moral development in which people make decisions that conform to societal expectations

postconventional level of moral development
third level of moral development in which people make decisions based on internalized principles

In part, according to Lawrence Kohlberg, the decision will be based on your level of moral development. Kohlberg identified three phases of moral development, with two stages in each phase (see Exhibit 3.2).[28] At the **preconventional level of moral development**, people decide based on selfish reasons. For example, if you were in Stage 1, the punishment and obedience stage, your primary concern would be not to get in trouble. So you wouldn't copy the software. Yet, in Stage 2, the instrumental exchange stage, you make decisions that advance your wants and needs. So you copy the software.

People at the **conventional level of moral development** make decisions that conform to societal expectations. In Stage 3, the good boy–nice girl stage, you normally do what the other "good boys" and "nice girls" are doing. If everyone else is illegally copying software, you will, too. In the law and order stage, Stage 4, you do whatever the law permits, so you wouldn't copy the software.

People at the **postconventional level of moral development** always use internalized ethical principles to solve ethical dilemmas. In Stage 5, the legal contract stage, you would refuse to copy the software because, as a whole, society is better off when the rights of others—in this case, the rights of software authors and manufacturers—are not violated. In Stage 6, the universal principle stage, you might or might not copy the software, depending on your principles of right and wrong. Moreover, you will stick to your principles even if your decision conflicts with the law (Stage 4) or what others believe is best for society (Stage 5). For example, someone with socialist or communist beliefs would always choose to copy the software, because they view goods and services as owned by society rather than by individuals and corporations. (For information about the legal issues concerning software piracy, see the Software Information and Industry Association site at www.spa.org.)

Kohlberg originally predicted that people would progress sequentially from earlier stages to later stages. We now know that one's level of moral maturity can change, depending on individual and situational factors. As people age, become more educated, or deal with dilemmas high in ethical intensity, they are more likely to make ethical decisions using a higher level of moral maturity.

EXHIBIT 3.2
Kohlberg's Stages of Moral Development

PRECONVENTIONAL LEVEL
Stage 1: Punishment and Obedience
Stage 2: Instrumental Exchange
CONVENTIONAL LEVEL
Stage 3: Good Boy–Nice Girl
Stage 4: Law and Order
POSTCONVENTIONAL LEVEL
Stage 5: Legal Contract
Stage 6: Universal Principle

Source: W. Davidson III & D. Worrell, "Influencing Managers to Change Unpopular Corporate Behavior Through Boycotts and Divestitures," *Business & Society* 34 (1995): 171–196.

Principles of Ethical Decision-Making

Besides an issue's ethical intensity and a manager's level of moral maturity, the particular ethical principles that managers use will also affect how they solve ethical dilemmas. Unfortunately, there is no one "ideal principle" by which to make ethical business decisions.

According to Professor Larue Hosmer, a number of different ethical principles can be used to make business decisions: long-term self-interest, personal virtue, religious injunctions, government requirements, utilitarian benefits, individual rights, and distributive justice.[29] What these ethical principles have in common is that they encourage managers and employees to take others' interests into account when making ethical decisions. At the same time, however, these principles can lead to very different ethical actions. This is illustrated by using these principles to decide whether to award full benefits to Joan Addessi and her children.

According to the **principle of long-term self-interest**, you should never take any action that is not in your or your organization's long-term self-interest. While it sounds as if the principle of self-interest promotes selfishness, it doesn't. What we do to maximize our long-term interests (save more, spend less, exercise every day, watch what we eat) is often very different from what we do to maximize short-term interests (max out our credit cards, be a couch potato, eat whatever we want). At any single time, IBM has nearly 1000 employees who are just months away from retirement. Thus, because of the costs involved, it serves IBM's long-term interest to pay full benefits only after employees have put in their 30 years.

The **principle of personal virtue** holds that you should never do anything that is not honest, open, and truthful, and which you would not be glad to see reported in the newspapers or on TV. Using the principle of personal virtue, IBM should have quietly awarded Joan Addessi her husband's full benefits. Had it done so, it could have avoided the publication of an embarrassing newspaper article on this topic.

The **principle of religious injunctions** holds that you should never take an action that is unkind or that harms a sense of community, such as the positive feelings that come from working together to accomplish a commonly accepted goal. Using the principle of religious injunctions, IBM would have been concerned foremost with compassion and kindness. Thus, it would have awarded full benefits to Joan Addessi.

According to the **principle of government requirements**, the law represents the minimal moral standards of society, so you should never take any action that violates the law.

The **principle of utilitarian benefits** states that you should never take any action that does not result in greater good for society. In short, you should do whatever creates the greatest good for the greatest number. At first, this principle suggests that IBM should award full benefits to Joan Addessi. However, if IBM did this with any regularity, the costs would be enormous, profits would shrink, and IBM's stock price would drop, harming countless shareholders, many of whom rely on IBM stock dividends for retirement income. So, in this case, the principle does not lead to a clear choice.

The **principle of individual rights** holds that you should never take any action that infringes on others' agreed-on rights. Using the principle of individual rights, IBM would deny Joan Addessi full benefits. If it carefully followed the rules specified in its pension plan, and if it permitted Mrs. Addessi due process, meaning the right to appeal the decision, then IBM would not be violating Mrs. Addessi's rights. In fact, it could be argued that providing full benefits to Mrs. Addessi would violate the rights of employees who had to wait 30 years to receive full benefits.

Finally, the **principle of distributive justice** is that you should never take any action that harms the least among us in some way. This principle is designed to protect the poor, the uneducated, and the unemployed. While Joan Addessi could probably find a job, it's unlikely, after 20 years as a stay-at-home mom, that she could easily find one that would support herself and her daughters in the manner to which they were accustomed. Using the principle of distributive justice, IBM would award her full benefits.

principle of long-term self-interest
ethical principle that holds that you should never take any action that is not in your or your organization's long-term self-interest

principle of personal virtue
ethical principle that holds that you should never do anything that is not honest, open, and truthful, and which you would not be glad to see reported in the newspapers or on TV

principle of religious injunctions
ethical principle that holds that you should never take any action that is not kind and that does not build a sense of community; a sense of everyone working together for a commonly accepted goal

principle of government requirements
ethical principle that holds that you should never take any action that violates the law, for the law represents the minimal moral standard

principle of utilitarian benefits
ethical principle that holds that you should never take any action that does not result in greater good for society. Instead, do whatever creates the greatest good for the greatest number

principle of individual rights
ethical principle that holds that you should never take any action that infringes on others' agreed-on rights

principle of distributive justice
ethical principle that holds that you should never take any action that harms the least among us: the poor, the uneducated, the unemployed

As stated at the beginning of this chapter, one of the "real world" aspects of ethical decisions is that no matter what you decide, someone or some group will be unhappy with the decision. This corollary is also true: No matter how you decide, someone or some group will be unhappy. Consequently, despite the fact that all of these different ethical principles encourage managers to balance others' needs against their own, they can also lead to very different ethical actions. So, even when managers strive to be ethical, there are often no clear answers when it comes to doing "the" right thing.

Review 3: Influences on Ethical Decision-Making

Three factors influence ethical decisions: the ethical intensity of the decision, the moral development of the manager, and the ethical principles used to solve the problem. Ethical intensity is strong when decisions have large, certain, immediate consequences, and when we are physically or psychologically close to those affected by the decision. There are three phases of moral maturity and two steps within each phase. At the preconventional level, decisions are made for selfish reasons. At the conventional level, decisions conform to societal expectations. At the postconventional level, internalized principles are used to make ethical decisions. Finally, managers can use a number of different principles when making ethical decisions: self-interest, personal virtue, religious injunctions, government requirements, utilitarian benefits, individual rights, and distributive justice.

4 PRACTICAL STEPS TO ETHICAL DECISION-MAKING

Let's examine how managers can encourage more ethical decision-making in their organizations. They can do this by carefully selecting and hiring new employees, establishing a specific code of ethics, training employees to make ethical decisions, and creating an ethical climate.

Selecting and Hiring Ethical Employees

overt integrity test written test that estimates employee honesty by directly asking job applicants what they think or feel about theft or about punishment of unethical behaviours

As an employer, you can increase your chances of hiring honest people if you give job applicants integrity tests. **Overt integrity tests** estimate employee honesty by directly asking job applicants what they think or feel about theft or about punishment of unethical behaviours.[30] For example, an employer might ask an applicant, "Do you think you would ever consider buying something from somebody if you knew the person had

PHIL DATE/SHUTTERSTOCK

Job interviews are ideal situations to assess ethical attitudes of employees.

stolen the item?" or "Don't most people steal from their companies?" Surprisingly, because they believe that the world is basically dishonest and that dishonest behaviour is normal, unethical people will usually answer yes to such questions.[31]

Personality-based integrity tests indirectly estimate employee honesty by measuring psychological traits such as dependability and conscientiousness. For example, prison inmates serving time for white-collar crimes (counterfeiting, embezzlement, and fraud) scored much lower than a comparison group of middle-level managers on scales measuring reliability, dependability, honesty, and being conscientious and rule-abiding.[32] These results show that companies can selectively hire and promote people who will be more ethical.[33]

personality-based integrity test
written test that indirectly estimates employee honesty by measuring psychological traits such as dependability and conscientiousness

For more on integrity testing, see the "What Really Works" feature on page 70.

Codes of Ethics

As shown in Exhibit 3.3, Shell Canada (www.shell.ca) has had in place a set of business principles and code of ethics for over 30 years.[36]

Today, nine out of ten large corporations have an ethics code in place.[37] However, two things must happen if those codes are to encourage ethical decision-making and behaviour. First, companies must communicate the codes to others both within and outside the company. An excellent example of a well-communicated code of ethics can be

EXHIBIT 3.3
Shell Canada's Statement of General Business Principles

Shell's Statement of General Business Principles sets out the company's objectives and its responsibilities to various stakeholders—shareholders, customers, employees, those individuals or organizations with whom it does business and society in general. The code of ethics covers

- Business integrity (including conflict of interest; gifts, entertainment, and bribery; the integrity of the company's financial information; protection and use of property; business controls; confidential information; insider trading; and timely disclosure).
- Health, safety, and the environment.
- Competition law.
- Political activities.

The conduct required by this code means that all employees will

- Act with honesty and integrity and be open in dealings with all stakeholders;
- Treat others with fairness, dignity, and respect to create and protect a trusting environment free from harassment and discrimination; and
- Strive for excellence and professionalism, taking pride in what they do individually and as part of a team.

Although the code of ethics provides some specific examples of ethical conduct, employees are cautioned that the examples are not exhaustive and that they must use their best judgment in the application of Shell's Business Principles and Code of Ethics. They are also encouraged to consult with their supervisor. In assessing whether a situation might contravene the principles or code, employees should consider whether

- The conduct is legal.
- The conduct violates Shell's policies or procedures.
- The conduct is within Shell's authorized system of business controls.
- The results of the conduct would be fair in both the short and long term.
- The conduct would meet Shell's responsibilities to its stakeholders.
- The disclosure of such conduct, internally, would not be of concern.
- The public would consider the conduct to be honest and ethical.

Source: Courtesy Shell Canada Limited. Available www.shell.ca, 21 October 2002.

WHAT REALLY WORKS

Integrity Tests[34]

In some cases and in some countries, unethical employee behaviour can lead to multimillion-dollar fines for corporations. Moreover, workplace deviance, such as stealing, fraud, and vandalism, can cost companies billions of dollars every year. One way to reduce workplace deviance and the chance of a large fine for unethical employee behaviour is to use overt and personality-based integrity tests to screen job applicants.

One hundred eighty-one studies, with a combined total of 576 460 study participants, have examined how well job performance and various kinds of workplace deviance are predicted by integrity tests. Not only do these studies show that integrity tests can help companies reduce workplace deviance, but they have the added bonus of helping companies hire workers who are better performers in their jobs.

WORKPLACE DEVIANCE (COUNTERPRODUCTIVE BEHAVIOURS)

Compared to job applicants who score poorly, there is an 82 percent chance that job applicants who score well on overt integrity tests will participate in less illegal activity, unethical behaviour, drug abuse, or workplace violence.

Overt Integrity Tests & Workplace Deviance

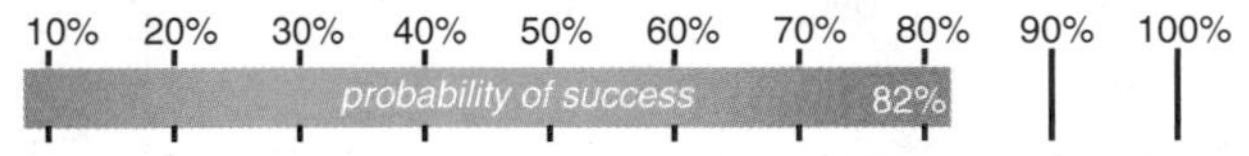

Personality-based integrity tests also do a good job of predicting who will engage in workplace deviance. Compared to job applicants who score poorly, there is a 68 percent chance that job applicants who score well on personality-based integrity tests will participate in less illegal activity, unethical behaviour, excessive absences, drug abuse, or workplace violence.

Personality-Based Integrity Tests & Workplace Deviance

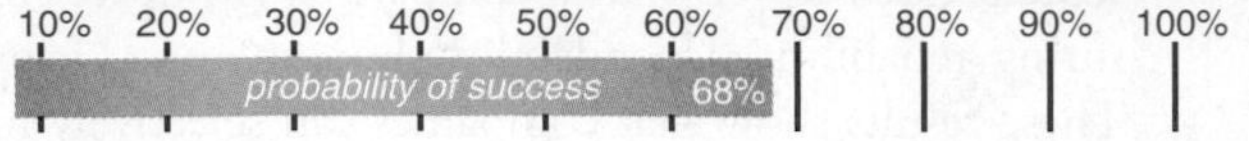

JOB PERFORMANCE

Integrity tests not only reduce unethical behaviour and workplace deviance, but they also help companies hire better performers. Compared to employees who score poorly, there is a 69 percent chance that employees who score well on overt integrity tests will be better performers.

Overt Integrity Tests & Job Performance

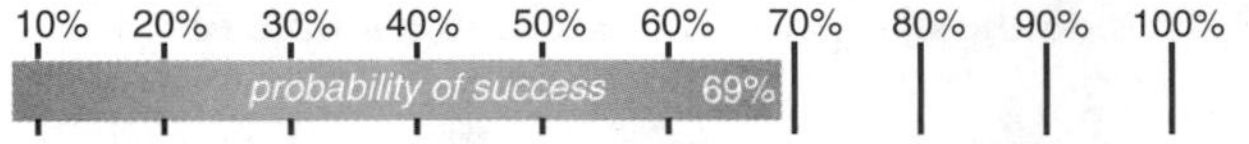

The figures are nearly identical for personality-based integrity tests. Compared to those who score poorly, there is a 70 percent chance that employees who score well on personality-based integrity tests will be better at their jobs.

Personality-Based Integrity Tests & Job Performance

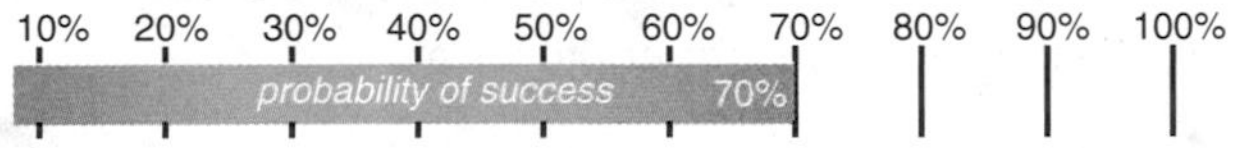

THEFT

While integrity tests can help companies decrease most kinds of workplace deviance and increase employees' job performance, they have a smaller effect on a specific kind of workplace deviance: theft. Compared to employees who score poorly, there is a 57 percent chance that employees who score well on overt integrity tests will be less likely to steal. No theft data were available to assess personality-based integrity tests.

found at Nortel Networks' Internet site (www.nortelnetworks.com). Anyone inside or outside the company can quickly and easily obtain detailed information about the company's core values, specific ethical business practices, and much more.

Second, in addition to general guidelines and ethics codes such as "Do unto others as you would have others do unto you," management must also develop practical ethical standards and procedures specific to the company's line of business. Visitors to Nortel Networks' Internet site can instantly access references to 36 specific ethics codes, ranging from bribes and kickbacks to expense vouchers and illegal copying of software. For example, most business people believe that it is wrong to take bribes or other gifts from a company that wants your business. Therefore, one of Nortel Networks' ethical guidelines is "Under no circumstances is it acceptable to offer, give, solicit, or receive any form of bribe, kickback, or inducement. This principle applies to Nortel Networks transactions everywhere in the world, even where the practice is widely considered 'a way of doing business.'" Specific codes of ethics such as these make it much easier for employees to decide what they should do when they want to do the "right thing." They also help Nortel's current president and CEO, Mike Zafirovski, move the company away from an era plagued by scandals toward a future full of opportunities.

DOING THE RIGHT THING

IF YOU CHEAT IN SCHOOL, WILL YOU CHEAT IN THE WORKPLACE?

Studies show that university students who cheat once are likely to cheat again. Students who cheat on exams are likely to cheat on assignments and projects. Furthermore, tolerance of cheating is widespread, as 70 percent of university students don't see cheating as a problem. So, with relaxed attitudes toward cheating, and on-campus cheating at all-time highs, employers want to know if you cheat in school, will you cheat in the workplace? Studies generally indicate that the answer is "yes." The best predictor of cheating in medical school was cheating in high school or college. Likewise, students who cheated in school were much more likely to cheat on their taxes, in politics, or in sports. And, when students cheated in university, they were much more likely to cheat on the job. Why is this the case? Because people who cheat and then cheat again see their behaviour as normal. And, they rationalize that cheating isn't wrong. In fact, 60 percent of the people who cheat employers don't feel guilty about it. So if you want to do the right thing, don't cheat in school or tolerate others cheating. Cheating isn't situation specific. Once you decide that cheating is acceptable, you're likely to cheat in most areas of your life. Don't slide down the slippery slope of cheating.[35]

Ethics Training

The first objective of ethics training is to develop employee awareness about ethics.[38] This means helping employees recognize what issues are ethical issues, and then avoid the rationalization of unethical behaviour: "This isn't really illegal or immoral" or "No one will ever find out."

The second objective for ethics training programs is to achieve credibility with employees. Not surprisingly, employees can be highly suspicious of management's reasons for offering ethics training. At one telecommunications company, employees initially assumed that management instituted the program to get employees to "rat" on each other. So they labelled the program "1-800-SNITCH."[39] One of the ways in which companies mistakenly hurt the credibility of their ethics programs is by having outside instructors and consultants conduct the classes. Employees often complain that outside instructors and consultants are teaching theory that has nothing to do with their jobs and the "real world." Seeking to regain credibility with its workers, this company avoided this problem by having supervisors conduct 30-minute "tailgate" sessions in which they could literally begin the training by talking to their workers from atop a truck tailgate rather than a classroom.

The third objective of ethics training is to teach employees a practical model of ethical decision-making. A basic model should help them think about the consequences their choices will have on others and consider how they will choose between different solutions. Exhibit 3.4 presents a basic model of ethical decision-making.

Ethical Climate

In study after study in which researchers have asked, "What is the most important influence on your ethical behaviour at work?" the answer comes back, "My manager." The first step in establishing an ethical climate is for managers to act ethically themselves. Managers who decline to accept lavish gifts from company suppliers; who use the company phone, fax, and copier only for business and not personal use; or who keep their promises to employees, suppliers, and customers encourage others to believe that ethical behaviour is normal and acceptable. Although transgressions such as these may appear to be obvious to many readers, thousands of former Enron and Tyco employees may have reason to suspect that a number of their former senior managers did not take the idea of an ethical work climate very seriously.

A second step in establishing an ethical climate is for top management to be active in the company ethics program. Shell Canada believes that its reputation and credibility are based on its total commitment to ethical business practices.[40] Top management must play an active leadership role in the establishment of an ethical climate. For example, one executive is the "custodian" of Shell Canada Limited's business principles and code of ethics. However this executive assumes this role on behalf of the entire senior management team. As a member of the Royal Dutch/Shell Group of companies, Shell Canada shares one of the world's most recognizable emblems. Former president and chief executive officer Tim Faithfull sent an annual letter of assurance to the group's

1.	Identify the problem. What makes it an ethical problem? Think about rights, obligations, fairness, relationships, and integrity. How would you define the problem if you stood on the other side of the fence?
2.	Identify the constituents. Who has been hurt? Who could be hurt? Who could be helped? Are they willing players, or are they victims? Can you negotiate with them?
3.	Diagnose the situation. How did it happen in the first place? What could have prevented it? Is it going to get worse or better? Can the damage now be undone?
4.	Analyze your options. Imagine the range of possibilities. Limit yourself to the two or three most manageable. What are the likely outcomes of each? What are the likely costs? Look to the company mission statement or code of ethics for guidance.
5.	Make your choice. What is your intention in making this decision? How does it compare with the probable results? Can you discuss the problem with the affected parties before you act? Could you disclose without qualm your decision to your boss, the CEO, the board of directors, your family, or society as a whole?
6.	Act. Do what you have to do. Don't be afraid to admit errors. Be as bold in confronting a problem as you were in causing it.

EXHIBIT 3.4
A Basic Model of Ethical Decision-Making

Source: L.A. Berger, "Train All Employees to Solve Ethical Dilemmas," *Best's Review-Life-Health Insurance Edition* 95 (1995): 70–80.

London office stating that Shell Canada Limited had conducted its business ethically and in accordance with its business principles. "We established a set of business principles and code of ethics almost 30 years ago and today, perhaps more than ever, these standards for ethical behaviour are our best safeguard against wrongdoing," Faithfull said. "By knowing and following these standards, we protect our own individual reputation and the reputation of the company. We actively encourage openness at all levels through an annual employee survey, which includes questions about the ethical standards of the individual work groups. We have also created an ombuds position to whom employees can take their concerns in complete confidence."

whistle-blowing
reporting others' ethics violations to management or legal authorities

A third step is to put in place a reporting system that encourages managers and employees to report potential ethics violations. **Whistle-blowing**—that is, reporting others' ethics violations, is a difficult step for most people to take and occasionally results in unwanted public visibility for the whistle blower. One example of a high-profile Canadian case involved accusations by the former chief financial officer of Livent Inc. of accounting audit irregularities of Livent's books by the accounting firm Deloitte & Touche.[41]

Potential whistle blowers often fear that they will be punished rather than the ethics violators.[42] Managers who have been interviewed about whistle-blowing have said, "In every organization, someone's been screwed for standing up." "If anything, I figured that by taking a strong stand I might get myself in trouble. People might look at me as a 'goody two shoes.' Someone might try to force me out." Today, some companies, like Northrup Grumman, a defence contractor, have made it easier to report possible violations by establishing anonymous toll-free corporate ethics hotlines. However, the factor that does the most to discourage whistle blowers is lack of company action on their complaints.[43] Thus, the final step in developing an ethical climate is for management to fairly and consistently punish those who violate the company's code of ethics.

Review 4: Practical Steps to Ethical Decision-Making

Employers can increase the chances of hiring more ethical employees by administering overt integrity tests and personality-based integrity tests to all job applicants. Most large companies now have corporate codes of ethics. But for those codes to affect ethical decision-making, they must be known both inside and outside the organization. In addition to offering general rules, ethics codes must also offer specific, practical advice. Ethics training seeks to make employees aware of ethical issues, to make ethics a serious, credible factor in organizational decisions, and to teach employees a practical model of ethical decision-making. The most important factors in creating an ethical business climate are the personal examples set by company managers, involvement of management in the company ethics program, a reporting system that encourages whistle blowers to report potential ethics violations, and fair but consistent punishment of violators.

DOING THE RIGHT THING

FINDING AN ETHICAL EMPLOYER

Rather than struggling in an unethical workplace, use these steps to discover whether a prospective employer is ethical *before* you accept a job:

- Check the company's financial history.
- Meet with current and past employees, as well as your personal business contacts, to explore the company reputation.
- Do an Internet search for complaints from employees, customers, or suppliers.
- During job interviews, ask interviewers and others about the importance of ethics in the company. Ask "Are means as well as ends important?" "How do employees get guidance on ethical issues?" "Is there an ethics code?" "Is there an ethics officer and does that person report to the board and the CEO?" "How are ethics formally incorporated into performance appraisal and promotions?"[44]

What Is Social Responsibility?

Social responsibility is a business's obligation to pursue policies, make decisions, and take actions that benefit society.[45] Unfortunately, because there are strong disagreements over to whom and for what in society organizations are responsible, it can be difficult for managers to know what is or will be perceived as socially responsible corporate behaviour. One example involves many Canadian retail organizations such as London Drugs, Pharmaprix, and Shoppers Drug Mart that are struggling with the issue of selling tobacco products alongside other store offerings intended to promote and preserve good health. If you are reading this while sitting in a Canadian university lecture hall, you are probably concerned about tuition hikes. A challenge for almost all Canadian university administrators is deciding where to draw the line with tuition levels given the financial constraints imposed on academic institutions because of government funding cutbacks. At what point does education no longer remain affordable for the masses?

social responsibility
a business's obligation to pursue policies, make decisions, and take actions that benefit society.

Alcan Inc. is another example of a well-known Canadian company that is striving to manage its image. At a recent shareholder meeting, its reputation as a socially responsible corporation was challenged by activists, workers, and politicians who were troubled by Alcan's plans to expand to India, lay off workers, and sell excess electricity.[46] Interestingly, despite these woes, Canadian companies are generally well respected when it comes to their capacity to behave in a socially responsible manner. According to KPMG's 2005 *International Survey of Corporate Social Responsibility Reporting*, Canada ranks third (after Japan and the United States) among 16 countries who companies issue corporate social responsibility reports separate from their annual reports.[47]

After reading the next four sections, you should be able to

5 explain to whom organizations are socially responsible.

6 explain for what organizations are socially responsible.

7 explain how organizations can choose to respond to societal demands for social responsibility.

8 explain whether social responsibility hurts or helps an organization's economic performance.

5 TO WHOM ARE ORGANIZATIONS SOCIALLY RESPONSIBLE?

There are two perspectives on to whom organizations are socially responsible: the shareholder model and the stakeholder model. According to Nobel Prize–winning economist Milton Friedman, the only social responsibility that organizations have is to satisfy their owners, that is, company shareholders. This view—called the **shareholder model**—holds that the only social responsibility that businesses have is to maximize

shareholder model
view of social responsibility that holds that an organization's overriding goal should be profit maximization for the benefit of shareholders

profits. By maximizing profit, the firm maximizes shareholder wealth and satisfaction. More specifically, as profits rise, the company stock owned by company shareholders generally increases in value. For example, the year after Microsoft (www.microsoft.com) released its Windows 95 operating software, company earnings increased by 45 percent over the previous year. During this time, Microsoft's stock rebounded from a low of $58.25 to $90, increasing the wealth of Microsoft shareholders by 54.5 percent.

Friedman argues that it is socially irresponsible for companies to divert their time, money, and attention from maximizing profits to social causes and charitable organizations. The first problem he sees is that organizations cannot act effectively as moral agents for all company shareholders. While shareholders are likely to agree on investment issues concerning a company, it's highly unlikely that they possess common views on what social causes a company should or should not support. Rather than act as moral agents, Friedman argues that companies should maximize profits for shareholders. Shareholders can then use their time and increased wealth to contribute to the social causes, charities, or institutions they want, rather than those that companies want.

The second major problem, according to Friedman, is that the time, money, and attention diverted to social causes undermine market efficiency. In competitive markets, companies compete for raw materials, talented workers, customers, and investment funds. Spending money on social causes means there is less money to purchase quality materials or to hire talented workers who can produce a valuable product at a good price. If customers find the product less desirable, sales and profits will fall. If profits fall, stock prices will decrease and the company will have difficulty attracting investment funds that could be used to fund long-term growth. In the end, Friedman argues, diverting the firm's money, time, and resources to social causes hurts customers, suppliers, employees, and shareholders.

stakeholder model
theory of corporate responsibility that holds that management's most important responsibility, long-term survival, is achieved by satisfying the interests of multiple corporate stakeholders

stakeholders
persons or groups with a "stake" or legitimate interest in a company's actions

primary stakeholder
any group on which an organization relies for its long-term survival

By contrast, under the **stakeholder model**, management's most important responsibility is long-term survival (not just maximizing profits), which is achieved by satisfying the interests of multiple corporate stakeholders (not just shareholders). **Stakeholders** are people or groups with a legitimate interest in a company.[48] Since stakeholders are interested in and affected by the organization's actions, they have a "stake" in what those actions are. Consequently, stakeholder groups may try to influence the firm to act in their own interests. Exhibit 3.5 shows the various stakeholder groups that the organization must satisfy to ensure long-term survival.

Being responsible to multiple stakeholders raises two basic questions. First, how does a company identify organizational stakeholders? Second, how does a company balance the needs of different stakeholders? Distinguishing between primary and secondary stakeholders can answer these questions.[49]

Some stakeholders are more important to the firm's survival than others. **Primary stakeholders** are groups, such as shareholders, employees, customers, suppliers, governments, and local communities, on which the organization depends for long-term survival. So when managers are struggling to balance the needs of different stakeholders, the stakeholder model suggests that the needs of primary stakeholders take precedence over the needs of secondary stakeholders. However, contrary to the shareholder model, no primary stakeholder group is more or less important than another, since all are critical to the firm's success and survival. So managers must try to satisfy the needs of all primary stakeholders. The issues important to primary stakeholders are noted in Exhibit 3.6. For example, responding to concerns from car manufacturers, consumers, environmental groups, and proposed government legislation, Irving Oil Ltd. of Saint John, New Brunswick, "became the first gasoline refiner in the country to get a thumbs-up from the Canadian Vehicle Manufacturers Association for its new 'green' gas."[50] Irving Oil (www.irvingoil.com) reduced the sulphur content in its gas to 150 parts per million (ppm) down from the Canadian average of 360 ppm and an Ontario average of 560 ppm. Despite significant refinery upgrading costs, this and other improvements positioned the company as the first in Canada to offer consumers cleaner-burning fuel that does not clog the sophisticated pollution-control devices in newer vehicles.[51]

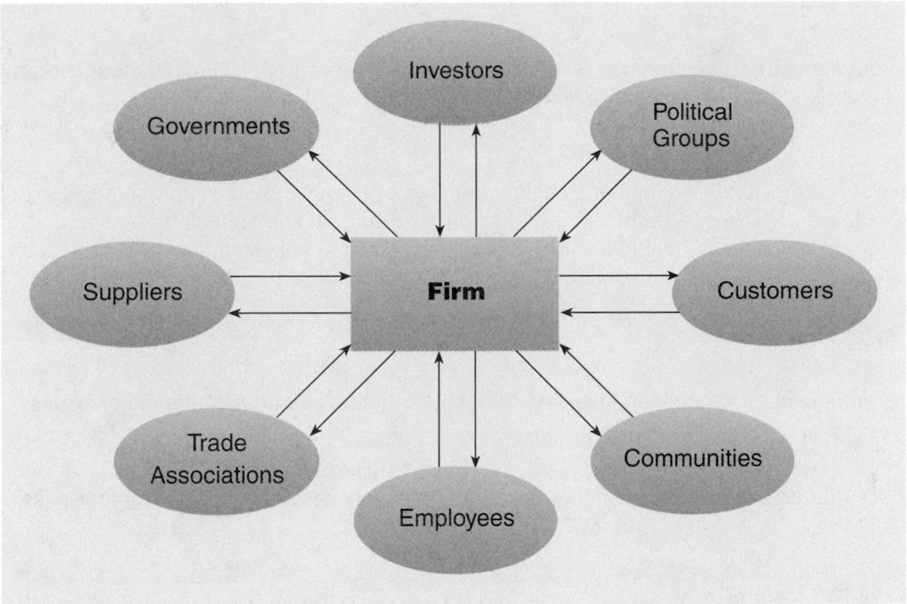

Source: Academy of Management Review by T. Donaldson & L.E. Preston. Copyright 1995 by Academy of Management. Reproduced with permission of the publisher via Copyright Clearance Center.

EXHIBIT 3.5
Stakeholder Model of Corporate Social Responsibility

Secondary stakeholders, such as the media and special interest groups, can influence or be influenced by the company. Yet in contrast to primary stakeholders, they do not engage in regular transactions with the company and are not critical to its long-term survival. Consequently, meeting the needs of primary stakeholders is usually more important than meeting the needs of secondary stakeholders. While not critical to long-term survival, secondary stakeholders are still important, because they can affect public perceptions and opinions about socially responsible behaviour. For instance, many Canadians wore fur coats up until the early 1980s. However, soon after that, public perceptions about the treatment of animals and the fur industry in general had turned negative as a result of environmental groups publicizing the cruel manner by which many animals were being trapped in the wilderness, clubbed on ice floes, or raised on farms. Consequently, many stores stopped selling furs.

secondary stakeholder any group that can influence or be influenced by the company and can affect public perceptions about its socially responsible behaviour

So to whom are organizations socially responsible? Many, especially economists and financial analysts, continue to argue that organizations are responsible only to shareholders. However, many top managers have increasingly come to believe that they and their companies must be socially responsible to their stakeholders.[52] Surveys show that as many as 80 percent of top-level managers believe that it is unethical to focus just on shareholders. So while there is not complete agreement, a majority of opinion makers would make the case that companies must be socially responsible to their stakeholders.

Review 5: To Whom Are Organizations Socially Responsible?

Social responsibility is a business's obligation to benefit society. Who are organizations socially responsible to? According to the shareholder model, the only social responsibility that organizations have is to maximize shareholder wealth by maximizing company profits. According to the stakeholder model, companies must satisfy the needs and interests of many corporate stakeholders, not just shareholders. However, the needs of primary stakeholders, on which the organization relies for its existence, take precedence over those of secondary stakeholders.

6 FOR WHAT ARE ORGANIZATIONS SOCIALLY RESPONSIBLE?

If organizations are to be socially responsible to stakeholders, just what are they to be socially responsible for? As illustrated in Exhibit 3.7, companies can best benefit their stakeholders by fulfilling their economic, legal, ethical, and discretionary responsibilities.[53]

Company	Company history, industry background, organization structure, economic performance, competitive environment, mission or purpose, corporate codes, stakeholder and social-issues management systems.
Employees	Benefits, compensation and rewards, training and development, career planning, employee assistance programs, health promotion, absenteeism and turnover, leaves of absence, relationships with unions, dismissal and appeal, termination, layoffs, retirement and termination counselling, employment equity and discrimination, women in management and on the board, daycare and family accommodation, employee communication, occupational health and safety, and part-time, temporary, or contract employees.
Shareholders	Shareholder communications and complaints, shareholder advocacy, shareholder rights, and other shareholder issues.
Customers	Customer communications, product safety, customer complaints, special customer services, and other customer issues.
Suppliers	Relative power, general policy, and other supplier issues.
Public Stakeholders	Public health, safety, and protection, conservation of energy and materials, environmental assessment of capital projects, other environmental issues, public policy involvement, community relations, social investment and donations.

Source: M.B.E. Clarkson, "A Stakeholder Framework for Analyzing and Evaluating Corporate Social Performance," *Academy of Management Review* 20 (1995): 92–117.

EXHIBIT 3.6
Issues Important to Primary Stakeholders

Exhibit 3.7 indicates that economic and legal responsibilities play a larger part in a company's social responsibility than do ethical and discretionary responsibilities. However, the relative importance of economic, legal, ethical, and discretionary responsibilities depends on the expectations that society has toward corporate social responsibility at a particular point in time.[54] A century ago, society expected businesses to meet their eco-

AP/WIDE WORLD PHOTOS

Environmentalists from Rainforest Relief and Wetlands Rainforest Action Group hold up a banner outside a Home Depot store. Protesters convinced the company to quit selling wood and wood products from threatened old-growth forests.

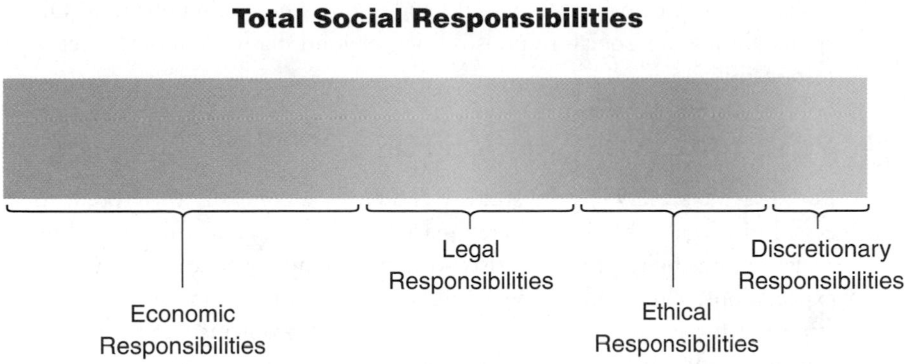

EXHIBIT 3.7
Social Responsibilities

Source: Academy of Management Review by A.B. Carroll. Copyright 1979 by Academy of Management. Reproduced with permission of the publisher via Copyright Clearance Center.

nomic and legal responsibilities and little else. Today, however, when society judges whether businesses are socially responsible, ethical and discretionary responsibilities are considerably more important than they used to be.

Historically, economic responsibility, making a profit by producing a product or service valued by society, has been a business's most basic social responsibility. Organizations that don't meet their financial and economic expectations come under tremendous pressure. For example, company boards are very, very quick these days to fire CEOs. Typically, all it takes is two or three bad quarters in a row. William Rollnick, who became acting chairman of Mattel after the company fired CEO Jill Barad, said, "There's zero forgiveness. You screw up and you're dead." Indeed, at least 38 of the largest 200 firms in North America have got rid of their CEOs between 2000 and 2003.[55]

Historically, **economic responsibility**, making a profit by producing a product or service valued by society, has been a business's most basic social responsibility. Organizations that don't meet their financial and economic expectations come under tremendous pressure. **Legal responsibility** is the expectation that companies will obey a society's laws and regulations as they try to meet their economic responsibilities.

economic responsibility
the expectation that a company will make a profit by producing a valued product or service

legal responsibility
the expectation that a company will obey society's laws and regulations

Ethical responsibility is society's expectation that organizations will not violate accepted principles of right and wrong when conducting their business. Because different stakeholders may disagree about what is or is not ethical, meeting ethical responsibilities is more difficult than meeting economic or legal responsibilities. **Discretionary responsibilities** pertain to the social roles that businesses play in society beyond their economic, legal, and ethical responsibilities. For example, MasterCard and its cardholders have teamed up with Canadian organizations such as the Juvenile Diabetes Research Foundation (www.jdrf.org), the Ontario Soccer Association (www.soccer.on.ca), and Scouts Canada (www.scouts.ca), to support research, minor soccer, and the scouting movement respectively.[56] Every time someone uses a MasterCard credit card to make a purchase, MasterCard donates a small percentage of the purchase to the designated affinity partners. While the amounts per transaction may be small, the thousands of purchases made yearly by affinity cardholders (3000 in the case of Scouts Canada[57]) can prove to be extremely valuable to any organization over time. Discretionary responsibilities are voluntary. Companies will not be considered unethical if they don't perform them. However, today, corporate stakeholders expect companies to do much more than in the past to meet their discretionary responsibilities.

ethical responsibility
the expectation that a company will not violate accepted principles of right and wrong when conducting its business

discretionary responsibilities
the expectation that a company will voluntarily serve a social role beyond its economic, legal, and ethical responsibilities

Review 6: For What Are Organizations Socially Responsible?

Companies can best benefit their stakeholders by fulfilling their economic, legal, ethical, and discretionary responsibilities. Being profitable, or meeting one's economic responsibility, is a business's most basic social responsibility. Legal responsibility consists of following a society's laws and regulations. Ethical responsibility means not violating accepted principles of right and wrong when doing business. Discretionary responsibilities are social responsibilities beyond basic economic, legal, and ethical responsibilities.

7 RESPONSES TO DEMANDS FOR SOCIAL RESPONSIBILITY

social responsiveness the strategy chosen by a company to respond to stakeholders' economic, legal, ethical, or discretionary expectations concerning social responsibility

Social responsiveness is the strategy chosen by a company to respond to stakeholders' economic, legal, ethical, or discretionary expectations concerning social responsibility. A social responsibility problem exists whenever company actions do not meet stakeholder expectations. One model of social responsiveness, shown in Exhibit 3.8, identifies four strategies for responding to social responsibility problems: reactive, defensive, accommodative, and proactive. These strategies differ in the extent to which the company is willing to act to meet or exceed society's expectations.

reactive strategy a social responsiveness strategy where a company chooses to do less than society expects and to deny responsibility for problems

A company using a **reactive strategy** will do less than society expects. It may deny responsibility for a problem or "fight all the way" any suggestions that the company should solve a problem. For example, *Consumer Reports* magazine (www.consumerreports.org) came out with a report showing that the Suzuki Samurai would tip over when drivers changed lanes or went around corners at normal speeds. The Samurai, a four-wheel-drive vehicle, was easy to tip over because it was a lightweight vehicle with a high centre of gravity and a narrow wheelbase. Rather than admit this safety problem, Suzuki Corporation immediately embarked on a multimillion-dollar television advertising campaign to dispute *Consumer Reports*' findings.[58]

defensive strategy a social responsiveness strategy where a company chooses to admit responsibility for a problem but do the least required to meet societal expectations

By contrast, a company using a **defensive strategy** would admit responsibility for a problem, but would do the least required to meet societal expectations. For example, when the sudden and unpredictable tread separation problems associated with Firestone ATX tires first became public knowledge, Firestone's response was to deny that there were problems (a reactive strategy). However seven months later, when public fury over the problem grew intense, Firestone recalled 6.5 million of the 15-inch ATX tires. However, Firestone angered lawmakers by refusing to recall all the tires recommended by the U.S. National Highway Traffic Safety Administration (www.nhtsa.gov) (a defensive strategy).[59] Firestone also frustrated and angered consumers at that time by proposing a "phased rollout," in which it would first replace tires in southern and western states—where higher temperatures seemed to be related to the problems. Steven Fink, president of Lexicon Communications, a crisis management consulting firm, criticized Firestone's response: "After they announced the recall, they were not prepared to deal with it. They were telling consumers they will have to wait up to a year to get tires."[60] In fact, Firestone's crisis management firm was so frustrated with the company's refusal to admit the problem and quickly act to restore consumer confidence (by immediately apologizing and quickly recalling and replacing all tires) that it quit.[61]

EXHIBIT 3.8
Social Responsiveness

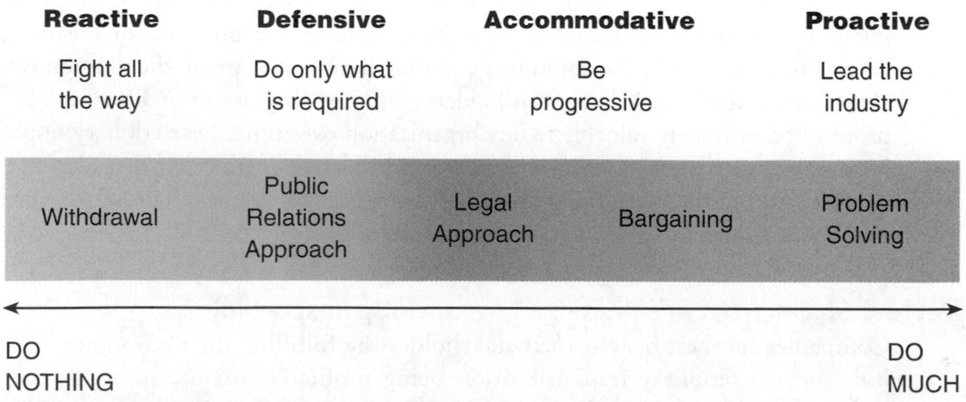

Source: Academy of Management Review by A.B. Carroll. Copyright 1979 by Academy of Management. Reproduced with permission of the publisher via Copyright Clearance Center.

A company using an **accommodative strategy** would accept responsibility for a problem and take a progressive approach by doing all that was expected to solve the problem. For example, in 1997 Noranda (www.noranda.com) was faced with the difficult task of having to close two mines in Quebec prior to opening a new mine two years later. A creative employment and benefits package constructed by Noranda and a number of government agencies allowed 70 employees to upgrade their skills and further their education while waiting for the new mine to re-open.[62] In contrast to Suzuki, Nissan Motors took an accommodative strategy when it voluntarily recalled 33 000 minivans sold in North America that were prone to catch fire when the engine's fan belt broke. Nissan spent approximately $70 million to fix the vans, installing a brand-new heavy-duty cooling system with warning lights in each vehicle. However, it also reimbursed customers for 900 vans that were beyond repair. Then it destroyed the 900 vans, so that they could not be resold to unsuspecting used-car buyers. To maintain customers' goodwill, Nissan also made other major repairs on the vans, such as air conditioning or transmission repairs, for free.[63]

accommodative strategy
a social responsiveness strategy where a company chooses to accept responsibility for a problem and do all that society expects to solve problems

Finally, a company using a **proactive strategy** would anticipate responsibility for a problem before it occurred, do more than expected to address the problem, and lead the industry in its approach. For example, Andrew Benedek, founder and CEO of Zenon Environmental Inc. (www.zenonenv.com), understood that much of the world's population has limited access to clean drinking water. Using cell membrane technology, his company developed water filtration products used in 40 countries that purify water without the use of harmful chemicals. His firm also "donated a micro filtration-based water purification plant to the Temagami First Bear Nation in Bear Island Ontario" which in turn "reduced high incidence of giardiasis or 'beaver fever.'"[64]

proactive strategy
a social responsiveness strategy where a company anticipates responsibility for a problem before it occurs and would do more than society expects to address the problem

Review 7: Responses to Demands for Social Responsibility

Social responsiveness is a company response to stakeholders' demands for socially responsible behaviour. There are four social responsiveness strategies. When a company uses a reactive strategy, it denies responsibility for a problem. When it uses a defensive strategy, it takes responsibility for a problem, but does the minimum required to solve it. When a company uses an accommodative strategy, it accepts responsibility for problems and does all that society expects to solve them. Finally, when a company uses a proactive strategy, it does much more than expected to solve social responsibility problems.

8 SOCIAL RESPONSIBILITY AND ECONOMIC PERFORMANCE

One question that managers often ask is "Does it pay to be socially responsible?" While this is an understandable question, asking whether social responsibility pays is a bit like asking if giving to your favourite charity will help you get a better-paying job. The obvious answer is no. There is not an inherent relationship between social responsibility and economic performance. Yet a number of ethical or socially responsible investment vehicles are available to Canadians. These include mutual funds such as the Meritas Fund, Manulife's Canadian Balance Ethics fund, and 12 funds from Ethical Funds Inc.[65] Not surprisingly, many investors do "put their money where their mouths are." In Canada alone, one recent estimate suggests Canadians support socially responsible investments to the tune of almost $50 billion or 3 percent of the Canadian mutual fund market.[66] Further, between 1998 and 2000, social investment assets grew at more than twice the rate of the Canadian mutual fund industry as a whole.[67] Supporters of corporate social responsibility also claim a positive relationship. For example, in Canada, the Jantzi Social Index (www.mjra-jsi.com), claims to have outperformed the TSE 60 in its first year of operation.[68] On the other hand, critics have plenty of facts to support their claim that social responsibility hurts economic performance. For example, another study of 42 socially responsible mutual funds found that the socially responsible companies underperformed the Standard and Poor's 500 by 8 percent.[69]

CP PHOTO/BORIS SPREMO

This recycled waste paper in Toronto is ready for shipment to a processing plant. Recycling is one example of social responsibility being profitable.

When it comes to social responsibility and economic performance, the first reality is that it can sometimes cost a company significantly if it chooses to be socially responsible. During the 1980s, American multinational corporations were under intense public pressure to withdraw their operations from South Africa. Political activists argued that if businesses withdrew from South Africa, the white-controlled government would be hurt economically. Thus it would be more difficult for it to maintain its system of apartheid against black South Africans. Many companies chose to pull their businesses out of South Africa. Yet when they did, they paid a steep price, selling corporate land, buildings, and equipment at a fraction of their value. Furthermore, within days of announcing that they were leaving South Africa, their company stock price dropped an average of 5.5 percent.[70] Here, socially responsible behaviour not only harmed the company financially, but harmed its shareholders financially, too. Nonetheless, hundreds of top managers still felt it was the right thing to do. In Canada one might argue that Petro-Canada (www.petrocanada.com) gave up potentially large future revenues when it chose to forfeit its undersea mineral rights in the vicinity of the Queen Charlotte Islands off the coast of British Columbia in order to help preserve the wildlife eco-system.[71]

The second reality of social responsibility and economic performance is that sometimes it does pay to be socially responsible. Zenon Environmental Inc.'s water-purification technology based on cell membranes was responsible for $125 million in revenues in 2001.[72] Another good example is Ben & Jerry's Homemade Ice Cream. Ben & Jerry's started in 1978 when founders Ben Cohen and Jerry Greenfield mailed away for a $5 course on how to make ice cream. Today, Ben & Jerry's is as well known for its super-premium ice cream as it is for its reputation as a socially responsible company. Ben & Jerry's donates 7.5 percent of its pretax profits to social causes: to charitable groups supporting AIDS patients, the homeless, and the environment.[73] The company buys brownies from a bakery that employs homeless workers and blueberries from Native North American Indian tribes. Moreover, customers buy Ben & Jerry's ice cream because it tastes great and because they want to support a socially responsible company. As Ben Cohen says, "We see ourselves as somewhat of a social service agency and somewhat of an ice cream company."[74]

The third reality of social responsibility and economic performance is that while socially responsible behaviour may be "the right thing to do," it does not guarantee profitability. Socially responsible companies experience the same ups and downs in economic performance that traditional businesses do. For example, after a year in which neither market share nor profits grew and the company's stock dropped 72 percent in value, Ben Cohen announced that he was stepping aside as Ben & Jerry's CEO. A "professional manager" who is now charged with turning around the company's financial performance replaced him. Ben & Jerry's is now owned by Unilever, a multinational consumer products company.

However, while Ben & Jerry's struggled, a Vancouver-based mining company, BHP Billiton Diamonds (www.bhpbilliton.com), has prospered while going the extra mile for its employees who are located at its remote Ekati Diamond mine in the Northwest Territories.[75] The firm hires locally, offers residences to its workers who live elsewhere in the North, sources its supplies as much as possible locally, has developed a well-received adult education program for its workers, and offers its employees a diamond purchase plan. While at work, employees benefit from a free 24-hour dining room as well as sporting facilities and private rooms. Edmonton-based power utility Epcor is another example of a profitable company giving back to its community.[76] In instances where an employee volunteers 50 hours or more per year, the company contributes $150 to that charity or community group.

In the end, if company management chooses a proactive or accommodative strategy toward social responsibility (rather than a defensive or reactive strategy), it should do so because it wants to benefit society and its corporate stakeholders, not because it expects a better financial return.

Review 8: Social Responsibility and Economic Performance

Does it pay to be socially responsible? Sometimes it costs and sometimes it pays. Overall, there is no clear relationship between social responsibility and economic performance. Consequently, managers should not expect an economic return from socially responsible corporate activities. If your company chooses to practise a proactive or accommodative social responsibility strategy, it should do so to better society and not to improve its financial performance.

What Really Happened?[77]

In the opening case, you learned that Gap Inc. has received intense negative publicity regarding how workers are treated in the overseas factories of the companies who make the clothes that it sells in its Gap, Banana Republic, and Old Navy stores. With the company losing money and protest groups calling for worldwide boycotts of its products and stores, Gap's new CEO found himself in a very difficult situation. Let's find out what really happened and see what steps Gap took to address these issues.

Since Gap is a publicly traded company, one of your most important responsibilities is to keep shareholders happy by making sure the company is profitable. And that means that your overseas suppliers have to keep their prices low. On the other hand, negative publicity and boycotts may lower sales and reduce profits. So how do you decide whose interests—stakeholders, suppliers, overseas workers, or protesters—take precedence?

According to the shareholder model, the only social responsibility that organizations have is to maximize shareholder wealth by maximizing company profits. By contrast, according to the stakeholder model, the primary responsibility of companies is to satisfy the needs and interests of multiple corporate stakeholders, meaning persons or groups with a legitimate interest in a company. Since it's impossible to please all stakeholders equally, how does a company decide which stakeholders' interests to address? In general, managers will usually try to satisfy the needs of primary stakeholders first. Organizations depend on primary stakeholders, such as employees, customers, suppliers, governments, and local communities for their survival. By contrast, companies usually try to meet the needs of secondary stakeholders, such as the media and special interest groups, after meeting the needs of primary stakeholders. Secondary stakeholders can affect public perceptions and opinions about companies, but they usually don't threaten their survival. However, if they do, corporations will clearly need to satisfy their needs, too.

In fact, this turned out to be the case for Gap. An economic downturn combined with negative worldwide news coverage, prompted by protests from special interest groups over the treatment of overseas workers, resulted in three straight unprofitable years for the company. While some argue that Gap's lack of profitability was due to poor economic conditions, the experience of Nike, the sports shoe and apparel maker, suggests that Gap had reason to be concerned. Indeed, Nike was targeted for nearly a decade by protestors for similar reasons—the poor conditions, treatment, and pay of workers in the factories of overseas suppliers who made its products. Eventually, after its stock price and market share dropped significantly and its profits plummeted by 50 percent, Nike CEO Phil Knight announced the company's anti-sweatshop programs (see www.nike.com/nikebiz/nikebiz.jhtml?page=25 or search for "workers & factories" at www.nike.com), while also publicizing the positive economic and personal effects that Nike's business had for foreign workers, their families, and their countries.

As for Gap, it has now adopted a multi-stakeholder approach to solving the problems in its overseas factories. The company has stated, "We are convinced that collaborative, multi-stakeholder engagement is the only way to create sustainable change industry wide. That's why we've been expanding our global partnerships and significantly broadening our work with outside groups. For example, we recently joined Social Accountability International's (SAI) Corporate Involvement Program, the Ethical Trading Initiative (ETI) and the United Nations' Global Compact." (See www.cepaa.org/ for more about Social Accountability International, www.ethicaltrade.org/ for more about the Ethical Trading Initiative, and www.un.org/Depts/ptd/global.htm for more about the UN's Global Compact.)

Furthermore, is Gap really responsible for the terrible treatment of overseas workers? In other words, is this your problem or is this a problem that the managers and owners of overseas factories need to address?

If organizations are to be socially responsible to stakeholders, for what are they to be socially responsible? In general, companies can best benefit their stakeholders by fulfilling their economic (making a profit by producing a product or service valued by society), legal (obeying society's laws and regulations), ethical (not violating accepted principles of right and wrong), and discretionary responsibilities (what companies choose to do to benefit society over and beyond their economic, legal, and ethical responsibilities). While economic and legal responsibilities play a larger part in a company's social responsibility than do ethical and discretionary responsibilities, the relative importance of these various responsibilities depends on society's expectations of corporate social responsibility at a particular point in time. A century ago, society expected businesses to meet their economic and legal responsibilities and little else. Today, when society judges whether businesses are socially responsible, ethical and discretionary responsibilities are considerably more important than they used to be. And, for Gap, that means that a large segment of society truly expects the company to take responsibility for the well-being of the workers in its suppliers' overseas factories. In other words, a large percentage of people believe that the foreign workers' problems *are* Gap's responsibility.

Over the last few years, Gap has accepted that responsibility. Paul Pressler, Gap's new CEO said, "We believe that garment and other manufacturing workers around the world deserve better than the reality that many unfortunately face. We recognize and embrace our duty to take a leadership role. While we know firsthand that positive change is possible, we also have learned that creating sustainable and scalable solutions across the retail apparel and garment manufacturing industries is immensely difficult. We are working to effect change in factories that produce apparel for many apparel retailers. And while some of these retailers share our commitment, others may not."

As evidence of its new-felt responsibility toward apparel manufacturing workers, Gap, in conjunction with the International Finance Corporation, which is part of the World Bank, is paying to train 650 Cambodian factory supervisors how to be better managers and how to improve labour relations. A similar program in Indonesia produced less worker absenteeism, fewer labour strikes, and better-quality clothes. Furthermore, all of Gap's garment manufacturers are required to meet its Code of Vendor Conduct, which prohibits child labour, forced labour, and discrimination, and protects other worker rights. The code is based on globally accepted labour standards and is published in 24 different languages. Moreover, each supplier must sign documents stating their agreement to comply with the Code of Vendor Conduct, pass an initial evaluation visit, and then await approval by Gap's global compliance staff. The evaluation and approval process can take anywhere from a week to a year to complete. In fact, 90 percent of suppliers fail their initial inspections, but most make changes, correct their problems, and subsequently pass and begin doing business with Gap. However, 16 percent of vendors are ultimately rejected. Furthermore, Gap uses outside agencies and 90 of its own vendor compliance officers to monitor ongoing adherence to the Code of Vendor Conduct so that garment factory workers producing its products continue to be treated fairly. Indeed, in one recent year, Gap's monitors made 8500 visits to inspect 94 percent of its current garment factories around the world.

Finally, how should Gap respond? Should you do nothing, make minimal changes, or aggressively tackle these issues no matter the effect on the company's bottom line?

Social responsiveness is a company's response to stakeholders' demands for socially responsible behaviour. There are four social responsiveness strategies. When a company uses a reactive strategy, it denies responsibility for a problem. When it uses a defensive strategy, it takes responsibility for a problem, but does the minimum required to solve it. When a company uses an accommodative strategy, it accepts responsibility for problems and does all that society expects to solve them. Finally, when a company uses a proactive strategy, it does much more than expected to solve social responsibility problems.

Over time, Gap has progressed from a reactive strategy to a proactive strategy. Dan Henkle, Gap's vice president of global compliance, said, "We have been reactive. The industry has been reactive. As a company, we needed to really start thinking about where we're headed with this work." Henkle continued, saying, "There was a lot of soul-searching within the company about who we are and where we wanted to go. We all understood that there was a real need for change [on this issue]."

However, with the recent release of its 40-page Social Responsibility Report (see http://ccbn.mobular.net/ccbn/7/645/696/print/print.pdf) in which it provided complete, unrestricted, detailed information regarding the problems it found in its suppliers' factories, it could be argued that Gap has become the most proactive retailer in the industry. In this report, Gap indicates the extent to which it found instance of forced labour (involuntary labour, prison labour, or debt bondage), child labour (employment of workers under 14 years old or local laws specifying particular working ages), problems with wages and hours (paying below minimum wage, insufficient or nonexistent overtime pay, work weeks greater than 60 hours, threats against workers who refuse overtime, not giving workers at least one day off per week, or ambiguous wage agreements that end up cheating workers out of the pay they've earned), and workplace conditions (physical punishment, coercion, verbal abuse, poor lighting or ventilation, obstructed aisles or exits, insufficient safety devices on machinery, lack of first-aid kits, or inadequate storage of hazardous materials), and so forth, in all of its apparel suppliers' factories.

The Wall Street Journal characterized the report this way: "The Gap report represents a dramatic change in strategy for a retailer that has long been on the defensive about working conditions at the factories that make its clothing. It may also represent a deft strategic move. At the same time that the report exonerates the majority of factories making Gap clothes, its frank discussion of violations at a minority of plants already is winning praise from some of the retailer's most vociferous critics." Anne Gust, Gap's chief administrative and compliance officer, said, "For us to be transparent [about our problems], we had to be willing to live with bad reactions to the report. We knew it was not going to be strictly, 'Gap is good.' It's more complicated than that."

Reaction to the report has been positive, even among Gap's strongest critics. Adam Kanzer, director of shareholder advocacy for Domini Social Investments, the manager of the Domini Social Equity Fund, which invests in socially responsible businesses, said, "Nearly a decade after major retailers began to develop codes of conduct for their supply chains to deter sweatshop conditions, it is virtually impossible to determine levels of compliance with these codes. To restore and maintain the confidence of consumers and investors, it is essential that retailers issue public reports detailing code compliance." Ruth Rosenbaum, executive director of the Center for Reflection, Education and Action, said, "In our view, corporate social compliance systems should exist to bring working conditions in line with internationally accepted human rights standards. These systems are critically important to helping workers protect their rights. We commend Gap for recognizing that its code of conduct sits within this broader context of international human rights norms. It is an important recognition of public accountability." Alya Kayal, senior international/human rights analyst for Calvert, a socially responsible investment company, said, "While companies say that they have been steadily improving the quality of their vendor standards enforcement, they have generally not been willing to share meaningful data to verify their assertions. Establishing a meaningful public benchmark that helps stakeholders and the general public understand and measure the company's progress is a valuable step forward on public disclosure."

And, in addition to releasing its candid, detailed Social Responsibility Report, Gap is backing up its statement with serious actions and consequences uncovered by its vendor monitoring system. In fact, Gap recently revoked the contracts of 136 suppliers because of persistent or severe violations, including violation of child labour laws. However, in most cases, it revoked the contracts only after first working with factory owners and managers to try to fix the problems and improve working conditions. In addition to working with factory managers and owners, Gap is also working with UNITE, the world's largest apparel and textiles workers union, to improve workers' lives and workplace conditions. Together, Gap and UNITE will open El Salvador's first independent and fully unionized clothing factory. UNITE's president, Bruce Raynor, said, "We've had our differences with Gap in the past, and we may in the future. But when we started talking with them about this situation [in El Salvador], and others like it, we realized we could work together and create positive change for workers in El Salvador and elsewhere. This industry is riddled with problems worldwide. We're excited about working with the Gap to create some positive examples that show garment factories can be successful and protect labor standards." Finally, Raynor said, "My daughter asked me if it was OK to shop at Gap now, and when I said 'yes,' it instantly cost me $80."

Key Terms

Self-Assessment

AN ETHICAL BASELINE

Most people think they are ethical, particularly when the right thing to do is seemingly obvious. But, as you read in the chapter, 75 percent of the respondents in a large survey indicated that they had witnessed unethical behaviour at work. In another study across multiple industries, 48 percent of the respondents admitted to actually committing an unethical or illegal act in the past year. And recall that with so many ways to approach ethical decision-making, ethical choices are not always obvious. To give you an idea of your ethical perspective, take the 25-question survey found on page 511 in the Assessment Appendix. The assessment will provide some baseline information as a foundation for your ethical development.

Management Decisions

TO LIE OR TO TELL THE TRUTH?

Ethical dilemmas in the workplace occur often. Some are completely obvious, while others are subtle. Suppose you are the purchasing agent for a large corporation. A supplier has approached you regarding a recently submitted bid and has stated that if you choose his company as the winning bidder, he will provide you and your spouse with round-trip airfare tickets to Hawaii. His company's bid is 25 percent higher than the lowest bid. Accepting his offer would clearly be an unethical response, since it provides you, the purchasing agent, with a gain (airline tickets for you and your spouse) and costs your company money by accepting the proposal from the supplier with the highest price. Additionally, since your company has a policy forbidding cash, gifts, and other entitlements from suppliers and vendors, you would most likely lose your job if anyone found out. Therefore, the only ethical choice is to refuse the supplier's offer and award the contract to the vendor with the best product and the best price.

Now look at a scenario that has less obvious challenges. Assume that you have recently been hired as an entry-level manager for a small marketing agency and your supervisor, Ms. Johnson, tells you that she is running behind on an advertising proposal for a client. Ms. Johnson states that the client will be dropping in this afternoon to discuss the proposal. She has asked that you intercept the client and tell him that she was called out of town for an emergency business meeting and to inform him that she will contact him when she returns from her trip. Delaying the client will buy Ms. Johnson the necessary time to finalize the client's proposal and allow her to appear more professional when she presents the proposal to him. In this dilemma, the gain is more time for Ms. Johnson to complete her assignment and the cost is that the client is delayed and deceived. There appears to be no personal gain for you.

Questions

1. Describe what you would do in the preceding scenario: accept the order from Ms. Johnson or refuse to cover for her.
2. Suppose a colleague tells you that your predecessor was fired for refusing to accommodate Ms. Johnson and her continual demands for unethical behaviour and unethical responses. Would that change your decision in question 1? Why or why not?
3. If you had to choose a principle of ethical decision-making to support your decision to this scenario, which principle would you choose and why?

Management Decisions[78]

SPEEDING TICKETS OR A POOR CREDIT RECORD?

Who is the poorer risk for an insurance company: someone who has been caught speeding numerous times or someone who has a bad credit record? Logically, it should be the speeder, because everyone knows that "speed kills," that speeders are in more accidents themselves, and that speeders cause other drivers to have accidents. In fact, government studies confirm that speed is one of the major causes of fatal car accidents. Everyone knows this to be true!

Surprisingly, however, the speeder is less likely to file benefit claims with an insurance company than someone with a poor credit record. Why? It is not exactly clear. However, insurance executives suspect that people who are good with their money are reliable and conscientious about driving (except for speeding). On the other hand, they speculate that people with poor credit records may be more likely to file false claims.

Regardless of the reasons, auto insurers have found that adding a request for credit information to a standard auto insurance application helps them do a better job of screening good insurance risks, that is, identifying people who will pay their premiums each month and those who will file claims for insurance benefits. "The data is absolutely overwhelming," says one insurance industry executive. "There is a very strong correlation between serious financial instability and future loss."

Critics charge that insurers who use credit records when deciding whether to offer insurance coverage are simply discriminating against the poor and minorities. Studies show that credit problems are inversely related to one's level of income. Others simply doubt that credit records are accurate predictors of insurance risk.

Questions

1. Is it unethical or socially irresponsible for auto insurers to use credit records to screen applicants for auto insurance? Explain.
2. There is often disagreement about what companies should be socially responsible for. Explain what an insurance company's economic, legal, ethical, and discretionary responsibilities should be.

Develop Your Management Potential

"It is only the farmer who faithfully plants seeds in the Spring, who reaps a harvest in the Autumn."

—B.C. Forbes, Founder of *Forbes* Magazine

The purpose of these assignments is to develop your present and future capabilities as a manager. Since stakeholders increasingly expect companies to do more to fulfill their discretionary responsibilities, chances are you and your company will be expected to support your community in some significant way. To begin learning about community needs and corporate social responsibility, visit a local charity or nonprofit organization of your choosing, perhaps a hospital, the Red Cross, a soup kitchen, or a homeless shelter. Talk to the people who work or volunteer there. Gather the information you need to answer the following questions.

Questions

1. What is the organization's mission?
2. Whom does the organization serve and how does it serve them?
3. What percentage of the organization's donations is used for administrative purposes? What percentage is used to directly benefit those served by the organization? What is the ratio of volunteers to paid workers?
4. What job or task does the "typical" volunteer perform for the organization? How much time per week does the typical volunteer give to the organization? For what jobs do they need more volunteers?
5. How does the business community support the organization?
6. Why are you interested in the activities of this organization?

Discussion Questions

1. Canadian Tire is one of the most Canadian and best-known retailers—for example, everyone knows immediately what is meant by "Canadian Tire money." As with all large organizations, managers may from time to time be faced with dealing with worker behaviour that fits under the heading of "workplace deviance." Think of a typical Canadian Tire store. What four categories of deviant behaviour might a typical manager need to be wary of as he or she leads the day-to-day operations? In this instance, what does deviant behaviour refer to?
2. Times are tough for CEOs. Recent evidence suggests that boards of directors are far less tolerant of wayward managers. Higher turnover rates means that more new faces are being found in the executive suite. For a newly hired CEO, what four steps might he or she take to encourage more ethical decision-making?
3. Picture yourself being offered a high-profile challenge. You have been asked to take over the reins of Worldcom (now known as MCI), reinvent the top management team, and create a work environment that will be the envy of the industry. What are the four most important factors that you should consider as you attempt to create an ethical business climate?
4. Food banks are a necessary but unfortunate part of many towns and cities. Newly graduated from the University of Alberta's undergraduate Business program, you have taken on the responsibility of managing one of Edmonton's food banks. Among your most important responsibilities is to ensure that your organization can respond to the needs of the unfortunate on a day-to-day basis. Unfortunately, as the administrator you also have to manage other issues. Recently, you have been feeling overwhelmed by the different tasks and have decided to start ranking issues. Before doing this, however, you recognize that the needs and requests of some stakeholders may be more important than others. If you were to categorize the various stakeholders, which would be considered primary and which would be categorized as secondary? In this instance, what would be the difference between a primary stakeholder and a secondary stakeholder?
5. As manager of the food bank, you are also given the task of ensuring that the organization behaves in a socially responsible manner. Which four areas of corporate social responsibility would be most relevant to the food bank's stakeholders? Briefly describe each.

Critical Thinking Video Case

CBC

Visit www.management2e.nelson.com to view this chapter's CBC video case.

Take Two

Biz Flix
Emperor's Club

William Hundert (Kevin Kline), a professor at Saint Benedict's preparatory school, believes in teaching his students about living a principled life as well as teaching them his beloved classical literature. Hundert's principled ways are challenged, however, by a new student, Sedgewick Bell (Emile Hirsch). Bell's behaviour during the 73rd annual Julius Caesar competition causes Hundert to suspect that Bell leads a less than principled life. Years later Hundert is the honoured guest of his former student Sedgewick Bell (Joel Gretsch) at Bell's estate. Depaak Mehta (Rahul Khanna), Bell, and Louis Masoudi (Patrick Dempsey) compete in a re-enactment of the Julius Caesar competition. Bell wins the competition, but Hundert notices that Bell is wearing an earpiece. Earlier in the film, Hundert had suspected that the young Bell also wore an earpiece during the competition, but Headmaster Woodbridge (Edward Herrmann) had pressed him to ignore his suspicion. This scene appears at the end of the film. It is an edited portion of the competition re-enactment. Bell announced his candidacy for the U.S. Senate just before talking to Hundert in the bathroom. He carefully described his commitment to specific values that he would pursue if elected.

What to Watch for and Ask Yourself

1. Does William Hundert describe a specific type of life that one should lead? If so, what are its elements?
2. Does Sedgewick Bell lead that type of life? Is he committed to any specific ethical view or theory?
3. What consequences or effects do you predict for Sedgewick Bell because of the way he chooses to live his life?

Management Workplace
Eco-Natural Solutions, Sundance, and Diversified Chemical

Ethical business and social responsibility have a different meaning for every organization. Eco-Natural Solutions (an organic candy company), Sundance (the artistic venture associated with Robert Redford), and Diversified Chemical (a conglomerate based in Detroit) all have a different perspective on what it means to be socially responsible. Nevertheless, they all agree that business and social responsibility do not have to be opposing forces. In fact, they view social responsibility as an impetus and rationale for starting, building, and growing a business enterprise.

What to Watch for and Ask Yourself

1. Compare the way that Eco-Natural, Sundance, and Diversified Chemical view social responsibility.
2. For these companies, has social responsibility been profitable?

Part 2

Making Things Happen

PHOTO: INDU GHUMAN

Chapter 4

Planning

CHAPTER OUTLINE

Planning

- **Benefits and Pitfalls of Planning**
  - Benefits of Planning
  - Planning Pitfalls
- **How to Make a Plan that Works**
  - Setting Goals
  - Developing Commitment to Goals
  - Developing Effective Action Plans
  - Tracking Progress
  - Maintaining Flexibility

Kinds of Plans

- **Planning from Top to Bottom**
  - Starting at the Top
  - Bending in the Middle
  - Finishing at the Bottom
- **Special-Purpose Plans**
  - Planning for Change
  - Planning for Contingencies
  - Planning for Product Development

LEARNING OBJECTIVES

After reading this chapter, you should be able to

1. discuss the costs and benefits of planning.
2. describe how to make a plan that works.
3. discuss how companies can use plans at all management levels, from top to bottom.
4. describe the different kinds of special-purpose plans that companies use to plan for change, contingencies, and product development.

WestJet Airlines (www.westjet.ca) began operating a no-frills air service in 1996 with three airplanes while its main competitors, Air Canada (www.aircanada.ca) and Canadian Airlines, had a combined fleet that approached 300. Tiny by comparison to the "friendly duopoly" of Canadian and Air Canada (see Chapter 2), WestJet concentrated on short-haul routes in western Canada and originally serviced only five cities. WestJet modelled itself on the very successful U.S.-based Southwest Airlines, a no-frills, low-fare airline and one of the few consistently profitable airlines in North America. After starting with a few destinations and a small fleet, it embarked on a model of slow and cautious growth. By the end of 2002, WestJet had turned a profit for 22 consecutive fiscal quarters, a great accomplishment given that the U.S. industry lost US$11 billion in 2001 and US$3.5 billion in 2002. Air Canada, WestJet's main Canadian competitor, lost money in 2000 and 2001 and the prospects did not look much better for 2002.[1]

Air Canada had controlled approximately 90 percent of the domestic market after it purchased and merged with Canadian Airlines in early 2000. By the first quarter of 2001, the airline held only 73 percent of the market, while WestJet's share climbed to 14 percent. Ticket prices were a major problem for Air Canada as in most cases Air Canada's ticket prices were significantly higher than WestJet's. Travellers who wanted to fly on short notice or not stay over a Saturday night could pay up to six times more to fly on Air Canada than on WestJet. Air Canada also relied heavily on business travellers who were willing to pay premium prices, but this market was in significant decline. WestJet was able to keep ticket prices low because it had a cost structure that was 40 percent lower than Air Canada's. There were several factors that contributed to its lower cost structure. One key item was that WestJet operated only one type of aircraft, the Boeing 737. Having only one type of airplane allowed the company to save on the cost of mechanics' and pilots' training and spare-part inventories. It also has a nonunionized, flexible work force that is motivated by profit sharing. On the other hand, Air Canada has a unionized work force with rigid work rules and strong unions. Another factor is that, as opposed to Air Canada, WestJet does not offer food service on its flights. All these factors lead to significant cost savings.

What Would You Do?

In 2002 WestJet started to service Hamilton, Ontario, a lower-cost alternative to Toronto, and there were also plans in the works to move into the Maritimes. Up to this point, Air Canada had a virtual stranglehold on central Canada and the Maritimes and these markets were essential to Air Canada's already-shaky bottom line. Now its key markets were being threatened. A further indication of trouble ahead was the fact that WestJet seemed to be constantly increasing the size of its fleet even faster than it had originally planned. The new airplanes were very fuel-efficient and would need less maintenance, which could cut WestJet's operating costs even further. It seemed like it would not take long for WestJet to compete nationwide directly with Air Canada as Canada's second national carrier.

Grey skies were clearly ahead for Air Canada but it took a bold and risky move. It launched two new no-frills airlines called Tango, launched in October 2001, and Zip, launched in September 2002. Air Canada hoped these two airlines would mimic the success of WestJet and Southwest Airlines. Zip was based in Calgary and focused on the western Canadian short haul market. It started with six planes and there were hopes it would grow to 20. It was intended that this service would complement longer-haul Air Canada flights and provide "seamless" service connecting to these flights. Tango, on the other hand, was intended to compete directly with Air Canada. It focused on the medium- and long-haul market and was also expected to grow to 20 aircraft. Each airline was intended to fly only one type of aircraft in order to cut costs. Tango would fly Boeing 737s while Zip would fly Airbus A320s.

These changes by no means guaranteed the resurrection of Air Canada's fortunes. Other large international airlines, such as British Airways, had launched low-cost subsidiaries and generally failed in the attempt, as the low-cost subsidiaries found it very difficult to disentangle themselves from the parent airline's high-cost structure. There was also the problem that Air Canada could cannibalize higher-paying passengers from itself to its lower-cost airlines, thereby reducing its overall revenue and possibly even profits. Also, attempts to reduce labour costs, while somewhat successful, have been fraught with troubles. Many of the unions at Air Canada resisted the launch of Tango and Zip and claimed that all employees of Tango and Zip should work under the same conditions as at Air Canada, resulting in no savings in labour costs. Air Canada wanted to pay employees at Tango less, while at Zip they wanted to merge three employee groups that have direct contact with customers into a single bargaining group (reservation agents, passenger agents, and flight attendants) to increase work force flexibility and also pay lower wages. Reduced wages at Tango were agreed to, and Tango's fleet was limited to only 20 planes in order to protect Air Canada jobs. Although unable to combine employee groups, the company was able to negotiate reduced wages at Zip.

Despite the rocky start, Air Canada turned a profit in the second and third quarters of 2002, something it attributed at least in part to the launch of Tango. It was also the first international North American carrier to turn a quarterly profit since the terrorist attacks on the World Trade Center. Despite what looked like a turning point, the company lost money in the last quarter of 2002 and was forced to seek bankruptcy protection in April 2003. It seems that having only 20 planes in Tango and 20 planes in Zip, out of a fleet of over 300, was not enough to change Air Canada's fortunes. The company was also carrying a heavy debtload and had an inefficient fleet of aircraft.

If you were the CEO of Air Canada, what would you do?

As Air Canada's troubles show, creating and executing a plan is one of the most important tasks a manager has. This chapter begins by examining the costs and benefits of planning. Next, you will learn how to make a plan that works. Then you will look at the different kinds of plans that are used from the top to the bottom in most companies. Finally, you will investigate the different kinds of special-purpose plans that managers use today.

Planning

planning
choosing a goal and developing a strategy to achieve that goal

Planning is choosing a goal and developing a method or strategy to achieve that goal. Although the price of energy may be much lower by the time you read this, the price of energy has skyrocketed over the last few years. Oil, gas and electricity are rising in price. As a result of this, many organizations are looking to cut the cost of heating and air conditioning. For example, Canadian Forces Base Kingston recently undertook a program to reduce its $9.1 million annual utility bill by $2.3 million. This was part of a nationwide strategy by the Department of National Defence to reduce the energy consumption of all Canadian Forces Bases. In order to do this, they installed more efficient lighting, upgraded thermostats, and plugged leaks in water pipes under the base to reduce water consumption.[2]

After reading the next two sections, you should be able to

1. discuss the costs and benefits of planning.
2. describe how to make a plan that works.

1 BENEFITS AND PITFALLS OF PLANNING

Are you one of those naturally organized people who always makes a daily to-do list, who always writes everything down so you won't forget, and who never misses a deadline because you keep track of everything with your handy time-management notebook or your Palm PC? Or are you one of those flexible, creative, go-with-the-flow people who dislikes planning and organizing because it restricts your freedom, energy, and performance? Some people are natural planners. They love it and can see only the benefits of planning. However, others dislike planning and can see only its disadvantages. It turns out that both views are correct.

Planning has advantages and disadvantages. Let's learn about the benefits of planning and the pitfalls of planning.

Benefits of Planning

Planning has several important benefits: intensified effort, persistence, direction, and creation of task strategies.[3] First, managers and employees put forth greater effort when following a plan. Take two workers. Instruct one to "do his or her best" to increase production, and instruct the other to achieve a 2 percent increase in production each month. Research shows that the one with the specific plan will work harder.[4] When Mike Weir started to play golf at the age of ten, he would often play 36 holes a day throughout the summer to improve his game. His mother often sent his meals to the golf course where he would be practising putting and chipping on the practice green—after playing his 36 holes. After winning his first professional golf tournament in 1999, he set a long-term goal of continuous improvement and started to plan his schedule and workout cycles so he would be in peak form for golf's major tournaments (the Masters, U.S. Open, British Open, and the PGA Championship). His hard work and planning seem to have paid off. In 2003, he became the first Canadian male to win a major golf championship and only the second left-handed golfer to win a major.[5]

Second, planning leads to persistence—that is, working hard for long periods. In fact, planning encourages persistence even when there may be little chance of short-term success.[6] Mary Kay Ash overcame numerous professional and personal obstacles before founding Mary Kay Cosmetics. For example, after 11 years as head of sales for a company (which she won't name), she was replaced by her assistant, a man whom she had spent the previous nine months training. Then, despite her proven track record and years of experience, the company paid him twice what they had been paying her. Frustrated, she quit to start her own company, only to have her 45-year-old husband suddenly die of a heart attack a month prior to the company's start-up. Today, because of her persistence and hard work, Mary Kay Cosmetics has almost 30 000 sales representatives in Canada and 1.3 million worldwide, with over $3.8 billion in annual sales.[7]

The third benefit of planning is direction. Plans encourage managers and employees to direct their persistent efforts toward activities that help accomplish their goals and away from activities that don't. For example, a large insurance company wanted to improve the way its managers gave employees performance evaluation feedback. To help managers improve, company trainers taught them 43 effective performance feedback behaviours. Examples included "I will give my subordinate a clear understanding of the results I expect him or her to achieve," or "During the performance appraisal interview, I will be very supportive, stressing good points before discussing needed improvement." However, during training, managers were instructed to choose just 12 behaviours (out of the 43) on which they wanted to make the most improvement. When subordinates rated their managers on the 43 effective feedback behaviours, it became clear that no matter which 12 behaviours different managers chose, they only improved on the 12 behaviours for which they had set improvement goals. Plans direct behaviour toward activities that lead to goal accomplishment and away from those that don't.

The fourth benefit of planning is that it encourages the development of task strategies. After selecting a goal, it's natural to ask, "How can it be achieved?" For example, Telus (www.telus.com), a Burnaby, B.C-based provider of data, Internet protocol, and voice and wireless communications, received an unfavourable ruling from the Canadian Radio-television and

CP PHOTO/DAVID J. PHILLIP

Mike Weir plans his schedule and workout cycles so he will be in peak form for golf's major tournaments, a factor in his success, he believes.

Telecommunications Commission that would reduce its operating income by about $45 million in 2002 and by $75 million in subsequent years. Coupled with an earlier ruling, Telus found itself in a position where it would see a substantial decline in revenue; its share price had slid to less than $6. In March 2001 share prices had peaked at $40. It set a goal to cut $300 million in annual costs. To reach this goal, Telus offered severance and early retirement packages to 11 000 employees, rationalized product offerings, and focused on its core business. By the end of 2002 the restructuring was nearly complete. Share prices in early 2003 rose to over $20, and by the end of 2006 share prices had reached almost $60.[8] As this example shows, not only does planning encourage people to work hard for extended periods and to engage in behaviours directly related to goal accomplishment, but it also encourages them to think of better ways to do their jobs.

Finally, perhaps the most compelling benefit of planning is that it has been proven to work for both companies and individuals. On average, companies with plans have larger profits and grow much faster than companies that don't.[9] The same holds true for individual managers and employees. There is no better way to improve the performance of the people who work in a company than to have them set goals and develop strategies for achieving those goals. (For more on the benefits of planning, see the "What Really Works?" feature on page 105.)

Planning Pitfalls

Despite the significant benefits associated with planning, planning is not a cure-all. Plans won't fix all organizational problems. In fact, many management authors and consultants believe that planning can harm companies in several ways.[10]

The first pitfall of planning is that it can impede change and prevent or slow needed adaptation. Sometimes companies become so committed to achieving the goals set forth in their plans or they become so intent on following the strategies and tactics spelled out in them, that they fail to see that their plans aren't working or that their goals need to change. Sony, which is famous for its Triniton (picture-tube) TVs, was ironically one of the last major TV manufacturers to develop a line of flat-screen TVs. Sony's TV-engineering group was so committed to the old—and now outdated—Triniton picture-tube technology that its engineers were reluctant to turn to Sony's audio, videogame, and computer monitor divisions for help and expertise in designing new flat-screen TVs. Makoto Kogure, who headed Sony's TV division, admitted the problem, saying, "We did everything inside the TV group."[11]

The second pitfall of planning is that it can create a false sense of certainty. Planners sometimes feel that they know exactly what the future holds for their competitors, their suppliers, and their companies. However, all plans are based on assumptions. "The price of gasoline will increase by 4 percent per year." "Exports will continue to rise." For plans to work, the assumptions on which they are based must hold true. If the assumptions turn out to be false, then plans based on them are likely to fail. For example, as cell phones became cheaper and more reliable, Nokia, a Finland-based manufacturer of cell phones, experienced tremendous growth in its business. So when sales suddenly dropped by 25 percent, Nokia was caught off guard. Officially, company management blamed "logistical hiccups." However, *The Wall Street Journal* concluded that "Nokia didn't see it coming and didn't know how to handle it [the drop in sales]."[12] Because Nokia assumed that its cellular phone sales would continue to grow, it bought parts at high prices and did a poor job of controlling its costs. When the assumption (i.e., continued growth) underlying its production plans turned out to be false, the result was a 30 percent decline in operating profits. Jorma Ollila, Nokia's CEO, said the problems were "driven by economic uncertainty, the ongoing technology transition, and less aggressive marketing by the operators [companies that sell mobile phone services]."[13]

The third pitfall of planning is the detachment of planners. In theory, strategic planners and top-level managers are supposed to focus on the big picture and not concern themselves with the details of implementation, that is, carrying out the plan. According to McGill management professor Henry Mintzberg, detachment leads planners to plan for things they don't understand.[14] Plans are not meant to be abstract theories. They are meant to be guidelines for action. Consequently, planners need to be familiar with the daily details of their businesses if they are to produce plans that can work.

For example, if you doubt that the "details" are important to good execution of a plan, imagine that you're about to have coronary bypass surgery to replace four clogged arteries. Rather than having an experienced cardiologist perform your surgery, you're going under the knife of a first-year medical intern. The intern is a fully qualified M.D. who clearly understands the theory and the plan behind bypass surgery, but has never performed such an operation. As you lie on the operating table, who is the last person you'd like to see as the anesthesia kicks in, the first-year intern who knows the plan but has never done a bypass, or the experienced cardiologist who has followed the plan hundreds of times? Planning works better when the people developing the plan are not detached from the process of executing the plan.

Review 1: Costs and Benefits of Planning

Planning is choosing a goal and developing a method to achieve that goal. Planning is one of the best ways to improve organizational and individual performance. It encourages people to work harder (intensified effort), to work hard for extended periods (persistence), to engage in behaviours directly related to goal accomplishment (directed behaviour), and to think of better ways to do their jobs (task strategies). But most important, companies that plan have larger profits and faster growth than companies that don't plan. However, planning also has three potential pitfalls. Companies that are overly committed to their plans may be slow to adapt to changes in their environment. Planning is based on assumptions about the future, and when those assumptions are wrong, plans are likely to fail. Finally, planning can fail when planners are detached from the implementation of plans.

2 HOW TO MAKE A PLAN THAT WORKS

Planning is a double-edged sword. If done right, planning brings about tremendous increases in individual and organizational performance. At Pixar Animation Studios (www.pixar.com), the plan is to produce one movie a year. Pixar, which makes digitally animated movies, produced only three movies, *Toy Story*, *A Bug's Life*, and *Toy Story 2*, in five years. So while making one movie a year is nothing for traditional movie studios, making a movie a year has been a significant, long-term goal for Pixar. To achieve this goal, Pixar has implemented a plan to hire more people (550 people now work at Pixar, up from 400), added new divisions to develop new movies (story creation) and to manage movie development (shot by shot), increased its computer capabilities (with a several hundredfold increase in computer power and storage), and moved into a new headquarters that fosters collaboration and creativity (compared to the four different locations in which people previously worked). The plan in place included four new movies. By the summer of 2006, Pixar had released four films in five years and started production of a fifth.[15] However, if planning is done wrong, it can have just the opposite effect and harm individual and organizational performance. Pixar's first three films, *Toy Story*, *A Bug's Life*, and *Toy Story 2*, were critical and box-office successes. The risk from Pixar's plan is that increasing the frequency of its films may lead to poorer quality. Paul Dergarabedian, president of a box-office tracking company, said, "The more movies you have, the greater the chance you'll falter once in awhile." Indeed, CEO Steve Jobs said that while Pixar's "priority is still to make films that are really great, not every one of our films will succeed."[16] Despite the risk, this didn't happen, and so far the films have been critical and box-office successes.

In this section, you will learn how to make a plan that works.

As depicted in Exhibit 4.1, planning consists of setting goals, developing commitment to goals, developing effective action plans, tracking progress, and maintaining flexibility.

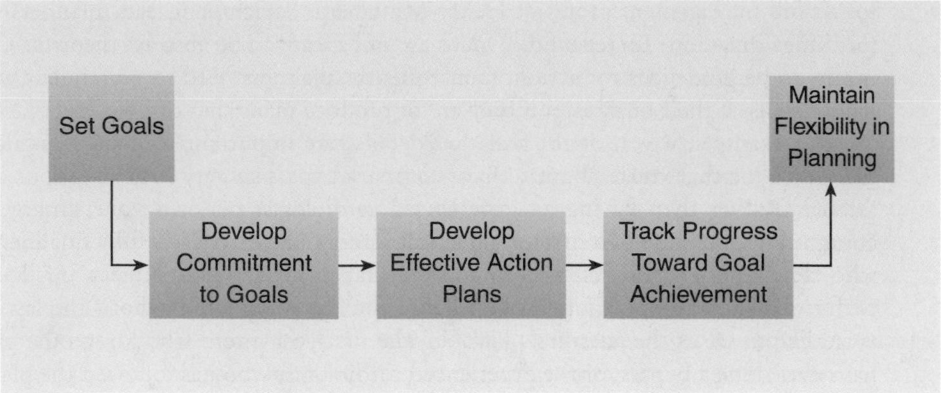

EXHIBIT 4.1
How to Make a Plan That Works

Setting Goals

Since planning is choosing a goal and developing a method or strategy to achieve that goal, the first step in planning is to set goals. To direct behaviour and increase effort, goals need to be specific and challenging.[17] For example, deciding to "increase sales this year" won't direct and energize workers as much as deciding to "increase Manitoba sales by 4 percent in the next six months." Likewise, choosing to "drop some weight" won't motivate you as much as choosing to "lose 10 kilograms." Specific, challenging goals provide a target for which to aim and a standard against which to measure success.

S.M.A.R.T. goals goals that are specific, measurable, attainable, results-oriented, and time-bounded

One way of writing effective goals for yourself, your job, or your company is to use the S.M.A.R.T. guidelines. **S.M.A.R.T. goals** are *specific, measurable, attainable, results-oriented,* and *time-bounded.*[18] Let's see how a heating, ventilation, and air-conditioning (HVAC) company might use S.M.A.R.T. goals in its business.

The HVAC business is cyclical. It's extremely busy at the beginning of summer, when homeowners find that their air-conditioning isn't working, and at the beginning of winter, when furnaces and heat pumps need repair. During these times, most HVAC companies have more business than they can handle. But at other times of year, business can be very slow. So a specific goal would be to increase sales by 50 percent during the fall and spring, when business is slower. This goal could be measured by keeping track of the number of annual maintenance contracts sold to customers. This goal of increasing sales during the off seasons is attainable, because maintenance contracts typically include spring tune-ups (air-conditioning systems) and fall tune-ups (furnace or heating systems). Moreover, a 50 percent increase in sales during the slow seasons is results-oriented. Since customers want their furnaces and air-conditioners to work the first time it gets cold (or hot) each year, they are likely to buy service contracts that ensure their equipment is in working order. Tune-up work can then be scheduled during the slow seasons, increasing sales at those times. Finally, this goal can be made time-bounded by asking the staff to push sales of maintenance contracts before Labour Day, the traditional end of summer, when people start thinking about the cold days ahead, and in March, when winter-weary people start longing for hot days in air-conditioned comfort. The result would be more work during the slow fall and spring seasons.

Developing Commitment to Goals

Just because a company sets a goal doesn't mean that people will try to accomplish it. If workers don't care about a goal, then the goal won't encourage them to work harder or smarter. Thus, the second step in planning is to develop commitment to goals.

goal commitment the determination to achieve a goal

Goal commitment is the determination to achieve a goal. Commitment to achieve a goal is not automatic. Managers and workers must choose to commit themselves to a goal. For example, Professor Edwin Locke, the foremost expert on how, why, and when goals work, told a story about an overweight friend. After not seeing him for years, Locke ran into his friend, who had finally lost 35 kilograms. Because of the change, he nearly walked by without recognizing him. Locke said, "So I asked him how he did it, knowing how hard it was for most people to lose so much weight." His friend responded, "Actually, it was quite simple. I simply decided that I really wanted to do it."[19] Said in another way, goal commitment is really wanting to achieve a goal.

So how can managers bring about goal commitment? The most popular approach is to set goals participatively. Rather than assigning goals to workers ("Johnson, you've got 'til Tuesday of next week to redesign the flex capacitor so it gives us 10 percent more output"), managers and employees choose goals together. The goals are more likely to be realistic and attainable if employees participate in setting them. Also, people are more likely to strive for a goal they feel they have a reasonable chance of attaining. For example, would you be more likely to stick to an exercise program that required one-half hour per day or one that required three hours per day?

Another technique for gaining commitment to a goal is to make the goal public. For example, college students who publicly communicated their semester grade goals ("This semester, I'm shooting for a 3.5") to significant others (usually a parent or sibling) were much more committed to achieving their grades. More importantly, students who told others about their goals earned grades that were nearly a half-grade higher than students who did not tell others about their grade goals.[21] So, one way to increase commitment to goals is to "go public" by having individuals or work units tell others about their goals. For example, work units could post their goals on a bulletin board for all to see.

Another way to increase goal commitment is to obtain top management's support. Top management can show support for a plan or program by providing funds, speaking publicly about the plan, or participating in the plan itself. When General Electric (GE) announced its new "six sigma" program in which it planned to improve quality by reducing the number of product or service errors to just 3.4 defects or errors per million, top management put an incredible amount of support behind the program. Every employee went through two weeks of intense training in statistical process control. At the end of training, they were expected to demonstrate what they had learned by completing two on-the-job projects that would increase quality or decrease costs. Statistical tools, formulas, guidelines, readings, and employee discussions were made available on the GE intranet to support six sigma efforts. Furthermore, 4500 six sigma project leaders, known internally at GE as "black belts" because of their advanced six sigma training, experience, and expertise, worked full-time throughout the company, managing various improvement projects. Finally, GE shared feedback on six sigma progress by tracking and measuring the results of six sigma projects worldwide. The results thus far indicate an internal savings of more than $3 billion a year. None of this would have happened without complete support from GE's top management, which invested $750 million and four years' time to make the program a success and to institutionalize it in GE's culture.[22]

DOING THE RIGHT THING

STRETCH GOALS: AVOID THE "15 PERCENT DELUSION"
Stretch goals are extremely ambitious goals that you don't know how to reach. The purpose of stretch goals is to achieve extraordinary improvements in company performance. Stretch goals are so demanding that they force managers and workers to throw away old comfortable solutions and adopt radical, never-used solutions. Though stretch goals may encourage large improvements, they may also pressure people to do anything to meet "the numbers." The most common stretch goal CEOs set is "15 percent annual growth," the magical number that doubles corporate earnings every five years. But with earnings growth averaging just 8 percent over the last 40 years, the chances of achieving 15 percent growth every year are extremely low. So instead of promising generally unobtainable results, managers should set more realistic stretch goals. When Bob Eckert became CEO of Mattel, he dumped the company's stated goals of 15 percent annual earnings growth and 10 percent revenue growth. Said Eckert, "They were not realistic. We were not going to play that game anymore."[20]

Developing Effective Action Plans

The third step in planning is to develop effective action plans. An **action plan** lists the specific steps, people, resources, and time period for accomplishing a goal. For example, for some time, at Severn Sound, one of Ontario's most popular water recreational areas, swimming and fishing had been restricted because of pollution and reduced oxygen levels in the water. Now, however, thanks to steps implemented over the last decade, the

action plan
the specific steps, people, and resources needed to accomplish a goal

ecosystem has been restored and walleye fish, once nearly eliminated, are abundant again. Cities and towns reduced and treated storm-water runoff, farmers and local residents reduced agricultural and yard fertilizer runoff, farmers reduced animal waste runoff by erecting fences to keep livestock away from streams that fed the sound, local residents reduced human waste runoff by connecting their homes to municipal sewer systems and better maintaining their septic systems, 129 000 trees and shrubs were planted to reduce erosion, and the Department of Fisheries and Oceans mapped fish habitats to determine which areas of the sound could be developed for housing without adversely affecting the sound or its fish population.[23]

Tracking Progress

proximal goals short-term goals or subgoals

distal goals long-term or primary goals

The fourth step in planning is to track progress toward goal achievement. There are two accepted methods of tracking progress. The first is to set proximal goals and distal goals. **Proximal goals** are short-term goals or subgoals, whereas **distal goals** are long-term or primary goals.[24] The idea behind setting proximal goals is that they may be more motivating and rewarding than waiting to achieve far-off distal goals. In a research study, Massachusetts Institute of Technology students were given a complex proofreading assignment and were paid ten cents for each error they found, but were penalized $1 a day for turning in their work late. One group of students was given a single deadline, that is, a distal goal, of turning in their proofreading work three weeks from the start of the study. A second group of students was given weekly deadlines, that is, a proximal goal, in which they were to turn in one-third of their work each week. A third group of students was allowed to set their own deadlines; that is, they set their own proximal goals. The single-deadline students (i.e., those with no proximal goals, just a distal goal) were the worst performers, as they turned their work in 12 days late and corrected only 70 errors. The students who were assigned weekly goals (i.e., proximal goals) were the best performers, as they only turned in their work one-half day late, and corrected 136 errors. The next best group was the students who set their own proximal goals, as they turned in their work 6.5 days late and corrected 104 errors.[25] The lesson for managers is clear. If you want people to do a better job of tracking the quality and timeliness of their work, use proximal goals to set multiple deadlines.[26]

The second method of tracking progress is to gather and provide performance feedback. Regular, frequent performance feedback allows workers and managers to track their progress toward goal achievement and make adjustments in effort, direction, and strategies.[27] For example, Exhibit 4.2 shows the result of providing feedback on safety behaviour to the makeup and wrapping workers in a large bakery company. The company had a worker safety record that was two and a half times worse than the industry average. During the baseline period, workers in the wrapping department, who measure and mix ingredients, roll the bread dough, and place it into baking pans, performed their jobs safely about 70 percent of the time. The baseline safety record for workers in the makeup department, who bag and seal baked bread and assemble, pack, and tape cardboard cartons for shipping, was a bit better at 78 percent.

Yet after the company gave workers 30 minutes of safety training, set a goal of 90 percent safe behaviour, and then provided daily feedback (such as a chart similar to Exhibit 4.2), performance improved dramatically. During the intervention period, the percentage of safely performed behaviours rose to an average of 95.8 percent for wrapping workers and 99.3 percent for workers in the makeup department, and never fell below 83 percent. Thus, the combination of training, a challenging goal, and feedback led to a dramatic increase in performance.

However, the importance of feedback alone can be seen in the reversal stage, when the company quit posting daily feedback on safe behaviour. Without daily feedback, the percentage of safely performed behaviour returned to baseline levels, 70.8 percent for the wrapping department and 72.3 percent for the makeup department. For planning to be effective, workers need a specific, challenging goal and regular feedback to track their progress.

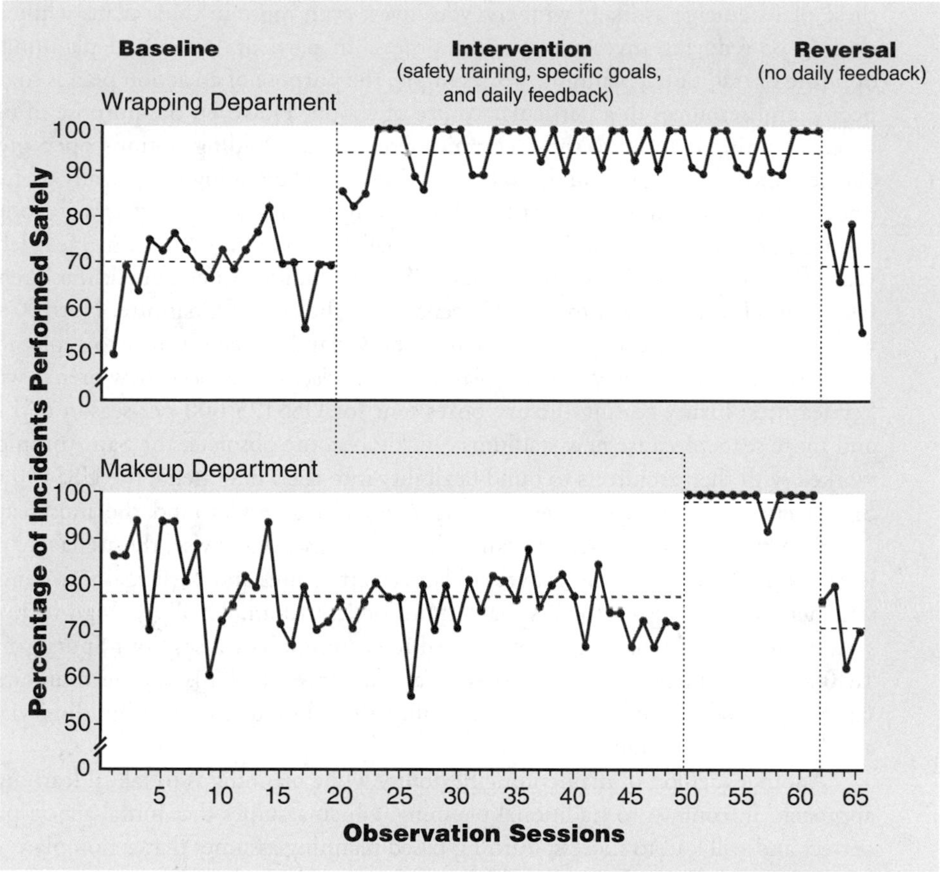

EXHIBIT 4.2
Effects of Goal-Setting, Training, and Feedback on Safe Behaviour in a Bread Factory

Source: Reprinted with permission of the Journal of Applied Psychology. "A Behavioral Approach to Occupational Safety: Pinpointing and Reinforcing Safe Performance in a Food Manufacturing Plant." Komaki, J., Barwick, K.D., and Scott, L.R., *Journal of Applied Psychology*, 1978, V63. Reproduced with permission of the publisher. Copyright © 1978 by the American Psychological Association.

Maintaining Flexibility

Because action plans are sometimes poorly conceived and goals sometimes turn out to not be achievable, the last step in developing an effective plan is to maintain flexibility. Claren Wooten and his partner started Metamorphosis Studios to build custom Web sites for companies. However, most of their customers got sticker shock and walked away because they couldn't believe that it would cost $4500 to $9000 to produce a Web site (more like $40 000 to $75 000 today). They wanted a sophisticated Web site, but not at that price. So rather than continue to struggle as a custom maker and designer of Web sites, Metamorphosis Studios morphed into an online store that allowed small businesses to buy predesigned, customizable Web sites. Wooten said that this "enabled us to reduce our price to only a couple of hundred dollars without sacrificing quality. No one had really taken that approach before—and we would never have thought to take it had we not listened to our small-business customers."[28] Today, Metamorphosis Studios has become Network Solutions (www.networksolutions.com), a one-stop Internet solution for building your own Web site, sending out personalized e-mail (for marketing), purchasing the domain name (e.g., mycompany.com) you want, and many other services at reasonable prices for small businesses. So when plans fail, it is far better to scrap the plan and start over than it is to ride the failing plan into the ground.

An even more desirable strategy is to build flexibility into planning from the start. One method of maintaining flexibility while planning is to adopt an options-based approach.[29] The goal of **options-based planning** is to keep options open by making small, simultaneous investments in many options or plans. Then when one or a few of

options-based planning maintaining planning flexibility by making small, simultaneous investments in many alternative plans

these plans emerge as likely winners, you invest even more in these plans while discontinuing or reducing investment in the others. In part, options-based planning is the opposite of traditional planning. For example, the purpose of an action plan is to commit people and resources to a particular course of action. However, the purpose of options-based planning is to leave those commitments open. Holding options open gives you choices, and choices give you flexibility. Options-based planning is especially useful when uncertainty is high and you don't know how things will change or what will work in the future. For example, in the National Basketball Association, the Miami Heat left a 12-year-old arena to play in the brand new US$280 million American Airlines arena. The Charlotte Hornets moved to New Orleans when the city of Charlotte, North Carolina, wouldn't replace their 14-year-old arena. The Orlando Magic wants to replace its 12-year-old arena with a new one. As player salaries rise, teams need new arenas with two key features: luxury seating (luxury boxes rent for US$125 000 per season and higher) and more seats. Because new stadiums quickly become obsolete, the San Antonio Spurs worked with their architects to build flexibility into their new arena, the US$190 million SBC Center. For instance, there are no physical barriers around the most expensive "club" seats so that prime seating can easily be increased. Likewise, the arena's 40 terrace-level luxury boxes can easily convert to larger party suites and back again, depending on whether high-paying customers want more or less room. Finally, a high-tech curtain system allows the arena to be reconfigured to accommodate a sold-out Spurs game with 18 000 in attendance or a concert with an audience of 5000. Says lead architect Bill Crockett, "We've built in a lot of flexibility that should keep the building viable for another 30 years without major changes."[30]

learning-based planning learning better ways of achieving goals by continually testing, changing, and improving plans and strategies

Another method of maintaining flexibility while planning is to take a learning-based approach. In contrast to traditional planning, which assumes that initial action plans are correct and will lead to success, learning-based planning assumes that action plans need to be continually tested, changed, and improved as companies learn better ways of achieving goals.[31] Because the purpose is constant improvement, **learning-based planning** not only encourages flexibility in action plans, but it also encourages frequent reassessment and revision of organizational goals.

Tupperware removed its products from Target stores after less than a year due to poor sales and the feeling that in-store sales were threatening its traditional home parties.

For example, Knight-Ridder Corporation, which owns the second-largest newspaper chain in the United States, continues to test a number of different plans as it tries to reverse the 9 percent decline in its newspaper circulation over the last decade.[32] To increase readership among young adults, only 41 percent of whom read newspapers, Knight-Ridder newspapers have added sections with music and movie reviews and a wide listing of entertainment events. They've also switched to shorter articles, more colour, and better layouts and indexes to make it easier for younger readers to find what they're looking for. So far, young adult readership hasn't budged, so four Knight-Ridder newspapers are experimenting with price cuts, slashing the cost of their papers to 25 cents on weekdays and $1 on Sundays. Since the price cuts, some papers have seen daily and Sunday circulation increase. The company will continue to test and revise its plans until it learns how to increase readership.[33]

Review 2: How to Make a Plan That Works

There are five steps to making a plan that works: (1) Set S.M.A.R.T. goals—goals that are *specific, measurable, attainable, results-oriented,* and *time-bounded.* (2) Develop commitment to the goal from the people who contribute to goal achievement. Managers can increase workers' goal commitment by encouraging worker participation in goal setting, making goals public, and getting top management to show their support for workers' goals. (3) Develop action plans for goal accomplishment. (4) Track progress toward goal achievement by setting both proximal and distal goals and by providing workers with regular performance feedback. (5) Maintain flexibility. Keeping options open through options-based planning and seeking continuous improvement through learning-based planning help organizations maintain flexibility as they plan.

Kinds of Plans

Planning is critical to organizational success and failure to plan can lead to its demise. Organizations need to respond to circumstances as they change and also attempt to anticipate change. In 1995 the Canadian government ended the Crow rate, which had subsidized grain shipments by rail across the prairies since the late 1880s. In turn, the major railway companies changed the way they hauled grain and abandoned many branch lines. They instead wanted to rely on long trains with up to 100 cars and haul grain from only a limited number of major grain-handling hubs. This created a major problem for the grain pools across the prairies as they had a very large number of old wooden elevators scattered across the countryside in every little town. The Saskatchewan Wheat Pool responded with a massive and expensive plan to respond to the changing environment. The pool shrunk the number of elevators from over 500 to 47. The new elevators, though, could handle ten times the amount of grain that the old elevators could. The plan paid off and the Saskatchewan Wheat Pool has made a successful transition to the new world of grain handling and shipping.[34]

As this example illustrates, companies use specialized plans to respond to change. Also, top-, middle-, and first-level managers can look at the same goals and plans in different ways because of their different perspectives and responsibilities.

After reading the next two sections, you should be able to

3 discuss how companies can use plans at all management levels, from top to bottom.

4 describe the different kinds of special-purpose plans that companies use to plan for change, contingencies, and product development.

3 PLANNING FROM TOP TO BOTTOM

Planning works best when the goals and action plans at the bottom and middle of the organization support the goals and action plans at the top of the organization. In other words, planning works best when everybody pulls in the same direction. Exhibit 4.3 illustrates this planning continuity, beginning at the top with a clear definition of the company vision and ending at the bottom with the execution of operational plans.

Let's see how top managers create the organizational vision and mission; how middle managers develop tactical plans and use management by objectives to motivate employee efforts toward the overall vision and mission; and how first-level managers use operational, single-use, and standing plans to implement the tactical plans in the following sections: starting at the top, bending in the middle, and finishing at the bottom.

Starting at the Top

As shown in Exhibit 4.4, top management is responsible for developing long-term **strategic plans** that make clear how the company will serve customers and position itself against competitors in the next two to five years. (The strategic planning and management

strategic plans
overall company plans that clarify how the company will serve customers and position itself against competitors over the next two to five years

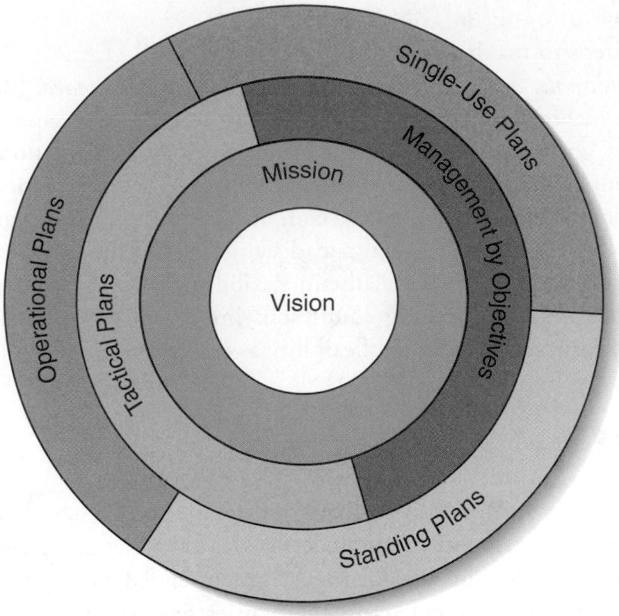

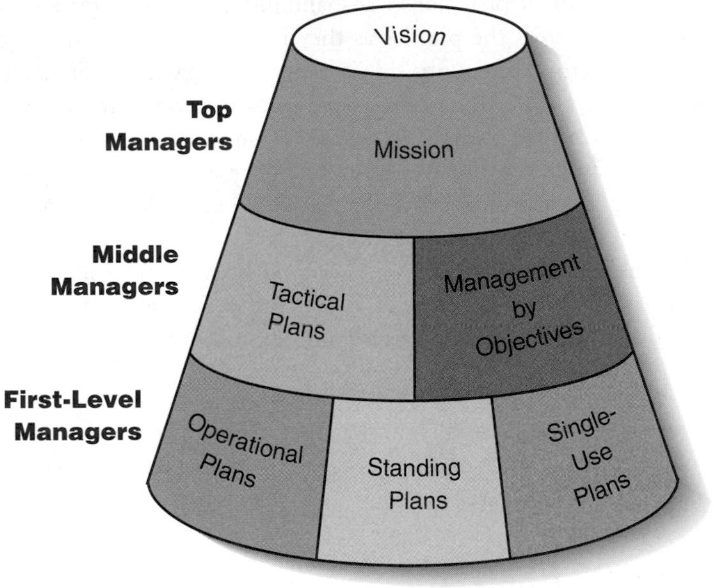

EXHIBIT 4.3
Planning from Top to Bottom

process is reviewed in its entirety in Chapter 9.) Strategic planning begins with the creation of an organizational vision and an organizational mission.

vision
inspirational statement of an organization's enduring purpose

A **vision** is a statement of a company's purpose or reason for existing.[35] Vision statements should be brief—no more than two sentences. They should also be inspirational, clear, and consistent with widely shared company beliefs and values. For example, Mountain Equipment Co-op (www.mec.ca), Canada's largest retail co-operative by membership, has a vision to be "an innovative, thriving co-operative that inspires excellence in products and services, passion for wilderness experiences, leadership for a just world, and action for a healthy planet." Mountain Equipment Co-op's vision is clear and inspirational and guides the company in its business practices. For example, MEC, as it is more commonly known, does not sell motorized vehicles and ensures that its new stores are built in an environmentally friendly way. When building a new store in Winnipeg, it used salvaged materials at considerable expense to reduce the environmental

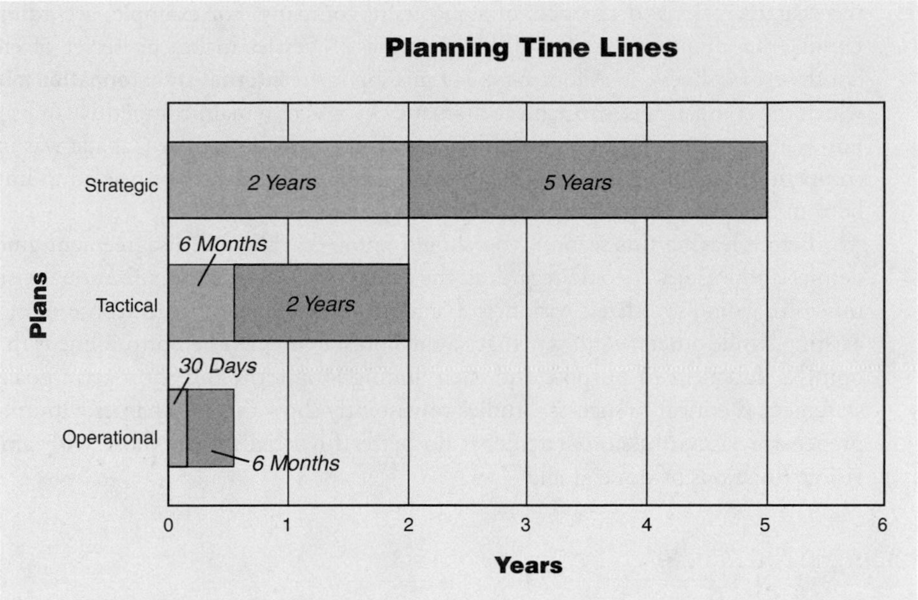

EXHIBIT 4.4
Timelines for Strategic, Tactical, and Operational Plans

impact of the new store.[36] Its Web site even hosts an equipment swap so that members don't have to buy new equipment and consume even more of the earth's resources. All these activities are intended to provide for a "healthy planet."[37] Other examples of organizational visions are Walt Disney Corporation's "to make people happy" and St. Michael's Hospital, a teaching hospital affiliated with the University of Toronto, to "be Canada's finest academic health care provider."[38]

The **mission**, which flows from the vision, is a more specific goal that unifies company-wide efforts, stretches and challenges the organization, and possesses a finish line and a timeframe. For example, in 1961, U.S. President John F. Kennedy established an organizational mission for NASA with this simple statement: "Achieving the goal, before this decade is out, of landing a man on the moon and returning him safely to earth."[39] NASA achieved this goal on 20 July 1969, when astronaut Neil Armstrong walked on the moon. Once a mission has been accomplished, a new one should be chosen. Again, however, the new mission must grow out of the organization's vision, which does not change over time. For example, NASA's vision statement is "As explorers, pioneers, and innovators, we boldly expand frontiers in air and space to inspire and serve America, and to benefit the quality of life on earth." NASA used this vision to develop the three-part mission statement. For each mission statement, NASA has created specific, challenging goals to be accomplished from 1998 to 2002, from 2003 to 2009, and from 2010 to 2023, and beyond. In September 2005 NASA announced a new goal—to put another human on the moon by 2018.[40]

mission
statement of a company's overall goal that unifies company-wide efforts toward its vision, stretches and challenges the organization, and possesses a finish line and a timeframe

Companies can set missions in four ways.[41] One is **targeting**, setting a clear, specific target and "aiming" for it. For example, WestJet announced in September 2005 that it wishes to raise its annual revenue from $1 billion in 2004 to $2 billion by 2007. It intends to do this by increasing its marketing in central and eastern Canada, increasing the number of business travellers, expanding its cargo service, and establishing a vacation package service.[42]

targeting
mission stated as a clear specific company goal

A second type of mission is the **common-enemy mission**, in which the company vows to defeat one of its corporate rivals. Pepsi's aspirations of beating Coke, Krispy Kreme's desire to defeat Tim Hortons, or Avis's hopes ("We're number two. We try harder.") to catch Hertz Rental Cars are all examples of common-enemy missions. At one point, when Honda was making only motorcycles, its mission was "We will crush, squash, and slaughter Yamaha." A third type of mission is the **role-model mission**. Here, rather than focusing on defeating specific competitors, as in the common-enemy mission, the company emulates

common-enemy mission
company goal of defeating a corporate rival

role-model mission
company goal of imitating the characteristics and practices of a successful company

the characteristics and practices of a successful company. For example, according to Ted Larkin, the airline analyst for HSBC securities, "WestJet makes no secret of emulating Southwest [Airlines]."[43] A fourth type of mission is the **internal-transformation mission**, in which the company aims to achieve dramatic changes to remain competitive in its markets. For example, at the beginning of the chapter, you learned that Air Canada was in serious competitive and financial trouble. A new direction would clearly be needed to improve its bottom line and halt the erosion of its market share.

internal-transformation mission
company goal of remaining competitive by making dramatic changes in the company

Before leaving this section, you should know that there is disagreement among academics and business people regarding the differences between organizational visions and missions. Some say that a vision is a statement of a company's purpose or reason for existing, while others would say that's a mission statement. The bottom line is that developing a statement of purpose and then linking long-term and short-term goals to that statement is critical to success. Studies consistently show that companies with more comprehensive vision/mission statements do better financially than those with ambiguous visions/missions or none at all.[44]

Bending in the Middle

Middle management is responsible for developing and carrying out tactical plans to accomplish the organization's mission. **Tactical plans** specify how a company will use resources, budgets, and people to accomplish specific goals within its mission. Whereas strategic plans and objectives are used to focus company efforts over the next two to five years, tactical plans and objectives are used to direct behaviour, efforts, and attention over the next six months to two years. For example, Craig Knouf, CEO of Associated Business Systems, a 110-person business that sells office equipment, re-examines his company's 30-page business plan on a monthly, semi-annual and annual basis. As a result of these reviews, in which he compares actual company performance to the goals set forth in his business plan, he noticed that over a six-month period the company had sold more high-volume scanners than before. So he changed his business plan to put a greater emphasis on scanners and scanning software. As a result, sales of scanning products now account for one-third of all sales. Working without his business plan, says Knouf, "would be like driving a car with no steering wheel."[45]

tactical plans
plans created and implemented by middle managers that specify how the company will use resources, budgets, and people over the next six months to two years to accomplish specific goals within its mission

Management by objectives (see the "What Really Works?" feature on page 105) is a management technique often used to develop and carry out tactical plans. **Management by objectives**, or **MBO**, is a four-step process in which managers and their employees (1) discuss possible goals, (2) participatively select goals that are challenging, attainable, and consistent with the company's overall goals, (3) jointly develop tactical plans that lead to accomplishment of tactical goals and objectives, and (4) meet regularly to review progress toward accomplishment of those goals. Lee Iacocca, the former CEO who brought Chrysler Corporation back from the verge of bankruptcy, credits MBO (though he called it a "quarterly review system") for his 30 years of extraordinary success as a manager. Iacocca said, "Over the years, I've regularly asked my key people—and I've had them ask their key people, and so on down the line—a few basic questions: 'What are your objectives for the next ninety days? What are your plans, your priorities, your hopes? And how do you intend to go about achieving them?'"[46]

management by objectives (MBO)
a four-step process in which managers and employees discuss and select goals, develop tactical plans, and meet regularly to review progress toward goal accomplishment

When done right, MBO is an extremely effective method of tactical planning. However, MBO is not without disadvantages.[48] Some MBO programs involve excessive paperwork, requiring managers to file annual statements of plans and objectives, plus quarterly or semi-annual written reviews assessing goal progress. Another difficulty is that managers are frequently reluctant to give employees feedback about their performance. A third disadvantage is that managers and employees sometimes have difficulty agreeing on goals. And when employees are forced to accept goals that they don't want, goal commitment and employee effort suffer. Last, because MBO focuses on quantitative, easily measured goals, employees may neglect important unmeasured parts of their jobs. In other words, if your job performance is judged only by whether you reduce costs by

Management by Objectives[47]

For years, both managers and management researchers have wondered how much of a difference planning made in organizational performance, or whether it really made any difference at all. While proponents argued that planning encouraged workers to work hard, to persist in their efforts, to engage in behaviours directly related to goal accomplishment, and to develop better strategies for achieving goals, opponents argued that planning impeded organizational change and adaptation, created the illusion of managerial control, and artificially separated thinkers and doers.

Now, however, the results from 70 different organizations strongly support the effectiveness of management by objectives (i.e., short-term planning).

MANAGEMENT BY OBJECTIVES (MBO)

Management by objectives is a process in which managers and subordinates at all levels in a company sit down together to jointly set goals, to share information and discuss strategies that could lead to goal achievement, and to regularly meet to review progress toward accomplishing those goals. Thus, MBO is based on goals, participation, and feedback. On average, companies that effectively use MBO will outproduce those that don't use MBO by an incredible 44.6 percent! And in companies where top management is committed to MBO, that is, where objective setting begins at the top, the average increase in performance is an even more astounding 56.5 percent. By contrast, when top management does not participate in or support MBO, the average increase in productivity drops to 6.1 percent. In all, though, there is a 97 percent chance that companies that use MBO will outperform those that don't! Thus, MBO can make a very big difference to the companies that use it.

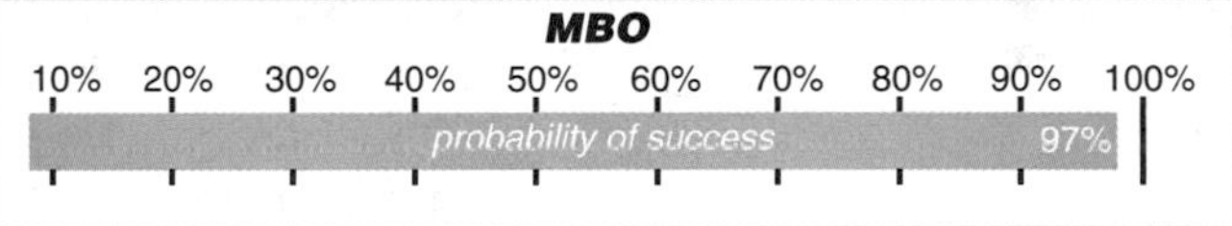

3 percent or raise revenues by 5 percent, then you are unlikely to give high priority to the unmeasured, but still important parts of your job, like mentoring new employees or sharing new knowledge and skills with co-workers.

Finishing at the Bottom

Lower-level managers are responsible for developing and carrying out **operational plans**, which are the day-to-day plans for producing or delivering the organization's products and services. Operational plans direct the behaviour, efforts, and priorities of operative employees for periods ranging from 30 days to six months. There are three kinds of operational plans: single-use plans, standing plans, and budgets.

operational plans
day-to-day plans, developed and implemented by lower-level managers, for producing or delivering the organization's products and services over a 30-day to six-month period

Single-use plans deal with unique, one-time-only events. Plans for mergers and acquisitions are prime examples of single-use plans. For example, in 2005 two of the largest Canadian movie theatre chains announced a merger. Cineplex Galaxy, which operates theatres under the Cineplex Odeon and Galaxy brands, announced it was buying the Famous Players chain for $500 million. As part of a deal with the federal Commissioner of Competition, the company will have to sell off 35 theatres.[49]

single-use plans
plans that cover unique, one-time-only events

Unlike single-use plans that are created, carried out, and then never used again, **standing plans** save managers time, because they are created once and then used repeatedly to handle frequently recurring events. If you encounter a problem that you've seen before, someone in your company has probably written a standing plan that explains how to address it. There are three kinds of standing plans: policies, procedures, and rules and regulations.

standing plans
plans used repeatedly to handle frequently recurring events

Policies indicate the general course of action that company managers should take in response to a particular event or situation. A well-written policy will also specify why the policy exists and what outcome the policy is intended to produce. For example, most Canadian employers have an employment equity policy. The Canadian Imperial Bank of

policy
standing plan that indicates the general course of action that should be taken in response to a particular event or situation

Commerce (www.cibc.com) has its employment equity policy posted on its careers page. It states that the "CIBC is an equal opportunity employer. It is the Company's policy to recruit and select applicants for employment solely on the basis of their qualifications, with emphasis on selecting the best-qualified person for the job. CIBC does not discriminate against applicants based on race, colour, religion, sex, national origin, disability or any other status or condition protected by applicable federal, [provincial] or local law."[50] Companies have these policies in place partly in response to federal and provincial law but also due to a growing recognition among companies that it is in their best interest to have a diversified work force and that it is a socially responsible thing to do. This policy is intended to provide guidance to managers as they handle many human resource functions.

procedure
standing plan that indicates the specific steps that should be taken in response to a particular event

Procedures are more specific than policies, because they indicate the series of steps that should be taken in response to a particular event. For example, when the Canadian Human Rights Commission (www.chrc-ccdp.ca) receives a complaint from an individual who claims to have been discriminated against, it follows very specific procedures. A complaints officer assesses the application to see if it meets certain criteria and in most cases sends the complaint on to mediation. If this fails, then an investigator is assigned and given the nature of the investigator's report, the complaint may go on to conciliation.[51]

rules and regulations
standing plans that describe how a particular action should be performed, or what must happen or not happen in response to a particular event

Rules and regulations are even more specific than procedures, because they specify what must happen or not happen. They describe precisely how a particular action should be performed. For instance, rules and regulations forbid many managers from writing job reference letters for employees who have worked at their firms. Companies insist on such rules because a negative reference letter may prompt a former employee to sue for defamation of character.[52]

Another area in which companies are struggling to create effective rules and regulations is the Internet. For example, several years ago, a study by Nielsen Media Research found that of the 54 million "hits" to *Penthouse* magazine's Web site during a two-month period, the most came from workers at IBM, Apple, Hewlett-Packard, and AT&T.[53] As a result of behaviours like these, more than 75 percent of major U.S. companies now block or monitor workers' Web use, while 38 percent review employees' e-mail. Canadian companies are following suit. For example, the Bank of Montreal blocks employee access to "high-risk" Web sites such as playboy.com.[54] Tim Carney, founder of a network security firm, said, "If you're going to supply a company car, you can dictate they won't drag-race it. The same thing holds with Internet access."[55] The Ontario Ministry of Natural Resources fired six employees and 40 Ontario police officers were disciplined in 2001 for inappropriate use of e-mail and the Internet.[56] In fact, one out of four companies has fired someone for inappropriate workplace use of the Internet. Why do companies need to take these steps? Because, says Roland Cloutier, at Brac Solutions, a network security firm, "you have Joe Schmoe going to some porno dot-com site while a female counterpart walks behind him, and it's a potential lawsuit."[57]

budgeting
quantitative planning through which managers decide how to allocate available money to best accomplish company goals

Budgets are the third kind of operational plan. **Budgeting** is quantitative planning, because it forces managers to decide how to allocate available money to best accomplish company goals. According to Jan King, author of *Business Plans to Game Plans*, "Money sends a clear message about your priorities. Budgets act as a language for communicating your goals to others."

Review 3: Planning from Top to Bottom

Proper planning requires that the goals at the bottom and middle of the organization support the objectives at the top of the organization. Top management develops strategic plans that indicate how a company will serve customers and position itself against competitors over a two- to five-year period. Strategic planning starts with the creation of an organizational vision and mission. There are four kinds of organization missions: targeting, common enemy, role model, and internal transformation. Middle managers use techniques such as management by objectives to develop tactical plans that direct behaviour, efforts, and priorities over the next six months to two years. Finally, lower-level managers develop operational plans that guide daily activities in producing or delivering an organization's products and services. Operational plans typically span periods ranging from 30 days to six months. There are three kinds of operational plans: single-use plans, standing plans (policies, procedures, and rules and regulations), and budgets.

4 SPECIAL-PURPOSE PLANS

You wouldn't use a hammer to flip your pancakes. You wouldn't hire a Ph.D. in archaeology to install a new hard drive in your computer. And you wouldn't light an acetylene torch to make popcorn. Everyone knows that a big part of getting a job done right is to hire people who know what they're doing. Or, if you're brave enough to try to fix something on your own, the secret to getting something done right is to use the right tools.

Plans are like tools and technicians. If you use the wrong one, your plan will fail. But if you use them for what they were intended, they'll serve you well. Let's examine how companies use special-purpose plans when they're planning for change, planning for contingencies, and planning for product development.

Planning for Change

People are creatures of habit. It's extremely difficult to get them to change. Therefore, managers and employees are more comfortable trying to achieve small incremental improvements than overhauling the way they do business. They know that if they work a little harder, plan a bit smarter, and don't catch any unlucky breaks, they should be able to hit 3 percent, 4 percent, or 5 percent improvement goals year after year.

However, sometimes doing more of the same won't improve business performance sufficiently to achieve the company's mission. When this is the case, companies use stretch goals. **Stretch goals**, by definition, are extremely ambitious goals that you don't know how to reach.[58] The purpose of stretch goals is to achieve extraordinary improvements in company performance. Stretch goals are so demanding that they force managers and workers to throw away old comfortable solutions and adopt radical, never-used solutions. Steve Kerr, former dean of the University of Southern California's Business School, who is now Morgan Stanley's "Chief Learning Officer," illustrates the idea of stretch goals with this story:

stretch goals
extremely ambitious goals that, initially, employees don't know how to accomplish

> You give a team an orange and say that each person must handle the orange—you can throw it to each other, do anything you want—but the orange has to end up in the hands of the person who started it. The group throws the orange back and forth, and you time it. The first time we did it, it took nine seconds. When asked to improve, they stood a little closer, threw it a little faster, and got it down to seven seconds. Then we said, "Many groups do this in less than a second, and it's possible to do it in less than half a second." In the third trial, the team did it in less than a second, by simply stacking up their hands. The guy with the orange dropped it, it went swoosh through everybody's hands, and he caught it at the bottom—that was it. It was a neat example of the power of a stretch goal.[59]

In 1991 Richmond Savings, a credit union located in Richmond, B.C., developed an ambitious ten-year business plan that set itself a goal of having 100 000 members and \$2.8 billion in assets. In order to do this, it undertook an ambitious marketing campaign using a fictitious bank known as "Humungous Bank." The idea was to target consumers who were tired of the poor service at the largest six Canadian banks by poking fun at them. Richmond Savings wanted to highlight its responsiveness to the needs of its customers, needs that it thought were not being met elsewhere. The ad campaign was credited with increasing membership by 55 percent to 80 000 and increasing the asset base to \$2.8 billion. Richmond Savings has now merged with Pacific Coast Savings,

Richmond Savings' stretch goals helped it grow to the second-largest credit union in Canada. It has merged with Pacific Coast Savings to form Coast Capital Savings.

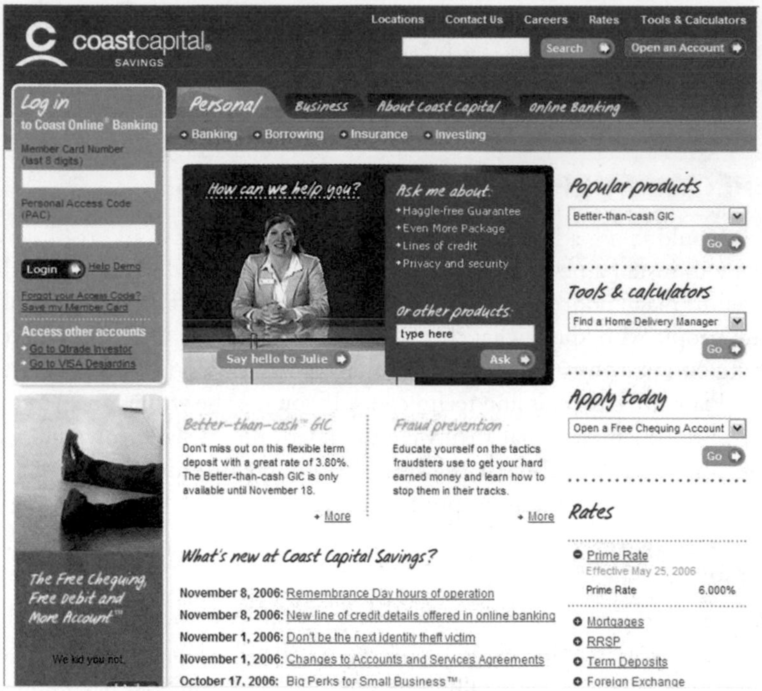

COURTESY OF COAST CAPITAL SAVINGS

headquartered in Victoria, B.C.[60] The two credit unions formed Coast Capital Savings and bought a third company, Surrey Metro Savings. Coast Capital now has assets of $7.2 billion, 45 branches, and 300 000 members, making it the second-largest credit union in Canada. Clearly Richmond Savings' stretch goals paid off.

Since the first reaction to most stretch goals is "You've got to be kidding," Kerr recommends setting "achievable" stretch goals. However, knowing what is too easy (and thus not a stretch goal) and what is too difficult (and thus not achievable) is difficult. One way companies choose a stretch goal of just the right difficulty is by benchmarking. **Benchmarking** is the process of identifying outstanding practices, processes, and standards in other companies and adapting them to your company.[61] For example, one of the biggest hassles associated with most hospital stays is the amount of paperwork and time it takes to complete the admissions process. If you were a hospital administrator, who would you benchmark to learn how to streamline your slow, cumbersome admissions process? What business or company would know how to handle admissions-like situations and paperwork faster than your hospital? Well, many U.S. hospitals actually benchmark their admissions processes against Marriott Hotels. Think about it. Both admit people to rooms, typically for no more than a couple of nights, but longer if necessary. Both collect basic information, such as your name, address, phone number, and how payment will be made (a credit card for the hotel and a medical insurance card for the hospital). And both try to determine your preferences upon admission (smoking or non-smoking room, the kind of room you desire, food preferences, etc.). The processes are nearly identical. Consequently, benchmarking helps employees realize that they can achieve extraordinary levels of performance; after all, it's being done at another company—in this case, Marriott.

benchmarking
the process of identifying outstanding practices, processes, and standards in other companies and adapting them to your company

Based on General Electric's experience, Kerr strongly recommends that companies not punish managers and workers when they fail to achieve stretch goals. Since the purpose of stretch goals is to achieve extraordinary improvements in performance, it is a mistake for companies to measure progress by assessing whether new levels of performance meet or fall short of the stretch goal. For example, Kerr would likely argue that it was wrong for DaimlerChrysler's board of directors to cut top management's annual bonuses by 18 percent because DaimlerChrysler failed to achieve stretch goals for improvements in car quality. Because of the inherent difficulty of stretch goals, companies need to assess progress by comparing new levels of performance to old levels. For example, though DaimlerChrysler's board punished top management by reducing its annual bonus, the punishment wasn't because quality didn't improve. DaimlerChrysler spokesperson Steve Harris said, "We just didn't reach the tough stretch goals we set," noting that DaimlerChrysler had made double-digit percentage improvements in quality in the last year.[62] What do you think? Did DaimlerChrysler managers fail because they didn't achieve their stretch goal? Or did they succeed because they achieved double-digit improvements in quality?

Planning for Contingencies

When senior managers from Duke Energy Corp., an electric utility company, met for a two-day meeting, their job was to confront three different scenarios about the future that might affect their business. In the first scenario, called the "economic treadmill," they assumed that economic growth would slow to just 1 percent a year. In this scenario, energy prices would drop, making it difficult for Duke to pay the significant debt it had accumulated in the last few years to build new electric plants. In the "market.com" scenario, the Internet would lead to fully deregulated market trading of electricity and gas, giving industrial and home buyers an advantage over energy producers and sellers. Finally, the "flawed competition" scenario assumes that deregulation will be uneven and inconsistent from place to place, producing volatile swings in energy demand, supply, and prices. Why is Duke considering these different planning scenarios? Because with $13.5 billion in debt to pay off, even small changes in growth, energy costs, or deregulation could affect the profitability of the company by tens of millions of dollars.[63]

scenario planning
the process of developing plans to deal with several possible future events and trends that might affect the business

Scenario planning is the process of developing plans to deal with events and trends that might affect a business in the future. It helps managers answer "what if" questions and prepare responses should those "what if" scenarios actually occur. You probably do scenario planning often in your own life. Your plans could go something like this: "If I get the scholarship I applied for, I won't work this term. If I don't get it, I'll apply to work in the library."

Scenario planning was first used extensively in World War II when teams of Allied military strategists created scenarios by assuming the role of enemy battle planners. Their job was to devise alternative strategies that enemy forces might use to attack Allied troops and to figure out the best way to defend against each strategy.[64] By anticipating possible enemy strategies and planning actions to counter each one, Allied commanders could be ready no matter which strategy the enemy actually employed. Currently, one of the biggest global developments driving scenario planning is the potential for a bird flu pandemic. The Canadian Manufacturers and Exporters trade association estimated that a major flu pandemic could keep up to half a firm's work force home at any given time and the pandemic could last a year.[65] How does a company operate under these circumstances? Developing a response to this threat falls under the topic of scenario planning.

Scenario planning can be broken down into these steps:[66]

1. *Define the scope of the scenario.* The scope might include a time frame, assumptions about the product, and a geographic area in which the scenario is to take place. For example, a hospital might create a scenario like this:

    > Ten years from now, most hospital care (the product) will be short-term or outpatient treatment, and rather than just treating local community residents, our hospital will serve a wider geographic area, as doctors use the Internet and teleconferencing to offer medical analysis and treatment to patients who currently live too far away to be treated by hospital staff.

2. *Identify the major stakeholders (customers, suppliers, competitors, government, etc.) and the roles you expect them to play in the scenario.*

3. *Identify basic political, economic, societal, technological, competitive, and legal trends that you expect to occur in the scenario.*
4. *Identify key uncertainties and the likely outcomes associated with them.* One of the key uncertainties is how hospitals will change if they primarily provide short-term and outpatient care. Will they become much smaller? If so, will they need fewer doctors, nurses, and staffers? Will this make it easier or more difficult for hospitals to be more efficient? Another set of uncertainties would be the legal questions surrounding "distant" care. Traditionally, medical care requires doctors to have face-to-face visits with their patients. However, with technology allowing doctors to recommend treatment without traditional face-to-face visits, would patients be more likely to sue if something went wrong? Would hospitals and doctors then deal with the threat of lawsuits by requiring patients to sign waivers in order to gain access to "distant" care?
5. *Using Steps 1 through 4, put together your initial scenarios.* A common technique is to write scenarios that use different combinations of key uncertainties. Another is to create best-case and worst-case scenarios.
6. *Check for consistency and plausibility of facts and assumptions in each scenario.* The key here is to make sure that the scenario holds together as a whole. There shouldn't be any obviously inconsistent facts. For example, if the scenario states that the use of "distant" care will increase, it wouldn't make sense to also write that hospitals would be spending less money on technology when, in fact, they'd probably be spending much more. Before being used, each scenario should be read and checked by a number of people within an organization and industry.
7. *Write the final scenarios and conduct a series of planning sessions for management teams to develop contingency plans for each scenario.*
8. *Develop measures or signposts for each scenario that allow managers to know when the events predicted in this scenario are occurring.* Once scenarios have been created, signposts or measures serve as triggers to let managers know when their business environments have changed (i.e., various scenarios) and when they should implement action plans to address those changes. For example, at Solutia, a chemical company, managers put together four different short-term outcomes for each scenario, with each set of outcomes containing short-term signposts that allow the company to abandon or embrace different scenarios or strategies in days. These signposts proved effective when Solutia was deciding whether to resell another company's chemical, one used in computer chip production. At first, said Mitch Pulwer, Solutia's chief scenario strategist, "We thought that because of our expertise, we'd have a wonderful new business opportunity here." But when one of the key signposts, prices for chip memory, dropped significantly, Solutia decided against the project within days.[67]

Planning for Product Development

Drip, drip, drip. Time to replace that leaky faucet? Just a few years ago, your only choice would have been chrome, not pretty, but functional. However, that changed when Moen, which manufactures plumbing fixtures, decided it was in the home decorating business, selling "jewelry for the bathroom and the kitchen." President Jeff Svoboda calls this Moen's "9 to 5" strategy, meaning that if customers had a choice of new styles, they would buy a new Moen faucet every five years instead of every nine years (www.moen.com). The only problem was that Moen averaged only one new product line per year. Today, though, Moen's 50 design engineers work on three to fifteen new faucet product lines per year. The speed-up was accomplished by using "ProjectNet," an online collaboration site where Moen's designers share product plans and designs with suppliers all over the world. When a supplier makes changes, those changes are then saved in a master Web file for later use, cutting development time by one-third. Likewise, Moen has used its Web site to even allow customers to design and customize their kitchens, bathrooms, and faucets. So with more products being developed at a faster pace, Moen's sales are up dramatically in the last several years, moving it from third in the industry to a tie for first.[68]

Product development is an increasingly important competitive tool. Like Moen, companies that are the first to market with new products or newly redesigned products that customers want can quickly increase market share, earn higher profits, and stay ahead of competitors who are forced to play catch-up.

The first step in effective product-development planning is to create an aggregate project plan.[69] Because very few companies can survive by relying on just one product, companies develop **aggregate product plans** to manage and monitor all new products in development at any one time. Aggregate product plans should indicate the resources (funds, equipment, facilities, materials, and employees) being used for each product and that product's place within the company's mission and strategic plan.

aggregate product plans plans developed to manage and monitor all new products in development at any one time

More than anything else, aggregate product plans help companies avoid the classic mistake of having too many products in development at any one time. For example, in one subsidiary of an American firm, a product-development staff of 40 people was responsible for almost 140 projects. Not surprisingly, the subsidiary's managing director complained that "nothing is getting done as well as we would like." And when asked if all 140 projects were equally important to the company, he replied, "We have no method of weighing the merits of one against another."[70] By contrast, after creating an aggregate product plan, a large manufacturer of scientific instruments and laboratory equipment reduced the number of products it planned to develop by nearly two-thirds. After topping out at a high of 30 products, it now has a much more manageable group of 11 products, all of which are consistent with the company's long-term strategic goals.

Besides keeping the overall set of products in balance and limited to a reasonable number, the second step is effective management of the product-development process itself. Four factors lead to a better, faster product-development process: cross-functional teams, internal and external communication, overlapping development phases, and frequent testing of product prototypes.[71]

Cross-functional teams, which are made up of individuals from different functional backgrounds (e.g., manufacturing, engineering, marketing), make better product-development decisions. The diversity of functional backgrounds means that cross-functional teams have a greater amount and variety of information, knowledge, and experience available as they develop new products. At food manufacturer Sara Lee, cross-functional teams test and bring new food products to market. Paul Bernthal, senior vice president of Research and Development, said, "One of our core competencies is the diverse background of our R&D group. Our staff has backgrounds in culinary arts, food science, meat science, grain science, animal science, package engineering, and chemical engineering, with varying degrees, including B.S., M.S., M.B.A. and Ph.D." He continued, "As a development company, cross-functional teams help bring us to market more quickly. And with all of us under one roof, there is a greater understanding of each group's functions."[72] According to Sandy Glatter, director of Bakery Research and Development, when Sara Lee was testing its new microwave calzone products (a calzone is pizza dough with meat, cheeses, or veggies baked in the middle), "We utilized our meat products group and combined their expertise with the bakery side to enter a category that we were not competing in—hand-held sandwiches." Then, "We leveraged our refrigerated folks to help determine the types of meats that should go inside and truly differentiate our product, making Calzone Creations live up to the Sara Lee name."[73]

Frequent internal and external communication is the second critical factor in the product-development process. Like cross-functional teams, frequent internal communication between product-development team members increases the amount of relevant information used to make decisions. It also builds group cohesion and reduces mistakes and misunderstandings that are commonplace in the product-development process. External communication with outsiders, such as customers and suppliers, broadens development team members' perspectives by helping them see their product and its uses through others' eyes. While communication with outsiders is typically beneficial, development teams may want to give more weight to what customers and suppliers do with new products (during product testing) than what they say they will do. For example, surveys and focus groups of fast-food restaurant customers usually result in the same conclusion: customers say they want healthier, low-fat food on the menu. However, Taco Bell's Border Lights, McDonald's McLean, Kentucky Fried Chicken's skinless chicken, and Pizza Hut's low-cal pizza all flopped and have been removed from restaurant menus. Not surprisingly, a National Restaurant Association study found a large difference between what people say they will eat (fruit, vegetables, etc.) and what they really eat (cheeseburgers and french fries).[74]

Overlapping development phases is the third critical factor when planning the product-development process. In contrast to a sequential design process, where each step (product plans and specs, product testing, product roll-out) must be completed before beginning the next step, overlapping development means multiple product-development steps and phases are started and completed at the same time. Exhibit 4.5 shows the development time line used by Silicon Graphics Incorporated (SGI) to develop one of its new "supercomputer" computer servers. The white rectangles indicate traditional planning processes. Here, SGI created the block diagram (the general plan) and the system specifications (the details behind the plan) that it wanted in its new computer. Notice, however, that product testing, indicated by the grey (computer software simulations) and black rectangles (prototype hardware testing), began long before SGI had completed its plans and detailed product specifications. The primary advantage of overlapping development is that it speeds up product development and makes the entire process much more flexible. In fact, SGI began software simulation testing just four months after product development began. And by having customers participate in product testing at an early stage, SGI had the flexibility to incorporate their feedback (and any last-minute changes in computer technology—which always occur at a rapid pace).[75]

product prototype
a full-scale, working model of a final product that is being tested for design, function, and reliability

The last critical component in the product-development process is frequent testing of product prototypes. A **product prototype** is a full-scale, working model that is being tested for design, function, and reliability. A good product plan or blueprint is essential.

EXHIBIT 4.5
Silicon Graphics: Overlapping Product-Development Phases for a New "Supercomputer" Server

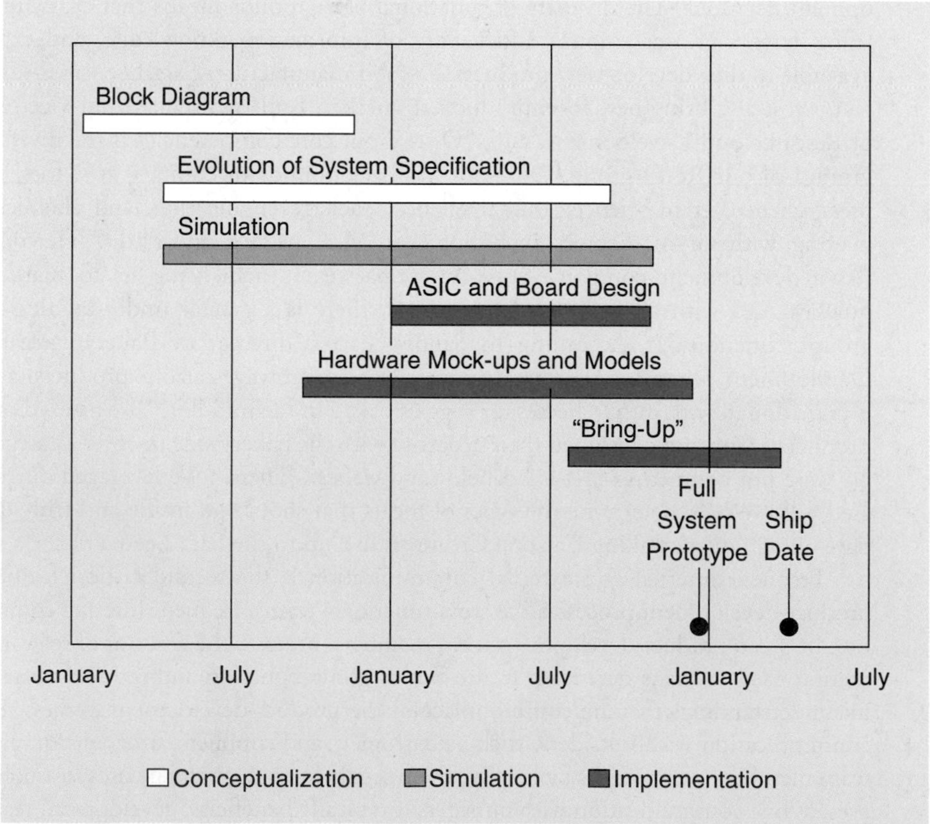

Source: Copyright © 1995, by The Regents of the University of California. Reprinted from the *California Management Review*, Vol. 38, no. 1. By permission of The Regents.

Very few new products succeed without them. But planning is no substitute for the hands-on learning that comes from frequent testing of product prototypes. At Lear Corporation, which designs and makes automotive interiors for companies such as General Motors, designers, engineers, and sculptors used to make initial design prototypes with 3D clay models of seats and doors. These days, however, with advanced CAD (computer-aided design) software, prototyping is as much "virtual" as it is "hands-on." In fact, Lear has constructed a special "reality centre" with a screen stretching 6 metres wide and 2.5 metres tall to view computerized prototypes. As the lights come down and the computerized 3D design is projected onto the screen, it feels as if you're actually sitting in a new car. Glance to the right and you view the centre console and controls. Turn to your right and view the passenger seat. Make the computer "glance" over your "right shoulder" and you can see what the back seat looks like, too.[76] Normally, it takes Lear three years to completely design the interior of a new car, but with its CAD-based virtual-reality prototypes, it has been able to cut that development time in half.

Prototype testing works best as a "hands-on" process. It begins by testing a prototype, making changes in the product based on what you learned, testing the new version of the prototype, and then making changes again, and so on. While Lear now makes many of these tests and changes on computers, it realized that there are limitations to completely relying on computer-based design prototypes. Leather seats have to be sat on. Real people need to try the steering wheel and controls for functionality and logic. Steven Allen, who designed interiors at Lear, said, "Our goal is always to get to market faster. But you've got to be able to put a qualified rear end in the seat. If you don't understand sculpture in the real world, you can't sculpt on a computer." So Lear always makes at least one physical product prototype of everything it develops in its design centre. In fact, to make its virtual prototypes more realistic, Lear builds "mistakes" into its computer models, such as leather textures with folds in the leather that mimic real seats. Steve Allen said, "My goal is to destroy the difference between what's real and what's perceived. I don't want any doubt that you're looking at a product, not a concept."[77]

Review 4: Special-Purpose Plans

Companies use special-purpose plans to deal with change, contingencies, and product development. Stretch goals are used to encourage workers to discover creative ways of doing their work. Benchmarking can be used to set challenging, achievable stretch goals. Managers and workers should not be punished for failing to achieve stretch goals. Scenario planning helps managers anticipate and prepare for future contingency factors that could influence their businesses. The steps of scenario planning are (1) define the scenario scope, (2) identify the major stakeholders, (3) identify trends, (4) identify key uncertainties, (5) create initial scenarios, (6) check for consistency and plausibility, (7) develop contingency plans for each scenario, and (8) develop measures or signposts that serve as triggers to let managers know when their business environments have changed. Aggregate product plans help companies manage all products in development at any one time and avoid developing too many low-priority products. Product-development processes can be accelerated by planning to use cross-functional teams, promoting internal and external communication, using overlapping development phases, and frequently testing product prototypes.

What Really Happened?[78]

Air Canada faced a serious problem at the beginning of the chapter. It had already lost market share in western Canada and had declared bankruptcy. Now WestJet was slowly marching eastward into markets that Air Canada dominated and contributed significantly to its bottom line. WestJet had a significantly lower cost structure and its growth seemed to be unstoppable. By contrast, Air Canada was stuck with a much higher cost structure and a stagnant or even shrinking market share. Attempts to cut labour costs, while somewhat successful, had come at a price—a limited number of planes would be allowed to fly for Tango and Zip, seriously limiting Air Canada's ability to cut costs. Remember Air Canada has over 300 airplanes in its fleet.

Given the current circumstances and constraints, what would improve Air Canada's competitive position? How could it possibly stop the continuous erosion of its market?

Planning is one of the best ways to improve organizational and individual performance. It encourages people to work harder (intensified effort), to work hard for extended periods (persistence), to engage in behaviours directly related to goal accomplishment (directed behaviour), and to think of better ways to do their jobs (task strategies). But most important, companies that plan have larger profits and faster growth than companies that don't plan. Further, because action plans are sometimes poorly conceived and goals sometimes turn out to not be achievable, the last step in developing an effective plan is to maintain flexibility and not escalate your commitment to a single course of action (see Chapter 6 for more on escalation of commitment). For Air Canada to have a successful plan, it needed to set specific goals, develop commitment to goals, develop action plans, track progress, and maintain flexibility. Air Canada's foremost goals were to keep WestJet from continuing to take away its market share and to reverse its financial losses. Its initial plan was not as successful as hoped. Air Canada's unions had limited the number of planes that the two discount carriers could fly, and the company had failed to achieve the level of labour cost savings in terms of wages and work-force flexibility.

Further, there is a danger for decision makers when it becomes widely believed that there is only one way to solve a problem. For example, when top management sits around a table and quickly decides that layoffs are the answer without considering any other options, this danger is called "groupthink" or "satisficing." Yet, regardless of the label you attach to it, premature definition of the problem ("We've got too many employees.") and limited consideration of alternative solutions ("We've got no choice. We have to start layoffs.") will almost always produce poor decisions and poor results. Air Canada had already laid off a substantial number of workers but the losses continued. It had attempted to launch two discount carriers, but with limited success. It had to address the three major cost items that were keeping ticket prices high: labour costs, service levels, and using multiple types of inefficient aircraft.

What alternatives were available that directly addressed the different cost structures? How could Air Canada address these key cost issues?

The first step in decision-making is defining the problem, that is, figuring out what's going wrong. The traditional way to do that is to look for gaps between desired states and existing states. If you remember from the beginning of the chapter, the higher cost structure was the result of the three main factors: labour costs, service levels, and use of multiple types of aircraft. Clearly, Air Canada had to focus on these issues. Limiting lower cost structures to a mere 40 planes out of over 300 would not be enough to stem the losses that Air Canada had suffered. Lower costs across its entire operation were desperately needed. In the wake of its bankruptcy, Air Canada began an aggressive round of negotiations with its labour unions. In May 2003 Air Canada announced that it wanted to slash $770 million in labour costs from its $3 billion annual labour costs. Air Canada wanted a 15 percent pay cut from pilots and managers and a 10 percent pay cut from the remainder of its workers. In turn, it wanted to introduce a profit-sharing plan just like WestJet's. It also announced that it was planning to purchase 85 new small jets with 90 to 100 seats in order to serve regional markets. It was also grounding larger less efficient aircraft and cutting back the number of routes it would fly. It also shut down Tango and Zip, recognizing that cost savings could not be limited to a small segment of their operation but had to be system-wide. In turn, it folded "Tango" fares into its mainline operations to mirror the fare structures of WestJet.

Although negotiations with its unions have been difficult and fraught with acrimony, Air Canada has been able to cut over $1 billion in annual labour costs. Air Canada was also able to reduce aircraft ownership and lease costs by $550 million and restructure its debt. Air Canada emerged from bankruptcy protection in late 2004 and all these activities have led ACE Aviation, the owner of Air Canada after its restructuring and emergence from bankruptcy, to a second quarter profit in 2005 of $168 million, compared to a loss of $510 million in the same period in 2004. Although Air Canada has shown marked improvement in its operations and ACE Aviation's share price has gone from $20 to almost $40, it is not necessarily out of the woods yet. Only time will tell.

Key Terms

action plan *(97)*
aggregate product plans *(111)*
benchmarking *(108)*
budgeting *(106)*
common-enemy mission *(103)*
distal goals *(98)*
goal commitment *(96)*
internal-transformation mission *(104)*
learning-based planning *(100)*
management by objectives *(104)*
mission *(103)*
operational plans *(105)*
options-based planning *(99)*
planning *(92)*
policy *(105)*
procedure *(106)*
product prototype *(112)*
proximal goals *(98)*
role-model mission *(103)*
rules and regulations *(106)*
S.M.A.R.T. goals *(96)*
scenario planning *(109)*
single-use plans *(105)*
standing plans *(105)*
strategic plans *(101)*
stretch goals *(107)*
tactical plans *(104)*
targeting *(103)*
vision *(102)*

Self-Assessment

SELF-MANAGEMENT

A key part of planning is setting goals and tracking progress toward their achievement. As a manager, you will be involved in some type of planning in an organization. But the planning process is also used in a personal context, where it is called self-management. Self-management involves setting goals for yourself, developing a method or strategy to achieve them, and then carrying it out. For some people, self-management comes naturally. Everyone seems to know someone who is highly organized, self-motivated, and disciplined. That someone may even be you. If that someone is not you, however, then you will need to develop your self-management skills as a means to becoming a better manager. To gain insights into your level of self-management, take the 35-question assessment on page 512 of the Assessment Appendix. That assessment will give you some baseline information as a foundation for your later self-management goals (i.e., where you are now so that you can see what you need to do to get where you want to be).

Management Decisions

WHAT'S YOUR POLICY?[79]

Ah, what's this, a Post-it note from the boss attached to a couple of newspaper articles? The first story is about a McDonald's manager who used the company voice-mail system to record "intimate exchanges" with a co-worker. For reasons that were not made clear in the article, McDonald's later played the tape for his wife. The manager sued, claiming that his voice-mail messages were private and protected because they could be accessed only by someone who possessed his voice-mail security password. McDonald's countered by claiming that since the voice-mail system was owned, run, and maintained by the company, nothing contained on the voice-mail system could be construed as personal or private.

The second news story is about Irene Wechselberg, a university librarian who works in the rare books department. Like most people, a large percentage of the e-mails that she sends and receives on her university e-mail account are business-related. However, some are personal. When Irene went on medical leave, her supervisor asked for her e-mail password so that the library staff could keep up with her responsibilities. (No doubt, Irene subscribed to several professional listserv groups that kept her informed on issues related to rare books.) When she refused, calling the request an "invasion of privacy," the university redirected all her e-mail to her supervisor's computer. The campus is now in an uproar over this issue. The article quoted Daniel Tsang, a biographer and host of a campus radio show, as saying, "Just because the university owns the public buildings, does that mean the state has the right to install cameras in the bathroom?"

Oh, here's a second Post-it note from the boss. "ASAP, write a policy that makes clear to all employees the appropriate and inappropriate uses of e-mail. Without a clear policy, we're leaving ourselves exposed to problems, controversies, and potential lawsuits. Have a draft in my e-mail account by 9:00 A.M. Monday."

Questions

1. Before writing a rough draft of the e-mail policy, specify, in writing, the purpose of the policy and its desired outcomes.
2. Write a rough draft of the new e-mail policy for your company. Be as specific as possible about appropriate and inappropriate uses of e-mail. Keep the policy short, no more than a page. Since it will be used to guide the actions of everyone in the company, make it easy to read and understand (no techno-speak).

Management Decisions

CELL PHONE DILEMMA[80]

You've just finished watching a CTV news item on Newfoundland's recent ban on using hand-held cell phones while driving, something that has happened in over 30 countries. You agree that talking on a cell phone while driving, along with other activities such as eating or searching for a radio station, is a distraction and can increase the probability of having an accident.

As you think about the implications the ban may have on individuals and companies, you begin to realize that most of your employees currently use cell phones on the job, many while driving. Suddenly, you find yourself subconsciously practising scenario planning. Questions immediately pop into your head, such as would your company be held liable if an employee injures or kills someone while talking on a company-issued cell phone while driving? Should you develop a policy regarding safe cell phone use while driving? As a manufacturer, your company certainly has plenty of other safety policies in place, so perhaps one concerning cell phones is needed. You decide to investigate the matter further before drafting a cell phone safety proposal.

In doing some basic research, you discover a case involving an investment broker who, while using a company-provided cell phone, ran a red light and killed the driver of a motorcycle. The family of the motorcycle rider sued the broker's employer, claiming that the employer encouraged the broker to use his cell phone after hours to maintain contact with clients. Although the investment-banking firm did not admit fault, it decided to avoid a jury trial by settling the suit for $750 000. Now you believe you have the ammunition needed to draft an operational plan about cell phone safety.

Questions

1. Do you need a policy, a set of procedures, or rules and regulations? Or maybe all three?
2. As the manager in question, draft the appropriate operational plan(s) for this situation.

Develop Your Management Potential

WHAT DO YOU WANT TO BE WHEN YOU GROW UP?[81]

What do you want to be when you grow up? Still not sure? Ask around. You're not alone. Chances are, your friends and relatives aren't certain either. Sure, they may have jobs and careers, but what you're likely to find out is that, professionally, many of them don't want to be where they are today. One reason this occurs is that people's interests change. Burnout is another reason that people change their minds about what they want to be when they grow up. For example, a former lawyer, Michael Stone, said, "I hated it." So he and a partner created a licensing agency that helps companies obtain licences to sell products bearing the names and logos of corporations such as Coca-Cola and Harley-Davidson. Another reason some people are unhappy with their current jobs or careers is that they were never in the right one to begin with. For example, lawyer Marsha Cohen said that it took the results of a personality test for her to realize why she disliked her jobs in large organizations. The reason? She was an introvert. Today, she runs her own small practice in international business and is much happier.

Getting the job and career you want is not easy. It takes time, effort, and persistence. Moreover, in today's ever-more-mobile society, it's common for people to have three to five fairly different career paths over the course of their working lives. No matter what you decide to be "when you grow up," your career-planning process will be easier (and more effective!) if you take the time to develop a personal career plan.

Write a personal career plan by answering the following questions. (Hint: Type it up. Treat this seriously. If you do it effectively, this plan could guide your career decisions for the next five to seven years.)

Questions

1. Describe your strengths and weaknesses. Don't just rely on your opinions of your abilities. Ask your parents, relatives, friends, and employers what they think, too. Encourage them to be honest and then be prepared to hear some things that you may not want to hear. Remember, though, this information can help you pick the right job or career.
2. Write an advertisement for the job you want to have five years from now. Be specific. Describe the company, title, responsibilities, required education, required experience, salary, and benefits that you desire. If you're not sure where to begin, model the advertisement for your ideal job after the employment ads appearing in the Sunday job listings.
3. Create a detailed plan to obtain this job. In the short term, what classes do you need to take? Do you need to change your major? Do you need to get a business major or minor or maybe a minor in a foreign language? What kind of summer work experience will move you closer to getting the job you want five years from now? What job do you need to get right out of university or college in order to get the work experience you need? At the very least, you should have a specific plan for each of the five years in your career plan.

Don't worry too much about locking in your fourth- and fifth-year plans. Those are likely to change anyway. The value in planning is that it forces you to think about what you want and what steps you can take now to help achieve those goals.

4. Decide when you will monitor and evaluate the progress you're making with your plan. Career experts suggest that every six months is about right. How about your birthday and six months after your birthday? Others prefer the beginning and middle of the calendar year. Whatever dates you choose, write them in your schedule. Furthermore, right now, before you forget, set five specific, challenging goals that you need to accomplish in the next six months in order to accomplish your career plans.

Discussion Questions

1. What activities can managers undertake to enhance goal commitment? What activities will detract from goal commitment?
2. Is there a difference between a company's vision and its mission? Give examples.
3. What is the difference between a policy and a procedure? Give examples.
4. How could you use management by objective to complete (a) this course, (b) this semester, (c) your diploma/degree?

Critical Thinking Video Case

CBC

Visit www.management2e.nelson.com to view this chapter's CBC video case.

Take Two

Biz Flix
The Bourne Identity

Jason Bourne (Matt Damon) cannot remember who he is, but others believe he is an international assassin. Bourne tries to learn his identity with the help of his new friend and lover Marie (Franka Potente). Meanwhile, while CIA agents pursue him across Europe trying to kill him, Bourne slowly discovers that he is an extremely well-trained and lethal agent. The story is loosely based on Robert Ludlum's 1981 novel. This scene is an edited version of the "Bourne's Game" sequence near the end of the film. Jason Bourne kills the hired assassin who tried to kill him the day after Jason and Marie arrived at the home of Eamon (Tim Dutton). Eamon is Marie's friend but is a stranger to Jason. Jason uses the dead man's cell phone after returning to his apartment in Paris, France. He presses the redial button, which connects him to Conklin (Chris Cooper), the CIA manager who is looking for him. Listen carefully to Jason's conversation with Conklin.

What to Watch for and Ask Yourself

1. Does Bourne describe a plan to Conklin? If he does, what are the plan's elements? What is Bourne's goal?
2. Does Bourne assess the plan's execution to determine if it conforms to his goal? If so, what does he do?
3. Was Bourne's plan successfully carried out? Why or why not? How does this scene relate to organizational strategic planning?

Management Workplace
Community Insurance Center

Planning is a crucial part of solid business practices. That's not to say that you won't be successful if you don't plan, but planning can bring clarity and focus to your operation. Community Insurance Center was launched in 1962 in a suburb of Chicago, and over the company's history, owner Milton Moses has had numerous opportunities to plan.

What to Watch for and Ask Yourself

1. When Milton Moses says, "We have a basic plan," what kind of plan is he talking about?
2. How does Community Insurance maintain flexibility in planning?

Managing Information

Chapter 5

CHAPTER OUTLINE

LEARNING OBJECTIVES

After reading this chapter, you should be able to

1. explain the strategic importance of information.
2. describe the characteristics of useful information.
3. explain the basics of capturing, storing, processing, and protecting information.
4. describe how companies can share and access information and knowledge.

London, England, has had serious traffic problems for more than a century. In the early 1900s, roads were so crowded with horses and wagons that traffic stood still for up to five hours a day. In 1935, a witness testifying for the Royal Commission on London Traffic said, "Unless we do provide some very far-reaching system, London will be almost unbearable in a few years." In 1951, the London & Home Counties Traffic Advisory Committee concluded that the "saturation point has been reached ... traffic has outgrown the capacity of the streets...." In 1959, the Ministry of Transport advised that the "traffic crisis will soon overtake the Metropolis." And then again in 1988, the British secretary of state for transport said, "If we don't act, London will seize up in the next decade."[1]

With a history like this, it's no surprise that London has the worst traffic in Europe, as London drivers spend 50 percent of the time in their vehicles *not* moving. In 1903, with horse-drawn carriages, traffic moved at an understandable pace of 19 km per hour. But, today, with cars and trucks, traffic has slowed to 14 kilometres per hour! The reasons are straightforward. First, most of central London's street patterns are 400 to 600 years old, and are therefore narrow, cramped, and not designed for car and truck traffic. Unlike the straight roads in most of today's cities, London's roads zig, zag, and confuse even the most experienced Londoners. In fact, it takes the average London taxi driver two years to learn the city's streets in preparation for the licensing exam! Second, with a population of 7.2 million people, there are just too many people in cars and trucks trying to get through central London's narrow streets. Consequently, streets and bridges resemble parking lots, and on many streets, pedestrians move faster than vehicles. Russ Kane, a long-time London traffic reporter says, "It's just sheer weight of traffic. It happens all the time—you get to the end of a massive traffic jam and there's nothing there at all. It's just congestion. Pure and simple."

What Would You Do?

The question, of course, is what to do with it. Over time, London has tried Bobbies (police officers splattered with mud and horse droppings), the world's first traffic lights, and then coordinated, computerized traffic lights designed to keep traffic flowing. But, nothing has worked. So this time, rather than trying to control the traffic, London's mayor has decided to shrink the traffic by charging a "Congestion Zone" fee of £5 (about $10) per day for any vehicle that enters the eight square miles (about 21 square kilometres) of central London between 7 A.M. and 6:30 P.M. on weekdays. Your job is to use information technology to create an inexpensive, reliable, fair method for imposing and collecting the congestion charge. Never mind that you've only got a year to do it, that there are 174 ways in and out of the congestion zone, that no other city has ever attempted this, that the mayor has staked his job (and yours) on this, and that it will be incredibly difficult from a technological standpoint to get this done.

To impose the fee, you have to accurately determine which vehicles are entering the congestion zone. With 250 000 vehicles doing so each day, how can you accurately capture that information? Next, once you've collected data showing which vehicles have entered—however it is you do that—you've got to process those data into useful information so you can charge the companies and people that own those vehicles. Finally, you have to make the charges accessible to everyone—from truck drivers, to corporate accountants, to taxi drivers—and do so in a way that makes it quick and easy to pay the congestion zone charge, so drivers don't incur late payment penalties (the equivalent of roughly US$75 to US$200).

If you were in charge of managing this information, what would you do?

A generation ago, computer hardware and software had little to do with managing business information. Rather than storing information on hard drives, managers stored it in filing cabinets. Instead of uploading daily sales and inventory levels by satellite to corporate headquarters, they mailed hard-copy summaries to headquarters at the end of each month. Instead of word processing, there was the electric typewriter. Instead of spreadsheets, there were adding machines. Managers didn't communicate by e-mail; they communicated by sticky notes. Phone messages weren't left on voice-mail; assistants and co-workers wrote them down. Workers didn't use desktop or laptop computers as a daily tool to get work done; they scheduled limited access time to run batch jobs on the mainframe computer (and prayed that the batch job computer code they wrote would work—it often didn't).

Moore's law
prediction that every 18 months, the cost of computing will drop by 50 percent as computer-processing power doubles

Today, a generation later, computer hardware and software are an integral part of managing business information. In large part, this is due to something called **Moore's law**. Gordon Moore is one of the founders of Intel Corporation (www.intel.com), which makes 80 percent of the integrated processors used in personal computers. In 1966, Moore predicted that every 18 months, the cost of computing would drop by 50 percent as computer-processing power doubled.[2] As shown in Exhibit 5.1, Moore was right. Every few years, computer power, as measured by the number of transistors per computer chip, has more than doubled. Consequently, the computer sitting on your lap or your desk is not only smaller, but also much cheaper and more powerful than the large mainframe computers used by Fortune 500 companies in the early 1990s. In fact, if car manufacturers had achieved the same power increases and cost decreases attained by computer manufacturers, a fully outfitted Lexus or Mercedes sedan would cost less than $1500!

Why Information Matters

raw data
facts and figures

information
useful data that can influence people's choices and behaviour

Raw data are facts and figures. For example, 11, $363, 128, and 6100 are some data used the day this section of the chapter was written. However, facts and figures aren't particularly useful unless they have meaning. For example, you probably can't guess what these four pieces of raw data represent, can you? And if you can't, these data are useless. That's why researchers make the distinction between raw data and information. While raw data consist of facts and figures, **information** is useful data that can influence someone's choices and behaviour. So what did those four pieces of data mean? Well, 11 stands for

EXHIBIT 5.1
Moore's Law

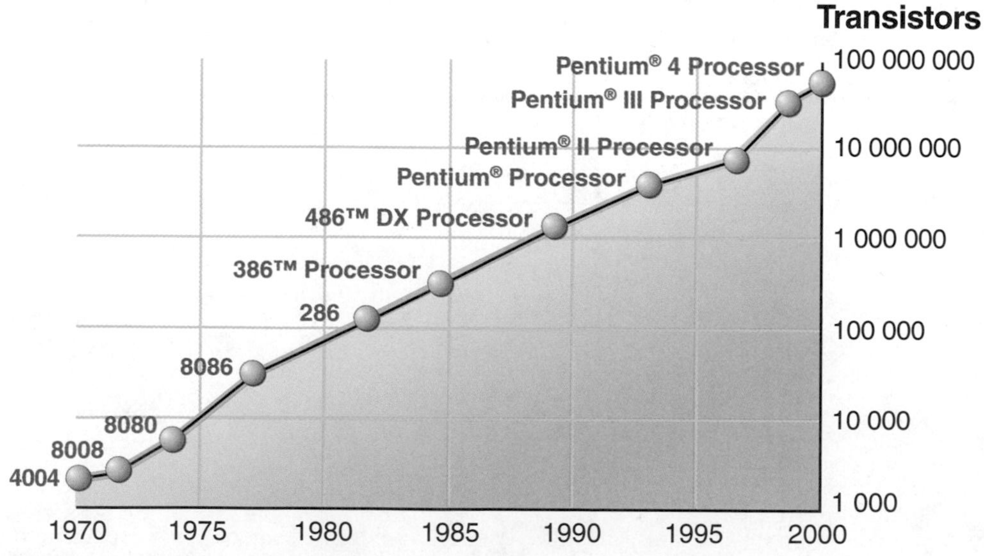

Source: Reprinted by permission of Intel Corporation, copyright Intel Corporation 2003.

channel 11, the local Global affiliate on which the author of this chapter watched part of the men's Canadian Open golf tournament; $363 is how much it would cost him to rent a minivan for a week of skiing over spring break; 128 is for the 128 megabytes of memory needed by the laptop computer this chapter was written on (prices are low right now—a good time to act); and 6100 means that it's time to get the car's oil changed.

After reading the next two sections, you should be able to

1 explain the strategic importance of information.

2 describe the characteristics of useful information.

1 STRATEGIC IMPORTANCE OF INFORMATION

If you ask most top managers whether they thought real estate (i.e., office space, factory space, etc.) was critical to their businesses, most would say no. By contrast, Charles Woznick, CEO of Facility Information Systems (www.fisinc.com), said, "If you talk to somebody who manufactures automobiles, they can tell you what each of 40 000 parts costs down to the penny, and how many they will need to make cars this year."[3] However, according to Woznick, top managers should be paying attention to their real estate costs and gathering critical information to manage it. Using FIS's software, companies and government agencies operating in Canada and abroad can determine how much vacant space they have, which workers are sitting at which desks, even if those desks are in New York, Toronto, or Edmonton, and whether they can move workers into the spaces they have or need to rent or build new space. Paul Savastano, director of information technology, said, "You can say I have this many workstations nationwide, how many are vacant, and where they are. If I can find 100 workstations in the appropriate city or combination of buildings, I can save the company several million dollars over the term of a new lease."[4]

In today's hypercompetitive business environments, information, whether it's about real estate, product inventory, pricing, or costs, is as important as capital (i.e., money) for business success. It takes money to get businesses started, but businesses can't survive and grow without the right information. Information has strategic importance for organizations, because it can be used to obtain first-mover advantage and to sustain a competitive advantage once it has been created.

Information and information technology are important for other reasons. Among the most important are the flattening of boundaries related to time and geography. Information can now be shared almost instantly across the globe, allowing companies to take advantage of time zone differences. Web-accessible information databases allow knowledge workers access to the same information on an as-needed basis, thus significantly reducing costs and allowing business to be conducted from almost anywhere in the world where an Internet connection can be found. The use of online information databases also increases trust within companies and beyond simply by making information easily available through the Web. This can serve to smooth business relations, making it less difficult to come to agreement on issues. While it may be a cliché that our world is becoming more complex, advances in information technology truly do offer managers many tools to do their jobs more effectively.

First-Mover Advantage

First-mover advantage is the strategic advantage that companies earn by being the first in an industry to use new information technology to substantially lower costs or to differentiate a product or service from competitors. For example, cable TV companies have taken a surprising lead over telephone companies in providing high-speed Internet access to people's homes. As this is written, 1.8 million Canadian homes have high-speed cable modems, compared to just 1.15 million that have high-speed digital subscriber lines (DSL) from phone companies.[5] These figures suggest that of the 75 percent of the Canadian population that has Internet access in the home, almost half have a broadband

first-mover advantage
the strategic advantage that companies earn by being the first in an industry to use new information technology to substantially lower costs or to differentiate a product or service from competitors

connection. Cable companies outflanked the phone companies initially by spending billions over four years to rewire their systems, replacing copper coaxial lines with 750 mHz digital lines that feed high-speed cable modems and digital TV cable channels alike (to compete with satellite TV, such as Bell ExpressVu or StarChoice). By contrast, the phone companies, having run into unexpected technical difficulties and high expenses, had until recently moved at a slower pace in bringing high-speed DSL service to people's homes. A recent poll, however, suggests that DSL providers are now moving more quickly to close the gap, having gone from 29 percent of Canadian households with broadband in 2000 to a 2005 figure of just under 49 percent.[6]

In all, first-mover advantages can be sizable. On average, first movers earn 30 percent market share, compared to 19 percent for companies that follow.[7] For example, banks that were early adopters of ATM technology were able to increase both market share and profits by 26 percent over nonadopters of ATM technology.[8] Likewise, over 70 percent of today's market leaders started as first movers.[9]

Sustaining a Competitive Advantage

Sustaining a competitive advantage through information technology is not easy to do. For example, smaller banks with fewer ATMs eventually caught up with larger banks by forming ABM networks such as Plus and Cirrus. Because these networks allow ATM machines to process transactions on most bank cards (as long as you're willing to pay a small fee), it didn't matter whether a bank had two or 2000 ATM machines. Furthermore, because new information technology always costs more when it is new, first-mover strategies are typically much more expensive than adopting technology after it has been established (and prices have fallen). This means that companies that establish first-mover advantage and then lose it can lose substantial amounts of money and market share. In many instances, this can put the company that had first-mover advantage out of business, such as failed Web companies such as Pets.com and Webvan (a defunct Internet grocery store).[10]

According to the resource-based view of information technology shown in Exhibit 5.2, companies need to address three critical issues in order to sustain a competitive advantage through information technology. First, does the information technology create value for the firm by lowering costs or providing a better product or service? If an information technology doesn't add value, investing in it would put a firm at a competitive disadvantage to companies that choose information technologies that do add value.

Second, is the information technology the same or different across competing firms? If all the firms have access to the same information technology and use it in the same way, no firm has an advantage over another (i.e., competitive parity).

Third, is the firm's use of information technology difficult for another company to create or buy? If so, a firm has established a sustainable competitive advantage over competitors through information technology. If not, the competitive advantage is just temporary, and competitors should eventually be able to duplicate the advantages the leading firm has gained from information technology. You'll learn more about sustainable competitive advantage and its sources in Chapter 9.

In short, the key to sustaining a competitive advantage is not faster computers, more memory, and larger hard drives. The key is using information technology to continuously improve and support the core functions of a business. For instance, every time someone goes through the register, Wal-Mart (www.walmart.com) collects "market-basket data" to better figure out what products customers are likely to purchase together. Because of these data, stored in the second-largest database in the world (only the U.S. government's is larger), Wal-Mart knows that bananas are the most common item in shoppers' grocery carts. However, because these data indicated that people tend to buy bananas and cereal at the same time, it now places bananas near the cereal aisle, in addition to the fruits and vegetables aisle. Likewise, Kleenex can be found in the paper goods aisle, but also near cold medicine.[11] Measuring spoons are in the housewares aisle, but also next to the

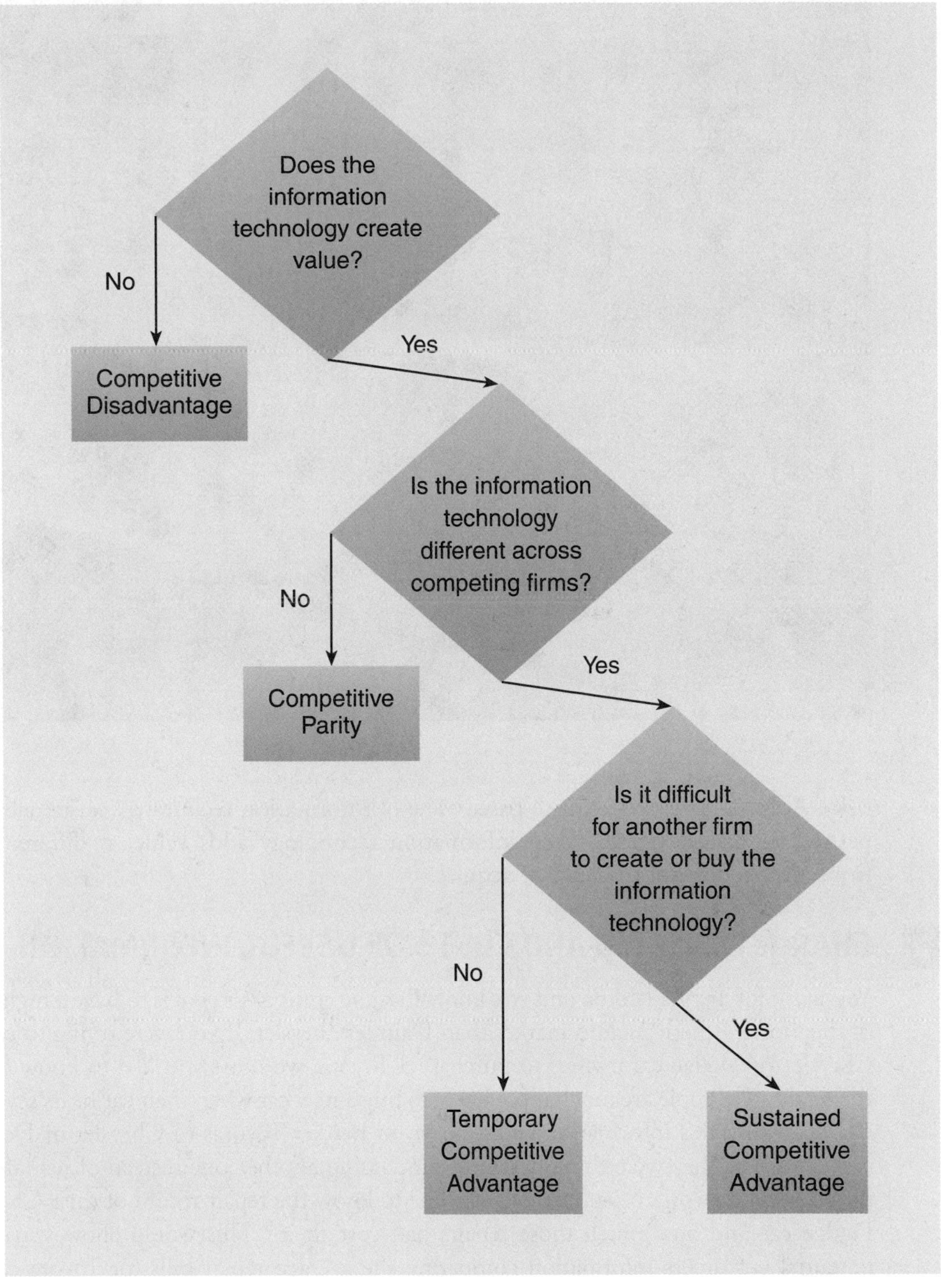

Source: Adapted from F.J. Mata, W.L. Fuerst, & J.B. Barney, "Information Technology and Sustained Competitive Advantage: A Resource-Based Analysis," *MIS Quarterly*, December 1995, 487–505. Copyright © 1995 by the Management Information Systems Research Center (MISRC) of the University of Minnesota.

EXHIBIT 5.2
Using Information Technology to Sustain a Competitive Advantage

Crisco shortening. Every chance it gets, Wal-Mart digs farther into this database to improve sales by making it easier for customers to find and buy what they want. Companies such as Wal-Mart that achieve first-mover advantage with information technology and then sustain it with continued investment create a moving target that competitors have difficulty hitting.

Review 1: Strategic Importance of Information

The first company to use new information technology to substantially lower costs or differentiate products or services often gains first-mover advantage, higher profits, and larger market share. However, creating a first-mover advantage can be difficult, expensive, and

© SUSAN VAN ETTEN

Wal-Mart's information collection is second only to the U.S. government. Knowing what people are likely to purchase together helps the company place products throughout the store. Any parent who has purchased a toy whose batteries weren't included would appreciate having some placed in the toy aisle.

risky. According to the resource-based view of information technology, sustainable competitive advantage occurs when information technology adds value, is different across firms, and is difficult to create or acquire.

2 CHARACTERISTICS AND COSTS OF USEFUL INFORMATION

You work for Toyota Motor, and you know that the company's goal is to have a higher share of the North American auto market than DaimlerChrysler. If you were trying to convince Chrysler or Dodge car owners to purchase a Toyota, wouldn't you like to know how old their cars are? People are much more likely to buy a new car when their car nears seven years old. Knowing this information could help you market Toyotas to Chrysler or Dodge car owners just as they were thinking about purchasing another one instead of just after they purchased a new one. Wouldn't you also like to know the repair record of their Chrysler or Dodge car and how much those repairs had cost them? This would allow you to send potential customers information comparing the average repair bills for Toyota cars they might buy to the actual repair bills they had been paying on their Chrysler or Dodge cars.

The answer to both questions is obviously "Yes!" Yes, you'd like to know how old people's Chrysler or Dodge cars are and what they pay for repairs for those cars. Information can influence people's choices and behaviour, and you'd want to use this information to improve the chance that they would buy a Toyota instead of a Chrysler or Dodge. While this information would be fantastic to have, more than likely it would be difficult, expensive, or impossible to obtain. And if you somehow managed to get hold of it, the data would probably be so out of date that it would be of little use.

Information is useful when it is accurate, complete, relevant, and timely. However, there can be significant costs—acquisition, processing, storage, retrieval, and communication—associated with useful information.

Accurate Information

Information is useful when it is accurate. To be accurate, information must be reliable and valid. For instance, airline maintenance crews can't service and fix passenger jets unless they receive accurate information from plane crews or from the plane's own information system. In fact, at one time, the information systems on Boeing's 747 passenger jets indicated a large number of false problems—problems that didn't really exist.[12] If, for example, a member of the crew accidentally flipped a circuit breaker off, the 747's information system would indicate that the plane needed to be taken out of service to be fixed. However, simply resetting the circuit breaker switch would fix the problem. Since maintenance costs represent 20 percent of the cost of running an airline, inaccurate information can lead to expensive mistakes.

Complete Information

Information is useful when it is complete. To be complete, the amount of information must be sufficient to identify the problem and begin to identify potential solutions. Aircraft manufacturers recognized the importance of providing flight crews and maintenance personnel with more information about how their jets were running. Consequently, new-generation planes, such as Boeing's 777, contain 600 computer sensors that airlines can use to fix problems and schedule maintenance. United Airlines (www.ual.com), an Air Canada Star Alliance partner, feeds this information into a system called AMIS, Aircraft Maintenance Information System. In turn, ground crews use laptop computers to run diagnostic tests on information gleaned from AMIS, while flight crews use computer monitors to access hundreds of colour graphs that continuously monitor and display the plane's performance.[13]

Relevant Information

Information is useful when it is relevant. Information is relevant when it pertains to the problem, so that decision makers can use it to define the problem and begin to identify potential solutions. The U.S. Federal Aviation Administration (FAA) classifies maintenance problems on planes into three categories.[14] Once a priority-one problem has been identified, it must be fixed after the plane lands or before it is allowed to take off. Anything that could lead to engine failure would be a priority-one problem. A priority-two problem does not require immediate action. The FAA (www.faa.gov) allows planes with priority-two problems to take off, fly, and land for a specified time period. But the plane must be fixed within this timeframe, or the FAA will ground the plane. Priority-three problems are minor maintenance problems, such as broken refrigerators or video monitors that airlines can fix at their own discretion. Since the new information systems, like United's AMIS system, provide information on all three kinds of problems, flight crews and maintenance crews are much more likely to have the relevant information they need to make good decisions. Although the FAA is a U.S. government regulator, its classifications and decisions matter to most of the world's major airlines, airplane manufacturers, and air transport authorities, including those located in Canada such as Air Canada, WestJet, and Bombardier. Failure to adhere to FAA safety rules can result in foreign carriers being barred from travel to American destinations and American carriers being barred from travel to unsafe destinations.

Timely Information

Finally, information is useful when it is timely. To be timely, the information must be available when needed to define a problem or begin to identify possible solutions. If you've ever thought, "I wish I'd known that ahead of time," you understand the importance of timely information and the opportunity cost of not having it. For the airlines, the information that can now be obtained on plane performance is not only more accurate, more complete, and more relevant, but also more timely. In fact, United Airlines' maintenance crews track the performance and problems of their planes while they're en route to their destinations. For example, if you're 8000 metres over upper New York State on the way back to New York City from your business trip to Toronto, United's ground crews are tracking the performance of your plane on their computer workstations. And because problems can be identified while planes are in the air, ground crews now have several hours to gather the tools, parts, and mechanical expertise needed to begin repairs as soon as the plane stops at the passenger gate. The timeliness of this information greatly increases the chances of keeping planes in service and on time.[15]

Acquisition Costs

acquisition cost
the cost of obtaining data that you don't have

Acquisition cost is the cost of obtaining data that you don't have. For example, Acxiom Inc. (www.acxiom.com) gathers and processes data for direct-mail marketing companies. Competitors offering similar services for the Canadian market include Equifax Canada Inc. (www.equifax.com) and InfoUSA.com. If you've received an unsolicited, "pre-approved" credit card application recently (and who hasn't?), chances are one of these three companies helped the credit card company gather information about you. Where does a firm such as Acxiom get that information? The first place it turns is to companies that sell consumer credit reports at a wholesale cost of $1 each. Acxiom also obtains information from retailers. Each time you use your credit card, retailers' checkout scanners gather information about your spending habits and product preferences. Many retailers sell this information to companies such as Acxiom that use it for market research. So why pay for this information? Because acquiring it can help credit card companies do a better job of identifying who will mail back a signed credit card application and who will rip the credit card application in half and toss it in the wastebasket.[16]

Processing Costs

processing cost
the cost of turning raw data into usable information

Processing cost is the cost of turning raw data into usable information. As the chief technology officer of one large North American insurance company said, "We have massive amounts of data. But whether we have massive amounts of information is another question."[17] Often, companies already have the data they want, but it's not in the form or combination that they need it to be in. When one large U.S. insurer wanted to build a better customer database, it realized that it had good information on more than 10 million households, information that could help it do a better job of targeting its insurance, money market, and real estate services to those customers. However, the processing costs were enormous, because the raw data had to be processed from 15 different computer systems that stored the data in incompatible formats.

Storage Costs

storage cost
the cost of physically or electronically archiving information for later use and retrieval

Storage cost is the cost of physically or electronically archiving information for later use and retrieval. One of the reasons that credit card companies hire companies such as Equifax Canada or Acxiom to help them identify good customer prospects is that they maintain databases of extremely useful information. For instance, in Acxiom's database one can find the following information on about 195 million North Americans: age, estimated income, home ownership, cars owned, occupation, children, number of credit cards, and so on. All of that information is stored in Acxiom's "data warehouse" at its corporate headquarters. Acxiom uses 16 mainframes and 600 000 computer tapes to process and store all that information. In all, Acxiom has 350 terabytes (a terabyte is the equivalent of 500 million pages of single-spaced text) of information in storage in its data warehouse. And it intends to store even more. Acxiom's CEO said, "Our customers today are saying, 'Save everything, because we might find a use for this information a year from now.'"[18]

Retrieval Costs

retrieval cost
the cost of accessing already-stored and processed information

Retrieval cost is the cost of accessing already-stored and processed information. One of the most common misunderstandings about information is that it is easy and cheap to retrieve once the company has it. Not so. First, you have to find the information. Then, you've got to convince whoever has it to share it with you. Then the information has to be processed into a form that is useful for you. By the time you get the information you need, it may not be timely anymore.

© DON MASON/CORBIS

There are probably better places for these old computers than a dumpster.

For example, R.R. Donnelley & Sons (www.rrdonnelley.com), which is headquartered in Chicago, is the largest printer of phonebooks in the world and has offices in Montreal, Toronto, Ottawa, and Calgary, as well as around the world. Donnelley designed software that would make it easier to convert electronic information into the metal printing plates that are used to print each page of the phonebook. When the software didn't work the way it was supposed to, the printers who used the software to make the metal printing plates called the software designers to get the information they needed to fix the problem. An assistant then forwarded the request for information. However, it often took several weeks (sometimes months!) for the software designers to provide the information that fixed the problem.[20] Because phonebook information is "perishable" (people move, numbers change, new numbers are added), the printers not only lost production time, but they also frequently had to start over in order to print the most up-to-date information in the phonebook. In theory, retrieval should be quick and easy. In practice, it often isn't.

communication cost
the cost of transmitting information from one place to another

Communication Costs

Communication cost is the cost of transmitting information from one place to another. For example, the most important information that an electric utility company collects each month is the information from the electric meter attached to the side of your house. Traditionally, electric companies have employed meter readers to walk from house to house to gather information that would then be entered into company computers. However, meter readers are losing their jobs to radio networks that work by placing a small transceiver in your electric meter. Every five minutes, the transceiver uses radio waves to transmit data indicating how much electricity was used at your house. The data are transmitted to a

DOING THE RIGHT THING

RECYCLING AND DISPOSING OF COMPUTER EQUIPMENT

With most companies replacing computers every four years, an estimated 270 million computers were discarded in North America in 2004. Computers and computer monitors contain hazardous materials, however, so you can't just toss them in the trash. Doing that is not just wrong—it's against the law. Instead, contact your province's ministry of environmental protection for help in finding a recycling company. Or, donate your old computers to deserving individuals or charitable organizations. Or, sell the computers at a steep discount to your employees. And, when you buy your new corporate computers, bargain with the vendor to make it responsible for recycling those computers the next time around.[19]

nearby electric pole that holds a small computer. The small computer forwards the information to a somewhat larger computer within a 400-metre range, which then sends the information to a base-station computer that is no more than 14 kilometres away. The base-station computer completes the communication process by forwarding the information via phone lines or microwave towers to company headquarters. The cost: less than $1.50 per month for each household.[21]

Review 2: Characteristics and Costs of Useful Information

Raw data are facts and figures. Raw data don't become information until they are in a form that can affect decisions and behaviour. For information to be useful, it has to be reliable and valid (accurate), of sufficient quantity (complete), pertinent to the problems you're facing (relevant), and available when you need it (timely). Useful information does not come cheaply. The five costs of obtaining good information are the costs of acquiring, processing, storing, retrieving, and communicating information.

Getting and Sharing Information

In 1907, Metropolitan Life Insurance built a huge office building for its brand-new, state-of-the-art information technology system. What was the system that represented such a breakthrough in information management? The advanced system was card files. That's right, the same card file systems that every library in Canada and the United States used before computers. Metropolitan Life's information "technology" consisted of 20 000 separate file drawers that sat in hundreds of file cabinets more than 4.5 metres tall. This filing system held 20 million insurance applications, 700 000 accounting books, and 500 000 death certificates. Metropolitan Life employed 61 workers who did nothing but sort, file, and climb ladders to pull files as needed.[22]

Less than a century later, the cost, inefficiency, and ineffectiveness of using this system that was previously state of the art would put a contemporary insurance company out of business within months. Today, if storms, fire, or accidents damage policyholders' property, insurance companies write cheques on the spot to cover the losses. When policyholders buy a car, they call their insurance agent from the car dealership to activate their insurance before driving off in their new car. And now, insurance companies are marketing their products and services to customers directly from the Internet.

Wow! From card files to Internet files in 95 years. The rate of change in information technology is spectacular.

After reading the next two sections, you should be able to

3 explain the basics of capturing, processing, and protecting information.

4 describe how companies can share and access information and knowledge.

3 CAPTURING, PROCESSING, AND PROTECTING INFORMATION

In many instances, when you go to your local pharmacy to pick up a prescription, the pharmacist reviews an electronic file that shows all the medications you're now taking. That same system automatically checks to make sure that your new prescription won't create adverse side effects by interacting with the other medications you take. When you pay for your prescription, the point-of-sale information system determines whether you've written any bad cheques lately (to the pharmacy or other stores), records your payment, and then checks with the computer of the pharmaceutical company that makes your prescription drugs to see if it's time to reorder. Finally, the system protects your information to make sure that your data are readily available to only you, your physician, and your pharmacist.

In this section, you will learn about the information technologies that companies use for capturing information, processing information, and protecting information.

Capturing Information

There are two basic methods of capturing information: manual and electronic. Manual capture of information is a labour-intensive process by which data are recorded and entered by hand into a data storage device. For example, when you applied for a driver's licence, you probably recorded personal information about yourself by filling out a form. Then, after passing your driver's test, someone typed your handwritten information into the department of motor vehicles' computer database so that local and provincial police could access it from their patrol cars when they pulled you over for speeding. (Isn't information great?) The problem with manual capture of information is that it is slow, expensive, and often inaccurate.

Consequently, companies are relying more on electronic capture, in which data are electronically recorded and entered into electronic storage devices. For example, scientists are now using a software program called WinWedge 32 to capture research data electronically. By connecting their scientific instruments (scales, thermometers, etc.) directly to the computer, WinWedge 32 can automatically record the data from these instruments into a computer spreadsheet (such as Lotus 1-2-3 or Microsoft Excel). For researchers, this software allows data to be quickly dumped directly into a computer database with no hand-entry errors.[23]

Bar codes and document scanners are the most common methods of electronically capturing data. **Bar codes** represent numerical data by varying the thickness and pattern of vertical bars. The primary advantage that bar codes offer is that the data they represent can be read and recorded in an instant with a hand-held or pen-type scanner. One pass of the scanner (okay, sometimes several) and "Beep!" The information has been captured. Bar codes were invented in 1952 and were first used to track parts inventory in factories in 1961. In 1967, railroad companies began using bar codes for tracking railroad cars. In 1973, the grocery business adopted the Universal Product Code, which required product manufacturers to place bar codes on their products or product labels. However, it took nearly two decades for bar code scanners to become standard equipment in most retail and grocery stores. Once adopted, bar codes cut checkout times in half, reduced data entry errors by 75 percent, and saved stores money because stockers didn't have to go through the labour-intensive process of placing a price tag on each item in the store.[24]

bar code
a visual pattern that represents numerical data by varying the thickness and pattern of vertical bars

Because they are inexpensive and easy to use, **electronic scanners**, which convert printed text and pictures into digital images, have become an increasingly popular method of electronically capturing data. However, text that has been digitized cannot be searched or edited like the regular text in your word-processing software. Therefore, companies can use **optical character recognition** software to scan and convert original or digitized documents into ASCII text (American Standard Code for Information Interchange). ASCII text can be searched, read, and edited in standard word-processing, e-mail, desktop publishing, database management, and spreadsheet software. Once data have been captured, they have to be stored before they are accessed and shared. Exhibit 5.3 describes the advantages and disadvantages of different kinds of data storage media.

electronic scanner
an electronic device that converts printed text and pictures into digital images

optical character recognition
software to convert digitized documents into ASCII text (American Standard Code for Information Interchange) that can be searched, read, and edited by word-processing and other kinds of software

Processing Information

Processing information means transforming raw data into meaningful information that can be applied to business decision-making. Evaluating sales data to determine the best- and worst-selling products, examining repair records to determine product reliability, or monitoring the cost of long-distance phone calls are all examples of processing raw data into meaningful information. And, with automated, electronic capture of data, increased processing power, and cheaper and more plentiful ways to store data, managers no longer worry about getting data. Instead, they scratch their heads about how to use the overwhelming amount of data that pours into their businesses every day. Furthermore, most managers know little about statistics and have neither the time nor the inclination to learn how to use them to analyze data.

processing information
transforming raw data into meaningful information

DATA STORAGE MEDIUM	ADVANTAGES	DISADVANTAGES
1. Paper	• Most common form of data storage	• Expensive • Takes tremendous space • Manual search processes • Only one person can access at a time
2. Microfilm—picture of the data is stored on a small photographic slide	• Reel of microfilm can store hundreds of pages of data • Inexpensive and cheaper than paper • Requires little storage space • Good for storing infrequently accessed data	• Only one person can access at a time • Access only available where microfilm is stored • Slow searches
3. CDs—hold 650 megabytes of data	• Inexpensive • Nearly all computers have CD drives • Easy	• Need CD-burner to put data on CD • Easily lost or misplaced
4. DVDs—hold 4.7 gigabytes of data	• Becoming less expensive • Easy • DVD drives can read CDs	• Need special DVD-burner to put data on DVD • Easily lost or misplaced • Not all computers have DVD drives; CD drives cannot read DVDs
5. Data Storage Tapes—magnetic tapes used to archive data for long-term storage	• Holds huge amounts of data • Not much larger than floppy disks • Portable, used to transport large files	• Requires special tape device for accessing and recording data • Easily lost or misplaced
6. Hard Drives—magnetic disks that read and write (store) data	• Primary storage for data used most often in performing jobs • Fastest data retrieval • Holds huge amounts of data • Cheap storage	• Only one person can access at a time, unless drive is networked • Access only available where drive is located, unless accessed via network or Internet • Unreliability—drives can crash
7. RAID—redundant array inexpensive disk system	• Uses a series of small disk drives together to act as a large disk drive (i.e., combining 10 20-gig hard drives to act as a 200-gig hard drive) • More reliable since data are duplicated across small drives • If one disk fails, backup data are immediately retrieved from another drive in the series • Good for mission-critical data	• More expensive • Typically must be networked to justify additional cost

EXHIBIT 5.3
Advantages and Disadvantages of Different Kinds of Data Storage Devices

data mining
the process of discovering unknown patterns and relationships in large amounts of data

One promising tool to help managers dig out from under the avalanche of data is data mining. **Data mining** is the process of discovering unknown patterns and relationships in large amounts of data.[25] Data mining works by using complex algorithms such as neural networks, rule induction, and decision trees. If you don't know what those are, that's okay. With data mining, you don't have to. Most managers only need to know that data mining looks for patterns that are already in the data but are too complex for them to spot on their own. For example, IBM has provided 25 National Basketball Association teams with data mining software called Advanced Scout. Advanced Scout allows basketball coaches to ask "What if?" questions such as "What if I start a certain lineup or run certain plays?" "When should we go for more three-pointers?" and "Does this strategy lead to victory?" Dr. Inderpal Bhandari, a computer scientist at IBM, said, "The beauty of Advanced Scout is that it requires little computer training or data analysis background. It was written with the coach in mind."[26] As well, Advanced Scout is easy to use. It asks users simple questions and makes suggestions that may help them find what they're looking for.

Data mining typically splits a data set in half, finds patterns in one half, and then tests the validity of those patterns by trying to find them again in the second half of the data set. The data typically come from a **data warehouse** that stores huge amounts of data that have been prepared for data mining analysis by being cleaned of errors and redundancy.

data warehouse stores huge amounts of data that have been prepared for data mining analysis by being cleaned of errors and redundancy

The data in a data warehouse can then be analyzed using two kinds of data mining. **Supervised data mining** usually begins with the user telling the data mining software to look and test for specific patterns and relationships in a data set. For instance, a grocery store manager might instruct the data mining software to determine if coupons placed in the Sunday paper increase or decrease profits. By contrast, with **unsupervised data mining**, the user simply tells the data mining software to uncover whatever patterns and relationships it can find in a data set.

supervised data mining user tells the data mining software to look and test for specific patterns and relationships in a data set

unsupervised data mining user simply tells the data mining software to uncover whatever patterns and relationships it can find in a data set

Unsupervised data mining is particularly good at identifying association or affinity patterns, sequence patterns, and predictive patterns. It can also identify what data mining "techies" call data clusters.[27] **Association or affinity patterns** occur when two or more database elements tend to occur together in a significant way. Earlier in the chapter, you learned how Wal-Mart discovered that people tend to buy the following items at the same time: bananas and cereal, Kleenex and cold medicine, and Crisco and measuring spoons. These items are an example of an association or affinity pattern. **Sequence patterns** occur when two or more database elements occur together in a significant pattern, but with one of the elements preceding the other. For example, by analyzing Web site registration and car purchasing behaviour, a car company such as Acura might find out that people who first register on the www.acura.ca site are then more likely to purchase an Acura car. Or a credit card company may find people who have been denied a request to raise their credit card limit are more likely to change credit card companies in the next few months.

association or affinity patterns when two or more database elements tend to occur together in a significant way

sequence patterns when two or more database elements occur together in a significant pattern, but one of the elements precedes the other

By contrast, predictive patterns are just the opposite of association or affinity patterns. While association or affinity patterns look for database elements that seem to go together, **predictive patterns** help identify database elements that are different. For example, mortgage companies can make more accurate lending decisions by studying a database that contains people who make their mortgage payments each month and those who don't, and then asking the data mining software to look for differences between the two. If reliable differences are found, those differences can then be used when approving or denying mortgage applications.

predictive patterns help identify database elements that are different

Data clusters are the last kind of pattern found by data mining. **Data clusters** occur when three or more database elements occur together (i.e., cluster) in a significant way. For example, after analyzing several years' worth of repair and warranty claims, Ford might find that, compared to cars built in its Oakville plant, the cars it builds in Atlanta (first element) are more likely to have problems with overtightened fan belts (second element) that break (third element) and result in overheated engines (fourth element), ruined radiators (fifth element), and payments for tow trucks (sixth element), which are paid for by Ford's three-year, 60 000-kilometre warranty.

data clusters when three or more database elements occur together (i.e., cluster) in a significant way

Traditionally, data mining has been very expensive and very complex. Today, however, with services and analysis provided by companies such as Digimine.com, data mining is much more affordable and within reach of most companies' budgets. And, if it follows the path of most technology, it will become even easier and cheaper to use in the future.

Protecting Information

Protecting information is the process of insuring that data are reliably and consistently retrievable in a usable format for authorized users, but no one else. For instance, when you place an order online, your personal information and credit card information are encrypted using SSL (Secure Sockets Layer) encryption technology before being sent over the Internet, making it virtually impossible for your information to be stolen or intercepted while being transferred to the vendor. Your credit card information is always

protecting information the process of insuring that data are reliably and consistently retrievable in a usable format for authorized users, but no one else

stored in encrypted form in a database that is away from the Web site database so it isn't connected to the Internet and is therefore safe from hackers.

Many companies find it necessary to protect information because of the numerous security threats to data and data security listed in Exhibit 5.4. From denial-of-service Web server attacks that can bring down some of the busiest and best-run sites on the Internet (e.g., Yahoo.com), to e-mail viruses that spread quickly and result in data loss and business disruption, to keystroke monitoring in which every mouse and keystroke you make is unknowingly monitored, stored, and sent to unauthorized users, there are many ways for people inside and outside of companies to steal or destroy company data.

As shown in the right-hand column of Exhibit 5.4, there are numerous steps to properly securing data and data networks. Some of the most important are using firewalls, anti-virus software for PCs and e-mail servers, data encryption, and virtual private networks.[28]

If you have an Internet service provider such as Microsoft Network (MSN), Sympatico, or AOL Canada, any time you make a dial-up connection, there's literally nothing between your personal computer and the Internet. Data files and Web site information are downloaded directly to your PC. By contrast, **firewalls** are hardware or software devices that sit between the computers in an internal organizational network and outside networks, such as the Internet. Firewalls filter and check incoming and outgoing data.

firewall
hardware or software device that sits between the computers in an internal organizational network and outside networks, such as the Internet

A **virus** is a program or piece of code that attaches itself to other programs on your computer and can trigger anything from a harmless flashing message to the reformatting of your hard drive to the system-wide network shutdown.[29] Anti-virus software for personal computers scans e-mail, downloaded files, and computer hard drives and memory to detect and stop computer viruses from doing damage. However, it is effective only to the extent that users of individual computers have and use up-to-date versions of anti-virus software. With new viruses appearing all the time, users should update their anti-virus software at least once a month. By contrast, anti-virus software for e-mail servers automatically scans e-mail attachments, such as Microsoft Word documents, graphics, or text files, which contain viruses as they come across the company e-mail server.

virus
a program or piece of code that attaches itself to other programs on your computer and can trigger anything from a harmless flashing message to the reformatting of your hard drive to the system-wide network shutdown

Another way of protecting information is to encrypt sensitive data. **Data encryption** transforms data into complex, scrambled digital codes that can be unencrypted only by authorized users who possess unique decryption keys. One method of data encryption is to use products such as PGP Desktop Security (www.pgp.com) to encrypt the files stored on personal computers. This is especially important with laptop computers, which are easily stolen. For example, the CEO of Qualcomm (www.qualcomm.com), a maker of chips and technologies used in mobile phones and wireless communication, had his laptop computer stolen after providing a presentation at a journalism conference. The stolen laptop contained megabytes of confidential corporate information, including several years of financial and strategic data.[30]

data encryption
transforms data into complex, scrambled digital codes that can be unencrypted only by authorized users who possess unique decryption keys

The Internet works by cutting data into smaller packets that are numbered and reassembled in order after being transported from one location to another. Imagine a high-speed video of a finished, 1000-piece jigsaw puzzle, with all the pieces numbered for easy assembly, which is quickly taken apart, moved from one place to another, and then quickly reassembled. The Internet does the same thing with software, text, data, or graphic files as it moves data files from one place to another. Unfortunately, since Internet data are not encrypted, "packet sniffer" software easily allows hackers to read everything you send or receive. For most of us, this is not a high-security risk. Hackers are not especially interested in what millions of ordinary people are doing on the Internet. However, there is a security risk for people away from their offices (e.g., sales people, business travellers, telecommuters who work at home) who interact with their company networks via the Internet. For them, packet sniffing can represent a substantial risk and an easy target for hackers. Previously, the only practical solution was to have employees dial in to secure company phone lines for direct access to the company network. Of course, with international and long-distance phone calls, the costs quickly add up. However, **virtual private networks** (VPN) solve this problem by encrypting Internet data at both ends of the transmission process. Instead of making long-distance calls, employees dial an Internet

virtual private network
encrypts Internet data at both ends of the transmission process

SECURITY PROBLEM	SOURCE	AFFECTS	SEVERITY	THE THREAT	THE SOLUTION
Denial-of-service Web server attacks and corporate network attacks	Internet hackers	All servers	High	Loss of data, disruption of service, and theft of service.	Implement firewall, password control, server-side review, threat monitoring, and bug fixes.
Unauthorized access to PCs	Local area network, Internet	All users, especially digital subscriber line and cable Internet users	High	Hackers take over PCs. Privacy can be invaded. Corporate users' systems are exposed to other machines on the network.	Close ports and firewall, disable file and print sharing, and use strong passwords.
Viruses, worms, Trojan horses	E-mail, downloaded and distributed software	All users	Moderate to high	Monitor activities and cause data loss, file deletion, and compromise security.	Use anti-virus and firewalls, and control Internet access.
Malicious scripts and applets	Rogue Web pages	All users	Mild, overestimated	Invade privacy, intercept passwords, and damage files or file system	Disable browser script support, and use security and blocking software.
E-mail snooping	Hackers on your network and the Internet	All users	Moderate to high	People read your e-mail from intermediate servers or packets, or they physically access your machine.	Encrypt message, ensure strong password protection, and limit physical access to machines.
Keystroke monitoring	Trojan horses, people with direct access to PCs	All users	High	Records everything typed at the keyboard and intercepts keystrokes before password masking or encryption occurs.	Use anti-virus software to catch Trojan horses, control Internet access, implement system monitoring and physical access control.
Referrers	Websites you visit	Individual users	Mild	Send e-mail notification of your Web activity.	Use ad blockers and security packages.
Spam	E-mail	All users and corporations	Mild	Clogs e-mail servers and inboxes with junk mail. HTML-based spam may be used for profiling and identifying users.	Filter known spam sources and senders, block Internet access by HTML messages.
Cookies	Web sites you visit	Individual users	Mild to moderate	Trace Web usage and permit the creation of personalized Web pages that track behaviour and interest profiles.	Use cookie managers to control and edit cookies, and use ad blockers.

Source: "Protect & Defend," B. Machrone, *PC Magazine*, 27 June 2000, 168–181.

EXHIBIT 5.4
Security Threats to Data and Data Networks

service provider, such as MSN or AOL, that provides local service all over the world. Unlike typical Internet connections in which Internet data packets are unencrypted, the virtual private network encrypts the data sent by employees outside the company network, decrypts the data when they arrive within the company computer network, and does the same when data are sent back to the computer outside the network.

One major company that is looking to VPNs, wireless Internet access, and paying attention to security is Nortel Networks. The company "is investing millions of dollars to roll out ubiquitous wireless local area network (LAN) coverage across its 250 offices worldwide.... Nortel estimates that overall productivity gains from the current in-office W-Lab deployment are US$3.1 million a year, yielding a one-year payback on the investment.... Even bigger benefits are emerging as voice over Internet protocol (VoIP) is tied into W-LANs."[31]

Review 3: Capturing, Processing, and Protecting Information

Electronic data capture (bar codes, scanners, optical character recognition, and devices that record data straight into structured data sets) is much faster, easier, and cheaper than manual data capture. Processing information means transforming raw data into meaningful information that can be applied to business decision-making. Data mining helps managers with this transformation by discovering unknown patterns and relationships in data. Supervised data mining looks for patterns specified by managers, while unsupervised data mining looks for four general kinds of data patterns: association/affinity patterns, sequence patterns, predictive patterns, and data clusters. Protecting information insures that data are reliably and consistently retrievable in a usable format for authorized users, but no one else. Firewalls, anti-virus software for PCs and e-mail servers, data encryption, and virtual private networks are some of the best ways to protect information.

4 ACCESSING AND SHARING INFORMATION AND KNOWLEDGE

Imagine a situation in which the only way customers could contact your company would be to fax a company in Switzerland, which would then fax the customer faxes to you. A company would have to be crazy to do that, right? Well, that's exactly the situation that Ingersoll-Rand (www.irco.com), a $5 billion manufacturing company, put itself in with its international customers. For example, Sermatec (www.sermatec.com), which sells Ingersoll-Rand air compressors in Santiago, Chile, would fax its order for more air compressors to Ingersoll-Rand's international trading company in Switzerland, which would then fax the order to factories in North America. Sermatec's general manager said, "It would take up to two weeks just to get confirmation that I'd placed an order." With no direct contact and no way to discover order status, distributors might as well have put a message in a bottle and dropped it in the ocean with the hope that Ingersoll-Rand would someday get the message and respond.

It didn't take long for Ingersoll-Rand's manager of global business systems to realize that "we had to make a change, and we had to make it quickly." So the company installed a US$1.5 million system that lets customers make orders and check on pricing, inventory, and the status of previous orders from their own office computers. With instant access to this information, Sermatec increased its sales. Now when a customer calls about the price and availability of an Ingersoll-Rand part or product, Sermatec logs onto the system to provide an immediate answer. Moreover, Ingersoll-Rand has reduced product delivery times to distributors like Sermatec from well over a month to three days.[32]

Today, information technologies are letting companies communicate, share, and provide data access to workers, managers, and customers in ways that were unthinkable just a few years ago. After reading this section, you should be able to explain how companies use information technology to improve communication, internal access, and external access, and to share knowledge and expertise.

Communication

E-mail, voice messaging, and conferencing systems are changing how managers, workers, and customers communicate and work with each other. E-mail, the transmission of messages via computers, is the fastest growing form of communication in organizations. E-mail is the cheapest way to send a message and is substantially faster, usually appearing in the receiver's electronic mailbox within seconds.[33] Because of its similarity to regular mail (which devoted e-mail users call "snail mail"), e-mail is easy to learn and use.

Of course, the ease and simplicity of e-mail create their own disadvantages: too much e-mail! Patricia Baldwin, director of business simplification for Sun Microsystems (www.sun.com), makers of Unix-based computers and the Java software language, gets more than 250 e-mails a day. Of those 250 messages, no more than 20 have any significant impact on her job.[34] Unfortunately, the volume of e-mail that Patricia receives is not unusual.

Voice messaging, or "voice-mail," is a telephone answering system that records audio messages. Surveys indicate that 89 percent of respondents believe that voice messaging is critical to business communication, 78 percent believe that it improves productivity, and 58 percent would rather leave a message on a voice messaging system than with a receptionist.[35] Voice messaging systems are easy to use and cut costs because workers don't have to spend their time recording and forwarding messages. However, handling voice messages can take a considerable amount of time. By contrast, because people read six times faster than they can listen, 30 e-mail messages can usually be handled in 10 to 15 minutes.[36] As well, some companies have found that customers prefer to talk to "real" people, even if only to leave a message. Winguth, Dohahue & Co., a North American executive search firm, scrapped its $28 000 voice messaging system. Owner Ed Winguth said, "At first clients said it was terrific that we were in the 21st century. But soon customers started saying it was too cold and annoying. These were CEOs and VPs calling in. Our repeat customers really got annoyed."[37]

Unlike e-mail and voice-mail, which permit users only to leave messages, **conferencing systems** allow two or more users in different locations to see and talk to each other as if they were working side by side in the same room. There are three kinds of conferencing systems: document conferencing, application sharing, and video conferencing.[38] The key similarity across all three is that time and space don't matter when it comes to getting work done. No matter where people are, conferencing systems allow them to work together.

Document conferencing, also called "white boarding," allows two or more people to use computers to simultaneously view and make comments about a document. **Application sharing** takes document conferencing several steps further by allowing two or more people in different locations to actually make changes in a document by sharing control of the software application running on one computer. Here's how it works. A lawyer in Halifax and her client, a businessperson in Calgary, are making the final changes on a contract for the businessperson's company. Step one: The lawyer and the businessperson talk on the phone while they work. Step two: Both use a second phone line or a company network to connect their computers as they talk. Step three: The lawyer opens the contract in word-processing software and then starts the application sharing software. (Several companies make this software: Netscape's Conference, www.netscape.com, and Microsoft's NetMeeting, www.microsoft.com/windows/netmeeting/.) Seconds later, the first page of the contract appears on the lawyer's computer in Halifax, and a few seconds after that, it appears on the businessperson's computer in Calgary. Now both can make changes to the document. For example, the lawyer could change $5000 to $50 000 on the first page while the businessperson is correcting a misspelling on page 20.[39] As the changes are being made, the computers communicate the changes over the phone line or network, so that both parties can work on identical versions of the file at all times.

There are numerous advantages to application sharing. Companies save an enormous amount of money and time by eliminating or reducing travel. Unlike videoconferencing, which is discussed next, document sharing runs well over standard phone lines. Thus, most companies and businesspeople can use it now without having to invest funds for additional equipment.

Desktop videoconferencing allows two or more people in different locations to use video cameras and computer monitors to see and hear each other and to share documents. Also, like document sharing, participants can see the files they are sharing.

Internal Access and Sharing

Two kinds of information technology are used by executives, managers, and workers inside the company to access and share information: executive information systems and intranets. An **executive information system (EIS)** uses internal and external sources of data

conferencing system
communications system that lets two or more users in different locations see and talk to each other as if they were in the same room

document conferencing
communications system that allows two or more people in different locations to simultaneously view and make comments about a document

application sharing
communications system that allows two or more people in different locations to make changes in a document by sharing control of the software application running on one computer

desktop videoconferencing
communications system that allows two or more people in different locations to use video cameras and computer monitors to see and hear each other and share documents

executive information system (EIS)
data processing system that uses internal and external data sources to provide the information needed to monitor and analyze organizational performance

Research in Motion's BlackBerry. An important technology? Just ask politicians, executives, and police forces throughout North America. It is a lifestyle-altering technology for many individuals.

MARIO ANZUONI/REUTERS/LANDOV

to provide managers and executives the information they need to monitor and analyze organizational performance.[40] For example, with the click of a mouse, senior and middle managers at United Cigar Stores can pull up graphs and charts of weekly and monthly sales on their computers to see if they're on target. If they're not, they can "drill down" for more information to help them figure out whether the problem is at the divisional, regional, or district level.

Since most managers are not computer experts, EISs must be easy to use and must provide information that managers want and need. Consequently, most EIS programs use touch screens, "point and click" commands, and easy-to-understand displays, such as colour graphs, charts, and written summaries so that little learning or computer experience is required. Exhibit 5.5 describes the capabilities of two of the best-selling products that companies use for EIS programs.

EXHIBIT 5.5
Characteristics of Best-Selling Executive Information Systems

EASE OF USE

- Few commands to learn. Simply drag-and-drop or point-and-click to create charts and tables or get the information you need.
- Important views saved. Need to see weekly sales by store every Monday? Save that "view" of the data, and it will automatically be updated with new data every week.
- 3-D charts to display data. Column, square, pie, ring, line, area, scatter, bar, cube, etc.
- Geographic dimensions. Different geographic areas are automatically colour-coded for easy understanding.

ANALYSIS OF INFORMATION

- Sales tracking. Track sales performance by product, region, account, and channel.
- Easy-to-understand displays. Information is displayed in tabular and graphical charts.
- Time periods. Data can be analyzed by current year, prior year, year to date, quarter to date, and month to date.

IDENTIFICATION OF PROBLEMS AND EXCEPTIONS

- Compare to standards. Compares actual company performance (actual expenses versus planned expenses, or actual sales by sales quotas).
- Trigger exceptions. Allows users to set triggers (5 percent over budget, 3 percent under sales quota), which then highlights negative exceptions in red and positive exceptions in green.
- Drill down. Once exceptions have been identified, users can drill down for more information to determine why the exception is occurring.
- Detect and alert newspaper. When things go wrong, the EIS delivers a "newspaper" via e-mail to alert managers to problems. The newspaper offers an intuitive interface for easily navigating and further analyzing the alert content.
- Detect and alert robots. Detect and alert robots keep an extra "eye" out for events and problems. Want to keep an eye out for news about one of your competitors? Use a news robot to track stories on Dow Jones News Retrieval. Robots can also be used to track stock quotes, internal databases, and e-mail messages.

Sources: "Business Intelligence: Overview: Enterprise Services from Pilot Software," Accrue Software. [Online] Available www.pilotsw.com/Products/Accrue Pilot Suite/business intelligence.html, 9 February 2002. Comshare home page. [Online] Available www.comshare.com, February 2002.

Intranets are private company networks that allow employees to easily access, share, and publish information using Internet software. Intranet Web sites are just like external Web sites, but the firewall separating the internal company network from the Internet only permits authorized internal access.[41] At Boeing (www.boeing.com), employees can access messages from top company leaders, information bulletins, and the doctor and hospital directory wherever they live. Boeing's intranet also helps its engineers work together to design planes wherever they're located. Intranets are exploding in popularity. One source suggests that 90 percent of U.S. corporations now have an intranet up and running in some form. Further, corporate spending worldwide on Intranets is supposed to grow to US$200 billion annually by 2010.[42] The reasons for this phenomenal growth, as shown in Exhibit 5.6, are many. First, executive information systems can cost as much as several hundred thousand dollars to install for a small group of managers. In comparison, intranets, which can be used by everyone in the company, are inexpensive. Much of the software required to set up an intranet is either **freeware** (no cost) or **shareware** (try before you buy, usually less expensive than commercial software).

intranets
private company networks that allow employees to easily access, share, and publish information using Internet software

freeware
computer software that is free to whoever wants it

shareware
computer software that you can try before you buy, but if you keep it beyond the trial period, usually 30 days, you must buy it

Second, intranets reduce costs, increase efficiencies, and save organizations money. Companies can save millions of dollars every year from using their intranets to purchase office supplies, handle reimbursement forms, and displace the paper-based forms their employees use. With 1000 internal Web sites and more than 2 million pages of information, Microsoft probably has one of the most advanced and used intranets in the world, with one-third of its 30 000 employees using it every day. In fact, MSWeb, Microsoft's intranet, is so advanced, that nearly all company paperwork, forms, and paper documents have been moved onto it.[43]

Third, using Intranets is intuitive and easy. As a result, companies are rushing to put as much information as they can on their Intranets. Indeed, a study of 323 companies in 10 different industries found that 23 percent of company intranets contained information on company benefits; 18 percent have information about savings plans, profit sharing, or company stock plans; 70 percent have information about jobs; 6 percent allow managers to conduct performance appraisals online; 24 percent are used for training; and 57 percent are used for corporate communications.[44]

Fourth, it doesn't matter if the people in marketing use the Macintosh operating system, the finance folks use Windows, and the information systems people use Unix systems—everyone can easily access information if it's available on the company intranet.[45] Intranets work across all kinds of computers and computer operating systems.

Fifth, if you already have a computer network in place, chances are your company already has the computer equipment and expertise to quickly and easily roll out an intranet.

Sixth, while it's not seamless, many software programs easily convert electronic documents from proprietary word processing (WordPerfect, Microsoft Word, etc.), spreadsheet (Lotus 1-2-3, Microsoft Excel), or graphics (Lotus Freelance or Microsoft PowerPoint) formats to the hypertext markup language (HTML) used to display text and graphics on the Internet and intranets. Indeed, many HTML software editors are now as easy to use as word processors. Boeing's intranet contains everything from corporate-policy material to maintenance manuals, and Boeing encourages its employees to publish any information that others might find useful.[46]

EXHIBIT 5.6
Why 90 Percent of Companies Use Intranets

1.	Intranets are inexpensive.
2.	Intranets increase efficiencies and reduce costs.
3.	Intranets are intuitive and easy to use (Web-based).
4.	Intranets work across all computer systems and platforms (Web-based).
5.	Intranets can be built on top of existing computer networks.
6.	Intranets work with software programs that easily convert electronic documents to HTML files for intranet use.

External Access and Sharing

Historically, companies have been unable or reluctant to let outside groups have access to corporate information. However, three information technologies—electronic data interchange, extranets, and the Internet—are making it easier to share company data with external groups such as suppliers and customers. They're also reducing costs, increasing productivity, improving customer service, and speeding communications. As a result, managers are scrambling to find ways to use them in their own companies.

electronic data interchange (EDI)
the direct electronic transmission of purchase and ordering information from one company's computer system to another company's computer system

Electronic data interchange, or **EDI**, is the direct electronic transmission of purchase and ordering information from one company's computer system to another company's computer system. For example, when a Wal-Mart checkout clerk drags a CD across the checkout scanner, Wal-Mart's computerized inventory system automatically reorders another copy of that CD through the direct EDI connection that its computer has with the manufacturing and shipping computer at the company that published the CD, say Atlantic Records. No one at Wal-Mart or Atlantic Records fills out paperwork. No one makes phone calls. There are no delays to wait to find out whether Atlantic has the CD in stock. The transaction takes place instantly and automatically.

EDI saves companies money by eliminating step after step of manual information processing. One study found that EDI could save manufacturing companies $25 per transaction, retail companies $32 per transaction, and wholesalers $15 per transaction.[47] Of course, those are just averages. Some companies save more. R.J. Reynolds, which deals with more than 1400 suppliers and tens of thousands of orders per year, said that EDI reduced the cost of orders from between $105 and $175 to just $1.30![48] And when you consider that 70 percent of the data output from one company, such as a purchase order, ends up as data input at another company, such as a sales invoice or shipping order, EDI also reduces data entry errors. Finally, EDI reduces order and delivery times. Hotel and motel chains such as Marriott and Hilton have found that EDI has reduced the average time for food and beverage orders to their kitchens by half, from six days to three days.[49]

extranet
allows companies to exchange information and conduct transactions with outsiders by providing them direct, Web-based access to authorized parts of a company's intranet or information system

While EDI directly transmits information from one company's computer system to another's, an **extranet**, by contrast, allows companies to exchange information and conduct transactions with outsiders by providing them direct, Web-based access to authorized parts of a company's intranet or information system. Typically, user names and passwords are required to access an extranet.[50] For example, to make sure that its distribution trucks don't waste money by running half empty (or produce late deliveries to customers because it waited to ship until its trucks were full), General Mills (www.generalmills.com) uses an extranet to provide Web-based access to its trucking database to 20 other companies that ship their products over similar distribution routes. When other companies are ready to ship products, they log on to General Mills' trucking database, check the availability, and then enter the shipping load, place, and pickup time. Thus, by sharing shipping capacity on its trucks, General Mills' trucks run fully loaded all the time. In several test areas, General Mills saved 7 percent on shipping costs, or nearly US$2 million in the first year. Cost savings will be even larger when the program is expanded company-wide.[51]

Internet
a global network of networks that allows users to send and retrieve data from anywhere in the world

Similar to the way in which extranets are used to handle transactions with suppliers and distributors, companies are reducing paperwork and manual information processing by using the Internet to electronically automate transactions with customers. The **Internet** is a global network of networks that allows users to send and retrieve data from anywhere in the world. Companies such as Air Canada (www.aircanada.com), United Airlines (www.ual.com), and American Airlines (www.aa.com), as well as independent travel sites such as Microsoft Expedia (www.expedia.ca), have Internet sites where customers can purchase tickets without calling a ticket agent or the airline's toll-free number. However, most airlines have further automated the ticketing process by eliminating tickets altogether. Simply buy an e-ticket via the Internet and then show the airport ticket agent your driver's licence or passport. The ticket agent then checks the database, confirms your e-ticket, issues you your boarding pass, and you're on your way. Together,

Internet purchases and ticketless travel have the potential to fully automate the purchase of airline tickets. By eliminating the recording, printing, handling, and mailing costs of tickets and the commission that would have been paid to travel agents, the airlines save an estimated $35 to $50 per ticket.[52]

So, in the end, why should companies try to connect Internet sites for customers to company intranets, EDIs, and extranets? Because companies that use information technologies in these ways achieve increases in productivity 2.7 times larger than those that don't.[53]

Sharing Knowledge and Expertise

At the beginning of the chapter, we distinguished between raw data, which consists of facts and figures, and information, which consists of useful data that influence someone's choices and behaviour. One more important distinction needs to be made—namely, that data and information are not the same as knowledge. **Knowledge** is the understanding that one gains from information. Importantly, knowledge does not reside in information. Knowledge resides in people. That's why companies hire consultants or why family doctors refer patients to specialists. Unfortunately, it can be quite expensive to employ consultants, specialists, and experts. So companies have begun using two information technologies, decision-support systems and expert systems, to capture and share the knowledge of consultants, specialists, and experts with other managers and workers.

knowledge
the understanding that one gains from information

Unlike executive information systems that speed up and simplify the acquisition of information, **decision support systems (DSS)** help managers understand problems and potential solutions by acquiring and analyzing information with sophisticated models and tools.[54] DSS programs have been developed to help managers pick the shortest and most efficient routes for delivery trucks, to pick the best combination of stocks for investors, and to schedule the flow of inventory through complex manufacturing facilities.

decision support system (DSS)
an information system that helps managers to understand specific kinds of problems and potential solutions and to analyze the impact of different decision options using "what if" scenarios

It's important to understand that DSS programs don't replace managerial decision-making; they improve it by furthering managers' and workers' understanding of the problems they face and the solutions that might work. For example, Apache Medical Systems [now owned by Cerner Corporation (www.cerner.com)] makes a DSS for emergency room physicians that is sold throughout Canada.[55] Apache's DSS collects data on 17 different physiological signs, such as blood pressure, respiratory rates, temperature, white blood counts, and so on. Then, using a database containing the medical records of more than 400 000 people (with 100 diseases) who received treatment at more than 200 different emergency rooms, Apache's DSS gives a diagnosis and then rates the chances of a patient's survival using various treatment procedures. For a patient with heart problems, the Apache DSS would create a graph showing the likelihood (from zero to 100 percent) of surviving five more years, depending on whether the patient had coronary bypass surgery, an angioplasty, or drug treatment.

Apache's DSS also helps physicians analyze the impact of different decision options by using "What if?" scenarios. The ability to analyze "What if" scenarios is a key capability of all DSS systems. What if we continue with our current strategy, would that work? What if we tried something else? Apache's DSS helps physicians pose and answer "What if?" questions by processing the latest information regarding a patient's health status three times a day and then printing out an unbiased, statistically based estimate of whether a given treatment is working. For example, if a nurse receives two printouts, one in the morning, and then another in the afternoon, indicating that a patient's chances of survival have dropped from 75 percent to 55 percent, the nurse has a very good reason to contact the doctor to reconsider treatment options. Apache is not only helping doctors save lives, but it is also giving doctors the confidence to move patients out of intensive care earlier. With intensive care costs in the United States running about US$2500 a day, Apache helped one major U.S. medical centre save US$2.5 million a year in unnecessary treatments.[56]

expert system information system that contains the specialized knowledge and decision rules used by experts and experienced decision makers, so that nonexperts can draw on this knowledge base to make decisions

Expert systems are created by capturing the specialized knowledge and decision rules used by experts and experienced decision makers. They permit nonexpert employees to draw on this expert knowledge base to make decisions. For example, when two companies draw up a contract, it usually takes at least two lawyers, one for each company. However, at one major North American telecommunications service provider, company purchasing agents are drafting long-term, multimillion-dollar contracts without using lawyers. Instead, they use an expert system designed and created by company lawyers to automate the creation of company contracts.[57]

Most expert systems work by using a collection of "if-then" rules to sort through information and recommend a course of action. For example, let's say that you're using your American Express card to help your spouse celebrate a promotion. You buy dinner and then some movie tickets. After the movie, you and your spouse stroll by a travel office that displays a Lake Louise poster in its window. Thirty minutes later, caught up in the moment, you find yourselves at the Pearson airport ticket counter trying to purchase last-minute tickets to Calgary. But there's just one problem. American Express didn't approve your purchase. In fact, the ticket counter agent is on the phone with an American Express (www.americanexpress.com) customer service agent. So what put a temporary halt to your weekend escape to Lake Louise? An expert system that American Express calls "Authorizer's Assistant." The first "if-then" rule that prevented your purchase was the rule "if a purchase is much larger than the cardholder's regular spending habits, then deny approval of the purchase." This rule is built into American Express's transaction-processing system that handles thousands of purchase requests per second. Now that the American Express customer service agent is on the line, he or she is prompted by the Authorizer's Assistant to ask the ticket counter agent to examine your identification. You hand over your driver's licence and another credit card to prove you're you. Then the ticket agent asks for your address, phone number, social insurance number, and your mother's maiden name, and relays the information to American Express. Finally, your ticket purchase is approved. Why? Because you met the last series of "if-then" rules. If the purchaser can provide proof of identity and if the purchaser can provide personal information that isn't common knowledge, then approve the purchase.

REVIEW 4: ACCESSING AND SHARING INFORMATION AND KNOWLEDGE

E-mail, voice messaging, and conferencing systems are changing how we communicate and work with each other. E-mail is cheap, fast, and easy to use. Though also easy to use, voice messages take more time to process than e-mail. Application sharing and document and videoconferencing let people in different locations work as if they were together in the same room. Executive information systems and intranets facilitate internal sharing and access to company information. Electronic data interchange and the Internet allow external groups, such as suppliers and customers, to easily access company information. Both decrease costs by reducing or eliminating data entry, data errors, and paperwork, and by speeding up communication. Organizations use decision support systems and expert systems to capture and share specialized knowledge with nonexpert employees.

What Really Happened?[58]

In the opening case, you learned that for over a century, London has had the worst traffic in Europe. Drivers spend half of their time in their vehicles not moving, and the average speed is only 14 kilometres per hour, down from 19 kilometres per hour in 1903 when traffic consisted of horses and carriages instead of cars and trucks. To improve traffic, London's mayor has imposed a "Congestion Zone" fee of £5 per day for any vehicle that enters the eight square miles (about 21 square kilometres) of central London between 7 A.M. and 6:30 P.M. on weekdays. Drivers who come into the zone, but who don't pay, will be fined the equivalent of US$75 to US$200. Let's see how the city of London used information technology to fairly and accurately charge drivers who used the congestion zone, and then whether those charges had the desired effect on London's terrible traffic.

To impose the fee, you have to accurately determine which vehicles are entering the congestion zone. With 250 000 vehicles doing so each day,

how can you accurately capture that information?

There are two basic methods of capturing information: manual and electronic. Manual capture of information is a labour-intensive process, which entails recording and entering data by hand into a data storage device. The problem with manual capture of information is that it is slow, expensive, and often inaccurate. For example, if the city of London relied on the manual capture of information for its traffic congestion zone charge, it would most likely have to rely on manned tollbooths. But with 174 different streets in and out of London's congestion zone, it would require 174 tollbooths, 174 toll takers, and drivers would have to stop long enough to pay the toll, or to show they had already paid it that day. Obviously, this would be enormously expensive in terms of time and payroll, and it would slow traffic rather than speed it up.

Those clear disadvantages of manual capture are why companies rely on electronic capture, in which data are electronically recorded and entered into electronic storage devices, whenever they can. Bar codes, radio frequency identification tags, and document scanners are methods of electronically capturing data. But, could those methods be used to determine which cars entered the London congestion zone? The answer was yes, but you couldn't decide what data to capture or how to capture those data without first determining how the entire information system would be managed. With that in mind, the Transport for London and the consultants it hired broke the project into five different "packages." Package 1 consists of the cameras to be used to take pictures of cars entering the congestion zone. Package 2 consists of the "image management store" on which the images of each vehicle can be stored, processed into registered licence numbers, and then condensed (so cars entering the zone multiple times in one day wouldn't be charged more than once). Package 3 is the telecommunication link between the cameras and the servers on which the images were stored. (Would that link be wireless, a dedicated line, or a secure Internet connection? We'll talk more about packages 2 and 3 when we answer the next question.) Package 4 links the car registration data to the owners of the vehicles and then to the payments those owners make to pay the congestion charge via the Web, phone, or mail. Package 5 consists of the network of retails stores, such as shops, kiosks, or gas stations, where congestion charges could also be paid. (Packages 4 and 5 will be discussed further in the answer to the last question.)

Let's return to package 1. How were cameras used to take pictures of cars entering the congestion zone? The first step was simply deciding where cameras were needed. As mentioned, there were 174 entrances and exits in and out of the congestion zone. However, because of the strange angles of London's streets, high concentrations of pedestrians within the zone (Hey bud, can ya move while I take this car's picture?), and the difficulty of getting straight-on pictures of the licence plates on the front and back of various cars and trucks (at various heights), 688 cameras were used in 203 locations to take accurate pictures of vehicles entering the congestion zone. At each camera site, a colour camera and a black-and-white camera were used for each lane of traffic that was being monitored. How accurate are the cameras? In general, the cameras are 90 percent accurate in reading the licence plate numbers on the cars. Is 90 percent good enough? No, not if you just relied on a few cameras. But, with 688 cameras in total, multiple pictures are taken of each car, and partial pictures of licence plates are matched with complete pictures, with the former tossed and the latter retained.

Next, once you've collected data showing which vehicles have entered—however it is you do that—you've got to process those data into useful information so you can charge the companies and people that own those vehicles.

Companies often have massive amounts of data, but not in the form or combination they need. Consequently, processing cost is the cost of turning raw data into usable information. More specifically, processing information means transforming raw data into meaningful information that can be applied to business decision-making (in this case, charging a fee to people who have driven into London's congestion zone). For Transport of London, that meant taking complete pictures of vehicles with good shots of licence plates (i.e., data), and turning those data into accurate information—meaning registered licence plate numbers.

As summarized above for packages 2 and 3, the pictures from the cameras would be taken and then sent via a dedicated fibre-optic cable to an image management store. Why fibre-optic cable? Because, compared to most data files (word processing, spreadsheets, etc.), graphics files are huge and data intensive. Fibre-optic cable was needed because they're the biggest and fastest "pipes" available for sending data from one place to another. The lines were also dedicated so that the system was completely closed and secure. If other systems or networks went down, the congestion zone network would be unaffected. Why an "image management store?" Well, an image management store is basically a huge farm of networked, redundant servers. If one server goes down, you've got multiple backup servers running live with the same data. A "huge farm" of network servers was needed because the city anticipated processing a million pictures a day (again, remember that multiple pictures are taken of the 250 000 cars entering the zone each day).

Once the pictures arrive at the image management store, the next step is "reading" the licence plate in the picture and then turning that image into readable text that actually matches licence plate records already stored in government databases. Basically, this is a form of optical character recognition (OCR) software that scans digitized documents, in this case, digital pictures, into ASCII text. While OCR software is common, the existing OCR software wasn't able to match and compare multiple pictures of the same licence plate. For example, imagine that a license plate is 12345678, and that the congestion cameras get three partial pictures, 12345, 34567, and 5678, and one complete picture of 12345678. The software had to be able to know that all four pictures were from the same vehicle, and then it had to know that it should use the last picture, 12345678, and not the partial pictures, when converting the picture to text.

Finally, once the licence plate was converted to text, the license plate number would then be matched with an existing licence plate already recorded in a government database. At that point, congestion zone charges are linked with whoever owns the vehicles. Let's turn to the last question to see how that was done.

Finally, you have to make the charges accessible to everyone, from truck drivers, to corporate accountants, to taxi drivers, and do so in a way that makes it quick and easy to pay the congestion zone charge, so they don't incur late payment penalties.

The key to making the congestion charge work is a quick and easy payment system that gives Londoners multiple places and ways to pay. Each time you enter the congestion zone, you've got until 10 P.M. that night to pay the £5 congestion fee (note, as we write this, London is raising the fee from £5 to £8 per day). If you don't pay by 10 P.M., then you must pay a £5 late fee. If you don't pay by midnight, the fine rises to £100. If you pay within the next 14 days, that fine is reduced to £50. But, if you fail to pay within 28 days, the fine increases to £150. If you fail to pay the congestion charge three or more times, your vehicle is "booted," rendering it undrivable. To "unboot" your car, you must pay your outstanding congestion charges and late fees, as well as a booting fee of £65 and an unbooting fee of £150. In short, you'll go broke if you don't pay the congestion fee by 10 P.M. or midnight. And that means that making the payments has to be quick and painless.

Historically, companies have been unable or reluctant to let outside groups have access to their information. For organizations like Transport for London, that would mean that city workers would be in charge of collecting the congestion fees. However, with 250 000 cars per day and essentially no staff to collect those fees, Transport for London had to be able to share the congestion fee data with outsiders, such as shops, kiosks, gas stations, or Web sites, where congestion charges could also be paid. In fact, Londoners can pay their congestion charges online, via cell phone text messaging, at standalone kiosks, at 229 retail stores within the congestion zone, and at over 10 000 retails stores nationwide (for those who drive into London for the day and then return home).

How well has the system worked? Incredibly well! Congestion has dropped by 30 percent, more than double what was expected. It's estimated the reduced congestion saves Londoners 2 to 3 million hours a year. Furthermore, accidents have dropped 9 percent within the zone. And, traffic has dropped so much that buses, once unable to meet their schedules because of slow traffic, are unable to meet their schedules because they're always running ahead. In fact, Transport for London is having to redo bus schedules as a result.

And while the congestion charge and monitoring system is an unqualified success when it comes to traffic, reduced congestion has sometimes hurt businesses located within the congestion zone. John Lewis, a well-known department store in England, says that sales at its large Oxford Street store are down 5.5 percent. Plus, 42 percent of 334 retailers who were surveyed blame the congestion charge for sales declines at their businesses. Still, says Mayor Ken Livingston who championed the congestion zone fee, "The congestion charge is the only thing I've done in 33 years in public life that turned out better than I hoped."

Key Terms

acquisition cost *(128)*
application sharing *(137)*
association/affinity patterns *(133)*
bar code *(131)*
communication cost *(129)*
conferencing system *(137)*
data clusters *(133)*
data encryption *(134)*
data mining *(132)*
data warehouse *(133)*
decision support system (DSS) *(141)*
desktop videoconferencing *(137)*
document conferencing *(137)*
electronic data interchange (EDI) *(140)*
electronic scanner *(131)*
executive information system (EIS) *(138)*
expert system *(142)*
extranet *(140)*
firewall *(134)*
first-mover advantage *(123)*
freeware *(139)*
information *(122)*
Internet *(140)*
intranets *(139)*
knowledge *(141)*
Moore's law *(122)*
optical character recognition *(131)*
predictive patterns *(133)*
processing cost *(128)*
processing information *(131)*
protecting information *(133)*
raw data *(122)*
retrieval cost *(128)*
sequence patterns *(133)*
shareware *(139)*
storage cost *(128)*
supervised data mining *(133)*
unsupervised data mining *(133)*
virtual private network *(135)*
virus *(134)*

Self-Assessment

COMPUTER COMFORT

Computers are ubiquitous fixtures of modern society, but that does not mean that everyone embraces computer technology. As with any innovation, there are people who are reluctant to adopt it for whatever reason. How comfortable are you with computer technology? The Assessment Appendix has a survey designed to reveal how anxious or confident you are with computers. Wherever you fall on the spectrum you can use the results as a baseline for developing (or enhancing) your computer skills. Turn to page 513 and get started!

Management Decisions

LEASE OR BUY?

It has been over four years since your company last upgraded any of its computers or peripherals. Unfortunately, system outages and hardware malfunctions are beginning to disrupt worker performance. You are the chief information officer (CIO) of a medium-sized accounting and consulting firm, and maintaining an operational and efficient computer system is one of your main priorities. Over the last year, you have reported the need for newer computers and have presented several proposals toward upgrading the system in phases. Unfortunately, every time you broached the subject, the owner's response was "if it isn't broken, don't fix it." Now he is singing a different tune. Because of a recent system glitch, the company lost one of its biggest and oldest clients. As a result, the owner now agrees that the entire system needs to be upgraded immediately. In fact, just yesterday, he told you "to spare no expense, just buy it and have it up and running as soon as possible. We can't afford to lose another client because of our dilapidated information system."

You want to purchase machines from a name-brand, quality computer manufacturer. The previous machines, also produced by a well-known manufacturer, have only recently begun to exhibit hardware malfunctions. Therefore, due to advances in technology and improvements in quality, you reasonably expect that the new system will have a useful life of at least four years, possibly more. You have been on the phone all morning contacting vendors and requesting price quotes. All the vendors you spoke to have similar purchase plans and most have lease arrangements. After analyzing the differences between leasing and purchasing, you have identified the advantages and disadvantages associated with each.

Although purchasing the computer system will result in a higher monthly payment compared to leasing, the units will belong to the company when paid off, a clear advantage. Additionally, the entire cost of purchasing and maintaining the computer system will be tax deductible, an element the owner will certainly approve of. The main disadvantage associated with purchasing the computer system includes having to pay for computer-related maintenance and repairs once the warranty period expires. An extended policy can be purchased to provide technical support and repairs after the warranty period; however, the monthly fee for this type of service is rather expensive. A second disadvantage associated with purchasing the computer system, one that you will soon face, is determining what to do with the old computer system. It was once common for many businesses to donate old computers to local school districts after an upgrade; however, due to recent technology initiatives within the local school system, most public schools in your area have better computers than your firm currently does. Therefore, disposing of the obsolete machines will be somewhat difficult.

The advantages of leasing a computer system include a smaller monthly payment; free 24-hour technical support and repair services; and the ability to upgrade to newer, faster machines when the lease period expires, approximately 24 months from now. Disposing of old computers is not a problem under the lease option since leased computers can be traded in on new computers when the lease expires. One of the biggest disadvantages of leasing is that it is very similar to renting. At the end of the lease period, you have two choices. Either pay a huge balloon payment and keep the two-year-old (outdated) computer system, or renew the lease and upgrade the system again. Given the owner's previous track record, you feel it will be difficult to convince the owner to upgrade the system again after only 24 months. You yourself doubt the need for replacing computers every two years since the majority of employees are currently using less than 20 percent of their computer's processing power at any given time. Additionally, after discussing the leasing option with several accountants within the firm, one accountant informed you that certain computer leases, specifically operational leases, are not tax deductible and cannot be depreciated.

As you jot down the minimum system requirements on your legal pad, you ask yourself, should we buy or lease?

Questions

1. Acting as the CIO mentioned above, which method would you recommend to the owner and why?
2. Go online to a well-known computer manufacturer such as Dell computers at www.dell.ca or Gateway computers at www.gateway.com and compare their purchase/lease options. Re-evaluate your recommendation. Did your decision change after viewing the two options? Why or why not?

3. Use the Internet Resources listed below to further your information-gathering. Once you have done all your research, review your decision again. Did it change after more extensive research? Why or why not?

ADDITIONAL INTERNET RESOURCES

- Evaluate various machines by consulting several non–marketing-controlled (i.e., independent) sources of information. Consumer Reports (www.consumerreports.org) is an example. You may also wish to consult computer magazines such as PC World (www.pcworld.com), PC Magazine (www.pcmag.com), and Computer World (www.computerworld.com). They regularly review hardware and software systems and may provide you with a more detailed analysis of the systems you are considering than you can find anywhere else.
- Consider checking shopping bots—any script or program such as MySimon.com and cnet.com that is designed to perform automated actions on behalf of the owner, usually without the owner's direct intervention—and comparing features and prices. Other good price comparison tools are PriceScan.com and Bizrate.com. Streetprices.com is also a good resource for price shopping.
- If you're thinking of trying to get a deal, review auction sites. A popular site that specializes in electronics is www.ubid.com. Also try www.pcbuyer.com.
- And don't forget to check offers at retailers such as Best Buy (www.bestbuy.ca). Even office supply retailers such as Office Depot (www.techdepot.com) and Staples (www.staples.ca) may have what you're looking for. At the very least, you will have something to compare your hot Internet deal to!

Management Decisions

HACK ATTACK[59]

As you clear off your desk, getting ready to leave for the night, the phone rings. The voice on the other end of the line is Sue, your company's network administrator. She informs you that a hacker has just broken into the company's e-commerce site. One of the databases entered by the intruder contains personal customer data, including names, addresses, and credit card information. You immediately ask questions, attempting to determine the potential damage caused by this attack. According to Sue, approximately 3.3 million customer files, both past and present, could have been compromised. Upon noticing the intrusion, Sue immediately closed down the network and ordered her staff to get on the phone with the software company's technical support to begin repairing the breach. She informs you that she and her staff will do everything to repair the network and get it back online as soon as possible, but she asks about the information that might have been compromised. Should we tell someone? As the chief information officer (CIO) of Egghead.com, an Internet-based retailer, you assure her that you will notify the proper constituencies.

As you hang up the phone, you begin to calculate the different options of attempting to resolve this current problem. Attempted hacking is not new to your firm. Research shows that most well-known sites face up to five or six attempted intrusions on any given day. Unfortunately, this is the first successful attempt on Egghead.com's site. The fact that they were able to not only get in, but also enter a secure database is disturbing. Currently, Egghead.com has no policy and procedures manual to turn to when a network compromise has occurred. Questions begin to race through your mind. Do you risk notifying all your customers, suppliers, and other stakeholders? Doing so might diminish customer confidence and result in decreased sales. Do you notify the press? Doing so would most likely advertise to would-be hackers that your site has serious security issues. You think to yourself, "We might as well put up a billboard saying, 'We're open, hack away.'"

Questions

1. As the CIO of Egghead.com, would you alert all affected parties and inform them of the breach, or keep the information internal? What is the rationale behind your decision?
2. What policies and procedures could be implemented to keep this problem from recurring?

Develop Your Management Potential

WEB PRIVACY POLICY[60]

With the advent of the Internet and its explosive growth, the need to protect an individual's privacy has increased dramatically in recent years. Many Internet sites require that personal information such as name, address, phone number(s), social insurance number, and credit card information be submitted before allowing a consumer to conduct any type of e-commerce transactions. Most Web-based companies have policies stating the extent to which this information will be used, the length of time the information will be kept, and what will happen to the information if the company folds. However, with the recent crash of many dot-coms, the industry has discovered that a significant portion of these policies are not worth the paper that they are printed on. For instance, Toysmart.com, a recent casualty of the dot-com bust, sought to gain approval from a bankruptcy court to auction off their database despite promising to never do so in their Web privacy policy. As more and more dot-coms fail, the opportunity to sell customer information, possibly the only tangible asset that an Internet-based firm owns, will most likely rise. One example of the detrimental effects of sensitive information being publicly released was recently observed when pharmaceutical company Eli Lilly accidentally released the e-mail addresses of more than 600 people currently taking Prozac, a common antidepressant medication. In order to combat the problems caused by the release of sensitive and confidential information, privacy advocates are pushing for more stringent legislation to protect consumers and their personal information. In order to appease legislators and to promote self-regulation as opposed to government regulation, one industry body is proposing several recommendations for Internet-based businesses to adopt in constructing or strengthening their privacy policies. These recommendations are as follows:

1. The word "never" should be taken literally. If a firm promises to never sell customer information, it should abide by its promise. Additionally, this promise should survive and remain true even if the firm's assets are parcelled out as a result of bankruptcy hearings.
2. Consumers should be given a choice. If a firm decides to sell confidential customer information, customers should be given a choice before that information is released. Although this rule is currently being enforced through current legislation, privacy laws require the customer to "opt out" if they wish their information not be released. This places the burden on the consumer to contact the retailer and inform them of their wish to keep their personal information private. Privacy advocates want the rule to be changed so that consumers must "opt in," thereby placing the burden on retailers by requiring them to obtain the consumer's approval before information can be released.
3. Companies should restrict the type of information disclosed. Should a company sell information, it should limit the information disclosed to only names and addresses, typical of information found on most mailing lists. This would require companies to maintain separate databases, one for information that can be sold or disclosed, and the other, a secure database that contains more private information such as age, ethnicity, income, social insurance number, credit information, and so forth.

As a manager charged with constructing a privacy policy for your firm, you are instructed to visit a well-known company Web site and inspect its Web-privacy policy. As you read the policy, compare its policy with the information proposed above. What elements of its policy could be improved and what elements would you include in developing your own firm's Web-privacy policy? Using the information presented above and another firm's Web-privacy policy as a guide, draft a Web-privacy policy for your firm.

Discussion Questions

1. What is the difference between raw data and useful information?
2. Two years into your position with a major multinational consulting firm, your boss has approached you with an interesting assignment. She has asked you to find out as much as you can about a competitor's new product launch. You are excited about the prospect of pursuing this challenge but you also realize that not all the information you will need will be found in-house. Prior to accepting the assignment, you would like to discuss with her the five costs of obtaining information. What are they? Describe each briefly.
3. Sitting at home one night, an interesting thought pops into your mind. It is that you have extreme good fortune to have joined a small firm upon graduation and stuck with it for a few years while it grew and prospered. Personally you have gained from this experience—a healthy bi-weekly paycheque, numerous promotions, and interesting work. Unfortunately, with growth has also come challenges. One challenge is that your company now faces the need to store large amounts of data for long periods of time. You have been asked to give a presentation in the morning on the kinds of data storage devices available for use by your organization. What are your options in this regard?
4. A good friend of yours has just been offered a position as head of marketing of a small manufacturing company. Oddly, within his portfolio of responsibilities is the IT function for his company. Admittedly, he has a few things to learn to get up to speed with this function. He invites you to join him for coffee to share any insight you might be able to offer him given your stature as a business student. In particular, he is interested in learning how his company can protect information and why it is important to do so. What can you tell him?
5. As a favour to a parent, you have agreed to take the daughter of a business client out for coffee. Although you

dreaded the occasion, once underway you found yourself fascinated by the curiosity of this 20-year-old. It soon became apparent that you both shared a common interest—information technology. Unfortunately, your actual experiences far outweighed those of your new friend. Of particular interest to her was the function of an intranet and the reasons behind their popularity with companies. What might you tell her?

Critical Thinking Video Case

CBC

Visit www.management2e.nelson.com to view this chapter's CBC video case.

Take Two

Biz Flix
Lorenzo's Oil

This film tells the true story of young Lorenzo Odone who suffers from adrenoleukodystrophy (ALD), an incurable degenerative brain disorder. (Six actors and actresses play Lorenzo throughout the film.) Physicians and medical scientists offer little help to Lorenzo's desperate parents, Michaela (Susan Sarandon) and Augusto (Nick Nolte). They use their resources to learn about ALD to try to save their son. Director George Miller co-wrote the script, which benefited from his medical training as a physician. Six months after Lorenzo's ALD diagnosis, his condition fails to improve with a restricted diet. Michaela and Augusto continue their research at the National Institutes of Health library in Bethesda, Maryland. Michaela finds a report of a critical Polish experiment that showed positive effects of fatty acid manipulation in rats. Convinced that a panel of experts could systematically focus on their problem, they help organize the First International ALD Symposium. This scene is an edited version of the symposium sequence that appears about midway through the film. The film continues with the Odones' efforts to save their son.

What to Watch for and Ask Yourself

1. Do the scientists present data or information during the symposium?
2. If it is information, who transformed the data into information? Speculate about how such data become information.
3. What do you predict will be the next course of action for the Odones?

Management Workplace
Data Management

Have you ever thought of data as money? Probably not in your personal life, but in business, information has a cost and therefore a related value. Businesses across the world that rely heavily on computer technology understand the value of their data and implement ways to protect their data and data networks from theft, damage, or incompetence. Still, it is easy to be lulled into overconfidence (or sheer laziness) when it comes to computer upgrades or simple virus protection. Nevertheless, data management should be a priority for all companies. In this video, managers from some of the largest names in data protection (Symantec, Trend Micro, McAfee) talk about the threats to data and data networks and the ways you can safeguard your computer against attacks.

What to Watch for and Ask Yourself

1. According to the video, are upgrades really necessary?
2. Describe the nature of data protection.
3. Explain the paradox of ubiquitous computing described in the video. That is, how has the pervasiveness of computer technology made our lives easier and more difficult at the same time?

COURTESY OF INCO

Chapter 6

Decision-Making

CHAPTER OUTLINE

LEARNING OBJECTIVES

After reading this chapter, you should be able to

1. explain the steps to rational decision-making.
2. discuss the limits to rational decision-making.
3. describe how individual decision-making can be improved.
4. explain how group decisions and group decision-making techniques can improve decision-making.

In 1994, Inco, whose head office is located in Toronto, supplied more than 30 percent of the western world's nickel (235 million kilograms). Inco had purchased 25 percent of the Voisey's Bay project on the northern Labrador coast at a cost of over $500 million. The northern Labrador coast is a cold and remote location, and in the early 1990s it was one of the few remaining places in North America left unexplored for its mineral wealth. In September 1993, two men, Chris Verbiski and Albert Chislett, were prospecting over 25 000 square kilometres of the Labrador coast, searching for diamonds. They didn't find any diamonds, but they did find a high-grade deposit of nickel that also had some copper and cobalt in it. As they looked around the surrounding areas, they began to discover more and more deposits. The vast size of the Voisey's Bay deposit was only beginning to dawn upon them and the industry.[1]

The discovery was in many ways ideal. If developed, it would be a big project that would allow it to amortize any development costs over a large production base. The deposit was also close to the surface and therefore a lot of it could be mined by the inexpensive open-pit method. It was only 10 kilometres from tidewater, making shipping via the ocean a viable, inexpensive method for transporting the ore to any part of the world. Finally, the mine was located in a province hungry for work, as Newfoundland had an unemployment rate of about 20 percent.

What Would You Do?

Despite the huge advantages that the deposit had, the possibility to develop it faced many challenges. The area was subject to overlapping land claims from the Innu and Inuit peoples of Labrador, and they would likely demand a financial stake in a mine that covered part of their traditional hunting grounds. The provincial and federal governments have been unsuccessfully attempting to settle claims in the area for a number of years and legal tactics from the affected bands could delay the project indefinitely. Also, in response to the find, the provincial government was also looking to amend the provincial Mining and Mineral Rights Act to change the tax status of mining companies. The amendment would reduce the number of tax breaks to mining operations and therefore reduce the possible profits (or increase the losses) for the potential project. The provincial government had also passed a law that required companies, where economically feasible, to process the ore in the province where it was mined. This development could add substantial costs to the project, as using smelters in Ontario and Manitoba probably would be cheaper. In addition, projects of this magnitude were subject to protracted public hearings and environmental assessments, which could significantly delay any mine development or even possibly prevent its development entirely.

Further, the size of the deposit made the potential cost of purchasing it substantial (billions of dollars) but also ensured that the life of the mine would probably be decades. John Redstone, a mining analyst with Midland Walwyn Capital Inc., was quoted as saying that getting this deposit into production was like "giving birth to an elephant," and he was probably right. Giving birth to this elephant could be a risky proposition. Although, on the one hand, the sheer size of the deposit would be good; on the other hand, what would the price of nickel, copper, and cobalt be 10, 20, or 50 years from now? Although nickel prices had been firm, some experts were predicting that there would be a surplus by 1998. And, of course, with a surplus, prices would be likely to slide, but how far? If you discover more deposits of ore at Voisey's Bay, as many expect, how will this increase in potential supply affect the price of nickel? After all, Voisey's Bay is expected to produce about 12 percent of the world's total nickel production. Some experts were predicting that the market would maintain a price of US$3.50 a pound (US$7.70 per kilogram), enough to make the project viable, but of course there are no guarantees. After the discovery of the Voisey's Bay deposit in 1994, the Newfoundland government saw 287 000 prospecting stakes filed in the province. Everyone was looking for the next mother lode. On the other hand, if prices rise substantially, as other analysts predict, the deposit could be a metaphorical goldmine.

Inco's nickel production has been flat for 10 years, and its stock price was almost the same as it was 20 years earlier ($30). Given the fact that the Voisey's Bay deposit seems so large, Inco felt it could not ignore the deposit and has already paid over $500 million to purchase 25 percent of the Voisey's Bay project and is looking to purchase an even larger stake—risking even more of the company's capital—possibly purchasing enough of the project to have a controlling interest. If Inco purchases a controlling share of Voisey's Bay and all goes according to plan, production could start by 1999 and significantly boost Inco's nickel production. Part of the problem is that as a number of other companies are interested in buying a stake in the project, the price seems to keep going up and up (it was rumoured that the owners of the Voisey's Bay site had signed 20 nondisclosure agreements covering the project with mining and investment companies). The next 25 percent interest in the project could possibly cost Inco five to ten times the price it paid for the first 25 percent. On the other hand, some mining and investment companies are being lured by Bre-X's estimated gold find of 2 million ounces (about 55 million grams), at the time one of the biggest estimated finds of all time (if you don't know what happened to Bre-X, ask your instructor). In addition to the potential spiralling purchase price, the company would have to risk billions of dollars to develop the project. Given the uncertainty in the price of nickel (and copper and cobalt), the unknown size of the deposit, the land claims situation, the changing demands of the provincial government, and the magnitude of the project and the associated costs, **if you were the president of Inco, what would you do?**

CP PHOTO/ HO-INCO

Inco had to deal with uncertainty when deciding whether to develop Voisey's Bay.

Even inexperienced managers know that decision-making and problem-solving are central parts of their jobs. Figure out what the problem is. Generate potential solutions. Pick the best solution. Make it work. Experienced managers, however, know how hard it really is to make good decisions and solve problems. One seasoned manager said, "I think the biggest surprises are the problems. Maybe I had never seen it before. Maybe I was protected by my management when I was in sales. Maybe I had delusions of grandeur, I don't know. I just know how disillusioning and frustrating it is to be hit with problems and conflicts all day and not be able to solve them very cleanly."[2] Undoubtedly, the managers in charge of making a decision about whether or not to buy more of the Voisey's Bay project feel the same frustration and uncertainty. The project appears to hold fantastic potential that might, just might, pay off. However, the project is incredibly expensive and fraught with potential problems. And unlike its iffy payoffs, there's no uncertainty about its high costs. Any way you look at it, it's a tough decision for Inco to make.

decision-making
the process of choosing a solution from available alternatives

rational decision-making
a systematic process of defining problems, evaluating alternatives, and choosing optimal solutions

Decision-making is the process of choosing a solution from available alternatives.[3] We begin the chapter by reviewing **rational decision-making**, a systematic process in which managers define problems, evaluate alternatives, and choose optimal solutions that provide maximum benefits to their organizations. We discuss the steps of rational decision-making as well as its limitations. In the second part of the chapter, we look at how managers can improve their decisions. Here we discuss methods for improving rational decision-making and how managers can use groups and group decision techniques to improve decisions.

What Is Rational Decision-Making?

Imagine that you've been away on business. On your first day back at the office, you sort through your phone messages and find this voice-mail from the boss:

> You're an information technology specialist, aren't you? Well, you know more about this stuff than anyone else in the office. Here's what I need from you. You've got three weeks to get it done. I want you to

> prepare a presentation and write a report that details the problems we've been having with our computers. It should also summarize our current and future computer needs. Talk to everyone. Find out what they need and want. Be sure to consider upgrade options. I don't want to spend a ton of money to improve our systems only to have them be obsolete in two years. Finally, come up with at least five plans or options for getting us where we need to be. Hey, almost forgot, you're probably going to have to do some educating here. Most of us in management don't speak "computer geek." Heck, half of the dinosaurs we've got in upper management think computers are $1500 paperweights—don't repeat that, okay? So be sure to explain in everyday language how we can decide which plans or options are best. Have a rough draft on my desk in three weeks.

When your boss delegated this "computer problem," what he really wanted from you is a rational decision. In other words, you need to define and analyze the problem, and explore alternatives. Furthermore, the solution has to be "optimal," since the department is going to live with the computer equipment you recommend for the next three years.

After reading the next two sections, you should be able to

1 explain the steps to rational decision-making.
2 discuss the limits to rational decision-making.

1 STEPS TO RATIONAL DECISION-MAKING

Exhibit 6.1 shows the six steps of the rational decision-making process.

The steps in rational decision-making are defining the problem, identifying decision criteria, weighting the criteria, generating alternative courses of action, evaluating each alternative, and computing the optimal decision.

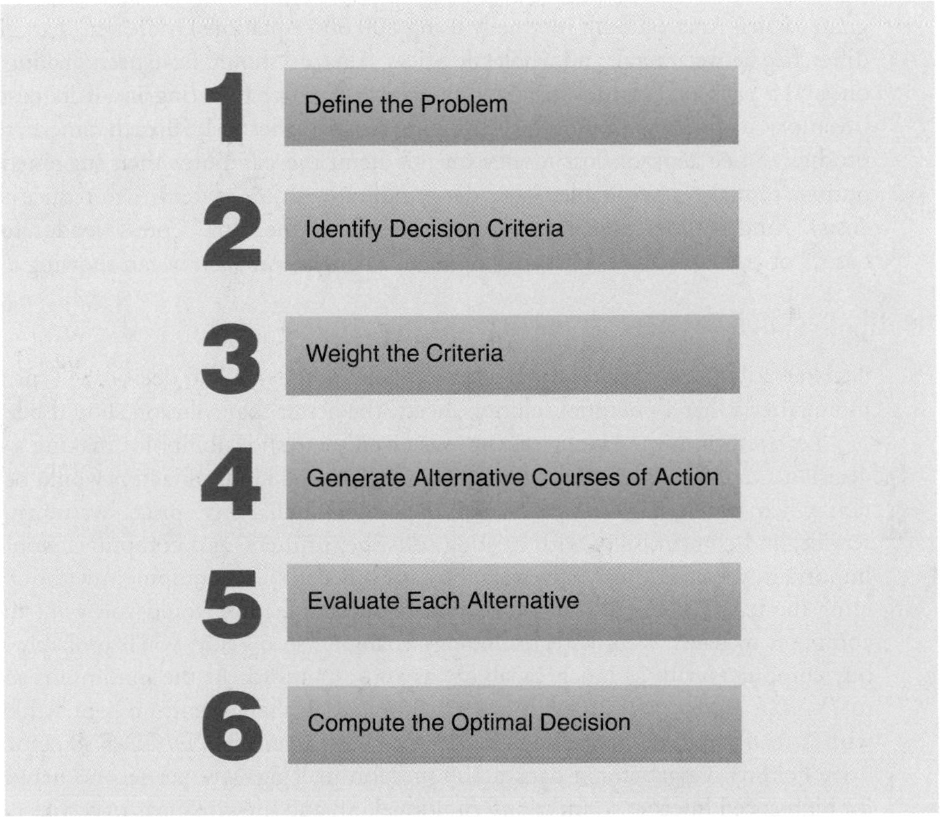

EXHIBIT 6.1
Steps of the Rational Decision-Making Process

Define the Problem

problem
a gap between a desired state and an existing state

The first step in decision-making is identifying and defining the problem. A **problem** exists when there is a gap between a desired state—what managers want—and an existing state—the situation that the managers are facing. For example, Shell Canada's last expansion in the Alberta oilsands was slated for 155 000 barrels per day of production and projected to cost $3.8 billion. The project actually ran to $5.7 billion, a massive cost overrun. Costs in the Alberta oilpatch are generally spiralling upward, as the cost of labour and materials is under extreme pressure because of the fast growth. Now Shell Canada wants to undertake another expansion of a further 300 000 barrels per day and is faced with the task of trying to figure out how to control its costs.[4]

The presence of a gap between an existing state and a desired state is no guarantee that managers will make decisions to solve problems. Three things must occur for this to happen.[5] First, managers have to be aware of the gap. They have to know there is a problem before they can begin solving it. For example, after noticing that people were spending more money on their pets, a new dog food company created an expensive, high-quality dog food. To emphasize the quality of the product, the dog food was sold in cans and bags with gold labels, red letters, and detailed information about product benefits and nutrients. However, the product didn't sell very well, and the company was out of business in less than a year. Company founders didn't understand why. When they asked a manager at a competing dog food company what their biggest mistake had been, the answer was "Simple. You didn't have a picture of a dog on the package."[6] This problem would have been easy to solve, if management had only been aware of it.

Being aware of the gap between a desired state and an existing state isn't enough to begin the decision-making process. Managers also have to be motivated to reduce the gap. Finally, it's not enough to be aware of a problem and be motivated to solve it. Managers must also have the knowledge, skills, abilities, and resources to fix the problem. Amazon.com is now going "full out" to reverse the gap between its oversized expenses and its undersized revenues. It has a new accounting system that uses product and shipping costs, the frequency with which products are returned, and 47 other factors to show how much money Amazon makes or loses on each product it sells. For example, this program (which Amazon built internally using 800 000 equations) indicated that, given the difference between retail and wholesale prices, Amazon should have been making a profit on a $15 pack of Polaroid instant film. However, after factoring in all its costs, from inventory to packing to billing to shipping, Amazon lost $1.50 each time it sold this product. Since Amazon lost money on this item, the computer then suggested several options to make it profitable: "consider bundling with other items" (to reduce shipping costs), "find another merchant to handle and ship the film," "press vendor for lower costs," or "raise prices."[7] After making many changes, Amazon began showing a profit.[8]

Identify Decision Criteria

decision criteria
the standards used to guide judgments and decisions

Decision criteria are the standards used to guide judgments and decisions. Typically, the more criteria that a potential solution meets, the better that solution should be.

Let's return to the employee who was given the responsibility for making a rational decision about the office computer setup. What general kinds of factors would be important when purchasing computers for the office? Reliability, price, warranty, on-site service, and compatibility with existing software, printers, and computers would all be important, wouldn't they? However, you can't buy computer equipment without considering the technical details. So what kinds of specific factors would you want the office computer to have? Well, with technology changing so quickly, you'll probably want to buy computers with as much capability as you can afford. At the minimum, according to *PC Magazine,* you'll probably want a 64-bit 3-gigahertz Pentium 4 or Athlon chip, with 2 to 4 gigabytes of memory, a 160-gig hard drive, a DVD/CD-RW combination drive holding 8 gigabytes of data, a 100 megabit to 1 gigabyte per second network card for high-speed Internet connections, multiple USB and firewire ports to connect external devices like digital cameras and flash drives, and a 19-inch flat-screen monitor—all for a price of $1000 or less![9] These general and specific factors represent the criteria that could guide the purchase of computer equipment.

Weight the Criteria

After identifying decision criteria, the next step is deciding which criteria are more or less important. For example, despite *PC Magazine's* advice, a 19 inch monitor and a DVD ROM drive aren't that important for business computers. In most cases, a lower-cost 17-inch monitor would suffice for office work (word processing, e-mail, and spreadsheets). And, as long as someone on the office network has a DVD-ROM drive that can be accessed from any other computer on the network, then most office computers don't have to have a DVD-ROM drive. A CD-ROM drive in each computer will do. On the other hand, 64-bit 3-gigahertz Pentium 4 or Athlon chip, with 2 to 4 gigabytes of memory, a 160-gig hard drive, a DVD/CD-RW combination drive holding 8 gigabytes of data, a 100 megabit to 1 gigabyte per second network card for high-speed Internet connections and multiple USB and firewire ports to connect external devices like digital cameras and flash drives are "must haves" for today's desktop corporate computers. (These specifications may be outdated by the time you read this.)

While there are numerous mathematical models for weighting decision criteria, all require the decision maker to provide an initial ranking of the decision criteria. Some use **absolute comparisons**, in which each criterion is compared to a standard or ranked on its own merits. For example, *Consumer's Digest* uses a 12-point checklist when it rates and recommends new cars. Six points address the car's performance (starting and acceleration, fuel economy, handling and steering, shifting/transmission, ride quality, and braking), and six address the car's design (overall design, interior ergonomics, seating, accessories and amenities, cargo space, and fit and finish).[10]

absolute comparisons
a process in which each criterion is compared to a standard or ranked on its own merits

Exhibit 6.2 shows the absolute weights that someone buying a car might use. Because these weights are absolute, each criterion is judged on its own importance, using a five-point scale, with "5" representing "critically important" and "1" representing "completely unimportant." In this instance, fuel economy, seating, and cargo space were rated most important, while shifting/transmission, accessories, and amenities were rated least important.

EXHIBIT 6.2
Absolute Weighting of Decision Criteria for a Car Purchase

5 critically important
4 important
3 somewhat important
2 not very important
1 completely unimportant

PERFORMANCE CHARACTERISTICS					
1. starting and acceleration	1	2	3	**4**	5
2. fuel economy	1	2	3	4	**5**
3. handling and steering	1	2	**3**	4	5
4. shifting/transmission	1	**2**	3	4	5
5. ride quality	1	2	**3**	4	5
6. braking	1	2	3	**4**	5
DESIGN CHARACTERISTICS					
1. overall design	1	2	3	**4**	5
2. interior ergonomics	1	2	**3**	4	5
3. seating	1	2	3	4	**5**
4. accessories and amenities	**1**	2	3	4	5
5. cargo space	1	2	3	4	**5**
6. fit and finish	1	2	**3**	4	5

relative comparisons
a process in which each decision criterion is compared directly to every other criterion

Another method is **relative comparisons**, in which each criterion is compared directly to every other criterion.[11] For example, moving down the first column of Exhibit 6.3, we see that starting/acceleration has been rated less important (−1) than fuel economy; more important (+1) than handling and steering, shifting/transmission, and ride quality; but just as important as braking (0). Total weights, which are obtained by summing the scores in each column, indicate that fuel economy and starting/acceleration are the most important factors to this car buyer, while handling and steering, shifting/transmission, and ride quality are the least important.

Generate Alternative Courses of Action

After identifying and weighting the criteria that will guide the decision-making process, the next step is to identify possible courses of action that could solve the problem. In general, at this step, the idea is to generate as many alternatives as possible. For instance, let's assume that your high-tech manufacturing company wants to reduce costs by moving its headquarters out of Toronto. Why? Because real-estate costs are astronomical, congested roadways lead to long commuting times, and housing costs make it difficult to attract talented employees from other parts of the country. Not surprisingly, the location of your new headquarters would have to meet the following criteria: high quality of life (easy commutes), low operating costs, low corporate tax rates, a highly educated work force, low cost of labour, and a low cost of living (low real-estate costs). After meeting with your staff, you generate a list of alternative locations: Calgary, Edmonton, Halifax, Ottawa, Regina, Saskatoon, St. John, and Winnipeg.

Evaluate Each Alternative

The next step is to systematically evaluate each alternative against each criterion. Because of the amount of information that must be collected, this step can take much longer and be much more difficult than other steps in the decision-making process. Chapter 5 discusses methods for collecting information from a firm's operations but information can be gathered from secondary sources external to the firm. For example, in order to evaluate the quality of locations, one has to find information from such organizations as Statistics Canada (www.statcan.ca). In addition, KPMG has done extensive work on such things as tax rates, operating costs, and cost of labour (www.competitivealternatives.com). Their data were based on the cost averages for the last ten years and looked at more than 30 000 cost items.

Once the necessary information has been gathered, it is used to evaluate each alternative against each criterion. Exhibit 6.4 shows how each of the eight cities fared on each criterion (higher scores are better). For example, Ottawa has some of the highest costs in all categories (housing, labour, and operating), while Halifax has the lowest labour costs.

Compute the Optimal Decision

The final step in the decision-making process is to compute the optimal decision by determining each alternative's value. This is done by multiplying the rating for each criterion (Step 5) by the weight for that criterion (Step 3), and then summing those scores

EXHIBIT 6.3
Relative Comparison for Car Performance Characteristics

CAR PERFORMANCE CHARACTERISTICS	STARTING/ ACCELERATION	FUEL ECONOMY	HANDLING AND STEERING	SHIFTING/ TRANSMISSION	RIDE QUALITY	BRAKING
starting/acceleration		+1	−1	−1	−1	0
fuel economy	−1		−1	−1	−1	−1
handling and steering	+1	+1		0	0	+1
shifting/transmission	+1	+1	0		0	0
ride quality	+1	+1	0	0		0
braking	0	+1	−1	0		0
Total weight	+2	+5	−3	−2	−2	0

	COMMUTING DISTANCE	OPERATING COSTS	TAX RATES	EDUCATION LEVEL	LABOUR COSTS	HOUSING COSTS
Calgary	3	2	7	7	2	2
Edmonton	2	3	6	3	6	3
Halifax	6	4	3	7	8	4
Regina	8	7	5	4	4	7
Ottawa	1	1	8	8	1	1
Saskatoon	7	6	4	5	5	5
Saint John	3	8	1	1	7	8
Winnipeg	5	5	2	3	3	6

Sources: www.statcan.ca, www.competitivealternatives.com.

EXHIBIT 6.4
Criteria Ratings Used to Evaluate the Best Company Locations

for each alternative course of action that you generated (Step 4). For example, your company rated the six criteria in the following manner: commuting time (15 percent), operating costs (25 percent), tax rates (15 percent), education level (10 percent), labour costs (15 percent), and housing costs (20 percent). Those weights are then multiplied by the ratings in each category. For example, Regina's optimal value of 6.10 (i.e., weighted average) is determined using the following calculation:

$$(.15 \times 8) + (.25 \times 7) + (.15 \times 5) + (.10 \times 4) + (.15 \times 4) + (.15 \times 7) = 6.10$$

Exhibit 6.5 shows that Regina is clearly the best location for your company, no doubt because of its extremely short commuting distances, low housing cost, and low labour costs. By contrast, Ottawa is the worst location by virtue of its high commuting distances and high labour, housing, and operating costs.

Review 1: Steps to Rational Decision-Making

Rational decision-making is a six-step process in which managers define problems, evaluate alternatives, and compute optimal solutions. The first step is identifying and defining the problem. Problems exist where there is a gap between desired and existing states. Managers won't begin the decision-making process unless they are aware of the gap, are motivated to reduce it, and possess the necessary resources to fix it. The second step is defining the decision criteria that are used when judging alternatives. In Step 3, an absolute or relative comparison process is used to rate the importance of decision criteria. Step 4 involves generating as many possible courses of action (i.e., solutions) as possible. Potential solutions are assessed in Step 5 by systematically gathering information and evaluating each alternative against each criterion. In Step 6, criterion ratings and weights are used to compute the optimal value for each alternative course of action. Rational managers then choose the alternative with the highest optimal value.

2 LIMITS TO RATIONAL DECISION-MAKING

In general, managers who diligently complete all six steps of the rational decision-making model will make better decisions than those who don't. So, when they can, managers should try to follow the steps in the rational decision-making model, especially for big decisions with long-range consequences.

However, it's highly doubtful that rational decision-making can help managers choose optimal solutions that provide maximum benefits to their organizations. The terms "optimal" and "maximum" suggest that rational decision-making leads to perfect or near-perfect decisions. Of course, for managers to make perfect decisions, they have to operate in perfect worlds with no real-world constraints. For example, in

EXHIBIT 6.5
Cities Ranked by Selection Criteria

VALUES		
1.	Regina	6.10
2.	Saskatoon	5.40
3.	Saint John	5.35
4.	Halifax	5.05
5.	Winnipeg	4.25
6.	Edmonton	3.75
7.	Calgary	3.40
8.	Ottawa	2.75

an optimal world, the manager who was given three weeks to define, analyze, and fix computer problems in the office would have followed *PC Magazine's* advice to buy all employees the "perfect personal computer" (i.e., 3-gigahertz chip, 2 to 4 gigabytes of memory, etc.). And in arriving at that decision, our manager would not have been constrained by price ("$1000 per computer? Sure, no problem.") or time ("Need six more months to decide? Sure, take as long as you need."). Furthermore, without any constraints, our manager could identify and weight an extensive list of decision criteria, generate a complete list of possible solutions, and then test and evaluate each computer against each decision criterion. Finally, our manager would have to have the necessary experience and knowledge with computers to easily make sense of all these sophisticated tests and information (see Chapter 5 for a description of some methods of analyzing information).

Of course, it never works like that in the real world. Managers face time and money constraints. They often don't have time to make extensive lists of decision criteria. And they often don't have the resources to test all possible solutions against all possible criteria.

Let's see how bounded rationality, risk and risky decisions, and common decision-making mistakes make it difficult for managers to make completely rational, optimal decisions.

DOING THE RIGHT THING

PLUS—A PROCESS FOR ETHICAL DECISION MAKING

People are often unsure how to include ethics in their decision-making processes. To help them, the Ethics Resource Center recommends using the following PLUS guidelines throughout the various steps of the rational decision-making model:

- P is for policies. Is your decision consistent with your organization's policies, procedures, and guidelines?
- L is for legal. Is your decision acceptable under applicable laws and regulations?
- U is for universal. Is your decision consistent with your organization's values and principles?
- S is for self. Does your decision satisfy your personal sense of right, good, and fair?

The PLUS guidelines can't guarantee ethical decisions, but they can help employees be more attentive to ethical issues as they define problems, evaluate alternatives, and choose solutions.[12]

Bounded Rationality

The rational decision-making model describes the way decisions should be made. In other words, decision makers wanting to make optimal decisions should not have to face time and cost constraints. They should have unlimited resources and time to generate and test all alternative solutions against all decision criteria. And they should be willing to recommend any decision that produces optimal benefits for the company, even if that decision would harm their own jobs or departments. Of course, very few managers actually make rational decisions the way they should. The way in which managers actually make decisions is more accurately described as "bounded (or limited) rationality."

bounded rationality decision-making process restricted in the real world by limited resources, incomplete and imperfect information, and managers' limited decision-making capabilities

Bounded rationality means that managers try to take a rational approach to decision-making, but are restricted by real-world constraints, incomplete and imperfect information, and their own limited decision-making capabilities. More specifically, as shown in Exhibit 6.6, at least four problems prevent managers from making rational decisions.[13] First, as described above, limited resources often prevent managers from making rational decisions. Managers only have so much time, so much money, and so many people, machines, or offices to devote to a specific problem. When resources increase or decrease, managers change their decisions. For example, when the economy slowed down, Jiffy-Tite, an auto parts manufacturer, cut back on capital spending for expensive new product testing equipment. CEO Jeff Zillig said, "We had planned on the worst ... and cut the spending budget for testing equipment in half to $100 000." Less than a year later, however, finances improved, so Zillig said, "We're going back to our original budget." Therefore, Jiffy-Tite bought the new testing equipment.[14] Because of limited resources, there is almost always a difference between what managers would like to do (i.e., rational decision-making) and what they can do (i.e., bounded rationality).

information overload situation in which decision makers have too much information to attend to

Second, attention problems limit the information that a decision maker can pay attention to at any one time. Chapter 5 discussed the gathering of information with the belief that more information was always better. Often, attention problems stem from **information overload**, or too much information. For example, since *PC Magazine* uses 24 specific decision criteria to describe the "perfect PC," and since it typically tests approximately 50 computers every time it conducts a review, our rational decision maker would have to process 1200 different pieces of information. This is simply too much information for one person to make sense of. Even 10 decision criteria and 10 computers would

EXHIBIT 6.6
Problems Associated with Bounded Rationality

be too much. Ever since supermarkets and other retailers began using scanners and affinity cards (membership cards), they have been collecting huge amounts of information on their customers' buying behaviour. The question becomes, what do you do with massive amounts of information? Data mining (Chapter 5) is a result of this gathering of large amounts of information.

Third, memory problems make it difficult to recall or retrieve stored information. Managers forget important facts and details. Companies don't always keep the best records (see Chapter 5 for a discussion of different methods for storing data). Since the new computer equipment has to be compatible with the old computer equipment, our manager's first task would be to find out what equipment the company already owns. However, if detailed records have not been kept, and if employees don't know the configuration of their computers ("Does it have an Athlon, or a Pentium chip? What speed is the chip, 1.5 or 3-gigahertz ?"), then each computer will have to be manually inspected to gather this information. Furthermore, information retrieval is not free. It costs time and money.

Fourth, expertise problems make it difficult for decision makers to organize, summarize, and fully comprehend all the information that is available for making the decision. Realistically, even though our manager is a self-professed computer "geek," he or she probably doesn't have the required experience or knowledge to make sense of all the test results and determine which computer is the "perfect PC." The difficulty of this task is illustrated by the fact that *PC Magazine* employs 30 full-time staffers in two research labs stuffed with hundreds of thousands of dollars of equipment to make such decisions. No one, not even managers, can possess expert knowledge about everything.

In theory, fully rational decision makers **maximize** decisions by choosing the optimal solution. However, limited resources, along with attention, memory, and expertise problems, make it nearly impossible for managers to maximize decisions. Consequently, most managers don't maximize—they "satisfice." Whereas maximizing is choosing the best alternative, **satisficing** is choosing a "good enough" alternative. With 24 decision criteria, 50 alternative computers to choose from, two computer labs with hundreds of thousands of dollars of equipment, and unlimited time and money, our manager could test all alternatives against all decision criteria and choose the "perfect PC." However, our manager's

maximizing
choosing the best alternative

satisficing
choosing a "good enough" alternative

limited time, money, and expertise mean that only a few alternatives will be assessed against a few decision criteria. In practice, our manager will visit two or three computer or electronic stores, read a couple of recent computer reviews, and then get three or four bids from local computer stores that sell complete computer systems at competitive prices, as well as from Dell, Gateway, and Hewlett-Packard. The decision will be complete when our manager finds a "good enough" computer that meets a few of the key decision criteria.

Risk and Decision-Making under Risky Conditions

conditions of certainty
conditions in which decision makers have complete information and knowledge of all possible outcomes

conditions of risk
conditions in which decision makers face a very real possibility of making the wrong decisions

Step 5 of the rational decision-making model assumes that managers can gaze into their crystal balls and accurately predict how well a potential solution will fix a problem. Furthermore, it assumes that managers make decisions under **conditions of certainty**, with complete information and knowledge of all possible outcomes. It's like knowing who won the Stanley Cup the last 10 times and then travelling 10 years back in time with $1000 in your pocket. Because you already know who won, deciding which team to bet on is easy. You're a guaranteed winner.

Of course, if decision-making were this easy, companies wouldn't need very many managers. In most situations, managers make decisions under **conditions of risk**, with a very real possibility of losing (making the wrong decision). Thus, risk and risky conditions make it difficult for managers to make completely rational, optimal decisions.

Furthermore, risk has a significant effect on how decision makers define and solve problems. Consider this problem from Max Bazerman's book *Judgment in Managerial Decision Making*:

> A large car manufacturer has recently been hit with a number of economic difficulties, and it appears as if three plants need to be closed and 6000 employees laid off. The vice president of production has been exploring alternative ways to avoid this crisis. She has developed two plans:
>
> Plan A: This plan will save one of three plants and 2000 jobs.
>
> Plan B: This plan has a one-third probability of saving all three plants and 6000 jobs, but has a two-thirds probability of saving no plants and no jobs.

Did you choose Plan A? According to Bazerman, 80 percent of people given these choices choose Plan A rather than Plan B. What would you have done if you were faced with the following choices to the same problem?

> Plan C: This plan will result in the loss of two of the three plants and 4000 jobs.
>
> Plan D: This plan has a two-thirds probability of resulting in the loss of all three plants and all 6000 jobs, but has a one-third probability of losing no plants and no jobs.

This time, did you choose Plan D? Again, according to Bazerman, 80 percent choose Plan D. However, if you look closely at both sets of choices, you can see that Plans A and C both save 2000 jobs, and Plans B and D both provide a two-thirds chance of losing all 6000 jobs. So why would 80 percent of decision makers choose Plan A in the first context, while only 20 percent chose its equivalent, Plan C, in the second? Likewise, why would 20 percent of decision makers choose Plan B in the first context, while 80 percent chose its equivalent, Plan D, in the second?

positive frame
couching a problem in terms of a gain, thus influencing decisions makers toward becoming risk-averse

The critical difference is how the problem is framed. A **positive frame** is the presentation of a problem in terms of a gain. When you begin with the belief that 6000 people will lose their jobs, Plan A's ability to keep 2000 jobs is clearly a gain. When faced with the prospect of a gain, decision makers tend to become risk-averse. In gambling terms, it's like quitting while you're ahead. You don't want to risk losing what you've already won. And in this situation, you start with 6000 lost jobs, but Plan A helps you win 2000 back. So most decision makers don't want to put that gain at risk.

By contrast, a **negative frame**, such as that shown in Plan D, is the presentation of a problem in terms of a loss. With nothing left to lose (i.e., there's already a two-thirds chance of losing all 6000 jobs), most decision makers become risk-seeking. In other words, if it's your last night in Las Vegas, and you've lost $900 of the $1000 you brought to town, why not put your last $100 in a $100 slot machine? You only get one chance, but if it pays off, you'll get all your money back and more. And if you lose, it doesn't really matter—you were going to lose that money anyway. In sum, risk not only affects how decision makers define problems, but it also affects the solutions they choose to fix those problems.

negative frame couching a problem in terms of a loss, thus influencing decision makers toward becoming risk-seeking

Managers also make decisions under **conditions of uncertainty**. How is uncertainty different from risk? With risk, any serious Texas hold 'em (a form of poker) player knows there is a 1 in 221 chance of being dealt a pair of aces, the best possible starting hand. But with uncertainty, you don't know how many cards there are, and you don't know how many aces are in the deck or whether the deck even has any aces. So under conditions of uncertainty, you can lose, but you don't even know the odds of winning or losing.[15]

conditions of uncertainty conditions in which decision makers don't know the odds of winning or losing

Very few people are willing to bet years of their lives and their own money under conditions of uncertainty. After all, why make the bet if you have no idea what your odds of success are? However, people differ in their willingness to embrace risks. For example, would you be willing to bungee jump off a bridge? Some, including at least one author of this book, wouldn't do it for all the money in the world. However, others would do it in a heartbeat. **Risk propensity** is a person's tendency to take or avoid risks. And it usually takes an individual with a high risk propensity to be willing to take risks under conditions of uncertainty. One such person is Bill Gross, founder and CEO of Idealab, an

risk propensity a person's tendency to take or avoid risk

MATT HENRY GUNTHER/STONE/GETTY IMAGES

Managers make decisions under conditions of uncertainty just as poker players do.

Internet business incubator that started the Internet companies eToys, Citysearch, Netzero, CarsDirect, Cooking.com, FreePC, Tickets.com, and GoTo.com. Idealab generates ideas for new businesses (mostly from Bill Gross), specs out the business plans and the business models, hires the managers to run the new businesses, gets the company Web sites running, gets venture capital funding to get the businesses running, and then takes the companies public with an initial public offering of stock. For the first few years, as the Internet took off, Idealab and its companies were wildly successful. But as dot-coms turned into dot-bombs, Gross and Idealab burned through US$800 million in funding in eight months! Even then, as eToys went bankrupt, CarsDirect blew through US$200 million, and Gross's companies' stock prices fell 90 percent in value, Gross was undeterred. Idealab, he proclaimed, would bounce back with "several multibillion-dollar ideas." GoTo.com, whose stock had fallen from $120 to $15, "could be a $100 stock if they show profitability." Only someone like Gross, who started all these companies and managed to nurse Idealab through all those failures, could be comfortable in the face of such uncertainties.[16]

Common Decision-Making Mistakes

Another reason that managers have difficulty making rational decisions is that, like all decision makers, they are susceptible to the common mistakes shown in Exhibit 6.7: overreliance on intuition, availability bias, representative bias, and anchoring and adjustment bias.[17]

Have you ever had an "Aha!" experience, in which the solution to a problem you've been working on jumps into your head when you weren't thinking about it? If so, you've experienced intuition. While it's widely believed that scientists and businesspeople use only logical, analytical, research-based methods, it's actually quite common for intuition to play a large role in the decisions and discoveries of both professions. For example, physicist Albert Einstein, discoverer of the law of relativity, claimed, "I did not arrive at my understanding of the fundamental laws of the universe through my rational mind." Henry Mintzberg, a leading management professor at McGill University, says that intuition and the underlying knowledge of your business are very important in decision-making, while spreadsheets and other decision-making tools aren't nearly as important.[18]

Intuition works best for experienced decision makers who can quickly analyze patterns of problems that they've seen before and apply "rules of thumb" to solve problems. In addition, ambiguity, interdependencies, complexity, response to crises and the speed with which decisions have to be made also force decision makers to rely on intuition.[19] Some even consider expertise a combination of analysis and intuition. Unfortunately, overreliance on intuition can lead even experienced decision makers to become overconfident, careless, and inconsistent. For example, nine radiologists participated in a study

EXHIBIT 6.7
Common Decision-Making Mistakes

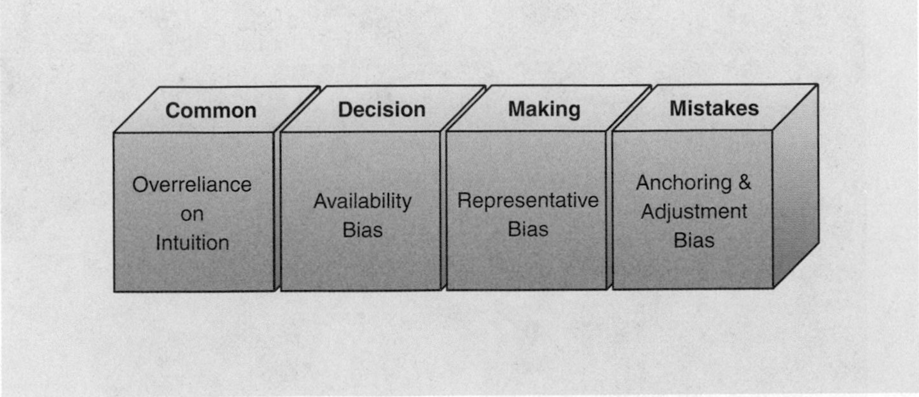

in which they examined 96 cases of possible stomach ulcers. Their task was to determine the likelihood that the ulcers were malignant. One week after initially reviewing these cases, the radiologists were shown the same cases again, but in a different order. Amazingly, these highly trained professionals, who knew that the purpose of the research was to study their diagnostic skills, arrived at different conclusions (malignant versus benign) for nearly one out of four patients in the second week of the study.[20] Put another way, if all 96 patients actually had cancer, 22 of the 96 would have been wrongly diagnosed as disease-free in the second week of the study.

The second common mistake occurs because decision makers have an availability bias when judging the frequency, probability, or causes of an event. The **availability bias** is the tendency of decision makers to give preference to recent information, vivid images that evoke emotions, and specific acts and behaviours that they personally observed. For example, in the last decade, there has been a steady significant decline in the total number of murders committed in Canada. In fact, the murder rate in Canada is about two-thirds of what it was in the 1970s and 1980s.[21] Nonetheless, people in some towns are feeling less safe despite the decline in crime, What accounts for this discrepancy? Possibly television and the availability bias. Television coverage of sensational violent crime can influence people's perceptions.[22] So, despite the fact that most people are actually much safer today than they were 20 years ago, people are increasingly fearful because their minds are filled with the vivid images of murders that are televised to their homes via the local news.

availability bias unrecognized tendency of decision makers to give preference to recent information, vivid images that evoke emotions, and specific acts and behaviours that they personally observed

The third common decision-making mistake is the **representative bias**, in which decision makers judge the likelihood of an event's occurrence based on its similarity to previous events and their likelihood of occurrence. For example, if a manager hired a graduate of ABC University, and that person just didn't work out, that manager might tend to avoid hiring any other ABC graduates. In other words, in the manager's mind, one ABC graduate represents all ABC graduates. If one didn't succeed in the job, the manager's unconscious expectation may be that others likely wouldn't succeed in the job either.

representative bias unrecognized tendency of decision makers to judge the likelihood of an event's occurrence based on its similarity to previous events

As another example, consider this riddle:

> A father and son are en route to a baseball game when their car stalls on the railroad tracks. The father can't restart the car. An oncoming train hits the car. The father dies. An ambulance rushes the boy to a nearby hospital. In the emergency room, the surgeon takes one look and says: "I can't operate on this child; he's my son."[23]

Researchers have found that it's common for people to invent strange scenarios—some involving extraterrestrials—to explain how this scenario could happen. However, since most surgeons are male, the representative bias prevents most people from considering the simple explanation that the surgeon is the boy's mother.

The fourth common decision-making mistake is the **anchoring and adjustment bias**, in which judgment (good-bad, large-small, yes-no, etc.) is "anchored" by an initial value. Once the anchor is "dropped," two things happen: (1) all subsequent experiences are judged by their similarity to the anchor, and (2) all possible decision alternatives tend to cluster around the anchor. For example, if you were accidentally bumped up from economy to first-class seating the first time you flew to Europe on business, the fine food, free drinks, attentive service, and fully reclining seats would make every subsequent trans-Atlantic trip in economy-class seating seem miserable. Likewise, when negotiating salaries or selling prices, the first number discussed tends to serve as the anchor for the entire negotiation. For example, in house shopping, the "listing price" stated by the house seller is typically the anchor value for negotiations. Consequently, buyers and sellers tend to judge whether they got a "good deal" by how close the selling price was to the listing price.

anchoring and adjustment bias unrecognized tendency of decision makers to use an initial value or experience as a basis of comparison throughout the decision process

Review 2: Limits to Rational Decision-Making

The rational decision-making model describes how decisions should be made in an ideal world without limits. However, bounded rationality recognizes that in the real world, managers' decision-making processes are restricted by limited resources, incomplete and imperfect information, and managers' limited decision-making capabilities. These limitations often prevent managers from being rational decision makers. So do common decision-making mistakes, such as overreliance on intuition and the availability, representative, and anchoring and adjustment biases. The rational decision-making model assumes that decisions are made under conditions of certainty. However, most managerial decisions are made under conditions of risk, where there is limited information and knowledge and a very real chance of making a bad decision. Risk also affects how decision makers define and solve problems. Positive frames encourage decision makers to be risk averse, whereas negative frames encourage them to be risk-seeking. Finally, managers also make decisions under conditions of uncertainty, in which the odds of winning or losing are unknown. It takes a high risk propensity to be willing to take risks under conditions of uncertainty.

Improving Decision-Making

What's the biggest decision you've ever made? Was it choosing where to go to university? Was it choosing a major? Or was it a personal decision, such as deciding whether to get married, where to live, or which car or house to buy? Considering the lasting effect that decisions like these have on our lives, wouldn't it be great if we could learn how to make them better? Managers struggle with decisions, too. They wring their hands over who to hire or promote, or when and how somebody should be fired. They fret about which suppliers the company should do business with. They lose sleep over who should get how much for pay raises or how to change the company strategy to respond to aggressive competitors. And, considering the lasting effect that these decisions have on themselves and their companies, managers also want to learn how to make better decisions.

After reading the next two sections, you should be able to

3 describe how individual decision-making can be improved.

4 explain how group decisions and group decision-making techniques can improve decision-making.

3 IMPROVING INDIVIDUAL DECISION-MAKING

In theory, rational decision-making leads to optimal decisions. However, in practice, we know that real-world constraints, common decision-making mistakes, and risky situations make fully rational decisions difficult to achieve. Consequently, in the business world, managers are much more likely to satisfice and make "good enough" decisions than they are to maximize and make "optimal" decisions.

Managers can make better decisions by using decision rules, multivariable testing, and decision software, and by avoiding a common post-decision-making error called escalation of commitment.

Decision Rules

decision rule
set of criteria that alternative solutions must meet to be acceptable to the decision maker

A **decision rule** is a set of criteria that alternative solutions must meet to be acceptable to the decision maker.[24] If an alternative doesn't meet the criteria in the decision rule, it is rejected. Nearly every kind of business uses basic decision rules. In restaurants, the general pricing decision rule is to price food at three times its cost, beer at four times its cost, and hard liquor at six times its cost. In many clothing stores, the rule is to sell clothing for 60 percent over wholesale, and then reduce that price by 20 percent every two weeks until the clothing has been sold. Decision rules improve decision-making because they are easy to understand and simple to follow. Managers who don't have the time or resources to use the complete rational decision-making model can use simpler decision rules instead.

There are two general kinds of decision rules: the dictionary rule and the threshold rule. In much the same way that a dictionary sorts words by their first letter and then their second letter, and so forth, the **dictionary rule** encourages decision makers to rank their criteria in order of importance and then assess alternative solutions against these criteria in rank order. Specifically, alternatives that meet the most important criterion must then meet the second most important criterion, and so on. For example, the first house a friend and his wife owned had a living room and a family room. They found that the living room went basically unused, except when they had guests. So as their family grew and they started shopping for a larger house, the first thing they told the realtor was "Don't show us any houses with two living areas. We want a house with one large living room." Second, because they had three children, "It would be great to have four bedrooms." They were willing to look at any houses that met those criteria.

dictionary rule
decision rule that requires decision makers to rank criteria in order of importance and then test alternative solutions against those criteria in rank order, so that alternatives that meet the most important criterion must then meet the second most important criterion, and so on

Sometimes decision makers need to make yes/no or accept/reject decisions. Should a bank accept or reject a mortgage application? Should MasterCard approve or deny a jeweller's request to charge your card $3500 for a jewellery purchase? When these kinds of decisions must be made, companies often use the **minimum threshold rule**, which requires an alternative to pass all the established minimum decision criteria. For example, one of the most common problems seen in emergency rooms is injured ankles. However, only 15 percent of ankle x-rays taken indicate fractures. In other words, doctors are ordering expensive x-rays much more than they need to. Recently, clinical research has resulted in the development of the "Ottawa rule," which states that physicians should send patients with ankle injuries for confirmatory x-rays only if there is (1) pain near the ankle joint, and (2) bone tenderness, and (3) an inability to bear weight on the ankle. All three criteria must be met before sending patients to have their ankles x-rayed. Studies showed that physicians using the Ottawa rule correctly ordered x-rays for 100 percent of the patients who fractured their ankles. Also, the Ottawa rule helped reduce the overall number of ankle x-rays by 34 percent.[25]

minimum threshold rule
decision rule that requires alternative solutions to meet all the established minimum decision criteria

Multivariable Testing

In practice, analyzing alternatives is one of the weakest steps in the decision-making process. Much of the "analysis" that gets done is based on guesswork ("We think that Plan E has a 90 percent chance of working") rather than on actual tests of possible solutions. Because it is based on data from small experiments rather than guesswork, **multivariable testing (MVT)** helps managers take a much more systematic approach to analyzing and evaluating potential solutions. Dwight Glover, CEO of Evans Clay, a small manufacturing company, said, "What I like about [MVT] is it provides data instead of opinions. It involves employees throughout the organization. You are using the brainpower that you have."[26]

multivariable testing (MVT)
a systematic approach of experimentation used to analyze and evaluate potential solutions

Multivariable testing improves decision-making in a number of important ways. First, instead of letting arguments determine what the best solution is ("I really like that plan that manufacturing came up with because ... "), MVT encourages managers to conduct small-scale experiments and let the data decide. Says MVT consultant and trainer Charles Holland, "The power of experimental design is not only its efficiency with data, but that it forces a team to make decisions based on facts. Hierarchy, politics, or emotions are refuted with data."[27] For example, the marketing team of a mail-order catalogue company wanted to improve sales. Rather than debating what might or might not increase sales, the team came up with 12 ideas that might work, such as adding more expensive white fibrefill in pillows, adding a price grid for easy reference on each page, or printing the background of the catalogue with white ink (instead of just using the natural colour of the paper for the catalogue background). Instead of arguing about what might work, the marketing team tested all 12 ideas separately by printing up 16 different catalogue inserts for one mailing.[28]

Second, traditional scientific experimentation typically relies on controlled testing, in which all potential influences, except the ones you want to test, are controlled. This sounds simple enough, but the 12 ideas that the marketing team came up with to improve mail-order catalogue sales would require 4096 different experiments to test all possible combinations of those 12 variables (i.e., ideas). The advantage of MVT is that it saves time and money by using a mathematical shortcut so that just a few quick tests can get you 70 percent of the information that you'd get if you tested all possible combinations of variables. Rather than running 4096 possible combinations of ideas that would improve catalogue sales, the marketing team only had to use 16 different tests for their 12 ideas. After mailing out 386 000 catalogues, they found that 7 of the 12 ideas made a difference. For instance, it turns out that the more expensive white fibrefill in pillows made no difference in sales. The company saved $450 000 by switching back to cheaper, grey fibrefill. However, the price grid on each page allowed more photo space to feature items, resulting in an increase of $750 000 in sales. In all, by quickly testing all meaningful combinations of their 12 ideas in one printing of the catalogue, MVT earned the company more than a million dollars in increased sales and lower costs.[29]

Exhibit 6.8 shows a simple multivariable testing experiment that a small amusement park might use to increase park attendance on Tuesdays, typically the slowest day in the park. On the first Tuesday, Test 1, no changes are made. The park earns a profit of $4000. On the next Tuesday, Test 2, the park runs a 2-for-1 admission special and gives everyone who enters the park a coupon for a free hot dog and a Coke between 11:00 A.M. and 1:00 P.M. The park earns just $2000, losing money on all the free lunches it gave away to all those people who were admitted for free. On the next Tuesday, Test 3, parking is free and everyone who enters the park gets a free lunch coupon. The park makes $9000. Finally, on the fourth Tuesday, the park again offers 2-for-1 admission, but this time with free parking. Profits this time are $5000. What's the answer? It's obvious: Offer free parking and free lunch on Tuesdays.

MVT can be used in all kinds of businesses for many kinds of decisions. However, managers and employees will need to be trained how to design simple experiments and how to gather and analyze basic statistical data. Nonetheless, despite its cost, MVT allows managers to test and evaluate potential solutions before committing large amounts of money to their use. So instead of arguing about what you "think" the best solution might be, use MVT to test alternative solutions.

Staying Rational: Decision Software

Most decision makers satisfice, accepting the first "good enough" solution that comes to mind. Furthermore, because of time pressures and situational limitations, intuitive, unstructured decision-making is the norm rather than the exception. Together, these factors make it nearly impossible for managers and business people to "stay rational" and maximize decisions.

Computer software, however, may do for decision-making what it did for the nasty tasks of balancing your chequebook and doing your taxes—make it simpler, faster, and easier. If you've got a computer, you probably use Quicken (or a similar program) to balance your chequebook and stick to a budget. Likewise, if you do your own taxes, you probably use QuickTax (www.intuit.com/canada/quicktax/) or TAXWHIZ (or a similar program) to figure out how much money you owe the government (or, if you're lucky,

EXHIBIT 6.8
Multivariable Testing to Increase Amusement Park Attendance on Tuesdays

TEST	2-FOR-1	FREE LUNCH	FREE PARKING	PROFITS
Test 1				$4000
Test 2	X	X		$2000
Test 3		X	X	$9000
Test 4	X		X	$5000

how much they owe you). Millions of people swear by these programs. According to Walter Mossberg, who writes the Personal Technology column for *The Wall Street Journal*, one such program, DecideRight, "does a far better job of organizing your options in a decision, and then ranking them by criteria you choose, than the traditional yellow legal pad with columns labeled 'pro' and 'con'—the method used by millions."[30]

Here's how it works. DecideRight starts with its QuickBuild tool, which, in an interview-like style, walks decision makers through the decision-making process. Step 1, label the decision. "What bank should we choose for the business?" Step 2, enter the decision criteria. "Location, hours, fees, and so forth." Step 3, enter the options you're considering. "Bank One, Credit Union Two, Treasury Branch Three, and so on." Step 4, weight the decision criteria. For example, click on "location" and then drag and drop it on the high-, medium-, or low-importance button on your screen. Step 5, rate each option against each decision criterion. Again, all you do is drag and drop. If Central Bank & Trust is just right around the corner from your business, click on "Central Bank & Trust" and then drag and drop it onto the "excellent" button on your screen for location. Step 6, the ranking of alternatives is performed automatically. There's no math involved (unless you choose this option).

Not only does DecideRight automatically rank alternatives, it also generates a report with charts and tables that explains why and how the decision was made. The report even explains why one alternative was chosen over another. Decision-making software such as DecideRight is no guarantee of good decisions. After all, Quicken can't guarantee that you'll always have money in the bank, and TAXWHIZ can't guarantee a tax refund. But to the extent that decision software tools such as DecideRight (www.performancesolutionstech.com), iDecide (www.definitivesoftware.com), and ExpertChoice (www.expertchoice.com) encourage managers to work through the steps of the rational decision-making model, it should help them make better decisions.[31]

After the Decision: Avoiding Escalation of Commitment

Earlier in the chapter you learned about the common mistakes that occur when managers are in the process of making decisions: overreliance on intuition, availability bias, representative bias, and the anchoring and adjustment bias. However, individuals and organizations often make a serious post-decision mistake called "escalation of commitment." **Escalation of commitment** is the tendency for a person who has already made a decision to more strongly support that original decision despite negative information that clearly indicates it was wrong.[32] For example, one of the reasons that Montgomery Ward's closed after more than a century in business is that it sat on $911 million in on-hand cash and never opened a new store—not one—between 1941 and 1957. Ward's chairman at the time, Sewell Avery, had created a chart that showed that every world war since the time of Napoleon had been followed by a major economic depression. After World War II ended in 1945, Sewell declared, "Who am I to argue with history? Why build $14-per-foot buildings when we soon can do it for $3 per foot?" So, as post-war Americans moved in mass from the cities to the suburbs, Ward's sat back and watched Sears and JCPenney build hundreds of new stores in suburbs and malls.

escalation of commitment the tendency for a person who has already made a decision to more strongly support that original decision despite negative information that clearly indicates it was wrong

Montgomery Ward's tried to catch up by building similar stores in the 1970s and 1980s, but unlike Sears and Penney's, it never had enough stores in enough good locations to survive. Avery's obviously wrong decision to not build any new stores, which he stuck to for 16 years, eventually led to Ward's closing half a century later.[33]

Besides committing to a failing course of action, like Ward's chairman Sewell Avery, escalation of commitment often involves an increased commitment of resources (i.e., time, money, and people) to try to save the failed effort or decision. The problems associated with B.C. Ferry Corp.'s ill-fated launch of three PacifiCat ferries illustrates this problem well. In June 1994, then-B.C. premier Glen Clark announced that B.C. Ferry Corp. would build three high-speed ferries. The intent was to create shipbuilding jobs and to provide new and faster ferries. The first ferry was intended to be launched in April

1997 at a cost of $70 million. In April 1995 a marine engineer warned B.C. Ferries that the project was economically unfeasible, it could endanger the public, and there could be difficulties building the ships because shipyard workers had to learn new and difficult shipbuilding techniques. B.C. Ferries ignored these warnings and proceeded anyway. The first ferry was not launched until June 1998 and because of technical difficulties did not see service until July 1999, two years late. The total cost had risen to $210 million and the entire project looked like it would cost $400 million. This, despite the fact Glen Clark, then the premier of B.C., bragged that "it's budgeted right down to the toilet paper."[34] After it was finally put in service, the new ferry was immediately plagued by more technical difficulties, operating costs were higher than expected, and there were serious concerns raised about public safety due to the speed and size of the wake created. Given the operational problems, cost overruns, and public safety issues seen with the first ferry, B.C.'s Liberal opposition urged the government to stop building the next two ferries. By this time, the level of commitment had gone too far. The project was completed at a cost of $454 million, although one columnist estimated the total cost as closer to $1 billion. The three ferries were finally pulled from service and sold for $19.2 million, a fraction of their cost.[35] Professor Barry Staw, a leading researcher on escalation of commitment, said, "Typically the leader is defensive and doesn't want to hear that he might be wrong. Then comes a social process in which other people's careers get staked to his course of action—even if it's wrong, they think they have to defend it or they'll lose their jobs. It's like propping up a defunct government."[36]

While nothing is failsafe, here are a few suggestions for avoiding the traps associated with escalation of commitment. To minimize escalation of commitment from the start, organizations should require frequent, detailed progress reports to make managers compare actual and planned spending, performance, and progress. If there are differences, they should explain why.[37] A second way to minimize escalation from the start is to hire an independent auditor to provide an objective assessment. Independent auditors have no psychological or financial investment in the decisions or projects they audit and are generally not directly affected by internal company politics. Their job is to provide a fresh set of eyes and to communicate a third-party perspective. And, if a project is failing, seriously behind schedule, or over cost, auditors should also be asked to suggest alternative courses of action to continued funding or investment in the project. Furthermore, the presence of an auditor is often enough to encourage managers to be more realistic about the progress or success of their decisions.[38]

Finally, several things can be done to minimize the damage and cost if escalation of commitment does occur. One of the most effective is to change managers. Like independent auditors, new managers with a fresh perspective are much more likely to discontinue decisions resulting in huge cost overruns or unproductive returns. For example, B.C. Ferry Corp. did not shut down its PacifiCat service and decide to sell the ferries until a new premier was in place and significant turnover of senior management at B.C. Ferries had occurred, including the firing of the entire board of directors of B.C. Ferries.[39] A second way to deal with escalation of commitment is to label the decision as an "experiment." Calling a failed decision or project an "experiment" indicates that failure was a possibility, that the project was designed to help the company learn something, and that there was no permanent commitment to the decision. This gets the company off the hook, permits managers associated with the failed decision to save face, and in general makes it easier to stop or shut down a failed decision or project.[40] For example, after the Priceline WebHouse Club lost $545 million selling gasoline and groceries using Priceline's "name your price" strategy, Priceline.com announced that it was shutting down the Priceline WebHouse Club.[41] Jay Walker, Priceline founder, said this about the closing:[42]

- "In scale and scope the WebHouse Club was a business opportunity with great potential but with real risks." [Translation: "We weren't sure it would work."]
- "We specifically structured the WebHouse Club as a separate company from Priceline .com so that private investors, not Priceline.com shareholders, would bear that risk."

[Translation: "Because we weren't sure it would work, we kept it separate from the main business, Priceline.com."]

- "All of us here at WebHouse Club are terribly disappointed, but I am proud of what we accomplished since we commenced operations." [Translation: "We tried our best, but we're hemorrhaging money, so we're going to close this down."]
- "In light of the weakness of the current capital market environment, the WebHouse Club executive team has reluctantly concluded that it was unlikely to be able to raise the additional capital the WebHouse Club would need next year to achieve the necessary scale and our goal of profitability. Accordingly, we have determined that the prudent course of action is to wind down our operations on an orderly basis while fully satisfying all of the WebHouse Club's obligations to customers, employees, and suppliers." [Translation: "We didn't have enough money to keep absorbing these tremendous losses. WebHouse is no more."]

Review 3: Improving Individual Decision-Making

Decision rules are a relatively simple method of improving decision-making. The dictionary rule helps decision makers choose among multiple alternative solutions, whereas the threshold rule helps decision makers make yes/no or accept/reject decisions. Managers use multivariable testing to do a better job of analyzing and evaluating potential solutions. The basic idea is to experimentally test several potential solutions at the same time and let data, rather than beliefs, guide decision-making. While most decision makers "satisfice," accepting the first "good enough" solution that comes to mind, decision software (such as DecideRight, which prompts managers to identify and weight decision criteria, generate alternative solutions, and then rank those solutions by their decision weights) can help them be better decision makers by working through the steps of the rational decision-making model. Escalation of commitment occurs when someone continues to strongly support a decision with funding and resources despite negative information that shows the decision was wrong. The damage and costs associated with escalation of commitment can be minimized by asking managers to make detailed progress reports comparing actual and planned spending and progress, hiring independent auditors, replacing managers who made the original decisions with new managers, and being willing to label the failed decision an "experiment," thus making it easier to end support for that decision.

4 USING GROUPS TO IMPROVE DECISION-MAKING

Using teams, task forces, or groups is a common method that companies choose for solving complex problems. For example, Celestica Inc., with headquarters in Toronto, used a group process to implement a widespread redesign of work practices in order to increase productivity. A steering committee was formed that had senior managers from all functional areas. A central design team and a resource team were also put together, and they in turn formed 21 design teams, one for each of the functions being redesigned. Further subteams were formed to complete detailed implementation plans. Despite the fact that Celestica was already a successful and profitable company, these undertakings managed to double the company's productivity.[43]

When done properly, as at Celestica, group decision-making can lead to much better decisions than individual decision-making. In fact, numerous studies show that groups consistently outperform individuals on complex tasks.

Let's explore the advantages and pitfalls of group decision-making and see how the following group decision-making methods—structured conflict, the nominal group technique, the Delphi technique, the stepladder technique, and electronic brainstorming—can be used to improve decision-making.

Advantages and Pitfalls of Group Decision-Making

Groups can do a much better job than individuals in two important steps of the decision-making process: defining the problem and generating alternative solutions. Four reasons explain why.

First, because group members usually possess different knowledge, skills, abilities, and experiences, groups will be able to view problems from several perspectives. Being able to view problems from several perspectives, in turn, can help groups perform better on complex tasks and make better decisions than individuals.[44] In fact, groups made up of members with greater diversity of knowledge, skills, abilities, and experiences will typically outperform groups with less diversity on those dimensions. For example, companies with more women in top management had better financial performance during initial public offerings (IPOs)—that is, the very first time a company publicly sells stock to investors. Companies with top management groups composed of at least 10 percent females had IPO stock prices 4.6 percent higher than companies with no women in top management jobs. And when women held at least half the top management positions in a company, IPO stock prices were 23 percent higher. Company performance and stock prices were higher after the initial public offering, too. Professor Theresa Welbourne, who conducted the study, said, "When you have diversity in top management, you have people looking at data differently, and that brings better decision-making overall."[45]

Second, groups can find and access much more information than can individuals. For example, Clough, Harbour & Associates, an engineering consulting firm, uses a hiring team for interviewing potential employees. The company's director of human resources said, "We think we make better hiring decisions when we get a number of people involved. It's like working a crossword puzzle. If you get four people together, their chances of solving the puzzle are greater than if the four work separately."[46]

Third, the increased knowledge and information available to groups make it easier for them to generate more alternative solutions. Studies show that generating lots of alternative solutions is a critical part of improving the quality of decisions. Fourth, if groups are involved in the decision-making process, group members will be more committed to making chosen solutions work.

groupthink
a barrier to good decision-making caused by pressure within the group for members to agree with each other

Although groups can do a better job of defining problems and generating alternative solutions, group decision-making is subject to some pitfalls that can quickly erase these gains. One possible pitfall is groupthink. **Groupthink** occurs in highly cohesive groups when group members feel intense pressure to agree with each other, so that the group can approve a proposed solution.[47] Because groupthink leads to consideration of a limited number of solutions and because it restricts discussion of any considered solutions, it usually results in poor decisions. Groupthink is most likely to occur under the following conditions:

- The group is insulated from others with different perspectives.
- The group leader begins by expressing strong preference for a particular decision.
- There is no established procedure for systematically defining problems and exploring alternatives.
- Group members have similar backgrounds and experiences.[48]

NASA's decision to launch the ill-fated space shuttle *Challenger* is an example of groupthink. Despite cold weather conditions that would normally have postponed a launch, NASA placed heavy pressure on Morton Thiokol (maker of the o-rings) and other engineering firms involved in the launch decision to give their approval to launch. After being told twice that a launch was not recommended, NASA administrators pressured Morton Thiokol one last time for an okay. Because of the pressure and time constraints, Thiokol reversed its decision. Tragically, as Thiokol had originally feared, the o-rings failed, and the shuttle exploded, killing all aboard.[49]

A second potential problem with group decision-making is that it takes considerable time. It takes time to reconcile schedules (so that group members can meet). Furthermore, it's a rare group that consistently holds productive task-oriented meetings to effectively work through the decision process. Some of the most common complaints about meetings (and thus decision-making) are that the meeting's purpose is unclear, meeting participants are unprepared, critical people are absent or late, conversation doesn't stay focused on the problem, and no one follows up on the decisions that were made.

A third possible pitfall is that sometimes just one or two people, perhaps the boss or a strong-willed, vocal group member, dominate group discussion, restricting consideration of different problem definitions and alternative solutions. Another possible problem is that, unlike their own decisions and actions, group members often don't feel accountable for the decisions made and actions taken by the group.

While these pitfalls can lead to poor decision-making, this doesn't mean that managers should avoid using groups to make decisions. When done properly, group decision-making can lead to much better decisions. The pitfalls of group decision-making are not inevitable. Most of them can be overcome through good management; Chapter 12 discusses more aspects of managing teams. Let's see how structured conflict, the nominal group technique, the Delphi technique, the stepladder technique, and electronic brainstorming help managers improve group decision-making.

Structured Conflict

Most people view conflict negatively. However, the right kind of conflict can lead to much better group decision-making. **C-type conflict**, or "**cognitive conflict**," focuses on problem- and issue-related differences of opinion.[50] In c-type conflict, group members disagree because their different experiences and expertise lead them to different views of the problem and its potential solutions. However, c-type conflict is also characterized by a willingness to examine, compare, and reconcile those differences to produce the best possible solution. Alteon WebSystems, now a division of Nortel Networks, makes critical use of c-type conflict. Top manager Dominic Orr described Alteon's c-type conflict this way:

c-type conflict (cognitive conflict) disagreement that focuses on problem- and issue-related differences of opinion

> There's no silent disagreement, and no getting personal, and definitely no "let's take it offline" mentality. Our goal is to make each major decision in a single meeting. People arrive with a proposal or a solution—and with the facts to support it. After an idea is presented, we open the floor to objective, and often withering, critiques. And if the idea collapses under scrutiny, we move on to another: no hard feelings. We're judging the idea, not the person. At the same time, we don't really try to regulate emotions. Passionate conflict means that we're getting somewhere, not that the discussion is out of control. But one person does act as referee—by asking basic questions like "Is this good for the customer?" or "Does it keep our time-to-market advantage intact?" By focusing relentlessly on the facts, we're able to see the strengths and weaknesses of an idea clearly and quickly.[51]

By contrast, **a-type conflict**, meaning "**affective conflict**," refers to the emotional reactions that can occur when disagreements become personal rather than professional. A-type conflict often results in hostility, anger, resentment, distrust, cynicism, and apathy. Unlike c-type conflict, a-type conflict undermines team effectiveness by preventing teams from engaging in the activities characteristic of c-type conflict that are critical to team effectiveness. Examples of a-type conflict phrases are "your idea," "our idea," "my department," "you don't know what you are talking about," or "you don't understand our situation." Rather than focusing on issues and ideas, these statements focus on individuals.[52]

a-type conflict (affective conflict) disagreement that focuses on individual or personally oriented issues

Devil's advocacy and dialectical inquiry are two methods that introduce structured c-type conflict into the group decision-making process. **Devil's advocacy** creates c-type conflict by assigning an individual or a subgroup the role of critic. The following five steps establish a devil's advocacy program:

devil's advocacy a decision-making method in which an individual or a subgroup is assigned the role of a critic

1. Generate a potential solution.
2. Assign a devil's advocate to criticize and question the solution.
3. Present the critique of the potential solution to key decision makers.
4. Gather additional relevant information.
5. Decide whether to use, change, or not use the originally proposed solution.[53]

WHAT REALLY WORKS

Devil's Advocacy and Dialectical Inquiry[56]

Ninety percent of the decisions managers face are well-structured problems that recur frequently under conditions of certainty. For example, showing up at an airline ticket counter without your ticket is a well-structured problem. It happens every day (recurs frequently), and it's easy to determine if you have your ticket or not (conditions of certainty).

Well-structured problems are solved with programmed decisions, in which a policy, procedure, or rule clearly specifies how to solve the problem. Thus, there's no mystery about what to do when someone shows up without a ticket. After you present identification to prove who you are, and after you pay a transaction fee (around $120), the airline gives you another ticket.

In some sense, programmed decisions really aren't decisions, because anyone with any experience knows what to do. There's no thought involved. What keeps managers up at night is the other 10 percent of problems. Ill-structured problems that are novel (no one's seen them before) and exist under conditions of uncertainty are solved with nonprogrammed decisions. Nonprogrammed decisions do not involve standard methods of resolution. Every time managers make a nonprogrammed decision, they have to figure out a new way of handling a new problem. That's what makes them so tough.

Both the devil's advocacy and dialectical inquiry approaches to decision-making can be used to improve nonprogrammed decision-making. Both approaches work because they force decision makers to identify and criticize the assumptions underlying the nonprogrammed decisions that they hope will solve ill-structured problems.

DEVIL'S ADVOCACY

There is a 58 percent chance that decision makers who use the devil's-advocacy approach to criticize and question their solutions will produce better-quality decisions than decisions based on the advice of experts.

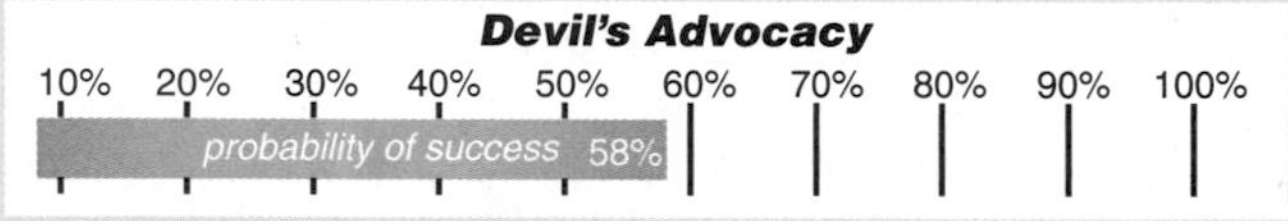

DIALECTICAL INQUIRY

There is a 55 percent chance that decision makers who use the dialectical-inquiry approach to criticize and question their solutions will produce better-quality decisions than decisions based on the advice of experts.

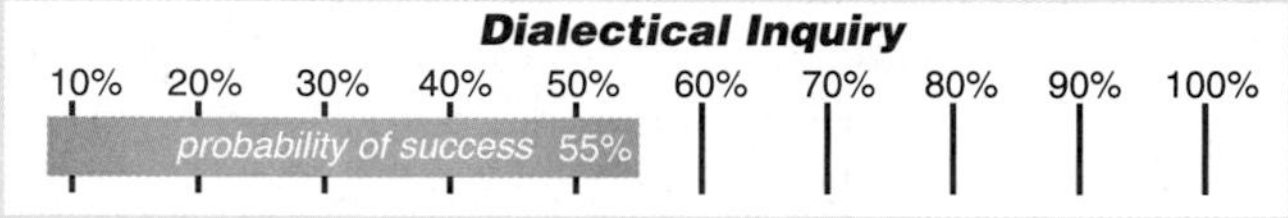

Note that each technique has been compared to decisions obtained by following experts' advice. So, while these probabilities of success, 58 percent and 55 percent, seem small, they very likely understate the effects of both techniques. In other words, the probabilities of success would have been much larger if both techniques had been compared to unstructured decision-making processes.

dialectical inquiry
a decision-making method in which decision makers state the assumptions of a proposed solution (a thesis) and generate a solution that is the opposite (antithesis) of that solution

Dialectical inquiry creates c-type conflict by forcing decision makers to state the assumptions of a proposed solution (a thesis) and to then generate a solution that is the opposite (antithesis) of the proposed solution. The following are the five steps of the dialectical inquiry process:

1. Generate a potential solution.
2. Identify the assumptions underlying the potential solution.
3. Generate a conflicting counterproposal based on the opposite assumptions.
4. Have advocates of each position present their arguments and engage in a debate in front of key decision makers.
5. Decide whether to use, change, or not use the originally proposed solution.[54]

When properly used, both the devil's advocacy and dialectical inquiry approaches introduce c-type conflict into the decision-making process. Further, contrary to the common belief that conflict is bad, studies show that these methods lead to less a-type conflict, improved decision quality, and greater acceptance of decisions once they have been made.[55] See the "What Really Works" feature for more information on both techniques.

Nominal Group Technique

"Nominal" means "in name only." Accordingly, the **nominal group technique** received its name because it begins with "quiet time," in which group members independently write down as many problem definitions and alternative solutions as possible. In other words, the nominal group technique begins by having group members act as individuals. After the "quiet time," the group leader asks each group member to share one idea at a time with the group. As they are read aloud, ideas are posted on flipcharts or wallboards for all to see. This step continues until all ideas have been shared. The next step involves a discussion of the advantages and disadvantages of these ideas. The nominal group technique closes with a second "quiet time," in which group members independently rank the ideas presented. Group members then read their rankings aloud, and the idea with the highest average rank is selected.[57]

nominal group technique decision-making method that begins and ends by having group members quietly write down and evaluate ideas to be shared with the group

The nominal group technique improves group decision-making by decreasing a-type conflict. However, in doing so, it also restricts c-type conflict. Consequently, the nominal group technique typically produces poorer-quality decisions than do the devil's advocacy or dialectical inquiry approaches. Nonetheless, more than 80 studies have found that nominal groups produce better-quality ideas than traditional group decisions.[58]

Delphi Technique

The **Delphi technique** is a decision-making method in which a panel of experts responds to questions and to each other until reaching agreement on an issue. The first step is to assemble a panel of experts. However, unlike other approaches to group decision-making, it isn't necessary to bring the panel together in one place. Since the Delphi technique does not require the experts to leave their offices or disrupt their schedules, they are more likely to participate in the process. For example, two colleagues were asked to conduct a Delphi technique assessment of the "10 most important steps for small businesses." With the help of the dean of a nearby business school and a former mayor of the city, they assembled a panel of local top-level managers and CEOs.

Delphi technique a decision-making method in which a panel of experts responds to questions and to each other until reaching agreement on an issue

The second step is to create a questionnaire consisting of a series of open-ended questions for the experts. For example, the panel was asked to answer these questions: "What is the most common mistake made by small-business persons?" "Right now, what do you think is the biggest threat to the survival of most small businesses?" "If you had one piece of advice to give to the owner of a small business, what would it be?"

In Step 3, panel members' written responses are analyzed, summarized, and fed back to the panel for reactions until panel members reach agreement. In the Delphi study described above, it took about a month to get the panel members' written responses to the first three questions. Then their written responses were summarized and typed into a brief report (no more than two pages). The summary was sent to the panel members and were asked to explain why they agreed or disagreed with these conclusions from the first round of questions. Asking why they agreed or disagreed is important, because it helps uncover panel members' unstated assumptions and beliefs. Again, this process of summarizing panel feedback and obtaining reactions to that feedback continues until panel members reach agreement. For this study, it took just one more round for panel members' views to reach a consensus. In all, it took approximately three and a half months to complete this Delphi study.

The Delphi technique is not an approach that managers should use for common decisions. Because it is a time-consuming, labour-intensive, and expensive process, the Delphi technique is best reserved for important long-term issues and problems. Nonetheless, the judgments and conclusions obtained from it are typically better than those you would get from one expert.

Stepladder Technique

stepladder technique
when group members are added to a group discussion one at a time (i.e., like a stepladder), the existing group members first take the time to listen to each new member's thoughts, ideas, and recommendations, and then the group, in turn, shares the ideas and suggestions that it had already considered, discusses the new and old ideas, and then makes a decision

The **stepladder technique** improves group decision-making by making sure that each group member's contributions are independent, are considered, and are discussed. As shown in Exhibit 6.9, the stepladder technique begins with discussion between two group members, each of whom presents to the other their thoughts, ideas, and recommendations before jointly making a tentative decision. At each step, as other group members are added to the discussion one at a time, like a stepladder, the existing group members take the time to listen to each new member's thoughts, ideas, and recommendations. The group then shares the ideas and suggestions that it had already considered, discusses the new and old ideas, and then makes a tentative decision. This process (new member's ideas are heard, group shares previous ideas and suggestions, discussion is held, tentative group decision is made) continues until each group member's ideas have been discussed.

For the stepladder technique to work, group members must have enough time to consider the problem or decision on their own, to present their ideas to the group, and to thoroughly discuss all ideas and alternatives with the group at each step. Rushing through each step destroys the advantages of this technique. Also, groups must make sure that subsequent group members are completely unaware of previous discussions and suggestions. This will ensure that each member who joins the group brings truly independent thoughts and suggestions, thus greatly increasing the chances of making better decisions.

One study found that compared to traditional groups in which all group members are present for the entire discussion, groups using the stepladder technique produced significantly better decisions. Moreover, the stepladder groups performed better than the best individual member of their group 56 percent of the time, while traditional groups outperformed the best individual member of their group only 13 percent of the time.[59] Besides better performance, groups using the stepladder technique also generated more ideas and were more satisfied with the decision-making process.

Electronic Brainstorming

brainstorming
a decision-making method in which group members build on each other's ideas to generate as many alternative solutions as possible

Brainstorming, in which group members build on others' ideas, is a technique for generating a large number of alternative solutions. Brainstorming has four rules:

1. The more ideas, the better.
2. All ideas are acceptable, no matter how wild or crazy they might be.

EXHIBIT 6.9
Stepladder Technique for Group Decision-Making

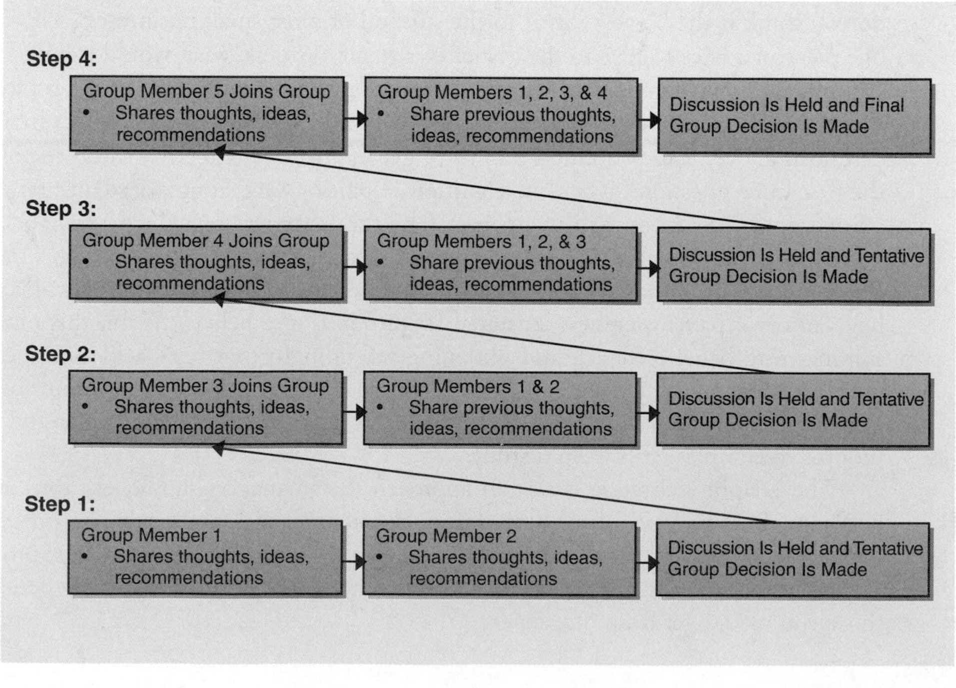

3. Other group members' ideas should be used to come up with even more ideas.
4. Criticism or evaluation of ideas is not allowed.

While brainstorming is great fun and can help managers generate a large number of alternative solutions, it does have a number of disadvantages. Fortunately, **electronic brainstorming**, in which group members use computers to communicate and generate alternative solutions, overcomes the disadvantages associated with face-to-face brainstorming.[60] Tom Corcoran, vice president of group insurance at Canada Life, is a big advocate of electronic brainstorming and regularly uses the brainstorming facilities at the Queen's University Executive Decision Centre, one of the first of its kind to be made accessible to the public. He brings employees together to deal with such issues as product development and strategic planning. He feels it avoids big debates and allows the discussion to converge, rather than having long debates.[61]

electronic brainstorming a decision-making method in which group members use computers to build on each other's ideas and generate many alternative solutions

The first disadvantage that electronic brainstorming overcomes is **production blocking**, which occurs when you have an idea, but you have to wait to share it because someone else is already describing an idea to the group. This short delay may make you forget your idea or decide that it really wasn't worth sharing. But with electronic brainstorming, production blocking doesn't happen. With all group members seated at computers, everyone can type in their ideas whenever they occur. There's no "waiting your turn" to be heard by the group.

production blocking a disadvantage of face-to-face brainstorming in which a group member must wait to share an idea because another member is presenting an idea

The second disadvantage that electronic brainstorming overcomes is **evaluation apprehension**, that is, being afraid of what others will think of your ideas. With electronic brainstorming, all ideas are anonymous. When you type in an idea and hit the "Enter" key to share it with the group, group members see only the idea. Furthermore, many brainstorming software programs also protect anonymity by displaying ideas in random order. So, if you laugh maniacally when you type "Cut top management's pay by 50 percent!" and then hit the "Enter" key, it won't show up immediately on everyone's screen. This makes it doubly difficult to determine which comments belong to whom.

evaluation apprehension fear of what others will think of your ideas

The photo on this page shows the typical layout for electronic brainstorming. All participants sit in front of computers around a U-shaped table. This configuration allows them to see their computer screens, each other, and a large main screen. Exhibit 6.10 shows what the typical electronic brainstorming group member will see on his or her computer screen. The first step in electronic brainstorming is to anonymously generate

Queen's Executive Decision Centre has an electronic brainstorming facility.

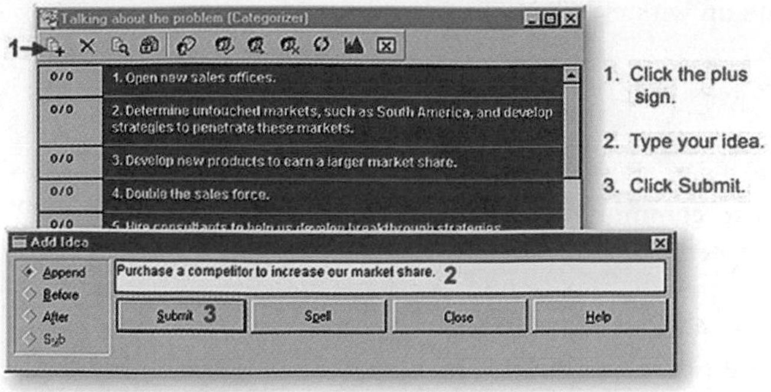

Source: "GroupSystems Tour Stop 2: Generating a List of Ideas," Ventana Web site. [Online] Available www.ventana.com/html/vc_tour_stop_2_categorizer.html, 12 January 1999.

EXHIBIT 6.10
What You See on the Computer During Electronic Brainstorming

as many ideas as possible. It's common for groups to generate 100 ideas in a half-hour period. Step 2 is to edit the generated ideas, categorize them, and eliminate redundancies. Step 3 is to rank-order the categorized ideas based on their quality. Step 4, the last step, has three parts: generate a series of action steps, decide the best order for accomplishing these steps, and identify who is responsible for each step. All four steps are accomplished with computers and electronic brainstorming software.[62]

Studies show that electronic brainstorming is much more productive than face-to-face brainstorming. Compared to regular four-person brainstorming groups, the same-sized electronic brainstorming groups produce 25 percent to 50 percent more ideas. Compared to regular 12-person brainstorming groups, the same-sized electronic brainstorming groups produce 200 percent more ideas! In fact, because production blocking (i.e., waiting your turn) is not a problem for electronic brainstorming, the number and quality of ideas generally increases with group size.[63]

Even though it works much better than traditional brainstorming, electronic brainstorming has disadvantages, too. An obvious problem is the expense of computers, networks, software, and so on. As these costs continue to drop, however, electronic brainstorming will become cheaper.

Another problem is that the anonymity of ideas may bother people who are used to having their ideas accepted by virtue of their position (i.e., the boss). On the other hand, one CEO said, "Because the process is anonymous, the sky's the limit in terms of what you can say, and as a result it is more thought-provoking. As a CEO, you'll probably discover things you might not want to hear but need to be aware of."[64]

A third disadvantage is that outgoing individuals who are more comfortable expressing themselves verbally may find it difficult to express themselves in writing. Finally, the most obvious problem is that participants have to be able to type. Those who can't type, or who type slowly, may be easily frustrated and find themselves at a disadvantage to experienced typists. For example, one meeting facilitator was tipped off that an especially fast typist was pretending to be more than one person. Said the facilitator, "He'd type 'Oh, I agree' and then 'Ditto, ditto' or 'What a great idea,' all in quick succession, using different variations of uppercase and lowercase letters and punctuation. He tried to make it seem like a lot of people were concurring, but it was just him." Eventually, the person sitting next to him got suspicious and began watching his screen.[65]

Review 4: Using Groups to Improve Decision-Making

When groups view problems from several perspectives, use more information, have a diversity of knowledge and experience, and become committed to solutions they help choose, they can produce better solutions than individual decision makers. However, group decisions suffer from these disadvantages: groupthink, slowness, discussions dominated by just a few individuals, and unfelt responsibility for decisions. Group decisions work best when group members encourage c-type conflict. However, group decisions don't work as well when groups become mired in a-type conflict. The devil's-advocacy and dialectical-inquiry approaches improve group decisions because they bring structured c-type conflict into the decision-making process. By contrast, the nominal group technique and the Delphi technique both improve decision-making by reducing a-type conflict through limited interactions between group members. The stepladder technique improves group decision-making by adding each group member's independent contributions to the discussion one at a time. Finally, because it overcomes the problems of production blocking and evaluation apprehension, electronic brainstorming is a more effective method of generating alternatives than face-to-face brainstorming.

What Really Happened?[66]

The cleanliness of the rational decision-making model (defining the problem, defining and weighting decision criteria, generating and evaluating alternative courses of action, and computing the optimal decision) rarely matches up with the messiness of real-world decision-making. Indeed, at the beginning of this chapter, you heard one manager say, "I just know how disillusioning and frustrating it is to be hit with problems and conflicts all day and not be able to solve them very cleanly." In 1996 Inco was faced with a difficult decision. The company's nickel production had been flat for 10 years and its stock price was almost at the same level it had been 20 years earlier. It had already invested over $500 million in a 25 percent stake in the Voisey's Bay project and was looking at a bidding war to purchase more.

Is management willing to purchase more of Voisey's Bay? Risk propensity is a person's tendency to take or avoid risks. And it usually takes an individual with a high risk propensity to be willing to take risks under conditions of uncertainty.

In most situations, managers make decisions under conditions of risk, with a very real possibility of losing (making the wrong decision). Thus, risk and risky conditions make it difficult for managers to make completely rational, optimal decisions. If Inco purchases controlling interest in Voisey's Bay and everything goes according to plan, production could start as early as 1999. On the other hand, the demands of the provincial government, the Innu and Inuit peoples, and environmental and public hearings could delay the project, significantly increasing costs, or could even scuttle the project entirely, thereby rendering the entire project worthless. The rational decision-making model assumes that managers can gaze into crystal balls and accurately predict whether a potential solution will fix a problem. The model also assumes that managers make decisions under conditions of certainty, with complete information and knowledge of all possible outcomes and their likelihood. Under those assumptions, it should be easy to demonstrate that investing in Voisey's Bay is the right thing to do. In fact, under conditions of certainty (you know precisely whether various alternatives will work), it should be self-evident what course of action you should take. Clearly, given the level of uncertainty, this is not the case. In the end, Inco purchased Voisey's Bay outright for an additional cost of about $4.5 billion. In many ways, this is just where the story begins.

Bounded rationality recognizes that in the real world, managers' decision-making processes are restricted by limited resources, incomplete and imperfect information, and managers' limited decision-making capabilities. These limitations often prevent managers from being rational decision makers. So do common decision-making mistakes, such as overreliance on intuition, and the availability, representative, and anchoring and adjustment biases.

The rational decision-making model assumes that decisions are made under conditions of certainty. However, most managerial decisions are made under conditions of risk, where there is limited information and knowledge, and a very real chance of making a bad decision. Soon after buying Voisey's Bay, it looked like Inco had made a bad decision—a very bad decision. Everything that could go wrong probably did. In 1997, a protest by the Innu and Inuit against the building of an airstrip and a road to the site turned from peaceful to violent. For two days demonstrators threw rocks at police, broke windows, and cut power lines. Two days later, a court enjoined the company from proceeding any further with construction work. Negotiation with Aboriginal groups over land claims compensation had essentially ground to a halt and the price of nickel was falling. It had been as high as US$6.25 a pound in early 1995 but was now just barely over US$4. Then the provincial government became insistent that the company had to build a smelter in the province, despite the fact that doing so was becoming increasingly uneconomic as the price of nickel fell. And the price kept falling—it had fallen to about US$1.70 a pound in late 1998, rendering a smelter uneconomic and maybe making the entire project uneconomic. Also, after further testing, the company had discovered that the mineral deposits were smaller than they originally thought. The price of its stock had fallen 65 percent, from a high of $50 down to $15, and it was looking like the company would have to take a massive write-down in the value of Voisey's Bay.

It wasn't until 2002, after the price of nickel had recovered substantially, and after lengthy and acrimonious negotiations with the provincial government that it was decided that Inco would build a mill concentrator in Argentia, Newfoundland. About the same time the company came to an agreement over compensation to the Aboriginal groups with land claims in the area, and the company was finally able to address environmental concerns.

Despite all the problems, the Voisey's Bay project finally began production in late 2005 (six years late!) and with the price of nickel hovering above the US$7 mark, the decision to buy and develop Voisey's Bay looks like a good one. Nickel demand, driven in a large part by China's phenomenal economic growth, is growing and it appears that it will be strong for years to come. Only time will really tell whether or not it was a good decision, but at the time of writing it looks like a very good decision despite the rocky, almost disastrous, start. Clearly, the stock market likes Inco's position, as the stock price has rebounded from its low of $15 and has traded over $90 in 2006.

Key Terms

absolute comparisons *(155)*
anchoring and adjustment bias *(163)*
a-type conflict (affective conflict) *(171)*
availability bias *(163)*
bounded rationality *(158)*
brainstorming *(174)*
conditions of certainty *(160)*
conditions of risk *(160)*
conditions of uncertainty *(161)*
c-type conflict (cognitive conflict) *(171)*
decision criteria *(154)*
decision-making *(152)*
decision rule *(164)*
Delphi technique *(173)*
devil's advocacy *(171)*
dialectical inquiry *(172)*
dictionary rule *(165)*
electronic brainstorming *(175)*
escalation of commitment *(167)*
evaluation apprehension *(175)*
groupthink *(170)*
information overload *(158)*
maximizing *(159)*
minimum threshold rule *(165)*
multivariable testing (MVT) *(165)*
negative frame *(161)*
nominal group technique *(173)*
positive frame *(160)*
problem *(154)*
production blocking *(175)*
rational decision-making *(152)*
relative comparisons *(156)*
representative bias *(163)*
risk propensity *(161)*
satisficing *(159)*
stepladder technique *(174)*

Self-Assessment

CHECK YOUR DECISION-MAKING SKILLS

When you face problems, do you usually try to act promptly, or do you delay as long as possible? When pressed for a decision, do you often act too hastily, or do you seem to function best when under pressure? Do you often agonize both before and after making important decisions, or do you deal with such decisions calmly with no subsequent brooding?

The ability to make decisions sensibly, calmly, and with reasonable speed is helpful in any aspect of life, and especially so for managers. One way to distinguish between good and inadequate managers is by the way they cope with decision-making. Effective, reasonable, and prompt decision-making is important to win the respect of one's superiors and subordinates.

To gain insights into your decision-making skills, do the assessment on page 514 of the Assessment Appendix. Answer yes or no to each question. To ensure an accurate score and to receive feedback that is applicable to you, truthfully answer the questions—even though you know which answers will increase your score.

Management Decisions

SUGAR-FREE KOOL-AID: LET'S BRAINSTORM!

What comes to mind when you think of Kool-Aid? Summer? Pool parties and picnics? Third grade? Kool-pops that you made, poured into moulds, and froze in the freezer? Was one of these flavours your favourite: Black Cherry, Cherry, Grape, Incrediberry, Kickin'-Kiwi-Lime, Lemonade, Lemon-Lime, Man-o-Mangoberry, Oh-Yeah Orange-Pineapple, Orange, Pina-Pineapple, Pink Lemonade, Pink Swimmingo, Purplesaurus Rex, Raspberry, Rock-a-dile Red, Slammin' Strawberry-Kiwi, Strawberry, Strawberry-Raspberry, Tropical Punch, or Watermelon-Cherry?

When most people think of Kool-Aid, they think of kids. Just over a decade ago, Kool-Aid sales started to decline. In part, this was due to long-term demographic changes. Families were simply having fewer children. Since the makers of Kool-Aid obviously couldn't do anything to change demographic trends, the next best thing was to encourage groups other than kids, such as teens and adults, to drink more Kool-Aid. With the explosion in popularity of diet drinks, the answer seemed simple: Sugar-Free Kool-Aid. However, Kool-Aid's management knew that it would still have a tough time convincing teens and adults to make Sugar-Free Kool-Aid their drink of choice. So, to figure out how they might do this, Kool-Aid sponsored a contest for MBA students at major business schools. MBA student teams submitted their ideas, and the teams with the most promising proposals were flown to New York to make formal presentations. Unfortunately, their suggestions were not very creative. Kool-Aid management was extremely disappointed with the results.

The purpose of this in-class management-decision activity is to correct that problem by using brainstorming to generate as many ideas as possible for selling Sugar-Free Kool-Aid to teens and adults. Keep in mind the following rules of brainstorming:

- The more ideas, the better.
- All ideas are acceptable, no matter how wild or crazy they might be.

- Other group members' ideas should be used to come up with even more ideas.
- Criticism or evaluation of ideas is not allowed.

Remember, creativity requires playfulness. Make this fun! Be wild and crazy! And, most important, don't criticize others' ideas. No moaning, groaning, or commenting allowed (or aloud). The first step in brainstorming is to generate as many different ideas as possible. Evaluation comes later.

Question

1. Think of as many ways as possible to get teens and adults to buy and use Sugar-Free Kool-Aid.

Management Decisions

CAFETERIA OR GYM?[67]

Due to a record-breaking year, your company posted profits 24 percent above analysts' expectations. In an attempt to retain qualified employees and to continue to provide an atmosphere of innovation and creativity, a decision was made to allot $1 million of retained earnings toward improving employee incentives. Upon announcing the program, a memo was circulated describing the rationale behind this decision. The memo encouraged employees to submit proposals for ideas regarding the type of incentives to spend money on. A minimum threshold rule was imposed on all proposals to be submitted. In order to be considered, the proposal must provide a tangible return for the organization through an increase in productivity, aesthetic beauty, functionality, morale, or profitability. Additionally, the proposal must benefit a majority of stakeholders within the company.

A total of 36 ideas were submitted. After analyzing each of the proposals, determining their feasibility, and weighing them against the minimum threshold rule, 10 ideas were chosen to be further reviewed, discussed, and ranked. Several meetings were held discussing the pros and cons of each proposal, and a second memo was circulated asking all employees to rank the proposals from least to most desired. The results showed that the two proposals favoured most by employees appear to be the construction of a cafeteria and the construction of a gymnasium/workout centre. Both ideas received an equal ranking of importance. You have been chosen to decide which proposal should be implemented.

The cafeteria, as described in the proposal, would include both working and nonworking areas for employees. The working areas would have, in addition to the normal tables and chairs, erasable marker boards, flipcharts, networked computer workstations and projection devices, telephones, and teleconferencing equipment. The nonworking area, separated by a glass partition, would house the normal tables and chairs, along with a big-screen television and a CD-jukebox. The cafeteria would serve a daily special in addition to "on-demand" items, such as hamburgers, hot dogs, salads, burritos, and other common food items. Food would be provided at a reduced price for all employees. Additionally, employees who regularly take clients and representatives out for business lunches would be allowed to charge their meals to their expense account, thus providing a savings for the company through reduced meal expenses.

Proponents of this plan claim that innovativeness, creativity, and profitability would be increased because most employees (whether they realize it or not) would be inclined to discuss work-related matters during their lunch hour. By assembling diverse groups of employees in a common area, these discussions could evolve into new projects or the improvement of existing ones. Having technology-enhanced components available in the working area would provide employees with the tools necessary to perform further research of their ideas during active discussions. The ideas could then be presented and discussed on markerboards or through the computer's LCD projector. Proponents also stated that the cafeteria could improve employee morale since having an on-site cafeteria would reduce the hassle of fighting traffic and crowds during the lunch-time rush and would increase productivity by ensuring that employees do not spend more than their allotted time during lunch.

The proposed gymnasium/workout centre would include a half-court basketball area with goal, two racquetball courts, and a complete workout area, containing items such as Stairmasters, rowing machines, stationary bikes, Nautilus equipment, locker rooms, showers, and hot tubs. Proponents of this plan state that employee morale and productivity would be enhanced as studies show that exercise helps eliminate stress and boosts energy levels. Proponents further claim that the increased productivity would, in time, translate into increased profits for the firm. In addition, healthier employees would reduce health insurance costs over the long run. To avoid congestion, time slots for the use of the workout centre would be available by reservation. In order not to affect work time, employees would be encouraged to use the workout centre before work, during their lunch break, or after work.

Questions

1. If you were the manager in question, which proposal would you choose to implement and why?
2. Looking back at the proposal not chosen, did you fall prey to one of the common decision-making mistakes (intuition, availability bias, representative bias, or anchoring and adjustment bias) in not choosing this proposal? Explain.

Develop Your Management Potential

MAKING BETTER DECISIONS[68]

Modern research shows that managers who make the best decisions don't overanalyze things by relying on rational decision-making models, nor do they oversimplify them by relying solely on their intuition. Instead, many managers utilize a concept referred to as "recognitional decision-making." Recognitional decision-making leads to quicker decisions than rational decision-making because it integrates the use of memory in connection with the context of a situation in order to develop an immediate feel of the current situation. Recurrences from previous experiences help provide sample solutions to current problems. Managers then subconsciously combine these recurrences with their intuition and imagination to help develop potential solutions for the current dilemma. Once a manager has a potential solution(s) in mind, he or she then begins to practise a mental game to see how the situation will play out. This approach is often compared to the strategies used by professional chess players when analyzing their next move. Professional chess players calculate each possible move and the subsequent move(s) of their opponents in their heads. By analyzing the opponent's expected move, chess players narrow their options for moves until one results in the best possible option (or least negative consequence), given the current situation. Unfortunately, making good decisions, like becoming a master chess player, requires a lot of experience and practice. Managers and potential managers can improve their decision-making skills by practising the following activities.

First, define your decision criteria for a given situation. For example, if when making decisions under the pressure of a deadline, you often underestimate the length of time it takes to accomplish a task, you should begin by dissecting the situation to see if certain patterns exist. By knowing the components of the decision and by determining which components give you the most trouble, chances are that you can determine the best approach to simplify your choices should this type of decision recur. To reinforce your decision-making ability, intentionally place yourself into situations where these commonalities exist. Doing so will provide further experience and help strengthen your decision-making ability.

Second, obtain feedback regarding current and previous decisions you have made. For example, if part of your job involves scheduling tasks, you can obtain feedback concerning your decisions by logging the expected time to complete a task and comparing that to the actual time taken. Analyzing the factors that contributed to the difference will help you recall them in the future, thus increasing your accuracy. Keep in mind that in most cases, feedback will not occur on its own; it has to be collected.

Third, practise decision-making by reading case studies of actual problems and placing yourself in the shoes of the decision maker. This textbook reinforces this approach by offering a "What Would You Do?" case scenario for each chapter. The scenarios build on information presented in the text and discuss current problems of real-world situations. By comparing your answer to the "What Really Happened" answer, you can determine your decision-making ability and see if you understood and retained the information from the chapter.

Fourth, practise decision-making under conditions of uncertainty. Recall some previous decisions that you have made. Was uncertainty present, and if so, how did you handle it? What steps did you take, or could you have taken, that would have helped reduce the uncertainty or ambiguity involved?

Lastly, improve recognitional decision-making by using the expertise of others. If you respect and admire others for their ability to make quick, competent decisions, approach those people and ask them how they were able to arrive at their decisions. Also, ask what clues directed them to the solution that they chose.

Making decisions is a skill not unlike many other skills you have learned. The more you practise, the better decisions you will make. As your skill progresses, you'll notice that you now quickly and effortlessly make decisions that previously caused you grief. Additionally, you will be able to recognize patterns and recall potential solutions due to your increased decision-making experience.

Exercise

Recall a tough decision involving conditions of uncertainty that you recently made. Some examples include finding a roommate, buying a car, or picking your classes for next semester. The decision you select for this exercise should be one that you felt could have been improved. Analyze that decision using the five activities discussed above. After you analyze the decision, determine what steps you might take in the future to improve your decision-making ability, should this type of situation arise again.

Discussion Questions

1. What are the costs and benefits of planning? Give examples of situations when planning has been either advantageous or disadvantageous.
2. If you were buying a new car, what decision criteria would you rely on and why?
3. What is the relationship among bounded rationality, satisficing, and information overload? Give examples where bounded rationality, satisficing and information overload have affected decisions you have made.
4. Define and give examples of common decision-making mistakes (intuition, availability bias, representative bias, or anchoring and adjustment bias).

Critical Thinking Video Case

CBC

Visit www.management2e.nelson.com to view this chapter's CBC video case.

Take Two

Biz Flix
The Bourne Identity

Jason Bourne (Matt Damon) cannot remember who he is, but others believe he is an international assassin. Bourne tries to learn his identity with the help of his new friend and lover Marie (Franka Potente). Meanwhile, while CIA agents pursue him across Europe trying to kill him, Bourne slowly discovers that he is an extremely well-trained and lethal agent. The story is loosely based on Robert Ludlum's 1981 novel. This scene is an edited version of the "Bourne's Game" sequence near the end of the film. Jason Bourne kills the hired assassin who tried to kill him the day after Jason and Marie arrived at the home of Eamon (Tim Dutton). Eamon is Marie's friend but is a stranger to Jason. Jason uses the dead man's cell phone after returning to his apartment in Paris, France. He presses the redial button, which connects him to Conklin (Chris Cooper), the CIA manager who is looking for him. Listen carefully to Jason's conversation with Conklin.

What to Watch for and Ask Yourself

1. Does Bourne employ the steps of the rational decision-making process in coming up with his plan in relation to Conklin? Why or why not?
2. Are there conditions of risk inherent in Bourne's plan? What are they?
3. Did Bourne make any common decision-making mistakes in this scenario? Explain your answer.

Management Workplace
Community Insurance Center

Planning is a crucial part of solid business practices. That's not to say that you won't be successful if you don't plan, but planning can bring clarity and focus to your operation. Community Insurance Center was launched in 1962 in a suburb of Chicago, and over the company's history, owner Milton Moses has had numerous opportunities to make decisions.

What to Watch for and Ask Yourself

1. At one point, Milton Moses fired roughly 70 percent of his staff. Using the steps to rational decision-making outlined in the chapter, re-create the process Moses likely used to make this risky decision.

Activity

1. Use the decision regarding the music and headphones as a base for practising the devil's advocacy approach to group decision-making. Put together a team of four to five students and assign one team member to play Milton Moses in the role of devil's advocate, arguing for quiet so people can concentrate. Compare the outcome of your group decision with what happened at Community Insurance.

MARCOS TOWNSEND/BLOOMBERG NEWS/LANDOV

Control

Chapter 7

CHAPTER OUTLINE

LEARNING OBJECTIVES

After reading this chapter, you should be able to

1 describe the basic control process.

2 discuss the various methods that managers can use to maintain control.

3 describe the behaviours, processes, and outcomes that managers are choosing to control in today's organizations.

Control is a word that is used in many contexts. A teenager might think of his or her parents when the word is mentioned. A prisoner might think of a jail guard if asked about what control means. Control might come to the mind of a referee when stepping on to the ice before a hockey game. A jockey might also have thoughts of control as the gate opens to start a horse race.[1]

In the world of corporations and organizations, control can also mean different things. As defined in the following pages, it can refer to "a regulatory process of establishing standards that will achieve organizational goals, comparing actual performance to those standards, and then, if necessary, taking corrective action to restore performance to those standards." In practice, means of control include top-down hierarchies, regulating worker results or behaviour with rewards and incentives, shaping the belief and values of individuals, allowing groups or teams to create norms, and self-management by individuals. What can be controlled? Well, looking ahead in this text, answers include financial performance, economic value added, customer defections, and product and service quality.

What Would You Do?

But, do all managers think of control in these terms? Picture yourself as a member of a senior management team. You have worked for 20 years to get to where you are. As part of a team, you and your colleagues have been offered a vote of confidence by shareholders and the board of directors to guide the corporation and its many employees. The task is simple. Keep the share price moving in accordance with analyst predictions and everything will be all right. Well, maybe not.

Analyst predictions originate in the marketplace. The market has its own means of controlling behaviour and performance. That means takes the form of takeovers or acquisitions. It is termed the market for *corporate control*. How can it be explained? We asked Karyn Brooks, controller of Bell Canada Enterprises (BCE), the same questions. Her thoughts are timely given BCE's history:

> The company was started originally in 1880 as Bell Canada as a result of Alexander Graham Bell's invention of telephony. At the time it just provided local telephone service. It now provides local and long-distance services, wireless services, paging services, high-speed Internet, dial-up Internet, and satellite television. The development of Internet protocol or IP technology platforms has allowed it to deliver most of those services over an IP platform while also allowing other companies to enter its business arena. These include cable companies offering local telephone services. Historically, Bell Canada and the other incumbent telecommunications providers have never had the competition they now do from these cable companies.

If you were trying to maintain control of Bell Canada, what would you do?

control
a regulatory process of establishing standards to achieve organizational goals, comparing actual performance against the standards, and taking corrective action, when necessary

Control is a regulatory process of establishing standards that will achieve organizational goals, comparing actual performance to those standards, and then, if necessary, taking corrective action to restore performance to those standards.

Control is achieved when behaviour and work procedures conform to standards, and company goals are accomplished.[2] For example, control at airport security has become tighter as authorities try to guarantee the goal of personal safety of the flying public by making sure strict security procedures are followed. To review, making things happen is a function of planning what you want to accomplish (Chapter 4), gathering and managing the information needed to make good decisions (Chapter 5), deciding how to achieve those plans (Chapter 6), and controlling behaviour and processes through preventive or corrective action (Chapter 7).

We begin this chapter by examining the basic control process used in organizations. In the second part of the chapter, we go beyond the basics to an in-depth examination of the different methods that companies use to achieve control. We finish the chapter by taking a look at the things that companies choose to control (e.g., finances, product quality, customer retention, etc.).

Basics of Control

If you wanted to control traffic speeds in your town, how would you do it? Well, most municipalities put in speed bumps, lower speed limits, put up traffic lights, or write more speeding tickets. However, the city of Culemborg in the Netherlands is planning to use sheep to slow down speeding cars on its neighbourhood streets. Why sheep? One of the city council members, who had observed the driving patterns on country roads in rural England, said, "After all, it's impossible to speed past the sheep [in the middle of the road] if you drive in the Yorkshire Dales." When animal rights groups complained that this was a bad idea, the city responded by erecting a special kind of fence to prevent the sheep from wandering onto busier, high-speed roads where they would clearly be endangered. However, Culemborg's city leaders were apparently not familiar with the tradition of some Yorkshire locals who "accidentally" hit sheep, hoping to make off with a free supply of lamb chops.[3] The city plans to release five or six sheep at first. If motorists actually do slow down, as many as 100 sheep may eventually be released onto city streets.

After reading the next section, you should be able to

1 describe the basic control process.

1 THE CONTROL PROCESS

The basic control process involves standards; comparison to standards; corrective action; dynamic process; and feedback, concurrent, and feedforward control.

Standards

standards
a basis of comparison when measuring the extent to which various kinds of organizational performances are satisfactory or unsatisfactory

The control process begins when managers set goals, such as satisfying 90 percent of customers, or increasing sales by 5 percent. Companies then specify the performance standards that must be met to accomplish those goals. **Standards** are a basis of comparison for measuring the extent to which organizational performance is satisfactory or unsatisfactory. For example, many pizzerias use 30 minutes as the standard for delivery times. Since anything longer than that is viewed as unsatisfactory, they'll typically reduce their prices if they can't deliver a hot pizza to you in 30 minutes or less.

So how do managers set standards? How do they decide which levels of performance are satisfactory and which are unsatisfactory? The first criterion for a good standard is that it must enable goal achievement. If you're meeting the standard, but still not achieving company goals, then the standard may have to be changed. Companies also determine standards by listening to customers or observing competitors. After receiving feedback from consumers that they were interested in machines that would automate routine household tasks, iRobot, a manufacturer of industrial and government (military) robots, created the Scooba, a robot that washes floors. Founder Colin Angle says, "People just hated to mop, so we saw a real opportunity."[4] The Scooba vacuums up dirt and debris, sprays a bleach cleaning solution, and then squeegees and sucks up the dirty water from the floor. At about $250, the Scooba can mop a typical kitchen in 45 minutes.

Standards can also be determined by benchmarking other companies. **Benchmarking** is the process of determining how well other companies (though typically not competitors) perform business functions or tasks. In other words, benchmarking is the process of determining other companies' standards. So the first step in setting standards is to determine what to benchmark. Companies can benchmark anything, from cycle time (how fast) to quality (how well). The next step is to identify the companies against which to benchmark your standards. Since this can require a significant commitment on the part of the benchmarked company, it can take time to identify and get agreement from them to be benchmarked. The last step is to collect data to determine other companies' performance standards. Sometimes data that can be used for benchmarking can be found from secondary sources (e.g., magazines or newspapers). For example, Certicom, a Mississauga, Ontario–based data encryption company, recently announced that its elliptic curve digital signatures algorithm (ECDSA), which is quickly becoming the U.S. and Canadian cryptographic standard used to verify electronic signatures, has shortened its verification time from 221 milliseconds to 158 milliseconds, a 40 percent improvement. Although this does not seem like a lot of time, if you are processing millions of transactions a day, this could significantly reduce costs by reducing the number or servers a company has to run. Other companies that wish to compete for data encryption business could set this as their benchmark standard.[5] Another method for setting standards is to look to external standard-setting processes. For example, this can be done by implementing the ISO 9000 series of standards, which is discussed in more detail in Chapter 14.

benchmarking
the process of identifying outstanding practices, processes, and standards in other companies and adapting them to your company

Comparison to Standards

The next step in the control process is to compare actual performance to performance standards. While this sounds straightforward, the quality of the comparison largely depends on the measurement and information systems a company uses to keep track of performance. The better the system, the easier it is for companies to track their progress and identify problems that need to be fixed.

For example, because it is so difficult to gather detailed information about how customers are treated when they interact with employees, retail stores and restaurants spend millions a year to hire "secret shoppers," who visit their stores or restaurants to determine whether their employees provide helpful customer service. In fact, the "secret shoppers" aren't shoppers at all. They're hired consultants who, acting like customers, make detailed observations of the service provided (or not) by employees. For instance, on visiting a grocery store, a "secret shopper" gave a bagboy positive points for hustle, but negative points for wearing his hat backwards. More negative points are tallied when the store clerk in the produce department fails to greet the "secret shopper," when a service counter employee is chewing gum, and when a cashier enters an incorrect price code for an item that the scanner couldn't pick up.[6] Companies such as Calgary-based Service Intelligence Inc. (www.serviceintelligence.com) specialize in providing secret shoppers to the retail and service sectors. In 2002, McDonald's signed the company on to help it improve its customer service, and Service Intelligence has

At Lululemon Athletica, head office employees work one day a week on the sales floor to increase customer feedback.

PHOTO: INDU GHUMAN

been sending secret shoppers to locations all over North America.[7] Vancouver-based Lululemon Athletica takes a novel approach. Most head office employees work one day a week on the sales floor of one of their retail outlets, thus allowing customer feedback to reach the head office very quickly.[8]

Corrective Action

The next step in the control process is to identify performance deviations, analyze those deviations, and then develop and implement programs to correct them. This is similar to the planning process discussed in Chapter 4: Regular, frequent performance feedback allows workers and managers to track their performance and make adjustments in effort, direction, and strategies. For example, Microsoft uses a program called Dr. Watson to generate feedback whenever something goes wrong on your Windows-based computer. You've probably seen it at one time or another. Something freezes up on your computer, and then a dialogue box pops up, asking if you want to send a report to Microsoft so they can use your information, along with information from others' computers, to figure out what went wrong. Microsoft used a version of Dr. Watson when developing its latest version of Microsoft Office software. Beta copies of Office went out to 600 000 testers, and the Dr. Watson feedback generated from problems they experienced prompted Microsoft to spend an additional three months working the bugs out of the software before releasing an official version for sale.[9]

Dynamic Process

As shown in Exhibit 7.1, control is a continuous, dynamic process. It begins with actual performance and measures of that performance. Managers then compare performance to the pre-established standards. If they identify deviations from standard performance, they analyze the deviations and develop corrective programs. Then implementing the programs (hopefully) achieves the desired performance. To maintain performance levels at standard, managers must repeat the entire process again and again in an endless feedback loop. So control is not a one-time achievement or result. It continues over time (a dynamic process) and requires daily, weekly, and monthly attention from managers.

For example, at Pepsi, when the weekly Nielsen numbers come in, indicating the popularity of the television shows on which Pepsi bought commercial time, 70 people immediately begin analyzing and questioning the numbers to see if Pepsi got the audiences it wanted for its advertising dollar. If it didn't, the company may cancel its advertising on shows that didn't measure up and purchase advertising time on shows that appear to hold more promise.[10]

Sure, it's a cliché, but it's just as true in business as it is in sports: If you take your eye off the ball, you're going to strike out. Control is an ongoing, dynamic process.

EXHIBIT 7.1
Cybernetic Control Process

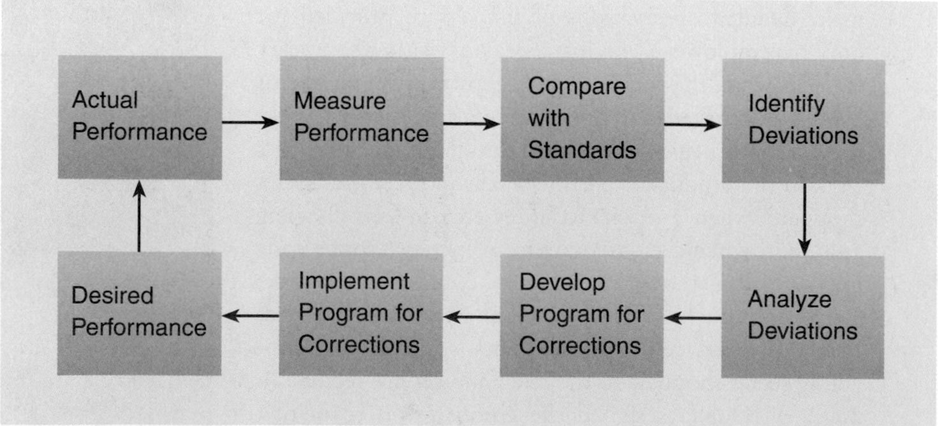

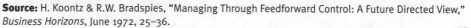

Source: H. Koontz & R.W. Bradspies, "Managing Through Feedforward Control: A Future Directed View," *Business Horizons*, June 1972, 25–36.

Feedback, Concurrent, and Feedforward Control

There are three basic control methods: feedback control, concurrent control, and feedforward control.[11] **Feedback control** is a mechanism for gathering information about performance deficiencies after they occur. This information is then used to correct or prevent performance deficiencies. Study after study has clearly shown that feedback improves both individual and organizational performance. In most instances, any feedback is better than no feedback. However, if there is a downside to feedback, it is that it sometimes occurs too late. Sometimes it comes after big mistakes have been made or after it is too late.

feedback control
a mechanism for gathering information about performance deficiencies after they occur

For example, 90 percent of the time an electrical transformer malfunctions on a neighbourhood utility pole, a squirrel caused the problem. Unfortunately, electrical utilities have had little success keeping squirrels away from their equipment. In general, utilities like Pepco Holdings, which experiences nearly a thousand squirrel-related outages a year, don't find out about the problem until after a squirrel stands atop a utility pole, touches a live wire, and fries itself and the transformer, creating a huge power surge that blows out computers, televisions, and appliances in nearby homes. Power goes out in the neighbourhood and customer complaints pour in with no advance warning. Sheila Frazier, a senior project manager for Energy Consulting Group LLC says, "You've got to drive forever to some place, replace the transformer—and the worst problem is you know in your heart it's a squirrel, but you don't often have a fried carcass to show anybody because predators have already snatched it, and customers are crying bloody murder."[12]

Concurrent control is a mechanism for gathering information about performance deficiencies as they occur. Thus, it is an improvement over feedback, because it attempts to eliminate or shorten the delay between performance and feedback about the performance. Aircraft manufacturers have recognized the importance of providing flight crews and maintenance personnel with more information about how their jets are running. Consequently, new-generation planes contain hundreds of computer sensors that airlines can use to monitor an airplane's systems while it is in flight. For instance, according to Lou Mancini, vice president of maintenance services for Boeing's Commercial Airplane Group, Boeing's Airplane Health Management service "is designed to increase the airplane's availability, since the carrier will be able to identify a problem [while the flight is in the air] and be prepared to fix it, as soon as the airplane arrives at the gate."[13]

concurrent control
a mechanism for gathering information about performance deficiencies as they occur, eliminating or shortening the delay between performance and feedback

Feedforward control is a mechanism for gathering information about performance deficiencies before they occur. In contrast to feedback and concurrent control, which provide feedback on the basis of outcomes and results, feedforward control provides information about performance deficiencies by monitoring inputs, not outputs. Thus, feedforward seeks to prevent or minimize performance deficiencies before they occur. In addition to using the Dr. Watson tool on your computer to provide feedback *after* customers have experienced problems on their computers, Microsoft also uses feedforward to try to prevent software problems *before* they occur. For example, when developing the latest version of its Windows Server software (for network and Internet computer servers), Microsoft taught 8500 experienced programmers new methods for writing more reliable software code *before* having them develop new features for Windows Server software. Microsoft has also developed new software testing tools that let each programmer thoroughly test the code they've written (i.e., input) before passing the code on to others to be used in beta and then final products.[14] Exhibit 7.2 lists guidelines that companies can follow to get the most out of feedforward control.

feedforward control
a mechanism for monitoring performance inputs rather than outputs to prevent or minimize performance deficiencies before they occur

Control Isn't Always Worthwhile or Possible

Control is achieved when behaviour and work procedures conform to standards and goals are accomplished. By contrast, **control loss** occurs when behaviour and work procedures do not conform to standards.[15] John Caudwell, owner of Phones4U, one of the United Kingdom's largest mobile phone chains, felt that his company had control loss with respect to e-mail. Managers and employees were averaging three hours per day on

control loss
situation in which behaviour and work procedures do not conform to standards

EXHIBIT 7.2
Guidelines for Using Feedforward Control

1.	Thorough planning and analysis are required.
2.	Careful discrimination must be applied in selecting input variables.
3.	The feedforward system must be kept dynamic.
4.	A model of the control system should be developed.
5.	Data on input variables must be regularly collected.
6.	Data on input variables must be regularly assessed.
7.	Feedforward control requires action.

Source: H. Koontz & R.W. Bradspies, "Managing Through Feedforward Control: A Future Directed View," *Business Horizons*, June 1972, 25–36.

e-mail and, according to Caudwell, not spending enough time with customers. So he completely banned e-mail. "The policy came from me. The staff was initially slightly shocked that I should make such a revolutionary move." Said Caudwell, "We have e-mail paralysis. If you have a cancer, you have to cut it out. That's what I've done."[16]

Maintaining control is important because control loss prevents goal achievement (in the Phones4U example, not spending enough time with customers). When control loss occurs, managers need to find out what, if anything, they could have done to prevent it. Usually, as just discussed, that means identifying deviations from standard performance, analyzing the causes of those deviations, and taking corrective action. Implementing controls, however, isn't always worthwhile or possible. For example, it's debatable whether, in the long run, Phones4U's e-mail ban is a net plus or minus for the company. Indeed, Tanno Massar, director of media relations at TPG, a logistics company, said, "It would be a serious setback for the company if we could no longer use e-mail, and we are not considering it."[17] Let's look at regulation costs and cybernetic feasibility to see why implementing controls isn't always worthwhile or possible.

regulation costs
the costs associated with implementing or maintaining control.

To determine whether control is worthwhile, managers need to carefully assess **regulation costs**—that is, whether the costs and unintended consequences of control exceed its benefits. For example, one of the reasons that the number of U.S. pharmaceutical companies producing major vaccines has dropped significantly is that the *cost of controlling* legal risk (through liability insurance and in-house legal staffs) is just too high. In the 1960s, 37 U.S. companies produced 380 licensed vaccines. In 1984, 15 U.S. companies produced 88 licensed vaccines. Today, because of legal costs, just five U.S. companies produce vaccines.[18] As a result, parents and doctors face severe shortages in 8 of the 11 recommended vaccines that prevent children from contracting diseases like diphtheria, tetanus, whooping cough, measles, mumps, rubella, and chickenpox.[19] Before choosing to implement control, managers should be confident that the benefits exceed the costs.

An often-overlooked factor in determining the cost of control is the set of *unintended consequences* that sometimes accompany increased control. Control systems help companies, managers, and workers accomplish their goals, but at the same time that control systems help solve some problems, they can create others. Hewlett-Packard (H-P) became the market leader by manufacturing high-quality, reliable computer printers. But, as competition grew and prices dropped, H-P printers grew relatively more expensive for consumers, and H-P began losing market share. The problem was that H-P, where product quality and functionality always came first, was overengineering its printers. They were too expensive because they were made too well. To convince H-P's computer engineers that this was the problem, manager Tom Alexander put a $150 H-P printer on a conference table and then stood on top of it. His point? Consumers want printers that print, so don't add unnecessary costs by making them strong enough to use as step stools.[20]

cybernetic feasibility
the extent to which it is possible to implement each step in the control process

Another factor to consider is **cybernetic feasibility**, the extent to which it is possible to implement each step in the control process: clear standards of performance, comparison of performance to standards, and corrective action. If one or more steps cannot be implemented, then maintaining effective control may be difficult or impossible. For example, in 2004 Visa Canada and MasterCard Canada wrote off $163.2 million in fraudulent credit card transactions. Almost two hundred thousand of the more than one million credit cards reported lost or stolen in Canada were used fraudulently. In response to this well-known problem, merchants and card issuers have been building and installing a new system to stem credit and debit card fraud. These "smart" cards will replace magnetic strips with computer chips. The chips have their own operating system, software, and memory. These new cards provide much greater security and will hopefully significantly reduce debit and credit card fraud.[21]

Review 1: The Control Process

The first step in the control process is to set goals and performance standards and comparing actual performance to performance standards. The better a company's information and measurement systems, the easier it is to make these comparisons. The control process continues by identifying and analyzing performance deviations, and then developing and implementing programs for corrective action. However, control is a continuous, dynamic process, not a one-time achievement or result. Control requires frequent managerial attention. The three basic control methods are feedback control (after-the-fact performance information), concurrent control (simultaneous performance information), and feedforward control (preventive performance information). Control, however, has regulation costs and unanticipated consequences, and isn't always possible.

How and What to Control

Midnight-shift employees at about 10 percent of Sam's Club and Wal-Mart stores are locked in to keep out robbers, and some say, to also prevent employee theft. Mona Williams, Wal-Mart's vice president for communications, said, "Wal-Mart secures these stores just as any other business does that has employees working overnight. Doors are locked to protect associates and the store from intruders."[22] However, many employees dislike the policy. Michael Rodriguez, whose ankle was injured at 3 A.M. and who had to wait an hour for a store manager to show up to unlock the doors, said, "Being locked in in an emergency like that, that's not right."[23] Wal-Mart's Mona Williams responded,

© JAMES LEYNSE/CORBIS

Wal-Mart locks employees in their stores to prevent robberies.

saying, "Fire doors are always accessible [and unlocked from the inside] for safety, and there will always be at least one manager in the store with a set of keys to unlock the doors."[24]

If you managed a Wal-Mart store, would you lock-in your midnight employees? Would doing so jeopardize or improve their safety? Kmart, Sears, Home Depot, and Costco don't lock in employees, so is Wal-Mart's policy overly restrictive? Or is it a reasonable response to preventing employee theft, which can often exceed a store's profits. Regarding the lock-in practice, former Sam's Club manager Tom Lewis says, "They're concerned about the bottom line, and the bottom line is affected by shrinkage in the store."[25] If you were a Wal-Mart or Sam's Club store manager, what would you do?

After reading the next two sections, you should be able to

2 discuss the various methods that managers can use to maintain control.

3 describe the behaviours, processes, and outcomes that managers are choosing to control in today's organizations.

2 CONTROL METHODS

There are five different methods that managers can use to achieve control in their organizations: bureaucratic control, objective control, normative control, concertive control, and self-control.

Bureaucratic Control

bureaucratic control use of hierarchical authority to influence employee behaviour by rewarding or punishing employees for compliance or noncompliance with organizational policies, rules, and procedures

When most people think of managerial control, what they have in mind is bureaucratic control. **Bureaucratic control** is top-down control, in which managers try to influence employee behaviour by rewarding or punishing employees for compliance or noncompliance with organizational policies, rules, and procedures. However, most employees would argue that bureaucratic managers emphasize punishment for noncompliance much more than rewards for compliance. For instance, when visiting the company's regional offices and managers, the president of a training company, who was known for his temper and for micromanaging others, would get some toilet paper from the restrooms and aggressively ask, "What's this?" When the managers answered, "Toilet paper," he would scream that it was two-ply toilet paper that the company couldn't afford. When told of a cracked toilet seat in one of the women's restrooms, he said, "If you don't like sitting on that seat, you can stand up like I do!"[26]

Ironically, bureaucratic management and control were created to prevent just this type of managerial behaviour. By encouraging managers to apply well-thought-out rules, policies, and procedures in an impartial, consistent manner to everyone in the organization, bureaucratic control is supposed to make companies more efficient, effective, and fair. Perversely, it frequently has just the opposite effect. Managers who use bureaucratic control often put following the rules above all else. When an employee collapsed from chest pains, her boss, fearing a heart attack, helped carry her to an ambulance. Yet, when the employee was thankfully diagnosed with indigestion and not a heart attack and returned to work several hours later, her boss filed a disciplinary action accusing her of an unexcused absence. Employees complained to the company CEO, who then took steps to correct the situation. The boss subsequently apologized to the employee and to his entire 25-person staff, explaining that he was wrong for taking the company's absence policy "too literally."[27]

Another characteristic of bureaucratically controlled companies is that due to their rule- and policy-driven decision-making, they are highly resistant to change and slow to respond to customers and competitors. Even Max Weber, the German philosopher who is largely credited with popularizing bureaucratic ideals in the late 19th century, referred to bureaucracy as the "iron cage." He said, "Once fully established, bureaucracy is among those social structures which are the hardest to destroy."[28]

Objective Control

In many companies, bureaucratic control has evolved into **objective control**, which is the use of observable measures of employee behaviour or outputs to assess performance and influence behaviour. Objective control differs from bureaucratic control in that managers focus on the observation or measurement of worker behaviour or outputs rather than policies and rules. For example, determining whether sales representatives filed expense reports within 30 days, as specified by company policy, is an example of bureaucratic control, while measuring whether they met their sales quotas or returned phone calls in a timely manner is an example of objective control. There are two kinds of objective control: behaviour control and output control. Total quality management (TQM) and various statistical quality control techniques can be used to objectively measure organizational performance. These topics are dealt with in Chapter 14.

objective control
use of observable measures of worker behaviour or outputs to assess performance and influence behaviour

Behaviour control is the regulation of the behaviours and actions that workers perform on the job. The basic assumption of behaviour control is that if you do the right things (i.e., the right behaviours) every day, then those things should lead to goal achievement. However, behaviour control is still management-based, which means that managers are responsible for monitoring, rewarding, and punishing workers for exhibiting desired or undesired behaviours. Companies that use global positioning satellite (GPS) technology to track where workers are and what they're doing are using behaviour control. For example, after getting complaints that his officers weren't always on the job, Sergeant John Kuczynsky quietly put GPS tracking devices in his officers' cars. Contrary to reports written by the officers indicating they were patrolling streets or using radar to catch speeding drivers, GPS tracking software soon showed that five officers were sitting for long periods in parking lots or taking long breaks for meals. All five are now barred from law-enforcement jobs.[30] Likewise, some organizations, worried that employees are wasting time on nonproductive behaviours, are removing Solitaire and Mine Sweeper games from employees' computers. Why do so? Because research shows that half the time that employees use computers they're playing games, gambling, or shopping on the Internet.[31]

behaviour control
regulation of the behaviours and actions that workers perform on the job

output control
regulation of worker results or outputs through rewards and incentives

Instead of measuring what managers and workers do, **output control** measures the results of their efforts. Whereas behaviour control regulates, guides, and measures how workers behave on the job, output control gives managers and workers the freedom to behave as they see fit as long as it leads to the accomplishment of prespecified, measurable results. Output control is often coupled with rewards and incentives. However, three things must occur for output control and rewards to lead to improved business results.

First, output control measures must be reliable, fair, and accurate. Second, employees and managers must believe that they can produce the desired results. Third, the rewards or incentives tied to outcome control measures must truly be dependent on achieving established standards of performance. For example, it seems that each year *The Globe and Mail* or *Canadian Business* runs a story about some CEO who racked up another multimillion-dollar bonus. Nonetheless, this is not always the case. Hank Swartout, CEO of Precision Drilling, Canada's largest oilfield services company, received no bonus in 2002 after receiving a $2.2 million bonus in 2001. His bonus is tied to a strict formula based on company earnings and return on capital. Because company performance was poor, he received no bonus in 2002.[32] So for output control to work with rewards, the rewards must truly be at risk if performance doesn't measure up.

DOING THE RIGHT THING

DON'T CHEAT ON TRAVEL EXPENSE REPORTS

Workers are often tempted to pad their travel expense reports. As one put it, "After a while you feel that they owe it to ya, so the hell with 'em. I'm going to expense it." Frank Navran of the Ethics Resource Center says that people justify this by telling themselves, "I'm not really stealing from the company—I'm just getting back what I feel I'm entitled to." However, Joel Richards, executive vice president and chief administrative officer of El Paso Corporation, says, "You learn a lot about people from their expense reports. If you can't trust an employee to be truthful on an expense report, if you can't trust them with small dollars, how can you trust them with making decisions involving millions of dollars?" So, do the right thing, don't cheat on your travel expense reports.[29]

Normative Control

normative control regulation of workers' behaviour and decisions through widely shared organizational values and beliefs

Rather than monitoring rules, behaviour, or outputs, another way to control what goes on in organizations is to shape the beliefs and values of the people who work there through normative control. With **normative controls**, a company's widely shared values and beliefs guide workers' behaviour and decisions. For example, at Mountain Equipment Co-op (MEC), an outdoor equipment retailer based in Vancouver, one value permeates the entire work force from top to bottom: environmental responsibility.[33] MEC (www.mec.ca) builds environmentally friendly buildings and used salvage materials when building a new store in Winnipeg. It also monitors the safety and environmental practices of its suppliers and prints its catalogue on recycled paper.

Normative controls are created in two ways. First, companies that use normative controls are very careful about whom they hire. While many companies screen potential applicants on the basis of their abilities, normatively controlled companies are just as likely to screen potential applicants based on their attitudes and values. For example, the CEO of MEC, Peter Robinson, was a park ranger in British Columbia, indicating his interest in the environment began before his stint as president of MEC. Second, with normative controls, managers and employees learn what they should and should not do by observing experienced employees and by listening to the stories they tell about the company.

Concertive Control

concertive control regulation of workers' behaviour and decisions through work group values and beliefs

Whereas normative controls are based on the strongly held, widely shared beliefs throughout a company, **concertive controls** are based on beliefs that are shaped and negotiated by work groups.[34] So while normative controls are driven by strong organizational cultures, concertive controls usually arise when companies give autonomous work groups

Mountain Equipment Co-op's store in Winnipeg is partly built from salvaged materials, an example of its environmental responsibility.

COURTESY OF MOUNTAIN EQUIPMENT CO-OP

complete responsibility for task completion. **Autonomous work groups** are groups that operate without managers and are completely responsible for controlling work group processes, outputs, and behaviour. These groups do their own hiring, firing, worker discipline, work schedules, materials ordering, budget making and meeting, and decision-making.

autonomous work groups groups that operate without managers and are completely responsible for controlling work group processes, outputs, and behaviour

Concertive control is not established overnight. Autonomous work groups evolve through two phases as they develop concertive control. In phase one, autonomous work group members learn to work with each other, supervise each other's work, and develop the values and beliefs that will guide and control their behaviour. And because they develop these values and beliefs themselves, work group members feel strongly about following them.

For example, a member of an autonomous team at ISE Electronics, a small manufacturer of electronic boards, said, "I feel bad, believe it or not. Last Friday, we missed a shipment. I feel like *I* missed the shipment since I'm the last person that sees what goes to ship. But Friday we missed the shipment by two boards and it shouldn't have been missed. But it was and I felt bad because it's me, it's a reflection on me, too, for not getting the boards out the door."[35]

The second phase in the development of concertive control is the emergence and formalization of objective rules to guide and control behaviour. The beliefs and values developed in phase one usually develop into more objective rules as new members join teams. The clearer those rules, the easier it becomes for new members to figure out how and how not to behave.

For example, a team member at ISE Electronics described how the team dealt with members showing up late to work: "Well, we had some disciplinary thing, you know. We had a few certain people who didn't show up on time and made a habit of coming in late. So the team got together and kinda set some guidelines and we told them, you know, 'If you come in late the third time and you don't wanna do anything to correct it, you're gone.' That was a team decision that this was a guideline that we were gonna follow."[36] Again, the key difference in concertive control is that the teams and not management enforced these rules.

Self-Control

Self-control, also known as **self-management**, is a control system in which managers and workers control their own behaviour.[37] However, self-control is not anarchy in which everyone gets to do whatever they want. In self-control or self-management, leaders and managers provide workers with clear boundaries within which they may guide and control their own goals and behaviours.[38] Leaders and managers also contribute to self-control by teaching others the skills they need to maximize and monitor their own work effectiveness. In turn, individuals who manage and lead themselves establish self-control by setting their own goals, monitoring their own progress, rewarding or punishing themselves for achieving or for not achieving their self-set goals, and constructing positive thought patterns that remind them of the importance of their goals and their ability to accomplish them.[39]

self-control (self-management) control system in which managers and workers control their own behaviour by setting their own goals, monitoring their own progress, and rewarding themselves for goal achievement

One technique for reminding yourself of your goals is daily affirmation, in which you write down or speak your goals aloud to yourself several times a day. Skeptics contend that daily affirmations are nothing more than positive thinking. However, an affirmation is just a simple way to help control what you think about and how you spend your time. Basically, it's a technique to prevent (i.e., control) yourself from getting sidetracked on unimportant thoughts and activities.

Scott Adams, creator of the cartoon strip "Dilbert," was skeptical that affirmations would work, but he gave them a try. His first affirmations were to see the price of a company's stock rise and to impress a particular woman. Both happened. Then when he was getting ready to take the GMAT test to get into an MBA program, every day he wrote that he wanted a score of 94. His score was 94. When he began affirming, "I will be the best cartoonist on the planet," "Dilbert" ballooned in popularity. Where it once appeared in only 100 newspapers, it now appears in more than 1100. What's he affirming now? "I will win a Pulitzer Prize."[40] Okay, start writing, "I will get an 'A' in Management. I will get an 'A' in Management...."

Review 2: Control Methods

There are five methods of control: bureaucratic, objective, normative, concertive, and self-control (self-management). Bureaucratic and objective controls are top-down, management- and measurement-based. Normative and concertive controls represent shared forms of control, because they evolve from company-wide or team-based beliefs and values. Self-control, or self-management, is a control system in which managers largely, but not completely, turn control over to the individuals themselves.

Bureaucratic control is based on organizational policies, rules, and procedures. Objective controls are based on reliable measures of behaviour or outputs. Normative control is based on strong corporate beliefs and careful hiring practices. Concertive control is based on the development of values, beliefs, and rules in autonomous work groups. Self-control is based on individuals' setting their own goals, monitoring themselves, and rewarding or punishing themselves with respect to goal achievement.

We end this section by noting that there are more or less appropriate circumstances for using each of these control methods. Examine Exhibit 7.3 to find out when each of these five control methods should be used.

3 WHAT TO CONTROL

Earlier in the chapter we asked, "Is control necessary or possible?" Then we asked, "How should control be obtained?" In this section, we ask the equally important question "What should managers control?" The way their managers answer this question has critical implications for most businesses. In the midst of an economic slowdown, a medium-sized financial company created a huge upheaval when it tried to cut costs by eliminating company-paid-for cell phones. Salespeople were furious, claiming, "No other group in the company had their cell phone use restricted." Lynda Ford, a consultant who was working with the company at the time, said that cancelling cell phones "became the straw that broke the camel's back." As a result, salespeople started quitting and productivity dropped significantly. Several months later, after realizing it was wrong, the company reinstated company cell phones.[41] After reading this section, you should be able to explain the balanced scorecard approach to control, and how companies can achieve balanced control of company performance by choosing to control economic value added, customer defections, quality, and waste and pollution.

The Balanced Scorecard

balanced scorecard measurement of organizational performance in four equally important areas: finances, customers, internal operations, and innovation and learning

In most companies, performance is measured using standard financial and accounting measures, such as return on capital, return on assets, return on investments, cash flow, net income, net margins, and so on. The **balanced scorecard** encourages managers to look beyond traditional financial measures to four different perspectives on company performance. How do customers see us (the customer perspective)? What must we excel at (the internal perspective)? Can we continue to improve and create value (the innovation and learning perspective)? How do we look to shareholders (the financial perspective)?[42]

The balanced scorecard has several advantages over traditional control processes that rely solely on financial measures. First, it forces managers at each level of the company to set specific goals and measure performance in each of the four areas. For example, Exhibit 7.4 shows that Southwest Airlines, the company upon which WestJet models itself, uses nine different measures in its balanced scorecard. Of those, only three—market value, seat revenue, and plane lease costs (at various rates of compounded annual growth, or

BUREAUCRATIC CONTROL
• When it is necessary to standardize operating procedures
• When it is necessary to establish limits
BEHAVIOUR CONTROL
• When it is easier to measure what workers do on the job than what they accomplish on the job
• When "cause–effect" relationships are clear, that is, when companies know which behaviours will lead to success and which won't
• When good measures of worker behaviour can be created
OUTPUT CONTROL
• When it is easier to measure what workers accomplish on the job than what they do on the job
• When good measures of worker output can be created
• When it is possible to set clear goals and standards for worker output
• When "cause–effect" relationships are unclear
NORMATIVE CONTROL
• When organizational culture, values, and beliefs are strong
• When it is difficult to create good measures of worker behaviour
• When it is difficult to create good measures of worker output
CONCERTIVE CONTROL
• When responsibility for task accomplishment is given to autonomous work groups
• When management wants workers to take "ownership" of their behaviour and outputs
• When management desires a strong form of worker-based control
SELF-CONTROL
• When workers are intrinsically motivated to do their jobs well
• When it is difficult to create good measures of worker behaviour
• When it is difficult to create good measures of worker output
• When workers have or are taught self-control and self-leadership skills

Sources: L.J. Kirsch, "The Management of Complex Tasks in Organizations: Controlling the Systems Development Process," *Organization Science* 7 (1996): 1–21. S.A. Snell, "Control Theory in Strategic Human Resource Management: The Mediating Effect of Administrative Information," *Academy of Management Journal* 35 (1992): 292–327.

EXHIBIT 7.3
When to Use Different Methods of Control

CAGR)—are standard financial measures of performance. But Southwest also measures its FAA (U.S. Federal Aviation Administration) on-time arrival rating and the cost of its airfares compared to competitors (customer perspective), how much time each plane spends on the ground after landing and the percentage of planes that depart on time (internal business perspective), and the percentage of its ground-crew workers, such as mechanics and luggage handlers, who own company stock and have received job training (learning perspective).

The second major advantage of the balanced scorecard approach to control is that it minimizes the chances of **suboptimization**, where performance improves in one area, but only at the expense of decreased performance in others.

suboptimization performance improvement in one part of an organization but only at the expense of decreased performance in another part

Let's examine some of the ways in which companies are controlling the four basic parts of the balanced scorecard: the financial perspective (economic value added), the customer perspective (customer defections), the internal perspective (total quality management), and the innovation and learning perspective (waste and pollution).

	OBJECTIVES	MEASURES	TARGETS	INITIATIVES
FINANCIAL	Profitability	Market Value	30% CAGR	
	Increased Revenue	Seat Revenue	20% CAGR	
	Lower Costs	Plane Lease Cost	5% CAGR	
CUSTOMER	On-time Flights	FAA On-Time Arrival Rating	#1	Quality Management, Customer Loyalty Program
	Lowest Prices	Cutomer Ranking (Market Survey)	#1	
INTERNAL	Fast Ground Turnaround	Time on Ground	30 Minutes	Cycle Time Optimization Program
		On-Time Departure	90%	
LEARNING	Ground Crew Alignment with Company Goals	% Ground Crew Shareholders	Year 1 70% Year 3 90% Year 5 100%	Employee Stock Option Plan Ground Crew Training
		% Ground Crew Trained		

Source: G. Anthes, "ROI Guide: Balanced Scorecard," *Computer World*, [Online] available at www.computerworld.com/managementtopics/roi/story/0,1081,78512,00.html, 5 May 2003.

EXHIBIT 7.4
Example of a Balanced Scorecard

The Financial Perspective: Controlling Economic Value Added

The traditional approach to controlling financial performance focuses on measures such as analysis of financial ratios, cash flow, capital budgets, balance sheets, and income statements. For years, management textbooks have recommended that managers use these measures to monitor and control the financial performance of their companies. In reality, though, most managers don't (but should) have a good understanding of accounting measures.[43] (If you struggle with these, you might find help in the following books: *Accounting the Easy Way* by Peter J. Eisen, *Accounting for Dummies* and *How to Read a Financial Report: Wringing Vital Signs Out of the Numbers*, both by John A. Tracy.) Furthermore, the complexity and sheer amount of information contained in these measures can shut down the brains and glaze over the eyes of even the most experienced managers.[44]

On the other hand, the balanced scorecard focuses on one simple question when it comes to finances: How do we look to shareholders? One of the best ways to answer that question is through something called economic value added.

economic value added (EVA)
the amount by which company profits (revenues minus expenses minus taxes) exceed the cost of capital

Conceptually, **economic value added (EVA)** is fairly easy for managers and workers to understand. It is the amount by which profits (after expenses) exceed the cost of capital in a given year. It is based on the simple idea that it takes capital to run a business, and capital comes at a cost. While most people think of capital as cash, capital is more likely to be found in a business in the form of computers, manufacturing plants, employees, raw materials, and so forth. And just like the interest that a homeowner pays on a mortgage or that a university student pays on a student loan, there is a cost to that capital.

The most common costs of capital are the interest paid on long-term bank loans used to buy all those resources, the interest paid to bondholders (who lend organizations their money), and the dividends (cash payments) and growth in stock value that accrue to shareholders. EVA is positive when company profits (revenues minus expenses minus taxes) exceed the cost of capital in a given year. In other words, if a business is to truly grow, its revenues must be large enough to cover both short-term costs (annual expenses and taxes) and long-term costs (the cost of borrowing capital from bondholders and shareholders). If you're a bit confused, Robert Goizueta, the former CEO of Coca-Cola, explained it this way: "You borrow money at a certain rate and invest it at a higher rate and pocket the difference. It is simple. It is the essence of banking."[45]

So why is EVA so important? First and most important, since it includes the cost of capital, it shows whether a business, division, department, or profit centre is really paying for itself. Second, because EVA can easily be determined for subsets of a company, such as divisions, regional offices, manufacturing plants, and sometimes even departments, it makes managers at all levels pay much closer attention to how they run their segment of the business. For example, at Coke, when the managers of the fountain business realized that they weren't even covering the cost of capital (i.e., a negative EVA), they looked for ways to do more with less capital. They determined that instead of delivering Coke concentrate in thousands of small 20-gallon steel containers, they could save money by delivering it to restaurants in huge tanker trucks.[46] In other words, EVA motivates all managers to think like small business owners who must scramble to contain costs and generate enough business to meet their bills each month.

Finally, unlike many kinds of financial controls, EVA doesn't specify what should or should not be done to improve performance. Thus, it encourages managers and workers to be creative as they try to find ways to improve EVA performance.

Exhibit 7.5 shows the capital, return on capital, and cost of capital, for some major companies. Remember that EVA is the amount by which profits (after expenses) exceed the cost of capital in a given year. So the more that return on capital exceeds the cost of capital, the better a company is using investors' money.

The Customer Perspective: Controlling Customer Defections

The second aspect of organizational performance that the balanced scorecard helps managers monitor is customers. It does so by forcing managers to address the question "How do customers see us?" Unfortunately, most companies try to answer this question through customer satisfaction surveys that are often misleadingly positive. Most customers are reluctant to talk about their problems, because they don't know whom to complain to, or they don't think that complaining will do any good. Indeed, a study by the Strategic Planning Institute indicated that 96 percent of unhappy customers never complain to anyone in the company and nine out of ten of the people who didn't complain never did business with the company again.[47] Another reason that customer satisfaction surveys can be misleading is that sometimes even very satisfied customers will leave to do business with competitors. Dave Nichol, founder of the President's Choice brand and former president of Loblaws, explained why: "Customer loyalty is the absence of something better."[48] So even if customers are pleased, they may go elsewhere if they believe they can get a better product or service.

Rather than poring over customer satisfaction surveys from current customers, studies indicate that companies may do a better job of answering the question "How do customers see us?" by closely monitoring **customer defections**, that is, by identifying

customer defections performance assessment in which companies identify which customers are leaving and measure the rate at which they are leaving

EXHIBIT 7.5
Leading Companies by Market Value Added and Economic Value Added

MVA RANKING IN 2004	MVA RANKING IN 2003	COMPANY	MARKET VALUE ADDED (US$ MILLIONS)	ECONOMIC VALUE ADDED (US$ MILLIONS)
1	1	General Electric	$299 810	$5 288
2	9	ExxonMobil	197 782	14 456
3	3	Microsoft	178 032	6 426
4	2	Wal-Mart	161 693	4 972
5	10	Johnson & Johnson	138 199	5 655
6	15	United Health Group	112 755	1 897
7	7	Procter & Gamble	105 858	3 951
8	4	Citigroup	99 485	4 536
9	5	Intel	97 468	1 720
10	13	Dell	88 086	1 891

Source: R. Grizzetti, "U.S. Performance 1000," Stern Stewart & Co, [Online] available by request, www .sternstewart.com, 20 June 2005.

which customers are leaving the company and measuring the rate at which they are leaving. In contrast to customer satisfaction surveys, customer defections and retention have a much greater effect on profits.

For example, very few managers realize that it costs five times as much to obtain a new customer as it does to keep a current one. In fact, the cost of replacing old customers with new ones is so great that most companies could double their profits by increasing the rate of customer retention by just 5 to 10 percent per year.[49] And, if a company can keep a customer for life, the benefits are even larger. For Taco Bell, keeping a customer is worth $16 500 in lifetime sales. For a Cadillac dealer, the value is $498 000. For a grocery store, it can approach $300 000.[50]

Beyond the clear benefits to the bottom line, the second reason to study customer defections is that customers who have defected to other companies are much more likely than current customers to tell you what you are doing wrong. Perhaps the best way to tap into this source of good feedback is to have top-level managers from various departments talk directly to customers who have left. Some might argue that it's a waste of valuable executive time to have upper-level managers make these calls, but there's no faster way to get the people in charge to realize what needs to be done than to hear it directly from customers who decided that their company's performance was lacking.

Finally, companies that understand why customers leave can not only take steps to fix ongoing problems, but can also identify which customers are likely to leave and make changes to prevent them from leaving. For example, a large bank discovered that departing customers would send signals that they were getting ready to leave. A small business that made regular overnight deposits would make them less frequently. Or a customer with a personal bank account who withdrew money each Friday might withdraw money only once or twice a month. Since these changes usually occurred before customers left, the bank used its computers to create a daily "retention alert" that would identify customers whose regular interaction patterns had changed. Then, each of those customers would receive a personal phone call from bank account managers to determine what could be done to solve their problems and keep their business.[51]

The Internal Perspective: Controlling Quality

The third part of the balanced scorecard, the internal perspective, consists of the processes, decisions, and actions that managers and workers make within the organization. So, in contrast to the financial perspective of EVA and the outward-looking customer perspective, the internal perspective asks the question "What must we excel at?" For McDonald's, the answer would be quick, low-cost food. For an Internet service provider, the answer would be reliability—when your modem dials, the network should be up and running and you should be able to connect without getting a busy signal. Yet no matter what area a company chooses, the key is to excel in that area. Consequently, the internal perspective of the balanced scorecard usually leads managers to a focus on quality.

Quality is typically defined and measured in three ways: excellence, value, and conformance to expectations.[52] When the company defines its quality goal as *excellence*, then managers must try to produce a product or service of unsurpassed performance and features. For example, by almost any count, Singapore International Airlines (SIA) is "the best" airline in the world. It has been named so numerous times by the readers of *Conde Nast Traveler* magazine.[53] Even SIA's competitors recognize its excellence. *Air Transport World*, the magazine read by those who work in the airline industry, stated, "SIA aimed to be the best and most successful airline in the world."[54] SIA was the first airline to introduce a choice of meals, and complementary drinks and earphones in coach class in the 1970s. Today, it continues to innovate, introducing the first worldwide video, news, telephone, and fax service on any airline. This system offers 22 video channels with movies, news, and documentaries, 12 audio channels, and 10 different Nintendo games.

value
customer perception that the product quality is excellent for the price offered

Value is the customer perception that the product quality is excellent for the price offered. At a higher price, for example, customers may perceive the product to be less of a value. When a company emphasizes value as its quality goal, managers must simulta-

Principle 1.	We do everything we can to make our products better. We improve material, add back features and construction details that others have taken out over the years. We never reduce the quality of a product to make it cheaper.
Principle 2.	We price our products fairly and honestly. We do not, have not, and will not participate in the common retailing practice of inflating mark-ups to set up a future phony "sale."
Principle 3.	We accept any return for any reason, at any time. Our products are guaranteed. No fine print. No arguments. We mean exactly what we say: GUARANTEED. PERIOD.
Principle 4.	We ship faster than anyone we know of. We ship items in stock the day after we receive the order. At the height of the last Christmas season the longest time an order was in the house was 36 hours, excepting monograms which took another 12 hours.
Principle 5.	We believe that what is best for our customer is best for all of us. Everyone here understands that concept. Our sales and service people are trained to know our products, and to be friendly and helpful. They are urged to take all the time necessary to take care of you. We even pay for your call, for whatever reason you call.
Principle 6.	We are able to sell at lower prices because we have eliminated middlemen; because we don't buy branded merchandise with high protected mark-ups; and because we have placed our contracts with manufacturers who have proven that they are cost conscious and efficient.
Principle 7.	We are able to sell at lower prices because we operate efficiently. Our people are hard-working, intelligent, and share in the success of the company.
Principle 8.	We are able to sell at lower prices because we support no fancy emporiums with their high overhead. Our main location is in the middle of a 40-acre cornfield in rural Wisconsin.

Source: "The Lands' End Principles of Doing Business," Lands' End Web site. [Online] Available www.landsend .com/cd/fp/help/0,2471,1_26215_26859_26906_,00.html?sid=0999527403537, 3 September 2001.

EXHIBIT 7.6
The Lands' End Principles of Doing Business

neously control excellence, price, durability, or other features of a product or service that customers strongly associate with value. One company that has put value at the core of everything it does is Lands' End, the catalogue company that sells quality clothing and accessories at reasonable prices. In its advertising, Lands' End said, "Value is more than price. Value is the combination of product quality, world class customer service and a fair price." Lands' End puts its commitment to value into practice through its eight principles of doing business, which are shown in Exhibit 7.6.

When a company defines its quality goal as conformance to specifications, employees must base decisions and actions on whether services and products measure up to standard specifications. In contrast to excellence and value-based definitions of quality that can be somewhat ambiguous, measuring whether products and services are "in spec" is relatively easy. Furthermore, while conformance to specifications is usually associated with manufacturing, it can be used equally well to control quality in nonmanufacturing jobs. Exhibit 7.7 shows a quality checklist that a cook or restaurant owner would use to ensure quality when buying fresh fish.

The way in which a company defines quality affects the methods and measures that workers use to control quality. Accordingly, Exhibit 7.8 shows the advantages and disadvantages associated with the excellence, value, and conformance to specification definitions of quality.

The Innovation and Learning Perspective: Controlling Waste and Pollution

The last part of the balance scorecard, the innovation and learning perspective, addresses the question "Can we continue to improve and create value?" Thus, the innovation and learning perspective is concerned with new product development, continuous improvement in ongoing products and services (discussed in Chapter 14), and relearning and

QUALITY CHECKLIST FOR BUYING FRESH FISH		
FRESH WHOLE FISH	**ACCEPTABLE**	**NOT ACCEPTABLE**
Eyes	clear, bright, bulging, black pupils	dull, sunken, cloudy, grey pupils
Gills	bright red, free of slime, clear mucus	brown to greyish, thick, yellow mucus
Flesh	firm and elastic to touch, tight to the bone	soft and flabby, separating from the bone
Smell	inoffensive, slight ocean smell	ammonia, putrid smell
Skin	opalescent sheen, scales adhere tightly to skin	dull or faded colour, scales missing, or easily removed
Belly cavity	no viscera or blood visible, lining intact, no bone protruding	incomplete evisceration, cuts or protruding bones, off-odour

EXHIBIT 7.7
Conformance to Specifications Checklist for Buying Fresh Fish

Sources: "A Closer Look: Buy It Fresh, Keep It Fresh," *Consumer Reports Online*. [Online] www.seagrant.sunysb.edu/SeafoodTechnology/SeafoodMedia/CR02-2001/CR-SeafoodII020101.htm, 3 September 2001. Philipps, "Turn to Pros for Fish Buying Tips," *Cincinnati Post*, 2 September 2000, 3C. "How to Purchase: Buying Fish," AboutSeaFood Web site. [Online] www.aboutseafood.com/faqs/purchase1.html, 3 September 2001.

redesigning the processes by which products and services are created (discussed in Chapter 10). Since all three categories are discussed in more detail elsewhere in the text, this section reviews an increasingly important topic, waste and pollution minimization, that is affected by all three of these issues.

As shown in Exhibit 7.9, there are four levels of waste minimization, with waste prevention and reduction producing the greatest minimization of waste and waste disposal producing the smallest minimization of waste.[55] It should also be noted that many of these activities will be performed under a comprehensive occupational health and safety (OH&S) program, which is required under law and discussed further in Chapter 13. The top level is *waste prevention and reduction*, in which the goals are to prevent waste and

EXHIBIT 7.8
Advantages and Disadvantages of Different Measures of Quality

QUALITY AS EXCELLENCE	
ADVANTAGES	**DISADVANTAGES**
Promotes clear organizational vision.	Provides little practical guidance for managers.
Being/providing the "best" motivates and inspires managers and employees.	Excellence is ambiguous. What is it? Who defines it?
Appeals to customers, who "know excellence when they see it."	Difficult to measure and control.
QUALITY AS VALUE	
ADVANTAGES	**DISADVANTAGES**
Customers recognize differences in value.	Can be difficult to determine what factors influence whether a product/service is seen as having value.
Easier to measure and compare whether products/services differ in value.	Controlling the balance between excellence and cost (i.e., affordable excellence) can be difficult.
QUALITY AS CONFORMANCE TO SPECIFICATIONS	
ADVANTAGES	**DISADVANTAGES**
If specifications can be written, conformance to specifications is usually measurable.	Many products/services cannot be easily evaluated in terms of conformance to specifications.
Should lead to increased efficiency.	Promotes standardization, so may hurt performance when adapting to changes is more important.
Promotes consistency in quality.	May be less appropriate for services, which are dependent on a high degree of human contact.

Source: Academy of Management Review by C.A. Reeves and D.A. Bednar. Copyright 1994 by Academy of Management Review. Reproduced with permission of the publisher via Copyright Clearance Center.

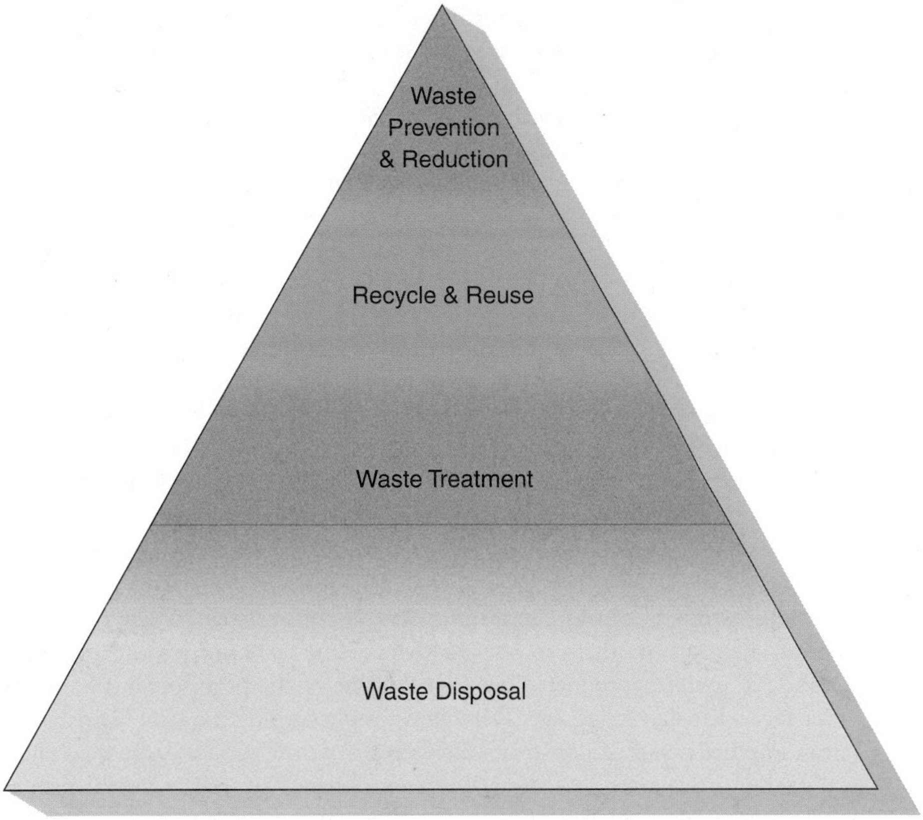

Source: D.R. May & B.L. Flannery, "Cutting Waste with Employee Involvement Teams," *Business Horizons*, September–October 1995, 25–38. Reprinted with permission from Business Horizons, September–October 1995. Copyright 1995 by The Trustees at Indiana University, Kelley School of Business.

EXHIBIT 7.9
Four Levels of Waste Minimization

pollution before they occur, or to reduce them when they do occur. There are three strategies for waste prevention and reduction:

1. *Good housekeeping*—regularly scheduled preventive maintenance for offices, plants, and equipment. Quickly fixing leaky valves and making sure machines are running properly so they don't use more fuel than necessary are examples of good housekeeping. For example, Doug Goulding, a maintenance supervisor at Canada Cordage, a producer of synthetic and natural fibre ropes, reduced the water bills at the company's factory in Kitchener, Ontario, from $1200 to $200 per month by systematically plugging leaks in machines and pipes and installing water-saving devices.[56]
2. *Material/product substitution*—replacing toxic or hazardous materials with less harmful materials. As part of its Pollution Prevention Pays program over the last 30 years, 3M eliminated 1 billion kilograms of pollutants and saved US$1 billion by using benign substitutes for toxic solvents in its manufacturing processes.[57]
3. *Process modification*—changing steps or procedures to eliminate or reduce waste. Cargill Dow has developed a way to use corn to make biodegradable plastic that is used in carpets, T-shirts, and the plastic baskets in which strawberries are sold. Compared to plastic made from oil, corn-made plastic reduces greenhouse gas emissions by 20 to 60 percent.[58]

The second level of waste minimization is *recycle and reuse*. At this level, wastes are reduced by reusing materials as long as possible, or by collecting materials for on- or off-site recycling. Sears recycles the 90 million clothes hangers used at its 860 stores each year. The hangers are collected and shipped to Sears' distribution centres where they are reused or processed for recycling. In a recent year, Sears also recycled 44 000 tonnes of corrugated cardboard, 910 tonnes of plastic bags and coverings, and 995 000 plastic ratchets. Over the preceding eight years, Sears reduced waste by 60 percent. Now, 48 percent of its waste is recycled.[59]

A growing trend in recycling is *design for disassembly*, where products are designed from the start for easy disassembly, recycling, and reuse once they are no longer usable. For example, the European Union (EU) is moving toward prohibiting companies from selling products unless most of the product and its packaging can be recovered for recycling.[60] Since companies, not consumers, will be held responsible for recycling the products they manufacture, they must design their products from the start with recycling in mind.[61] At reclamation centres throughout Europe, companies will have to be able to recover and recycle 80 percent of the parts that go into their original products.[62] Already, under the EU's end-of-life vehicle program, all cars built in Europe since June 2002 are subject to the 80 percent requirement, which will rise to 85 percent in 2006 and 95 percent by 2015 for autos. Moreover, beginning in 2007, the EU will require auto manufacturers to pay to recycle all the cars they made between 1989 and 2002.[63] One company that already does this in part is Bosch in Germany, which takes back old auto alternators, remanufactures them, and then resells them, certifying that they are as good as new.[64]

The third level of waste minimization is *waste treatment*, where companies use biological, chemical, or other processes to turn potentially harmful waste into harmless compounds or useful byproducts. For example, one of the processes in the manufacture of steel sheets is called "pickling." Pickling is simply bathing the steel in an acid solution to clean impurities and oxides (that would rust) from the surface of the steel sheet. Getting rid of the "pickle juice" has always been a problem. Not only is the juice an acid, but it also contains ferric chloride and other metals that prevent steel makers from dumping it into local water supplies. Fortunately, Magnetics International has found a safe, profitable way to treat the pickle juice. It sprays the juice into a 30-metre high chamber at 650°C. The iron chloride in the juice reacts with oxygen at that temperature to form pure iron oxide, which can be transformed into a useful magnetic powder. Inland Steel is now using this process to transform pickle juice into 23 000 tonnes of magnetic powder that can be reused in electric motors, stereo speakers, and refrigerator gaskets.[65]

The fourth and last level of waste minimization is *waste disposal*. Wastes that cannot be prevented, reduced, recycled, reused, or treated should be safely disposed of in environmentally secure landfills that prevent leakage and damage to soil and underground water supplies. Contrary to common belief, all businesses, not just manufacturing firms, have waste-disposal problems. For example, although the fluorescent lights used in most businesses are environmentally friendly because they last longer and use less electricity, burned-out fluorescent bulbs contain mercury, a hazardous waste.[66]

Review 3: What to Control

Deciding what to control is just as important as deciding whether to control or how to control. In most companies, performance is measured using financial measures alone. However, the balanced scorecard encourages managers to measure and control company performance from four perspectives: financial, customers, internal operations, and innovation and learning. One way to measure financial performance is through economic value added (EVA). Unlike traditional financial measures, EVA helps managers assess whether they are performing well enough to pay the cost of the capital needed to run the business. Instead of using customer satisfaction surveys to measure customer performance, companies should pay attention to customer defectors, who are more likely to speak up about what the company is doing wrong. Performance of internal operations is often measured in terms of quality, which is defined in three ways: excellence, value, and conformance to expectations.[67] Minimization of waste has become an important part of innovation and learning in companies. The four levels of waste minimization are waste prevention and reduction, recycle and reuse, waste treatment, and waste disposal.

What Really Happened?[68]

In the opening case, we learned about issues of corporate control. What does an executive in the front lines have to say about this important topic? We asked Karyn Brooks, controller of Bell Canada Enterprises for her thoughts. Here is what she had to say.

What internal governance mechanisms does BCE use to align the interests of its managers with those of its shareholders?

You can look at this in two ways. What the board does is it participates in the activities of management and how management is compensated. If we look at the board with respect to management's activities, it participates in strategy development and it reviews policies and procedures. Participating in strategy development in my mind is a key part of corporate governance in the broad sense. They are then ensuring that management is taking the company in the appropriate direction. When you think about corporate governance in a more financial sense, aligning management views with shareholders is typically done through compensation. BCE has changed its compensation in the last year because there has been all of this fuss over stock options, specifically whether stock options are the appropriate way to compensate management, even as a long-term incentive plan. We have changed our incentive plan so it is now composed of a stock option piece, which is called restricted share units [RSUs]. The difference is that stock options are driven off financial performance. That may generate inappropriate behaviour and perhaps we have seen some of that in some of these company failures in the last few years. The restricted share units are granted on the basis of operating performance not financial performance. You do need to get those two things aligned to be successful in the long term. We have what is called a short term incentive program, which is just a bonus program. BCE and many Canadian companies have put in share ownership guidelines for its senior executives. If you are a VP you have to own one times your salary in BCE common shares so that if you're not doing something in the best interest of a shareholder then there is a personal price to be paid for that as well. I should say that these restricted share units, to the extent that the performance measures are met, can be paid out in either cash or shares. If one of the senior executives hasn't met his or her share ownership guidelines, the RSUs are automatically paid in shares. There is a personal financial interest in ensuring that the decisions you make in the office are good for the shareholder because they impact personal wealth.

An external mechanism useful for aligning the interests of executives with shareholders is the market for corporate control or the "threat of takeover." How does this mechanism constrain executives' decisions and actions?

In a financial context and it's the context I speak best from, it certainly constrains managers from taking too much risk. Weak companies get taken over when they have weak financial performance. You either have to put yourself on the market or someone comes after you. Once a target, you will be bought—maybe not by the guy who made you a target. But you will be bought. The company philosophy, and particularly public companies that do not wish to be taken over, then motivates management to keep the company strong, which is then in the best interest of the shareholders.

From time to time the market for corporate control arises. Why might this occur?

Some of it is being weak. If you're weak, you don't have a strong strategy. Your products are performing poorly and you become a target because someone thinks that they can do a better job of managing your business than you do. I think there is the pure "lets get bigger for bigger sake," and I think we've seen a lot of that recently in the past few years. If you get bigger, you can't be a takeover target because you become too big. Many companies want to keep their corporate identity. Some companies want to stay Canadian. One company I worked for felt it was very important to get bigger for bigger sake because then we wouldn't be taken over by a U.S. company. I think the motivations or the reasons are different depending on the economic circumstances the company finds itself in. Sometimes it's to do with vertical or horizontal diversification. You want more control over your inputs or your outputs, so every situation I think is different.

What mechanisms might executives put in place to counter the threat of an external takeover?

It's really about strength of strategy, market position, and financial position. Those are the three things you can do to keep your company safe from that threat other than somebody just wanting to buy you to get bigger.

Key Terms

autonomous work groups *(195)*
balanced scorecard *(196)*
behaviour control *(193)*
benchmarking *(187)*
bureaucratic control *(192)*
concertive control *(194)*
concurrent control *(189)*
control *(186)*
control loss *(189)*
customer defections *(199)*
cybernetic feasibility *(190)*
economic value added (EVA) *(198)*
feedback control *(189)*
feedforward control *(189)*
normative control *(194)*
objective control *(193)*
output control *(193)*
regulation costs *(190)*
self-control (self-management) *(195)*
standards *(186)*
suboptimization *(197)*
value *(200)*

Self-Assessment

TOO MUCH INFORMATION?

Imagine that your professor handed back term papers, and the only mark on yours was the grade. Would you be content, or would you feel short-changed? People have different comfort levels about receiving feedback: Some thrive on it; others are ambivalent. What about you? Would you rather see comments in the margins of your term paper or not? The Assessment Appendix contains a 32-question survey to give you insights into your perceptions of feedback. Understanding your references in this area will help you develop the skills you'll need as a manager. Turn to page 514 to find out more about your interest in feedback.

Management Decisions

CONTROLLING EMPLOYEE HEALTH COSTS[69]

In Canada, an increasing portion of health-care costs are falling to employers in the form of increased costs for group insurance policies. The trend is only expected to get worse as Canada's population ages. For example, Canadians spent 13 percent more on prescription drugs in 2002 than they did in 2001. Not surprisingly, companies are doing everything they can to cut medical costs.

In the last decade, more companies have turned to wellness programs, which have roots in preventive medicine. Instead of reducing the costs of current medical treatments, or encouraging doctors and hospitals to use lower-cost treatments, wellness programs try to reduce costs by preventing employees from getting sick in the first place. Since nearly 70 percent of all illnesses are preventable, wellness programs encourage employees to exercise more, quit smoking, eat a low-fat diet, and manage stress in hopes that these lifestyle changes will help them lose weight, lower cholesterol, lower blood pressure, and reduce the incidence of strokes, heart attacks, cancer, diabetes, and other illnesses. Furthermore, studies show that wellness programs work. Low-risk employees who exercise regularly, avoid smoking, eat right, and manage their stress average $300 a year in health claims, compared to over $2400 a year on average for high-risk employees who don't practise these preventive guidelines. For example, it was found that obese employees who claim short-term disability benefits average $13 000 per claim versus an average of $5800 per claim. Indeed, of the 48 studies on work-site wellness programs in the last decade, only one failed to show a cost savings for the company.

Ironically, while studies show that wellness programs do exactly what they're supposed to when employees join them, they also show that it's very difficult to get most employees to actually join and continue to participate in wellness programs. David Anderson, vice president of operations at StayWell Health Management Systems, said, "One of the real problems [confronting] wellness programs is that the healthier employees are the ones more interested in getting involved." Of course, this does little to reduce costs, since these employees are already healthier than most.

Questions

1. Explain how you could use bureaucratic control ideas to encourage more employees, especially those who really need it, to participate in wellness programs.
2. Explain how you could use self-control ideas to encourage more employees, especially those who really need it, to participate in wellness programs.
3. Explain how you could use objective control ideas to encourage more employees, especially those who really need it, to participate in wellness programs.

Management Decisions

PREVENTING PIRACY[70]

Point, click, and pirate. Software piracy, which includes the unauthorized copying, use, or distribution of software, costs the computer industry approximately $18 billion each year in lost licensing revenue. Software piracy is a problem in the United States and Canada. In Canada it is estimated that in 2002 38 percent of business applications didn't have proper licences, compared with 25 percent in the United States. It is estimated that illegal software cost the Canadian economy $289 million in 2001. However, it appears to be worse in other parts of the world such as South America and Asia. According to a recent study by the Business Software Alliance (BSA), six out of ten computers operating in Mexico contain pirated software. Unfortunately, the numbers are just as dreary in China and elsewhere across the globe. As the director of piracy for Microsoft, you feel as though your job is a never-ending battle. In order to crack down on piracy in North America, you and your staff have begun discussions aimed at coming up with solutions to the piracy problem. Piracy occurs in both private homes and in businesses, yet a recent study by the Software & Information Industry Association (SIIA) suggests that one-quarter of piracy committed in the United States occurs in high-tech companies.

One factor that leads to piracy among businesses today is expansion. Most businesses start out by purchasing legal copies of software for their firms. As a firm grows, however, some businesses choose to purchase additional computers and copy their existing software onto the new machines. For example, Microsoft allows companies to sign volume agreements that allow for unlimited copying of their software with the expectation that the company will pay for each copy made. Some firms unintentionally do not keep accurate records and end up underpaying Microsoft. Another common act of piracy involves "soft-loading." Soft-loading occurs when a firm purchases one legal copy of software and installs it on the local area network (LAN). By installing the software on the server, one copy can support hundreds of machines through a network connection.

Although the SIIA and the BSA conduct routine audits in large companies looking for piracy violations, you and your staff want to step up efforts to identify companies engaging in piracy. Some of the computer manufacturers to which you supply software have notified you recently that there has been an increase in the number of "naked" computer system orders. A computer system is "naked" when it is ordered without any operating system software. Although there are several reasons for ordering a naked system (e.g., perhaps a company wants to use a competitor's operating software, such as Linux), you suspect that companies are beginning to pirate operating software in addition to application software. Software piracy not only costs your company money through a loss of revenue, but is also a violation of copyright law, and is therefore illegal.

Questions

1. What policies or plans could you implement that might help control or diminish piracy of your operating system software within North American businesses?
2. How vigorously will you pursue offenders once you identify them? Remember, there is a cost to control.

Develop Your Management Potential

LEARNING FROM FAILURE[71]

> "There is the greatest practical benefit of making a few failures early in life."
>
> —T.H. Huxley

No one wants to fail. Everyone wants to succeed. However, some businesspeople believe that failure can have enormous value. At Microsoft, founder and former CEO Bill Gates encouraged his managers to hire people who have made mistakes in their jobs or careers. A Microsoft vice president said, "We look for somebody who learns, adapts, and is active in the process of learning from mistakes. We always ask, what was a major failure you had? What did you learn from it?" Another reason that failure is viewed positively is that it is often a sign of risk taking and experimentation, both of which are in short supply in many companies. John Kotter, a Harvard Business School professor, says, "I can imagine a group of executives 20 years ago discussing a candidate for a top job and saying, 'This guy had a big failure when he was 32.' Everyone else would say, 'Yep, yep, that's a bad sign.' I can imagine that same group considering a candidate today and saying, 'What worries me about this guy is that he's never failed.'" Jack Matson, who teaches a class at the University of Michigan called Failure 101, says, "If you are doing something innovative, you are going to trip and fumble. So the more failing you do faster, the quicker you can get to success."

One of the most common mistakes that occur after failure is the *attribution error*. An *attribution* is to assign blame or credit. When we succeed, we take credit for the success by owning up to our strategies, how we behaved, and how hard we worked. However, when we fail, we ignore our strategies, or how we behaved, or how hard we worked (or didn't). Instead, when we fail, we assign the blame to other people, or to the circumstances, or to bad luck. In other words, the basic attribution error is that success is our fault but failure isn't. The disappointment we feel when we fail often prevents us from learning from our failures.

What this means is that attribution errors disrupt the control process. The three basic steps of control are to set goals and performance standards, to compare actual performance to performance standards, and to identify and correct performance deviations. When we put all the blame on external forces rather than our own actions, we stop ourselves from identifying and correcting performance deviations. Furthermore, by not learning from our mistakes, we make it even more likely that we will fail again.

Your task in this Developing Your Management Potential is to begin the process of learning from failure. This is not an easy thing to do. When *Fortune* magazine writer Patricia Sellers wrote an article called "So You Fail," she found most of the people she contacted reluctant to talk about their failures. She wrote,

> Compiling this story required months of pleading and letter writing to dozens of people who failed and came back. "If it weren't for the 'F' word, I'd talk," lamented one senior executive who got fired twice, reformed his know-it-all management style, and considered bragging about his current hot streak. Others cringed at hearing the word "failure" in the same breath as "your career."

Questions

1. Identify and describe a point in your life when you failed. Don't write about simple or silly mistakes. The difference between a failure and a mistake is how badly you felt afterwards. Years afterwards, a real failure still makes you cringe when you think about it. What was the situation? What were your goals? And how did it turn out?
2. Describe your initial reaction to the failure. Were you shocked, surprised, angry, or depressed? Initially, who or what did you blame for the failure? Explain.
3. One purpose of control is to identify and correct performance deviations. With that in mind, describe three mistakes that you made that contributed to your failure. Now that you've had time to think about it, what would you have done differently to prevent these mistakes? Finally, summarize what you learned from your mistakes that will increase your chances of success the next time around.

Discussion Questions

1. What sort of strategies could a company use to reduce customer defections? Why do they work?
2. There are five different methods that managers (managerial control) can use to achieve control in their organizations. What are they and when would they be most appropriate to use? Give examples.
3. What kinds of organizations have a great deal of control over their resource flows? Which have little control and why? How can organizations increase control over their resource flows?
4. There are three basic control methods: feedback control, concurrent control, and feedforward control. Define each and give examples of when they might be most appropriate to use.

Critical Thinking Video Case

CBC

Visit www.management2e.nelson.com to view this chapter's CBC video case.

Take Two

Biz Flix
Brazil

Brazil takes place in a retro-futuristic world where automation pervades every facet of life, but paperwork, inefficiency, and mechanical failures are the rule. The film stars Jonathan Pryce in the role of Sam, a low-level bureaucrat. In this scene, Sam inadvertently gets wrapped up in an intrigue surrounding the so-called terrorist Harry Tuttle (played by Robert DeNiro), who is actually a renegade heating technician for whom the Ministry of Central Services has issued an arrest order.

What to Watch for and Ask Yourself

1. What kind of control is being used by Central Services?
2. Tuttle describes a paradox of control. What is it?
3. What kind of control does Tuttle seem to prefer? Explain.

Management Workplace
Wahoo's Fish Taco

Wahoo's Fish Taco is the brainchild of three brothers who grew up in the restaurant business. Because of their extensive experience in the industry, they spent many years managing from "between the ears." That is, they never had any paperwork in place. They simply remembered everything they needed to do. By the time they had three stores, however, it was clear that they needed more formal control measures.

What to Watch for and Ask Yourself

1. Based on the video, what methods of control seem most prevalent at Wahoo's?
2. How does Steve Karfaridis use the cybernetic control process at Wahoo's?
3. What does Wahoo's need to control to be successful? In other words, what would Wahoo's balanced scorecard potentially look like?

Part 3

Meeting the Competition

PHOTO: NEELAM KAUR

Global Management

Chapter 8

CHAPTER OUTLINE

LEARNING OBJECTIVES

After reading this chapter, you should be able to

1. describe the impact of global business on Canada.
2. discuss the trade rules and agreements that govern global trade.
3. explain why companies choose to standardize or adapt their business procedures.
4. explain the different ways that companies can organize to do business globally.
5. explain how to find a favourable business climate.
6. discuss the importance of identifying and adapting to cultural differences.
7. explain how to prepare workers for international assignments.

If you were around in the 1980s, you might remember the words from the Dire Straits song "Money for Nothing": "*I want my, I want my, I want my MTV..*" You grew up on MTV. But, then again, in the '80s, '90s, and even today, who didn't? MTV, and its sister station, VH1, revolutionized the music business and pioneered some of the first reality shows (*The Real World, The Osbournes*, etc.) on TV. In the early '90s, MTV created an international division, MTV International, to take MTV to the rest of the world. The initial format was simple—hire local English-speaking VJs (video disk jockeys) and have them talk in between introducing Western videos (e.g., Michael Jackson and Phil Collins). The problem? It didn't work. Divya Gupta, president of Media Edge, which helps companies buy advertising in India, said, "MTV, when it first entered the country [India], made the mistake of coming in as MTV. No changes. They didn't go anywhere." While the world's youth clamoured for Western artists and videos, they also wanted to see and hear some artists from their countries, too.[1]

What Would You Do?

The difficulty with doing that, though, is that while the international youth TV market is huge, industry revenues are low, costs are high, and competition is intense. For example, in terms of revenues, while MTV can command tens of thousands of dollars for a 30-second commercial in the United States, it only gets between US$175 and US$250 per commercial in developing markets like India. With respect to costs, if MTV has to develop local programming (which can cost from US$200 000 to US$350 000 per half-hour) to appeal to potential viewers, hire local VJs with whom local viewers will connect, find and sell to local, lower-paying advertisers, and then buy or create local broadcasting facilities in each major market or country, it basically ends up duplicating itself at very high costs in each of the markets it enters. Finally, MTV International faces incredible competition across the globe. For example, in the United Kingdom, MTV UK battles with Emap Performance Television, whose seven music television channels are just as popular MTV UK. In Canada, the recently launched MTV Canada faces stiff competition from MuchMusic. In India, however, MTV doesn't just compete with other music television stations (and there are a number of alternative national and regional music channels already in India)—it also competes with soap operas, sports, and news. Why? Because in India, most households have only one TV and families tend to watch TV shows together. Consequently, popular shows like *Pimp My Ride, Punk'd*, and *MTV Spring Break*, which appeal to Western youths, are unlikely to help MTV gain viewers in more conservative India, at least not with the entire family sitting around the TV set.

With an estimated 2.8 billion people worldwide between the ages of 10 and 34 by 2010, exponential growth in the number of low-income families purchasing TVs in China, Brazil, Russia, and India, and only 62 percent of the population outside the United States having cable or satellite TV, there are tremendous opportunities to grow MTV International. The question is how? Should MTV International be consistent across countries, or should it be completely different in each culture? How should MTV International expand internationally? Should it license its MTV brand to local businesspeople in each area, form a strategic alliance with key foreign business partners, or should it bear the risk itself and completely own and control each MTV station throughout the world? Finally, deciding where to take your company global is always an important decision. But, with so many good foreign markets to enter, the question for MTV International isn't where it should expand, but how it can expand successfully in so many different places at the same time?

If you were in charge of MTV International, what would you do?

MTV's international expansion is an example of the key issue in global business: How can you be sure that the way you run your business in one country is the right way to run that business in another? This chapter discusses how organizations make those decisions. We will start by examining global business in two ways: first, by exploring its impact on Canadian businesses, and second, by reviewing the basic rules and agreements that govern global trade. Next, we will examine how and when companies go global by examining the trade-off between consistency and adaptation and by discussing how to organize a global company. Finally, we will look at how companies decide where to expand globally. Here, we will examine how to find the best business climate, how to adapt to cultural differences, and how to better prepare employees for international assignments.

What Is Global Business?

Business is the buying and selling of goods or services. Buying this textbook was a business transaction. So was selling your first car. So was getting paid for babysitting or for mowing lawns. **Global business** is the buying and selling of goods and services by people from different countries. The Timex watch the author of this chapter wears was purchased at a Zellers in Nova Scotia. But since it was made in the Philippines, he participated in global business when he wrote Zellers a cheque. Zellers, in turn, paid Timex, which then paid the company that employs the Filipino managers and workers who made the watch. Of course, there is more to global business than buying imported products at Zellers.

global business
the buying and selling of goods and services by people from different countries

After reading the next two sections, you should be able to

1 describe the impact of global business on Canada.
2 discuss the trade rules and agreements that govern global trade.

1 IMPACT OF GLOBAL BUSINESS

Foreign direct investment (FDI) is a method of investment in which a company builds a new business or buys an existing business in a foreign country. Kao Corporation, maker of Japanese laundry detergent and body soaps and shampoos, made a foreign direct investment when it purchased Andrew Jergens Company, which makes hair- and skin-care products.

foreign direct investment (FDI)
a method of investment in which a company builds a new business or buys an existing business in a foreign country

The United States is an especially large investor in Canada. Exhibit 8.1 shows which countries have the largest foreign direct investment in the Canada. Recent figures[2] suggest that the United States accounts for 72 percent of FDI in Canada, while the

EXHIBIT 8.1
Regional Distribution of Inward FDI, 1999

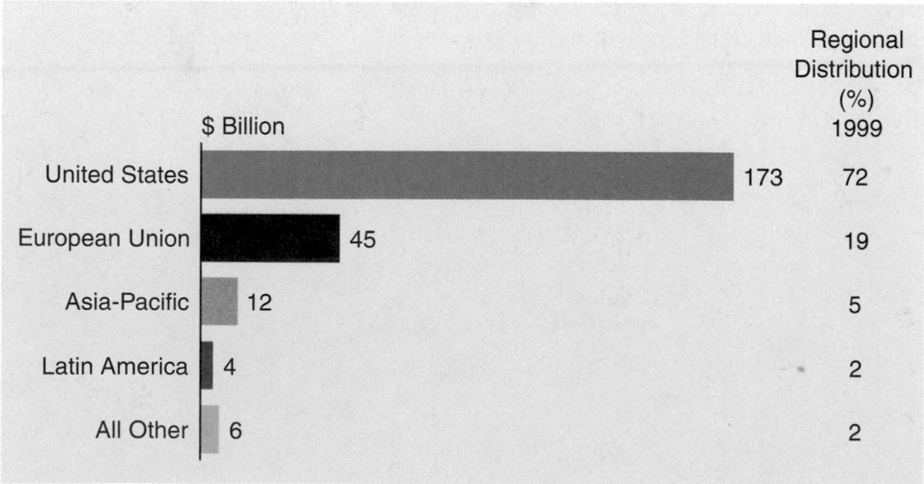

Source: Document: Trends in Canada's Inward FDI Oct. 2000 prepared by Strategic Investment Analysis, Micro-Economic Policy Analysis Branch, Industry Canada. http://strategis.ic.gc.ca/sc_ecnmy/mera/engdoc/11.html.

European Union countries account for about 19 percent. Approximately 5 percent of FDI in Canada originates with Japan, while the next largest contributor is Latin America with 2 percent. All other countries account for 2 percent of the total foreign direct investment in Canada. Which areas of the Canadian economy have benefited the most from these investments? Over the decade of the 1990s, the big winners were companies operating in the petroleum and natural gas sector, insurers, chemical producers, electronic equipment manufacturers, computer service providers, and motor vehicle manufacturers. In what areas has FDI been growing the most? Three areas in particular stand out: railway transportation, electronic equipment manufacturers and computer service providers, and financing intermediaries.

However, foreign direct investment in Canada is just half the picture. Canadian companies also have made large foreign direct investments in businesses throughout the world.[3] Exhibit 8.2 shows that Canadian companies have made their largest foreign direct investments, $134 billion, in the United States, followed by the European Union and Latin America. Up until recently, the United States was the destination for just over 52 percent of Canadian investment abroad while the latter regions accounted for 19 percent of FDI outflow. Despite the liberalization of the Chinese economy and the great size of the Japanese marketplace, these two regions accounted for only 6 percent of all Canadian outward-bound FDI. Into what industries did Canadian money flow? Just over 20 percent or $42 billion was invested in the foreign banking sector. At the same time, 14 percent of all outflowing FDI was made up of nonferrous metals and primary metal products while 11 percent was invested in foreign insurance operations.

Overall, foreign direct investment throughout the world has more than doubled in the last decade. So whether foreign companies invest in Canada or Canadian companies invest abroad, foreign direct investment is an increasingly important and common method of conducting global business.

North American companies face stiff competition in the world market, especially in high-tech industries. One survey suggests many North Americans consider this a serious problem. However, data from the U.S. National Science Board show that North American companies lead Japan, Germany, France, the United Kingdom, China, and South Korea in global high-technology market share. Furthermore, the North American share of the global high-technology markets has increased, not decreased, since 1980. By 2003, almost 40 percent of the world's high technology output originated from North America.[4]

Despite these gains, U.S. and Canadian companies are not alone in their quest for a share of global markets. The economies of France, Germany, Italy, Japan, Russia, and the

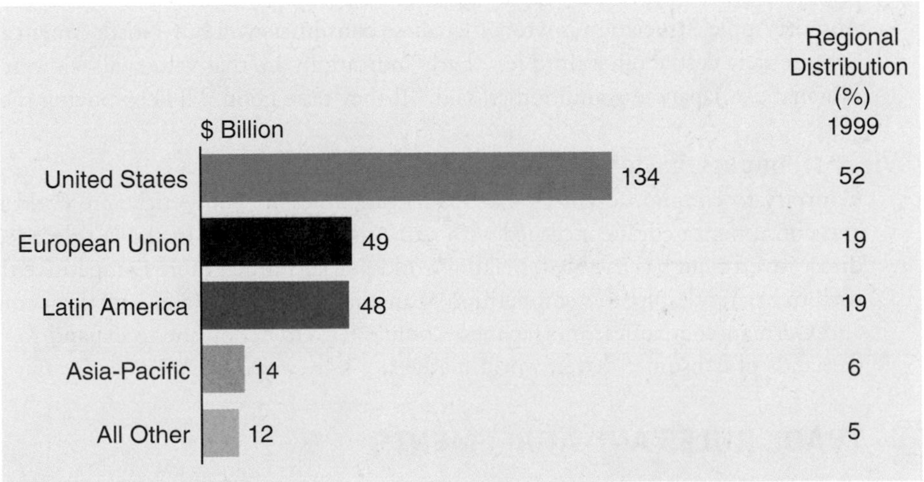

EXHIBIT 8.2
Regional Distribution of Outward FDI, 1999

Source: Document: Trends in Canada's Inward FDI Oct. 2000 prepared by Strategic Investment Analysis, Micro-Economic Policy Analysis Branch, Industry Canada. http://strategis.ic.gc.ca/sc_ecnmy/mera/engdoc/11.html.

world gross national product the value of all the goods and services produced annually worldwide

United Kingdom, which were decimated by World War II, are now part of a group of eight countries that account for more than 70 percent of the **world gross national product** (Canada and the United States are the other two members). This is roughly the same portion of world GNP controlled by the United States alone following World War II. Add to these countries the economy of China and it is easy to see how the playing field is increasingly crowded.

multinational corporation corporation that owns businesses in two or more countries

Another sign of increased competition in world markets is the number of multinational corporations and where those multinational corporations are headquartered. **Multinational corporations** are corporations that own businesses in two or more countries. In 1970, more than half the world's 7000 multinational corporations were headquartered in just two countries, the United States and Britain. Today, there are more than 60 000 multinational companies headquartered around the world.[5]

country of manufacture country where product is made and assembled

It might be said that if given the choice many Canadians would prefer to "buy Canadian," but if so, why does the demand for imported products remain strong? There are a number of potential explanations. The first is that consumers often don't know or pay attention to **country of manufacture** when making purchases. Stop reading for a minute. Take your shoes off. Where were they made? What about the VCR in your house, or your computer, or your backpack? Did you learn where these products were manufactured before you purchased them? Chances are you didn't. Many consumers don't know or care about country of manufacture.

country of origin the home country for a company, where its headquarters is located

A second explanation for strong imports is that consumers want to buy Canadian and think they are buying Canadian but, in fact, are unknowingly buying imported products. For example, take your cousin Fred who lives near the Ford Canada manufacturing facility in Oakville, Ontario. Many of his neighbours work at that plant. Fred feels that he is helping them out by buying a Ford product. Further, he also likes Ford cars. However, Ford's assembly and distribution operations are integrated on both sides of the border. The chances are that his new purchase may be an import as opposed to one manufactured in Oakville. Cousin Fred may have confused the country of manufacture, where the product is made, with the **country of origin**, which is the company's home country, which for Ford Canada is Canada. However, this is an easy mistake to make in today's global marketplace.

The third explanation for the continued increases in sales of imported products is that consumers know that many products they purchase are imported, but they just don't care. For example, until recently, Japan had closed its markets to foreign-grown apples, claiming that imported apples contained insects that would infest Japanese orchards. With no foreign competition, Japanese apples were expensive, about $7 for a bag of six "bargain" apples, and about $8.50 for a flawless, gourmet apple. The president of the Aomori Apple Association said, "This is Japanese culture. Japanese don't want apples with scratches or uneven colour, even if they taste fine." However, Japan is now allowing apples to be imported from "approved" apple orchards in North America. If the president of the Aomori Apple Association is wrong, Japanese consumers will buy North American apples because they cost about a third less. Early indications are that value will win out. Sadako Watanabe, a Japanese grandmother, said, "If they taste good, I'll keep buying them."[6]

Review 1: Impact of Global Business

Contrary to common opinion, Canadian companies are competitive in world markets, and consumers are less concerned with patriotism than value. In the last decade, foreign direct investment has doubled, making world markets much more competitive than they used to be. Yet despite this competition, Canadian companies (and American companies, and German companies, and Japanese companies, etc.) continue to expand to meet the demands of consumer-driven world markets.

2 TRADE RULES AND AGREEMENTS

The rules governing global trade are many and complex and have changed tremendously in the last few years. In the next two sections, we'll look at trade barriers and trade agreements.

Trade Barriers

Although most consumers don't especially care where the products they buy come from, national governments have preferred that consumers buy domestically made products in hopes that such purchases would increase the number of domestic businesses and workers. However, governments have done much more than hope that you buy from domestic companies. For most of the last century, governments have actively used **trade barriers** to make it much more difficult or expensive (or sometimes impossible) for their citizens to buy imported goods. For example, the U.S. government placed a 27 percent excise tax on Canadian softwood lumber. By establishing this tax, the U.S. government engaged in **protectionism**, which is the use of trade barriers to protect local companies and their workers from foreign competition.[7]

Governments have used two general kinds of trade barriers: tariff and nontariff barriers. A **tariff** is a direct tax on imported goods. Like the U.S. excise tax on Canadian softwood lumber, tariffs increase the cost of imported goods relative to domestic goods. **Nontariff barriers** are nontax methods of increasing the cost or reducing the volume of imported goods. There are five types of nontariff barriers: quotas, voluntary export restraints, government standards, government subsidies, and customs valuation/classification. Because there are so many different kinds of nontariff barriers, they can be an even more potent method of shielding domestic industries from foreign competition.

Quotas are specific limits on the number or volume of imported products. Canada sets quotas for the importation of a number of products, including textiles, apparel, and fabrics, and agricultural products, especially dairy, poultry, and milk.

Voluntary export restraints are similar to quotas in that there is a limit on how much of a product can be imported annually. The difference is that the exporting country rather than the importing country imposes the limit. However, the "voluntary" offer to limit imports usually occurs because of the implicit threat of forced trade quotas by the importing country. For example, the European Union holds yearly "monitoring talks" with Japanese auto manufacturers to discuss limits on the number of imported Japanese cars. When the sales of European-made cars fell significantly, the Japanese "voluntarily" agreed to cut their exports by 100 000 cars.[8] However, according to the World Trade Organization (see the discussion on the General Agreement on Trade and Tariffs following), countries should have phased out voluntary export restraints after 1999.[9]

In theory, government standards are specified for imports to protect the health and safety of citizens. In reality, government standards are often used to restrict or ban imported goods. For example, China is the only nation in the world that requires North American–grown grain to be 100 percent fungus free. Although preventing the importation of a fungus-infected agricultural product sounds reasonable enough, having a very small percentage of fungus is normal for harvested wheat. Since there is no chance that the fungus will spread once wheat has been harvested, and since China is the only nation to insist on this standard, the Chinese government is actually using this government standard to protect the economic health of its wheat farmers, rather than the physical health of its consumers.[10]

Many nations also use **subsidies**, such as long-term, low-interest loans, cash grants, and tax deferments, to develop and protect companies in special industries. European governments have invested billions of dollars to develop a commercial airplane manufacturing industry to support Airbus Industries (www.airbus.com), a manufacturer of commercial airplanes. Japan has historically supported domestic rice producers. The Canadian government has provided subsidies for many firms, including some of those operating in the auto industry; Bombardier, a manufacturer of trains and airplanes, has received subsidies from the Canadian government. Not surprisingly, businesses complain about unfair trade practices when other companies receive government subsidies. For example, efforts by the Canadian government to enhance economic growth by supporting specific companies in certain regions of the country through agencies such as the Atlantic Canada Opportunities Agency (ACOA) have been criticized for offering an

trade barriers
government-imposed regulations that increase the cost and restrict the number of imported goods

protectionism
a government's use of trade barriers to shield domestic companies and their workers from foreign competition

tariff
a direct tax on imported goods

nontariff barriers
nontax methods of increasing the cost or reducing the volume of imported goods

quota
limit on the number or volume of imported products

voluntary export restraints
voluntarily imposed limits on the number or volume of products exported to a particular country

subsidies
government loans, grants, and tax deferments given to domestic companies to protect them from foreign competition

unfair advantage to some companies at the expense of others. Boeing Corporation (www.boeing.com), the world's largest manufacturer of commercial airplanes, frequently complains to U.S. government officials about the millions of dollars in direct government subsidies that Airbus receives each year from European governments.[11]

The last nontariff barrier is customs classification. As products are imported into a country, they are examined by customs agents, who must decide into which thousands of categories they should classify a product. Classification is important, because the category assigned by customs agents can affect the size of the tariff and consideration of import quotas.

Trade Agreements

Thanks to the trade barriers described above, buying imported goods has often been much more expensive and difficult than buying domestic goods. However, the regulations governing global trade were transformed in the 1990s. The most significant change was that 124 countries agreed to adopt the **General Agreement on Tariffs and Trade (GATT)**.

General Agreement on Tariffs and Trade (GATT) worldwide trade agreement that will reduce and eliminate tariffs, limit government subsidies, and protect intellectual property

Through tremendous decreases in tariff and nontariff barriers, GATT will make it much easier and cheaper for consumers in all countries to buy foreign products. First, GATT will cut average tariffs worldwide. Second, GATT will eliminate tariffs in ten specific industries: beer, alcohol, construction equipment, farm machinery, furniture, medical equipment, paper, pharmaceuticals, steel, and toys. Third, GATT puts stricter limits on government subsidies. For example, GATT places limits on how much national governments can subsidize company research in electronic and high-technology industries. Fourth, GATT protects intellectual property such as trademarks, patents, and copyright. Protection of intellectual property has been an increasingly important issue in global trade because of widespread product piracy. For example, Chinese bootleggers were selling illegal copies of Disney's *The Lion King* and *Mulan* videos even before Disney could get its official copies to stores in North America.[12] Product piracy like this costs companies billions in lost revenue each year. Finally, trade disputes between countries will be fully settled by arbitration panels from the World Trade Organization. For more information about GATT and the World Trade Association (WTO), go to the WTO Web site at www.wto.org.

regional trading zones areas in which tariff and nontariff barriers on trade between countries are reduced or eliminated

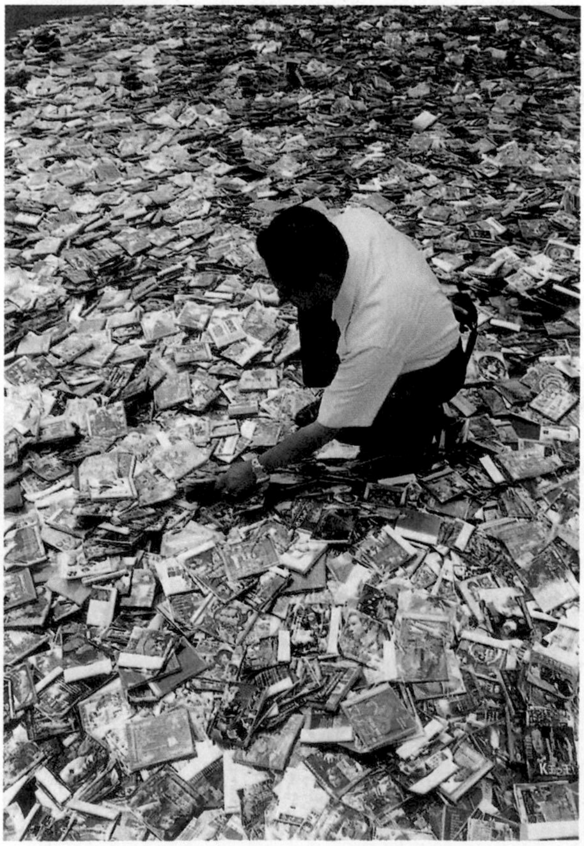

AP/WIDE WORLD PHOTOS

In Kuala Lumpur, a city hall worker spreads millions of pirated DVDs, software, and CDs on the floor before destroying them. Malaysia has been escalating its crackdown on pirated software.

The second major development in the historic move toward reduction of trade barriers has been the creation of **regional trading zones**, in which tariff and nontariff barriers are reduced or eliminated for countries within the trading zone. The largest and most important trading zones are in Europe (the Maastricht Treaty), North America (the North American Free Trade Agreement, NAFTA), South America (the Free Trade Area of the Americas, FTAA), and Asia (ASEAN, Association of South East Nations, and APEC, Asia-Pacific Economic Cooperation). The map in Exhibit 8.3 shows the extent to which free trade agreements govern global trade.

In 1992, the countries of Belgium, France, Germany, Italy, Luxembourg, the Netherlands, Denmark, Ireland,

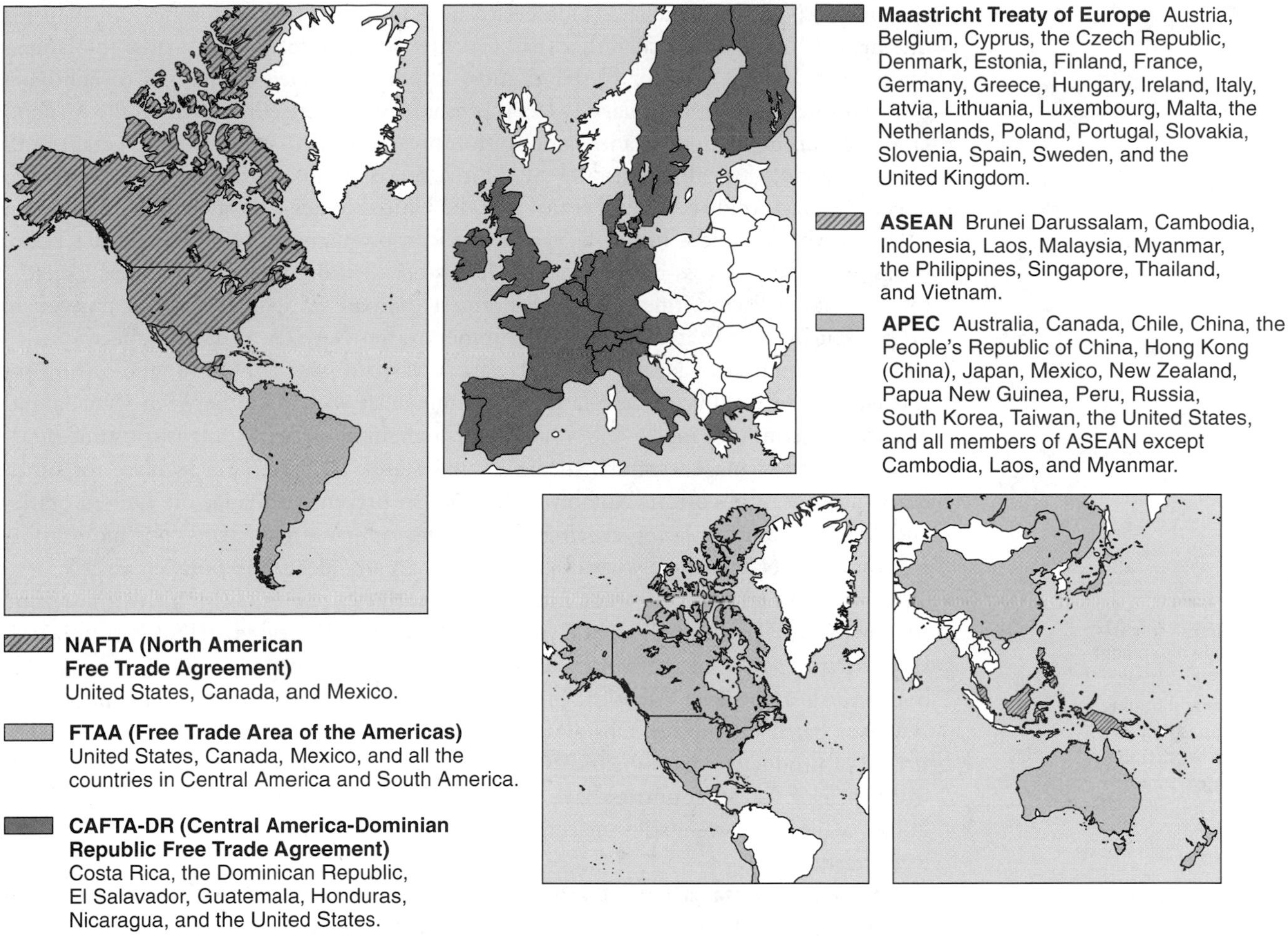

EXHIBIT 8.3
Global Map of Regional Agreements

United Kingdom, Greece, Portugal, and Spain implemented the **Maastricht Treaty of Europe**. The purpose of this treaty was to transform their 15 different economies and 15 currencies into one common economic market, called the European Union, and one common currency, the euro. Austria, Finland, and Sweden became members in 1995.[13] In 2004, membership grew to 25, with the addition of Cyprus, the Czech Republic, Estonia, Latvia, Lithuania, Hungary, Malta, Poland, Slovakia, and Slovenia.[14]

Maastricht Treaty of Europe regional trade agreement between most European countries

Prior to the treaty, trucks carrying products were stopped and inspected by customs agents at each border. Furthermore, since the required paperwork, tariffs, and government product specifications could be radically different in each country, companies often had to file 12 different sets of paperwork, pay 12 different tariffs, and produce 12 different versions of their basic product to meet various government specifications.

Likewise, open business travel, which we take for granted in Canada as we travel from province to province, was complicated by inspections at each border crossing. For example, if you lived in Germany, but worked across the border in Luxembourg, your car was stopped and your passport was inspected twice a day, every day, as you travelled to and from work. Also, every business transaction required a currency exchange (e.g., from German deutsche marks to Italian lira, or from French francs to British pounds). Imagine all of this happening to millions of trucks, cars, and businesspeople, and you can begin to appreciate the difficulty and cost of conducting business across Europe before the Maastricht Treaty.

For more information about the European Union, go to http://europa.eu/. For more about Europe's new currency, the euro, which has replaced the currencies of many of its member countries, see http://ec.europa.eu/economy_finance/euro/our_currency_en.htm.

NAFTA, the **North American Free Trade Agreement** between Canada, the United States, and Mexico, went into effect January 1, 1994. More than any other regional trade

North American Free Trade Agreement (NAFTA) regional trade agreement between Canada, the United States, and Mexico

agreement, NAFTA liberalizes trade between countries so that businesses can plan for one market, North America, rather than for three separate markets, Canada, the United States, and Mexico. One of NAFTA's most important achievements was to eliminate most product tariffs. On January 1, 1994, product tariffs were eliminated on the first and largest group of products traded among the three countries. The result? Overall, both Canadian and Mexican exports to the United States doubled after NAFTA went into effect.[15] In fact, trade between Mexico and the United States is so strong that more than 2500 18-wheeler trucks full of U.S. and Mexican products cross the border at Laredo, Texas, each day.[16] Cross-border traffic is heavy between the United States and Canada, too. Canadian Pacific, one of Canada's largest railroad companies, saw an immediate 10 percent increase in its north–south shipments after NAFTA went into effect.

The second set of NAFTA product tariffs was eliminated in 1998, and a third set was eliminated in 2003. These tariff reductions dealt with trade between Canada and Mexico. In terms of Canada–U.S. trade, tariffs remain in place in Canada for some products in supply-managed sectors. In the United States, tariffs remain in place for sugar, dairy, peanuts, and cotton. Notably, NAFTA also prevents Canada, the United States, and Mexico from increasing existing tariffs or introducing new tariffs. For more information about NAFTA, see www.dfait-maeci.gc.ca/nafta-alena/questions-en.asp?#5.

Free Trade Area of the Americas (FTAA) regional trade agreement that, when signed, will create a regional trading zone encompassing 36 countries in North and South America

The goal of **FTAA, Free Trade Area of the Americas**, is to establish a free trade zone similar to NAFTA throughout the western hemisphere. If created, FTAA would be the largest trading zone in the world, consisting of 850 million people in 36 countries in both North and South America. Similar to NAFTA, FTAA pledges to support trade "without barriers, without subsidies, without unfair practices, and with an increasing stream of productive investments."[17] Negotiations may take a decade. However, leaders from each of the 36 countries have agreed to finish FTAA negotiations, but as of late 2006, negotiations were still not complete. For more information about the FTAA, see www.ftaa-alca.org.

Association of Southeast Asian Nations (ASEAN) regional trade agreement between Brunei Darussalam, Cambodia, Indonesia, Laos, Malaysia, Myanmar, the Philippines, Singapore, Thailand, and Vietnam

Asia-Pacific Economic Cooperation (APEC) regional trade agreement between Australia, Canada, Chile, China, Hong Kong, Japan, Mexico, New Zealand, Papua New Guinea, Peru, Russia, South Korea, the United States, and all members of ASEAN except Cambodia, Laos, and Myanmar

ASEAN, the **Association of Southeast Asian Nations**, and **APEC**, **Asia-Pacific Economic Cooperation**, are the two largest and most important regional trading groups in Asia. ASEAN is a trade agreement between Brunei Darussalam, Cambodia, Indonesia, Laos, Malaysia, Myanmar, the Philippines, Singapore, Thailand, and Vietnam that, together, form a market of more than 330 million people. APEC is a broader agreement between Australia, Canada, Chile, China, Hong Kong, Japan, Mexico, New Zealand, Papua New Guinea, Peru, Russia, South Korea, the United States, and all members of ASEAN except Cambodia, Laos, and Myanmar. APEC countries began reducing trade barriers in the year 2000, though it will take until 2020 for all trade barrier reductions to be completely phased in. For more information about ASEAN, see www.aseansec.org. For more information about APEC, see www.apecsec.org.sg/.

Review 2: Trade Rules and Agreements

Tariffs and nontariff trade barriers, such as quotas, voluntary export restraints, government standards, government subsidies, and customs classifications, have made buying foreign goods much harder or expensive than buying domestically produced products. However, worldwide trade agreements, such as GATT, along with regional trading agreements such as the Maastricht Treaty of Europe, NAFTA, FTAA, ASEAN, and APEC, substantially reduced tariff and nontariff barriers to international trade. Companies have responded by investing in growing markets in Asia, Eastern Europe, and Latin America. Consumers have responded by purchasing products based on value, rather than geography.

How to Go Global

Once a company has decided that it will go global, it must decide how to go global. For example, if you decide to sell in Singapore, should you try to find a local business partner who speaks the language, knows the laws, and understands the customs and norms of

Singapore's culture, or should you simply export your products from your home country? What do you do if you are also entering Eastern Europe, perhaps starting in Hungary? Should you use the same approach in Hungary that you used in Singapore?

After reading the next two sections, you should be able to

3 explain why companies choose to standardize or adapt their business procedures.

4 explain the different ways that companies can organize to do business globally.

3 CONSISTENCY OR ADAPTATION?

In this section, we return to a key issue in the chapter: How can you be sure that the way you run your business in one country is the right way to run that business in another? In other words, how can you strike the right balance between global consistency and local adaptation?

Global consistency means that when a multinational company has offices, manufacturing plants, and distribution facilities in different countries, it will run those offices, plants, and facilities based on the same rules, guidelines, policies, and procedures. Managers at company headquarters value global consistency, because it simplifies decisions. For example, IBM's international sales used to be organized by country. Under this system, if a multinational company with offices in ten different countries wanted to purchase IBM personal computers, it would deal with ten different IBM offices and would likely get different prices and levels of service from each one. Today, multinational customers have to deal with IBM's central sales office only. Once a deal has been cut, they can expect similar prices and service in each location.[18]

Local adaptation is a company policy to modify its standard operating procedures to adapt to differences in foreign customers, governments, and regulatory agencies. Surprisingly, even aspects of the U.S. market need to be closely examined by Canadian firms seeking to pursue export opportunities. For instance, Tilano Fresco is a Canadian manufacturer and distributor of decorative tile-making kits. To understand the local business practices of potential customers operating in the Atlanta, Georgia, area of the United States, it needed to work hand in hand with Canadian consular representatives. The result was placement of its products in over 400 stores in just under a year.[19] Local adaptation is typically more important to local managers who are charged with making the international business successful in their countries. In his book *Blunders in International Business*, David Ricks describes an ill-fated advertising theme used by Sumitomo Corporation of Japan (www.sumitomo.com), to introduce a new kind of steel pipe to the North American market. Following the advice of a Japanese advertising agency, the steel was named "Sumitomo High Toughness" and was advertised in full-page advertisements with nearly full-page letters as SHT, the steel "made to match its name." Sumitomo could probably have prevented this mistake if it had given some control of its advertising to local managers who understood the culture and language.

Multinational companies struggle to find the correct balance between global consistency and local adaptation. If they lean too much toward global consistency, they run the risk of using management procedures poorly suited to particular countries' markets,

DOING THE RIGHT THING

FAIR AND SAFE WORKING CONDITIONS IN FOREIGN FACTORIES[20]

Requiring workers to work 15-hour days or to work seven days a week with no overtime pay, beating them for arriving late, requiring workers to apply toxic materials with their bare hands, charging them excessive fees for food and lodging—these are just a few of the workplace violations found in the overseas factories that make shoes, clothes, bicycles, and other goods for large multinational companies. The Fair Labor Association, which now inspects these factories for Adidas-Salomon, Levi Strauss, Liz Claiborne, Nike, Reebok, Polo Ralph Lauren, and others, recommends the following workplace standards for foreign factories:

- Make sure there is no forced labour or child labour; no physical, sexual, psychological, or verbal abuse or harassment; and no discrimination.
- Provide a safe and healthy working environment to prevent accidents.
- Respect the right of employees to freedom of association and collective bargaining. Compensate employees fairly by paying the legally required minimum wage or the prevailing industry wage, whichever is higher.
- Provide legally required benefits. Employees should not be required to work more than 48 hours per week and 12 hours of overtime (for which they should receive additional pay), and they should have at least one day off per week.

Do the right thing. Investigate and monitor the working conditions of overseas factories where the goods sold by your company are made. Insist that improvements be made. Find another supplier if they aren't.

cultures, and employees. However, if companies focus too much on local adaptation, they run the risk of losing the cost efficiencies and productivity that result from using standardized rules and procedures throughout the world.

Review 3: Consistency or Adaptation?

Global business requires a balance between global consistency and local adaptation. Global consistency means using the same rules, guidelines, policies, and procedures in each foreign location. Managers at company headquarters like global consistency, because it simplifies decisions. Local adaptation means adapting standard procedures to differences in foreign markets. Local managers prefer a policy of local adaptation, because it gives them more control. Not all businesses need the same combinations of global consistency and local adaptation. Some thrive by emphasizing global consistency and ignoring local adaptation. Others succeed by ignoring global consistency and emphasizing local adaptation.

4 FORMS FOR GLOBAL BUSINESS

Besides determining whether to adapt organizational policies and procedures, a company must also determine how to organize itself for successful entry into foreign markets. Historically, companies have generally followed the phase model of globalization.

This means that companies made the transition from a domestic company to a global company in sequential phases, through exporting, cooperative contracts, strategic alliances, wholly owned affiliates,[21] and global new ventures.[22]

Exporting

exporting
selling domestically produced products to customers in foreign countries

When companies produce products in their home countries and sell those products to customers in foreign countries, they are **exporting**. For example, Canadian wine producers are active in their efforts to export wine around the world. Recently, Canadian companies such as Andres Wine, Colio Estate, Vineland, Hillebrand Estates, and Creekside Estate Winery presented their wines to an invited group of high-end restaurants and hotel chains in Stockholm, Sweden. After an initial introduction of these products at the Canadian Embassy and a follow-up by European-based agents, at least one of the Canadian company's products has been listed with the Swedish alcohol retail monopoly.[23]

When thinking exporting, it is difficult to ignore China:

> Among Canadian companies participating in China's explosive growth are Inco, Alcan, Noranda, Falconbridge, Dorel Industries, Nortel Networks, and Potash Corp. of Saskatchewan.... Canada's top four export categories, which account for 46 per cent of total exports to China, are wood pulp, automotive parts, fertilizers, and organic chemicals. Alcan and Inco are both beneficiaries of the increase in demand for basic materials.[24]

Exporting has many advantages as a form of global business. It makes the company less dependent on sales in its home market and provides a greater degree of control over research, design, and production decisions. While advantageous in a number of ways, exporting also has its disadvantages.

The primary disadvantage is that many exported goods are subject to tariff and nontariff barriers that can substantially increase their final cost to consumers. A second disadvantage of exporting is that transportation costs can significantly increase the price of an exported product. For example, a 22-kilogram box of Nicaraguan sweet onions costs about $24, but shipping those onions to North America costs $7, adding more than 29 percent to the price.[25] Another disadvantage of exporting is that companies that export are dependent on foreign importers for distribution of their products. For example, if the

© JOHN HILLERY/REUTERS/CORBIS

A Hybrid car produced by Toyota. Good ideas and good products find customers around the world.

foreign importer makes a mistake on the paperwork that accompanies a shipment of imported goods, those goods can be returned to the foreign manufacturer at the manufacturer's expense.

Cooperative Contracts

When an organization decides to expand its business globally, but does not want to make large financial commitments to do so, it will sign a **cooperative contract** with a foreign business owner, who pays the company a fee for the right to conduct that business in his or her country. There are two kinds of cooperative contracts: licensing and franchising.

cooperative contract an agreement in which a foreign business owner pays a company a fee for the right to conduct that business in his or her country

Under a **licensing** agreement, a domestic company, the licensor, receives royalty payments for allowing another company, the licensee, to produce its product, sell its service, or use its brand name in a particular foreign market.

licensing agreement in which a domestic company, the licensor, receives royalty payments for allowing another company, the licensee, to produce its product, sell its service, or use its brand name in a specified foreign market

One of the most important advantages of licensing is that it allows companies to earn additional profits without investing more money. As foreign sales increase, the royalties paid to the licensor by the foreign licensee increase. Moreover, the licensee, not the licensor, invests in production equipment and facilities to produce the licensed product. Licensing also helps companies avoid tariff and nontariff barriers. Since the licensee manufactures the product within the foreign country, tariff and nontariff barriers don't apply. For example, Arctic Beverages is licensed to bottle and distribute Pepsi-Cola in northern Manitoba and parts of Saskatchewan. Because it bottles Pepsi in Canada, tariff and nontariff barriers do not affect the price or supply of these products.

The biggest disadvantage associated with licensing is that the licensor gives up control over the quality of the product or service sold by the foreign licensee. Other than specific restrictions in the licensing agreement, the licensee controls the entire business, from production to marketing to final sales. Many licensors include inspection clauses in their licence contracts, but closely monitoring product or service quality from thousands of kilometres away can be difficult. An additional disadvantage is that licensees can eventually become competitors, especially when a licensing agreement includes access to important technology or proprietary business knowledge.

A **franchise** is a collection of networked firms in which the manufacturer or marketer of a product or service, the franchisor, licenses the entire business to another person or organization, the franchisee. For the price of an initial franchise fee plus royalties, franchisors provide franchisees training, help with marketing and advertising, and give an exclusive right to conduct business in a particular location. Most franchise fees run between $7000 and $50 000. Atlantic Canada success story Greco Pizza (www.greco.ca) is currently accepting franchise applications for its expansion into Quebec. Its Web site suggests you would need a minimum of $30 000 to be eligible for serious consideration as a franchisee.

franchise a collection of networked firms in which the manufacturer or marketer of a product or service, the franchisor, licenses the entire business to another person or organization, the franchisee

Overall, franchising is a fast way to enter foreign markets. During the 1980s, North American franchisors increased their global franchises by an astronomical 79 percent, for a total of almost 40 000 global franchise units! Because it gives the franchisor additional cash flows from franchisee fees and royalties, franchising can be a good strategy when a company's domestic sales have slowed. For example, since 1990, McDonald's (www.mcdonalds.com) has nearly doubled its number of overseas stores. Further, Pizza Hut (www.pizzahut.com) has opened over 200 restaurants in China alone over the last few years.[26]

Despite its many advantages, franchisors face a loss of control when they sell businesses to franchisees who are thousands of kilometres away. Although there are successful exceptions, franchising success may be somewhat culture-bound. In other words, because most global franchisors begin by franchising their businesses in similar countries or regions (Canada is by far the first choice for American companies taking their first step into global franchising), and because 65 percent of franchisors make absolutely no change in their business for overseas franchisees, that success may not generalize to cultures with different lifestyles, values, preferences, and technological infrastructures. Because of this, simple things taken for granted in one's own country can trip up the most successful businesses when they franchise overseas.

Strategic Alliances

strategic alliance
agreement in which companies combine key resources, costs, risk, technology, and people

joint venture
a strategic alliance in which two existing companies collaborate to form a third, independent company

Companies forming **strategic alliances** combine key resources, costs, risks, technology, and people. The most common strategic alliance is a **joint venture**, which occurs when two existing companies collaborate to form a third company. The two founding companies remain intact and unchanged, except that, together, they now own the newly created joint venture. A recent example of a high-profile Canadian alliance involves Nortel Networks and IBM Corp. The companies created a development centre in Research Triangle Park, North Carolina, to collaborate on new products and services, such as improving broadband, voice over Internet protocol, multimedia services, and wireless technology.[27]

One of the advantages of global joint ventures is that, like licensing and franchising, they help companies avoid tariff and nontariff barriers to entry. Another advantage is that companies participating in a joint venture bear only part of the costs and the risks of that business. Many companies find this attractive, because of how expensive it is to enter foreign markets or develop new products.

Global joint ventures can be especially advantageous to smaller, local partners that link up with larger, more experienced foreign firms that can bring advanced technology, management, and business skills to the joint venture. After the Berlin Wall fell, General Motors (www.gm.com), the world's largest auto manufacturer, committed to a joint venture with German Automobil Werke Eisenach, an automobile manufacturer in Eisenach, Germany (formerly East Germany). Together, General Motors and GEW-Eisenach built a brand-new factory that allowed General Motors to introduce the most up-to-date manufacturing machines, teamwork-based assembly, and just-in-time inventory systems, none of which had been used in the antiquated factory that GEW-Eisenach used to manufacture East German cars.[28]

Global joint ventures are not without problems, though. Because companies share costs and risk with their joint venture partners, they must also share their profits. Setting up global joint ventures is also complex, often requiring detailed contracts that specify the obligations of each party. Toshiba (www.toshiba.com), which participated in its first global joint ventures in the early 1900s by making light bulb filaments with General Electric (www.ge.com), treats joint ventures like a marriage of two companies and views the contract as a prenuptial agreement.[29] In other words, the joint venture contract specifies how much each company will invest, what its rights and responsibilities are, and what it is entitled to if the joint venture does not work out. These steps are important, because it is estimated that the rate of failure for global joint ventures is as high as 33 percent to 50 percent.[30] Global joint ventures can also be difficult to manage, because they represent a merging of four cultures: the country and the organizational cultures of the first partner, and the country and the organizational cultures of the second partner.

Wholly Owned Affiliates (Build or Buy)

Approximately one-third of multinational companies enter foreign markets through **wholly owned affiliates.** Unlike licensing, franchising, or joint ventures, wholly owned affiliates are 100 percent owned by the parent company. For example, Honda Canada, located in the Greater Toronto Area of Ontario, is 100 percent owned by Honda Motors of Japan. The Ford Motor Company of Canada, in Oakville, Ontario, is 100 percent owned by the Ford Motor Company in Detroit, Michigan.

wholly owned affiliates foreign office, facilities, and manufacturing plants that are 100 percent owned by the parent company

The primary advantage of wholly owned businesses is that they give parent companies all the profits and complete control over foreign facilities. The biggest disadvantage is the expense of building new operations or buying existing businesses. While the payoff can be enormous if wholly owned affiliates succeed, the losses can be immense if they fail. For example, when Volkswagen (www.volkswagen.com) spent over US$250 million to purchase and modernize an American auto manufacturing plant from Chrysler, everyone, including the state of Pennsylvania that lured Volkswagen to Pennsylvania with a US$63 million tax break, thought Volkswagen would be wildly successful. However, nearly a decade later, Volkswagen sales had dropped and the plant, which was running at only 40 percent of capacity, was losing US$120 million a year. Twenty-five hundred workers lost their jobs when Volkswagen closed the plant for good.[31]

Global New Ventures

It used to be that companies slowly evolved from being small and selling in their home markets to being large and selling to foreign markets. Furthermore, as companies went global, they usually followed the phase model of globalization. However, three trends have combined to allow companies to skip the phase model when going global. First, quick, reliable air travel can transport people to nearly any point in the world within one day. Second, low-cost communication technologies, such as the Internet, e-mail, teleconferencing, and phone conferencing, make it easier to communicate with global customers, suppliers, managers, and employees. Third, there is now a critical mass of business people with extensive personal experience in all aspects of global business.[32] This combination of events has made it possible to start companies that are global from inception. With sales, employees, and financing in different countries, **global new ventures** are new companies founded with an active global strategy.[33]

global new ventures new companies with sales, employees, and financing in different countries that are founded with an active global strategy

While there are several different kinds of global new ventures, they share two common factors. First, the company founders successfully develop and communicate the company's global vision. Second, rather than going global one country at a time, new global ventures bring a product or service to market in several foreign markets at the same time. National GYP-Chipper, based in Texas, manufactures and sells a $10 000 machine that crushes scrap gypsum (drywall) into a recyclable powder.[34] It is cheaper and faster for building contractors to grind up used or leftover drywall board into a recyclable powder than it is to pay to have it hauled to the dump. Because National Gyp-Chipper feared that potential overseas competitors would copy its machine, it established licensing contracts with companies in Canada, Britain, and Japan and was seeking other relationships in Europe and the Middle East. By entering so many markets so quickly, National Gyp-Chipper hoped to get ahead of and deter any copycat competitors.

Review 4: Forms for Global Business

The phase model of globalization says that as companies move from a domestic to a global orientation, they use these organizational forms in sequence: exporting, cooperative contracts (licensing and franchising), strategic alliances, and wholly owned affiliates. Yet not all companies follow the phase model. For example, global new ventures are global from their inception.

Where to Go Global

Deciding where to go global is just as important as deciding how your company will go global.

After reading the next three sections, you should be able to

5 explain how to find a favourable business climate.
6 discuss the importance of identifying and adapting to cultural differences.
7 explain how to successfully prepare workers for international assignments.

5 FINDING THE BEST BUSINESS CLIMATE

When deciding where to go global, companies try to find countries or regions with promising business climates. An attractive global business climate positions the company for easy access to growing markets, is an effective but cost-efficient place to build an office or manufacturing site, and minimizes the political risk to the company.

Positioning for Growing Markets

purchasing power
a comparison of the relative cost of a standard set of goods and services in different countries

The most important factor in an attractive business climate is access to a growing market. Two factors help companies determine the growth potential of foreign markets: purchasing power and foreign competitors. **Purchasing power** is measured by comparing the relative cost of a standard set of goods and services in different countries. For instance, if a Coke costs about the same price in Tokyo as in Toronto, but significantly less in the United States, then the average Canadian would have similar purchasing power to a Japanese person while an American would have more purchasing power. Purchasing power is surprisingly strong in countries such as Mexico, India, and China, which have low average levels of income. This is because consumers still have money to spend after paying for basic living expenses, such as food, shelter, and transportation, which are very inexpensive in those countries. Because basic living expenses are so small, purchasing power is strong, and millions of Chinese, Mexican, and Indian consumers increasingly have extra money to spend on what they want, in addition to what they need.

Consequently, countries with high levels of purchasing power are good choices for companies looking for attractive global markets. Coke has found that the per capita consumption of Coca-Cola—how many Cokes a person drinks per year—rises directly with purchasing power. In Eastern Europe, as countries began to embrace capitalism after the fall of communism, per capita consumption of Coke increased from 20 to 31 Cokes in just two years. Today, the average has tripled to 93 drinks per year.[35]

The second part of assessing growing global markets is to analyze the degree of global competition, which is determined by the number and quality of companies that already compete in foreign markets. Canadians who have shopped from time to time in the United States will recognize the name JCPenney (www.jcpenney.com). Before JCPenney began developing stores in foreign markets, it sent a small team of experienced retailers to scout its global competition. In East Berlin, the team found display windows with nothing more than one dusty shirt on display. In Istanbul, they found retail stores with plumbing supplies next to the women's lingerie and clothing. Because its top-selling stores were right on the U.S.–Mexican border, Penney's managers didn't even have to leave the United States to assess its competition in Mexico. Studies confirmed that 60 percent of the sales in these U.S. stores came from Mexicans who crossed the border to shop.[36] Because its foreign competitors were weak in marketing, customer service, and product distribution, JCPenney followed through on its plan to expand into global markets.

Choosing an Office/Manufacturing Location

Companies do not have to establish an office or manufacturing location in each country they enter. They can license, franchise, or export to foreign markets, or they can serve a larger region from one country. Thus, the criteria for choosing an office/manufacturing location are different from the criteria for entering a foreign market.

Rather than focusing on costs alone, companies should consider both qualitative and quantitative factors. Two key qualitative factors are work force quality and company strategy. Work force quality is important because it is often difficult to find workers with the specific skills, abilities, and experience that a company needs to run its business.

Quantitative factors, such as the kind of facility being built, tariff and nontariff barriers, exchange rates, and transportation and labour costs, should also be considered when choosing an office/manufacturing location. Exhibit 8.4 shows *Fortune* magazine's rankings for the world's top cities for global business. This information is a good starting point if your company is trying to decide where to put an international office or manufacturing plant.

One example of a company that understands where it should compete is the Four Seasons Hotels and Resorts:

> Four Seasons operates 54 luxury hotels and resorts in 24 countries around the world. ... Four Seasons' goal was to develop a brand name synonymous with an unparalleled customer experience. To meet these aspirations, it chose to focus exclusively in serving high-end travellers. A second choice was to pursue a truly global strategy with its growing portfolio of hotels and resorts in key destinations around the world.

EXHIBIT 8.4
World's Best Cities for Business

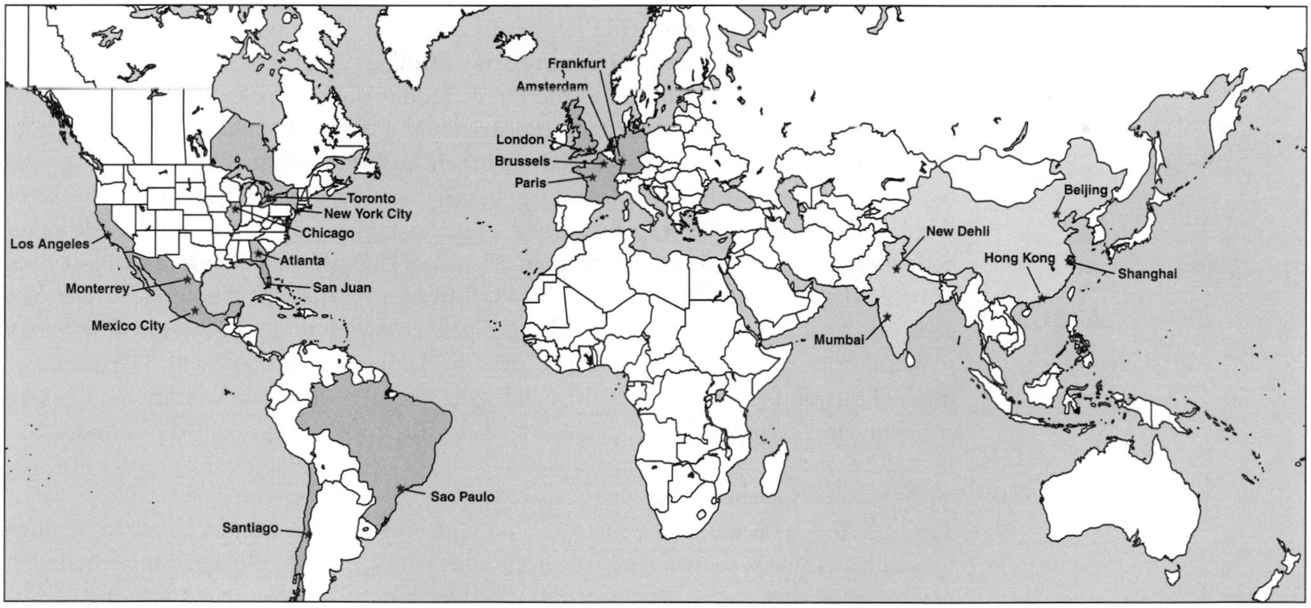

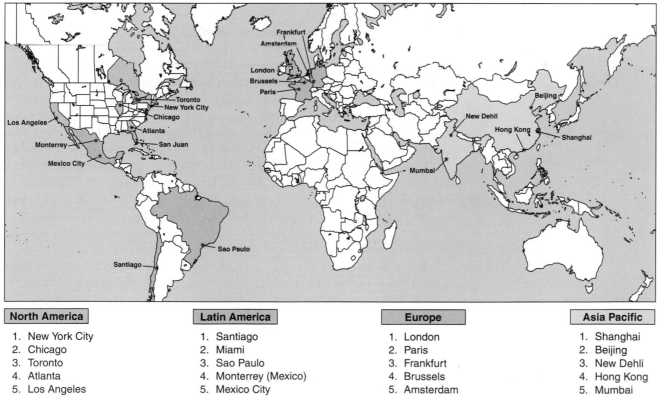

North America	Latin America	Europe	Asia Pacific
1. New York City	1. Santiago	1. London	1. Shanghai
2. Chicago	2. Miami	2. Paris	2. Beijing
3. Toronto	3. Sao Paulo	3. Frankfurt	3. New Dehli
4. Atlanta	4. Monterrey (Mexico)	4. Brussels	4. Hong Kong
5. Los Angeles	5. Mexico City	5. Amsterdam	5. Mumbai

Sources: M. Borden, "The Best Cities for Business: Big, Established, Monied Metropolises—With a Tech Twist—Top *Fortune's* Annual Ranking at the Turn of the Century," *Fortune*, 27 November 2000, 218. C. Murphy, "Winners of the World," *Fortune*, 27 November 2000, 232. "Miami Is the Best City for Doing Business in Latin America, According to AmericaEconomia Magazine," *PR Newswire*, 24 April 2003. "Shanghai Takes Top Position as Destination for Future Worldwide Expansion in 'European Cities Monitor,'" *Cushman & Wakefield Asia Pacific*, 30 September 2004, [Online] available at www.cushwakeasia.com/aboutus/pdf/news/ECM%20PR%20asia%20version%202004%20release%20on%203009.pdf

This distinguished Four Seasons from the bulk of smaller high-end competitors. The final key choice, which was made in 1985, was to specialize as a hotel manager, not a developer and owner.[37]

Minimizing Political Risk

When managers think about political risk in global business, they envision burning factories and riots in the streets. Although political events such as these receive dramatic and extended coverage from the press, the political risks that most companies face usually will not be covered as breaking stories on CTV Newsnet (www.ctv.ca), or CBC Newsworld (www.cbc.ca/newsworld/). However, the negative consequences of ordinary political risk can be just as devastating to companies that fail to identify and minimize those risks.

When conducting global business, companies should attempt to identify two types of political risk: political uncertainty and policy uncertainty.[38] **Political uncertainty** is associated with the risk of major changes in political regimes that can result from war, revolution, death of political leaders, social unrest, or other influential events. **Policy uncertainty** refers to the risk associated with changes in laws and government policies that directly affect the way foreign companies conduct business. This is the most common form of political risk in global business and perhaps the most frustrating. For example, the busiest McDonald's in the world used to be in a prime location in Wangfujing, China—that is, until the Chinese government broke McDonald's 20-year lease after only two years, telling McDonald's that it would have to build a brand-new store just blocks away from the original location. The Chinese government broke McDonald's lease so that a Hong Kong billionaire could develop the location. Ironically, after agreeing to let him build on the site, the Chinese government retracted that permission, too.[39]

political uncertainty
the risk of major changes in political regimes that can result from war, revolution, death of political leaders, social unrest, or other influential events

policy uncertainty
the risk associated with changes in laws and government policies that directly affect the way foreign companies conduct business

Several strategies can be used to minimize or adapt to the political risk inherent to global business. An *avoidance strategy* is used when the political risks associated with a foreign country or region are viewed as too great. If firms are already invested in high-risk areas, they may divest or sell their businesses. If they have not yet invested, they will likely postpone their investment until the risk shrinks.

Control is an active strategy to prevent or reduce political risks. Firms using a control strategy will lobby foreign governments or international trade agencies to change laws, regulations, or trade barriers that hurt their business in that country.

Another method for dealing with political risk is *cooperation*, which makes use of joint ventures and collaborative contracts, such as franchising and licensing. Although cooperation does not eliminate the political risk of doing business in a country, it does limit the risk associated with foreign ownership of a business. For example, a German company forming a joint venture with a Chinese company to do business in China may structure the joint venture contract so that the Chinese company owns 51 percent or more of the joint venture. Doing so qualifies the newly formed joint venture as a Chinese company and exempts it from Chinese laws that apply to foreign-owned businesses.[40]

Review 5: Finding the Best Business Climate

The first step in deciding where to take your company global is finding an attractive business climate. Be sure to look for a growing market where consumers have strong purchasing power and foreign competitors are weak. When locating an office or manufacturing facility, consider both qualitative and quantitative factors. In assessing political risk, be sure to examine political uncertainty and policy uncertainty. If the location you choose has considerable political risk, you can avoid it, try to control the risk, or use a cooperation strategy.

6 BECOMING AWARE OF CULTURAL DIFFERENCES

Some of the more interesting and amusing aspects of global business are the unexpected confrontations that people have with cultural differences, "the way they do things over there." For example, as part of a class assignment in global business, an American high school class and a high school class in Valle, Spain, agreed to form a global "joint venture." The two classes agreed that the American students would buy Spanish products from the Spanish high school students and resell them at a profit to other American students. Likewise, the Spanish students would purchase American products from the American students and then resell them at a profit to their Spanish friends. Now, what to buy from each other? The American students decided to buy giant beach towels showing teenaged Spanish lovers. One of the towels showed a boy helping his girlfriend remove her shirt. Another showed him unzipping her jeans. In Spain's culture, which is much more relaxed about sexuality than American culture, no one gives these towels a second thought. Of course, despite protestations of censorship, the American high school teacher vetoed the towels as too suggestive.[41]

national culture
the set of shared values and beliefs that affect the perceptions, decisions, and behaviour of the people from a particular country

National culture is the set of shared values and beliefs that affects the perceptions, decisions, and behaviour of the people from a particular country. The first step in dealing with culture is to recognize that there are meaningful differences in national cultures. Psychologist Geert Hofstede (http://geert-hofstede.international-business-center.com/index.shtml) has spent over 20 years studying cultural differences in 53 different countries. His research shows that there are five consistent differences across national cultures: power distance, individualism, short-term versus long-term orientation, masculinity, and uncertainty avoidance.[42]

Power distance is the extent to which people in a country accept that power is distributed unequally in society and organizations. In countries where power distance is weak, such as Denmark and Sweden, employees don't like their organizations or their bosses to have power over them or to tell them what to do. They want to have a say in

AP/WIDE WORLD PHOTOS

A veiled Muslim woman travels past a large billboard advertising a film that catalogues the plight of a middle-class Cairo family as it tries to come to terms with the pregnancy of its teenage daughter. The film captures the prevailing mood of contemporary urban Egypt struggling to balance tradition and modernity, religion, and science.

decisions that affect them. As shown in Exhibit 8.5, Russia and China, with scores of 95 and 80, are much stronger in power distance than Germany (35), the Netherlands (38), and the United States (40). Canada's rating is 39; the world average is 55.

Individualism is the degree to which societies believe that individuals should be self-sufficient. In individualistic societies, employees put loyalty to themselves first, and loyalty to their company and work group second. The United States (91), the Netherlands (80), France (71), and Germany (67) are the strongest in individualism, while West Africa (20), China (20), and Indonesia (14) are the weakest. Like many other English-speaking countries such as Britain, New Zealand, and Australia, Canada ranks individualism highly—at 80, it's the highest ranking of all the dimensions.

Masculinity and *femininity* capture the difference between highly assertive and highly nurturing cultures. Masculine cultures emphasize assertiveness, competition, material success, and achievement, whereas feminine cultures emphasize the importance of relationships, modesty, caring for the weak, and quality of life. Japan (95), Germany (66), and the United States (62) have the most masculine orientations, while the Netherlands (14) has the most feminine orientation. Canada ranks it at about 47.

The cultural difference of *uncertainty avoidance* is the degree to which people in a country are uncomfortable with unstructured, ambiguous, unpredictable situations. In countries with strong uncertainty avoidance, such as Greece and Portugal, people are aggressive, emotional, and seek security (rather than uncertainty). Japan (92), France (86), West Africa (90), and Russia (90) are strongest in uncertainty avoidance, while Hong Kong (29) is the weakest. Canada's ranking is about 42.

Short-term/long-term orientation addresses whether cultures are oriented to the present and seek immediate gratification, or to the future and defer gratification. Not surprisingly, countries with short-term orientations are consumer driven, whereas countries with long-term orientations are savings driven. China (118) and Hong Kong (96) have very strong long-term orientations, while West Africa (16), Indonesia (25), the United States (29), and Germany (31) have very strong short-term orientations. Canada gives it the lowest ranking of all the dimensions, at 23.

Cultural differences affect perceptions, understanding, and behaviour. Recognizing cultural differences is critical to succeeding in global business. However, Hofstede said we should recognize that these cultural differences are based on averages—the average

EXHIBIT 8.5
Hofstede's Five Cultural Dimensions

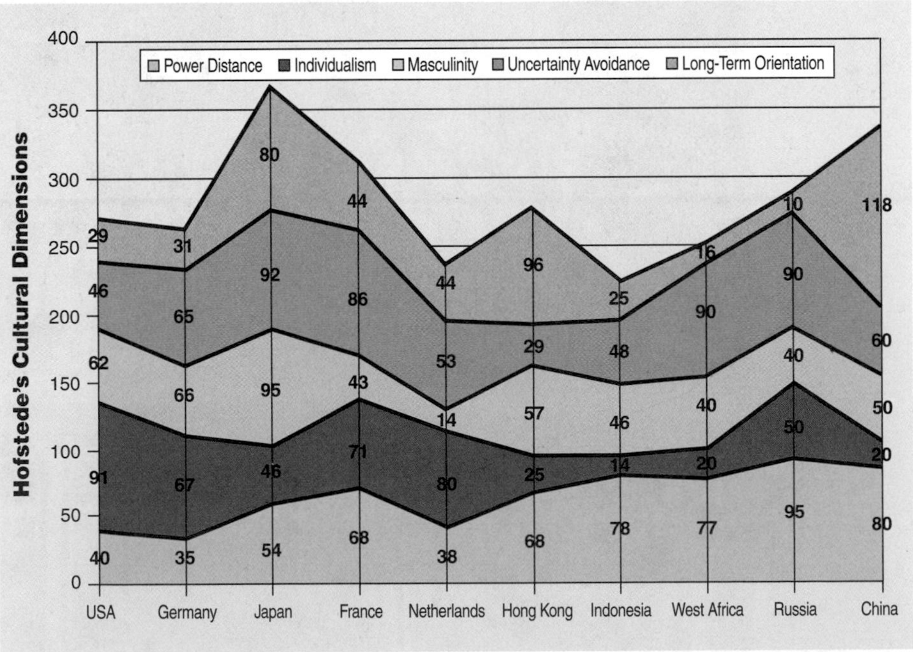

Source: Geert H. Hofstede, "Cultural Constraints in Management Theories," *Academy of Management Executive* 7, no. 1 (1993): 81–94.

level of uncertainty avoidance in Portugal, or the average level of power distance in Argentina, and so forth. Hofstede said, "If you are going to spend time with a Japanese colleague, you shouldn't assume that overall cultural statements about Japanese society automatically apply to this person."[43]

After becoming aware of cultural differences, the second step is deciding how to adapt your company to those cultural differences. Unfortunately, studies investigating the effects of cultural differences on management practice point more to difficulties than to easy solutions. One problem is that different cultures will probably perceive management policies and practices differently. For example, blue-collar workers in France and Argentina, all of whom performed the same factory jobs for the same multinational company, perceived the company's corporate-wide safety policy differently.[44] French workers perceived that safety wasn't very important to the company, but Argentine workers thought that it was. The fact that something as simple as a safety policy can be perceived differently across cultures shows just how difficult it can be to standardize management practices across different countries and cultures.

Another difficulty is that cultural values are changing, albeit slowly, in many parts of the world. The fall of communism in Eastern Europe and the former Soviet Union and the broad economic reforms in China have combined to produce sweeping changes on two continents. Thanks to increased global trade resulting from GATT and other regional free trade agreements, major economic transformations are also under way in India, Mexico, Central America, and South America. The difficulty that companies face when trying to adapt management practices to cultural differences is that they may be adapting the way they run their businesses based on outdated and incorrect assumptions about a country's culture.

Review 6: Becoming Aware of Cultural Differences

National culture is the set of shared values and beliefs that affect the perceptions, decisions, and behaviour of the people from a particular country. The first step in dealing with culture is to recognize meaningful differences, such as power distance, individualism, short-term/long-term orientation, masculinity, and uncertainty avoidance. Cultural differences should be carefully interpreted, because they are based on averages, not individuals. Adapting managerial practices to cultural differences is difficult, because policies and practices can be perceived differently in different cultures. Another difficulty is that cultural values may be changing in many parts of the world. Consequently, when companies try to adapt management practices to cultural differences, they need to be sure that those changes are not based on outdated assumptions about a country's culture.

7 PREPARING FOR AN INTERNATIONAL ASSIGNMENT

Around a conference table in a large American office tower, three American executives sat with their new boss, Mr. Akiro Kusumoto, the newly appointed head of a Japanese firm's American subsidiary, and two of his Japanese lieutenants. The meeting was called to discuss ideas for reducing operating costs. Mr. Kusumoto began by outlining his company's aspiration for its long-term continental presence. He then turned to the budgetary matter. One Japanese manager politely offered one suggestion, and an American then proposed another. After gingerly discussing the alternatives for quite some time, the then exasperated American blurted out: "Look, that idea is just not going to have much impact. Look at the numbers!" In the face of such bluntness, uncommon and unacceptable in Japan, Mr. Kusumoto fell silent. He leaned back, drew air between his teeth, and felt a deep longing to return East. He realized his life in this country would be filled with many such jarring encounters, and lamented his posting to a land of such rudeness.[45]

expatriate
someone who lives outside his or her native country

Mr. Kusumoto is a Japanese **expatriate**, someone who lives outside his or her native country. The cultural shock that he was experiencing is common. The difficulty of adjusting to language, cultural, and social differences is the primary reason that so many expatriates fail in overseas assignments. For example, it is estimated that 10 percent to 45 percent of North American expatriates sent abroad by their companies will return home before they have successfully completed their international assignments.[46] Of those who do complete their international assignments, as many as 30 percent to 50 percent are judged by their companies to be no better than marginally effective.[47] Since the cost of sending an employee on an international assignment can be in the hundreds of thousands of dollars, failure in those assignments can be extraordinarily expensive.[48]

However, the chances for a successful international assignment can be increased through language and cross-cultural training; and considering spouse, family, and dual-career issues.

Language and Cross-Cultural Training

The purpose of pre-departure language and cross-cultural training is to reduce the uncertainty that expatriates feel, the misunderstandings that take place between expatriates and natives, and the inappropriate behaviours that expatriates unknowingly commit when they travel to a foreign country. Indeed, simple things like using a phone, finding a public toilet, asking for directions, knowing how much things cost, exchanging greetings, or ordering in a restaurant can become tremendously complex when expatriates don't know a foreign language or a country's customs and cultures. In his book *Blunders in International Business*, David Ricks tells the story of a North American couple in Asia. After a walk with their dog, the couple had dinner at a local restaurant. Since the waiters and waitresses did not speak English, they ordered by pointing to items on the menu. Because their dog was hungry, they pointed to the dog and to the kitchen. The waiter had trouble understanding, but finally took the dog to the kitchen. The couple assumed that this meant the dog could not be fed in the dining room, but was going to be fed in the kitchen. Unfortunately, to the couple's dismay, the waiter and the chef returned later to proudly show them how well they had cooked the poodle.

Expatriates who receive pre-departure language and cross-cultural training make faster adjustments to foreign cultures and perform better on their international assignments (and are better at ordering in foreign restaurants).[49] Unfortunately, only a third of the managers who go on international assignments receive any kind of pre-departure training. This is somewhat surprising given the failure rates for expatriates and the high cost of those failures. It is also surprising because, with the exception of some language courses, pre-departure training is not particularly expensive or difficult to provide.

For example, a Canadian electronics manufacturer prepared workers for assignments in South Korea by using a combination of documentary training, cultural simulations, and field experiences. Documentary training focuses on identifying the critical specific differences between various cultures. Trainees learned that Canadian subordinates will normally look their bosses in the eye, whereas Korean subordinates avoid eye contact unless their bosses ask them questions. Trainees also learned about other Canadian–South Korean differences, such as how to greet businesspeople, how to behave toward South Korean women or elders, and how to respect privacy.

After learning critical specific differences in documentary training, trainees participated in a cultural simulation, in which they had the opportunity to practise adapting to cultural differences. For example, the trainees participated in a simulated cocktail party in which company managers who had spent time in South Korea posed as South Korean businesspeople and their spouses. Trainees practised South Korean greetings, introductions, and communication styles, and then received feedback on their performance.

WHAT REALLY WORKS

Cross-Cultural Training[50]

Most expatriates will tell you that cross-cultural training helped them adjust to foreign cultures. However, anecdotal data are not as convincing as systematic studies. Twenty-one studies, with a combined total of 1611 participants, have examined whether cross-cultural training affects the self-development, perceptions, relationships, adjustment, and job performance of expatriates. Overall, they show that cross-cultural training works extremely well in most instances.

SELF-DEVELOPMENT

When you first live in another country, you must learn how to make decisions that you took for granted in your home country: how to get to work, how to get to the grocery store, how to pay your bills, and so on. If you've generally been confident about yourself and your abilities, an overseas assignment can challenge that sense of self. However, cross-cultural training helps expatriates deal with these and other challenges. Expatriates who receive cross-cultural training are 79 percent more likely to report healthy psychological well-being and self-development than those who don't receive training.

Psychological Well-Being & Self Development

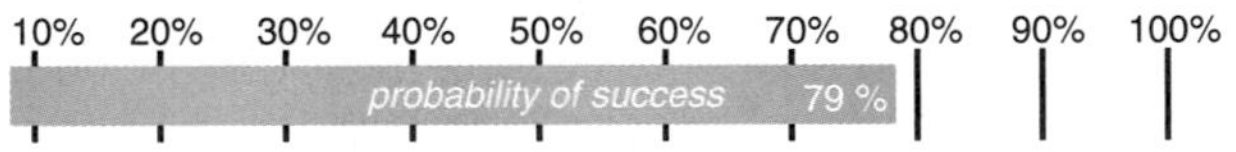

FOSTERING RELATIONSHIPS

One of the most important parts of an overseas assignment is establishing and maintaining relationships with host nationals. If you're in Brazil, you need to make friends with Brazilians. However, many expatriates make the mistake of making friends only with expatriates from their home country. In effect, they become social isolates in a foreign country. They work and live there, but as much as they can, they speak their native language, eat their native foods, and socialize with other expatriates from their home country. Cross-cultural training makes a big difference in whether expatriates establish relationships with host nationals. Expatriates who receive cross-cultural training are 74 percent more likely to have established such relationships.

Fostering Relationships with Native Citizens

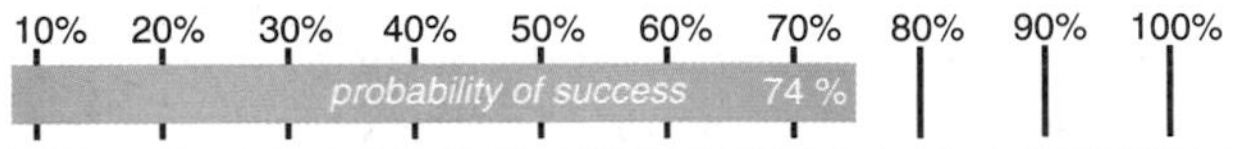

ACCURATE PERCEPTIONS OF CULTURE

Another thing that distinguishes successful from unsuccessful expatriates is that they understand the cultural norms and practices of the host country. For example, many Americans do not understand pictures that many of them may have seen of Japanese troops turning their backs to American military commanders on V-J day, the day that Japan surrendered to the United States in World War II. Americans viewed this as a lack of respect, when in fact in Japan, turning one's back in this way is a sign of respect. Cross-cultural training makes a big difference in the accuracy of perceptions concerning host country norms and practices. Expatriates who receive cross-cultural training are 74 percent more likely to have accurate perceptions.

Accurate Cultural Perceptions

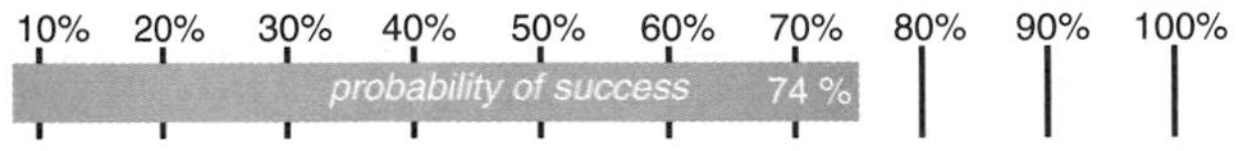

RAPID ADJUSTMENT

New employees are most likely to quit in the first six months, because this initial period requires the most adjustment: learning new names, new faces, new procedures, and new Information. It's tough. Of course, expatriates have a much tougher time making a successful adjustment, because besides learning new names, faces, procedures, and information, expatriates are learning new languages, new foods, new customs, and often new lifestyles. Expatriates who receive cross-cultural training are 74 percent more likely to make a rapid adjustment to a foreign country.

Rapid Adjustment to Foreign Cultures and Countries

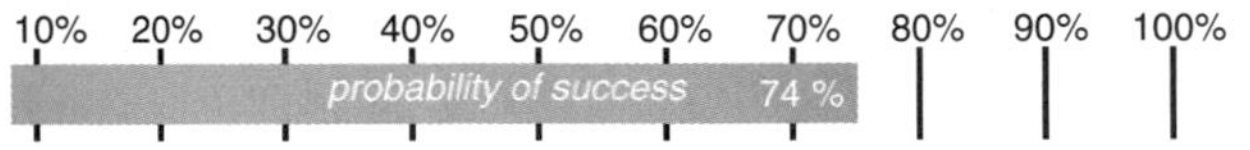

JOB PERFORMANCE

It's good that cross-cultural training improves self-development, fosters relationships, improves the accuracy of perceptions, and helps expatriates make rapid adjustments to foreign cultures. However, from an organizational standpoint, the ultimate test of cross-cultural training is whether it improves expatriates' job performance. The evidence shows that cross-cultural training makes a significant difference in expatriates' job performance. This is not quite as big a difference as for the other factors. However, it is estimated that cross-cultural training for 100 managers could bring

WHAT REALLY WORKS

about $500 000 worth of benefits to a company, nearly $5600 per manager. This is an outstanding return on investment, especially when you consider the high rate of failure for expatriates. Expatriates who have received cross-cultural training are 71 percent more likely to have better on-the-job performance than those who did not receive cross-cultural training.

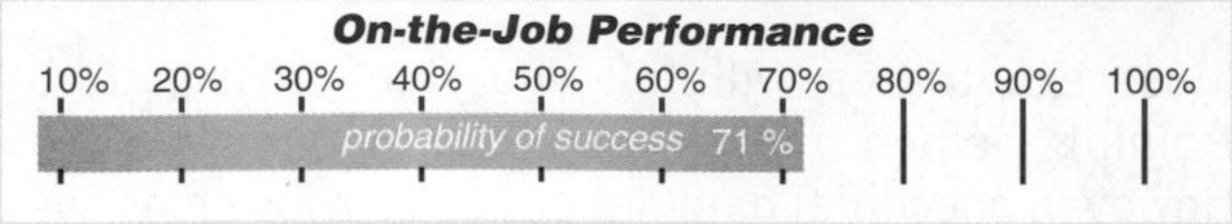

Consideration of Spouse, Family, and Dual-Career Issues

The evidence clearly shows that how well an expatriate's spouse and family adjust to the foreign culture is the most important factor in determining the success or failure of an international assignment.[51] Unfortunately, despite its importance, there has been little systematic research on what does and does not help expatriates' families successfully adapt. However, a number of companies have found that adaptability screening and intercultural training for families can lead to more successful overseas adjustment.

Adaptability screening is used to assess how well managers and their families are likely to adjust to foreign cultures. For example, one large North American multinational has developed an "Overseas Assignment Inventory" to assess the spouse and family's open-mindedness, respect for others' beliefs, sense of humour, and marital communication. But adaptability screening is not just companies assessing employees; it can also mean that employees screen international assignments for desirability. Since more employees are becoming aware of the costs of international assignments (spouses having to give up or change jobs, children having to change schools, having to learn a new language, etc.), some companies are willing to pay for a pre-assignment trip for the employee and his or her spouse to investigate the country before accepting the international assignment.[52]

Language and cross-cultural training for families is just as important as language and cross-cultural training for expatriates. In fact, it may be more important, because unlike expatriates, whose professional jobs often shield them from the full force of a country's culture, spouses and children are often fully immersed in foreign neighbourhoods and schools. Households must be run, shopping must be done, and bills must be paid. Likewise, children and their parents must deal with different cultural beliefs and practices about discipline, alcohol, dating, and other issues. Language and cross-cultural training can help reduce uncertainty about how to act and decrease misunderstandings between expatriates, their families, and locals.

Review 7: Preparing for an International Assignment

Many expatriates return prematurely from international assignments because of poor performance. However, this is much less likely to happen if employees receive language and cross-cultural training, such as documentary training, cultural simulations, or field experiences, before going on assignment. Adjustment of expatriates' spouses and families, which is the most important determinant of success in international assignments, can be improved through adaptability screening and intercultural training.

What Really Happened?[53]

In the opening case you learned that with certain demographic and economic trends throughout the world, there are tremendous opportunities to grow MTV International. However, you also learned that today's international youth TV market is characterized by low revenues, high costs, and intense competition, which should make it incredibly difficult for MTV to expand internationally. Let's find out what really happened and see how MTV International expanded to become one of the largest, truly global TV companies in the world.

There are tremendous opportunities to grow MTV International. The question is how? Should MTV International be consistent across countries, or should it be completely different in each culture?
One of the key issues in global business is determining whether the way you run your business in one country is the right way to run that business in another. In other words, how can you strike the right balance between global consistency and local adaptation? Global consistency means that when a multinational company like MTV has offices and facilities in different countries, it will use the same rules, guidelines, policies, and procedures to run them all. Managers at company headquarters value global consistency because it simplifies decisions. Local adaptation is typically more important to local managers who are charged with making the international business successful in their countries.

If companies focus too much on local adaptation, they run the risk of losing the cost efficiencies and productivity that result from using standardized rules and procedures throughout the world. (We'll return to this issue in the answer to the last question.) However, if companies lean too much toward global consistency, they run the risk of their business being poorly suited to particular countries' markets, cultures, and employees (i.e., a lack of local adaptation). This was the mistake that MTV International made when it first went global. According to Divya Gupta, president of Media Edge, which helps companies buy advertising in India, "MTV, when it first entered the country, made the mistake of coming in as MTV. No changes." So beginning in the late 1990s, MTV quit feeding nothing but Western videos to its international locations and started featuring music and shows adapted to local cultures and languages. In Russia, MTV developed *12 Angry Viewers*, where Russian celebrities and teens discuss music videos interspersed with dancing and "hitting" each other with inflatable objects. The show's producer, Piotr Sheksheyev, says, "MTV trusts that we Russians know best what works." Now *12 Angry Viewers* is one of the top three talk shows in Russia. In Brazil, MTV developed *Mochilao*, in which a popular model hosts a travel show where she backpacks through the country visiting famous sites. In China, there's *Mei Mei Sees MTV*, in which an animated, "virtual" video disc jockey hosts the program and introduces music videos. And, in India, there's *Silly Point*, a humour show that takes a lighthearted view of India's most popular sport, cricket.

However, giving local MTV managers and producers control was also not without risks. Bill Roedy, who runs MTV International, mentions that he had to "intervene" when MTV Taiwan crossed over the line by airing a nude wrestling show. Likewise, at first in India, the local music programmers refused to play the music from incredibly popular Bollywood films, because they felt it wasn't cool enough to be on MTV. So, for a second time, MTV International had to force a change. After Bollywood music videos began playing, ratings increased by 700 percent.

In general, though, the move toward airing local music and artists has been incredibly successful. According to Roedy, "We've had very little resistance once we explain that we're not in the business of exporting American culture." And because less than 10 percent of the 2500 people who work for MTV International are American, that makes it easier for the company to pour effort, time, and money into mining local markets for top music talent. Shakira, who is now globally known, was "discovered" locally after recording an MTV Unplugged CD in Latin America. Today, MTV International follows a policy of 70 percent local content and 30 percent shared content that is shown on most MTV International channels. As a result, MTV is different from country to country.

How should MTV international expand internationally? Should it license its MTV brand to local businesspeople in each area, form a strategic alliance with key foreign business partners, or should it bear the risk itself and completely own and control each MTV station throughout the world?
When an organization decides to expand its business globally, but does not want to make a large financial commitment to do so, it will sign a cooperative contract with a foreign business owner, who pays the company a fee for the right to conduct that business in his or her country. Licensing is one kind of cooperative contract. Under a licensing agreement, a domestic company, the licensor, receives royalty payments for allowing another company, the licensee, to produce its product, sell its service, or use its brand name in a particular foreign market. When MTV first entered India, it had a licensing agreement with a company called Asia to Star. MTV provided the television programming and Asia to Star sold the local advertising (commercials), worked with Indian cable TV providers (to get MTV included as part of their cable TV packages), and split the revenues with MTV. Unfortunately, this licensing agreement failed for two reasons. First, at that time, MTV was feeding Western programming into the country, while viewers wanted programming that reflected their values, tastes, and culture. Second, Asia to Star was purchased by News Corp., one of MTV's key competitors. MTV's parent company is Viacom, and Viacom's primary competitor is New Corp., a global content provider on five continents. News Corp., which is owned by billionaire Rupert Murdoch, has 175 newspapers, 20th Century Fox movies, satellite TV provider DirecTV, and 35 TV stations around the world. Indeed, one of the disadvantages of licensing is that international licensees, in this case Asia to Star, can eventually become competitors.

After licensing failed, MTV expanded internationally by using wholly owned affiliates, which are 100 percent owned by the parent company. For example, MTV Australia, Brazil, Canada, China, and others (see www.mtv.com/

mtvinternational/ for a complete list) are all 100 percent owned by MTV International, a division of MTV. The primary advantage of wholly owned businesses is that the parent company receives all of the profits and has complete control over foreign facilities. The biggest disadvantage is the expense of building new operations or buying existing businesses. While the payoff can be enormous if wholly owned affiliates succeed, the losses can be immense if they fail because the parent company assumes all of the risk. At this point in its development, MTV International is profitable, but not by much. While it has access to huge markets—in fact, 80 percent of MTV viewers are *outside* the United States—access to those markets has yet to translate into large profits. Bill Roedy says, "The epicenter [of MTV International] is shifting to the Far East and India. They are amazing markets, but it's important to not get too euphoric about the numbers."

Finally, deciding where to take your company global is always an important decision. But, with so many good foreign markets to enter, the question for MTV International isn't where it should expand, but how it can expand successfully in so many different places at the same time?

Companies used to evolve slowly from small operations selling in their home markets to large businesses selling to foreign markets. Furthermore, as companies went global, they usually followed the phase model of globalization (in which a company makes the transition from a domestic company to a global company in the following sequential phases: exporting, cooperative contracts, strategic alliances, and wholly owned affiliates). Recently, however, three trends have combined to allow companies to skip the phase model when going global. First, quick, reliable air travel can transport people to nearly any point in the world within one day. Second, low-cost communication technologies, such as international e-mail, teleconferencing, phone conferencing, and the Internet, make it easier to communicate with global customers, suppliers, managers, and employees. Third, there is now a critical mass of businesspeople with extensive personal experience in all aspects of global business. This combination of developments has made it possible to start companies that are global from inception. With sales, employees, and financing in different countries, global new ventures are new companies founded with an active global strategy.

While MTV wasn't global from inception (it was around for a decade before it got serious about global expansion) its international division is very much like a global new venture. First, MTV International's has a truly global vision. For example, MTV Europe (part of MTV International) alone now has 45 regional channels. MTV Europe's latest startup is MTV Africa, which will be MTV International's 100th channel.

Second, like a new global venture, rather than going global one country at a time, MTV International expanded in numerous foreign markets at the same time. Bill Roedy indicates that the company's global expansion will keep up this quick pace because, "Whenever I'm asked to forecast our expansion around the world, I get it wrong. I always underestimate it." But, for now, "We see in excess of 30 percent growth internationally."

With a global vision and expansion in so many places at the same time, how can MTV international expand successfully and grow profits at the same time? With MTV in so many foreign markets, and with local music, shows, and artists comprising 70 percent of the content on most of MTV International's channels, Roedy believes that it's time for MTV International to focus on global consistency—that is, using similar shows or content to a somewhat larger extent than it has in the past. What's driving this change is the opportunity to improve revenues and share costs across a larger base of channels. In other words, rather than viewing each MTV International channel as a standalone operation, Roedy wants the company to take advantage of their combined synergies.

One way it intends to do this is through regional and global sales teams who serve as one easy point of contact for companies that want to advertise simultaneously in dozens of different markets. The second way is to spread development costs for original programming, which can cost US$200 000 to US$350 000 per half-hour show, across different markets. By spreading the cost and, hopefully, revenues across multiple markets, MTV International should be able to develop such programming. Whether it will work or not is another matter, but MTV International clearly believes that it will, as it has set aside "tens of millions" of dollars to develop such programming. However, to make sure that it doesn't stray from the strategy that made it a global success, local managers will still be in charge of local programming decisions, and local content will still comprise 70 percent of channel programming.

Key Terms

Asia-Pacific Economic Cooperation (APEC) *(220)*
Association of Southeast Asian Nations (ASEAN) *(220)*
cooperative contract *(223)*
country of manufacture *(216)*
country of origin *(216)*
expatriate *(232)*
exporting *(222)*
foreign direct investment (FDI) *(214)*
franchise *(223)*
Free Trade Area of the Americas (FTAA) *(220)*
General Agreement on Tariffs and Trade (GATT) *(218)*
global business *(214)*
global new ventures *(225)*
joint venture *(224)*
licensing *(223)*
Maastricht Treaty of Europe *(219)*
multinational corporation *(216)*
North American Free Trade Agreement (NAFTA) *(219)*
national culture *(229)*
nontariff barriers *(217)*
policy uncertainty *(228)*
political uncertainty *(228)*
protectionism *(217)*
purchasing power *(226)*
quota *(217)*
regional trading zones *(218)*
strategic alliance *(224)*
subsidies *(217)*
tariff *(217)*
trade barriers *(217)*
voluntary export restraints *(217)*
wholly owned affiliates *(225)*
world gross national product *(216)*

Self-Assessment

ARE YOU NATION-MINDED OR WORLD-MINDED?

Attitudes about global business are as varied as managers are numerous. It seems that the business press can always find someone who is for globalization and someone who is against it. But regardless of your opinion on the subject, managers will increasingly confront issues related to the globalization of the business environment. It is probably that, as a manager, you will need to develop global sensibilities (if you don't already have them). Understanding your own cultural perspective is the first step in doing so. The Assessment Appendix contains a detailed survey that will reveal your global perspective and provide you with a baseline as you develop your managerial skills. Turn to page 515 to see if you tend to be more nation-minded or world-minded.

Management Decisions

WHEN IN CHINA, NEGOTIATE LIKE THE CHINESE DO?[54]

You are the chief executive officer of a medium-sized machine manufacturing company in Mississauga, Ontario. Twelve months ago, one of your best customers referred a Chinese manufacturer to you for business. Since then, a delegation of Chinese managers has twice visited your Ontario factory. You, your sales manager, and your plant manager took a ten-day trip to China to visit the Chinese company and to investigate shipping, banking, and customs procedures. After months of preparation, you are ready to begin formal negotiations. In ten days, representatives from your company will meet in Hong Kong with representatives from the Chinese company to negotiate a contract specifying the size, price, and delivery date of what you believe will be the largest overseas shipment your company has ever made.

You're concerned, however, because no one on your team has any experience negotiating with the Chinese, who are patient and skilled negotiators. As you were considering your options, some questions occurred to you.

Questions

1. Should you, the CEO, attend and be part of the negotiations?
2. North Americans and Chinese typically have very different negotiating styles. Since the Chinese are unlikely to adopt a North American style of negotiating, would negotiations go better if your team was prepared to negotiate "Chinese-style"?
3. Your sales manager feels that you should hire a Hong Kong consultant with extensive experience dealing with the Chinese to negotiate for your company. You can see the merit in this, but you also know that "guanxi," or personal relationships, is one of the most important parts of doing business in China. If you hired a Hong Kong consultant to do the negotiations, would you damage the "guanxi" that it has taken you six months to establish?

Management Decisions

HEARTS AT HOME AND GOING NATIVE[55]

In the last five years, your company has considerably improved the way in which it prepares employees for international assignments. Except in emergencies, employees are typically given four to five months' notice before being sent abroad. Employees, their spouses, and their families are carefully screened and selected. Moreover, all employees and their families receive two months of extensive language and cultural training before beginning an international assignment. Although these steps have greatly improved the success and performance of your company's expatriates, you're still running into two serious problems.

Problem number one is the expatriate who "goes native." Expatriates who go native are strongly committed to doing what is right for the foreign office, even at the expense of ignoring parent company policy. For example, Gary, a manager who had spent half his 15 years with a company on three different overseas assignments, stated, "My first commitment is to the unit here [in France]. In fact, half the time I feel as if corporate is a competitor I must fight rather than a benevolent parent I can look to for support." While he had only six months remaining on his French assignment, Gary had already asked the home office for an extended stay.

Problem number two is the expatriate whose heart is still at home. Consider Earl, who, after two decades with the parent company, was promoted to managing director of European headquarters. This was Earl's first international assignment. Consequently, his allegiance was first and foremost to the parent company rather than the European office. In fact, when his two years as managing director are up, he is going straight back home.

Expatriates who go native make it very difficult for companies to achieve global consistency in their operations. Expatriates whose hearts are at home ignore the importance of local adaptation. As one senior manager put it, "How can we get expatriate managers who are committed to the local overseas operation during their international assignments, but who remain loyal to the parent firm?"

Questions

1. What steps would you take to reduce the chances that an expatriate would go native?
2. What steps would you take to reduce the chances that an expatriate would leave his or her heart at home?
3. What steps could be taken to encourage expatriates to develop a dual allegiance to the parent company and the overseas operation?

Discussion Questions

1. Explain what is meant by trade barriers and identify two general kinds of trade barriers used by government.
2. IBM, Microsoft, Sony, and Nokia are examples of companies that operate and sell products around the world. How they sell their products and services often differs from country to country. Yet surprisingly, they often standardize their basic business procedures regardless of location. Why do they do this?
3. Briefly explain the phase model of globalization and list its stages in the appropriate order.
4. Convi Ltd. is a small Nova Scotia exporter of apple products including jams, sauces, and dried fruit. Recently, its CEO has been considering the potential of Sweden as a market for its products. Faced with limited human resources, she has asked your firm to prepare a consulting report to determine the growth potential of this market. How will you and your colleagues assess this new market opportunity for her?
5. Japan is an important market for Canadian firms that sell mineral sands products. You work in the Montreal offices of one of these firms. A request has come from your firm's Tokyo office asking for another employee to be hired to aid in the sales effort in Asia. The immediate reaction of a number of your colleagues is to question the need for a new body and to wonder aloud about what is so different about selling in Japan. Sympathizing with your colleague in Japan, you suggest that he might prepare a brief presentation regarding the differences in national culture for his trip to Montreal in the upcoming weeks. You agree to help him and offer to send by e-mail a brief discussion of the five dimensions that one might use to differentiate one national culture from another. What will you put in the e-mail message?

Critical Thinking Video Case

CBC

Visit www.management2e.nelson.com to view this chapter's CBC video case.

Take Two

Biz Flix
Mr. Baseball

The New York Yankees trade aging baseball player Jack Elliot (Tom Selleck) to the Chunichi Dragons, a Japanese team. This light-hearted comedy traces Elliot's bungling entry into Japanese culture where he almost loses everything, including Hiroko Uchiyama (Aya Takanashi). As Elliot slowly begins to understand Japanese culture and Japanese baseball, he finally is accepted by his teammates. This film shows many examples of Japanese culture, especially the Japanese love for baseball. Unknown to Hiroko's father, she and Jack develop an intimate relationship. Meanwhile, Jack does not know that Hiroko's father is "The Chief" (Ken Takakura), the manager of the Chunichi Dragons. This scene takes place after "The Chief" has removed Jack from a baseball game. The scene shows Jack dining with Hiroko and her grandmother (Mineko Yorozuya), grandfather (Jun Hamamura), and father.

What to Watch for and Ask Yourself

1. Does Jack Elliot behave as if he had had cross-cultural training before arriving in Japan?
2. Is he culturally sensitive or insensitive?
3. What do you propose that Elliot do for the rest of his time in Japan?

Management Workplace
King Company

David Arnold began his career as a wristwatch salesman, keeping excess inventory in his garage. He developed a strong customer base, expanded his business, and became a powerhouse in wristwatches. Watch the video to see how King Company used global management techniques to grow and prosper.

What to Watch for and Ask Yourself

1. King Company is headquartered in the United States and sells products online in the United States. Is it a global business? Why or why not?
2. What forms of global business has King Company used to grow?
3. Given that King Company is based in the United States, does David Arnold have to contend with cultural issues? Explain.

IMAGE COURTESY OF DOMAINE DE GRAND PRÉ

Organizational Strategy

Chapter 9

CHAPTER OUTLINE

LEARNING OBJECTIVES

After reading this chapter, you should be able to

1. explain the components of sustainable competitive advantage and why it is important.
2. describe the steps involved in the strategy-making process.
3. explain the different kinds of corporate-level strategies.
4. describe the different kinds of industry-level strategies.
5. explain the components and kinds of firm-level strategies.

Careers and passion can lead individuals in interesting directions. Hanspeter Stutz is a case in point. Stutz has come a long way from his days running an electric power company in Switzerland. Having immigrated to Canada with his family in the late 1990s, he had a dream—to establish a successful wine operation in Canada. Yet, this dream was not a life-long one. His introduction to the wine industry began in the 1980s and from Switzerland, when he discovered Vineland, a winery that had been abandoned following a bankruptcy and was then available at a sheriff's sale. Vineland, in operation since the 1970s had a special place in Nova Scotia history. It was the first estate operation in the province with its own grown wines. Following a short period of success internationally, it was put up for sale in 1988. Stutz says his interest "happened more by accident than design. I'd never heard of Niagara wines and never thought about making wine in Nova Scotia," he admits. "But, when I visited the winery, I saw the potential."[1]

The decision to make the purchase was not an easy one. The winery had an interesting history. Its founder, Roger Dial, began his work in 1978, and after many years of intense effort, he was able to bring prosperity to the winery, having conquered the challenges of a cool climate. His strategy in terms of grapes was fascinating and for a while successful. Russian Grape varieties Severnyi and Michurinetz were his choice. He planted and cared for them for years. Unfortunately, Nova Scotia had a reputation as a province where good wine could not be produced, and the long-term costs associated with operating a winery and the impact of time got the better of Dial and his Vineland winery.

What Would You Do?

As Stutz looked out over the winery, a number of concerns rested heavily on his shoulders.

Nova Scotia was beautiful. Every year, it was a destination to thousands of tourists, and the land of lobster, Lunenberg, and beautiful windswept beaches. It was also famous for the Cabot Trail of Cape Breton. Behind him at a distance of just a few kilometres were the world's highest tides of the Bay of Fundy. Unfortunately, Nova Scotia was not known for its wines.

In all of Canada, slightly more than 1000 individuals were employed in the wine industry. Only a small fraction of that number could be found in the Maritimes, let alone Nova Scotia. By world standards, the industry was tiny. Even with an initial 12 hectares of land under cultivation, his winery operation would be small. He was aware that new world wine-growing countries such as Australia and Chile were placing vast tracts of land under cultivation. These imported wines and many others were increasing their presence in Canadian market and were very popular. Indeed, imports captured almost 60 percent of the Canadian wine market in 1991. In terms of relative per capita wine consumption, Canadians drank only a small fraction of wine as compared to most Europeans. And then there was that image thing to consider. Canadian wines did not have a great reputation in the marketplace.

There was, however, an upside to consider. Ontario wine producers had recently developed the Vintners Quality Alliance (VQA) standards to help consumers identify high-quality wines based on the origin of the grapes. These standards were subsequently adopted in British Columbia. Unfortunately, the VQA was not even on the horizon in terms of Nova Scotia wine production. This led to another thought. What variety of grape should Stutz cultivate? Knowledge regarding types of grapes that might grow well in the Annapolis Valley was limited. Indeed, it was really only in the last decade that serious research began on this topic and only a few different types of grape varieties had been identified as logical candidates for planting or cultivation.

On that late summer day in 1993, Hanspeter Stutz's mind was racing with too much information. He wanted to make a good decision regarding purchasing the winery and vineyard. But how might he make sense of all these issues and do so in a systemic manner? **If you were Hanspeter Stutz, what would you do?**

In Chapter 4, you learned that strategic plans are overall company plans that clarify how a company intends to serve customers and position itself against competitors over the next two to five years. Picking the wrong strategic plan can have devastating consequences. This chapter begins with an in-depth look at how managers create and use strategies to obtain a sustainable competitive advantage. Then you will learn the three steps of the strategy-making process. Next, you will learn about corporate-level strategies that help managers answer the question: What business or businesses should we be in? You will then examine the industry-level competitive strategies that help managers determine how to compete successfully within a particular line of business. The chapter finishes with a review of the firm-level strategies of direct competition and entrepreneurship.

Basics of Organizational Strategy

Strategy is a term used frequently when discussing the behaviour of corporations. Unfortunately, it occasionally suffers from overuse and often the term is not well understood. Even when conceived by the brightest of minds, strategies often fail. The reasons for this are that strategies are carried out within competitive environments, are designed by humans and thus subject to our own inherent frailties, can occur at different levels, and take different forms. Efforts to improve the effectiveness of strategies will most often include planning. Planning helps to reduce uncertainty, thus increasing the probability that an implemented strategy will be successful. Planning, as you may recall, was the subject of Chapter 4. Strategy is the subject of this chapter.

After reading the next two sections, you should be able to

1. explain the components of sustainable competitive advantage and why it is important.
2. describe the steps involved in the strategy-making process.

resources
the assets, capabilities, processes, information, and knowledge that an organization uses to improve its effectiveness and efficiency and to create and sustain an advantage over competitors

competitive advantage
providing greater value for customers than competitors can

sustainable competitive advantage
a competitive advantage that other companies have tried unsuccessfully to duplicate and have, for the moment, stopped trying to duplicate

valuable resource
a resource that allows companies to improve efficiency and effectiveness

rare resource
a resource that is not controlled or possessed by many competing firms

imperfectly imitable resource
a resource that is impossible or extremely costly or difficult for other firms to duplicate

1 SUSTAINABLE COMPETITIVE ADVANTAGE

An organization's **resources** are the assets, capabilities, processes, information, and knowledge that the organization controls. Firms use their resources to improve organizational effectiveness and efficiency. Resources are critical to organizational strategy because they can help companies create and sustain an advantage over competitors.[2]

Organizations can achieve a **competitive advantage** by using their resources to provide greater value for customers than competitors can. A competitive advantage becomes a **sustainable competitive advantage** when other companies cannot duplicate the value a firm is providing to customers. Importantly, sustainable competitive advantage is not the same as a long-lasting competitive advantage, though companies obviously want a competitive advantage to last a long time. Instead, a competitive advantage is sustained if that advantage still exists after competitors have tried unsuccessfully to duplicate the advantage and have, for the moment, stopped trying to duplicate it.

Four conditions must be met if a firm's resources are to be used to achieve a sustainable competitive advantage. The resources must be valuable, rare, imperfectly imitable, and nonsubstitutable.

Valuable resources allow companies to improve their efficiency and effectiveness. Unfortunately, changes in customer demand and preferences, competitors' actions, and technology can make once-valuable resources much less valuable. For sustained competitive advantage, valuable resources must also be rare resources. Think about it. How can a company sustain a competitive advantage if all of its competitors have similar resources and capabilities? Consequently, **rare resources**, resources that are not controlled or possessed by many competing firms, are necessary to sustain a competitive advantage. For sustained competitive advantage, other firms must be unable to imitate or find substitutes for those valuable, rare resources. **Imperfectly imitable resources** are impossible or extremely costly or difficult to duplicate. Finally, valuable, rare, imperfectly imitable resources can produce sustainable competitive advantage only if they are also **nonsubstitutable resources**, meaning that no other resources can replace them and produce similar value or competitive advantage.

nonsubstitutable resource a resource, without equivalent substitutes or replacements, that produces value or competitive advantage

Review 1: Sustainable Competitive Advantage

Firms can use their resources to create and sustain a competitive advantage—that is, to provide greater value for customers than competitors can. A competitive advantage becomes sustainable when other companies cannot duplicate the benefits it provides and have, for now, stopped trying. To provide a sustainable competitive advantage, the firm's resources must be valuable (capable of improving efficiency and effectiveness), rare (not possessed by many competing firms), imperfectly imitable (extremely costly or difficult to duplicate), and nonsubstitutable (competitors cannot substitute other resources to produce similar value).

2 STRATEGY-MAKING PROCESS

Companies use a strategy-making process to create strategies that produce sustainable competitive advantage.[3] Exhibit 9.1 displays the three steps of the strategy-making process.

The three steps of the strategy-making process are listed below. Let's examine each of these steps in more detail: assessing the need for strategic change, situational analysis, and choosing strategic alternatives.

Assessing the Need for Strategic Change

The external business environment is much more turbulent than it used to be. With customers' needs constantly growing and changing, and with competitors working harder, faster, and smarter to meet those needs, the first step in strategy-making is determining the need for strategic change. In other words, the company needs to determine whether or not it needs to change its strategy to sustain a competitive advantage.[5]

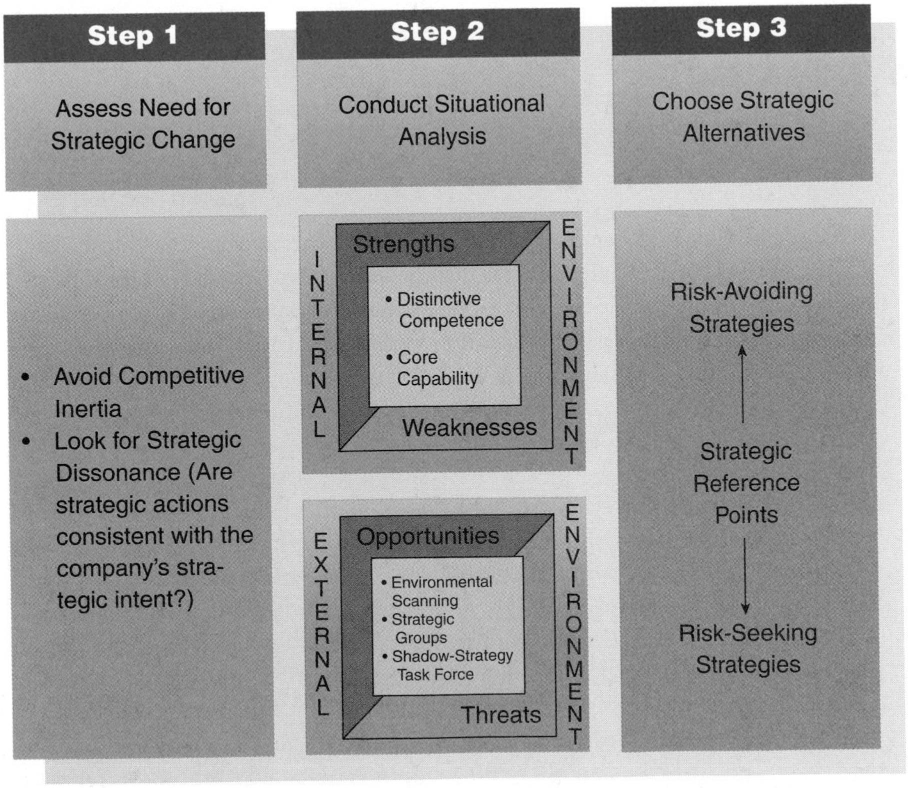

EXHIBIT 9.1 Three Steps of the Strategy-Making Process

WHAT REALLY WORKS

Strategy-Making for Firms, Big and Small[4]

The strategy-making process (assessing the need for strategic change, conducting a situational analysis, and choosing strategic alternatives) is the method by which companies create strategies that produce sustainable competitive advantage. For years, it had been thought that strategy-making was something that only large firms could do well. It was believed that small firms did not have the time, knowledge, or staff to do a good job of strategy-making. However, two meta-analyses indicate that strategy-making can improve the profits, sales growth, and return on investment of both big and small firms.

STRATEGY-MAKING FOR BIG FIRMS

There is a 72 percent chance that big companies that engage in the strategy-making process will be more profitable than big companies that don't. However, strategy-making not only improves profits, but also helps companies grow. Specifically, there is a 75 percent chance that big companies that engage in the strategy-making process will have greater sales and earnings growth than big companies that don't. Thus, in practical terms, the strategy-making process can make a significant difference in a big company's profits and growth.

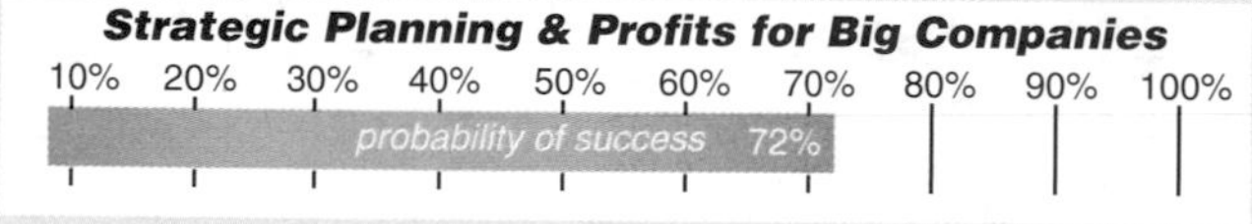

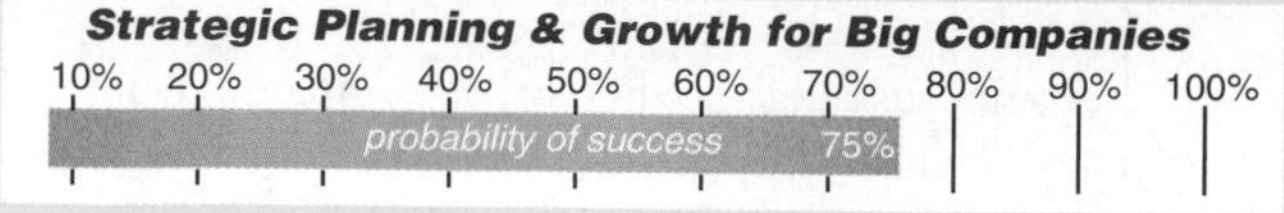

STRATEGY-MAKING FOR SMALL FIRMS

However, strategy-making can also improve the performance of small firms. There is a 61 percent chance that small firms that engage in the strategy-making process will have more sales growth than small firms that don't. Likewise, there is a 62 percent chance that small firms that engage in the strategy-making process will have a larger return on investment than small companies that don't. Thus, in practical terms, the strategy-making process can make a significant difference in a small company's profits and growth, too.

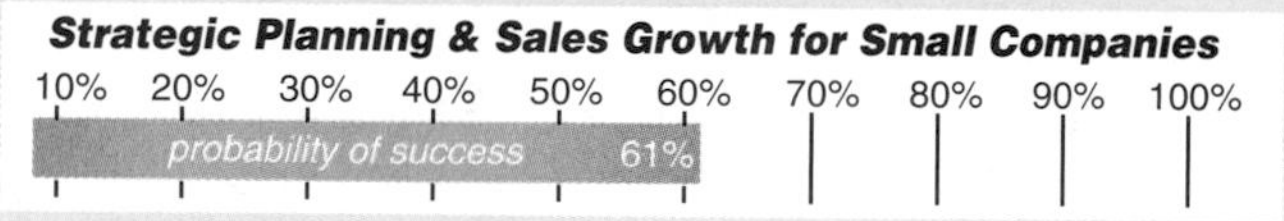

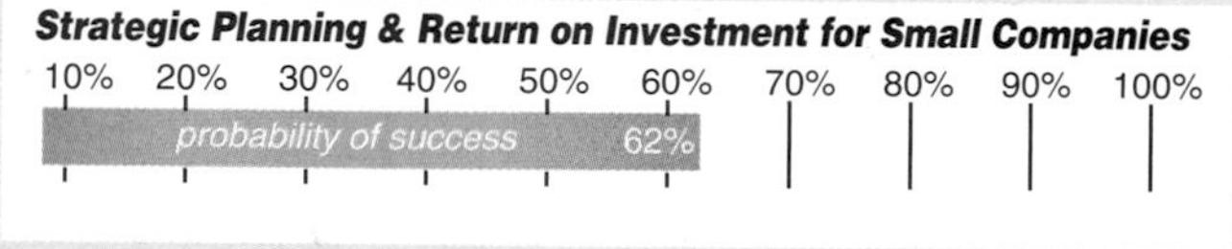

It might seem that determining the need for strategic change would be easy to do, but in reality, it's not. There's a great deal of uncertainty in strategic business environments. Furthermore, top-level managers are often slow to recognize the need for strategic change, especially at successful companies that have created and sustained competitive advantages. Because they are acutely aware of the strategies that made their companies successful, they continue to rely on them, even as the competition changes. In other words, success often leads to **competitive inertia**—a reluctance to change strategies or competitive practices that have been successful in the past.

competitive inertia
a reluctance to change strategies or competitive practices that have been successful in the past

For example, just a few years ago, no one in the cable TV industry believed that direct broadcast satellite dishes would threaten their business. With huge satellite dishes costing over $1000, why would the millions of Canadians who already had cable TV in their homes pay more than $1500 to install an unsightly 3-metre satellite dish in their yard to get the same number of channels that they could get from their local cable company for an installation fee of less than $100 and a moderate monthly charge? Managers of cable TV companies would laugh that "DBS" (direct broadcast satellite) really stood for "Don't Be Stupid." However, now that satellite dishes are smaller (60 cm in diameter), cost less than $200, and offer 200 channels (compared to the 60 or fewer channels

CP PHOTO/LARRY MACDOUGAL

OptiCanada is a Canadian success story. In less than five years it has created and brought to market one of the most important technologies driving the development of Alberta's Oilsands.

available on most cable systems), no one who manages a cable company is laughing anymore. Indeed, the number of subscribers to satellite TV service providers such as Bell ExpressVu and Star Choice is predicted to increase dramatically in the next few years.[6]

So, besides being aware of the dangers of competitive inertia, what can managers do to improve the speed and accuracy with which they determine the need for strategic change? One method is to actively look for signs of strategic dissonance. **Strategic dissonance** is a discrepancy between upper management's intended strategy and the strategy actually implemented by the lower levels of management. Upper management sets overall company strategy, but middle and lower-level managers must carry out the strategy. Middle and lower-level managers are held directly responsible for meeting customers' needs and responding to competitors' actions. While strategic dissonance can indicate that these managers are not doing what they should to carry out company strategy, it can also mean that the intended strategy is out of date and needs to be changed.

strategic dissonance
a discrepancy between upper management's intended strategy and the strategy actually implemented by lower levels of management

Situational Analysis

A situational analysis can also help managers determine the need for strategic change. A **situational analysis**, also called a **SWOT analysis** for *strengths, weaknesses, opportunities,* and *threats,* is an assessment of the strengths and weaknesses in an organization's internal environment and the opportunities and threats in its external environment.[7] Ideally, a SWOT analysis helps a company determine how to increase internal strengths and minimize internal weaknesses while simultaneously maximizing external opportunities and minimizing external threats. However, a basic situational analysis of Apple Computer (www.apple.com) shows this is not always easy to do. One of Apple's strengths used to be that its computers were much easier to learn and use than others on the market. Indeed, millions of customers were willing to pay much more for an Apple because this was so. However, there have been key changes in Apple's external environment. One of the most important was the introduction of Microsoft's Windows 95 (followed by Windows 98) software, which made IBM-compatible computers much easier to use. Consequently, Apple's strength, coupled with the much higher prices that Apple charged for its computers, eventually became a tremendous weakness. The result: Apple's share of the personal computer market plummeted from 16 percent to 4 percent in less than three years.[8]

situational (SWOT) analysis
an assessment of the strengths and weaknesses in an organization's internal environment and the opportunities and threats in its external environment

What are specific examples of strengths and weaknesses or opportunities and threats? If one thinks of strength, what comes to mind is preferential access to natural resources, patents, facility locations that are advantageous, well-known brands, and distinctive knowledge of production processes. Weaknesses may arise from ineffective marketing, inconsistent access to distribution channels, corporate image problems, and inferior goods and services. Opportunities can take the form of the opening up of new international markets, the formation of strategic alliances, the existence of a weak market leader, legislation that weakens regulation, and the reduction of international trade barriers. Finally, threats include (but are not limited to) legislation that bring about new regulations, increased trade barriers, powerful new industry entrants, and price wars among competitors.

distinctive competence
what a company can make, do, or perform better than competitors

core capabilities
the internal decision-making routines, problem-solving processes, and organizational cultures that determine how efficiently inputs can be turned into outputs

strategic group
a group of companies within an industry that top managers choose to compare, evaluate, and benchmark strategic threats and opportunities

As Apple's experience shows, competitive advantages can erode over time if internal strengths eventually become weaknesses. Consequently, an analysis of an organization's internal environment—that is, a company's strengths and weaknesses—begins with an assessment of distinctive competencies and core capabilities. A **distinctive competence** is something that a company can make, do, or perform better than its competitors. For example, *Consumer Reports* magazine (www.consumerreports.org) consistently ranks Toyota cars number one in quality and reliability.

While distinctive competencies are tangible—for example, a product or service is faster, cheaper, or better—the core capabilities that produce distinctive competencies are not. **Core capabilities** are the less visible, internal decision-making routines, problem-solving processes, and organizational cultures that determine how efficiently inputs can be turned into outputs.[10] Distinctive competencies cannot be sustained for long without superior core capabilities.

After examining internal strengths and weaknesses, the second part of a situational analysis is to look outside the company and assess the opportunities and threats in the external environment. In Chapter 2, you learned that environmental scanning is searching the environment for important events or issues that might affect the organization. With environmental scanning, managers usually scan the environment to stay up to date on important factors in their environment, such as pricing trends and changes in technology in the industry. However, in a situational analysis, managers use environmental scanning to identify specific opportunities and threats that can either improve or harm the company's ability to sustain its competitive advantage. Identification of strategic groups and formation of shadow-strategy task forces are two ways to do this.

Strategic groups are not "actual" groups, but are selected for study by managers. A strategic group is a group of other companies within an industry that top managers choose for comparing, evaluating, and benchmarking their company's strategic threats and opportunities.[11] Typically, managers include companies as part of their strategic group if they compete directly with those companies for customers or if those companies use strategies similar to theirs. For example, it's likely that the managers at CanWest Global, the largest Canadian newspaper publisher (over 30 daily newspapers, including the *National Post*, the *Montreal Gazette*, the *Calgary Herald*, and the *Ottawa Citizen*), assess strategic threats and opportunities by comparing themselves to a strategic group consisting of the other major newspaper companies. This would probably include Quebecor Inc. through its Sun Media subsidiary (the *Toronto Sun*, the *Calgary Sun*, the *Ottawa Sun*, and many other newspapers), BellGlobe Media (the *Globe and Mail*), and Torstar Corporation (the *Toronto Star*). Indeed, CanWest links its newspapers together online through the Canada.com Web site (www.canada.com) while the Sun Media papers may be found by browsing the Canoe.ca site (www.canoe.ca). By contrast, given that millions of Canadians read CanWest publications, it's

DOING THE RIGHT THING

IS ETHICS AN OVERLOOKED SOURCE OF COMPETITIVE ADVANTAGE?[9]

Volvo's reputation for selling safe cars has been a source of competitive advantage for years. You didn't buy a boxy Volvo for its looks; you bought it because your family would be well protected in an accident. If safety can be a source of competitive advantage, could ethics be one, too? While competitive advantage usually comes from physical capital (plant, equipment, finances), organizational capital (structure, planning, systems), and human capital (skills, judgment, adaptability of your work force), Johnson & Johnson is still widely admired, more than two decades later, for the way it quickly pulled Tylenol from store shelves (several people died after someone put cyanide in Tylenol caplets) and introduced tamper-proof packaging. The move cost the company about US$500 million, but protected consumers from further harm. Should ethics be your first source of competitive advantage? Probably not. It makes more sense to start with low costs, good service, or unique product capabilities. But when you're looking for another way to create or sustain a competitive advantage, consider that a reputation as an ethical corporation may be a way to differentiate your company from the competition.

unlikely that its management worries much about student newspapers such as the *McGill Daily* or Acadia University's *The Atheneum*. The *McGill Daily* is a fine paper, but with a total circulation of less than 5000, mostly within the McGill University community, managers at CanWest would probably not include it in their strategic group.

In fact, when scanning the environment for strategic threats and opportunities, managers tend to categorize the different companies in their industries into core and secondary strategic groups.[12] The first kind of strategic group consists of **core firms**—that is, central companies in a strategic group. CanWest's core firms would be Quebecor Media and BellGlobe Media. When most managers scan their environments for strategic threats and opportunities, they do so by primarily scanning the strategic actions of core firms. **Secondary firms** are firms that use related but somewhat different strategies from core firms. For CanWest, this might be Torstar, which publishes the *Toronto Star* and other daily newspapers. However, Torstar is somewhat different, in that it is also a book publisher with little presence in the television market; CanWest, BellGlobe Media, and Quebecor Media all own and operate television stations. Managers are aware of the potential threats and opportunities posed by secondary firms. However, they spend more time assessing the threats and opportunities associated with core firms.

core firms
the central companies in a strategic group

secondary firms
the firms in a strategic group that follow related but somewhat different strategies than do the core firms

Because top managers tend to limit their attention to the core firms in their strategic group, some companies have started using shadow-strategy task forces to more aggressively scan their environments for strategic threats and opportunities. The goal of a **shadow-strategy task force** is to actively seek out its own company's weaknesses and then, thinking like a competitor, determine how other companies could exploit them for competitive advantage.[13] Furthermore, to make sure that the task force challenges conventional thinking, its members should be independent-minded, come from a variety of company functions and levels, and have the access and authority to question the company's current strategic actions and intent. An interesting example relates to a manufacturer of pharmaceutical drugs, agricultural chemicals, plastics, pigments, and additives that had a large operation in Canada—Ciba-Geigy. Its industrial chemicals division made dyes used in carpet manufacturing. One of the difficulties in this business is ensuring colour consistency, that is, making sure that the dark grey carpet manufactured today looks the same colour as the dark grey carpet manufactured next week. Ciba-Geigy's shadow-strategy task force determined that if its competitors could find ways to consistently, precisely, and cheaply match colour carpet dyes (so that carpet colours looked the same regardless of when and where they were manufactured), Ciba-Geigy would be at a considerable competitive disadvantage. After the shadow-strategy task force challenged top management with its conclusions, the company went about developing distinctive competencies in dye research and manufacturing, which allowed it to make dyes with scientific preciseness.[14]

shadow-strategy task force
a committee within the company that analyzes the company's own weaknesses to determine how competitors could exploit them for competitive advantage

In short, there are two basic parts to a situational analysis. The first is to examine internal strengths and weaknesses by focusing on distinctive competencies and core capabilities. The second is to examine external opportunities and threats by focusing on environmental scanning, strategic groups, and shadow-strategy task forces.

Choosing Strategic Alternatives

After determining the need for strategic change and conducting a situational analysis, the last step in the strategy-making process is to choose strategic alternatives that will help the company create or maintain a sustainable competitive advantage. According to Strategic Reference Point Theory, managers choose between two basic alternative strategies. They can choose a conservative, risk-avoiding strategy that aims to protect an existing competitive advantage. Or they can choose an aggressive, risk-seeking strategy that aims to extend or create a sustainable competitive advantage.

The choice to be risk-seeking or risk-avoiding typically depends on whether top management views the company as falling above or below strategic reference points. **Strategic reference points** are the targets that managers use to measure whether their

strategic reference points
the strategic targets managers use to measure whether a firm has developed the core competencies it needs to achieve a sustainable competitive advantage

firms have developed the core competencies that they need to achieve a sustainable competitive advantage. For example, if a hotel chain decided to compete by providing superior quality and service, then top management would track the success of this strategy through customer surveys or published hotel ratings, such as those provided by the prestigious *Mobil Travel Guide* (http://exxonmobiltravel.com). By contrast, if a hotel chain decided to compete on price, it would regularly conduct market surveys that checked the prices of other hotels. The competitors' prices are the hotel managers' strategic reference points against which to compare their own pricing strategy. If competitors can consistently underprice them, then the managers need to determine whether their staff and resources have the core competencies to compete on price.

As shown in Exhibit 9.2, when companies are performing above or better than their strategic reference points, top management will typically be satisfied with company strategy. Ironically, this satisfaction tends to make top management conservative and risk-averse. After all, since the company already has a sustainable competitive advantage, the worst thing that could happen would be to lose it. Consequently, new issues or changes in the company's external environments are viewed as threats. But when companies are performing below or worse than their strategic reference points, top management will typically be dissatisfied with company strategy. However, in this instance, managers are much more likely to choose a daring, risk-taking strategy. After all, if the current strategy is producing substandard results, what does the company have to lose by switching to risky new strategies in the hopes that it can create a sustainable competitive advantage? Consequently, for companies in this situation, new issues or changes in external environments are viewed as opportunities for potential gain.

However, Strategic Reference Point Theory is not deterministic. Managers are not predestined to choose risk-averse or risk-seeking strategies for their companies. Indeed, one of the most important points in Strategic Reference Point Theory is that managers can influence the strategies chosen at their companies by actively changing and adjusting the strategic reference points they use to judge strategic performance. To illustrate, if a company has become complacent after consistently surpassing its strategic reference

EXHIBIT 9.2
Strategic Reference Points

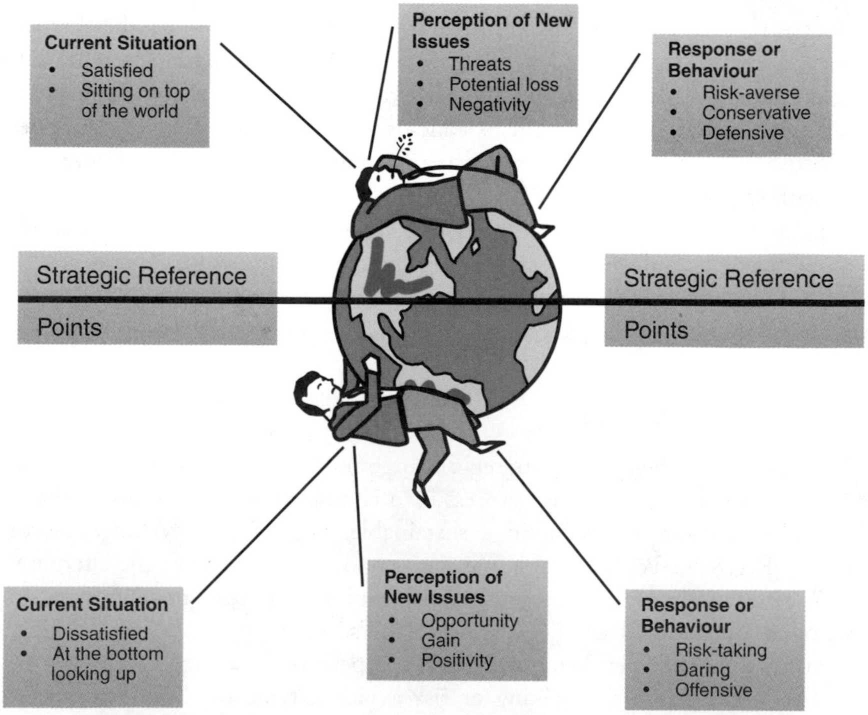

Source: A. Fiegenbaum, S. Hart, & D. Schendel, "Strategic Reference Point Theory," *Strategic Management Journal* 17 (1996): 219–235.

points, then top management can change the company's strategic risk orientation from risk-averse to risk-taking by raising the standards of performance (i.e., strategic reference points).

So even when (perhaps especially when) companies have achieved a sustainable competitive advantage, top managers may adjust or change strategic reference points to challenge themselves and their employees to develop new core competencies for the future. In the long run, effective organizations will frequently revise their strategic reference points to better focus managers' attention on the new challenges and opportunities that occur in their ever-changing business environments.

Review 2: Strategy-Making Process

The first step in strategy-making is determining whether a strategy needs to be changed in order to sustain a competitive advantage. Because uncertainty and competitive inertia make this difficult to determine, managers can improve the speed and accuracy of this step by looking for differences between top management's intended strategy and the strategy actually implemented by lower-level managers (i.e., strategic dissonance). The second step is to conduct a situational analysis that examines internal strengths and weaknesses (distinctive competencies and core capabilities), as well as external threats and opportunities (environmental scanning, strategic groups, and shadow-strategy task forces). In the third step of strategy-making, Strategic Reference Point Theory suggests that when companies are performing better than their strategic reference points, top management will typically choose a risk-averse strategy. When performance is below strategic reference points, risk-seeking strategies are more likely to be chosen. Importantly, however, managers can influence the choice of strategic alternatives by actively changing and adjusting the strategic reference points they use to judge strategic performance.

Corporate-, Industry-, and Firm-Level Strategies

What business are we in? How should we compete in this industry? Who are our competitors and how should we respond to them? These simple but powerful questions are at the heart of corporate-, industry-, and firm-level strategies.

After reading the next three sections, you should be able to

3 explain the different kinds of corporate-level strategies.

4 describe the different kinds of industry-level strategies.

5 explain the components and kinds of firm-level strategies.

Exhibit 9.3 provides an overview of the various corporate-, industry-, and firm-level strategies that you'll learn about in these sections.

3 CORPORATE-LEVEL STRATEGIES

Corporate-level strategy is the overall organizational strategy that addresses the question "What business or businesses are we in or should we be in?"

Let's learn more about how companies decide which businesses they should be in by examining the two major approaches to corporate-level strategy: portfolio strategy and grand strategies.

corporate-level strategy the overall organizational strategy that addresses the question "What business or businesses are we in or should we be in?"

diversification a strategy for reducing risk by buying a variety of items (stocks or, in the case of a corporation, types of businesses), so that the failure of one stock or one business does not doom the entire portfolio

Portfolio Strategy[15]

One of the standard strategies for stock market investors is **diversification**: buy stocks in a variety of companies in different industries. The purpose of this strategy is to reduce risk in the overall stock portfolio (i.e., the entire collection of stocks). The basic idea is simple: If you invest in ten companies in ten different industries, you won't lose your entire investment if one company performs poorly. Furthermore, because they're

CORPORATE-LEVEL STRATEGIES	

Portfolio Strategy
• Acquisitions, unrelated diversification, related diversification, single businesses
• Boston Consulting Group Matrix
  • Stars
  • Question marks
  • Cash cows
  • Dogs
Grand Strategies
• Growth
• Stability
• Retrenchment/recovery
	Positioning Strategies
	• Cost leadership
	• Differentiation
	• Focus
	Adaptive Strategies
	• Defenders
	• Prospectors
	• Analyzers
	• Reactors

INDUSTRY-LEVEL STRATEGIES	**FIRM-LEVEL STRATEGIES**
Five Industry Forces • Character of rivalry • Threat of new entrants • Threat of substitute products or services • Bargaining power of suppliers • Bargaining power of buyers	*Direct Competition* • Market commonality • Resource similarity *Strategic Moves of Direct Competition* • Attack • Response *Entrepreneurial Orientation* • Autonomy • Innovativeness • Risk-taking • Proactiveness • Competitive aggressiveness

EXHIBIT 9.3
Corporate-, Business-, and Firm-Level Strategies

in different industries, one company's losses are likely to be offset by another company's gains. Portfolio strategy is based on these same ideas.

portfolio strategy corporate-level strategy that minimizes risk by diversifying investment among various businesses or product lines

Portfolio strategy is a corporate-level strategy that minimizes risk by diversifying investment among various businesses or product lines. Like an investor who invests in a variety of stocks, portfolio strategy guides the strategic decisions of corporations that compete in a variety of businesses. For example, it could be used to guide the strategy of a company such as 3M, which makes 50 000 products for 16 different industries. Similarly, it could be used by Johnson & Johnson, which has 190 divisions making health-care products for the pharmaceuticals, diagnostics, consumers, and health-care professionals markets. And, just as investors consider the mix of stocks in their stock portfolio when deciding which stocks to buy or sell, portfolio strategy provides the following guidelines to help managers acquire companies that fit well with the rest of their corporate portfolio and sell those that don't.

acquisition purchase of a company by another company

unrelated diversification creating or acquiring companies in completely unrelated businesses

First, the more businesses in which a corporation competes, the smaller its overall chances of failing. Think of a corporation as a stool and its businesses as the legs of the stool. The more legs or businesses added to the stool, the less likely it is to tip over. Using this analogy, portfolio strategy reduces 3M's risk of failing, because the corporation's survival depends on essentially 16 different businesses. Because the emphasis is on adding "legs to the stool," managers who use portfolio strategy are often on the lookout for **acquisitions**—that is, other companies to buy.

Second, beyond adding new businesses to the corporate portfolio, portfolio strategy can reduce risk even more through **unrelated diversification**—creating or acquiring companies in completely unrelated businesses. If the businesses are unrelated, then losses in one business or industry will have minimal effect on the performance of other companies in the corporate portfolio. Bell Canada Enterprises (BCE) offers an example of a firm that toyed with a strategy of unrelated diversification:

> For decades, BCE has had but one goal—to escape the regulatory clutches of the Canadian Radio-television and Telecommunications Commission. The CRTC had (and still has) final say on what services could be offered to whom at what price in Bell's local markets.... The return on equity of BCE's main business, Bell Canada, while reasonable, could never be prodigious. Since that was no fun, BCE bought many unregulated businesses. The diversification exercises were flops for the most part.[17]

Because most internally grown businesses tend to be related to existing products or services, acquiring new businesses is the preferred method of unrelated diversification.

Third, investing the profits and cash flows from mature, slow-growth businesses into newer, faster-growing businesses can reduce long-term risk. The best-known portfolio strategy for guiding investment in a corporation's businesses is the Boston Consulting Group (BCG) matrix. The **BCG matrix** is a portfolio strategy that managers use to categorize their corporation's businesses by growth rate and relative market share, helping them decide how to invest corporate funds. The matrix, shown in Exhibit 9.4, separates businesses into four categories, based on how fast the market is growing (high growth or low growth) and the size of the business's share of that market (small or large). **Stars** are companies that have a large share of a fast-growing market. To take advantage of a star's fast-growing market and its strength in that market (large share), the corporation must invest substantially in it. However, the investment is usually worthwhile, because many stars produce sizable future profits. **Question marks** are companies that have a small share of a fast-growing market. If the corporation invests in these companies, they may eventually become stars, but their relative weakness in the market (small share) makes investing in question marks more risky than investing in stars. **Cash cows** are companies that have a large share of a slow-growing market. Companies in this situation are often highly profitable, hence the name "cash cow." Their profits should be reinvested in stars. Finally, **dogs** are companies that have a small share of a slow-growing market. As the name "dogs" suggests, having a small share of a slow-growth market is often not profitable. These companies should be divested.

While the BCG matrix and other forms of portfolio strategy are relatively popular among managers, portfolio strategy has some drawbacks. The most significant is that the evidence does not support the usefulness of acquiring unrelated businesses. As shown in Exhibit 9.5, there is a U-shaped relationship between diversification and risk. The left side of the curve shows that single businesses with no diversification are extremely risky (if the single business fails, the entire business fails). So, in part, the portfolio strategy of diversifying is correct—competing in a variety of different businesses can lower risk. However, portfolio strategy is partly wrong, too—the right side of the curve shows that conglomerates composed of completely unrelated businesses are even riskier than single, undiversified businesses.

The second set of problems with portfolio strategy has to do with the dysfunctional consequences that occur when companies are categorized as stars, cash cows, question marks, or dogs. Contrary to expectations, the BCG matrix often yields incorrect judgments about a company's future potential. This is because it relies on past performance

---

DOING THE RIGHT THING

ACQUISITION LUST: DON'T BE SEDUCED BY THE "DEAL"[16]

Dennis Kozlowski, the former CEO of Tyco Corporation, was called "deal-a-month-Dennis," because he grew Tyco by doing "deals" to acquire hundreds of companies in such diverse businesses as undersea fibre-optic cable, security alarm systems, medical supplies, and valves and pipes. Why do some companies and CEOs become seduced by the "deal"? Certainly, one reason is that deals generate media coverage, make you CEO of a larger company, increase your pay (CEOs of larger companies make more money), and generate "immediate" results. But, before spending millions, if not billions, to acquire another company, don't forget that studies repeatedly show there's only a 50-50 chance that a merger or acquisition will succeed. So, before "doing the deal," ask these tough questions: Will the acquisition increase productivity, improve service, cut costs, lead to better product design, generate and sustain a competitive advantage, and, in the end, pay for itself? Do the right thing. Don't be seduced by the "deal." Merge with or acquire other companies for the right reasons.

BCG matrix
a portfolio strategy, developed by the Boston Consulting Group, that managers use to categorize the corporation's businesses by growth rate and relative market share, helping them decide how to invest corporate funds

star
a company with a large share of a fast-growing market

question mark
a company with a small share of a fast-growing market

cash cow
a company with a large share of a slow-growing market

dog
a company with a small share of a slow-growing market

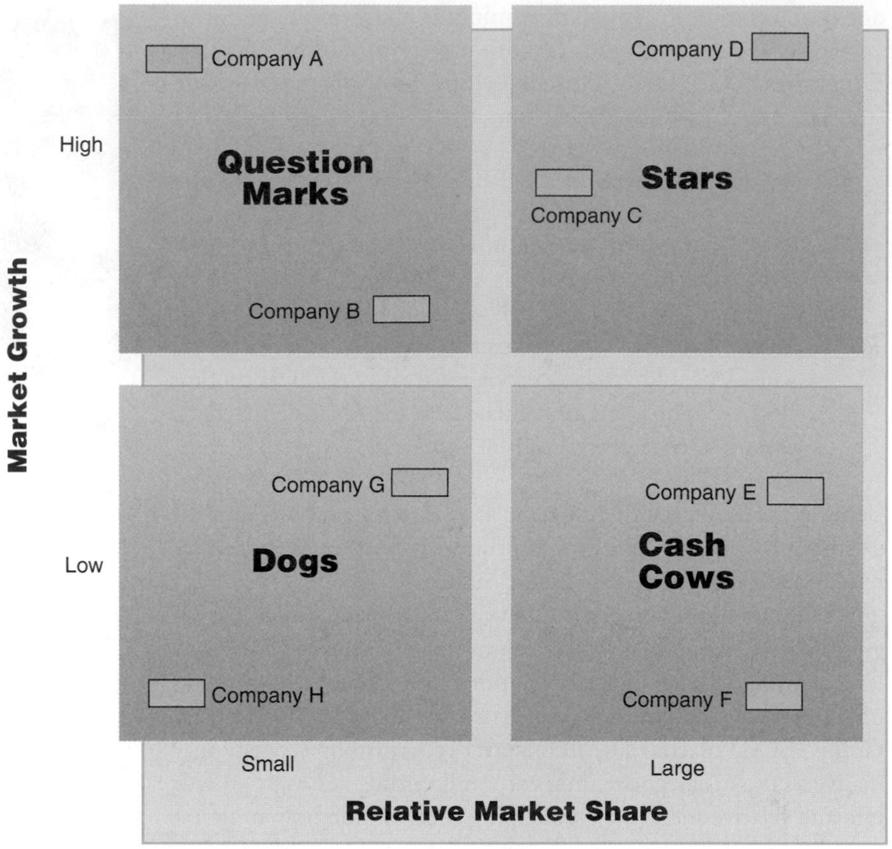

EXHIBIT 9.4
Boston Consulting Group Matrix

(i.e., previous market share and previous market growth), which is a notoriously poor predictor of future company performance.

Furthermore, using the BCG matrix can also weaken the strongest performer in the corporate portfolio, the cash cow. As funds are redirected from cash cows to stars, corporate managers essentially take away the resources needed to take advantage of the cash cow's new business opportunities. The result is that the cash cow becomes less aggressive in seeking new business or in defending its present business. Finally, labelling a top performer as a cash cow can harm employee morale. Instead of working for themselves, cash cow employees realize that they have inferior status because their successes are now being used to fund the growth of stars and question marks.

related diversification creating or acquiring companies that share similar products, manufacturing, marketing, technology, or cultures

So, what kind of portfolio strategy does the best job of helping managers decide which companies to buy or sell? The U-shaped curve in Exhibit 9.5 indicates that the best approach is probably **related diversification**, in which the different business units share similar products, manufacturing, marketing, technology, or cultures. The key to related diversification is to acquire or create new companies with core capabilities that complement the core capabilities of businesses already in the corporate portfolio. We began this section with the example of 3M (www.3m.com) and how its 50 000 products are sold in over 16 different industries. While seemingly different, most of 3M's product divisions are based in some fashion on its distinctive competencies in adhesives and tape (e.g., wet or dry sandpaper, Post-it notes, Scotchgard fabric protector, transdermal skin patches, reflective material used in traffic signs, etc.). Furthermore, divisions share a strong corporate culture that promotes and encourages risk-taking and innovation. In sum, in contrast to single, undiversified businesses or unrelated diversification, related diversification reduces risk, because the different businesses can work as a team, relying on each other for needed experience, expertise, and support.

Exhibit 9.6 details the problems associated with portfolio strategy and recommends ways that managers can increase their chances of success through related diversification.

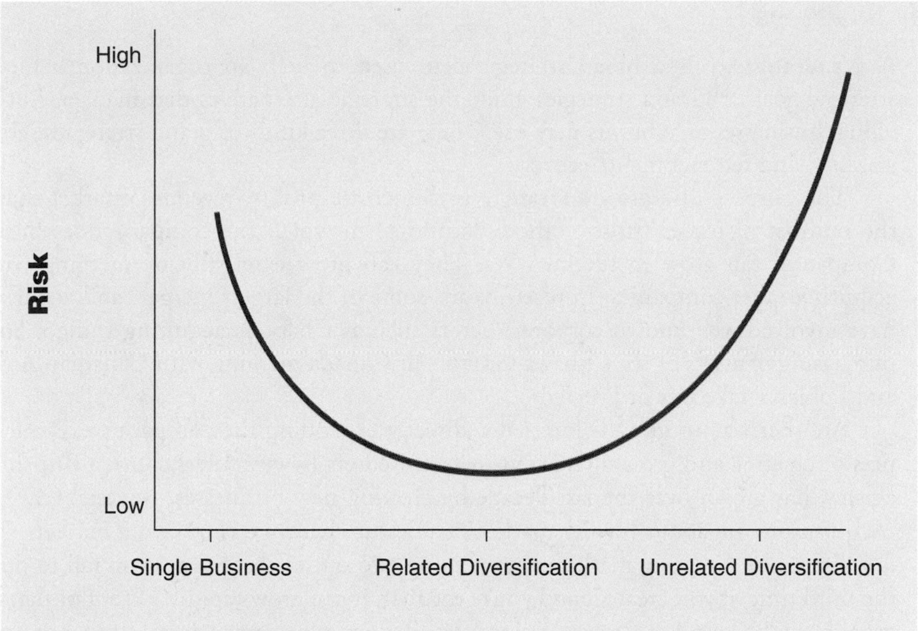

Source: "Psst ... The Merger Mavins Still Have It Wrong." (Figure) M. Lubatkin and P.J. Lane, *Academy of Management Executive*, 1996. Vol. 10.

EXHIBIT 9.5
U-Shaped Relationship Between Diversification and Risk

EXHIBIT 9.6
Portfolio Strategy: Problems and Recommendations

PROBLEMS WITH PORTFOLIO STRATEGY

- Unrelated diversification does not reduce risk.
- Uses present performance to predict future performance.
- Assessments of a business's growth potential are often inaccurate.
- Cash cows fail to aggressively pursue opportunities and defend themselves from threats.
- Being labelled a "cash cow" can hurt employee morale.
- Companies often overpay to acquire stars.
- Acquiring firms often treat acquired stars as "conquered foes." Key stars' managers, who once controlled their own destinies, often leave because they are now treated as relatively unimportant middle managers.

RECOMMENDATIONS FOR MAKING PORTFOLIO STRATEGY WORK

- Don't be so quick to sell dogs or question marks. Instead, management should commit to the markets in which it competes by strengthening core capabilities.
- Put your "eggs in similar (not different) baskets," by acquiring companies in related businesses.
- Acquire companies with complementary core capabilities.
- Encourage collaboration and cooperation between related firms and businesses within the company.
- "Date before you marry." Work with a business before deciding to acquire it.
- When in doubt, don't acquire new businesses. Mergers and acquisitions are inherently risky and difficult to make work. Acquire only firms that can help create or extend a sustainable competitive advantage.

Sources: M. Lubatkin, "Value-Creating Mergers: Fact or Folklore?" *Academy of Management Executive* 2 (1988): 295–302. M. Lubatkin & S. Chatterjee, "Extending Modern Portfolio Theory into the Domain of Corporate Diversification: Does It Apply?" *Academy of Management Journal* 37 (1994): 109–136. M.H. Lubatkin & P.J. Lane, "Psst ...The Merger Mavens Still Have It Wrong!" *Academy of Management Executive* 10 (1996): 21–39.

Grand Strategies

grand strategy
a broad corporate-level strategic plan used to achieve strategic goals and guide the strategic alternatives that managers of individual businesses or subunits may use

growth strategy
strategy that focuses on increasing profits, revenues, market share, or the number of places in which the company does business

stability strategy
strategy that focuses on improving the way a company sells the same products or services to the same customers

retrenchment strategy
strategy that focuses on turning around very poor company performance by shrinking the size or scope of the business

recovery
the strategic actions taken after retrenchment to return to a growth strategy

A **grand strategy** is a broad strategic plan used to help an organization achieve its strategic goals.[18] Grand strategies guide the strategic alternatives that managers of individual businesses or subunits may use. There are three kinds of grand strategies: growth, stability, and retrenchment/recovery.

The purpose of a **growth strategy** is to increase profits, revenues, market share, or the number of places (stores, offices, locations) in which the company does business. Companies can grow in several ways. They can grow externally by merging with or acquiring other companies. In recent years, some of the largest mergers and acquisitions have involved well-known corporate actors such as Chapters acquiring Indigo, Sobeys' purchasing of assets of the Oshawa Group, Air Canada merging with Canadian Airlines, and Loblaws' takeover of Provigo.

Another way to grow is internally, directly expanding the company's existing business or creating and growing new businesses. Reuters (www.reuters.com), a British news agency, has grown over the last decade by creating new businesses. Reuters' CEO said, "Acquisitions are about buying market share. Our challenge is to create markets. There is a difference. Creating markets is something two out of three times you fail to do. But the third time, if you create it and you're the first, it can grow rapidly." Proof of that rapid growth can be found in Reuters' rising sales. Reuters expects to achieve similar growth by expanding many of its new businesses on the Internet. For now, Reuters is the leading news provider on the Internet, with its news reports available at 900 different Web sites. However, Reuters' Reality Online division also designs transaction-based sites for stock brokerage companies that allow customers to research, buy, and sell investments via the World Wide Web.[19]

The purpose of a **stability strategy** is to continue doing what the company has been doing, but just do it better. Consequently, companies following a stability strategy try to improve the way they sell the same products or services to the same customers. For example, Danzas Corporation (www.danzas.com), an international air and sea freight company with 13 offices in Canada, is pursuing a stability strategy. Danzas, using what it calls its "core carriers strategy," has decided to limit the number of customers it serves and the number of air hubs and seaports where it will handle freight. The reason? To improve the quality of service it provides to its four core customers, Hapag-Lloyd, DSR-Senator Lines, Cho Yang, and Mediterranean Shipping Company, each of which has a long-term contract with the company.[20] Companies often choose a stability strategy when their external environment doesn't change much, or after they have struggled with periods of explosive growth.

The purpose of a **retrenchment strategy** is to turn around very poor company performance by shrinking the size or scope of the business. The first step of a typical retrenchment strategy might include significant cost reductions, layoffs of employees, closing of poorly performing stores, offices, or manufacturing plants, or closing or selling entire lines of products or services.[21]

After cutting costs and reducing a business's size or scope, the second step in a retrenchment strategy is recovery. **Recovery** consists of the strategic actions that a company takes to return to a growth strategy. This two-step process of cutting and recovery is analogous to pruning roses. Prior to each growing season, roses should be cut back to two-thirds of their normal size. However, pruning doesn't damage the roses; it makes them stronger and more likely to produce beautiful, fragrant flowers. The retrenchment-and-recovery process is similar. Cost reductions, layoffs, and plant closings are sometimes necessary to restoring companies to "good health." But like pruning, those cuts are intended to allow companies to eventually return to growth strategies (i.e., recovery). For example, to restore its profitability, Canadian label and business form maker Moore Corporation (www.moore.com) cut 4000 jobs and reduced annual expenses by over $100 million during 2001.[22] The effect in 2002 was a return to profitability in the second and third quarters.[23] So when company performance drops significantly, a strategy of retrenchment and recovery may help companies return to a successful growth strategy.

Review 3: Corporate-Level Strategies

Corporate-level strategies, such as portfolio strategy and grand strategies, help managers determine what businesses they should be in. Portfolio strategy focuses on lowering business risk by being in multiple, unrelated businesses and by investing the cash flows from slow-growth businesses into faster-growing businesses. One portfolio strategy, the BCG matrix, suggests that cash flows from cash cows should be reinvested in stars and in carefully chosen question marks. Dogs should be sold or liquidated. However, portfolio strategy has several problems. Acquiring unrelated businesses actually increases risk rather than lowering it. The BCG matrix is often wrong when predicting companies' (e.g., dogs, cash cows) future potential. And redirecting cash flows can seriously weaken cash cows. The most successful way to use the portfolio approach to corporate strategy is to reduce risk through related diversification.

The three kinds of grand strategies are growth, stability, and retrenchment/recovery. Companies can grow externally by merging with or acquiring other companies, or they can grow internally through direct expansion or creating new businesses. Companies choose a stability strategy—selling the same products or services to the same customers—when their external environment changes very little or after they have dealt with periods of explosive growth. Retrenchment strategy, shrinking the size or scope of a business, is used to turn around poor performance. If retrenchment works, it is often followed by a recovery strategy that focuses on increasing the business again.

4 INDUSTRY-LEVEL STRATEGIES

Industry-level strategy is a corporate strategy that addresses the question "How should we compete in this industry?" For example, the strategy of most nursing homes has been to provide medical care for elderly people who were no longer able to physically take care of themselves. However, in recent years, nursing homes have had to compete with assisted-living facilities. Assisted-living facilities don't offer the medical support available at most nursing homes. Although they provide assistance with things such as bathing and dressing, they have a different goal: to help residents be independent and active for as long as possible. Consequently, assisted-living facilities are much more livable than traditional nursing homes.

industry-level strategy
corporate strategy that addresses the question "How should we compete in this industry?"

Let's find out more about industry-level strategies by discussing five industry forces, positioning strategies, and adaptive strategies.

Five Industry Forces

According to Harvard professor Michael Porter, five industry forces—character of rivalry, threat of new entrants, threat of substitute products or services, bargaining power of suppliers, and the bargaining power of buyers—determine an industry's overall attractiveness and potential for long-term profitability. The stronger these forces, the less attractive the industry becomes to corporate investors, because it is more difficult for companies to be profitable. Let's examine how these industry forces are bringing changes to several kinds of industries.

Character of the rivalry is a measure of the intensity of competitive behaviour between companies in an industry. Is the competition among firms aggressive and cutthroat, or do competitors focus more on serving customers than attacking each other? Both industry attractiveness and profitability decrease when rivalry is cutthroat. For example, selling cars is a highly competitive business. Pick up a local newspaper on Friday, Saturday, or Sunday morning, and you'll find dozens of pages of car advertising ("Anniversary Sale-A-Bration," "Ford March Savings!" and "$99 Down, You Choose!"). In fact, competition is so intense that if it weren't for used car sales, repair work, and replacement parts, many auto dealers would actually lose money.

character of the rivalry
a measure of the intensity of competitive behaviour between companies in an industry

The **threat of new entrants** is a measure of the degree to which barriers to entry make it easy or difficult for new companies to get started in an industry. If it is easy for new companies to get started in the industry, competition will increase and prices and profits

threat of new entrants
a measure of the degree to which barriers to entry make it easy or difficult for new companies to get started in an industry

will fall. However, if there are sufficient barriers to entry, such as large capital requirements to buy expensive equipment or plant facilities or the need for specialized knowledge, competition will be weaker and prices and profits will generally be higher. For example, anyone wanting to start a new car dealership would have to give a large sum of money to one of the major auto manufacturers (e.g., GM, Ford) to become an official dealer. Then, on top of that, they would have to spend millions more to purchase sufficient land and construct buildings to showcase cars, hold dealership offices, and house repair bays and parts inventory. Not surprisingly, the number of new auto dealerships has steadily declined over the last two decades. However, the Internet has now made it possible for Internet sites such as Autobytel (www.autobytel.com) to bypass these barriers to entry, increase competition, and drive down auto prices (but Autobytel no longer operates in Canada).

So how does Internet-based auto-buying work? Well, on Autobytel's free Web site, customers indicate when and what they plan to buy. Autobytel then contacts a participating local car dealer who phones the customer (within 48 hours) with a low, no-haggle price for the car model the customer wants. One Autobytel customer said, "When he [car salesman] quoted me a price, I nearly fell over—[it was] nearly [US]$7000 less than what we were quoted earlier in the week at the dealership down the road." Another said, "I filled out your query and was contacted by the same dealership I had haggled with before. They found a vehicle, quoted a price (which was [US]$1500 less than the one we had agreed to two weeks prior), and we reached a financing plan in 20 minutes."[24] Autobytel earns money by charging dealers an annual fee of US$, and US$500 to US$1500 a month per car brand (e.g., Ford, Chevy). In return, dealers receive exclusive territories, low costs (by not having to advertise in local papers or on local radio and TV stations), and customers who are much more likely to buy.[25] As for the threat to car dealers who are not aligned with these Internet car-selling sites, it's likely to grow.

threat of substitute products or services
a measure of the ease with which customers can find substitutes for an industry's products or services

The **threat of substitute products or services** is a measure of the ease with which customers can find substitutes for an industry's products or services. If customers can easily find substitute products or services, the competition will be greater and profits will be lower. If there are few or no substitutes, competition will be weaker and profits will

DIGITAL VISION/GETTY IMAGES

Intel is one of many suppliers of chips to the consumer electronics industry, so it has less bargaining power in that industry than in personal computers, where it is the dominant supplier.

be higher. Generic medicines are some of the best-known examples of substitute products. Under Canadian patent law, a company that develops a drug has exclusive rights to produce and market that drug for 20 years. During this time, if the drug sells well, prices and profits are generally high. However, at the end of 20 years, after the patent has expired, any pharmaceutical company can manufacture and sell the same drug. When this happens, drug prices drop substantially, and the company that developed the drug typically sees its revenues drop sharply. For example, Capoten, a heart drug sold by Bristol-Myers Squibb, sold for 80 cents a pill while under patent, and just 4 cents a pill as a generic brand when produced by Bristol-Myers Squibb's competitors.[26]

Bargaining power of suppliers is a measure of the influence that suppliers of parts, materials, and services to firms in an industry have on the prices of these inputs. If an industry has numerous suppliers from whom to buy parts, materials, and services, companies will be able to bargain with suppliers to keep prices low. On the other hand, if there are few suppliers, or if a company is dependent on a supplier with specialized skills and knowledge, suppliers will have the bargaining power to dictate price levels.

bargaining power of suppliers
a measure of the influence that suppliers of parts, materials, and services to firms in an industry have on the prices of these inputs

Bargaining power of buyers is a measure of the influence that customers have on the firm's prices. If a company is dependent on just a few high-volume buyers, those buyers will typically have enough bargaining power to dictate prices. By contrast, if a company sells a popular product or service to multiple buyers, the company has more power to set prices.

bargaining power of buyers
a measure of the influence that customers have on a firm's prices

Positioning Strategies

After analyzing industry forces, the next step in industry-level strategy is to effectively protect your company from the negative effects of industry-wide competition and to create a sustainable competitive advantage. According to Michael Porter, there are three positioning strategies: cost leadership, differentiation, and focus.

Cost leadership means producing a product or service of acceptable quality at consistently lower production costs than competitors, so that the firm can offer the product or service at the lowest price in the industry. Cost leadership protects companies from industry forces by deterring new entrants, who will have to match low costs and prices. Cost leadership also forces down the prices of substitute products and services, attracts bargain-seeking buyers, and increases bargaining power with suppliers, who have to keep their prices low if they want to do business with the cost leader.

cost leadership
the positioning strategy of producing a product or service of acceptable quality at consistently lower production costs than competitors can, so that the firm can offer the products or service at the lowest price in the industry

Differentiation means making your product or service sufficiently different from competitors' offerings that customers are willing to pay a premium price for the extra value or performance that it provides. Differentiation protects companies from industry forces by reducing the threat of substitute products. It also protects companies by making it easier to retain customers and more difficult for new entrants trying to attract new customers. Anyone who has been to the movies lately should recognize that the major theatre companies are using differentiation to steal customers from each other. For example, some Empire Theatres located throughout Atlantic Canada have party facilities and video game rooms to broaden their appeal to families.

differentiation
the positioning strategy of providing a product or service that is sufficiently different from competitors' offerings that customers are willing to pay a premium price for it

A **focus strategy** means that a company uses either cost leadership or differentiation to produce a specialized product or service for a limited, specially targeted group of customers in a particular geographic region or market segment. Focus strategies typically work in market niches that competitors have overlooked or have difficulty serving. BMC Software (www.bmc.com), with offices in Calgary, Mississauga, Montreal, and Ottawa, is an example of a firm pursuing a focus strategy. It provides e-business systems management software with an emphasis on ensuring availability of information, on performance, and on recovery of information technology resources for both mainframe and distributed systems.

focus strategy
the positioning strategy of using cost leadership or differentiation to produce a specialized product or service for a limited, specially targeted group of customers in a particular geographic region or market segment

Adaptive Strategies

Adaptive strategies are another set of industry-level strategies. While the aim of positioning strategies is to minimize the effects of industry competition and build a sustainable competitive advantage, the purpose of adaptive strategies is to choose an industry-level strategy that is best suited to changes in the organization's external environment. There are four kinds of adaptive strategies: defenders, analyzers, prospectors, and reactors.[27]

defenders
an adaptive strategy aimed at defending strategic positions by seeking moderate, steady growth and by offering a limited range of high-quality products and services to a well-defined set of customers

Defenders seek moderate, steady growth by offering a limited range of products and services to a well-defined set of customers. In other words, defenders aggressively "defend" their current strategic position by doing the best job they can to hold on to customers in a particular market segment. However, despite the best intentions, sometimes, even the best plans don't work out. Consider the case of drug manufacturer Biovail, which attempted to defend its revenue stream:

> After months of high hopes, Biovail Corp. failed to impress analysts about its growth strategy for the second half of the decade.... [T]he overriding issue for analysts is whether Biovail ... can replace its blockbuster antidepressant Wellbutrin XL, which is generating a third of total company revenue but faces generic competition as early as mid-2007. The Street's consensus: No.... And a potential financial meltdown if it can't replace Wellbutrin XL continues to depress Biovail's stock price.[28]

prospectors
an adaptive strategy that seeks fast growth by searching for new market opportunities, encouraging risk-taking, and being the first to bring innovative new products to market

analyzers
an adaptive strategy that seeks to minimize risk and maximize profits by following or imitating the proven successes of prospectors

Prospectors seek fast growth by searching for new market opportunities, encouraging risk-taking, and being the first to bring innovative new products to market. Prospectors are analogous to gold miners who "prospect" for gold nuggets (i.e., new products) in hopes that it will lead them to a mine that has a rich deposit of gold (i.e., fast growth).

Analyzers are a blend of the defender and prospector strategies. Analyzers seek moderate, steady growth and limited opportunities for fast growth. Analyzers are rarely first to market with new products or services. Instead, they try to simultaneously minimize risk and maximize profits by following or imitating the proven successes of prospectors. For example, while 75 percent of personal computers are made by the 20 largest PC manufacturers (Compaq, Dell, IBM, Gateway, etc.), the remaining 25 percent are made by 100 000 small manufacturers, most of whom use an analyzer strategy. Rather than trying to design new computer products (a prospector strategy), smaller manufacturers may typically make computers with the same options and configurations as the large PC manufacturers offer. However, they may also distinguish themselves by offering personal service. Instead of impersonal Web sites and 24-hour phone support, small manufacturers can frequently send service technicians to customers' homes to make repairs. Likewise, when customers call with questions, they can often talk directly to the technicians who manufactured their computers.[29]

reactors
an adaptive strategy of not following a consistent strategy, but instead reacting to changes in the external environment after they occur

Finally, unlike defenders, prospectors, or analyzers, **reactors** do not follow a consistent strategy. Furthermore, rather than anticipating and preparing for external opportunities and threats, reactors tend to "react" to changes in their external environment after they occur. Not surprisingly, reactors tend to be poorer performers than defenders, prospectors, or analyzers.

Review 4: Industry-Level Strategies

Industry-level strategies focus on how companies choose to compete in their industry. Five industry forces determine an industry's overall attractiveness to corporate investors and potential for long-term profitability. Together, a high level of new entrants, substitute products or services, bargaining power of suppliers, bargaining power of buyers, and rivalry between competitors combine to increase competition and decrease profits. Three positioning strategies can help companies protect themselves from the negative effects of industry-wide competition. Under a cost leadership strategy, firms try to keep production costs low, so that they can sell products at prices lower than competitors'.

Differentiation is a strategy aimed at making a product or service sufficiently different from those of competitors that it can command a premium price. Using a focus strategy, firms seek to produce a specialized product or service for a limited, specially targeted group of customers. The four adaptive strategies help companies adapt to changes in the external environment. Defenders want to "defend" their current strategic positions. Prospectors look for new market opportunities by bringing innovative new products to market. Analyzers minimize risk by following the proven successes of prospectors. Reactors do not follow a consistent strategy, but instead react to changes in their external environment after they occur.

5 FIRM-LEVEL STRATEGIES

Firm-level strategy addresses the question "How should we compete against a particular firm?" For example, over the last two decades, McDonald's (www.mcdonalds.com) has dominated its nearest rival, Burger King, in sales, profits, market share, and growth. Consequently, McDonald's is twice Burger King's size. However, over the last few years, Burger King (www.burgerking.com) has become the attacker and McDonald's the nervous follower. Burger King started its attack by heavily advertising that its Whopper sandwich was bigger than McDonald's Big Mac. McDonald's responded by creating larger, more expensive Deluxe sandwiches such as the Arch Deluxe hamburger. When it did, Burger King's sales (not McDonald's) increased by 11 percent. To keep weight and health-conscious customers coming in, Burger King created a grilled chicken sandwich. Several years later, McDonald's did the same. Then Burger King attacked McDonald's stranglehold on the fast-food breakfast business, introducing its own croissant and biscuit breakfast sandwiches and selling them for 27 to 34 cents less than McDonald's better-known Egg McMuffin and Sausage McMuffin sandwiches. Moreover, Burger King was able to lower prices on items across its entire menu at the same time that McDonald's food prices increased.[30]

firm-level strategy
corporate strategy that addresses the question "How should we compete against a particular firm?"

All told, Burger King's aggressive attacks have worked. Burger King's sales are increasing while McDonald's are decreasing. Indeed, an internal McDonald's memo indicated that price cuts might be needed because of an "overt competitive attack by BK."[31]

Let's find out more about firm-level competition between companies by reading about direct competition, strategic moves of direct competition, and entrepreneurship: a firm-level strategy.

Direct Competition

While Porter's five industry forces indicate the overall level of competition in an industry, most companies do not compete directly with all the firms in their industry. For example, McDonald's and Olive Garden are both in the restaurant business, but no one would characterize them as competitors. McDonald's offers low-cost, convenient fast food in a "seat yourself" restaurant, while Olive Garden offers mid-priced, sit-down dinners complete with servers and a bar.

Instead of "competing" with the industry, most firms compete directly with just a few companies. **Direct competition** is the rivalry between two companies offering similar products and services that acknowledge each other as rivals and take offensive and defensive positions as they act and react to each other's strategic actions.[32] Two factors determine the extent to which firms will be in direct competition with each other: market commonality and resource similarity. **Market commonality** is the degree to which two companies have overlapping products, services, or customers in multiple markets. The more markets in which there is product, service, or customer overlap, the more intense the direct competition between the two companies. **Resource similarity** is the extent to which a competitor has similar amounts and kinds of resources, that is, similar assets, capabilities, processes, information, and knowledge used to create and sustain an advantage over competitors. From a competitive standpoint, resource similarity means that the strategic actions your company takes can probably be matched by your direct competitors.

direct competition
the rivalry between two companies that offer similar products and services, acknowledge each other as rivals, and act and react to each other's strategic actions

market commonality
the degree to which two companies have overlapping products, services, or customers in multiple markets

resource similarity
the extent to which a competitor has similar amounts and kinds of resources

Exhibit 9.7 shows how market commonality and resource similarity interact to determine when and where companies are in direct competition.[33] The overlapping area (between the triangle and the rectangle or between the differently coloured rectangles) in

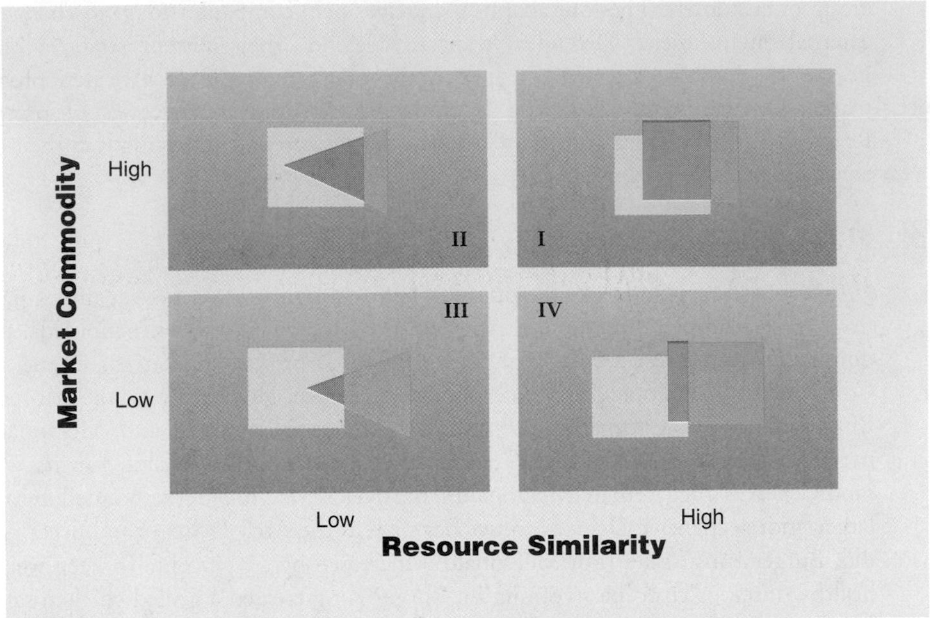

EXHIBIT 9.7
A Framework of Direct Competition

Source: Academy of Management Review by M. Chen. Copyright 1996 by Academy of Management. Reproduced with permission of the publisher via Copyright Clearance Center.

each quadrant depicts market commonality. The larger the overlap, the greater the market commonality. Shapes depict resource similarity, with rectangles representing one set of competitive resources and triangles representing another. Quadrant I shows two companies in direct competition, because they have similar resources at their disposal and a high degree of market commonality as they try to sell similar products and services to similar customers. McDonald's and Burger King would clearly fit here as direct competitors.

In Quadrant II, the overlapping parts of the triangle and rectangle show two companies going after similar customers with some similar products or services, but doing so with different competitive resources. McDonald's and Wendy's restaurants would fit here. Wendy's is after the same lunchtime and dinner crowds that McDonald's is. However, it is less of a direct competitor to McDonald's than Burger King is, because Wendy's hamburgers, fries, and shakes are more expensive. A representative from Wendy's said, "We believe you win customers by consistently offering a better product at a strong, everyday value." As well, Wendy's is now competing less with McDonald's as it expands its Tim Hortons chain of coffee shops that also serve doughnuts, baked goods, bagels, soups, deli sandwiches, cookies, and soft drinks.[34]

In Quadrant III, the very small overlap shows two companies with different competitive resources and little market commonality. McDonald's and Subway fit here. Although both are in the fast-food business, there's almost no overlap in products and customers. For example, Subway (www.subway.com) sells submarine sandwiches, a food type not available at McDonald's. Furthermore, Subway customers aren't likely to eat at McDonald's.

Finally, in Quadrant IV, the small shaded overlap between the two rectangles shows two companies competing with similar resources but with little market commonality. Surprisingly, McDonald's and Burger King fit here too. However, the major difference from Quadrant I is that Quadrant IV represents direct competition between McDonald's and Burger King in Japan, not Canada or the United States. Both sell burgers and fries in Japan (i.e., similar products). However, unlike the North American market, market commonality is low, because of Burger King's small size and because few Japanese fast-food customers have ever heard of it. Jun Fujita, an assistant manager at a Tokyo McDonald's, said, "We don't see them as a threat at all. Who has ever heard of Burger

King?"[35] This example also illustrates the point that even between direct competitors, competition in each market (e.g., geographic regions, particular products or services) is unique. Furthermore, direct competitors have different strengths and weaknesses in different markets. For example, although Burger King has been gaining on McDonald's in North America, McDonald's is clearly dominant in Japan. McDonald's has been in Japan for 25 years and has over 2000 restaurants. By contrast, Burger King hopes to open 200 restaurants in Japan over the next five years.

Strategic Moves of Direct Competition

While corporate-level strategies help managers decide what business to be in and business-level strategies help them determine how to compete within an industry, firm-level strategies help managers determine when, where, and what strategic actions should be taken against a direct competitor. There are two basic strategic moves in direct competition between firms: attacks and responses.

An **attack** is a competitive move designed to reduce a rival's market share or profits. For example, with its Pampers and Luv's brands, Procter & Gamble (www.pg.com) is the largest maker of disposable baby diapers. However, Procter & Gamble's market share is being attacked by Paragon Trade Brands (www.paragontradebrands.com). Paragon, which manufactures the cheaper, private-label diapers that grocery and discount stores in Canada and the United States sell under their own store brand names, now has a 16 percent share of the disposable-diaper market.[36]

attack
a competitive move designed to reduce a rival's market share or profits

A **response** is a countermove, prompted by a rival's attack, designed to defend or improve a company's market share or profit. For example, in an extremely aggressive response, Procter & Gamble sued Paragon for damages and lost profits, alleging that Paragon violated the patents it has for putting elastic in diapers to prevent leaking around a baby's legs. To those unfamiliar with the diaper business, "elastic around the legs" may not sound like an especially important thing. However, Andrew Urban, a diaper-technology consultant, called this design "one of the most important advances in diapers" since the invention of tight-fitting hourglass-shaped diapers.[37] Consequently, Procter & Gamble's intent was to force Paragon to stop making diapers with elastic in the legs or to make it pay a royalty for each diaper. Either would have greatly reduced Paragon's profitability. Luckily, for Paragon, the two parties settled the lawsuit.

response
a competitive countermove, prompted by a rival's attack, to defend or improve a company's market share or profit

Attacks and responses can include smaller, more tactical moves, such as price cuts, specially advertised sales or promotions, or improvements in service. However, they can also include resource-intensive strategic moves, such as expanding service and production facilities, introducing new products or services within the firm's existing business, or entering a completely new line of business for the first time. Of these, market entries and exits are probably the most important kinds of attacks and responses. Entering a new market is a clear offensive signal to an attacking or responding firm that your company is committed to gaining or defending market share and profits at their expense. By contrast, exiting a market is an equally clear defensive signal that your company is retreating.[38]

Exhibit 9.8 shows that market commonality and resource similarity determine the likelihood of an attack or response, that is, whether a company is likely to attack a direct competitor or to strike back with a strong response when attacked. When market commonality is strong and companies have overlapping products, services, or customers in multiple markets, there is less motivation to attack and more motivation to respond to an attack. The reason for this is straightforward: when firms are direct competitors in a large number of markets, there is much more at stake.

While market commonality affects the likelihood of an attack or a response to an attack, resource similarity largely affects response capability, that is, how quickly and forcefully a company can respond to an attack. When resource similarity is strong, the responding firm will generally be able to match the strategic moves of the attacking firm. Consequently, firms are less likely to attack firms with similar levels of resources, because they're unlikely to gain any sustained advantage when the responding firm strikes back.

EXHIBIT 9.8
Likelihood of Attacks and Responses in Direct Competition

Competitor Analysis	Interfirm Rivalry: Action and Response
Strong Market Commonality →	Less Likelihood of an Attack
Weak Market Commonality →	Greater Likelihood of an Attack
High Resource Similarity →	Greater Likelihood of a Response
Low Resource Similarity →	Less Likelihood of a Response

Source: M. Chen, "Competitor Analysis and Interfirm Rivalry: Toward a Theoretical Integration," *Academy of Management Review* 21 (1996): 100–134.

On the other hand, if one firm is substantially stronger than another (i.e., low resource similarity), a competitive attack is more likely to produce sustained competitive advantage.

In general, the greater the number of moves (i.e., attacks) a company initiates against direct competitors, and the greater a firm's tendency to respond when attacked, the better its performance. More specifically, attackers and early responders (companies that are quick to launch a retaliatory attack) tend to gain market share and profits at the expense of late responders. This is not to suggest that a "full-attack" strategy always works best. In fact, attacks can provoke harsh retaliatory responses. Consequently, when deciding when, where, and what strategic actions to take against a direct competitor, managers should always consider the possibility of retaliation.

Entrepreneurship: A Firm-Level Strategy

Firm-level strategy addresses how one company should compete against another. Furthermore, of the various kinds of attacks and responses used in direct competition, market entry is perhaps the most forceful attack or response, because it sends the clear signal that the company is committed to gaining or defending market share and profits at a direct competitor's expense.

entrepreneurship
the process of entering new or established markets with new goods or services

Since **entrepreneurship** is the process of entering new or established markets with new goods or services, entrepreneurship is also a firm-level strategy. In fact, the basic strategic act of entrepreneurship is new entry—creating a new business from a brand-new start-up firm or from an existing firm.

entrepreneurial orientation
the set of processes, practices, and decision-making activities that lead to new entry, characterized by five dimensions: autonomy, innovativeness, risk-taking, proactiveness, and competitive aggressiveness

While the goal of an entrepreneurial strategy is new entry, the process of carrying out an entrepreneurial strategy depends on the ability of the company's founders or existing managers to foster an entrepreneurial orientation. An **entrepreneurial orientation** is the set of processes, practices, and decision-making activities that lead to new entry. Five key dimensions characterize an entrepreneurial orientation: autonomy, innovativeness, risk-taking, proactiveness, and competitive aggressiveness.[39] Without these, an entrepreneurial strategy is unlikely to succeed.

1. *Autonomy.* If a firm wants to successfully develop new products or services to enter new markets, it must foster creativity among employees. To be creative, employees need the freedom and control to develop a new idea into a new product or service opportunity without interference from others. In other words, they need autonomy. For example, when IBM was developing its first personal computer in the early 1980s, it created a dozen design teams, gave them complete freedom to design what they wanted, and sent them to different locations away from IBM's regular offices. In fact, the winning team worked out of an old rundown manufacturing plant. Furthermore, to prevent interference or influence from IBM's existing business, almost no one in the company knew these teams existed.
2. *Innovativeness.* Entrepreneurial firms also foster innovativeness by supporting new ideas, experimentation, and creative processes that might produce new products,

services, or technological processes. One example is Great Plains Software, which makes accounting software for small companies. Recently it was acquired by Microsoft. Prior to this, along with 63 other firms also producing accounting software, the obvious question was how to make the company's accounting software stand out in a crowded market. The answer was to provide extensive phone support to customers who purchased the software. The innovation was to charge for that support, something that no software company had dared try. In fact, Great Plains found that customers were more than willing to pay a fixed amount for unlimited support, because Great Plains was not only helping them learn to use its software, but was also helping them set up their accounts and ledgers correctly. Indeed a major selling point was its promise to customers who paid a fixed annual fee for support, to have their own personal support representative call back within 30 minutes of a support request.[40]

3. *Risk-taking.* Entrepreneurial firms are also willing to take some risks, by making large resource commitments that may result in costly failure.[41] Another way to conceptualize risk-taking is to think of it as managers' preferences for bold rather than cautious acts.
4. *Proactiveness.* Entrepreneurial firms have the ability to anticipate future problems, needs, or changes by developing new products or services that may not be related to their current business, by introducing new products or services before the competition does, and by dropping products or services that are declining (and likely to be replaced by new products or services).[42] Internet Security Systems (ISS) (www.iss.net) anticipated the security risks associated with corporate e-mail, Internet access, and company intranets by developing software that helps companies protect company data and computer systems. For example, ISS's software scans company password databases, looking for 25 000 easy-to-crack account passwords, such as "Spot," "Steelers," and "Startrek." When it finds them, users must then submit a more secure password. In all, ISS's software can shut down over 200 computer hacker tricks that compromise corporate computer security. Christopher Klaus, the company founder, said, "We make sure all the windows are closed and the doors are locked."[43]
5. *Competitive aggressiveness.* Because new entrants are more likely to fail than are existing firms, they must be aggressive if they want to succeed. A new firm often must be willing to use unconventional methods to directly challenge competitors for their customers and market share.

Review 5: Firm-Level Strategies

Firm-level strategies are concerned with direct competition between firms. Market commonality and resource similarity determine whether firms are in direct competition and thus likely to attack each other or respond to each other's attacks. In general, the more markets in which there is product, service, or customer overlap, and the greater the resource similarity between two firms, the more intense the direct competition between them. When firms are direct competitors in a large number of markets, attacks are less likely, because responding firms are highly motivated to quickly and forcefully defend their profits and market share. By contrast, resource similarity affects response capability, meaning how quickly and forcefully a company responds to an attack. When resource similarity is strong, attacks are much less likely to produce a sustained advantage, because the responding firm is capable of striking back with equal force. Market entries and exits are the most important kinds of attacks and responses.

Entering a new market is a clear offensive signal, while exiting a market is a clear signal that a company is retreating. In general, attackers and early responders gain market share and profits at the expense of late responders. However, attacks must be carefully planned and carried out, because they can provoke harsh retaliatory responses. Firm-level strategy addresses how one company should compete against another. Of the various kinds of attacks and responses used in direct competition, market entry is perhaps the most forceful attack or response, because it sends the clear signal that the company is committed to gaining or defending market share and profits at a direct competitor's expense. Finally, the basic strategic act of entrepreneurship is new entry. To carry out an entrepreneurial strategy, a company must create an entrepreneurial orientation by encouraging autonomy, innovativeness, risk-taking, proactiveness, and competitive aggressiveness.

What Really Happened?[44]

At the beginning of this chapter, you learned about the issues facing Hanspeter Stutz as he thought through a potential acquisition. It turns out to be a good news story. But what really happened? What was the situation facing Hanspeter Stutz and how might he have organized the information facing him in order to make a good decision? One suggestion is to make use of a SWOT analysis. What were the features of the situation facing Hanspeter in 1993? An online search for characteristics of the Nova Scotia wine industry, Domaine de Grand Pre, and Hanspeter Stutz offers a wealth of information.

What strengths were associated with this business idea?

At least three stood out. Hanspeter understood wine and how to operate a winery. He also had access to the financial resources to launch a winery. The location of the winery was also good. It would be located on a busy road leading into a university town, in the heart of a tourist region close to the Bay of Fundy.

What were the weaknesses underlying this initiative?

There were a number of weaknesses. As an immigrant whose first language was not English, Hanspeter was not well versed in provincial or federal government regulations related to the wine business. He was also not aware of the various sources of financial resources available to him from government departments and granting agencies. Finally, upon purchase, the physical infrastructure of the winery was poor.

What opportunities faced this entrepreneur?

A number of opportunities were evident. To begin, the climate, soil, and topography of the Annapolis Valley of Nova Scotia remains conducive to grape growing. Global wine consumption was and continues to trend upwards. There appeared to be an underserved market of Atlantic Canadian wine consumers who had few locally produced wine products to choose from. Nova Scotia is also a traditional summer tourist destination, a state of affairs that suggested a relatively untapped market. Hanspeter also had access to abundant scientific help in the form of an Agriculture Canada research station that was located nearby in Kentville.

What threats lay in the way of a successful venture?

Along with opportunities came threats. At the time of the purchase, few wineries existed in Nova Scotia. As a result, wine making know-how and human resource skills related to this industry were in short supply. The positioning of Nova Scotia wineries was suspect. They were not members of the Vinters Quality Alliance (VQA), an industry association present in British Columbia and Ontario that has developed an accepted Canadian standard for wines recognized around the world. Nova Scotia wines also had an image problem. There were few of them, they were not that well known, and they were not associated with high quality.

What were the key milestones on this journey?

In 1993 Hanspeter purchased the land and buildings where one can now find Domaine de Grand Pre. During that same year, he commenced work to clean up the existing 12 hectares of vineyards. In 1995, he came to the conclusion that the vines would not allow him to produce an acceptable quality of wine and replanted the same 12 hectares. In 1999, he and his family celebrated the first harvest of wine-quality grapes, leading to the grand opening of his wine operation in 2000. While this was occurring, the physical infrastructure of his winery was completely refurbished. Buildings were renovated and significant financial and human resources were put in place to alter the landscape surrounding the main buildings. In addition, a restaurant aimed at casual and high-end diners was opened.

As the owner and proprietor of Domaine de Grand Pre, Stutz has come a long way from his days in Switzerland. Having immigrated to Canada with his family in the 1990s, he can now proudly point to the fruits of his family's efforts—a successful, established, wine operation in the heart of the Annapolis Valley that is increasingly on the travel itineraries of many tourists to the region.

Key Terms

acquisition *(252)*
analyzers *(260)*
attack *(263)*
bargaining power of buyers *(259)*
bargaining power of suppliers *(259)*
BCG matrix *(253)*
cash cow *(253)*
character of the rivalry *(257)*
competitive advantage *(244)*
competitive inertia *(246)*
core capabilities *(248)*
core firms *(249)*
corporate-level strategy *(251)*
cost leadership *(259)*
defenders *(260)*
differentiation *(259)*
direct competition *(261)*
distinctive competence *(248)*
diversification *(251)*
dog *(253)*
entrepreneurial orientation *(264)*
entrepreneurship *(264)*
firm-level strategy *(261)*
focus strategy *(259)*
grand strategy *(256)*
growth strategy *(256)*
imperfectly imitable resource *(244)*
industry-level strategy *(257)*
market commonality *(261)*
nonsubstitutable resource *(245)*
portfolio strategy *(252)*
prospectors *(260)*
question mark *(253)*
rare resource *(244)*
reactors *(260)*
recovery *(256)*
related diversification *(254)*
resources *(244)*
resource similarity *(261)*
response *(263)*
retrenchment strategy *(256)*
secondary firms *(249)*
shadow-strategy task force *(249)*
situational (SWOT) analysis *(247)*
stability strategy *(256)*
star *(253)*
strategic dissonance *(247)*
strategic group *(248)*
strategic reference points *(249)*
sustainable competitive advantage *(244)*
threat of new entrants *(257)*
threat of substitute products or services *(258)*
unrelated diversification *(252)*
valuable resource *(244)*

Self-Assessment

STRATEGY QUESTIONNAIRE

Generally speaking, a strategy is a plan of action that is designed to help you achieve a goal. Strategies are not limited to grand plans that help you accomplish grand goals. You probably use strategies every day in simple ways. For example, think of a route you regularly drive. Do you know how fast (or slow) you need to go to catch all the lights on green? Or where to swerve to avoid a pothole? Or even when to take a side street to shave a few minutes off your commute? Speeding up for one block in order to catch the green lights at the next five intersections is a strategy. Strategy, then, involves thinking ahead of how you are going to accomplish what you set out (i.e., have planned) to do. On page 516 of the Assessment Appendix, you will find a survey that will provide some baseline information you can use as you develop your strategic managerial skills.

Management Decisions

HOW ABOUT A "CUPPA?"[45]

In Great Britain, when someone asks, "How about a cuppa?" they're asking if you want a cup of tea. And with an average of 3.6 "cuppas" a day per person, Great Britain, which has a population approximately twice the size of Canada's, consumes an amazing 10 percent of the world's tea each year—more than North America and Europe put together. In Great Britain, people of all ages and economic levels drink tea. Indeed, the British drink so much tea that market researchers estimate that tea accounts for 42 percent of all liquid intake in Great Britain.

Yet even in tea-crazed Britain, tea is not as popular as it once was. Tea still outsells coffee and soft drinks combined, but tea sales are no longer growing. By contrast, coffee sales, especially among young professionals, are increasing approximately 4 percent per year. Mark Beales, a coffee marketing manager at Nestlé Foods, said, "It's seen to be more sophisticated than tea now. Out-of-home consumption is being driven by the increasing number of quality café bars, which improves the perception of coffee and makes it more widely available." With sales of soft drinks increasing, too, especially among children and teens, the long-term prospects for tea don't look promising.

Questions

1. Using Michael Porter's Industry Forces model, explain how each of the five forces will affect the tea industry's overall attractiveness and potential for long-term profitability.

2. If you worked for one of the leading tea companies in Britain (tea bags account for 83 percent of all tea sold by these companies), what industry-level strategy would you recommend to the company? Would it be focus, cost-leadership, differentiation, defender, prospector, analyzer, reactor, or a combination of these strategies? Explain which you recommend, why you recommend it, and how the company should use that strategy to gain competitive advantage.

Management Decisions

ABSOLUTELY, POSITIVELY OVERNIGHT[46]

It begins at 11:00 each night. Every 90 seconds an orange, blue, and white FedEx cargo plane lands at the Memphis airport. By 1:00 A.M., all the planes have arrived. As FedEx workers scurry between planes, loading and unloading packages and cargo containers, activity is everywhere. The scene is not unlike a busy colony of ants lucky enough to find itself underneath a park picnic table. Before the planes return to the runway several hours later, stuffed to the cockpit with packages guaranteed to be delivered to their final destinations "absolutely, positively overnight," FedEx's 9000 Memphis workers will have sorted 1 million packages in less than four hours. However, the daily numbers for the entire company are even more impressive: 637 cargo planes and 43 500 vans delivering 4.5 million packages in 211 countries, including Canada.

Thanks to the increasing pace of the business world (and the human tendency to want immediate gratification, despite determined procrastination), FedEx has had unparalleled growth over the last three decades. Revenues have grown from zero, when FedEx invented the overnight delivery business more than 30 years ago, to more than $33 billion a year. But can FedEx achieve the same explosive growth in the next 30 years that it had in its first few decades? Unlike 1973, when founder and CEO Fred Smith started the company, FedEx faces numerous competitors, as well as technology (e.g., faxes and the Internet) that no one had even imagined back then.

Questions

1. Conduct a situational analysis for FedEx. What are its internal strengths (i.e., core competencies) and weaknesses? What strategic opportunities and threats does it face?
2. Assume that CEO Fred Smith has made you head of FedEx's shadow-strategy task force. Thinking like a competitor, actively determine FedEx's weaknesses and how a competitor could exploit them for competitive advantage.

Develop Your Management Potential

STRATEGIC PLANNING, PROTEAN CAREERS, AND PSYCHOLOGICAL SUCCESS[47]

For most of the 20th century, planning for a career has been as simple as planning for your next job. This is because most 20th-century careers have been linear—a progressive series of upward job promotions in the same field. For example, university and college graduates might begin a marketing career by starting as sales representatives. Then, over time, as they acquired knowledge and experience, they could expect to be promoted to marketing jobs with more authority and responsibility, perhaps sales manager or account manager. Eventually, they would retire, having spent their entire career in marketing-related jobs.

Today, however, careers are much more likely to be protean than linear. The term "protean" comes from the mythical Greek god Proteus, who would change shapes to keep others from finding him and obtaining his knowledge about all things past, present, and future. So, by contrast to linear careers in which the next job was simply a step up from one's previous job, protean career paths change frequently. If the ladder is the appropriate symbol for linear careers, then a parachute is the best symbol for protean careers, as people jump from one set of jobs to a completely different set of jobs. Instead of a job path that heads straight up the same career ladder, the job path in protean careers zigs and zags as "career jumpers" land their job parachutes far away from their original targets.

Of course, this creates a problem. How do you plan for a protean career when it's highly likely that what you do in your current job will be completely unrelated to what you do in your next job or the job after that? Fortunately, there is something you can do to plan for a protean career.

Since there's no way to know when a significant job change may present itself, career experts recommend that you focus on psychological success rather than that next job or promotion. A common reaction to this advice is that the "experts" have got it backwards. It's widely believed that you can't achieve career success, happiness, or wealth without keeping an eye on that next promotion. The "experts" have two responses. First, several decades of research clearly indicate that there's only a tiny positive relationship between money (which, for most of us, comes from getting promoted) and happiness. In fact, only 2 percent of the differences between happy and miserable people stem from money. Second, many businesspeople don't achieve real success until they let go of their "careerist" goals (i.e., promotion after promotion) and focus on enjoying and excelling at their jobs. Ironically, after this occurs, promotions and other career opportunities tend to take care of themselves. In other words, over the long run, that is, from a strategic perspective, it makes more sense to worry about whether you enjoy what you're doing than when and where that next promotion will come from and how much more money you'll earn when you get it.

Begin your plan for a protean career by answering the following questions.

Questions

1. Of all the jobs you've had, which made you feel the best about yourself as a person? What did you enjoy most about this job? Be specific. Now, of all the jobs you've had, which made you feel the worst about yourself as a person? What was the worst part of this job? Finally, describe three significant differences between your best and worst jobs.
2. What do you do in your free time? Do you have any hobbies or interests in which you become readily absorbed? Describe your favourite outside interest or hobby. List three reasons why this activity or interest is so much fun for you.

Discussion Questions

1. Sony and Sanyo are two well-known manufacturers of DVD players and other home entertainment products. Every few months, they place on vendor shelves new versions of their products that are priced and appear quite similar to each other. If one puts an innovative product on the market, the other soon has its own version on the shelves. Evidently, when referring to DVD players, neither firm possesses a sustainable competitive advantage relative to the other. In this light, differentiate competitive advantage from sustainable competitive advantage.
2. With thousands of Canadians flying on its planes daily, Air Canada is a company of interest to many of us. Along with other competitors in the global aviation industry, it faces a number of interesting challenges, including the existence of powerful unions, a decreasing customer base, an aging fleet of airplanes, costly government regulations and taxes, unstable fuel prices, and a business model designed for a different operating environment. Solutions to these challenges are not simple. A form of analysis may, however, clarify needed steps forward. In this light, identify the roles and basic components of a situational analysis.
3. Briefly explain what the BCG matrix is, and what its basic recommendations are.
4. When one thinks of business in Canada, industries such as lumber, oil and gas, wheat, automobiles, pharmaceuticals, financial services, aeronautics, and fish products often come to mind. Despite being distinct from one another, each can be described in terms of a number of generic forces. Choose one particular industry and list the five industry forces that determine overall levels of competition in that industry. Next, identify what happens to competition as these forces increase in strength.
5. Canadian Pacific and CN compete in the North American transportation industry. These two rail carriers face two major challenges: competition from other railroaders and the trucking industry and changes to their overall operating environments due to altered macro-economic forces, new regulations, new technologies, or stakeholder pressures. In order to respond to these pressures, both CN and Canadian Pacific will need to implement specific strategies. Differentiate between the position strategies and the adaptive strategies available to these two important players.

Critical Thinking Video Case

CBC

Visit www.management2e.nelson.com to view this chapter's CBC video case.

Take Two

Biz Flix
Seabiscuit

Seabiscuit is a 2003 American drama film based on the best-selling book *Seabiscuit: An American Legend* by Laura Hillenbrand. The film stars Tobey Maguire as Red Pollard, the jockey for Seabiscuit, an undersized and overlooked thoroughbred racehorse whose unexpected successes made him a popular sensation in the United States near the end of the Great Depression. In this scene, a hospitalized Pollard is unable to ride during the final leg of the Triple Crown, so he tries to communicate to his friend and replacement jockey Charley Kurtsinger (played by Chris McCarron) what he needs to do to win the race.

What to Watch for and Ask Yourself

1. What aspects of strategic planning can you identify in the clip?
2. Which strategic alternative (risk seeking or risk avoiding) does Red Pollard advocate that his friend use during the race? Explain.

Management Workplace
Texas Jet

Even the most enthusiastic, determined managers encounter strategic difficulties when environments change and their businesses expand, contract, or are stuck in the status quo. Reed Pigman, owner of Texas Jet, was already experiencing crippling and debt stagnating sales in a commodity market when the competitive environment changed, pushing him to the brink of going out of business. By stepping back to rethink his strategy, he was able to save his company and turn it into a prosperous enterprise in a difficult industry.

What to Watch for and Ask Yourself

1. Describe Reed Pigman's use of strategic reference points.
2. Explain how moving from a firm-level strategy to an industry-level strategy helped Texas Jet to achieve a competitive advantage.
3. Do you think Texas Jet's competitive advantage is sustainable? Explain.

GETTY IMAGES

Innovation and Change

Chapter 10

CHAPTER OUTLINE

LEARNING OBJECTIVES

After reading this chapter, you should be able to

1. explain why innovation matters to companies.
2. discuss the different methods that managers can use to effectively manage innovation in their organizations.
3. discuss why change occurs and why it matters.
4. discuss the different methods that managers can use to better manage change as it occurs.

Nancy Garapick. Victor Davis. Alex Bauman. Mark Tewkesbury. If you followed competitive swimming in Canada over the last two decades, then you would recognize the names. Whether it be the World Aquatic Championships, the Commonwealth Games, or the Olympic Games, the success of these four swimmers and many others helped to create a global swimming powerhouse that for many years challenged Americans, Australians, and other leading swimming nations on medal podiums throughout the world.[1]

The success that characterized the Canadian swimming scene throughout much of the 1980s and 1990s did not carry on into the new millennium. If the 1984 Olympic Games represented the pinnacle of success for Canada in terms of medal performance, the 2004 Athens Games were its low point. Few medals were won and few personal best times attained. Sadly, the entire team's performance was epitomized by a well-publicized squabble between members of the men's relay team. The incident involved one member, Rick Say, being caught on camera venting his frustration. In response, 1992 gold medallist Mark Tewkesbury lashed out publicly at the Olympic coaching staff.

What Would You Do?

The 2004 Olympics represented yet another controversy for Swimming Canada, an organization that increasingly was featured in the news, not for the achievements of swimmers from coast to coast but rather for a seeming unending series of missteps. While the nation celebrated a number of medal successes at the 2000 Sydney Olympics, many were also aware of the legal proceedings initiated by one high-profile swimmer not chosen for the team. While Swimming Canada proclaimed the virtues of its eight National Swim Centres, the media focused its attention on the infighting surrounding the hiring of a young female coach for the national team. While the team prepared for the Athens Olympics, a growing cadre of former national team swimmers began to publicly discuss the failings of the once-proud program and its head coach. Coupled with these problems was a growing concern that the club system in Canada was no longer producing enough swimmers who might excel at the national and international levels. Further, swimming was becoming an expensive sport—too expensive for many families.

The performance of Canadian swimmers at the 2004 Olympics proved to be a catalyst for change. Unaccustomed to such negative publicity, reeling from the mediocre outcomes of the national swim team, and pressured by increasingly important stakeholders, Swimming Canada's head coach and CEO was fired within days. The issue now became what should board members of Swimming Canada do? What steps needed to be taken in order to return to the glory years of the '90s and '80s?

If you were on the board of Swimming Canada, what would you do?

How might an organization like Swimming Canada become more creative and use innovation to promote change? How can an organization walk the walk when it comes to being more innovative? Heather Fraser of the Rotman School of Business has some ideas. She labels these "design doing." According to Fraser, organizations really need to do three things. First, they need to "examine their existing business model" in order "to make the most of their current capabilities and capacity in the form of line extensions and expansions." They then need to "explore many prototypes, with an open mind to feedback and reconfiguration along the way." Finally, these same organizations need to be concerned about "strategic business design." They need to "create a unique network of business activities that not only deliver value to the user, but also competitive advantage and profit to the company." Fraser cites examples such as Apple's computer mouse as one where extensive prototyping was used and Apple's iPod as an example that changed our definition of mobile entertainment and represented a new business model.[2]

organizational innovation the successful implementation of creative ideas in organizations

creativity the production of novel and useful ideas

organizational change a difference in the form, quality, or condition of an organization over time

We begin this chapter by reviewing the issues associated with **organizational innovation** and **creativity**. You will learn why innovation matters and how to manage innovation to create and sustain a competitive advantage.

In the second half of this chapter, you will learn about **organizational change** and why changes occur. You will also learn about the risk of not changing, the different kinds of change, and the ways in which companies can manage change.

Organizational Innovation

Do you remember the first time, probably as a child, that you saw a blimp floating overhead? It moved slowly, was clearly visible for kilometres, and held your attention as it got closer, passed overhead, and then floated away. Interestingly, the things that make blimps fascinating to kids also make them great for advertising (e.g., slow, visible, holds attention). Company names are clearly displayed on the side of blimps at sporting events that are attended by thousands and seen by millions on TV. Blimps are so commonplace that major sporting events such as the Grey Cup, the Super Bowl, and the World Series would seem incomplete without traditional overhead camera shots from the blimp.

Today, however, the "Lightship," an innovative new blimp made by the American Blimp Company (www.americanblimp.com), is revolutionizing the blimp business and the advertising revenues that go with it. Lightships have several advantages over traditional blimps. To start, they're much smaller and cheaper. A typical, full-size blimp costs about $420 000 a month to operate. Most of that cost is for the 24 people who work in the blimp's ground and flight crews. Because American Blimp's Lightships are smaller, it takes only 14 people to staff the ground and flight crews. Consequently, monthly costs run around $280 000, one-third less than full-size blimps. Another advantage is that Lightships are lighted from the inside. So when it gets dark, the company name and logo on the side of the blimp are still visible! This is critical since most sporting events take place at night to maximize the size of their TV audience.[3]

Organizational innovation, like American Blimp's new Lightships, is the successful implementation of creative ideas in an organization.[4] This chapter focuses largely on innovation with regard to changes in technology or design. Innovation can of course take other forms. Innovation can refer to changes in an organization as a whole. It can refer to specific products. It can also refer to business processes. These latter three innovation types are addressed indirectly in this chapter.

After reading the next two sections, you should be able to

1. explain why innovation matters to companies.
2. discuss the different methods that managers can use to effectively manage innovation in their organizations.

1 WHY INNOVATION MATTERS

We can only guess what changes technological innovations will bring in the next 20 years. Maybe we'll be listening to compact chips rather than compact discs. Maybe cars won't need tune-ups. Maybe we'll use the Internet to have cookies delivered hot to our homes like pizza. And maybe TVs will be voice-activated, so it doesn't matter if you lose the remote (just don't lose your voice). Who knows? The only thing we do know about the next 20 years is that innovation will continue to change our lives. The Government of Canada agrees. It has developed a national innovation strategy[5] and has committed millions of dollars to ensuring that innovation is supported throughout the private and educational sectors. Through two programs, it supports innovative behaviour by Canadians. One program, *Achieving Excellence: Investing in People, Knowledge and Opportunity*, recognizes the need to consider knowledge as a strategic national asset and has introduced a variety of programs to meet its goals. It focuses on how to strengthen our science and research capacity and on how to ensure that this knowledge contributes to building an innovative economy that benefits all Canadians. Industry Canada is the department implementing this program. The other program, *Knowledge Matters: Skills and Learning for Canadians*, recognizes that a country's greatest resource in the knowledge society is its people. It looks at what can be done to strengthen learning in Canada, to develop people's talent, and to provide opportunity for all to contribute to and benefit from the new economy. Human Resources and Social Development Canada is the department responsible for implementing this program. Programs such as these help to foster innovation. But what does this term innovation mean? Let's begin our discussion of innovation by learning about technology cycles and innovation streams.

Technology Cycles

In Chapter 2, you learned that technology is the knowledge, tools, and techniques used to transform inputs (raw materials, information, etc.) into outputs (products and services). A **technology cycle** begins with the "birth" of a new technology and ends when that technology reaches its limits and "dies" as it is replaced by a newer, substantially better technology.[6] For example, technology cycles occurred when air conditioning supplanted fans and when Henry Ford's Model T replaced horse-drawn carriages.

technology cycle
cycle that begins with the "birth" of a new technology and ends when that technology reaches its limits and is replaced by a newer, substantially better technology

From Gutenberg's invention of the printing press in the 1400s to the rapid advance of the Internet in the last few years, studies of hundreds of technological innovations have shown that nearly all technology cycles follow the typical **S-curve pattern of innovation** shown in Exhibit 10.1.[7] Early in a technology cycle, there is still much to learn and progress is slow, as depicted by point A on the S-curve. The flat slope indicates that increased effort (i.e., money, research and development) brings only small improvements in technological performance. Intel's technology cycles have followed this pattern. Intel spends billions to develop new computer chips and to build new production facilities to produce them. Intel has found that the technology cycle for its integrated circuits (that power personal computers) is about three years. In each three-year cycle, Intel introduces a new chip, improves the chip by making it a little bit faster each year, and then replaces that chip at the end of the cycle with a brand-new chip that is substantially faster than the old chip. But at first, those billions typically produce only small improvements in performance. For instance, as shown in Exhibit 10.2, Intel's first 60 megahertz (MHz) Pentium processors ran at a speed of 51 based on the iComp Index.[8] (The iComp Index is a benchmark test for measuring relative computer speed. For example, a computer with an iComp score of 200 is twice as fast as a computer with an iComp score of 100.) Yet, six months later, Intel's new 75 MHz Pentium was only slightly faster, with an iComp speed of 67.

S-curve pattern of innovation
a pattern of technological innovation characterized by slow initial progress, then rapid progress, and then again by slow progress as a technology matures and reaches its limits

Fortunately, as the technology matures, researchers figure out how to get better performance from the new technology. This is represented by point B of the S-curve in Exhibit 10.1. The steeper slope indicates that small amounts of effort will result in

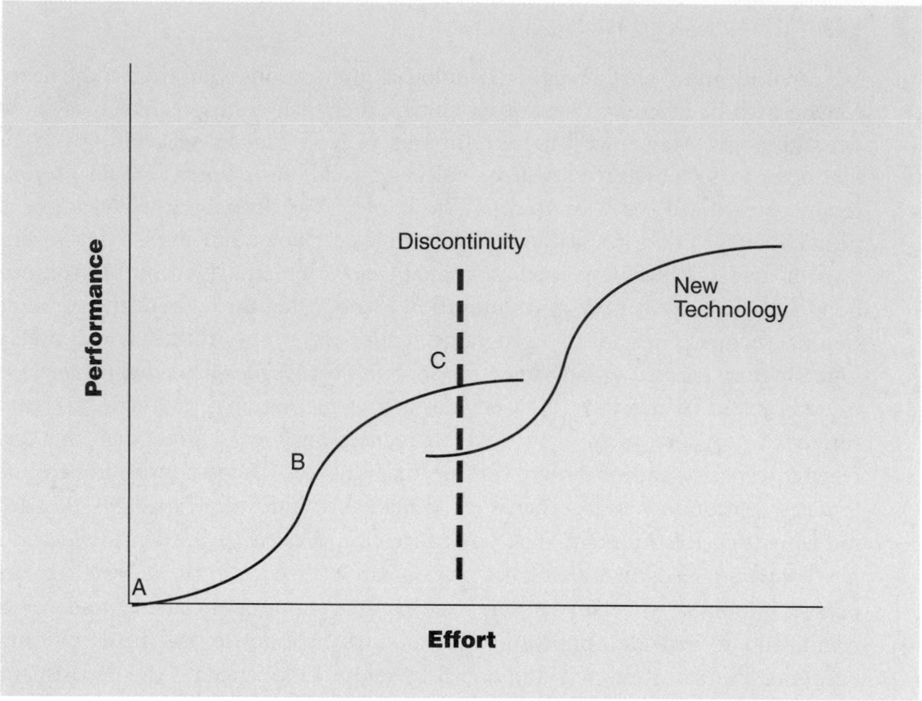

EXHIBIT 10.1
S-Curves and Technological Innovation

Source: R.N. Foster, *Innovation: The Attacker's Advantage* (New York: Summit, 1986).

significant increases in performance. Again, Intel's technology cycles have followed this pattern. In fact, after six months to a year with a new chip design, Intel's engineering and production people have typically figured out how to make the new chips much faster than they were initially. For example, as shown in Exhibit 10.2, Intel soon rolled out 100 MHz, 120 MHz, 133 MHz, 150 MHz, and 166 MHz Pentium chips that were 76 percent, 117 percent, 124 percent, 149 percent, and 178 percent faster than its original 60 MHz speed.

At point C, the flat slope again indicates that further efforts to develop this particular technology will result in only small increases in performance. More importantly, however, point C indicates that the performance limits of that particular technology are being reached. In other words, additional significant improvements in performance are highly unlikely. For example, Exhibit 10.2 shows that with iComp speeds of 127 and 142, Intel's 166 MHz and 200 MHz Pentiums were 2.49 and 2.78 times faster than its original 60 MHz Pentiums. Yet, despite these impressive gains in performance, Intel was unable to make its Pentium chips run any faster, because the basic Pentium design had reached its limits.

After a technology has reached its limits at the top of the S-curve, significant improvements in performance usually come from radical new designs or new performance-enhancing materials. In Exhibit 10.1, that new technology is represented by the second S-curve. The changeover or discontinuity between the new and old technologies is represented by the dotted line. At first, the new and old technologies will likely co-exist. Eventually, however, the new technology will replace the old technology. When that happens, the old technology cycle will be complete and a new one will have started. The changeover between Intel's Pentium processors, the old technology, and its Pentium II processors, the new technology (these chips are significantly different technologies despite their similar names), took approximately a year. Exhibit 10.2 shows this changeover or discontinuity between the two technologies. With an iComp speed of 267, the first Pentium II (233 MHz) was 88 percent faster than the last and fastest 200 MHz Pentium processor. And because their design and performance are significantly different (and faster) than Pentium II chips, Intel's Pentium III chips represented the beginning of yet another

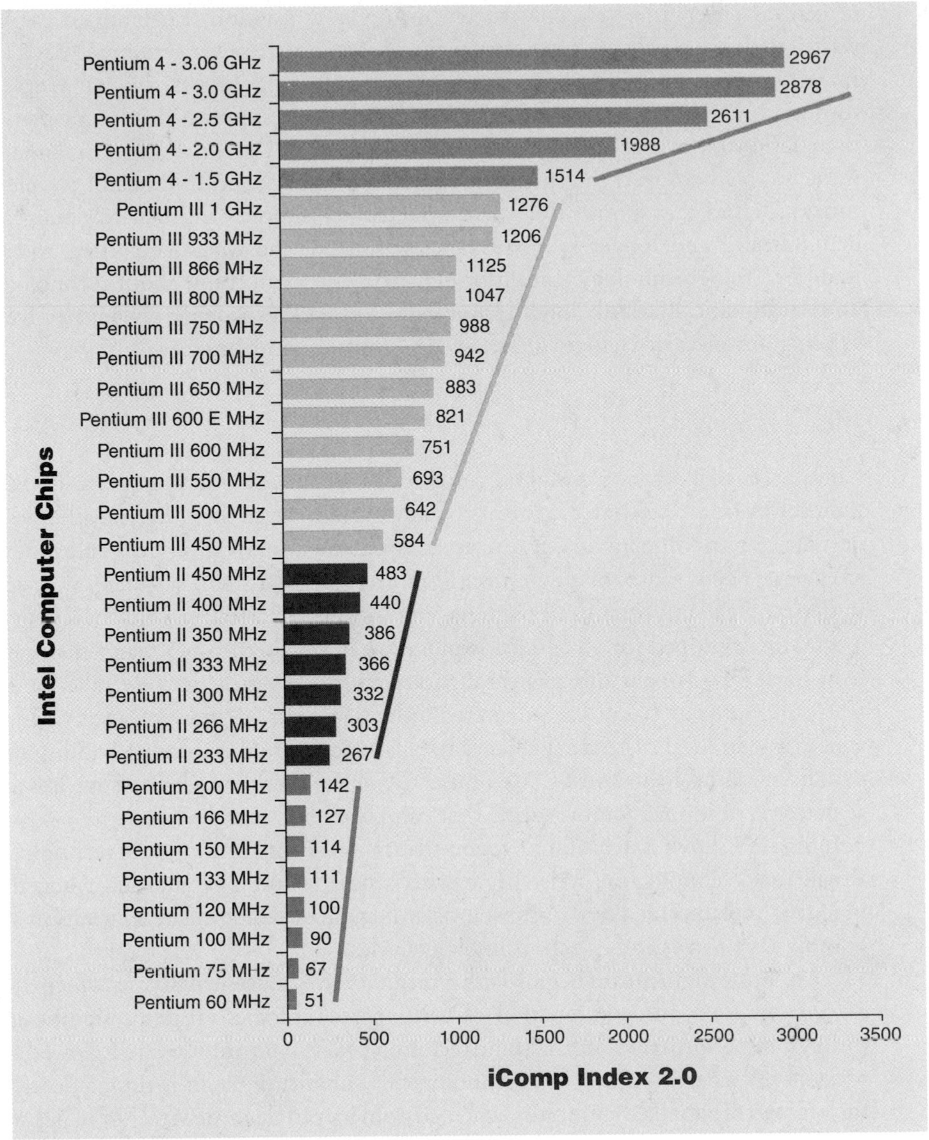

EXHIBIT 10.2
iComp Index 2.0 Comparing the Relative Performance of Different Intel Microprocessors

Sources: "Intel iComp (Full List)," Ideas International, [Online] available at www.ideasinternational.com/benchmark/intel/icomp.html, 16 May 2002. "Benchmark Resources: iComp Index3.0," Intel, [Online] available at http://developer.intel.com/procs/perf/icomp/index.htm, 13 October 2001. "PC CPU Benchmarks, News, Prices and Reviews," CPU Scorecard, [Online] available at www.cpuscorecard.com, 17 March 2003.

S-curve technology cycle in integrated circuits. A 450 MHz Pentium III processor was 21 percent faster than a 450 MHz Pentium II chip. Over time, improving existing technology (tweaking the performance of the current technology cycle), combined with replacing old technology with new technology cycles (i.e., the Pentium 4 replacing the Pentium III replacing the Pentium II replacing the Pentium), has increased the speed of Pentium computer processors by a factor of 58 in just 17 years and all computer processors by a factor of 300!

Though the evolution of Intel's Pentium chips has been used to illustrate S-curves and technology cycles, it's important to note that technology cycles and technological innovation don't necessarily mean "high technology." Remember, technology is simply the knowledge, tools, and techniques used to transform inputs into outputs. So a technology cycle occurs whenever there are major advances or changes in the knowledge, tools, and techniques of a field or discipline. For example, one of the most important technology cycles in the history of civilization occurred in 1859, when 3400 kilometres of central sewer line were constructed throughout London, England, to carry human waste to the sea nearly 30 kilometres away. This extensive sewer system replaced the widespread practice of dumping raw sewage directly into streets, where people walked through it and where it drained into public wells that supplied drinking water. Though the relationship wasn't known at the time, preventing waste runoff from contaminating water supplies stopped the spread of cholera that had killed millions of people for centuries in cities throughout the world.[9] Safe water supplies immediately translated into better health and longer life expectancies. Indeed, the water you drink today is safe thanks to this "technology" breakthrough. So, when you think about technology cycles, don't automatically think "high technology." Instead, broaden your perspective by considering advances or changes in knowledge, tools, and techniques.

Innovation Streams

Companies that want to sustain a competitive advantage must understand and protect themselves from the strategic threats of innovation. Over the long run, the best way to do that is for a company to create a stream of its own innovative ideas and products year after year. Focus Corp. of Edmonton is an example of a small company that appears to understand the importance of ongoing innovation. It has taken land surveying software originally developed for oil and gas exploration in northern Alberta and customized it to help local government officials throughout North America manage civic emergencies. The same software has also been altered to help law enforcement officials track and prevent crime in local districts. The keys to this success are the software's ability to present data in graphical form and its ease of use.[10] Consequently, we define **innovation streams** as patterns of innovation over time that can create sustainable competitive advantage.[11] Exhibit 10.3 shows a typical innovation stream consisting of a series of technology cycles. Recall that technological cycles begin with a new technology and end when that technology is replaced by a newer, substantially better technology. The innovation stream in Exhibit 10.3 shows three such technology cycles.

innovation streams
patterns of innovation over time that can create sustainable competitive advantage

An innovation stream begins with a **technological discontinuity**, in which a scientific advance or a unique combination of existing technologies creates a significant breakthrough in performance or function. Technological discontinuities are followed by an **era of ferment** characterized by technological substitution and design competition. **Technological substitution** occurs when customers purchase new technologies to replace older technologies. For example, in the first half of the 1800s, letters, messages, and news travelled slowly by boat, train, or horseback, such as the famous Pony Express that, using a large number of fresh riders and fresh horses, could deliver mail from one part of the continent to another in 10 days.[12] However, between 1840 and 1860, many businesses began using the telegraph, because it allowed messages and news to be sent cross-country (or even around the world) in minutes rather than days, weeks, or months.[13] Indeed, telegraph companies were so successful that the Pony Express went out of business almost immediately after the completion of the transcontinental telegraph, which linked telegraph systems from coast to coast.

technological discontinuity
scientific advance or unique combination of existing technologies that creates a significant breakthrough in performance or function

era of ferment
phase of a technology cycle characterized by technological substitution and design competition

technological substitution
purchase of new technologies to replace older ones

An era of ferment is also characterized by **design competition** in which the old technology and several different new technologies compete to establish a new technological standard or dominant design. Because of large investments in old technology, and because the new and old technologies are often incompatible with each other, companies and consumers are reluctant to switch to a different technology during design competition. Indeed, the telegraph was so widely used as a means of communication in the late 1800s that, at first, almost no one understood why telephones would be a better way to communicate. In his book *Interactive Excellence: Defining and Developing New Standards for the Twenty-First Century*, Edwin Schlossberg wrote, "People could not imagine why they would want or need to talk immediately to someone who was across town or, even more absurdly, in another town."[14] Also, during design competition, the changeover from older to newer technologies is often

design competition
competition between old and new technologies to establish a new technological standard or dominant design

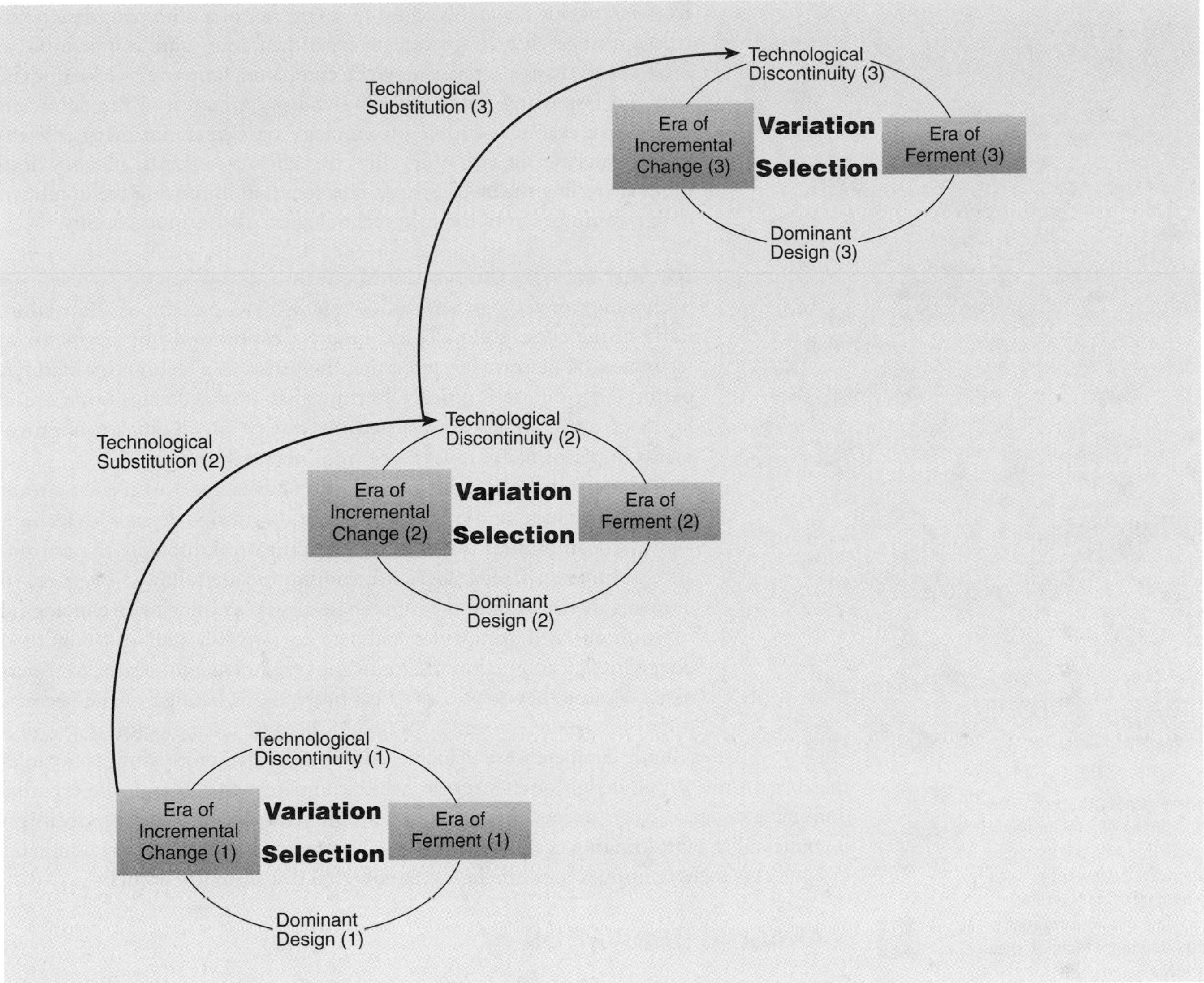

Source: From *Managing Strategic Innovation and Change: A Collection of Readings* by Michael L. Tushman & Philip C. Anderson, copyright © 1997 by Oxford University Press, Inc. Used by permission of Oxford University Press, Inc.

EXHIBIT 10.3
Innovation Streams: Technology Cycles over Time

slowed by the fact that older technology usually improves significantly in response to the competitive threat from the new technologies.

An era of ferment is followed by the emergence of a **dominant design**, which becomes the accepted market standard for technology.[16] Dominant designs emerge in several ways. One is critical mass, meaning that a particular technology can become the dominant design simply because most people use it. Since millions more people bought VCRs that used VHS tapes, VHS tapes beat out Sony's Beta format to become the dominant design for VCRs. Likewise, a design can become dominant if it solves a practical problem. For example, the QWERTY keyboard (look at the top left line of letters on a keyboard) became the dominant design for typewriters, because it slowed typists who, by typing too fast, caused mechanical typewriter keys to jam.

dominant design
a new technological design or process that becomes the accepted market standard

Yet, no matter how they occur, the emergence of a dominant design is a key event in an innovation stream. First, emergence of a dominant design indicates that there are winners and losers. Technological innovation is both competence enhancing and competence destroying. Companies that bet on the wrong design or on the old technology often struggle, while companies that bet on the now-dominant design usually prosper. In fact, more companies are likely to go out of business in an era of ferment than in an economic recession or slowdown. Second, the emergence of a dominant design signals a change away from design experimentation and competition to **incremental change**, a phase in which companies innovate by lowering the cost and improving the functioning and performance of the dominant design. For example, during a technology cycle, manufacturing efficiencies let Intel cut the cost of its chips by half to two-thirds, all while doubling or tripling the chips' speed. This focus on improving the dominant design continues until the next technological discontinuity occurs.

DOING THE RIGHT THING

GIVE CREDIT, DON'T TAKE IT[15]

You came up with a great idea and ran it by your boss, who loved it. Next thing you know, the office is buzzing about this "great new idea." But instead of giving you the credit, your boss took the credit and shamelessly sold the idea as his own. Not only is stealing others' ideas wrong, but nothing kills a creative work environment faster than not giving people credit for their ideas. So, if you're the boss, no matter who comes up with "the" idea, give them credit. Spread the recognition and acknowledgment around so that their coworkers and your boss's boss know about your employees' great ideas. Do the right thing. Give credit where it's due. You'll be rewarded with more great ideas.

Review 1: Why Innovation Matters

Technology cycles typically follow an S-curve pattern of innovation. Early in the cycle, technological progress is slow and improvements in technological performance are small. However, as a technology matures, performance improves quickly. Finally, small improvements occur as the limits of a technology are reached. At this point, significant improvements in performance must come from new technologies.

The best way to protect a competitive advantage is to create a stream of innovative ideas and products. Innovation streams begin with technological discontinuities that create significant breakthroughs in performance or function. Technological discontinuities are followed by an era of ferment, in which customers purchase new technologies (technological substitution) and companies compete to establish the new dominant design (design competition). Dominant designs emerge because of critical mass, because they solve a practical problem, or because of the negotiations of independent standards bodies. Because technological innovation is both competence enhancing and competence destroying, companies that bet on the wrong design often struggle, while companies that bet on the eventual dominant design usually prosper. Emergence of a dominant design leads to a focus on incremental change, lowering costs, and small, but steady improvements in the dominant design. This focus continues until the next technological discontinuity occurs.

incremental change
the phase of a technology cycle in which companies innovate by lowering costs and improving the functioning and performance of the dominant technological design

2 MANAGING INNOVATION

The previous discussion of technology cycles and innovation streams showed that managers must be equally good at managing innovation in two very different circumstances. First, during eras of ferment, companies must find a way to anticipate and survive the technological discontinuities that can suddenly transform industry leaders into losers and industry unknowns into industry powerhouses. Companies that can't manage innovation following technological discontinuities risk quick organizational decline and dissolution. Second, after a new dominant design emerges following an era of ferment, companies must manage the very different process of incremental improvement and innovation. Companies that can't manage incremental innovation slowly deteriorate as they fall farther behind industry leaders.

Unfortunately, what works well when managing innovation after technological discontinuities doesn't work well when managing innovation during periods of incremental change (and vice versa). Consequently, to successfully manage innovation streams, companies need to be good at two things: managing innovation during discontinuous change, and managing innovation during incremental change.

Managing Innovation During Discontinuous Change

A study of 72 product development projects (i.e., innovation) in 36 computer companies across North America, Europe, and Asia found that companies that succeeded in periods of discontinuous change (in which a technological discontinuity created a significant breakthrough in performance or function) typically followed an experiential approach to innovation.[17] The experiential approach to innovation assumes that innovation is occurring within a highly uncertain environment, and that the key to fast product innovation is to use intuition, flexible options, and hands-on experience to reduce uncertainty and accelerate learning and understanding. There are five parts to the **experiential approach to innovation**: design iterations, testing, milestones, multifunctional teams, and powerful leaders.[18]

experiential approach to innovation
an approach to innovation that assumes a highly uncertain environment, and uses intuition, flexible options, and hands-on experience to reduce uncertainty and accelerate learning and understanding

An "iteration" is a repetition. So a **design iteration** is a cycle of repetition in which a company tests a prototype of a new product or service, improves on the design, and then builds and tests the improved product or service prototype. As you learned in Chapter 4, a product prototype is a full-scale working model that is being tested for design, function, and reliability. **Testing** is a systematic comparison of different product designs or design iterations. Companies that want to create a new dominant design following a technological discontinuity quickly build, test, improve, and retest a series of different product prototypes.

design iteration
a cycle of repetition in which a company tests a prototype of a new product or service, improves on that design, and then builds and tests the improved prototype

testing
systematic comparison of different product designs or design iterations

For example, it took a number of design iterations for Starbucks and its suppliers to successfully create a paper coffee cup that would keep coffee hot but not burn customers' hands. To prevent customers from burning themselves, Starbucks had either stacked two paper cups together or used cardboard sleeves that slid over the outside of the cup. However, customers complained that sleeves fell off or prevented cups from fitting into cup holders and that using two cups was wasteful. As a result, Starbucks and its suppliers worked for three years to come up with a paper cup that was light, cheap, environment friendly, and heat insulating. Prototypes ranged from a layered cup that folded and wrapped one long piece of paper into three layers of paper, to a Japanese-designed cup coated with a special plastic. Testing was both practical, using human hands to pick up different cups filled with steaming coffee, and scientific, using an infrared temperature gauge to test cups' external temperatures. The breakthrough cup design, now being tested in Starbucks stores, sandwiches a thin air layer between an inner polyethylene liner and outer layer of brown recycled paper.[19]

By trying a number of very different designs, or by making successive improvements and changes in the same design, frequent design iterations reduce uncertainty and improve understanding. Simply put, the more prototypes you build, the more likely you are to learn what works and what doesn't. Plus, building a number of prototypes also means that designers and engineers are less likely to "fall in love" with a particular prototype. Instead, they'll be more concerned with improving the product or technology as much as they can. Testing speeds up and improves the innovation process, too. Testing two very different design prototypes against each other, or testing the new design iteration against the previous iteration, quickly makes product design strengths and weaknesses apparent. Likewise, testing uncovers errors early in the design process when they are easiest to correct. Finally, testing accelerates learning and understanding by forcing engineers and product designers to examine hard data about product performance. An example of an innovation involving a number of different design iterations originates with Pro Mac Manufacturing Ltd., of Courtney, British Columbia. An added bonus of its innovation is that it will inevitably save lives. So what is it? The company has developed a blast-proof excavator for removing land mines from war zones.[20]

Milestones are formal project review points used to assess progress and performance. For example, a company that has put itself on a 12-month schedule to complete a project might schedule milestones at the three-month, six-month, and nine-month points on the schedule. By making people regularly assess what they're doing, how well they're performing, and whether they need to take corrective action, milestones provide structure to the general chaos that follows technological discontinuities. Milestones also shorten the innovation process by creating a sense of urgency that keeps everyone on task. For example, when one electrical utility was building its first nuclear power facility, the company's construction manager passed out 2000 desk calendars to company employees, construction contractors, vendors, and suppliers, so that everyone involved in the project was aware of the construction timeline. Contractors that regularly missed deadlines were replaced.[21] Finally, milestones are beneficial for innovation, because meeting regular milestones builds momentum by giving people a sense of accomplishment.

milestones
formal project review points used to assess progress and performance

© JEFF SCIORTINO

Multifunctional work teams are a key part of generating new ideas. When Kellogg's realized that it was experiencing a dearth of new ideas and products, it implemented multifunctional work teams. In their first month, the teams generated 65 new product ideas, including the now-popular prepackaged Rice Krispie Treat.

multifunctional teams
work teams composed of people from different departments

Multifunctional teams are work teams composed of people from different departments. Multifunctional teams accelerate learning and understanding by mixing and integrating technical, marketing, and manufacturing activities. By involving all key departments in development from the start, multifunctional teams speed innovation through early identification of problems that would typically not have been identified until much later.

Powerful leaders provide the vision, discipline, and motivation to keep the innovation process focused, on time, and on target. Powerful leaders are able to get resources when they are needed, are typically more experienced, have high status in the company, and are held directly responsible for product success or failure. On average, powerful leaders can get innovation-related projects done nine months faster than leaders with little power or influence.

Managing Innovation During Incremental Change

compression approach to innovation
an approach to innovation that assumes that incremental innovation can be planned using a series of steps, and that compressing those steps can speed innovation

While the experiential approach is used to manage innovation during periods of discontinuous change, a compression approach can be used during periods of incremental change, in which the focus is on systematically improving the performance and lowering the cost of the dominant technological design. A **compression approach to innovation** assumes that innovation is a predictable process, that incremental innovation can be planned using a series of steps, and that compressing the time it takes to complete those steps can speed up innovation. There are five parts to the compression approach to innovation: planning, supplier involvement, shortening the time of individual steps, overlapping steps, and multifunctional teams.[22]

In Chapter 4, planning was defined as choosing a goal and a method or strategy to achieve that goal. When planning for incremental innovation, the goal is to squeeze or compress development time as much as possible, and the general strategy is to create a series of planned steps to accomplish that goal. Planning for incremental innovation helps avoid unnecessary steps. In addition, planning allows developers to sequence steps in the right order to avoid wasted time and shorten the delays between steps. Planning also reduces misunderstandings and decreases coordination problems regarding when and how things are to be done.

Most planning for incremental innovation is based on the idea of generational change. **Generational change** occurs when incremental improvements are made to a dominant technological design such that the improved version of the technology is fully backward compatible with the older version.[23] So unlike technological discontinuities that result in the replacement of older technologies, generational change allows the old and newer versions of the same technological design to co-exist in the marketplace. For example, Sony (www.sony.com) used the idea of generational change to extend the life of its Sony Walkman products. After inventing the Walkman tape player in 1978, Sony introduced 250 different kinds of Walkmans over the next decade. However, there were few significant changes in the basic Walkman over that time. In fact, 85 percent of the new models simply represented small improvements such as adding AM/FM stereo radio, auto reverse, Dolby sound, water resistance, TV audio band, digital tuning, and enhanced bass. Together, these generational changes have helped Sony maintain above-average profits and a 50 percent share of this market.[24]

generational change change based on incremental improvements to a dominant technological design such that the improved technology is fully backward compatible with the older technology

Because the compression approach assumes that innovation can follow a series of preplanned steps, one of the ways to shorten development time is supplier involvement. Delegating some of the preplanned steps in the innovation process to outside suppliers reduces the amount of work that internal development teams must do. As well, suppliers provide an alternative source of ideas and expertise that can lead to better designs. Supplier involvement also takes advantage of distinctive competencies by allowing both the development team and the suppliers to do what they do best. In general, the earlier suppliers are involved, the quicker they are to catch and prevent future problems, such as unrealistic designs or mismatched product specifications.

Another way to shorten development time is to simply shorten the time of individual steps in the innovation process. One of the most common ways to do that is through computer-aided design (CAD). CAD speeds up the design process by allowing designers and engineers to make and test design changes using computer models. In many steps of the design process, Ford (www.ford.com) found that CAD models and computer simulations can replace physical testing of expensive automobile prototypes. And since computer-based CAD systems store design specifications and characteristics in computer files (the same way that a personal computer stores word processing files), CAD speeds innovation by making it easy to access and reuse previous designs. At Ford, product designers and engineers use desktop and laptop computers to access a design knowledge base containing standard parts, standard design guides (that walk designers through the process of creating new parts), and detailed performance and testing information. The design knowledge base is accessible to any computer connected to Ford's company network. Finally, CAD systems improve communication and organization by making sure that all design team members work with the latest design iteration. If the engineers in charge of engine design change the size of an engine from four to six cylinders, those changes are automatically registered in what Ford calls the "common total vehicle data model." So when the designers in charge of the car's suspension system log on, they'll find that the engine has been changed and can make the necessary changes to the car's suspension system.[25]

In a sequential design process, each step must be completed before the next step begins. But sometimes multiple development steps can be performed at the same time. Overlapping steps shorten the development process by reducing the delays or waiting time between steps. By using overlapping rather than sequential steps, most car companies have reduced the time it takes to develop a brand-new car from five years to three years. However, they still develop new models sequentially. First they design and build, say, a four-door sedan. Then, after perfecting the design and manufacture of the sedan, two or three years later they introduce the two-door coupe. A couple of years after that, they introduce the station wagon version of the same model.

Review 2: Managing Innovation

To successfully manage innovation streams, companies must manage the sources of innovation and learn to manage innovation during both discontinuous and incremental change. Since innovation begins with creativity, companies can manage the sources of innovation by supporting a creative work environment, in which creative thoughts and ideas are welcomed, valued, and encouraged. Creative work environments provide challenging work; offer organizational, supervisory, and work group encouragement; allow significant freedom; and remove organizational impediments to creativity.

Companies that succeed in periods of discontinuous change typically follow an experiential approach to innovation. The experiential approach assumes that intuition, flexible options, and hands-on experience can reduce uncertainty and accelerate learning and understanding. This approach involves frequent design iterations, frequent testing, regular milestones, creation of multifunctional teams, and use of powerful leaders to guide the innovation process.

A compression approach to innovation works best during periods of incremental change. This approach assumes that innovation can be planned using a series of steps, and that compressing the time it takes to complete those steps can speed up innovation. The five parts to the compression approach are planning (generational change), supplier involvement, shortening the time of individual steps (computer-aided design), overlapping steps, and multifunctional teams.

Organizational Change

"Ding-dong. Avon calling." When people think of Avon, they think of their local "Avon Lady." In North America alone, Avon (www.avon.com) has more than 450 000 Avon Ladies who, using the company's distinctive one-on-one marketing approach, have been selling Avon products directly to customers for decades. Now, however, Avon management is testing the idea of selling Avon products through Avon retail stores. This strategy has been successful overseas, particularly in Malaysia, where 145 Avon stores now account for half of Avon's Malaysian sales. The company is also testing a direct-mail catalogue. Early results indicate that catalogue customers spend twice as much per order as customers who place orders through Avon Ladies. While these changes look promising, they are also risky, because they're likely to cut into the sales and earnings of Avon's North American sales force, which accounts for almost all of their North American sales! Avon hopes to keep its Avon Ladies happy by giving them franchising opportunities with its new Avon stores. Or it may try to refer store customers to them for additional sales. However, when Avon has tried to make changes before, its Avon Ladies have responded angrily. For example, when management tried to cut costs by eliminating sales representative discounts on a limited number of Avon products, 25 000 Avon Ladies quit their jobs in protest.[26]

Why would a company like Avon consider such drastic changes in the way it does business? And with the strong resistance it expects from its sales force, how can it implement these changes successfully?

After reading the next two sections, you should be able to

3 discuss why change occurs and why it matters.

4 discuss the different methods that managers can use to better manage change as it occurs.

3 WHY CHANGE OCCURS AND WHY IT MATTERS

Businesses operate in a constantly changing environment. Recognizing and adapting to internal and external changes can mean the difference between continued success and going out of business.

Let's learn about change forces and resistance forces, and organizational decline: the risk of not changing.[27]

Change Forces and Resistance Forces

According to social psychologist Kurt Lewin, change is a function of the forces that promote change and the opposing forces that slow or resist change.[28] **Change forces** lead to differences in the form, quality, or condition of an organization over time. By contrast, **resistance forces** support the status quo—that is, the existing state of conditions in organizations.

change forces
forces that produce differences in the form, quality, or condition of an organization over time

resistance forces
forces that support the existing state of conditions in organizations

Exhibit 10.4 illustrates how the relative strengths of resistance and change forces interact to bring about different levels of change. Change can be nonexistent, sporadic, continuous, or discontinuous, depending on whether change forces are stronger or weaker than resistance forces. At one extreme, when resistance forces are strong and change forces are weak, there is no change. When resistance and change forces are both weak, chance events can lead to sporadic change that occurs in random patterns or for accidental reasons.

When change forces are strong and resistance forces are weak, continuous change occurs, as organizations are forced to adapt to ongoing change forces. If both change and resistance forces are strong, and the resistance forces can no longer hold back the change forces, sudden discontinuous change can occur. Discontinuous change is similar to an arm-wrestling match between two very strong men. Both men are physically powerful, but after a while, one is likely to lose his grip or tire. When that happens, the match will end seconds later, as the winner suddenly overpowers the loser.

Organizational Decline: The Risk of Not Changing

Organizational decline occurs when companies don't anticipate, recognize, neutralize, or adapt to the internal or external pressures that threaten their survival.[29] In other words, decline occurs when organizations don't recognize the need for change. GM's loss of market share in the automobile industry (from 60 percent to 30 percent) is an example

organizational decline
a large decrease in organizational performance that occurs when companies don't anticipate, recognize, neutralize, or adapt to the internal or external pressures that threaten their survival

EXHIBIT 10.4
How Change and Resistance Forces Create Change

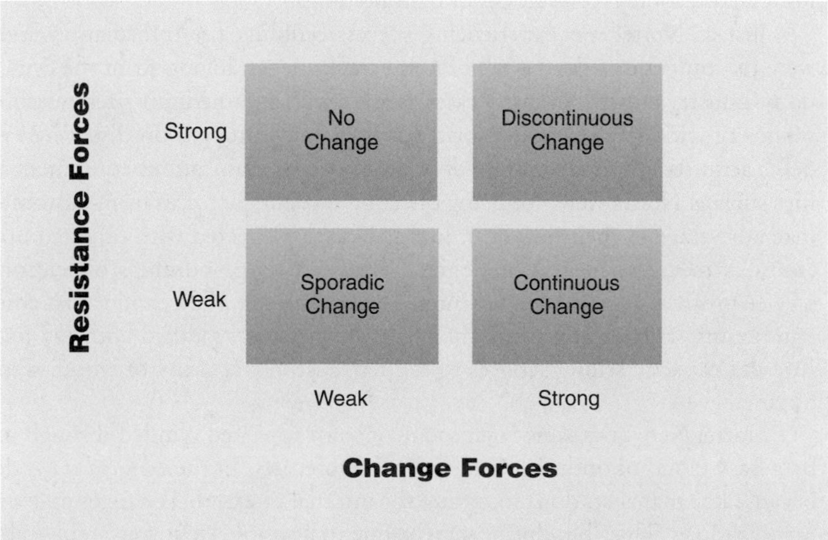

Source: P. Strebel, "Choosing the Right Change Path," *California Management Review*, Winter 1994, 29–51

CP PHOTO/JOHN WOODS

Following its defeat in the 2006 federal election, the Liberal Party of Canada faces a series of daunting challenges that include picking a new leader, rebuilding an image torn apart by a disastrous sponsorship scandal, and recreating its party organization in Quebec.

of organizational decline. There are five stages of organizational decline: blinded, inaction, faulty action, crisis, and dissolution.[30]

GM's concerns are well known. Yet few organizational declines have been as dramatic as that of Nortel Networks. One estimate suggests that in early 2000, 75 percent of North America's Internet traffic was carried by Nortel equipment. Over 90 000 individuals were employed by Nortel, most of them in high-paying jobs, much of this the result of a multi-year corporate acquisition spree that cost well over $28 billion. Throughout the world, the Nortel insignia could be found on 24 production facilities. Its 2000 revenues alone were greater than $40 billion, a double-digit increase from the year before and the year before that.[31] At its pinnacle during the summer of 2000, the price of Nortel's shares had peaked at $124.50 while the company stock value was almost $400 billion. Nortel's impact on many Canadians was enormous. During the same period, Nortel's value was equal to 36 percent of the value of the entire TSE 300, an index fund that held 300 major stocks traded on the Toronto Stock Exchange. Few Canadian pension or mutual funds did not contain some Nortel stocks in their holdings.[32]

Just as Nortel was experiencing success building the information highway, so too were its competitors. In the fall of 2000 cracks began to appear in the mirage of continuous industry growth. In many cases, large, small, and medium-sized telecommunication service providers throughout North America and Europe soon discovered that the large debts acquired to purchase state-of-the-art telecommunications equipment from companies such as Nortel were not being offset by revenue increases from customers seeking to take advantage of their new gear. Just as Nortel competed with other equipment manufacturers to create new technologies, so too did large numbers of telecommunication service providers compete to lay Internet pipe into the home, and across cities, countries, and oceans. The result was too many service providers saddled with too much debt and Internet capacity selling services to too few customers, many of whom were simply not buying.

Nortel Network's senior management team appeared blinded through much of 2000 by a hazy cloud of optimism and rosy sales forecasts. In the *blinded stage,* decline begins because key managers don't recognize the internal or external changes that will harm their organizations. This "blindness" may be due to a simple lack of awareness about changes. It may stem from an inability to understand the significance of changes. Or it may simply come from the overconfidence that can develop when companies have been successful.

In this case, success may have been the villain. While Nortel executives were forecasting future industry growth in the double digits during the early fall of 2000, a prominent New York–based analyst, Paul Sagawa, was predicting a dramatic fall in telecommunication carrier spending throughout 2001.[33]

The reaction to these signals by Nortel Networks could best be described for a long time as "inaction." Up until October of 2001, it still employed 55 000 people with many of its facilities still in operation and its CEO, John Roth, still the architect of its growth. In the *inaction stage,* as organizational performance problems become more visible, management may recognize the need to change but still take no action. The managers may be waiting to see if the problems will correct themselves. Or they may find it difficult to change previous practices and policies that once led to success. Another possible reason is that they wrongly assume that they can make changes to correct problems, so they don't feel the problems are urgent. It is here where Nortel Networks sat in 2006. With employment levels near 35 000 and revenues of just over $10 billion, its product lines have been reorganized and it has a new CEO in the person of Mike Zafirovski, a former chief operating officer of Motorola. The jury is still out as to whether Nortel's actions will be labelled in the future as "faulty actions," or whether this is the stage where Nortel halts and turns around its decline.

In the *faulty action stage,* due to rising costs and decreasing profits and market share, management will announce "belt-tightening" plans designed to cut costs, increase efficiency, and restore profits. In other words, rather than recognizing the need for fundamental changes, managers assume that if they just run a "tighter ship," company performance will return to previous levels.

In the *crisis stage,* bankruptcy or dissolution (i.e., breaking up and selling the different parts of the company) is likely to occur unless the company completely reorganizes the way it does business. At this point, however, companies typically lack the resources needed to fully change how they run their businesses. Cutbacks and layoffs will have reduced the level of talent among employees. Furthermore, talented managers who were savvy enough to see the crisis coming will have begun taking jobs with other companies (often with competitors). Because of rising costs and lower sales, cash is tight. And lenders and suppliers are unlikely to extend further loans or credit to ease the cash crunch.

In the *dissolution stage,* after failing to make the changes needed to sustain the organization, the company is dissolved through bankruptcy proceedings or by selling assets in order to pay suppliers, banks, and creditors. At this point, a new CEO may be brought in to oversee the closing of stores, offices, and manufacturing facilities; the final layoff of managers and employees; and the sale of assets to pay bills and loans.

Finally, because decline is reversible at each of the first four stages, not all companies in decline reach final dissolution. For example, after nearly a decade in decline, GM has cut costs, stabilized its market share, and had several consecutive years of small profits.

Review 3: Why Change Occurs and Why It Matters

Change is a function of the relative strength of the change forces and resistance forces that occur inside and outside of organizations. Change can be nonexistent, sporadic, continuous, or discontinuous, depending on whether change forces are stronger or weaker than resistance forces. The five-stage process of organizational decline begins when organizations don't recognize the need for change. In the blinded stage, managers don't recognize the changes that threaten their organization's survival. In the inaction stage, management recognizes the need to change, but doesn't act, hoping that the problems will correct themselves. In the faulty action stage, management focuses on cost cutting and efficiency rather than facing up to fundamental changes needed to insure survival. In the crisis stage, failure is likely unless fundamental reorganization occurs. Finally, in the dissolution stage, the company is dissolved through bankruptcy proceedings, by selling assets to pay creditors, or through the closing of stores, offices, and facilities. However, if companies recognize the need to change early enough, dissolution may be avoided.

4 MANAGING CHANGE

resistance to change
opposition to change resulting from self-interest, misunderstanding and distrust, or a general intolerance for change

Resistance to change is caused by self-interest, misunderstanding and distrust, and a general intolerance for change.[34] People resist change out of self-interest, because they fear that change will cost or deprive them of something they value. For example, resistance might stem from a fear that the changes will result in a loss of pay, power, responsibility, or even perhaps one's job. People also resist change because of misunderstanding and distrust—that is, they don't understand the change or the reasons for it, or they distrust the people, typically management, behind the change. Ironically, when this occurs, some of the strongest resisters may support the changes in public, nodding and smiling their agreement, but then ignore the changes in private and just do their jobs as they always have.

Resistance may also come from a generally low tolerance for change. Some people are simply less capable of handling change than others. People with a *low tolerance for change* are threatened by the uncertainty associated with change and worry that they won't be able to learn the new skills and behaviours needed to successfully negotiate change in their companies.

Because resistance to change is inevitable, successful change efforts require careful management. Change efforts need to be well thought out. At Calgary-based Enmax, president and CEO Bob Nicolay said the city-owned utility believes that superior treatment of employees provides a competitive advantage in Calgary's red-hot employment market—as well as just making good business sense. That's particularly advantageous in the newly deregulated and increasingly competitive environment the enterprise operates in. "The best way to change or to evolve a culture is to tend to the development and the needs of employees," said Nicolay, noting Enmax's employee leadership programs, its new $60 million headquarters building, flexible work hours, fitness centre, education sponsorship programs and extended health benefits. "Anyone can match salaries ... so if you're going to differentiate yourself as an employer and become an employer of choice, you're going to have to develop a strategy that's more difficult for others to emulate," said Nicolay.[35]

In this section you will learn about managing resistance to change, change tools and techniques, managing conversations to promote change, and what not to do when leading change.

Managing Resistance to Change

unfreezing
getting the people affected by change to believe that change is needed

change intervention
the process used to get workers and managers to change their behaviour and work practices

refreezing
supporting and reinforcing the new changes so they "stick"

According to Kurt Lewin, managing organizational change is a basic process of unfreezing, change intervention, and refreezing. **Unfreezing** is getting the people affected by change to believe that change is needed. During the **change intervention** itself, workers and managers change their behaviour and work practices. **Refreezing** is supporting and reinforcing the new changes so they "stick."

Resistance to change is an example of frozen behaviour. Given the choice between changing and not changing, most people would rather not change. Because resistance to change is natural and inevitable, managers need to unfreeze resistance to change to create successful change programs. The following methods can be used to manage resistance to change: education and communication, participation, negotiation, top management support, and coercion.

When resistance to change is based on insufficient, incorrect, or misleading information, managers should *educate* employees about the need for change and *communicate* change-related information to them. Managers must also supply the information and funding or other support employees need to make changes.

Another way to reduce resistance to change is to have those affected by the change *participate in planning and implementing the change process.* Employees who participate have a better understanding of change and the need for it. Furthermore, employee concerns about change can be addressed as they occur if employees participate in the planning and implementation process. For example, in 1996, when Acadia University incorporated IBM laptops into its educational program, its administrators realized that a challenge lay before them. Its faculty members were unionized. Tenure and promotion decisions were based primarily on publication record as opposed to teaching effectiveness. There were few if any other universities to learn from. Classroom pedagogy for fully wired classroom settings was virtually nonexistent. Future bandwidth and server usage needs were at best educated guesses given the continual improvements to Internet-related technologies and applications such as video-streaming, file swapping software, and MP3 technology. Finally, an in-house capacity to service a campus of 4200 laptops was yet to be fully developed and tested. So how was the laptop program implemented, given these concerns? To begin, implementation committees were formed and staffed by volunteers. The laptops were phased in over four years with pilot initiatives occurring in the first year. Standard technologies and laptops were adopted. A User Support Centre (USC) was established to support the operation and maintenance of laptop technologies both in the classroom and beyond. The Acadia Institute for Teaching Technology (AITT) was formed to support faculty efforts to develop technology-related pedagogy. Funding and student support for faculty-initiated projects to improve teaching were made available on an annual basis for development each summer. Finally, the union agreements were altered to recognize the importance of teaching and innovation in promotion and tenure.[36]

Employees are less likely to resist change if they are allowed to *discuss and agree on who will do what after change occurs.* For example, construction projects are notoriously hard to manage. It's difficult to get clients, architects, contractors, and subcontractors to agree on things such as prices, materials, schedules, or who should be held responsible for unexpected changes and expenses. Often, lawsuits have to be filed to force reluctant parties to fulfill their responsibilities. Resistance to change also decreases when change efforts receive *significant managerial support.* Top managers must do more than talk about the importance of change. They must provide the training, resources, and autonomy needed to make change happen.

coercion
use of formal power and authority to force others to change

Finally, use of formal power and authority to force others to change is called **coercion**. Because of the intense negative reactions it can create (e.g., fear, stress, resentment, sabotage of company products), coercion should be used only when a crisis exists or when all other attempts to reduce resistance to change have failed. Exhibit 10.5 summarizes some additional suggestions for what managers can do when employees resist change.

EXHIBIT 10.5
What to Do When Employees Resist Change

UNFREEZING

- Share Reasons: Share the reason for change with employees.
- Emphasize: Be empathetic to the difficulties that change will create for managers and employees.
- Communicate: Communicate the details simply, clearly, extensively, verbally, and in writing.

CHANGE

- Benefits: Explain the benefits, "What's in it for them."
- Champion: identify a highly respected manager to manage the change effort.
- Input: Allow the people who will be affected by change to express their needs and offer their input.
- Timing: Don't begin change at a bad time, for example, during the busiest part of the year or month.
- Security: if possible, maintain employees' job security to minimize fear of change.
- Training: Offer training to ensure that employees are both confident and competent to handle new requirements.
- Pace: Change at a manageable pace. Don't rush.

REFREEZING

- Top Management Support: Send consistent messages and free resources.
- Publicize Success: Let others know when and where change is working.
- Employee Services: Offer counselling or other services to help employees deal with the stress of change.

Source: G.J. Iskat & J. Liebowitz, "What to Do When Employees Resist Change," *Supervision*, 1 August 1996.

Change Tools and Techniques

If your boss came to you and said, "All right, genius, you wanted it. You're in charge of turning around the division," how would you start? Where would you begin? How would you encourage change-resistant managers to change? What would you do to include others in the change process? How would you get the change process off to a quick start? Finally, what long-term approach would you use to promote long-term effectiveness and performance? Results-driven change, the General Electric Workout, transition management teams, and organizational development are different change tools and techniques that can be used to address these issues.

One of the reasons that organizational change efforts fail is that they are activity oriented, meaning that they primarily focus on changing company procedures, management philosophy, or employee behaviour. Typically, there is much build-up and preparation as consultants are brought in, presentations are made, books are read, and employees and managers are trained. There's a tremendous emphasis on "doing things the new way." But for all the focus on activities, on "doing," there's almost no focus on results, on seeing if all this activity has actually made a difference.

By contrast, **results-driven change** supplants the sole emphasis on activity with a laser-like focus on quickly measuring and improving results.[38] Another advantage of results-driven change is that managers introduce changes in procedures, philosophy, or behaviour only if they are likely to improve measured performance. In other words, managers actually test to see if changes make a difference.

A third advantage of results-driven change is that quick, visible improvements motivate employees to continue to make additional changes to improve measured performance. Are these ideas used throughout the corporate world? It appears so. Indeed, consultants have introduced the results-driven change programs in such important institutions as Bell Canada, Pfizer Canada, the Industrial Accident Prevention Association of Ontario, Dupont Canada, and Pitney Bowes Canada.[39] For example, at one company, a team used cross-training to reduce the number of job categories from 120 to 32. Another, encouraged by the success of 90 other problem-solving teams, trained machine operators to enter production data directly into the computer on the factory floor, eliminating the 7600 hours of staff work that it used to take to enter those data from paper records. Consequently, unlike most change efforts, the quick successes associated with results-driven change were particularly effective at reducing resistance to change. Exhibit 10.6 describes the basic steps of results-driven change.

DOING THE RIGHT THING

ORGANIZATIONAL LIES ABOUT THE "PROGRAM OF THE MONTH"[37]

It's common for companies to announce new company-wide change programs, such as "six sigma quality" on an annual basis. But that's much too often if you want change to "stick." It takes several years at a minimum to produce systematic change in an organization. According to consultant Susan Cramm, "People don't hate change; they hate the promise of change unfulfilled. That is, everybody hates le grand programme du jour that starts with a bang and ends with a whimper. With each successive program launch, workers become increasingly more cynical and, over time, stop listening and lose hope." In effect, management lies to employees about the importance and changes ostensibly associated with each program of "the month." So, do the right thing. Limit company-wide change programs to once every three to five years. Then, fully implement and use each program. If you do, the next time you call for change, people might believe you.

results-driven change change created quickly by focusing on the measurement and improvement of results

EXHIBIT 10.6
Results-Driven Change Programs

1.	Create measurable, short-term goals to improve performance.
2.	Use action steps only if they are likely to improve measured performance.
3.	Management should stress the importance of immediate improvements.
4.	Consultants and staffers should help managers and employees achieve quick improvements in performance.
5.	Managers and employees should test action steps to see if they actually yield improvements. Action steps that don't should be discarded.
6.	It takes few resources to get results-driven change started.

Source: R.H. Schaffer & H.A. Thomson, J.D., "Successful Change Programs Begin with Results," *Harvard Business Review on Change* (Boston: Harvard Business School Publishing, 1998), 189–213.

The **General Electric Workout** is a special kind of results-driven change. It is a three-day meeting that brings together managers and employees from different levels and parts of an organization to quickly generate and act on solutions to specific business problems.[40] On the first morning of a workout, the boss discusses the agenda and targets specific business problems that the group is to try to solve. Then the boss leaves, and an outside facilitator breaks the group, typically 30 to 40 people, into five or six teams and helps them spend the next day and a half discussing and debating solutions. On day three, in what GE calls a "town meeting," the teams present specific solutions to their boss, who has been gone since day one. As each team spokesperson makes specific suggestions, the boss has only three options: agree on the spot, say no, or ask for more information so that a decision can be made by a specific agreed-on date. Prior to its merger with TransCanada Pipelines Ltd., Calgary-based Nova Gas Transmission Ltd. used a GE Workout to help improve the operating conditions of its gas plant maintenance workers operating throughout Alberta.

General Electric Workout
a three-day meeting in which managers and employees from different levels and parts of an organization quickly generate and act on solutions to specific business problems

While the GE Workout clearly speeds up change, it may fragment change, as different managers approve different suggestions in different town meetings across a company. By contrast, a transition management team provides a way to coordinate change throughout an organization. A **transition management team (TMT)** is a team of 8 to 12 people whose full-time job is to manage and coordinate a company's change process.[41] Exhibit 10.7 outlines the primary responsibilities of the TMT. One member of the TMT is assigned the task of anticipating and managing the emotions and behaviours related to resistance to change. Despite their importance, many companies overlook the impact that negative emotions and resistant behaviours can have on the change process. Also, TMTs report to the CEO every day, decide which change projects are approved and funded, select and evaluate the people in charge of different change projects, and make sure that different change projects complement one another. For example, entertainment company Viacom used a TMT to handle the changes that occurred when it acquired two much larger companies, Paramount Communications (TV and films) and Blockbuster Entertainment. The TMT reported directly to the CEO and included managers from Viacom, Paramount, and Blockbuster. Furthermore, Viacom's TMT was charged with eliminating duplication in television production, distribution and sales, and overhead and administrative costs in order to cut $280 million in expenses.[42]

transition management team (TMT)
a team of 8 to 12 people whose full-time job is to completely manage and coordinate a company's change process

Organizational development is a philosophy and collection of planned change interventions designed to improve an organization's long-term health and performance. Organizational development takes a long-range approach to change; assumes that top management support is necessary for change to succeed; creates change by educating workers and managers to change ideas, beliefs, and behaviours so problems can be solved in new ways; and emphasizes employee participation in diagnosing, solving, and evaluating problems.[43] As shown in Exhibit 10.8, organizational development interventions begin with recognition of a problem. Then the company designates a change agent to be

organizational development
a philosophy and collection of planned change interventions designed to improve an organization's long-term health and performance

EXHIBIT 10.7
The Primary Responsibilities of Transition Management Teams

1.	Establish context for change and provide guidance.
2.	Stimulate conversation.
3.	Provide appropriate resources.
4.	Coordinate and align projects.
5.	Ensure congruence of messages, activities, policies, and behaviours.
6.	Provide opportunities for joint creation.
7.	Anticipate, identify, and address people problems.
8.	Prepare the critical mass.

Source: J.D. Duck, "Managing Change: The Art of Balancing," *Harvard Business Review on Change* (Boston: Harvard Business School Publishing, 1998), 55–81.

1.	Entry	A problem is discovered and the need for change becomes apparent. Search begins for someone to deal with the problem and facilitate change.
2.	Start-up	A change agent enters the picture and works to clarify the problem and gain commitment to a change effort.
3.	Assessment and Feedback	The change agent gathers information about the problem and provides feedback about it to decision makers and those affected by it.
4.	Action Planning	The change agent works with decision makers to develop an action plan.
5.	Intervention	The action plan, or organizational development intervention, is carried out.
6.	Evaluation	The change agent helps decision makers assess the effectiveness of the intervention.
7.	Adoption	Organizational members accept ownership and responsibility for the change, which is then carried out through the entire organization.
8.	Separation	The change agent leaves the organization after first ensuring that the change intervention will continue to work.

EXHIBIT 10.8
General Steps for Organizational Development Interventions

Source: W.J. Rothwell, R. Sullivan, & G.M. McLean, *Practicing Organizational Development: A Guide for Consultants* (San Diego: Pfeiffer & Company, 1995).

change agent
the person formally in charge of guiding a change effort

formally in charge of guiding the change effort. This person can be someone from the company or a professional consultant. The **change agent** clarifies the problem, gathers information, works with decision makers to create and implement an action plan, helps to evaluate the plan's effectiveness, implements the plan throughout the company, and then leaves only after making sure the change intervention will continue to work.

Organizational development interventions are aimed at changing large systems, small groups, or people.[44] More specifically, the purpose of *large system interventions* is to change the character and performance of an organization, business unit, or department. The purpose of a *small group intervention* is to assess how a group functions and help it work more effectively toward the accomplishment of its goals. The purpose of a *person-focused intervention* is to help people become aware of their attitudes and behaviours and acquire new skills and knowledge to increase interpersonal effectiveness. Exhibit 10.9 describes the most frequently used organizational development interventions for large systems, small groups, and people.

EXHIBIT 10.9
Different Kinds of Organizational Development Interventions

LARGE SYSTEM INTERVENTIONS	
Sociotechnical Systems	An intervention designed to improve how well employees use and adjust to the work technology used in an organization.
Survey Feedback	An intervention that uses surveys to collect information from organizational members, reports the results of that survey to organizational members, and then uses those results to develop action plans for improvement.
SMALL GROUP INTERVENTIONS	
Team Building	An intervention designed to increase the cohesion and cooperation of work group members.
Unit Goal Setting	An intervention designed to help a work group establish short- and long-term goals.
PERSON-FOCUSED INTERVENTIONS	
Counselling/Coaching	An intervention designed so that a formal helper or coach listens to managers or employees and advises them how to deal with work or interpersonal problems.
Training	An intervention designed to provide individuals the knowledge, skills, or attitudes they need to become more effective at their jobs.

Source: W.J. Rothwell, R. Sullivan, & G.M. McLean, *Practicing Organizational Development: A Guide for Consultants* (San Diego: Pfeiffer & Company, 1995).

WHAT REALLY WORKS

Change the Work Setting or Change the People? Do Both![45]

Let's assume that you believe that your company needs to change. Congratulations! Just recognizing the need for change puts you ahead of 80 percent of the companies in your industry. But now that you've recognized the need for change, how do you make change happen? Should you focus on changing the work setting or the behaviour of the people who work in that setting? It's a classic chicken or egg type of question. Which would you do?

A recent meta-analysis based on 52 studies and a combined total of 29 611 study participants indicated that it's probably best to do both!

CHANGING THE WORK SETTING

An organizational work setting has four parts: organizing arrangements (control and reward systems, organizational structure), social factors (people, culture, patterns of interaction), technology (how inputs are transformed into outputs), and the physical setting (the actual physical space in which people work).

Overall, there is a 55 percent chance that organizational change efforts will successfully bring changes to a company's work setting. While the odds are still 55-45 in your favour, this is undoubtedly a much lower probability of success than you've seen with the management techniques discussed in other chapters. This simply reflects how strong resistance to change is in most companies.

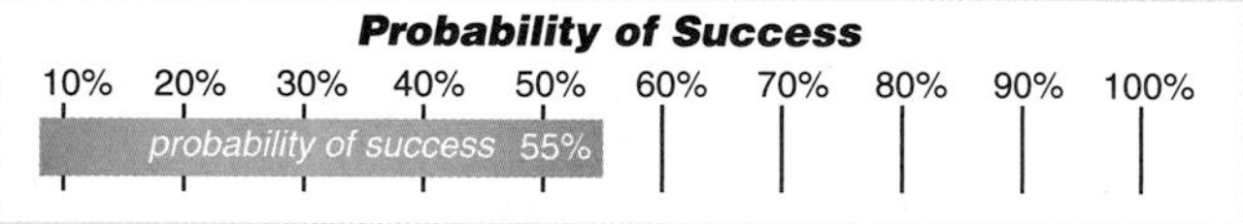

CHANGING THE PEOPLE

Changing people means changing individual work behaviour. The idea is powerful. Change the decisions people make. Change the activities they perform. Change the information they share with others. And change the initiatives they take on their own. Change these individual behaviours and collectively you change the entire company. Overall, there is a 57 percent chance that organizational change efforts will successfully change people's individual work behaviour. If you're wondering why the odds aren't higher, consider how difficult it is to simply change personal behaviour. It's incredibly difficult to quit smoking, change diet, or maintain a daily exercise program. Not surprisingly, changing personal behaviour at work is also difficult. Thus, viewed in this context, a 57 percent chance of success is a notable achievement.

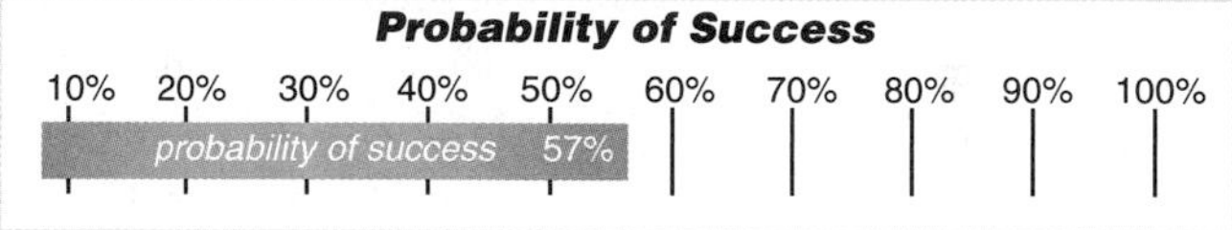

CHANGING INDIVIDUAL BEHAVIOUR AND ORGANIZATIONAL PERFORMANCE

The point of changing individual behaviour is to improve organizational performance (i.e., higher profits, market share, and productivity, and lower costs). Overall, there is a 76 percent chance that changes in individual behaviour will produce changes in organizational outcomes. So if you want to improve your company's profits, market share, or productivity, focus on changing the way that your people behave at work.

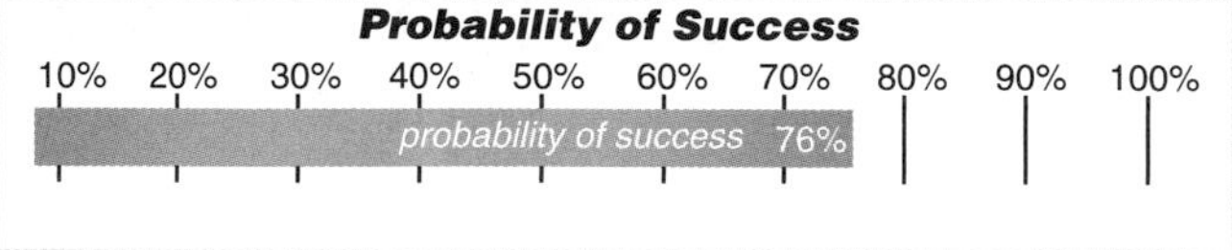

Managing Conversations to Promote Change

Think about where you have worked. How well and often did managers, especially top management, talk to you and other employees? Was it one-way, top-down communication, or did management listen and respond to the ideas of lower-level managers and employees? How did people from different parts of the company talk to each other? Did they try to understand each other, or did they talk past each other by using terms and ideas particular to their jobs or departments?

organizational dialogue the process by which people in an organization learn to talk effectively and constructively with each other

Organizational dialogue is the process by which people in an organization learn to talk effectively and constructively with each other.[46] Unfortunately, in most companies, the quality of organizational dialogue isn't very good. But when change forces are strong and managers and workers are stressed, organizational dialogue can be nonexistent. Consequently, the way managers and workers talk (or don't talk) to each other can be a significant barrier to successful change efforts.

According to this line of thinking, talk is not cheap. Conversations shape attitudes, intentions, and actions. What is said or not said really matters. So when organizational dialogue breaks down, change efforts break down, too. From this perspective, managing change is akin to managing the conversations that make up organizational dialogue.

What Not to Do When Leading Change

So far, you've learned about the basic change process (unfreezing, change, refreezing), managing resistance to change, the four kinds of change tools and techniques (results-driven change, the GE Workout, transition management teams, and organizational development), and using conversations to promote change. However, John Kotter of the Harvard Business School argues that knowing what not to do is just as important as knowing what to do when it comes to achieving successful organizational change.[47]

Exhibit 10.10 shows the most common errors that managers make when they lead change. The first two errors occur during the unfreezing phase, in which managers try to get the people affected by change to believe that change is really needed. The first and potentially most serious of these errors is *not establishing a great enough sense of urgency.* Indeed, Kotter estimates that more than half of all change efforts fail because the people affected by change are just not convinced that change is necessary. However, people will feel a greater sense of urgency about change if a leader in the company makes a public, candid assessment of the company's problems and weaknesses.

The second mistake that occurs in the unfreezing process is *not creating a powerful enough coalition.* Change often starts with one or two people, but in order to build enough momentum to change an entire department, division, or company, change has to be supported by a critical and growing group of people. Besides top management, Kotter recommends that key employees, managers, board members, customers, and even union leaders be members of a core change coalition, which guides and supports organizational change. Furthermore, it's important to strengthen this group's resolve by periodically bringing its members together for off-site retreats.

The next four errors that managers make occur during the change phase, in which a change intervention is used to try to get workers and managers to change their behaviour and work practices.

EXHIBIT 10.10
Errors Managers Make When Leading Change

UNFREEZING
1. Not establishing a great enough sense of urgency.
2. Not creating a powerful enough guiding coalition.
CHANGE
3. Lacking a vision.
4. Undercommunicating the vision by a factor of ten.
5. Not removing obstacles to the new vision.
6. Not systematically planning for and creating short-term wins.
REFREEZING
7. Declaring victory too soon.
8. Not anchoring changes in the corporation's culture.

Source: J.P. Kotter, "Leading Change: Why Transformation Efforts Fail," *Harvard Business Review* 73, no. 2 (March–April 1995): 59.

Lacking a vision for change is a significant error at this point. As you learned in Chapter 4, a vision is a statement of a company's purpose or reason for existing. A vision for change makes clear where a company or department is headed and why the change is occurring. Change efforts that lack vision tend to be confused, chaotic, and contradictory. By contrast, change efforts guided by visions are clear, easy to understand, and can be effectively explained in five minutes or less.

Undercommunicating the vision by a factor of ten is another mistake in the change phase. According to Kotter, companies mistakenly hold just one meeting to announce the vision. Or, if the new vision receives heavy emphasis in executive speeches or company newsletters, senior management then undercuts the vision by behaving in ways contrary to it. Successful communication of the vision requires that top managers link everything the company does to the new vision and that they "walk the talk" by behaving in ways consistent with the vision. Furthermore, even companies that begin change with a clear vision sometimes make the mistake of *not removing obstacles to the new vision.* Insisting on change, but then failing to redesign jobs, pay plans, and technology to support the new way of doing things leaves formidable barriers to change in place.

Similar to results-driven change, another error in the change phase is *not systematically planning for and creating short-term wins.* Most people don't have the discipline and patience to wait two years to see if the new change effort works. Change is threatening and uncomfortable, so for people to continue to support it, they need to see an immediate payoff. Kotter recommends that managers create short-term wins by actively picking people and projects that are likely to work extremely well early in the change process.

The last two errors that managers make occur during the refreezing phase, when attempts are made to support and reinforce changes so they "stick."

Declaring victory too soon is a tempting mistake in the refreezing phase. Managers typically declare victory right after the first large-scale success in the change process. Ironically, declaring success too early has the same effect as draining the gasoline out of a car. It stops change efforts dead in their tracks. With success declared, supporters of the change process stop pushing to make change happen. After all, why "push" when success has been achieved? Rather than declaring victory, managers should use the momentum from short-term wins to push for even bigger or faster changes. This maintains urgency and prevents change supporters from slacking off before the changes are frozen into the company's culture.

The last mistake that managers make is *not anchoring changes in the corporation's culture.* An *organization's culture* is the set of key values, beliefs, and attitudes shared by organizational members that determines the "accepted way of doing things" in a company. As you learned in Chapter 2, cultures are extremely difficult and slow to change. Kotter said that two things help anchor changes in a corporation's culture. The first is directly showing people that the changes have actually improved performance. The second is to make sure that the people who get promoted fit the new culture. If they don't, it's a clear sign that the changes were only temporary.

Review 4: Managing Change

The basic change process is unfreezing, change, and refreezing. Resistance to change, which stems from self-interest, misunderstanding and distrust, and a general intolerance for change, can be managed through education and communication, participation, negotiation, coercion, and top management support.

Managers can use a number of change techniques. Results-driven change and the GE Workout reduce resistance to change by getting change efforts off to a fast start. Transition management teams, which manage a company's change process, coordinate change efforts throughout an organization. Organizational development is a collection of planned change interventions (large system, small group, person-focused) guided by a change agent that are designed to improve an organization's long-term health and performance. Finally, knowing what not to do is as important as knowing what to do to achieve successful change. Managers should avoid these errors when leading change: not establishing urgency, not creating a guiding coalition, lacking a vision, undercommunicating the vision, not removing obstacles to the vision, not creating short-term wins, declaring victory too soon, and not anchoring changes in the corporation's culture.

What Really Happened?[48]

In the opening case, you learned about the struggles facing Swimming Canada. Read the answers to the opening case to find out how it is addressing these problems.

What were the main challenges facing Swimming Canada?

In 2004, Swimming Canada was perceived as an organization in decline, bouncing from scandal to scandal. At the 2004 Athens Olympics, it experienced its lowest medal count in 40 years. Its swimming alumni wanted a change in leadership and went to the press demanding it. Its swimmers fought among themselves and its former CEO was accused of being biased against swimmers from one province in particular. The same CEO was also embroiled in controversy surrounding the hiring of a national team coach deemed to be inexperienced. The swimming program in the largest province, Ontario, was labelled a shambles, with its representation of swimmers on the national team being nowhere near its 40 percent share of the Canadian population. Ontario's swimming infrastructure was also considered to be inadequate with some of the blame being placed on Swimming Canada's decision to establish and maintain eight separate Centres of Excellence across the country. One observer of Canada's swimming scene captured the state of affairs as follows: "Ontario's aquatic infrastructure is lacking in many areas. Even in many cities of 300 000-plus, there is no 50-metre pool. The only two 50-metre pools in the [greater Toronto area] are at [the University of Toronto], which is overcrowded, and the Etobicoke Olympium, which is not aging well." Clearly, something was wrong with Swimming Canada and many were pointing the finger at its former CEO. Something needed to be done.

What steps were taken initially to turn the situation around?

Immediately following the 2004 Athens Olympics, Swimming Canada's CEO was fired and the hunt for a new leader began. A number of steps were taken to initiate a turnaround. In November of that year, a new Swimming Canada board was elected. In March of 2005, a strategic plan was then created by a series of working groups. This led to the selection of Quebec-born Pierre Lafontaine as CEO. Lafontaine brought with him almost 30 years of experience in competitive swimming, the most recent being with the Australian Institute of Sport. He also brought with him a philosophy suggesting that success will follow effective organization and planning. So what would be his overarching theme? Rebuild at the grassroots level. To do so, Lafontaine realized that he would need to dramatically increase the resources available to Swimming Canada. A first step was to shut down all eight national swimming centres, lay off the coaches, and disband the existing national training program. He would centralize his organizations structure and move it away from its established decentralized setup. He would also have to play the role of visionary and cheerleader and spend time criss-crossing the country to build enthusiasm for his ideas with important stakeholders, such as Canada Summer Games coaches and provincial swim officials, while delivering coaching clinics. Among those who Lafontaine would visit would be corporate sponsors—witting or unwitting recipients of a pitch conceived as part of a new marketing program.

What objectives did Pierre Lafontaine initially set to move Swimming Canada forward?

In his first few months in office, Lafontaine and his colleagues set a series of objectives for the national swim program. Underlying the objectives was a belief that the core of swimming in Canada had to return to its rightful home—the local swim club and the youngsters who swim on a daily basis. What would be the specific objectives that would guide the efforts of Lafontaine and his team? Win three Olympic swimming medals in London; double the number of registered swimmers in Canada to deepen the talent pool (that's about 5000 per year for seven years to about 70 000); break every existing provincial and Canadian record, some a quarter-century old; double Swimming Canada's operating budget to roughly $7 million; and provide swimmers, coaches, and officials with a plan to promote progression and development.

What have been the initial results of these efforts?

Well to begin, one result has been a positive change in the organization of Swimming Canada. "What we've seen here is a cultural shift in our organization," said Dan Thompson, Swimming Canada's volunteer president and a former butterfly world-record-holder from Toronto. "It's been about believing in ourselves, in our kids and in our country. But we all have to remember there's a lot of work to do. We're up for that challenge and we want to be the pre-eminent summer sport for Canada." Second, the image of the organization in the media has dramatically improved. One indicator was the inclusion of Pierre Lafontaine on *The Globe and Mail*'s list of the 25 most influential people in sport for 2005. Finally, just a few months after taking the job, Canada's swim team returned to medal glory at World Aquatic Championships in Montreal, winning five medals. In the short term, Swimming Canada was back on track in terms of performance.

Key Terms

change agent *(292)*
change forces *(285)*
change intervention *(288)*
coercion *(289)*
compression approach to innovation *(282)*
creativity *(274)*
design competition *(278)*
design iteration *(281)*
dominant design *(279)*
era of ferment *(278)*
experiential approach to innovation *(281)*
General Electric Workout *(291)*
generational change *(283)*
incremental change *(280)*
innovation streams *(278)*
milestones *(281)*
multifunctional teams *(282)*
organizational change *(274)*
organizational decline *(285)*
organizational development *(291)*
organizational dialogue *(293)*
organizational innovation *(274)*
refreezing *(288)*
resistance forces *(285)*
resistance to change *(288)*
results-driven change *(290)*
S-curve pattern of innovation *(275)*
technological discontinuity *(278)*
technological substitution *(278)*
technology cycle *(275)*
testing *(281)*
transition management team (TMT) *(291)*
unfreezing *(288)*

Self-Assessment

MIND-BENDERS

Innovation is a key to corporate success. Companies that innovate and embrace the changes presented by fluctuations in the business environment tend to outperform those that stand still. Even so, innovative companies don't simply rely on the creativity of their own work force. They often contract with outside providers to generate new ideas for everything from operations to new products. In other words, innovative companies fill gaps in their own creativity by looking outside the organization. As a manager, you will benefit from understanding how you are creative. And just important as your creativity is your attitude toward creative endeavours. The Assessment Appendix has a questionnaire that can give you insight into your own perspective on creativity and innovation, which will form a baseline for you as you develop your managerial skills. Turn to page 517 and get started!

Management Decisions

HEADS, YOU CHANGE. TAILS, YOU CHANGE

You are the general manager of a medium-sized appliance manufacturing facility in Mississauga, Ontario. You've just received a phone call that you have been expecting for some time now. Your boss just informed you that if your plant doesn't show markedly better results (in productivity, profitability, etc.) within six months, it will be closed down and relocated to Ciudad Juarez, an industrial Mexican city across the border from El Paso, Texas. Of course, this news is no surprise to you. Your plant is one of only a few left producing appliances in Canada. Due to lower wages, closer proximity to suppliers, and favourable tax treatments, a few Canadian factories have closed their Canadian doors and reopened as Maquiladoras within Mexico's borders. If your plant follows the same road, most of the production workers will lose their jobs. The supervisory, middle, and top-level management positions, however, will be transferred to the new location.

Moving your managers would be a challenge. Even the carrot of job security may not be enough to overcome resistance. Many of your management staff have lived in or around Mississauga their whole lives, have close family ties to the area, or have children who are entrenched in their schools and social lives. The alternative—turning the plant around in six months—is no more attractive. This would require all employees to rethink how work is done and to re-engineer work processes, in short to change the very way they all think about working at your company.

The typical employee at your plant is like Tom, your assistant and best friend, who would probably be very resistant to any kind of change. Tom eats the same kind of sandwich every day. He is never receptive to new ideas or radical change. And he has worked at the plant since he returned to Mississauga after university.

You really don't want to move to Mexico, and you'd like to keep the 500 production jobs at your plant in Mississauga. But there are so many ways to implement change. Which one would be best suited to your situation?

Questions

1. Jot down the pros and cons of each change tool and technique presented in the chapter and determine what seems to fit this situation the best. Which one(s) did you choose and why?
2. You are going to have to internally promote whatever option you chose. Outline change conversations that you might have with the typical employee, say Tom, for example. How can you avoid breakdowns in change initiatives during your conversations?
3. If your change initiatives fail to bring the plant into corporate expectations, you will have to handle the equally tough situation of convincing managers to follow the company to Mexico. How will you do this? What can you do as their supervisor to calm their fears and minimize their resistance to this type of change?

Management Decisions

FREEDOM NOT TO WORRY ABOUT PRODUCTS AND PROFITS?[49]

What a great opportunity! Head of company research and development for a Fortune 100 high-tech company. This is the job you've been wanting for years. And what better time to get it? Thanks to the innovative products and technology produced by your R&D labs, profits are strong and market share is growing. There's only one downside. Its success has attracted numerous competitors and dozens of new start-up companies, all intent on taking a substantial chunk of your customers and profits. If the company doesn't maintain its stream of innovative products, it's sure to lose its competitive advantage to one of these hungry competitors. This morning, when you met with the CEO, you were given one directive: "Find a way to increase the level of innovation we get from our R&D labs. How you do it is up to you. Just make it happen." Your reply was quick and confident, "You can count on me." But as you were leaving the office, you really weren't sure just how to improve on the company's already fine record of innovation.

In general, there are two lines of thought about how to get the most out of R&D labs. The first is to focus on basic research and give researchers the freedom they need to pursue the ideas that intrigue them. This is the model that Bell Labs followed for over 60 years. During that time, Bell Labs researchers came up with more than 25 000 patents, more than one per day, as they invented motion pictures with sound, long-distance transmission of TV signals, stereo recording, transistors, solar power cells, lasers, communications satellites, and cellular phones. Not surprisingly, seven Bell Labs scientists won Nobel Prizes for science during that time, more than any other lab in the world. Under the basic research model, leading scientists study what they want and never have to worry about profits. Furthermore, they have "signatory authority," meaning that they control their own research budgets and have the ability (within that budget) to purchase whatever equipment they need to conduct their research.

The second line of thought is that innovation can be improved by holding researchers accountable for developing marketable ideas that can be turned into practical products. For example, at ICL PLC, the British computer company owned by Fujitsu of Japan, researchers are expected to maintain close contact with customers. When ICL PLC developed a new computer system for Cathay Pacific Airlines, management told the researchers to "get out of their Jesus sandals and into business suits ... we're going to transfer you (to Asia) along with the technology." In general, moves like this are designed to make researchers aware of three questions: What can the company do with your idea/technology/product? How big is the market for it? And how much money can the company make from it?

Questions

1. Both approaches have trade-offs. After reviewing the chapter discussion concerning innovation streams and technology cycles, describe two important advantages and two serious disadvantages for the "basic research" model described above.
2. Describe two important advantages and two serious disadvantages for the "profits and products" model described above.
3. If you were running this company's R&D lab, which would you choose, the "basic research" model or the "profits and products" model? Explain your choice and the reasons for it.

Develop Your Management Potential

A PERSONAL FORCE FIELD ANALYSIS

In the "What Really Works" feature of this chapter (page 293), you learned that when people change their behaviour in the workplace, there is a 76 percent chance that organizational profits, market share, and productivity can be improved. However, you also learned that organization-wide change efforts have only a 57 percent chance of successfully changing people's work behaviour. So changing people's behaviour works great.

The hard part is figuring out how to get them to change their behaviour. This "Develop Your Management Potential" assignment reviews how you can use a personal force field analysis to change your behaviour at work.

At the beginning of this chapter, you learned that organizational change is a function of change forces and resistance forces. Change forces lead to differences in the form, quality, or condition of an organization over time. Resistance forces support the status quo—that is, the existing state of conditions in organizations. One of the ways that managers prepare for specific organizational change is to carefully conduct an organizational force field analysis by listing the change and resistance forces that support and oppose that change. For example, Exhibit 10.11 lists the resistance forces and change forces that oppose and support the possibility of changing a company's corporate headquarters from Toronto to Calgary.

EXHIBIT 10.11
Resistance and Change Forces

POSSIBLE CHANGE: MOVING CORPORATE HEADQUARTERS FROM TORONTO TO CALGARY	
RESISTANCE FORCES	**CHANGE FORCES**
• Many employees may not want or be able to move.	• Much lower cost of living and no provincial sales tax will make it easier to attract and retain a talented work force.
• Large expense of making the move, buying or building a new headquarters, and selling old headquarters.	• Lower real estate and energy costs will significantly lower the cost of maintaining corporate headquarters.
• Negative publicity from local press generated by just considering the move.	• Significant customer base has developed in the western regions of the country.
• Toronto city officials may offer incentives to encourage firm to stay.	• Calgary city officials may offer incentives to encourage firm to move.

Listing resistance and change forces is also a useful way to conduct a personal force field analysis. The first step of a personal force field analysis is to clearly describe how or what behaviour you intend to change. For example, if you're always late with your expense reports, you might write, "I will turn in my expense reports within three days of returning from a business trip." In Chapter 4, you learned that to be effective, goals need to be S.M.A.R.T.—specific, measurable, attainable, realistic, and timely. Descriptions of the behaviours you intend to change should follow the S.M.A.R.T. guidelines, too.

The second step of a personal force field analysis is to list and describe resistance forces—that is, the reasons that make it difficult for you to change your behaviour. Since resistance to change is caused by self-interest, misunderstanding and distrust, and a general intolerance for change, be sure to assess whether these factors are making it difficult for you to change your behaviour. For example, are you turning your expense reports in late because turning them in on time will cost or deprive you of something of value (i.e., self-interest)? Probably not, because if you turned the expense reports in on time, you'd get your money back sooner.

Are you turning in your expense reports late because you misunderstand or distrust the reasons for turning in your expense report on time or distrust the people who review the expenses? Well, we might be on to something here. Misunderstanding probably isn't the problem. What's to misunderstand about an expense report? You fill it out, turn it in, and get reimbursed. In this case, it's more likely that your resistance stems from distrust of the people who review the reports. Perhaps, in the past, you felt that you weren't fairly reimbursed. If so, why turn in your expense report on time when you don't expect to get back all the money you're owed?

Finally, are you turning in your expense reports late because you have a low tolerance for change? In this case, however, a low tolerance for change probably has more to do with habitual behaviour than with any uncertainty associated with the change process.

The final step of a personal force field analysis is to list the change forces—that is, the reasons prompting you to consider changing your behaviour. At this step, it can be useful to separate your reasons by category, such as personal or organizational benefits, or personal or organizational consequences (i.e., the negative consequences associated with not changing your behaviour). For example, turning in your expense report on time gets you your money faster, a personal benefit; helps the organization stay current with its expenses, an organizational benefit; and helps you avoid getting yelled at by your boss for being late with the expense report, which is a personal negative consequence.

Now use these steps to conduct a personal force field analysis.

Questions

1. Clearly describe how or what behaviour you intend to change. Be sure your description is S.M.A.R.T.—specific, measurable, attainable, realistic, and timely.
2. List and describe the resistance forces that make it difficult for you to change this behaviour. Do these reasons have anything to do with

- Self-interest? Will the change cost or deprive you of something you value?
- Misunderstanding and distrust? Do you not understand the change or the reasons for it? Do you distrust the people behind the change? In other words, is someone other than yourself pressuring you to make this change?
- A general intolerance for change? Are you simply less capable of handling change than others? Are you worried that you won't be able to learn the new skills and behaviours needed to successfully negotiate this behaviour change?

3. List and describe the change forces that are leading you to consider changing your behaviour. Separate your reasons into personal or organizational benefits, or personal or organizational consequences (i.e., the negative consequences associated with not changing your behaviour).

Discussion Questions

1. Define innovation streams and list the basic phases in the process.
2. The personal computer (PC) industry is an interesting one to watch these days. Overall, sales in the industry are down as are sales for all major manufacturers with the exception of Dell. Dell is bucking industry trends and has actually increased its sales and market share. One firm particularly hard hit by reduced PC sales is Gateway Inc. In this context, explain what is meant by organizational decline and list its five stages.
3. Identify and briefly explain the three steps involved in the process of managing organizational change according to Kurt Lewin.
4. For many undergraduates, a sign of success upon completion of a degree is a job with a world-class organization. Especially difficult to capture are positions with some of the world's leading consulting firms such as McKinsey and Co. and Bain and Co. These companies are famous for the rigour of their interview process. As graduation approaches, you set your eyes on one of these cherished positions and are granted an interview. As you begin your preparation for your encounter, a number of questions swirl through your mind. One of them is "What are the tools and techniques available to you as a change agent when seeking to foster change in an organization?"

Critical Thinking Video Case

CBC

Visit www.management2e.nelson.com to view this chapter's CBC video case.

Take Two

Biz Flix
October Sky

October Sky is a 1999 movie based on the autobiographical book *Rocket Boys* by Homer Hickam. An all-star cast is led by Jake Gyllenhaal, who plays Homer Hickam. As a teenager, Homer is facing a dreary future as a coal-miner until he sees the Soviet satellite Sputnik pass over his small mining town of Coalwood, West Virginia. A new interest in rockets infects Homer, who begins to experiment with model rockets in the summer of 1957. Soon, Homer has convinced several of his friends to join him in designing a rocket to enter in the National Science Fair, where they hope to win college scholarships as a result.

What to Watch for and Ask Yourself

1. Are Homer and his friends working toward discontinuous change or incremental change? Explain.
2. Which approach to innovation best describes what the "Rocket Boys" are doing? Identify the elements of the approach you choose that are evident in the clip.

Management Workplace
Ziba Designs

Do you ever wonder who designs all the gadgets and gizmos you see and use every day? Ziba Designs, one of the most renowned industrial design companies, is based in Portland, Oregon; it was started by Sohrab Vossoughi, an Iranian immigrant, more than 20 years ago. No industrial design firm in the world has won as many awards per employee as Ziba, which has won as many as four prestigious awards in one year. Ziba's success is a tribute to the culture of innovation nurtured by its founder.

What to Watch for and Ask Yourself

1. Describe the elements of Ziba's creative work environment.
2. In what ways does Ziba use an experiential approach to innovation? In what ways does the company use a compression approach?
3. Based on what you saw in the video, how well do you think Ziba manages change?

JUPITER IMAGES

Organizational Structures and Processes

Chapter 11

CHAPTER OUTLINE

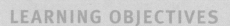

LEARNING OBJECTIVES

After reading this chapter, you should be able to

1. describe the departmentalization approach to organizational structure.
2. explain organizational authority.
3. discuss the different methods for job design.
4. explain the methods that companies are using to redesign internal organizational processes (i.e., intraorganizational processes).
5. describe the methods that companies are using to redesign external organizational processes (i.e., interorganizational processes).

Grant Thornton International is one of the world's leading organizations of independently owned and managed accounting and consulting firms providing assurance, tax, and specialist advice to independent businesses and their owners. Member firms operate in 111 countries in around 600 offices worldwide.[1] As with almost all professional services firms, it is different from most other more traditional organizations. Along with firms such as KPMG, PricewaterhouseCoopers, and Ernst & Young, it is a well-known name in the world of smaller corporations. In Canada, its CEO and executive partner is Alex MacBeath. In a recent interview he was asked about the history of this company. Here are his thoughts:

> Grant Thornton started in Atlantic Canada. It was formed in 1939 in Halifax and it was a sole practitioner that began the firm, Harvey Doane. At that time it was known as H.R. Doane and Company. From the initial base in Halifax, it expanded across Atlantic Canada, initially, through a series of mergers and the opening of new offices to respond to opportunities in different parts of Atlantic Canada and to respond to the expanding needs of clients as they expanded through Atlantic Canada. As it moved into the '60s and '70s, it began to expand into Ontario and eventually the West, mainly through a series of mergers with local firms. That created a presence in Western Canada and Ontario building on the strong base that we had in Atlantic Canada at that time. There were two major events in the '80s and the '90s that helped create the firm that we have today and really built on the early success that Harvey Doane started. The first was in 1981 when we associated with a firm in Quebec, the largest firm in Quebec, called Robichaud Martin St. Pierre. That created a firm that had a presence in every part of the country. In 1991 we did another merger with a firm called Panel Kerr McGillivary. Panel Kerr McGillivary had a very strong presence in Western Canada and in Ontario but not in the East nor in Quebec, so it was a very complementary merger and really created the firm we have today, with a presence across the country and in all the major markets of the country. In 1981, at the same time we associated with the firm in Quebec, we joined a new international organization called Grant Thornton. Grant Thornton was created at that time and we were the third member firm to join the international organization and in fact are the third largest member firm of the international organization.
>
> I think one key success variable for our firm, and the fundamental motivator for the firm's founding partner, Harvey Doane, was our early recognition that we were first and foremost a professional services firm. In terms of providing strong professional services, maintenance of high standards was critical. A second key factor in our growth and success was our strict attention to client service and to understanding evolving client needs. To a large degree, building the capacity in the firm that some clients needed really drove some of our growth and expansion. All of which is to say that almost from its inception the firm's focus was on developing, expanding, and growing itself to ensure a critical mass of capacity and capability sufficient to meet its clients' dynamic needs. At the same time, the firm's partners also worked to ensure that its core principles of high standards, independence, and objectivity were not sacrificed for growth and expansion.
>
> Of course, responding to clients' needs and growing the business was not possible without a real focus on people. We are a professional services firm and the key input in any services firm is its people. At the same time that the firm was responding to client needs, we also needed to be able to respond to the needs of our professional and administrative staff. In short, we needed to be able to provide them an opportunity to grow professionally to continue to meet the needs of our clients. In the face of rapid growth and expansion and a very dynamic professional services environment, we were able to develop and grow our own human resources, and I think if you look back over the 65 years that we've been in this country, that was another of our key success variables.

What Would You Do?

MacBeath's repeated references to clients and the use of professionals suggest that something is different about firms like Grant Thornton. The way that these organizations are organized, the role of executives, the means by which they are promoted, and the way that knowledge is shared within the firm may be different from the norm. **How are they different and what does this mean for Alex MacBeath?**

No one builds a house without first looking at the design. Put a window there. Take out a wall here. Soon you've got the design you want. Only then do you start building. These days, the design of a company is just as important as the design of a house. As the Grant Thornton case shows, getting the right design is not necessarily a simple task.

In the first half of the chapter, you will learn about the traditional vertical and horizontal approaches to **organizational structure**, including departmentalization, organizational authority, and job design. In the second half of the chapter, you will learn how companies are using re-engineering, empowerment, and behaviour informality to redesign their internal **organizational processes**. The chapter ends with a discussion about the ways in which companies are redesigning their external processes—that is, how they are changing to improve their interactions with those outside the company. In that discussion, you will explore the basics of modular, virtual, and boundaryless organizations.

organizational structure the vertical and horizontal configuration of departments, authority, and jobs within a company

organizational process the collection of activities that transforms inputs into outputs that customers value

Designing Organizational Structures

Reynolds Wrap is a name you may recognize. It is the brand name of the aluminum foil that you may use to keep leftovers fresh in your fridge. It is also a product of Reynolds Metals, an integrated manufacturer, distributor, and marketer of processed and unprocessed aluminum products. Prior to its merger with ALCOA (www.alcoa.com), Reynolds had been organized geographically, with separate regional operations around the world. One day, it announced that it was restructuring. Jeremiah Sheehan, Reynolds' chairman and CEO at the time, said that "as part of our Portfolio Review process, we have streamlined our business focus and assessed new organization structures appropriate for managing our businesses in the future. As a result, we are reorganizing the structure of the company into six worldwide, market-focused businesses...."[2] So instead of having geographic divisions, Reynolds will now use a product structure, with separate divisions focusing on aluminum cans, building and construction, consumer products, infrastructure, packaging, and transportation.

Why would a large company like Reynolds, with 29 000 employees and US$4.8 billion in annual revenues, completely restructure its global organizational design? What did it expect to gain as a result of this massive change?

After reading the next three sections, you should be able to

1. describe the departmentalization approach to organizational structure.
2. explain organizational authority.
3. discuss the different methods for job design.

1 DEPARTMENTALIZATION

Traditionally, organizational structures have been based on some form of departmentalization. **Departmentalization** is a method of subdividing work and workers into separate organizational units that take responsibility for completing particular tasks.[3] For example, the Sony Corporation has separate departments or divisions for electronics, music, movies, television, games, and theatres.[4] Likewise, Bayer, a German-based company, has separate departments or divisions for health care, agriculture, polymers, chemicals, and photography.[5] Why is the idea of departmentalization important? Well, consider the impact on employees. In most instances, responsibility for attaining corporate goals and objects is shared. Often a boss or manager is also shared, as are important resources. Further, departments often form the basis of distinct corporate subcultures and environments where collaboration occurs.[6]

departmentalization subdividing work and workers into separate organizational units responsible for completing particular tasks

Traditionally, organizational structures have been created by departmentalizing work according to five methods: functional departmentalization, product departmentalization, customer departmentalization, geographic departmentalization, and matrix departmentalization.

Functional Departmentalization

The most common organizational structure is functional departmentalization. Companies tend to use this structure when they are small or just starting out. **Functional departmentalization** organizes work and workers into separate units responsible for particular business functions or areas of expertise. For example, a common set of functions would consist of accounting, sales, marketing, production, and human resources departments. However, not all functionally departmentalized companies have the same functions. For example, Exhibit 11.1 shows functional structures for an insurance company and an advertising agency. The light-coloured boxes indicate that both companies have sales, accounting, human resources, and information systems departments. The darker boxes are different for each company. As would be expected, the insurance company has separate departments for life, auto, home, and health insurance. By contrast, the advertising agency has departments for artwork, creative work, print advertising, and radio advertising. So the kind of functional departments in a functional structure depends, in part, on the business or industry a company is in. Functional departmentalization has some advantages. First, it allows work to be done by highly qualified specialists. Second, it lowers costs by reducing duplication. Third, with everyone in the same department having similar work experience or training, communication and coordination are less problematic for departmental managers. However, functional departmentalization has a number of disadvantages, too. To start, cross-department coordination can be difficult. Managers and employees are often more interested in doing what's right for their function than in doing what's right for the entire organization. As companies grow, functional departmentalization may also lead to slower decision-making and produce managers and workers with narrow experience and expertise.

functional departmentalization organizing work and workers into separate units responsible for particular business functions or areas of expertise

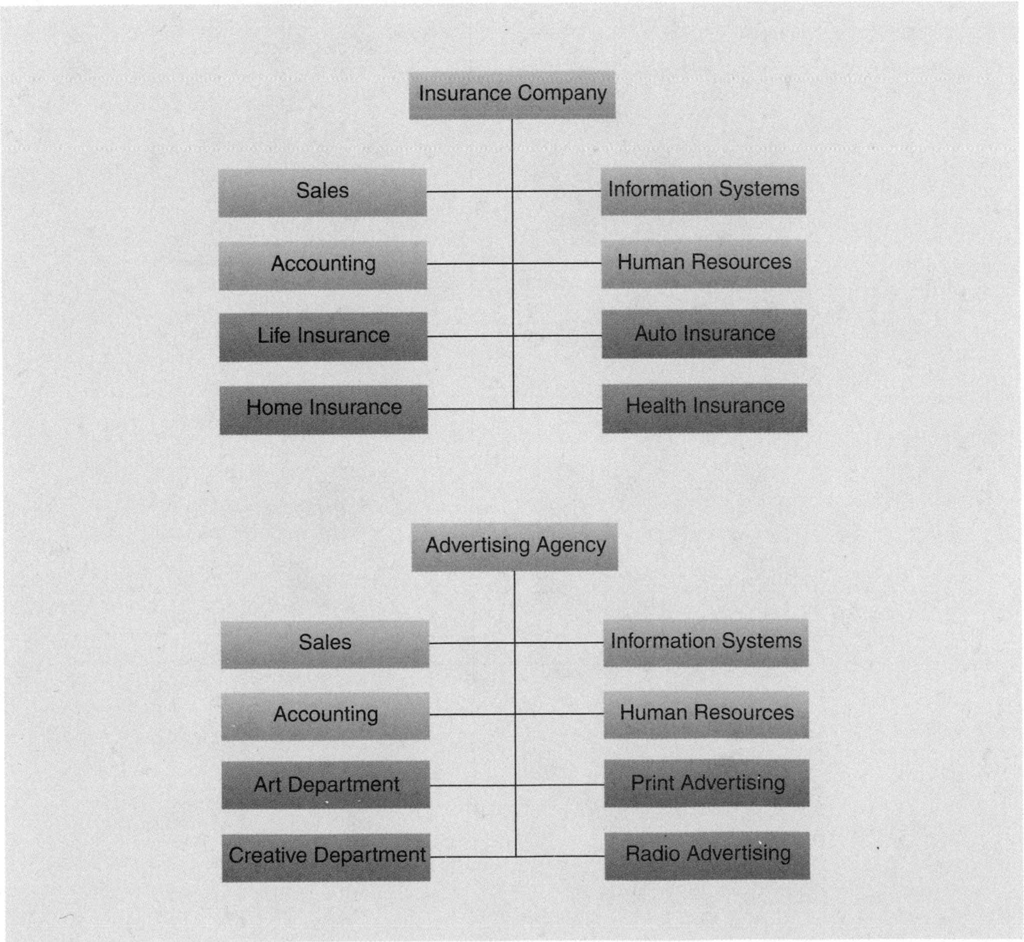

EXHIBIT 11.1
Functional Departmentalization

Product Departmentalization

product departmentalization
organizing work and workers into separate units responsible for producing particular products or services

Product departmentalization organizes work and workers into separate units responsible for producing particular products or services. Exhibit 11.2 shows the product departmentalization structure used by the General Electric Corporation. GE is organized along 12 different product lines: aircraft engines, appliances, capital services, lighting, medical systems, NBC television, plastics, power systems, electrical distribution and control, information services, industrial control systems, and transportation systems. One of the advantages of product departmentalization is that, like functional departmentalization, it allows managers and workers to specialize in one area of expertise. However, unlike the narrow expertise and experiences in functional departmentalization, managers and workers develop a broader set of experiences and expertise related to an entire product line. Likewise, product departmentalization makes it easier for top managers to assess work-unit performance. For example, because of their clear separation, it is a relatively straightforward process for GE's top managers to evaluate the performance of their 12 different product divisions. For instance, GE's Aircraft Engines product division outperformed GE's Power Systems product division. Both had similar revenues, US$10.78 billion for Aircraft Engines and US$11.85 billion for Power Systems, but Aircraft Engines had a profit of US$2.46 billion, while Power Systems had a profit of US$2.19 billion.[7] Finally, because managers and

EXHIBIT 11.2
Product Departmentalization: General Electric Corporation

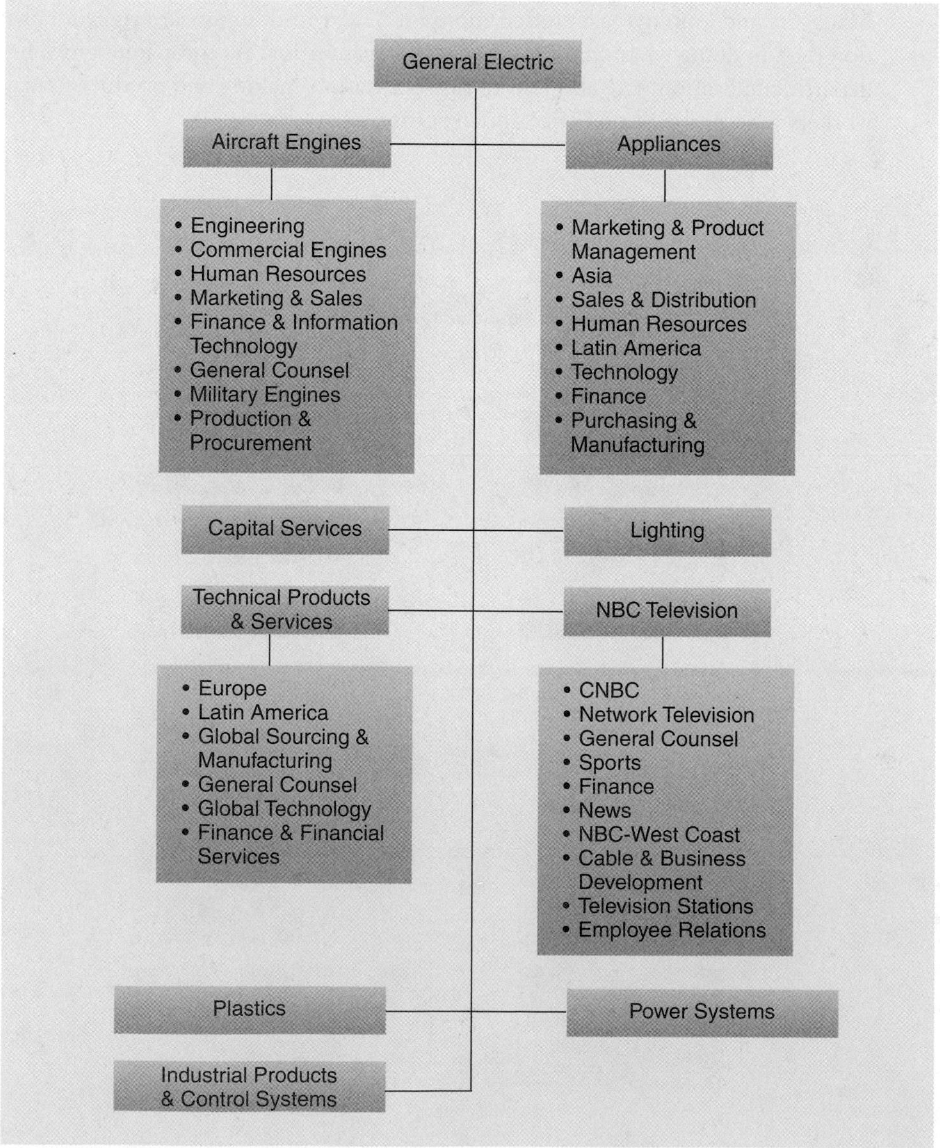

Source: GE Annual Report. [Online] Available www.ge.com/, 3 November 2001.

workers are responsible for the entire product line rather than for separate functional departments, decision-making should be faster because there are fewer conflicts (compared to functional departmentalization). The primary disadvantage of product departmentalization is duplication as this often results in higher costs. A second disadvantage is that it can be difficult to achieve coordination across the different product departments.

customer departmentalization organizing work and workers into separate units responsible for particular kinds of customers

Customer Departmentalization

Customer departmentalization organizes work and workers into separate units responsible for particular kinds of customers. For example, Exhibit 11.3 shows that American Express (www.americanexpress.com) is organized into departments that cater to consumers

EXHIBIT 11.3
Customer Departmentalization: American Express Corporation

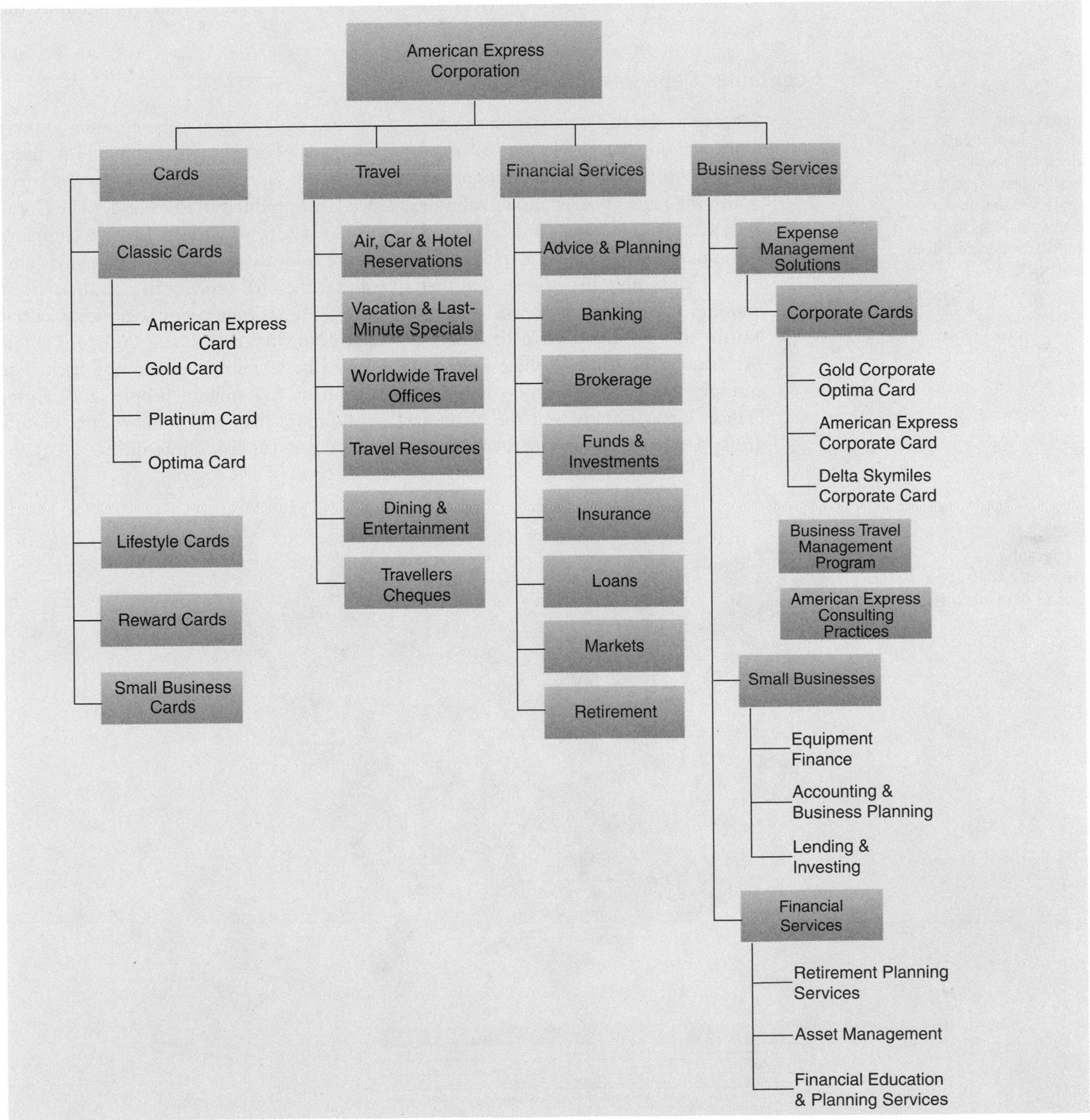

Source: "About American Express," American Express Web site. [Online] Available www.americanexpress.com/corp/?aexp_nav=hp_corp, 11 January 1999.

(Cards: credit and charge cards), travellers (Travel: travellers' cheques, airline tickets, vacations, and worldwide travel offices), investors (Financial Services: advisors, mutual and money market funds, etc.), shoppers (Shopping: catalogue, gift, and online shopping), and businesspeople (Business Services: business travel, corporate cards, and financing, accounting, planning, and lending for small businesses). The primary advantage to customer departmentalization is that it focuses the organization on customer needs rather than on products or business functions. Furthermore, creating separate departments to serve specific kinds of customers allows companies to specialize and adapt their products and services to customer needs and problems. The primary disadvantage of customer departmentalization is that, like product departmentalization, it leads to duplication of resources. Furthermore, like product departmentalization, it can be difficult to achieve coordination across different customer departments. Finally, the emphasis on meeting customers' needs may lead workers to make decisions that please customers but hurt the business.

Geographic Departmentalization

geographic departmentalization organizing work and workers into separate units responsible for doing business in particular geographical areas

Geographic departmentalization organizes work and workers into separate units responsible for doing business in particular geographical areas. For example, Exhibit 11.4 shows the geographic departmentalization used by Coca-Cola Enterprises (CCE) (www.cokecce.com), the largest bottler and distributor of Coca-Cola products in the world. (The Coca-Cola Company develops and advertises soft drinks. CCE, which is a separate company with its own stock, buys the soft drink concentrate from the Coca-Cola Company, combines it with other ingredients, and then distributes the final product in cans, bottles, or fountain containers.) As shown in Exhibit 11.4, CCE has four regional groups: Central North America, Eastern North America, Western North America, and Europe. Exhibit 11.4 shows that each of these four regions would be a sizable company by itself. For example, the European group serves a population of 137 million people in Belgium, France, Great Britain, and the Netherlands, sells more than 825 million cases of soft drinks a year, employs more than 7907 people, and runs 28 bottling facilities.

EXHIBIT 11.4
Geographic Departmentalization Coca-Cola Enterprises

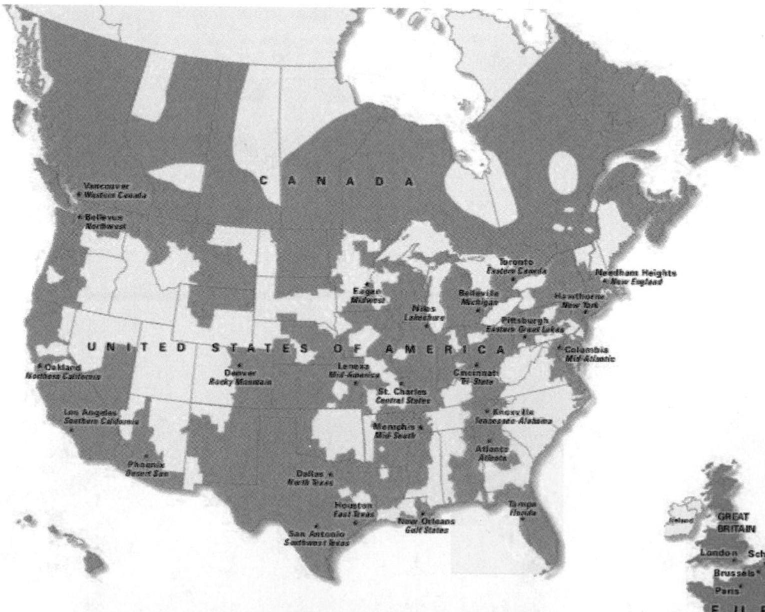

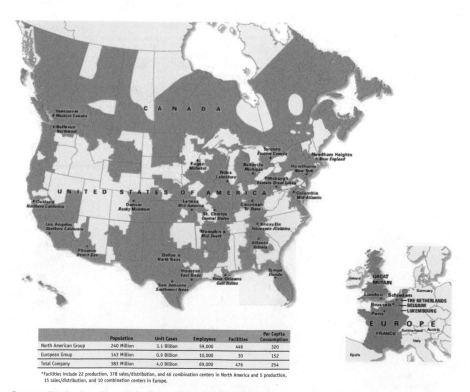

	Population	Unit Cases	Employees	Facilities	Per Capita Consumption
North American Group	240 Million	3.1 Billion	59,000	446	320
European Group	143 Million	0.9 Billion	10,000	30	152
Total Company	383 Million	4.0 Billion	69,000	476	254

*Facilities include 22 production, 378 sales/distribution, and 46 combination centers in North America and 5 production, 15 sales/distribution, and 10 combination centers in Europe.

Source: Territories. Coca-Cola Enterprises. [Online] Available www.cokecce.com, 4 November 2001.

The primary advantage of geographic departmentalization is that it helps companies respond to the demands of different markets. This can be especially important when selling in different countries. For example, CCE's geographic divisions sell products suited to the taste preferences in different countries. CCE bottles and distributes the following products in Europe but not in the United States or Canada: Aquarius, Bonaqua, Buxton Mineral Water, Coca-Cola light, Cresta flavours, Finley, Kia-Ora, Kinley, Lilt, Oasis, and Roses. Another advantage is that geographic departmentalization can reduce costs by locating unique organizational resources closer to customers. The primary disadvantage of geographic departmentalization is that it can lead to duplication of resources. Also, even more so than with the other forms of departmentalization, it can be especially difficult to coordinate departments that are literally thousands of kilometres from each other and whose managers have very limited contact with each other.

matrix departmentalization
a hybrid organizational structure in which two or more forms of departmentalization, most often product and functional, are used together

Matrix Departmentalization

Matrix departmentalization is a hybrid structure in which two or more forms of departmentalization are used together. In Canada, CAE Inc. (www.cae.com) makes extensive use of a matrix structure to build flight simulators. The most common matrix combines product and functional forms of departmentalization. Exhibit 11.5 shows the matrix structure used by Pharmacia & Upjohn, a pharmaceutical company. Across the top of Exhibit 11.5, you can see that the company uses a functional structure (research, development, manufacturing, and marketing) within each of its three largest geographic markets, the United States, Europe, and Japan. However, down the left side of the exhibit, notice that the company is using a product structure to research and develop drugs for the central nervous system, infectious diseases, metabolic and inflammatory diseases, as well as thrombosis, women's health, ophthalmology, critical care, urology, and oncology.

EXHIBIT 11.5
Matrix Departmentalization: Pharmacia & Upjohn

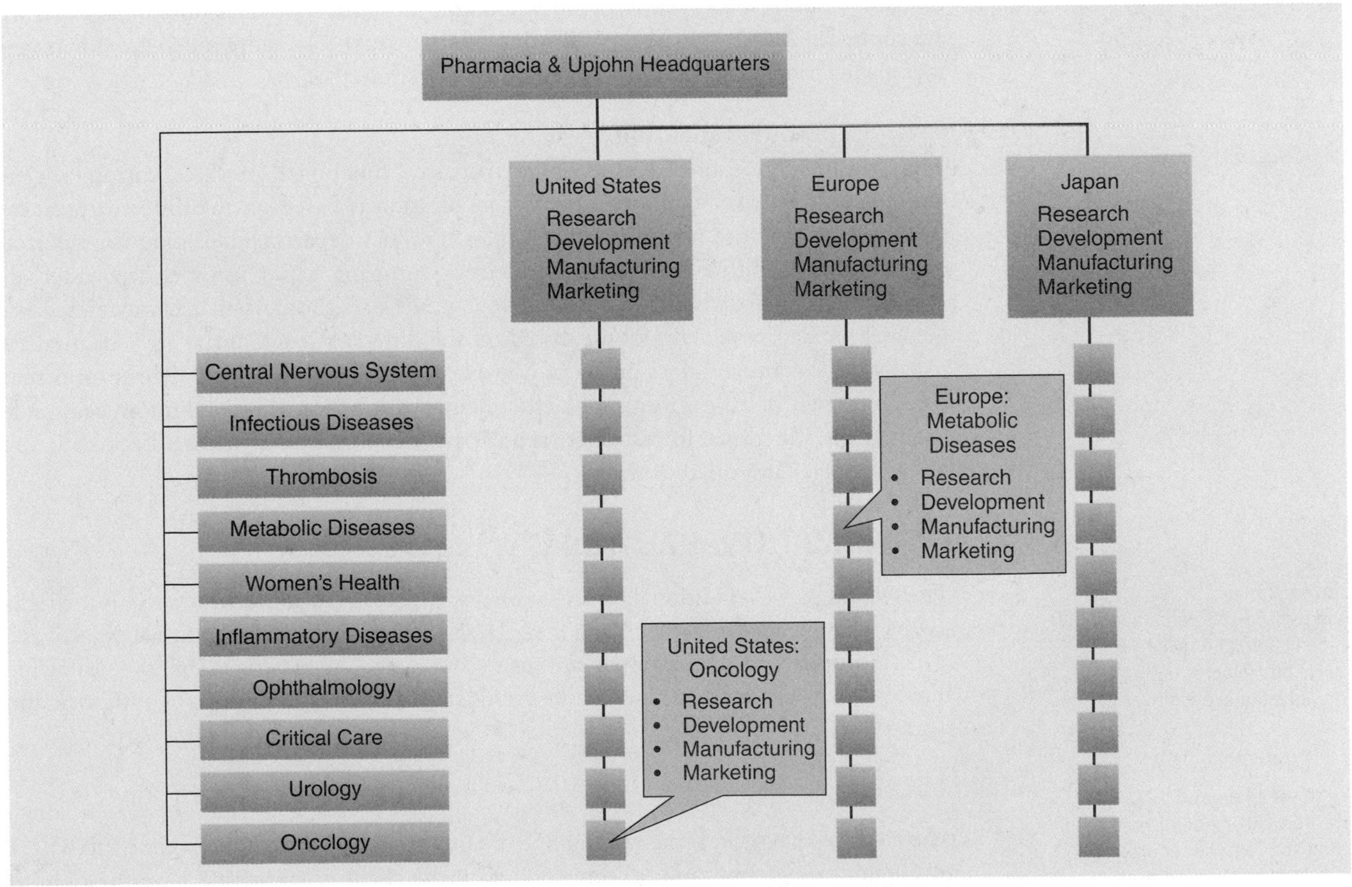

Source: "Financial Reports," Pharmacia & Upjohn Annual Report. [Online] Available www.upjohn.com, 11 January 1999.

The boxes in the exhibit represent the matrix structure, created by the combination of the functional/geographic and product structures. For example, in Europe, the Metabolic Diseases group has four functional departments: Research, Development, Manufacturing, and Marketing. In the United States, the Oncology group has the same set of functional departments.

Several things distinguish matrix departmentalization from the other traditional forms of departmentalization.[8] First, most employees report to two bosses, a functional boss and a project or product boss. Second, by virtue of the function-by-project design, matrix structures lead to much more cross-functional interaction than other forms of departmentalization. In fact, while matrix workers are members of only one functional department (based on their work experience and expertise), it is common for them to be members of several ongoing project groups. Third, because of the high level of cross-functional interaction, matrix departmentalization requires significant coordination between functional and project managers. In particular, these managers have the complex job of tracking and managing the multiple project and functional demands on employees' time.

The primary advantage of matrix departmentalization is that it allows companies to efficiently manage large, complex tasks such as researching, developing, and marketing pharmaceuticals. Efficiency comes from avoiding duplication. Another advantage is the ability to carry out large, complex tasks. Because of the ability to quickly pull in expert help from all the functional areas of the company, matrix project managers have a much more diverse set of expertise and experience at their disposal than do managers in the other forms of departmentalization. The primary disadvantage of matrix departmentalization is the high level of coordination required to manage the complexity involved with running large, ongoing projects at various levels of completion. Matrix structures are notorious for confusion and conflict between project bosses, or between project and functional bosses. Disagreements or misunderstandings about project schedules, budgets, available resources, and the availability of employees with particular functional expertise are common. Another disadvantage is that matrix structures require much more management skill than the other forms of departmentalization.

Review 1: Departmentalization

There are five traditional departmental structures: functional, product, customer, geographic, and matrix. Functional departmentalization is based on the different business functions or expertise used to run a business. Product departmentalization is organized according to the different products or services a company sells. Customer departmentalization focuses its divisions on the different kinds of customers that companies have. Geographic departmentalization is based on the different geographical areas or markets in which the company does business. Matrix departmentalization is a hybrid form that combines two or more forms of departmentalization, the most common being the product and functional forms. There is no "best" departmental structure. Each structure has advantages and disadvantages.

2 ORGANIZATIONAL AUTHORITY

authority
the right to give commands, take action, and make decisions to achieve organizational objectives

The second part of traditional organizational structures is authority. **Authority** is the right to give commands, take action, and make decisions to achieve organizational objectives.[9]

Traditionally, organizational authority has been characterized by the following dimensions:[10] chain of command, line versus staff authority, delegation of authority, and degree of centralization.

Chain of Command

chain of command
the vertical line of authority that clarifies who reports to whom throughout the organization

The **chain of command** is the vertical line of authority that clarifies who reports to whom throughout the organization. People higher in the chain of command have the right, if they so choose, to give commands, take action, and make decisions concerning activities

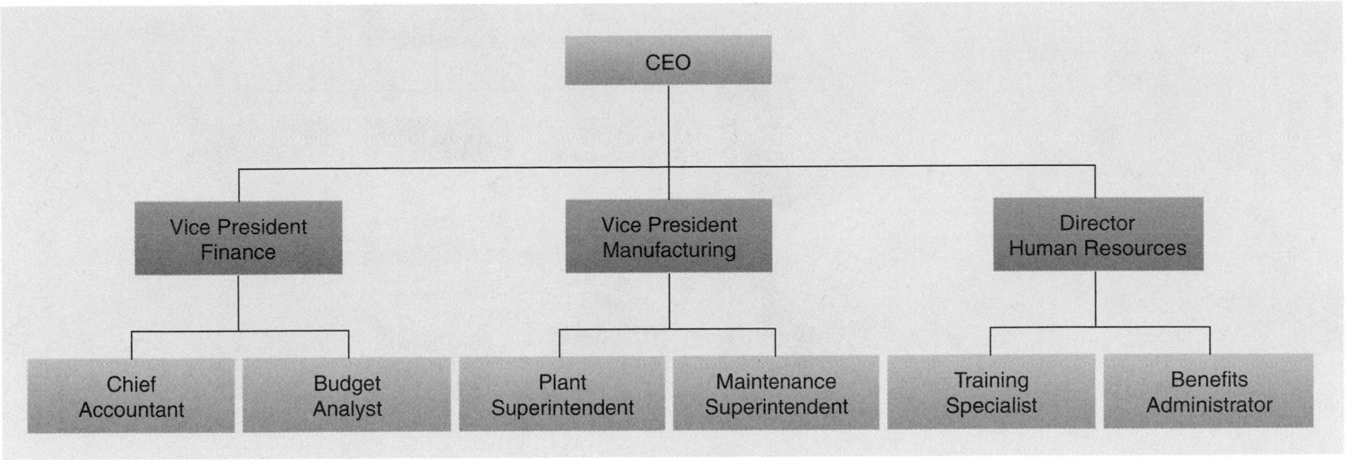

EXHIBIT 11.6
Organization Chart for a Manufacturing Firm

occurring anywhere below them in the chain. Exhibit 11.6 offers an example of an organization chart for a manufacturing company. In this instance, two vice presidents (one of finance and the other of manufacturing) along with a director of human resources, report to the CEO. Two positions report to each of these latter three offices. More specifically, a chief accountant and budget analyst report to the VP finance, while a maintenance superintendent and a plant superintendent report to the VP manufacturing. In the case of the director of human resources, direct reports include a training specialist and a benefits administrator.

Organizational charts or structures can differ in many ways, as shown in Exhibit 11.7. It illustrates the top level reporting relationships for organizations that are structured in a functional, divisional, multi-functional, horizontal, or modular fashion.

One of the key assumptions underlying the chain of command is **unity of command**, which means that workers should report to just one boss.[11] In practical terms, this means that only one person can be in charge at a time. Matrix organizations, in which employees have two bosses, automatically violate this principle. This is one of the primary reasons that matrix organizations are difficult to manage. The purpose of unity of command is to prevent the confusion that might arise when an employee receives conflicting commands from two different bosses. For example, someone walks into an emergency room, describing

unity of command
a management principle that workers should report to just one boss

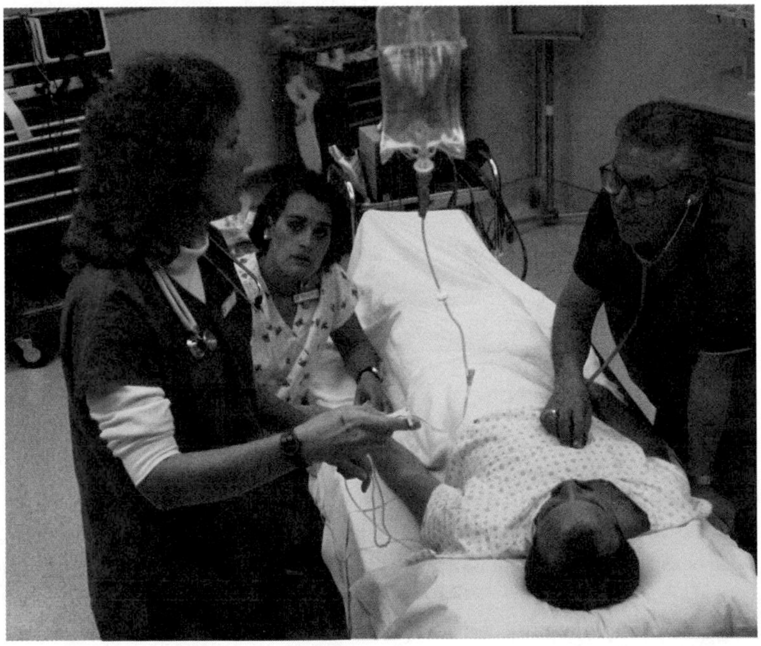

© WARREN MORGAN/CORBIS

At first glance, many emergency rooms appear chaotic. However, a well-understood command structure passing from nurse to emergency room physician to specialist ensures patients receive the best available care.

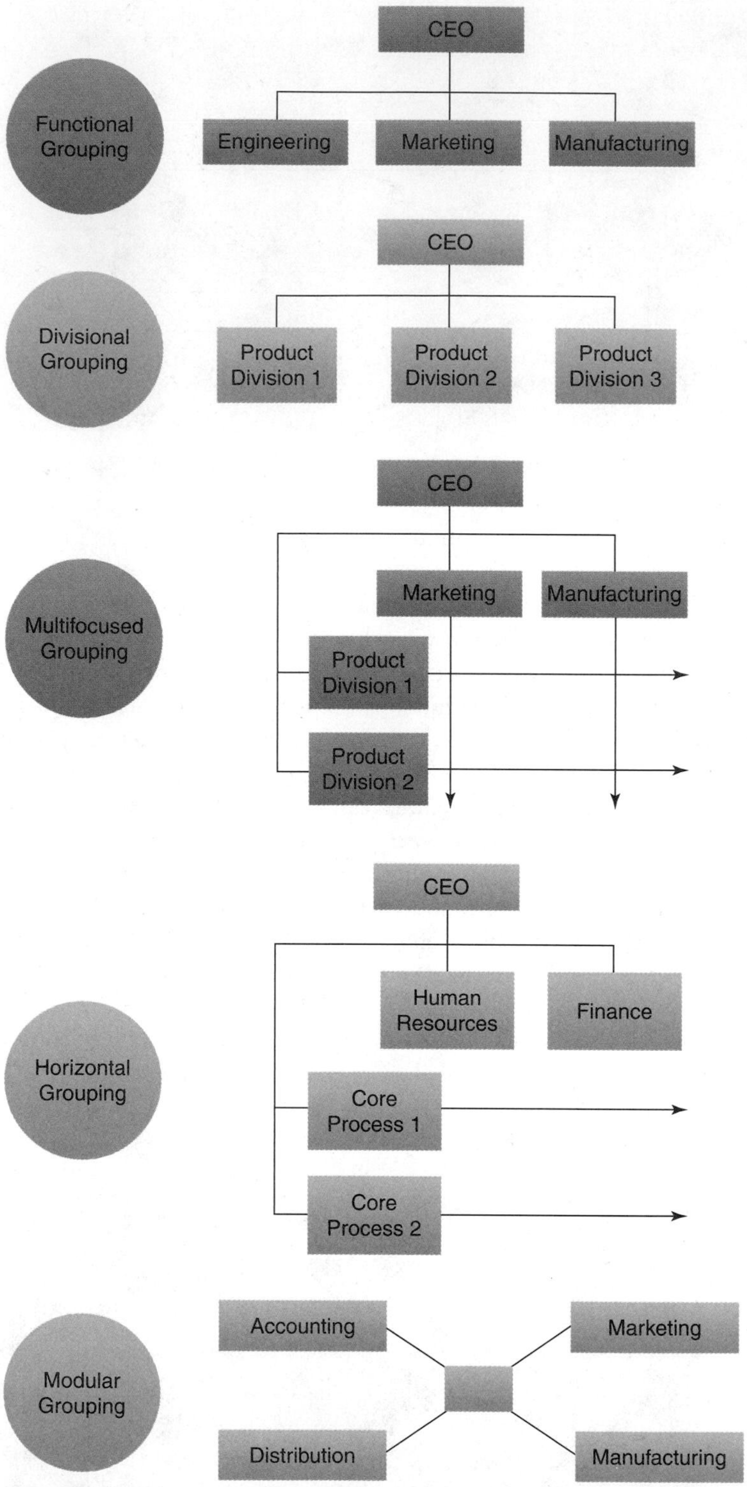

EXHIBIT 11.7
Organization Chart Options

symptoms similar to a heart attack. The first person in charge, most likely a nurse, makes the initial assessment, assigns the patient to a treatment room, and gets the necessary doctors, nurses, and equipment to begin evaluation and treatment. Then the emergency room physician, who is higher than the nurse in the chain of command, takes charge and begins the process of determining whether the patient is really having a heart attack by conducting an examination, ordering tests, and taking the patient's medical history. If the physician calls in a cardiologist for consultation, the cardiologist becomes the person in charge and makes the final treatment decision. Despite the number of people involved in the process, it's clear who is in charge at each point because the emergency room follows the principle of unity of command.

A second key assumption is the idea termed "**span of control**" or the number of individuals who report to any one supervisor. It is probably not surprising to learn that the fewer the individuals being supervised by any one manager, the easier it is to control the behaviour of subordinates. The reason is quite simple—more time will be available to spend with each subordinate. Is there a magic number when considering how many individuals should report to any one supervisor? The research suggests six or seven.

span of control
the number of people reporting to a specific supervisor

Line Versus Staff Authority

A second dimension of authority is the distinction between line and staff authority. **Line authority** is the right to command immediate subordinates in the chain of command. This person can issue orders to that division manager and expect them to be carried out.

Staff authority is the right to advise but not command others who are not subordinates in the chain of command. The terms "line" and "staff" are also used to describe different functions within the organization. A **line function** is an activity that contributes directly to creating or selling the company's products. A **staff function** is one that does not contribute directly to creating or selling the company's products, but instead supports line activities. Typical staff functions within an organization are accounting, human resources, and legal services.

line authority
the right to command immediate subordinates in the chain of command

staff authority
the right to advise but not command others who are not subordinates in the chain of command

line function
an activity that contributes directly to creating or selling the company's products

staff function
an activity that does not contribute directly to creating or selling the company's products, but instead supports line activities

Delegation of Authority

Managers can exercise their authority directly by completing the tasks themselves, or they can choose to pass on some of their authority to subordinates. **Delegation of authority** is the assignment of direct authority and responsibility to a subordinate to complete tasks for which the manager is normally responsible.

delegation of authority
the assignment of direct authority and responsibility to a subordinate to complete tasks for which the manager is normally responsible

How authority is passed on is not always as intended. Consider the following:

> Switching to specialist from jack of all trades is helping administrative professionals gain recognition as experts in their field. As a result of specializing, administrative professionals are enjoying more authority and decision-making clout in the workplace than ever before, said Tracy Heslop, president of the Calgary chapter of the International Association of Administrative Professionals (IAAP). As such, the role of today's administrative professional is more reminiscent of the middle-management positions of the late 1980s than the early days, when administrative assistants were known as secretaries and considered worker bees, she said.[12]

When a manager delegates work, three transfers occur, as illustrated in Exhibit 11.8. First, the manager transfers full responsibility for the assignment to the subordinate. Many managers find giving up full responsibility somewhat difficult. Indeed, most managers have way too much to do. So, from a practical perspective, they can't assume new responsibilities that come with change and growth until they fully delegate old ones. Another problem is that managers often fear that the task won't be done as well if they don't do it themselves. Sometimes managers delegate "full responsibility" only to later interfere with how the employee is performing the task: "Why are you doing it that way? That's not the way I do it." In short, delegating full responsibility means that the employee—not the manager—is now completely responsible for task completion. Second, delegation transfers to the subordinate full authority over the budget, resources, and personnel needed to do the job. To do the job effectively, subordinates must have the same tools and information at their disposal that managers had when they were responsible for the same task. In other words, for delegation to work, delegated authority must be commensurate with delegated responsibility.

EXHIBIT 11.8
Delegation: Responsibility, Authority, and Accountability

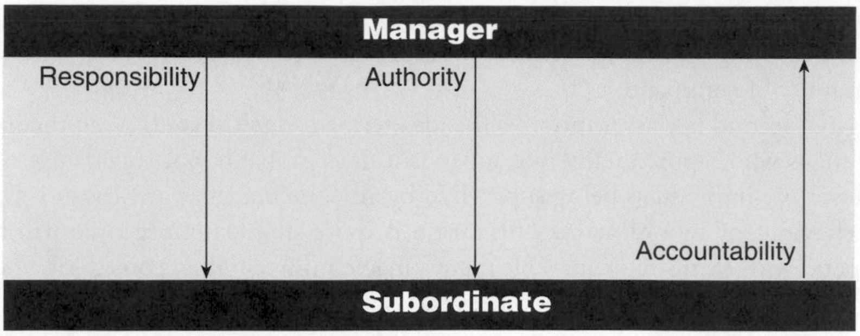

Source: Pringle, *Managing Organizations: Functions and Behaviors*, 1st Edition, © 1988. Reprinted by permission of Pearson Education, Inc., Upper Saddle River, NJ.

The third transfer that occurs with delegation is the transfer of accountability. The subordinate now has the authority and responsibility to do the job, and is then accountable for getting the job done. In other words, managers give subordinates their managerial authority and responsibility in exchange for results. Exhibit 11.9 gives some tips on how to be an effective delegator.

Degree of Centralization

centralization of authority the location of most authority at the upper levels of the organization

decentralization the location of a significant amount of authority in the lower levels of the organization

Centralization of authority is the location of most authority at the upper levels of the organization. In a centralized organization, managers make most decisions, even the relatively small ones. **Decentralization** is the location of a significant amount of authority in the lower levels of the organization. An organization is decentralized if it has a high degree of delegation at all levels. In a decentralized organization, workers closest to problems are authorized to make the decisions necessary to solve the problems on their own.

Decentralization has a number of advantages. It develops employee capabilities throughout the company and leads to faster decision-making and more satisfied customers and employees. Furthermore, a study of 1000 large companies found that companies with a high degree of decentralization outperformed those with a low degree of decentralization with regard to return on assets (6.9 percent versus 4.7 percent), return on investment (14.6 percent versus 9 percent), return on equity (22.8 percent versus 16.6 percent), and

EXHIBIT 11.9
How to Be a More Effective Delegator

1. Trust your staff to do a good job. Recognize that others have the talent and ability to complete projects.
2. Avoid seeking perfection. Establish a standard of quality and provide a time frame for reaching it.
3. Give effective job instructions. Make sure employees have enough information to complete the job successfully.
4. Know your true interests. Delegation is difficult for some people who actually prefer doing the work themselves rather than managing it.
5. Follow up on progress. Build in checkpoints to help identify potential problems.
6. Praise the efforts of your staff.
7. Don't wait to the last minute to delegate. Avoid crisis management by routinely delegating work.
8. Ask questions, expect answers, and assist employees to help them complete the work assignments as expected.
9. Provide the resources you would expect if you were doing an assignment yourself.
10. Delegate to the lowest possible level to make the best possible use of organizational resources, energy, and knowledge.

Source: S.B. Wilson, "Are You an Effective Delegator?" *Female Executive*, 1 November 1994, 19.

return on sales (10.3 percent versus 6.3 percent). Ironically, however, the same study found that few large companies are actually decentralized. Specifically, only 31 percent of employees in these 1000 companies were responsible for recommending improvements to management. Overall, just 10 percent of employees received the training and information needed to support a truly decentralized approach to management.[13]

With results like these, the key question is no longer whether companies should decentralize, but where they should decentralize. One rule of thumb is to stay centralized where standardization is important and to decentralize where standardization is unimportant. **Standardization** is solving problems by consistently applying the same rules, procedures, and processes.

standardization
solving problems by consistently applying the same rules, procedures, and processes

Review 2: Organizational Authority

Organizational authority is determined by the chain of command, line versus staff authority, delegation, and the degree of centralization in a company. The chain of command vertically connects every job in the company to higher levels of management and makes clear who reports to whom. Managers have line authority to command employees below them in the chain of command, but have only staff or advisory authority over employees not below them in the chain of command. Managers delegate authority by transferring to subordinates the authority and responsibility needed to do a task, and, in exchange, subordinates become accountable for task completion. In centralized companies, most authority to make decisions lies with managers in the upper levels of the company. In decentralized companies, much of the authority is delegated to the workers closest to problems, who can then make the decisions necessary for solving the problems themselves. Centralization works best for tasks that require standardized decision-making. When standardization isn't important, decentralization can lead to faster decisions, greater employee and customer satisfaction, and significantly better financial performance.

3 JOB DESIGN

Imagine that McDonald's (www.mcdonalds.com) decided to pay $50 000 a year to its drive-through window cashiers. Fifty thousand dollars for saying, "Welcome to McDonald's. May I have your order please?" Would you take the job? Sure you would. Work a couple of years. Make a hundred grand. Why not? However, let's assume that to get this outrageous salary, you have to be a full-time drive-through McDonald's window cashier for the next 10 years. Would you still take the job? Just imagine, 40 to 60 times an hour you repeat the same basic process:

1. "Welcome to McDonald's. May I have your order please?"
2. Listen to the order. Repeat it for accuracy. State the total cost. "Please drive to the second window."
3. Take the money. Make change.
4. Give customers drinks, straws, and napkins.
5. Give customers food.
6. "Thank you for coming to McDonald's."

Could you stand to do the same simple tasks an average of 50 times per hour, 400 times per day, 2000 times per week, or 8000 times per month? Few can. It's rare for fast-food workers to stay on the job more than six months. Indeed, McDonald's and other fast-food restaurants have well over 100 percent employee turnover each year.[14]

In this next section, you will learn about **job design**—the number, kind, and variety of tasks that individual workers perform in doing their jobs. You will learn about job specialization, job rotation, enlargement, and enrichment.

job design
the number, kind, and variety of tasks that individual workers perform in doing their jobs

The importance of job design can be found in the Canadian government. It has had to compete with the private sector for top talent and more often than not has not come

DOING THE RIGHT THING

JOB SPECIALIZATION AND WORKER SAFETY[16]

When redesigning specialized jobs to make them more interesting, don't overlook the need to redesign these jobs to make them safer. Specialized jobs, such as factory work, extensive computer usage, or even grocery store work (scanning items at checkout, stocking items on shelves), often require the same tasks or motions to be repeated over and over. As a result, the most common workplace injuries are carpal tunnel syndrome, back injuries, sprains, and strains that come from lifting, repetitive motion, or overexertion. To protect workers and reduce the number of lost workdays from such injuries (on average, 25 days for carpal tunnel and 6 days for sprains and strains), redesign tools or tool handles to put user wrists in neutral positions, reduce vibrations from tool handles, redesign workstations to reduce lifting or twisting, make tools and workstations adjustable to fit each employee, provide lifting devices, and keep most work at elbow height. Do the right thing. Protect the health of employees who do specialized work.

out on top. Indeed, it is not considered an employer of choice for many individuals. This is now becoming a problem as it faces a large number of retirements in the next few years, many of whom will have to be replaced. Graham Lowe, a member of the Canadian Policy Research Networks, suggests that "governments have started to scramble to devise strategies to attract the future generation of public servants.... They are trying to figure out how to position themselves to deal with the change." What are some of the solutions suggested by Lowe and his colleagues? Create flexible practices, encourage collaboration, create flexible job designs, and deal with compensation and human resource practices.[15]

Job Specialization

Job specialization is a job composed of a small part of a larger task or process. Specialized jobs are characterized by simple, easy-to-learn steps, low variety, and high repetition, like the McDonald's drive-through window job described above. One of the clear disadvantages of specialized jobs is that, being so easy to learn, they quickly become boring. This, in turn, can lead to low job satisfaction and high absenteeism and employee turnover, all of which are very costly to organizations. Why, then, do companies continue to create and use specialized jobs? The primary reason is that specialized jobs are very economical. Once a job has been specialized, it takes little time to learn and master. Consequently, when experienced workers quit or are absent, the company loses little productivity when replacing them with a new employee.

job specialization
a job composed of a small part of a larger task or process

Job Rotation, Enlargement, and Enrichment

Because of the efficiency of specialized jobs, companies are often reluctant to eliminate them. Consequently, job redesign efforts have focused on modifying jobs to keep the benefits of specialized jobs, but to reduce their obvious costs and disadvantages. Three methods, job rotation, job enlargement, and job enrichment, have been used to try to improve specialized jobs.[17]

In factory work, or even some office jobs, many workers perform the same task all day long. For example, if you attach side mirrors in an auto factory, you probably complete this task 45 to 60 times an hour. If you work as the cashier at a grocery store, you check out a different customer every two to three minutes. And if you work as an office receptionist, you may answer and direct phone calls up to 200 times an hour.

Job rotation attempts to overcome the disadvantages of job specialization by periodically moving workers from one specialized job to another to give them more variety and the opportunity to use different skills. For example, the office receptionist who does nothing but answer phones could be systematically rotated to a different job, such as typing, filing, or data entry, every day or two. Because employees simply switch from one specialized job to another, job rotation allows companies to retain the economic benefits of specialized work. However, the greater variety of tasks makes the work less boring and more satisfying for workers. A slightly different example of job rotation can be found in academic institutions. In many departments, the role of academic head is not one that is fought over. Preferring to focus on teaching and research, many scholars shy away from administrative duties whenever possible. As a result, some academic units work on the basis of a voluntary rotation of department heads where an individual assumes the duty for a year and then passes the responsibilities on to a colleague who, after a year, passes the role on to another colleague, and so on. The Management Department of Saint Mary's University in Halifax uses this type of job rotation.

job rotation
periodically moving workers from one specialized job to another to give them more variety and the opportunity to use different skills

Another way to counter the disadvantages of specialization is to enlarge the job. **Job enlargement** is increasing the number of different tasks that a worker performs within one particular job. So, instead of having to perform just one task, workers with enlarged

job enlargement
increasing the number of different tasks that a worker performs within one particular job

© ROYALTY-FREE/CORBIS

Specialized jobs are found in most companies. Interestingly, companies are increasingly using job rotation to add variety to the tasks faced by workers such as this assembly-line worker. Job rotation also allows workers to add to their repertoire of skills and retain other skills.

jobs would be given several tasks to perform. For example, an enlarged "mirror attacher" job might include attaching the mirror, checking to see that the mirror's power adjustment controls work, and then cleaning the mirror's surface. While job enlargement increases variety, many workers report feeling more stress when their jobs are enlarged. Consequently, many workers view enlarged jobs as simply "more work," especially if they are not given additional time to complete the additional tasks.

Job enrichment attempts to overcome the deficiencies in specialized work by increasing the number of tasks and by giving workers the authority and control to make meaningful decisions about their work.[18]

job enrichment
increasing the number of tasks in a particular job and giving workers the authority and control to make meaningful decisions about their work

Review 3: Job Design

Companies use specialized jobs because they are economical and easy to learn and don't require highly paid workers. However, specialized jobs aren't motivating or particularly satisfying for employees. Companies have used job rotation, job enlargement, and job enrichment to make specialized jobs more interesting and motivating. With job rotation, workers move from one specialized job to another. Job enlargement simply increases the number of different tasks within a particular job. Job enrichment increases the number of tasks in a job and gives workers authority and control over their work.

Designing Organizational Processes

More than 40 years ago, Tom Burns and G.M. Stalker described how two kinds of organizational designs, mechanistic and organic, are appropriate for different kinds of organizational environments.[19] **Mechanistic organizations** are characterized by specialized jobs and responsibilities; precisely defined, unchanging roles; and a rigid chain of command based on centralized authority and vertical communication. This type of organization works best in stable, unchanging business environments. By contrast, **organic organizations** are characterized by broadly defined jobs and responsibility; loosely defined, frequently changing roles; and decentralized authority and horizontal communication based on task knowledge. This type of organization works best in dynamic, changing business environments.

mechanistic organization
organization characterized by specialized jobs and responsibilities; precisely defined, unchanging roles; and a rigid chain of command based on centralized authority and vertical communication

organic organization
organization characterized by broadly defined jobs and responsibility; loosely defined, frequently changing roles; and decentralized authority and horizontal communication based on task knowledge

The key difference between these approaches is that while mechanistic organizational designs focus on organizational structure, organic organizational designs are concerned with organizational processes—the collection of activities that transform inputs into outputs valued by customers.

After reading the next two sections, you should be able to

4 explain the methods that companies are using to redesign internal organizational processes (i.e., intraorganizational processes).

5 describe the methods that companies are using to redesign external organizational processes (i.e., interorganizational processes).

4 INTRAORGANIZATIONAL PROCESSES

intraorganizational process
the collection of activities that take place within an organization to transform inputs into outputs that customers value

An **intraorganizational process** is the collection of activities that take place within an organization to transform inputs into outputs that customers value. The steps involved in an automobile insurance claim are a good example of an intraorganizational process:

1. Document the loss (i.e., the accident).
2. Assign an appraiser to determine the dollar amount of damage.
3. Make an appointment to inspect the vehicle.
4. Inspect the vehicle.
5. Write an appraisal and get the repair shop to agree to the damage estimate.
6. Pay for the repair work.
7. Return the repaired car to the customer.

Let's take a look at how companies are using re-engineering, empowerment, and behavioural informality.

Re-engineering

re-engineering
fundamental rethinking and radical redesign of business processes to achieve dramatic improvements in critical measures of performance, such as cost, quality, service, and speed

In their best-selling book *Reengineering the Corporation*, Michael Hammer and James Champy defined **re-engineering** as "the *fundamental* rethinking and *radical* redesign of business *processes* to achieve *dramatic* improvements in critical, contemporary measures of performance, such as cost, quality, service and speed."[20] Hammer and Champy further explained the four key words shown in italics in this definition. The first key word is "fundamental." When re-engineering organizational designs, managers must ask themselves, "Why do we do what we do?" and "Why do we do it the way we do?" The usual answer is "Because that's the way we've always done it." The second key word is "radical." Re-engineering is about significant change, about starting over by throwing out the old ways of getting work done. The third key word is "processes." Hammer and Champy noted that "most business people are not process oriented; they are focused on tasks, on jobs, on people, on structures, but not on processes." The fourth key word is "dramatic." Re-engineering is about achieving "quantum" improvements in company performance.

An example from IBM's credit operation illustrates how work can be re-engineered.[21] "IBM Credit" loans businesses money to buy IBM computers. Previously, the loan process would begin when an IBM salesperson called needing credit approval for a customer's purchase. The first department involved in the process would take the credit information over the phone from the salesperson and record it on the credit form. Then, the credit form was sent to a separate credit checking department, and then to a separate pricing department (where the interest rate was determined), and so on. In all, it would take five departments six days to approve or deny the customer's loan. Of course, this delay cost IBM business. Some customers got their loans elsewhere. Others, frustrated by the wait, simply cancelled their orders.

Finally, two IBM managers decided to walk a loan straight through to each of the five departments involved in the process. At each step, they asked the workers to stop what they were doing to immediately process their loan application. They were shocked by what they found. From start to stop the entire process took just 90 minutes! It turns out that the average time of six days was created by delays that occurred in handing off the work from one department to another. The solution: IBM redesigned the process so that one person, not five in five separate departments, handled the entire loan approval process alone without any handoffs. The results were "dramatic." Re-engineering the credit process reduced approval time from six days to four hours and allowed "IBM Credit" to increase the number of loans it handled by a factor of 100!

A second example involves the Acadia University (www.acadiau.ca) bookstore. Previously, books were ordered by professors for each course and the books would be stored on the shelves. Students needing textbooks would march into the store, find the books they needed on the shelves, walk to the cash, pay, and then leave. Early in each semester, lineups would be long and tempers short. Shelf space was also limited but, for the most part, stocked with textbooks that were going to be sold one way or another. Shelf space for higher-profit nonacademic book items was limited, with the result that sales of this nature were stagnant and had been for years. To alter this situation, Acadia developed an online ordering system for students. With a connection to the Internet, students could order all their textbooks from the convenience of their rooms. The orders were filled and packed for pickup or delivery by university football players for a small fee. Putting the student ordering system on the Web allowed the bookstore to increase revenue possibilities by taking books off valuable shelf space. (They were stored in a room adjoining the bookstore.) Cash register mistakes were drastically reduced and lineups were cut dramatically. The bookstore was also able to collect valuable data about the products it sold and the buying habits of its main clients—students.

Re-engineering changes an organization's orientation from vertical to horizontal. Instead of "taking orders" from upper management, lower- and middle-level managers and workers "take orders" from a customer who is at the beginning and end of each process. Instead of running independent functional departments, managers and workers in different departments take ownership of cross-functional processes. Instead of simplifying work so that it becomes increasingly specialized, re-engineering complicates work by giving workers increased autonomy and responsibility for complete processes.

In essence, re-engineering changes work by changing **task interdependence**, the extent to which collective action is required to complete an entire piece of work. As shown in Exhibit 11.10, there are three kinds of task interdependence.[22] In **pooled interdependence**, each job or department independently contributes to the whole. In **sequential interdependence**, work must be performed in succession, as one group's or job's outputs become the inputs for the next group or job. Finally, in **reciprocal interdependence**, different jobs or groups work together in a back-and-forth manner to complete the process. By reducing the handoffs between different jobs or groups, re-engineering decreases sequential interdependence. Likewise, re-engineering decreases pooled interdependence by redesigning work so that formerly independent jobs or departments now work together to complete processes. Finally, re-engineering increases reciprocal interdependence by making groups or individuals responsible for larger, more complete processes in which several steps may be accomplished at the same time.

As an organizational design tool, re-engineering promises big rewards. However, it has come under severe criticism, too. The most serious complaint is that, since it allows a few workers to do the work formerly done by many, re-engineering is simply a corporate code word for cost cutting and worker layoffs. Likewise, for that reason, detractors claim that re-engineering hurts morale and performance. For example, despite reducing ordering times from three weeks to three days, Levi Strauss (www.levistrauss.com) ended a US$850 million re-engineering project because of the fear and turmoil it created in its work force. One of the low points occurred when Levi management, encouraged by its re-engineering consultants, told 4000 workers that they would have to "reapply for their jobs" as the company shifted from its traditional vertical structure to a "process-based form of organizing."[23]

task interdependence
the extent to which collective action is required to complete an entire piece of work

pooled interdependence
work completed by having each job or department independently contribute to the whole

sequential interdependence
work completed in succession, with one group or job's outputs becoming the inputs for the next group or job

reciprocal interdependence
work completed by different jobs or groups working together in a back-and-forth manner

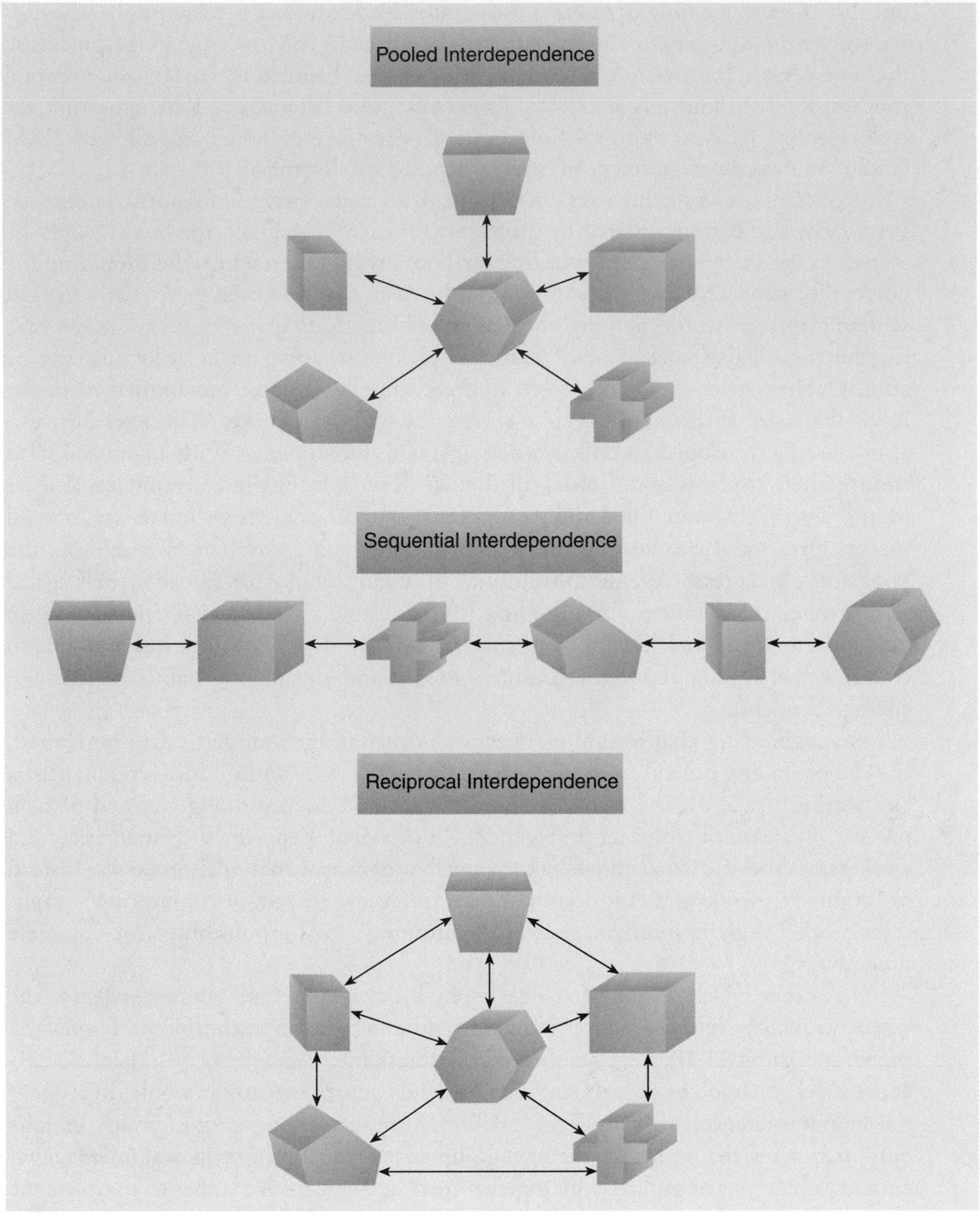

EXHIBIT 11.10
Re-engineering and Task Interdependence

Empowerment

empowering workers permanently passing decision-making authority and responsibility from managers to workers by giving them the information and resources they need to make and carry out good decisions

Another way of redesigning interorganizational processes is through empowerment. **Empowering workers** means permanently passing decision-making authority and responsibility from managers to workers. However, for workers to be fully empowered, companies must give them the information and resources they need to make and carry out good decisions, and then reward them for taking individual initiative.[24]

Behavioural Informality

How would you describe the atmosphere in the office in which you last worked? Was it a formal, by-the-book, follow-the-rules, address-each-other-by-last-names atmosphere? Or was it more informal, with an emphasis on results rather than rules, casual business dress rather than suits, and first names rather than last names and titles? Or was it somewhere in between?

Behavioural informality (or formality) is a third influence on intraorganizational processes. **Behavioural informality** refers to workplace situations characterized by spontaneity, casualness, and interpersonal familiarity. By contrast, **behavioural formality** refers to workplace situations characterized by routine and regimen, specific rules about how to behave, and impersonal detachment. Exhibit 11.11 shows that behavioural formality and informality are characterized by four factors: language usage, conversational turn-taking and topic selection, emotional and proxemic gestures, and physical and contextual cues. Let's examine each in more detail.[25]

behavioural informality workplace atmosphere characterized by spontaneity, casualness, and interpersonal familiarity

behavioural formality workplace atmosphere characterized by routine and regimen, specific rules about how to behave, and interpersonal detachment

Compared to formal work atmospheres, the language in informal workplaces is often slurred ("Whatcha doin'?"), elliptical ("Coffee?" rather than "Would you like some coffee?"), and filled with slang terms and vivid descriptions. People use first names and perhaps nicknames to address each other, rather than Mr., Ms., Dr., or formal titles. As an example, next time you are in a Tim Hortons coffee shop, watch the interaction of the employees behind the counter. For the most part, the interaction is informal. When it comes to conversations in informal workplaces, people jump right in when they have something to say (i.e., unregulated turn-taking), conversations shift from topic to topic, many of which are unrelated to business, and joking and laughter are common. From joy to disappointment, people show much more emotion in informal workplaces. In addition, relaxed expressions, such as putting your feet on your desk, or congregating in hallways for impromptu discussions, are more common, too. With regard to physical and contextual cues, informal workplaces de-emphasize differences in hierarchical status or rank to encourage more frequent interaction between organizational members. Consequently, to make their organizations feel less formal, many companies have eliminated what used

EXHIBIT 11.11 Differences Between Formal and Informal Workplaces

FORMAL	INFORMAL
LANGUAGE USAGE	
Fully articulated speech ("What are you doing?")	Phonological slurring ("Whatcha doin'?")
Grammatically complete phrasing ("Would you like some coffee?")	Use of elliptical expressions ("Coffee?")
Use of formal word choices ("Would you care to dine?")	Use of colloquial and slang expressions ("Wanna grab a bite to eat?")
Use of honorifics ("Ms.," "Sir," "Dr.")	Use of the vivid present ("So I come down the stairs, and she says...")
Elimination of "I" and "you" ("It is requested that...")	First name, in-group names ("Mac," "Bud")
CONVERSATIONAL TURN-TAKING AND TOPIC SELECTION	
Turn-taking well regulated	Turn-taking relatively unregulated
Few interruptions or overlaps	Many interruptions or overlaps
Few changes of topic	Many shifts of topic possible
Seriousness of topic	Joking or conversational levity possible
EMOTIONAL AND PROXEMIC GESTURES	
Sober facial demeanour	Greater latitude of emotional expression
Much interpersonal distance	Small interpersonal distance
No touching, postural attention	Touching, postural relaxation allowed
PHYSICAL AND CONTEXTUAL CUES	
Formal clothing, shoes, etc.	Informal clothing, shoes, etc.
Central focus of attention possible	Decentralized, multiple centres of attention
Symmetric arrangement of chairs/furniture	Asymmetric arrangement of chairs/furniture
Artifacts related to official status	Informal trappings: flowers, art, food, soft furniture
Hushed atmosphere, little background noise	Background noise acceptable

Source: Academy of Management Review by D.A. Morland. Copyright 1995 by Academy of Management. Reproduced with permission of the publisher via Copyright Clearance Center.

to be considered "management perks," things such as executive dining rooms, reserved parking spaces, and large corner offices separated from most workers because they were located on a higher floor of the company building (the higher the floor, the greater one's status).

Casual dress policies and open office systems are two of the most popular methods for increasing behavioural informality. While casual dress increases behavioural informality by having managers and workers at all levels dress in a more relaxed manner, open office systems such as those found in some Nortel Networks facilities increase behavioural informality by significantly increasing the level of communication and interaction among employees. By definition, **open office systems** try to increase interaction by removing physical barriers that separate workers. One characteristic of open office systems is that they have much more shared space than private space. **Shared spaces** are used by and open to all employees. Cubicles with low-to-the-ground partitions, offices with no doors or with glass walls, collections of comfortable furniture that encourage people to congregate, and common areas with tables and chairs that encourage people to meet, work, or eat together are examples of shared space. **Private spaces**, such as a private office with a door, are used by and open to just one employee. Before Steelcase (www.steelcase.com), a leading office furniture manufacturer, switched to open systems, 80 percent of its executive office space was private space used for individual offices, whereas 20 percent was shared space. However, after switching to open offices, 80 percent is shared space and 20 percent is private space. After the change, CEO Jim Hackett went from a private, 700-square-foot office to a 48-square-foot enclosure that sits out in the open of a 22 000-square-foot environment that workers have dubbed "The Leadership Community."[27]

open office systems
offices in which the physical barriers that separate workers have been removed in order to increase communication and interaction

shared spaces
spaces used by and open to all employees

private spaces
spaces used by and open to just one employee

The advantage of this much-shared space in open offices is that it dramatically increases the amount of unplanned, spontaneous, and chance communication among employees.[28] People are much more likely to plan meetings and work together when numerous "collaboration spaces" with conference tables, white boards, and computers are readily available. With no office walls, with inviting common areas, and with different departments mixed together in large open spaces, spontaneous communication occurs more often. Also, open office systems increase chance communication by making it much more likely that people from different departments or areas will run into each other. However, not all companies are enthusiastic about open offices. Microsoft gives employees private offices so they can concentrate on their work.

DOING THE RIGHT THING

DON'T SCAVENGE THAT OFFICE IF SOMEBODY IS STILL IN IT[26]

It's like roadkill in the animal kingdom. As soon as the word gets out that someone is leaving the company, the remaining co-workers start scheming to scavenge the office leftovers—chairs, computer monitors, filing cabinets, and even staplers. Mary Wong, president of a human resources consulting company, says, "This issue is practically everywhere ... , professionals—anyone you and I would normally consider to be very adult—turn into children" over the prospect of picking an empty office clean of its 'goodies.'" Sometimes, however, and this is where it gets disrespectful, office scavengers move in before the employee, who's often been laid off, has left. Ethics consultant Steve Lawler tells the story of a laid-off manager who, just hours after hearing the bad news, was already getting requests for the expensive Herman Miller Aeron chair in which he was still sitting. Office scavenging is a strange and predictable aspect of office life. It happens everywhere. But, if you're going to scavenge, and you probably will, do the right thing by maintaining the dignity of departing co-workers: wait until the office is empty before you strike.

Review 4: Intraorganizational Processes

Today, companies are using re-engineering, empowerment, and behavioural informality to change their intraorganizational processes. Through fundamental rethinking and radical redesign of business processes, re-engineering changes an organization's orientation from vertical to horizontal. Re-engineering changes work processes by decreasing sequential and pooled interdependence, and by increasing reciprocal interdependence. Re-engineering promises dramatic increases in productivity and customer satisfaction, but has been criticized as simply an excuse to cut costs and lay off workers. Empowering workers means taking decision-making authority and responsibility from managers and giving it to workers. Empowered workers develop feelings of competence and self-determination and believe their work to have meaning and impact. Workplaces characterized by behavioural informality are spontaneous and casual. The formality or informality of a workplace depends on four factors: language usage, conversational turn taking and topic selection, emotional and proxemic gestures, and physical and contextual cues. Casual dress policies and open office systems are two of the most popular methods for increasing behavioural informality.

5 INTERORGANIZATIONAL PROCESSES

What do "Voodoo Lounge," "$100 million," and an "interorganizational process" have in common? "Voodoo Lounge" is the name of a Rolling Stones tour. "$100 million" is the profit the Stones earned from the Voodoo Lounge tour.[29] And an "interorganizational process" is the method the Stones' business manager used to organize the tour.

An **interorganizational process** is a collection of activities that occur among companies to transform inputs into outputs that customers value. In other words, many companies work together to create a product or service that keeps customers happy. For example, in the interorganizational process used to manage the Voodoo Lounge tour, the Stones did one thing, play music. Everything else in the tour—recording, transportation, marketing, and construction—was farmed out to other companies.

interorganizational process
a collection of activities that take place among companies to transform inputs into outputs that customers value

In this section, you'll explore interorganizational processes by learning about modular organizations, virtual organizations, and boundaryless organizations.[30]

Modular Organizations

Except for the core business activities that they can perform better, faster, and cheaper than others, **modular organizations** outsource all remaining business activities to outside companies, suppliers, specialists, or consultants. The term "modular" is used because the business activities purchased from outside companies can be added and dropped as needed, much like adding pieces to a three-dimensional puzzle. Exhibit 11.12 depicts a modular organization in which the company has chosen to keep training, human resources, sales, research and development, information technology, product design, customer service, and manufacturing as core business activities. However, it has chosen to outsource noncore activities of product distribution, Web page design, advertising, payroll, accounting, and packaging.

modular organization
an organization that outsources noncore business activities to outside companies, suppliers, specialists, or consultants

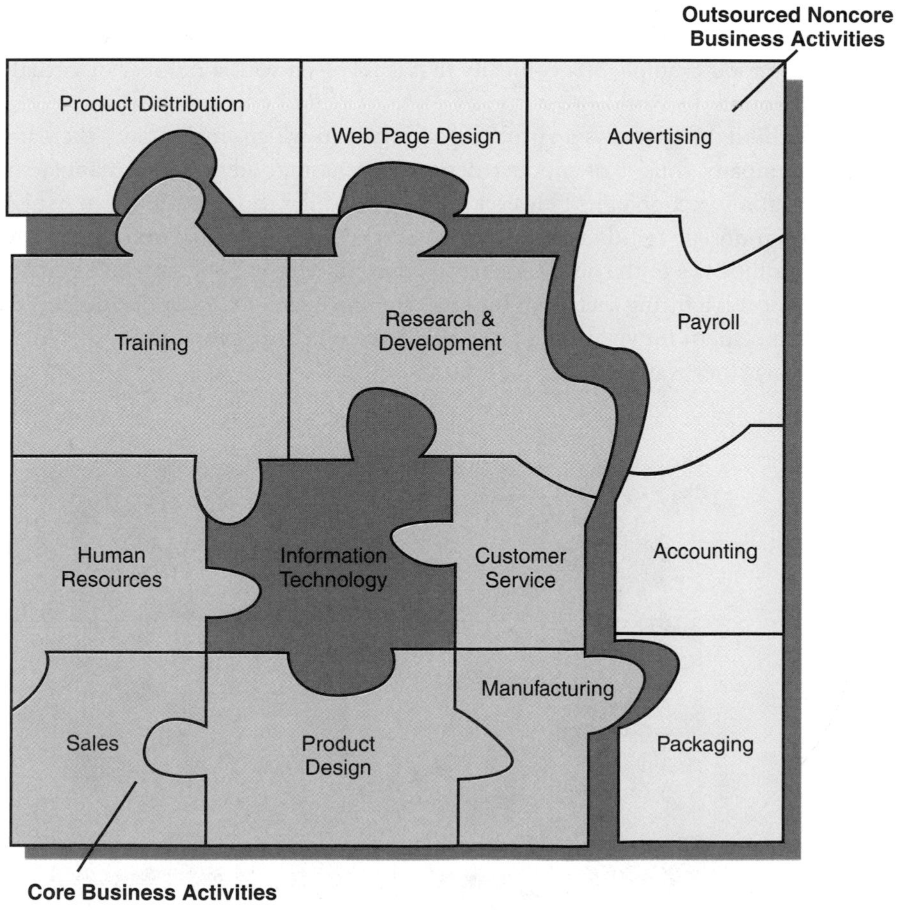

EXHIBIT 11.12
Modular Organization

Modular organizations have several advantages. First, because modular organizations pay for outsourced labour, expertise, or manufacturing capabilities only when needed, they can cost significantly less to run than traditional organizations. For example, of the "big three" auto makers in the United States, DaimlerChrysler, which outsources 70 percent of its parts manufacturing to suppliers, has by far the lowest costs.[31] Second, outsourcing allows both modular companies, and the companies to whom they outsource, to focus on the core activities they do best. However, to obtain these advantages, modular organizations need to work closely with reliable partners—that is, vendors and suppliers that they can trust.

However, modular organizations have disadvantages, too. The primary disadvantage is the loss of control that occurs when key business activities are outsourced to other companies. Also, companies may reduce their competitive advantage in two ways if they mistakenly outsource a core business activity. First, competitive and technological change may produce a situation in which the noncore business activities a company has outsourced suddenly become the basis for competitive advantage. Second, related to that point, companies to whom work is outsourced can sometimes become competitors.

Virtual Organizations

virtual organization
an organization that is part of a network in which many companies share skills, costs, capabilities, markets, and customers to collectively solve customer problems or provide specific products or services

By contrast to modular organizations in which the interorganizational process revolves around a central company, a **virtual organization** is part of a network in which many companies share skills, costs, capabilities, markets, and customers with each other. For example, Puma (www.puma.com), the athletic shoe company, is a virtual organization. Puma takes care of strategy and marketing in Herzogenaurach, Germany. A small network of firms in Asia handles the purchasing and distribution of the materials used to make Puma shoes. Separate companies in China, Taiwan, Indonesia, and Korea manufacture Puma shoes. Separate sales and distribution networks operate in Africa, Asia, Australia, Europe, North America, and South America. In all, 80 different companies throughout the world help make and sell Puma shoes.[32] As a contract manufacturer of electronic parts for different industries, Celestica Inc. (www.celestica.com) of Toronto is another good example of a company that is involved with a number of virtual organizations around the world.

Exhibit 11.13 shows a virtual organization in which, for "today," the parts of a virtual company consist of product design, purchasing, advertising, manufacturing, and information technology. However, unlike modular organizations, in which outside organizations are tightly linked to one central company, virtual organizations work with some companies in the network alliance, but not with all. So, whereas a puzzle with various pieces is a fitting metaphor for modular organizations, a potluck dinner is an appropriate metaphor for virtual organizations. Everyone brings their finest food dish, but eats only what they want.

Puma running shoes are a creation of a virtual organization.

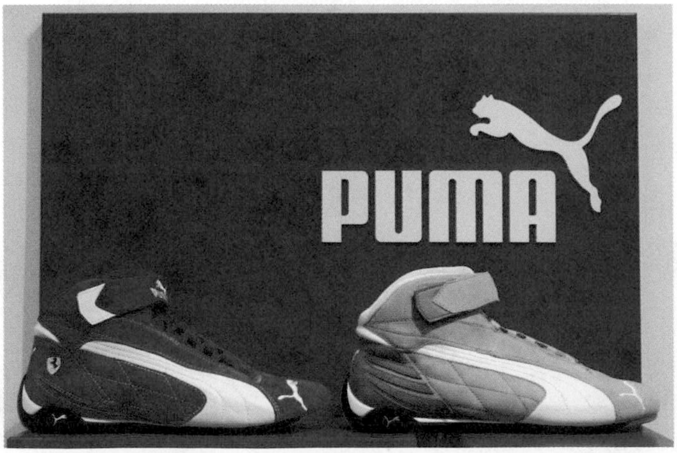

AP PHOTO/CHRISTOF STACHE

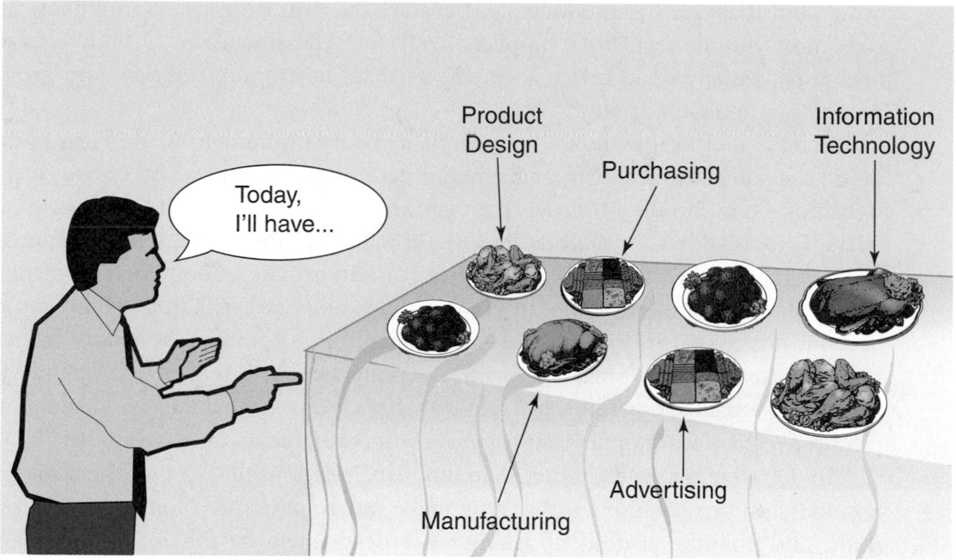

EXHIBIT 11.13
Virtual Organization

Another difference is that the working relationships between modular organizations and outside companies tend to be more stable and longer lasting than the shorter, often temporary relationships found among the virtual companies in a network alliance. Thus, the composition of a virtual organization is always changing. The combination of network partners that a virtual corporation has at any one time simply depends on the expertise needed to solve a particular problem or provide a specific product or service. This is why the businessperson in the network organization shown in Exhibit 11.13 said, "Today, I'll have ..." Tomorrow, the business could want something completely different. In this sense, the term "virtual organization" means the organization that exists "at the moment."

Virtual organizations have a number of advantages. They let companies share costs. And, because members can quickly combine their efforts to meet customers' needs, they are fast and flexible. Finally, because each company in the network alliance is the "best" at what it does, in theory, virtual organizations should provide better products and services in all respects.

Like modular organizations, a disadvantage of virtual organizations is that once work has been outsourced, it can be difficult to control the quality of work done by network partners. However, the greatest disadvantage is that it requires tremendous managerial skills to make a network of independent organizations work well together, especially since their relationships tend to be shorter and task or project based. However, virtual organizations are using two methods to solve this problem. The first is to use a broker whose job is to create and assemble the knowledge, skills, and resources from different companies for outside parties, such as customers.[33] The second way to make networks of virtual organizations more manageable is to use a virtual organization agreement that, somewhat like a contract, specifies the schedules, responsibilities, costs, and payouts to participating organizations.[34]

Boundaryless Organizations

General Electric (www.ge.com) CEO Jack Welch coined the term "boundaryless organization" in an annual letter to GE shareholders. Welch wrote, "Our dream is a boundaryless company, a company where we knock down the walls that separate us from each other on the inside and from our constituencies on the outside." Why was Welch, arguably one of the most effective CEOs ever, so concerned with boundaries? Steve Kerr, GE's vice president of leadership development, explained: "Boundaries determine how an organization operates. There are vertical boundaries like floors and ceilings that separate levels of the organization; there are inside walls that separate departments from each other; and there are outside walls that separate the firm from its environment, from its customers, outside regulators, suppliers, and other constituencies."[35] Thus, a **boundaryless organization** would break down the vertical, horizontal, external, and geographic boundaries in organizations.[36]

boundaryless organization a speedy, responsive, and flexible organization in which vertical, horizontal, external, and geographic boundaries are removed or minimized

Exhibit 11.14 shows how a boundaryless organization might work. First, notice that inside the company, in the internal environment, there are no vertical or horizontal relationships. Now, this doesn't mean that there are literally no bosses in boundaryless organizations. It also doesn't mean that lower-level managers and workers aren't responsible to upper-level managers. They are. What it does mean is that in boundaryless organizations the emphasis is on speed, responsiveness, and flexibility rather than to whom you report. Second, notice that in Exhibit 11.14, the organization's external boundary, represented by the dotted line, is permeable. Again, the point here is to remove the boundary separating the organization's internal environment from its external environment (i.e., industry regulation, suppliers, customers, competitors, and advocacy groups).

By focusing on results rather than reporting relationships, one of the advantages of boundaryless organizations is that they make much better use of employee knowledge, skills, and abilities. Instead of asking what department or job is "responsible" for a problem, the question that gets asked is "Who inside or outside the company can best solve this problem?" Another advantage is that they lead to much closer relationships with the components of the company's external environment. For example, one of the ways that GE has made external boundaries more permeable is by putting key managers "on loan" to outside companies. So, instead of reporting to work at a GE office in a GE building, these "on loan" managers report to work at offices that are permanently located in customers' or suppliers' offices or buildings.

EXHIBIT 11.14
Boundaryless Organization

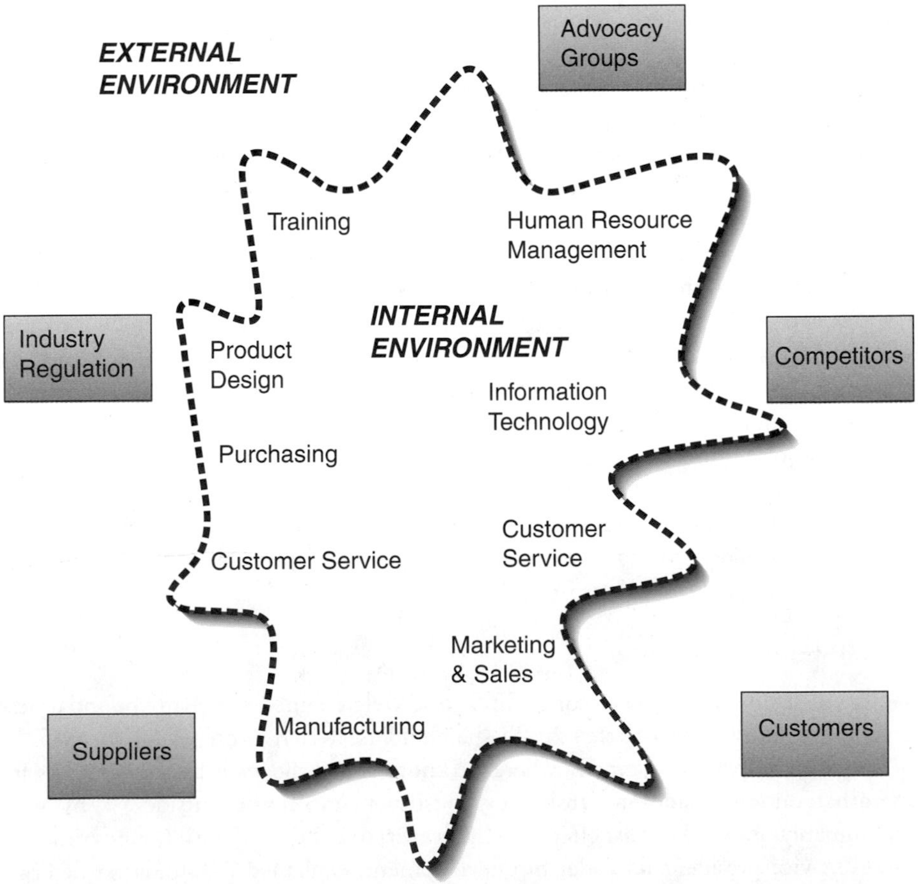

Source: Adapted from G.G. Dess, A.M.A. Rasheed, K.J. McLaughlin, & R.L. Priem, "The New Corporate Architecture," *Academy of Management Executive* 9 (1995): 7–18.

However, boundaryless organizations have significant disadvantages as well. To start, managers and employees often find the transition to boundaryless organizations threatening. Managers and workers who are used to the clear accountability and reporting relationships of vertical hierarchies often struggle with the new emphasis on speed and flexibility. However, the biggest disadvantage to boundaryless organizations is that there is no clear way to achieve them. The suggested methods read like a list of ingredients: create interdivisional committees, establish communication flows, create mutually beneficial relationships with suppliers and customers, build trust with employees, and so forth. Unfortunately, there is little advice on how best to combine and "cook" them.[37]

Review 5: Interorganizational Processes

Organizations are using modular, virtual, and boundaryless organizations to change interorganizational processes. Because modular organizations outsource all noncore activities to other businesses, they are less expensive to run than traditional companies. However, modular organizations require extremely close relationships with suppliers, may result in a loss of control, and could create new competitors if the wrong business activities are outsourced. Virtual organizations participate in a network in which they share skills, costs, capabilities, markets, and customers. As customer problems, products, or services change, the combination of virtual organizations that work together changes. Virtual organizations reduce costs, respond quickly, and, if they can successfully coordinate their efforts, can produce outstanding products and service. By breaking down internal and external boundaries, boundaryless organizations try to increase organizational speed, flexibility, and responsiveness. However, boundaryless organizations are threatening to managers and workers and are difficult to create.

What Really Happened?[38]

At the beginning of the chapter, you learned about Grant Thornton and how, as a professional service firm, it might be different. But what does different mean? In an interview with Ian Hutchinson and Conor Vibert, professors at the Manning School of Business of Acadia University, Alex MacBeath, executive partner and CEO of Grant Thornton, offers insight into its structure, the roles of partners, the means by which professionals are promoted, and the manner by which knowledge is shared within this well known organization. So, in the following paragraphs, let's find out what's really happening at Grant Thornton.

Hutchinson and Vibert: How is Grant Thornton structured differently than a traditional corporation?

MacBeath: Professional services firms are really unique forms of organization. If you think about a partnership, the partners are the owners, the partners are the managers, and the partners are the producers of work. So it's almost as if all the shareholders of a corporate entity show up for work every day and they make the decisions and they decide what they are going to do. It is in that sense that the partner represents and takes on a number of different rolls. For someone in my role or someone else in a formal leadership role there is not a lot of authority. Indeed, it is a role without authority so you lead and you manage through influence not through the position itself. You do not have a corporate structure or style or role that gives you power. It comes through influence. If you have a partnership where the owners are there every day working on par with the management of the firm, it does make change on one hand difficult because you really need to get the active buy-in of the partnership. On the other hand, when you do get that buy-in there is a tremendous opportunity to leverage the power of the partners. Once they accept and buy in to the change and agree about what you want to do or where the firm is going to go, then the leverage that they bring is really quite phenomenal. It allows you to move ahead with change more quickly than you might in a corporate environment.

Hutchinson and Vibert: What is the role of a senior partner, a junior partner, and a principal?

MacBeath: A senior partner is who we would term an equity partner. That is the real owner of the firm. As I mentioned before, each owner, each partner, has one vote. They may not receive the same income, but in terms of equity or voting power they are one. That position has the risks and rewards of ownership—risk if their results are lower, risk around claims, risk around litigation, but with the rewards of distributive income. When the firm does well, then the owners and the partners do well. To look at the role of an equity partner, what we did about three years ago was articulate the role, the expectation, or the competencies of a partner in a document we call the "vision partner document." I could summarize that in perhaps the three roles of an equity partner or a partner in our firm. First would be a preferred advisor to clients. They have the business partner relationship with the client, they have a knowledge of the industry or sector that they bring to the client, they have a technical competence that they bring to the client, and they deliver the services. Second, you have the entrepreneurial co-owner. That is someone who acts in an entrepreneurial manner to build the business, who helps to build the practice, who helps to build a profitable practice in their area, and who is highly effective in a personnel and communication role. So that's what we would look for in a partner. A junior partner is someone who has been admitted from a senior staff level to partnership with the full expectations that they will become an equity partner. This is an opportunity for them to grow into the partner role and that is normally about a three-year period, at which point they are admitted as an equity partner. We have a third position which is a principal. This is a senior practitioner who is usually based in a local office and who has a more local office perspective. You might term the occupant of the position, a *local office partner*. They would be very strong leaders but usually fill a specific role and perhaps do not have the national scope that you would expect of an equity partner.

Hutchinson and Vibert: How does an accountant become a partner in your firm?

MacBeath: In terms of the admission process what we look for is an individual who has the ability or capability to achieve the expectations that we have set out in the vision partner document. It starts with a good knowledge of who the senior staff are that have this capability. We have, in the firm, a leadership development program or leadership development initiative. All senior staff who are within three to four years of being eligible for partnership enter the leadership program, so we have a chance to work with them over that period of time. When they are ready to be nominated, usually seven, eight, or maybe nine years after their gaining their CA, their office or business unit will nominate them. There is a panel of six partners and myself that interview them. It is really to test their readiness, to test whether they are at the point that they're capable of being a partner. Then there is an approval of the board. In our firm all partners get to vote on the new admissions to the partnership, so there's a partnership vote. This is, on one hand, an informal process of getting to know the senior staff and who is capable of working with them to develop their skills so that they are ready to join the partnership. Then there is a formal part, which revolves around the process itself.

Hutchinson and Vibert: How do professionals in your firm transfer and share knowledge in different geographically dispersed offices?

MacBeath: We have, first of all, a very collaborative culture and that certainly facilitates a sharing of knowledge. We have an intranet within the firm so we have been able to establish communities of practice. We have shared workspaces which allow groups working on a specific client, within an industry, or within a sector, to collaborate. We are in the process of expanding that. There will be a shared workspace with our clients where we can collaborate on the work we're doing for a specific client offering them access to a lot of the resources and knowledge that we have in the firm. So I think we are using technology quite effectively to be able to share it across the firm. A big part of our practice is obviously audit. We have a common audit methodology that every office and every practitioner in the firm uses. That allows us to share this knowledge across the firm. We can do a file in Halifax. All our files are electronic, so it can be developed in Halifax and reviewed by an expert in Vancouver or some other part of the country.

Key Terms

authority *(310)*
behavioural formality *(321)*
behavioural informality *(321)*
boundaryless organization *(326)*
centralization of authority *(314)*
chain of command *(310)*
customer departmentalization *(307)*
decentralization *(314)*
delegation of authority *(313)*
departmentalization *(304)*
empowering workers *(320)*
functional departmentalization *(305)*
geographic departmentalization *(308)*
interorganizational process *(323)*
intraorganizational process *(318)*
job design *(315)*
job enlargement *(316)*
job enrichment *(317)*
job rotation *(316)*
job specialization *(316)*
line authority *(313)*
line function *(313)*
matrix departmentalization *(309)*
mechanistic organization *(317)*
modular organization *(323)*
open office systems *(322)*
organic organization *(317)*
organizational process *(304)*
organizational structure *(304)*
pooled interdependence *(319)*
private spaces *(322)*
product departmentalization *(306)*
reciprocal interdependence *(319)*
re-engineering *(318)*
sequential interdependence *(319)*
shared spaces *(322)*
span of control *(313)*
staff authority *(313)*
staff function *(313)*
standardization *(315)*
task interdependence *(319)*
unity of command *(311)*
virtual organization *(324)*

Self-Assessment

FLEXIBILITY AND STRUCTURE

Every organization needs some degree of flexibility and standardization. In other words, companies need to have enough flexibility in their organizations to respond to changes in their business environment but also must have certain structures in place ensure smooth operations. For example, if someone gets hurt on company property, clear procedures about what to do in case of an accident help managers respond quickly and confidently. But being overly committed to following rules can hamstring an organization and keep it from growing. As a manager, you will probably encounter both types of situations, and to respond appropriately, you will need to have an idea of how comfortable you are in a formal environment versus a more loosely structured workplace. On page 517 of the Assessment Appendix is a survey that can give you baseline information on your preferences for structure.

Management Decisions

OUTSOURCE OR NOT?[39]

As you gaze out the windshield of your car while stopped at a red light, you think back on how simple life used to be. Several years ago when you started your small manufacturing company, life was tough, but it wasn't as hectic as it is today. You started your company, which builds partially assembled furniture and components, on a shoestring with only a few employees. Even though everyone worked 15-hour days, six or seven days a week, things still seemed easier back then. Now that your firm has grown and is finally turning a healthy profit, your average workday has dropped to around 10 hours per day. Because of sustained growth, you have distanced yourself from the physical production of the product. Instead, you now spend your time wandering around the factory, looking for ways to streamline the production process, speed up delivery time, improve quality, and solve any other logistical or systems problems that crop up.

One area that is in need of immediate attention is the customer service department. It seems that customer service issues and questions quadrupled overnight. In the beginning, you and your spouse used to take turns returning the occasional customer complaint, question, or request for additional information. When the volume of customer service requests began to consume a large portion of both your work routines, you hired a full-time customer service representative to take over. Today, the company has four full-time customer service reps on staff and is still experiencing long periods of delays and complaints because customers can't get through in a timely basis.

Of course, one easy solution is to outsource the customer service function to an outside agency. An external agency that specializes in customer service is likely better prepared to handle the ever-increasing number of customer service calls and could possibly do so for the same cost you are paying now. Outsourcing is not new to you. During the enormous growth cycle your company has experienced over the last two years, you have outsourced a number of functions within the firm, including accounting, personnel, payroll, and maintenance. You thought those were easy decisions because each required only a little time each month to perform. In addition, the cost to you of staffing and performing those functions internally significantly outweighed any benefits received. Since you made your decision to outsource those areas, you have been delighted with the service that you receive and have not had to micromanage the providers' results.

Unfortunately, you believe customer service is different. It is a daily activity—sometimes a 24/7 activity—not to mention that it requires specific and detailed knowledge of the 115 products you produce. Your customer service reps are not only well-versed in your product lines, but they are also able to decipher the sometimes-incomprehensible instructions that accompany your products, a critical part of resolving many customer-related issues. You take pride in the fact that two of the four customer service reps have been with you from the start and are good at defusing potentially bad situations. These two individuals can usually turn a disgruntled customer into a happy one and do it without giving away the store. You're afraid that if you outsource the CS department, you'll lose that ability and jeopardize the loyalty of these two employees. On the other hand, you see your market share declining as frustrated customers flock to the competition. You've got to decide.

Questions

1. What factors would you consider before determining whether to outsource the customer service department or not? What advantages and disadvantages are there to outsourcing activities?
2. What would you do? Why?
3. If you choose to outsource the customer service department, how could you control the performance of the outsourcing agency?

Management Decisions

PLUSH MANAGEMENT PERKS: PARTAKING OR PRUNING?[40]

"They do, too!" "They do not!" "You don't know what you're talking about." "See, it's attitudes like yours that prove my point!"

Ah, nothing like watching your top two executives argue during lunch to raise your blood pressure. You knew that Sam, the VP of sales, was going to get mad when Catherine, the VP of human resources, suggested getting rid of executive perks (the private dining room, company cars, first-class air travel, etc.). It took Sam 25 years to become a vice president and nobody, including Sam, wants to see his or her perks and rewards reduced. However, you didn't think it was possible for someone to get that mad that fast. Given the way Sam's face instantly turned beet red when Catherine suggested that the reserved parking spaces be eliminated, it's a good thing she caught him between bites or he might have choked on his shrimp salad.

Well, with executive perks topping the agenda for the annual executive retreat next weekend, Sam and Catherine's argument has given you something to think about. Is Catherine right? Do all executive perks need to be eliminated? Or is Sam right? Do the executive perks need to be left alone? After all, even Catherine got defensive when Sam asked her how happy she'd be if the company closed its on-site daycare. When she responded, "They wouldn't dare do that," Sam barked, "That's exactly the way I feel about your recommendations!"

Well, you need to get your thoughts sorted out. A good place to start is with the list of executive perks currently being offered by the company:

- company cars
- reserved parking spaces
- company cellular phones
- personal financial counselling
- personal liability insurance
- executive dining room
- first-class air travel
- spouse travel on extended business trips
- signing bonuses
- stock options
- country club memberships
- large, expensively furnished private offices
- home security systems
- home computer/office equipment

Questions

1. Of the perks listed above, choose three that your managers are most likely to desire. In other words, which three executive perks would your managers scream the most about if you took them away? Explain why for each of the three perks.
2. Of the perks listed above, which three probably create the most resentment among your work force (i.e., nonmanagers)? In other words, which three executive perks anger your work force the most? Explain why for each of the three perks.
3. Choose the option (a, b, or c) that is likely to benefit the company most in the long run:
   a. eliminate all executive perks
   b. retain all executive perks
   c. selectively eliminate perks

Explain the reasoning behind your choice. If you choose option c, specify the perks you kept and why you kept them.

Develop Your Management Potential

"WORK" IN SOMEONE ELSE'S SHOES[41]

Why is learning to see things from someone else's perspective one of the most difficult things to do in today's workplace? Sometimes, the inability to see things as others see them has to do with the people involved. Inexperience, ignorance, and selfishness can all play a role. However, in most organizations, the inability to see things from someone else's perspective results from the jobs themselves, not the people who do them. Because jobs limit who we talk to, what we talk about, what we think about, and what we care about at work, it should not be a surprise that people who perform different jobs have very different views about each other and the workplace.

For example, in the airline industry the pilots who fly the planes and the ground crews who unload, load, and refuel them may have little appreciation for each other. The ground crews may feel that the pilots treat them like second-class citizens. The pilots may not understand why the ground crews aren't doing more to get their planes out of the gates and in the air as fast as possible. To improve understanding and help them see things from each other's perspective, one company created a program in which the captains and ground crews learn a lot about each other's jobs. For example, the pilots bring the ground crews into their cockpits and show them the detailed processes they are required to follow to get planes ready for departure. The pilots, on the other hand, gain appreciation and understanding by actually working as members of a ground crew. After several days of demanding ground crew work, one pilot said:

> I remember one time when I was working the ramp [as a member of a ground crew]. I was dead tired. I had flown that morning and had a couple of legs in, so I got out of

my uniform and jumped into my ramp clothes. That afternoon was very hot. It was in the 30s, I was tired and hungry and hadn't had a break. Then I saw this pilot sitting up there in the cockpit eating his frozen yogurt. I said to myself, "Man, I'd like to be up there now." Then I caught myself. I'm up there every day. Now, I know that pilot has been up since 3:00 in the morning. I know that he's been flying an airplane since 6:00 A.M. I know it's 3:00 in the afternoon and he hasn't had a chance to get off and have a meal yet today. I know all that, and yet, the yogurt still looks really good to me. Then I thought, "How can a ramp agent [on the ground crew] who works his butt off for two or three years, working double shifts two or three times a week, understand this?" It hit me that there's a big gap in understanding here.

The misunderstandings between pilots and ground crews are not unique. All organizations experience them. Nurses and doctors, teachers and students, and managers and employees all have difficulty seeing things from each other's perspective. However, as this program shows, you can minimize differences and build understanding by "working" in someone else's shoes.

Questions

1. Describe the job-related differences or tensions where you work. Who is involved? What jobs do they do? Explain why the job-related differences or tensions exist.
2. Since the best way to see things from someone else's perspective is to "work" in his or her shoes, see if you can spend a day, a morning, or even two hours performing one of these jobs. If that's not possible, spend some time carefully observing the jobs and then interview several people who perform them. Describe your boss's reaction to this request. Was he or she supportive or not? Why?
3. Answer the following questions after you have worked the job or conducted your interviews. What most surprised you about this job? What was easiest? What was hardest? Explain. Now that you've had the chance to see things as others see them, what do you think would happen, good or bad, from letting other people in your organization work in someone else's shoes? Explain.

Discussion Questions

1. Manulife, Shell Canada, CAE Inc., Emera, Loblaws, and CN are all important Canadian companies. None operate in the same industry and all offer different products. In each instance, designers have numerous options to choose from when seeking to build effective organizational structures. Which five traditional approaches to organizational structure are available to these designers and which one is best for use by each company?
2. Explain what standardization means and how this concept is relevant to the degree of centralization.
3. IBM, Aliant, Petro Canada, Pfizer, and McGraw-Hill are all well-known companies that experienced large-scale internal change during the last decade. Change efforts of this nature are massive and leave few areas of a company untouched. A number of methods are available to change consultants seeking to redesign internal organizational processes. Identify these methods and briefly describe each.
4. Over the course of your degree program, you have decided to enter into the co-op program for your university. Your first posting is with a small apple exporter in the Annapolis Valley of Nova Scotia. One slow day at work, you were glancing through your textbook with the intention of obtaining a few ideas that might help this company. Your boss noticed your diligence and was curious about the terms "modular," "virtual," and "boundaryless" organization. In the context of the apple industry, how might you define these terms?

Critical Thinking Video Case

CBC

Visit www.management2e.nelson.com to view this chapter's CBC video case.

Take Two

Biz Flix
Reality Bites

Reality Bites is an American film starring Winona Ryder, Ethan Hawke, Ben Stiller, Steve Zahn, Janeane Garofalo, and David Spade. The plot follows the life of recent college graduate Lelaine Pierce (Ryder), who wants to make a documentary about her friends as away to capture the strife and problems confronting her generation. In this scene, she is applying for a job at Wiener Schnitzel, a fast-food restaurant managed by David Spade.

What to Watch for and Ask Yourself

1. Using the terms from the chapter, outline the job of cashier as Spade is describing it in the clip.
2. Is the cashier position a line or staff function?
3. Describe the atmosphere at the restaurant.

Management Workplace
Black Diamond

Organizational structure should imitate the culture and purpose of the organization—at least, according to Peter Metcalf, founder of Black Diamond, a manufacturer of mountain climbing equipment. A company that started with 50 employees has grown to over 200 people who generate over $20 million in annual revenue. Black Diamond is now the leading maker of high-end climbing equipment, and paradoxically, it got there by creating a flat organization.

What to Watch for and Ask Yourself

1. What evidence do you see in the video that Black Diamond is an informal work environment?
2. Describe organizational authority at Black Diamond.
3. Why do you think a loose organizational structure is successful at Black Diamond?

Part 4

Organizing People, Projects, Processes

AP PHOTO/GEORGE WIDMAN

Managing Teams

Chapter 12

CHAPTER OUTLINE

LEARNING OBJECTIVES

After reading this chapter, you should be able to

1. explain the good and bad of using teams.
2. recognize and understand the different kinds of teams.
3. understand the general characteristics of work teams.
4. explain how to enhance work team effectiveness.

What Would You Do?

The words "Cessna Skyhawk" have special meaning for anyone who has ever wanted to learn to fly. More people have learned to fly in a Cessna Skyhawk than in any other plane in aviation history. In fact, the Skyhawk, with its 11-metre wingspan, 220 kph cruising speed, and room for two adults and their luggage, is the best-selling plane of all time. Since 1911, Cessna has been a storied name in aviation. Cessna built gliders for the army in World War II, introduced the Skyhawk in 1956, produced the first turbocharged and cabin-pressurized single-engine planes in the 1960s, delivered its first business jet in the 1970s, and topped US$1 billion in sales in the 1980s. Then in the 1990s, as the aviation industry experienced one of its worst downturns ever, Cessna nearly went out of business. Sales of general aviation aircraft for the entire industry, which had reached 17 000 planes per year, hit rock bottom at 928 planes in 2001. During the same period, sales of Cessna's piston-engine planes, like the Skyhawk, dropped from 8000 planes per year to just 600. Cessna laid off 75 percent of the employees at its piston-engine plane factories and, eventually, stopped making piston-engine planes altogether. Now, however, positive changes in the external environment have prompted Cessna to start building its legendary Skyhawks again.[1]

This is where you come in. You have been with the company nearly 20 years and have just been made the vice president of Cessna's "new" single-engine business. It's your job to rebuild this part of the business from scratch. Pilots tend to remain loyal to the kind of airplane on which they learned to fly, so if you can rebuild Cessna's single-engine business today, pilots who learn to fly on today's Skyhawks will still be buying and flying Cessna jets 20 years from now.

One of the advantages of starting over completely is that you get to design the entire production facility—everything from its location, to the new workers, to the suppliers. Furthermore, instead of using a standard production line where each worker does just one task, you have tentatively decided to use teams to assemble the planes.

You're aware that switching to teams may strike some people as radical, particularly at conservative Cessna where, as one of your fellow managers admitted, "we probably got into a mode of doing things for the future based on how we'd always done things in the past." But the more you think about it, the more you believe you've made the right decision.

You expect to see several benefits from a team-based approach: increased customer satisfaction from improved product quality; faster, more efficient production; and higher employee job satisfaction. A few things worry you, however. Despite all of their promise, teams and teamwork are also prone to significant disadvantages: they're expensive to implement, they require significant training, and they work only about a third of the time they're used. So, despite their promise, you can't ignore the reality that using teams would be quite risky for Cessna.

Still, you can't help thinking that teams could pay off and that there might be ways for you to minimize the risk of failure. For example, since the plant will be in a new location, you get to start with a brand new work force. What kinds of people should you hire for teamwork? What kinds of skills and experience will they need to succeed in a team environment? How much authority and responsibility should you give them? Should they be limited to just advising management, or should they be totally responsible for quality, costs, and productivity?

Finally, are there other places where you might use teams besides the assembly line? How could teams contribute to the success of Cessna's "new" single-engine plane manufacturing facility in other ways?

If you were in charge of Cessna's "new" single-engine factory, what would you do?

Like Cessna, a growing number of organizations are significantly improving their effectiveness by establishing work teams. Nonetheless, teams really haven't been in place at most Canadian companies for more than 10 to 15 years, if that long. In other words, teams are a relatively new phenomenon in companies, and there's still much for organizations to learn about managing them.

We begin this chapter by reviewing the advantages and disadvantages of teams and exploring when companies should use them over more traditional approaches. Next, we discuss the different types of work teams and the characteristics common to all teams. The chapter ends by focusing on the practical steps to managing teams—team goals and priorities and organizing, training, and compensating teams.

Why Work Teams?

work team
a small number of people with complementary skills who hold themselves mutually accountable for pursuing a common purpose, achieving performance goals, and improving interdependent work processes

Work teams consist of a small number of people with complementary skills who hold themselves mutually accountable for pursuing a common purpose, achieving performance goals, and improving interdependent work processes.[2]

When compared with 116 other refineries, Imperial Oil's refinery in Dartmouth, Nova Scotia, used to perform in the bottom 25 percent of the group. Managers worried that the plant would be shut down. After making lists of things that needed to be done, they finally hit on a new solution: teams. The refinery shifted to a team arrangement and formed groups of 40 to 50 workers who took responsibility for entire processes within the plant such as fraction and catalytic conversion (the breaking down of crude oil in to more useful products). As teams took responsibility for processes in the plant, a layer of supervision was eliminated. In less than a year, they found ways to reduce staffing by 46 percent and identified a number of other cost savings. Overall costs fell by 30 percent and the refinery was approaching the top 25 percent. The work teams were clearly a success.[3]

The success that Imperial Oil's Dartmouth refinery experienced with teams is not uncommon. In many industries, teams are growing in importance because they help organizations respond to specific problems and challenges. While work teams are not the answer for every situation or organization, if the right teams are used properly and in the right settings, teams can dramatically improve company performance over more traditional management approaches and instill a sense of vitality in the workplace that is otherwise difficult to achieve.

After reading the next two sections, you should be able to

1 explain the good and bad of using teams.

2 recognize and understand the different kinds of teams.

1 THE GOOD AND BAD OF USING TEAMS

Let's begin our discussion of teams by learning about the advantages of teams, the disadvantages of teams, and when to use teams.

The Advantages of Teams

Companies are making greater use of teams because teams have been shown to increase customer satisfaction, product and service quality, speed and efficiency in product development, and employee job satisfaction.[4] Teams help businesses increase *customer satisfaction* in several ways. One way is to create work teams that are trained to meet the needs of specific customer groups. When Eastman Kodak re-engineered its customer service centre, it created specific teams to field calls from the general public (based on the geographic location of the caller), scientific users, and corporate users. Under this system, customers are immediately directed to the team trained to meet their needs. Within a year, the work teams doubled the rate at which Kodak solved customer problems on the first phone call.[5]

Teams also help firms improve *product and service quality* in several ways.[6] Here, in contrast to traditional organizational structures where management is responsible for organizational outcomes and performance, one of the primary advantages is that teams take direct responsibility for the quality of the products and service they produce. At Texas Instruments, production teams are directly responsible for resolving quality issues, and even visit suppliers when necessary to track down quality problems.[7] At Whole Foods, a supermarket chain that sells groceries and health foods, the ten teams that manage each store are not only responsible for store quality and performance, but they are also directly accountable, since the size of their team bonus depends on it.[8] And making teams directly responsible for service and production quality pays off. A survey by *Industry Week* indicates that 42 percent of the companies that use teams report revenues of more than US$250 000 per employee compared to only 25 percent of the companies that don't use teams.[9]

A third reason that teams are increasingly popular is *the need for speed and efficiency when designing and manufacturing products.*[10] Traditional product design proceeds sequentially, meaning that one department has to finish its work on the design of a product before the next department can start. Unfortunately, this is not only slow, but it also encourages departments to work in isolation from one another.[11] For example, with sequential design processes, it's common for different departments, such as manufacturing, to work for months on their part of the product design only to have it rejected by another department, such as marketing, which was never consulted as the work was being done. *Overlapping development phases* is a faster and better way to design products and is often made possible through the use of teams. With overlapping development phases, teams of employees, consisting of members from the different functional areas in a firm (i.e., engineering, manufacturing, and marketing), work on the product design at the same time. Because each of the different functional areas is involved in the design process from the start, the company can avoid most of the delays and frustration associated with sequential development.

Another reason for using teams is that teamwork often leads to increased job satisfaction.[12] One reason that teamwork can be more satisfying than traditional work is that it gives workers a chance to improve their skills. This is often accomplished through **cross training**, in which team members are taught how to do all or most of the jobs performed by the other team members. The advantage for the organization is that cross training allows teams to function normally when one member is absent or a team member quits or is transferred. The advantage for workers is that cross training broadens their skills and makes them more capable while also making their work more varied and interesting. Village Food Markets, located on Vancouver Island, cross trains its employees to improve service and make employees' work more interesting.[13] Employees will stock shelves, run cash registers, or deliver to customers' homes, depending on the need at any given time.

cross training
training team members how to do all or most of the jobs performed by the other team members

A second reason that teamwork is satisfying is that work teams often receive proprietary business information that is available only to managers at most companies. For example, at Whole Foods, the supermarket chain that sells groceries and health foods, team members are given full access to their store's financial information and everyone's salaries, including the store manager and the CEO.[14] Each day, next to the time clock, Whole Foods employees can see the previous day's sales for each team, as well as the sales on the same day from the previous year. Each week, team members can examine the same information, broken down by team, for all of the Whole Foods stores in their region. And each month, store managers review information on profitability, including sales, product costs, wages, and operating profits, with each team in the store. Since team members decide how much to spend, what to order, what things should cost, and how many team members should work each day, this information is critical to making teams work at Whole Foods.[15]

Participation in work teams also increases job satisfaction by providing team members unique opportunities that would otherwise not be available to them. At Chaparral Steel, employee work teams routinely visit customers' production facilities to discuss

© ERIK FREELAND/CORBIS

At Whole Foods, employees work in teams and receive company information that normally would only be shared with managers.

quality-related issues. Team members often gain job satisfaction from unique leadership responsibilities that would typically not be available in traditional organizations. For example, at Colgate-Palmolive work teams are responsible for determining their own work assignments, scheduling overtime, making out vacation schedules, performing preventive equipment maintenance, and ensuring quality control. For each work team, the position of team leader rotates, giving different team members the opportunity to build leadership skills.[16]

Teams share many of the advantages of group decision-making discussed in Chapter 4. For instance, because team members possess different knowledge, skills, abilities, and experiences, teams will be able to view problems from multiple perspectives. This diversity of viewpoints increases the odds that team decisions will solve the underlying causes of problems rather than simply address the symptoms. The increased knowledge and information available to teams also make it easier for them to generate more alternative solutions, which is a critical part of improving the quality of decisions. Finally, because teams members are involved in decision-making processes, they should be more committed to making those decisions work. In short, teams can do a much better job than individuals in two important steps of the decision-making process: defining the problem and generating alternative solutions.

The Disadvantages of Teams

Although teams can significantly increase customer satisfaction, product and service quality, speed and efficiency in product development, and employee job satisfaction, using teams does not guarantee these positive outcomes. In fact, if you've ever participated in team projects in your classes, you're probably already aware of some of the problems inherent in work teams. So despite all of their promise, teams and teamwork are also prone to these significant disadvantages: initially high turnover, social loafing, and legal risk.

The first disadvantage of work teams is *initially high turnover.* Teams aren't for everyone, and some workers will balk at the responsibility, effort, and learning required in team settings. When General Electric's Salisbury plant switched to teams, the turnover rate, which was near zero, jumped to 14 percent. Plant manager Roger Gasaway said of teams and teamwork, "It's not all wonderful stuff."[17]

Social loafing is another disadvantage of work teams. **Social loafing** occurs when workers withhold their efforts and fail to perform their share of the work. A 19th-century German scientist named Ringleman first documented social loafing when he found that one person pulling on a rope by himself or herself exerted an average of 63 kg of force on the rope. In groups of three, the average force dropped to 53 kg. In groups of eight, the average dropped to just 31 kg. Ringleman concluded that the larger the team, the smaller the individual effort. In fact, social loafing is more likely to occur in larger groups where it can be difficult to identify and monitor the efforts of individual team members.[18] In other words, social loafers count on being able to blend into the background so that their lack of effort isn't easily spotted. Because of team-based class projects, most students already know about social loafers or "slackers," who contribute poor, little, or no work whatsoever. Not surprisingly, research with 250 student teams clearly shows that the most talented students are typically the least satisfied with team-work because of having to carry "slackers" and having to do a disproportionate share of their team's work.[19]

social loafing
behaviour in which team members withhold their efforts and fail to perform their share of the work

How prevalent is social loafing on teams? One study found that when team activities were not mandatory, only 25 percent of manufacturing workers volunteered to join problem-solving teams, 70 percent were quiet, passive supporters (i.e., not putting forth effort), and 5 percent were actively opposed to these activities.[20] Another study found that on management teams, 56 percent of the managers, or more than half, withheld their effort in one way or another.

Finally, teams share many of the disadvantages of group decision-making discussed in Chapter 4. This includes *groupthink,* in which, in highly cohesive groups, group members feel intense pressure not to disagree with each other so that the group can approve a solution that has been proposed. Because groupthink restricts discussion and leads to consideration of a limited number of alternative solutions, it usually results in poor decisions. Also, team decision-making takes considerable time. Furthermore, it's the rare team that consistently holds productive task-oriented meetings to effectively work through the decision process. Another possible pitfall is that sometimes just one or two people dominate team discussions, restricting consideration of different problem definitions and alternative solutions. Last, team members may not feel accountable for the decisions and actions taken by the "team."

DOING THE RIGHT THING

DON'T BE A TEAM SLACKER—DO YOUR SHARE.
Given the amount of teamwork required in business classes, most of you have encountered slackers in student groups. Perhaps you've even "slacked" yourself from time to time. But, from an ethical perspective, slacking is clearly wrong. In reality, it's no different than cheating on an exam. When you slack, you're relying on others to do your work. You benefit without putting forth effort. And "your" team's project, paper, or presentation hasn't benefited from your contributions. In fact, it's very likely that your slacking may have significantly hurt "your" team's performance. Furthermore, in the real world, the consequences of team slacking, such as lost sales, poorer decisions, lower-quality service or products, or poorer productivity, are much larger. So, do the right thing. Whether it's in class or in business, don't be a slacker. Don't cheat your teammates. Pull your share of the "rope."

When to Use Teams

The two previous subsections make clear that teams come with significant advantages *and* disadvantages. Therefore, the question is not whether to use teams, but when and where to use teams for maximum benefit and minimum cost. Doug Johnson, associate director at the Center for the Study of Work Teams, said, "Teams are a means to an end, not an end in themselves. You have to ask yourself questions first. Does the work require interdependence? Will the team philosophy fit company strategy? Will management make a long-term commitment to this

USE TEAMS WHEN ...	DON'T USE TEAMS WHEN ...
1. There is a clear, engaging reason or purpose.	1. There isn't a clear, engaging reason or purpose.
2. The job can't be done unless people work together.	2. The job can be done by people working independently.
3. Rewards can be provided for teamwork and team performance.	3. Rewards are provided for individual effort and performance.
4. Ample resources are available.	4. The necessary resources are not available.
5. Teams will have clear authority to manage and change how work gets done.	5. Management will continue to monitor and influence how work gets done.

Source: R. Wageman, "Critical Success Factors for Creating Superb Self-Managing Teams," *Organizational Dynamics* 26, no. 1 (1997): 49–61.

EXHIBIT 12.1
When to Use or Not Use Teams

process?"[21] Exhibit 12.1 provides some additional guidelines on when to use or not use teams.[22]

First, teams should be used where there is a clear, engaging reason or purpose for using them. Too many companies use teams because they're popular or because they assume that teams can fix all problems but forming teams does not guarantee improved performance. But teams are much more likely to succeed if they know why they exist and what they are supposed to accomplish.

Second, teams should be used when the job can't be done unless people work together. This typically means that teams are required when tasks are complex, require multiple perspectives, or require repeated interaction with others to complete. For example, contrary to stories of legendary programmers who write software programs by themselves, Microsoft uses teams to write computer code because of the enormous complexity of today's software. Most software simply has too many options and features for one person (or even one team) to complete it all. Likewise, Microsoft uses teams because writing good software requires repeated interaction with others. Microsoft ensures this interaction by having its teams "check in" their computer code every few days. The different pieces of code written by the different teams are then compiled to create an updated working build or prototype of the software. Then, beginning the next day, all the teams and team members begin testing and debugging the new build. Over and over again, the computer code is compiled, then sent back to the teams to be tested and improved, and then compiled and tested again.[23]

However, if tasks are simple and don't require multiple perspectives or repeated interaction with others, teams should not be used. For instance, production levels dropped by 23 percent when Levi Strauss introduced teams in its factories. Levi's mistake was assuming that teams were appropriate for garment work, where workers performed single, specialized tasks, like sewing zippers or belt loops. Because this kind of work does not require interaction with others, Levi's unwittingly pitted the faster workers against the slower workers in each team. Arguments, infighting, insults, and threats were common between faster workers and the slower workers who held back team performance. One seamstress even had to physically restrain an angry co-worker who was about to throw a chair at a faster worker who constantly nagged her about her slow pace.[24]

Third, teams should be used when rewards can be provided for teamwork and team performance. Team rewards that depend on team performance rather than individual performance are the key to rewarding team behaviours and efforts. You'll read more about team rewards later in the chapter, but for now it's enough to know that if the level of rewards (individual vs. team) is not matched to the level of performance (individual vs. team), groups won't work. As discussed above, this was the case with Levi's, where a team structure was superimposed on individual jobs that didn't require interaction between workers. After the switch to teams, faster workers placed tremendous pressure on slower workers to increase their production speed. And since pay was determined by team performance, top individual performers saw their pay drop by several dollars an hour, while slower workers saw their pay increase by several dollars an hour, all while overall productivity dropped in the plant.[25]

Fourth, teams should be used when ample resources are available. The resources that teams need include training (discussed later in the chapter), sufficient time and a place or method to work together, job-specific tools, and consistent information and feedback concerning team work processes and job performance. Susan Cohen, a professor at the University of Southern California's Center for Effective Organizations, said, "People keep doing it [teams] because it is popular, a fad, a thing to do. But then they find that they run into problems because these things do require considerable care and feeding. Companies have to invest some resources in making them succeed."[27] At Levi's, team members complained that there were few resources, such as training, to support the transition from independent, individual-based work to team-based work. They also complained about not being given enough time to learn how to run the new machines to which they were assigned on the team system.

Another key problem with resources is management resistance. Managers who have been in charge are often reluctant to help teams or turn over resources to them. At Levi's, when team members would ask supervisors for assistance, a common reaction was that they should handle problems and make decisions for themselves.[28]

Finally, teams should be used when they have clear authority to manage and change how the work gets done. This means that teams—not managers—decide what problem to tackle next, when to schedule time for maintenance or training, or how to solve customer problems. Research clearly shows that teams with the authority to manage their own work strongly outperform teams that don't.[29] Unfortunately, managers can undermine teams' authority by closely monitoring their work, asking teams to change their decisions, or directly ignoring or overruling team decisions. Jeffrey Pfeffer, a Stanford professor and management consultant/author, said, "The fact is, the people doing the work know better how to do it. Get the managers out of the way and you will do better."[30]

DOING THE RIGHT THING

DON'T CREATE TEAMS AND THEN KILL THEM WITH A LACK OF RESOURCES

"Have we got a place to meet?" "No." "Do we have a budget?" "No, not that either." "Well, what have we got?" "Not much." There's no surer way to kill a team than to give it responsibility *without* the money, space, equipment, information, training, and authority it needs to complete its assignments. Professor Richard Hackman, a group expert, says, "Teams that start with great enthusiasm can quickly become disillusioned as they encounter frustration after frustration while trying to get the support they need." So, if you create a team, do the right thing. Give it the resources and authority it needs to get the job done.[26]

Review 1: The Good and Bad of Using Teams

In many industries, teams are growing in importance because they help organizations respond to specific problems and challenges. Teams have been shown to increase customer satisfaction (specific customer teams), product and service quality (direct responsibility), speed and efficiency in product development (overlapping development phases), and employee job satisfaction (cross training, unique opportunities, and leadership responsibilities). While teams can produce significant improvements in these areas, using teams does not guarantee these positive outcomes. Teams and teamwork have the disadvantages of initially high turnover, social loafing (especially in large groups), and groupthink. Teams also share many of the advantages (multiple perspectives, generation of more alternatives, and more commitment) and disadvantages (groupthink, time, poorly run meetings, domination by a few team members, and weak accountability) of group decision-making. Finally, teams should be used for a clear purpose, when the work requires that people work together, when rewards can be provided for both teamwork and team performance, when ample resources can be provided, and when teams can be given clear authority over their work.

2 KINDS OF TEAMS

Workers at the Honeywell plant in Scarborough, Ontario, used to have dull and routine jobs until the plant turned to teams as part of its reorganization. Its 320 workers were placed into 35 teams and given control of different parts of the production process, including quality control of the products they were making. As a result of these changes, they were able to eliminate most of its quality control inspectors, all the jobs assigned to rework, and one-third of the managers. The plant now has 40 percent fewer workers and productivity has almost doubled.[31]

Let's start by looking at autonomy, the key dimension, and special kinds of teams.

Autonomy, the Key Dimension

Teams can be classified in a number of ways, such as whether they are permanent or temporary, or functional or cross-functional. However, studies indicate that the amount of autonomy possessed by a team is the key dimension that makes teams different from each other.[32] *Autonomy* is the degree to which workers have the discretion, freedom, and independence to decide how and when to accomplish their jobs.

Exhibit 12.2 displays an autonomy continuum that shows how five kinds of teams differ in their autonomy. Moving left to right at the top of Exhibit 12.2, notice that traditional work groups and employee involvement groups have the lowest levels of autonomy, followed by semi-autonomous work groups, which have a higher level of autonomy, and then self-managing teams and self-designing teams, which have the highest levels of autonomy. Moving from top to bottom along the left side of Exhibit 12.2, note that the number of responsibilities given to each kind of team increases directly with that team's autonomy. Let's review each of these teams and their autonomy and responsibilities in more detail.

traditional work group group composed of two or more people who work together to achieve a shared goal

The smallest amount of autonomy is found in **traditional work groups**, where two or more people work together to achieve a shared goal. In these groups, workers do not have direct responsibility or control over their work, but are responsible for doing the work or "executing the task." Workers report to managers, who are responsible for their performance and have the authority to hire and fire them, make job assignments, and control resources. For instance, take the situation of an experienced worker who blatantly refuses to do his share of the work, saying, "I've done my time. Let the younger employees do the work." In a team with high autonomy, the responsibility of getting this employee to put forth his fair share of effort would belong to his teammates. But in traditional work

EXHIBIT 12.2
Team Autonomy Continuum

LOW TEAM AUTONOMY ⟵⟶ HIGH TEAM AUTONOMY

RESPONSIBILITIES	TRADITIONAL WORK GROUPS	EMPLOYEE INVOLVEMENT GROUPS	SEMI-AUTONOMOUS WORK GROUPS	SELF-MANAGING TEAMS	SELF-DESIGNING TEAMS
Execute Task	√	√	√	√	√
Give Advice/ Make Suggestions		√	√	√	√
Information			√	√	√
Major Production/ Service Tasks:					
Make Decisions			√	√	√
Solve Problems			√	√	√
All Production/ Service Tasks:					
Make Decisions				√	√
Solve Problems				√	√
Control Design:					
Team					√
Tasks					√
Membership					√

Sources: R.D. Banker, J.M. Field, R.G. Schroeder, & K.K. Sinha, "Impact of Work Teams on Manufacturing Performance: A Longitudinal Field Study," *Academy of Management Journal* 39 (1996): 867–890. J.R. Hackman, "The Psychology of Self-Management in Organizations," in *Psychology and Work: Productivity, Change, and Employment*, eds. M.S. Pallak & R. Perloff (Washington, D.C.: American Psychological Association), 85–136.

groups, the responsibility of telling this employee that his "sitting days are over" belongs to the boss or supervisor. In fact, the supervisor in this situation calmly confronted this employee and told him, "We need your talent, [and] your knowledge of these machines. But if you won't work, you'll have to go elsewhere." Within days, the employee's behaviour improved.[33]

Employee involvement teams, which have somewhat more autonomy, meet on company time on a weekly or monthly basis to provide advice or make suggestions to management concerning specific issues, such as plant safety, customer relations, or product quality.[34] And while they offer advice and suggestions, they do not have the authority to make decisions. Membership on these teams is often voluntary, but members may be selected because of their expertise. The idea behind employee involvement teams is that the people closest to the problem or situation are best able to recommend solutions.

employee involvement team
team that provides advice or makes suggestions to management concerning specific issues

Semi-autonomous work groups not only provide advice and suggestions to management, but they also have the authority to make decisions and solve problems related to the major tasks required to produce a product or service. Semi-autonomous groups regularly receive information about budgets, work quality, and performance, as well as competitors' products. Furthermore, members of semi-autonomous work groups are typically cross trained in a number of different skills and tasks. In short, semi-autonomous work groups give employees the autonomy to make decisions that are typically made by supervisors and managers.

semi-autonomous work group
group that has the authority to make decisions and solve problems related to the major tasks of producing a product or service

However, that authority is not complete. Managers still play a role, though much reduced compared to traditional work groups, in supporting the work of semi-autonomous work groups. At the Ritz-Carlton, Kansas City, where semi-autonomous work groups were implemented, long-time manager Sandi Shartzer, director of housekeeping, said, "I had attendants who for 22 years had been told where to go, what to do. Now they're being told to do it on their own. Sure, the staff still runs to me occasionally, but they're learning to 'own' their own responsibility. I even had one worker tell me today that she's setting goals for herself." Hotel manager Bob Schrader reinforced Shartzer's view of the Ritz's semi-autonomous work groups. Schrader said, "My role is to be out on the floor, not sit in my office and look at paperwork. I attend team meetings and try to get people comfortable about approaching me on issues, but then a lot of my job is directing people back to their teams for solutions. A lot of what I should be doing now is asking questions instead of dictating methods."[35]

Self-managing teams are different from semi-autonomous work groups in that team members manage and control all the major tasks directly related to production of a product or service without first getting approval from management. This includes managing and controlling the acquisition of materials, making a product or providing a service, and ensuring timely delivery. For example, Alcoa uses self-managing teams at its aluminum smelter in Deschambault, Quebec. Each team has 10 to 15 people and the management of the team rotates amongst the members. The team leader is responsible for matters such as training, budgeting, vacation scheduling, performance appraisal, and accident prevention.[36]

self-managing team
team that manages and controls all the major tasks of producing a product or service

Self-designing teams have all the characteristics of self-managing teams, but they can also control and change the design of the teams themselves, the tasks they do and how they do them, and who belongs to the teams. At the GE Aerospace Engines manufacturing plant in Durham, North Carolina, which makes jet engines, all workers have e-mail addresses, access to the Internet, their own voicemail boxes, business cards, and their own desks, all of which are extremely uncommon for factory workers. Team member Duane Williams said, "We had to come up with a schedule. We had the chance to order tools, tool carts, and so on. We had to figure out the *flow of the assembly line* [emphasis added] that makes the engine. We were put on councils for every part of the business." Williams went on to say, "I was never valued that much as an employee in my life. I had never been at the point where I couldn't wait to get to work. Here, I couldn't wait to get to work every day."[37]

self-designing team
team that has the characteristics of self-managing teams but that also controls team design, work tasks, and team membership

Special Kinds of Teams

There are a number of other kinds of teams that can't be easily categorized with regard to autonomy. In other words, depending on how these teams are designed, they can be either low- or high-autonomy teams. Nonetheless, companies are increasingly using these teams. These special kinds of teams are cross-functional teams, virtual teams, and project teams.

cross-functional team
team composed of employees from different functional areas of the organization

Cross-functional teams are purposively composed of employees from different functional areas of the organization.[38] Because their members have different functional backgrounds, education, and experience, cross-functional teams usually attack problems from several perspectives and generate more ideas and alternative solutions, all of which are especially important when trying to innovate or do creative problem solving.[39] Cross-functional teams can be used almost anywhere in an organization and are often used in conjunction with matrix and product organizational structures. They can also be used with either part-time or temporary team assignments, or they can be used with full-time, long-term teams.

virtual team
team composed of geographically and/or organizationally dispersed co-workers who use telecommunications and information technologies to accomplish an organizational task

Virtual teams are groups of geographically and/or organizationally dispersed co-workers who use a combination of telecommunications and information technologies to accomplish an organizational task.[40] In other words, members of virtual teams rarely meet face to face. The idea of virtual teams is relatively new and has been made possible by advances in communications and technology, such as e-mail, the World Wide Web, videoconferencing, and other products. Virtual teams can be employee involvement teams, self-managing teams, or nearly any kind of team discussed in this chapter. Virtual teams are often (but not necessarily) temporary teams that are set up to accomplish a specific task.[41] At Nortel, permanent virtual teams are used. The director of human resources at Nortel uses teleconferencing and a variety of computer software to hold same-time meetings with her international management team, which is located around the world.[42] She can talk to her staff while simultaneously displaying information on their individual computer screens.

The principal advantage of virtual teams is that they are very flexible. Employees can work with each other, regardless of physical location, time zone, or organizational affiliation.[43] In addition, virtual teams have certain efficiency advantages over traditional team structures. Because the teammates do not meet face to face, the time commitment involved in participating in a virtual team is typically not as great as for a traditional team. Moreover, employees can fulfill the responsibilities of their virtual team membership from the comfort of their own offices, without the travel time or downtime typically required by "real" face-to-face meetings.[44]

A drawback of virtual teams is that the team members must learn to express themselves in new contexts. For example, the give-and-take that naturally occurs in face-to-face meetings is more difficult to achieve through videoconferencing or other methods of virtual teaming. In addition, several studies have shown that physical proximity enhances information processing.[45] Virtual teams have to devise ways to overcome these shortcomings.

project team
team created to complete specific, one-time projects or tasks within a limited time

Project teams are created to complete specific, one-time projects or tasks within a limited time.[46] Project teams are often used to develop new products, to significantly improve existing products, to roll out new information systems, or to build new factories or offices. The project team is typically led by a project manager, who has the overall responsibility for planning, staffing, and managing the team. For example, Montreal-based Au Dragon Forge formed a project team to help develop a new manufacturing process for walkway components for Toronto's new airport terminals that had to be manufactured to very high specifications.[47]

Because project tasks are often unique, project teams are often staffed by employees from different functional areas and may also include members from the company's suppliers or customers.

One advantage of project teams is that drawing employees from different functional areas can reduce or eliminate communication barriers. In turn, free-flowing communication encourages cooperation among separate departments and typically speeds up the design process. Another advantage of project teams is their flexibility. When projects are finished, project team members either move on to the next project or return to their functional units. For example, publication of this book required designers, editors, graphic artists, and Web designers, among others. When the task was finished, these people applied their skills to other text assignments. Because of this flexibility, project teams are often used with the matrix organizational designs discussed in Chapter 11.

Review 2: Kinds of Teams

Companies use different kinds of teams to make themselves more competitive. Autonomy is the key dimension that makes teams different. Traditional work groups (that execute tasks) and employee involvement groups (that make suggestions) have the lowest levels of autonomy. Semi-autonomous work groups (that control major, direct tasks) have more autonomy, followed by self-managing teams (that control all direct tasks) and self-designing teams (that control membership and how tasks are done), which have the highest levels of autonomy. Cross-functional, virtual, and project teams are common, but not easily categorized with regard to autonomy. Cross-functional teams combine employees from different functional areas to help teams attack problems from several perspectives and generate more ideas and solutions. Virtual teams use telecommunications and information technologies to bring co-workers "together," regardless of physical location or time zone. Virtual teams reduce travel and work time, but communication may suffer since team members don't work face-to-face. Finally, project teams are used for specific, one-time projects or tasks that must be completed within a limited time. Project teams reduce communication barriers and promote flexibility, as teams and team members are reassigned to their departments or new projects as old projects are completed.

Managing Work Teams

Operations manager: Why did I ever let you talk me into teams? They're nothing but trouble. I have to spend all my time in training and meetings, and we're behind on our production schedule.

Human resources manager: Hey, you were the one who wanted to try teams, remember? We went to visit that car company and you fell in love with their program.

Operations manager: I know, but obviously there's something wrong here. Maybe the car people were giving us a song and dance.

HR manager: I don't know about that. Maybe we ought to look at ourselves. What is it we're doing that's causing the problem?[48]

"Why did I ever let you talk me into teams?" Lots of managers have this reaction after making the move to teams. However, many don't realize that this reaction is normal, both for them and for workers. In fact, such a reaction is characteristic of the storming stage of team development. Managers who are familiar with these stages and with the other important characteristics of teams will be better prepared to manage the predictable changes that occur when companies make the switch to team-based structures.

After reading the next two sections, you should be able to

3 understand the general characteristics of work teams.

4 explain how to enhance work team effectiveness.

3 WORK TEAM CHARACTERISTICS

Understanding the characteristics of work teams is a requirement for making teams an effective part of an organization.

Therefore, in this section you'll learn about team norms, team cohesiveness, team size, team conflict, and stages of team development.

Team Norms

norms
informally agreed-on standards that regulate team behaviour

Over time, teams develop **norms**, informally agreed-on standards that regulate team behaviour.[49] Norms are valuable because they let team members know what is expected of them. Studies indicate that norms are one of the most powerful influences on work behaviour. Team norms are often associated with positive outcomes, such as stronger organizational commitment, more trust in management, and stronger job and organizational satisfaction.[50] In general, effective work teams develop norms about the quality and timeliness of job performance, absenteeism, safety, and honest expression of ideas and opinions. The power of norms also comes from the fact that they regulate the everyday kinds of behaviours that allow teams to function effectively. For example, when General Motors changed its Oshawa plant from a traditional production line to one that used a team-based approach, the various teams quickly established and accepted a standard production pace, or team norm.[51]

However, norms can also influence team behaviour in negative ways. For example, most people would agree that "damaging organizational property," "saying or doing something to hurt someone at work," "purposively doing one's work badly, incorrectly, or slowly," "griping about co-workers," "deliberately bending or breaking rules," or "doing something to harm the company or your boss" are negative behaviours. However, a study of workers from 34 teams in 20 different organizations found that teams with negative norms strongly influenced their team members to engage in these negative behaviours. In fact, the longer they were a member of a team with negative norms, and the more frequently they interacted with their teammates, the more likely individual team members were to perform negative behaviours. Since team norms typically develop early in the life of a team, these results indicate how important it is for teams to establish positive norms from the outset.[52]

Team Cohesiveness

cohesiveness
the extent to which team members are attracted to a team and motivated to remain in it

Cohesiveness is another important characteristic of work teams. **Cohesiveness** is the extent to which team members are attracted to a team and motivated to remain in it.[53] Burlington Northern Railroad's intermodal team, which was charged with finding efficient ways to combine transportation through trucks and trains, was a particularly cohesive team. Dave Burns, a member of that team, said, "In my mind, the key word to this team was 'shared.' We shared everything. There was a complete openness among us. And the biggest thing that we shared was an objective and a strategy that we had put together jointly. That was our benchmark every day. Were we doing things in support of *our* plan."[54]

The level of cohesiveness that exists in a group is important for several reasons. To start, cohesive groups have a better chance of retaining their members. As a result, cohesive groups typically experience lower turnover.[55] In addition, team cohesiveness promotes cooperative behaviour, generosity, and a willingness on the part of team members to assist each other.[56] When team cohesiveness is high, team members are more motivated to contribute to the team, because they want to gain the approval of other team members. As a result of these reasons and others, studies have clearly established that cohesive teams are consistently better performing teams.[57] Furthermore, cohesive teams quickly achieve high levels of performance. By contrast, it takes teams low in cohesion much longer to reach the same levels of performance.[58]

What can be done to promote team cohesiveness? First, make sure that all team members are present at team meetings and activities. Team cohesiveness suffers when

© PHOTODISC/GETTY IMAGES

Participation in nonwork activities, such as sports and recreation, helps build team cohesiveness.

members are allowed to withdraw from the team and miss team meetings and events.[59] Second, create additional opportunities for teammates to work together by rearranging work schedules and creating common workspaces. When task interdependence is high and team members have lots of chances to work together, team cohesiveness tends to increase.[60] Third, engaging in nonwork activities as a team can help build cohesion.

Team Size

There appears to be a curvilinear relationship between team size and performance. In other words, very small or very large teams may not perform as well as moderately sized teams. For most teams, the right size is somewhere between six and nine members.[62] This size is conducive to high team cohesion, which has a positive effect on team performance as discussed above. Teams of this size are small enough for the team members to get to know each other, and for each member to have an opportunity to contribute in a meaningful way to the success of the team. However, they're also large enough to take advantage of team members' diverse skills, knowledge, and perspectives. It is also easier to instill a sense of responsibility and mutual accountability in teams of this size.[63]

By contrast, when teams get too large, team members find it difficult to get to know one another and may splinter into smaller subgroups. When this occurs, subgroups sometimes argue and disagree, weakening overall team cohesion. As teams grow, there is a greater chance of *minority domination,* where just a few team members dominate team discussions. Even if minority domination doesn't occur, there still isn't as much time in larger groups for all team members to share their input. And when team members feel that their contributions are unimportant or not needed, the result is less involvement, effort, and accountability to the team.[64] Large teams also face logistical problems, such as finding an appropriate time or place to meet. Finally, the incidence of social loafing, discussed earlier in the chapter, is much higher in large teams. All these factors indicate how large teams can have a negative impact on team performance.

While teams should not be too large, it's also important that they not be too small. Teams with just a few people may lack the diversity of skills and knowledge found in larger teams. Also, teams that are too small are unlikely to gain the advantages of team decision-making (i.e., multiple perspectives, generating more ideas and alternative solutions, and stronger commitment) found in larger teams.

WHAT REALLY WORKS

Cohesion and Team Performance[61]

Have you ever worked in a really cohesive group where everyone really liked and enjoyed each other and was glad to be part of the group? It's great. By contrast, have you ever worked in a group where everyone really disliked each other and was unhappy to be a part of the group? It's terrible. Anyone who has had either of these experiences can appreciate how important group cohesion is and the effect it can have on team performance. Indeed, 46 studies based on 1279 groups confirm that cohesion does matter.

TEAM PERFORMANCE

On average, there is a 66 percent chance that cohesive teams will outperform less cohesive teams.

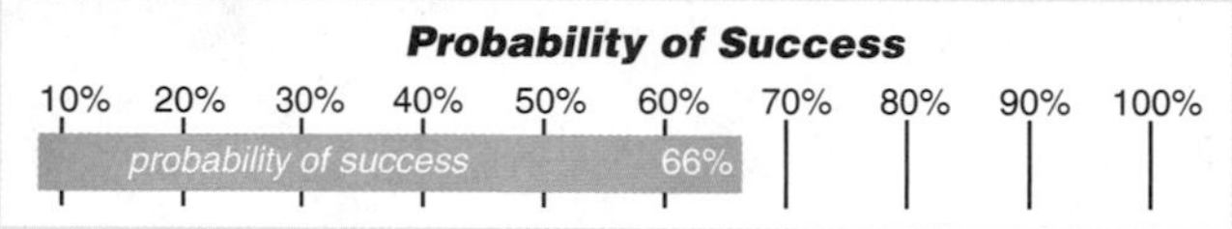

TEAM PERFORMANCE WITH INTERDEPENDENT TASKS

Teams work best for interdependent tasks that require people to work together to get the job done. When teams perform interdependent tasks, there is a 73 percent chance that cohesive teams will outperform less cohesive teams.

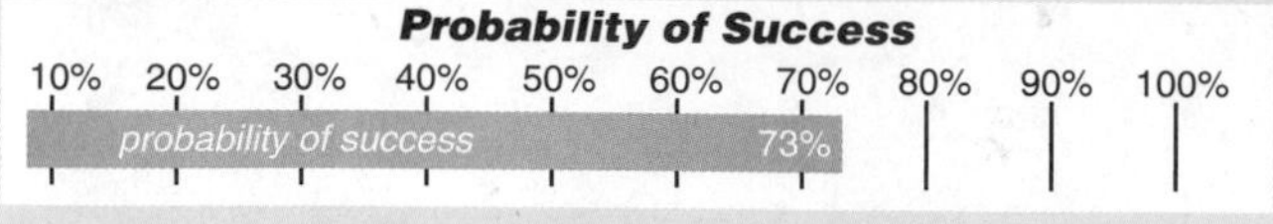

TEAM PERFORMANCE WITH INDEPENDENT TASKS

Teams are generally not suited for independent tasks in which people can accomplish the job by themselves. When teams perform independent tasks, there is only a 60 percent chance that cohesive teams will outperform less cohesive teams.

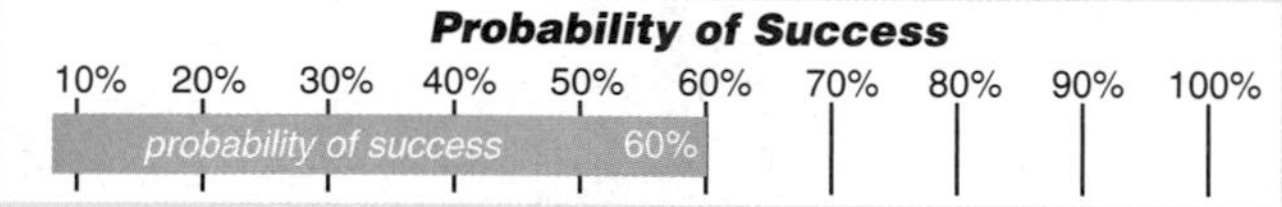

Some caution is warranted in interpreting these results. For example, there is always the possibility that a team could become so cohesive that its team goals become more important than organizational goals. Also, teams sometimes unite around negative goals and norms that are harmful rather than helpful to organizations. However, there is also room for even more optimism about cohesive teams. Teams that are cohesive and committed to the goals they are asked to achieve should have an even higher probability of success than the numbers shown here.

What signs indicate that a team's size needs to be changed? If decisions are taking too long, if it is difficult for the team to make decisions or take action, if the team is dominated by a few members, or if the commitment or efforts of team members are weak, chances are the team is too big. However, if a team is having difficulty coming up with ideas or generating solutions, or if the team does not have the expertise to address a specific problem, chances are the team is too small.

Team Conflict

Conflict and disagreement are inevitable in most teams. But this shouldn't surprise anyone. From time to time, people who work together are going to disagree about what and how things get done. What causes conflict in teams? While almost anything can lead to conflict—casual remarks that unintentionally offend a team member or fighting over scarce resources—the primary cause of team conflict is disagreement over team goals and priorities.[65] Other common causes of team conflict include disagreements over task-related issues, interpersonal incompatibilities, and simple fatigue.

While most people view conflict negatively, the key to dealing with team conflict is not avoiding conflict, but making sure that teams experience the right kind of conflict. In Chapter 6, you learned about *c-type conflict*, or cognitive conflict, which focuses on problem-related differences of opinion, and *a-type conflict*, or affective conflict, which refers to the emotional reactions that can occur when disagreements become personal rather than professional.[66] Cognitive conflict is strongly associated with improvements in team performance, while affective conflict is strongly associated with decreases in team performance.[67] Why does this happen? With cognitive conflict, team members disagree because their different experiences and expertise lead them to different views of the problem and solutions. Indeed, managers who participated on teams that emphasized cognitive conflict described their teammates as "smart," "team players," and "best in the business." They described their teams as "open," "fun," and "productive." One manager summed up the positive attitude that team members had about cognitive conflict by saying, "We scream a lot, then laugh, and then resolve the issue."[68] Thus, cognitive conflict is also characterized by a willingness to examine, compare, and reconcile differences to produce the best possible solution.

By contrast, affective conflict often results in hostility, anger, resentment, distrust, cynicism, and apathy. Managers who participated on teams that emphasized affective conflict described their teammates as "manipulative," "secretive," "burned out," and "political."[69] Not surprisingly, affective conflict can make people uncomfortable and cause them to withdraw and decrease their commitment to a team.[70] Affective conflict also lowers the satisfaction of team members, may lead to personal hostility between co-workers, and can decrease team cohesiveness.[71] So, unlike cognitive conflict, affective conflict undermines team effectiveness by preventing teams from engaging in the kinds of activities that are critical to team effectiveness.

So what can managers do to manage team conflict? First, managers need to realize that emphasizing cognitive conflict alone won't be enough. Studies show that cognitive and affective conflicts often occur together in the same teams! Therefore, sincere attempts to reach agreement on a difficult issue can quickly deteriorate from cognitive to affective conflict if the discussion turns personal and tempers and emotions flare. So while cognitive conflict is clearly the better approach to take, efforts to engage in cognitive conflict should be approached with caution.

Can teams disagree and still get along? Fortunately, they can. In an attempt to study this issue, researchers examined team conflict in 12 high-tech companies. In 4 of the 12 companies, work teams used cognitive conflict to address work problems but did so in a way that minimized the occurrence of affective conflict. Exhibit 12.3 shows what steps these teams took to be able to have a "good fight."[72]

Stages of Team Development

As teams develop and grow, they pass through four stages of development. As shown in Exhibit 12.4, those stages are forming, storming, norming, and performing.[73] While not every team passes through each of these stages, teams that do tend to be better performers.[74] This holds true even for teams composed of seasoned executives. However, after a period of time, if not managed well, performance may start to deteriorate as teams begin a process of decline, in which they progress through the stages of de-norming, de-storming, and de-forming.[75]

forming
the first state of team development in which team members meet each other, form initial impressions, and begin to establish team norms

Forming is the initial stage of team development. This is the getting-acquainted stage, where team members first meet each other, form initial impressions, and try to get

EXHIBIT 12.3
How Teams Can Have a Good Fight

1.	Work with more, rather than less, information.
2.	Develop several alternatives to enrich debate.
3.	Establish common goals.
4.	Inject humour into the workplace.
5.	Maintain a balance of power.
6.	Resolve issues without forcing a consensus.

Source: K.M. Eisenhardt, J.L. Kahwajy, & L.J. Bourgeois III, "How Management Teams Can Have a Good Fight," *Harvard Business Review* 75, no. 4 (July/August 1997): 77–87.

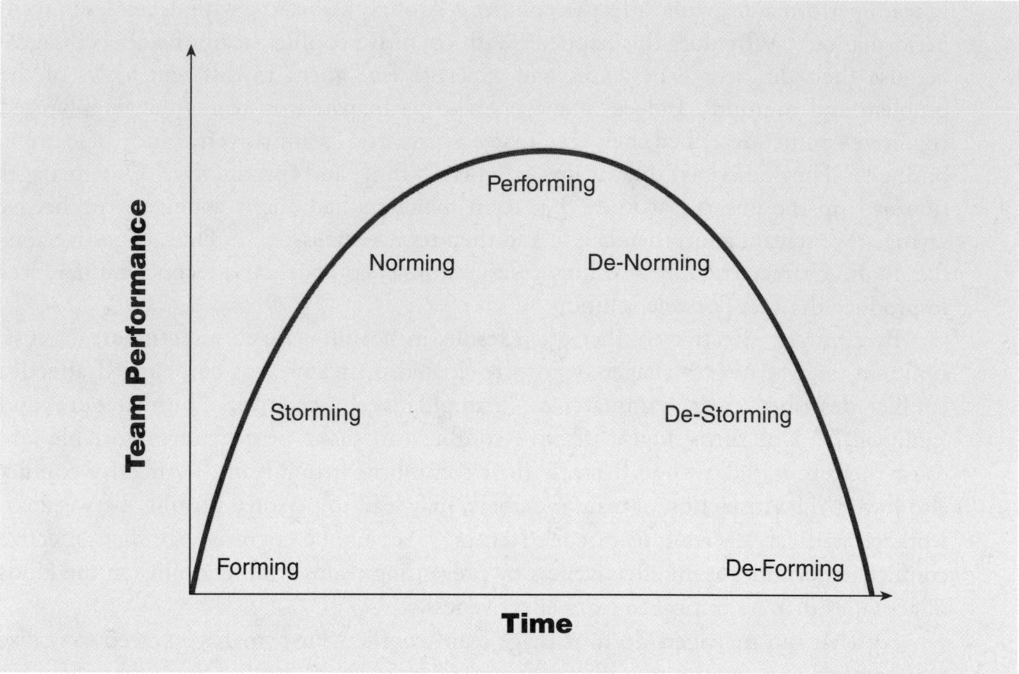

EXHIBIT 12.4
Stages of Team Development

Sources: J.F. McGrew, J.G. Bilotta, & J.M. Deeney, "Software Team Formation and Decay: Extending the Standard Model for Small Groups," *Small Group Research* 30, no. 2 (1999): 209–234. B.W. Tuckman, "Development Sequence in Small Groups," *Psychological Bulletin* 63, no. 6 (1965): 384–399.

a sense of what it will be like to be part of the team. Some of the first team norms will be established during this stage, as team members begin to find out what behaviours will and won't be accepted by the team. Team leaders should allow enough time for team members to get to know each other during this stage and should set early ground rules and begin to set up a preliminary team structure.

storming
the second stage of team development, characterized by conflict and disagreement, in which team members disagree over what the team should do and how it should do it

Conflicts and disagreements often characterize the second stage of team development, **storming**. As team members begin working together, different personalities and work styles may clash. Team members become more assertive at this stage and more willing to state opinions. This is also the stage when team members jockey for position and try to establish a favourable role for themselves in the team. In addition, team members are likely to disagree about what the group should do and how it should do it. Team performance is still relatively low, given that team cohesion is weak and team members are still reluctant to support each other. Since teams that get stuck in the storming stage are almost always ineffective, it is important for team leaders to focus the team on team goals and on improving team performance. Team members need to be particularly patient and tolerant with each other in this stage.

norming
the third stage of team development, in which team members begin to settle into their roles, group cohesion grows, and positive team norms develop

During **norming**, the third stage of team development, team members begin to settle into their roles as team members. Positive team norms will have developed by this stage, and teammates should know what to expect from each other. Petty differences should also have been resolved, friendships will have developed, and group cohesion will be relatively strong. At this point, team members will have accepted team goals, will be operating as a unit, and, as indicated by the increase in performance, will be working together effectively. This stage can be very short and is often characterized by someone in the team saying, "I think things are finally coming together." However, teams may also cycle back and forth between storming and norming several times before finally settling into norming.

performing
the fourth stage of team development, in which performance improves because the team has matured into an effective, fully functioning team

In the last stage of team development, **performing**, performance improves because the team has finally matured into an effective, fully functioning team. At this point, members should be fully committed to the team and think of themselves as "members of a team" and not just "employees." Team members often become intensely loyal to one another at this stage and feel mutual accountability for team successes and failures. Trivial disagreements, which can take time and energy away from the work of the team, should be rare. At this stage, teams get a lot of work done, and it is fun to be a team member.

However, after a period of time, if not managed well, performance may begin to decline, as teams progress through the stages of de-norming, de-storming, and de-forming.[76] Indeed, John Puckett, manufacturing vice president for circuit board maker XEL Communications, said, "The books all say you start in this state of chaos and march through these various stages, and you end up in this state of ultimate self-direction, where everything is going just great. They never tell you it can go back in the other direction, sometimes just as quickly."[77]

In **de-norming**, which is a reversal of the norming stage, team performance begins to decline as the size, scope, goal, or members of the team change. With new members joining the group, older members may become defensive as established ways of doing things are questioned and challenged. Expression of ideas and opinions becomes less open. New members change team norms by actively rejecting or passively neglecting previously established team roles and behaviours.

de-norming
a reversal of the norming stage, in which team performance begins to decline as the size, scope, goal, or members of the team change

In **de-storming**, which is a reversal of the storming phase, the team's comfort level decreases. Team cohesion weakens as more group members resist conforming to team norms and quit participating in team activities. Angry emotions flare as the group explodes in conflict and moves into the final stage of de-forming.

de-storming
a reversal of the storming phase, in which the team's comfort level decreases, team cohesion weakens, and angry emotions and conflict may flare

In **de-forming**, which is a reversal of the forming stage, team members position themselves to gain control of pieces of the team. Team members begin to avoid each other and isolate themselves from team leaders. Team performance rapidly declines as the team quits caring about even minimal requirements of team performance.

de-forming
a reversal of the forming stage, in which team members position themselves to control pieces of the team, avoid each other, and isolate themselves from team leaders

If teams are actively managed, decline is not inevitable. However, managers need to recognize that the forces at work in the de-norming, de-storming, and de-forming stages represent a powerful, disruptive, and real threat to teams that have finally made it to the performing stage. Getting to the performing stage is half the battle. Staying there is the second half.

Review 3: Work Team Characteristics

The most important characteristics of work teams are team norms, cohesiveness, size, conflict, and development. Norms let team members know what is expected of them and can influence team behaviour in positive and negative ways. Positive team norms are associated with organizational commitment, trust, and job satisfaction. Team cohesiveness helps teams retain members, promotes cooperative behaviour, increases motivation, and facilitates team performance. Attending team meetings and activities, creating opportunities to work together, and engaging in nonwork activities can increase cohesiveness. Team size has a curvilinear relationship with team performance, such that very small or very large teams do not perform as well as moderately sized teams of six to nine members. Teams of this size are cohesive and small enough for team members to get to know each other and contribute in a meaningful way, but are large enough to take advantage of team members' diverse skills, knowledge, and perspectives. Conflict and disagreement are inevitable in most teams. The key to dealing with team conflict is to maximize cognitive conflict, which focuses on issue-related differences, and minimize affective conflict, the emotional reactions that occur when disagreements become personal rather than professional. As teams develop and grow, they pass through four stages of development: forming, storming, norming, and performing. However, after a period of time, if not managed well, performance may decline, as teams progress through the stages of de-norming, de-storming, and de-forming.

4 ENHANCING WORK TEAM EFFECTIVENESS

Making teams work is a challenging and difficult process. However, companies can increase the likelihood that teams will succeed by carefully setting team goals and priorities, selecting people for teamwork, training the team, and addressing team compensation and recognition.[78]

Setting Team Goals and Priorities

In Chapter 4 you learned that specific, measurable, attainable, results-oriented, and time-bounded (i.e., S.M.A.R.T.) goals are one of the most effective means for improving individual job performance. Fortunately, team goals also improve team performance. In fact, team goals lead to much higher team performance 93 percent of the time.[79] For example, Nucor Steel sets specific, challenging goals for each of its production teams, which consist of first-line supervisors and production and maintenance workers. Each day these teams are challenged to produce a specific amount of high-quality steel.[80] Teams that meet their goals earn daily bonuses that can double their base salaries.

Why is the setting of specific, challenging team goals so critical to team success? One reason is that increasing a team's performance is inherently more complex than just increasing one individual's job performance. For instance, consider that for any team there are likely to be at least four different kinds of goals: each member's goal for the team, each member's goal for himself or herself on the team, the team's goal for each member, and the team's goal for itself.[81] In other words, without a specific, challenging goal for the team itself (the last of the four goals listed), these other goals may encourage team members to head off in 12 different directions at once. Consequently, setting a specific, challenging goal *for the team* clarifies team priorities by providing a clear focus and purpose.

Specific, challenging team goals also regulate how hard team members work. In particular, challenging team goals greatly reduce the incidence of social loafing. When faced with difficult goals, team members simply expect everyone to contribute. Consequently, they are much more likely to notice and complain if a teammate isn't doing his or her share. In fact, when teammates know each other well, when team goals are specific, when team communication is good, and when teams are rewarded for team performance (discussed below), there is only a 1 in 16 chance that teammates will be social loafers.[82]

What can companies and teams do to ensure that team goals lead to superior team performance? One increasingly popular approach is to give teams stretch goals. *Stretch goals*, as discussed in Chapter 4, are extremely ambitious goals that workers don't know how to reach.[83] The purpose of stretch goals is to achieve extraordinary improvements in performance by forcing managers and workers to throw away old comfortable solutions and adopt radical, never-used solutions. Home Depot's CEO, Bob Nardelli, who set a stretch goal to double revenues from $50 to $100 billion in just five years, explains stretch goals this way: "I think what has served us well [at Home Depot] is setting not unrealistic goals but challenging goals. If you set aggressive stretch goals and develop a plan and put the right leadership in place, you start to see realization. Now, will we get there as fast as we want to? Maybe not. But we will get there faster than we would have."[84]

Four things must occur for stretch goals to effectively motivate teams.[85] First, teams must have a high degree of autonomy or control over how they achieve their goals. Second, teams must be empowered with control resources, such as budgets, workspaces,

Home Depot employs stretch goals to improve its performance.

computers, or whatever they need to do their jobs. Steve Kerr, General Electric's "chief learning officer," said, "We have a moral obligation to try to give people the tools to meet tough goals. I think it's totally wrong if you don't give employees the tools to succeed, then punish them when they fail."[86]

Third, teams need structural accommodation. **Structural accommodation** means giving teams the ability to change organizational structures, policies, and practices if it helps them meet their stretch goals. When Hewlett-Packard imposed tough goals on its customer service teams, one of the unintended consequences was a big increase in work stress from being called to customer sites on weekends and at all hours of the night. As a result, overworked customer service engineers began quitting their jobs, making it unlikely that the teams could achieve their stretch goals. HP responded by giving teams the ability to "reinvent work" in a way that would meet the stretch goals, but reduce worker stress. The teams decided to throw out existing policies on employee work hours and simply asked who would be willing to work Fridays through Mondays and who would be willing to work Tuesdays through Fridays. Stress dropped immediately, and employees stopped quitting their jobs.[87]

structural accommodation the ability to change organizational structures, policies, and practices

Finally, teams need bureaucratic immunity. **Bureaucratic immunity** means that teams no longer have to go through the frustratingly slow process of multilevel reviews and signoffs to get management approval before making changes. Once granted bureaucratic immunity, teams are immune from the influence of various organizational groups and are only accountable to top management. Therefore, teams can act quickly and even experiment with little fear of failure. KI Pembroke, a small Canadian filing-cabinet manufacturer, operates with 11 self-directed work teams with 10 members each. These teams have complete control over the area they are responsible for, whether health and safety, scheduling, or cost control. With no middle managers, each team must report to senior management, thereby providing them with bureaucratic immunity.[88]

bureaucratic immunity the ability to make changes without first getting approval from managers or other parts of an organization

Selecting People for Teamwork

University of Southern California Professor Edward Lawler said, "People are very naive about how easy it is to create a team. Teams are the Ferraris of work design. They're high performance but high maintenance and expensive."[89] It's almost impossible to make effective work teams without carefully selecting people who are suited for teamwork or for working on a particular team. A preference for teamwork, team elevation, and team diversity can help companies choose the right team members.[90]

Are you more comfortable working alone or with others? If you strongly prefer to work alone, you may not be well suited for teamwork. Indeed, studies show that job satisfaction is higher in teams when team members prefer working with others.[91] An indirect way to measure someone's *preference for teamwork* is to assess the person's degree of individualism or collectivism. **Individualism-collectivism** is the degree to which a person believes that people should be self-sufficient and that loyalty to one's self is more important than loyalty to one's team or company.[92] *Individualists,* who put their welfare and interests first, generally prefer independent tasks in which they work alone. On the other hand, *collectivists,* who put group or team interests ahead of self-interests, generally prefer interdependent tasks in which they work with others. Collectivists would also rather cooperate than compete and are fearful of disappointing team members or of being ostracized from teams. Given these differences, it makes sense to select team members who are collectivists rather than individualists. Indeed, many companies use individualism-collectivism as an initial screening device for team members. However, as discussed below, individualists may be appropriate if team diversity is desired. To determine your preference for teamwork, take the Team Player Inventory shown in Exhibit 12.5.

individualism-collectivism the degree to which a person believes that people should be self-sufficient and that loyalty to one's self is more important than loyalty to one's team or company

Team level is the average level of ability, experience, personality, or any other factor on a team. For example, a high level of team experience means that a team has particularly experienced team members. This does not mean that every member of the team has considerable experience, but that enough team members do to significantly raise the average level of experience on the team. Team level is used to guide selection of teammates when

team level the average level of ability, experience, personality, or any other factor on a team

	STRONGLY DISAGREE 1	2	3	4	5 STRONGLY AGREE
1. I enjoy working on team/group projects.	1	2	3	4	5
2. Team/group project work easily allows others to not "pull their weight."	1	2	3	4	5
3. Work that is done as a team/group is better than the work done individually.	1	2	3	4	5
4. I do my best work alone rather than in a team/group.	1	2	3	4	5
5. Team/group work is overrated in terms of the actual results produced.	1	2	3	4	5
6. Working in a team/group gets me to think more creatively.	1	2	3	4	5
7. Team/groups are used too often, when individual work would be more effective.	1	2	3	4	5
8. My own work is enhanced when I am in a team/group situation.	1	2	3	4	5
9. My experiences working in team/group situations have been primarily negative.	1	2	3	4	5
10. More solutions/ideas are generated when working in a team/group situation than when working alone.	1	2	3	4	5
Reverse score items 2, 4, 5, 7, and 9. Then add the scores for items 1–10.					
Higher scores indicate a preference for teamwork, while lower total scores indicate a preference for individual work.					

Source: T.J.B. Kline, "The Team Player Inventory: Reliability and Validity of a Measure of Predisposition toward Organizational Team-Working Environments," *Journal for Specialists in Group Work* 24, no. 1 (1999): 102–112.

EXHIBIT 12.5
The Team Player Inventory

teams need a particular set of skills or capabilities to do their jobs well. For example, at GE's Aerospace Engines manufacturing plant in Durham, North Carolina, everyone hired had to have a U.S. Federal Aviation Administration–certified mechanic's license. Following that, all applicants were tested in 11 different areas, only one of which involved those technical skills. Keith McKee, who works at the plant, said, "You have to be above the bar in all 11 of the areas: helping skills, team skills, communication skills, diversity, flexibility, coaching ability, work ethic, and so forth. Even if just one thing out of the 11 knocks you down, you don't come to work here."[93]

team diversity
the variances or differences in ability, experience, personality, or any other factor on a team

While team level represents the average level or capability on a team, **team diversity** represents the variances or differences in ability, experience, personality, or any other factor on a team. For example, teams with strong team diversity on job experience would have a mix of team members, ranging from seasoned veterans to people with three or four years of experience to rookies with little or no experience. Team diversity is used to guide selection of teammates when teams are asked to complete a wide range of different tasks or when tasks are particularly complex. Even demographic diversity can improve team performance. One study from 1995 to 2001 by the Conference Board of Canada found that Canadian companies with at least two female members on their board of directors were leaders in company revenue and profit.[94]

Team Training

Organizations that create work teams often underestimate the amount of training required to make teams effective. This mistake occurs frequently in successful organizations, where managers assume that if employees can work effectively on their own, they can work effectively in teams. However, companies that successfully use teams provide thousands of hours of training to make sure that teams work. When General Motors successfully changed its Oshawa plant to a team environment, it invested extensively in training in teamwork and problem-solving skills.[95]

The most common type of training provided to members of work teams is training in interpersonal skills. **Interpersonal skills**, such as listening, communicating, questioning, and providing feedback, enable people to have effective working relationships with others. When Super Sack, a maker of heavy-duty plastic bags for the food and pharmaceutical industries, first used teams, it failed. David Kellenberger, Super Sack's vice president of manufacturing, said, "One of our greatest mistakes at the beginning was our failure to recognize how important training was. You need to make a huge commitment of time and resources for training people in communication, goal-setting, and general team-building skills to make a successful transition [to teams]...."[96] Experiences like these are why Wilson Sporting Goods provides all of its first-year team members 26 hours of training on team interaction skills and how to run meetings.[97]

interpersonal skills
skills, such as listening, communicating, questioning, and providing feedback, that enable people to have effective working relationships with others

Because of their autonomy and responsibility, many companies give teams training in decision-making and problem-solving skills to help them do a better job of cutting costs and improving quality and customer service. Stacy Myers, a consultant who helps companies implement teams, said, "When we help companies move to teams, we also require that employees take basic quality and business knowledge classes as well. Teams must know how their work affects the company, and how their success will be measured."[98] Many organizations also teach teams conflict resolution skills. Consider the case of Delta Faucet:

> Teams at Delta Faucet have specific protocols for addressing conflict. For example, if an employee's behavior is creating a problem within a team, the team is expected to work it out without involving the team leader. Two team members will meet with the "problem" team member and work toward a resolution. If this is unsuccessful, the whole team meets and confronts the issue. If necessary, the team leader can be brought in to make a decision, but ... it is a rare occurrence for a team to reach that stage.[99]

Firms must also provide team members the technical training they need to do their jobs, particularly if they are expected to perform all the different jobs on the team (i.e., cross training). Before teams were created at Milwaukee Mutual Insurance, separate employees performed the tasks of rating, underwriting, and processing insurance policies. However, after extensive cross training, each team member can now do all three jobs.[100] Cross training is less appropriate for teams of highly skilled workers. For instance, it is unlikely that a group of engineers, computer programmers, and systems analysts would be cross-trained for each other's jobs.

Finally, companies need to provide training for team leaders, who often feel unprepared for their new duties. Exhibit 12.6 shows the top ten problems reported by new team leaders. These range from confusion about their new roles as team leaders (compared to their old jobs as managers or employees) to not knowing where to go for help when their teams have problems. The solution is extensive training for team leaders.

Team Compensation and Recognition

Compensating teams correctly is very difficult. For instance, one survey found that only 37 percent of companies were satisfied with their team compensation plans and even fewer, just 10 percent, reported being "very positive."[101] One of the problems, according to Monty Mohrman of the Center for Effective Organizations, is that "there is a very strong set of beliefs in most organizations that people should be paid for how well they do. So when people first get put into team-based organizations, they really balk at being paid for how well the team does. It sounds illogical to them. It sounds like their individuality and their sense of self-worth are being threatened."[102] Consequently, companies need to carefully choose a team compensation plan and then fully explain how teams will be rewarded. One basic requirement is that the level of rewards (individual vs. team)

1.	Confusion about their new roles and about what they should be doing differently.
2.	Feeling they've lost control.
3.	Not knowing what it means to coach or empower.
4.	Having personal doubts about whether the team concept will really work.
5.	Uncertainty about how to deal with employees' doubts about the team concept.
6.	Confusion about when a team is ready for more responsibility.
7.	Confusion about how to share responsibility and accountability with the team.
8.	Concern about promotional opportunities, especially about whether the "team leader" title carries any prestige.
9.	Uncertainty about the strategic aspects of the leader's role as teams mature.
10.	Not knowing where to turn for help with team problems, since few if any of their organization's leaders have led teams.

EXHIBIT 12.6
Top Ten Problems Reported by Team Leaders

Source: B. Filipczak, M. Hequet, C. Lee, M. Picard, & D. Stamps, "More Trouble with Teams," *Training*, October 1996, 21.

must match the level of performance (individual vs. team) for team compensation to work.

There are three methods of compensating employees for team participation and accomplishments. The first is called skill-based pay. **Skill-based pay** programs pay employees for learning additional skills or knowledge.[103] These programs encourage employees to acquire the additional skills they will need to perform several jobs within a team. For example, at XEL Communications, the number of skills each employee has mastered determines his or her individual pay. An employee who takes a class in advanced soldering (XEL makes circuit boards) followed by on-the-job training will earn 30 cents more per hour. Passing a written test or satisfactorily performing a skill or job for a supervisor or trainer certifies mastery of new skills and results in increased pay.[104]

skill-based pay
compensation system that pays employees for learning additional skills or knowledge

The second approach to compensating employees for team participation is through **gainsharing** programs, in which companies share the financial value of performance gains, such as productivity, cost savings, or quality, with their workers.[105] The first month that gainsharing was used at Rogan Corporation, a maker of plastic handles and knobs, employee teams saved the company $35 136, earning an additional $17 568 for themselves. They earned slightly more the second month. Since its inception, gainsharing has added 16 percent to 22 percent to the salaries of Rogan's employees, typically $4500 to $7500 per employee per year. But the company has benefited as well. Before gainsharing, employees produced an average of 95 000 knobs per employee each year. But after gainsharing, employees produced at more than twice that rate, turning out an average of 206 000 knobs per employee per year.[106]

gainsharing
compensation system in which companies share the financial value of performance gains, such as productivity, cost savings, or quality, with their workers

Nonfinancial rewards are another way to reward teams for their performance. These awards, which can range from vacation trips to T-shirts, plaques, and coffee mugs, are especially effective when coupled with management recognition.[107] At Motorola, each year several thousand teams enter a company-wide competition in which work teams review their past accomplishments and discuss their future goals. The final 24 teams make presentations to a panel of top managers at company headquarters. Becoming a finalist is quite prestigious and gives those employees unique exposure to Motorola's top managers. Likewise, NCR has a "Great Performance Award" that recognizes its top teams.[108]

Which team plan should your company use? In general, skill-based pay is most effective for self-managing and self-directing teams performing complex tasks. In these situations, the more each team member knows and can do, the better the whole team performs. By contrast, gainsharing works best in relatively stable environments where employees can focus on improving the productivity, cost savings, or quality of their current work system.

Finally, given the level of dissatisfaction with most team compensation systems, what compensation plans would today's managers like to use with the teams in their companies? Forty percent of managers would directly link merit pay increases to team performance, but allow adjustments within teams for differences in individual performance. By contrast, 13.7 percent would link merit-based increases directly to team performance, but would give each team member an equal share of the team's merit-based reward. Nineteen percent would use gainsharing plans based on quality, delivery, productivity, or cost reduction, and then provide equal payouts to all teams and team members. Fourteen and a half percent would use gainsharing, but would vary the team gainsharing award, depending on how much money the team saved the company. Payouts would still be equally distributed within teams. Finally, 12.2 percent of managers would opt for plantwide profit-sharing plans tied to overall company or division performance. In this case, there would be no payout distinctions between or within teams.[109]

Review 4: Enhancing Work Team Effectiveness

Companies can make teams more effective by setting team goals and managing how work team members are selected, trained, and compensated. Team goals provide a clear focus and purpose, reduce the incidence of social loafing, and lead to higher team performance 93 percent of the time. Extremely difficult stretch goals can be used to motivate teams as long as teams have autonomy, control over resources, structural accommodation, and bureaucratic immunity. Not everyone is suited for teamwork. When selecting team members, companies should select people who have a preference for teamwork (individualism-collectivism) and should consider the importance of team level (average ability on a team) and team diversity (different abilities on a team). Organizations that successfully use teams provide thousands of hours of training to make sure that teams work. The most common types of team training are for interpersonal decision-making and problem-solving skills, conflict resolution, technical training to help team members learn several jobs (i.e., cross training), and training for team leaders. There are three methods of compensating employees for team participation and accomplishments: skill-based pay, gainsharing, and nonfinancial rewards.

What Really Happened?[110]

It's almost impossible to make effective work teams without carefully selecting people who are suited for teamwork or for working on a particular team. When selecting team members, companies should select people who have a preference for teamwork (collectivism versus individualism) and should consider the importance of team level (average ability on a team) and team diversity (different abilities on a team).

For example, since the plant will be in a new location, you get to start with a brand new work force. What kinds of people should you hire for teamwork? What kinds of skills and experience will they need to succeed in a team environment?

In selecting workers for its team-based approach to manufacturing single-engine planes like the Skyhawk, Cessna focused exclusively on team skills. If tests indicated that you weren't a "team player" with an aptitude and willingness to take on responsibility and work with others, Cessna didn't hire you. However, because it is located in a small town, there was trouble finding experienced manufacturing workers. In fact, most of the people Cessna hired to work in the plant had never worked in a manufacturing setting before. In terms of team level, the average ability on a team, Cessna's production teams were extraordinarily good in terms of being strong team players, but extraordinarily bad in terms of manufacturing experience. Cessna was hoping it could quickly train its workers about manufacturing, but that took much longer than expected. For instance, Cessna hoped to produce 1000 single-engine planes in the factory's first year. But because of worker inexperience, it only produced 360 planes that year. In fact, it took four years for its inexperienced workers to produce 1000 planes per year. John Daniel, who directs assembly at the plant, said, "What we did was kick off the team concept with a whole new work force." It is because of that, "... every time we hit a new situation, it was grounds to shut everything down."

So, Cessna dealt with the problem by increasing team diversity, the variances or differences in ability, experience, personality, or any other factor on a team. For example, teams with strong team diversity on job experience would have a mix of team members, ranging from seasoned veterans to people with three or four years of experience to rookies with little or no experience. Since Cessna's single-engine production teams had no experience whatsoever, Cessna infused them with diversity by bringing in 60 retirees who had built Skyhawks before. Said Daniel, "We decided, 'Let's take a break from this team thing and make sure we know how to build the product.'" The mentors worked with teams, teaching them basic manufacturing skills, and instilling confidence. Slowly, production speed increased, without sacrificing quality, and the focus shifted back to teams and learning how to resolve conflict, solve problems, and increase flexibility. Eventually, Cessna's production teams will be highly skilled manufacturing workers and extraordinarily good at teamwork. With teams taking nearly twice as long as planned to build each single-engine plane, it will be some time before the plant is profitable and before it hits its long-term goal of producing 1500 planes per year. Clearly, teams can produce phenomenal results, but it takes time, training, and patience to achieve them. Moreover, good team skills aren't enough. It takes good team skills and experienced, capable workers for teams to produce their best.

If you decide to take the plunge and use teams, just how much authority and responsibility should you give them? Should they be limited to just advising management or should you make them totally responsible for quality, costs, and productivity?

Autonomy is the key dimension that makes teams different. Traditional work groups (that execute tasks) and employee involvement groups (that make suggestions) have the lowest levels of autonomy. Semi-autonomous work groups (that control major, direct tasks) have more autonomy, followed by self-managing teams (that control all direct tasks) and self-designing teams (that control membership and how tasks are done), which have the highest levels of autonomy.

Traditionally at Cessna, manufacturing employees were graded under a productivity system called "standard-hour attainment," in which industrial engineers would conduct time studies to determine how long it should take each worker to complete their job on an assembly line. Then actual production time was compared to those standards. If the standards were met, it was called "standard-hour attainment." If standards weren't met, workers were blamed for poor performance, even if the standards were unreasonable, or even if slowing down one's work would lead to higher quality. Even though Cessna's regular factory workers weren't organized as teams, we can still say that their autonomy was equivalent to traditional work groups because they only had authority to execute their tasks (see Exhibit 12.2, the Team Autonomy Continuum, on page 342).

When Cessna chose a team approach at its single-engine plane factory, its goal was to change from a "people-blaming" culture to a "process-oriented" culture, in which teams would have much more authority, and would own and control their work. It did that by creating semi-autonomous work teams that had the authority to execute tasks, give advice and make suggestions, and make decisions and solve problems on their own. Now, rather than engineers deciding the "standard" time that it takes to complete a task, teams decide the standard. More importantly, they don't just determine the time standards—they determine how the work gets done to best improve quality and lower costs.

Finally, while you're considering using teams on the assembly line, are there other places in which you might use teams? Not all teams are alike. Maybe there's someplace else in which teams could contribute to the success of Cessna's "new" single-engine plane manufacturing facility?

Besides traditional, employee-involvement, semi-autonomous, self-managing teams, and self-designing teams, which vary in degrees of autonomy (that control membership and how tasks are done), companies also use cross-functional teams, which combine employees from different functional areas to help teams attack problems from multiple perspectives and generate more ideas and solutions; virtual teams, which use telecommunication and information technologies to bring co-workers together regardless of physical location or time zone; and project teams, which are used for specific, one-time projects or tasks that must be completed within a limited time. So, in addition to production teams, where else might Cessna use teams?

Other than manufacturing, Cessna has used more teams in purchasing than any place else. In particular, it created cross-functional commodity teams with workers from seven different areas, purchasing, manufacturing engineering, quality engineering, product design engineering, reliability engineering, product support, and finance. Each commodity team created strategic plans dealing with make versus buy decisions, sourcing (who to buy from), plant and quality improvements, and training suppliers to reduce costs and increase quality. For example, Cessna has long been one of the most vertically integrated aviation manufacturers, meaning that it has typically produced most of the parts for its planes, rather than buying those parts from suppliers. Because of the cross-functional commodities teams, it began re-examining that strategy.

Mike Crabtree, Cessna's director of sustaining procurement, said, "We had to back up and look at ourselves from the standpoint of understanding what our key competencies were. It seemed that we were just doing too much. We had no idea what our real costs were. All that seemed to matter was that business was good and we were selling a ton of airplanes." So, when the cross-functional commodities teams examined make versus buy decisions, they worked for a year to determine what Cessna's core competencies were. In other words, what did Cessna build or do best? The committees looked at every major category of parts, from engines, to wings, to electronics, and took a hard look at Cessna's areas of expertise and production capabilities. In the end, they came up with groups of parts that could be completely outsourced to suppliers at a lower cost and higher quality. One of the first groups of parts to be outsourced was sheet and plate aluminum, which Cessna determined that Alcoa, the leading manufacturer of aluminum products, could do better and more cheaply than it could. Thanks to this agreement, Cessna got rid of its aluminum shearing division, and now pays less to buy aluminum precut to its rigorous specifications directly from Alcoa.

How well have the cross-functional commodities teams worked? Since their inception, quality is up 86 percent, on-time delivery performance has risen 28 percent, and inventories are down 52 percent, saving Cessna tens of millions of dollars in inventory costs each year.

Key Terms

bureaucratic immunity *(353)*
cohesiveness *(346)*
cross-functional team *(344)*
cross training *(337)*
de-forming *(351)*
de-norming *(351)*
de-storming *(351)*
employee involvement team *(343)*
forming *(349)*
gainsharing *(356)*
individualism-collectivism *(353)*
interpersonal skills *(355)*
norming *(350)*
norms *(346)*
performing *(350)*
project team *(344)*
self-designing team *(343)*
self-managing team *(343)*
semi-autonomous work group *(343)*
skill-based pay *(356)*
social loafing *(339)*
storming *(350)*
structural accommodation *(353)*
team diversity *(354)*
team level *(353)*
traditional work group *(342)*
virtual team *(344)*
work team *(336)*

Self-Assessment

WORKING IN GROUPS

From sports to school to work to civic involvement, working in teams is increasingly part of our experience. Even though teams are more and more common ways of getting work done, people still have widely varying opinions of their value. Think of your own situation. When a professor divides the class into groups to complete a project, do you respond with an inward smile or a heavy sigh? Do you enjoy team projects, or would you rather just do your own work? The Assessment Appendix has a 20-question survey that can give you insights into your thoughts about working in teams. Turn to page 518 and complete the assessment for some baseline information on your attitudes toward group work.

Management Decisions

A TEAM LEADER'S WORST NIGHTMARE[111]

"Okay, Ted, tell me one more time what happened." Ted Knight, a new employee just assigned to the Hard Disk Assembly Team, is sitting in your office on a Friday afternoon, and you can't believe what you're hearing.

Each member of the Hard Disk Assembly Team is responsible for assembling and testing hard disks that go into PCs. As a way of creating healthy competition among the team's six members, you've been recording each member's production output each day and posting it near the team's work area. At the end of each week, the team member who has assembled the most hard disks without a quality failure receives a $50 bonus.

You always thought that the competition had worked well. Several different team members had won the $50 bonus, production numbers were inching up, and no one had complained about the availability of extra cash. But Ted's story was making you heartsick. Ted joined the Hard Disk Assembly Team three weeks ago. His first two weeks were primarily training. But this week, Ted had a workstation of his own on the factory floor. Ted is a quick learner, which is one of the reasons you hired him. According to Ted, two of his teammates cornered him in a quiet corner of the snack room during his afternoon break. They told him that under no circumstances was he to assemble more than 30 hard disks during a single day. One of the employees, whom Ted was not willing to identify, told him, "We all work at a comfortable pace around here. If you assemble more than 30 hard disks a day, the team leader will expect us all to." Ted went on to say that the second employee told him, "And by the way, no one gets to win the weekly production award until they've been around for a while. If you are leading toward the end of the week, I'll let you know so you can slow down some."

You took a deep breath and looked Ted straight in the eye. "Ted, thanks for letting me know what's going on. I honestly had no idea that anything like this was happening. Give me the weekend, and on Monday morning I'll let you know what I am going to do."

Questions

1. If you were the team leader, what would you do? Would you call a team meeting and deal directly with this problem, or would you try a more subtle approach?
2. What about Ted? If you go to Ted's teammates and reveal what he told you, will he ever be accepted as a member of the team? Also, what about the weekly production award? Should you cancel it, allow it to continue as is, or change it in some way?

Management Decisions

YOU THOUGHT THAT AWARDING BONUSES WOULD BE EASY. THINK AGAIN.[112]

You've just reread the fifth e-mail message this month about the new team bonus plan. None of them has been positive. Two years ago, you switched your Credit Card Customer Service Centre to a team-based design. Prior to the switch, your employees had been assigned to traditional functional areas. But hoping to increase customer service and decrease costs, you eliminated the traditional departments and put your employees into teams. Now you have five teams to service your credit card customers. The teams are as follows:

Team 1	Handles routine requests for personal accounts
Team 2	Handles routine requests for corporate accounts
Team 3	Investigates requests for credit line increases
Team 4	Sells credit card protection insurance
Team 5	Investigates disputed charges

After you created work teams, your employees complained about the lack of team incentives. Basically, you were still paying employees an individually based merit increase plus a cost-of-living adjustment. Six months ago you decided to give team incentives a try. You challenged each team to increase its productivity by 5 percent per month. According to the new plan, teams that increased productivity by that amount would receive a $500 bonus to split among its team members.

But it hasn't worked. Here's the problem. Teams 1, 2, and 3 have won the bonus for each of the six months that the bonus has been in existence. Teams 4 and 5 have never won the bonus. You're getting the same complaint from every member of Teams 4 and 5 that you talk to. What they keep telling you is that it is easier for Teams 1, 2, and 3 to increase their productivity than it is for them. Teams 1 and 2 handle hundreds of routine calls every day. To increase productivity, all they have to do is move more quickly through their calls. Team 3 investigates requests for credit line increases. Because interest rates have been going down, they have gotten numerous requests and have been able to approve the majority of them. So these teams have been steadily increasing their productivity and have been awarded the $500 bonus each month.

However, according to members of Teams 4 and 5, it is not as easy for them to increase their productivity. Team 4 sells credit card protection insurance, which is a tough product to sell. Team 5 investigates disputed charges. It can sometimes take weeks to get to the bottom of a disputed charge. It is not a process that is easily rushed. As a result, despite their efforts, Teams 4 and 5 have never won the award. Instead, they continue to complain that the bonus program just isn't fair.

As you look up from your desk, a group of employees from Team 4 is waiting to see you. They had called earlier in the day and asked if they could stop by to talk about the bonus program. You are really tiring of this. You thought that awarding bonuses would be easy. What should you tell them?

Questions

1. Is the bonus compensation program fair? If not, would you scrap the program or revise it in some way?
2. Was the implementation of the bonus compensation plan handled appropriately in the first place? What could have been done initially to create a more equitable plan?

Develop Your Management Potential

A QUICK CHECK OF YOUR TEAM SKILLS[113]

To be part of an effective team, you have to be a good team member. However, sometimes it's hard to objectively judge our contributions in a team or group effort. Think about one of your most important team experiences. Were you an effective team member? Take the following test to find out. After you take the test, answer the questions below to begin thinking about how you can improve.

Instructions:

Step 1: Answer the following questions the way that you think other members of your team would if they were describing your actions.

Step 2: Total your score for each section. Then transfer all totals to the "Quick Check of My Team Skills" section at the conclusion of the exercise.

Scale:

1 = Almost never
2 = Seldom
3 = Sometimes
4 = Usually
5 = Almost always

I. Honour team values and agreements.

As a team member, I **Your score:**

a. Show appreciation for other team members' ideas. ______
b. Help other team members cope with change. ______
c. Encourage others to use their strengths. ______
d. Help the team develop a productive relationship with other teams. ______
e. Willingly assume a leadership role when needed. ______

Total: ______

II. Promote team development.

As a team member, I **Your score:**

a. Volunteer for all types of tasks, including the hard ones. ______
b. Help orient and train new team members. ______
c. Help organize and run effective meetings. ______
d. Help examine how we are doing as a team and make any necessary changes in the way we work together. ______
e. Help identify milestones and mini-successes to celebrate. ______

Total: ______

III. Help make team decisions.

As a team member, I **Your score:**

a. Analyze what a decision entails. ______
b. Ensure that the team selects and includes the appropriate people in the decision process. ______
c. Clearly state my concerns. ______
d. Search for common ground when team members have different views. ______
e. Actively support the team's decisions. ______

Total: ______

IV. Coordinate and carry out team tasks.

As a team member, I **Your score:**

a. Help identify the information, skills, and resources necessary to accomplish team tasks. ______
b. Help formulate and agree on a plan to meet performance goals. ______
c. Stay abreast of what is happening in other parts of the organization and bring that information to the team. ______
d. Find innovative ways to meet the needs of the team and of others in the organization. ______
e. Maintain a win-win outlook in all dealings with other teams. ______

Total: ______

V. Handle difficult issues with the team.

As a team member, I **Your score:**

a. Bring team issues and problems to the team's attention. ______
b. Encourage others on the team to state their views. ______
c. Help build trust among team members by speaking openly about the team's problems. ______
d. Give specific, constructive, and timely feedback to others. ______
e. Admit when I've made a mistake. ______

Total: ______

A Quick Check of My Team Skills

Category	Total Score
Honour team values and agreements.	______
Promote team development.	______
Help make team decisions.	______
Coordinate and carry out team tasks.	______
Handle difficult issues with the team.	______

Interpreting Scores

- A score of 20 or above in any activity indicates an area of strength.
- A score of 19 or below in any activity indicates an area that needs more attention.

Question

1. Looking at your scores, what areas are strengths? How can you maintain these strengths? What areas are weaknesses? What steps can you take to turn these areas into strengths?

Discussion Questions

1. Teams have both positive and negative aspects. When working in groups in your courses at college/university, what was good about working in groups? What was bad about working in groups? What could be done to improve group work processes?
2. In what sort of work environments do you think teams would work well? When wouldn't they work well?
3. What strategies might a manager use to overcome the problem of social loafing?
4. Why might employees resist the formation of teams? Why might managers resist the formation of teams?

Critical Thinking Video Case

CBC

Visit www.management2e.nelson.com to view this chapter's CBC video case.

Take Two

Biz Flix
Apollo 13

This film re-creates the heroic efforts of astronaut Jim Lovell (Tom Hanks), his crew, NASA, and Mission Control to return the damaged Apollo spacecraft to earth. Examples of both problem-solving and decision-making occur in almost every scene.

This scene takes place during day five of the mission, about two-thirds of the way through the film. Early in Apollo 13's mission, Jack Swigert (Kevin Bacon) stirred the oxygen tanks at the request of Mission Control. After this procedure, an explosion occurred, causing unknown damage to the command module. Before the scene takes place, the damage has forced the crew to move into the LEM (Lunar Exploration Module), which becomes their lifeboat for return to earth.

What to Watch for and Ask Yourself

1. What triggers the conflict in this scene?
2. Is this intergroup conflict or intragroup conflict? What effects can such conflict have on the group dynamics on board Apollo 13?
3. Does mission commander Jim Lovell successfully manage the group dynamics to return the group to a normal state?

Management Workplace
Orange Tree Imports

As you read in the chapter, the number of companies using teams is growing, but despite the popularity of teams, the challenges in managing teams are not diminishing. Carol and Dean Schroeder own Orange Tree Imports, a specialty gift shop with 30 employees, which generates nearly $2 million in annual sales. To get such outstanding results, the Schroeders have experimented with various techniques as they define team structures at their company.

What to Watch for and Ask Yourself

1. Does the video describe teams of workgroups? Explain.
2. Classify the employees at Orange Tree Imports using the team autonomy continuum. Why did you put it where you did?
3. Is a retail store an appropriate place for using teams?

CP PHOTO/ADRIAN WYLD

Managing Human Resource Systems

Chapter 13

CHAPTER OUTLINE

LEARNING OBJECTIVES

After reading this chapter, you should be able to

1. describe the basic steps involved in human resource planning.
2. explain how different employment laws affect human resource practice.
3. explain how companies use recruiting to find qualified job applicants.
4. describe employee selection techniques and procedures.
5. describe how to determine training needs and select the appropriate training methods.
6. discuss how to use performance appraisal to give meaningful performance feedback.
7. describe basic compensation strategies.
8. discuss the four kinds of employee separations.

What Would You Do?

Charles Fipke, a geologist from British Columbia, had been prospecting since the age of 17 in the farthest reaches of the world. He had travelled to New Guinea, Africa, and the Amazon in search of a buried fortune. Looking a little closer to home, he headed for Canada's arctic shield. Canada's North has long been considered a potential source for gas, oil, and minerals. In 1981 Fipke began looking for something else—diamonds. In 1983 he formed Dia Met Minerals to fund exploration for diamonds in Canada's North and took a crew into the Northwest Territories to search for rocky outcrops that had trace minerals such as garnets, which are associated with kimberlite. Kimberlite is known to be potentially diamond bearing. Fipke and another geologist, Stewart Blusson, spent ten years scrambling around the Lac de Gras region of the Northwest Territories. They almost ran out of money before they finally discovered a kimberlite pipe in 1991. They drilled a core hole 120 metres down and removed a 59-kilogram core sample. When analyzed, it was found to contain 81 diamonds. After further exploration and many more core samples, it was estimated that the site had 65.9 million tonnes of ore that would yield an average of over one carat per tonne. Following the announcement, a diamond prospecting rush ensued in the Northwest Territories. It was clear that the site had immense potential and could make everyone involved a great deal of money, if only they could make it all work.[1]

Despite the immense potential of the discovery, there were many hurdles to overcome. Dia Met Minerals was joined by BHP Billiton, which eventually bought out Dia Met Minerals, and they started a long and difficult process of trying to build and operate a mine 300 kilometres northeast of Yellowknife, essentially in the middle of nowhere, which would be large enough to yield about 4 percent of the world's total diamond production. Planning and building a mine is a difficult task at the best of times. There are endless difficulties in meeting environmental concerns both at the provincial/territorial level and at the federal level. This task was made even more difficult as the planned mine site was closer to the artic circle than to Yellowknife. The winters were long, dark, and cold, with temperatures dropping below −50°C and the wind-chill reaching −70°C. Watching bears and caribou and getting bitten by mosquitoes were the primary summer activities, while staying warm was the sole winter concern. Despite the daunting location and the obvious challenges created by it, almost $1 billion was spent over seven years on successfully developing a mine on the site.

The question now becomes, how do you staff a mine in the middle of nowhere? There is no town site, no major local population base, and there are only about 40 000 people in the entire Northwest Territories. Locally, there are scattered bands of Inuit and the only access to the mine site is by air. You need to find almost 1000 workers, the majority of them skilled, to run a mine 24 hours a day, 365 days of the year. In addition, you are not the only game in town, so to speak. Canada's northern regions were being scoured from east to west, from north to south for other natural resources. The likelihood of more mining and oil and gas operations operating in Canada's north was pretty high. They too would be looking for large numbers of highly skilled workers. If this wasn't enough of a challenge, other circumstances made the immediate difficulties of staffing the mine even more complicated.

If you cast your mind back to Chapter 6 and the challenges that Inco faced in the early stages of Voisey's Bay, this project faced similar issues. Although the negotiations with the territorial government and the local Aboriginal peoples were less problematic and took a lot less time, the results created certain new challenges. Part of the agreement was that the mine's work force would be 62 percent northern residents, with 31 percent of them Aboriginal. In addition, the Aboriginal portion of the work force must be always at least half of the northern resident total. You might ask yourself, why is this a problem? Approximately 30 percent of all northern workers have less than a grade-nine education, and functional literacy is a requirement for almost all of the jobs at the mine. In addition, the Northwest Territories has only one postsecondary institution, Aurora College, and Aboriginal education levels are even lower than the general population.

Given the shortage of skilled workers in the Northwest Territories, the difficult requirement to hire a large number of Aboriginal workers, the growing competition for skilled workers across Canada, and the isolation of the mine site, the human resource challenges were immense.

If you were a human resource manager for the Ekati mine, what would you do to hire and retain a qualified work force?

Unfortunately, "personnel problems" like those at the Ekati mine are all too common. For example, when Erler Industries, a small industrial painting and finishing company, signed a contract for a large amount of work with Dell Computer, it grew from 6 to 175 people almost overnight to meet the increased workload. Co-owner Linda Erler said, "We were so desperate for employees that if we could see the whites of your eyes and it looked as if blood was running through your veins, [you were offered a job]." Linda explained that this approach didn't always translate into successful hiring, like the time that a group of new hires all came to work with "whiskey in their soda cans." And even though new employees could earn bonuses if they stayed for just 30 days, she said, "we had tremendous turnover. Everyone had to be replaced five or six times before we found a person who really wanted to work."[2]

human resource management
the process of finding, developing, and keeping the right people to form a qualified work force

The experiences of Ekati mine and Erler Industries indicate that **human resource management**, the process of finding, developing, and keeping the right people to form a qualified work force, remains one of the most difficult and important of all management tasks. This chapter is organized around the four parts of the human resource management process shown in Exhibit 13.1: determining human resource needs and attracting, developing, and keeping a qualified work force.

Accordingly, the chapter begins by reviewing how human resource planning determines human resource needs, such as the kind and number of employees a company requires to meet its strategic plans and objectives. Next, we explore how companies use recruiting and selection techniques to attract and hire qualified employees to fulfill those needs. The third part of the chapter reviews how training and performance appraisal can

EXHIBIT 13.1
The Human Resource Management Process

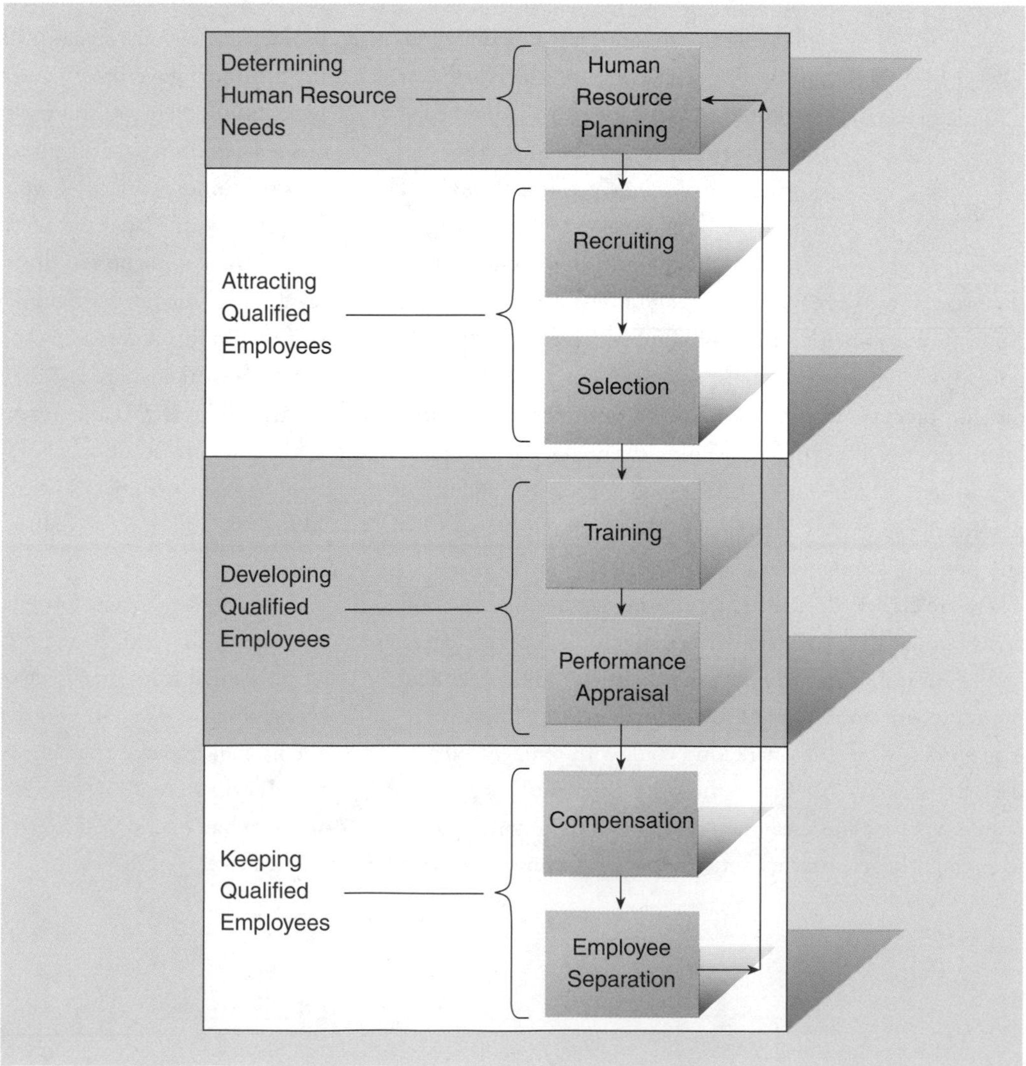

develop the knowledge, skills, and abilities of the work force. The chapter concludes with a review of compensation and employee separation—that is, how companies can keep their best workers through effective compensation practices, and how they can manage the separation process when employees do leave the organization.

Determining Human Resource Needs

Should we hire more workers? What should we pay our current employees to slow employee turnover? What kinds of training do our new employees need to be prepared to do a good job, and what's the best way to deliver that training? In other words, what are our human resource needs and what's the best way to address them?

Managers often treat these questions as separate issues. However, the human resource process illustrated in Exhibit 13.1 shows that attracting (recruiting and selecting), developing (training and appraising performance), and keeping or losing employees (compensating and separating) are interdependent issues. You can't solve one problem without considering its impact on the others. More specifically, Exhibit 13.1 indicates that human resource needs affect how the company uses recruiting and selection to attract employees. In turn, the kind and number of employees hired influence the orientation, training, performance appraisal, and compensation strategies the company uses, which then affect who stays and who leaves. Finally, as indicated by the feedback loop, the process comes full circle, as the number and kind of employees who leave the company affect its human resource needs and planning.

You can see how the HR process works by examining what high-tech companies had to do to deal with the acute shortage of qualified workers in Canada prior to the downturn in the technology sector. For instance, because of the shortage, a number of Canadian software companies had been very aggressive in their recruitment. Many companies in Ottawa, including Cognos and Mitel, developed employee referral programs to help recruit qualified employees. Employees received up to $5000 for a successful referral.[3] During this period they also had to actively compete with U.S. companies, some of whom were offering phenomenal benefits, such as four-star restaurant-quality food in company cafeterias; pool and ping pong tables for recreation; massage therapists; free soft drinks, juice, popcorn, and snacks; dry-cleaning drop-off and pickup; car detailers; dog walkers; and special staffers to run personal errands.[4] Finally, some high-tech companies dealt with the demand for workers by doing less recruiting, hoping instead that retraining current workers would be an effective way to reduce recruiting needs. It is predicted that there will again be a shortage of information technology workers in the near future.[5] Ideally, companies should be developing strategies to deal with the shortage now so that they will be prepared when it happens. Some companies have gone to the extreme of moving provinces in the face of labour shortages. Calgary-based Raydan Manufacturing, which modifies truck chassis, expanded its work force in Ontario as it was having great difficulties in recruiting qualified staff in Calgary as a result of the booming economy. "We just got tired of fighting for labour with Syncrude and the other megaprojects," Ray English, the CEO, said.[6]

Fortunately, there are steps that companies can take to begin to address expected employee shortfalls.

After reading the next two sections, you should be able to

1. describe the basic steps involved in human resource planning.
2. explain how different employment laws affect human resource practice.

1 HUMAN RESOURCE PLANNING

Human resource planning (HRP) is the process of using an organization's goals and strategy to forecast the organization's human resource needs in attracting, developing, and keeping a qualified work force.[7] Companies that don't use HRP or that do HRP

human resource planning (HRP)
using an organization's goals and strategy to forecast the organization's human resource needs in attracting, developing, and keeping a qualified work force

poorly may end up with either a surplus of employees and have to lay off some to correct the surplus, or a shortage of employees that leads to increased overtime costs and an inability to meet demand for the company's product or service.

The HRP process begins with a consideration of the organization's mission, strategy, and objectives. Therefore, HRP is directly related to and should be considered part of an organization's strategic planning process.[8] Dell Computer makes sure that the HRP process is tied to its mission and strategy by splitting its HR function into two departments. "HR Operations" has a service centre that takes care of all "transactional" activities for Dell employees, such as benefits and compensation. HR Operations rarely has direct contact with Dell's business units. Its job is to serve Dell's individual employees. By contrast, the HR staffers in Dell's "HR Management" department report directly to the vice president of HR and the vice president of a Dell business unit (e.g., procurement, higher education sales). The HR staffers then attend that business unit's staff meetings, help to develop that unit's leadership team, and then create a specific HR strategy for that part of Dell's business.[9] Dell's HR Management team also helps business units identify personnel needs, assess training needs, and determine the best organizational structure for reporting relationships (i.e., the organizational chart).

Let's explore human resource planning by examining how to forecast demand and supply and to use human resource information systems.

Forecasting Demand and Supply

work-force forecasting the process of predicting the number and kind of workers with specific skills and abilities that an organization will need in the future

Work-force forecasting is the process of predicting the number and kind of workers with specific skills and abilities that an organization will need in the future.[10] There are two kinds of work-force forecasts, internal and external forecasts, and three kinds of forecasting methods, direct managerial input, best guess, and statistical/historical ratios.

Internal forecasts are projections about factors within the organization that affect the supply and demand for human resources. These factors include the financial performance of the organization, productivity, the organization's mission, changes in technology or the way the work is performed, and the termination, promotion, transfer, retirement, resignation, and death of current employees. For example, Telus Corporation, which merged with B.C. Telecom and provides local service in both British Columbia and Alberta, offered 11 000 employees early retirement and voluntary departure packages as part of plan to reduce the size of its work force and increase its work-force productivity.[11] *External forecasts* are projections about factors outside the organization that affect the supply and demand for human resources. These factors include the labour supply for specific types of workers, the economy (unemployment rate), labour unions, demographics of the labour force (i.e., proportion of labour force in various age groups), geographic movement of the labour force, strength of competitors, and growth in particular businesses and markets. For example, Nortel eliminated more than 50 000 jobs worldwide as it struggled with a downturn in demand for its products.[12] Exhibit 13.2 provides a more complete list of factors that influence internal and external forecasts.

Three kinds of forecasting methods—direct managerial input, best guess, and statistical/historical ratios—are often used to predict the number and kind of workers with specific skills and abilities that an organization will need in the future.[13] The most common forecasting method, *direct managerial input,* is based on straightforward projections of cash flows, expenses, or financial measures, such as return on capital. While financial indicators are relatively quick to calculate and can help managers determine how many workers they might need, they don't help managers decide which critical skills new employees should possess.

The *best guess* forecasting method is based on managers' assessment of current head count, plus a best guess of how internal factors and external factors would affect that head count. Summing these together produces the total projection.

Finally, the *statistical/historical ratios* forecasting method uses statistical methods, such as multiple regression, in combination with historical data, to predict the number and

INTERNAL FACTORS	EXTERNAL FACTORS
• New positions	• Demographics of labour supply
• New equipment and technology	• Geographic population shifts
• Eliminated positions	• Shift from manufacturing- to service- to information-based economy
• Terminations	• General economic conditions
• Retirements	• Unemployment rate
• Resignations	• Labour unions
• Turnover	• Availability of applicants with specific skills and education
• Transfers	• Technological advances
• Deaths	• Strength and number of competitors
• Promotions	• Growth in particular businesses and markets
• Organization's mission	
• Productivity of current employees	
• Skills/education of current employees	

EXHIBIT 13.2
Internal and External Factors That Influence Work-Force Forecasting

kind of workers a company should hire. For example, a manager might run a regression analysis using data from the last two years. In that regression equation, the number of employees that need to be hired is the dependent (predicted) variable, and the number of items manufactured, number of clients, or average increase in sales, and so forth, are the independent (predictor) variables. The regression analysis produces a simple equation that indicates how many more employees should be added for each increase in the independent variables, such as items manufactured or increased sales. This approach takes advantage of existing data and can be much more accurate than best guess predictions, but only if a company's internal and external environments have not changed significantly.

Dell also uses statistical/historical ratios to help predict its work-force needs. Andy Esparza, vice president of staffing for Dell's company-wide staffing function, said, "One of the things this [HR planning process] maps into is a set of key job openings that we can use to start forecasting and sourcing people in advance." More specifically, Dell's Web-based HR planning process allows managers to play "what if?" with work-force predictions. Kathleen Woodhouse, an HR manager who supports Dell's preferred accounts division, said, "Managers use our intranet to complete HR functions, like appraisals; our appraisal system also feeds into the financial system so they can play with figures if they need to."[14]

Human Resource Information Systems

Human resource information systems (HRIS) are computerized systems for gathering, analyzing, storing, and disseminating information related to attracting, developing, and keeping a qualified work force.[15] Exhibit 13.3 shows some of the data that are commonly used in HR information systems, such as personal and educational data, company employment history, performance appraisal information, work history, and promotions.

human resource information systems (HRIS)
computerized systems for gathering, analyzing, storing, and disseminating information related to the HRM process

Human resource information systems can be used for transaction processing, employee self-service, and decision support. *Transaction processing* is a centralized computer system, often a mainframe, that records the thousands of routine daily transactions involved in running a business. For HRIS systems, transaction processing usually involves employee payroll cheques, taxes, and benefit deductions. HRISs can also reduce administrative costs by preparing certain routine reports that are required of many companies.

PERSONAL DATA	EDUCATIONAL DATA
• Name • Address/Telephone Number • Employee Identification Number • Social Insurance Number • Medical Plan/Coverage • Retirement/Investment Plan	• High School Diploma • College Diplomas/University Degrees • Special Courses/Training
COMPANY EMPLOYMENT HISTORY	**PERFORMANCE APPRAISAL**
• Previous Job Assignments • Current Position • Date of Initial Employment • Seniority Date • Salary/Pay History • Current Salary/Pay • Fringe Benefit Package • Last Pay Raise	• Date of Last Performance Appraisal • Productivity Measures • Disciplinary Action • Tardiness • Absenteeism • Last Performance Rating • Quality Measures
WORK HISTORY	**PROMOTION DATA**
• Previous Employers • Previous Positions • Duties in Previous Positions • Supervisory Experience	• Geographic Preferences • Personal Interests • Awards • Job Preferences • Special Skills/Knowledge • Foreign Language(s)

EXHIBIT 13.3
Common Data Categories in Human Resource Information Systems

While human resource information systems are typically used to give managers and HR staffers access to human resource data, the flip side of today's Web-based HRISs is that they can also give employees immediate, 24-hour *self-service* access to personal data, such as benefits and retirement packages. With secure, Web-based systems, employees need to enter only a user name and password to access and change their medical insurance plan, fill out time sheets, or check on the status of medical or child-care reimbursements.[16] For example, Ontario Power Generation, which is one of North America's largest power generators and has 11 500 employees, implemented a Web-based system that allows employees to change their personal information and check the status of their pension plans.[17] According to benefits coordinator Priscilla Craven, the primary advantage of self-service systems is that "you no longer need to call a person when an office is open to get a form or make an enrolment choice." And with access available 24 hours a day, companies have also begun eliminating restricted "open enrolment" periods, in which employees have to make (and then not change) all their benefit decisions for the entire year at one time.[18] With Web-based systems, employees can make changes whenever they want.

Human resource information systems are not only useful for gathering and storing information, but they also help managers by serving as decision support systems for critical human resource decisions.[19] In Chapter 5, you learned that *decision support systems* (DSS) help managers understand problems and potential solutions by acquiring and analyzing information with sophisticated models and tools. For instance, an HRIS can help managers make human resource decisions from the moment that job applicants submit résumés to the company. Those résumés are scanned, turned into text via optical character recognition software, and then fed into the HRIS, where they are analyzed for the quality of the writing and for key words that match the organization's job database. John Reese, founder of Interactive Search, an Internet recruiting site, said, "Whatever the media—paper, e-mail, the Web or fax—we can scan a résumé into a database, re-format it according to our specifications, and then make it available to the hiring manager or HR manager anywhere in a company, anywhere in the world. An applicant can send in an application on Thursday and have an interview by Monday."[20]

An HRIS can even be used to do pre-employment testing or background screening. Elaine Daily, marketing director for Qwiz, Inc., which sells computerized employment tests to companies, said, "We can do remote testing through a website or through software installed on a PC. This saves the company from having to bring in a candidate to headquarters before deciding whether the person is technically competent."[21]

HRISs can also be used effectively to screen internal applicants on particular qualifications, to match the qualifications of external applicants against those of internal applicants, to compare salaries within and between departments, and to review and change employees' salaries instantaneously without lengthy paperwork. In short, today's HRISs can help managers make any number of critical human resource decisions.

Review 1: Human Resource Planning

Human resource planning (HRP) uses organizational goals and strategies to determine what needs to be done to attract, develop, and keep a qualified work force. Work-force forecasts are used to predict the number and kind of workers with specific skills and abilities that an organization needs. Work-force forecasts consider both internal and external factors that affect the supply and demand for workers and can be formulated using three kinds of forecasting methods: direct managerial input, best guess, and statistical/historical ratios. Computerized human resource information systems improve human resource planning by gathering, analyzing, storing, and disseminating information (personal, educational, work history, performance, and promotions) related to human resource management activities. Human resource information systems can be used for transaction processing (payroll cheques and routine reports), employee self-service (24-hour Web access allowing instant changes to benefit and retirement packages), and decision support for human resource decisions (analyzing résumés, background screening, and pre-employment testing).

2 EMPLOYMENT LEGISLATION

One of the most challenging aspects of managing human resources is complying with legislation that regulates the employment relationship. There are two reasons for this. The first is that there is a lot of legislation that an employer has to comply with. The second is that legislation and how it is enforced changes often. The combination of these two factors means that human resource management can be a difficult task. Further complicating matters is that the employment relationship is regulated by both the federal and provincial governments. The federal government has jurisdiction over federally regulated industries. These include such industries as banking, airlines, shipping, and telecommunications. Together these industries account for less than 10 percent of the Canadian work force. Most employers and employees fall under provincial jurisdiction. This means that most companies that operate in more than one province would have to comply with legislation in each province. Many Canadian companies also operate in the United States, where similar laws exist.

Federal and provincial governments all pass human rights laws that affect employment as well as occupational health and safety laws (see www.ccohs.ca/oshanswers/information/govt.html) and laws that set minimum standards of work for matters such as vacation pay, parental leave, wages, and hours of work. In addition, the federal government has imposed pay equity and employment equity on federally regulated employers and imposed a federal contractors program (see www.hrsdc.gc.ca/en/gateways/topics/wzp-pxp.shtml), which all companies that have at least 100 employees and wish to bid on contracts over $200 000 must comply with. Some provinces also have pay equity and employment equity legislation.

Let's explore employment legislation by reviewing federal and provincial employment laws, employment discrimination, and sexual harassment.

Federal and Provincial Employment Laws

Exhibit 13.4 lists the major federal employment laws as well as the Web sites where you can find more detailed information on federal law. It should be remembered that for each of the federal acts listed in Exhibit 13.4, each of the provinces has similar acts that cover workers under provincial jurisdiction (90 percent of the work force). Human rights laws are some of the most challenging laws, as it can be difficult to ensure that you do not breach them. Although all human rights laws are not the same across all provinces and the federal government, they are quite similar. Exhibit 13.5 shows the prohibited grounds for discrimination across the various Canadian jurisdictions. The general result of this body of law, which is still evolving through human rights commission and court decisions, is that employers may not discriminate in employment decisions on the basis of gender, age, religion, colour, national origin, race, or disability. The intent is to make these factors irrelevant in employment decisions. Stated another way, employment decisions should be based on factors that are "job related," "reasonably necessary," or a "business necessity" for successful job performance. The only time that gender, age, religion, and so on, can be used to make employment decisions is when they are considered a *bona fide occupational qualification* or *requirement* (BFOQ or BFOR). For example, a Baptist church hiring a new minister can reasonably specify that being a Baptist rather than a Catholic or Presbyterian minister is a BFOQ for Baptist ministers. However, it's unlikely that a church could specify race or national origin as a BFOQ. In general, the courts and the human rights commissions take a hard look when a business claims that gender, age, religion, colour, national origin, race, or disability are BFOQs.

It is important to understand, however, that these laws don't just apply to selection decisions (i.e., hiring and promotion), but rather to the entire HRM process. Thus, these laws cover all training and development activities, performance appraisals, terminations, and compensation decisions.

The Canadian Human Rights Act is administered and enforced by the Canadian Human Rights Commission (CHRC) (www.chrc-ccdp.ca), which also provides useful guidelines for employers. Each province has its own human rights commission to administer its human rights legislation. Links can be found to them on provincial government

EXHIBIT 13.4
Summary of Major Federal Employment Laws

CANADA LABOUR CODE—PART III
Minimum wage, parental leave, hours of work, vacation entitlements. http://laws.justice.gc.ca/en/L-2/index.html
CANADA LABOUR CODE—PART II
Occupational health and safety. http://laws.justice.gc.ca/en/L-2/index.html
CANADA LABOUR CODE—PART I
Guarantees the right to form and join unions. http://laws.justice.gc.ca/en/L-2/index.html
CANADIAN HUMAN RIGHTS ACT
Prohibits discrimination on the basis of race, origin, gender, religion, etc. http://laws.justice.gc.ca/en/H-6/index.html

Jurisdiction	Federal	Alberta	British Columbia	Manitoba	New Brunswick	Newfoundland	Nova Scotia	Ontario	Prince Edward Island	Quebec	Saskatchewan	Northwest Territories	Nunavut	Yukon Territory
Place of Origin		●	●		●			●			●	●	●	
Creed		●				●	●	●	●	●	●	●	●	●
Social Condition					●					●		●		
Social Origin						●								
Source of Income				●			●		●		●		●	●
Language										●				
Civil Status										●				
Sexual Orientation**	●	●	●	●	●	●	●	●	●	●	●	●	●	●
Gender Identity												●		
Family Status	●			●				●			●	●	●	
Family Affiliation												●		
Political Beliefs****			●	●	●	●			●	●		●		●
Ancestry		●	●		●			●			●	●	●	●
Physical Disability	●	●	●	●	●	●	●	●	●	●	●	●	●	●
Mental Disability	●	●	●	●	●	●	●	●	●	●	●	●	●	●
Conviction Criminal	●		●					●	●	●			●	●
Marital Status	●	●	●	●	●	●	●	●	●	●	●	●	●	●
Pregnancy/ Childbirth*	●	●						●		●			●	●
Sex	●	●	●	●	●	●	●	●	●	●	●	●	●	●
Age	●	● (18+)	● (19–65)	●	● (19+)	● (19–65)	●	● (18–65)	●	●	● (18–65)	●	●	●
Religion	●	●	●	●	●	●	●		●	●	●	●	●	●
Nationality/ Citizenship				●				●			●		●	
Colour	●	●	●	●	●	●	●	●	●	●	●	●	●	●
National/Ethnic Origin	●			●	●	●	●	●	●	●		●	●	●
Race	●	●	●	●	●	●	●	●	●	●	●	●	●	●
Dependence on Alcohol/Drug	●													

* In Alberta discrimination on the basis of pregnancy is deemed to be discrimination on the basis of sex. In Ontario, Manitoba, Nova Scotia and the Yukon discrimination on the basis of pregnancy in included in discrimination on the basis of sex.

** The Supreme Court decision in *Vriend v. Alberta* "read in" sexual orientation as a prohibited ground of discrimination in Alberta.

*** Harassment is barred on all proscribed grounds of discrimination except in New Brunswick and Nova Scotia where it refers only to sexual harassment.

**** In New Brunswick, political activity is a prohibited ground of discrimination as well as political belief.

EXHIBIT 13.5
Prohibited Grounds of Discrimination in Employment in Canada

Source: Reproduced with permission from *The Canadian Master Labour Guide*, 12th ed., published by and copyright CCH Canadian Limited, Don Mills, ON, 1998, p. 339.

sites (http://canada.gc.ca/othergov/prov_e.html) and on the CHRC Web site. Employers who use factors such as gender, age, race, or religion, among others, to make employment-related decisions when those factors are unrelated to an applicant's or employee's ability to perform a job may face charges of discrimination from provincial or federal human rights commissions. The Canada Labour Code is administered by the Canada Industrial Relations Board (www.cirb-ccri.gc.ca) and Human Resources and Social Development Canada (http://www.hrsdc.gc.ca/en/home.shtml). As with human rights laws, each province has commissions and boards to administer provincial employment legislation.

Federal and provincial labour laws regulate the interaction between management and labour unions that represent groups of employees. These laws guarantee employees the right to form and join unions of their own choosing. Labour unions can have a significant impact on the terms and conditions of employment by constraining an employer's ability to set pay levels, discipline employees, and set shift assignments, among other things. Federal and provincial occupational health and safety laws require that employers provide employees with a place of employment that is free from recognized hazards that are causing or are likely to cause death or serious physical harm. Occupational health and safety laws set health and safety standards for employers, and the departments conduct inspections to determine whether those standards are being met. Employers who do not meet occupational health and safety standards may be fined. For example, the Toronto District School Board was fined $150 000 after one of its workers died as a result of a workplace accident after it was determined that the board was not in compliance with occupational health and safety laws.[22] At the federal level, these laws are administered by the Canada Industrial Relations Board and there are corresponding commissions and boards to administer provincial legislation.

Employment Discrimination

Federal and provincial human rights commissions have investigatory, enforcement, and informational responsibilities. Therefore, they investigate charges of discrimination, enforce the provisions of these laws, and publish guidelines that organizations can use to ensure they are in compliance with the law. One of the key issues that must be dealt with is ensuring that all hiring, promotion, or other employment decisions are based on bona fide occupational requirements. This is best done by ensuring the reliability and validity of all selection techniques and qualifications required for a job. The **reliability** of a selection technique refers to the degree to which the test is free from random measurement error and provides consistent results. **Validity** of selection techniques refers to the degree to which a selection technique accurately predicts future job performance. Required qualifications must reflect the actual needs of the job. Failure to ensure the reliability and validity of selection techniques or employment qualifications can lead to charges of discrimination.[23]

reliability
the degree to which a measure (test) is free from random error and is consistent

validity
the degree to which a measure (selection technique) is shown to accurately predict what it is expected to measure (job performance)

In addition to the above-mentioned laws, all employers regulated by the federal government must also comply with the Employment Equity Act (http://laws.justice.gc.ca/en/E-5.401/). The act compels federally regulated employers to remove employment barriers against persons in designated groups, make reasonable accommodation for des-

Employment equity legislation is intended to have a company's work force mirror larger work-force diversity.

ignated groups, and set goals for the hiring of designated groups, where they are underrepresented in an employer's work force. Under the law, the designated groups are women, Aboriginals, persons with disabilities, and visible minorities. The goal of the legislation is to have an employer's work force mirror the work force at large by matching the appropriate pool of qualified workers (e.g., accountants) with the employer's work force. For example, if 35 percent of accountants are female, an employer would be expected to have, over time, approximately 35 percent female accountants.[24] Employers can be fined up to $50 000 for failure to comply with the legislation.

Sexual Harassment

Sexual harassment is a form of discrimination in which unwelcome sexual advances, requests for sexual favours, or other verbal or physical conduct of a sexual nature occur. From a legal perspective, there are two kinds of sexual harassment—quid pro quo and hostile work environment.[25]

sexual harassment
form of discrimination in which unwelcome sexual advances, requests for sexual favours, or other verbal or physical conduct of a sexual nature occur while performing one's job

Quid pro quo sexual harassment occurs when employment outcomes, such as hiring, promotion, or simply keeping one's job, depend on whether an individual submits to being sexually harassed. For example, in a quid pro quo sexual harassment lawsuit against Prudential Insurance, a female employee alleged that she was repeatedly propositioned for sexual favours by her boss, and that when she refused, he said that "she would not amount to anything in this business without his help."[26] By contrast, a **hostile work environment** occurs when unwelcome and demeaning sexually related behaviour creates an intimidating, hostile, and offensive work environment. One example of a hostile work environment was a Sears manager who would ask his female subordinates to step into his office to look at close-up photos of women's breasts and bottoms that he had taken while on vacation at a beach.[27] Inappropriate sexual comments or jokes and the displaying of pornographic material on company property are also prime examples of a hostile work environment.

quid pro quo sexual harassment
form of sexual harassment in which employment outcomes, such as hiring, promotion, or simply keeping one's job, depend on whether an individual submits to sexual harassment

hostile work environment
form of sexual harassment in which unwelcome and demeaning sexually related behaviour creates an intimidating and offensive work environment

What common mistakes do managers make when it comes to sexual harassment laws?[28] First, many assume that the victim and harasser must be of the opposite sex and only women can be victims. According to human rights commissions, this assumption is incorrect. Sexual harassment can occur between people of the same sex and men are often the victims of sexual harassment.[29] Second, it is assumed that sexual harassment can occur only between co-workers or between supervisors and subordinates. Not so. Sexual harassers can also include agents of employers, such as consultants, and can even include nonemployees such as customers.[30] The key is not employee status but whether the harassment takes place while conducting company business. Third, it is often assumed that only people who have themselves been harassed can file complaints or lawsuits. In fact, especially in hostile work environments, anyone affected by offensive conduct can file a complaint.

Finally, what should companies do to make sure that sexual harassment laws are followed and not violated?[31] First, respond immediately when sexual harassment is reported. A quick response encourages victims of sexual harassment to report problems to management rather than to lawyers or the human rights commission. Furthermore, a quick and fair investigation may serve as a deterrent to future harassment. Next, take the time to write a clear, understandable sexual harassment policy that is strongly worded, gives specific examples of what constitutes sexual harassment, spells outs sanctions and punishments, and is widely publicized within the company. This lets potential harassers and victims know what will not be tolerated and how the firm will deal with harassment should it occur.

Next, clear reporting procedures that indicate how, where, and to whom incidents of sexual harassment can be reported should also be established. The best procedures ensure a quick response, that impartial parties will handle the complaint, and that the privacy of the accused and accusers will be protected. For example, the Canadian Armed Forces set up a 1-800 hotline to report cases of sexual harassment.[32]

Review 2: Employment Legislation

Human resource management is regulated by both the federal and provincial governments. Each jurisdiction has passed human rights legislation that is administered and enforced by a human rights commission. In general, these laws indicate that gender, age, religion, colour, national origin, race, disability, and pregnancy may not be considered in employment decisions unless these factors reasonably qualify as a BFOQ. In addition, the federal government under the Employment Equity Act requires federally regulated employers to set goals to match designated groups with work-force availability.

The two kinds of sexual harassment are quid pro quo and hostile work environment. Managers often wrongly assume that the victim and harasser must be of the opposite sex, that sexual harassment can only occur between co-workers or between supervisors and their employees, that all victims are female, and that only people who have themselves been harassed can file complaints. To make sure that sexual harassment laws are followed, companies should respond immediately when harassment is reported, write a clear, understandable sexual harassment policy, establish clear reporting procedures, and be aware of and follow provincial or federal laws concerning sexual harassment.

Finding Qualified Workers

Finding qualified workers can be very difficult. For example, Fort McMurray, Alberta, has gone through a number of cycles of labour shortages with the current one looking as if it may continue for a long time. Recently, both Shell Canada and Suncor saw huge cost overruns due to a shortage of qualified workers. One of Suncor's projects had a cost overrun of almost 50 percent, which amounted to $1.25 billion, and less than a year after Shell Canada announced its newest project it had to revise its cost estimate upwards from $4 billion to $7.3 billion, possibly learning from its last experience.[33] Meanwhile, many jobs in the service industry go unfilled, leaving the service sector with significant staffing shortages.[34] The results can be extreme. For example, a 20-year-old Dairy Queen franchise and a brand new Burger King franchise in Nisku, a suburb of Edmonton, were forced to shut down in 2005 due to a lack of staff.[35] With a strong economy, these difficulties are experienced by employers across Canada. A 2005 Conference Board of Canada survey found that 67 percent of employers report difficulty in attracting and retaining qualified workers.[36]

As these examples illustrate, finding qualified workers in today's tight labour market is an increasingly difficult task. However, finding qualified applicants is just the first step. Selecting which applicants to hire is the second. CEO John Chambers of Cisco Systems, the leading designer and manufacturer of high-tech equipment that serves as the backbone of the Internet, said, "Cisco has an overall goal of getting the top 10 percent to 15 percent of people in our industry. Our philosophy is very simple—if you get the best people in the industry to fit into your culture and you motivate them properly, then you're going to be an industry leader."[37]

After reading the next two sections, you should be able to

3 explain how companies use recruiting to find qualified job applicants.

4 describe the selection techniques and procedures that companies use when deciding which applicants should receive job offers.

3 RECRUITING

recruiting
the process of developing a pool of qualified job applicants

Recruiting is the process of developing a pool of qualified job applicants. Let's examine job analysis and recruiting, internal recruiting, and external recruiting.

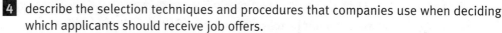

Job Analysis and Recruiting

Job analysis is a "purposeful, systematic process for collecting information on the important work-related aspects of a job."[38] Typically, a job analysis collects four kinds of information:

- work activities, such as what workers do and how, when, and why they do it,
- the tools and equipment used to do the job,
- the context in which the job is performed, such as the actual working conditions or schedule, and
- the personnel requirements for performing the job, meaning the knowledge, skills, and abilities needed to do a job well.[39]

job analysis
a purposeful, systematic process for collecting information on the important work-related aspects of a job

Job analysis information can be collected by having job incumbents and/or supervisors complete questionnaires about their jobs, by direct observation, by interviews, or by filming employees as they perform their jobs.

Job descriptions and job specifications are two of the most important results of a job analysis. A **job description** is a written description of the basic tasks, duties, and responsibilities required of an employee holding a particular job. **Job specifications**, which are often included as a separate section of a job description, are a summary of the qualifications needed to successfully perform the job.

job description
a written description of the basic tasks, duties, and responsibilities required of an employee holding a particular job

job specifications
a written summary of the qualifications needed to successfully perform a particular job

Because a job analysis clearly specifies what a job entails, as well as the knowledge, skills, and ability that are needed to do a job well, companies must complete a job analysis *before* beginning to recruit job applicants. Exhibit 13.6 shows that job analysis, job descriptions, and job specifications are the foundation on which all critical human resource activities are built. They are used during recruiting and selection to match applicant qualifications with the requirements of the job. They are used throughout the staffing process to ensure that selection devices and the decisions based on these devices are job related. For example, the questions asked in an interview should be based on the most important work activities identified by a job analysis. Likewise, during performance appraisals, employees should be evaluated in areas that a job analysis has identified as the most important in a job.

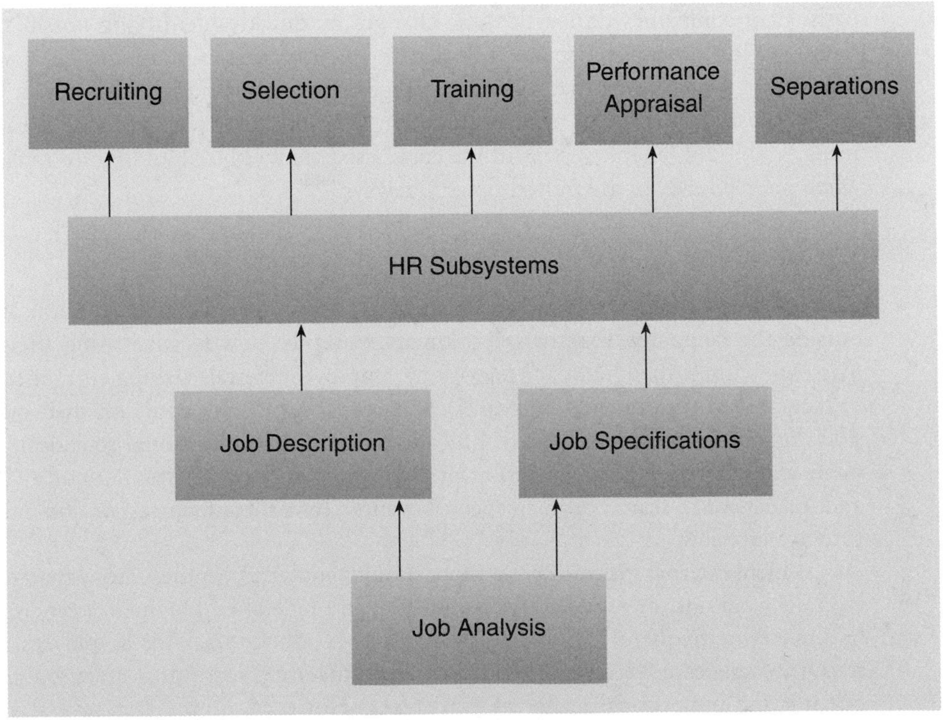

EXHIBIT 13.6
Importance of Job Analysis to Human Resource Management

Job analyses, job descriptions, and job specifications also help companies meet the legal requirement that their human resource decisions be job related. To be judged *job related*, recruitment, selection, training, performance appraisals, and employee separations must be valid and be directly related to the important aspects of the job, as identified by a careful job analysis. For example, the Canadian Human Rights Commission has taken the position that except in limited circumstances pre-employment testing for drugs and alcohol is prohibited.[40]

Internal Recruiting

internal recruiting
the process of developing a pool of qualified job applicants from people who already work in the company

Internal recruiting is the process of developing a pool of qualified job applicants from people who already work in the company. Internal recruiting, sometimes called "promotion from within," improves employee commitment, morale, and motivation. Recruiting current employees also reduces recruitment start-up time and costs and, because employees are already familiar with the company's culture and procedures, generally increases workers' chances of success in new jobs. Job posting and career paths are two methods of internal recruiting.

Job posting is a procedure for advertising job openings within the company to existing employees. A job description and requirements are typically posted on a bulletin board, in a company newsletter, or in an internal computerized job bank that is accessible only to employees. Job posting helps organizations discover hidden talent, allows employees to take responsibility for career planning, and makes it easier for companies to retain talented workers who are dissatisfied in their current jobs and would otherwise leave the company.[41] Baxter Health Care calls its job posting program the "Inside Advantage Program." Baxter employees can access this program via an automated telephone prompting system.[42]

A *career path* is a planned sequence of jobs through which employees may advance within an organization. For example, many of the managers of Calgary Co-op stores started out bagging groceries for the company.[43] Career paths help employees focus on long-term goals and development while also helping companies do succession or replacement planning. For instance, one of the disadvantages of internal recruitment is that it sets off a domino effect of job changes. When an internal employee changes jobs within a company, this person fills one job opening but automatically creates another. Career paths help companies deal with these changes by quickly identifying possible replacements as job openings ricochet through an organization. Coca-Cola deals with this problem by making sure that all of its managers are developing replacements at least two levels below their current position. Ian Pinto, senior HR manager for Coca-Cola of India, said, "This enables us to cut the costs associated with scrambling for replacements when people leave, or are moved up or sideways."[44]

External Recruiting

external recruiting
the process of developing a pool of qualified job applicants from outside the company

External recruiting is the process of developing a pool of qualified job applicants from outside the company. External recruitment methods include advertising (newspapers, magazines, direct mail, radio, or television), employee referrals (asking current employees to recommend possible job applicants), walk-ins (people who apply on their own), outside organizations (universities, technical/trade schools, professional societies), employment services (federal, provincial, or private employment agencies, temporary agencies, and professional search firms), special events (career conferences or job fairs), and Internet job sites.

Which external recruiting method should you use? Studies show that employee referrals, walk-ins, newspaper advertisements, and federal employment agencies tend to be used most frequently for office/clerical and production/service employees. By contrast, newspaper advertisements and college/university recruiting are used most frequently for professional/technical employees. However, in the last several years the biggest changes in external recruiting have come as a result of the Internet. For example,

Cisco Systems no longer runs newspaper help-wanted ads. Instead, it takes out simple newspaper ads that direct recruits to its Web site (www.cisco.com/jobs), where they can see hundreds of job descriptions, learn in detail about Cisco's highly competitive benefits, and submit an online résumé.[45] In addition to extensive job information on corporate Web sites, some companies have begun subscribing to Internet job sites such as Monster (www.monster.ca) and CareerBuilder (www.careerbuilder.com). For just $3000 to $4000 per month, companies can advertise up to 100 job openings and reach millions of job applicants worldwide at a fraction of the cost of newspaper advertising.[46] One advantage of online recruiting is the ability to reach large numbers of people. For example, Computer Sciences Corporation listed 200 jobs on its Web site and received over 8000 résumés.[47]

Despite its promise, there are some disadvantages to Internet recruiting. The main drawback (which some companies consider a plus) is that Internet recruiting is unlikely to reach recruits who don't use or have access to the Internet. And, since it is so easy for applicants to apply, companies may receive hundreds, if not thousands, of applications from unqualified applicants, which increases the importance of proper screening and selection. Furthermore, if the proper security precautions aren't taken, there is also the danger of violating employee/applicant privacy.[48] Still, despite these disadvantages, companies are expected to make even more use of the Internet for external recruiting. Today, between 82 percent and 92 percent of companies use the Internet to fill job openings. In fact, Internet recruiting is now second to newspaper advertising in terms of the number of applicants it generates.[49] And, with the addition of a new ".jobs" Internet suffix (e.g., Nortel could use, www.nortel.jobs for job psotings at Nortel), more and more companies will now use their Web sites to attract, recruit, and screen job applicants.[50]

Review 3: Recruiting

Recruiting is the process of finding qualified job applicants. The first step in recruiting is to conduct a job analysis to collect information about the important work-related aspects of the job. The job analysis is then used to write a job description of basic tasks, duties, and responsibilities and to write job specifications indicating the knowledge, skills, and abilities needed to perform the job. Job analyses, descriptions, and specifications help companies meet the legal requirement that their human resource decisions be job related. Internal recruiting, finding qualified job applicants from inside the company, can be done through job posting and career paths. External recruiting, finding qualified job applicants from outside the company, is done through advertising, employee referrals, walk-ins, outside organizations, employment services, special events, and Internet job sites. The Internet is a particularly promising method of external recruiting because of its low cost, wide reach, and ability to communicate and receive unlimited information.

4 SELECTION

Once the recruitment process has produced a pool of qualified applicants, the selection process is used to determine which applicants have the best chance of performing well on the job. Tom Blangiardo, president of Basic Education and Training Associations (BETA Group), uses a fairly typical selection process to hire telemarketers to sell the company's educational videos. "For every ad we place, we get about 100 applicants. I interview everyone over the phone, because the way you come across on the phone is very important here. I evaluate voice tone, friendliness, and persuasiveness." Around 30 to 40 candidates are then chosen for group interviews. Managers explain BETA Group's philosophy and benefits and show the candidates examples of the videos they'll be selling. After the group interviews, 9 candidates are typically eliminated, 6 receive job offers, and 15 go on to individual interviews with human resource director John Brown. During the individual interview, candidates are asked to role-play a sales call. Another 7 applicants are lost at this stage. The 10 to 15 survivors are hired and put through a one-week orientation program that includes product and technology training, practice taking live

selection
the process of gathering information about job applicants to decide who should be offered a job

validation
the process of determining how well a selection test or procedure predicts future job performance. The better or more accurate the prediction of future job performance, the more valid a test is said to be.

calls, and more role-playing. "We put people on the hot seat to see how they behave," says Kara O'Connor, BETA Group's employee training manager. After 30 to 60 days, about half of these survivors leave because it's either too intense for them, or they're just not selling enough.[51]

As this example illustrates, **selection** is the process of gathering information about job applicants to decide who should be offered a job. To make sure that selection decisions are accurate and legally defendable, all selection procedures should be validated. **Validation** is the process of determining how well a selection test or procedure predicts future job performance. It is important to note that a test must first be reliable before one can even consider the question of validity (see page 374 for a definition of reliability). The better or more accurate the prediction of future job performance, the more valid a test is said to be. See the "What Really Works" feature on page 385 for more on the validity of common selection tests and procedures.

Let's examine common selection procedures, such as application forms and résumés, references and background checks, selection tests, and interviews.

DOING THE RIGHT THING

DON'T EMBELLISH YOUR RÉSUMÉ

Your résumé is supposed to help you get the interview that can get you a job. So where do you draw the line between making yourself look attractive to a potential employer and lying? Despite the strong temptation to improve your odds of getting a job, embellishing your résumé is wrong. Moreover, the information on your résumé is legally binding. If you misrepresent information or lie on your résumé, and many do, you're breaking the law and can be fired. But where should you draw the line? In general, if what you put on your résumé feels wrong, don't do it. More specifically, don't embellish job titles, responsibilities, employment dates, college degrees, certifications, general qualifications, or previous experience in any way. Do the right thing: Tell the truth on your résumé.[53]

Application Forms and Résumés

The first selection devices that most job applicants encounter when they seek a job are application forms and résumés. Both contain similar information about job applicants, such as name, address, and job and educational history. While an organization's application form often asks for information already provided by the résumé, most organizations prefer to collect this information in their own format for entry into a human resource information system.

Employment-related laws apply to application forms, as they do to all selection devices. Application forms may ask applicants about only valid, job-related information. However, application forms commonly ask applicants to report non–job-related information, such as marital status, maiden name, age, or date of high school graduation. Exhibit 13.7 presents a list of the kinds of information that companies may not request in application forms, during job interviews, or in any other part of the selection process. Attorney Tiberio Trimmer said, "Your objective is to hire someone qualified to perform the requirements of the job. Not asking things that are peripheral to the work itself helps you to stay on the right side of the law."[52] Consequently, most companies should closely examine their application forms for compliance with provincial and federal human rights legislation.

Résumés also pose problems for companies, but in a different way. Studies show as many as one out of every three job applicants falsifies some information on his or her résumé. A study of 200 000 job applicants found that 20 percent of applicants listed college degrees they hadn't earned, 30 percent changed the dates of their employment, 40 percent reported much higher salaries, 30 percent incorrectly described their previous jobs, 27 percent falsified their references, and 25 percent reported working at nonexistent or no-longer-existing companies, where the fact that they never worked there couldn't be discovered.[54] Therefore, managers should verify the information collected via résumés and application forms by comparing it with additional information collected during interviews and other stages of the selection process, such as references and background checks, which are discussed next.

employment references
sources such as previous employers or co-workers who can provide job-related information about job candidates

background checks
procedures used to verify the truthfulness and accuracy of information that applicants provide about themselves and to uncover negative, job-related background information not provided by applicants

References and Background Checks

Nearly all companies ask applicants to provide **employment references**, such as previous employers or co-workers, which they can contact to learn more about job candidates. **Background checks** are used to verify the truthfulness and accuracy of information that applicants provide about themselves and to uncover negative, job-related background information not provided by applicants. Background checks are conducted by contacting "educational institutions, prior employers, court records, police and governmental agencies and other informational sources, either by telephone, mail, remote computer access or through in-person investigations."[55]

EXHIBIT 13.7
A Guide to Screening and Selection in Employment

SUBJECT	AVOID ASKING	PREFERRED QUESTION	COMMENT
Name	about name change: whether it was changed by court order, marriage, or other reason; maiden name.	Ask after selection if needed to check on previously held jobs or educational credentials.	
Address	for addresses outside Canada.	Ask place and duration of current or recent address.	
Age	for birth certificates, baptismal records, or about age in general.	Ask applicants if they are eligible to work under Canadian laws regarding age restrictions.	If precise age is required for benefits plans or other legitimate purposes, it can be determined after selection.
Sex	males or females to fill in different applications; about pregnancy, child-bearing plans, or child-care arrangements.	Can ask applicant if the attendance requirements can be met.	During interview or after selection, the applicant, for purposes of courtesy, may be asked which of Mr., Mrs., Miss, Ms. is preferred.
Marital Status	whether applicant is single, married, divorced, engaged, separated, widowed, or living common-law.	If transfer or travel is part of the job, the applicant can be asked if he or she can meet these requirements.	Ask whether there are any circumstances that might prevent completion of a minimum service commitment. Information on dependants can be determined after selection, if necessary.
Family Status	number of children or dependants; about child-care arrangements.	Ask if the applicant would be able to work the required hours and where applicable, overtime.	Contacts for emergencies and/or details on dependants can be determined after selection.
National or Ethnic Origin	about birthplace, nationality of ancestors, spouse, or other relatives; whether born in Canada; for proof of Canadian citizenship.	Since those who are entitled to work in Canada must be citizens, permanent residents, or holders of valid work permits, applicants can be asked if they are legally entitled to work in Canada.	Documentation of eligibility to work (papers, visas, etc.) can be requested after selection.
Military Service	about military service in other countries.	Inquiry about Canadian military service is permitted where employment preference is given to veterans by law.	
Language	mother tongue; where language skills obtained.	Ask if applicant understands, reads, writes, or speaks languages required for the job.	Testing or scoring applicants for language proficiency is not permitted unless job-related.
Race or Colour	any inquiry into race or colour, including colour of eyes, skin, or hair.		
Photographs	for photo to be attached to applications sent to interviewer before interview.		Photos for security passes or company files can be taken after selection.
Religion	about religious affiliation, church membership, frequency of church attendance; if applicant will work a specific religious holiday; for references from clergy or religious leader.	Explain the required work shift, asking if such a schedule poses problems for the applicant.	Reasonable accommodation of an employee's religious beliefs is the employer's duty.
Height and Weight	No inquiry unless there is evidence they are genuine occupational requirements.		

SUBJECT	AVOID ASKING	PREFERRED QUESTION	COMMENT
Disability	for listing of all disabilities, limitations, or health problems; whether applicant drinks or uses drugs; whether applicant has ever received psychiatric care or been hospitalized for emotional problems; whether applicant has received workers' compensation.	Ask if applicant has any condition that could affect ability to do the job. Ask if the applicant has any condition that should be considered in selection.	A disability is only relevant to job ability if it threatens the safety or property of others; prevents the applicant from carrying out safe and adequate job performance even when reasonable efforts are made to accommodate the disability.
Medical Information	if currently under physician's care; name of family doctor; if receiving counselling or therapy.		Medical exams should be conducted after selection and only if an employee's condition is related to job duties.
Pardoned Conviction	whether an applicant has a criminal record.		
Sexual Orientation	any inquiry about the applicant's sexual orientation.		Contacts for emergencies and/or details on dependants can be determined after selection.
References			The same restrictions that apply to questions asked of applicants apply when asking for employment references.

Source: "A Guide to Screening and Selection in Employment," Canadian Human Rights Commission. Copyright © 2001 Canadian Human Rights Commission.

EXHIBIT 13.7
A Guide to Screening and Selection in Employment, Cont'd

Unfortunately, previous employers are increasingly reluctant to provide references or background check information for fear of being sued by previous employees for defamation. If former employers provide unsubstantiated information to potential employers that damages applicants' chances of being hired, applicants can (and do) sue for defamation. As a result, many employers are reluctant to provide information about previous employees. Many provide only dates of employment, positions held, and date of separation.

With previous employers generally unwilling to give full, candid references, companies don't get full, candid references and background information. What can companies do? Dig deeper for more information. Ask references to provide references. Next, ask in writing before checking references or running a background check.

Always document all reference and background checks, who was called, and what information was obtained. And to reduce the success of negligent hiring lawsuits, it's particularly important to document which companies and people refused to share reference check and background information. Finally, consider hiring private investigators to conduct background checks. A background check might have saved Sunbeam Corp. a lot of embarrassment. Albert "Chainsaw Al" Dunlap was appointed CEO in 1996 and was known as a successful business executive who even wrote a best-selling memoir about his experiences. He manipulated Sunbeam's earnings and helped drive the company into bankruptcy. What was not known by Sunbeam's board of directors was that he had been fired twice before for similar behaviour, a fact that he had left off his résumé and that might have been revealed by private investigators.[56]

Selection Tests

Why do some people do well on jobs while other people do poorly? If only you could know before deciding who to hire! Selection tests give organizational decision makers a chance to know who will likely do well in a job and who won't. The basic idea behind selection testing is to have applicants take a test that measures something directly or indirectly related to doing well on the job. The selection tests discussed here are specific ability tests, cognitive ability tests, biographical data, personality tests, work sample tests, and assessment centres. Again, as with any selection method, all tests need to be reliable and valid in order to successfully screen candidates and protect a company from human rights complaints.

Specific ability tests are tests that measure the extent to which an applicant possesses the particular kind of ability needed to do a job well. Specific ability tests are also called **aptitude tests**, because they measure aptitude for doing a particular task well. For example, if you were to take the GMAT to get into a graduate business program, you've taken the aptly named Graduate Management Admission Test, which is one predictor of how well students will do in graduate business school (i.e., scholastic performance). Specific ability tests also exist for mechanical, clerical, sales, and physical work. For example, Cambridge, Ontario–based Prudential Grand Valley Realty used a sales simulator after it received 249 applications for only two real estate agent positions. The simulator used Web-based software that allowed applicants to go on simulated cold calls, with real-life video, audio, and customer reactions. The simulation was based on thousands of hours of research and development. Fifty-five people took the test and two of the highest scorers were hired, both of whom turned out to be excellent real estate agents.[57]

specific ability tests (aptitude tests)
tests that measure the extent to which an applicant possesses the particular kind of ability needed to do a job well

cognitive ability tests
tests that measure the extent to which applicants have abilities in perceptual speed, verbal comprehension, numerical aptitude, general reasoning, and spatial aptitude

biographical data (biodata)
extensive surveys that ask applicants questions about their personal backgrounds and life experiences

Cognitive ability tests measure the extent to which applicants have abilities in perceptual speed, verbal comprehension, numerical aptitude, general reasoning, and spatial aptitude. In other words, these tests indicate how quickly and how well people understand words, numbers, logic, and spatial dimensions. While specific ability tests predict job performance in only particular types of jobs, cognitive ability tests accurately predict job performance in almost all kinds of jobs.[58] Why is this so? Because people with strong cognitive or mental abilities are usually good at learning new things, processing complex information, and solving problems and making decisions, and these abilities are important in almost all jobs to some extent. And not only do cognitive ability tests predict job performance well in almost all kinds of jobs, but they are almost always the best predictors of job performance. Consequently, if you were allowed to use just one selection test, a cognitive ability test would be the one to use. (In practice, though, companies use a battery of different tests, which can lead to much more accurate selection decisions.)

Biographical data, or **biodata**, are extensive surveys that ask applicants questions about their personal backgrounds and life experiences. The basic idea behind biodata is that past behaviour (personal background and life experience) is the best predictor of future behaviour. For example, the Canadian life insurance industry has used biodata since 1942 in the selection of applicants.[60]

Most biodata questionnaires have over 100 items that gather information about habits and attitudes, health, interpersonal relations, money, what it was like growing up in your family (parents, siblings, childhood years, teen years), personal habits, current home (spouse, children), hobbies, education and training, values, preferences, and work.[61] In general, biodata are very good predictors of future job performance, especially in entry-level jobs.

You may have noticed that some of the information requested in biodata surveys also appears in Exhibit 13.7 (page 381) as topics employers should avoid in application blanks, interviews, or other parts of the selection process. This information can be requested in biodata questionnaires provided that companies can demonstrate that the information is job-related (i.e., valid) and does not result in discrimination against protected groups of job applicants. Although legal in Canada, biodata surveys should be

DOING THE RIGHT THING

DON'T USE PSYCHICS, LIE DETECTORS, OR HANDWRITING ANALYSIS TO MAKE HR DECISIONS

The Coronado Bay Resort in San Diego hired a psychic to work with its 18-member management team as a way of "moving the managers to the next step." Seventy-five percent of the organizations in France and Switzerland use handwriting analysis for hiring and promotion decisions. In the past, employers like the Canadian Security Intelligence Service regularly used polygraphs (lie detectors) for pre-employment screening. What do these methods have in common? Companies use them, but they don't work. For example, there is no scientific evidence that handwriting analysis works, yet managers continue to use it. Lie detectors are no more accurate than a coin flip in screening out unethical employees. As for psychics at work, well, enough said. So, when you're hiring and promoting people, do the right thing. Stay away from fads. Use the reliable, valid, scientifically proven selection and assessment procedures discussed here to hire the right workers and promote the right people into management.[59]

very carefully validated and tested before using them to make selection decisions; the onus remains on employers to validate any questions that might violate human rights legislation.[62]

personality tests
tests that measure the extent to which applicants possess different kinds of job-related personality dimensions

Personality is the relatively stable set of behaviours, attitudes, and emotions displayed over time that makes people different from each other. **Personality tests** measure the extent to which applicants possess different kinds of job-related personality dimensions. Research indicates that five major personality dimensions (the Big 5)—extroversion, emotional stability, agreeableness, conscientiousness, and openness to experience—are related to work behaviour.[63] Of these, only conscientiousness—the degree to which someone is organized, hard-working, responsible, persevering, thorough, and achievement oriented—predicts job performance across a wide variety of jobs. Conscientiousness works especially well in combination with cognitive ability tests, allowing companies to select applicants who are organized, hard-working, responsible, and smart!

work sample tests
tests that require applicants to perform tasks that are actually done on the job

Work sample tests, also called *performance* tests, require applicants to perform tasks that are actually done on the job. So unlike specific ability, cognitive ability, biographical data, and personality tests, which are indirect predictors of job performance, work sample tests directly measure job applicants' capability to do the job. Work sample tests generally do a very good job of predicting future job performance; however, they can be expensive to administer and can be used for only one kind of job. For example, at an auto dealership, a work sample test for mechanics could not be used as a selection test for sales representatives.

assessment centres
a series of managerial simulations, graded by trained observers, that are used to determine applicants' capability for managerial work

Assessment centres use a series of job-specific simulations that are graded by several trained observers to determine the extent to which applicants can perform managerial work. So unlike the previously described selection tests commonly used for specific jobs or entry-level jobs, assessment centres are most often used to select applicants who have high potential to be good managers. Assessment centres often last two to five days and require participants to complete a number of tests and exercises that simulate managerial work.

Are tests perfect predictors of job performance? No, they aren't. Some people who do well on selection tests will do poorly in their jobs. Likewise, some people who do poorly on selection tests (and should have been hired, but weren't) would have been very good performers. However, valid tests will minimize these selection errors (hiring people who should not have been hired, and not hiring people who should have been hired) while maximizing correct selection decisions (hiring people who should have been hired, and not hiring people who should not have been hired). In short, tests increase the chances that you'll hire the right person for the job—that is, someone who turns out to be a good performer. So while tests aren't perfect, almost nothing predicts future job performance as well as the selection tests discussed here. For more on how well selection tests increase the odds of hiring the right person for the job, see the "What Really Works" feature on page 385.

Interviews

interviews
selection tool in which company representatives ask job applicants job-related questions to determine whether they are qualified for the job

In **interviews**, company representatives ask job applicants job-related questions to determine whether they are qualified for the job. Interviews are probably the most frequently used and relied-on selection device. There are several basic kinds of interviews: unstructured, structured, and semi-structured.

In *unstructured interviews,* interviewers are free to ask applicants anything they want, and studies show that they do. For instance, because interviewers often disagree about which questions should be asked during interviews, different interviewers tend to ask applicants very different questions.[65] Furthermore, individual interviewers even seem to have a tough time asking the same questions from one interview to the next. This high level of inconsistency lowers the validity of unstructured interviews as a selection device, because it becomes difficult to compare applicant responses. As a result, unstructured interviews do about half as well as structured interviews in accurately predicting which job applicants should be hired.

WHAT REALLY WORKS

Using Selection Tests to Hire Good Workers[64]

Hiring new employees always seems like a gamble. When you speak the words "We'd like to offer you a job," you never know how it's going to turn out. However, the selection tests discussed in this chapter and reviewed in this section go a long way toward helping employers take the gambling aspect out of the hiring process. Indeed, more than 1000 studies based on over 100 000 study participants strongly indicate that selection tests can give employers a much better than average (50–50) chance of hiring the right workers. In fact, if you had odds like these working for you in Las Vegas, you'd make so much money the casinos wouldn't let you in the door.

COGNITIVE ABILITY TESTS

There is a 76 percent chance that workers who did well on cognitive ability tests will be much better performers in their jobs than employees who did not do well on such tests.

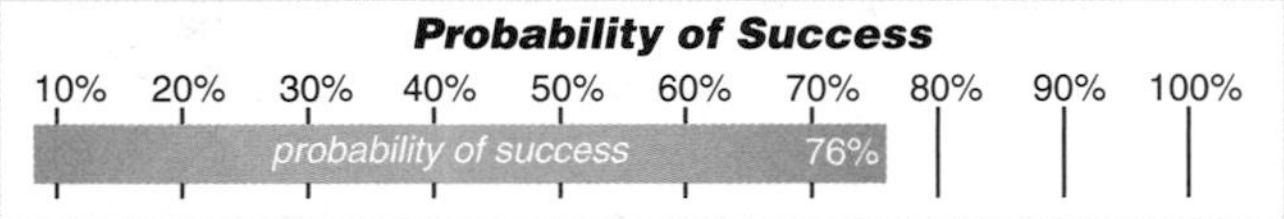

WORK SAMPLE TESTS

There is a 77 percent chance that workers who did well on work sample tests will be much better performers in their jobs than employees who did not do well on such tests.

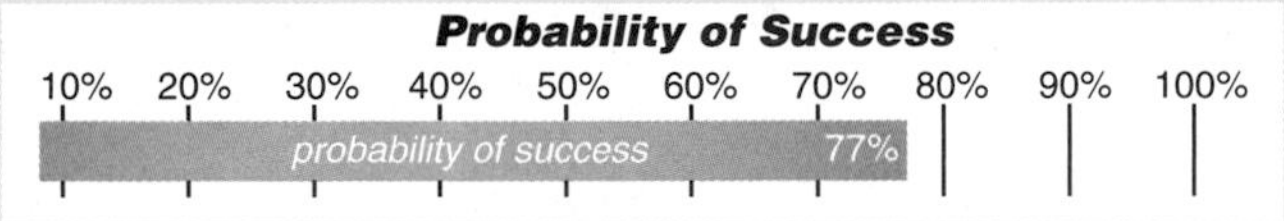

ASSESSMENT CENTRES

There is a 69 percent chance that workers who did well on assessment centre exercises will be much better managers than employees who did not do well on such exercises.

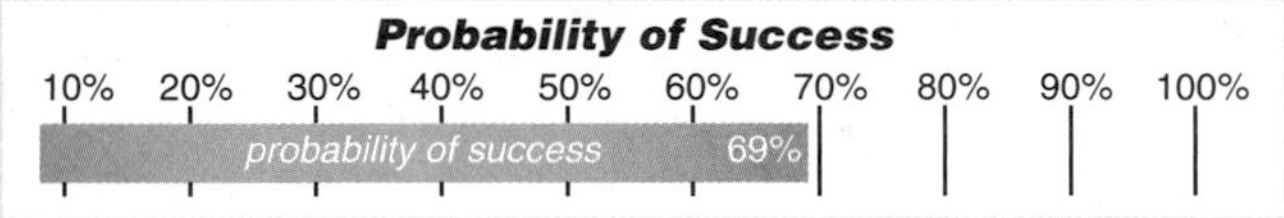

STRUCTURED INTERVIEWS

There is a 76 percent chance that workers who did well in structured interviews will be much better performers in their jobs than employees who did not do well in structured interviews.

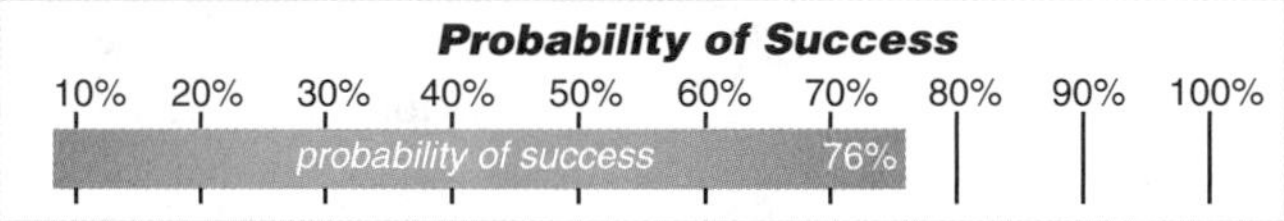

COGNITIVE ABILITY + WORK SAMPLE TESTS

When deciding whom to hire, most companies use a number of tests together to make even more accurate selection decisions. There is an 82 percent chance that workers who did well on a combination of cognitive ability tests and work sample tests will be much better performers in their jobs than employees who did not do well on both tests.

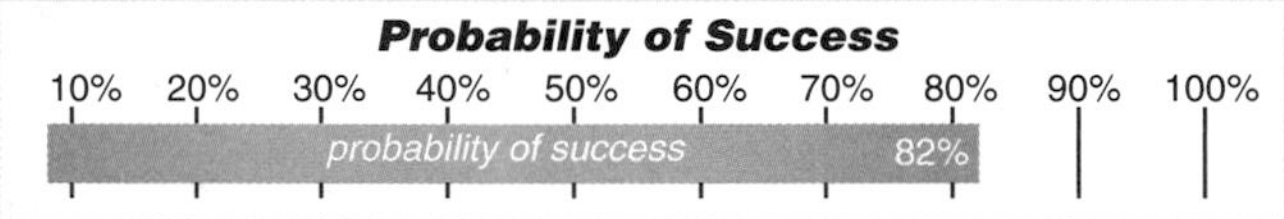

COGNITIVE ABILITY + INTEGRITY TESTS

There is an 83 percent chance that workers who did well on a combination of cognitive ability tests and integrity tests (see Chapter 3 for a discussion of integrity tests) will be much better performers in their jobs than employees who did not do well on both tests.

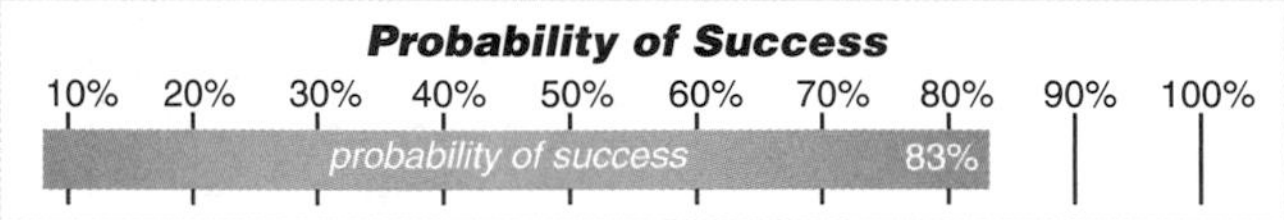

COGNITIVE ABILITY + STRUCTURED INTERVIEWS

There is an 82 percent chance that workers who did well on a combination of cognitive ability tests and structured interviews will be much better performers in their jobs than employees who did not do well on both tests.

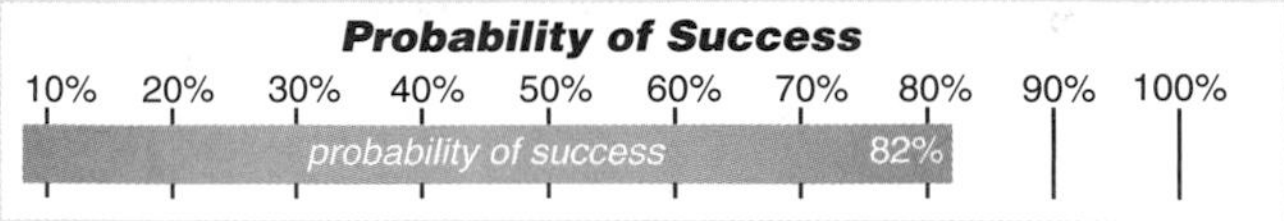

structured interviews interviews in which all applicants are asked the same set of standardized questions, usually including situational, behavioural, background, and job-knowledge questions

By contrast, with **structured interviews**, standardized interview questions are prepared ahead of time, so that all applicants are asked the same job-related questions. Four kinds of questions are typically asked in structured interviews:

- *situational questions*, which ask applicants how they would respond in a hypothetical situation (e.g., "What would you do if ...?").
- *behavioural questions*, which ask applicants what they did in previous jobs that were similar to the job for which they are applying (e.g., "In your previous jobs, tell me about ...").
- *background questions*, which ask applicants about their work experience, education, and other qualifications (e.g., "Tell me about the training you received at ...").
- *job-knowledge questions*, which ask applicants to demonstrate their job knowledge (e.g., for nurses, "Give me an example of a time when one of your patients had a severe reaction to a medication. How did you handle it?").[66]

The primary advantage of structured interviews is that asking all applicants the same questions makes comparing applicants a much easier process. Structuring interviews also ensures that interviewers ask only for important, job-related information. These advantages not only improve the accuracy, usefulness, and validity of the interview, but also reduce the chances that interviewers will ask questions about topics that violate employment laws (go back to Exhibit 13.7 on page 381 for a list of these topics).

Semi-structured interviews lie somewhere in between structured and unstructured interviews. A major part of the semi-structured interview (perhaps as much as 80 percent) is based on structured questions. However, some time is set aside for unstructured interviewing to allow interviewers to probe into ambiguous or missing information uncovered during the structured portion of the interview.

How well do interviews predict future job performance? Contrary to what you've probably heard, recent evidence indicates that even unstructured interviews do a fairly good job. However, when conducted properly, structured interviews can lead to much more accurate hiring decisions than unstructured interviews. In some cases, the validity of structured interviews can rival that of cognitive ability tests. But even more important, since interviews are especially good at assessing applicants' interpersonal skills, they work especially well together with cognitive ability tests. The combination (i.e., smart people who work well with others) leads to even better selection decisions than using either alone. Exhibit 13.8 provides a set of guidelines for conducting effective structured employment interviews.

Review 4: Selection

Selection is the process of gathering information about job applicants to decide who should be offered a job. Accurate selection procedures are valid, are legally defendable, and improve organizational performance. Application forms and résumés are the most common selection devices. Because many application forms request illegal, non–job-related information, and because as many as one-third of job applicants falsify information on résumés, these procedures can sometimes be of little value when making hiring decisions. References and background checks can also be problematic, given that previous employers are reluctant to provide such information for fear of being sued for defamation. Unfortunately, the lack of this information puts other employers at risk of negligent hiring lawsuits. Selection tests generally do the best job of predicting applicants' future job performance. In general, cognitive ability tests, work sample tests, biographical data, and assessment centres are the most valid tests, followed by personality tests and specific ability tests, which are still good predictors. Selection tests aren't perfect predictors of job performance, but almost nothing predicts future job performance as well as selection tests. The three kinds of job interviews are unstructured, structured, and semi-structured interviews. Of these, structured interviews work best, because they ensure that all applicants are consistently asked the same situational, behavioural, background, or job-knowledge questions.

PLANNING THE INTERVIEW
• Identify and define the knowledge, skills, abilities, and other (KSAO) characteristics needed for successful job performance.
• For each essential KSAO, develop key behavioural questions that will elicit examples of past accomplishments, activities, and performance.
• For each KSAO, develop a list of things to look for in applicants' responses to key questions.
CONDUCTING THE INTERVIEW
• Create a relaxed, nonstressful interview atmosphere.
• Review applicants' application blanks, résumés, and other information.
• Allocate enough time to complete the interview without interruption.
• Put the applicant at ease; don't jump right into heavy questioning.
• Tell the applicant what to expect. Explain the interview process.
• Obtain job-related information from the applicant by asking those questions prepared for each KSAO.
• Describe the job and the organization to applicants. Applicants need adequate information to make a selection decision about the organization.
AFTER THE INTERVIEW
• Immediately after the interview, review your notes and make sure they are complete.
• Evaluate applicants on each essential KSAO.
• Determine each applicant's probability of success and make a hiring decision.

Source: B.M. Farrell, "The Art and Science of Employment Interviews," *Personnel Journal* 65 (1986): 91–94.

EXHIBIT 13.8
Guidelines for Conducting Effective Structured Interviews

Developing Qualified Workers

Harmon Industries, which makes signalling and communications equipment for the railway and transit industries, has a new training centre where its employees learn engineering, safety, teamwork, time management, and other workplace skills. Ron Breshears, Harmon's vice president of human resources and safety, said, "Training is an investment, not a cost. Once you see that, you see that you get a good return on your investment."[67] At Sprint, the telecommunications company, over 80 percent of employees participate in its training program. Sprint's University of Excellence has 400 employees, who provide classroom and on-the-job training in 20 cities. Said Brad Harsha, assistant vice president of Sprint's University of Excellence, "Our philosophy is that Sprint supports continuous learning. Our training doesn't stop with orientation to the company. It's a lifelong learning commitment."[68]

Why are Harmon Industries and Sprint spending so much time and money to train their workers? Because, according to the American Society for Training and Development, an investment in training increases productivity by an average of 17 percent, reduces employee turnover, and makes companies more profitable; Toronto Dominion Bank estimates that it gets a 15 percent return from its extensive training programs.[69]

However, giving employees the knowledge and skills they need to improve their performance is just the first step in developing employees. The second step is giving employees formal feedback about their actual job performance. A CEO of a large telecommunications company hired an outside consultant to assess and coach (i.e., provide feedback) the company's top 50 managers. To the CEO's surprise, 75 percent of those managers indicated that the feedback they received from the consultant regarding their strengths and weaknesses was the only substantial feedback they had received about their performance in the last five years. On a more positive note, as a result of that feedback, two-thirds of the managers then took positive steps to improve their skills, knowledge, and job performance and expressed a clear desire for more feedback, especially from their boss, the CEO.[70] So, in today's competitive business environment, even CEOs understand the importance of formal performance feedback.

After reading the next two sections, you should be able to

5 describe how to determine training needs and select the appropriate training methods.

6 discuss how to use performance appraisal to give meaningful performance feedback.

5 TRAINING

training
developing the skills, experience, and knowledge employees need to perform their jobs or improve their performance

Training means providing opportunities for employees to develop the job-specific skills, experience, and knowledge they need to do their jobs or improve their performance. On average, Canadian firms spent $914 per employee on training in 2004.[71]

To make sure those training dollars are well spent, companies need to evaluate their procedures of determining training needs, training methods, and evaluating training.

Determining Training Needs

needs assessment
the process of identifying and prioritizing the learning needs of employees

Needs assessment is the process of identifying and prioritizing the learning needs of employees. Needs assessments can be conducted by identifying performance deficiencies, listening to customer complaints, surveying employees and managers, or formally testing employees' skills and knowledge.

Needs assessment usually begins with a job analysis to determine the knowledge and skill levels required to perform a job successfully. For example, Exhibit 13.9 shows that the job of customer service representative requires strong listening, reading, and writing skills, but only moderate capabilities in locating information, applied technology, and teamwork. Following the job analysis, employees are tested and their skill levels are compared to the requirements for the job. The greater the difference between an employee's skill levels and those required by the job, the greater the need for training. Exhibit 13.9 shows the current skill levels in each area for one individual. Based on the needs assessment, this employee needs some training in listening and locating information.

Note that training should never be conducted without first performing a needs assessment. Sometimes, training isn't needed at all, or it isn't needed for all employees. Since the needs assessment shown in Exhibit 13.9 indicates that the customer service representative has reading, applied technology, and teamwork skills that exceed those required for the job, it would be a waste of time and money to send this employee for training in these skills. Unfortunately, however, many organizations simply require all employees to attend training, whether they need to or not. The result is that employees who are not interested or don't need the training may react negatively during or after training. Likewise, employees who should be sent for training but aren't may also react negatively. Consequently, a needs assessment is an important tool for deciding who should or should not attend training. Just like hiring decisions, the selection of training participants should be based on job-related information.

Training Methods

Assume that you're a training director for a bank and that you're in charge of making sure that all bank employees know what to do in case of a robbery.[72] Exhibit 13.10 lists a number of training methods you could use: films and videos, lectures, planned readings, case studies, coaching and mentoring, group discussions, on-the-job training, role playing, simulations and games, vestibule training, and computer-based learning. Which method would be best? Vancouver-based Purdy's Chocolates, for example, emphasizes training and primarily uses mentoring. "It's about allowing people to learn along the way and watch what others are doing and ask questions," says Carmen Grant, their director of human resources.[73]

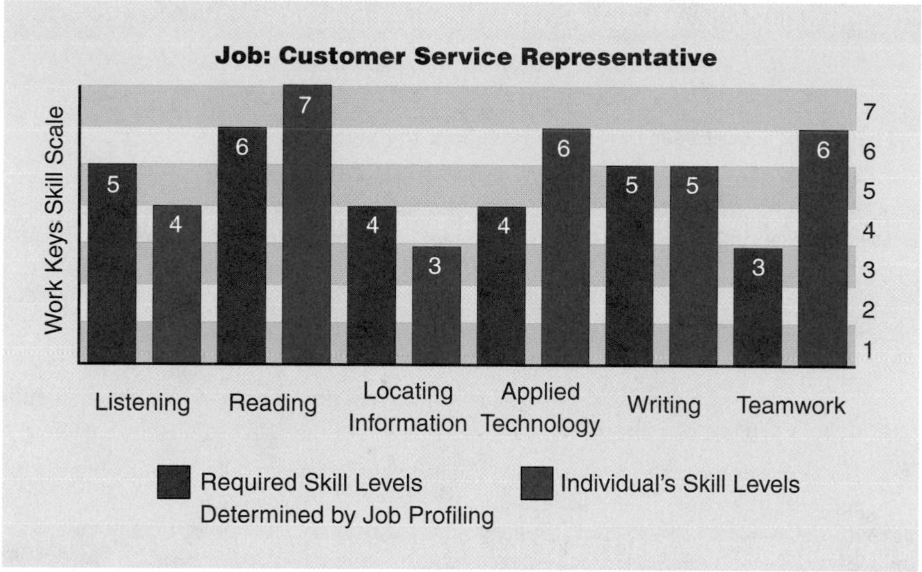

Source: "Work Keys in Action," Introduction to Work Keys. [Online] Available www.act.org/workkeys/, 31 May 1999.

EXHIBIT 13.9
Needs Assessment for a Customer Service Representative Job

To choose the best method, you should consider a number of factors, such as the number of people to be trained, the cost of training, and the objectives of the training. For instance, if the training objective is to impart information or knowledge to trainees, you should use films and videos, lectures, and planned readings. In the robbery training example, trainees would hear, see, or read about what to do in case of a robbery.

If developing analytical and problem-solving skills is the objective, use case studies, group discussions, and coaching and mentoring. In our example, trainees would read about a real robbery, discuss what to do, and then talk to people who had been through robberies before.

PHOTODISC/GETTY IMAGES

In on-the-job training, new employees learn by watching and working alongside experienced employees. Gradually, the trainee does more and more of the job on his or her own.

TRAINING OBJECTIVE: IMPART INFORMATION OR KNOWLEDGE
• *Films and Videos:* Films and videos share information, illustrate problems and solutions, and do a good job of holding trainees' attention. • *Lecture:* Instructors make oral presentations to trainees. • *Planned Readings:* Trainees read about concepts or ideas before attending training.
TRAINING OBJECTIVE: DEVELOP ANALYTICAL AND PROBLEM-SOLVING SKILLS
• *Case Studies:* Cases are analyzed and discussed in small groups. The cases present a specific problem or decision and trainees develop methods for solving the problem or making the decision. • *Coaching and Mentoring:* Coaching and mentoring of trainees by managers involves informal advice, suggestions, and guidance. This method is helpful for reinforcing other kinds of training and for trainees who benefit from support and personal encouragement. • *Group Discussions:* Small groups of trainees actively discuss specific topics. Instructor may perform the role of discussion leader.
TRAINING OBJECTIVE: PRACTISE, LEARN, OR CHANGE JOB BEHAVIOURS
• *On-the-Job Training (OJT):* New employees are assigned to experienced employees. The trainee is expected to learn by watching the experienced employee perform the job, and eventually by working alongside the experienced employee. Gradually, the trainee is left on his or her own to perform the job. • *Role Playing:* Trainees assume job-related roles and practise new behaviours by acting out what they would do in job-related situations. • *Simulations and Games:* Experiential exercises that place trainees in realistic job-related situations and give them the opportunity to experience a job-related condition in a relatively low-cost setting. The trainee benefits from "hands-on experience" before actually performing the job where mistakes may be more costly. • *Vestibule Training:* Procedures and equipment similar to those used in the actual job are set up in a special area called a vestibule. The trainee is then taught how to perform the job at his or her own pace without disrupting the actual flow of work, making costly mistakes, or exposing the trainee and others to dangerous conditions.
TRAINING OBJECTIVE: IMPART INFORMATION OR KNOWLEDGE; DEVELOP ANALYTICAL AND PROBLEM-SOLVING SKILLS; PRACTISE, LEARN, OR CHANGE JOB BEHAVIOURS
• *Computer-Based Learning:* Interactive videos, software, CD-ROMs, personal computers, teleconferencing, and the Internet may be combined to present multimedia-based training.

EXHIBIT 13.10
Training Objective and Methods

Source: A. Fowler, "How to Decide on Training Methods," *People Management* 25, no. 1 (1995): 36.

If practising, learning, or changing job behaviours is the objective, use on-the-job training, role-playing, simulations and games, and vestibule training. In the robbery example, trainees would learn about robbery situations on the job, pretend that they were in a robbery situation, or participate in a highly realistic mock robbery. If training is supposed to meet more than one of these objectives, your best choice may be to combine one of the previous methods with computer-based training.

Evaluating Training

After selecting a training method and conducting the training, the last step is to evaluate the training. Training can be evaluated in four ways: on *reactions*, how satisfied trainees were with the program; on *learning*, how much employees improved their knowledge or skills; on *behaviour*, how much employees actually changed their on-the-job behaviour because of training; or on *results*, how much training improved job performance, such as increased sales or quality, or decreased costs.[74]

Review 5: Training

Training is used to give employees the job-specific skills, experience, and knowledge they need to do their jobs or improve their job performance. To make sure training dollars are well spent, companies need to determine specific training needs, select appropriate training methods, and then evaluate the training. Needs assessments can be conducted by identifying performance deficiencies, listening to customer complaints, surveying employees and managers, or formally testing employees' skills and knowledge. Selection of an appropriate training method depends on a number of factors, such as the number of people to be trained, the cost of training, and the objectives of the training. If the objective is to impart information or knowledge, films and videos, lectures, and planned readings should be used. If developing analytical and problem-solving skills is the objective, case studies, group discussions, and coaching and mentoring should be used. If practising, learning, or changing job behaviours is the objective, on-the-job training, role-playing, simulations and games, and vestibule training should be used. If training is supposed to meet more than one of these objectives, it may be best to combine one of the previous methods with computer-based training. Training can be evaluated on reactions, learning, behaviour, or results.

6 PERFORMANCE APPRAISAL

performance appraisal the process of assessing how well employees are doing their jobs

Performance appraisal is the process of assessing how well employees are doing their jobs. Most employees and managers intensely dislike the performance appraisal process. One manager said, "I hate annual performance reviews. I hated them when I used to get them, and I hate them now that I give them. If I had to choose between performance reviews and paper cuts, I'd take paper cuts every time. I'd even take razor burns and the sound of fingernails on a blackboard."[75] Unfortunately, attitudes like this are all too common. One study of small businesses in the Halifax area found that less than 38 percent performed regular, formal performance appraisals of their employees, indicating just how unpopular and undervalued the process is.[76] Another found that seven out of ten employees are dissatisfied with the performance appraisal process in their companies.[77] In another study, unhappiness with performance appraisal systems were cited as their number one human resource management issue with 34 percent of companies planning to make changes to improve their systems.[78]

Because they are used for so many important purposes, companies with poor performance appraisal systems face tremendous problems. For example, performance appraisals are used as a basis for compensation, promotion, and training decisions. In human resource planning, performance appraisals are used for career planning and for making termination decisions.[79] And because of their key role in so many organizational decisions, performance appraisals are also central to many of the lawsuits that employees (or former employees) file against employers.

Let's explore how companies can avoid some of these problems with performance appraisals by accurately measuring job performance, and sharing performance feedback.

Accurately Measuring Job Performance

Workers often have strong doubts about the accuracy of their performance appraisals. And they may be right. For example, it's widely known that assessors are prone to rater errors when rating worker performance. Three of the most common rater errors are central tendency, halo, and leniency. *Central tendency* error occurs when assessors rate all workers as average or in the middle of the scale. *Halo error* occurs when assessors rate all workers as performing at the same level (good, bad, or average) in all parts of their jobs. *Leniency error* occurs when assessors rate all workers as performing particularly well. One of the reasons that managers make these errors is they often don't spend enough time gathering or reviewing performance data. Winston Connor, the former vice president of human resources at Huntsman Chemical, said, "Most of the time, it's just a ritual that managers go through. They pull out last year's review, update it and do it quickly."[80]

What can be done to minimize rater errors and improve the accuracy with which job performance is measured? In general, two approaches have been used: improving performance appraisal measures themselves and training performance raters to be more accurate.

One of the ways in which companies try to improve performance appraisal measures is to use as many objective performance measures as possible. **Objective performance measures** are measures of performance that are easily and directly counted or quantified. Common objective performance measures include output, scrap, waste, sales, customer complaints, or rejection rates.

objective performance measures
measures of job performance that are easily and directly counted or quantified

But when objective performance measures aren't available, and frequently they aren't, subjective performance measures have to be used instead. **Subjective performance measures** require that someone judge or assess a worker's performance. The most common kind of subjective performance appraisal measure is the trait rating scale shown in Exhibit 13.11. **Trait rating scales** ask raters to indicate the extent to which a worker possesses a particular trait or characteristic, such as reliability or honesty. However, trait rating scales, also called *graphic rating scales*, are typically inaccurate measures of performance. To start, managers are notoriously poor judges of employee traits. Second, traits are not related to job performance in any meaningful way.

subjective performance measures
measures of job performance that require someone to judge or assess a worker's performance

trait rating scales
a rating scale that indicates the extent to which a worker possesses particular traits or characteristics

So instead of using trait rating scales, subjective performance should be measured using behavioural observation scales. **Behavioural observation scales (BOS)** ask raters to rate the frequency with which workers perform specific behaviours representative of the job dimensions that are critical to successful job performance. Exhibit 13.11 shows a BOS for two important job dimensions for a retail salesperson: customer service and handling money. Notice that each dimension lists several specific behaviours characteristic of a worker who excels in that dimension of job performance. (Normally, the scale would list 7 to 12 items, not 3 as shown in the table.)

behavioural observation scales (BOS)
rating scales that indicate the frequency with which workers perform specific behaviours that are representative of the job dimensions critical to successful job performance

Not only do BOSs work well for rating critical dimensions of performance, but studies also show that managers strongly prefer BOSs for giving performance feedback; accurately differentiating between poor, average, and good workers; identifying training needs; and accurately measuring performance. And in response to the statement "If I were defending a company, this rating format would be an asset to my case," lawyers strongly preferred BOSs over other kinds of subjective performance appraisal scales.[81]

EXHIBIT 13.11
Subjective Performance Appraisal Scales

TRAIT RATING SCALE							
	Strongly Disagree	***1***	***2***	***3***	***4***	***5***	***Strongly Agree***
1. Employee is a hard worker.		1	2	3	4	5	
2. Employee is reliable.		1	2	3	4	5	
3. Employee is trustworthy.		1	2	3	4	5	
BEHAVIOURAL OBSERVATION SCALE							
Dimension: Customer Service	***Almost Never***	***1***	***2***	***3***	***4***	***5***	***Almost Always***
1. Greets customers with a smile and a "hello."		1	2	3	4	5	
2. Calls other stores to help customers find merchandise that is not in stock.		1	2	3	4	5	
3. Promptly handles customer concerns and complaints.		1	2	3	4	5	
Dimension: Money Handling	***Almost Never***	***1***	***2***	***3***	***4***	***5***	***Almost Always***
1. Accurately makes change from customer transactions.		1	2	3	4	5	
2. Accounts balance at the end of the day, no shortages or surpluses.		1	2	3	4	5	
3. Accurately records transactions in computer system.		1	2	3	4	5	

The second approach to improving the measurement of workers' job performance appraisal is rater training, an activity that is not done enough. In the previously mentioned study of small Halifax employers, less than half of the 38 percent who actually did formal performance appraisal actually trained raters.[82] In **rater training**, performance raters are trained to avoid rating errors (i.e., central tendency, halo, strictness, and leniency) and to improve rating accuracy. In rater training designed to minimize rating errors, trainees view videotapes of managers observing an employee performing some aspect of a job. Following each video, trainees are asked how they would have rated the worker's performance and how the manager on the tape would have rated it. Each videotape, however, is an example of the different kinds of rating errors. So trainees have a chance to actually observe rating errors being made (by the manager in the videotape) and then discuss how to avoid those errors.

rater training
training performance appraisal raters in how to avoid rating errors and increase rating accuracy

Another common form of rater training stresses rater accuracy (rather than minimizing errors). Here, raters closely examine the key dimensions of job performance (e.g., customer service and handling money for the retail salesperson in our example) and discuss specific behaviours representative of each dimension. Trainees may then be asked to role-play examples of these behaviours or to watch videos containing behavioural examples of each dimension of job performance. Both kinds of rater training are effective.[83]

Sharing Performance Feedback

After gathering accurate performance data, the next step is to share performance feedback with employees. Unfortunately, even when performance appraisal ratings are accurate, the appraisal process often breaks down at the feedback stage. Employees become defensive and dislike hearing any negative assessments of their work, no matter how small. Managers become defensive, too, and dislike giving appraisal feedback as much as employees dislike receiving it. One manager said, "I myself don't go as far as those who say performance reviews are inherently destructive and ought to be abolished, but I agree that the typical annual-review process does nothing but harm. It creates divisions. It undermines morale. It makes people angry, jealous, and cynical. It unleashes a whole lot of negative energy, and the organization gets nothing in return."[84]

So what can be done to overcome the inherent difficulties in performance appraisal feedback sessions? Since performance appraisal ratings have traditionally been the judgments of just one person, the boss, one approach is to use **360-degree feedback**. In this approach, feedback comes from four sources: the boss, subordinates, peers and co-workers, and the employees themselves. The data, which are obtained anonymously (except for the boss), are then compiled into a feedback report comparing the employee's self-ratings to those of the boss, subordinates, and peers and co-workers. Usually, a consultant or human resource specialist discusses the results with the employee. The advantage of 360-degree programs is that negative feedback ("You don't listen") is often more credible if heard from several people. For example, one boss who received 360-degree feedback thought he was a great writer, so he regularly criticized and corrected his subordinates' reports. Though the subordinates never discussed it among themselves, they all complained about his writing in the 360-degree feedback and mentioned that he should quit rewriting their reports. After receiving the feedback, he apologized and stopped.[85]

360-degree feedback
a performance appraisal process in which feedback is obtained from the boss, subordinates, peers and co-workers, and the employees themselves

A word of caution, though. About half the companies using 360-degree feedback for performance appraisal now use the feedback only for developmental purposes. For example, Sofia Theodorou, director of organizational development at Rogers Communications says, "With us, although it was positioned for developmental purposes only, you can bet we received a lot of calls asking to see reports. We responded that we would never break confidentiality because we could never re-earn the trust of our employees. That element is absolutely crucial."[86] They found that sometimes with raises and promotions on the line, peers and subordinates would distort ratings to harm competitors or help people they liked, and that sometimes people would give high ratings in order to get high ratings from others. On the other hand, studies clearly show that ratees prefer to receive feedback from several raters, so 360-degree feedback is likely to continue to grow in popularity.[87] A study of large Canadian firms found that 43 percent use 360-degree feedback in their performance appraisal process.[88]

Herbert Meyer, who has been studying performance appraisal feedback for more than 30 years, made the following specific recommendations for sharing performance feedback with employees.[89] First, managers should separate developmental feedback, which is designed to improve future performance, from administrative feedback, which is used as a reward for past performance, such as for raises. When managers give developmental feedback, they're acting as coaches, but when they give administrative feedback, they're acting as judges. These roles, coaches and judges, are clearly incompatible. As coaches, managers are encouraging, pointing out opportunities for growth and improvement, and employees are typically open and receptive to feedback. But as judges, managers are evaluative, and employees are typically defensive and closed to feedback. Jean Gatz, a training expert, said, "Most of us don't like to sit down and hear where we're lacking and where we need to improve. It's like sitting down with your mom and dad and they're telling you, 'We know what's best.'"[90]

Second, Meyer suggests that performance appraisal feedback sessions be based on self-appraisals, in which employees carefully assess their own strengths, weaknesses, successes, and failures in writing. Because employees play an active role in the review of their performance, managers can be coaches rather than judges. Also, because the focus is on future goals and development, both employees and managers are likely to be more satisfied with the process and more committed to future plans and changes. See Exhibit 13.12 for the list of topics that Meyer recommends for discussion in performance appraisal feedback sessions.

One concern about self-appraisals is that employees will be overly positive when evaluating their performance. However, when the focus is on development and not administrative assessment, studies show that self-appraisals lead to more candid self-assessments than traditional supervisory reviews.[91]

Third, Meyer suggests eliminating the "grading" aspect of performance appraisal, in which employees are ranked on a 1–5 scale or are scored as below average, average, above average, or exceptional. He says that "assigning a numerical or adjectival grade, such as 'satisfactory,' 'excellent,' 'adequate,' 'outstanding,' or 'poor,' to overall performance or specific performance tends to obstruct rather than facilitate constructive discussion. It treats a mature person like a schoolchild. The administrative action taken, such as the amount of salary increase or a promotion, will communicate an overall appraisal better than will a grade."[92]

Review 6: Performance Appraisal

Most employees and managers intensely dislike the performance appraisal process. However, some of the problems associated with appraisals can be avoided by accurately measuring job performance and effectively sharing performance feedback with employees. Managers are prone to three kinds of rating errors: central tendency, halo, and leniency error. One way to minimize rating errors is to use better appraisal measures,

EXHIBIT 13.12
What to Discuss in a Performance Appraisal Feedback Session

1.	Overall progress—an analysis of accomplishments and shortcomings.
2.	Problems encountered in meeting job requirements.
3.	Opportunities to improve performance.
4.	Long-range plans and opportunities—for the job and for the individual's career.
5.	General discussion of possible plans and goals for the coming year.

Source: H.H. Meyer, "A Solution to the Performance Appraisal Feedback Enigma," *Academy of Management Executive* 5, no. 1 (1991): 68–76.

such as objective measures of performance or behavioural observation scales. Another method is to directly train performance raters to minimize errors and more accurately rate the important dimensions of job performance.

After gathering accurate performance data, the next step is to share performance feedback with employees. One way to overcome the inherent difficulties in performance appraisal feedback is to provide 360-degree feedback, in which feedback is obtained from four sources: the boss, subordinates, peers and co-workers, and the employees themselves. Feedback tends to be more credible if heard from several sources. Traditional performance appraisal feedback sessions can be improved by separating developmental and administrative feedback, by basing feedback discussions on employee self-appraisals, and by eliminating the "grading" aspect.

Keeping Qualified Workers

Retaining qualified workers is a major challenge for today's employers. The best employees always have options, and during boom times it seems that everyone has options. Think back to Chapter 2 when we discussed how difficult it was for software firms to obtain qualified employees. Although we often associate employee retention problems with skilled workers, given a hot enough economy even unskilled workers have options. For example, because of the tremendous boom and the associated shortage of workers, many fast-food outlets in Fort McMurray, Alberta, have to pay $14 an hour to retain employees.[93] Employees are not simply looking for better wages but also quality of working life. Issues such as length of holidays and flexible workdays can help companies retain their employees. And with acute labour shortages in many industries occurring nationwide, nearly all employers now understand the effect that compensation has on their ability to keep qualified workers.

After reading the next two sections, you should be able to

7 describe basic compensation strategies and how they affect human resource practice.

8 discuss the four kinds of employee separations: termination, downsizing, retirements, and turnover.

7 COMPENSATION

Compensation includes both the financial and nonfinancial rewards that organizations give employees in exchange for their work.

Let's learn more about compensation by examining the compensation decisions and employment benefits.

compensation
the financial and nonfinancial rewards that organizations give employees in exchange for their work

Compensation Decisions

There are four basic kinds of compensation decisions: pay level, pay variability, pay structure, and employment benefits. We'll discuss employment benefits in the next subsection.[94]

Pay-level decisions are decisions about whether to pay workers at a level that is below, above, or at current market wages. Companies use job evaluation to set their pay structures. **Job evaluation** determines the worth of each job by determining the market value of the knowledge, skills, and requirements needed to perform it. After conducting a job evaluation, most companies try to pay the "going rate," meaning the current market wage.

job evaluation
a process that determines the worth of each job in a company by evaluating the market value of the knowledge, skills, and requirements needed to perform it

Some companies choose to pay above-average wages to attract and keep employees. Above-market wages can attract a larger, more qualified pool of job applicants, increase the rate of job acceptance, decrease the time it takes to fill positions, and increase how long employees stay.[95] Some government agencies and departments that typically pay well below market wages find that it can take months and sometimes years to fill job openings, as applicants go to the private sector for much more money.[96] Service industries, which typically also pay low wages, can have a great deal of difficulty obtaining and retaining employees. For example, a bagel franchise in Banff (a town that finds it notoriously difficult to retain employees) that had 12 employees hired 60 people in one year, an incredible turnover rate of 500 percent![97]

Pay-variability decisions are decisions concerning the extent to which employees' pay varies with individual and organizational performance. Linking pay to organizational performance is intended to increase employee motivation, effort, and job performance. Piecework, sales commission, profit sharing, employee stock ownership plans, and stock options are common pay-variability options. For instance, under **piecework** pay plans, employees are paid a set rate for each item produced up to some standard (e.g., $0.35 per item produced for output up to 100 units per day). Once productivity exceeds the standard, employees are paid a set amount for each unit of output over the standard (e.g., $0.45 for each unit above 100 units). For example, Canadian tree planting operations (reforestation) typically pay an individual for each tree planted. Ontario-based PRT Frontier Resource Management pays $0.08 to $0.10 per tree.[98] Sales **commission** is another kind of pay variability, in which salespeople are paid a percentage of the purchase price of items they sell. The more they sell, the more they earn.

piecework
a compensation system in which employees are paid a set rate for each item they produce

commission
a compensation system in which employees earn a percentage of each sale they make

Because pay plans such as piecework and commissions are based on individual performance, they can reduce the incentive that people have to work together. Therefore, companies also use group incentives and organizational incentives, such as profit sharing, employee stock ownership plans, and stock options, to encourage teamwork and cooperation.

Profit sharing is the payment of a portion of the organization's profits to employees over and above their regular compensation. The more profitable the company, the more profit is shared. WestJet is one company that has traditionally relied on profit sharing to motivate employees. By 2004 WestJet had distributed $56 million in profits.[99]

profit sharing
a compensation system in which a percentage of company profits is paid to employees in addition to their regular compensation

DAVID FRAZIER/STONE/GETTY IMAGES

Tree planting is an example of a job that is usually paid by piecework.

Employee stock ownership plans (ESOPs) compensate employees by awarding them shares of the company stock in addition to their regular compensation. Castek Software Factory, a Toronto-based software developer, has had an ESOP since 1995. The CFO, Fay Wu, credits this plan with substantially reducing the firm's level of employee turnover, which in the software industry can be quite high.[100]

employee stock ownership plans (ESOPs)
a compensation system that awards employees shares of company stock in addition to their regular compensation

Stock options give employees the right to purchase shares of stock at a set price, which is another program offered by WestJet.[101] It works like this. If you are awarded the right (or option) to 100 shares of stock valued at $5 a share and the stock price rises to $15 a share, you can exercise your options and make $1000 (100 shares which have increased $10 in value, from $5 to $15). Of course, as company profits and share values increase, stock options become even more valuable to employees.

stock options
a compensation system that gives employees the right to purchase shares of stock at a set price, even if the value of the stock increases above that price

Pay-structure decisions are concerned with internal pay distributions, meaning the extent to which people in the company receive very different levels of pay.[102] With *hierarchical pay structures*, there are big differences from one pay level to another. The largest pay levels are for people near the top of the pay distribution. The basic idea behind hierarchical pay structures is that large differences in pay between jobs or organizational levels should motivate people to work harder to obtain those higher-paying jobs.

By contrast, with *compressed pay structures*, there are typically fewer pay levels and smaller differences in pay between pay levels. Pay is less dispersed and more similar across jobs in the company. The basic idea behind compressed pay structures is that similar pay levels should lead to higher levels of cooperation, feelings of fairness and a common purpose, and better group and team performance.

So should companies choose hierarchical or compressed pay structures? The evidence isn't straightforward, but studies seem to indicate that there are significant problems with the hierarchical approach. The most damaging is that there appears to be little link between organizational performance and the pay of top managers.[103] Furthermore, studies of professional athletes indicate that hierarchical pay structures (e.g., paying superstars 40 to 50 times more than the lowest-paid athlete on the team) hurt the performance of teams and individual players.[104] For now, the key seems to be that hierarchical pay structures work best for independent work, where it's easy to determine the contributions of individual performers and where little coordination with others is needed to get the job done. In other words, hierarchical pay structures work best when clear links can be drawn between individual performance and individual rewards. By contrast, compressed pay structures (i.e., paying everyone similar amounts of money) seem to work best for interdependent work, in which employees must work with each other. But some companies are pursuing a middle ground, in which they try to balance hierarchical and compressed pay structures by giving ordinary workers the chance to earn more through ESOPs, stock options, and profit sharing.

Employment Benefits

Employment benefits include virtually any kind of compensation other than direct wages paid to employees.[105] Three employee benefits are mandated by law: Canada Pension Plan, worker's compensation, and employment insurance. However, to attract and retain a good work force, most organizations offer a wide variety of benefits, including retirement plans and pensions, paid holidays, paid vacations, sick leave, health insurance, life insurance, dental care, eye care, daycare facilities, paid personal days, legal assistance, physical fitness facilities, educational assistance, and discounts on company products and services. In 2004 KPMG estimated that benefits cost Canadian organizations about 27 percent of an employer's payroll costs, indicating that they are a key element in compensation packages.[106]

employment benefits
a method of rewarding employees that includes virtually any kind of compensation other than wages or salaries

Managers should understand that benefits are not likely to improve employee motivation and performance. However, benefits do affect job satisfaction, employee decisions about staying or leaving the company, and the company's attractiveness to job applicants.[107] One way in which organizations make their benefit plans more attractive to

cafeteria benefit plans (flexible benefit plans) plans that allow employees to choose which benefits they receive, up to a certain dollar value

employees is through **cafeteria benefit plans** or **flexible benefit plans**, which allow employees to choose which benefits they receive, up to a certain dollar value.[108] Many cafeteria or flexible benefit plans start with a core of benefits, such as health insurance and life insurance that are available to all employees. Then employees are allowed to select other benefits that best fit their needs, up to a predetermined dollar amount. Some organizations provide several packages of benefits from which employees may choose. Each package is of equivalent value; however, the mix of benefits differs. For example, older employees may prefer more benefit dollars spent on retirement plans, while younger employees may prefer additional vacation days. Flexible benefits plans are becoming increasingly popular. In a study conducted in 2005 in Canada, 55 percent of employers had flexible benefit plans or planned to have in the near future.[109]

The drawback to flexible benefit plans has been the high cost of administering these programs. However, with advances in information processing technology and HRISs, the cost of administering benefits has begun to drop in recent years.

Review 7: Compensation

Compensation includes both the financial and nonfinancial rewards that organizations give employees in exchange for their work. There are four basic kinds of compensation decisions: pay level, pay variability, pay structure, and employment benefits. Pay-level decisions determine whether workers will receive wages below, above, or at current market levels. Pay-variability decisions concern the extent to which pay varies with individual and organizational performance. Piecework, sales commission, profit sharing, employee stock ownership plans, and stock options are common pay-variability options. Pay-structure decisions concern the extent to which people in the company receive very different levels of pay. Hierarchical pay structures work best for independent work, while compressed pay structures work best for interdependent work.

Employee benefits include virtually any kind of compensation other than direct wages paid to employees. Flexible or cafeteria benefit plans, which offer employees a wide variety of benefits, improve job satisfaction, increase the chances that employees will stay with companies, and make organizations more attractive to job applicants. The cost of administering benefits has begun to drop in recent years.

8 EMPLOYEE SEPARATIONS

employee separation the voluntary or involuntary loss of an employee

Employee separation is a broad term covering the loss of an employee for any reason. *Involuntary separation* occurs when employers decide to terminate or lay off employees. *Voluntary separation* occurs when employees decide to quit or retire. Because employee separations affect recruiting, selection, training, and compensation, organizations should forecast the number of employees they expect to lose through terminations, layoffs, turnover, or retirements when doing human resource planning.

Let's explore employee separation by examining terminating employees, downsizing, retirement, and employee turnover.

Terminating Employees

Hopefully, the words "You're fired!" have never been directed at you, but lots of people hear them. Getting fired is a terrible thing, but many managers make it even worse by bungling the firing process, needlessly provoking the people who were fired, and unintentionally inviting lawsuits. For example, one worker found out he had been fired after a restaurant told him that his company credit card was no longer active. A manager found out that she had been fired when she came back from lunch and found a note on her desk chair. And workers at a high-tech company know that they've been fired when their security codes no longer open their office doors or the front door to their office buildings.[110] How would you feel if you had been fired in one of these ways? While firing is never pleasant (and managers hate firings nearly as much as employees do), there are several things managers can do to minimize the problems inherent in firing employees.

First, in most firing situations, firing should not be the first option. Instead, employees should be given a chance to change their behaviour. So when problems arise, employees should have ample warning and must be specifically informed as to the nature and seriousness of the trouble they're in. After being notified, they should be given sufficient time to change. If the problems continue, they should again be counselled about their job performance, what could be done to improve it, and the possible consequences if things don't change (e.g., written reprimand, suspension without pay, or firing). Sometimes, this is enough to solve the problem. Outplacement specialist Laurence Stybel tells the story about a large hospital that was getting ready to fire its director of radiology because of his bad attitude and increasing rudeness to co-workers. Rather than fire him, hospital management put him on probation and hired a consultant to counsel him about working with others. Within weeks, his attitude and behaviour changed, and the hospital avoided firing him and the expense of replacing him (which could have included a lawsuit).[111] However, after several rounds of warnings and discussions, if the problem isn't corrected, the employee may be terminated.[112]

Second, employees should be fired for a good reason, which is referred to as just cause. Employers used to hire and fire employees under the legal principle of "termination at will," which allowed them to fire employees for a good reason, a bad reason, or no reason at all. However, as employees began contesting their firings in court, the principle of wrongful dismissal emerged. **Wrongful dismissal** is a legal doctrine that requires employers to have a job-related reason to terminate employees. In other words, just like other major human resource decisions, termination decisions should be made on the basis of job-related factors, such as violating company rules or consistently poor performance. Managers should record the job-related reasons for the termination, document specific instances of rule violations or continued poor performance, and keep notes and documents from the counselling sessions held with employees.[113] If an employer does not have just cause for terminating an employee, the employer must compensate the employee in lieu of the notice period to which they would normally be entitled. The minimum entitlement under provincial and federal laws varies and employees can obtain up to two years' pay under common law, depending on the circumstances.

wrongful dismissal
a legal doctrine that requires employers to have a job-related reason to terminate employees

Third, companies need to pay attention to reactions of remaining employees after someone has been fired. Jenai Lane of Respect, Inc., a maker of jewellery and accessories, believes it is important to consider the employees who remain after someone is terminated. After she fires someone, she holds an "emergency pow-wow" and encourages employees to speak their minds. "It takes a little prodding, but it's good to get people's feelings out in the open."[114] However, managers should be careful not to criticize the employee who has just been fired, as this could lead to a wrongful dismissal or defamation lawsuit.

Downsizing

Downsizing is the planned elimination of jobs in a company. Whether it's because of cost cutting, declining market share, or overaggressive hiring and growth, downsizing is a common strategy.[115] A recent study found that two-thirds of U.S. companies that downsize will downsize a second time within a year. For example, Applied Materials, based in California's Silicon Valley, let 1500 workers go the first time it downsized, followed by another 2000 workers less than three months later.[116] In Canada, Nortel and Air Canada have gone through repeated rounds of downsizing.

downsizing
the planned elimination of jobs in a company

Does downsizing work? In theory, downsizing is supposed to lead to higher productivity and profits, better stock performance, and increased organizational flexibility. However, numerous studies demonstrate that it doesn't. For instance, a 15-year study of downsizing found that downsizing 10 percent of a company's work force only produces a 1.5 percent decrease in costs, that firms that downsized increased their stock price by 4.7 percent over three years compared to 34.3 percent for firms that didn't, and that profitability and productivity were generally not improved by downsizing.[117] These results make it clear that the best strategy is to conduct effective human resource planning and avoid downsizing altogether. Indeed, downsizing should always be used as a measure of last resort and there are a number of alternative strategies such as reducing hours, job sharing, leaves of absence, and employee buy-outs.[118]

However, if companies do find themselves in financial or strategic situations where downsizing is required for survival, they should train managers how to break the news to downsized employees, have senior managers explain in detail why downsizing is necessary, and time the announcement so employees hear it from the company and not from other sources, such as TV or newspaper reports.[119] Finally, companies should do everything they can to help downsized employees find other jobs. One of the best ways to do this is to use **outplacement services** that provide employment-counselling services for employees faced with downsizing. Outplacement services often include advice and training in preparing résumés and getting ready for job interviews, and even identifying job opportunities in other companies.

outplacement services
employment-counselling services offered to employees who are losing their jobs because of downsizing

When Victoria's JDS Uniphase decided that it needed to downsize, it went to great lengths to find each laid-off employee a new job. It put together a 112-page directory of employees' biographical sketches and mailed it to 400 employers. They offered added incentives to employees to remain until the last day that JDS wanted them to work, and most stayed on. They also offered employees job-hunting training such as résumé writing, job search techniques, and where to find "hidden jobs." Other training was also made available such as computer skills. Job fairs were organized and speakers were brought in to provide information to employees about a number of helpful issues.[120] Extensive outplacement programs not only help laid-off employees, but also help the company maintain a positive image in the community affected by downsizing. Steps such as these also help employees remain productive during their final days at the company.

Retirement

early retirement incentive programs (ERIPs)
programs that offer financial benefits to employees to encourage them to retire early

Early retirement incentive programs (ERIPs) offer financial benefits to employees to encourage them to retire early. Companies use ERIPs to reduce the number of employees in the organization, to lower costs by eliminating positions after employees retire, to lower costs by replacing high-paid retirees with lower-paid, less-experienced employees, or to create openings and job opportunities for people inside the company. For example, in 2001 DaimlerChrysler agreed on a $90 million retirement package with the Canadian Auto Workers, the union that represents the majority of its employees. It was hoped that this package would reduce the need for layoffs by up to 60 percent. Each package was worth about $52 500, which included a one-time payment of $26 000 and a credit of $16 000 toward the purchase of a Chrysler vehicle.

The biggest problem with most ERIPs is accurately predicting who and how many will accept early retirement. The company will likely lose good as well as poor performers, and sometimes more workers than they expect. For example, Ameritech Corporation, the largest telephone company in the Midwest U.S., offered an ERIP consisting of a US$5000 educational assistance program to retrain workers, financial planning counselling, and outplacement advice and guidance. Since most pension benefits are based on a formula including years of service and employee age, the core of Ameritech's program was the "three-plus-three enhancement," which added three years to the employees' age and three years to their years of service to help them qualify for greater retirement benefits. Ameritech carefully identified the number of employees near retirement age and estimated that 5000 to 6000 of its 48 000 employees would take advantage of the program. Instead, nearly 22 000 employees accepted the ERIP offer and applied for early retirement![121]

Employee Turnover

employee turnover
loss of employees who voluntarily choose to leave the company

Employee turnover is the loss of employees who voluntarily choose to leave the company. In general, most companies try to keep the rate of employee turnover low to reduce recruiting, hiring, training, and replacement costs. However, not all kinds of employee turnover are bad for organizations. In fact, some turnover can actually be good. For instance, **functional turnover** is the loss of poor-performing employees who choose to leave the organization.[122] Functional turnover gives the organization a chance to replace poor performers with better replacements. In fact, one study found that simply replacing poor-performing leavers with average replacements would increase the revenues produced by retail salespeople in an upscale department store by US$112 000 per person per year.[123] By contrast, **dysfunctional turnover**, the loss of high performers who choose to leave, is a costly loss to the organization.

functional turnover
loss of poor-performing employees who voluntarily choose to leave a company

dysfunctional turnover
loss of high-performing employees who voluntarily choose to leave a company

Employee turnover should be carefully analyzed to determine exactly who is choosing to leave the organization, good or poor performers. If the company is losing too many high performers, managers should determine the reasons and find ways to reduce the loss of valuable employees. The company may have to raise salary levels, offer enhanced benefits, or improve working conditions to retain skilled workers. One of the best ways to influence functional and dysfunctional turnover is to link pay directly to performance. A study of four sales forces found that when pay was strongly linked to performance via sales commissions and bonuses, poor performers were much more likely to leave (i.e., functional turnover). By contrast, poor performers were much more likely to stay when paid large, guaranteed monthly salaries and small sales commissions and bonuses.[124] Companies often perform exit interviews to determine the reasons why employees have left. For example, Community Hospital in O'Leary, P.E.I., was experiencing very high nursing staff turnover. After conducting exit interviews, it identified numerous concerns over working conditions.[125]

Review 8: Employee Separations

Employee separation is the loss of an employee, which can occur voluntarily or involuntarily. Before firing or terminating employees, managers should give employees a chance to improve. If firing becomes necessary, it should be done because of job-related factors, such as violating company rules or consistently poor performance. Downsizing is supposed to lead to higher productivity and profits, better stock performance, and increased organizational flexibility, but studies show that it doesn't. The best strategy is to downsize only as a last resort. Companies that do downsize should offer outplacement services to help employees find other jobs. Companies use early retirement incentive programs to reduce the number of employees in the organization, lower costs, and create openings and job opportunities for people inside the company. The biggest problem with ERIPs is accurately predicting who and how many will accept early retirement. Companies generally try to keep the rate of employee turnover low to reduce costs. However, functional turnover can be good for organizations, because it offers the chance to replace poor performers with better replacements. Managers should analyze employee turnover to determine who is resigning and take steps to reduce the loss of good performers.

What Really Happened?[126]

Remember the daunting task that the human resource manager for the Ekati mine was facing at the beginning of the chapter? The company had overcome significant challenges and constructed a large mine in the Northwest Territories and had to hire a permanent work force of almost 1000. Given that there were a limited number of qualified employees in the Northwest Territories, that the demand for skilled workers across Canada was increasing, that the mine had to hire a large number of Aboriginals, and that the company really wanted to hire and retain good employees, this was a genuinely challenging task.

How do you go about obtaining qualified applicants?

Finding qualified workers in today's job market is an increasingly difficult task. Successful selection decisions begin by recruiting to develop a pool of qualified job applicants. What if there are a limited number of qualified applicants? Companies are often faced with a classic "make or buy" decision with regard to component parts that they use in the production of their products. For example, a car company can decide to buy a bumper from another company and put it on its car. This is what Magna International does; it makes car parts for major car manufacturers. Companies also face this issue with regard to their skilled work force. Do they "buy" a skilled work force? In other words, do they hire workers who already have the skills required or do they "make" skilled employees by hiring unskilled or semi-skilled workers and train them for more skilled work.

Clearly, as this was an entirely new company and project, it initially had to rely exclusively on external recruiting. One of the first things it did was start an aggressive recruiting campaign across the Northwest Territories. Despite an aggressive campaign, it became clear that the company would have a great deal of difficulty meeting its human resource needs by relying on external recruiting.

What do you do when you cannot recruit qualified employees?

The management of the Ekati mine decided to "make" employees by developing a qualified applicant pool. Internal recruiting is the process of developing a pool of qualified job applicants from people who already work in the company. Internal recruiting, sometimes called "promotion from within," improves employee commitment, morale, and motivation. Recruiting current employees also reduces recruitment start-up time and costs and, because employees are already familiar with the company's culture and procedures, generally increases workers' chances of success in new jobs. In addition, career paths help employees focus on long-term goals and development while also helping companies do succession or replacement planning. A career path is a planned sequence of jobs through which employees may advance within an organization. In order to get employees onto a career path, they first have to be hired. Ekati mine managers decided to relax their initial hiring standards. As mentioned, a significant portion of the work force in the Northwest Territories has less than a grade-nine education. The relaxed entry standards gained the company a pool of workers, but they weren't fully qualified and they had no skills to progress beyond entry-level jobs.

Now that it had hired individuals lacking many basic skills, what did Billiton do to create a qualified work force?

Billiton created specific programs at the Ekati mine to develop employees to build a qualified pool of workers. The program was named the Workplace Learning Program. Given the fact that basic numeracy and literacy skills were required for almost all jobs, this was a clear area to focus on. This was critical, given that 24 percent of their entry-level employees could only read and understand the word "stop" if it was written on stop sign. In addition to basic numeracy and literacy skills, they also needed to develop their critical-thinking and problem-solving abilities. The mine divides its entry-level employees into three groups: those with less that a grade three education, those with grade three to six, and those with at least a sixth grade education. The mine then hired a number of adult educators to work with employees. Training is not mandatory but employees are generally very eager to participate in training programs. Over 100 people per year participate in the training programs, and the company also encourages employees to undertake training when not at the mine site. The mine's goal is to move employees from these basic skills and get them into higher-level training in order for them to qualify for promotion. Employees work on their skills from four to six hours per work rotation (employees work for two weeks straight and then are flown out of the camp for two weeks). In addition, the mine is participating in a number of trades training programs and has over 80 apprentices in seven trades. The mine also developed a skills profile for four entry-level positions: heavy equipment operator, process plant technician, maintenance helper, and warehouse technician. The mine used these skill profiles to direct training programs at these specific jobs.

Another strategy that it employed was to participate in a number of stay-in-school programs. Over time, these would help increase the number of local people available for immediate employment and would also increase the number of people eligible for training in the skilled trades. The mine also sponsored a number of scholarships and provided summer employment for Aboriginal and northern students so that they could gain some work experience. Clearly, it wanted to have a long-term influence on the demographics of the labour supply in the Northwest Territories. Although the company has yet to meet all its hiring goals, it has been named one of the best employers in Canada and is working diligently toward meeting its commitments. Only time will tell if these efforts will be enough, but Billiton appears to be moving in the right direction.

Key Terms

assessment centres *(384)*
background checks *(380)*
behavioural observation scales (BOS) *(392)*
biographical data (biodata) *(383)*
cafeteria benefit plans (flexible benefit plans) *(398)*
cognitive ability tests *(383)*
commission *(396)*
compensation *(395)*
downsizing *(399)*
dysfunctional turnover *(401)*
early retirement incentive programs (ERIPs) *(400)*
employee separation *(398)*
employee stock ownership plans (ESOPs) *(397)*
employee turnover *(400)*
employment benefits *(397)*
employment references *(380)*
external recruiting *(378)*
functional turnover *(401)*
hostile work environment *(375)*
human resource information systems (HRIS) *(369)*
human resource management *(366)*
human resource planning (HRP) *(367)*
internal recruiting *(378)*
interviews *(384)*
job analysis *(377)*
job description *(377)*
job evaluation *(395)*
job specifications *(377)*
needs assessment *(388)*
objective performance measures *(392)*
outplacement services *(400)*
performance appraisal *(391)*
personality tests *(384)*
piecework *(396)*
profit sharing *(396)*
quid pro quo sexual harassment *(375)*
rater training *(393)*
recruiting *(376)*
reliability *(374)*
selection *(380)*
sexual harassment *(375)*
specific ability tests (aptitude tests) *(383)*
stock options *(397)*
structured interviews *(386)*
subjective performance measures *(392)*
360-degree feedback *(393)*
training *(388)*
trait rating scales *(392)*
validation *(380)*
validity *(374)*
work-force forecasting *(368)*
work sample tests *(384)*
wrongful dismissal *(399)*

Self-Assessment

INTERVIEW ANXIETY

How would you feel if you got a call to interview for your dream job? Excited? Nervous? Or downright panicked? It's not uncommon to get some "butterflies" in your stomach at the prospect of a job interview, but some candidates have more than weak knees and sweaty palms. On page 518 of the Self-Assessment Appendix, you'll find a 30-question survey designed to give you insights into your own reactions. Your score will be a baseline as you begin working on the skills you'll need during a job hunt.

Management Decisions

A BEHAVIOURAL INTERVIEW FOR YOUR PROFESSOR?

Interviews are by far the most frequently used selection procedure. In fact, it's rare for people to be hired without first being interviewed. But as you learned in the chapter, most managers conduct unstructured interviews, in which they are free to ask applicants anything they want, and studies show that they do. Indeed, studies show that because interviewers often disagree about which questions should be asked during interviews, different interviewers tend to ask applicants very different questions. However, individual interviewers even seem to have a tough time asking the same questions from one interview to the next. This high level of inconsistency lowers the validity of interviews as a selection device, because it becomes difficult to compare applicant responses. As a result, unstructured interviews do about half as well as structured interviews in accurately predicting which job applicants should be hired.

By contrast, with structured interviews, standardized interview questions are prepared ahead of time, so that all applicants may be asked the same job-related questions. The primary advantage of structured interviews is that asking all applicants the same questions makes comparing applicants a much easier process. Also, structuring interviews ensures that interviewers will ask for only important, job-related information. These advantages significantly improve the accuracy, usefulness, and validity of interviews as a selection procedure. Since you're likely to use interviewing more than any other selection procedure, the purpose of this assignment is to give you some experience creating questions for structured interviews.

You'll be writing questions for the job of university professor, a job with which all of you should be familiar (having observed each of your instructors for an average of 40 hours per college class). Your job is to write 12 questions that you would ask applicants who wanted to teach at your university. Remember, four kinds of questions are typically asked in structured interviews. You'll be writing three questions for each of the four kinds of questions shown below.

- *Situational questions* ask applicants how they would respond in a hypothetical situation (e.g., "What would you do if ...?").
- *Behavioural questions* ask applicants what they did in previous jobs that were similar to the job for which they are applying (e.g., "In your previous jobs, can you tell me about ...?").
- *Background questions* ask applicants about their work experience, education, and other qualifications (e.g., "Tell me about the training you received at ...").
- *Job-knowledge questions* ask applicants to demonstrate their job knowledge (e.g., for nurses, "Give me an example of a time in which one of your patients had a severe reaction to a medication. How did you handle it?").

Always ask open-ended questions, not closed-ended questions that can be answered with a "yes" or a "no." The point of the interview is to get applicants to talk about themselves, so that you can make a good hiring decision. Also, make sure your questions are job related. Finally, remember that if you were actually using this interview to hire college instructors, every person interviewing for the job would be asked these 12 questions. So try to pick questions that would help you differentiate good instructors from bad instructors. For example, asking candidates where they received their Ph.D., which is a research degree, would probably not help you determine which candidates are most qualified to teach.

Assignment

Write three questions of each type (situational, behavioural, background, and job-knowledge) that you would like to ask someone who wanted to teach at your university.

Management Decisions

JOB ANALYSIS

Job analysis is a foundation for many of the HRM subsystems. Even though you may never have to actually conduct a job analysis and write job descriptions, you should be familiar with the process to better understand how to use this information in selection decisions. Pick a relatively simple job that you can observe without interrupting the employee. You should observe this job at least twice at different times (e.g., once in the morning and once in the afternoon) for approximately 30 minutes each time. The goal is to observe a representative performance of this job.

Copy or recreate the form below and use it to perform a job analysis of this job. Remember, your goal is to identify the most important activities, responsibilities, and duties, as well as any special equipment or tools that are used or any significant customer/client/co-worker contact. If you are working in teams, have two or three team members observe the same job. When you've finished, write a job description and job specifications for this job.

On the job analysis form below, the column headings stand for I = Importance of the activity, T = Time spent performing the activity (e.g., percentage of each day on average), and D = Difficulty of this activity. Use the following rating scales for these factors:

Importance of Activity
1 Very Unimportant
2 Slightly Unimportant
3 Slightly Important
4 Fairly Important
5 Very Important

Time Spent on Average
1 0–19% of each day
2 20–39% of each day
3 40–59% of each day
4 60–79% of each day
5 80–100% of each day

Difficulty of Activity
1 Extremely Easy
2 Fairly Easy
3 Average Difficulty
4 Above Average Difficulty
5 High Difficulty

After rating each activity, add the scores in each column and the total score. These scores can be used to compare relative values of different jobs to the company. If you are working in teams, average the scores from your group members to come up with a total for the job.

Activity	I	T	D	I + T + D
TOTAL				

Job Description:

Job Specifications:

Develop Your Management Potential

360-DEGREE FEEDBACK

While most performance appraisal ratings have traditionally come from just one person, the boss, 360-degree feedback is obtained from four sources: the boss, subordinates, peers and co-workers, and the employees themselves. In this assignment, you will be gathering 360-degree feedback from people whom you work with or from a team or group that you're a member of for a class.

Here are some guidelines for obtaining your 360-degree feedback:

- *Carefully select respondents.* One of the keys to good 360-degree feedback is getting feedback from the right people. In general, the people you ask for feedback should interact with you on a regular basis and have the chance to regularly observe your behaviour. Also be sure to get a representative sample of opinions from a similar number of co-workers and subordinates (assuming you have some).
- *Get a large enough number of responses.* Except for the boss, you should have a minimum of three respondents to give you feedback in each category (peers and subordinates). Five or six respondents per category is even better.
- *Ensure confidentiality.* Respondents are much more likely to be honest if they know that their comments are confidential and anonymous. So when you ask respondents for feedback, have them return their comments to someone other than yourself. Have this person (we'll call the person your "feedback facilitator") remove the names and any other information that would identify who made particular comments.
- *Explain how the 360-degree feedback will be used.* In this case, explain that the feedback is for a class assignment, that the results will be used for your own personal growth and development, and that the feedback they give you will not affect your grade or formal assessment at work.
- *Ask them to make their feedback as specific as possible.* For instance, writing "bad attitude" isn't very good feedback. However, writing "won't listen to others' suggestions" is much better feedback, because it would let you know how to improve your behaviour. Have your respondents use the feedback form shown below to provide your feedback.

Here's what you need to turn in for this assignment:

1. The names and relationships (boss, peers, subordinates, classmates, teammates) of those you've asked for feedback.
2. The name of the person you've asked to be your feedback facilitator.
3. Copies of all written feedback that was returned to you.
4. A one-page summary of the written feedback.
5. A one-page plan in which you describe specific goals and action plans for responding to the feedback you received.

360-Degree Feedback Form

As part of a class assignment, I, ______________________________, am collecting feedback from you about my performance. What you say or write will not affect my grade. The purpose of this assignment is for me to receive honest feedback from the people I work with in order to identify the things I'm doing well and the things upon which I need to improve. So please be honest and direct in your evaluation.

When you have completed this feedback form, please return it to ______________________________. He/She has been selected as my feedback facilitator and is responsible for ensuring that your confidentiality and anonymity are maintained. After all feedback forms have been returned to ______________________________, he/she will make sure that your particular responses cannot be identified. Only then will the feedback be shared with me.

Please provide the following feedback.

Continue doing...

Describe 3 things that ______________________________ is doing that are a positive part of his/her performance and that you want him/her to continue doing.

1.

2.

3.

Start doing...

Describe 3 things that ______________________________ needs to start doing that would significantly improve his/her performance.

1.

2.

3.

Please make your feedback as specific and behavioural as possible. For instance, writing "needs to adjust attitude" isn't very good feedback. However, writing "needs to begin listening to others' suggestions" is much better feedback because the group member now knows exactly what behaviour should change. So please be specific. Also please write more than one sentence per comment. This will help feedback recipients better understand your comments.

Discussion Questions

1. What role does job analysis play in recruiting and selection?
2. What type of recruiting strategies can be undertaken to attract workers when qualified workers are in short supply?
3. What are the advantages and disadvantages of internal recruiting? What are the advantages and disadvantages of external recruiting?
4. What are the advantages of having employees access personal information from a company's human resource information system? Are there any disadvantages?
5. What are the advantages and disadvantages of 360-degree feedback?

Critical Thinking Video Case

CBC

Visit www.management2e.nelson.com to view this chapter's CBC video case.

Take Two

Biz Flix
Bowfinger

This film, which brought Steve Martin and Eddie Murphy together for the first time, offers a funny look at Hollywood filmmaking. Bobby Bowfinger (Martin), perhaps the least successful director in films, wants to produce a low-budget film with top star Kit Ramsey (Murphy). Bowfinger's problem: recruit a crew and cast with almost no budget and trick Kit into appearing in his film. Bowfinger interviews several candidates for the Kit Ramsey look-alike role. He rejects everyone until Jifferson (Jiff) Ramsey (also played by Murphy) auditions. This scene is an edited version of the "The Lookalike" sequence early in the film. It includes Jiff's audition, interview, and a brief look at his first day at work.

What to Watch for and Ask Yourself

1. Does Bobby Bowfinger have a set of valid selection criteria for filling the role of a Kit Ramsey look-alike? Does Bowfinger apply the criteria uniformly to each applicant?
2. Is there a good person-job fit of Jiff Ramsey in the screen role of Kit Ramsey?
3. Do you predict that Jiff Ramsey will be successful as a Kit Ramsey substitute?

Management Workplace
AMCI, Ziba Designs, Wahoo's Fish Taco

Managing human resource (HR) systems is as complex an undertaking as any in business. AMCI is a manufacturer's rep firm that sells things like glow-in-the-dark cockroaches, Groucho Marx glasses, and specialty gift items; Ziba Designs is an industrial design firm that develops innovative products for its clients; and Wahoo's Fish Taco is a chain of surfer-themed restaurants in Southern California. As diverse as these three companies are, they all need to find qualified employees, train them for specific tasks and responsibilities, and then implement tools to keep them on the payroll long term.

What to Watch for and Ask Yourself

1. What HR tools from the chapter are mentioned in the video?
2. Compare how the three companies in the video find qualified employees.
3. What retention strategies do these companies use? Why have Ziba and Wahoo's focused on retention?

CP PHOTO/STEVE WHITE

Managing Service and Manufacturing Operations

Chapter 14

CHAPTER OUTLINE

Managing for Productivity and Quality
- **Productivity**
  - Why Productivity Matters
  - Kinds of Productivity
- **Quality**
  - Quality-Related Product Characteristics
  - Quality-Related Service Characteristics
  - ISO 9000
  - Total Quality Management

Managing Operations
- **Service Operations**
  - The Service-Profit Chain
  - Service Recovery and Empowerment
- **Manufacturing Operations**
  - Amount of Processing in Manufacturing Operations
  - Flexibility of Manufacturing Operations
- **Inventory**
  - Types of Inventory
  - Measuring Inventory
  - Costs of Maintaining an Inventory
  - Managing Inventory

LEARNING OBJECTIVES

After reading this chapter, you should be able to

1. discuss the kinds of productivity and their importance in managing operations.
2. explain the role that quality plays in managing operations.
3. explain the essentials of managing a service business.
4. describe the different kinds of manufacturing operations.
5. describe why and how companies should manage inventory levels.

Ever since *Tonight Show* host Jay Leno joked that a Hyundai car is like a luge sled—it "has no room, you have to push it to get going, and it only goes downhill"—the jokes just haven't stopped. Another popular joke goes "How do you double the value of a Hyundai? Fill it with gas!" They're even repeating these jokes in South Korea![1]

What Would You Do?

It's not funny. As one of your top managers said, "Car buyers have long memories and it takes a while to change their perceptions, especially when they're bad." And, with problematic electrical systems, rusting bumpers, poor-fitting doors, and broken air conditioners, those perceptions were clearly reflected in the well-known and influential J.D Power Survey of Initial Car Quality. Recently, Hyundai cars ranked 26th out of 35 in terms of initial car quality, while Kia, a bankrupt South Korean car company that Hyundai had paid US$8 billion to acquire, finished dead last. Not surprisingly, because of terrible quality Hyundai's U.S. sales had also recently dropped. As a result, even car dealers who put up thousands of dollars to have the chance to sell Hyundais began to abandon their Hyundai franchises as fast as they could. When customers leave in droves, it can't be good. But when the dealers start jumping like rats off a sinking ship, it's deadly. And why shouldn't they, especially with corporate managers telling them that "With such low prices, we don't need higher quality."

Hoping to expand its North American presence, Hyundai is also spending US$1 billion to build a new auto plant in Alabama. But customers won't buy Hyundais just because they're built in North America. Daewoo Motors, another South Korean auto company, followed a similar strategy in the 1990s, spending billions to build plants around the world. But because it never fixed its quality problems, it lost billions and filed for bankruptcy. Amazingly, Hyundai made the same mistake in Canada, where it spent US$1 billion to build a manufacturing plant, only to close it three years later. If Hyundai repeats that mistake with the new plant, it just might put the company under. Hyundai, which recently experienced its first loss, is short on cash and high on debt, which is six times more than Hyundai's stock market capitalization of US$1 billion. Plus, labour-management relations are still tenuous after settling a 47-day worker strike in Hyundai's South Korean factories. During the strike, which cost the company US$1 billion in disrupted production, workers living in tents on factory grounds threw Molotov cocktails to express their frustration. However, they gained a huge 8.6 percent pay increase that will put even more strain on company finances. And those finances are likely to come under more pressure now that the South Korean government has for the first time lifted its ban on Japanese car imports.

If the company is to survive, if car buyers' perceptions are to change, and if the US$1 billion investment in the new auto plant is to pay off, then quality must improve. Of course, the question is how? Your first goal is to change the mindset in the company, to convince managers and factory workers that quality comes first. What's the best way to do that? Next, what steps do you need to take to actually improve quality? It won't be easy and it won't be quick, but it can be done. Where do you start? Finally, you've got to convince customers that you're responsive to their complaints, that you care, and that you're listening. If you can't do that, there won't be any improvements in those all-important quality rankings. **If you were in charge at Hyundai, what would you do?**

The problems that *Hyundai faces* are not unique to the auto industry. Airlines, publishers, hospitals, restaurants, and many other kinds of businesses also struggle to find ways to efficiently produce quality products and services and then deliver them in a timely manner.

operations management
managing the daily production of goods and services

In this chapter, you will learn about **operations management**—managing the daily production of goods and services. You will begin by learning about the basics of operations management: productivity and quality. Next, you will read about managing operations, beginning with service operations, turning next to manufacturing operations, and finishing with an examination of the types, measures, costs, and methods for managing inventory.

Managing for Productivity and Quality

Brothers Hank and Bucky Kashiwa started Volant, Inc., a manufacturer of skis and snowboards. Combining Hank's experience as an Olympic and professional skier and Bucky's Ph.D. in fluid mechanics, the Kashiwas designed a less expensive, more stable, easier-to-turn ski. In contrast to standard skis made of a composite of several materials layered atop each other, the top and sides of Volant skis were made from a single sheet of steel. Ski shops and customers loved the skis, and sales soared. However, despite their superior design and performance, Volant's skis literally started falling apart on the slopes soon after skiers started using them. The company finally fixed this problem, but because of other problems with quality control in its manufacturing facility, it still had to throw away more than 40 percent of the skis it was producing! This led to sky-high costs and an inability to ship product orders on time. So, even though sales were taking off, productivity and quality levels were so bad that Volant was losing money on every pair of skis it sold.[2]

The Kashiwas eventually solved Volant's problems by hiring a manufacturing consultant, who taught company managers and employees how to improve the quality of their products and the productivity of their factory. Today, Volant skis don't fall apart on the slopes, the company ships orders early, and Volant is profitable for the first time in its history.

After reading the next two sections, you should be able to

1. discuss the kinds of productivity and their importance in managing operations.
2. explain the role that quality plays in managing operations.

1 PRODUCTIVITY

productivity
a measure of performance that indicates how many inputs it takes to produce or create an output

At their core, organizations are production systems. Companies combine inputs, such as labour, raw materials, capital, and knowledge, to produce outputs in the form of finished products or services. **Productivity** is a measure of performance that indicates how many inputs it takes to produce or create an output.

$$\text{Productivity} = \frac{\text{Outputs}}{\text{Inputs}}$$

The fewer inputs it takes to create an output (or the greater the output from one input), the higher the productivity. For example, a car's gas consumption is a common measure of productivity. A car that gets 25 kilometres (output) per litre (input) is more productive and fuel efficient than a car that gets 12 kilometres per litre.

Let's examine why productivity matters and kinds of productivity.

Why Productivity Matters

Why does productivity matter? For companies, higher productivity—that is, doing more with less—results in lower costs. In turn, lower costs can lead to lower prices, higher market share, and higher profits. For countries, productivity matters because it produces a higher standard of living. One way productivity leads to a higher standard of living is through increased wages. When companies can do more with less, they can raise employee wages without increasing prices or sacrificing normal profits. For example, because a Motorola (www.motorola.com) plant makes 200 percent more pagers now with only 22 percent more employees, it can give those employees better benefits and wages and still make good profits. Being able to offer higher wages also helps the company by attracting and retaining good workers.

Rising income stemming from increased productivity creates numerous other benefits. For example, during the productive 1980s, charitable giving increased 5.1 percent per year, compared to an average of 3.5 percent per year during the previous 25 years.

Another way that productivity increases the standard of living is by making products more affordable. For example, while inflation has pushed the average cost of a car to more than $20 000, increases in productivity have actually made cars cheaper. In 1960, the average family needed 26 weeks of income to pay for the average car. Today, the average family needs only 23 weeks of income—and today's car is loaded with accessories, such as airbags, power steering and brakes, power windows, cruise control, stereo/CD players, and air conditioning, features that weren't even available in 1960.[3] So, in terms of real purchasing power, productivity gains have actually made the $20 000 car of today cheaper than the $2000 car of 1960.

Kinds of Productivity

Two common measures of productivity are partial productivity and multifactor productivity. **Partial productivity** indicates how much of a particular kind of input it takes to produce an output.

partial productivity
a measure of performance that indicates how much of a particular kind of input it takes to produce an output

$$\text{Partial Productivity} = \frac{\text{Outputs}}{\text{Single Kind of Input}}$$

Labour is one kind of input that is frequently used when determining partial productivity. Labour productivity typically indicates the cost or number of hours of labour it takes to produce an output. In other words, the smaller the cost of the labour to produce a unit of output, or the less time it takes to produce a unit of output, the higher the labour productivity. For example, the automobile industry often measures labour productivity by determining the average number of hours of labour it takes to completely assemble a car. The three most productive auto manufacturers can assemble a car with 31 or fewer hours of labour. Nissan (www.nissan.com) assembles a car in only 27 hours of labour. Toyota (www.toyota.com) does it in 29 hours, and Honda (www.honda.com) assembles a car in 31 hours. By comparison, Nissan, Toyota, and Honda have much higher labour productivity than Ford, which needs 38 hours of labour to assemble a car, or Chrysler, which needs 43 hours, or General Motors, which needs 46.[4] In terms of labour costs, this means that Nissan pays $1332 less for labour per car than does Ford. In turn, Ford pays $507 less for labour per car than does General Motors.[5]

Partial productivity assesses how efficiently companies use only one input, such as labour, when creating outputs. **Multifactor productivity** is an overall measure of productivity that assesses how efficiently companies use all the inputs it takes to make outputs. More specifically, multifactor productivity indicates how much labour, capital, materials, and energy it takes to produce an output.[6]

multifactor productivity
an overall measure of performance that indicates how much labour, capital, materials, and energy it takes to produce an output

$$\text{Multifactor Productivity} = \frac{\text{Outputs}}{\text{Labour} + \text{Capital} + \text{Materials} + \text{Energy}}$$

Exhibit 14.1 shows the trends in multifactor productivity across a number of different U.S. industries since 1987. With a six-fold increase (from the starting point scaled at 100 in 1987 to a productivity level of 631 in 1999), the growth in multifactor productivity in the electronics components and accessories industry far exceeded the productivity growth in the railroad, cement, beverage, and paint products industries, as well as most other

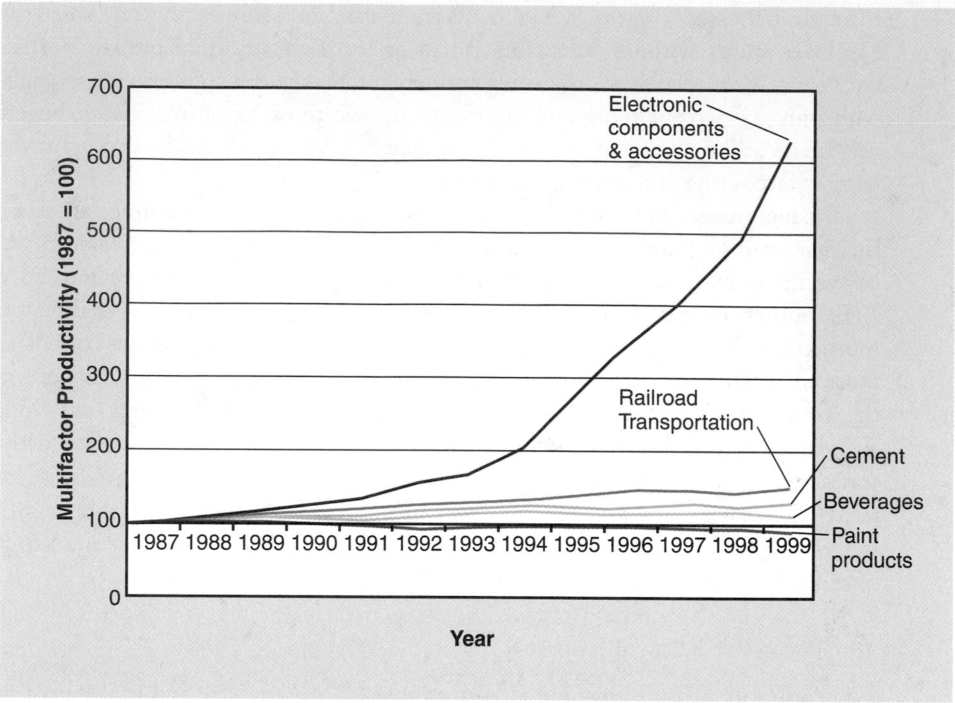

EXHIBIT 14.1
Multifactor Productivity Growth Across Industries

Source: "Industry Multifactor Productivity Indexes (1987=100)," Bureau of Labor Statistics. [Online] Available ftp://ftp.bls.gov/put/special.requests/opt/dipts/indmfp2.txt, 21 February 2002.

industries tracked. On the other hand, multifactor productivity growth in Canada's business sector in 2002 of 1.9 percent was six times the pace of growth compared to 0.3 percent in 2001. Only productivity growth of 2.3 percent in both 1999 and 2000 was better. For most of the 1980s and 1990s Canadian multifactor productivity growth trailed that of the United States. Only in 2001 was this trend reversed, with Canadian performance ahead of that in the United States.[7]

Should managers use multiple or partial productivity measures? In general, they should use both. Multifactor productivity indicates a company's overall level of productivity relative to its competitors. In the end, that's what counts most. However, multifactor productivity measures don't indicate the specific contributions that labour, capital, materials, or energy make to overall productivity. To analyze the contributions of these individual components, managers need to use partial productivity measures.

REVIEW 1: PRODUCTIVITY

At their core, companies are production systems that combine inputs, such as labour, raw materials, capital, and knowledge, to produce outputs, such as finished products or services. Productivity is a measure of how many inputs it takes to produce or create an output. The greater the output from one input, or the fewer inputs it takes to create an output, the higher the productivity. Partial productivity measures how much of a single kind of input, such as labour, is needed to produce an output. Multifactor productivity is an overall measure of productivity that indicates how much labour, capital, materials, and energy are needed to produce an output. Increased productivity helps companies lower costs, which can lead to lower prices, higher market share, and higher profits. Increased productivity helps countries by leading to higher wages, lower product prices, and a higher standard of living.

2 QUALITY

With the average car costing more than $20 000, car buyers want to make sure that they're getting good quality for their money. Fortunately, as indicated by the number of problems per 100 cars (PP100), today's cars are of much higher quality than earlier models. In 1981, Japanese cars averaged 240 PP100. GM (www.gm.com) averaged 670, Ford (www.ford.com), averaged 740, and Chrysler (www.daimlerchrysler.com) averaged 870 PP100! In other words, as measured by PP100, the quality of North American cars was three to four times worse than Japanese cars. However, by 1992, North American carmakers had made great strides, reducing the number of problems to 155 PP100. Japanese vehicles had improved, too, averaging just 125 PP100. By 1997, overall car quality had improved so much that the average number of problems for all kinds of cars was just 100 PP100. In fact, after three months of ownership, half of new car buyers report no problems whatsoever with their cars![8]

The American Society for Quality gives two meanings for **quality**. First, it can mean a product or service free of deficiencies, such as the number of problems per 100 cars. Consumer products that are not free of deficiencies are often not too difficult to spot. They are frequently recalled from the market by government regulators in Canada and the United States. Listings of such products may be found on the Web sites of the CBC consumer show *Marketplace* (www.cbc.ca/consumers/market/) and the U.S. Consumer Product Safety Commission (www.cpsc.gov). Second, quality can mean the characteristics of a product or service that satisfy customer needs.[9] In this sense, today's cars are of higher quality because of the additional standard features (power brakes and steering, stereo/CD player, power windows and locks, rear defrosters, cruise control, etc.) they have compared to 20 years ago.

quality
a product or service free of deficiencies, or the characteristics of product or service that satisfy customer needs

In this part of the chapter, you will learn about quality-related product characteristics, quality-related service characteristics, ISO 9000, and total quality management.

Quality-Related Product Characteristics

As shown in Exhibit 14.2, quality products usually possess three characteristics: reliability, serviceability, and durability.[10] A breakdown occurs when a product quits working or doesn't do what it was designed to do. The longer it takes for a product to break down, or the longer the time between breakdowns, the more reliable the product. Consequently, many companies define product reliability by the average time between breakdowns.

Serviceability refers to how easy or difficult it is to fix a product. The easier it is to maintain a working product or fix a broken product, the more serviceable that product is. For example, Ford redesigned its cars to make them easier for mechanics to fix and owners to maintain. On the Ford Escort and Mercury Tracer, if a bulb burns out in the dashboard, the entire instrument cluster (gauges and speedometer) can be accessed by removing a few simple screws. This process now takes minutes instead of hours. Likewise, a two-piece bracket now holds the car's alternator in a spot that is easy for mechanics to reach. Before, mechanics had to empty and remove the car's radiator to reach the alternator.[11]

A product breakdown assumes that a product can be repaired. However, some products don't break down—they fail. Product failure means these products can't be repaired. They can only be replaced. Thus, durability is a quality characteristic that applies to products that can't be repaired. Durability is defined as the mean time to failure. For example, most household light bulbs have an estimated time to failure of between 750 and 1000 hours. By contrast, the durability of fluorescent light bulbs is as long as 10 000 hours.[12]

Quality-Related Service Characteristics

Reliability, serviceability, and durability characterize high-quality products. However, services and products are different. With services, there's no point in assessing durability. Unlike products, services don't last. Services are consumed the minute they're performed. For example, once a lawn service has mowed your lawn, the job is done until the mowers come back next week to do it again. Likewise, services don't have serviceability. You

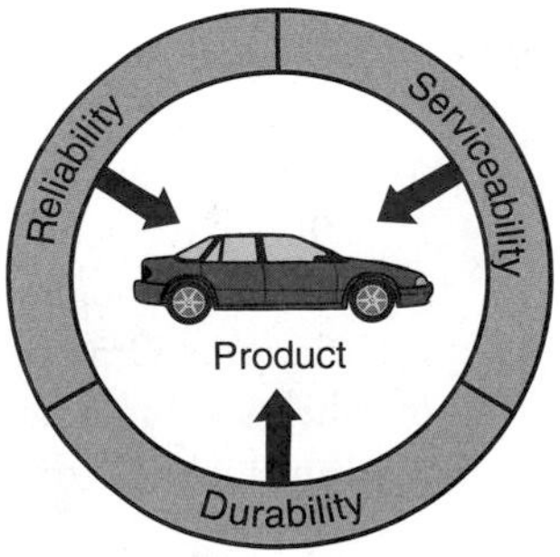

EXHIBIT 14.2
Characteristics of Product Quality

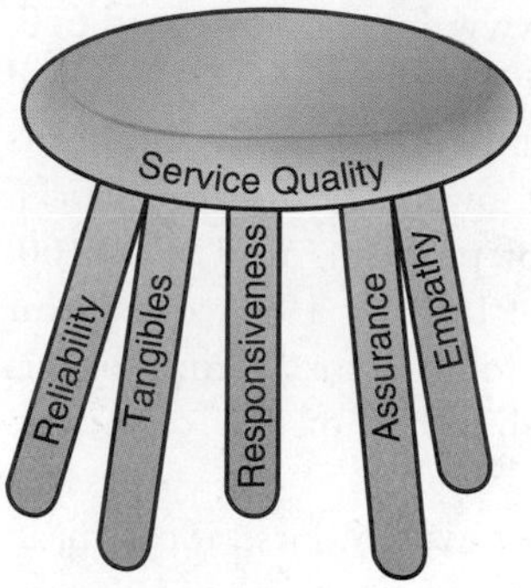

EXHIBIT 14.3
Characteristics of Service Quality

can't maintain or fix a service. If a service wasn't performed correctly, all you can do is perform the service again. Finally, the quality of service interactions often depends on how the service provider interacts with the customer. Was the service provider friendly, rude, or helpful? Consequently, as shown in Exhibit 14.3, five characteristics—reliability, tangibles, responsiveness, assurance, and empathy—typically distinguish a quality service.[13]

Service reliability is the ability to consistently perform a service well. Studies clearly show that reliability matters more to customers than anything else when buying services. Also, while services themselves are not tangible (you can't see or touch them), services are provided in tangible places. Thus, tangibles refer to the appearance of the offices, equipment, and personnel involved with the delivery of a service. Responsiveness is the promptness and willingness with which service providers give good service. Assurance is the confidence that service providers are knowledgeable, courteous, and can be trusted. Empathy is the extent to which service providers give individual attention and care to customers' concerns and problems.

Newark International Airport (www.panynj.gov/aviation/ewrframe.HTM) is a good example of quality service. Many Canadians may recognize it, as Air Canada (www.aircanada.com) flies into and out of this airport. If you're thinking to yourself, "Newark Airport and quality?" you're not alone. In the past, Newark was known for dirty terminals, auto theft, and delayed departures and arrivals. However, in the last several years, Newark has improved the quality of the services it provides to the airlines and passengers that use it.[14] For example, with respect to reliability, both flight delays and auto thefts have been greatly reduced. As a result, passenger traffic increased 32 percent over a six-year period.

With respect to tangibles, Newark is much cleaner than it used to be. Standards were set and enforced for the cleanliness of the parking lots and the terminals. Airport manager Benjamin Decosta said, "My philosophy is that if the place appears to be well managed, people looking to break the rules will go elsewhere."

As part of improved responsiveness, Decosta holds monthly meetings with Newark's airlines, giving them a say on things ranging from snow removal to police staffing. Decosta even asks the airlines how he should spend the airport's money.

To improve assurance, Decosta launched a customer-service training program to instill a "customer-first orientation." The mission, now embossed on all airport employees' caps, is "to be the best by putting the customer first."

Decosta also found ways to improve empathy in the airport's service. Continental Airlines had long sought space in a building used by airport management. This building overlooked Newark's tarmac, where planes sit before heading to and from the runways. From this location, Continental could direct its own ground traffic and more easily prevent ground delays, such as a jumbo jet sitting at a gate where its size prevents other planes from getting to and from their terminals. Previously, this request had been denied, because airport managers would have to give up the great view in their cafeteria. Decosta quickly approved the change after taking charge of the airport, deeming Continental's needs much more important than his managers'.[15]

ISO 9000

ISO 9000
a series of five international standards, from ISO 9000 to ISO 9004, for achieving consistency in quality management and quality assurance in companies throughout the world

ISO, pronounced *ice-o,* comes from the Greek word *isos,* meaning equal, similar, alike, or identical. Thus, **ISO 9000** is a series of five international standards, from ISO 9000 to ISO 9004, for achieving consistency in quality management and quality assurance in companies throughout the world. The ISO 9000 standards were created by the International Organization of Standards (www.iso.org), which is an international agency that helps set standards for 91 countries. The purpose of this agency is to develop and publish standards that facilitate the international exchange of goods and services.[16]

The ISO 9000 standards publications are general and can be used for manufacturing any kind of product or delivering any kind of service. Importantly, the ISO 9000 standards don't describe how to make a better-quality car, computer, or widget. Instead, they describe how companies can extensively document (and thus standardize) the steps they take to create and improve the quality of their products.

Why should companies go to the trouble to achieve ISO 9000 certification? Because, increasingly, their customers want them to. Indeed, DuPont, General Electric, Eastman Kodak, British Telecom, and Philips Electronics are some of the Fortune 500 companies that are telling their suppliers to achieve ISO 9000 certification. John Yates, GE's general manager of global sourcing, said, "There is absolutely no negotiation. If you want to work with us, you have to get it."[17] Are these companies listening? If Toronto-based electronics manufacturing service company Celestica Inc. is a good example, then yes, they are listening. Among the many services that it offers, Celestica manufactures products for other companies on a contract basis. A glance at its Web site (www.celestica.com) suggests that fully 36 of its 38 global manufacturing facilities are ISO 9000 compliant, with two others meeting ISO 9002 standards.

Typically, "getting" ISO 9000 means having your company certified for ISO 9000 registration by an accredited third party. The process is similar to having a certified accountant indicate that a company's financial accounts are up-to-date and accurate. But in this case, the certification is for quality, not accounting procedures. To become certified, a process that can take months to prepare for, companies must show that they are following their own procedures for improving production, updating design plans and specifications, keeping machinery in top condition, educating and training workers, and satisfactorily dealing with customer complaints.[18]

Once a company has been certified as ISO 9000 compliant, the accredited third party will issue an ISO 9000 certificate that the company can use in its advertising and publications. This is the quality equivalent of the "Good Housekeeping Seal of Approval." However, ISO 9000 certification is not guaranteed. Accredited third parties typically conduct periodic audits to make sure quality procedures continue to be followed. Companies that don't follow their quality systems have their certifications suspended or cancelled.

In Canada, the National Quality Institute (www.nqi.ca) recognizes exceptional quality-related performance by private- and public-sector organizations. It offers the Canada Awards for Excellence to Canadian companies who meet the criteria for demonstrating outstanding achievement across major functions of the organization. Recent award winners have included the Cardiac Care Network of Ontario, Diversicare Canada Management Services Co., Dana Canada Inc., and the Gleneagle Elementary School of West Vancouver.[19]

Total Quality Management

Total quality management (TQM) is an integrated organization-wide strategy for improving product and service quality. TQM is not a specific tool or technique. Rather, TQM is a philosophy or overall approach to management that is characterized by three principles: customer focus and satisfaction, continuous improvement, and teamwork.[20]

Contrary to most economists, accountants, and financiers, who argue that companies exist to earn profits for shareholders, TQM suggests that customer focus and customer satisfaction should be a company's primary goals. **Customer focus** means the entire organization, from top to bottom, should be focused on meeting customers' needs. **Customer satisfaction** is an organizational goal to make products or deliver services that meet or exceed customers' expectations. And at companies where TQM is taken seriously, such as Cisco Systems (www.ciscosystems.com), a leading provider of the routers used to run the Internet, paycheques depend on keeping customers satisfied. For example, Cisco surveys clients each year about 60 different performance criteria. CEO John Chambers said, "If a manager improves his [customer satisfaction] scores, he can

total quality management (TQM)
an integrated, principle-based, organization-wide strategy for improving product and service quality

customer focus
an organizational goal to concentrate on meeting customers' needs at all levels of the organization

customer satisfaction
an organizational goal to provide products or services that meet or exceed customers' expectations

get a fair amount [of a financial bonus]. But if the scores go down, we'll take money out of the manager's pocket."[21] Not surprisingly, this emphasis on quality increased the number of completely satisfied Cisco customers from 81 percent to 85 percent in just one year.

continuous improvement an organization's ongoing commitment to constantly assess and improve the processes and procedures used to create products and services

variation a deviation in the form, condition, or appearance of a product from the quality standard for that product

teamwork collaboration between managers and nonmanagers, across business functions, and between the companies, customers, and suppliers

Continuous improvement is an ongoing commitment to increase product and service quality by constantly assessing and improving the processes and procedures used to create those products and services. How do companies know whether they're achieving continuous improvement? Besides higher customer satisfaction, continuous improvement is usually associated with a reduction in variation. **Variation** is a deviation in the form, condition, or appearance of a product from the quality standard for that product. The less a product varies from the quality standard, or the more consistently a company's products meet a quality standard, the higher the quality.

The third principle of TQM is teamwork. **Teamwork** means collaboration between managers and nonmanagers, across business functions, and between the company and its customers and suppliers. In short, quality improves when everyone in the company is given the incentive to work together and the responsibility and authority to make improvements and solve problems. For example, Johnson Controls (www.johnsoncontrols.com) manufactures and sells auto parts in Canada and throughout the world. At one of its factories, 230 workers provided 631 suggestions in one year for improving how the plant is run. In particular, one employee, Jason Moncer, came up with 30 different suggestions. Moncer, who said, "I go on sprees," is now trying to figure out how best to organize the metal parts that are used to make car seats.[22]

Together, customer focus and satisfaction, continuous improvement, and teamwork mutually reinforce each other to improve quality throughout a company. Customer-focused continuous improvement is necessary to increase customer satisfaction. However, continuous improvement depends on teamwork from different functional and hierarchical parts of the company.

REVIEW 2: QUALITY

Quality can mean a product or service free of deficiencies or the characteristics of a product or service that satisfy customer needs. Quality products usually possess three characteristics: reliability, serviceability, and durability. Quality service means reliability, tangibles, responsiveness, assurance, and empathy. ISO 9000 is a series of five international standards for achieving consistency in quality management and quality assurance. The ISO 9000 standards can be used for any product or service, because they ensure that companies carefully document the steps they take to create and improve quality. ISO 9000 certification is awarded following a quality audit from an accredited third party. Total quality management (TQM) is an integrated organization-wide strategy for improving product and service quality. TQM is based on three mutually reinforcing principles: customer focus and satisfaction, continuous improvement, and teamwork.

Managing Operations

At the start of this chapter, you learned that operations management means managing the daily production of goods and services. Then you learned that to manage production, you must oversee the factors that affect productivity and quality. In this half of the chapter, you will learn about managing operations in service and manufacturing businesses. The chapter ends with a discussion of inventory management, a key factor in a company's profitability.

After reading the next three sections, you should be able to

3 explain the essentials of managing a service business.
4 describe the different kinds of manufacturing operations.
5 describe why and how companies should manage inventory levels.

3 SERVICE OPERATIONS

Imagine that your trusty five-year-old VCR breaks down as you try to record your favourite TV show. You've got two choices. You can run to Wal-Mart or Zellers and spend about $120 to purchase a new VCR. Or you can spend somewhere between $50 and $100 (you hope) to have it fixed at a repair shop. With either choice, you end up with the same thing, a working VCR. However, the first choice, getting a new VCR, involves buying a physical product (a "good"), while the second, dealing with a repair shop, involves buying a service.

Services are different from goods in several ways. First, goods are produced or made, but services are performed. In other words, services are almost always labour intensive. Someone typically has to perform the service for you. A repair shop could give you the parts needed to repair your old VCR, but without the technician to perform the repairs, you're still going to have a broken VCR. Second, goods are tangible, but services are intangible. You can touch and see that new VCR from Zellers, but you can't touch or see the service provided by the technician who fixed your old VCR. All you can "see" is that the VCR works. Third, services are perishable and unstorable. If you don't use them when they're available, they're wasted. For example, if your VCR repair shop is backlogged on repair jobs, you'll just have to wait until next week to get your VCR repaired. You can't store an unused service and use it when you like. By contrast, you can purchase a good, such as motor oil, and store it until you're ready to use it.

Because services are different from goods, managing a service operation is different from managing a manufacturing or production operation. Let's look at the service-profit chain, and service recovery and empowerment.

The Service-Profit Chain

One of the key assumptions in the service business is that success depends on how well employees—that is, service providers—deliver their services to customers. However, the concept of the service-profit chain, depicted in Exhibit 14.4, suggests that in service businesses, success begins with how well management treats service employees.[23]

The first step in the service-profit chain is internal service quality, meaning the quality of treatment that employees receive from a company's internal service providers, such as management, payroll and benefits, and human resources.

As depicted in Exhibit 14.4, good internal service leads to employee satisfaction and service capability. Employee satisfaction occurs when companies treat employees in a way that meets or exceeds their expectations. In other words, the better employees are treated, the more satisfied they are, and the more likely they are to give high-value service to satisfy customers.

Service capability is an employee's perception of his or her ability to serve customers well. When an organization serves its employees in ways that help them to do their jobs well, employees, in turn, are more likely to believe that they can and ought to provide high-value service to customers.

Finally, according to the service-profit chain shown in Exhibit 14.4, high-value service leads to customer satisfaction and customer loyalty, which, in turn, lead to long-term profits and growth. What's the link between customer satisfaction and loyalty and profits? To start, the average business keeps only 70 percent to 90 percent of its existing customers each year. No big deal, you say? Just replace leaving customers with new customers. Well,

> **DOING THE RIGHT THING**
>
> **PROTECT YOUR FRONT-LINE STAFF: THE CUSTOMER ISN'T ALWAYS RIGHT**
>
> In 1909, Harry Gordon Selfridge, an American who founded London's famous Selfridge's department store, coined the phrase "The customer is always right." Though managers and employees should do what they can to provide great service and make up for mistakes with great service recovery, the customer isn't *always* right. Companies should fire customers who use foul language, make threats against employees or other customers, lie, demand unethical or illegal service, try to bully front-line employees into granting special favours, or are just generally belligerent. Management consultant John Curtis says, "If you don't [fire these customers], you're telling your employees and your other customers that you care more about money than the safety of the people in the business." So, do the right thing. Protect your front-line staff by telling bad customers that you won't tolerate these kinds of behaviour. Ask them to leave. Close their accounts. Inform them that they'll need to go elsewhere.[25]

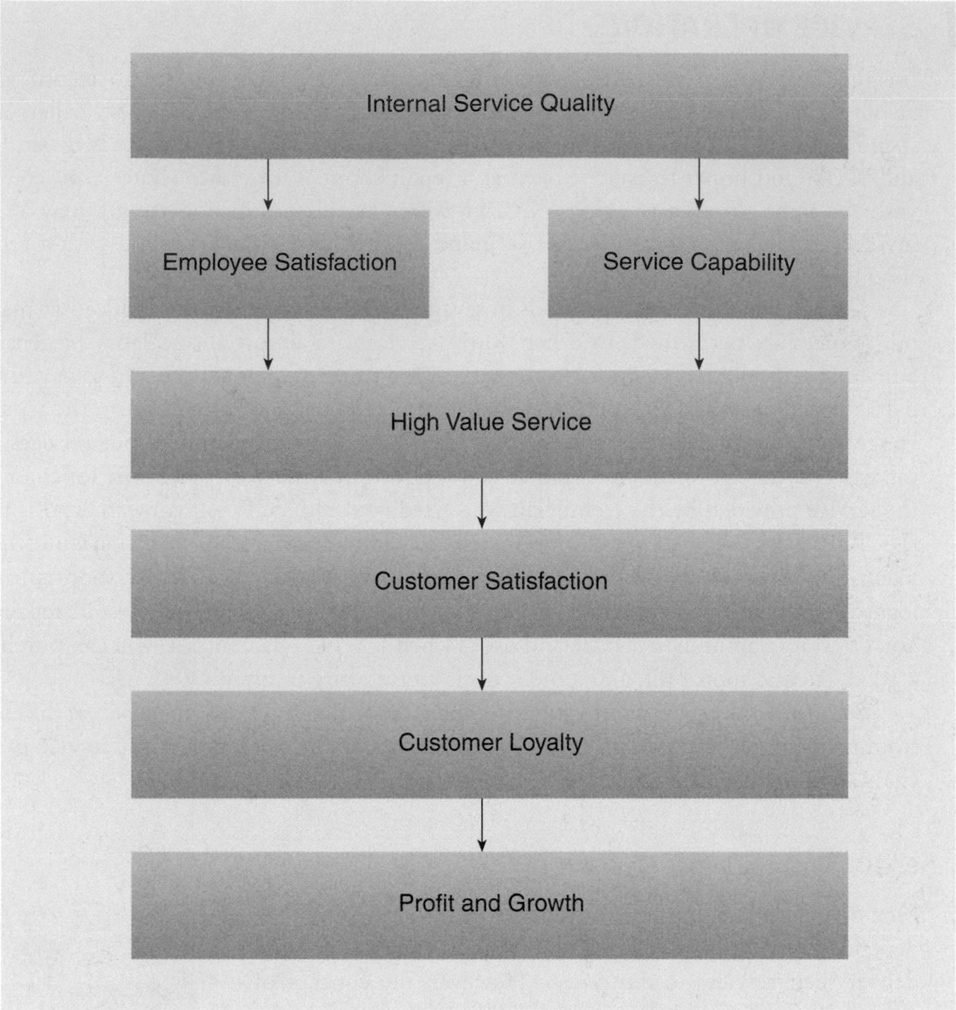

EXHIBIT 14.4
Service-Profit Chain

Sources: R. Hallowell, L.A. Schlesinger, & J. Zornitsky, "Internal Service Quality, Customer and Job Satisfaction: Linkages and Implications for Management," *Human Resource Planning* 19 (1996): 20-31. J.L. Heskett, T.O. Jones, G.W. Loveman, W.E. Sasser, Jr., & L.A. Schlesinger, "Putting the Service-Profit Chain to Work," *Harvard Business Review,* March–April 1994, 164–174.

there's one significant problem with that solution. It costs five times as much to find a new customer as it does to keep an existing customer. Also, new customers typically buy only 20 percent as much as established customers. In fact, keeping existing customers is so cost-effective that most businesses could double their profits by simply keeping 5 percent more customers per year![24]

Service Recovery and Empowerment

Many service businesses organize themselves like manufacturing companies. Tasks and jobs are simplified and separated, creating a clear division of labour. Equipment and technology are substituted for people whenever possible. Strict guidelines and rules take the place of employee authority and discretion. This production-line approach to running a service business is still widely used today in businesses that sell a high-volume, low-cost service in which there is a brief, simple transaction between customers and service providers.[26]

service recovery
restoring customer satisfaction to strongly dissatisfied customers

While the production-line model excels at efficiency and low costs, it doesn't work well when mistakes are made and customers have become dissatisfied with the service they've received. When this occurs, service businesses must switch from the process of service delivery to the process of **service recovery**—that is, restoring customer satisfaction to strongly dissatisfied customers.[27] Sometimes, service recovery requires service employees to not only fix whatever mistake was made, but also perform "heroic" service acts that "delight" highly dissatisfied customers by far surpassing their expectations of fair treatment. For example, at Delta Hotels (www.deltahotels.com), if a guest tells a member of the house-cleaning staff that there were no towels in the room, that guest will not only receive fresh towels as quickly as possible, but may also receive a complimentary fruit basket. Likewise, if guests complain that they were mistakenly given a room reserved for smokers, the front desk will transfer them to a nonsmoking room and may also arrange for a free night's stay to make up for the inconvenience.[28] In both instances, Delta Hotels' service employees fixed the original problem and then performed service recovery by surpassing guests' expectations with an additional act meant to make up for the poor service.

Unfortunately, when mistakes occur under a production-line system, service employees typically don't have the discretion to resolve customer complaints. Customers who want service employees to correct or make up for poor service are frequently told, "I'm not allowed to do that," "I'm just following company rules," or "I'm sorry, only managers are allowed to make changes of any kind." In other words, the production-line system prevents them from engaging in acts of service recovery meant to turn dissatisfied customers back into satisfied customers. The result is frustration for customers and service employees and lost customers for the company.

Because production-line systems make it difficult for service employees to do service recovery, many companies are now empowering their service employees.[29] In Chapter 10, you learned that empowering workers means permanently passing decision-making authority and responsibility from managers to workers. With respect to service recovery, empowering workers means giving service employees the authority and responsibility to make decisions that immediately solve customer problems.[30] For example, at Marriott Hotels (www.marriott.com), doormen like Tony Prsyszlak are now empowered to check in guests if lines are long or solve other problems that guests mention to him. Says Prsyszlak, "I'm a bellman, a doorman, a front-desk clerk, and a concierge all rolled into one. I have more responsibilities. I feel better about my job, and the guest gets better service."[31] In short, the purpose of empowering service employees is zero customer defections—that is, to turn dissatisfied customers back into satisfied customers who continue to do business with the company.

Empowering service workers does entail some costs. Exhibit 14.5 describes some costs and benefits of empowering service workers to act in ways that they believe will accomplish service recovery. The savings to the company of retaining customers usually exceed the costs of empowering workers.

Review 3: SERVICE OPERATIONS

Services are different from goods. Goods are produced, tangible, and storable. Services are performed, intangible, and perishable. Likewise, managing service operations is different from managing production operations. The service-profit chain indicates that success begins with internal service quality, meaning how well management treats service employees. Internal service quality leads to employee satisfaction and service capability, which, in turn, lead to high-value service to customers, customer satisfaction, customer loyalty, and long-term profits and growth. Many service businesses are organized like manufacturers. While this "production-line" approach is efficient and inexpensive, its strict rules and guidelines make it difficult for service workers to perform service recovery, restoring customer satisfaction to strongly dissatisfied customers. To resolve this problem, some companies are empowering service employees to perform service recovery by giving them the authority and responsibility to immediately solve customer problems. The hope is that empowered service recovery will prevent customer defections.

4 MANUFACTURING OPERATIONS

Let's play word association. What do the words "Chicken and Stars," "Chicken Noodle," "Cream of Mushroom," and "Cream of Tomato" make you think of? Well, soup, of course! And, chances are, you thought of Campbell's soup (www.campbellsoup.com), the

BENEFITS

1. Quicker responses to customer complaints and problems.
2. Employees feel better about their jobs and themselves.
3. Employee interaction with customers will be warm and enthusiastic.
4. Employees are more likely to offer ideas for improving service or preventing problems.

COSTS OF EMPOWERING SERVICE WORKERS

1. Increased cost of selection to find service workers who are capable of solving problems and dealing with upset customers.
2. Increased cost to train service workers how to solve different kinds of problems.
3. Higher wages to attract and keep talented service workers.
4. A focus on service recovery may lead to less emphasis on service reliability, doing it right the first time. Ultimately, this could lead to slower delivery of services.
5. In their quest to please customers, empowered service workers may cost the company money by being too eager to provide "giveaways" to make up for poor or slow service.
6. Empowered service workers may unintentionally treat customers unfairly by occasionally being overly generous to make up for poor or slow service.

Source: D.E. Bowen & E.E. Lawler III, "The Empowerment of Service Workers: What, Why, How, and When," *Sloan Management Review* 33 (Spring 1992): 31–39.

EXHIBIT 14.5
Costs and Benefits of Empowering Service Workers for Service Recovery

world's best-selling soup brand. In fact, Campbell's soup can be found in over 90 percent of North American households. While Campbell's effective "hmmm-mmmm good" advertisements bring to mind images of home cooking, Campbell's obviously doesn't make its soups in small kitchens. It makes them in large factories. One measures 1.4 million square feet (130 000 square metres) and produces 4.9 million cans of soup per day! It alone can make over 200 different kinds of soup, as well as Spaghetti Os, pork and beans, and different kinds of gravy.

Like the Campbell's soup manufacturing plant described above, all manufacturing operations produce physical goods. But not all manufacturing operations are the same. Even those that produce food are often quite different.

Let's learn how various manufacturing operations differ in the amount of processing in manufacturing operations and in the flexibility of manufacturing operations.

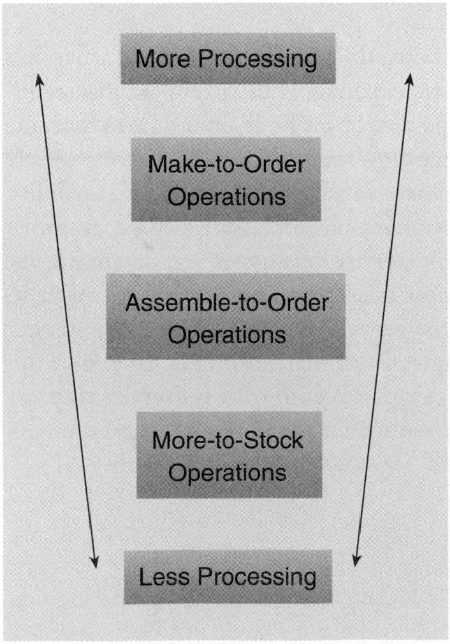

EXHIBIT 14.6
Processing in Manufacturing Operations

Amount of Processing in Manufacturing Operations

As Exhibit 14.6 shows, manufacturing operations can be classified according to the amount of processing or assembly that occurs after receiving an order from customers. The highest degree of processing occurs in **make-to-order operations**. A make-to-order operation does not start processing or assembling products until it receives a customer order. In fact, some make-to-order operations may not even order parts until that customer order is received. Not surprisingly, these practices permit make-to-order operations to produce or assemble highly specialized or customized products for customers.

make-to-order operation manufacturing operation that does not start processing or assembling products until a customer order is received

GETTY IMAGES

Dell computers are created using a make-to-order operation.

For example, Dell Computer (www.dell.com) has one of the most advanced make-to-order operations in the computer business. Dell has no finished-goods inventory—it does not build a computer until someone buys it. Because Dell doesn't order parts from suppliers until machines are purchased, its computers always have the latest, most advanced computer components. No one who buys a Dell computer gets stuck with old technology. Also, because prices of computer components tend to fall, Dell's make-to-order operation can pass on price cuts to customers. As well, Dell can customize all its orders, big and small. For example, it took Dell just six weeks to make and ship 2000 personal computers and 4000 network servers for Wal-Mart. Furthermore, Dell pre-loaded each of these 6000 machines with proprietary software that Wal-Mart uses in its stores and offices.[32]

A moderate degree of processing occurs in **assemble-to-order operations**. A company using an assemble-to-order operation divides its manufacturing or assembly process into separate parts or modules. They order parts and assemble modules ahead of customer orders. Then, on the basis of actual customer orders or on research forecasting what customers will want, those modules are then combined to create semi-customized products. For example, when a customer orders a new car, Ford may have already ordered the basic parts or modules it needs from suppliers. In other words, on the basis of sales forecasts, Ford may already have ordered enough tires, air-conditioning compressors, brake systems, and seats from suppliers to accommodate nearly all customer orders on a particular day. However, special orders from customers and car dealers are then used to determine the final assembly checklist for particular cars as they move down the assembly line.

assemble-to-order operation
manufacturing operation that divides manufacturing processes into separate parts or modules that are combined to create semi-customized products

The lowest degree of processing occurs in make-to-stock operations. A company using a **make-to-stock operation** starts ordering parts and assembling finished products before receiving customer orders. These standardized products are typically purchased by consumers at retail stores or directly from the manufacturer. Because parts are ordered and products are assembled before customers order the products, make-to-stock operations are highly dependent on the accuracy of sales forecasts. If sales forecasts are incorrect, make-to-stock operations may end up building too many or too few products, or they may make products with the wrong features or lacking the features that customers want.

make-to-stock operation
manufacturing operation that orders parts and assembles standardized products before receiving customer orders

These disadvantages led Wilkerson Corporation (www.wilkersoncorp.com), a manufacturer of pneumatic devices such as air compressors, with distributors throughout Canada, to switch to a make-to-order assembly operation. Under its old make-to-stock system, Wilkerson would make large batches of its best-selling products and store them on shelves that reached all the way to the ceiling of its manufacturing plant. Storing

Auto manufacturers are usually assemble-to-order operations because they create semi-customized products (e.g., the Ford Explorer XL or XLT) with different options and features.

unsold inventory was not only expensive (costs ran as high as 30 percent of sales), but it also sometimes took 6 to 18 months to sell off the unsold finished inventory. And because the company was spending all its time producing large batches of its best-selling products, it was frequently unable to make special, customized products for customers who required them. With a product catalogue of more than 50 000 items, it was almost impossible under the make-to-stock system for Wilkerson to have all its products in stock and ready for delivery.[33]

Flexibility of Manufacturing Operations

manufacturing flexibility degree to which manufacturing operations can easily and quickly change the number, kind, and characteristics of products they produce

A second way to categorize manufacturing operations is by **manufacturing flexibility**, meaning the degree to which manufacturing operations can easily and quickly change the number, kind, and characteristics of products they produce. Flexibility allows companies to respond more quickly to changes in the marketplace (i.e., competitors and customers) and to reduce the lead time between ordering and final delivery of products. However, there is often a trade-off between flexibility and cost, with the most flexible manufacturing operations frequently having higher costs per unit and the least flexible operations having lower costs per unit.[34] As shown in Exhibit 14.7, the least to most flexible manufacturing operations are continuous-flow production, line-flow production, batch production, job shops, and project manufacturing.

Most production processes generate finished products at a discrete rate. A product is completed, and then, perhaps a few seconds, minutes, or hours later, another is completed, and so on. For instance, if you stood at the end of an automobile assembly line, it would appear as if nothing much was happening for 55 seconds of every minute. However, in that last 5 seconds, a new car would be started and driven off the assembly line, ready for its new owner. By contrast, in **continuous-flow production**, products are produced at a continuous, rather than discrete, rate, in which production of the final product never stops. It's sort of like a water hose that is never turned off. The water (or product) just keeps on flowing. In other words, the product is always and continuously being produced. Liquid chemicals and petroleum products are examples of continuous-flow production. If you're still struggling with this concept (and it can be confusing), think of PlayDoh. Continuous-flow production is similar to squeezing PlayDoh into a toy press and watching the various shapes ooze out of the "PlayDoh Machine." But with continuous-flow production, the PlayDoh machine would never quit oozing or producing rectangle- or triangle-shaped PlayDoh. Because of their complexity, continuous-flow production processes are the most standardized and least flexible manufacturing operations.

continuous-flow production manufacturing operation that produces goods at a continuous, rather than a discrete, rate

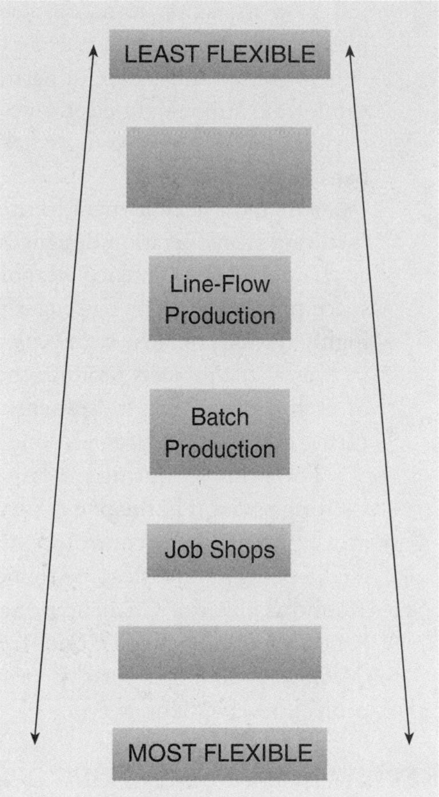

EXHIBIT 14.7
Flexibility of Manufacturing Operations

Line-flow production processes are pre-established, occur in a serial or linear manner, and are dedicated to making one type of product. In this way, the 10 different steps required to make product X can be completed in a separate manufacturing process (with separate machines, parts, treatments, locations, and workers) from the 12 different steps required to make product Y. Line-flow production processes are inflexible, because they are typically dedicated to the manufacture of one kind of product. Breweries are often built in this fashion with processes or steps that are serial, meaning they must occur in a particular order. For example, in some companies, after empty bottles are sterilized, they are filled with beer using a special dispenser that distributes the beer down the inside walls of the bottle. This fills the bottle from the bottom up and displaces the air that was in the bottle. The bottles are then crowned or capped, checked for under-filling and missing caps, labelled, inspected a final time for fill levels and missing labels, and then placed in cases that are shrink-wrapped on pallets and put on trucks for delivery.[35]

line-flow production manufacturing processes that are pre-established, occur in a serial or linear manner, and are dedicated to making one type of product

The next most flexible manufacturing operation is **batch production**, which involves the manufacture of large batches of different products in standard lot sizes. Consequently, a worker in a batch production operation will perform the same manufacturing process on 100 copies of product X, followed by 200 copies of product Y, and then 50 copies of product Q. Furthermore, these "batches" move through each manufacturing department or process in identical order. So, if the paint department follows chemical treatment, and chemical treatment is now processing a batch of 50 copies of product Q, then the paint department's next task will be to paint 50 copies of product Q. One example of the use of batch production would be found in the creation of Mega Bloks (www.megabloks.com), children's toys developed in Montreal that compete directly with Lego. Popular Mega Blok kits such as Alien Agency D.N.A. Lab or Dragons Man O' War each have hundreds of pieces, many of them identical. If we multiply these kits by the tens of thousands, it is easy to see the need for this style of production.

batch production manufacturing operation that produces goods in large batches in standard lot sizes

The next most flexible manufacturing operation is called a job shop. **Job shops** are typically small manufacturing operations that handle special manufacturing processes or jobs. By contrast to batch production, which handles large batches of different products, job shops typically handle very small batches, some as small as one product or process per "batch." Basically, each "job" in a job shop is different, and once a job is done, the

job shops manufacturing operations that handle customer orders or small batch jobs

job shop moves on to a completely different job or manufacturing process for, most likely, a different customer. For example, some job shops specialize in assembling products for other firms. One in particular has 12 full-time employees who assemble everything from strobe-light electronics, laser light-show equipment, personal air-monitoring devices, speed-boat steering wheels, and automated chemical dispensers to hand-held bar-code readers.[36]

project manufacturing
manufacturing operations designed to produce large, expensive, specialized products

The most flexible manufacturing operation is project manufacturing. **Project manufacturing** is an operation designed to produce large, expensive, specialized products such as custom homes, defence weapons such as aircraft carriers and submarines, and aerospace products such as passenger planes and the space shuttle. Project manufacturing is highly flexible, because each project is usually significantly different from the one before it, even if the projects produce the same type of product, such as a submarine. Because of each project's size and expense and high degree of customization, project manufacturing can take an extremely long time to complete.

For example, during the last few decades CAE Inc. (www.cae.com) has built itself a strong position in the power plant simulator niche. CAE manufactures simulators that are duplicates of the control rooms of major coal, hydroelectric, and nuclear generation facilities. Its products can be found in electrical utilities throughout North America and around the world. Challenging to CAE and its engineers is a quirky feature of North American nuclear generation facilities. No two are the same, so every time CAE develops a simulator for this market, it has to start from scratch in its planning and project development.

REVIEW 4: MANUFACTURING OPERATIONS

Manufacturing operations produce physical goods. Manufacturing operations can be classified according to the amount of processing or assembly that occurs after receiving an order from customers. Make-to-order operations have the highest degree of processing, in which assembly doesn't begin until products are ordered. The next-highest degree of processing occurs in assemble-to-order operations, in which pre-assembled modules are combined after orders are received to produce semi-customized products. The lowest degree of processing occurs in make-to-stock operations, in which, on the basis of sales forecasts, standard parts are ordered and assembled before orders occur.

Manufacturing operations can also be classified by flexibility, the degree to which the number, kind, and characteristics of products can easily and quickly be changed. Flexibility allows companies to respond quickly to competitors and customers and to reduce order lead times, but can also lead to higher unit costs. The least to most flexible manufacturing operations are continuous-flow production, line-flow production, batch production, job shops, and project manufacturing.

5 INVENTORY

In February 1998, Ford shut down one of its North American assembly plants for two weeks. The plant, which assembles Ford Escorts and Mercury Tracers, laid off 3500 workers during that time. According to Jim Bright, a Ford spokesperson, the plant was closed to "maintain dealer inventories at reasonable levels." Said Bright, "We have a 117-day supply on Escort and a 103-day supply on Tracer and that's higher than we'd like to have, which is ideally about a 72-day supply."[37]

inventory
the amount and number of raw materials, parts, and finished products that a company has in its possession

Inventory is the amount and number of raw materials, parts, and finished products that a company has in its possession. Ford made the mistake of having too much inventory on hand and had to close its factories to let existing sales draw down inventory levels to an acceptable and affordable level.

In this section, you will learn about types of inventory, measuring inventory, costs of maintaining an inventory, and managing inventory.

Types of Inventory

Exhibit 14.8 shows the four kinds of inventory a manufacturer stores: raw materials, component parts, work-in-process, and finished goods. The flow of inventory through a manufacturing plant begins when the purchasing department buys raw materials from vendors. **Raw material inventories** are the basic inputs in the manufacturing process. For example, to begin making a car, automobile manufacturers purchase raw materials such as steel, iron, aluminum, copper, rubber, and unprocessed plastic.

raw material inventories
the basic inputs in a manufacturing process

Next, raw materials are fabricated or processed into **component parts inventories**, meaning the basic parts used in manufacturing a product. For example, in an automobile plant, steel is fabricated or processed into a car's body panels, and steel and iron are melted and shaped into engine parts such as pistons or engine blocks. Component parts inventories are sometimes purchased directly from vendors.

component parts inventories
the basic parts used in manufacturing that are fabricated from raw materials

The component parts are then assembled to make unfinished **work-in-process inventories**, which are also known as partially finished goods. This process is also called initial assembly. For example, steel body panels are welded to each other and to the frame of the car to make a "unibody," which comprises the unpainted interior frame and exterior structure of the car. Likewise, pistons, camshafts, and other engine parts are inserted into the engine block to create a working engine.

work-in-process inventories
partially finished goods consisting of assembled component parts

EXHIBIT 14.8
Types of Inventory

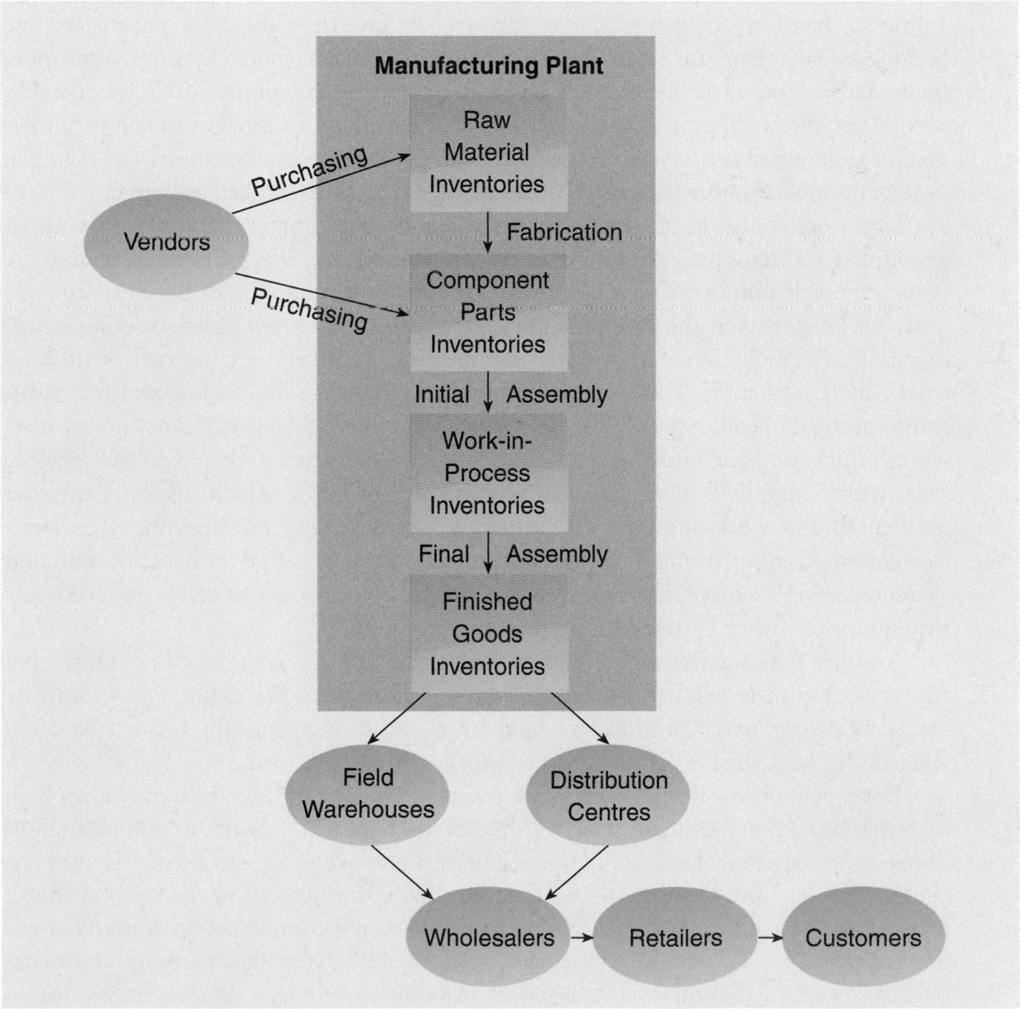

Source: Adapted from *Operations Management* by Markland/Vickery. (c) 1998. Reprinted with permission of South-Western, a division of Thomson Learning: www.thomsonrights.com. Fax 800-730-2215.

finished goods inventories
the final outputs of manufacturing operations

Next, all the work-in-process inventories are assembled to create **finished goods inventories**, which are the final outputs of the manufacturing process. This process is also called final assembly. So, for a car, the engine, wheels, brake system, suspension, interior, and electrical system are assembled into a car's painted unibody to make the working automobile, which is the factory's finished product. In the last step in the process, the finished goods are sent to field warehouses or distribution centres or wholesalers, and then to retailers for final sale to consumers.

Measuring Inventory

As you'll learn below, uncontrolled inventory can lead to huge costs for a manufacturing operation. Consequently, managers need good measures of inventory to prevent inventory costs from becoming too large. Three basic measures of inventory are average aggregate inventory, weeks of supply, and inventory turnover.

If you've ever worked in a retail store and have had to "take inventory," you probably weren't too excited about the process of counting every item in the store and storeroom. It's an extensive process. Fortunately, "taking inventory" is somewhat easier today because of bar codes that mark items and computers that can count and track them. However, if you took inventory at the beginning of the month, the inventory count would likely be different from the count at the end of the month. Similar differences in inventory count might occur if inventory was taken on a Friday rather than a Monday. Because of day-to-day differences in inventories, companies often measure **average aggregate inventory**, which is the average overall inventory during a particular time period. Average aggregate inventory for a month can be determined by simply averaging the inventory counts at the end of each business day for that month. One way companies know whether they're carrying too much or too little inventory is to compare their average aggregate inventory to the industry average for aggregate inventory. For example, in the automobile industry, 60 to 65 days of inventory is the industry average.

average aggregate inventory
average overall inventory during a particular time period

Inventory is also measured by weeks of supply, meaning the number of weeks it would take for a company to run out of its current supply of inventory. In general, there is an acceptable number of weeks of inventory for a particular kind of business. Too few weeks of inventory on the one hand, and a company risks a **stockout**—running out of inventory. Too many weeks of inventory on the other hand, and the business incurs high costs (discussed below). For example, companies that make linerboard used for corrugated cardboard boxes typically have too much inventory when they have more than six weeks' supply on hand and about the right amount of inventory when the level drops to four weeks' supply.[38] Likewise, 3Com (www.3com.com), which makes computer modems and network cards, aims for a four- to six-week supply of network cards, a six- to eight-week supply of modems, and a five- to seven-week supply of network hubs and switches. Anything more than that results in excess inventory, which can be reduced only through price cuts or by temporarily stopping production.[39]

stockout
situation in which a company runs out of finished product

Another common inventory measure, **inventory turnover**, is the number of times per year that a company sells or "turns over" its average inventory. For example, if a company keeps an average of 100 finished widgets in inventory each month, and it sold 1000 widgets this year, then it "turned" its inventory 10 times this year.

inventory turnover
the number of times per year that a company sells or "turns over" its average inventory

In general, the higher the number of inventory "turns," the better. In practice, a high turnover means that a company can continue its daily operations with just a small amount of inventory on hand. For example, let's take two companies, A and B, which, over the course of a year, have identical inventory levels (520 000 widget parts and raw materials). If company A turns its inventories 26 times a year, it would completely replenish its inventory every two weeks and have an average inventory of 20 000 widget parts and raw materials. By contrast, if company B turned its inventories only two times a year, it would completely replenish its inventory every 26 weeks and have an average inventory of 260 000 widget parts and raw materials. So by turning its inventory more often, company A has 92 percent less inventory on hand at any one time than company B.

Across all kinds of manufacturing plants, the average number of inventory turns is approximately seven per year. However, food manufacturing plants, which have an obvious need for fresh ingredients, average 25 inventory turns per year, while auto and truck makers, which aggressively manage their inventories, can average inventory turns as high as 52 per year![40]

Costs of Maintaining an Inventory

Maintaining an inventory incurs four kinds of costs: ordering, setup, holding, and stockout. **Ordering cost** is not the cost of the inventory itself, but the costs associated with ordering the inventory. It includes the costs of completing paperwork, manually entering data into a computer, making phone calls, getting competing bids, correcting mistakes, and simply determining when and how much new inventory should be reordered. For example, ordering costs are relatively high in the restaurant business, because 80 percent of food service orders (in which restaurants reorder food supplies) are processed manually. However, it's estimated that the North American food industry could save more than $9 billion if all restaurants converted to electronic data interchange (see Chapter 5), in which purchase and ordering information from one company's computer system is automatically relayed to another company's computer system. In fact, a number of restaurants and food service trade groups have formed an interest group called Efficient Foodservice Response to encourage restaurants and food suppliers to use EDI and other methods of electronic commerce.[41]

ordering cost
the costs associated with ordering inventory, including the cost of data entry, phone calls, obtaining bids, correcting mistakes, and determining when and how much inventory to order

Setup cost is the cost of changing or adjusting a machine so it can produce a different kind of inventory.[42] For example, 3M (www.3m.com) uses the same production machinery to make several kinds of industrial tape. However, different adjustments have to be made to the machines for each kind of tape. There are two kinds of setup costs, downtime and lost efficiency. *Downtime* occurs anytime a machine is not being used to process inventory. So if it takes five hours to switch a machine from processing one kind of inventory to another, then five hours of downtime have occurred. Downtime is costly, because companies earn an economic return only when machines are actively turning raw materials into parts or parts into finished products. The second setup cost is *lost efficiency.* Typically, after a switchover, it takes some time to recalibrate a machine to its optimal settings. It may take several days of fine-tuning before a machine finally produces the number of high-quality parts that it is supposed to.

setup cost
the costs of downtime and lost efficiency that occur when changing or adjusting a machine to produce a different kind of inventory

Holding cost, also known as carrying or storage cost, is the cost of keeping inventory until it is used or sold. Holding costs include the cost of storage facilities, insurance to protect inventory from damage or theft, inventory taxes, the cost of obsolescence (holding inventory that is no longer useful to the company), and the opportunity cost of spending money on inventory that could have been spent elsewhere in the company.

holding cost
the cost of keeping inventory until it is used or sold, including storage, insurance, taxes, obsolescence, and opportunity costs

Stockout costs are the costs incurred when a company runs out of a product. There are two basic kinds of stockout costs. The first is the transaction costs of overtime work, shipping, and so forth, that are incurred in trying to quickly replace out-of-stock inventories with new inventories. The second and perhaps most damaging cost is the loss of customers' goodwill when a company cannot deliver the products that it promised. Marc Pritchard, vice president and general manager for Procter & Gamble, said, "Research shows the number-one complaint of mass shoppers is product availability. Twenty-five percent of shoppers walk out of the mass store without a purchase. What's worse is what you'd find in the back of stores and in manufacturers' warehouses—[US]$1.3 billion in inventory, think of that—but we still can't keep the right product in stock."[43]

stockout costs
the costs incurred when a company runs out of a product, including transaction costs to replace inventory and the loss of customers' goodwill

Managing Inventory

Inventory management has two basic goals. The first is to avoid running out of stock and angering and dissatisfying customers. Consequently, this goal seeks to increase inventory levels to a "safe" level that won't risk stockouts. The second is to efficiently reduce inventory levels and costs as much as possible without impairing daily operations. Thus, this goal seeks a minimum level of inventory. The following inventory management techniques—economic order quantity (EOQ), just-in-time inventory (JIT), and materials requirement planning (MRP)—are different ways of balancing these competing goals.

economic order quantity (EOQ)
a system of formulas that minimizes ordering and holding costs and helps determine how much and how often inventory should be ordered

Economic order quantity (EOQ) is a system of formulas that helps determine how much and how often inventory should be ordered. EOQ takes into account the overall demand (D) for a product while trying to minimize ordering costs (O) and holding costs (H). The formula for EOQ is

$$EOQ = \sqrt{\frac{2DO}{H}}$$

For example, if a factory uses 40 000 litres of paint a year (D), and ordering costs (O) are $75 per order, and holding costs (H) are $4 per litre, then the optimal quantity to order is 1225 litres.

$$EOQ = \sqrt{\frac{2(40\,000)(75)}{4}} = 1.225$$

And, with 40 000 litres of paint being used per year, the factory uses approximately 110 litres per day.

$$EOQ = \frac{40\,000 \ liters}{365 \ days} = 110$$

Consequently, the factory would order 1225 new litres of paint approximately every 11 days.

$$EOQ = \frac{1225 \ liters}{110 \ liters \ per \ day} = 11.1 \ days$$

just-in-time (JIT) inventory system
inventory system in which component parts arrive from suppliers just as they are needed at each stage of production

While EOQ formulas try to minimize holding and ordering costs, the just-in-time (JIT) approach to inventory management attempts to eliminate holding costs by reducing inventory levels to near zero. A **just-in-time (JIT) inventory system** is a system in which component parts arrive from suppliers just as they are needed at each stage of production. By having parts arrive "just in time," the manufacturer has little inventory on hand, avoiding the costs associated with holding inventory. For example, thanks to its JIT inventory system, one of Toyota's North American car factories has only 2.8 hours' worth of inventory on hand at any one time. This low level of inventory saves Toyota millions of dollars a year in inventory expenses.[44] When Ford needs more seats at its Taurus plant, it uses an electronic system to give its seat supplier two hours' notice to make its next delivery of seats to the factory.[45]

To have just the right amount of inventory arrive at just the right time requires a tremendous amount of coordination between manufacturing operations and suppliers. One way to promote tight coordination under JIT is close proximity. At the Toyota plant noted above, most parts suppliers are located within 300 kilometres of the plant. Furthermore, parts are picked up from suppliers and delivered to Toyota as often as 16 times a day.[46]

A second way to promote close coordination under JIT is shared information systems. These systems allow manufacturers and their suppliers to know the quantity and kinds of parts inventory the other has in stock. One way to facilitate information sharing is for factories and suppliers to use the same parts numbers and names. Ford's seat supplier accomplishes this by sticking a bar code on each seat. Ford then uses the same bar code in its factories to determine when the seat is needed, which car the seat is installed in, and which workstation on the assembly line will install the seat.

Another way to facilitate close coordination between manufacturing operations and their parts suppliers is the Japanese system of kanban. **Kanban**, which is Japanese for "sign," is a simple ticket-based system that indicates when it is time to reorder inventory. Suppliers attach kanban cards to batches of parts. Then when an assembly line worker uses the first part out of a batch, the kanban card is removed. The cards are then collected, sorted, and quickly returned to the supplier, who begins resupplying the factory with parts that match the order information on the kanban cards. And, because prices and batch sizes are typically agreed to ahead of time, kanban tickets greatly reduce paperwork and ordering costs.[47]

kanban
a ticket-based system that indicates when to reorder inventory

A third method for managing inventory is **materials requirement planning (MRP)**. MRP is a production and inventory system that, from beginning to end, precisely determines the production schedule, production batch sizes, and inventories needed to complete final products. The three key parts of MRP systems are the master production schedule, the bill of materials, and inventory records. The master production schedule is a detailed schedule that indicates the quantity of each item to be produced, the planned delivery dates for those items, and the time by which each step of the production process must be completed in order to meet those delivery dates. Based on the quantity and kind of products set forth in the master production schedule, the bill of materials identifies all the necessary parts and inventory, the quantity or volume of inventory to be ordered, and the order in which the parts and inventory should be assembled. Inventory records indicate the kind, quantity, and location of inventory that is on hand or that has been ordered. When inventory records are combined with the bill of materials, the resulting report indicates what to buy, when to buy it, and what it will cost to order. Today, nearly all MRP systems are available in the form of powerful, flexible computer software.[48]

materials requirement planning (MRP)
a production and inventory system that determines the production schedule, production batch sizes, and inventory needed to complete final products

Which inventory management system should you use? Economic order quantity (EOQ) formulas are intended for use with **independent demand systems**, in which the level of one kind of inventory does not depend on another. For example, because inventory levels for automobile tires are unrelated to the inventory levels of ladies' dresses, Sears could use EOQ formulas to calculate separate optimal order quantities for dresses and tires. By contrast, JIT and MRP are used with **dependent demand systems**, in which the level of inventory depends on the number of finished units to be produced. For example, if Yamaha makes 1000 motorcycles a day, then it will need 1000 seats, 1000 gas tanks, and 2000 wheels and tires each day. So when optimal inventory levels depend on the number of products to be produced, use a JIT or MRP management system.

independent demand system
inventory system in which the level of one kind of inventory does not depend on another

dependent demand system
inventory system in which the level of inventory depends on the number of finished units to be produced

REVIEW 5: INVENTORY

There are four kinds of inventory: raw materials, component parts, work-in-process, and finished goods. Because companies incur ordering, setup, holding, and stockout costs when handling inventory, inventory costs can be enormous. To control those costs, companies measure and track inventory in three ways: average aggregate inventory, weeks of supply, and turnover. Companies meet the basic goals of inventory management (avoiding stockouts and reducing inventory without hurting daily operations) through economic order quantity (EOQ) formulas, just-in-time (JIT) inventory systems, and materials requirement planning (MRP). EOQ formulas minimize holding and ordering costs by determining how much and how often inventory should be ordered. By having parts arrive just when they are needed at each stage of production, JIT systems attempt to minimize inventory levels and holding costs. JIT systems often depend on proximity, shared information, and the Japanese system of kanban. MRP precisely determines the production schedule, production batch sizes, and the ordering of inventories needed to complete final products. The three key parts of MRP systems are the master production schedule, the bill of materials, and inventory records. Use EOQ formulas when inventory levels are independent, and JIT and MRP when inventory levels are dependent on the number of products to be produced.

What Really Happened?[49]

In the opening case, you learned that Hyundai, the butt of talk show jokes because of the poor quality of its cars, had seen U.S. sales drop from 264 000 cars to 90 000 cars in just two years. Hyundai cars ranked 26th out of 35 car brands in terms of initial car quality as measured by the influential J.D. Power Initial Car Quality survey, and Kia, which Hyundai had paid US$8 billion to acquire, was ranked 35th—dead last. With US$6.6 million in debt, a US$1 billion investment for a new manufacturing plant, and the company's first-ever loss, Hyundai's new chairman declared that improving quality was the only way to fix the company. Let's see what really happened and what steps Hyundai took to address to improve the quality of its cars.

If the company is to survive, if car buyers' perceptions are to change, and if the US$1 billion investment in the new plant is to pay off, then quality must improve. Of course, the question is "how?" Your first goal is to change the mindset in the company—to convince managers and factory workers that quality comes first. What's the best way to do that?

The challenge for Hyundai's new chairman and CEO, Chung Mong Koo, was to get his managers to put quality, and not costs, first. The first thing that Chung did was to send a visible, meaningful message that poor quality would no longer be tolerated. During a surprise visit to a Hyundai manufacturing plant, he peeked under the hood of a new Sonata. Seeing a mess, he ordered the assembly line stopped and all the nuts and bolts painted black on that car. The message was clear: No car would leave the plant until all the parts under the hood were organized appropriately. He then stated that Hyundai's goal was to build higher-quality cars than Toyota, the industry leader.

And, to drive this message home to top managers, each workweek starts with a demanding three-hour meeting that begins at 9 A.M. Managers, engineers, designers, and suppliers all attend. And instead of reviewing reports and data or listening to PowerPoint presentations, Chung brings Hyundai's quality problems to life in his large boardroom by having Hyundai cars displayed on rotating turntables or mechanical lifts, whatever is required for those in attendance to see up close what problems need to be fixed. With management convinced and paying close attention, the next move was to make changes on the factory floor to consistently improve quality.

Next, what steps do you need to take to actually improve quality? It won't be easy and it won't be quick, but it can be done. Where do you start?

Quality can mean two things. It can mean a product or service free of deficiencies (perhaps based on the number of problems per 100 cars) or it can mean the characteristics of a product or service that satisfy customer needs. We'll address the first definition here and the second in the next question.

Quality products usually possess three characteristics: reliability, serviceability, and durability. A breakdown occurs when a product quits working or doesn't do what it was designed to do. The longer it takes for a product to break down, or the longer the time between breakdowns, the more reliable the product. Consequently, many companies define product reliability in terms of the average time between breakdowns. Serviceability refers to how easy or difficult it is to fix a product. The easier it is to maintain a working product or fix a broken product, the more serviceable that product is. However, some products don't break down—they fail. Product failure means products can't be repaired. They can only be replaced. Thus, durability is a quality characteristic that applies to products that can't be repaired. Durability is defined as the mean time to failure. Of these three characteristics, Hyundai focused the most on reliability (increasing how long it takes the various parts of a car to break), and then, secondarily, on serviceability (making repairs easy if and when they occurred). So, what steps did Hyundai take on the factory floor to improve the quality of its cars?

The first step was to reduce variation. Variation is a deviation in the form, condition, or appearance of a product from the quality standard for that product. The less a product varies from the quality standard, or the more consistently a company's products meet a quality standard, the higher the quality. And the best way to control variation is to measure it. So in every Hyundai factory you'll find hundreds of charts on the wall that measure the number of times and the degree to which a process has produced parts that vary meaningfully from the quality standards for those parts. For example, stamping presses are huge machines into which are fed flat pieces of steel that are literally stamped into shape to become body parts in your car. For instance, to create the rear quarter panel for a Hyundai car, a flat piece of stainless steel might literally be stamped by 25 or 30 different stamping machines, each bending the steel a little bit more each time until it assumes the shape of a finished rear quarter panel. The oiling of stamping presses is critical because it affects the quality of the parts and the rate at which the stamping machines have to be shut down for maintenance. Over the course of four years, Hyundai workers consistently improved the oiling of the stamping machines. In the past, they had to redo the oiling 11 percent of the time to get it right. But over the next four years, that percentage was reduced to 7 percent, 4 percent, 2.5 percent, and 1.5 percent.

Step two was to increase the size of the quality department. Chairman and CEO Chung Mong Koo increased the quality department at Hyundai from 100 to 1000 people. And, so no one would mistake the message he was sending, he had the quality department report directly to him as CEO. When Hyundai released its new Sonata in Korea, the launch of the car was delayed for two months, as Chung's quality department identified 50 problems that needed to be fixed. And rather than focusing on getting the Sonata to market on time, no matter the cost, Chung stood behind the quality department, declaring that the Sonata would not go to market unto those problems were fixed. For instance, using precise measuring tools, quality manager Sang Kil Han found a 0.1 millimetre discrepancy between the specified gap between two pieces of sheet metal—the same sheet metal shaped by stamping machines. No one could see the discrepancy, and the discrepancy had no effect on how well the car ran. Still, Sang and his workers and his engineers worked for 25 days to determine how to eliminate the 0.1 millimetre discrepancy. The answer? Special training for the workers who put those parts together.

The third step was to encourage all employees to share their ideas about how to improve quality. Chung communicated to workers that their ideas were critical and welcomed, and he rewarded them with bonuses. Knowing that the quality department reported directly to Chung, employees knew that they would be listened to and responded by the thousands. At Hyundai's new factory in Seoul, South Korea, workers have suggested 25 000 ideas for improving quality, 30 percent of which have been made in the factory. For instance, a worker noticed that the Hyundai Sonata and SG 350 sedans had identically sized spare tires, but different sized spare-tire covers. Though it sounds trivial, using the same spare tire cover for both cars saves Hyundai US$100 000 a year.

Finally, you've got to convince customers that you're responsive to their complaints, that you care, and that you're listening. If you can't do that, there won't be any improvements in those all-important quality rankings.

As mentioned above, quality can mean a product or service free of deficiencies or it can mean the characteristics of a product or service that satisfy customer needs. We'll address the latter issue in this question.

Historically, at most car companies, unless the quality problems are severe, once a car has been launched, the company doesn't act on customer complaints and feedback right away. Automakers will wait a few months to see what needs to be fixed and will then work on all the problems at once. Some will even wait until the model year is over and then address the major issues during the next model year. However, Hyundai realized that since customers had such strong negative perceptions about the quality of its cars, it had to address customer complaints as quickly as possible. For instance, after Hyundai Santa Fe owners complained about wind noise, engineers immediately began tackling the problem. After redesigning the aerodynamics of the side view mirrors and changing the position of a crossbar on the luggage rack on top of the Santa Fe's roof, the cars were much quieter. Quick responses to customer complaints like this reduced the Santa Fe's score in J.D. Power's Initial Car Quality survey from 149 problems per 100 cars (PP100) to 93 PP100 in just one year.

Another indication of the extent to which Hyundai now goes to address customer concerns is the "concept clinic" that it held before introducing the Sonata. At this concept clinic, 200 potential Sonata customers told Hyundai managers and researchers precisely what they liked or didn't like (and why) about the Toyota Camry, Honda Accord, Ford Taurus, and Audi A6 that Hyundai had brought to the clinic. Since the Sonata is supposed to compete with these cars, Hyundai wanted to know directly from customers what it should or shouldn't build into the Sonata's design. The customers particularly liked Audi's A6, so Hyundai began designing the Sonata to be an "affordable A6." But, since the Toyota Camry is the market leader in this segment, Hyundai has also focused on building a "better Camry," too.

Have customers noticed the improvements that Hyundai is making and that Hyundai is doing a better job of listening to their complaints? Indeed they have, and they're telling their friends. Bill Miller who bought a Hyundai Santa Fe said, "We had read good things about Hyundai, but what really convinced us was several of our friends who had Santa Fes were very pleased and satisfied." Why does this matter? Because it indicates that Hyundai is having success changing the perceptions that customers have about the quality of its cars.

Some of the strongest reasons to buy a Hyundai are found in J.D. Power's and *Consumer Reports*' quality ratings. Once ranked 26th in quality out of 35 car brands, the quality of Hyundai cars now approaches Toyota's. In a recent J.D. Power survey of initial car quality, Hyundai cars averaged just 110 problems per 100 cars (PP100) compared to 105 for Toyota. Hyundai cars still rank toward the bottom of J.D. Power's quality survey for older cars, but that's to be expected, since the initial quality of those older cars was poorer, too. The real test is whether it can keep close to Toyota when these new cars are three years old. Further, Hyundai has made remarkable progress, with *Consumer Reports* indicating that the Hyundai Sonata was the most reliable car made in 2004.

Finally, if the greatly improved quality isn't enough to convince you to buy a Hyundai, the company believes that its 10-year/100 000 mile (161 000 km) warranty may be enough. And, that warranty probably won't cost Hyundai much either, as the improved quality of its cars has dramatically cut the cost of warranty repairs, which are paid for by headquarters.

Other signs also point to Hyundai customers being much more satisfied with their cars. One of the most important is that 52 percent of the people buying a Hyundai today already own a Hyundai. For Toyota, that number is 50 percent. Likewise, when customers buy a new Hyundai, four of the top five cars traded in are Hyundais. Michael Chung, an analyst at Edmunds.com, a leading automobile Web site, said, "Before, Hyundai was a springboard to other makes." But not anymore.

Key Terms

assemble-to-order operation *(421)*
average aggregate inventory *(426)*
batch production *(423)*
component parts inventories *(425)*
continuous-flow production *(423)*
continuous improvement *(416)*
customer focus *(415)*
customer satisfaction *(415)*
dependent demand system *(429)*
economic order quantity (EOQ) *(428)*
finished goods inventories *(426)*
holding cost *(427)*
independent demand system *(429)*
inventory *(424)*
inventory turnover *(426)*
ISO 9000 *(414)*
job shops *(423)*
just-in-time (JIT) inventory *(428)*
kanban *(429)*
line-flow production *(423)*
make-to-order operation *(420)*
make-to-stock operation *(421)*
manufacturing flexibility *(422)*
materials requirement planning (MRP) *(429)*
multifactor productivity *(411)*
operations management *(410)*
ordering cost *(427)*
partial productivity *(411)*
productivity *(410)*
project manufacturing *(424)*
quality *(413)*
raw material inventories *(425)*
service recovery *(418)*
setup cost *(427)*
stockout *(426)*
stockout costs *(427)*
teamwork *(416)*
total quality management (TQM) *(415)*
variation *(416)*
work-in-process inventories *(425)*

Self-Assessment

HOW TO HANDLE DISGRUNTLED CUSTOMERS

Even though the "zero-defects" approach to service is a laudable goal, it will forever be unattainable. Mistakes happen (after all, people are not robots—and even robots malfunction from time to time), and service recovery will be the accepted response. To practise effective service recovery, companies need to implement a customer service orientation. But much like ethical decision-making, service recovery can be perceived differently depending on the situation. How would you handle service recovery? The Assessment Appendix contains a questionnaire based on several customer service scenarios. Turn to page 519 to gain insights into how you would respond to customer service snafus.

Management Decisions

CONTINUOUS QUALITY IMPROVEMENT, YEAH, RIGHT![50]

You've just been promoted as the manager of customer service for a medium-sized general merchandise retailer. Your boss, the former customer service manager, resigned yesterday, when she realized that her department was not going to meet the company's mandate of increasing customer satisfaction by 15 percent for the quarter. You are glad to get the chance to head up the department; however, you realize that your time may also be limited.

Your company has been suffering from low customer satisfaction since you began working there three years ago. Although customer satisfaction has increased during that time period, the company currently holds a 73 percent satisfaction rate, compared to its closest competitor's satisfaction rate of 92 percent. This rate suggests that only 7.3 out of 10 people are satisfied with their shopping experience. The company has tried many tactics to improve satisfaction in the store, ranging from training sales associates to be more customer-friendly, providing bonuses and pay raises for those who receive favourable evaluations from customers, and demoting or terminating sales associates who receive unfavourable evaluations from customers. Despite these programs, the overall customer satisfaction rate has yet to achieve top management's expectations. As the newly appointed customer service manager, what factors might you consider when attempting to solve the current customer satisfaction dilemma?

Management Decisions

CYCLE TIME AND QUALITY IMPROVEMENT

In the pursuit of quality improvement, many service organizations attempt to reduce the cycle time of key processes. "Cycle time" refers to the time taken to complete a key step in the delivery of a service or good. For example, cycle time can be the amount of time it takes the purchasing department to approve a purchase request. The cycle time begins when the purchasing department receives the request and ends when the request has been processed and returned to the individual.

Many organizations attempt to improve cycle time by looking at the processes involved in each department and removing any redundant steps or steps that do not create value for the organization. One organization that seems to have a negative image regarding cycle time is the government. At the local motor vehicle department (MVD), it seems that no matter what time of day or what day of the week you visit, you will end up spending a majority of your time standing in line. Likewise, receiving a tax refund or a passport traditionally have not been quick transactions. Wouldn't it be great if governmental agencies took steps to improve quality and decrease the cycle time of the services that they offer!

Another situation in which customers spend time waiting is at the local college, especially during registration. Many colleges tend to send students from one location to another in order for them to complete the registration process. For example, at one school, new students are required to fill out the admissions application and request for transcripts in the registrar's office. Then students must go down the hall to the business office in order to pay their admission fee. Once the fee has been paid, they must return to the registrar's office and show their receipt in order to complete the admission process. Once admitted, they must then go to an advisor's office to set an appointment in order to register for classes. Since they are new students, the advisor typically wants to see a copy of their transcript, which they typically don't have. If a transcript is on file, they have to return to the registrar's office in order to get a copy. Hopefully, with a copy of their transcript in hand, students are now ready to go back to the advisor's office and register for classes. All of these steps take time and confuse and frustrate the customer (in this case the student). If the whole process were inspected and improved, the majority of this confusion and frustration could be prevented.

Your assignment for this management decision is to think back to your last visit to the MVD, registrar, or other place where you had to either wait for a long time or go through several steps before completing the process. Think about ways to decrease the cycle time between steps, improve the overall flow, and increase customer satisfaction with the entire process.

Begin this exercise by describing the situation that you faced. Then list the steps you would take or the changes you would implement to improve the overall quality and outcome of the situation.

Develop Your Management Potential

TAKE A FACTORY TOUR[51]

Imagine that you're watching the final game of the Stanley Cup final series. As it ends, the camera zooms in on the game's most valuable player. The on-air announcer says to the MVP, "You've just won another championship. What are you going to do next?" And the player responds, "I'm going to Spamtown!" Spamtown? Actually, the winning athlete is supposed to say, "I'm going to Disney World," not Spamtown, the museum that Hormel Corporation established for its best-known product, Spam (www.spam.com).

Well, Spamtown isn't about to displace Disney World, but 60 000 people actually visit Spamtown each year. Thousands more also visit these corporate facilities:

- The BMW Factory Tour (www.bmwusfactory.com) guides viewers through the production process of its top-of-the-line cars.
- Hershey's Chocolate World (www.hersheys.com/chocolateworld/), Hershey Food Corporation's free visitor's centre with a Disney-like ride through a simulated chocolate factory.
- The Everett Tour Center (www.boeing.com/companyoffices/aboutus/tours/), where Boeing makes its 747, 767, and 777 passenger jets.
- The Vaughn Hockey factory (www.vaughnhockey.com) where hockey goalie equipment is custom made.

Your assignment for this Develop Your Management Potential is to take a factory tour. Do a quick Web search on the keywords "factory tour," or just ask around about a good factory tour near you. When on your tour, gather some literature and ask about the following issues.

Questions

1. What steps or procedures does the company take to ensure the quality of its products?

2. How does the company measure productivity and how does its productivity compare to others in the industry?
3. Describe the basic steps used to make the finished products in this factory. As you do this, be sure to describe the raw material inventories, component parts inventories, and work-in-process inventories used to create the finished products.
4. What did you find most impressive about the factory or manufacturing processes? Also, using the material from the chapter, describe one thing that the company could do differently to improve quality, increase productivity, or reduce inventory.

Discussion Questions

1. Define productivity and provide an everyday example of a measure of productivity that consumers sometimes use in selecting a car to purchase.
2. A rite of passage of many adults is participation, at one time or another, on an elementary or high school PTA. As a caring aunt or uncle, you have agreed to help out your sister by serving on the PTA for your nephew's school. Welcomed with open arms, you have been asked to use PTA funds to buy $200 worth of basketballs and $500 worth of chairs for one classroom. The only real stipulation suggested to you is that the products purchased are of high quality. In this instance, briefly identify the two possible meanings of the term *quality*.
3. Briefly describe what is meant by TQM.
4. Once a year, the college where you are studying offers a trip to a high-technology manufacturing facility. You are fortunate enough to go to school on the West Island of Montreal, which is also home to a number of pharmaceutical operations. Your professor confirms to you and your classmates that, indeed, tomorrow you will be touring a drug manufacturing facility. In preparation for the visit, she asks you to explain what the term "manufacturing flexibility" means and list the five types of manufacturing operations. Prepare a brief response for your professor.
5. The next day, during the visit, you notice that inventory in this facility consists of small piles of flour-like additives that occupy very little physical space. This strikes your curiosity and that of your professor. As an assignment, she asks you to hand in a one-page assignment in which you briefly identify the different methods of inventory management, and specify the circumstances under which each should be used. What does your response look like?

Critical Thinking Video Case

CBC

Visit www.management2e.nelson.com to view this chapter's CBC video case.

Take Two

Biz Flix
Casino

Martin Scorsese's lengthy, complex, and beautifully filmed *Casino* offers a close look at the gambling casinos of Las Vegas and their organized crime connections in the 1970s. It completes his trilogy that began with *Mean Streets* (1973) and continued with *Goodfellas* (1990). In *Casino*, ambition, greed, drugs, and sex ultimately destroy the mob's gambling empire. The film includes strong performances by Robert De Niro, Joe Pesci, and Sharon Stone. The violence and expletive-filled dialogue give *Casino* an R rating. This scene, which comes from the beginning of "The Truth about Las Vegas" sequence, opens the film and establishes important background about casino operations. Listen carefully to Sam Rothstein's (De Niro) voice-over. He quickly describes the casino's operation and explains how it tries to reach its goals.

What to Watch for and Ask Yourself

1. What type of operations management does this scene show—manufacturing operations management or service operations management?
2. Are the customers directly involved in this operation? If they are, in what way? What likely effects does their involvement have on the casino's operation and its management?
3. Does the casino have independent or interdependent demand systems?

Management Workplace
Texas Nameplate

Winning the Baldrige Award is a tremendous feat. Texas Nameplate did it twice. Facing environmental cleanup lawsuits, razor-thin margins, and the likely loss of a key account, Dale Crownover figured his company had nothing to lose by trying to win the National Quality Award. The simple act of applying for the award started Texas Nameplate down a path to profitability unprecedented in the company's history.

What to Watch for and Ask Yourself

1. What effect has improved quality had on Texas Nameplate?
2. Describe how Texas Nameplate uses total quality management.
3. What kind of manufacturing operation is Texas Nameplate?

Part 5

Leading

CP PHOTO/ADRIAN WYLD

Motivation and Leadership

Chapter 15

CHAPTER OUTLINE

LEARNING OBJECTIVES

After reading this chapter, you should be able to

1. explain the basics of motivation
2. use equity theory to explain how employees' perceptions of fairness affect motivation.
3. use expectancy theory to describe how workers' expectations about rewards, effort, and the link between rewards and performance influence motivation.
4. explain what leadership is.
5. describe who leaders are and what effective leaders do.
6. explain Fiedler's contingency theory.
7. discuss Hersey and Blanchard's situational theory.
8. explain how visionary leadership (i.e., charismatic and transformational leadership) helps leaders achieve strategic leadership.

What Would You Do?

Although Nortel Networks can trace its lineage back to the 1880s (it used to manufacture sleigh bells), Nortel emerged in the late 1990s and early 2000s as one of Canada's leading technology companies and was seen as the darling of the industry. It purchased many other emerging companies to retain its leading industry position and grew to become a very large company. It was big, not just by Canadian standards but by international standards. In 2000 its stock reached the lofty price of $120 a share and it had annual revenues of over $30 billion. It had the largest stock market capitalization of any company in Canada at almost $370 billion, almost three times the next largest company, Bell Canada, and ten times the size of third place Seagram, and it represented over 30 percent of the value of the TSE 300 index (now called the TSX 300). During this period, the company's CEO was John Roth. He had taken over the company in October of 1997 and changed the name from Northern Telecom to the now-familiar Nortel. He led the company through its frenzy of acquisitions and phenomenal growth and was credited with its meteoric rise in share price. All seemed to be going Nortel's way until it hit a bump in the road, and the bump was more like a wall.[1]

Despite its impressive rise, Nortel soon fell from its lofty perch and within a year the stock was under $25. This was only the start of the company's problems. Sales began to lag, falling by about two-thirds. John Roth, once lauded as someone with great vision who had led Nortel to the position it was in, was quietly replaced in 2001 by Frank Dunn, who had spent a quarter century working his way up through the ranks of the company and had previously held the post of chief financial officer (CFO). This was done amid swirling rumours that there were problems with Nortel's financial reporting and there was even talk that the company would go bankrupt. This led to pointed questions about why the man in charge of the purse strings during a period of financial irregularities was now placed in charge of the entire company.

In 2002 in the midst of rumours, Nortel's stock price fell to less than $1 and the company was being subjected to a number of class-action suits over its revenue forecasts (historical share prices of Canadian and U.S. stocks can be viewed at http://finance.yahoo.com). It soon began slashing tens of thousands of jobs and abandoning buildings. It would be a long climb out of the woods. The Ontario Securities Commission and the U.S. Securities and Exchange Commission had begun investigating Nortel's accounting practices while the RCMP was making its own inquiries. Although Nortel soon stepped back from the brink of bankruptcy, it was hit by a new challenge, a full-blown public accounting scandal. The rumours appeared to be true. In 2003 the company announced that it would be restating its financial statements back to 2000, as auditors had found that the company had been overstating its sales and profits. Nortel was in good company as this was the era of the accounting scandal. Enron, WorldCom, and Tyco were in turmoil, stock market investors were leery about every company, regulators were scrutinizing everyone's activity more closely, and the United States was implementing the Sarbanes-Oxley Act, which increased the due diligence requirements of U.S. firms and those that did business in the United States. Meanwhile, Nortel's auditors were conducting an internal review, which would go on to uncover numerous problems with Nortel's corporate culture and accounting standards.

It seemed that Nortel encouraged executives to be extremely loose when applying accounting standards in order to ensure that high sales and profit targets were met. Executives received very large—some would even say excessive—bonuses when profit targets were met (or were they?). These lofty profit targets could only be met if the company used "aggressive" accounting methods. It seemed that these methods did not comply with generally accepted accounting principles, creating a great deal of turmoil for the company and uncertainty in the minds of investors. Former CFO, now CEO, Frank Dunn appeared to lead by example. Mr. Dunn had been the CFO during some of Nortel's very best years in the late 1990s and now was CEO, but the bloom was off the rose. After a long investigation by its auditors, Nortel had to remove $3.4 billion in sales that were placed on the books prior to 2001, erasing much of the company's earlier profits. Many executives had received their large bonuses based on these inflated numbers, and Nortel attempted to get its money back. It was able to recoup about $9 million from executives that were still with the company but many were no longer employed at Nortel. In April of 2004, the board of directors fired Mr. Dunn and nine other senior executives, including the CFO and the controller, leaving the company without several key executives—most importantly, without a CEO. Something had to be done to get Nortel back on track and restore investor confidence in the company.

If you were on Nortel's board of directors, what would you do?

Nortel was facing a leadership crisis and while such crises normally don't occur in such dire circumstances, leadership-related issues create severe problems for all kinds of companies each year. Leadership, motivating employees, and working with teams are all key elements of management.

This chapter begins by reviewing the basics of motivation—effort, needs, and intrinsic and extrinsic motivation. We will start with a basic model of motivation and add to it as we progress through each section in the chapter. Next, we will explore how employees' equity perceptions and reward expectations affect their motivation. If you're familiar with the phrase "perception is reality," you're off to a good start in understanding the importance of perceptions and expectations in motivation. We then discuss what leadership is, who leaders are (meaning their traits and characteristics), and what leaders do that makes them different from people who aren't leaders. Next we examine two major contingency theories of leadership that specify which leaders are best suited for which situations or how leaders should change their behaviour to lead different people in different circumstances. The chapter ends by reviewing strategic leadership issues, such as charismatic and transformational leadership, that are concerned with working with others to meet long-term goals and creating a viable future for an organization.

What Is Motivation?

motivation
the set of forces that initiates, directs, and makes people persist in their efforts to accomplish a goal

Motivation is the set of forces that initiates, directs, and makes people persist in their efforts to accomplish a goal.[2] Based on this definition, *initiation of effort* is concerned with the choices that people make about how much effort to put forth in their jobs. ("Gosh, I hate writing performance appraisals, so maybe I'll just add a paragraph to last year's appraisals" rather than "Performance feedback is important. I'm going to schedule an hour to review each file and an hour to write each appraisal.") *Direction of effort* is concerned with the choices that people make in deciding where to put forth effort in their jobs. ("I'm really excited about the new computer system and can't wait to get started" rather than "Yeah, yeah, another new computer system. I'll do what I need to get by with it, but I think my time is better spent working directly with employees and customers.") *Persistence of effort* is concerned with the choices that people make about how long they will put forth effort in their jobs before reducing or eliminating those efforts. ("We're only halfway to our goal with three months to get it done. We'll never make it, so I'm not going to work at this anymore" rather than "We're only halfway to our goal with three months to go, but if we all keep working hard, we can do it.") As shown in Exhibit 15.1, initiation, direction, and persistence are at the heart of motivation.

EXHIBIT 15.1
The Components of Motivation

After reading the next section, you should be able to

1 explain the basics of motivation.

1 BASICS OF MOTIVATION

Take your right hand and point the palm toward your face. Keep your thumb and pinky finger straight and bend the three middle fingers so the tips are touching your palm. Now rotate your wrist back and forth. If you were in the Regent Square Tavern, that hand signal would tell waitress Marjorie Landale that you wanted a Yeungling beer. However, Marjorie, who isn't deaf, would not have understood that sign a few years ago. But with a school for the deaf nearby, the tavern always had its share of deaf customers, so she decided on her own to take classes to learn how to sign. She said, "It occurred to me that I could learn their language more easily than they could learn mine." At first, deaf customers would signal for a pen and paper to write out their orders. But after Marjorie signalled that she was learning to sign, she said, "Their eyes [would] light up, and they [would] finger-spell their order and [then] we've made a connection." The tavern's regular deaf customers teased her in a friendly way about her poor signing skills, but word quickly spread as the students started bringing in their friends, classmates, teachers, and hearing friends as well. Said Marjorie, "The deaf customers are patient with my amateur signing. They appreciate the effort."[3]

What would motivate an employee like Marjorie to voluntarily learn a new language like sign language? (Sign language is every bit as much a language as French or Spanish.) She wasn't paid to take classes in her free time. She chose to do it on her own. And while she undoubtedly makes more tip money with a full bar than with an empty one, it's highly unlikely that she began her classes with the objective of making more money. Just what is it that motivates employees like Marjorie Landale?

Let's learn more about motivation by building a basic model of motivation out of these parts: effort and performance, need satisfaction, extrinsic and intrinsic rewards, and motivation with the basics.

Effort and Performance

When most people think of work motivation, they think that working hard (effort) should lead to doing a good job (performance). Exhibit 15.2 shows a basic model of work motivation and performance, displaying this process.

The first thing to notice about Exhibit 15.2 is that this is a basic model of work motivation and performance. In practice, it's almost impossible to talk about one without mentioning the other. Not surprisingly, managers often confuse the two, saying things such as "Your performance was really terrible last quarter. What's the matter? Aren't you

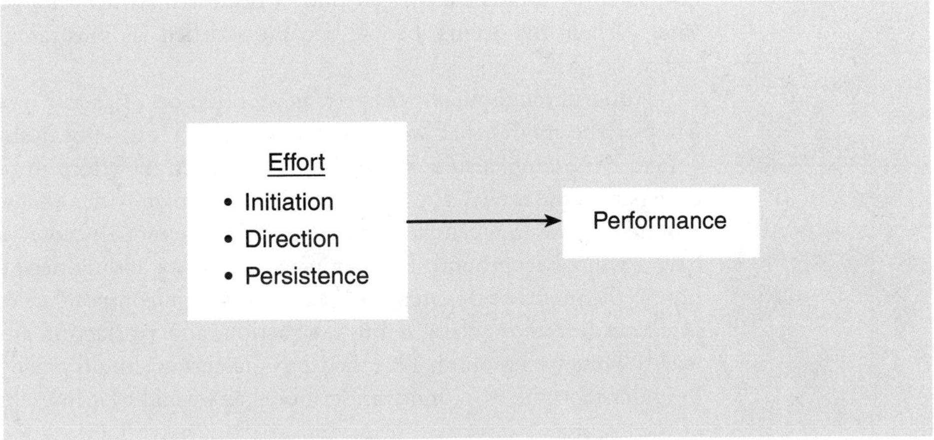

EXHIBIT 15.2
A Basic Model of Work Motivation and Performance

as motivated as you used to be?" In fact, motivation is just one of three primary determinants of job performance. In industrial psychology, job performance is frequently represented by this equation:

$$\text{Job Performance} = \text{Motivation} \times \text{Ability} \times \text{Situational Constraints}$$

In this formula, *job performance* is how well someone performs the requirements of the job. Motivation, as defined above, is effort, the degree to which someone works hard to do the job well. *Ability* is the degree to which workers possess the knowledge, skills, and talent needed to do a job well. And *situational constraints* are factors beyond the control of individual employees, such as tools, policies, and resources that have an effect on job performance. Since job performance is a multiplicative function of motivation times ability times situational constraints, job performance will suffer if any one of these components is weak.

Does this mean that motivation doesn't matter? No, not at all. It just means that all the motivation in the world won't translate into high performance when you have little ability and high situational constraints.

needs
the physical or psychological requirements that must be met to ensure survival and well-being

Need Satisfaction

In Exhibit 15.2, we started with a very basic model of motivation in which effort leads to job performance. However, managers want to know, "What leads to effort?" And they will try almost anything they can to find the answer to this question. For example, a Vancouver-based mining company, BHP Billiton Diamonds, has a long list of unusual workplace benefits that include foosball, billiards, squash courts, and even an indoor driving range and putting green.[5] Employees at Intuit Canada, in Edmonton, can use one of the napping rooms or enjoy the company's big-screen TV or go to the company's gym and get instruction from a personal trainer. Maritime Life, based in Halifax, provides an on-site masseuse and daycare facilities. At Motorola, employees receive $5000 after they have reached 10 years of service.[6] So which of these techniques will motivate employees and lead to increased effort? The answer is all of them and none of them: It depends on employees' needs.

Needs are the physical or psychological requirements that must be met to ensure survival and well-being.[7] As shown on the left side of Exhibit 15.3, a person's unmet need creates an uncomfortable, internal state of tension that must be resolved. For example, if you normally skip breakfast, but then get stuck working through lunch, chances are you'll be so hungry by late afternoon that the only thing you'll be motivated to do is find something to eat. So, according to needs theories, people are motivated by unmet needs. But once a need is met, it no longer motivates. When this occurs, people become satisfied, as illustrated on the right side of Exhibit 15.3.

Note: Throughout the chapter, as we build on this basic model, the parts of the model that we've already discussed will appear shaded in colour. For example, since we've already discussed the effort → performance part of the model, those components are shown with a shaded background. However, when we add new parts to the model, those parts will have a white background. For instance, since we're adding need satisfaction to the model at this step, the need-satisfaction components of unsatisfied need, tension, energized to take action, and satisfaction are shown with a white background. This shading convention should make it easier to understand the work motivation model as we add to it in each section of the chapter.

DOING THE RIGHT THING

FAKING IT, NOT MAKING IT

With technology these days, you may be tempted to engage in "impression management" to try to convince your boss and co-workers that you're working hard when you're really not. For instance, a tech support worker who enjoyed three-hour lunches used a program on his Palm personal computer to remotely control his office computer. He would open, close, and move files to make it look like he had just stepped away from his desk. Other employees write e-mails before they go home and then "send" them after midnight (we won't tell you how this is done) to make it look as though they are still at work. Another trick is to leave early, but then send e-mails on the way home via your BlackBerry device to make it look as if you are still at the office. You may be thinking that these ruses are harmless, but 59 percent of human resource managers and 53 percent of supervisors have caught employees lying about the hours they work. Furthermore, if you're using technology to fake it, you're usually leaving high-tech "tracks" and "footprints" along the way. That tech worker who controlled his office computer with his Palm PC at lunch was fired for "habitual lateness." Motivation is all about effort. So, do the right thing. Work hard for your company, your customers, and yourself.[4]

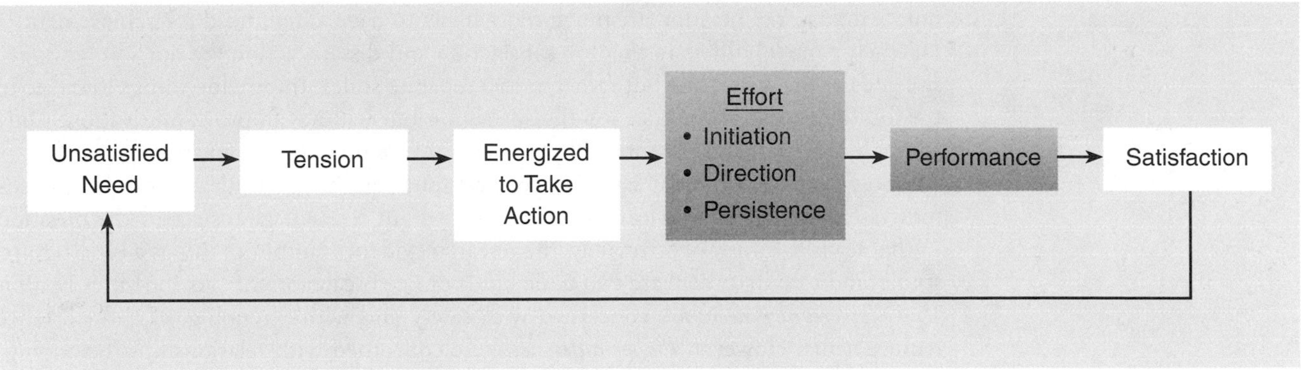

EXHIBIT 15.3
Adding Need Satisfaction to the Model

Since people are motivated by unmet needs, managers must learn what those unmet needs are and address them. However, this is not always a straightforward task, since different needs theories suggest different needs categories. Exhibit 15.4 shows needs from four well-known needs theories. Maslow's Hierarchy of Needs suggests that people are motivated by *physiological* (food and water), *safety* (physical and economic), *belongingness* (friendship, love, social interaction), *esteem* (achievement and recognition), and *self-actualization* (realizing your full potential) needs.[8] Alderfer's ERG theory collapses Maslow's five needs into three: *existence* (safety and physiological needs), *relatedness* (belongingness), and *growth* (esteem and self-actualization).[9] McClelland's Learned Needs Theory suggests that people are motivated by the need for *affiliation* (to be liked and accepted), the need for *achievement* (to accomplish challenging goals), or the need for *power* (to influence others).[10] Herzberg's Motivator-Hygiene theory has two basic components. Motivators are gained from doing a job well and receiving rewards such as recognition, advancement, and personal growth. Hygiene factors are associated with the nature of the job and workplace and include job security, working conditions, and supervisory policies.[11]

Things become even more complicated when we consider the different predictions made by these theories. According to Maslow, needs are arranged in a hierarchy from low (physiological) to high (self-actualization). Within this hierarchy, people are motivated by their lowest unsatisfied need. And, as needs are met, they work their way up the hierarchy from physiological to self-actualization needs. By contrast, Alderfer says that people can be motivated by more than one need at a time. Furthermore, he suggests that people are just as likely to move down the needs hierarchy as up, particularly when unable to achieve satisfaction at the next-higher need level. McClelland, on the other hand, argues that the degree to which particular needs motivate varies tremendously from person to person, with some people being motivated primarily by achievement, and others by power or affiliation. Moreover, McClelland says that needs are learned, not innate. For instance, studies show that children whose fathers own a small business or

	MASLOW'S HIERARCHY	ALDERFER'S ERG	MCCLELLAND'S LEARNED NEEDS	HERZBERG'S MOTIVATOR-HYGIENE THEORY
Higher-Order Needs	Self-Actualization Esteem Belongingness	Growth Relatedness	Power Achievement Affiliation	Motivators
Lower-Order Needs	Safety Physiological	Existence		Hygiene

EXHIBIT 15.4
Needs Classification of Different Theories

hold a managerial position are much more likely to have a high need for achievement.[12] Herzberg's model differs in that job satisfaction and dissatisfaction are not seen as opposite ends of the same scale but rather as two separate scales. Improving things extrinsic to the job (hygienes) will reduce job dissatisfaction but will not improve motivation. Only through improving motivators will you increase an employee's motivation.

So with three different sets of needs and four very different ideas about how needs motivate, where does this leave managers who want a practical answer to the question "What leads to effort?" Fortunately, the research evidence simplifies things a bit. To start, studies indicate that there are two basic kinds of needs categories.[13] As shown in Exhibit 15.4, *lower-order needs* are concerned with safety and with physiological and existence requirements. However, *higher-order needs* are concerned with relationships (belongingness, recognition, relatedness, and affiliation); challenges and accomplishments (esteem, self-actualization, growth, and achievement); and influence (power). Studies generally show that higher-order needs will not motivate people as long as lower-order needs remain unsatisfied.

So, what leads to effort? In part, needs do. Later we'll discuss how managers can use what we know from need-satisfaction theories to motivate workers.

Extrinsic and Intrinsic Rewards

No discussion of motivation would be complete without considering rewards. Let's add two kinds of rewards, extrinsic and intrinsic, to the model, as shown in Exhibit 15.5.[14]

extrinsic reward
a reward that is tangible, visible to others, and given to employees contingent on the performance of specific tasks or behaviours

Extrinsic rewards are tangible and visible to others and are given to employees contingent on the performance of specific tasks or behaviours.[15] External agents (managers, for example) determine and control the distribution, frequency, and amount of extrinsic rewards, such as pay, company stock, benefits, and promotions. At Research in Motion, stock options are a key extrinsic reward that attracts and keeps people at the company. New employees are awarded options to buy shares at a fixed price. So if the stock was selling for $1, but is now worth $10, employees who exercise their stock options can earn $9 per share. One 20-something employee was very excited when Research in Motion's shares spiked at over $225. She was worth almost $1 million on paper. Of course, what can go up can come down, as the shares fell to about a tenth of what they used to be, although they have since rebounded.[16]

intrinsic reward
a natural reward associated with performing a task or activity for its own sake

Why do companies need extrinsic rewards? To get people to do things they wouldn't otherwise do. Companies use rewards to motivate people to perform three basic behaviours: joining the organization, regularly attending their jobs, and performing their jobs well.[17]

By contrast, **intrinsic rewards** are the natural rewards associated with performing a task or activity for its own sake. For example, aside from the external rewards management offers for doing something well, employees often experience a sense of interest and

EXHIBIT 15.5
Adding Rewards to the Model

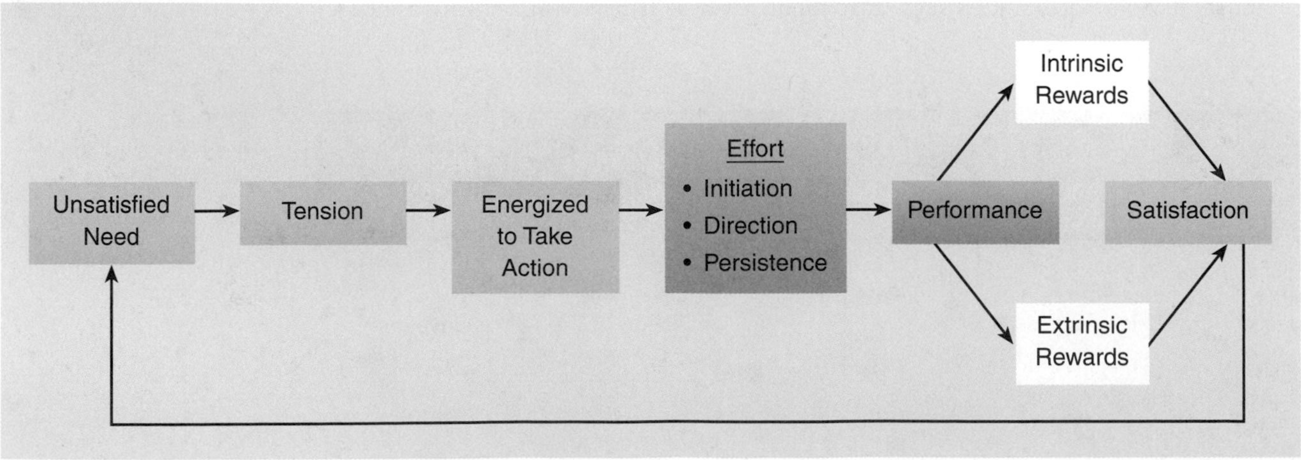

© ROYALTY-FREE/CORBIS

Extrinsic rewards can help motivate employees and can take many forms.

enjoyment from the activities or tasks they perform. Examples of intrinsic rewards include a sense of accomplishment or achievement, a feeling of responsibility, the chance to learn something new or interact with others, or simply the fun that comes from performing an interesting, challenging, and engaging task. For instance, researcher Mark Rise works for Medtronic, a leading medical technology company. Rise, one of Medtronic's most creative inventors, could have a more prestigious job at a university or make more money starting his own company. However, Rise doesn't want to test theory or develop marketing plans or raise venture capital. What matters most to him is developing products that make a difference in people's lives. Says Rise, "That's what keeps me tied to what I'm doing now." Indeed, Rise thrives on the intrinsic aspects of his work such as being able to work with physicians, medical researchers, software developers, and engineers to identify new treatments and design and manufacture new products.[18]

Which types of rewards are most important to workers in general? A number of surveys suggest that both extrinsic and intrinsic rewards are important. One survey found that the most important rewards were good benefits and health insurance, job security, having a week or more of vacation (all extrinsic rewards) and interesting work, the opportunity to learn new skills, and being able to work independently (all intrinsic rewards). And employee preferences for intrinsic and extrinsic rewards appear to be relatively stable. Studies conducted over the last three decades have consistently found that employees are twice as likely to indicate that "important and meaningful work" matters more to them than what they are paid.[19] Remember from Chapter 11 the thought of working at a McDonald's drive-though window for years on end? Clearly, the nature of a job can have significant impact on a person's motivation.

Motivating with the Basics

So, given the basic model of work motivation in Exhibit 15.5, what practical things can managers do to motivate employees to increase their effort?

Start by asking people what their needs are. If managers don't know what workers' needs are, they won't be able to provide them the opportunities and rewards that can satisfy those needs. Linda Connor, vice president of corporate culture at Technology Professionals Corp (TPC), keeps careful notes about TPC employees' needs. She says, "I sit down at employees' 30-day reviews and ask specific questions about hobbies and interests for each member of their families."[20] For instance, her notes about top performer Phil Mayrose indicated that he loves football, oldies music, and, more than anything else, golf. Armed with this information, Connor and TPC rewarded Mayrose with a weekend vacation at a dude ranch with a great golf course. Sometimes meeting employees' needs also means helping them deal with stress. Here again, Connor's notes helped TPC take care of an employee. Connor's notes read, "During stressful periods [she] loses confidence in her ability as a mom, housekeeper, sister, daughter, friend, and aunt. Ideas during high-stress times: lawn-mowing service, housekeeping, hot meals, day away with her son."[21] So, if you want to meet employees' needs, do what Linda Connor does and just ask.

Next, satisfy lower-order needs first. Since higher-order needs will not motivate people as long as lower-order needs remain unsatisfied, companies should satisfy lower-order needs first. In practice, this means providing the equipment, training, and knowledge to create a safe workplace free of physical risks, paying employees well enough to provide financial security, and offering a benefits package that will protect employees and their families through good health and disability insurance. In a Canadian survey, 73 percent of employees said they would not likely work for a company that did not have benefits.[22] A survey based on a representative sample of Americans found that when people choose jobs or organizations, three of the four most important factors—starting pay/salary (62 percent), employee benefits (57 percent), and job security (47 percent)—are lower-order needs.[23]

Expect people's needs to change. As other needs are satisfied, or situations change, managers should expect that employees' needs will change. In other words, what motivated people before may not motivate them again.

Finally, as needs change and lower-order needs are satisfied, satisfy higher-order needs by looking for ways to allow employees to experience intrinsic rewards. Recall that intrinsic rewards, such as accomplishment, achievement, learning something new, and interacting with others, are the natural rewards associated with performing a task or activity for its own sake. And with the exception of influence (power), intrinsic rewards correspond very closely to higher-order needs that are concerned with relationships (belongingness, relatedness, and affiliation) and challenges and accomplishments (esteem, self-actualization, growth, and achievement). Therefore, one way for managers to meet employees' higher-order needs is to create opportunities for employees to experience intrinsic rewards by providing challenging work, encouraging employees to take greater responsibility for their work, and giving employees the freedom to pursue tasks and projects they find naturally interesting. For example, we began this section by asking, "What would motivate an employee like Marjorie Landale to voluntarily learn sign language?" Marjorie wasn't paid to do this. In fact, she even spent her own money and free time to learn how to sign. The reason that Marjorie learned how to sign is that doing so met her higher-order needs. It gave her a sense of accomplishment, and it allowed her to interact with deaf customers with whom she had been previously unable to interact. And Marjorie learned how to sign because her boss was smart enough to realize that there was no downside to giving her the freedom to pursue a task or project that she found naturally interesting.

REVIEW 1: BASICS OF MOTIVATION

Motivation is the set of forces that initiates, directs, and makes people persist in their efforts over time to accomplish a goal. Managers often confuse motivation and performance. However, since job performance is a multiplicative function of motivation times ability times situational constraints, job performance will suffer if any one of these components is weak. Needs are the physical or psychological requirements that must be met to ensure survival and well-being. When needs are not met, people experience an internal state of tension. But once a particular need is met, it no longer motivates. When this occurs, people become satisfied and are then motivated by other unmet needs. Different motivational theories, such as Maslow's Hierarchy of Needs (physiological, safety, belongingness, esteem, and self-actualization); Alderfer's ERG Theory (existence, relatedness, and growth); McClelland's Learned Needs Theory (affiliation, achievement, and power); and Herzberg's Motivator-Hygiene theory, specify a number of different needs. However, studies generally show that there are only two general kinds of needs, lower-order needs and higher-order needs, and that higher-order needs will not motivate people as long as lower-order needs remain unsatisfied. Both extrinsic and intrinsic rewards motivate people. Extrinsic rewards, which include pay, company stock, benefits, and promotions, are used to motivate people to join organizations and attend and perform their jobs. The basic model of motivation suggests that managers can motivate employees by asking them what their needs are, satisfying lower-order needs first, expecting people's needs to change, and satisfying higher-order needs through intrinsic rewards.

How Perceptions and Expectations Affect Motivation

Europe's new currency, the euro, replaced the currencies of 12 countries (Austria, Belgium, Finland, France, Germany, Greece, Ireland, Italy, Luxembourg, Netherlands, Portugal, and Spain). Consumers can now easily compare the prices of goods from one country to those of another without having to make cumbersome currency translations. ("Let's see, 100 deutsche marks are worth 335 French francs, and 100 Spanish pesetas are worth 1164 Italian lira, so that means it's cheaper if I buy it in....") But consumers won't be the only ones making cross-border euro comparisons. Companies and employees will, too, as they compare salaries and benefits from one country to those of another. For example, salaries tend to be much higher in northern than in southern Europe. In Germany, a sales and marketing director in a medium-sized company would be paid about 160 000 euros ($225 000) a year. But in Spain, the same job pays about 100 000 euros ($140 000). Yet even after taxes, which are higher in Germany, the German sales and marketing director takes home 80 000 euros a year ($112 000), while the Spanish sales and marketing director takes home 55 000 euros ($77 000). The difference is a whopping 45 percent.[24]

Companies are expecting to have to make significant wage adjustments now that much of Europe's work force is being paid in euros. William Scott, who heads the Paris office of Hewitt Associates, a human resources consulting company, said, "We're doing many more cross-border [pay] comparisons. The need to compete and pay on a European-wide basis is quite significant. There will be a pay extravaganza for some folks." And if companies don't make salary adjustments, they can expect some employees to leave for higher pay in other companies or countries, especially multilingual employees who possess technical skills. Although it is expected that it will take many years for salaries to converge, a recent study by Hay Group, a consulting firm specializing in executive pay, has found that salaries for senior executives have already converged significantly.[25]

After reading the next two sections, you should be able to

2 use equity theory to explain how employees' perceptions of fairness affect motivation.

3 use expectancy theory to describe how workers' expectations about rewards, effort, and the link between rewards and performance influence motivation.

2 EQUITY THEORY

Equity theory says that people will be motivated when they perceive that they are being treated fairly. In particular, equity theory stresses the importance of perceptions. So, regardless of the actual level of rewards people receive, they must also perceive that, relative to others, they are being treated fairly. For instance, by any objective measure it's hard to make the argument that the best professional athletes, who make upwards of $25

equity theory
theory states that people will be motivated when they perceive that they are being treated fairly

million a year (and no doubt more by the time you read this), are treated unfairly, given that this is about 500 times what the average Canadian with a full-time job earns. But, as is explained below, equity theory doesn't focus on objective equity. Instead, equity, like beauty, is in the eye of the beholder. So, according to equity theory, if people truly perceive that they are being treated unfairly, then inequity exists, regardless of the "objective equity." Witness the inclusion of escalator clauses in top athletes' contracts that specify that if another player at the same position receives a larger contract, then their contract will automatically be revised to that higher amount. So, despite their already enormous paycheques, top athletes still want to be paid as much as or more than other top athletes.

Let's learn more about equity theory by examining the components of equity theory, people's reaction to perceived inequity, and motivating with equity theory.

Components of Equity Theory

inputs
in equity theory, the contributions employees make to the organization

outcomes
in equity theory, the rewards employees receive for their contributions to the organization

referents
in equity theory, others with whom people compare themselves to determine if they have been treated fairly

outcome/input (O/I) ratio
in equity theory, an employee's perception of the comparison between the rewards received from an organization and the employee's contributions to that organization

underreward
when the referent you compare yourself to is getting more outcomes relative to inputs than you are

overreward
when you are getting more outcomes relative to your inputs than the referent to whom you compare yourself

The basic components of equity theory are inputs, outcomes, and referents. **Inputs** are the contributions employees make to the organization. Inputs include education and training, intelligence, experience, effort, number of hours worked, and ability. **Outcomes** are the rewards employees receive in exchange for their contributions to the organization. Outcomes include pay, fringe benefits, status symbols, job titles and assignments, and even the leadership style of their superiors. And since perceptions of equity depend on how you are being treated compared to others, **referents** are others with whom people compare themselves to determine if they have been treated fairly. Usually, people choose to compare themselves to referents who hold the same or similar jobs, or are otherwise similar to themselves in some way, such as in gender, race, age, or tenure.[26]

According to the equity theory process shown in Exhibit 15.6, employees compare inputs, their contributions to the organization, to outcomes, the rewards they received from the organization in exchange for those inputs. This comparison of outcomes to inputs is called the **outcome/input (O/I) ratio**. After an internal comparison in which they compare their outcomes to their inputs, employees then make an external comparison in which they compare their O/I ratio with the O/I ratio of a referent.[27] When people perceive that their O/I ratio is equal to the referent's O/I ratio, they conclude that they are being treated fairly. But when people perceive that their O/I ratio is different from their referent's O/I ratio, they conclude that they have been treated inequitably or unfairly.

There are two kinds of inequity—underreward and overreward. **Underreward** occurs when a referent's O/I ratio is better than your O/I ratio. In other words, the referent you compare yourself to is getting more outcomes relative to his or her inputs than you are. When people perceive that they have been underrewarded, they tend to experience anger or frustration. For example, when a manufacturing company received notice that some important contracts had been cancelled, management cut employees' pay by 15 percent in one plant but not in another. Just as equity theory predicts, theft doubled in the plant that received the pay cut. This was not surprising, as the Retail Council of Canada found that companies that paid 20 percent more than their competition had substantially lower employee theft rates.[28] Also, at the manufacturing plant that cut pay employee turnover increased from 5 percent to 23 percent.[29]

By contrast, **overreward** occurs when a referent's O/I ratio is worse than your O/I ratio. In this case, you are getting more outcomes relative to your inputs than your referent is. In theory, when people perceive that they have been overrewarded, they experience guilt. Not surprisingly, people have a very high tolerance for overreward. It takes a tremendous amount of overpayment before people decide that their pay or benefits are more than they deserve.

EXHIBIT 15.6
Outcome/Input Ratios

$$\frac{\text{OUTCOMES}_{\text{SELF}}}{\text{INPUTS}_{\text{SELF}}} = \frac{\text{OUTCOMES}_{\text{REFERENT}}}{\text{INPUTS}_{\text{REFERENT}}}$$

How People React to Perceived Inequity

What happens when people perceive that they have been treated inequitably? Exhibit 15.7 shows that perceived inequity affects satisfaction. In the case of underreward, this usually translates into frustration or anger, while with overreward the reaction is guilt. In turn, these reactions lead to tension and a strong need to take action to restore equity in some way. At first, a slight inequity may not be strong enough to motivate an employee to take immediate action. However, if the inequity continues or there are many inequities, tension may build over time until a point of intolerance is reached, and the person is energized to take action.[30]

There are five ways in which people try to restore equity when they perceive that they have been treated unfairly: reducing inputs, increasing outcomes, rationalizing inputs or outcomes, changing the referent, or simply leaving. These will be discussed in relation to the inequity associated with underreward, which is much more common than the inequity associated with overreward.

People who perceive that they have been underrewarded may try to restore equity by decreasing or withholding their inputs (i.e., effort). Increasing outcomes is another way in which people try to restore equity. This might include asking for a raise or pointing out the inequity to the boss and hoping that he or she takes care of it. Sometimes, however, employees may go to external organizations, such as labour unions or provincial labour boards, to get some help in increasing outcomes to restore equity. Joining a union is another way to increase outcomes. Service industries are noted for not paying high wages. As a result, workers in the restaurant industry are increasingly turning to unions. In March 1999, the McDonald's restaurant in Squamish, British Columbia, became the first in North America to be unionized.[31] The Canadian Auto Workers have been successful in unionizing a number of fast-food restaurants across

EXHIBIT 15.7
Adding Equity Theory to the Model

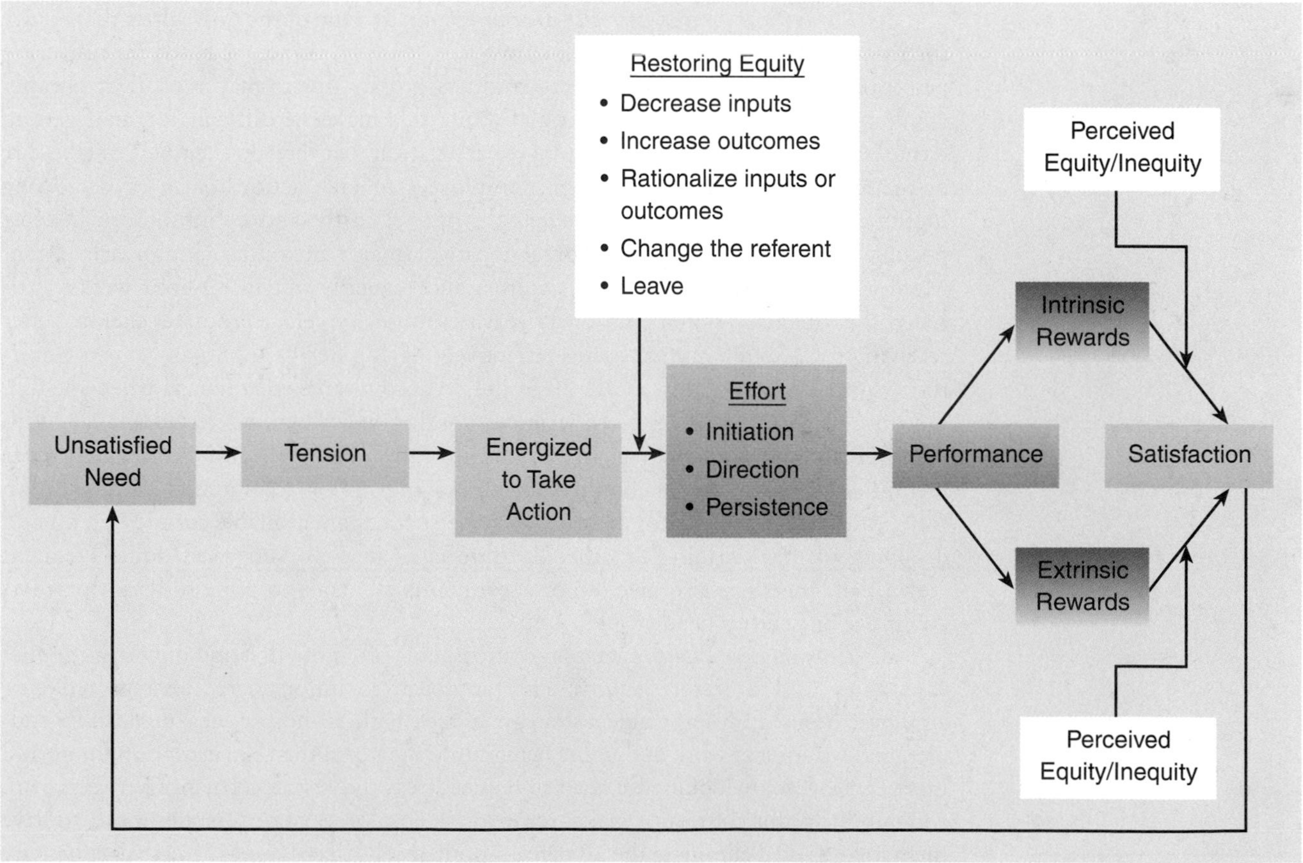

British Columbia, including 50 KFC outlets.[32] Low pay is often a key issue in these unionizing drives.

Another method of restoring equity is to rationalize or distort inputs or outcomes. So instead of actually decreasing inputs or increasing outcomes, employees restore equity by making mental or emotional "adjustments" in their O/I ratios or the O/I ratios of their referents. For example, say a company downsizes 10 percent of its work force. It's likely that the survivors, the people who still have jobs, will be angry or frustrated with company management because of the layoffs. However, if alternative jobs are difficult to find, the employees who are still with the company may rationalize or distort their O/I ratios and conclude, "Well, things could be worse. At least I still have my job." Rationalizing or distorting outcomes may be used when other ways to restore equity aren't available.

Changing the referent is another way of restoring equity. In this case, people compare themselves to someone other than the referent they had been using for previous O/I ratio comparisons. Since people usually choose to compare themselves to others who hold the same or similar jobs or are otherwise similar, they may change referents to restore equity when their personal situations change, such as a decrease in job status or pay.

Finally, when reducing inputs, increasing outcomes, rationalizing inputs or outcomes, or changing referents doesn't restore equity, employees may leave by quitting their jobs, transferring, or increasing absenteeism.[33] For example, Disney Corporation's Internet divisions have had a very difficult time keeping their top talent. Disney is well managed and pays very well but, because it's an established company, it hasn't been able to offer the stock options that Internet start-up companies are able to offer their employees. Both former Disney Online President Richard Wolpert and Winney Wechsler, head of Disney.com, left to take jobs with start-up companies.[34]

Motivating with Equity Theory

What practical things can managers do to use equity theory to motivate employees?

Start by looking for and correcting major inequities. One of the difficulties that equity theory makes us aware of is that an employee's sense of fairness is based on subjective perceptions. So what one employee considers grossly unfair may not affect another employee's perceptions of equity at all. While this makes it difficult for managers to create conditions that satisfy all employees, it's critical that they do their best to take care of major inequities that can energize employees to take actions, such as decreasing inputs or leaving, that can be extremely disruptive, costly, and harmful. So, whenever possible, managers should look for and correct major inequities. Junior accountant Monica DiCenso supervised three auditors and regularly put in 80-hour weeks certifying the financial statements of PriceWaterhouseCoopers' corporate clients. After receiving a US$2000 annual bonus (effectively paying her US$2.86 an hour for overtime work), DiCenso quit, as did 20 of the 35 accountants who started when she did. DiCenso said, "I could have made more working at a fast-food restaurant."[35] With turnover up significantly, major accounting firms have begun addressing those inequities by paying bigger bonuses and by giving junior accountants more vacation time. And, to help with long hours, concierge services are available for picking up and dropping off dry cleaning or other daytime tasks that workers need done. Frequent "town hall" meetings also give junior accountants a chance to gripe to senior partners about the difficulties in their jobs.

Reduce employees' inputs. Increasing outcomes is often the first and only strategy that companies use to restore equity. This approach is unfortunate, because reducing employee inputs is just as viable a strategy. In fact, with 50-hour weeks, dual-career couples, and working at work and home being more the norm than the exception, more and more employees are looking for ways to reduce stress and restore a balance between work and family. In this context, it makes sense to ask employees to do less, not more, to have them identify and eliminate the 20 percent of their jobs that doesn't increase productivity or add value for customers, and to have managers eliminate company-imposed requirements that really aren't critical to managers', employees', or companies' performance (e.g., unnecessary meetings, reports, etc.). To help address these issues, Markham, Ontario–based Pfizer Consumer Healthcare Canada instituted its "Freedom 6 to 6" policy, which bans work phone calls and e-mails from 6 P.M.. to 6 A.M., without any negative effect on its financial performance. The company also has meeting-free days and has provided employees with massage chairs and a gym. It's all part of an overall strategy to provide employees with a greater work–life balance.[36]

Make sure decision-making processes are fair. Equity theory focuses on **distributive justice**, the degree to which outcomes and rewards are fairly distributed or allocated. However, **procedural justice**, the fairness of the process used to make reward allocation decisions, is just as important.[37] Procedural justice matters because even when employees are unhappy with their outcomes (i.e., low pay), they're much less likely to be unhappy with company management if they believe that the procedures used to allocate outcomes were fair. For example, employees who are laid off tend to be hostile toward their employer when they perceive that the procedures leading to the layoffs were unfair. By contrast, employees who perceive layoff procedures to be fair tend to continue to support and trust their employers.[38] Also, if employees perceive that their outcomes are unfair (i.e., distributive injustice), but that the decisions and procedures leading to those outcomes were fair (i.e., procedural justice), they are much more likely to seek constructive ways of restoring equity, such as discussing these matters with their managers. In contrast, if employees perceive both distributive and procedural injustice, they may resort to more destructive tactics, such as withholding effort, absenteeism, tardiness, or even sabotage and theft.[39]

distributive justice
the perceived degree to which outcomes and rewards are fairly distributed or allocated

procedural justice
the perceived fairness of the process used to make reward allocation decisions

REVIEW 2: EQUITY THEORY

The basic components of equity theory are inputs, outcomes, and referents. After an internal comparison in which employees compare their outcomes to their inputs, they then make an external comparison in which they compare their O/I ratio with the O/I ratio of a referent, a person who works in a similar job or is otherwise similar. When their O/I ratio is equal to the referent's O/I ratio, employees perceive that they are being treated fairly. But when their O/I ratio is different from their referent's O/I ratio, they perceive that they have been treated inequitably or unfairly. There are two kinds of inequity, underreward and overreward. Underreward occurs when a referent's O/I ratio is better than the employee's O/I ratio. Underreward leads to anger or frustration. Overreward occurs when a referent's O/I ratio is worse than the employee's O/I ratio. Overreward can lead to guilt, but only when the level of overreward is extreme. When employees perceive that they have been treated inequitably (i.e., underreward), they may try to restore equity by reducing inputs, increasing outcomes, rationalizing inputs or outcomes, changing the referent, or simply leaving. Managers can use equity theory to motivate workers by looking for and correcting major inequities, reducing employees' inputs, and emphasizing procedural as well as distributive justice.

3 EXPECTANCY THEORY

How attractive would you find the following rewards? A company concierge service that sends someone to be at your house when the cable guy or repair person shows up, or picks up your car from the mechanic? A "7 to 7" travel policy that stipulates that no one has to leave home for business travel before 7 A.M. on Mondays and that everyone should return home from their business travels by 7 P.M. on Fridays? The opportunity to telecommute so that you can feed your kids breakfast, pick them up after school, and then tuck them into bed at night? A "circle of excellence" award, in which employees nominate co-workers for outstanding work, and the winners get company-paid trips to Hawaii and the Bahamas? A full-sized basketball court with a real wooden floor? Or a sabbatical program that gives employees the chance to take a paid leave so they can work for local charities?[40]

If you had kids, you might love the chance to telecommute; but if you didn't, you might not be interested. If you didn't travel much on business, you wouldn't be interested in the "7 to 7" travel policy; but if you did, you'd probably love it. One of the hardest things about motivating people is that rewards that are attractive to some employees are unattractive to others. **Expectancy theory** says that people will be motivated to the extent to which they believe that their efforts will lead to good performance, that good performance will be rewarded, and that they are offered attractive rewards.[41]

expectancy theory
theory that states that people will be motivated to the extent to which they believe that their efforts will lead to good performance, that good performance will be rewarded, and that they will be offered attractive rewards

Let's learn more about expectancy theory by examining the components of expectancy theory and motivation with expectancy theory.

Components of Expectancy Theory

Expectancy theory holds that people make conscious choices about their motivation. The three factors that affect those choices are valence, expectancy, and instrumentality.

Valence is simply the attractiveness or desirability of various rewards or outcomes. Expectancy theory recognizes that the same reward or outcome—say, a promotion—will be highly attractive to some people, highly disliked by others, and for some may not make much difference one way or the other. Accordingly, when people are deciding how much effort to put forth, expectancy theory says that they will consider the valence of all possible rewards and outcomes that they can receive from their jobs. The greater the sum of those valences, each of which could be positive, negative, or neutral, the more effort people will choose to put forth on the job.

valence
the attractiveness or desirability of a reward or outcome

Expectancy is the perceived relationship between effort and performance. When expectancies are strong, employees believe that their hard work and efforts will result in good performance, so they work harder. By contrast, when expectancies are weak, employees figure that no matter what they do or how hard they work, they won't be able to perform their jobs successfully, so they don't work as hard.

expectancy
the perceived relationship between effort and performance

Instrumentality is the perceived relationship between performance and rewards. When instrumentality is strong, employees believe that improved performance will lead to better and more rewards, and they will choose to work harder. When instrumentality is weak, employees don't believe that better performance will result in more or better rewards, so they will choose not to work as hard.

instrumentality
the perceived relationship between performance and rewards

Expectancy theory holds that for people to be highly motivated, all three variables—valence, expectancy, and instrumentality—must be high. Thus, expectancy theory can be represented by the following simple equation:

$$\text{Motivation} = \text{Valence} \times \text{Instrumentality} \times \text{Expectancy}$$

So if any one of these variables (valence, instrumentality, or expectancy) declines, overall motivation will decline, too.

Exhibit 15.8 incorporates the expectancy theory variables into our motivation model. Valence and instrumentality combine to affect employees' willingness to put forth effort (i.e., the degree to which they are energized to take action), while expectancy transforms intended effort ("I'm really going to work hard in this job") into actual effort. If you're offered rewards that you desire, and you believe that you will in fact receive these rewards for good performance, you're highly likely to be energized to take action. However, you're not likely to actually exert effort unless you also believe that you can do the job (i.e., that your efforts will lead to successful performance).

Motivating with Expectancy Theory

What practical things can managers do to use expectancy theory to motivate employees?

Systematically gather information to find out what employees want from their jobs. In addition to individual managers' directly asking employees what they want from their jobs (see "Motivating with Equity Theory" on page 450), companies still need to survey their employees regularly to determine their wants, needs, and dissatisfactions. Since

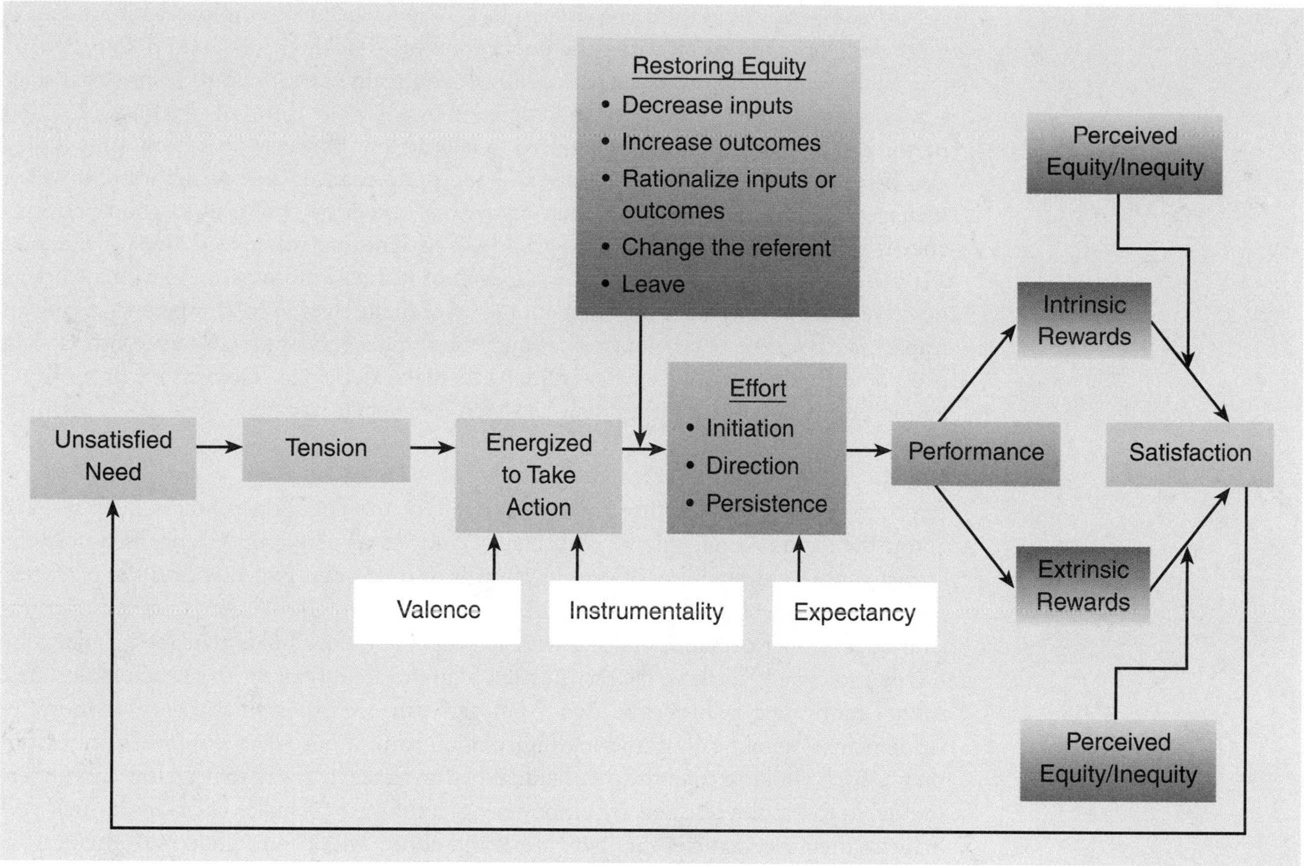

EXHIBIT 15.8
Adding Expectancy Theory to the Model

people consider the valence of all the possible rewards and outcomes that they can receive from their jobs, regular identification of wants, needs, and dissatisfaction gives companies the chance to turn negatively valent rewards and outcomes into positively valent rewards and outcomes, thus raising overall motivation and effort. Marc Albin, CEO of Albin Engineering, says, "My experience in managing people is, they're all different. Some people want to be recognized for their cheerful attitude and their ability to spread their cheerful attitude. Some want to be recognized for the quality of their work, some for the quantity of their work. Some like to be recognized individually; others want to be recognized in groups."[42] Therefore, at the end of each employee orientation session (during the first week on the job), he asks new employees to identify the rewards they want. The new employees appreciate his interest in what they want or need. Says Albin, "No one has ever said, 'Just recognize me for anything I do well.'"[43]

Second, managers can take clear steps to link rewards to individual performance in a way that is clear and understandable to employees. Unfortunately, most employees are extremely dissatisfied with the link between pay and performance in their organizations. One Canadian survey found that less than half of Canadian workers were happy with their compensation. Of even more concern is that the same study found that only 19 percent of employees surveyed were happy with pay-for-performance systems in their companies.[44] Other than making sure there is a connection between pay and performance in their companies (see Chapter 13 for a discussion of compensation strategies), another way for managers to establish a clearer link between pay and performance is to publicize the way in which pay decisions are made. For example, at Allstate Insurance, the company compensation team wrote a pamphlet called "Tracking the Clues to Your Pay," which explained how Allstate carefully used market value surveys and analyses to determine employee pay. Importantly, this helped counter the widespread belief that employee pay was determined in some random way. When asked "To what extent does the pay system competitively reward you for results?" 27 percent more employees responded "A great deal" or "Quite a bit" after the publication of "Tracking the Clues to Your Pay."[45]

Empower employees to make decisions if you really want them to believe that their hard work and effort will lead to good performance. If valent rewards are linked to good performance, people should be energized to take action. However, this works only if they also believe that their efforts will lead to good performance. One of the ways in which managers destroy the expectancy that hard work and effort will lead to good performance is by restricting what employees can do or by ignoring employees' ideas. In Chapter 11, you learned that empowerment is a feeling of intrinsic motivation, in which workers perceive their work to have meaning and perceive themselves to be competent, having an impact, and capable of self-determination.[46] So if managers want workers to have strong expectancies, they should empower them to make decisions. Doing so will motivate employees to take active rather than passive roles in their work.

REVIEW 3: EXPECTANCY THEORY

Expectancy theory holds that three factors affect the conscious choices people make about their motivation: valence, expectancy, and instrumentality. Valence is simply the attractiveness or desirability of various rewards or outcomes. Expectancy is the perceived relationship between effort and performance. Instrumentality is the perceived relationship between performance and rewards. Expectancy theory holds that for people to be highly motivated, all three factors must be high. So if any one of these factors declines, overall motivation will decline, too. Managers can use expectancy theory to motivate workers by systematically gathering information to find out what employees want from their jobs, by linking rewards to individual performance in a way that is clear and understandable to employees, and by empowering employees to make decisions, which will increase their expectancies that hard work and efforts will lead to good performance.

What Is Leadership?

When Cynthia Danaher became general manager of Hewlett-Packard's Medical Products Group, she told her 5300 employees, "I want to do this job, but it's scary and I need your help." And you finally have a boss who "knows how to make coffee." After three years of experience as a leader, she now regrets that choice of words. If she had a chance to hold that meeting again, she says that she would emphasize goals and challenge her people to find ways to meet them. She said, "People say they want a leader to be vulnerable just like them, but deep down they want to believe you have the skill to move and fix things they can't. And while anyone who starts something new is bound to feel some anxiety, you don't need to bare your soul." Moreover, she says that for leaders, setting a direction is more important than making employees feel comfortable.[47]

As H-P's Cynthia Danaher discovered, **leadership** is the process of influencing others to achieve group or organizational goals.

leadership
the process of influencing others to achieve group or organizational goals

After reading the next two sections, you should be able to

4 explain what leadership is.

5 describe who leaders are and what effective leaders do.

4 LEADERSHIP

Southwest Airlines, the airline that WestJet has modelled itself on, flies two to three times as many passengers per employee as other U.S. airlines at a cost 25 percent to 40 percent below its competitors.[48] A key part of Southwest's performance is that it empties its planes, refills them with passengers, crews, fuel, and food (snacks and soft drinks), and has them back on the runway in 20 minutes, compared to an hour for most airlines. This allows Southwest to keep each of its planes filled with paying passengers about three more hours a day. Why is Southwest able to achieve such incredible results? Herb Kelleher, Southwest's CEO and co-founder, answered the question this way: "We pay just as good wages and benefits as other airlines, but our costs are lower because our productivity is higher, which is achieved through the dedicated energy of our people. It's sheer willpower—no mechanical tricks. We've got exactly the same equipment. The difference is, when a plane pulls into a gate, our people run to meet it. Ponce de León was looking for the Fountain of Youth in the wrong place—he should have come to Southwest Airlines." In other words, the people of Southwest Airlines have been successfully influenced to achieve company goals (i.e., leadership).

Let's learn more about leadership by exploring leaders versus managers, and substitutes for leadership.

Leaders versus Managers

In Chapter 1, we defined *management* as getting work done through others. In other words, managers don't do the work themselves. Managers help others do their jobs better. By contrast, *leadership* is the process of influencing others to achieve group or organizational goals. So what are the key differences between leadership and management?

According to Professor Warren Bennis, the primary difference, as shown in Exhibit 15.9, is that leaders are concerned with doing the right thing, while managers are concerned with doing things right.[49] In other words, leaders will begin with the question "What should we be doing?" while managers start with "How can we do what already we're doing better?" Leaders focus on visions, missions, goals, and objectives, while managers focus solely on productivity and efficiency. Managers see themselves as preservers of the status quo, while leaders see themselves as promoters of change, as challengers of the status quo in that they encourage creativity and risk taking. According to Bill Black, president of Halifax-based Maritime Life Assurance, "At the senior levels it's more important to be a good leader than a good manager. My feeling is that the person who is a good leader is able to identify a long-term direction for the organization."[50] Carol Bartz, CEO of Autodesk, Inc., a software company, said managers "know how to write business plans, while leaders get companies—and people—to change." She went on to say that "human nature says cling to what you have, whether that's an old coat, a boyfriend, or a way of doing business," but that leaders have to "leave that behind."[51] Managers have a relatively short-term perspective, while leaders take a long-term view. Managers are more concerned with means, how to get things done, while leaders are more concerned with

EXHIBIT 15.9
Managers versus Leaders

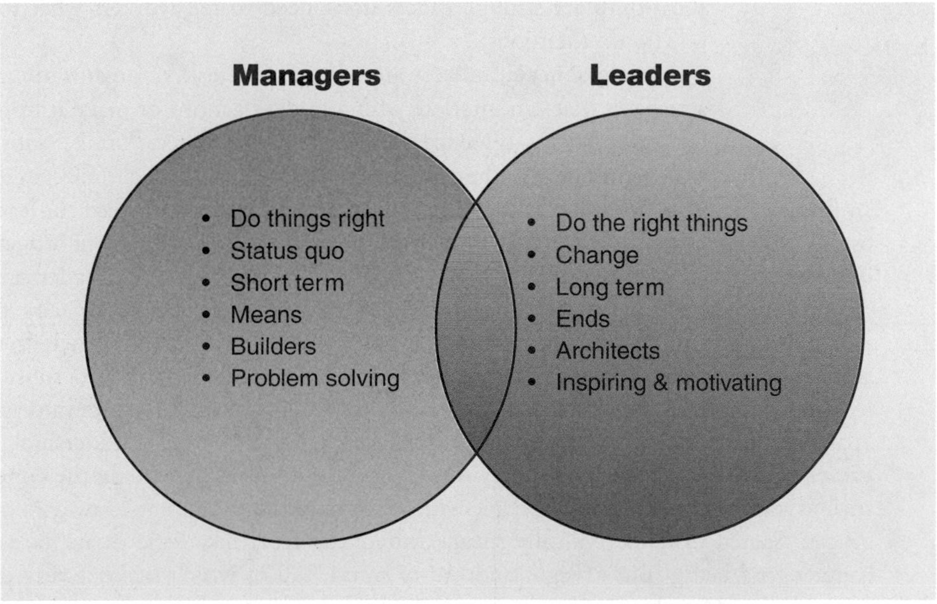

DOING THE RIGHT THING

THE THREE M'S: MISSION, MENTOR, AND MIRROR

Doctors take the Hippocratic oath. Lawyers swear to protect and enforce the law. Leaders ... Well, there's no equivalent for business leaders. That's why Harvard professor Howard Gardner says that business leaders can develop personal ethics by focusing on their mission, a mentor, and the mirror:

- First, leaders need to develop a personal mission statement by asking themselves these questions: Why are you doing what you're doing? What do you want from work? What are your personal goals? Let your personal mission statement, and not the company's, guide your ethical behaviour.
- Second, take care in choosing a mentor. An interesting study compared 20 business leaders selected at random with 20 "good" business leaders nominated by businesspeople, and business school professors, and deans. The randomly selected business leaders focused on short-term goals exclusively, worrying only about next quarter's results. By contrast, 18 of the 20 "good" executives focused on the long term, on doing what was right for the company in the long run. So, when choosing a mentor, choose a "good" one.
- Third, periodically stand in front of the mirror to assess your ethical performance as business leader. Are you proud or ashamed of what you accomplished and how you accomplished it? Are you proud or ashamed of your company? What needs to change to make you proud?

So, do the right thing. Develop a personal mission statement. Choose the right mentor. And look hard at yourself in the mirror.[54]

ends, what gets done. Managers are concerned with control and limiting the choices of others, while leaders are more concerned with expanding people's choices and options.[52] Finally, managers solve problems so that others can do their work, while leaders inspire and motivate others to find their own solutions.

While leaders are different from managers, in practice, organizations need them both. Managers are critical to getting out the day-to-day work, and leaders are critical to inspiring employees and setting the organization's long-term direction. The key issue is the extent to which organizations are properly led or properly managed. Warren Bennis summed up the difference between leaders and managers by noting that "organizations ... are underled and overmanaged. They do not pay enough attention to doing the right thing, while they pay too much attention to doing things right."[53]

Substitutes for Leadership: Do Leaders Always Matter?

One of the basic assumptions about leadership is that leaders always matter. The thinking goes that without sound leadership, organizations are sure to fail. In fact, when companies struggle, their leaders are almost always blamed for their poor performance.

However, there are situations and circumstances in which leadership isn't necessary, or is unlikely to make much of a difference, or where leaders aren't to blame for poor performance. These are known as leadership substitutes and leadership neutralizers.[55] Exhibit 15.10 lists a number of subordinate, task, or organizational characteristics that can act as leadership substitutes or neutralizers for either task-related or people-related leader behaviours.

Leadership substitutes are subordinate, task, or organizational characteristics that make leaders redundant or unnecessary. For instance, when leadership substitutes such as ability and performance feedback are present, task-related leader behaviour that specifies goals, task assignments, and how to do the job aren't likely to improve a subordinate's work performance. Think about it. Workers already have the capability to do their jobs. And the job itself provides enough information to let them know how well they're doing their jobs or what they might do to correct performance problems. In situations like this, where leadership substitutes are strong, leaders don't need to tell workers what to do or how to do their jobs.

Leadership neutralizers are subordinate, task, or organizational characteristics that can interfere with a leader's actions or make it impossible for a leader to influence followers' performance. Unlike substitutes, which simply take the place of leaders, leadership neutralizers create an "influence vacuum." In other words, leadership neutralizers create a need for leadership by ironically preventing leadership from working. For example, when subordinates are indifferent toward organizational rewards, there may be nothing that a leader can do to reward them for good performance. Likewise, union contracts that specify that all employees be paid the same, organizational policies that reward employees by seniority, and salary and raise processes that don't give leaders enough money to substantially reward good performers effectively neutralize the ability of leaders to reward workers. Spatial distance (an organizational characteristic) can also neutralize leadership. *Spatial distance* is a situation in which supervisors and subordinates don't work in the same place, such as with telecommuters or people working thousands of kilometres away in overseas offices. Spatial distance typically means infrequent feedback, little or no face-to-face contact, and being "out of sight and out of mind," all of which make it very difficult for leaders to lead. In fact, some companies find telecommuting to be so disruptive to

leadership substitutes subordinate, task, or organizational characteristics that make leaders redundant or unnecessary

leadership neutralizers subordinate, task, or organizational characteristics that can interfere with a leader's actions or make it impossible for a leader to influence followers' performance

CHARACTERISTIC	PEOPLE-RELATED LEADERSHIP BEHAVIOURS	TASK-RELATED LEADERSHIP BEHAVIOURS
SUBORDINATE CHARACTERISTICS		
• Ability, experience, training, knowledge	Neutralize	Substitute, Neutralize
• Need for independence	Neutralize	Neutralize
• Professional orientation	Substitute, Neutralize	Substitute, Neutralize
• Indifference toward organizational rewards	Neutralize	Neutralize
TASK CHARACTERISTICS		
• Unambiguous and routine tasks	No effect	Substitute, Neutralize
• Performance feedback provided by the work itself	No effect	Substitute, Neutralize
• Intrinsically satisfying work	Substitute, Neutralize	Neutralize
ORGANIZATIONAL CHARACTERISTICS		
• Formalization, meaning specific plans, goals, and areas of responsibility	No effect	Neutralize
• Inflexibility, meaning rigid, unbending rules and procedures	No effect	Neutralize
• Highly specified staff functions	No effect	Neutralize
• Cohesive work groups	Substitute, Neutralize	Substitute, Neutralize
• Organizational rewards beyond a leader's control	Neutralize	Neutralize
• Spatial distance between supervisors and subordinates	Neutralize	Neutralize

Source: S. Kerr & J.M. Jermier, "Substitutes for Leadership: Their Meaning and Measurement," Organizational Behavior and Human Performance 22 (1978): 375–403.

EXHIBIT 15.10
Leadership Substitutes and Neutralizers

leadership processes that they require their telecommuters to come into the office at least once or twice a week.

So do leaders *always* matter? Leadership substitutes and neutralizers indicate that sometimes they don't. However, this doesn't mean that leaders don't matter at all. Quite the opposite. Leaders do matter, but they're not superhuman. They can't do it all by themselves. And they can't fix every situation. In short, leadership is very important. But poor leadership isn't the cause of every organizational crisis, and changing leaders isn't the solution to every company problem.

REVIEW 4: LEADERSHIP

Leadership is the process of influencing others to achieve group or organizational goals. Leaders are different from managers. The primary difference is that leaders are concerned with doing the right thing, while managers are concerned with doing things right. Furthermore, managers have a short-term focus and are concerned with the status quo, with means rather than ends, and with solving others' problems. By contrast, leaders have a long-term focus and are concerned with change, with ends rather than means, and with inspiring and motivating others to solve their own problems. Organizations need both managers and leaders. But, in general, companies are overmanaged and underled. While leadership is important, leadership substitutes and neutralizers create situations in which leadership isn't necessary or is unlikely to make much of a difference. Leadership substitutes are subordinate, task, or organizational characteristics that make leaders redundant or unnecessary. By contrast, leadership neutralizers are subordinate, task, or organizational characteristics that interfere with a leader's actions or make it impossible for a leader to influence followers' performance.

5 WHO LEADERS ARE AND WHAT LEADERS DO

Every year, *Fortune* magazine conducts a survey to determine corporate America's "most admired" companies. And, every year, as part of that study, it takes a look at the leaders of those companies. However, the last time it did this, it found that the CEOs of its ten most admired companies were surprisingly different. In fact, *Fortune* wrote that "every conceivable leadership style is represented by these CEOs."[56] General Electric's Jack Welch was described as "combative," as someone who "tilts his head, and thrusts out his chin as if to say, 'Go ahead, take your best shot'—and is never happier than when you do." Southwest Airlines' Herb Kelleher was described as "a prankster and a kisser so unabashedly affectionate that his company's ticker symbol is LUV, so hands-on he has loaded baggage and served peanuts to passengers."

So if the CEOs of *Fortune*'s "most admired" corporations are all different, just what makes a good leader? Let's learn more about who leaders are by investigating leadership traits and behaviours.

Leadership Traits

trait theory
leadership theory that holds that effective leaders possess a similar set of traits or characteristics

traits
relatively stable characteristics, such as abilities, psychological motives, or consistent patterns of behaviour

Trait theory is one way to describe who leaders are. **Trait theory** says that effective leaders possess a similar set of traits or characteristics. **Traits** are relatively stable characteristics, such as abilities, psychological motives, or consistent patterns of behaviour. For example, according to trait theory, leaders were commonly thought to be taller, more confident, and have greater physical stamina (i.e., higher energy levels). Trait theory is also known as the "great person" theory, because early versions of trait theory stated that leaders were born, not made. In other words, you either had the "right stuff" to be a leader, or you didn't. And if you didn't, there was no way to get "it."

Until recently, studies indicated that trait theory was wrong, that there were no consistent trait differences between leaders and nonleaders, or between effective and ineffective leaders. However, more recent evidence shows that "successful leaders are not like other people," that successful leaders are indeed different from the rest of us.[57] More specifically, leaders are different from nonleaders on the following traits: drive, the desire to lead, honesty/integrity, self-confidence, emotional stability, cognitive ability, and knowledge of the business.[58]

Drive refers to high levels of effort and is characterized by achievement, motivation, ambition, energy, tenacity, and initiative. When Frank Stronach, the founder of Magna International, arrived in Canada, he had $40 in his pocket. He worked hard at a number of menial jobs before he trained as a tool-and-die maker. When he started his own business, he slept on a cot by his lathe.[59] Now the company sells tens of billions of dollars worth of car parts a year and has a market value of about $8 billion. With regard to achievement and ambition, leaders always try to make improvements or achieve success in what they're doing and have strong desires to "get ahead." Leaders typically have more energy, and they have to, given the long hours they put in year after year. Furthermore, leaders don't have the luxury of being "down." Since we tend to take our cues from leaders, we expect them to be positive and "up." As the Toronto-based billionaire and chair of Midland Group, Alex Shnaider says, "I'm always optimistic.... You cannot not be optimistic if you're in business."[60] Thus, leaders must have physical, mental, and emotional vitality. Leaders are also more tenacious than nonleaders and are better at overcoming obstacles and problems that would deter most of us. Most change takes place slowly, and leaders need to have a "stick-to-it-iveness" to see changes through. Leaders also show more initiative. For example, GE's former CEO Jack Welch said, "Some CEOs think the day they become CEO is the high point of their careers. They ought to feel they're just beginning." Indeed, legendary investor Warren Buffett once said, "Jack [felt] there [had been] more to do at GE than when he started," more than 15 years before.[61] So rather than waiting for others to take action, leaders move forward quickly to promote change or solve problems.

CP PHOTO/ADRIAN WYLD

Frank Stronach slept on a cot by his lathe as he built Magna International and his fortune.

Successful leaders also have a stronger *desire to lead.* They want to be in charge and think about ways to influence or convince others about what should or shouldn't be done. *Honesty/integrity* is also important to leaders. *Honesty,* that is, being truthful with others, is a cornerstone of leadership. Without honesty, leaders won't be trusted. But with it, subordinates are willing to overlook other flaws. For example, one follower said this about the leadership qualities of his manager: "I don't like a lot of the things he does, but he's basically honest. He's a genuine article and you'll forgive a lot of things because of that. That goes a long way in how much I trust him."[62] *Integrity* is the extent to which leaders do what they said they would do. Leaders may be honest and have good intentions, but if they don't consistently deliver on what they promise, they won't be trusted.

Self-confidence, believing in one's abilities, also distinguishes leaders from nonleaders. Self-confidence is critical to leadership. Leaders make risky, long-term decisions and must convince others of the correctness of those decisions. Self-confident leaders are more decisive and assertive and more likely to gain others' confidence. Moreover, self-confident leaders will admit mistakes, because they view them as learning opportunities rather than a refutation of their leadership capabilities. This also means that leaders have *emotional stability.* Even when things go wrong, they remain even-tempered and consistent in their outlook and the way in which they treat others. Leaders who can't control their emotions, who anger quickly or attack and blame others for mistakes, are unlikely to be trusted.

Leaders are also smart. Leaders typically have strong cognitive abilities. This doesn't mean that leaders are geniuses—far from it. But it does mean that leaders have the capacity to analyze large amounts of seemingly unrelated, complex information and can see patterns or opportunities or threats where others might not see them. Finally, leaders also "know their stuff," which means they have superior technical knowledge about the businesses they run. Leaders who have a good *knowledge of the business* understand the key technological decisions and concerns facing their companies. More often than not, studies indicate that effective leaders have long, extensive experience in their industries.

How does Anne Mulcahy, the CEO who turned around Xerox, measure up on these traits? In general, quite well. *Fortune* magazine said this about her:

> She is straightforward, hard-working, disciplined. She is fiercely loyal to Xerox—the company, the brand, the people. She has the integrity of the Catholic schoolgirl she was for 16 years. Her co-workers describe her as both compassionate and tough. She is not afraid of bad news. "Part of her DNA is to tell you the good, the bad, and the

WHAT REALLY WORKS

Leadership Traits Do Make a Difference[63]

For decades, researchers assumed that leadership traits, such as drive, emotional stability, cognitive ability, and charisma were not related to effective leadership. However, more recent evidence shows that there are reliable trait differences between leaders and nonleaders. In fact, 54 studies based on more than 6000 people clearly indicate that with regard to leadership traits, "successful leaders are not like other people."

TRAITS AND PERCEPTIONS OF LEADERSHIP EFFECTIVENESS

Several leadership models argue that successful leaders will be viewed by their followers as good leaders. (This is completely different from determining whether leaders actually improve organizational performance.) Consequently, one test of trait theory is whether leaders with particular traits are viewed as more or less effective leaders by their followers.

Intelligence.

On average, there is a 75 percent chance that intelligent leaders will be seen as better leaders than less intelligent leaders.

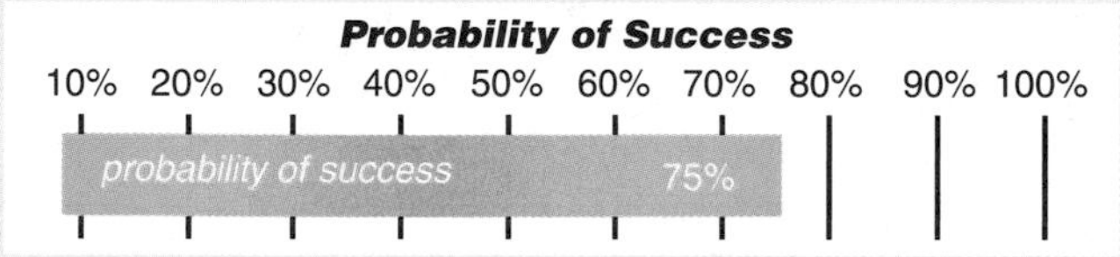

Dominance.

On average, there is only a 57 percent chance that leaders with highly dominant personalities will be seen as better leaders than those with less dominant personalities.

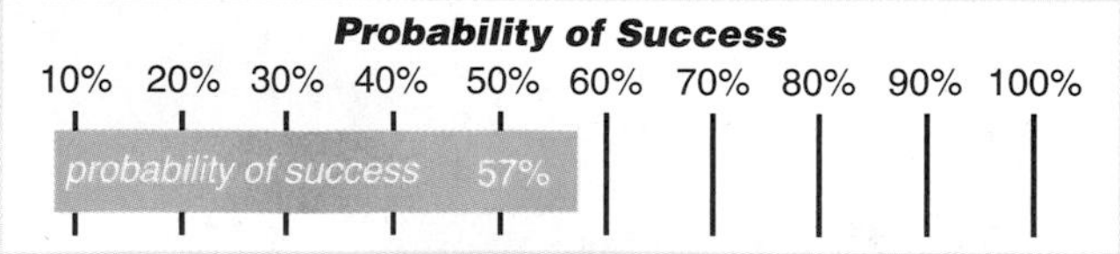

Extroversion.

On average, there is a 63 percent chance that extroverts will be seen as better leaders than introverts.

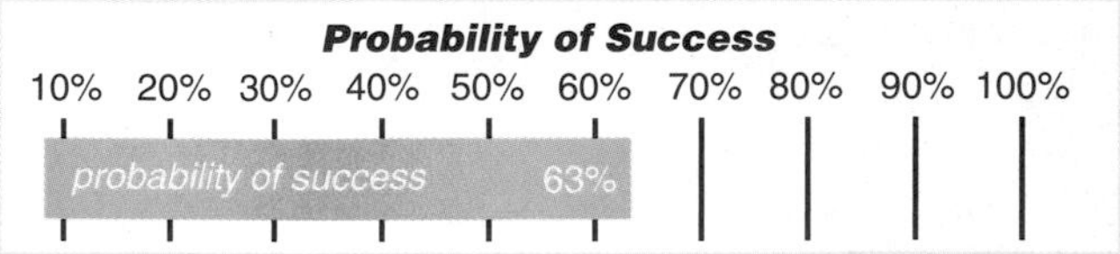

CHARISMA AND LEADERSHIP EFFECTIVENESS

As discussed at the end of the chapter, charismatic leadership is the set of behavioural tendencies and personal characteristics of leaders that creates an exceptionally strong relationship between leaders and their followers. More specifically, charismatic leaders articulate a clear vision for the future that is based on strongly held values or morals, model those values by acting in a way consistent with the vision, communicate high performance expectations to followers, and display confidence in followers' abilities to achieve the vision.

Performance and Charisma.

On average, there is a 72 percent chance that charismatic leaders will have better performing followers and organizations than less charismatic leaders.

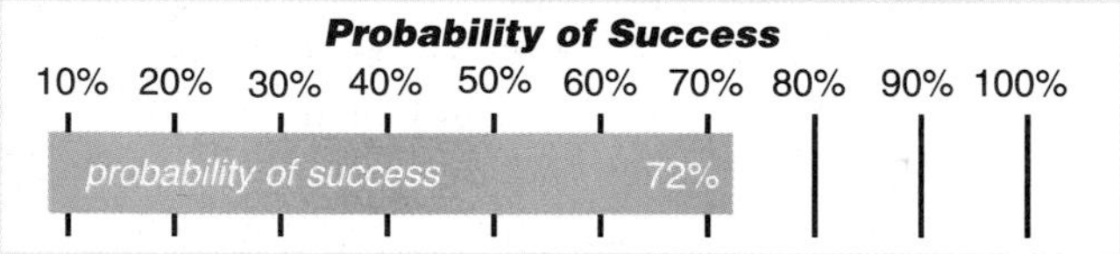

Charisma and Perceived Leader Effectiveness.

On average, there is an 89 percent chance that charismatic leaders will be perceived as more effective leaders than less charismatic leaders.

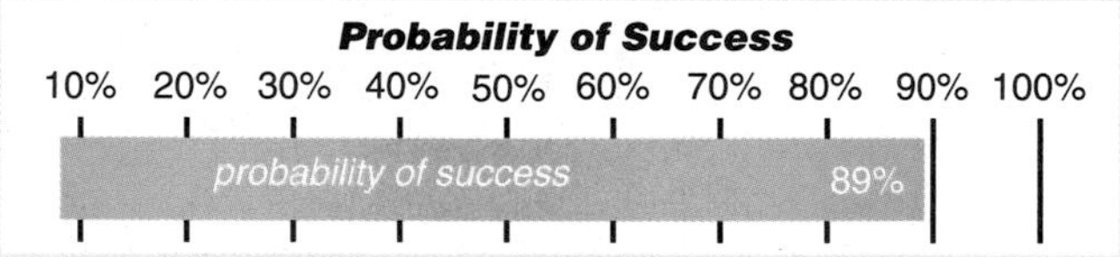

Charisma and Leader Satisfaction.

On average, there is a 90 percent chance that the followers of charismatic leaders will be more satisfied with their leaders than the followers of less charismatic leaders.

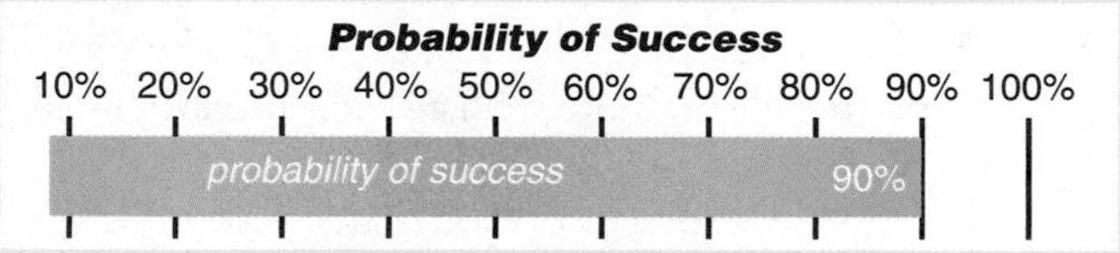

> ugly," says a colleague. Her willingness to work shoulder to shoulder with subordinates gives her unusual credibility and the ability to galvanize her team.[64]

However, because her experience was limited to sales, Mulcahy's clear initial weakness was a lack of knowledge of the entire business. And since Xerox was US$14.1 billion in debt, with only US$154 million in cash on hand, she had to learn fast. So she asked Joe Mancini, Jr., the director of corporate financial analysis to give her a course in "Balance Sheet 101." Mulcahy said, "It was an unusual situation for him—tutoring the CEO. But there wasn't a lot of time for false pride."[65] So she took home binders full of information to study each night, and eventually turned her knowledge of the business from a weakness into a strength.

Leadership Behaviours

Thus far, you've read about who leaders are. However, traits alone are not enough to be a successful leader. Traits are a precondition for success. After all, it's hard to imagine a truly successful leader who lacks all these qualities. Leaders who have these traits (or many of them) must then take actions that encourage people to achieve group or organizational goals.[66] Accordingly, we now examine what leaders do, meaning the behaviours they perform or the actions they take to influence others to achieve group or organizational goals.

Research at the University of Michigan, Ohio State University, and the University of Texas examined the specific behaviours that leaders use to improve subordinate satisfaction and performance. Hundreds of studies were conducted and hundreds of leader behaviours were examined. At all three universities, two basic leader behaviours emerged as central to successful leadership: initiating structure (called *job-centred leadership* at the University of Michigan and *concern for production* at the University of Texas) and considerate leader behaviour (called *employee-centred leadership* at the University of Michigan and *concern for people* at the University of Texas).[67] In fact, these two leader behaviours form the basis for many of the leadership theories discussed in this chapter.

Initiating structure is the degree to which a leader structures the roles of followers by setting goals, giving directions, setting deadlines, and assigning tasks. A leader's ability to initiate structure primarily affects subordinates' job performance. In helping to turn around Xerox, Ursula Burns, head of manufacturing, focused on nuts-and-bolts initiating structure issues. She granted freedom and authority to those meeting goals and paid personal visits to those who didn't. CEO Anne Mulcahy described Burns's approach this way: "She'd say, 'Jim, you blew it; tell us what happened,'"[68] The message was clear, meet your goals and you control your destiny. Meet them late or fail to meet them, and you'll have to defend your actions. With Xerox near bankruptcy, Burns had time for little else. After all, Mulcahy had given Burns a tough goal of her own to meet, increase manufacturing productivity while cutting US$1 billion in costs.

initiating structure
the degree to which a leader structures the roles of followers by setting goals, giving directions, setting deadlines, and assigning tasks

Consideration is the extent to which a leader is friendly, approachable, supportive, and shows concern for employees. Consideration primarily affects subordinates' job satisfaction. Specific leader consideration behaviours include listening to employees' problems and concerns, consulting with employees before making decisions, and treating employees as equals. Bill Aziz discussed how he would do this when he was president of Interlink Freight Systems:

consideration
the extent to which a leader is friendly, approachable, supportive, and shows concern for employees

> Getting face-to-face with people tells them that you are sincere. I used to go to the docks at 2 in the morning at Interlink Freight Systems. I was the first president that they had seen in the dock in the middle of the night, and the reason I went there was to see what goes on. I went one time on a truck trip from Toronto to Kingston, switched trucks in Kingston and drove to Montreal. I learned what the truck drivers were talking about, their worries, and found out that if you're a truck driver and you sit in a truck eight hours a day, with a rattle beside your

> head in the truck, you come out of that truck furious. I came out of that truck in Montreal and I went down to the basement where they had a place where these guys eat breakfast and I sat down by myself, ordered some bacon and eggs. Suddenly one guy came over and he wanted to know who I was. Pretty soon I had about a 100 guys around me, all truck drivers and dock workers who wanted to talk. They'd never seen a president of this company in their little cafeteria.[69]

While researchers at all three universities generally agreed on the two kinds of basic leader behaviours, initiating structure and consideration, they differed on the interaction and effectiveness of these behaviours. The University of Michigan studies indicated that initiating structure and consideration were mutually exclusive behaviours on opposite ends of the same continuum. In other words, leaders who wanted to be more considerate would have to do less initiating of structure (and vice versa). The University of Michigan studies also indicated that only considerate leader behaviours (i.e., employee-centred) were associated with successful leadership. By contrast, researchers at Ohio State University and the University of Texas found that initiating structure and consideration were independent behaviours, meaning that leaders can be considerate and initiate structure at the same time. Additional evidence confirms this finding.[70] The same researchers also concluded that the most effective leaders were strong on both initiating structure and considerate leader behaviours.

This "high-high" approach can be seen in the upper right corner of the Blake and Mouton Leadership Grid shown in Exhibit 15.11. Blake and Mouton used two leadership behaviours, concern for people (i.e., consideration) and concern for production (i.e.,

EXHIBIT 15.11
Blake/Mouton Leadership Grid

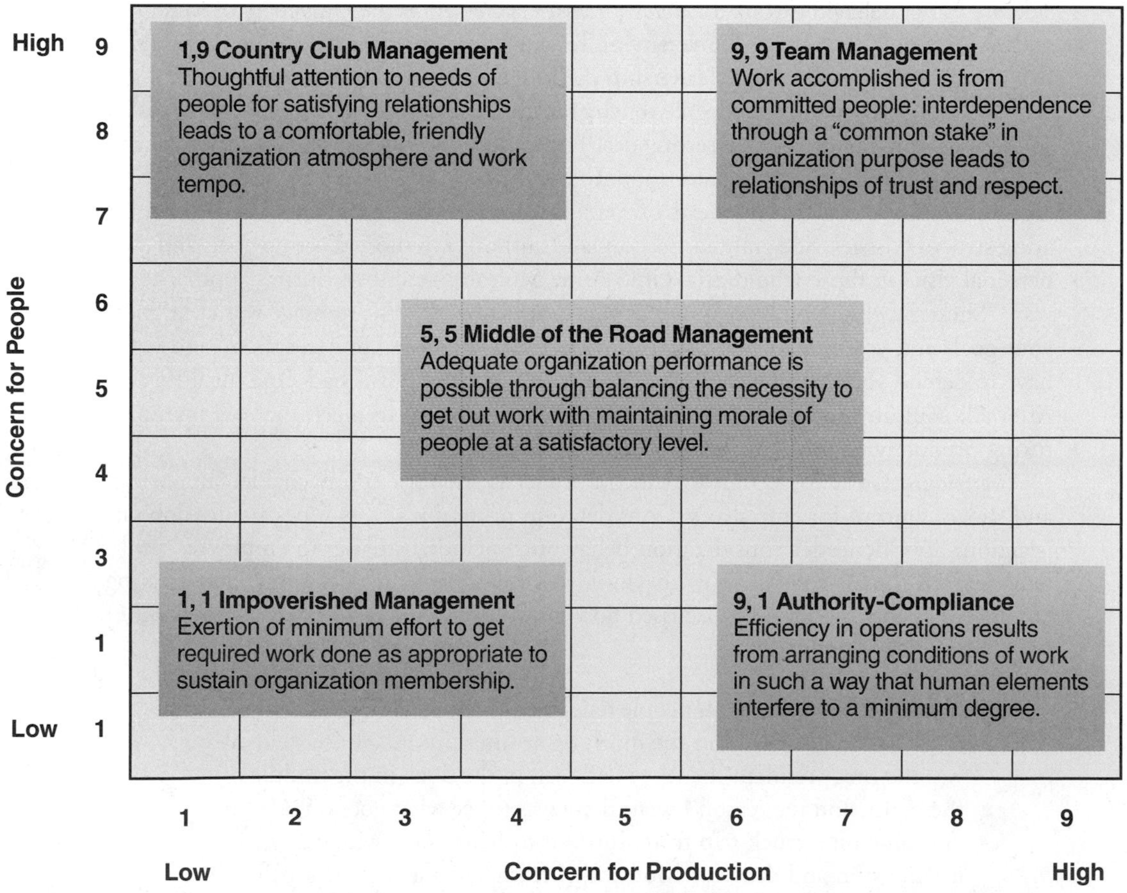

Source: R.R. Blake and A. A. McCanse, "The Leadership Grid," *Leadership Dilemmas—Grid Solutions* (Houston: Gulf Publishing Company), 29. Copyright 1991, by Scientific Methods, Inc.

initiating structure), to categorize five different leadership styles. Both behaviours are rated on a 9-point scale, with 1 representing "low" and 9 representing "high." Blake and Mouton suggest that a "high-high" or 9-9 leadership style is the best. They call this style *team management* because leaders who use it display a high concern for people (9) and a high concern for production (9). By contrast, leaders use a 9-1 *authority-compliance* leadership style when they have a high concern for production and a low concern for people. A 1-9 *country club* style occurs when leaders really care about producing a friendly and enjoyable work environment but don't really pay much attention to production or performance. The worst leadership style, according to the grid, is the 1-1 *impoverished* leader, who shows little concern for people or production and does the bare minimum needed to keep his or her job. Finally, the 5-5 *middle-of-the-road* style occurs when leaders show a moderate amount of concern for people and production.

Is the team management style, with a high concern for production and a high concern for people, the "best" leadership style? Logically, it would seem so. Why wouldn't you want to show high concern for both people and production? However, nearly 50 years' worth of research indicates that there isn't one "best" leadership style. The "best" leadership style depends on the situation. In other words, no one leadership behaviour by itself and no one combination of leadership behaviours works well across all situations and employees.

REVIEW 5: WHO LEADERS ARE AND WHAT LEADERS DO

Trait theory says that effective leaders possess traits or characteristics that differentiate them from nonleaders. Those traits are drive, the desire to lead, honesty/integrity, self-confidence, emotional stability, cognitive ability, and knowledge of the business. However, traits aren't enough for successful leadership. Leaders who have these traits (or many of them) must behave in ways that encourage people to achieve group or organizational goals. Two key leader behaviours are initiating structure, which improves subordinate performance, and consideration, which improves subordinate satisfaction. There is no "best" combination of these behaviours. The "best" leadership style depends on the situation.

Situational Leadership

After leader traits and behaviours, situational leadership is the third major approach to the study of leadership. Two major situational leadership theories—Fiedler's contingency theory and Hersey and Blanchard's situational theory—both assume that the effectiveness of any leadership style, the way a leader generally behaves toward followers, depends on the situation.[71] Accordingly, there is no one "best" leadership style. However, these theories differ in one significant way. Fiedler's contingency theory assumes that leadership styles are consistent and difficult to change. Therefore, leaders must be placed in or "matched" to a situation that fits their leadership style. However, Hersey and Blanchard's situational theory assumes that leaders are capable of adapting and adjusting their leadership styles to fit the demands of different situations.

After reading the next two sections, you should be able to

6 explain Fiedler's contingency theory.

7 discuss Hersey and Blanchard's situational theory.

6 PUTTING LEADERS IN THE RIGHT SITUATION: FIEDLER'S CONTINGENCY THEORY

contingency theory leadership theory that states that in order to maximize work group performance, leaders must be matched to the situation that best fits their leadership style

Fiedler's **contingency theory** states that in order to maximize work group performance, leaders must be matched to the right leadership situation.[72] More specifically, as shown in Exhibit 15.12, the first basic assumption of Fiedler's theory is that leaders are effective

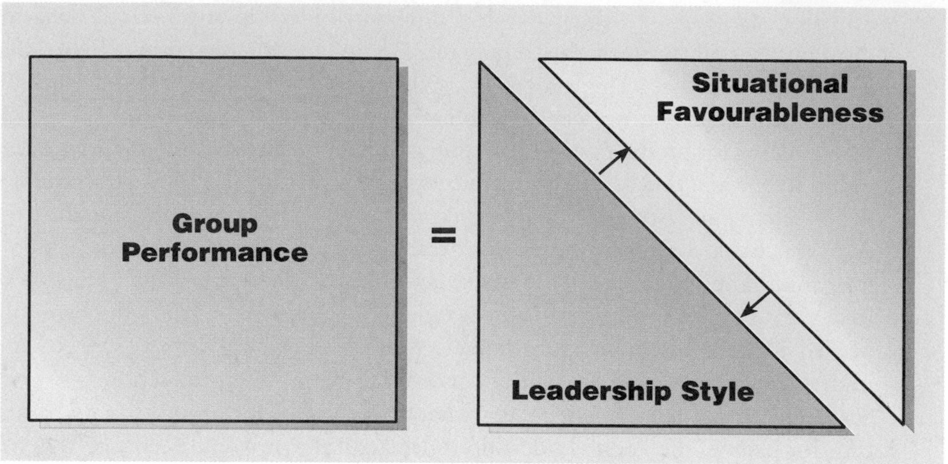

EXHIBIT 15.12
Fiedler's Contingency Theory

when the work groups they lead perform well. So instead of judging leader effectiveness by what a leader does (i.e., initiating structure and consideration) or who the leader is (i.e., trait theory), Fiedler assesses leaders by the conduct and performance of the people they supervise. Second, Fiedler assumes that leaders are generally unable to change their leadership styles and that leaders will be more effective when their leadership styles are matched to the proper situation. The third assumption is that the favourableness of a situation for a leader depends on the degree to which the situation permits the leader to influence the behaviour of group members. Thus, Fiedler's third assumption is consistent with our definition of leadership, which is the process of influencing others to achieve group or organizational goals.

Let's learn more about Fiedler's contingency theory by examining leadership styles, situational favourableness, and matching leadership styles to situations.

Leadership Style: Least Preferred Co-worker

When Fiedler refers to *leadership style,* he means the way in which leaders generally behaves toward followers. Do they yell and scream and blame others when things go wrong? Or, do they correct mistakes by first listening and then quietly, but directly make their point? Do they take credit for others' work when things go right? Or, do they make sure that those who did the work receive the credit they rightfully deserve? Do they let others make their own decisions and hold them accountable for results? Or, do they micromanage, insisting that others' decisions be approved first by them? Fiedler also assumes that leadership styles are tied to leaders' underlying needs and personalities. And since personality and needs are relatively stable, he assumes that leaders are generally incapable of changing their leadership styles. In other words, the way that leaders treat people now is probably the way they've always treated others. So, according to Fiedler, if your boss's first instinct is to yell and scream and blame others, chances are he or she has always done that.

Fiedler uses a questionnaire called the Least Preferred Co-worker (LPC) scale to measure leadership style. When completing the LPC scale, people are instructed to consider all the people with whom they have ever worked and then to choose the one person with whom they "least preferred" to work. Take a second yourself to identify your LPC. It's usually someone you had a big disagreement with, or, for whatever reason, you couldn't get along with or didn't like. After identifying their LPC, people use the LPC scale shown in Exhibit 15.13 to "describe" their LPC.

Complete the LPC yourself. Did you describe your LPC as pleasant, friendly, helpful, supportive, interesting, and cheerful? Or did you describe the person as unpleasant, unfriendly, frustrating, hostile, boring, and gloomy? People who describe their LPC in a positive way (scoring 64 and above) have *relationship-oriented* leadership

Pleasant	8	7	6	5	4	3	2	1	Unpleasant
Friendly	8	7	6	5	4	3	2	1	Unfriendly
Rejecting	1	2	3	4	5	6	7	8	Accepting
Helpful	8	7	6	5	4	3	2	1	Frustrating
Unenthusiastic	1	2	3	4	5	6	7	8	Enthusiastic
Tense	1	2	3	4	5	6	7	8	Relaxed
Distant	1	2	3	4	5	6	7	8	Close
Cold	1	2	3	4	5	6	7	8	Warm
Cooperative	8	7	6	5	4	3	2	1	Uncooperative
Supportive	8	7	6	5	4	3	2	1	Hostile
Boring	1	2	3	4	5	6	7	8	Interesting
Quarrelsome	1	2	3	4	5	6	7	8	Harmonious
Self-assured	8	7	6	5	4	3	2	1	Hesitant
Efficient	8	7	6	5	4	3	2	1	Inefficient
Gloomy	1	2	3	4	5	6	7	8	Cheerful
Open	8	7	6	5	4	3	2	1	Guarded

Source: Least Preferred Co-worker Scale, F.E. Fiedler & M.M. Chemers, *Improving Leadership Effectiveness: The Leader Match Concept*, 2nd Edition (New York: John Wiley and Sons, 1984). Reprinted by permission of the authors.

EXHIBIT 15.13
Least Preferred Co-worker Scale

styles. After all, if they can still be positive about their least preferred co-worker, they must be people-oriented. By contrast, people who describe their LPC in a negative way (scoring 57 or below) have *task-oriented* leadership styles. Given a choice, they'll focus first on getting the job done and second on making sure everyone gets along. Finally, there is a third group with moderate scores (from 58 to 63) who are somewhat more flexible in their leadership style and can be somewhat relationship-oriented or somewhat task-oriented.

Situational Favourableness

Fiedler assumes that leaders will be more effective when their leadership styles are matched to the proper situation. More specifically, Fiedler defines **situational favourableness** as the degree to which a particular situation either permits or denies a leader the chance to influence the behaviour of group members.[73] In highly favourable situations, leaders find that their actions influence followers. However, in highly unfavourable situations, leaders have little or no success influencing them.

situational favourableness the degree to which a particular situation either permits or denies a leader the chance to influence the behaviour of group members

leader-member relations the degree to which followers respect, trust, and like their leaders

task structure the degree to which the requirements of a subordinate's tasks are clearly specified

Three situational factors determine the favourability of a situation: leader-member relations, task structure, and position power. **Leader-member relations**, which is the most important situational factor, is how well followers respect, trust, and like their leaders. When asked about business success, Tim Fowler, vice president of Pepsi-QTG Canada, said, "Work hard—I don't believe in shortcuts—make time for other people, build relationships and listen to people. At the end of the day, that's how to get things done."[74] When leader-member relations are good, followers trust the leader and there is a friendly work atmosphere. **Task structure** is the degree to which the requirements of a subordinate's tasks are clearly specified. With highly structured tasks, employees have clear job responsibilities, goals, and procedures. Position power is the degree to which leaders are able to hire, fire, reward, and punish workers. The more influence leaders have over hiring, firing, rewards, and punishments, the greater their power.

Exhibit 15.14 shows how leader-member relations, task structure, and position power can be combined into eight different situations that differ in their favourability to leaders. In general, Situation I is the most favourable leader situation. Followers like and trust their leaders and know what to do because their tasks are highly structured. Also, the leader has the formal power to influence workers through hiring, firing, rewarding, and punishing them. Therefore, in Situation I it's relatively easy for a leader to influence followers. By contrast, Situation VIII is the least favourable situation for leaders. Followers don't like or trust their leaders. As well, followers are not sure what they're supposed to be doing, given that their tasks or jobs are highly unstructured. Finally, leaders find it difficult to influence followers since they don't have the ability to hire, fire, reward, or punish the people who work for them. In short, it's very difficult to influence followers given the conditions found in Situation VIII.

Matching Leadership Styles to Situations

After studying thousands of leaders and followers in hundreds of different situations, Fiedler found that the performance of relationship- and task-oriented leaders followed the pattern displayed in Exhibit 15.15. Relationship-oriented leaders with high LPC scores were better leaders (i.e., their groups performed more effectively) under moderately favourable situations. In moderately favourable situations, the leader may be liked somewhat, tasks may be somewhat structured, and the leader may have some position power. In this situation, a relationship-oriented leader improves leader-member relations, which is the most important of the three situational factors. In turn, morale and performance improve. By contrast, task-oriented leaders with low LPC scores were better leaders in highly favourable and unfavourable situations. Task-oriented leaders do well in favourable situations where leaders are liked, tasks are structured, and the leader has the power to hire, fire, reward, and punish. In these favourable situations, task-oriented leaders effectively step on the gas of a highly tuned car that's in perfect running condition. Their focus on performance sets the goal for the group, which then charges forward to meet it. But task-oriented leaders also do well in unfavourable situations where leaders are disliked, tasks are unstructured, and the leader doesn't have the power to hire, fire, reward, and punish. In these unfavourable situations, the task-oriented leader sets goals, which focuses attention on performance, and clarifies what

EXHIBIT 15.14
Situational Favourableness

Leader—Member Relations	Good	Good	Good	Good	Poor	Poor	Poor	Poor
Task Structure	High	High	Low	Low	High	High	Low	Low
Position Power	Strong	Weak	Strong	Weak	Strong	Weak	Strong	Weak
Situation	I	II	III	IV	V	VI	VII	VIII
	Favourable		**Moderately Favourable**				**Unfavourable**	

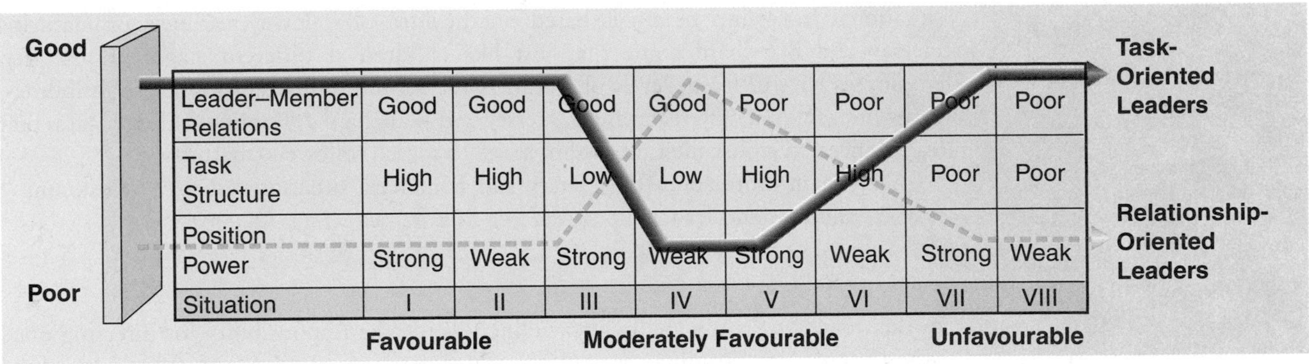

EXHIBIT 15.15
Matching Leadership Styles to Situations

needs to be done, thus overcoming low task structure. This is enough to jump-start performance, even if workers don't like or trust the leader.

Recall, however, that Fiedler assumes that leaders are incapable of changing their leadership styles. Accordingly, the key to making Fiedler's contingency theory practical in the workplace is to accurately measure and match leaders to situations or to teach leaders how to change situational favourableness by changing leader-member relations, task structure, or position power. While matching or placing leaders in appropriate situations works particularly well, practising managers have had little luck with "re-engineering situations" to fit their leadership styles. The primary problem, as you've no doubt realized, is the complexity of the theory. In a study designed to teach leaders how to re-engineer their situations to fit their leadership styles, Fiedler found that most of the leaders simply did not understand what they were supposed to do to change their leadership situations. Furthermore, if they didn't like their LPC profile (perhaps they felt they were more relationship-oriented than their scores indicated), they arbitrarily changed it to better suit their view of themselves. Of course, the theory won't work as well if leaders are attempting to change situational factors to fit their perceived leadership style rather than their real leadership style.[75]

REVIEW 6: PUTTING LEADERS IN THE RIGHT SITUATION: FIEDLER'S CONTINGENCY THEORY

Fiedler's theory assumes that leaders are effective when their work groups perform well, that leaders are unable to change their leadership styles, that leadership styles must be matched to the proper situation, and that favourable situations permit leaders to influence group members. According to the Least Preferred Co-worker (LPC) scale, there are two basic leader styles. People who describe their LPC in a positive way have relationship-oriented leadership styles. By contrast, people who describe their LPC in a negative way have task-oriented leadership styles. Situational favourableness occurs when leaders can influence followers and is determined by leader-member relations, task structure, and position power. In general, relationship-oriented leaders with high LPC scores are better leaders under moderately favourable situations, while task-oriented leaders with low LPC scores are better leaders in highly favourable and unfavourable situations. Since Fiedler assumes that leaders are incapable of changing their leadership styles, the key is to accurately measure and match leaders to situations or to teach leaders how to change situational factors. While matching or placing leaders in appropriate situations has worked well, "re-engineering situations" to fit leadership styles hasn't because of the complexity of the model, which people find difficult to understand.

7 ADAPTING LEADER BEHAVIOUR: HERSEY AND BLANCHARD'S SITUATIONAL THEORY

Have you ever had a new job that you didn't know how to do and the boss wasn't around to help you learn it? Or have you been in the other situation where you knew exactly how to do your job but your boss kept treating you like you didn't? Hersey and Blanchard's situational leadership theory is based on the idea of follower readiness or maturity. Hersey and Blanchard argue that just like children at different stages of maturity, employees have different levels of readiness for handling different jobs, responsibilities, and work assignments. Accordingly, Hersey and Blanchard's **situational theory** states that leaders need to adjust their leadership styles to match followers' maturity.[76]

situational theory
leadership theory that states that leaders need to adjust their leadership styles to match followers' maturity

Let's learn more about the Hersey and Blanchard situational theory by examining worker readiness and leadership styles.

Worker Readiness

worker readiness
the ability and willingness to take responsibility for directing one's behaviour at work

Worker readiness is the ability and willingness to take responsibility for directing one's behaviour at work. Readiness is made up of two components. *Job readiness* consists of the amount of knowledge, skill, ability, and experience people have to perform their jobs. As you would expect, people with greater skill, ability, and experience do a better job of supervising their own work. *Psychological readiness*, on the other hand, is a feeling of self-confidence or self-respect. Likewise, confident people do a better job of guiding their own work than do insecure people.

Job readiness and psychological readiness are combined to produce four different levels of readiness in Hersey and Blanchard's situational leadership theory. The lowest level, R1, represents insecure people who are neither willing nor able to take responsibility for guiding their own work. The second level, R2, represents people who are confident and are willing but not able to take responsibility for guiding their own work. The third level, R3, represents people who are insecure and are able but not willing to take responsibility for guiding their own work. And the highest level, R4, represents people who are confident and willing and able to take responsibility for guiding their own work. It's important to note that a follower's readiness is usually task specific. For example, you may be highly confident and capable when it comes to personal computers but know nothing about setting up budgets for planning purposes. Thus, you would possess readiness (R4) with computers but not (R1) with respect to budgets.

Leadership Styles

Similar to Blake and Mouton's managerial grid, situational theory defines leadership styles in terms of task behaviour (i.e., concern for production) and relationship behaviour (i.e., concern for people). These two behaviours can be combined to form four different leadership styles: telling, selling, participating, and delegating. Leaders choose one of these styles depending on the readiness a follower has for a specific task.

A *telling* leadership style (high task behaviour and low relationship behaviour) is based on one-way communication, in which followers are told what, how, when, and where to do particular tasks. Telling is used when people are insecure and neither willing nor able to take responsibility for guiding their own work (R1). For instance, someone using a telling leadership style might say, "We're going to start a company newsletter. I want you to contact three printers for cost estimates. Then get together with each manager and get a one-page update with the latest activities from each department. Don't write these yourself. Have the managers write them and we'll edit them as we see fit. Also, call the CEO's assistant to remind her that we need her comments. Finally, have this all assembled in a three-ring notebook for me next Friday."

A *selling* leadership style (high task behaviour and high relationship behaviour) involves two-way communication and psychological support to encourage followers to "own" or "buy into" particular ways of doing things. Selling is used when confident people are willing but not able to take responsibility for guiding their own work (R2). For instance, someone using a selling leadership style might say, "We're going to start a company newsletter. I really think that's a great idea, don't you? We're going to need some cost estimates from printers and some comments from each of the managers. But that's pretty straightforward. Oh, don't forget that we need the CEO's comments, too. She's expecting you to call. I know that you'll do a great job on this. We'll meet next Tuesday to see if you have any questions once you've dug into this. By the way, we need to have this done by next Friday."

A *participating* style (low task behaviour and high relationship behaviour) is based on two-way communication and shared decision-making. Participating is used when insecure people are able but not willing to take responsibility for guiding their own work (R3). Since the problem is with motivation and not ability, someone using a participating leadership style might say, "What do you think about starting a company newsletter? Uh-huh, uh-huh (listening)? Okay, I think so, too. What kind of stuff do you hate in company newsletters? Uh-huh (listening). Okay, I agree. That stuff drives me nuts, too. Well, what do you think we should put in our company newsletter? Uh-huh (listening). Those are great ideas. I'd like to see you implement them. We've got about 10 days to put it together. Why don't you put together a first draft, based on what we talked about here today, and we can meet on Tuesday to review those ideas. Great!"

A *delegating* style (low task behaviour and low relationship behaviour) is a style in which leaders basically let workers "run their own show" and make their own decisions. Delegating is used when people are willing and able to take responsibility for guiding their own work (R4). For instance, someone using a delegating leadership style might say, "We're going to start a company newsletter. You've got 10 days to do it. Run with it. Let me know when you've got it done. I'll e-mail you a couple of ideas, but other than that, do what you think is best. Thanks."

In general, Hersey and Blanchard's situational theory shows that at first, as people become more ready, and thus increasingly willing and capable of guiding their own behaviour, leaders should become less task oriented and more relationship oriented. However, after people become even more ready, leaders should become both less task-oriented and less relationship-oriented, as people eventually manage their own work with little input from their leaders.

How well does Hersey and Blanchard's situational theory work? Despite its intuitive appeal (managers and consultants tend to prefer it over Fiedler's contingency theory because of its underlying logic and simplicity), most studies don't support situational theory.[77] While managers generally do a good job of judging followers' readiness levels, the theory doesn't seem to work well, except at lower levels, where a telling style is recommended for people who are insecure and neither willing nor able to take responsibility for guiding their own work.[78]

REVIEW 7: ADAPTING LEADER BEHAVIOUR: HERSEY AND BLANCHARD'S SITUATIONAL THEORY

According to situational theory, leaders need to adjust their leadership styles to match follower's readiness, which is the ability (job readiness) and willingness (psychological readiness) to take responsibility for directing one's work. Job readiness and psychological readiness combine to produce four different levels of readiness (R1–R4) in which people vary in their confidence, ability, and willingness to guide their own work. Situational theory combines task and relationship behaviour to create four leadership styles: telling (R1), selling (R2), participating (R3), and delegating (R4), that are used with employees at different readiness levels.

Strategic Leadership

Thus far, you have read about two major leadership ideas: traits and behaviours. Leader traits are relatively stable characteristics, such as abilities or psychological motives. Traits capture who effective leaders are. Leader behaviours are the actions leaders take to influence others to achieve group or organizational goals. Behaviours capture what effective leaders do (i.e., initiate structure and consideration). This leadership topic of the chapter introduces a third major leadership idea—strategic leadership—and its components: visionary, charismatic, and transformational leadership.

strategic leadership the ability to anticipate, envision, maintain flexibility, think strategically, and work with others to initiate changes that will create a positive future for an organization

Strategic leadership is the ability to anticipate, envision, maintain flexibility, think strategically, and work with others to initiate changes that will create a positive future for an organization.[79] For example, General Electric's former CEO, Jack Welch, was one of the most successful CEOs ever, having increased GE's stock market value from US$12 billion when he took over in 1981 to more than US$400 billion 20 years later when he retired. From the start, Welch imparted strategic leadership by making it clear that every GE business (there are more than a dozen) needed to be "#1 or #2 in its industry." For two decades, he reinforced GE's strategic leadership by holding half-day "classes" with more than 15 000 GE managers and executives at GE's executive centre. Every week, Welch also used surprise visits to GE plants and offices to maintain connections with GE's lower- and middle-level managers. Brian Nailor, a GE marketing manager, said, "We're pebbles in an ocean, but he knows about us."[80]

Thus, strategic leadership captures how leaders inspire their followers to change and to give extraordinary effort to accomplish organizational goals.

After reading this next section, you should be able to

8 explain how visionary leadership (i.e., charismatic and transformational leadership) helps leaders achieve strategic leadership.

8 VISIONARY LEADERSHIP

visionary leadership leadership that creates a positive image of the future that motivates organizational members and provides direction for future planning and goal setting

In Chapter 4, we defined a vision as a statement of a company's purpose or reason for existing. Similarly, **visionary leadership** creates a positive image of the future that motivates organizational members and provides direction for future planning and goal setting.[81]

Two kinds of visionary leadership are charismatic leadership and transformational leadership.

Charismatic Leadership

Charisma is a Greek word meaning "gift from God." The Greeks saw people with charisma as divinely inspired and capable of incredible accomplishments. German sociologist Max Weber viewed charisma as a special bond between leaders and followers.[82] Weber wrote that the special qualities of charismatic leaders enable them to strongly influence followers. Weber also noted that charismatic leaders tended to emerge in times of crisis and that the radical solutions they propose enhance the admiration that followers feel for them. Indeed, charismatic leaders tend to have incredible influence over their followers, who become zealously inspired by and attracted to their leaders. From this perspective, charismatic leaders are often seen as bigger-than-life or uniquely special.

charismatic leadership the behavioural tendencies and personal characteristics of leaders that create an exceptionally strong relationship between them and their followers

Charismatic leaders have strong, confident, dynamic personalities that attract followers and enable them to create strong bonds between themselves and their followers. Followers trust charismatic leaders, are loyal to them, and are inspired to work toward the accomplishment of the leader's vision. Because of these qualities, followers become devoted to charismatic leaders and may go to extraordinary lengths to please them. Therefore, we can define **charismatic leadership** as the behavioural tendencies and personal characteristics of leaders that create an exceptionally strong relationship between them and their followers. Charismatic leaders also

- articulate a clear vision for the future that is based on strongly held values or morals,
- model those values by acting in a way consistent with the vision,
- communicate high performance expectations to followers, and
- display confidence in followers' abilities to achieve the vision.[83]

Orit Gadiesh, chairman of Bain & Co., a management consulting firm, is an example of charismatic leadership. Gadiesh led Bain out of serious financial problems, expanded the company from 990 to 1400 employees, and increased revenues by 25 percent a year. Gadiesh dresses with flair and is described as complex, intense, driven, painfully direct, and a lot of fun. Founder Bill Bain recalls interviewing Gadiesh for the

AP/WIDE WORLD PHOTOS

British billionaire adventurer Richard Branson dons a Virgin Cola costume and sprays the soft drink during a promotion in Tokyo. Branson's charismatic leadership has catapulted his business undertakings into the limelight and brought great success to his companies.

job: "The way she listened made my energy level go up. She asked the most thoughtful, original questions. There was nothing boilerplate about her." Bain managing director Tom Tierney says, "Her style comes from this intense passion about being true to herself and the client." Says James Morgan, CEO of Philip Morris USA, one of Bain's clients, "Orit has that talent for making you feel you're the most important person in the room."[84]

Does charismatic leadership work? Studies indicate that it often does. In general, the followers of charismatic leaders are more committed and satisfied, are better performers, are more likely to trust their leaders, and simply work harder.[85] However, the risks associated with charismatic leadership are at least as large as its benefits, particularly if ego-driven leaders take advantage of fanatical followers.

In general, there are two kinds of charismatic leaders, ethical charismatics and unethical charismatics.[86] **Ethical charismatics** provide developmental opportunities for followers, are open to positive and negative feedback, recognize others' contributions, share information, and have moral standards that emphasize the larger interests of the group, organization, or society. For example, Reuben Mark, the CEO of Colgate for two decades, is a very successful ethical charismatic (a $10 000 investment in the company when he became CEO would now be worth $335 000).[87] According to the *Wall Street Journal*, "He meets regularly with Colgate employees and is the corporate cheerleader, discussing Colgate's core values: caring, continuous improvement and teamwork. 'Love,' he has said, according to people who have worked for him, 'is a better motivator than fear.'"[88] As you would expect, ethical charismatics produce stronger commitment, higher satisfaction, more effort, better performance, and greater trust.

ethical charismatics charismatic leaders that provide developmental opportunities for followers, are open to positive and negative feedback, recognize others' contributions, share information, and have moral standards that emphasize the larger interests of the group, organization, or society

By contrast, unethical charismatics pose a tremendous risk for companies. Followers can be just as supportive and committed to unethical charismatics as they are to ethical charismatics. However, unethical charismatics control and manipulate followers, do what is best for themselves instead of their organizations, only want to hear positive feedback, only share information that is beneficial to themselves, and have moral standards that put their interests before everyone else's. John Thompson, a management consultant, said, "Often what begins as a mission becomes an obsession. Leaders can cut corners on values and become driven by self-interest. Then they may abuse anyone who makes a mistake."[89]

Exhibit 15.16 shows the stark differences between ethical and unethical charismatics on several leader behaviours: exercising power, creating the vision, communicating with followers, accepting feedback, stimulating followers intellectually, developing followers, and moral standards. For example, with regard to creating the vision, ethical charismatics include followers' concerns and wishes by having them participate in the development of the company vision. By contrast, unethical charismatics develop the vision by themselves solely to meet their personal agendas. One unethical charismatic said, "The key thing is that it is my idea; and I am going to win with it at all costs."[90]

So what can companies do to reduce the risks associated with unethical charismatics?[91] To start, they need a clearly written code of conduct that is fairly and consistently enforced for all managers. Next, companies should recruit, select, and promote managers with high ethical standards. Also, companies need to train leaders how to value, seek, and use diverse points of view. Leaders and subordinates also need training regarding ethical leader behaviours so abuses can be recognized and corrected. Finally, companies should celebrate and reward people who exhibit ethical behaviours, especially ethical leader behaviours.[92]

transformational leadership
leadership that generates awareness and acceptance of a group's purpose and mission and gets employees to see beyond their own needs and self-interest for the good of the group

Transformational Leadership

While charismatic leaders are able to articulate a clear vision, model values consistent with that vision, communicate high performance expectations, and establish very strong relationships between themselves and their followers, **transformational leadership** goes further by generating awareness and acceptance of a group's purpose and mission and by getting employees to see beyond their own needs and self-interest for the good of the group.[93] Transformational leaders, like charismatic leaders, are visionary. However, transformational leaders transform their organizations by getting their followers to accomplish

EXHIBIT 15.16
Ethical and Unethical Charismatics

CHARISMATIC LEADER BEHAVIOURS	ETHICAL CHARISMATICS	UNETHICAL CHARISMATICS
Exercising power	Power is used to serve others.	Power is used to dominate or manipulate others for personal gain.
Creating the vision	Followers help develop the vision.	Vision comes solely from leader and serves his or her personal agenda.
Communicating with followers	Two-way communication: Seek out viewpoints on critical issues.	One-way communication: Not open to input and suggestions from others.
Accepting feedback	Open to feedback. Willing to learn from criticism.	Inflated ego thrives on attention and admiration of yes-men. Avoid or punish candid feedback.
Stimulating followers intellectually	Want followers to think and question status quo as well as leader's views.	Don't want followers to think. Want uncritical, unquestioning acceptance of leader's ideas.
Developing followers	Focus on developing people with whom they interact. Express confidence in them and share recognition with others.	Insensitive and unresponsive to followers' needs and aspirations.
Moral standards	Follow self-guided principles that may go against popular opinion. Have three virtues: courage, a sense of fairness or justice, and integrity.	Follow standards only if they satisfy immediate self-interests. Manipulate impressions so that others think they are "doing the right thing." Use communication skills to manipulate others to support their personal agenda.

Source: J.M. Howell & B.J. Avolio, "The Ethics of Charismatic Leadership: Submission or Liberation?" *Academy of Management Executive* 6, no. 2 (1992): 43–54.

more than they intended and even more than they thought possible. Transformational leaders are able to make their followers feel as if they are a vital part of the organization and can help them see how their jobs fit with the organization's vision. By linking individual and organizational interests, transformational leaders encourage followers to make sacrifices for the organization, because they know that they will prosper when the organization prospers. There are four components of transformational leadership: charismatic leadership or idealized influence, inspirational motivation, intellectual stimulation, and individualized consideration.[94]

Charismatic leadership or *idealized influence* means that transformational leaders act as role models for their followers. Because transformational leaders put others' needs ahead of their own and share risks with followers, they are admired, respected, and trusted, and followers want to emulate them. Thus, in contrast to purely charismatic leaders (especially unethical charismatics), transformational leaders can be counted on to do the right thing and maintain high standards for ethical and personal conduct. For example, CEO Alan Lacy didn't hesitate to fire two top managers when they misled him about the revenue and profit outlook for Sears' credit business (i.e., credit cards and loans), which accounts for more than half of Sears' profits. Lacy explained his actions, saying, "There's a higher standard today. As a CEO, I've got to sign a certificate affirming that our financial reporting is not just in conformance with GAAP [generally accepted accounting principles] but that it fairly presents the business."[95]

Inspirational motivation means that transformational leaders motivate and inspire followers by providing meaning and challenge to their work. By clearly communicating expectations and demonstrating commitment to goals, transformational leaders help followers envision future states, such as the organizational vision. In turn, this leads to greater enthusiasm and optimism about the future.

Intellectual stimulation means that transformational leaders encourage followers to be creative and innovative, to question assumptions, and to look at problems and situations in new ways, even if they are different from the leader's ideas. CEO Anne Mulcahy encourages a questioning approach by regularly meeting with Xerox's 500 top managers. Gathering with 80 top managers at a time for several days, Mulcahy says, "The meetings are designed to be critical," to encourage honest, unfiltered discussions, and to realistically face up to problems that need solving. She asks them to tell her what Xerox's weaknesses are and what their major concerns are. In general, said Mulcahy, "They worry about growth, and whether our strategy is sufficient to deliver growth, especially with the economy we're in."[96] In return, Mulcahy also uses these meetings to be brutally candid with her managers regarding their performance where Xerox stands. Said one manager, "Part of her DNA is to tell you the good, the bad, and the ugly."[97]

Individualized consideration means that transformational leaders pay special attention to followers' individual needs by creating learning opportunities, accepting and tolerating individual differences, encouraging two-way communication, and being a good listener. Roy Pelaez supervises 426 Aramark employees who clean airplanes. He believes in attending to employees' needs, saying "Managers are not supposed to get involved with the personal problems of their employees, but I take the opposite view."[98] With morale low and turnover high, he hired a tutor to improve employees' English skills. To keep absences low, he found government programs that provided certified baby-sitters for his low-paid employees. And, he set up three computers so employees could teach each other how to use word processors and spreadsheets. Pelaez said, "All of these things are important, because we want employees who really feel connected to the company." Clearly, they did, as turnover, once near 100 percent per year, dropped to 12 percent after Pelaez paid attention to his employees' needs.

Finally, a distinction needs to be drawn between transformational leadership and transactional leadership. While transformational leaders use visionary and inspirational appeals to influence followers, **transactional leadership** is based on an exchange process, in which followers are rewarded for good performance and punished for poor performance. When leaders administer rewards fairly and offer followers the rewards that they

transactional leadership leadership based on an exchange process, in which followers are rewarded for good performance and punished for poor performance want, followers will often reciprocate with effort. However, transactional leaders often rely too heavily on discipline or threats to bring performance up to standards. While this may work in the short run, it's much less effective in the long run. Many leaders and organizations have difficulty successfully linking pay practices to individual performance. The result is that studies consistently show that transformational leadership is much more effective on average than transactional leadership. In Canada, the United States, Japan, and India, and at all organizational levels, from first-level supervisors to upper-level executives, followers view transformational leaders as much better leaders and are much more satisfied when working for them. Furthermore, companies with transformational leaders have significantly better financial performance.[99]

REVIEW 8: VISIONARY LEADERSHIP

Strategic leadership requires visionary, charismatic, and transformational leadership. Visionary leadership creates a positive image of the future that motivates organizational members and provides direction for future planning and goal setting. Charismatic leaders have strong, confident, dynamic personalities that attract followers, enable them to create strong bonds, and inspire followers to accomplish the leader's vision. Followers of ethical charismatic leaders work harder, are more committed and satisfied, are better performers, are more likely to trust their leaders. Followers can be just as supportive and committed to unethical charismatics, but these leaders can pose a tremendous risk for companies. Unethical charismatics control and manipulate followers and do what is best for themselves instead of their organizations. To reduce the risks associated with unethical charismatics, companies need to enforce a clearly written code of conduct; recruit, select, and promote managers with high ethical standards; train leaders how to value, seek, and use diverse points of view; teach everyone in the company to recognize unethical leader behaviours; and celebrate and reward people who exhibit ethical behaviours. Transformational leadership goes beyond charismatic leadership by generating awareness and acceptance of a group's purpose and mission and by getting employees to see beyond their own needs and self-interest for the good of the group. The four components of transformational leadership are charisma or idealized influence, inspirational motivation, intellectual stimulation, and individualized consideration.

What Really Happened?[100]

At the beginning of the chapter you read about Nortel's meteoric rise and subsequent fall from grace. The board of directors was faced with a huge challenge. They had just fired their CEO and nine other senior executives due to irregularities with the company's financial statements. Auditors had begun the long process of combing through Nortel's financial statements to see if there were further accounting irregularities. Now Nortel was left without a leader and shareholders didn't trust its financial numbers.

While leaders are different from managers, in practice, organizations need them both. Managers are critical to getting out the day-to-day work, and leaders are critical to inspiring employees and setting the organization's long-term direction. The key issue is the extent to which organizations are properly led. The "best" leadership style depends on the situation. In other words, no one leadership behaviour by itself and no one combination of leadership behaviours works well across all situations and employees. Leaders need different combinations of traits given varying circumstances.

Given the difficulties faced by Nortel what sort of leadership traits should the new CEO hold?

Managers have a short-term focus and are concerned with the status quo, with means rather than ends, and with solving others' problems. It could be argued that Nortel's previous CEO was more interested in short-term gains in order to maximize his bonuses and less interested in the longer term. Leaders need to have a long-term focus and be concerned with change, with ends rather than means, and with inspiring and motivating others to solve their own problems. Trait theory says that effective leaders possess a similar set of traits or characteristics. Traits are relatively stable characteristics, such as abilities, psychological motives, or consistent patterns of behaviour. More specifically, leaders are different from nonleaders on the following traits: drive, the desire to lead, honesty/integrity, self-confidence, emotional stability, cognitive ability, and knowledge of the business. Successful leaders also have a stronger desire to lead. They want to be in charge and think about ways to influence or convince others about what should or shouldn't be done. Honesty/integrity is also important to leaders. Honesty—being truthful with others—is a cornerstone of leadership. Without honesty, leaders won't be trusted. But with it, subordinates are willing to overlook other flaws. Integrity is the extent to which leaders do what they said they would do. Leaders may be honest and have good intentions, but if they don't consistently deliver on what they promise, they won't be trusted.

Two major situational leadership theories—Fiedler's contingency theory and Hersey and Blanchard's situational theory—both assume that the effectiveness of any leadership style, the way a leader generally behaves toward followers, depends on the situation. Accordingly, there is no one "best" leadership style. However, these theories differ in one significant way. Fiedler's contingency theory assumes that leadership styles are consistent and difficult to change. Therefore, leaders must be placed in or "matched" to a situation that fits their leadership style.

While charismatic leaders are able to articulate a clear vision, model values consistent with that vision, communicate high performance expectations, and establish very strong relationships between themselves and their followers, transformational leadership goes further by generating awareness and acceptance of a group's purpose and mission and by getting employees to see beyond their own needs and self-interest for the good of the group. Transformational leaders, like charismatic leaders, are visionary.

Unethical charismatics pose a tremendous risk for companies. Followers can be just as supportive and committed to unethical charismatics as they are to ethical charismatics. However, unethical charismatics manipulate followers, do what is best for themselves instead of their organizations, only want to hear positive feedback, only share information that is beneficial to themselves, and have moral standards that put their interests before everyone else's. It is arguable that this was the case at Nortel. Senior managers were interested in managing the company to ensure that the financial statements reflected positively on themselves (and in turn providing them with lucrative bonuses) rather than the long-term leadership of the company. They also fostered a culture that encouraged others to exaggerate Nortel's results.

Given that Nortel has just fired the CEO and other senior managers because of unethical behaviour, what traits should be most required by the CEO?

Clearly, the company was in dire need of leadership by someone with a clearly ethical orientation and undoubted integrity. Investor confidence was at an all-time low. There was a feeling that Nortel's financial statements could not be trusted. It seemed more important that ethics be a driving force rather than industry knowledge. Nortel's board of directors realized this and offered the job to Bill Owens.

Mr. Owens did not have any direct industry experience nor was he a turnaround specialist. His job was to clean up the company's image and restore investor confidence. He had grown up in a poor family and had joined the U.S. Navy after being accepted into the Naval Academy in Annapolis. He obtained an engineering degree and because he finished in the top 10 percent of his class, he was assigned to the Navy's new and growing elite nuclear submarine fleet. He became known for his intelligence, honesty, and forthrightness. In 1970, when he was selected by the Navy to attend Oxford University, he was summoned to a senior admiral's office. The admiral, known to be extremely tough and to always get his way, demanded that Owens study physics, a very useful subject for a nuclear submariner. Owens told him in no uncertain terms that he was going to study economics, philosophy, and politics. Owens got his way and exhibited the honesty and forthrightness that went on to mark his career.

Owens went on to rise through the ranks, ending up as the second highest-ranking officer in the U.S. military (not just the Navy) as the vice-chairman of the Joint Chiefs of Staff. He was known to encourage his subordinates and lead by example. He also led a cultural change in the military that broke down barriers between the branches of the armed services (Army, Navy, Air Force, and Marines), a very difficult task that met with a great deal of resistance.

Taking the CEO's job at Nortel was not an easy decision for him, but he felt a great deal of loyalty toward the organization, as he was on the board of directors and had seen first-hand the difficulties that the company was going through. He decided that for the sake of the company he needed to take the job. He set the tone at Nortel immediately when he hired Susan Shepard, a lawyer from New York, and a former federal U.S. prosecutor, to become the company's chief ethics officer. This provided a strong signal that ethical behaviour would be a key element of Nortel's expectations of employees' behaviour. It was a move widely welcomed by industry analysts and business professors. Ms. Shepard was not the first ethics czar at Nortel. The first was marginalized under former CEO John Roth, and the old ethics policy was largely collecting dust. The change in leadership and emphasis under Bill Owens symbolized a change in the direction of the company.

In addition, Mr. Owens supported a move to revisit Nortel's books for any misstatement of earnings and its accounting practices. There seemed to be systemic cultural problems that encouraged the aggressive accounting practices that got Nortel in trouble. He had to change the culture of the organization. He set firm deadlines for the restatement of financial numbers, which in many cases he ended up missing, but he was seen as injecting integrity back into Nortel's financial statements even if it took longer than anticipated. It was clear that investors needed the correct numbers rather than fast numbers. In many ways his vision and goal for the company was to restore trust, confidence, and integrity in the company. Shortly after Owens became the CEO, the company's share price stabilized in the $3 to $4 range and the company released new (revised) financial numbers that withstood investor scrutiny. Despite getting the company on stable footing, he was not seen as the person to do the job over the long term. With stability gained through Owens's leadership, the board of directors now felt it was time for someone with more industry experience to lead the company into a growth phase. Owens voluntarily stepped down in October 2005 to make way for Mike Zafiroski. He had helped turn around Motorola and had been a 25-year veteran of General Electric, which had seen phenomenal growth while he was there. Shortly after Zafiroski's appointment, he began tapping other former General Electric senior managers in an attempt yet again to return the company to its roots as industry leaders. At the time of writing, it is unclear how successful he will be, but the two changes in leadership demonstrate how leadership traits need to be matched to the circumstances of the job.

Key Terms

charismatic leadership *(470)*
consideration *(461)*
contingency theory *(463)*
distributive justice *(451)*
equity theory *(447)*
ethical charismatics *(471)*
expectancy *(452)*
expectancy theory *(452)*
extrinsic reward *(444)*
initiating structure *(461)*
inputs *(448)*
instrumentality *(452)*
intrinsic reward *(444)*
leader-member relations *(466)*
leadership *(454)*
leadership neutralizers *(456)*
leadership substitutes *(456)*
motivation *(440)*
needs *(442)*
outcome/input (O/I) ratio *(448)*
outcomes *(448)*
overreward *(448)*
procedural justice *(451)*
referents *(448)*
situational favourableness *(465)*
situational theory *(468)*
strategic leadership *(470)*
task structure *(466)*
trait theory *(458)*
traits *(458)*
transactional leadership *(473)*
transformational leadership *(472)*
underreward *(448)*
valence *(452)*
visionary leadership *(470)*
worker readiness *(468)*

Self-Assessment

WHAT DO YOU NEED?

What people want out of their jobs is as varied as the jobs themselves. And as you would expect, needs theory shows why not everyone wants to be CEO. Take the example of the woman who is extremely organized and efficient in her job as an assistant. She is so effective that she is offered a promotion to management, but she turns it down flatly, saying that she has no interest in moving up the ladder, that she is happy doing what she does. What she needs from work clearly differs from the needs of the person who jumps at every opportunity to move up the corporate hierarchy. Which needs most motivate you? The Assessment Appendix has a survey designed to give you insights into how strongly different needs motivate you. Go to page 520 and complete the questionnaire.

Management Decisions

SUBBING FOR LEADERS

Six months ago when you accepted the job as the president of a small marketing agency, you knew that it would be a tough task. You had no idea, however, that it would be nearly impossible. While interviewing, you conducted some basic research and found that even though the company was profitable, it had a bad reputation of not playing fair in the advertising industry. Many people that you talked to voiced their concerns about the firm, saying that its people were sneaky, backstabbing individuals who would stop at nothing to make a buck. Despite their concerns, you accepted the position, assuming that their perceptions were somewhat biased.

Unfortunately, soon after your arrival, you began to realize that many people's perceptions might not have been far off base. Initially, George, your assistant and the vice president of the company, seemed like a good guy—a little different, possibly even abrasive, but otherwise an okay person. At first his personality didn't pose a problem. Then you began to hear conversations about George's reliance on punishment and manipulation to ensure that the marketing sales force increased their sales revenue each quarter. In fact, the more you listened, the more you heard, and the uneasier you became.

As you began to watch George more closely, you realized that he was definitely an ends-versus-the-means person. His main focus was on increasing advertising dollars for the firm (and eventually for himself), regardless of the tactics used. You also began to notice that during important meetings discussing current customers' marketing strategies, George always did a majority of the talking. Anyone who attempted to interject ideas inconsistent with George's was immediately cut off and publicly scolded. In fact, this morning as you walked past one such meeting, you overheard John, a junior-level marketing agent, propose a new strategy for an important customer. George replied to John in front of the group, saying, "Now you folks see why John is only a junior-level agent after working over 12 years with this firm. Does anyone else have any stupid comments to offer, or can we move on with our meeting?"

As you stood outside the conference room, you realized that something must be done to change the culture, perception, and success of this firm. Clearly, things can't continue as is, but George is a valuable employee despite his shortcomings. Maybe you should have a talk with him about what you expect from leaders. Resolving the problem may mean better matching George's leadership style to another work group within the company. Is that even feasible? You really need to change the culture inside the firm and the perception of the firm from outside. If not, the very existence of the firm will be on the line.

Questions

1. What should your expectation be of George as a leader? Is he meeting this expectation?
2. What type of leadership style is George exhibiting? Do you move George out of the leadership role, or do you coach him to change? If you coach him, what leadership style do you try to cultivate in him?
3. Which leadership substitutes could you develop to insulate your company from leadership gaps, such as the one described above?

Management Decisions

EMPLOYEE OF THE MONTH!

As you get back to your desk with your third cup of coffee this morning, your boss stops at your desk in the middle of his morning rounds. He says, "Hey, you've got a degree in management, don't you? Heck, even if you don't, you're probably more up to date on all these new motivational theories and ideas than I am. Here's what I want. We need an employee-of-the-month award for our clerical employees. I want to boost their morale and motivate them to work harder and do their jobs better! So take a couple of weeks and design a basic employee award program, but make sure that it's got an employee-of-the-month award in it. That's the key. Have it on my desk two weeks from Friday." Before you can say yes, he's off to another co-worker's desk, to give her some other assignment that he brainstormed last night. You're not even sure he heard you say, "Sure, Mr. Smith, no problem."

However, what you really wanted to say was, "I don't know, Mr. Smith. I've never seen an employee-of-the-month award motivate anyone." In fact, no one really seemed to care about being employee-of-the-month in the places you had worked before, even when there was a small amount of cash involved. You think to yourself, "Well, if he wants an employee-of-the-month award, I'll make sure that's in there. But there have got to be better ways to motivate the clerical staff. I'm just going to have to figure out what those are."

Questions

1. What is wrong with many employee-of-the-month award programs? Why wouldn't they be particularly effective at motivating employees?
2. Describe the three most important steps you'd take to motivate the clerical staff in your office. Explain what the steps are, the reasoning behind them, and what they're meant to accomplish. Be specific.

Develop Your Management Potential

SHOW ME THE NONCASH REWARDS?

"Show me the money! Show me the money!" Lots of managers mistakenly assume that money is the primary motivator for most employees. However, studies regularly show that while money affects people's decisions to take or leave jobs, it is not one of the primary motivators once someone has a job.

New managers also assume that they'll have access to the money they need to "really motivate" their workers. This is wrong in two ways. First, most managers are given a pool of money to allocate among all employees as raises. So if they give one employee a large raise, they have less money for other raises. Second, psychological studies show that pay increases must be at least 15 to 20 percent before employees really feel that they've got a substantial increase in pay. In other words, with most annual pay raises between 2 and 4 percent, most managers simply aren't given the money they need to create the wow-what-a-great-raise reaction they want from their employees.

As a result of these factors, more and more managers are turning to noncash rewards to motivate their employees.

Questions

1. Develop a list of ten creative, noncash rewards that would be effective in motivating employees. If you're not sure what would be effective, think of the things that motivate you and your friends. You also might want to ask two or three managers about the noncash rewards they offer their employees.
2. Describe how you would administer each of these rewards. In other words, explain when and why you would give employees these particular rewards. Be specific.

Discussion Questions

1. Think back on the jobs that you have had. What sorts of things did the companies you worked for do to motivate you? Did they work? Why or why not?
2. Have you ever felt underrewarded in a job? Why did you feel underrewarded? What could have been done to address the perceived inequity?
3. What is the difference between a leader and a manager? Provide specific examples.
4. Provide examples of good leaders. What characteristics make them good leaders?

Critical Thinking Video Case

CBC

Visit www.management2e.nelson.com to view this chapter's CBC video case.

Take Two

Biz Flix
U-571

This action-packed thriller deals with a U.S. submarine crew's efforts to retrieve an Enigma encryption device from a disabled German submarine during World War II. After the crew gets the device, the U.S. submarine sinks, and they must use the German submarine to escape from enemy destroyers. The film's almost nonstop action and extraordinary special effects will look and sound best with a home theatre system. This scene is an edited composite of the "To Be a Captain" sequence early in the film. The S33, an older U.S. submarine, is embarking on a secret mission. Before departure, the S33's officers receive a briefing on their mission from Office of Naval Intelligence representatives on board. Executive officer Lt. Andrew Tyler (Matthew McConaughey) reports on the submarine's status to Lt. Commander Mike Dahlgren (Bill Paxton). The film continues with the S33 finding the disabled German submarine.

What to Watch for and Ask Yourself

1. What aspects of leadership does Dahlgren say are important for a submarine commander?
2. Which leadership behaviours or traits does he emphasize?
3. Are these traits or behaviours right for this situation? Why or why not?

Management Workplace
Modern Postcard

Modern Postcard prides itself in being able to turn around a customer's order in two days. That means designing the postcard, printing it, and mailing it out to the addresses on the customer's mailing list. For a company that produces 100 million postcards a year for some 150 000 customers, that's quite a feat, even for a company with a digital work flow. How can a company motivate 250 employees to act so quickly to serve customers? Founder Steve Hoffman and his management team use several techniques to encourage employees to always do their best work.

What to Watch for and Ask Yourself

1. Which motivational theory best describes the practices at Modern Postcard?
2. How is Steve Hoffman using path-goal theory? Are there elements of the theory for which Hoffman does not have related business practice? If so, how could Modern Postcard fill these gaps?
3. What role do the Image Awards play in motivating the employees at Modern Postcard?

© AMY ETRA/PHOTOEDIT

Managing Communication

Chapter 16

CHAPTER OUTLINE

Communication

- **Perception and Communication Problems**
  - Basic Perception Process
  - Perception Problems
  - Perceptions of Others
  - Self-Perception
- **Kinds of Communication**
  - The Communication Process
  - Formal Communication Channels
  - Informal Communication Channels
  - Coaching and Counselling: One-on-One Communication
  - Nonverbal Communication

Improving Communication

- **Managing One-on-One Communication**
  - Choosing the Right Communication Medium
  - Listening
  - Giving Feedback
  - Improving Cross-Cultural Communication
- **Managing Organization-Wide Communication**
  - Improving Transmission: Getting the Message Out
  - Improving Reception: Hearing What Others Feel and Think

LEARNING OBJECTIVES

After reading this chapter, you should be able to

1. explain the role that perception plays in communication and communication problems.
2. describe the communication process and the various kinds of communication in organizations.
3. explain how managers can manage effective one-on-one communication.
4. describe how managers can manage effective organization-wide communication.

What Would You Do?

Procter & Gamble, otherwise known as P&G, has been in business since 1837. P&G sells some of the world's best-known household and consumer brands, including Tide detergent, Folger's coffee, Crest toothpaste, Charmin toilet paper, Bounty paper towels, Head & Shoulders shampoo, Ivory soap, and Pampers diapers. You've worked for P&G for 25 years and just became its CEO a month ago. What an intense month it's been. Your predecessor, Durk Jager, had been CEO for only 17 months, the shortest tenure for any P&G CEO.[1]

Jager moved aggressively to change P&G, but the company struggled under his leadership. Hoping to find the next billion-dollar brand (like Tide), he encouraged departments to set "stretch goals" for big improvements (see Chapter 4). But then he allowed them to base their budgets on those targets, long before the targets were reached. Consequently, overspending was rife, as costs grew much faster than revenues. Jager also tried to "globalize" P&G's brands, for instance, by changing the name of P&G's dishwashing liquid in Germany from Fairy, as it was known there, to Dawn, as it was known in North America. Since German consumers weren't familiar with the Dawn brand, sales dropped drastically. Finally, Jager, who had a reputation for being hard driving and abrasive, had trouble getting P&G's 103 000 employees and managers to fully buy into his plans. One consultant said, "Durk tried to move too fast and didn't listen to his people." In the end, P&G's stock lost a total of US$70 billion in value while Jager was CEO.

Unfortunately, the "market" wasn't any happier when P&G announced that you would replace Jager. P&G's stock dropped US$4 from US$62 to US$58 on your first day on the job and was at US$53 at the end of your first month. However, the market wasn't reacting so much to you as to the serious problems facing P&G: encouraging talented managers to stay (25 percent of brand managers had left the company); calming upset brand managers in Europe (who had watched their sales dive thanks to the failed brand globalization efforts); finding ways to improve sales of P&G's leading brands; and simplifying P&G's organizational structure (which had assumed a confusing matrix structure over the last few years).

At this point, though, you feel you've got a fairly good plan to fix these problems. First, you're going to refocus P&G on its core, the ten billion-dollar brands, like Tide and Pampers, that account for most of its sales and revenues. That should simplify things for everyone. Next, globalization of brands is over. Although there will still be a focus on innovation, the company will try for smaller successes instead of trying to hit home runs by developing new blockbuster billion-dollar brands. The internal focus will be on innovating with existing products, while the external focus will be on acquiring innovative ideas and brands from outside the company. Finally, in a symbolic move, you're redoing P&G's legendary 11th floor, home to the company's top executives. Two-thirds of the space is being turned into a learning centre, and the rest will house those same top-level executives in open offices that, in theory, will make it easier for them to communicate with each other. Those changes should get you off to a good start and help turn around the company. The hard part, though, will be changing the pattern of communication throughout the company. People are still stinging from the hard-charging, combative approach of your predecessor, so you need to find a way to make regular P&G employees feel comfortable communicating with top management again. What's the best way to do that? And, with a history of centralized authority in which P&G management sent marching orders from headquarters, the traditional focus has been on "getting the message out." But that's only half the communication formula. These days, it's also important to "improve reception" by finding out what others feel and think. So how can P&G do a better job of hearing what people inside the company feel and think? Likewise, with an emphasis on its core brands and small-scale innovation, how can P&G do a better job of hearing what people outside the company feel and think?

If you were the new CEO of Procter & Gamble, what would you do?

It's estimated that managers spend over 80 percent of their day communicating with others.[2] Indeed, much of the basic management process—making things happen, meeting the competition, organizing people, projects, and processes, and leading—cannot be performed without effective communication. According to Bill Black, former president of Maritime Life, which is now part of Manulife Financial, "One of the three or four central jobs of the CEO is communications. A very substantial part of your accountability as a CEO is to communicate with stakeholders such as employees and customers. People want the CEO to communicate the strategic issues-the 'big picture' questions. For things happening at the corporate level, they want to hear it from the top."[3] If this weren't reason enough to study communication, consider that oral communication, such as listening, following instructions, conversing, and giving feedback, is the most important skill for college graduates who are entering the work force.[4] Furthermore, across all industries, poor communication skill is the single most important reason that people do not advance in their careers.[5] Finally, communication is especially important for top managers. In a study of Canadian CFOs, 64 percent said that the biggest challenge their companies face is a lack of communication with staff.[6] Without a doubt, the issue is one all managers should be concerned about.

This chapter begins by examining the role of perception in communication and how perception can make it difficult for managers to achieve effective communication. Next, you'll read about the communication process and the various kinds of communication found in most organizations. In the last half of the chapter, the focus is on improving communication in organizations. You'll learn about the significant barriers to effective one-on-one communication and organization-wide communication. But, more importantly, you'll learn ways to overcome those barriers, too.

Communication

Whenever Kristy Keith's boss would say, "Today is a good day for change," she knew that bad news, such as layoffs or losing a client, was sure to follow. Keith said that "It was comforting to some people who didn't know better," but that the experienced employees "got back to their offices and huddled" to discuss what her boss's news really meant (and it usually wasn't good).[7] Many bosses try to make bad news sound good with phrases like "rightsizing" for layoffs, "merger of equals" for another company has acquired ours, "pursuing other interests" for employees who were fired, and "cost efficiencies" for your job is being outsourced to India. Why do managers sugarcoat bad news when communicating? Because, says management professor Paul Argenti, they think, "They'll get less flak."

communication
the process of transmitting information from one person or place to another

Communication is the process of transmitting information from one person or place to another. While some bosses sugarcoat bad news, smart managers understand that in the end effective, straightforward communication between managers and employees is essential for success.

After reading the next two sections, you should be able to

1. explain the role that perception plays in communication and communication problems.
2. describe the communication process and the various kinds of communication in organizations.

1 PERCEPTION AND COMMUNICATION PROBLEMS

One study showed that when asked whether their supervisor gives recognition for good work, 13 percent of employees said that their supervisor gives a pat on the back, while 14 percent said that their supervisor gives sincere and thorough praise. But when the supervisors of these employees were asked if they give recognition for good work, 82 percent said they gave pats on the back, while 80 percent said that they give sincere and thorough praise.[8] Given that these managers and employees worked closely together, how could they have had such different perceptions of something as simple as praise?

Let's learn more about perception and communication problems by examining the basic perception process, perception problems, perceptions of others, and self-perception.

Basic Perception Process

As shown in Exhibit 16.1, **perception** is the process by which individuals attend to, organize, interpret, and retain information from their environments. And since communication is the process of transmitting information from one person or place to another, perception is obviously a key part of communication. However, perception can be a key obstacle to communication, as well.

perception
the process by which individuals attend to, organize, interpret, and retain information from their environments

As people perform their jobs, they are exposed to a wide variety of informational stimuli, such as e-mails, direct conversations with the boss or co-workers, rumours heard over lunch, stories about the company in the press, or a video broadcast of a speech from the CEO to all employees. However, exposure to an informational stimulus is no guarantee that an individual will pay attention or attend to that stimulus. People experience stimuli through their own **perceptual filters**—the personality-, psychology-, or experience-based differences that influence them to ignore or pay attention to particular stimuli. Because of filtering, people exposed to the same information will often disagree about what they saw or heard. For example, almost every major football stadium or hockey rink has a huge TV monitor on which fans can watch replays. As the slow-motion video is replayed on the monitor, you can often hear cheers and boos, as fans of both teams perceive the same replay in completely different ways. This happens because the fans' perceptual filters predispose them to attend to stimuli that support their team and not their opponents. And the same perceptual filters that affect whether we believe our favourite team was "robbed" by the referees also affect communication. As shown in Exhibit 16.1,

perceptual filters
the personality-, psychology-, or experience-based differences that influence people to ignore or pay attention to particular stimuli

EXHIBIT 16.1
Basic Perception Process

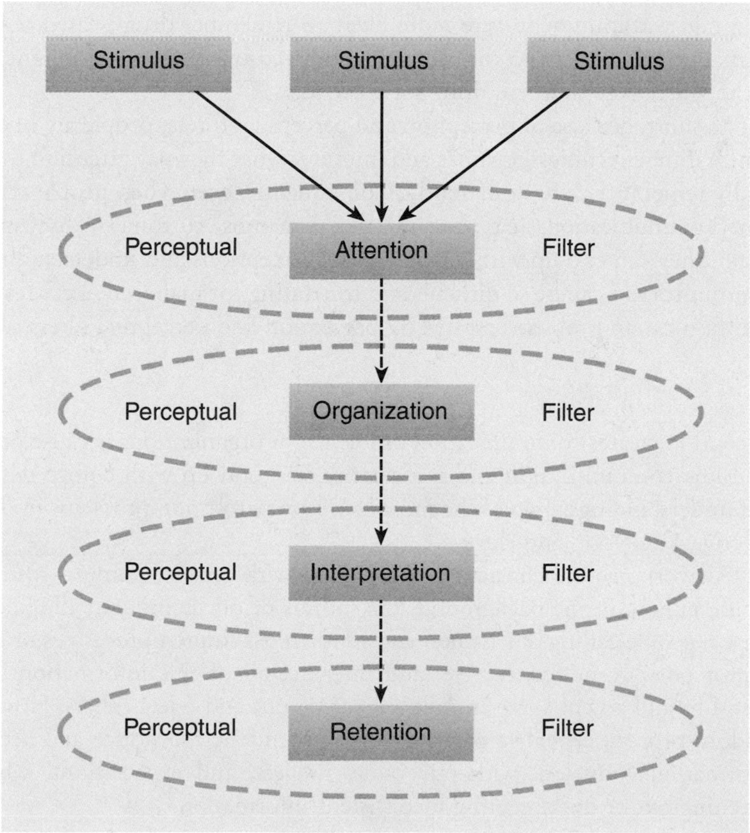

perceptual filters affect each part of the perception process: attention, organization, interpretation, and retention.

Attention is the process of noticing or becoming aware of particular stimuli. Because of perceptual filters, we attend to some stimuli and not others. *Organization* is the process of incorporating new information (from the stimuli that you notice) into your existing knowledge. Because of perceptual filters, we are more likely to incorporate new knowledge that is consistent with what we already know or believe. *Interpretation* is the process of attaching meaning to new knowledge. Because of perceptual filters, our preferences and beliefs strongly influence the meaning we attach to new information (e.g., "This must mean that top management supports our project"). Finally, *retention* is the process of remembering interpreted information. In other words, retention is what we recall and commit to memory after we have perceived something. Of course, perceptual filters also affect retention—that is, what we're likely to remember in the end.

For instance, imagine that you missed the first ten minutes of a TV show and that you turned on your TV to a scene in which two people were talking to each other in a living room. As they talked, they walked around the room and picked up and then put down various items, some of which were valuable, such as a ring, a watch, and a credit card, and some of which appeared to be drug related, such as a water pipe for smoking marijuana. In fact, this situation was depicted on videotape in a well-known study that manipulated people's perceptual filters.[9] One-third of the study participants were told that these people were there to rob the apartment. Another third of the participants were told that police were on their way to conduct a drug raid and that the people in the apartment were getting rid of incriminating evidence. The remaining third of study participants were told that these people were simply waiting for a friend to show up.

After watching the video, participants were asked to list all of the objects from the video that they could remember. Not surprisingly, the different perceptual filters (theft, drug raid, and waiting for a friend) affected what the study participants attended to, how they organized the information, how they interpreted the information, and ultimately what objects they remembered from the video. People who thought a theft was in process were more likely to remember the valuable objects in the video. Those who thought a drug raid was imminent were more likely to remember drug-related objects. There was no discernable pattern to the items remembered by those who thought that the people in the video were simply waiting for a friend.

In short, because of perception and perceptual filters, people are likely to pay attention to different things, organize and interpret what they pay attention to differently, and finally remember things differently. Consequently, even when people are exposed to the same communications (e.g., organizational memos, customers, discussions with managers), they can end up with very different perceptions and understandings. This is why communication can be so difficult and frustrating for managers. Let's review some of the communication problems created by perception and perceptual filters.

Perception Problems

Perception creates communication problems for organizations because people exposed to the same communication and information can end up with completely different ideas and understandings. Two of the most common perception problems in organizations are selective perception and closure.

selective perception
the tendency to notice and accept objects and information consistent with our values, beliefs, and expectations, while ignoring or screening out or not accepting inconsistent information

At work, we are constantly bombarded with sensory stimuli—the phone ringing, people talking in the background, the sounds of our computers dinging as new e-mail arrives, people calling our names, and so forth. As limited processors of information, we cannot possibly notice, receive, and interpret all of this information. As a result, we attend to and accept some stimuli but screen out and reject others. However, this isn't a random process. **Selective perception** is the tendency to notice and accept objects and information consistent with our values, beliefs, and expectations, while ignoring or screening out or not accepting inconsistent information.

Once we have initial information about a person, event, or process, **closure** is the tendency to fill in the gaps where information is missing, that is, to assume that what we don't know is consistent with what we already know. If employees are told that budgets must be cut by 10 percent, they may automatically assume that 10 percent of employees will lose their jobs, too, even if that isn't the case. Not surprisingly, when closure occurs, people sometimes "fill in the gaps" with inaccurate information, and this can create problems for organizations.

closure
the tendency to fill in gaps of missing information by assuming that what we don't know is consistent with what we already know

Perceptions of Others

Attribution theory says that we all have a basic need to understand and explain the causes of other people's behaviour.[10] In other words, we need to know why people do what they do. And, according to attribution theory, we use two general reasons or attributions to explain people's behaviour: an internal attribution, in which behaviour is thought to be voluntary or under the control of the individual, and an external attribution, in which behaviour is thought to be involuntary and outside the control of the individual.

attribution theory
theory that states that we all have a basic need to understand and explain the causes of other people's behaviour

For example, have you ever seen anyone changing a flat tire on the side of the road and thought to yourself, "What rotten luck—somebody's having a bad day"? If you did, you perceived the person through an external attribution known as the defensive bias. The **defensive bias** is the tendency for people to perceive themselves as personally and situationally similar to someone who is having difficulty or trouble.[11] And when we identify with the person in a situation, we tend to use external attributions (i.e., the situation) to explain the person's behaviour. For instance, since flat tires are fairly common, it's easy to perceive ourselves in that same situation and put the blame on external causes, such as running over a nail.

defensive bias
the tendency for people to perceive themselves as personally and situationally similar to someone who is having difficulty or trouble

Now, let's assume a different situation, this time in the workplace:

> A utility company worker puts a ladder on a utility pole and then climbs up to do his work. As he's doing his work, he falls from the ladder and seriously injures himself.[12]

Answer this question: Who or what caused the accident? If you thought, "It's not the worker's fault. Anybody could fall from a tall ladder," then you're still operating from a defensive bias in which you see yourself as personally and situationally similar to someone who is having difficulty or trouble. In other words, you made an external attribution and attributed the accident to an external cause, meaning the situation.

In reality, however, most accident investigations end up blaming the worker (i.e., an internal attribution) and not the situation (i.e., an external attribution) in which people do their jobs. Typically, 60 percent to 80 percent of workplace accidents that occur each year are blamed on "operator error," that is, the employees themselves. However, more complete investigations usually show that workers are really only responsible for 30 percent to 40 percent of all workplace accidents.[13] Why would accident investigators be so quick to blame workers? Because they are committing the **fundamental attribution error**, which is the tendency to ignore external causes of behaviour and to attribute other people's actions to internal causes.[14] In other words, when investigators examine the possible causes of an accident, they're much more likely to assume that the accident is a function of the person and not the situation.

fundamental attribution error
the tendency to ignore external causes of behaviour and to attribute other people's actions to internal causes

Which attribution, the defensive bias or the fundamental attribution error, are workers likely to make when something goes wrong? In general, workers are more likely to perceive events and explain behaviour from a defensive bias. Because they do the work themselves, and because they see themselves as similar to others who make mistakes, have accidents, or are otherwise held responsible for things that go wrong at work, workers are likely to attribute problems to external causes, such as failed machinery, poor support, or inadequate training. By contrast, because they are typically observers (who don't do the work themselves), and see themselves as situationally and personally different from workers, managers tend to commit the fundamental attribution error and blame mistakes, accidents, and other things that go wrong on workers (i.e., an internal attribution).

Consequently, in most workplaces, when things go wrong, the natural response is one in which workers and managers can be expected to take completely opposite views. Therefore, together, the defensive bias, which is typically used by workers, and the fundamental attribution error, which is typically made by managers, represent a significant challenge to effective communication and understanding in organizations.

Self-Perception

A manager at a large oil company decided that he wanted to find a way to help his poor-performing employees improve their performance. So he sat down with each one of them and, in a positive, nonconfrontational way, explained that "I'm here to help you improve." Most of his employees took his offer in the spirit it was meant and accepted his help. However, one employee burst into tears because no one had ever told her that her performance needed improvement. In fact, her hour-long outburst was so emotional that her manager decided that he would never "criticize" her again.[15]

self-serving bias
the tendency to overestimate our value by attributing successes to ourselves (internal causes) and attributing failures to others or the environment (external causes)

The **self-serving bias** is the tendency to overestimate our value by attributing successes to ourselves (internal causes) and attributing failures to others or the environment (external causes).[16] As the example with the upset oil company employee illustrates, the self-serving bias can make it especially difficult for managers to talk to employees about performance problems. In general, people have a need to maintain a positive self-image. This need is so strong that when people seek feedback at work, they typically want verification of their worth (rather than information about performance deficiencies) or assurance that mistakes or problems haven't been their fault.[17] And when managerial communication threatens people's positive self-image, they can become defensive and emotional. In turn, they quit listening, and communication becomes ineffective. In the second half of the chapter, which focuses on improving communication, we'll explain ways in which managers can minimize this self-serving bias and improve effective one-on-one communication with employees.

REVIEW 1: PERCEPTION AND COMMUNICATION PROBLEMS

Perception is the process by which people attend to, organize, interpret, and retain information from their environments. However, perception is not a straightforward process. Because of perceptual filters, such as selective perception and closure, people exposed to the same information stimuli often end up with very different perceptions and understandings. Perception-based differences can also lead to differences in the attributions (internal or external) that managers and workers make when explaining workplace behaviour. In general, workers are more likely to explain behaviour from a defensive bias, in which they attribute problems to external causes (i.e., the situation). Managers, on the other hand, tend to commit the fundamental attribution error, attributing problems to internal causes (i.e., the worker associated with a mistake or error). Consequently, when things go wrong, it's common for managers to blame workers and for workers to blame the situation or context in which they do their jobs. Finally, this problem is compounded by a self-serving bias that leads people to attribute successes to internal causes and failures to external causes. So when workers receive negative feedback from managers, they can become defensive and emotional and not hear what their managers have to say. In short, perceptions and attributions represent a significant challenge to effective communication and understanding in organizations.

2 KINDS OF COMMUNICATION

In a Toronto manufacturing plant a janitor accidentally mixed chemicals that produced a toxic cloud. As the fumes wafted through the building, workers thought that someone had pulled a stink bomb prank but as the chemical smell intensified, employees' eyes started to water and some had difficulty breathing. The occupational health and safety officer had not been told what the problem was and just recommended that the windows and doors be opened to provide some ventilation. Soon it became clear that the problem was serious and the supervisor had to clear the building, but not before many of the workers had been subjected to enough toxic fumes to be hospitalized. If there had been better communication, the janitor may not have mixed the chemicals that created the problem. If there had been better communication after the accident, no one would likely have been hospitalized.[18]

In this situation, the communication process between senders and receivers broke down at some point. However, this isn't surprising. Miscommunication is possible with every kind of communication, even simple things. For example, Americans travelling in Canada are often confused when asked by a waiter or waitress if they want "brown bread" with their meal (in the United States, they usually call it "whole wheat"), often leaving them puzzled over their breakfast toast.[19]

Let's learn more about the different kinds of communication by examining the communication process, formal communication channels, informal communication channels, one-on-one communication, and nonverbal communication.

The Communication Process

Earlier in the chapter, we defined communication as the process of transmitting information from one person or place to another. Exhibit 16.2 displays a model of the communication process and its major components: the sender (message to be conveyed, encoding the message, transmitting the message), the receiver (received message, decoded message, and the message that was understood), and noise, which interferes with the communication process.

The communication process begins when a sender thinks of a message he or she wants to convey to another person. This could be what the sender wants someone else to know ("The meeting has been changed to 3:00 P.M."), to do ("Make sure to include last quarter's financial information in the proposal"), or not to do ("Sorry, the budget is tight. You'll have to fly economy rather than business class"). The next step is to encode the message. **Encoding** means putting a message into a written, oral, or symbolic form that can be recognized and understood by the receiver. The sender then transmits the message via *communication channels*, such as the telephone or face-to-face communication, which allow the sender to receive immediate feedback; or e-mail (text messages and file attachments), fax, beepers, voice-mail, memos, and letters, in which senders must wait for receivers to respond.

encoding
putting a message into a written, oral, or symbolic form that can be recognized and understood by the receiver

If the message is received—and because of technical difficulties (e.g., fax down, dead battery on the mobile phone, inability to read e-mail attachments) or people-based

EXHIBIT 16.2
The Interpersonal Communication Process

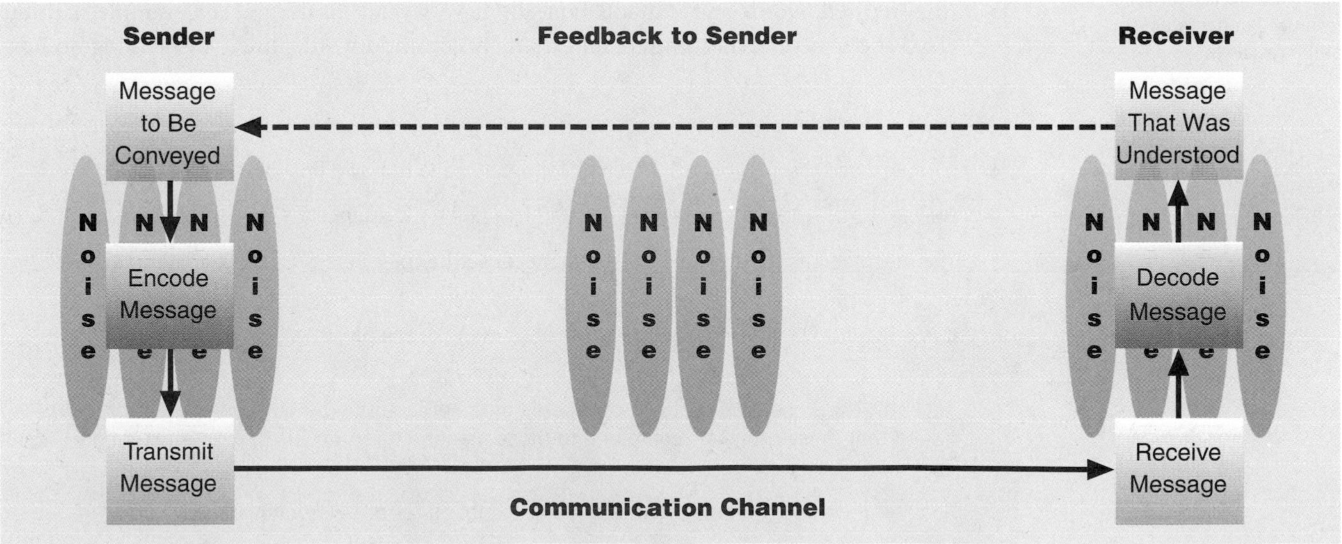

decoding
the process by which the receiver translates the written, oral, or symbolic form of a message into an understood message

feedback
in the communication process, a return message to the sender that indicates the receiver's understanding of the message

noise
anything that interferes with the transmission of the intended message

conduit metaphor
the mistaken assumption that senders can pipe their intended messages directly into the heads of receivers with perfect clarity and without noise or perceptual filters interfering with the receivers' understanding of the message

transmission problems (e.g., forgetting to pass on the message), messages often aren't received—the next step is for the receiver to decode the message. **Decoding** is the process by which the receiver translates the written, oral, or symbolic form of the message into an understood message. However, the message, as understood by the receiver, isn't always the same message that was intended by the sender. Because of different experiences or perceptual filters, receivers may attach a completely different meaning to a message than was intended. A North American baby food company tried to market its product in Africa where, due to the relatively high rate of illiteracy, the custom was to place a picture of the product on the label. They put a picture of a baby on the jar, leading the local population to think that the jars contained ground-up babies. Needless to say, sales were not great.[20] Something got lost in the decoding.

The last step of the communication process occurs when the receiver gives the sender feedback. **Feedback** is a return message to the sender that indicates the receiver's understanding of the message (of what the receiver was supposed to know, to do, or not to do). Feedback makes senders aware of possible miscommunications and enables them to continue communicating until the receiver understands the intended message.

Unfortunately, feedback doesn't always occur in the communication process. Complacency and overconfidence about the ease and simplicity of communication can lead senders and receivers to simply assume that they share a common understanding of the message and to not use feedback to improve the effectiveness of their communication. This is a serious mistake, especially since messages and feedback are always transmitted with and against a background of noise. **Noise** is anything that interferes with the transmission of the intended message. Noise can occur if

1. the sender isn't sure about what message to communicate.
2. the message is not clearly encoded.
3. the wrong communication channel is chosen.
4. the message is not received or decoded properly.
5. the receiver doesn't have the experience or time to understand the message.

When managers wrongly assume that communication is easy, they reduce communication to something called the "conduit metaphor."[21] Strictly speaking, a conduit is a pipe or tube that protects electrical wire. The **conduit metaphor** refers to the mistaken assumption that senders can pipe their intended messages directly into the heads of receivers with perfect clarity and without noise or perceptual filters interfering with the receivers' understanding of the message. However, this just isn't possible. Even if managers could telepathically direct their thoughts straight into receivers' heads, there would still be misunderstandings and communication problems because, depending on how they're used, words and symbols typically have several meanings. For example, Exhibit 16.3 shows several meanings of an extremely common word, "fine." Depending on how

EXHIBIT 16.3
Meanings of the Word "Fine"

1.	If you exceed the 100 km/h speed limit, you may have to pay a fine (meaning a penalty).
2.	During the playoffs, Mario Lemieux turned in a fine performance (meaning excellent).
3.	The machine has to run at a slow speed, because the tolerance is extremely fine (meaning delicate).
4.	It is difficult to put this puzzle together, since many of the pieces are so fine (meaning small).
5.	Recently, experiments have been conducted on manufacturing certain drugs in space. It is hoped that these drugs, as compared to those manufactured on Earth, will be extremely fine (meaning pure).
6.	Be careful when you handle that antique book. Its pages are extremely fine (meaning flimsy).

you use it, "fine" can mean a penalty, a good job, or that something is delicate, small, pure, or flimsy. Many years ago someone received a parking ticket for parking in an area with a sign saying, "Fine for Parking." He fought the ticket, arguing that the sign meant that it was a good place to park. The judge did not agree, although one can see the potential ambiguity of the language used on the sign.

In summary, the conduit metaphor causes problems in communication by making managers too complacent and confident in their ability to easily and accurately transfer messages to receivers. Managers who want to be effective communicators need to carefully choose words and symbols that will help receivers derive the intended meaning of a message. Furthermore, they need to be aware of all the steps of the communication process, beginning with the sender (message to be conveyed, encoding the message, transmitting the message) and ending with the receiver (received message, decoded message, understanding the message, and using feedback to communicate what was understood).

Formal Communication Channels

The **formal communication channel** is the system of official channels that carry organizationally approved messages and information. Organizational objectives, rules, policies, procedures, instructions, commands, and requests for information are all transmitted via the formal communication system or "channel." There are three formal communication channels: downward communication, upward communication, and horizontal communication.[22]

formal communication channel
the system of official channels that carry organizationally approved messages and information

Downward communication flows from higher to lower levels in an organization. Downward communication is used to issue orders down the organizational hierarchy, to give organizational members job-related information, to give managers and workers performance reviews from upper managers, and to make clear organizational objectives and goals.[23] When an economic downturn quickly produced a significant drop in sales at Agilent, a technology company, CEO Ned Barnholt pulled together his top managers. Together, they decided that their first strategy would be to freeze hiring, cut expenses, and cut temporary workers. Then, through e-mails, the twice-weekly company newsletter, and a speech played over the public-address system at all Agilent facilities, Barnholt explained why the cuts were necessary, how the cuts would help the company, and then encouraged the troops to cut costs any way they could. Agilent managers reinforced the message at "coffee talks," the regular brainstorming meetings that they hold with their employees. Employees responded by using Web sites to house data electronically (to avoid printing costs), by staying with friends and family when on company travel (to avoid hotel charges), and by bringing bags of potato chips to company recruiting events (to avoid costly catering charges). Within months, thanks to effective downward communicating, travel expenses dropped by 50 percent, whereas purchases of personal computers had dropped by 70 percent.[24]

downward communication
communication that flows from higher to lower levels in an organization

Upward communication flows from lower levels to higher levels in an organization. Upward communication is used to give higher-level managers feedback about operations, issues, and problems; to help higher-level managers assess organizational performance and effectiveness; to encourage lower-level managers and employees to participate in organizational decision-making; and to give those at lower levels the chance to share their concerns with higher-level authorities. Information can flow from lower levels to higher levels in a number of ways. Upward communication can occur through such methods as grievance procedures, open-door policies, ombudsman, suggestion boxes, and meetings.[25] Sundog Printing, based in Calgary, has become one of the largest privately owned commercial printers in western Canada. Dale Hodson, president, and Ray Remada, vice president, credit Sundog's growth and success to their employees. One key element they identify in their success in dealing with employees is their open-door policy, which both of them support and maintain. "You have to be open ... you have to be approachable," says Remada.[26]

upward communication
communication that flows from lower to higher levels in an organization

Horizontal communication flows among managers and workers who are at the same organizational level. For instance, horizontal communication occurs when the day-shift

horizontal communication
communication that flows among managers and workers who are at the same organizational level

supervisor comes in at 7:30 A.M. for a half-hour discussion with the midnight-shift supervisor who leaves at 8:00 A.M., or when the regional marketing director meets with the regional accounting director to discuss costs and plans for a new marketing campaign. Horizontal communication helps facilitate coordination and cooperation between different parts of a company and allows co-workers to share relevant information. It also helps people at the same level resolve conflicts and solve problems without involving high levels of management. For example, Siemens and Osram Sylvania have instituted formal communication at factory shift changes; supervisors from the departing work shift meet with the supervisors from the incoming shift to discuss problems and issues (e.g., parts that are needed, machines that are malfunctioning) that arose during the shift.[27]

In general, what can managers do to improve formal communication? First, decrease reliance on downward communication. Second, increase chances for upward communication by increasing personal contact with lower-level managers and workers. Third, like at Oracle software, encourage much greater use of horizontal communication.

Informal Communication Channels

informal communication channel ("grapevine") the transmission of messages from employee to employee outside of formal communication channels

The **informal communication channel**, sometimes called the "**grapevine**," is the transmission of messages from employee to employee outside of formal communication channels. The grapevine arises out of curiosity, that is, the need to know what is going on in an organization and how it might affect you or others. And to satisfy this curiosity, employees need a consistent supply of relevant, accurate, in-depth information about "who is doing what and what changes are occurring within the organization."[28] Employee Paul Haze agrees, saying, "If employees don't have a definite explanation from management, they tend to interpret for themselves."[29]

For example, at the University of Texas Medical Branch, any of the 13 000 employees wanting to know the truth about rumours working their way through the campus grapevine can log on to the school's Web site and click on "Rumors or Trumors." Campus administrators comment on each posted rumour and rate it using the "kernel of truth" system. One kernel of corn indicates a little bit of truth. Two kernels indicate that more of the rumour is accurate, but it's still not entirely true. Three kernels indicate that the rumour is accurate. Wildly inaccurate rumours are rated with a spaceship, indicating that they're too far out to be believed. Reaction thus far has been positive. Lecturer Sheryl

© ROB LEWINE/CORBIS

Gossip is an informal communication channel and is commonly referred to as the grapevine. This form of communication is usually faster than formal communication channels.

Prather says, "It looks sincere. I've found that everything thus far has been pretty factual. It at least shows that somebody's listening to some of the talk that goes on around here and [is] putting it down on the computer where we can all see it."[30]

Grapevines arise out of informal communication networks, such as the gossip or cluster chains shown in Exhibit 16.4. In the *gossip chain*, one "highly connected" individual shares information with many other managers and workers. By contrast, in the *cluster chain*, numerous people simply tell a few of their friends. The result in both cases is that information flows freely and quickly through the organization. Some believe that grapevines are a waste of employees' time, that they promote gossip and rumours that fuel political speculation, and that they are sources of highly unreliable, inaccurate information. Yet studies clearly show that grapevines are highly accurate sources of information for a number of reasons.[31] First, because grapevines typically carry "juicy" information that is interesting and timely, information spreads rapidly. At Meghan De Goyler Hauser's former company, the word on the grapevine was that her boss drank on the job, the company accountant was stealing the company blind, and that one of her co-workers was a nude model. She says, "The rumors all turned out to be true."[32] Second, since information is typically spread by face-to-face conversation, senders can seek feedback to make sure they understand the message that is being communicated. This reduces misunderstandings and increases accuracy. Third, since most of the information in a company moves along the grapevine, as opposed to formal communication channels, people can usually verify the accuracy of information by "checking it out" with others.

What can managers do to "manage" organizational grapevines? The very worst thing managers can do is withhold information or try to punish those who share information with others. The grapevine abhors a vacuum, and in the absence of information from company management, rumours and anxiety will flourish. Maureen Shaw, president of Ontario-based Industrial Accident Prevention Association, tries to prevent the grapevine from taking on a life of its own. She meets regularly with all employees for what she calls "water cooler chit-chats." Every three weeks she distributes a "Friday update," which is intended to discuss the most current rumours on the grapevine. "I collect things that I hear before the rumour mill gets started," she says. "I let people know what's really happening."[33] Clearly, she recognizes the power of the grapevine.

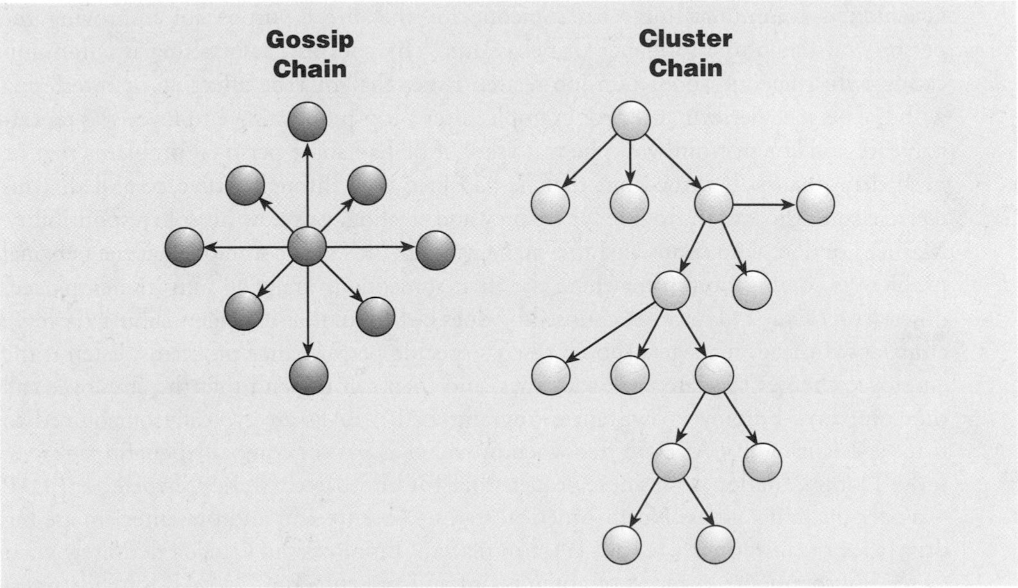

EXHIBIT 16.4
Grapevine Communication Networks

Source: Grapevine Communication Networks, K. Davis and J. W. Newstrom, *Human Behavior at Work: Organizational Behavior*, 8th ed. (New York: McGraw-Hill, 1989), p. 373. Reproduced with permission of the McGraw-Hill Companies.

A better strategy is to embrace the grapevine to keep employees informed about possible changes and strategies. Management consultant Arnold Brown said managers should "identify the key people in your company's grapevine and, instead of punishing them, feed them information. When a company issues a press release it knows what newspapers to contact, so why not know your internal media?"[34]

Finally, in addition to using the grapevine to communicate with others, managers should not overlook the fact that the grapevine can be a tremendous source of valuable information and feedback. In fact, information flowing through organizational grapevines is estimated to be 75 percent to 95 percent accurate.[35] For this reason, managers should gather their courage and be willing to read the anonymous comments that angry, frustrated employees post on Internet "gripe sites" like www.cibcsucks.com (about the Canadian Imperial Bank of Commerce), www.stainedapron.com (for griping restaurant workers), or www.vault.com, where employees post gripes about hundreds of different companies. Bob Rosner, who runs the gripe site www.workingwounded.com, suggests managers look for themes rather than responding to any particular message. Mark Oldman, cofounder of vault.com, says, "Most companies are delighted that we provide a forum to talk candidly for better or worse about a company. It [vault.com] basically just digitizes what already happens offline at the water cooler."[36] Jeff Jarvis, author of *The Blog BuzzMachine*, also recommends that "There should be someone at every company whose job is to put into Google and blog search engines the name of the company or the brand, followed by the word 'sucks,' just to see what customers [and employees] are saying."[37]

Coaching and Counselling: One-on-One Communication

In one study CEOs were asked, "If you could go back and change one thing, what would it be?" The answer? "The way we communicated with our employees." CEOs stated that instead of flashy videos, printed materials, or formal meetings, they would make greater use of one-to-one communication, especially with employees' immediate supervisors, and not higher-level executives that employees didn't know.[38] Hamilton-based AnswerPlus provides call centre services for other companies. Employee turnover in the industry often exceeds 100 percent per year, but AnswerPlus has instituted a number of strategies to reduce turnover to less than a quarter of the industry standard. Providing employees support through coaching is one of the key elements for this success.[39]

coaching
communicating with someone for the direct purpose of improving their on-the-job performance or behaviour

counselling
communicating with someone about non-job-related issues that may be affecting or interfering with their performance

There are two kinds of one-on-one communication: coaching and counselling. **Coaching** is communicating with someone for the direct purpose of improving the person's on-the-job performance or behaviour.[40] By contrast, **counselling** is communicating with someone about non-job-related issues that may be affecting or interfering with the person's performance. For example, after a top-performing employee was repeatedly late and absent from work, he was asked if he had some personal problems that he needed to discuss. It turned out that he had just gone through a divorce and that his teenage son, who was in trouble for truancy and stealing, was now his sole responsibility. Marina London, who counselled this manager, said, "It's very common that the personal problem is coming from somewhere else, that someone is dragging him [the employee] down with them."[41] However, counselling does not mean that managers should try to be clinicians. Instead, managers should discuss specific performance problems, listen if the employee chooses to share personal issues, and then recommend that the employee call the company's Employee Assistance Program (EAP). EAPs are typically outsourced to firms specializing in EAPs and free when provided as part of company benefit packages. Judy Plotkin, national business leader for Toronto-based WarrenShepell, an EAP provider operating across North America, states: "Absenteeism and presenteeism are big drivers for organizations who put EAPs in place.... Employers in Canada definitely want to see improvements in terms of absenteeism and presenteeism."[42] EAPs provide referrals to organizations and professionals that can help employees and their family members address personal issues. EAPs can provide immediate counselling and support in emergencies or times of crisis.

While we'll discuss a number of specific steps for effective one-on-one communication later in the chapter, you should know that, in general, openness is one of the most important factors in effective one-on-one communication. Consistent with our discussion of the communication model, *openness in message sending* is the candid disclosure of information. *Openness in message receiving* is encouraging employees to respond with candid, forthright opinions, even when they disagree.[43]

Nonverbal Communication

nonverbal communication
any communication that doesn't involve words

When people talk, they send verbal and nonverbal messages. Verbal messages are sent and received through the words we speak. "That was a great presentation." By contrast, nonverbal messages are sent through body language, facial expressions, or tone of voice. For instance, hearing "THAT was a GREAT presentation!" is very different from hearing "ahem (clearing throat), that was, ahem, ahem, a great presentation."

More specifically, **nonverbal communication** is any communication that doesn't involve words. Nonverbal communication and messages almost always accompany verbal communication and may support and reinforce the verbal message or contradict it. The importance of nonverbal communication is well established. Researchers have estimated that as much as 93 percent of any message is transmitted nonverbally, with 55 percent coming from body language and facial expressions and 38 percent coming from tone and pitch of voice.[45] And since many nonverbal cues are unintentional, receivers often consider nonverbal communication to be a more accurate representation of what senders are really thinking and feeling. If you have ever asked someone out on a date and been told "yes," but realized that the real answer was "no," then you understand the importance of paying attention to nonverbal communication.

Kinesics and paralanguage are two kinds of nonverbal communication.[46] **Kinesics** are movements of the body and face.[47] These movements include arm and hand gestures, facial expressions, eye contact, folding arms, crossing legs, and leaning toward or away from another person. For example, people tend to avoid eye contact when they are embarrassed or unsure of the message they are sending. Crossed arms and/or legs usually indicate defensiveness or that the person is not receptive to the message or the sender. Also, people tend to smile frequently when they are seeking someone's approval. Lawyers frequently use body language and facial movements to communicate nonverbal messages to jurors. Attorney and trial consultant Lisa Blue said, "If you want to show that the cross-examination of your witness was ridiculous or boring, you could start looking at your watch."[48]

> **DOING THE RIGHT THING**
>
> **PROTECT PERSONAL, CONFIDENTIAL INFORMATION**
>
> By virtue of their jobs, managers are privy to information that others aren't. Although much of that information will be about the company, some of it will be personal and confidential information about employees. As a manager, you have a moral and legal obligation to protect employees' privacy. Moreover, sharing others' personal, confidential information may dissuade employees from confiding in managers or seeking help from a company's employee assistance program. Does this mean that if employees confide in you that you can't tell anyone else? No, if you're a manager, sometimes you may have to inform your boss or human resources about a situation. But only inform those who have a need to know and who are also obligated to protect employee privacy. Furthermore, not all information that employees disclose to you should be protected. Information about discrimination, sexual harassment, potential workplace violence, or conflicts of interest between employees and the company may need to be shared with upper management to protect the rights and well-being of others. So, when employees disclose personal, confidential information, do the right thing. Don't discuss it with others unless it falls into one of the exceptions discussed here.[44]

kinesics
movements of the body and face

paralanguage
the pitch, rate, tone, volume, and speaking pattern (i.e., use of silences, pauses, or hesitations) of one's voice

Paralanguage includes the pitch, rate, tone, volume, and speaking pattern (i.e., use of silences, pauses, or hesitations) of one's voice. For example, when people are unsure what to say, they tend to decrease their communication effectiveness by speaking softly. By contrast, when people are nervous, they tend to talk faster and louder. These characteristics have a tremendous influence on whether listeners are receptive to what speakers are saying. Again, lawyers have long used the power of their voices to influence whether jurors were receptive to arguments that supported their clients. For instance, tobacco company lawyers complained about the dramatic way in which plaintiffs' attorney Stanley Rosenblatt would read secret company documents aloud to jurors. Rosenblatt, who would vary his voice from a slow whisper to a fast, loud voice that filled the entire courtroom, said that opposing attorneys always complained that "I should read in a very flat monotone."[49]

Nonverbal communication is equally, if not more, important than the words being spoken. In this photo, the man with his arms crossed could be considered as unreceptive to his co-worker's message.

© DENNIS COOPER/ZEFA/CORBIS

In short, since nonverbal communication is so informative, especially when it contradicts verbal communication, managers need to learn how to monitor and control their nonverbal behaviour.

REVIEW 2: KINDS OF COMMUNICATION

Organizational communication depends on the communication process, formal and informal communication channels, one-on-one communication, and nonverbal communication. The major components of the communication process are the sender, the receiver, noise, and feedback. The conduit metaphor refers to the mistaken assumption that senders can pipe their intended messages directly into receivers' heads with perfect clarity. However, with noise, perceptual filters, and little feedback, this just isn't possible. Formal communication channels, such as downward, upward, and horizontal communication, carry organizationally approved messages and information. By contrast, the informal communication channel, called the "grapevine," arises out of curiosity and is carried out through gossip or cluster chains. Managers should use the grapevine to keep employees informed and to obtain better, clearer information for themselves. Effective one-on-one communication, such as coaching and counselling, depends on openness in message receiving and message sending. Nonverbal communication, such as kinesics and paralanguage, account for as much as 93 percent of a message's content and understanding. Since nonverbal communication is so informative, managers need to learn how to monitor and control their nonverbal behaviour.

Improving Communication

An employee comes in late every day, takes long lunches, and leaves early. His co-workers resent his tardiness and having to do his share of the work. Another employee makes as many as ten personal phone calls a day on company time. Another employee has seen her job performance drop significantly in the last three months. How do you communicate with these employees to begin solving these problems? On the other hand, if you supervise a division of 50 or 100, or even 1000 people, how can you communicate effectively with everyone in that division? Moreover, how can top managers communicate effectively with everyone in the company when employees work in different offices, provinces, countries, and time zones? Turning that around, how can managers make themselves accessible so that they can hear what employees feel and think throughout the organization?

When it comes to improving communication, managers face two primary tasks—managing one-on-one communication and managing organization-wide communication.

After reading the next two sections, you should be able to

3 explain how managers can manage effective one-on-one communication.

4. describe how managers can manage effective organization-wide communication.

3 MANAGING ONE-ON-ONE COMMUNICATION

In Chapter 1, you learned that, on average, first-line managers spend 57 percent of their time with people, middle managers spend 63 percent of their time directly with people, and top managers spend as much as 78 percent of their time dealing with people.[50] These numbers make it clear that managers spend a great deal of time in one-on-one communication with others.

Learn more about managing one-on-one communication by reading how to improve communication by choosing the right communication medium, listening, giving feedback, and improving cross-cultural communication.

Choosing the Right Communication Medium

Sometimes messages are poorly communicated simply because they are delivered using the wrong **communication medium**, which is the method used to deliver a message. For example, the wrong communication medium is being used when an employee returns from lunch, picks up the note left on her office chair, and learns she has been fired. Or the wrong communication medium is being used when an employee pops into your office every ten minutes with a simple request.

communication medium the method used to deliver an oral or written message

There are two general kinds of communication media: oral and written communication. *Oral communication* includes face-to-face and group meetings, as well as telephone calls or other ways, such as videoconferencing, in which spoken messages are sent and received. Studies show that managers generally prefer oral communication, because it provides the opportunity to ask questions about parts of the message that they don't understand. Oral communication is also a rich communication medium because it allows managers to receive and assess the nonverbal communication that accompanies spoken messages (i.e., body language, facial expressions, or the voice characteristics associated with paralanguage). Furthermore, you don't need a personal computer and an Internet connection to conduct oral communication. Simply schedule an appointment, track someone down in the hall, or catch someone on the phone. In fact, management consultant Tom Durel worries that with voice-mail and e-mail, managers are not as willing to engage in meaningful face-to-face, oral communication as they once were. He said, "Why is it that the first thing people do in the morning is turn on their computers and send e-mail to a colleague in the office next door? What's wrong with getting up, walking over there, and actually talking to that person?"[51] However, oral communication should not be used for all communication. In general, when messages are simple, such as a quick request or presentation of straightforward information, memos, instant messaging or e-mail are often the better communication medium.

Written communication includes letters, e-mail, instant messaging, and memos. While most managers like and use oral communication, they are generally less receptive to using written communication. They may avoid written communication for a number of reasons, such as poor writing skills, being a poor typist, or not knowing (or refusing to learn) how to use Internet or corporate e-mail systems. However, written communication is well suited for delivering straightforward messages and information. Furthermore, with e-mail access available at the office, at home, and on the road (by laptop computer or Web-based e-mail), managers can use e-mail to stay in touch from anywhere at almost any time. And, since e-mail and other written communications don't have to be sent and received simultaneously, messages can be sent and stored for reading at any time. This allows managers to send and receive many more messages using e-mail than with oral communication, which requires people to get together in person or by phone or videoconference.

However, written communication is not well suited to ambiguous or emotionally laden topics, which are better delivered through oral communication. Management consultant Tom Durel said, "Don't assume that you did your part just because you sent out a bunch of memos. If you really want to communicate, you need to take the time to get real-time feedback."[52]

Listening

Are you a good listener? You probably think so. But, in fact, most people, including managers, are terrible listeners, retaining only about 25 percent of what they hear.[53] You qualify as a poor listener if you frequently interrupt others, jump to conclusions about what people will say before they've said it, hurry the speaker to finish his or her point, are a passive listener (not actively working at your listening), and simply don't pay attention to what people are saying.[54] On this last point, attentiveness, college students were periodically asked to record their thoughts during a psychology course. On average, 20 percent of the students were paying attention (only 12 percent were actively working at being good listeners), 20 percent were thinking about sex, 20 percent were thinking about things they had done before, and the remaining 40 percent thought about a number of things (worries, religion, lunch, daydreaming, etc.), none of which were related to the class.[55]

How important is it to be a good listener? In general, about 45 percent of the total time you spend communicating with others is spent listening. Furthermore, listening is particularly important for managerial success even for those at the top of an organization. According to *Fortune* magazine, listening is one of the reasons that CEO A.G. Lafley has been able to turn around Procter & Gamble so quickly:

> He's a listener, not a storyteller. He's likable but not awe inspiring. He's the type of guy who gets excited in the mop aisle of a grocery store. His plan to fix P&G isn't anything groundbreaking, but rather

Good listening skills require active, empathetic involvement.

PHOTODISC/GETTY IMAGES

> a straightforward, back-to-basics tack. And so far it's worked. He has rallied his troops not with big speeches and dazzling promises, but by *hearing them out* (practically) one at a time.[56]

In fact, managers with better listening skills are rated as better managers by their employees and are much more likely to be promoted.[57]

So what can you do to improve your listening ability? First, understand the difference between hearing and listening. According to *Webster's New World Dictionary*, **hearing** is the "act or process of perceiving sounds," whereas **listening** is "making a conscious effort to hear." In other words, we react to sounds, such as bottles breaking or music being played too loudly, because hearing is an involuntary physiological process. By contrast, listening is a voluntary behaviour. So if you want to be a good listener, you have to choose to be a good listener. Typically, that means choosing to be an active, empathetic listener.[58]

hearing
the act or process of perceiving sounds

listening
making a conscious effort to hear

active listening
assuming half the responsibility for successful communication by actively giving the speaker nonjudgmental feedback that shows you've accurately heard what he or she said

Active listening means assuming half the responsibility for successful communication by actively giving the speaker nonjudgmental feedback that shows you've accurately heard what he or she said. Active listeners make it clear from this behaviour that they are listening carefully to what the speaker has to say. Active listeners put the speaker at ease, maintain eye contact, and show the speaker that they are attentively listening by nodding and making short statements.

Several specific strategies can help you be a better active listener. First, *clarify responses* by asking the speaker to explain confusing or ambiguous statements. Second, when there are natural breaks in the speaker's delivery, use this time to paraphrase or summarize what has been said. *Paraphrasing* is restating what has been said in your own words. *Summarizing* is reviewing the speaker's main points or emotions. Paraphrasing and summarizing give the speaker the chance to correct the message if the active listener has attached the wrong meaning to it. Paraphrasing and summarizing also show the speaker that the active listener is interested in the speaker's message. Exhibit 16.5 lists specific statements that listeners can use to clarify responses, paraphrase, or summarize what has been said.

EXHIBIT 16.5
Clarifying, Paraphrasing, and Summarizing Responses for Active Listeners

CLARIFYING RESPONSES

- Could you explain that again?
- I don't understand what you mean.
- I'm confused, would you run though that again?
- I'm not sure how...

PARAPHRASING RESPONSES

- What you're really saying is...
- If I understand you correctly...
- So your perspective is that...
- In other words...
- Tell me if I'm wrong, but what you're saying is...

SUMMARIZING RESPONSES

- Let me summarize...
- Okay, your main concerns are...
- Thus far, you've discussed...
- To recap what you've said...

Source: E. Atwater, *I Hear You*, revised ed. (New York: Walker, 1992).

Active listeners also avoid evaluating the message or being critical until the message is complete. They recognize that their only responsibility during the transmission of a message is to accurately receive it and derive the intended meaning from it. Evaluation and criticism can take place after the message is accurately received. Finally, active listeners also recognize that a large portion of any message is transmitted nonverbally and thus pay very careful attention to the nonverbal cues transmitted by the speaker.

empathetic listening
understanding the speaker's perspective and personal frame of reference and giving feedback that conveys that understanding to the speaker

Empathetic listening means understanding the speaker's perspective and personal frame of reference and giving feedback that conveys that understanding to the speaker. Empathetic listening goes beyond active listening, because it depends on our ability to set aside our own attitudes or relationships to be able to see and understand things through someone else's eyes. Empathetic listening is just as important as active listening, especially for managers, because it helps build rapport and trust with others.

The key to being a more empathetic listener is to show your desire to understand and to reflect people's feelings. You can *show your desire to understand* by listening first, that is, by asking people to talk about what's most important to them and then giving them sufficient time to talk before responding or interrupting. Management consultant Neil Grammer said:

> One of the best sales meetings I've ever had taught me a valuable lesson about the importance of listening. The meeting was with an investment bank's managing director. The appointment lasted 30 minutes—28 of those minutes were spent by the director telling me everything about his business and personnel. I told him nothing more about my company and its services than I had in our initial phone conversation. As the meeting concluded, he enthusiastically shook my hand and proclaimed how much he was looking forward to working with me—someone who understood his business.[59]

Reflecting feelings is also an important part of empathetic listening, because it demonstrates that you understand the speaker's emotions. But unlike active listening, in which you would restate or summarize the informational content of what had been said, the focus is on the affective part of the message. As an empathetic listener, you can use the following statements to reflect the speaker's emotions:

- So, right now you're feeling...
- You seem as if you're...
- Do you feel a bit...?
- I could be wrong, but I'm sensing that you're feeling...

Giving Feedback

In Chapter 13, you learned that performance appraisal feedback (i.e., judging) should be separated from developmental feedback (i.e., coaching).[60] At this point, we now focus on the steps needed to communicate feedback one-on-one to employees.

destructive feedback
feedback that disapproves without any intention of being helpful and almost always causes a negative or defensive reaction in the recipient

constructive feedback
feedback intended to be helpful, corrective, and/or encouraging

To start, managers need to recognize that feedback can be constructive or destructive. **Destructive feedback** is disapproving without any intention of being helpful and almost always causes a negative or defensive reaction in the recipient. In fact, one study found that 98 percent of employees responded to destructive feedback from their bosses with either verbal aggression (two-thirds) or physical aggression (one-third).[61] By contrast, **constructive feedback** is intended to be helpful, corrective, and/or encouraging. It is aimed at correcting performance deficiencies and motivating employees. However, even when they want to give constructive rather than destructive feedback, managers still get nervous about discussing problems with employees. Joan Hill, president of human resource consulting firm Core Consulting, based in Mississauga, Ontario, said, "After many years in the business, even I don't enjoy them."[62]

In order for feedback to be constructive rather than destructive, it must be immediate, focused on specific behaviours, and problem oriented. Because the mistake or incident can be recalled more accurately and discussed in detail by the manager and the worker, *immediate feedback* is much more effective than delayed feedback. For example, if a worker is rude to a customer and the customer immediately reports the incident to management, and the manager, in turn, immediately discusses the issue with the employee, there should be little disagreement over what was said or done. By contrast, if the manager waits several weeks to discuss the incident, it's unlikely that either the manager or the worker will be able to accurately remember the specifics of what occurred. When that happens, it's usually too late to have a meaningful conversation.

Specific feedback focuses on particular acts or incidents that are clearly under the control of the employee. For instance, instead of telling an employee that he or she is "always late for work," it's much more constructive to say, "In the last three weeks, you have been 30 minutes late on four occasions and more than an hour late on two others." Furthermore, specific feedback isn't very helpful unless employees have control over the problems that the feedback addresses. Indeed, giving negative feedback about behaviours beyond someone's control is likely to be seen as unfair. Similarly, giving positive feedback about behaviours beyond someone's control may be viewed as insincere.

Last, *problem-oriented feedback* focuses on the problems or incidents associated with the poor performance rather than on the worker or the worker's personality. Giving feedback does not give managers the right to personally attack workers. While managers may be frustrated by a worker's poor performance, the point of problem-oriented feedback is to draw attention to the problem in a nonjudgmental way, so that the employee has enough information to correct it. So, rather than telling people that they're "idiots," focus on the problem. For instance, a shipping clerk at a restaurant had a bad case of body odour. Rather than telling him "You stink" or "You're doing a lousy job because you stink," the manager explained the specific ways in which his body odour was "getting in the way of doing his job." Because the manager's feedback was specific and problem oriented and didn't attack or blame the employee, the employee didn't get defensive and took steps to take care of his body odour.[63]

Improving Cross-Cultural Communication

As you know by now, effective communication is very difficult to accomplish. However, **cross-cultural communication**, which involves transmitting information from a person in one country or culture to a person from another country or culture, is much more difficult. But there are a number of things you can do to increase your chances for successful cross-cultural communication: familiarize yourself with that culture's work norms, address terms, and attitudes toward time.[64]

cross-cultural communication transmitting information from a person in one country or culture to a person from another country or culture

In Chapter 8, you learned that expatriates who receive predeparture language and cross-cultural training make faster adjustments to foreign cultures and perform better on their international assignments.[65] Therefore, *familiarizing yourself with cultural work norms* is the first step for successful cross-cultural communication.

Next, *know the address terms* that people in that culture use to address each other in the workplace. **Address terms** are the cultural norms that establish whether you address businesspeople by their first names, family names, or titles. When meeting for the first time, North Americans and Australians tend to be informal and address each other by first names, even nicknames. However, such immediate informality is not accepted in many cultures. For instance, an American manager working in one of his company's British subsidiaries introduced himself as "Chuck" to his British employees and co-workers. However, even after six months on the job, his British counterparts still referred to him as "Charles." And the more he insisted they call him "Chuck," the more they seemed to dig in their heels and call him "Charles."[66] So, to decrease defensiveness, know your address terms before addressing your international business counterparts.

address terms cultural norms that establish whether you should address businesspeople by their first names, family names, or titles

Understanding cultural attitudes toward time is another major consideration for effective one-on-one communication when conducting international business. Four important temporal concepts affect cross-cultural communication: appointment time, schedule time, discussion time, and acquaintance time.[67] **Appointment time** is concerned with how punctual you must be when showing up for scheduled appointments or meetings. In Canada, any amount beyond 5 minutes late is considered "late." However, Swedes don't even allow 5 minutes, expecting others to arrive by their appointment time. By contrast, in Latin countries, people can arrive 20 to 30 minutes after a scheduled appointment and still not be considered late. Nicholas Benedict, an MBA student from Toronto who took a two-month job in the United Arab Emirates, quickly learned the difference between meeting times in the UAE and Canada. He found that he had to grow "accustomed to setting business and personal meeting times at least a half hour before I planned to arrive."[68]

appointment time
cultural norm for how punctual you must be when showing up for scheduled appointments or meetings

Schedule time is the time by which scheduled projects or jobs should actually be completed. In North American and other Anglo cultures, a premium is placed on completing things on time. By contrast, more relaxed attitudes toward schedule time can be found throughout Asia and Latin America.

schedule time
cultural norm for the time by which scheduled projects or jobs should actually be completed

Discussion time concerns how much time should be spent in discussion with others. In North America, we carefully manage discussion time to avoid "wasting" time on nonbusiness topics. In Brazil, though, because of the emphasis on building relationships, as much as two hours of general discussion on nonbusiness topics can be required before moving on to business issues.

discussion time
cultural norm for how much time should be spent in discussion with others

Finally, **acquaintance time** is how much time you must spend getting to know someone before the person is prepared to do business with you. Again, in North America, people are quick to get down to business and are willing to strike a deal on the same day if the terms are good and initial impressions are positive. In the Middle East, however, it may take two or three weeks of meetings before reaching this comfort level. The French also have a different attitude toward acquaintance time. Polly Platt, author of *French or Foe*, a book that explains French culture and its people for travellers and businesspeople, says, "Know that things are going to take longer and don't resent it. Realize that the time system is different. Time is not a quantity for them. We save time, we spend time, we waste time; all this comes from money. The French don't. They pass time. It's a totally different concept."[69]

acquaintance time
cultural norm for how much time you must spend getting to know someone before the person is prepared to do business with you

REVIEW 3: MANAGING ONE-ON-ONE COMMUNICATION

One-on-one communication can be managed by choosing the right communication medium, being a good listener, giving effective feedback, and understanding cross-cultural communication. Managers generally prefer oral communication, because it provides the opportunity to ask questions and assess nonverbal communication. Oral communication is best suited to complex, ambiguous, or emotionally laden topics. Written communication is best suited for delivering straightforward messages and information. Listening is important for managerial success, but most people are terrible listeners. To improve your listening skills, choose to be an active listener (clarifying responses, paraphrasing, and summarizing) and an empathetic listener (show your desire to understand, reflect feelings). Feedback can be constructive or destructive. To be constructive, feedback must be immediate, focused on specific behaviours, and problem oriented. Finally, to increase chances for successful cross-cultural communication, familiarize yourself with the culture's work norms, address terms, and attitudes toward time (appointment time, schedule time, discussion time, and acquaintance time).

4 MANAGING ORGANIZATION-WIDE COMMUNICATION

While managing one-on-one communication is important, managers must also know how to effectively communicate to a larger number of people throughout an organization. For instance, Barry Salzman, president of DoubleClick International, an Internet advertising firm, spends 75 percent of his time travelling to 14 international offices. And every Monday, no matter where he is, he conducts a conference call with DoubleClick managers in Canada, Europe, and Asia. Says Salzman, "We try to maintain voice contact. We lose that with computers and e-mail."[70] While this is an effective method of managing a small group of geographically dispersed people, managers can't hold a conference call with everyone in the company. Thus, managers need additional methods for organization-wide communication and for making themselves accessible, so they can hear what employees throughout their organizations are feeling and thinking.

Learn more about organization-wide communication by reading the following sections about improving transmission, including getting the message out and improving reception.

Improving Transmission: Getting the Message Out

Several methods of electronic communication—e-mail, online discussion forums, televised/videotaped speeches and conferences, corporate talk shows, and broadcast voicemail—now make it easier for managers to communicate with people throughout the organization and "get the message out." Although we normally think of *e-mail*, the transmission of messages via computers, as a means of one-on-one communication, it also plays an important role in organization-wide communication. For example:

> Perot Systems Corporation publishes three online newsletters via e-mail. The internal communication department produces one every week and writes the others on an as-needed basis. Perot Systems chose this "low frills" approach for its simplicity and affordability. The department spends 15 hours a week collecting information. Copy approvals are completed within 24 hours, and the newsletters are distributed to its 2,400 associates (employees). The newsletters are typically no longer than three pages and include briefs about the latest company news.[71]

Also, with the click of a button, managers can send e-mail to everyone in the company via e-mail distribution lists. Many CEOs now use this capability regularly to keep employees up to date on changes and developments in the company. Also, many CEOs and top executives make their e-mail addresses public and encourage employees to contact them directly. There are of course drawbacks to e-mail. For example, a writer for the *National Post*, Jonathan Kay, received an e-mail that had Bill Gates's Christmas list by mistake. Pushing the wrong button can be hazardous.[72]

Another way to electronically promote organization-wide communication is through discussion forums. **Online discussion forums**, which are the in-house equivalent of Internet newsgroups, are Web- or software-based discussion tools that are available across the company to permit employees to easily ask questions and share knowledge with each other. The point is to share expertise and not duplicate solutions already "discovered" by others in the company. Furthermore, because online discussion forums remain online, they provide a historical database for people who are dealing with particular problems for the first time.

online discussion forums the in-house equivalent of Internet newsgroups; Web- or software-based discussion tools available across the company to permit employees to easily ask questions and share knowledge with each other

Online discussion forums are typically organized by topic. For example, at Ernst & Young, a major accounting and management-consulting corporation, consultants who have questions about multinational tax analysis can simply log on to the E & Y tax forum (or dozens of other forums, too). They can either post new questions and get help from others who respond with answers, or read previously posted questions and answers to see if the information they need has already been discussed. If either of those options fails, they can at least come away with the names of people in the organization that they can contact for help.[73] British Petroleum Amoco has taken this a step farther by creating "Connect," which is essentially a company Yellow Pages where more than 12 000 managers and workers have

1.	*Perform a "Knowledge" Audit*—to pinpoint your company's top intellectual assets; then spread that knowledge throughout the organization.
2.	*Create an Online Directory*—detailing the expertise of individual workers, and make it available to all employees.
3.	*Set Up Discussion Groups on the Net*—so that managers and workers can collaborate on problem-solving.
4.	*Reward Information Sharing*—make sharing knowledge online a key part of performance ratings.

Source: G. McWilliams & M. Stepanek, "Knowledge Management: Taming the Info Monster," *Business Week*, 22 June 1998, 170.

EXHIBIT 16.6
Establishing Online Discussion Forums

entered their contact information and listed their expertise to make it easier for others to find expert help for their problems.[74] Exhibit 16.6 lists the steps companies need to take to establish successful online discussion forums.

televised/videotaped speeches and meetings speeches and meetings originally made to a smaller audience that are either simultaneously broadcast to other locations in the company or videotaped for subsequent distribution and viewing

Televised/videotaped speeches and meetings are a third electronic method of organization-wide communication. **Televised/videotaped speeches and meetings** are simply speeches and meetings originally made to a smaller audience that are either simultaneously broadcast to other locations in the company or videotaped for subsequent distribution and viewing.

corporate talk shows televised company meetings that allow remote audiences (employees) to pose questions to the show's host and guests

Corporate talk shows are a variant on televised/videotaped speeches and meetings. But instead of simply watching a televised/videotaped speech or meeting, **corporate talk shows** allow remote audience members, all of whom are typically workers or managers, to pose questions to the show's host and guests. For example, Jim Rager, retired vice-chairman of personal and commercial banking at the Royal Bank of Canada, would hold quarterly town hall meetings but would also have satellite television broadcasts and interactive teleconferences to get his message out to those that could not attend in person. He felt that "It's an important way of ensuring that everyone understands the context in which we work and how the corporate priorities relate to their own team's objectives."[75]

Voice messaging, or "voice-mail," is a telephone answering system that records audio messages. Eighty-nine percent of respondents believe that voice messaging is critical to business communication, 78 percent believe that it improves productivity, and 58 percent would rather leave a message on a voice messaging system than with a receptionist.[76] However, most people are unfamiliar with the ability to broadcast voice-mail by sending a recorded message to everyone in the company. Broadcast voice-mail gives top managers a quick, convenient way to address their work forces via oral communication.

Improving Reception: Hearing What Others Feel and Think

When people think of "organization-wide" communication, they think of the CEO and top managers getting their message out to people in the company. However, organization-wide communication also means finding ways to communicate and stay in touch with people throughout the organization. Company hotlines, survey feedback, frequent informal meetings, and surprise visits are ways of accomplishing this.

organizational silence when employees withhold information about organizational problems or issues

Withholding information about organizational problems or issues is called **organizational silence**. Organizational silence occurs when employees believe that telling management about problems won't make a difference or that they'll be punished or hurt in some way for sharing such information.[77] For example, after the space shuttle *Columbia* exploded over east Texas in 2003, the investigation board charged with determining the cause of the accident that killed all seven people on board, concluded that, "the NASA organizational culture had as much to do with this accident as the foam [debris that damaged the shuttle's wing at lift-off]." How so? "Cultural traits and organizational practices detrimental to safety and reliability were allowed to develop, including ... organizational barriers which prevented effective communication of critical safety information and stifled professional differences of opinion ... when they did not speak up, safety personnel could not fulfill their stated mission to provide 'checks and balances.'"[78] In short, NASA's culture engineered organizational silence with deadly consequences. Fortunately, though, company hotlines, survey feedback, frequent informal meetings, surprise visits, and blogs are ways of overcoming organizational silence.

Company hotlines are phone numbers that anyone in the company can anonymously call to leave information for upper management. For instance, Toyota's employee handbook says, "Don't spend time worrying about something. Speak up!" The Toyota hotline is anonymous and available 24 hours a day, seven days a week. Every message is reviewed and fully investigated by Toyota's top human resources manager. Moreover, if the questions or statements left on the hotline would be of interest to others in the company, they are then posted on company bulletin boards (without sacrificing callers' anonymity).[79]

company hotlines
phone numbers that anyone in the company can anonymously call to leave information for upper management

Survey feedback is information collected by survey from organizational members that is then compiled, disseminated, and used to develop action plans for improvement. Many organizations make use of survey feedback by surveying their managers and employees several times a year. For example, Maritime Life, located in Halifax, surveys employees once or twice a year. Employees are asked about their job satisfaction and they can also anonymously evaluate their boss. The feedback from surveys helps Maritime Life maintain its rating as one of the top 50 companies in Canada to work for.[80]

survey feedback
information collected by survey from organizational members that is then compiled, disseminated, and used to develop action plans for improvement

Frequent, *informal meetings* between top managers and lower-level employees are one of the best ways for top managers to hear what others feel and think. Many people assume that top managers are at the centre of everything that goes on in organizations. However, it's common for top managers to feel isolated from most of the managers and employees in their companies. Consequently, more and more top managers are scheduling frequent, informal meetings with people throughout their companies. Remember Maureen Shaw, president of Industrial Accident Prevention Association? She met regularly with all her employees for her water cooler chats.

Have you ever been around supervisors when they found out that upper management was going to be paying a visit? First, there's shock. Next, there's anxiety. And then there's panic, as everyone is told to drop what he or she is doing to polish, shine, and spruce up the workplace, so it looks perfect for top management's visit. Of course, when visits are conducted under these conditions, top managers don't get a realistic look at what's going on in the company. Consequently, one of the ways to get an accurate picture is to pay *surprise visits* to various parts of the organization. However, surprise visits should not be surprise inspections. Instead, surprise visits should be used as an opportunity to increase the chances for meaningful upward communication from those who normally don't get a chance to work with upper management. Indeed, surprise visits like these are part of the culture at Enterprise Rent-a-Car. Fred Sorino, who manages an Enterprise office in Eatontown, New Jersey, said, "Once I was working at a branch in Cranbury, New Jersey, and a corporate vice president and a regional president showed up for a surprise visit. I was outside washing cars in 20-degree [−7°C] weather, and we were very busy. These two executives offered to help me clean the cars. I felt so awkward that I said I didn't need help, but they did it anyway." Enterprise's CEO, Andy Taylor, tells a similar story, saying, "We were visiting an office in Berkeley and it was mobbed, so I started cleaning cars. As it was happening, I wondered if it was a good use of my time, but the effect on morale was tremendous."[81]

Blogs are another way to hear what people are thinking and saying, both inside and outside of the organization. A **blog** is a personal Web site that provides personal opinions or recommendations, news summaries, and reader comments. At Google, which started Blogger.com, hundreds of employees are writing *internal blogs.* One employee even wrote a blog for posting all the notes from the brainstorming sessions used to redesign the search page used by millions each day. Staffer Marissa Mayer says, "Our legal department loves the blogs, because it basically is a written-down, backed-up, permanent time-stamped version of the scientist's notebook. When you want to file a patent, you can now show in blogs where this idea happened."[82]

blog
a personal Web site that provides personal opinions or recommendations, news summaries, and reader comments

REVIEW 4: MANAGING ORGANIZATION-WIDE COMMUNICATION

Managers need methods for organization-wide communication and for making themselves accessible, so they can hear what employees throughout their organizations are feeling and thinking. E-mail, online discussion forums, televised/videotaped speeches and conferences, corporate talk shows, and broadcast voice-mail make it much easier for managers to improve message transmission and "get the message out." By contrast, anonymous company hot lines, survey feedback, frequent informal meetings, and surprise visits help managers improve reception by hearing what others in the organization feel and think.

What Really Happened?[83]

At the beginning of the chapter, you read about the problems that Procter & Gamble was experiencing when A.G. Lafley, the manager portrayed in the case, became CEO. Expenses were out of control, profits were down, brand managers were leaving, and the total value of P&G's stock had dropped by more than US$70 billion. As a result of these problems and others, A.G. Lafley became CEO after his predecessor, Durk Jager, resigned. Lafley refocused P&G on its top ten brands, stopped globalization of brands, focused on small innovations, and turned two-thirds of the 11th floor of P&G's headquarters, where top executives are located, into a new learning centre.

The hard part, though, will be changing the pattern of communication throughout the company. People are still stinging from the hard-charging, combative approach of your predecessor, so you need to find a way to make regular P&G employees feel comfortable communicating with top management again. What's the best way to do that?

Listening is perhaps the best way for top managers to make regular employees comfortable and prove to them that top managers care about their thoughts and feelings. Active listening means assuming half the responsibility for successful communication by actively giving the speaker nonjudgmental feedback that shows you have accurately heard what he or she said. Active listeners make it clear from this behaviour that they are listening carefully to the speaker. Active listeners put the speaker at ease, maintain eye contact, and show the speaker that they are attentively listening by nodding and making short statements.

In an age of charismatic CEOs renowned for their overpowering personalities, P&G's A.G. Lafley is the exception. He's quiet, reserved, and most of all a listener. Stock analyst Ann Gillin-Lefever, who covers P&G, said, "If there were 15 people sitting around the conference table, it wouldn't be obvious that he was the CEO." P&G board member Jonathan Rodgers says, "He doesn't have that superstar CEO personality." *Fortune* magazine described him this way: "He's a listener, not a storyteller. He's likable but not awe inspiring. He's the type of guy who gets excited in the mop aisle of a grocery store. His plan to fix P&G isn't anything groundbreaking, but rather a straightforward, back-to-basics tack. And so far it's worked. He has rallied his troops not with big speeches and dazzling promises, but by hearing them out (practically) one at a time." Indeed, Lafley describes his management style this way: "I work by walking around. I like to have conversations with people."

And, with a history of centralized authority in which P&G management sent marching orders from headquarters, the traditional focus has been on "getting the message out." But that's only half the communication formula. These days, it's also important to "improve reception" by finding out what others feel and think. So how can P&G do a better job of hearing what people inside the company feel and think?

When people think of communication, they think of the CEO and top managers getting their message out to people in the company. But communication also means finding ways to hear what people throughout the organization are feeling and thinking. Despite what many people think, finding out what people are feeling and thinking in the organization isn't really that easy. In fact, most employees and managers are reluctant to share their thoughts and feelings with top managers. Surveys indicate that only 29 percent of first-level managers feel that their companies encourage employees to express their opinions openly. Another study of 22 companies found that 70 percent of the people surveyed were afraid to speak up about problems they knew existed at work. This phenomenon, known as organizational silence, occurs when people believe that telling management about problems won't make a difference, or that they'll somehow be punished for sharing such information. It takes time and patience to overcome organizational silence, especially when company management has a reputation for not listening.

Informal meetings are one of the best ways to overcome organizational silence and find out what people inside the company really think and feel. Unfortunately, when most CEOs meet with lower-level managers and employees, the meetings are fairly formal. The

CEO gives a speech, answers three or four prescreened questions, and leaves. Not surprisingly, top managers don't learn much about what's going on in the organization when this happens. By contrast, when A.G. Lafley meets with lower-level managers and employees, the meetings really are informal. For example, at a simple buffet lunch with 40 middle-level managers, he starts out by saying, "I don't have a speech planned. I thought we could talk. I'm searching for meaty issues. Give me some meaty issues." In most organizations, lower-level managers and employees are very guarded about what they say to the CEO because they don't want to make themselves or anyone else look bad. When that happens, CEOs get very little "meaty" information, and communication grinds to a halt. However, Lafley's quiet demeanour makes him approachable, and the managers and employees who meet with him invariably open up. Chris Start, a P&G vice president, said, "You can tell him bad news or things you'd be afraid to tell other bosses."

Another way in which Lafley finds out what people in the company are thinking and feeling is by encouraging discussions in which multiple perspectives and disagreements are shared. For example, P&G is considering the possibility of outsourcing a number of traditional staffing functions, such as information technology and human resource benefits. With P&G's history as a highly centralized, tightly controlled company, this is a very controversial proposal. Consequently, Lafley had P&G teams—one in favour of outsourcing, and the other against it—make arguments for their case to P&G's board of directors. Board member Scott Cook, co-founder of Intuit, the maker of Quicken software, said, "Boards typically don't see that level of debate. They're usually hidden by the CEOs."

Likewise, with an emphasis on its core brands and small-scale innovation, how can P&G do a better job of hearing what people outside the company feel and think?

Under CEO Durk Jager, P&G's innovation strategy was to hit home runs by trying to develop the company's next blockbuster billion-dollar brand. While innovation is still important under A.G. Lafley's leadership, the internal focus will be on innovating with existing products, while the external focus will be on acquiring innovative ideas and brands from outside the company. In both instances, there is a premium on obtaining information from outside the company, on finding out what people outside the company are thinking and feeling.

At P&G, which has a history of going it alone, looking outside the company for ideas is revolutionary. In the past, if the ideas weren't invented inhouse, they weren't any good. However, in the name of innovation, CEO Lafley is encouraging P&G'ers to find good ideas whenever they can. Lafley said, "Today, about 20% of our invention comes from outside. We'd like to get it up to 40% to 50% eventually. And if you think about that, that means we would double the productivity of our current investment in R&D. Half would come from inside, and half would come from connecting and developing outside." Some of those ideas can come simply by benchmarking what other companies are doing. For example, global marketing officer James Stengle now meets several times a year with his counterparts from other organizations like Kraft, Nestlé, Toyota, and Gucci. As simple as this sounds, Stengle and other P&G'ers weren't sharing and receiving ideas from "outsiders" just a few years ago. Likewise, in an effort to come up with innovative ideas for bathroom cleaners, P&G has brought in IDEO, the award-winning design firm, to study the way in which people clean their bathrooms. Tom Kelley, IDEO's general manager, said "In the old days, they kept us almost entirely in the dark." P&G is also turning to the Internet to do a better job of hearing what people outside the company are feeling and thinking. Similar to online discussion forums that can promote organization-wide communication, P&G is working with PlanetFeedback to find out what consumers are saying about P&G's two biggest brands—Tide detergent and Pampers diapers. PlanetFeedback will collect consumer comments on its Web site, from telephone hotlines, and faxes. It will also search online message boards, discussion Web sites, and Usenet user groups to find out what consumers are saying about P&G's brands.

Lafley's simple communication/listening methods have worked extremely well at P&G. The stock price, which dropped US$9 a share a month after he became CEO, is now up by 70 percent. At the time this was written, quarterly profits had risen to US$910 million from a US$320 million loss the previous year. Finally, net earnings were up 52 percent from a year earlier. In short, said stock analyst Ann Gillin-Lefever, Lafley has "restored our confidence" in P&G.

Key Terms

acquaintance time *(500)*
active listening *(497)*
address terms *(499)*
appointment time *(500)*
attribution theory *(485)*
blog *(503)*
closure *(485)*
coaching *(492)*
communication *(482)*
communication medium *(495)*
company hotlines *(503)*
conduit metaphor *(488)*
constructive feedback *(498)*
corporate talk shows *(502)*
counselling *(492)*
cross-cultural communication *(499)*
decoding *(488)*
defensive bias *(485)*
destructive feedback *(498)*
discussion time *(500)*
downward communication *(489)*
empathetic listening *(498)*
encoding *(487)*
feedback *(488)*
formal communication channel *(489)*
fundamental attribution error *(485)*
hearing *(497)*
horizontal communication *(489)*
informal communication channel (grapevine) *(490)*
kinesics *(493)*
listening *(497)*
noise *(488)*
nonverbal communication *(493)*
online discussion forums *(501)*
organizational silence *(502)*
paralanguage *(493)*
perception *(483)*
perceptual filters *(483)*
schedule time *(500)*
selective perception *(484)*
self-serving bias *(486)*
survey feedback *(503)*
televised/videotaped speeches and meetings *(502)*
upward communication *(489)*

Self-Assessment

HOW DO YOU LISTEN?

Have you ever been eager to tell someone a funny story, only to have that person interrupt you repeatedly to ask for details or clarification? And have you ever said in exasperation, "Will you just listen?" Some people prefer an inquisitive listening style, whereas others prefer a contemplative listening style. What listening style best describes you? The Assessment Appendix has a listening styles inventory on page 521. Take the 10-question survey to establish a baseline you can use as a foundation for developing your listening skills.

Management Decisions

SELLING IN LATIN AMERICA[84]

As you glance at the calendar on your desk, you realize that you have only two weeks left to prepare for your first international assignment. Since your recent promotion to the position of a regional sales manager for a mid-sized, multinational, telecommunications firm, you have spent the majority of your time working out of the home office. What time you did spend travelling was spent visiting customers and offices in and around your sales region. Your new job entails describing your firm's products and services; explaining the benefits, price, and terms; and, once the customer agrees, closing the sale by signing a formal contract containing the necessary information.

During last month's regional managers' meeting, your boss informed you that because of your ability to speak Spanish fluently and your recent success and promotion, you would soon assume part of the Latin American region and would be responsible for meeting and dealing with customers in Mexico and parts of South America, in addition to your current duties. Although you are excited at the prospect of travelling abroad, you are also a little nervous because, other than a week-long, school-sponsored trip to Ciudad Juarez, Mexico, you have never left the country before.

The company's travel office has helped relieve some of your anxiety by performing a majority of the paperwork involved, preparing your passport, making your travel arrangements, and putting you in touch with the former regional manager for Latin America. Even though she has been a tremendous asset by telling you which hotel chains and restaurants are "decent" and which are not, showing you how to avoid some of the customs inspection problems, and giving you an updated potential-customer database, she hasn't provided much information regarding the local culture of the area or your prospective customers' expectations. As a region, Latin America is less developed in the area of telecommunications than North America, so you are excited about the sales potential of the area. However, you also have some concerns.

One major area of concern is the myriad of cultural differences between North America and Latin America. You believe that one of the reasons that you were so successful in your region is because you really knew and understood your customers and their needs. Given the fact that you will be making cold calls, requesting appointments, making presentations to individuals and groups, and attempting to close on contractual agreements involving thousands of dollars, you feel your concerns are legitimate.

Questions

1. As the manager in question, what could you do to help put an end to your uneasiness?
2. Although you speak Spanish, you know that language is not the only element of cross-cultural fluency. What issues will you be confronting with regards to cross-cultural communication in your new Latin American position? What can you do to overcome the obstacles to cross-cultural communication?

Management Decisions

IS UPWARD COMMUNICATION WORTH THE RISK?

It's been 18 months now since the new CEO was hired, and what a breath of fresh air he's been. He's exciting and visionary, but also friendly and approachable, and has gone out of his way to meet as many people as possible, holding quarterly town hall meetings and doing lunch with lower-level managers and workers at least once a week. And every time you've heard him speak, he's announced his e-mail address and encouraged anyone who wanted to contact him directly.

In fact, people throughout the organization have been energized by his leadership and the changes he's made to bring about a more open, innovative culture. Of course, not everything can change at once. In fact, things haven't changed much in your division at all. Your division head, Tim Howard, hasn't really embraced the new leadership style. You might even say he's rejected it. Tim is short with subordinates, prone to yelling when things aren't done to his satisfaction, and, in the last year or so, incredibly indecisive. Each week, dozens of big and little decisions that need to be made aren't being made. The whole division just sits there with no direction and no momentum. And if you come up with an idea that might make the division more competitive and are brave enough to discuss it with Tim, you find out that he's not completely indecisive. Indeed, Tim has a bad case of "not invented here" syndrome, so if it's not his idea, the automatic answer is "no."

It's obvious to you and everyone else that Tim is burned out and that you need a new division head. You're tempted to e-mail the new CEO about the situation—after all, he's open to communication from anyone in the company. However, you worry about going around Tim to top management. And what if the CEO isn't quite as open as he makes himself out to be?

Questions

1. What risks do you incur if you e-mail the CEO about Tim's leadership of your division?
2. If you were going to e-mail the CEO, what would your opening paragraph say?
3. Would you e-mail the CEO about Tim? Yes or no? Explain your decision.

Develop Your Management Potential

I DON'T AGREE, BUT I'M LISTENING

Being a good listener is a critical part of effective communication. Without it, you're unlikely to be a good manager. Therefore, the purpose of this assignment is to help you develop your listening skills. And there's no better way to do that than to talk to someone whose views are quite different from yours.

In the best of situations, being a good listener is difficult. Because of perceptual filters, distractions, or daydreams, you retain only about 25 percent of what you hear. However, it can be almost impossible to be a good listener when you're talking to someone who has very different views and opinions. When you talk to people with different views, it's easy to interrupt, jump to conclusions about what they'll say, and hurry them to finish their points (which you don't want to listen to anyway), so you can "correct" their thinking with your opinions.

To complete this assignment, you'll have to find someone who has different views or opinions on some topic (gun control, abortion, and euthanasia are just some of the topics on which you can always find someone with a different viewpoint). Once you've found someone, conduct a ten-minute listening session, following this simple rule: Before stating your opinion, you must first accurately reflect or paraphrase the statement that your listening partner just made (be sure to reread the discussion on listening on page 496). So if your listening partner said, "Women shouldn't have to ask anyone for permission for what they do to their bodies. If they decide they want an abortion, they should go ahead and have it," you would have to accurately paraphrase that statement in your own words before being allowed to make your point or disagree with that of your partner. If you don't paraphrase it correctly, your listening partner will tell you. If you or your partner have difficulty accurately paraphrasing a statement, then ask the other person to repeat the statement, and try again. Also, don't parrot the response by repeating it word for word. Good listening isn't mimicry. It's capturing the essence of what others have said in your own words. And before your listening partner responds, he or she, too, has to accurately paraphrase what you say. Continue this listening-based discussion for ten minutes.

Questions

1. Was this different from the way in which you normally discuss contentious topics with other people? Why or why not?
2. Was it difficult to reflect or paraphrase your listening partner's perspectives? Explain and give an example.
3. What led to more effective listening for you—active listening techniques or empathetic listening techniques? Explain.

Discussion Questions

1. Identify a situation where you have misunderstood what someone was trying to tell you. What was the cause of the misunderstanding (relate it back to the theory in the chapter)?
2. Compare the advantages and disadvantages of e-mail and face-to-face communication. When are they the most appropriate to use?
3. What four skills are essential for managers to use during face-to-face communication? Give examples from your workplace.
4. What is the difference between coaching and counselling? Give examples.

Critical Thinking Video Case

CBC

Visit www.management2e.nelson.com to view this chapter's CBC video case.

Take Two

Biz Flix
The Paper

This engaging film shows the ethical dilemmas and stress of producing the *New York Sun*, a daily metropolitan newspaper. Metro editor Henry Hackett (Michael Keaton) races against the clock to publish a story about a major police scandal that could send two young African-American men to jail. He is in constant conflict with managing editor Alicia Clark (Glenn Close), who is more concerned about controlling the budget than about running accurate stories. Hackett is also under constant pressure from his wife Marty (Marisa Tomei), who is pregnant with their first child. While Hackett tries to get his story, Marty urges him to take a less demanding job at *The Sentinel*.

This scene is an edited version of the "The Managing Editor" sequence, which occurs early in *The Paper*. It shows a staff meeting that takes place the day after the *Sun* missed a story about a murder and other shootings with racial overtones. Instead, the *Sun* ran a front-page story about parking problems. At the meeting, senior editor Bernie White (Robert Duvall) discusses his preferences in front-page stories.

What to Watch for and Ask Yourself

1. Use the model of the communication process to diagram what is occurring in the clip.
2. What types of communication do you see in the video?
3. Discuss the paralanguage used in the clip. What mood or attitude does it convey?

Management Workplace
Tires Plus

Tires Plus started when Tom Gegax and Don Gullet left Royal Dutch Shell in 1976. The pair bought three gas stations, which they converted to tire stores that sold high-end tires and served cappuccino. The real competitive advantage of Tires Plus, however, was not the unique way the company delivered its service. Instead, Tom and Don thought their competitive advantage came from their employees, so they nurtured communication throughout the organization. After 25 years, Tires Plus has become a 150-store powerhouse that employs 2000 people and generates over US$200 million in annual sales.

What to Watch for and Ask Yourself

1. How do the leaders of Tires Plus work to avoid perception problems?
2. What kind of communication seems to be most important at Tires Plus? Why?
3. How do Tom Gegax and Don Gullet improve one-on-one communication?
4. Describe the technique Tom uses to hear what others in the organization feel and think.

self-assessment appendix

Chapter 1

As you learned in Chapter 1, many managers begin their careers in management with specific notions about what it means to be the boss. This assessment is meant to establish your baseline interests in the skills covered in the chapter. It will not tell you whether you should or should not be a manager, nor whether you have "what it takes" to be a manager. It will, however, give you feedback on whether you are interested in the kinds of things that managers do in their jobs. Be candid as you complete the assessment by circling the appropriate responses.[1]

ML = Most like me
SL = Somewhat like me
NS = Not sure
SU = Somewhat unlike me
MU = Most unlike me

1. I can get others to do what I want them to do.	ML	SL	NS	SU	MU
2. I frequently evaluate my job performance.	ML	SL	NS	SU	MU
3. I prefer not to get involved in office politics.	ML	SL	NS	SU	MU
4. I like the freedom that open-ended goals provide me.	ML	SL	NS	SU	MU
5. I work best when things are orderly and calm.	ML	SL	NS	SU	MU
6. I enjoy making oral presentations to groups of people.	ML	SL	NS	SU	MU
7. I am confident in my abilities to accomplish difficult tasks.	ML	SL	NS	SU	MU
8. I do not like to write.	ML	SL	NS	SU	MU
9. I like solving difficult puzzles.	ML	SL	NS	SU	MU
10. I am an organized person.	ML	SL	NS	SU	MU
11. I have difficulty telling others they made a mistake.	ML	SL	NS	SU	MU
12. I like to work set hours each day.	ML	SL	NS	SU	MU
13. I view paperwork as a trivial task.	ML	SL	NS	SU	MU
14. I like to help others learn new things.	ML	SL	NS	SU	MU
15. I prefer to work alone.	ML	SL	NS	SU	MU
16. I believe it is who you know, not what you know, that counts.	ML	SL	NS	SU	MU
17. I enjoy doing several things at once.	ML	SL	NS	SU	MU
18. I am good at managing money.	ML	SL	NS	SU	MU
19. I would rather back down from an argument than let it get out of hand.	ML	SL	NS	SU	MU
20. I am computer literate.	ML	SL	NS	SU	MU

Scoring

Start by reversing your scores for items 5, 8, 11, 15, and 16. For example, if you used ML, change it to MU, and vice versa; if you used SL, change it to SU, and vice versa. Now assign each answer a point value.

Number of MU answers _________ times 5 points each = _________

Number of ML answers _________ times 4 points each = _________

Number of SL answers _________ times 3 points each = _________

Number of NS answers _________ times 2 points each = _________

Number of SU answers _________ times 1 point each = _________

You can find the interpretation for your score at http://www.management2e.nelson.com/student/assessments.html

Chapter 2

Complete the following questionnaire to get a sense of your tolerance for ambiguity.[2] Indicate the extent to which you agree with the statements using the following scale:

1 Strongly disagree
2 Moderately disagree
3 Slightly disagree
4 Neutral
5 Slightly agree
6 Moderately agree
7 Strongly agree

_____ 1. I don't tolerate ambiguous situations well.

_____ 2. I find it difficult to respond when faced with an expected event.

_____ 3. I don't think new situations are any more threatening than familiar situations.

_____ 4. I am drawn to situations which can be interpreted more than one way.

_____ 5. I would rather avoid solving problems that must be viewed from several different perspectives.

_____ 6. I try to avoid situations which are ambiguous.

_____ 7. I am good at managing unpredictable situations.

_____ 8. I prefer familiar situations to new ones.

_____ 9. Problems which cannot be considered from just one point of view are a little threatening.

_____ 10. I avoid situations which are too complicated for me to easily understand.

_____ 11. I am tolerant of ambiguous situations.

_____ 12. I enjoy tackling problems which are complex enough to be ambiguous.

_____ 13. I try to avoid problems which don't seem to have only one "best" solution.

_____ 14. I often find myself looking for something new, rather than trying to hold things constant in my life.

_____ 15. I generally prefer novelty over familiarity.

_____ 16. I dislike ambiguous situations.

_____ 17. Some problems are so complex that just trying to understand them is fun.

_____ 18. I have little trouble coping with unexpected events.

_____ 19. I pursue problem situations which are so complex some people call them "mind-boggling."

_____ 20. I find it hard to make a choice when the outcome is uncertain.

_____ 21. I enjoy an occasional surprise.

_____ 22. I prefer a situation in which there is some ambiguity.

Scoring

Determine your score by entering your response to each survey item below, as follows. In blanks that say *regular score*, simply enter your response for that item. If your response was a 6, place a 6 in the *regular score* blank. In blanks that say *reverse score*, subtract your response from 8 and enter the result. So if your response was a 6, place a 2 (8 − 6 = 2) in the *reverse score* blank. Add up your total score.

1. regular score _____
2. regular score _____
3. reverse score _____
4. reverse score _____
5. regular score _____
6. regular score _____
7. reverse score _____
8. regular score _____
9. regular score _____
10. regular score _____
11. regular score _____
12. reverse score _____
13. regular score _____
14. reverse score _____
15. reverse score _____
16. regular score _____
17. reverse score _____
18. reverse score _____
19. reverse score _____
20. regular score _____
21. reverse score _____
22. reverse score _____

TOTAL = _____

You can find the interpretation for your score at http://www.management2e.nelson.com/student/assessments.html

Chapter 3

Answer each of the questions using the following scale:[3]

1 Strongly agree
2 Agree
3 Not sure
4 Disagree
5 Strongly disagree

_____ 1. Did you ever think about taking money from where you worked, but didn't go through with it?

_____ 2. Have you ever borrowed something from work without telling anyone?

_____ 3. There are times I've been provoked into a fist fight.

_____ 4. Is it okay to get around the law if you don't break it?

_____ 5. I've had fellow employees show me how to take things from where I work.

_____ 6. I will usually take someone up on a dare.

_____ 7. I've always driven insured vehicles.

_____ 8. If you were sent an extra item with an order, would you send it back?

_____ 9. Would you say everyone is a little dishonest?

_____ 10. Most supervisors treat their employees fairly.

_____ 11. I worry about getting hurt at work.

_____ 12. People say that I'm a workaholic.

_____ 13. I like to plan things carefully ahead of time.

_____ 14. Have you found a way a dishonest person in your job could take things from work?

_____ 15. I often act quickly without stopping to think things through.

_____ 16. It doesn't bother me what other people think.

_____ 17. I have friends who are a little dishonest.

_____ 18. I am not a thrill seeker.

_____ 19. I have had my driver's licence revoked.

_____ 20. Are you too honest to steal?

_____ 21. Do most employees take small items from work?

_____ 22. Do most employees get along well with their supervisors?

_____ 23. I'm lucky to avoid having accidents.

_____ 24. I always finish what I start.

_____ 25. I make sure everything is in its place before leaving home.

SCORING

Determine your average score for each category by entering your response to each survey item below, as follows. In blanks that say *regular score*, simply enter your response for that item. If your response was a 4, place a 4 in the *regular score* blank. In blanks that say *reverse score*, subtract your response from 6 and enter the result. So if your response was a 4, place a 2 ($6 - 4 = 2$) in the *reverse score* blank. Total your scores, and then compute your average score for each section.

Antisocial Behaviour:

1. regular score _____ 14. regular score _____
2. regular score _____ 15. regular score _____
3. regular score _____ 16. regular score _____
4. regular score _____ 17. regular score _____
5. regular score _____ 18. reverse score _____
6. regular score _____ 19. regular score _____
7. reverse score _____ 20. reverse score _____
8. reverse score _____

TOTAL = _____ ÷ 15 = _____ (your average for Antisocial Behaviour)

Orderliness/diligence:

12. regular score _____ 24. regular score _____
13. regular score _____ 25. regular score _____

TOTAL = _____ ÷ 4 = _____ (your average for Orderliness/diligence)

Positive Outlook:

9. reverse score _____ 21. reverse score _____
10. regular score _____ 22. regular score _____
11. reverse score _____ 23. regular score _____

TOTAL = _____ ÷ 6 = _____ (your average for Positive Outlook)

You can find the interpretation for your score at http://www.management2e.nelson.com/student/assessments.html

Chapter 4

A part of planning, and therefore, management, is setting goals and tracking progress toward goal achievement.[4] Answer each of the questions using the following scale:

1 Strongly disagree
2 Disagree
3 Not sure
4 Agree
5 Strongly Agree

_____ 1. I regularly set goals for myself.

_____ 2. I keep track of how well I've been doing.

_____ 3. I generally keep the resolutions that I make.

_____ 4. I often seek feedback about my performance.

_____ 5. I am able to focus on positive aspects of my work.

_____ 6. I'll sometimes deny myself something until I've set my goals.

_____ 7. I use a to-do list to plan my activities.

_____ 8. I have trouble working without supervision.

_____ 9. When I set my mind on some goal, I persevere until it's accomplished.

_____ 10. I'm a self-starter.

_____ 11. I make lists of things I need to do.

_____ 12. I'm good at time management.

_____ 13. I'm usually confident that I can reach my goals.

_____ 14. I am careful about how I manage my time.

_____ 15. I always plan my day.

_____ 16. I often find I spend my time on trivial things and put off doing what's really important.

_____ 17. Unless someone pushes me a bit, I have trouble getting motivated.

_____ 18. I reward myself when I meet my goals.

_____ 19. I tend to dwell on unpleasant aspects of the things I need to do.

_____ 20. I tend to deal with life as it comes rather than to try to plan things.

_____ 21. I generally try to find a place to work where I'll be free from interruptions.

_____ 22. I'm pretty disorganized.

_____ 23. The goals I set are quite specific.

_____ 24. Distractions often interfere with my performance.

_____ 25. I sometimes give myself a treat if I've done something well.

_____ 26. I am able to focus on positive aspects of my activities.

_____ 27. I use notes or other prompts to remind myself of schedules and deadlines.

_____ 28. I seem to waste a lot of time.

_____ 29. I use a day planner or other aids to keep track of schedules and deadlines.

_____ 30. I often think about how I can improve my performance.

_____ 31. I tend to lose track of the goals I've set for myself.

_____ 32. I tend to set difficult goals for myself.

_____ 33. I plan things for weeks in advance.

_____ 34. I try to make a visible commitment to my goals.

_____ 35. I set aside blocks of time for important activities.

Scoring

Determine your score by entering your response to each survey item below, as follows. In blanks that say *regular score*, simply enter your response for that item. If your response was a 4, place a 4 in the *regular score* blank. In blanks that say *reverse score*, subtract your response from 6 and enter the result. So if your response was a 4, place a 2 (6 − 4 = 2) in the *reverse score* blank. Add up your total score.

1. regular score _____
2. regular score _____
3 regular score _____
4. regular score _____
5. regular score _____
6. regular score _____
7. regular score _____
8. reverse score _____
9. reverse score _____
10. regular score _____
11. regular score _____
12. regular score _____
13. regular score _____
14. regular score _____
15. regular score _____
16. reverse score _____
17. reverse score _____
18. regular score _____
19. reverse score _____
20. reverse score _____
21. regular score _____
22. reverse score _____
23. regular score _____
24. reverse score _____
25. regular score _____

TOTAL = _____

26. regular score _____
27. regular score _____
28. reverse score _____
29. regular score _____
30. regular score _____
31. reverse score _____
32. regular score _____
33. regular score _____
34. regular score _____
35. regular score _____

You can find the interpretation for your score at http://www.management2e.nelson.com/student/assessments.html

Chapter 5

How do you feel about using computers and technology?[5] Be candid as you complete the assessment by circling the appropriate responses.

	Strongly disagree				Strongly agree
1. I hesitate to use a computer for fear of making mistakes that I cannot correct.	1	2	3	4	5
2. The challenge of learning about computers is exciting.	1	2	3	4	5
3. I feel apprehensive about using computers.	1	2	3	4	5
4. I am confident that I can learn computer skills.	1	2	3	4	5
5. I feel insecure about my ability to interpret a computer printout.	1	2	3	4	5
6. I look forward to using a computer on my job.	1	2	3	4	5
7. I have avoided computers because they are unfamiliar and somewhat intimidating to me.	1	2	3	4	5
8. Learning to operate computers is like learning any new skill—the more you practise, the better you become.	1	2	3	4	5
9. It scares me to think that I could cause the computer to destroy a large amount of information by hitting the wrong key.	1	2	3	4	5
10. If given the opportunity, I would like to learn about and use computers.	1	2	3	4	5
11. I have difficulty in understanding the technical aspects of computers.	1	2	3	4	5
12. I am sure that with time and practice, I will be as comfortable working with computers as I am working with a typewriter.	1	2	3	4	5
13. You have to be a genius to understand all the special keys contained on most computer terminals.	1	2	3	4	5
14. Anyone can learn to use a computer if they are patient and motivated.	1	2	3	4	5
15. I do not think I would be able to learn a computer programming language.	1	2	3	4	5
16. I feel computers are necessary tools in both educational and work settings.	1	2	3	4	5
17. I dislike working with machines that are smarter than I am.	1	2	3	4	5
18. I feel that I will be able to keep up with the advances happening in the computer field.	1	2	3	4	5
19. I am afraid that if I begin using computers, I will become dependent upon them and lose some of my reasoning skills.	1	2	3	4	5

TOTAL = ________

Scoring

Reverse scores on even-numbered items. Reverse means, for instance, a 1 becomes a 5; a 4 becomes a 2, and so on. Using the reversed scores and the remaining scores, compute your score for the 19 items by adding up the scores.

You can find the interpretation for your score at http://www.management2e.nelson.com/student/assessments.html

Chapter 6

In this exercise, you'll be asked some questions about your feelings about making decisions. Answer Yes or No to each question. To ensure an accurate score and to receive feedback that is applicable to you, answer the questions truthfully—even though you know which answers will increase your score.

_____ 1. Do you often try to avoid or delay making important decisions and even hope that problems will go away?

_____ 2. When required to make a decision fairly promptly, do you become flustered and fail to function at your best?

_____ 3. Would you consider it demeaning to consult your subordinates regarding a problem with which they have experience?

_____ 4. In deciding a complicated problem where strong arguments exist for either side, would you trust your "gut reaction"?

_____ 5. Do you often wish that you didn't have to make any decisions?

_____ 6. When faced with a serious decision, are your sleep and appetite usually adversely affected?

_____ 7. Do you secretly dislike making decisions because you lack self-confidence?

_____ 8. Are you uneasy even when required to make unimportant decisions?

_____ 9. Would you fire a friend if his or her continued employment were against the welfare of the organization in which you held a high position?

_____ 10. When baffled by a problem within your jurisdiction, would you try to get others to deal with it?

_____ 11. At home, do you participate in all or most of the important decisions?

_____ 12. Are you usually edgy both before and after making important decisions?

Scoring

1. Yes = 1 point, No = 4 points
2. Yes = 1 point, No = 4 points
3. Yes = 1 point, No = 4 points
4. Yes = 4 points, No = 1 point
5. Yes = 1 point, No = 4 points
6. Yes = 1 point, No = 4 points
7. Yes = 1 point, No = 4 points
8. Yes = 1 point, No = 4 points
9. Yes = 4 points, No = 1 point
10. Yes = 1 point, No = 4 points
11. Yes = 4 points, No = 1 point
12. Yes = 1 point, No = 4 points

Add together to compute your TOTAL _____.

You can find the interpretation for your score at http://www.management2e.nelson.com/student/assessments.html

Chapter 7

As you complete this feedback inventory, be candid as you circle the appropriate responses.[6]

	Extremely Untrue					Extremely True
1. It is important for me to obtain useful information about my performance.	1	2	3	4	5	6
2. If I receive negative feedback, I would have a negative attitude towards myself, so I try to avoid criticism.	1	2	3	4	5	6
3. I am not really worried about what people will think of me if I ask for feedback about my performance.	1	2	3	4	5	6
4. I like people to hear about my good performance at work (or at college).	1	2	3	4	5	6
5. Receiving feedback about my performance helps me to improve my skills.	1	2	3	4	5	6
6. Negative feedback doesn't really lower my self-worth, so I don't go out of my way to avoid it.	1	2	3	4	5	6
7. I'm concerned about what people would think of me if I were to ask for feedback.	1	2	3	4	5	6
8. Seeking feedback from my supervisor (instructor) is one way to show that I want to improve my performance.	1	2	3	4	5	6
9. I would like to obtain more information to let me know how I am performing.	1	2	3	4	5	6
10. Receiving negative feedback wouldn't really change the way I feel about myself.	1	2	3	4	5	6
11. I am worried about the impression I would make if I were to ask for feedback.	1	2	3	4	5	6
12. I want people to know when I ask for feedback so I can show my responsible nature.	1	2	3	4	5	6
13. I would like to receive more useful information about my performance.	1	2	3	4	5	6
14. It's hard to feel good about myself when I receive negative feedback.	1	2	3	4	5	6
15. I don't really worry about what others would think of me if I asked for feedback.	1	2	3	4	5	6
16. I don't really care if people hear the good feedback that is given to me.	1	2	3	4	5	6
17. I'm not really concerned about whether I receive useful information about my performance.	1	2	3	4	5	6
18. I don't really worry about getting negative feedback because I still feel I am a person of worth.	1	2	3	4	5	6
19. I don't really care if people know the type of feedback I get.	1	2	3	4	5	6

20. When I receive praise, I don't really want others to hear it.	1	2	3	4	5	6
21. Feedback is not really useful to help me improve my performance.	1	2	3	4	5	6
22. I try to avoid negative feedback because it makes me feel bad about myself.	1	2	3	4	5	6
23. If I sought feedback about my performance, I wouldn't want other people to know what type of feedback I received.	1	2	3	4	5	6
24. I don't care either way if people see me asking my supervisor (instructor) for feedback.	1	2	3	4	5	6
25. Obtaining useful feedback information is not very important to me.	1	2	3	4	5	6
26. I worry about receiving feedback that is likely to be negative because it hurts to be criticized.	1	2	3	4	5	6
27. I am usually concerned about other people hearing the content of the individual feedback I receive.	1	2	3	4	5	6
28. I hope positive feedback about my performance will make a good impression on others.	1	2	3	4	5	6
29. I don't really require more feedback to let me know how I am performing.	1	2	3	4	5	6
30. Negative feedback doesn't really worry me because I still have a positive attitude towards myself.	1	2	3	4	5	6
31. It doesn't worry me if people know how I've performed at something.	1	2	3	4	5	6
32. I don't really need to impress others by letting them know about the positive feedback I receive regarding my performance.	1	2	3	4	5	6

Scoring

Determine your average score for each category by entering your response to each survey item below, as follows. In blanks that say *regular score*, simply enter your response for that item. If your response was a 4, place a 4 in the *regular score* blank. In blanks that say *reverse score*, subtract your response from 7 and enter the result. So if your response was a 4, place a 3 (7 − 4 = 3) in the *reverse score* blank. Total your scores then compute each average score.

Desire for Useful Information:	*Ego Defence:*	*Defensive Impression Management:*	*Assertive Impression Management:*
1. regular score ___	2. regular score ___	3. reverse score ___	4. regular score ___
5. regular score ___	6. reverse score ___	7. regular score ___	8. regular score ___
9. regular score ___	10. reverse score ___	11. regular score ___	12. regular score ___
13. regular score ___	14. regular score ___	15. reverse score ___	16. reverse score ___
17. reverse score ___	18. reverse score ___	19. reverse score ___	20. reverse score ___
21. reverse score ___	22. regular score ___	23. regular score ___	24. reverse score ___
25. reverse score ___	26. regular score ___	27. regular score ___	28. regular score ___
29. reverse score ___	30. reverse score ___	31. reverse score ___	32. reverse score ___
TOTAL = ___	TOTAL = ___	TOTAL = ___	TOTAL = ___

You can find the interpretation for your score at http://www.management2e.nelson.com/student/assessments.html

Chapter 8

This assessment has three parts: Step 1, Complete the questionnaire shown below; Step 2, Determine your score; Step 3, Develop a plan to increase your global managerial potential.[7]

Step 1: Use the six-point rating scale to complete the 32-question inventory shown below.

Rating Scale

6 Strongly agree	3 Mildly disagree
5 Agree	2 Disagree
4 Mildly agree	1 Strongly disagree

____ 1. Our country should have the right to prohibit certain racial and religious groups from entering it to live.

____ 2. Our responsibility to people of other races ought to be as great as our responsibility to people of our own race.

____ 3. Immigrants should not be permitted to come into our country if they compete with our own workers.

____ 4. It would set a dangerous precedent if every person in the world had equal rights that were guaranteed by an international charter.

____ 5. All prices for exported food and manufactured goods should be set by an international trade committee.

____ 6. Our country is probably no better than many others.

____ 7. Race prejudice may be a good thing for us because it keeps many undesirable foreigners from coming into this country.

____ 8. It would be a mistake for us to encourage certain racial groups to become well educated because they might use their knowledge against us.

____ 9. We should be willing to fight for our country without questioning whether it is right or wrong.

____ 10. Foreigners are particularly obnoxious because of their religious beliefs.

____ 11. Immigration should be controlled by a global organization rather than by each country on its own.

____ 12. We ought to have a world government to guarantee the welfare of all nations irrespective of the rights of anyone.

____ 13. Our country should not cooperate in any global trade agreements that attempt to better world economic conditions at our expense.

____ 14. It would be better to be a citizen of the world than of any particular country.

____ 15. A global committee on education should have full control over what is taught in all countries about history and politics.

____ 16. Our country should refuse to cooperate in a total disarmament program even if some other nations agree to it.

____ 17. It would be dangerous for our country to make international agreements with nations whose religious beliefs are antagonistic to ours.

____ 18. Any healthy individual, regardless of race or religion, should be allowed to live wherever he or she wants to in the world.

____ 19. Our country should not participate in any global organization that requires that we give up any of our national rights or freedom of action.

____ 20. If necessary, we ought to be willing to lower our standard of living to cooperate with other countries in getting an equal standard for every person in the world.

____ 21. We should strive for loyalty to our country before we can afford to consider world brotherhood.

____ 22. Some races ought to be considered naturally less intelligent than ours.

____ 23. Our schools should teach the history of the whole world rather than of our own country.

____ 24. A global police force ought to be the only group in the world allowed to have armaments.

____ 25. It would be dangerous for us to guarantee by international agreement that every person in the world should have complete religious freedom.

____ 26. Our country should permit the immigration of foreign peoples, even if it lowers our standard of living.

____ 27. All national governments ought to be abolished and replaced by one central world government.

____ 28. It would not be wise for us to agree that working conditions in all countries should be subject to international control.

____ 29. Patriotism should be a primary aim of education so that our children will believe our country is the best in the world.

____ 30. It would be a good idea if all the races were to intermarry until there was only one race in the world.

____ 31. We should teach our children to uphold the welfare of all people everywhere, even though it may be against the best interests of our own country.

____ 32. War should never be justifiable, even if it is the only way to protect our national rights and honour.

Step 2: Determine your score by entering your response to each survey item below, as follows. In blanks that say *regular score*, simply enter your response for that item. If your response was a 4, place a 4 in the *regular score* blank. In blanks that say *reverse score*, subtract your response from 7 and enter the result. So if your response was a 4, place a 3 (7 − 4 = 3) in the *reverse score* blank.

1. reverse score	_____	17. reverse score	_____
2. reverse score	_____	18. regular score	_____
3. reverse score	_____	19. reverse score	_____
4. regular score	_____	20. regular score	_____
5. regular score	_____	21. reverse score	_____
6. reverse score	_____	22. reverse score	_____
7. reverse score	_____	23. regular score	_____
8. reverse score	_____	24. regular score	_____
9. reverse score	_____	25. reverse score	_____
10. regular score	_____	26. regular score	_____
11. regular score	_____	27. regular score	_____
12. reverse score	_____	28. reverse score	_____
13. regular score	_____	29. reverse score	_____
14. regular score	_____	30. regular score	_____
15. regular score	_____	31. regular score	_____
16. reverse score	_____	32. regular score	_____

Total your scores from items 1–16 _____

Total your scores from items 17–32 _____

Add together to compute TOTAL = _____

You can find the interpretation for your score at http://www.management2e.nelson.com/student/assessments.html

Chapter 9

This assessment will provide some baseline information on attitudes you might have that will relate to your management skills.[8] Answer each of the questions either true or false. Try not to spend too much time on any one item, and be sure to answer all the questions.

_____ 1. I get satisfaction from competing with others.

_____ 2. It's usually not important to me to be the best.

_____ 3. Competition destroys friendships.

_____ 4. Games with no clear-cut winners are boring.

_____ 5. I am a competitive individual.

_____ 6. I will do almost anything to avoid an argument.

_____ 7. I try to avoid competing with others.

_____ 8. I would like to be on a debating team.

_____ 9. I often remain quiet rather than risk hurting another person.

_____ 10. I find competitive situations unpleasant.

_____ 11. I try to avoid arguments.

_____ 12. In general, I will go along with the group rather than create conflict.

_____ 13. I don't like competing against other people.

_____ 14. I don't like games that are winner-take-all.

_____ 15. I dread competing against other people.

_____ 16. I enjoy competing against an opponent.

_____ 17. When I play a game, I like to keep score.

_____ 18. I often try to outperform others.

_____ 19. I like competition.

_____ 20. I don't enjoy challenging others even when I think they are wrong.

To determine your score, count the number of responses marked "True" and enter it here _____.

You can find the interpretation for your score at http://www.management2e.nelson.com/student/assessments.html

Chapter 10

This assessment will provide some baseline information you can use as you develop your managerial skills.[9] Indicate the extent to which each of the following statements is true of either your actual behaviour or your intentions at work. That is, describe the way you are or the way you intend to be on the job. Use this scale for your responses:

5 Almost always true	2 Seldom true
4 Often true	1 Almost never true
3 Not applicable	

_____ 1. I openly discuss with my supervisor how to get ahead.

_____ 2. I try new ideas and approaches to problems.

_____ 3. I take things or situations apart to find out how they work.

_____ 4. I welcome uncertainty and unusual circumstances related to my tasks.

_____ 5. I negotiate my salary openly with my supervisor.

_____ 6. I can be counted on to find a new use for existing methods or equipment.

_____ 7. Among my colleagues and co-workers, I will be the first or nearly the first to try out a new idea or method.

_____ 8. I take the opportunity to translate communications from other departments for my work group.

_____ 9. I demonstrate originality.

_____ 10. I will work on a problem that has caused others great difficulty.

_____ 11. I provide critical input toward a new solution.

_____ 12. I provide written evaluations of proposed ideas.

_____ 13. I develop contacts with experts outside my firm.

_____ 14. I use personal contacts to manoeuvre into choice work assignments.

_____ 15. I make time to pursue my own pet ideas or projects.

_____ 16. I set aside resources for the pursuit of a risky project.

_____ 17. I tolerate people who depart from organizational routine.

_____ 18. I speak out in staff meetings.

_____ 19. I work in teams to try to solve complex problems.

_____ 20. If my co-workers are asked, they will say I am a wit.

_____ = TOTAL

You can find the interpretation for your score at http://www.management2e.nelson.com/student/assessments.html

Chapter 11

Every organization needs some degree of flexibility to adapt to new situations, and some degree of standardization to make routine tasks and decisions as efficient and effective as possible.[10] In this assessment, indicate the extent to which you agree or disagree with the following statements. Use this scale for your responses:

7 Strongly agree	3 Slightly agree
6 Agree	2 Disagree
5 Slightly agree	1 Strongly disagree
4 Neutral	

_____ 1. If a written rule does not cover some situation, we make up informal rules for doing things as we go along.

_____ 2. I feel that I am my own boss in most matters.

_____ 3. There are many things in my business that are not covered by some formal procedure.

_____ 4. A person can make his or her own decisions without checking with somebody else.

_____ 5. Usually, my contact with my company and its representatives involves doing things "by the rule book."

_____ 6. How things are done here is left up to the person doing the work.

_____ 7. Contacts with my company and its representatives are on a formal, preplanned basis.

_____ 8. People here are allowed to do almost anything as they please.

_____ 9. I ignore the rules and reach informal agreements to handle some situations.

_____ 10. Most people here make their own rules on the job.

_____ 11. When rules and procedures exist in my company, they are usually written agreements.

_____ 12. The employees are constantly being checked on for rule violations.

_____ 13. People here feel as though they are constantly being watched, to see that they obey all the rules.

Scoring

Determine your score by entering your response to each survey item below, as follows. In blanks that say *regular score*, simply enter your response for that item. If your response was a 6, place a 6 in the *regular score* blank. In blanks that say *reverse score*, subtract your response from 8 and enter the result. So if your response was a 6, place a 2 ($8 - 6 = 2$) in the *reverse score* blank.

_____ 1. reverse score	_____ 8. reverse score
_____ 2. reverse score	_____ 9. reverse score
_____ 3. reverse score	_____ 10. reverse score
_____ 4. reverse score	_____ 11. regular score
_____ 5. regular score	_____ 12. regular score
_____ 6. reverse score	_____ 13. regular score
_____ 7. regular score	

Add together to compute your TOTAL _____ .

You can see where you fall on the formality continuum and find the interpretation of your score at http://www.management2e.nelson.com/student/assessments.html

Chapter 12

The following 20-question survey assesses your thoughts about working in teams.[11] Indicate the extent to which you agree with each of the following statements. Try not to spend too much time on any one item, and be sure to answer all the questions. Use this scale for your responses:

7 Strongly agree
6 Agree
5 Slightly agree
4 Neutral
3 Slightly disagree
2 Disagree
1 Strongly disagree

_____ 1. Only those who depend on themselves get ahead in life.

_____ 2. To be superior, a person must stand alone.

_____ 3. If you want something done right, you've got to do it yourself.

_____ 4. What happens to me is my own doing.

_____ 5. In the long run, the only person you can count on is yourself.

_____ 6. Winning is everything.

_____ 7. I feel that winning is important in both work and games.

_____ 8. Success is the most important thing in life.

_____ 9. It annoys me when other people perform better than I do.

_____ 10. Doing your best isn't enough; it is important to win.

_____ 11. I prefer to work with others in a group rather than working alone.

_____ 12. Given the choice, I would rather do a job where I can work alone rather than doing a job where I have to work with others in a group.

_____ 13. Working with a group is better than working alone.

_____ 14. People should be made aware that if they are going to be part of a group, then they are sometimes going to have to do things they don't want to do.

_____ 15. People who belong to a group should realize that they're not always going to get what they personally want.

_____ 16. People in a group should realize that they sometimes are going to have to make sacrifices for the sake of the group as a whole.

_____ 17. People in a group should be willing to make sacrifices for the sake of the group's well-being.

_____ 18. A group is more productive when its members do what they want to do rather than what the group wants them to do.

_____ 19. A group is most efficient when its members do what they think is best rather than doing what the group wants them to do.

_____ 20. A group is more productive when its members follow their own interests and desires.

Scoring

Determine your score by entering your response to each survey item below, as follows. In blanks that say *regular score*, simply enter your response for that item. If your response was a 3, place a 3 in the *regular score* blank. In blanks that say *reverse score*, subtract your response from 8 and enter the result. So if your response was a 3, place a 5 $(8 - 3 = 5)$ in the *reverse score* blank.

1. reverse score _____
2. reverse score _____
3. reverse score _____
4. reverse score _____
5. reverse score _____
6. reverse score _____
7. reverse score _____
8. reverse score _____
9. reverse score _____
10. reverse score _____
11. regular score _____
12. reverse score _____
13. regular score _____
14. regular score _____
15. regular score _____
16. regular score _____
17. regular score _____
18. reverse score _____
19. reverse score _____
20. reverse score _____

Add together to compute your TOTAL _____

You can find the interpretation for your score at http://www.management2e.nelson.com/student/assessments.html

Chapter 13

Complete the assessment below by indicating the extent to which you agree with each of the following statements.[12] Try not to spend too much time on any one item, and be sure to answer all the questions. Use this scale for your responses:

1 Strongly disagree
2 Disagree
3 Neutral
4 Agree
5 Strongly agree

_____ 1. I become so apprehensive in job interviews that I am unable to express my thoughts clearly.

_____ 2. I often feel uneasy about my appearance when I am being interviewed for a job.

_____ 3. While taking a job interview, I become concerned that the interviewer will perceive me as socially awkward.

_____ 4. In job interviews, I get very nervous about whether my performance is good enough.

_____ 5. During job interviews, my hands shake.

_____ 6. I get so anxious while taking job interviews that I have trouble answering questions that I know.

_____ 7. Before a job interview I am so nervous that I spend an excessive amount of time on my appearance.

_____ 8. I become very uptight about having to socially interact with a job interviewer.

_____ 9. I am overwhelmed by thoughts of doing poorly when I am in job interview situations.

_____ 10. My heartbeat is faster than usual during job interviews.

_____ 11. During job interviews, I often can't think of a thing to say.

_____ 12. In job interviews, I worry that the interviewer will focus on what I consider to be my least attractive physical features.

_____ 13. I get afraid about what kind of personal impression I am making on job interviews.

_____ 14. I worry that my job interview performance will be lower than that of other applicants.

_____ 15. It is hard for me to avoid fidgeting during a job interview.

_____ 16. I feel that my verbal communication skills are strong.

_____ 17. If I do not look my absolute best in a job interview, I find it very hard to be relaxed.

_____ 18. During a job interview, I worry that my actions will not be considered socially appropriate.

_____ 19. During a job interview, I am so troubled by thoughts of failing that my performance is reduced.

_____ 20. Job interviews often make me perspire (e.g., sweaty palms and underarms).

_____ 21. During job interviews, I find it hard to understand what the interviewer is asking me.

_____ 22. I feel uneasy if my hair is not perfect when I walk into a job interview.

_____ 23. I worry about whether job interviewers will like me as a person.

_____ 24. During a job interview, I worry about what will happen if I don't get the job.

_____ 25. My mouth gets very dry during job interviews.

_____ 26. I find it easy to communicate my personal accomplishments during a job interview.

_____ 27. During a job interview, I worry about whether I have dressed appropriately.

_____ 28. When meeting a job interviewer, I worry that my handshake will not be correct.

_____ 29. While taking a job interview, I worry about whether I am a good candidate for the job.

_____ 30. I often feel sick to my stomach when I am interviewed for a job.

_____ TOTAL (Reverse your score on items 16 and 26. That is, if you wrote in a "5," change it to a "1" and vice versa; if you wrote in a "4," change it to a "2" and vice versa.)

You can find the interpretation for your score at http://www.management2e.nelson.com/student/assessments.html

Chapter 14

The following assessment will evaluate your perspectives on the relationship a company has with its customers. Be candid as you respond to the questions using a scale from 1 to 9 in which 1 means you strongly disagree, 5 means you are neutral, and 9 means you strongly agree (other numbers indicate varying degrees of agreement or disagreement).[13]

_____ 1. I try to bring a customer with a problem together with a product/service that helps solve that problem.

_____ 2. I keep alert for weaknesses in a customer's personality so I can use them to put pressure on them to agree with me.

_____ 3. I try to influence a customer by information rather than pressure.

_____ 4. It is necessary to stretch the truth in describing a product to a customer.

_____ 5. I decide what product/service to offer on the basis of what I can convince customers to accept, not on the basis of what will satisfy them in the long run.

_____ 6. I paint too rosy a picture of my product/service to make them sound as good as possible.

_____ 7. I try to find out what kind of products/services will be most helpful to a customer.

_____ 8. I try to sell a customer all I can convince them to buy, even if I think it is more than a wise customer would buy.

_____ 9. I begin talking about the product/service before exploring a customer's need with him or her.

_____ 10. I try to help a customer achieve their goals.

_____ 11. I try to figure out what a customer's needs are.

_____ 12. A good employee has to have the customer's best interest in mind.

_____ 13. I try to sell as much as I can rather than to satisfy a customer.

_____ 14. I try to give customers an accurate expectation of what our product/service will do for them.

_____ 15. I imply to a customer that something is beyond my control when it is not.

_____ 16. I try to achieve my goals by satisfying customers.

_____ 17. If I am not sure if our product/service is right for a customer, I will still apply pressure to get him or her to buy.

_____ 18. I answer a customer's question about product/services as correctly as I can.

_____ 19. I offer the product/service that is best suited to the customer's problem.

_____ 20. I treat a customer as a rival.

_____ 21. I spend more time trying to persuade a customer to buy than I do trying to discover his or her needs.

_____ 22. I am willing to disagree with a customer in order to help him or her make a better decision.

_____ 23. I try to get the customer to discuss their needs with me.

_____ 24. I pretend to agree with a customer to please them.

Determine your score by entering your response to each survey item below, as follows. Total each column to derive two scores.

Customer Orientation	*Selling Orientation*
_____ 1. regular score	_____ 2. regular score
_____ 3. regular score	_____ 4. regular score
_____ 7. regular score	_____ 5. regular score
_____ 10. regular score	_____ 6. regular score
_____ 11. regular score	_____ 8. regular score
_____ 12. regular score	_____ 9. regular score
_____ 14. regular score	_____ 13. regular score
_____ 16. regular score	_____ 15. regular score
_____ 18. regular score	_____ 17. regular score
_____ 19. regular score	_____ 20. regular score
_____ 22. regular score	_____ 21. regular score
_____ 23. regular score	_____ 24. regular score

You can find the interpretation for your score at http://www.management2e.nelson.com/student/assessments.html

Chapter 15

Not everyone needs or wants the same things from their jobs.[14] Indicate the extent to which you agree with each of the following statements. Try not to spend too much time on any one item, and be sure to answer all the questions. Use this scale for your responses:

7 Strongly agree
6 Agree
5 Slightly agree
4 Neutral
3 Slightly disagree
2 Disagree
1 Strongly disagree

_____ 1. I get enough money from my job to live comfortably.

_____ 2. Our benefits cover many of the areas they should.

_____ 3. My boss encourages people to make suggestions.

_____ 4. I can count on my co-workers to give me a hand when I need it.

_____ 5. I always get the feeling of learning new things from my work.

_____ 6. I often think about how to improve my job performance.

_____ 7. My pay is adequate to provide for the basic things in life.

_____ 8. The benefit program here gives nearly all the security I want.

_____ 9. My boss takes account of my wishes and desires.

_____ 10. My co-workers will speak out in my favour if justified.

_____ 11. My job requires that a person use a wide range of abilities.

_____ 12. I will actively try to improve my job performance in the future.

_____ 13. Considering the work required, the pay is what it should be.

_____ 14. Compared to other places, our benefits are excellent.

_____ 15. My boss keeps me informed about what is happening in the company.

_____ 16. I can tell my co-workers how I honestly feel.

_____ 17. My job requires making one (or more) important decision(s) every day.

_____ 18. I intend to do a lot more at work in the future.

_____ 19. Compared to the rates for similar work, here, my pay is good.

_____ 20. The benefit program here is adequate.

_____ 21. My boss lets me know when I could improve my performance.

_____ 22. My co-workers welcome opinions different from their own.

_____ 23. I have the opportunity to do challenging things at work.

_____ 24. I will probably do my best to perform well on the job in the future.

Scoring

(A) Add together your scores for items 1, 2, 7, 8, 13, 14, 19, and 20: _____

(B) Add together your scores for items 3, 4, 9, 10, 15, 16, 21, and 22: _____

(C) Add together your scores for items 5, 6, 11, 12, 17, 18, 23, and 24: _____

You can find the interpretation for your score at http://www.management2e.nelson.com/student/assessments.html

Chapter 16

The following items relate to listening style.[15] Circle the appropriate responses. Please be candid. Use this scale for your responses:

	Almost Always	Often	Sometimes	Seldom	Almost Never
1. I want to listen to what others have to say when they are talking.	5	4	3	2	1
2. I do not listen at my capacity when others are talking.	1	2	3	4	5
3. By listening, I can guess a speaker's intent or purpose without being told.	5	4	3	2	1
4. I have a purpose for listening when others are talking.	5	4	3	2	1
5. I keep control of my biases and attitudes when listening to others speak so that these factors won't affect my interpretation of the message.	5	4	3	2	1
6. I analyze my listening errors so as not to make them again.	5	4	3	2	1
7. I listen to the complete message before making judgments about what the speaker has said.	5	4	3	2	1
8. I cannot tell when a speaker's biases or attitudes are affecting his or her message.	1	2	3	4	5
9. I ask questions when I don't fully understand a speaker's message.	5	4	3	2	1
10. I am aware of whether or not a speaker's meaning of words and concepts is the same as mine.	5	4	3	2	1
Subtotal	___	___	___	___	___
Grand Total	___	___	___	___	___

You can find the interpretation for your score at http://www.management2e.nelson.com/student/assessments.html

glossary

absolute comparisons
a process in which each criterion is compared to a standard or ranked on its own merits

accommodative strategy
a social responsiveness strategy where a company chooses to accept responsibility for a problem and do all that society expects to solve problems

acquaintance time
cultural norm for how much time you must spend getting to know someone before the person is prepared to do business with you

acquisition
purchase of a company by another company

acquisition cost
the cost of obtaining data that you don't have

action plan
the specific steps, people, and resources needed to accomplish a goal

active listening
assuming half the responsibility for successful communication by actively giving the speaker nonjudgmental feedback that shows you've accurately heard what he or she said

address terms
cultural norms that establish whether you should address businesspeople by their first names, family names, or titles

advocacy groups
groups of concerned citizens who band together to try to influence the business practices of specific industries, businesses, and professions

aggregate product plans
plans developed to manage and monitor all new products in development at any one time

analyzers
an adaptive strategy that seeks to minimize risk and maximize profits by following or imitating the proven successes of prospectors

anchoring and adjustment bias
unrecognized tendency of decision makers to use an initial value or experience as a basis of comparison throughout the decision process

application sharing
communications system that allows two or more people in different locations to make changes in a document by sharing control of the software application running on one computer

appointment time
cultural norm for how punctual you must be when showing up for scheduled appointments or meetings

Asia-Pacific Economic Cooperation (APEC)
regional trade agreement between Australia, Canada, Chile, China, Hong Kong, Japan, Mexico, New Zealand, Papua New Guinea, Peru, Russia, South Korea, the United States, and all members of ASEAN except Cambodia, Laos, and Myanmar

assemble-to-order operation
manufacturing operation that divides manufacturing processes into separate parts or modules that are combined to create semi-customized products

assessment centres
a series of managerial simulations, graded by trained observers, that are used to determine applicants' capability for managerial work

Association of Southeast Asian Nations (ASEAN)
regional trade agreement between Brunei Darussalam, Cambodia, Indonesia, Laos, Malaysia, Myanmar, the Philippines, Singapore, Thailand, and Vietnam

association or affinity patterns
when two or more database elements tend to occur together in a significant way

attack
a competitive move designed to reduce a rival's market share or profits

attribution theory
theory that states that we all have a basic need to understand and explain the causes of other people's behaviour

a-type conflict (affective conflict)
disagreement that focuses on individual or personally oriented issues

authority
the right to give commands, take action, and make decisions to achieve organizational objectives

autonomous work groups
groups that operate without managers and are completely responsible for controlling work group processes, outputs, and behaviour

availability bias
unrecognized tendency of decision makers to give preference to recent information, vivid images that evoke

emotions, and specific acts and behaviours that they personally observed

average aggregate inventory
average overall inventory during a particular time period

background checks
procedures used to verify the truthfulness and accuracy of information that applicants provide about themselves and to uncover negative, job-related background information not provided by applicants

balanced scorecard
measurement of organizational performance in four equally important areas: finances, customers, internal operations, and innovation and learning

bar code
a visual pattern that represents numerical data by varying the thickness and pattern of vertical bars

bargaining power of buyers
a measure of the influence that customers have on a firm's prices

bargaining power of suppliers
a measure of the influence that suppliers of parts, materials, and services to firms in an industry have on the prices of these inputs

batch production
manufacturing operation that produces goods in large batches in standard lot sizes

BCG matrix
a portfolio strategy, developed by the Boston Consulting Group, that managers use to categorize the corporation's businesses by growth rate and relative market share, helping them decide how to invest corporate funds

behaviour control
regulation of the behaviours and actions that workers perform on the job

behavioural addition
the process of having managers and employees perform new behaviours that are central to and symbolic of the new organizational culture that a company wants to create

behavioural formality
workplace atmosphere characterized by routine and regimen, specific rules about how to behave, and interpersonal detachment

behavioural informality
workplace atmosphere characterized by spontaneity, casualness, and interpersonal familiarity

behavioural observation scales (BOS)
rating scales that indicate the frequency with which workers perform specific behaviours that are representative of the job dimensions critical to successful job performance

behavioural substitution
the process of having managers and employees perform new behaviours central to the "new" organizational culture in place of behaviours that were central to the "old" organizational culture

benchmarking
the process of identifying outstanding practices, processes, and standards in other companies and adapting them to your company

benchmarking
the process of identifying outstanding practices, processes, and standards in other companies and adapting them to your company

biographical data (biodata)
extensive surveys that ask applicants questions about their personal backgrounds and life experiences

blog
a personal Web site that provides personal opinions or recommendations, news summaries, and reader comments

boundaryless organization
a speedy, responsive, and flexible organization in which vertical, horizontal, external, and geographic boundaries are removed or minimized

bounded rationality
decision-making process restricted in the real world by limited resources, incomplete and imperfect information, and managers' limited decision-making capabilities

brainstorming
a decision-making method in which group members build on each other's ideas to generate as many alternative solutions as possible

budgeting
quantitative planning through which managers decide how to allocate available money to best accomplish company goals

bureaucratic control
use of hierarchical authority to influence employee behaviour by rewarding or punishing employees for compliance or noncompliance with organizational policies, rules, and procedures

bureaucratic immunity
the ability to make changes without first getting approval from managers or other parts of an organization

business confidence indices
indices that show managers' level of confidence about future business growth

buyer dependence
degree to which a supplier relies on a buyer because of the importance of that buyer to the supplier and the difficulty of selling its products to other buyers

cafeteria benefit plans (flexible benefit plans)
plans that allow employees to choose which benefits they receive, up to a certain dollar value

cash cow
a company with a large share of a slow-growing market

centralization of authority
the location of most authority at the upper levels of the organization

chain of command
the vertical line of authority that clarifies who reports to whom throughout the organization

change agent
the person formally in charge of guiding a change effort

change forces
forces that produce differences in the form, quality, or condition of an organization over time

change intervention
the process used to get workers and managers to change their behaviour and work practices

character of the rivalry
a measure of the intensity of competitive behaviour between companies in an industry

charismatic leadership
the behavioural tendencies and personal characteristics of leaders that create an exceptionally strong relationship between them and their followers

closure
the tendency to fill in gaps of missing information by assuming that what we don't know is consistent with what we already know

coaching
communicating with someone for the direct purpose of improving their on-the-job performance or behaviour

coercion
use of formal power and authority to force others to change

cognitive ability tests
tests that measure the extent to which applicants have abilities in perceptual speed, verbal comprehension, numerical aptitude, general reasoning, and spatial aptitude

cognitive maps
graphic depictions of how managers believe environmental factors relate to possible organizational actions

cohesiveness
the extent to which team members are attracted to a team and motivated to remain in it

commission
a compensation system in which employees earn a percentage of each sale they make

common-enemy mission
company goal of defeating a corporate rival

communication
the process of transmitting information from one person or place to another

communication cost
the cost of transmitting information from one place to another

communication medium
the method used to deliver an oral or written message

company hotlines
phone numbers that anyone in the company can anonymously call to leave information for upper management

company vision
a company's purpose or reason for existence

compensation
the financial and nonfinancial rewards that organizations give employees in exchange for their work

competitive advantage
providing greater value for customers than competitors can

competitive analysis
a process for monitoring competitors that involves identifying competitors, anticipating their moves, and determining their strengths and weaknesses

competitive inertia
a reluctance to change strategies or competitive practices that have been successful in the past

competitors
companies in the same industry that sell similar products or services to customers

complex environment
an environment with many environmental factors

component parts inventories
the basic parts used in manufacturing that are fabricated from raw materials

compression approach to innovation
an approach to innovation that assumes that incremental innovation can be planned using a series of steps, and that compressing those steps can speed innovation

concentration of effect
the total harm or benefit that an act produces on the average person

conceptual skill
the ability to see the organization as a whole, how the different parts affect each other, and how the company fits into or is affected by its environment

concertive control
regulation of workers' behaviour and decisions through work group values and beliefs

concurrent control
a mechanism for gathering information about performance deficiencies as they occur, eliminating or shortening the delay between performance and feedback

conditions of certainty
conditions in which decision makers have complete information and knowledge of all possible outcomes

conditions of risk
conditions in which decision makers face a very real possibility of making the wrong decisions

conditions of uncertainty
conditions in which decision makers don't know the odds of winning or losing

conduit metaphor
the mistaken assumption that senders can pipe their intended messages directly into the heads of receivers with perfect clarity and without noise or perceptual filters interfering with the receivers' understanding of the message

conferencing system
communications system that lets two or more users in different locations see and talk to each other as if they were in the same room

consideration
the extent to which a leader is friendly, approachable, supportive, and shows concern for employees

constructive feedback
feedback intended to be helpful, corrective, and/or encouraging

contingency theory
leadership theory that states that in order to maximize work group performance, leaders must be matched to the situation that best fits their leadership style

continuous improvement
an organization's ongoing commitment to constantly assess and improve the processes and procedures used to create products and services

continuous-flow production
manufacturing operation that produces goods at a continuous, rather than a discrete, rate

control
a regulatory process of establishing standards to achieve organizational goals, comparing actual performance against the standards, and taking corrective action, when necessary

control loss
situation in which behaviour and work procedures do not conform to standards

controlling
monitoring progress toward goal achievement and taking corrective action when needed

conventional level of moral development
second level of moral development in which people make decisions that conform to societal expectations

cooperative contract
an agreement in which a foreign business owner pays a company a fee for the right to conduct that business in his or her country

core capabilities
the internal decision-making routines, problem-solving processes, and organizational cultures that determine how efficiently inputs can be turned into outputs

core firms
the central companies in a strategic group

corporate talk shows
televised company meetings that allow remote audiences (employees) to pose questions to the show's host and guests

corporate-level strategy
the overall organizational strategy that addresses the question "What business or businesses are we in or should we be in?"

cost leadership
the positioning strategy of producing a product or service of acceptable quality at consistently lower production costs than competitors can, so that the firm can offer the products or service at the lowest price in the industry

counselling
communicating with someone about non-job-related issues that may be affecting or interfering with their performance

country of manufacture
country where product is made and assembled

country of origin
the home country for a company, where its headquarters is located

creativity
the production of novel and useful ideas

cross training
training team members how to do all or most of the jobs performed by the other team members

cross-cultural communication
transmitting information from a person in one country or culture to a person from another country or culture

cross-functional team
team composed of employees from different functional areas of the organization

c-type conflict (cognitive conflict)
disagreement that focuses on problem- and issue-related differences of opinion

customer defections
performance assessment in which companies identify which customers are leaving and measure the rate at which they are leaving

customer departmentalization
organizing work and workers into separate units responsible for particular kinds of customers

customer focus
an organizational goal to concentrate on meeting customers' needs at all levels of the organization

customer satisfaction
an organizational goal to provide products or services that meet or exceed customers' expectations

cybernetic feasibility
the extent to which it is possible to implement each step in the control process

data clusters
when three or more database elements occur together (i.e., cluster) in a significant way

data encryption
transforms data into complex, scrambled digital codes that can be unencrypted only by authorized users who possess unique decryption keys

data mining
the process of discovering unknown patterns and relationships in large amounts of data

data warehouse
stores huge amounts of data that have been prepared for data mining analysis by being cleaned of errors and redundancy

decentralization
the location of a significant amount of authority in the lower levels of the organization

decision criteria
the standards used to guide judgments and decisions

decision rule
set of criteria that alternative solutions must meet to be acceptable to the decision maker

decision support system (DSS)
an information system that helps managers to understand specific kinds of problems and potential solutions and to analyze the impact of different decision options using "what if" scenarios

decision-making
the process of choosing a solution from available alternatives

decoding
the process by which the receiver translates the written, oral, or symbolic form of a message into an understood message

defenders
an adaptive strategy aimed at defending strategic positions by seeking moderate, steady growth and by offering a limited range of high-quality products and services to a well-defined set of customers

defensive bias
the tendency for people to perceive themselves as personally and situationally similar to someone who is having difficulty or trouble

defensive strategy
a social responsiveness strategy where a company chooses to admit responsibility for a problem but do the least required to meet societal expectations

de-forming
a reversal of the forming stage, in which team members position themselves to control pieces of the team, avoid each other, and isolate themselves from team leaders

delegation of authority
the assignment of direct authority and responsibility to a subordinate to complete tasks for which the manager is normally responsible

Delphi technique
a decision-making method in which a panel of experts responds to questions and to each other until reaching agreement on an issue

de-norming
a reversal of the norming stage, in which team performance begins to decline as the size, scope, goal, or members of the team change

departmentalization
subdividing work and workers into separate organizational units responsible for completing particular tasks

dependent demand system
inventory system in which the level of inventory depends on the number of finished units to be produced

design competition
competition between old and new technologies to establish a new technological standard or dominant design

design iteration
a cycle of repetition in which a company tests a prototype of a new product or service, improves on that design, and then builds and tests the improved prototype

desktop videoconferencing
communications system that allows two or more people in different locations to use video cameras and computer monitors to see and hear each other and share documents

de-storming
a reversal of the storming phase, in which the team's comfort level decreases, team cohesion weakens, and angry emotions and conflict may flare

destructive feedback
feedback that disapproves without any intention of being helpful and almost always causes a negative or defensive reaction in the recipient

devil's advocacy
a decision-making method in which an individual or a subgroup is assigned the role of a critic

dialectical inquiry
a decision-making method in which decision makers state the assumptions of a proposed solution (a thesis) and generate a solution that is the opposite (antithesis) of that solution

dictionary rule
decision rule that requires decision makers to rank criteria in order of importance and then test alternative solutions against those criteria in rank order, so that alternatives that meet the most important criterion must then meet the second most important criterion, and so on

differentiation
the positioning strategy of providing a product or service that is sufficiently different from competitors'

offerings that customers are willing to pay a premium price for it

direct competition
the rivalry between two companies that offer similar products and services, acknowledge each other as rivals, and act and react to each other's strategic actions

discretionary responsibilities
the expectation that a company will voluntarily serve a social role beyond its economic, legal, and ethical responsibilities

discussion time
cultural norm for how much time should be spent in discussion with others

disseminator role
the informational role managers play when they share information with others in their departments or companies

distal goals
long-term or primary goals

distinctive competence
what a company can make, do, or perform better than competitors

distributive justice
the perceived degree to which outcomes and rewards are fairly distributed or allocated

disturbance handler role
the decisional role managers play when they respond to severe problems that demand immediate action

diversification
a strategy for reducing risk by buying a variety of items (stocks or, in the case of a corporation, types of businesses), so that the failure of one stock or one business does not doom the entire portfolio

document conferencing
communications system that allows two or more people in different locations to simultaneously view and make comments about a document

dog
a company with a small share of a slow-growing market

dominant design
a new technological design or process that becomes the accepted market standard

downsizing
the planned elimination of jobs in a company

downward communication
communication that flows from higher to lower levels in an organization

dynamic environment
environment in which the rate of change is fast

dysfunctional turnover
loss of high-performing employees who voluntarily choose to leave a company

early retirement incentive programs (ERIPs)
programs that offer financial benefits to employees to encourage them to retire early

economic order quantity (EOQ)
a system of formulas that minimizes ordering and holding costs and helps determine how much and how often inventory should be ordered

economic responsibility
the expectation that a company will make a profit by producing a valued product or service

economic value added (EVA)
the amount by which company profits (revenues minus expenses minus taxes) exceed the cost of capital

effectiveness
accomplishing tasks that help fulfill organizational objectives

efficiency
getting work done with a minimum of effort, expense, or waste

electronic brainstorming
a decision-making method in which group members use computers to build on each other's ideas and generate many alternative solutions

electronic data interchange (EDI)
the direct electronic transmission of purchase and ordering information from one company's computer system to another company's computer system

electronic scanner
an electronic device that converts printed text and pictures into digital images

empathetic listening
understanding the speaker's perspective and personal frame of reference and giving feedback that conveys that understanding to the speaker

employee involvement team
team that provides advice or makes suggestions to management concerning specific issues

employee separation
the voluntary or involuntary loss of an employee

employee stock ownership plans (ESOPs)
a compensation system that awards employees shares of company stock in addition to their regular compensation

employee turnover
loss of employees who voluntarily choose to leave the company

employment benefits
a method of rewarding employees that includes virtually any kind of compensation other than wages or salaries

employment references
sources such as previous employers or co-workers who can provide job-related information about job candidates

empowering workers
permanently passing decision-making authority and responsibility from managers to workers by giving them the information and resources they need to make and carry out good decisions

encoding
putting a message into a written, oral, or symbolic form that can be recognized and understood by the receiver

entrepreneur role
the decisional role managers play when they adapt themselves, their subordinates, and their units to incremental change

entrepreneurial orientation
the set of processes, practices, and decision-making activities that lead to new entry, characterized by five dimensions: autonomy, innovativeness, risk-taking, proactiveness, and competitive aggressiveness

entrepreneurship
the process of entering new or established markets with new goods or services

environmental change
the rate at which a company's general and specific environments change

environmental complexity
the number of external factors in the environment that affect organizations

environmental munificence
degree to which an organization's external environment has an abundance or scarcity of critical organizational resources

environmental scanning
searching the environment for important events or issues that might affect an organization

equity theory
theory states that people will be motivated when they perceive that they are being treated fairly

era of ferment
phase of a technology cycle characterized by technological substitution and design competition

escalation of commitment
the tendency for a person who has already made a decision to more strongly support that original decision despite negative information that clearly indicates it was wrong

ethical behaviour
behaviour that conforms to a society's accepted principles of right and wrong

ethical charismatics
charismatic leaders that provide developmental opportunities for followers, are open to positive and negative feedback, recognize others' contributions, share information, and have moral standards that emphasize the larger interests of the group, organization, or society

ethical intensity
the degree of concern people have about an ethical issue

ethical responsibility
the expectation that a company will not violate accepted principles of right and wrong when conducting its business

ethics
the set of moral principles or values that defines right and wrong for a person or group

evaluation apprehension
fear of what others will think of your ideas

executive information system (EIS)
data processing system that uses internal and external data sources to provide the information needed to monitor and analyze organizational performance

expatriate
someone who lives outside his or her native country

expectancy
the perceived relationship between effort and performance

expectancy theory
theory that states that people will be motivated to the extent to which they believe that their efforts will lead to good performance, that good performance will be rewarded, and that they will be offered attractive rewards

experiential approach to innovation
an approach to innovation that assumes a highly uncertain environment, and uses intuition, flexible options, and hands-on experience to reduce uncertainty and accelerate learning and understanding

expert system
information system that contains the specialized knowledge and decision rules used by experts and experienced decision makers, so that nonexperts can draw on this knowledge base to make decisions

exporting
selling domestically produced products to customers in foreign countries

external environments
all events outside a company that have the potential to influence or affect it

external recruiting
the process of developing a pool of qualified job applicants from outside the company

extranet
allows companies to exchange information and conduct transactions with outsiders by providing them direct, Web-based access to authorized parts of a company's intranet or information system

extrinsic reward
a reward that is tangible, visible to others, and given to employees contingent on the performance of specific tasks or behaviours

feedback
in the communication process, a return message to the sender that indicates the receiver's understanding of the message

feedback control
a mechanism for gathering information about performance deficiencies after they occur

feedforward control
a mechanism for monitoring performance inputs rather than outputs to prevent or minimize performance deficiencies before they occur

figurehead role
the interpersonal role managers play when they perform ceremonial duties

finished goods inventories
the final outputs of manufacturing operations

firewall
hardware or software device that sits between the computers in an internal organizational network and outside networks, such as the Internet

firm-level strategy
corporate strategy that addresses the question "How should we compete against a particular firm?"

first-line managers
managers who train and supervise performance of nonmanagerial employees and who are directly responsible for producing the company's products or services

first-mover advantage
the strategic advantage that companies earn by being the first in an industry to use new information technology to substantially lower costs or to differentiate a product or service from competitors

focus strategy
the positioning strategy of using cost leadership or differentiation to produce a specialized product or service for a limited, specially targeted group of customers in a particular geographic region or market segment

foreign direct investment (FDI)
a method of investment in which a company builds a new business or buys an existing business in a foreign country

formal communication channel
the system of official channels that carry organizationally approved messages and information

forming
the first state of team development in which team members meet each other, form initial impressions, and begin to establish team norms

franchise
a collection of networked firms in which the manufacturer or marketer of a product or service, the franchisor, licenses the entire business to another person or organization, the franchisee

Free Trade Area of the Americas (FTAA)
regional trade agreement that, when signed, will create a regional trading zone encompassing 36 countries in North and South America

freeware
computer software that is free to whoever wants it

functional departmentalization
organizing work and workers into separate units responsible for particular business functions or areas of expertise

functional turnover
loss of poor-performing employees who voluntarily choose to leave a company

fundamental attribution error
the tendency to ignore external causes of behaviour and to attribute other people's actions to internal causes

gainsharing
compensation system in which companies share the financial value of performance gains, such as productivity, cost savings, or quality, with their workers

General Agreement on Tariffs and Trade (GATT)
worldwide trade agreement that will reduce and eliminate tariffs, limit government subsidies, and protect intellectual property

General Electric Workout
a three-day meeting in which managers and employees from different levels and parts of an organization quickly generate and act on solutions to specific business problems

general environment
the economic, technological, sociocultural, and political trends that indirectly affect all organizations

generational change
change based on incremental improvements to a dominant technological design such that the improved technology is fully backward compatible with the older technology

geographic departmentalization
organizing work and workers into separate units responsible for doing business in particular geographical areas

global business
the buying and selling of goods and services by people from different countries

global new ventures
new companies with sales, employees, and financing in different countries that are founded with an active global strategy

goal commitment
the determination to achieve a goal

grand strategy
a broad corporate-level strategic plan used to achieve strategic goals and guide the strategic alternatives that managers of individual businesses or subunits may use

groupthink
a barrier to good decision-making caused by pressure within the group for members to agree with each other

growth strategy
strategy that focuses on increasing profits, revenues, market share, or the number of places in which the company does business

hearing
the act or process of perceiving sounds

holding cost
the cost of keeping inventory until it is used or sold, including storage, insurance, taxes, obsolescence, and opportunity costs

horizontal communication
communication that flows among managers and workers who are at the same organizational level

hostile work environment
form of sexual harassment in which unwelcome and demeaning sexually related behaviour creates an intimidating and offensive work environment

human resource information systems (HRIS)
computerized systems for gathering, analyzing, storing, and disseminating information related to the HRM process

human resource management
the process of finding, developing, and keeping the right people to form a qualified work force

human resource planning (HRP)
using an organization's goals and strategy to forecast the organization's human resource needs in attracting, developing, and keeping a qualified work force

human skill
the ability to work well with others

imperfectly imitable resource
a resource that is impossible or extremely costly or difficult for other firms to duplicate

incremental change
the phase of a technology cycle in which companies innovate by lowering costs and improving the functioning and performance of the dominant technological design

independent demand system
inventory system in which the level of one kind of inventory does not depend on another

individualism-collectivism
the degree to which a person believes that people should be self-sufficient and that loyalty to one's self is more important than loyalty to one's team or company

industry regulation
regulations and rules that govern the business practices and procedures of specific industries, businesses, and professions

industry-level strategy
corporate strategy that addresses the question "How should we compete in this industry?"

informal communication channel ("grapevine")
the transmission of messages from employee to employee outside of formal communication channels

information
useful data that can influence people's choices and behaviour

information overload
situation in which decision makers have too much information to attend to

initiating structure
the degree to which a leader structures the roles of followers by setting goals, giving directions, setting deadlines, and assigning tasks

innovation streams
patterns of innovation over time that can create sustainable competitive advantage

inputs
in equity theory, the contributions employees make to the organization

instrumentality
the perceived relationship between performance and rewards

internal environment
the events and trends inside an organization that affect management, employees, and organizational culture

internal recruiting
the process of developing a pool of qualified job applicants from people who already work in the company

internal-transformation mission
company goal of remaining competitive by making dramatic changes in the company

Internet
a global network of networks that allows users to send and retrieve data from anywhere in the world

interorganizational process
a collection of activities that take place among companies to transform inputs into outputs that customers value

interpersonal skills
skills, such as listening, communicating, questioning, and providing feedback, that enable people to have effective working relationships with others

interviews
selection tool in which company representatives ask job applicants job-related questions to determine whether they are qualified for the job

intranets
private company networks that allow employees to easily access, share, and publish information using Internet software

intraorganizational process
the collection of activities that take place within an organization to transform inputs into outputs that customers value

intrinsic reward
a natural reward associated with performing a task or activity for its own sake

inventory
the amount and number of raw materials, parts, and finished products that a company has in its possession

inventory turnover
the number of times per year that a company sells or "turns over" its average inventory

ISO 9000
a series of five international standards, from ISO 9000 to ISO 9004, for achieving consistency in quality management and quality assurance in companies throughout the world

job analysis
a purposeful, systematic process for collecting information on the important work-related aspects of a job

job description
a written description of the basic tasks, duties, and responsibilities required of an employee holding a particular job

job design
the number, kind, and variety of tasks that individual workers perform in doing their jobs

job enlargement
increasing the number of different tasks that a worker performs within one particular job

job enrichment
increasing the number of tasks in a particular job and giving workers the authority and control to make meaningful decisions about their work

job evaluation
a process that determines the worth of each job in a company by evaluating the market value of the knowledge, skills, and requirements needed to perform it

job rotation
periodically moving workers from one specialized job to another to give them more variety and the opportunity to use different skills

job shops
manufacturing operations that handle customer orders or small batch jobs

job specialization
a job composed of a small part of a larger task or process

job specifications
a written summary of the qualifications needed to successfully perform a particular job

joint venture
a strategic alliance in which two existing companies collaborate to form a third, independent company

just-in-time (JIT) inventory system
inventory system in which component parts arrive from suppliers just as they are needed at each stage of production

kanban
a ticket-based system that indicates when to reorder inventory

kinesics
movements of the body and face

knowledge
the understanding that one gains from information

leader role
the interpersonal role managers play when they motivate and encourage workers to accomplish organizational objectives

leader-member relations
the degree to which followers respect, trust, and like their leaders

leadership
the process of influencing others to achieve group or organizational goals

leadership neutralizers
subordinate, task, or organizational characteristics that can interfere with a leader's actions or make it impossible for a leader to influence followers' performance

leadership substitutes
subordinate, task, or organizational characteristics that make leaders redundant or unnecessary

leading
inspiring and motivating workers to work hard to achieve organizational goals

learning-based planning
learning better ways of achieving goals by continually testing, changing, and improving plans and strategies

legal responsibility
the expectation that a company will obey society's laws and regulations

liaison role
the interpersonal role managers play when they deal with people outside their units

licensing
agreement in which a domestic company, the licensor, receives royalty payments for allowing another company, the licensee, to produce its product, sell its service, or use its brand name in a specified foreign market

line authority
the right to command immediate subordinates in the chain of command

line function
an activity that contributes directly to creating or selling the company's products

line-flow production
manufacturing processes that are pre-established, occur in a serial or linear manner, and are dedicated to making one type of product

listening
making a conscious effort to hear

Maastricht Treaty of Europe
regional trade agreement between most European countries

magnitude of consequences
the total harm or benefit derived from an ethical decision

make-to-order operation
manufacturing operation that does not start processing or assembling products until a customer order is received

make-to-stock operation
manufacturing operation that orders parts and assembles standardized products before receiving customer orders

management
getting work done through others

management by objectives (MBO)
a four-step process in which managers and employees discuss and select goals, develop tactical plans, and meet regularly to review progress toward goal accomplishment

manufacturing flexibility
degree to which manufacturing operations can easily and quickly change the number, kind, and characteristics of products they produce

market commonality
the degree to which two companies have overlapping products, services, or customers in multiple markets

materials requirement planning (MRP)
a production and inventory system that determines the production schedule, production batch sizes, and inventory needed to complete final products

matrix departmentalization
a hybrid organizational structure in which two or more forms of departmentalization, most often product and functional, are used together

maximizing
choosing the best alternative

mechanistic organization
organization characterized by specialized jobs and responsibilities; precisely defined, unchanging roles; and a rigid chain of command based on centralized authority and vertical communication

media advocacy
an advocacy group tactic of framing issues as public issues, exposing questionable, exploitative, or unethical practices, and forcing media coverage by buying media time or creating controversy that is likely to receive extensive news coverage

meta-analysis
a study of studies, a statistical approach that provides the best scientific estimate of how well management theories and practices work

middle managers
managers responsible for setting objectives consistent with top management's goals, and planning and implementing subunit strategies for achieving these objectives

milestones
formal project review points used to assess progress and performance

minimum threshold rule
decision rule that requires alternative solutions to meet all the established minimum decision criteria

mission
statement of a company's overall goal that unifies company-wide efforts toward its vision, stretches and challenges the organization, and possesses a finish line and a timeframe

modular organization
an organization that outsources noncore business activities to outside companies, suppliers, specialists, or consultants

monitor role
the informational role managers play when they scan their environment for information

Moore's law
prediction that every 18 months, the cost of computing will drop by 50 percent as computer-processing power doubles

motivation
the set of forces that initiates, directs, and makes people persist in their efforts to accomplish a goal

motivation to manage
an assessment of how enthusiastic employees are about managing the work of others

multifactor productivity
an overall measure of performance that indicates how much labour, capital, materials, and energy it takes to produce an output

multifunctional teams
work teams composed of people from different departments

multinational corporation
corporation that owns businesses in two or more countries

multivariable testing (MVT)
a systematic approach of experimentation used to analyze and evaluate potential solutions

national culture
the set of shared values and beliefs that affect the perceptions, decisions, and behaviour of the people from a particular country

needs
the physical or psychological requirements that must be met to ensure survival and well-being

needs assessment
the process of identifying and prioritizing the learning needs of employees

negative frame
couching a problem in terms of a loss, thus influencing decisions makers toward becoming risk-seeking

negotiator role
the decisional role managers play when they negotiate schedules, projects, goals, outcomes, resources, and employee raises

noise
anything that interferes with the transmission of the intended message

nominal group technique
decision-making method that begins and ends by having group members quietly write down and evaluate ideas to be shared with the group

nonsubstitutable resource
a resource, without equivalent substitutes or replacements, that produces value or competitive advantage

nontariff barriers
nontax methods of increasing the cost or reducing the volume of imported goods

nonverbal communication
any communication that doesn't involve words

normative control
regulation of workers' behaviour and decisions through widely shared organizational values and beliefs

norming
the third stage of team development, in which team members begin to settle into their roles, group cohesion grows, and positive team norms develop

norms
informally agreed-on standards that regulate team behaviour

North American Free Trade Agreement (NAFTA)
regional trade agreement between Canada, the United States, and Mexico

objective control
use of observable measures of worker behaviour or outputs to assess performance and influence behaviour

objective performance measures
measures of job performance that are easily and directly counted or quantified

online discussion forums
the in-house equivalent of Internet newsgroups; Web- or software-based discussion tools available across the company to permit employees to easily ask questions and share knowledge with each other

open office systems
offices in which the physical barriers that separate workers have been removed in order to increase communication and interaction

operational plans
day-to-day plans, developed and implemented by lower-level managers, for producing or delivering the organization's products and services over a 30-day to six-month period

operations management
managing the daily production of goods and services

opportunistic behaviour
transaction in which one party in the relationship benefits at the expense of the other

optical character recognition
software to convert digitized documents into ASCII text (American Standard Code for Information Interchange) that can be searched, read, and edited by word-processing and other kinds of software

options-based planning
maintaining planning flexibility by making small, simultaneous investments in many alternative plans

ordering cost
the costs associated with ordering inventory, including the cost of data entry, phone calls, obtaining bids, correcting mistakes, and determining when and how much inventory to order

organic organization
organization characterized by broadly defined jobs and responsibility; loosely defined, frequently changing roles; and decentralized authority and horizontal communication based on task knowledge

organizational ceremonies
planned activities or events that emphasize culturally consistent assumptions, decisions, and actions

organizational change
a difference in the form, quality, or condition of an organization over time

organizational culture
the values, beliefs, and attitudes shared by organizational members

organizational decline
a large decrease in organizational performance that occurs when companies don't anticipate, recognize, neutralize, or adapt to the internal or external pressures that threaten their survival

organizational development
a philosophy and collection of planned change interventions designed to improve an organization's long-term health and performance

organizational dialogue
the process by which people in an organization learn to talk effectively and constructively with each other

organizational heroes
people celebrated for their qualities and achievements within an organization

organizational innovation
the successful implementation of creative ideas in organizations

organizational process
the collection of activities that transforms inputs into outputs that customers value

organizational rituals
routine activities that emphasize the organization's culture

organizational silence
when employees withhold information about organizational problems or issues

organizational stories
stories told by organizational members to make sense of organizational events and changes, and to emphasize culturally consistent assumptions, decisions, and actions

organizational structure
the vertical and horizontal configuration of departments, authority, and jobs within a company

organizational symbols
something that represents another thing

organizing
deciding where decisions will be made, who will do what jobs and tasks, and who will work for whom

outcome/input (O/I) ratio
in equity theory, an employee's perception of the comparison between the rewards received from an organization and the employee's contributions to that organization

outcomes
in equity theory, the rewards employees receive for their contributions to the organization

outplacement services
employment-counselling service offered to employees who are losing their jobs because of downsizing

output control
regulation of worker results or outputs through rewards and incentives

overreward
when you are getting more outcomes relative to your inputs than the referent to whom you compare yourself

overt integrity test
written test that estimates employee honesty by directly asking job applicants what they think or feel about theft or about punishment of unethical behaviours

paralanguage
the pitch, rate, tone, volume, and speaking pattern (i.e., use of silences, pauses, or hesitations) of one's voice

partial productivity
a measure of performance that indicates how much of a particular kind of input it takes to produce an output

perception
the process by which individuals attend to, organize, interpret, and retain information from their environments

perceptual filters
the personality-, psychology-, or experience-based differences that influence people to ignore or pay attention to particular stimuli

performance appraisal
the process of assessing how well employees are doing their jobs

performing
the fourth stage of team development, in which performance improves because the team has matured into an effective, fully functioning team

personal aggression
hostile or aggressive behaviour toward others

personality tests
tests that measure the extent to which applicants possess different kinds of job-related personality dimensions

personality-based integrity test
written test that indirectly estimates employee honesty by measuring psychological traits such as dependability and conscientiousness

piecework
a compensation system in which employees are paid a set rate for each item they produce

planning
choosing a goal and developing a strategy to achieve that goal

planning (management functions)
determining organizational goals and the means for achieving them

policy
standing plan that indicates the general course of action that should be taken in response to a particular event or situation

policy uncertainty
the risk associated with changes in laws and government policies that directly affect the way foreign companies conduct business

political deviance
using one's influence to harm others in the company

political uncertainty
the risk of major changes in political regimes that can result from war, revolution, death of political leaders, social unrest, or other influential events

pooled interdependence
work completed by having each job or department independently contribute to the whole

portfolio strategy
corporate-level strategy that minimizes risk by diversifying investment among various businesses or product lines

positive frame
couching a problem in terms of a gain, thus influencing decisions makers toward becoming risk-averse

postconventional level of moral development
third level of moral development in which people make decisions based on internalized principles

preconventional level of moral development
first level of moral development in which people make

decisions based on selfish reasons

predictive patterns
help identify database elements that are different

primary stakeholder
any group on which an organization relies for its long-term survival

principle of distributive justice
ethical principle that holds that you should never take any action that harms the least among us: the poor, the uneducated, the unemployed

principle of government requirements
ethical principle that holds that you should never take any action that violates the law, for the law represents the minimal moral standard

principle of individual rights
ethical principle that holds that you should never take any action that infringes on others' agreed-on rights

principle of long-term self-interest
ethical principle that holds that you should never take any action that is not in your or your organization's long-term self-interest

principle of personal virtue
ethical principle that holds that you should never do anything that is not honest, open, and truthful, and which you would not be glad to see reported in the newspapers or on TV

principle of religious injunctions
ethical principle that holds that you should never take any action that is not kind and that does not build a sense of community; a sense of everyone working together for a commonly accepted goal

principle of utilitarian benefits
ethical principle that holds that you should never take any action that does not result in greater good for society. Instead, do whatever creates the greatest good for the greatest number

private spaces
spaces used by and open to just one employee

proactive strategy
a social responsiveness strategy where a company anticipates responsibility for a problem before it occurs and would do more than society expects to address the problem

probability of effect
the chance that something will happen and then result in harm to others

problem
a gap between a desired state and an existing state

procedural justice
the perceived fairness of the process used to make reward allocation decisions

procedure
standing plan that indicates the specific steps that should be taken in response to a particular event

processing cost
the cost of turning raw data into usable information

processing information
transforming raw data into meaningful information

product boycott
an advocacy group tactic of protesting a company's actions by convincing consumers not to purchase its product or service

product departmentalization
organizing work and workers into separate units responsible for producing particular products or services

product prototype
a full-scale, working model of a final product that is being tested for design, function, and reliability

production blocking
a disadvantage of face-to-face brainstorming in which a group member must wait to share an idea because another member is presenting an idea

production deviance
unethical behaviour that hurts the quality of work produced

productivity
a measure of performance that indicates how many inputs it takes to produce or create an output

profit sharing
a compensation system in which a percentage of company profits is paid to employees in addition to their regular compensation

project manufacturing
manufacturing operations designed to produce large, expensive, specialized products

project team
team created to complete specific, one-time projects or tasks within a limited time

property deviance
unethical behaviour aimed at the organization's property

prospectors
an adaptive strategy that seeks fast growth by searching for new market opportunities, encouraging risk-taking, and being the first to bring innovative new products to market

protecting information
the process of insuring that data are reliably and consistently retrievable in a usable format for authorized users, but no one else

protectionism
a government's use of trade barriers to shield domestic companies and their workers from foreign competition

proximal goals
short-term goals or subgoals

proximity of effect
the social, psychological, cultural, or physical distance between a decision maker and those affected by his or her decisions

public communications
an advocacy group tactic that relies on voluntary participation by the news media and the advertising industry to get an advocacy group's message out

punctuated equilibrium theory
theory that holds that companies go through long, simple periods of stability (equilibrium), followed by short periods of dynamic, fundamental change (revolution), and ending with a return to stability (new equilibrium)

purchasing power
a comparison of the relative cost of a standard set of goods and services in different countries

quality
a product or service free of deficiencies, or the characteristics of product or service that satisfy customer needs

question mark
a company with a small share of a fast-growing market

quid pro quo sexual harassment
form of sexual harassment in which employment outcomes, such as hiring, promotion, or simply keeping one's job, depend on whether an individual submits to sexual harassment

quota
limit on the number or volume of imported products

rare resource
a resource that is not controlled or possessed by many competing firms

rater training
training performance appraisal raters in how to avoid rating errors and increase rating accuracy

rational decision-making
a systematic process of defining problems, evaluating alternatives, and choosing optimal solutions

raw data
facts and figures

raw material inventories
the basic inputs in a manufacturing process

reactive strategy
a social responsiveness strategy where a company chooses to do less than society expects and to deny responsibility for problems

reactors
an adaptive strategy of not following a consistent strategy, but instead reacting to changes in the external environment after they occur

reciprocal interdependence
work completed by different jobs or groups working together in a back-and-forth manner

recovery
the strategic actions taken after retrenchment to return to a growth strategy

recruiting
the process of developing a pool of qualified job applicants

re-engineering
fundamental rethinking and radical redesign of business processes to achieve dramatic improvements in critical measures of performance, such as cost, quality, service, and speed

referents
in equity theory, others with whom people compare themselves to determine if they have been treated fairly

refreezing
supporting and reinforcing the new changes so they "stick"

regional trading zones
areas in which tariff and nontariff barriers on trade between countries are reduced or eliminated

related diversification
creating or acquiring companies that share similar products, manufacturing, marketing, technology, or cultures

relationship behaviour
mutually beneficial, long-term exchanges between buyers and suppliers

relative comparisons
a process in which each decision criterion is compared directly to every other criterion

reliability
the degree to which a measure (test) is free from random error and is consistent

representative bias
unrecognized tendency of decision makers to judge the likelihood of an event's occurrence based on its similarity to previous events

resistance forces
forces that support the existing state of conditions in organizations

resistance to change
opposition to change resulting from self-interest, misunderstanding and distrust, or a general intolerance for change

resource allocator role
the decisional role managers play when they decide who gets what resources

resource similarity
the extent to which a competitor has similar amounts and kinds of resources

resources
the assets, capabilities, processes, information, and knowledge that an organization uses to improve its effectiveness and efficiency and to create and sustain an advantage over competitors

response
a competitive countermove, prompted by a rival's attack, to defend or improve a company's market share or profit

results-driven change
change created quickly by focusing on the measurement and improvement of results

retrenchment strategy
strategy that focuses on turning around very poor company performance by shrinking the size or scope of the business

retrieval cost
the cost of accessing already-stored and processed information

risk propensity
a person's tendency to take or avoid risk

role-model mission
company goal of imitating the characteristics and practices of a successful company

rules and regulations
standing plans that describe how a particular action should be performed, or what must happen or not happen in response to a particular event

S.M.A.R.T. goals
goals that are specific, measurable, attainable, results-oriented, and time-bounded

satisficing
choosing a "good enough" alternative

scenario planning
the process of developing plans to deal with several possible future events and trends that might affect the business

schedule time
cultural norm for the time by which scheduled projects or jobs should actually be completed

S-curve pattern of innovation
a pattern of technological innovation characterized by slow initial progress, then rapid progress, and then again by slow progress as a technology matures and reaches its limits

secondary firms
the firms in a strategic group that follow related but somewhat different strategies than do the core firms

secondary stakeholder
any group that can influence or be influenced by the company and can affect public perceptions about its socially responsible behaviour

selection
the process of gathering information about job applicants to decide who should be offered a job

selective perception
the tendency to notice and accept objects and information consistent with our values, beliefs, and expectations, while ignoring or screening out or not accepting inconsistent information

self-control (self-management)
control system in which managers and workers control their own behaviour by setting their own goals, monitoring their own progress, and rewarding themselves for goal achievement

self-designing team
team that has the characteristics of self-managing teams but that also controls team design, work tasks, and team membership

self-managing team
team that manages and controls all the major tasks of producing a product or service

self-serving bias
the tendency to overestimate our value by attributing successes to ourselves (internal causes) and attributing failures to others or the environment (external causes)

semi-autonomous work group
group that has the authority to make decisions and solve problems related to the major tasks of producing a product or service

sequence patterns
when two or more database elements occur together in a significant pattern, but one of the elements precedes the other

sequential interdependence
work completed in succession, with one group or job's outputs becoming the inputs for the next group or job

service recovery
restoring customer satisfaction to strongly dissatisfied customers

setup cost
the costs of downtime and lost efficiency that occur when changing or adjusting a machine to produce a different kind of inventory

sexual harassment
form of discrimination in which unwelcome sexual advances, requests for sexual favours, or other verbal or physical conduct of a sexual nature occur while performing one's job

shadow-strategy task force
a committee within the company that analyzes the company's own weaknesses to determine how competitors could exploit them for competitive advantage

shared spaces
spaces used by and open to all employees

shareholder model
view of social responsibility that holds that an organization's overriding goal should be profit maximization for the benefit of shareholders

shareware
computer software that you can try before you buy, but if you keep it beyond the trial period, usually 30 days, you must buy it

shrinkage
employee theft of company merchandise

simple environment
an environment with few environmental factors

single-use plans
plans that cover unique, one-time-only events

situational (SWOT) analysis
an assessment of the strengths and weaknesses in an organization's internal environment and the opportunities and threats in its external environment

situational favourableness
the degree to which a particular situation either permits or denies a leader the chance to influence the behaviour of group members

situational theory
leadership theory that states that leaders need to adjust their leadership styles to match followers' maturity

skill-based pay
compensation system that pays employees for learning additional skills or knowledge

social consensus
agreement on whether behaviour is bad or good

social loafing
behaviour in which team members withhold their efforts and fail to perform their share of the work

social responsibility
a business's obligation to pursue policies, make decisions, and take actions that benefit society.

social responsiveness
the strategy chosen by a company to respond to stakeholders' economic, legal, ethical, or discretionary expectations concerning social responsibility

span of control
the number of people reporting to a specific supervisor

specific ability tests (aptitude tests)
tests that measure the extent to which an applicant possesses the particular kind of ability needed to do a job well

specific environment
the customer, competitor, supplier, industry regulation, and public pressure group trends that are unique to an industry and that directly affect how a company does business

spokesperson role
the informational role managers play when they share information with people outside their departments or companies

stability strategy
strategy that focuses on improving the way a company sells the same products or services to the same customers

stable environment
environment in which the rate of change is slow

staff authority
the right to advise but not command others who are not subordinates in the chain of command

staff function
an activity that does not contribute directly to creating or selling the company's products, but instead supports line activities

stakeholder model
theory of corporate responsibility that holds that management's most important responsibility, long-term survival, is achieved by satisfying the interests of multiple corporate stakeholders

stakeholders
persons or groups with a "stake" or legitimate interest in a company's actions

standardization
solving problems by consistently applying the same rules, procedures, and processes

standards
a basis of comparison when measuring the extent to which various kinds of organizational performances are satisfactory or unsatisfactory

standing plans
plans used repeatedly to handle frequently recurring events

star
a company with a large share of a fast-growing market

stepladder technique
when group members are added to a group discussion one at a time (i.e., like a stepladder), the existing group members first take the time to listen to each new member's thoughts, ideas, and recommendations, and then the group, in turn, shares the ideas and suggestions that it had already considered, discusses the new and old ideas, and then makes a decision

stock options
a compensation system that gives employees the right to purchase shares of stock at a set price, even if the value of the stock increases above that price

stockout
situation in which a company runs out of finished product

stockout costs
the costs incurred when a company runs out of a product, including transaction costs to replace inventory and the loss of customers' goodwill

storage cost
the cost of physically or electronically archiving information for later use and retrieval

storming
the second stage of team development, characterized by conflict and disagreement, in which team members disagree over what the team should do and how it should do it

strategic alliance
agreement in which companies combine key resources, costs, risk, technology, and people

strategic dissonance
a discrepancy between upper management's intended strategy and the

strategy actually implemented by lower levels of management

strategic group
a group of companies within an industry that top managers choose to compare, evaluate, and benchmark strategic threats and opportunities

strategic leadership
the ability to anticipate, envision, maintain flexibility, think strategically, and work with others to initiate changes that will create a positive future for an organization

strategic plans
overall company plans that clarify how the company will serve customers and position itself against competitors over the next two to five years

strategic reference points
the strategic targets managers use to measure whether a firm has developed the core competencies it needs to achieve a sustainable competitive advantage

stretch goals
extremely ambitious goals that, initially, employees don't know how to accomplish

structural accommodation
the ability to change organizational structures, policies, and practices

structured interviews
interviews in which all applicants are asked the same set of standardized questions, usually including situational, behavioural, background, and job-knowledge questions

subjective performance measures
measures of job performance that require someone to judge or assess a worker's performance

suboptimization
performance improvement in one part of an organization but only at the expense of decreased performance in another part

subsidies
government loans, grants, and tax deferments given to domestic companies to protect them from foreign competition

supervised data mining
user tells the data mining software to look and test for specific patterns and relationships in a data set

supplier dependence
degree to which a company relies on a supplier because of the importance of the supplier's product to the company and the difficulty of finding other sources of that product

suppliers
companies that provide material, human, financial, and informational resources to other companies

survey feedback
information collected by survey from organizational members that is then compiled, disseminated, and used to develop action plans for improvement

sustainable competitive advantage
a competitive advantage that other companies have tried unsuccessfully to duplicate and have, for the moment, stopped trying to duplicate

tactical plans
plans created and implemented by middle managers that specify how the company will use resources, budgets, and people over the next six months to two years to accomplish specific goals within its mission

targeting
mission stated as a clear specific company goal

tariff
a direct tax on imported goods

task interdependence
the extent to which collective action is required to complete an entire piece of work

task structure
the degree to which the requirements of a subordinate's tasks are clearly specified

team diversity
the variances or differences in ability, experience, personality, or any other factor on a team

team leaders
managers responsible for facilitating team activities toward goal accomplishment

team level
the average level of ability, experience, personality, or any other factor on a team

teamwork
collaboration between managers and nonmanagers, across business functions, and between the companies, customers, and suppliers

technical skills
the ability to apply the specialized procedures, techniques, and knowledge required to get the job done

technological discontinuity
scientific advance or unique combination of existing technologies that creates a significant breakthrough in performance or function

technological substitution
purchase of new technologies to replace older ones

technology
knowledge, tools, and techniques used to transform inputs (raw material) into outputs (finished products or services)

technology cycle
cycle that begins with the "birth" of a new technology and ends when that technology reaches its limits and is replaced by a newer, substantially better technology

televised/videotaped speeches and meetings
speeches and meetings originally made to a smaller audience that are either simultaneously broadcast to other locations in the company or videotaped for subsequent distribution and viewing

temporal immediacy
the time between an act and the consequences the act produces

testing
systematic comparison of different product designs or design iterations

threat of new entrants
a measure of the degree to which barriers to entry make it easy or difficult for new companies to get started in an industry

threat of substitute products or services
a measure of the ease with which customers can find substitutes for an industry's products or services

360-degree feedback
a performance appraisal process in which feedback is obtained from the boss, subordinates, peers and co-workers, and the employees themselves

top managers
executives responsible for the overall direction of the organization

total quality management (TQM)
an integrated, principle-based, organization-wide strategy for improving product and service quality

trade barriers
government-imposed regulations that increase the cost and restrict the number of imported goods

traditional work group
group composed of two or more people who work together to achieve a shared goal

training
developing the skills, experience, and knowledge employees need to perform their jobs or improve their performance

trait rating scales
a rating scale that indicates the extent to which a worker possesses particular traits or characteristics

trait theory
leadership theory that holds that effective leaders possess a similar set of traits or characteristics

traits
relatively stable characteristics, such as abilities, psychological motives, or consistent patterns of behaviour

transactional leadership
leadership based on an exchange process, in which followers are rewarded for good performance and punished for poor performance

transformational leadership
leadership that generates awareness and acceptance of a group's purpose and mission and gets employees to see beyond their own needs and self-interest for the good of the group

transition management team (TMT)
a team of 8 to 12 people whose full-time job is to completely manage and coordinate a company's change process

uncertainty
extent to which managers can understand or predict which environmental changes and trends will affect their businesses

underreward
when the referent you compare yourself to is getting more outcomes relative to inputs than you are

unfreezing
getting the people affected by change to believe that change is needed

unity of command
a management principle that workers should report to just one boss

unrelated diversification
creating or acquiring companies in completely unrelated businesses

unsupervised data mining
user simply tells the data mining software to uncover whatever patterns and relationships it can find in a data set

upward communication
communication that flows from lower to higher levels in an organization

valence
the attractiveness or desirability of a reward or outcome

validation
the process of determining how well a selection test or procedure predicts future job performance; the better or more accurate the prediction of future job performance, the more valid a test is said to be

validity
the degree to which a measure (selection technique) is shown to accurately predict what it is expected to measure (job performance)

valuable resource
a resource that allows companies to improve efficiency and effectiveness

value
customer perception that the product quality is excellent for the price offered

variation
a deviation in the form, condition, or appearance of a product from the quality standard for that product

virtual organization
an organization that is part of a network in which many companies share skills, costs, capabilities, markets, and customers to collectively solve customer problems or provide specific products or services

virtual private network
encrypts Internet data at both ends of the transmission process

virtual team
team composed of geographically and/or organizationally dispersed co-workers who use telecommunications and information technologies to accomplish an organizational task

virus
a program or piece of code that attaches itself to other programs on your computer and can trigger anything from a harmless flashing message to the reformatting of your hard drive to the system-wide network shutdown

visible artifacts
visible signs of an organization's culture, such as the office design and layout, company dress codes, and company benefits and perks such as stock options, personal parking spaces, or the private company dining room

vision
inspirational statement of an organization's enduring purpose

visionary leadership
leadership that creates a positive image of the future that motivates organizational members and provides direction for future planning and goal setting

voluntary export restraints
voluntarily imposed limits on the number or volume of products exported to a particular country

whistle-blowing
reporting others' ethics violations to management or legal authorities

wholly owned affiliates
foreign office, facilities, and manufacturing plants that are 100 percent owned by the parent company

work sample tests
tests that require applicants to perform tasks that are actually done on the job

work team
a small number of people with complementary skills who hold themselves mutually accountable for pursuing a common purpose, achieving performance goals, and improving interdependent work processes

worker readiness
the ability and willingness to take responsibility for directing one's behaviour at work

work-force forecasting
the process of predicting the number and kind of workers with specific skills and abilities that an organization will need in the future

work-in-process inventories
partially finished goods consisting of assembled component parts

workplace deviance
unethical behaviour that violates organizational norms about right and wrong

world gross national product
the value of all the goods and services produced annually worldwide

wrongful dismissal
a legal doctrine that requires employers to have a job-related reason to terminate employees

endnotes

Chapter 1

1. M. Kennedy, "Down, Yes, but Liberals Not Destroyed," *Winnipeg Free Press*, January 25, 2006, p. A11; J. Taber, "Liberal Campaign Leaves a Bitter Aftertaste; As Martin Exits, Grumblings About Boss's Inner Circle Feed Resentments in Fractious Party," *Globe and Mail*, January 28, 2006, p. A6; J. Simpson, "Why the Liberals Collapsed in Quebec," *Globe and Mail*, January 10, 2006, p. A17; "Federal Sponsorship Scandal," *CBC News Online*, November 1, 2005, www.cbc.ca/news/background/groupaction/; "Canada Dry; A Conservative Victory That Should Not Be Overinterpreted," *The Times* (London), January 25, 2006, p. 17; J. English, "Lessons for Liberals, and Some Advice," *Globe and Mail*, January 28, 2006; "Martin's Achievements" *The Toronto Star*, January 25, 2006, p. A22; J. Gray, "Whatever Became of Paul Martin?" *CBC.ca Reality Check*, January 24, 2006, www.cbc.ca/canadavotes/realitycheck/martin.html; "The Liberal Party, in Search of a Future," *Globe and Mail*, January 27, 2006, p. 14.
2. "U.S Dept. of Commerce Industry Sector Analysis: Canada, Mgt. Consulting Services," June 1998, [Online] available at http://strategis.ic.gc.ca/pics/bp/mgt.pdf. Quoted in March 2001, Industry Canada, *Management Consulting Industry*, Service Industries Overview Series.
3. "Management, Scientific and Technical Consulting." Table Four, Annual Survey of Management and *1998 Survey of Service Industries*, Statistics Canada, [Online] available at http://strategis.ic.gc.ca/pics/bp/mgt.pdf. Quoted in March 2001, Industry Canada, *Management Consulting Industry*, Service Industries Overview Series.
4. *Management Consulting Industry*. Services Industry Overview Series, Industry Canada. 2001, March, [Online] available at http://strategis.ic.gc.ca.
5. T. Peters, "The Leadership Alliance" (Pat Carrigan excerpt), *In Search of Excellence* (Northbrook, IL: Video Arts, distributor, 1985), videocassette.
6. R. Stagner, "Corporate Decision Making," *Journal of Applied Psychology* 53 (1969): 1–13.
7. D.W. Bray, R.J. Campbell, & D.L. Grant, *Formative Years in Business: A Long-Term AT&T Study of Managerial Lives* (New York: Wiley, 1993).
8. B. Dumaine, "The New Non-Manager Managers," *Fortune*, 22 February 1993, 80–84.
9. R.J. Grisson, "Probability of the Superior Outcome of One Treatment over Another," *Journal of Applied Psychology* 79 (1994): 314–316; J.E. Hunter & F.L. Schmidt, *Methods of Meta-analysis: Correcting Error and Bias in Research Findings* (Beverly Hills, CA: Sage, 1990).
10. B. Dumaine, "The New Non-Manager Managers," *Fortune*, 22 February 1993, 80–84
11. S.B. Garland, S. Hamm, & M. France. "The Cops Converge on Microsoft," *Business Week*, 18 May 1998, 34–37.
12. Anne Fisher, "Making Change Stick," *Fortune*, 17 April 1995, 121–127.
13. M. Carter, "Back from the Dead (Ford Revitalizes Jaguar Cars)," *The European*, 6 April 1998, 22–23.
14. A. Farnham, "Mary Kay's Lessons in Leadership," *Fortune*, 20 September 1993, 68–77.
15. M. MacDonald, "Legacy of Chrysler Canada Chief: A Revitalized Car Maker," *Canadian Press Newswire*, 16 March 1998.
16. H.S. Jonas, III, R.E. Fry, & S. Srivastva, "The Office of the CEO: Understanding the Executive Experience," *Academy of Management Executive* 4 (1990): 36–47.
17. J. Vardy, "CEO's Post Some Spectacular Departures: Boards Getting More Vigilant Less Tolerant of Mediocrity," *Financial Post*, 7 December 2001, 7.
18. K. Dorrell, "A Tough Act to Follow: The Death of Yves Landry Leaves a Large Void at Chrysler Canada Ltd. and in the Industry," *Plant* 57, no. 6 (1998): 42.
19. H.S. Jonas, III, R.E. Fry, & S. Srivastva, "The Office of the CEO: Understanding the Executive Experience," *Academy of Management Executive* 4 (1990): 36–47.
20. C. Hymowitz, "CEOs Work Hard to Maintain the Faith in the Corner Office," *The Wall Street Journal*, 9 July 2002, B1; L. Mitchell, "How to Do the Right Thing,"

Optimize, February 2002, [Online] available at www.optimizemag.com/issue/004/pr_ethics.fhtml, 1 February 2003.

21. "A CEO Who Delivers," *The Toronto Star,* 17 July 2005.
22. B.M. Bass, *Stogdill's Handbook of Leadership* (New York: Free Press, 1981).
23. S. Tully, "What Team Leaders Need to Know," *Fortune,* 20 February 1995.
24. K. Hultman, "The 10 Commandments of Team Leadership," *Training & Development,* 1 February 1998, 12–13.
25. S. Tully, "What Team Leaders Need to Know," *Fortune,* 20 February 1995.
26. J.S. Case, "What the Experts Forgot to Mention," *Inc.,* 1 September 1993, 66.
27. H. Mintzberg, *The Nature of Managerial Work* (New York: Harper & Row, 1973).
28. C.P. Hales, "What Do Managers Do? A Critical Review of the Evidence," *Journal of Management Studies* 23, no. 1 (1986): 88–115.
29. C. Vibert, personal correspondence, 17 October 2002.
30. R. Gibson, "McDonald's Makes Changes in Top Management," *The Wall Street Journal,* 1 May 1998, A3.
31. J. Vardy, "CEOs Post Some Spectacular Departures: Boards Getting More Vigilant, Less Tolerant of Mediocrity," *Financial Post,* 1 December 2001, 7.
32. "Latest Boss Eyes Growth Through Acquisition for 'Better Positioned' GEAC," *Canadian Press Newswire,* 5 December 2001; F. Sheikh, "The Turnaround: GEAC Has a New Blueprint for Growth. But Does the Blueprint Come with a New Mindset?" *Silicon Valley North—GTA* 7, no. 2 (January 2001): 5.
33. L.A. Hill, *Becoming a Manager: Mastery of a New Identity* (Boston, MA: Harvard Business School Press, 1992).
34. R.L. Katz, "Skills of an Effective Administrator," *Harvard Business Review,* September–October 1974, 90–102.
35. C.A. Bartlett & S. Ghoshal, "Changing the Role of Top Management: Beyond Systems to People," *Harvard Business Review,* May–June 1995, 132–142.
36. F.L. Schmidt & J.E. Hunter, "Development of a Causal Model of Process Determining Job Performance," *Current Directions in Psychological Science* 1 (1992): 89–92.
37. J.B. Miner, "Sentence Completion Measures in Personnel Research: The Development and Validation of the Miner Sentence Completion Scales," in *Personality Assessment in Organizations,* eds. H. J. Bernardin & D.A. Bownas (New York: Praeger, 1986), 147–146.
38. Wahl, M. McClearn, R. Robin, & D. Calleja, "Survivor, MBA Edition," *Canadian Business* 74, no. 21 (December 2001), 58–64.
39. M.W. McCall, Jr. & M.M. Lombardo, "What Makes a Top Executive?" *Psychology Today,* February 1983, 26–31; E. van Velsor & J. Brittain, "Why Executives Derail: Perspectives across Time and Cultures," *Academy of Management Executive,* November 1995, 62–72.
40. M.W. McCall, Jr. & M.M. Lombardo, "What Makes a Top Executive?" *Psychology Today,* February 1983, 26–31.
41. S. Stecklow, "Chief Prerequisite for College President's Job: Stamina," *The Wall Street Journal,* 1 December 1994, B1.
42. M.A. Huselid, "The Impact of Human Resource Management Practices on Turnover, Productivity, and Corporate Financial Performance," *Academy of Management Journal* 38 (1995): 635–672.
43. D. McDonald & A. Smith, "A Proven Connection: Performance Management and Business Results," *Compensation & Benefits Review* 27, no. 6 (1 January 1995): 59.
44. B. Schneider & D.E. Bowen, "Employee and Customer Perceptions of Service in Banks: Replication and Extension," *Journal of Applied Psychology* 70 (1985): 423–33; B. Schneider, J.J. Parkington, & V.M. Buxton, "Employee and Customer Perceptions of Service in Banks," *Administrative Science Quarterly* 25 (1980): 252–67.
45. "Martin's Achievements," *Toronto Star,* January 25, 2006, A22; J. Manley, "Comment: A Healing Prescription for Liberals," *Globe and Mail,* January 26, 2006; "The Liberal Party, in Search of a Future," *Globe and Mail,* January 27, 2006, A14; T. Axworthy, "Opinion: Time to Reflect on What Went Wrong," *Toronto Star,* January 25, 2006, p. A21; CBC.ca, "Liberal Leadership: Possible Candidates, Analysis & Commentary," www.cbc.ca/canadavotes/analysiscommentary/whither_liberals.html.
46. N. Gross, "Measuring the Muscle of R&D Spending," *Business Week,* 11 June 2001.
47. L.A. Hill, *Becoming a Manager: Mastery of a New Identity* (Boston, MA: Harvard Business School Press, 1992).

Chapter 2

1. "About the Movie," *Super Size Me: A Film of Epic Portions,* [Online] available at www.supersizeme.com/home.aspx?page=aboutmovie, 22 January 2005; Joel Baglole, "War of the Doughnuts," *The Wall Street Journal,* 23 August 2001, B1; Derek M. Boyle, "Can You Really Make Fast Food Healthy?" *Fortune,* 9 August 2004, 34; D. DeCloet, "How Krispy Got Creamed," *Globe and Mail,* 18 December 2004, F3; David Estok, "Timbit Nation," *Report on Business Magazine,* December 2000, 74–78; Jim Fox, "Wendy's 1,910 Tim Hortons Units Make Gains with Lunch Menus," *Nation's Restaurant News,* 22 May 2000, 288–290; Scott Gardiner, "In Praise of Saint Timmy," *Marketing Magazine,* 21 August 2000, 10; R. Givhan, "Lord of the Fries: Morgan Spurlock Got His Fill of Ailments Making 'Super Size Me,' But He's Been Fortified by Its Impact," *Washington Post,* 2 May 2004, N01; Chris Lambie, "Tim Hortons Heads to Sea," *The Ottawa Citizen,* 7 August 2004, A5; "Subway® Nutrition Facts—US, January 2005," *Subway,* [Online] available at http://subway.com/subwayroot/MenuNutrition/Nutrition/pdf/NutritionValues.pdf, 23 January 2005; "The Weight We Pack on Gets Heavier and Heavier," *Globe and Mail,* 11 July 2005, A12.
2. "U.S. Appeals WTO Report in Lumber Dispute," [Online] available at www.ctv.ca/servlet/ArticleNews/story/CTVNews/1126024104204_10, 07 September 2005; "Indepth Backgrounder: Softwood Lumber," [Online] available at http://cbc.ca/news/indepth/background/softwood_lumber.html, 18 August 2003; "Softwood Exports Plunge on 27% U.S. Duty," *Financial Post,* 8 July 2002.
3. "Loggers Say They've Been Burned by Liberals," [Online] available at www.ctv.ca/servlet/ArticleNews/story/CTVNews/1088111322805_83520522, 7 September 2005.
4. E. Romanelli & M.L. Tushman, "Organizational Transformation as Punctuated Equilibrium: An Empirical Test," *Academy of Management Journal* 37 (1994): 1141–1166.
5. E. G. Fisher & Alex Kondra, "Canada's Airlines: Recent Turbulence and Changing Flight Plans," in *Industrial Relations in Canadian Industry,* Richard P. Chaykowski & Anil Verma, eds.

(Toronto: Holt, Rinehart and Winston of Canada Limited, 1992) pp. 358–404; Statistics Canada, *Air Carrier Operations in Canada*, 1977–1994; "WestJet—About Us," [Online] available at http://c2dsp.westjet.com/ internet/sky/about/index.jsp, 21 August 2003.
6. G. Morgenson, "Denial in Battle Creek," *Forbes,* 7 October 1996, 44–46.
7. E. Ramstad, "I Want My Flat TV; Now!" *Wall Street Journal*, 27 May 2004, B1.
8. Statistics Canada, Table Number 3790017.
9. "Help-Wanted Index Unchanged in June," *Financial Post*, 9 July 1998, 6.
10. R. Norton, "Where Is This Economy Really Heading?" *Fortune,* 7 August 1995, 54–56.
11. B. Orwall, M. Peers, & E. Smith, "Stayin' Alive: Music Industry Presses 'Play' on Plan to Save Its Business," *Wall Street Journal*, 9 September 2003, A1.
12. C. Mann, "The Year the Music Dies," *Wired,* February 2003, [Online] available at www.wired.com/wired/archive/11.02/dirge_pr.html, 8 February 2003; T. Woody, "The Race to Kill Kazaa," *Wired,* February 2003, [Online] available at www.wired.com/wired/archive/11.02/kazaa_pr.html, 8 February 2003.
13. C. Mann, "The Year the Music Dies," *Wired,* February 2003, [Online] available at www.wired.com/wired/archive/11.02/dirge_pr.html, 8 February 2003.
14. *Women in Canada: Work Chapter Updates*, Statistics Canada, Cat. No.89F011XIE, 2003.
15. Sonya Felix, "Running on Empty: Tight Money Has Curtailed the Drive to Provide On-site Daycare Centres, but the Long-term Benefits to Employees and Employers Might Outweigh the Costs," *Benefits Canada*, 21, no. 6 (June 1997): 109, 111.
16. R. Sharpe, "Nannies on Speed Dial: There Is Growing Army of Domestic Help Out There, and More and More Families Are Picking Up the Phone," *Business Week,* 18 September 2000, 108.
17. R.J. Bies & T.R. Tyler, "The Litigation Mentality in Organizations: A Test of Alternative Psychological Explanations," *Organization Science* 4 (1993): 352–366.
18. Vicki Barnett, "Wrongful Dismissal Damages Rise," *Calgary Herald*, 7 August 1999, W1.
19. D. Smart & C. Martin, "Manufacturer Responsiveness to Consumer Correspondence: An Empirical Investigation of Consumer Perceptions," *Journal of Consumer Affairs* 26 (1992): 104.
20. David Estok, "Timbit Nation," *Report on Business Magazine*, 19 (December 2002): 78–84.
21. H. Appelman, "I Scream, You Scream: Consumers Vent over the Net," *New York Times,* 4 March 2001.
22. J. Pereira, "Trends (A Special Report)—It's a Whole New Game," *Wall Street Journal*, 22 November 2004, R9.
23. S.A. Zahra & S.S. Chaples, "Blind Spots in Competitive Analysis," *Academy of Management Executive* 7 (1993): 7–28.
24. J. M. Moran, "Getting Closer Together—Videophones Don't Deliver TV Quality Sound, Visuals, but They're Improving," *Seattle Times,* 15 March 1998.
25. A. Squeo, "FCC Is Poised to Clarify Future of Internet Phone Calls," *Wall Street Journal*, 22 January 2004, B1.
26. L. Fuld, "Chapter 1: Understanding Intelligence," *CI Strategies & Tools: The New Competitor Intelligence,* [Online] available at www.fuld.com/chap1.html, 15 February 2003.
27. K.G. Provan, "Embeddedness, Interdependence, and Opportunism in Organizational Supplier-Buyer Networks," *Journal of Management* 19 (1993): 841–856.
28. N. Gaouette, "Israel's Diamond Dealers Tremble: Diamond Colossus DeBeers Today Launches Fundamental Changes to $56 Billion Retail Market," *Christian Science Monitor,* 1 June 2001, [Online].
29. F. Shalom, "Clothing Firms Fight Wal-Mart Price Rollbacks," *Montreal Gazette,* 6 July 1995.
30. B.K. Pilling, L.A. Crosby, & D.W. Jackson, "Relational Bonds in Industrial Exchange: An Experimental Test of the Transaction Cost Economic Framework," *Journal of Business Research* 30 (1994): 237–251.
31. "Ethical Dangers Multiply," *Purchasing,* 17 October 1996; J. Dubinsky, "How to Foster Ethical Conduct: Companies Have a Clear Role in Preventing Conflicts of Interest," *Supplier Selection & Management,* 1 June 2001; "Amerinet Joins Groups Issuing Compliance Documents Based on Code of Conduct," *Hospital Materials Management,* 1 January 2003, 6; M. Lawson, "The Ethical Dilemma of Corporate Generosity," *Australian Financial Review,* 5 December 2002, 16.
32. M. Hudson, "PETA Doll Ruffles KFC's Feathers," *The Roanoke Times*, [Online] available at www.roanoke.com/extra%5C16581.html, 8 January 2005; "Animal Rights Protesters Shed Clothes on Rideau," [Online] available at www.ctv.ca/servlet/ArticleNews/story/CTVNews/1045520595249_72, 7 September 2005.
33. "KFC Canada CEO Asks Pam Anderson Out for Lunch," [Online] available at www.ctv.ca/servlet/ArticleNews/story/CTVNews/1115067858692_110477058, 7 September 2005.
34. J. Ball, "Detroit Fears Some Consumers May Be Souring on Big SUVs," *The Wall Street Journal Online,* http://online.wsj.com/article/0,SB1041979477724000464,00.html, 8 January 2003.
35. D.F. Jennings & J.R. Lumpkin, "Insights Between Environmental Scanning Activities and Porter's Generic Strategies: An Empirical Analysis," *Journal of Management* 4 (1992): 791–803.
36. Keith McArthur, "Digital Video Recorders Spur New TV Ad Model," *Globe and Mail*, 12 September 2005, B3.
37. S.E. Jackson & J.E. Dutton, "Discerning Threats and Opportunities," *Administrative Science Quarterly* 33 (1988): 370–387.
38. J.B. Thomas, S.M. Clark, & D.A. Gioia, "Strategic Sensemaking and Organizational Performance: Linkages among Scanning, Interpretation, Action, and Outcomes," *Academy of Management Journal 36* (1993): 239–270.
39. R. Daft, J. Sormunen, & D. Parks, "Chief Executive Scanning, Environmental Characteristics, and Company Performance: An Empirical Study," *Strategic Management Journal* 9 (1988): 123–139; D. Miller & P.H. Friesen, "Strategy-Making and Environment: The Third Link," *Strategic Management Journal* 4 (1983): 221–235.
40. S. Kraft, "Tradition under Siege/Supermarkets?Sacre Bleu!/A Shopping Revolution Imperils French Merchants," *Los Angeles Times,* 5 May 1996, D10.
41. "High Sales, Low Fat," *Financial Post*, 8 February 1996, 63.
42. K. Maney, "SAS Workers Won When Greed Lost," *USA Today*, 22 April 2004, B.01.
43. A. Harrington, N. Hira, C. Tkaczyk, "Hall of Fame: If Making the 100 Best List Is an Enormous Accomplishment,

Consider How Tough It Is to Repeat the Feat Every Single Year," *Fortune*, 24 January 2005, 94.
44. "SAS Makes the *Fortune* 'Hall of Fame'," *SAS Web Site*, [Online] available at www.sas.com/news/feature/16jan05/fortune.html, 20 January 2005.
45. W. Gulger, "Getting and Keeping Good People in the 21st Century," *Hardware and Home Centre Magazine* 24, no. 1 (January/February 2000): 37–38. Zena Olijynk, "The Farm Team," *Canadian Business,* 10–23 April 2006, 72.
46. P. Elmer-DeWitt, "Mine, All Mine; Bill Gates Wants a Piece of Everybody's Action. But Can He Get It?" *Time,* 5 June 1995.
47. D.M. Boje, "The Storytelling Organization: A Study of Story Performance in an Office-Supply Firm," *Administrative Science Quarterly* 36 (1991): 106–126.
48. S. Walton & J. Huey, *Sam Walton: Made in America* (New York: Doubleday, 1992).
49. D. Rushe, "Wal-martians," *Sunday Times–London,* 10 June 2001, 5.
50. M. Hayes, "Bowa Builders: NRS Excellence in Class, 50—Plus," *HousingZone.com*, [Online] available at www.housingzone.com/topics/pr/nrs/pr03ia009.asp, 19 January 2005.
51. Mark Stevens, "The Store to End All Stores," *Canadian Business Review* 67, no. 5 (May 1994): 20.
52. R.L. Daft, *Organizational Theory and Design* (Cincinnati, OH: South-Western College Publishing, 2001).
53. D.R. Denison & A.K. Mishra, "Toward a Theory of Organizational Culture and Effectiveness," *Organization Science* 6 (1995): 204–223.
54. L. Hays, "Gerstner Is Struggling as He Tries to Change Ingrained IBM Culture," *The Wall Street Journal,* 13 May 1994, A1.
55. A. Deutschman, "How H-P Continues to Grow and Grow," *Fortune,* 2 May 1994, 90–100.
56. "Company Profile," F. H. Faulding & Company, [Online] available at www.faulding.com.au/home/comp_profile/mission/mission.html, 21 June 2001.
57. E. Schein, *Organizational Culture and Leadership,* 2nd ed. (San Francisco: Jossey-Bass, 1992).
58. S. Albert & D.A. Whetten, "Organizational Identity," *Research in Organizational Behavior* 7 (1985): 263–295; C.M. Fiol, "Managing Culture as a Competitive Resource: An Identity-Based View of Sustainable Competitive Advantage," *Journal of Management* 17 (1991): 191–211.
59. Mary Rother, "The Will to Succeed: Besides a Good Product or Service, What Does It Take to Beat the Volatility of the IT Industry? Three Parables Provide Some Answers," *Financial Post Magazine*, March 1999, 44–50.
60. Claudia Cattaneo, "Petrocan Rids Itself of Pariah Legacy; Once Viewed as a Federal Government Invader, the Firm Is Now Accepted in Its Home Town," *Financial Post*, 17 November 1999, C8; David Olive, "The Brightest Stars in Canada's Oilpatch: This Generation of Executives Has Changed the Face of the Country's Oil Sector," *Financial Post*, 13 June 2000, C8, C9; James Sanford, "Oil Patch's Highest Perch Has a New View: Petro-Canada's Chief Stanford Has the Privatized Company in Fighting Trim and He's Ready to Lead It to New Conquests," *Financial Post*, 7/9 October 1995, 5.
61. "About the Movie," *Super Size Me: A Film of Epic Portions*, [Online] available at www.supersizeme.com/home.aspx?page=aboutmovie, 22 January 2005; Joel Baglole, "War of the Doughnuts," *The Wall Street Journal*, 23 August 2001, B1; Derek M. Boyle, "Can You Really Make Fast Food Healthy?" *Fortune*, 9 August 2004, 134; D. DeCloet, "How Krispy Got Creamed," *Globe and Mail*, 18 December 2004, F3. David Estok, "Timbit Nation," *Report on Business Magazine,* December 2000, 74–78; Jim Fox, "Wendy's 1,910 Tim Hortons Units Make Gains with Lunch Menus," *Nation's Restaurant News,* 22 May 2000, 288–290; Scott Gardiner, "In Praise of Saint Timmy," *Marketing Magazine*, 21 August 2000, 10; R. Givhan, "Lord of the Fries: Morgan Spurlock Got His Fill of Ailments Making 'Super Size Me,' But He's Been Fortified by Its Impact," *Washington Post*, 2 May 2004, N01; Chris Lambie, "Tim Hortons Heads to Sea," *The Ottawa Citizen*, 7 August 2004, A5; "Subway® Nutrition Facts—US, January 2005," *Subway*, [Online] available at http://subway.com/subwayroot/MenuNutrition/Nutrition/pdf/NutritionValues.pdf, 23 January 2005. "The Weight We Pack on Gets Heavier and Heavier," *Globe and Mail*, 11 July 2005, A12.
62. M. Roger, "How Culture Affects Mergers and Acquisitions," *Industrial Management*, September 2000 Vol. 42, No. 5: 22–26.
63. R. Karpinski, "Tandem Slates Web Server Product Line," *Interactive Age*, 10 April 1995, 24; T.J. Peters & N.K. Austin, *A Passion for Excellence* (New York: Random House, 1985); E. Ramstad & L. Gomes, "Compaq to Acquire Tandem Computers," *The Wall Street Journal*, 24 June 1997, A3; J.E. Rigdon, "Cruel World: Cannibalism Is a Virtue in Computer Business, Tandem's CEO Learns," *The Wall Street Journal*, 24 August 1994, A1; J. Ward, "The Thrill Is Gone," *Financial World*, 11 April 1995, 32; A.L. Wilkins & N.J. Bristow, "For Successful Organization Culture, Honor Your Past," *Academy of Management Executive* 1 (1987): 221–229.

Chapter 3

1. "Gap Inc. 2003 Social Responsibility Report," *Gap Inc.*, [Online] available at http://ccbn.mobular.net/ccbn/7/645/696/print/print.pdf, 12 February 2005; C. Dahle, "Gap's New Look: The See-Through," *Fast Company*, 1 September 2004, 69; D. Drickhamer, "Under Fire: Consumer Cries for Sweatshop-Free Products Drive Big-Name Brands to Extraordinary Lengths to Monitor Working Conditions at Contractor Plants," *Industry Week*, 1 June 2002, 30; P. Engardio, "Global Compact, Little Impact," *Business Week*, 12 July 2004, 86. F. Lawrence, "Sweatshop Campaigners Demand Gap Boycott," *The Guardian*, 22 November 2002, 10; A. Merrick, "Sweatshop' Tag, Retailer Details Problems Among Thousands of Plants," *Wall Street Journal*, 13 May 2004, A1; M. Perea, "Gap Reports Lower Sales than April 2001," *Associated Press Newswires*, 10 May 2002, 11:36; N. Stein, "No Way Out," *Fortune*, 20 January 2003, 102.
2. A. Losciale, "Survey Finds More than 75% of Workers Say They Have Seen Unethical Conduct," *The Salt Lake Tribune*, 27 May 2000, C2.
3. C. Smith, "The Ethical Workplace," *Association Management* 52 (2000): 70–73.
4. E. Petry, A. Mujica, & D. Vickery, "Sources and Consequences of Workplace Pressure: Increasing the Risk of Unethical and Illegal Business Practices," *Business & Society Review* 99 (1998): 25–30.
5. M. Jackson (Associated Press), "Workplace Cheating Rampant, Half of Employees Surveyed Admit They Take Unethical Actions," *Peoria Journal Star*, 5 April 1997.

6. Losciale, "Survey Finds More than 75% of Workers Say They Have Seen Unethical Conduct."
7. "Ethical Business Practices Come into Fashion," *National Post*, 30 April 2005, FW.09.
8. C. Smith, "The Ethical Workplace," *Association Management* 52 (2000): 70–73.
9. M. Maremont, "Blind Ambition: How the Pursuit of Results Got Out of Hand at Bausch & Lomb," *Business Week*, 23 October 1995.
10. M. Bordwin, "Don't Ask Employees to Do Your Dirty Work," *Management Review*, 1 October 1995.
11. L.S. Paine, "Managing for Organizational Integrity," *Harvard Business Review*, March–April 1994, 106–117.
12. K. Gibson, "Excuses, Excuses: Moral Slippage in the Workplace," *Business Horizons* 43, no. 6 (2000): 65; S.L. Robinson & R.J. Bennett, "A Typology of Deviant Workplace Behaviors: A Multidimensional Scaling Study," *Academy of Management Journal* 38 (1995): 555–572.
13. Peter Brieger, "Office Crime: Many Know, Few Tell: Huge Problem: Survey," *National Post*, 9 August 2002, FP5.
14. K. Gibson, "Excuses, Excuses: Moral Slippage in the Workplace," *Business Horizons* 43, no. 6 (2000): 65; S.L. Robinson & R.J. Bennett, "A Typology of Deviant Workplace Behaviors: A Multidimensional Scaling Study," *Academy of Management Journal* 38 (1995): 555–572.
15. L. Peek & B. Webster, "Sabotage Feared over Airliners' Cut Wires," *The Times of London*, 9 June 2001, 16; S. Gaudin, "Computer Sabotage Case Back in Court," *Network World Fusion*, 19 April 2001, 12.
16. Retail Council of Canada, *2001 Canadian Retail Security Report*, [Online] available at www.retailcouncil.org, 21 October 2002.
17. Marina Strauss, "Retailers Put Squeeze on Shrinkage," *Globe and Mail*, 13 July 2001, M1.
18. L. Lorek, "Sticky Fingers," *Interactive Week from ZDWire*, 27 March 2001.
19. David Ray, "Workplace Violence: Strategies for Prevention," *Law Now*, 26, no. 5, April–May 2002.
20. Shelley Boyles, "Workplace Violence: Coping in a Dangerous World," *The Canadian Consulting Engineer* 43, no. 1 (January–February 2002): 51–52.
21. Ibid.
22. Ibid.
23. "Work Rage," *BC Business Magazine* 29, no. 1 (January 2001): 23.
24. M.P. Coco, Jr., "The New War Zone: The Workplace," *SAM Advanced Management Journal* 63, no. 1 (1998): 15; M.G. Harvey & R.A. Cosier, "Homicides in the Workplace: Crisis or False Alarm?" *Business Horizons* 38, no. 10 (1995): 11.
25. L.A. Hays, "A Matter of Time: Widow Sues IBM over Death Benefits," *The Wall Street Journal*, 6 July 1995.
26. T.M. Jones, "Ethical Decision Making by Individuals in Organizations: An Issue-Contingent Model," *Academy of Management Review* 16 (1991): 366–395.
27. B. Mook, "Group Gets Tough on 'Software Piracy,'" *Denver Business Journal*, 6 March 1998, 19A.
28. L. Kohlberg, "Stage and Sequence: The Cognitive-Developmental Approach to Socialization," in *Handbook of Socialization Theory and Research*, ed. D.A. Goslin (Chicago: Rand McNally, 1969); L. Trevino, "Moral Reasoning and Business Ethics: Implications for Research, Education, and Management," *Journal of Business Ethics* 11 (1992): 445–459.
29. L.T. Hosmer, "Trust: The Connecting Link Between Organizational Theory and Philosophical Ethics," *Academy of Management Review* 20 (1995): 379–403.
30. M.R. Cunningham, D.T. Wong, & A.P. Barbee, "Self-Presentation Dynamics on Overt Integrity Tests: Experimental Studies of the Reid Report," *Journal of Applied Psychology* 79 (1994): 643–658.
31. H.J. Bernardin, "Validity of an Honesty Test in Predicting Theft among Convenience Store Employees," *Academy of Management Journal* 36 (1993): 1097–1108.
32. J.M. Collins & F.L. Schmidt, "Personality, Integrity, and White Collar Crime: A Construct Validity Study," *Personnel Psychology* (1993): 295–311.
33. W.C. Borman, M.A. Hanson, & J.W. Hedge, "Personnel Selection," *Annual Review of Psychology* 48 (1997).
34. D.S. Ones, C. Viswesvaran, & F.L. Schmidt, "Comprehensive Meta-Analysis of Integrity Test Validities: Findings and Implications for Personnel Selection and Theories of Job Performance," *Journal of Applied Psychology* 78 (1993): 679–703.
35. S. Nonis & C. Swift, "An Examination of the Relationship Between Academic Dishonesty and Workplace Dishonesty: A Multicampus Investigation," *Journal of Education for Business* (November 2001): 69–77.
36. Shell Canada Statement of General Business Principles and Corporate Ethics, [Online] available at www.shellcanada.com. With permission obtained: 22 October 2002.
37. P.E. Murphy, "Corporate Ethics Statements: Current Status and Future Prospects," *Journal of Business Ethics* 14 (1995): 727–740.
38. S.J. Harrington, "What Corporate America Is Teaching about Ethics," *Academy of Management Executive* 5 (1991): 21–30.
39. R. McGarver, "Doing the Right Thing," *Training* 30 (1993): 35–38.
40. Canada Statement of General Business Principles and Corporate Ethics, [Online] available at www.shellcanada.com. With permission obtained: October 22, 2002.
41. Diane Francis, "Livent: A Bean Counter Scandal: A Tale of Woes Raises Interesting Questions," *Financial Post*, 10 May 2001, 3.
42. M. Schwartz, "Business Ethics: Time to Blow the Whistle?" *Globe and Mail*, 5 March 1998, B2.
43. M.P. Miceli & J.P Near, "Whistleblowing: Reaping the Benefits," *Academy of Management Executive* 8 (1994): 65–72.
44. K. Maher, "Wanted: Ethical Employer—Job Hunters, Seeking to Avoid an Enron or an Andersen," *The Wall Street Journal*, 9 July 2002, B1.
45. H.R. Bower, *Social Responsibilities of the Businessman* (New York: Harper & Row, 1953).
46. "Alcan Comes under Fire by Activists; Company's Social Responsibility a Target," *Globe and Mail*, 29 April 2005.
47. "Canada Third in Corporate Responsibility Reporting," *Globe and Mail*, 16 June 2005.
48. S.L. Wartick & P.L. Cochran, "The Evolution of the Corporate Social Performance Model," *Academy of Management Review* 10 (1985): 758–769.
49. T. Donaldson & L.E. Preston, "The Stakeholder Theory of the Corporation: Concepts, Evidence, and Implications," *Academy of Management Review* 20 (1995): 65–91.
50. Donalee Moulton, "Irving Gets Auto Makers Choice Designation for Its Fuels," *Financial Post-National Post*, 19 November 1999, E15.

51. Michael MacDonald, "Automakers Encourage Clean Fuel Use," *Canadian Press Newswire*, 14 October 1999.
52. M. Silver, "Doing Your Bit to Save the Earth," *U.S. News & World Report*, 2 April 1990, 61–62.
53. E.W. Orts, "Beyond Shareholders: Interpreting Corporate Constituency Statutes," *The George Washington Law Review* 61 (1992): 14–135.
54. A.B. Carroll, "A Three-Dimensional Conceptual Model of Corporate Performance," *Academy of Management Review* 4 (1979): 497–505.
55. J. Lublin & M. Murray, "CEOs Leave Faster than Ever Before as Boards, Investors Lose Patience," *The Wall Street Journal Interactive,* 27 October 2000.
56. Google.ca key word search (Mastercard, Affinity), available at www.google.ca, retrieved 24 October 2002.
57. Scouts Canada, www.scouts.ca.
58. "T. Bryant, "Judge Rejects New Trial in Case of Woman Paralyzed in Suzuki Samurai Accident," *St. Louis Post-Dispatch,* 2 February 1998, C4; "Inclined to Roll, Suzuki Samurai Car Gets Unfavorable Rating Because of Tipping Tendency," *Time,* 13 June 1988, 51.
59. S. Power & N. Shirouzu, "Bridgestone Position Angers Lawmakers—Firm Balks at Wider Recall of Tires, Setting Stage for House Showdown," *The Wall Street Journal*, 5 September 2000, A3.
60. R. Silverman & K. Dunham, "Tire Recall: The Road Gets Rough—Consultants Split on Bridgestone's Crisis Management," *The Wall Street Journal*, 11 August 2000, A6.
61. K. Kranhold & E. White, "The Perils and Potential Rewards of Crisis Managing for Firestone," *The Wall Street Journal*, 8 September 2000, B1.
62. Toby Heaps, "Actions Speak Louder than Words," *Corporate Knights*, [Online] available at www .corporateknights.ca, June 2001.
63. N. Templin, "Nissan Recalls and Destroys Some Minivans," *The Wall Street Journal,* 9 December 1993, B1.
64. Paul Fengler & Toby Heaps, "Aqua Purus," *Corporate Knights*, [Online] available at www.corporateknights.ca, June 2002.
65. Socially Responsible Mutual Funds, Social Investment Organization, [Online] available at www.socialinvestment.ca, 17 October 2002.
66. Pablo Fuchs, "Real Assets Aims to Prove You Don't Have to Lose Money to Be Socially Responsible," *Canadian Business* 74, no. 13 (2001): 142–146.
67. Canadian Social Investment Review 2000, Social Investment Organization, [Online] available at www .socialinvestment.ca.
68. Pablo Fuchs, "Real Assets Aims to Prove You Don't Have to Lose Money to Be Socially Responsible," *Canadian Business* 74, no. 13 (2001): 142–146.
69. H. Haines, "Noah Joins Ranks of Socially Responsible Funds," *Dow Jones News Service,* 13 October 1995.
70. M.B. Meznar, D. Nigh, & C.Y. Kwok, "Effect of Announcements of Withdrawal from South Africa on Stockholder Wealth," *Academy of Management Journal* 37 (1994): 1633–1648.
71. Paul Fengler & Toby Heaps, "Aqua Purus," *Corporate Knights*, [Online] available at www.corporateknights.ca, June 2002.
72. Ibid.
73. D. Kadlec & B. Van Voorst, "The New World of Giving: Companies Are Doing More Good, and Demanding More Back," *Time*, 5 May 1997.
74. P. Carlin, "Will Rapid Growth Stunt Corporate Do-Gooders?" *Business and Society Review,* Spring 1995, 36–43.
75. Katherine Macklem, "Canada's Top 100 Employers," *Maclean's*, 28 October 2002, 26–34.
76. Ibid.
77. "Gap Inc. 2003 Social Responsibility Report," *Gap Inc.*, [Online] available at http://ccbn.mobular.net/ccbn/7/645/696/print/print.pdf, 12 February 2005; C. Dahle, "Gap's New Look: The See-Through," *Fast Company*, 1 September 2004, 69; D. Drickhamer, "Under Fire: Consumer Cries for Sweatshop-Free Products Drive Big-Name Brands to Extraordinary Lengths to Monitor Working Conditions at Contractor Plants," *Industry Week*, 1 June 2002, 30; P. Engardio, "Global Compact, Little Impact," *Business Week*, 12 July 2004, 86; F. Lawrence, "Sweatshop Campaigners Demand Gap Boycott," *The Guardian*, 22 November 2002, 10; A. Merrick, "Sweatshop Tag, Retailer Details Problems among Thousands of Plants," *Wall Street Journal*, 13 May 2004, A1; M. Perea, "Gap Reports Lower Sales than April 2001," *Associated Press Newswires*, 10 May 2002, 11; N. Stein, "No Way Out," *Fortune*, 20 January 2003, 102.
78. J. Barks, "Credit Reports Aid Underwriters, But Is It Worth the Controversy?" *Bests Review/Property-Casualty Insurance* 96 (1 August 1995): 44; K. Hoke, "Big Insurers Divide on Linking Auto Premiums to Credit History," *Business First-Columbus*, 8 January 1996; G. Sanders, "Arizona Probing Insurers on Redlining, Credit Checks," *Best Review/Property-Casualty Insurance* 95 (1 January 1995): 12. L. Scism, "Turned Down: A Bad Credit Record Can Get You Rejected for Auto Insurance," *The Wall Street Journal*, 11 November 1995.

Chapter 4

1. "Air Canada's Boss Worried about Competition from Discount Carriers," *Canadian Press Newswire*, 23 February 2001; "No Need for US Airlines to Fly in Canada for Competition, Says Collenette," *Canadian Press Newswire*, 18 January 2001; "Air Canada Reports Market Share Drop to 73%," *Canadian Press Newswire*, 25 April 2001; Joel Baglole, "Airlines in Turmoil: Air Canada Files for Protection from Creditors," *The Wall Street Journal*, 2 April 2003, A2; Frances Fiorino, "Air Canada Adds 'Zip' to Low-Fare Market," *Aviation Week and Space Technology* 156, no. 17; Peter Fitzpatrick, "WestJet Spends $1b Expanding Its Fleet: Company Adding 30 Planes in Bid to Grab Bigger Market," *Financial Post*, 2, no. 105, C1, C9; Peter Fitzpatrick, "Air Canada to Slash 6,000 Jobs, Cut Fleet in Bid to Save $500m: 'Industry in Freefall,'" *Financial Post*, 25 September 2001, B1, B4; Peter Fitzpatrick, "Leaner Air Canada Back in the Black," *Financial Post*, 2 August 2002, FP6; Perry Flint, "Interview: Zip President and CEO Steve Smith," *Air Transport World* 39, no. 6 (June 2002), 68; Gillian Livingston, "Air Canada CEO Says Discount Market Vital as Business Market Declines," *Canadian Press Newswire*, 1 August 2002. Allan Swift, "Air Canada Reports $125 Million Q3 Earning," *Canadian Press Newswire*, 25 October 2002; Peter Verburg, "Reach for the Bottom," *Canadian Business*, 73, no. 4, 42–48; http://c0dsp.westjet.com/internet/sky/about/index.jsp.
2. Craig Saunders, "New Energy Savings Contracts Cut Costs," *Globe and Mail*, 26 July 2005, B8.
3. E.A. Locke & G.P. Latham, *A Theory of Goal Setting and Task Performance* (Englewood Cliffs, NJ: Prentice Hall, 1990).
4. M.E. Tubbs, "Goal-Setting: A Meta-Analytic Examination of the Empirical Evidence," *Journal of Applied Psychology* 71 (1986): 474–83.

5. Michael Clarkson, "Weir Sets Major Goals: Canadian Golfer Hopes to Build on 2000 Success," *The Ottawa Citizen*, 11 January 2001, D5; Joe Scanlon, "Road to Success Filled with Bumps," *Calgary Herald*, 28 April 2003, C4.
6. J. Bavelas & E.S. Lee, "Effect of Goal Level on Performance: A Trade-Off of Quantity and Quality," *Canadian Journal of Psychology* 32 (1978): 219–240.
7. A. Farnham, "Mary Kay's Lessons in Leadership," *Fortune*, 20 September 1993; "Company Information: Products and Sales," Mary Kay Cosmetics, [Online] available at www.marykay.com/Home/Community/Headquarters/Company/Products.asp, 29 June 2001; "Earnings Representation" [Online] available at www.marykay.ca/display.asp?PageID=1484, 20 September 2005.
8. Mark Evans, "Telus Plans to Slash $300M in Operating Costs, 10% of Workforce May Go," *National Post*, 7 June 2002, FP1; Mark Evans, "Telus to Slash 6000 Jobs," *National Post*, 12 July 2002, FP1; Mark Evans, "Telus Chief Juggles Growth Strategy, Fiscal Responsibility," *National Post*, 14 November 2002, FP1.
9. C.C. Miller, "Strategic Planning and Firm Performance: A Synthesis of More than Two Decades of Research," *Academy of Management Performance* 37 (1994): 1649–1665.
10. H. Mintzberg, "Rethinking Strategic Planning," Part I: Pitfalls and Fallacies, *Long Range Planning* 27 (1994): 12–21; Part II: New Roles for Planners: 22–30; H. Mintzberg, "The Pitfalls of Strategic Planning," *California Management Review* 36 (1993): 32–47.
11. P. Dvorak, "Sony TVs Take Sibling Tips—Latest Machines Borrow from Videogame and Audio Technology," *Wall Street Journal*, 20 August 2004, B3.
12. K. Pope, "International: Runaway Growth at Phone Giant Nokia Humbles Newcomer after Early Success," *The Wall Street Journal*, 12 March 1996.
13. K. Capell, W. Echikson, & P. Elstrom, "Surprise! Nokia Doesn't Walk on Water: Its About-Face on Growth Will Hurt Credibility," *Business Week*, 25 June 2001, 30.
14. H. Mintzberg, "The Pitfalls of Strategic Planning," *California Management Review* 36 (1993): 32–47.
15. "Pixar," [Online] available at http://en.wikipedia.org/wiki/Pixar, 1 June 2006.
16. P. Tam, "Will Quantity Hurt Pixar's Quality?—Computer-Animation Studio Bets It Can Boost Output to One Feature a Year," *The Wall Street Journal*, 15 February 2001, B1.
17. E.A. Locke & G.P. Latham, *A Theory of Goal Setting and Task Performance* (Englewood Cliffs, NJ: Prentice Hall, 1990).
18. G.A. Bricker, "Performance Agreements: The Key to Increasing Motivation," *Sales and Marketing Management* (February 1992), 69; A. King, B. Oliver, B. Sloop, & K. Vaverek, *Planning and Goal Setting for Improved Performance, Participant's Guide* (Cincinnati, OH: Thomson Executive Press, 1995).
19. E.A. Locke & G.P. Latham, *A Theory of Goal Setting and Task Performance* (Englewood Cliffs, NJ: Prentice Hall, 1990).
20. S. Sherman, "Stretch Goals: The Dark Side of Asking for Miracles," *Fortune*, 13 November 1995, 231; C. Loomis, J. Schlosser, J. Sung, M. Boyle, & P. Neering, "The 15% Delusion Brash Predictions about Earnings Growth Often Lead to Missed Targets, Battered Stock, and Creative Accounting—And That's When Times Are Good. Why Can't CEOs Kick the Habit?" *Fortune*, 5 February 2001, 102; H. Paster, "Manager's Journal: Be Prepared," *The Wall Street Journal*, 24 September 2001, A24; P. Sellers, "The New Breed: The Latest Crop of CEOs Is Disciplined, Deferential, Even a Bit Dull," *Fortune*, 18 November 2002, 66.
21. J.R. Hollenbeck, C.R. Williams, & H.J. Klein, "An Empirical Examination of the Antecedents of Commitment to Difficult Goals," *Journal of Applied Psychology* 74 (1989): 18–23.
22. G. Lucier & S. Seshadri, "GE Takes Six Sigma Beyond the Bottom Line," *Strategic Finance* 82, no. 11 (2001): 40–46.
23. "Severn Sound Cleanup Cheered: Environmental Recovery of Vacationland 'Hot Spot' Emerged from Co-Operative Effort," *Globe and Mail*, 16 August 2002, D11.
24. A. Bandura & D.H. Schunk, "Cultivating Competence, Self-Efficacy, and Intrinsic Interest through Proximal Self-Motivation," *Journal of Personality and Social Psychology* 41 (1981): 586–598.
25. D. Ariely & K. Wertenboch, "Procrastination, Deadlines, and Performance: Self-Control by Precommitment," *Psychological Science* 13 (2002): 219–224.
26. N. Carr, "Curbing the Procrastination Instinct," *Harvard Business Review* (October 2001): 26.
27. E.A. Locke & G.P. Latham, *A Theory of Goal Setting and Task Performance* (Englewood Cliffs, NJ: Prentice Hall, 1990).
28. L. McCauley, "Relaunch! Unit of One," *Fast Company*, 1 July 2000, 97.
29. E.H. Bowman & D. Hurry, "Strategy through the Option Lens: An Integrated View of Resource Investments and the Incremental-Choice Process," *Academy of Management Review* 18 (1993): 760–782.
30. T. Poling, "Built to Modify; in the SBC the Athletes Aren't the Only Things That Can Flex," *San Antonio Express*, 2 November 2002, 01E.
31. N.A. Wishart, J.J. Elam, & D. Robey, "Redrawing the Portrait of a Learning Organization: Inside Knight-Ridder, Inc.," *Academy of Management Executive* 10 (1996): 7–20.
32. P. Callahan & K. Helliker, "Knight Ridder Loses Readers but Raises Rates for Advertisers—As Publisher's Profits Rise, Some Ad Buyers Fume or Switch to Other Media," *The Wall Street Journal*, 18 June 2001, A1.
33. J. Madore, "If You're 18 to 34 and Reading This, Your Secret's Safe with Us. Many Young Adults Are Rejecting the Traditional," *Newsday*, 3 February 2003, A27.
34. Derek DeCloet, "Elevator Up," *Report on Business*, May 2005, 59–70.
35. J.C. Collins & J.I. Porras, "Organizational Vision and Visionary Organizations," *California Management Review*, Fall 1991, 30–52.
36. Ken MacQueen, "The Anti-Retailer: Vancouver's Mountain Equipment Co-op Succeeds in Spite of Itself," *Maclean's*, 29 April 2002, 30.
37. Ibid.
38. J.C. Collins & J.I. Porras, "Organizational Vision and Visionary Organizations," *California Management Review*, Fall 1991, 30–52; "St. Michael's Hospital Vision Statement", [Online] available at www.stmichaelshospital.com/content/about_us/vision.asp, 22 September 2005.
39. J.C. Collins & J.I. Porras, "Organizational Vision and Visionary Organizations," *California Management Review*, Fall 1991, 30–52.
40. "NASA Unveils Moon Program," [Online] available at www.cnn.com/2005/TECH/space/09/19/space.moon.reut/index.html, 21 September 2005.

41. J.C. Collins & J.I. Porras, "Organizational Vision and Visionary Organizations," *California Management Review*, Fall 1991, 30–52.
42. Brent Jang, "WestJet Maps Out Ambitious Ontario Flight Plan," *Globe and Mail*, 16 September 2005, B1, B8.
43. Peter Morton, "Southwest Blazes Trail," *Financial Post*, 17 December 1999, C1, C9.
44. J.A. Pearce & F. David, "Corporate Mission Statements: The Bottom Line," *Academy of Management Executive* 1 (1987): 109–116.
45. N. Gull, "Plan B (And C And D And...)," *Inc.*, March 2004, 40.
46. L. Iococca, with W. Novak, *Iococca* (New York: Bantam, 1984).
47. R. Rodgers & J.E. Hunter, "Impact of Management by Objectives on Organizational Productivity," *Journal of Applied Psychology* 76 (1991): 322–336.
48. E. Marlow & R. Schilhavy, "Expectation Issues in Management by Objectives Programs," *Industrial Management* 33, no. 4 (1991): 29.
49. "Cineplex Galaxy Buying Famous Players for $500 Million," [Online] available at www.cbc.ca/story/business/national/2005/06/13/famouscineplex-050613.html, 22 September 2005.
50. CIBC, "Career Quest," [Online] available at www2.cibc.com/inside/careers/template/job_postings.html, 8 November 2002.
51. Canadian Human Rights Commission, "About the Canadian Human Rights Commission," [Online] available at www.chrc-ccdp.ca/AboutCHRC_AproposCCDP/about.asp, 8 November 2002.
52. N. Humphrey, "References a Tricky Issue for Both Sides," *Nashville Business Journal* 11 (8 May 1995): 1A.
53. M. Seminerio, "Nielsen: Penthouse Website Popular with PC Companies," *PC Week Online*, 2 April 1996.
54. Asha Tomlinson' "Heavy-Handed Net Policies Push Privacy Boundary," *Canadian HR Reporter*, 2 December 2002, 1–2.
55. M. Savage, "Keeping Watch—It's Not 1984, but Tools for Monitoring Employee Web Activity Are Catching On, Solution Providers Say," *Computer Reseller News*, 2 October 2000, 32.
56. Ian Mulgrew, "Powerful e-sheriffs Police Cyberspace," *Northern Daily News*, 26 April 2004, 7.
57. Savage, "Keeping Watch—It's Not 1984, but Tools for Monitoring Employee Web Activity Are Catching On, Solution Providers Say."
58. S. Sherman, "Stretch Goals: The Dark Side of Asking for Miracles," *Fortune*, 13 November 1995, 231.
59. lbid.
60. Julie MacLellan, "Locals Count Success," *Burnaby Now*, 10 August 2005, 11; "No Guts, No Glory: When Richmond Savings Took on the Humungous Bank(s) in a Cheeky Ad Campaign, the Big Six Were Not Amused," *B.C. Business Magazine*, September 1996, 30–34; "Richmond Savings Wins Ad Battle," *Marketing Magazine*, 2 October 2000, 1; Timothy Renshaw, "Credit Union Puts People First," *National Post*, 18 December 2002, SR3.
61. C. O'Dell, "Out-of-the-Box Benchmarking," *Management Review* 83 (1 January 1994): 63.
62. R. Vartabedian, "Chrysler Board Cuts Bonuses of Top Execs, Cites Lag in Quality," *Los Angeles Times*, 29 March 1996, D-1.
63. B. Wysocki, Jr., "Power Grid: Soft Landing or Hard? Firm Tests Strategy on 3 Views of Future—Most Likely, Duke Energy Decides, Is a Growth Era of 'Flawed Competition'—Retailing Gas on the Internet," *The Wall Street Journal*, 7 July 2000, A1.
64. G. Robbins, "Scenario Planning," *Public Management*, 1 March 1995, 4.
65. Andrew Nikiforuk, "Winging It? Smart Businesses Are Ready for a Bird-Flu Pandemic," *Canadian Business*, 24 April–7 May 2006, 55–57.
66. P.J. Schoemaker, "Scenario Planning: A Tool for Strategic Thinking," *Sloan Management Review* 36 (1995): 25.
67. M. Stepanke, "How Fast Is Net Fast? On the Internet, Companies Have to Be Ready to Change Goals or Strategy Virtually Overnight," *Business Week*, 1 November 1999, EB52.
68. F. Keenan, "Opening the Spigot: Faucet Maker Moen Uses the Web to Streamline Design. Rivals Are Eating Dust," *Business Week*, 4 June 2001, EB16.
69. S.C. Wheelwright & K.B. Clark, "Creating Project Plans to Focus Product Development," *Harvard Business Review*, March–April 1992, 70.
70. D. Dimancescu & K. Dwenger, "Smoothing the Product Development Plan," *Management Review* 85, no. 6 (1996): 36.
71. S.L. Brown, "Product Development: Past Research, Present Findings, and Future Directions," *Academy of Management Review* 20 (1995): 343–378.
72. L. Ohr, "Delivering Taste and Convenience," *Prepared Foods*, February 2001, 28.
73. Ibid.
74. J. Martin, "Ignore Your Customer," *Fortune*, 1 May 1995, 121.
75. M. Iansiti, "Shooting the Rapids: Managing Product Development in Turbulent Environments," *California Management Review* 38 (1995): 36–58.
76. F. Warner, "Lear Won't Take a Back Seat: For Decades, Lear Corp. Made Car Seats. Today, with the Help of Virtual Reality and Other Digital Technologies, Lear Makes a Whole Lot More—And Makes It a Whole Lot Faster. Along the Way, The Company Learned How to Get Real about What Technology Can and Cannot Do," *Fast Company*, 1 June 2000, 178.
77. Ibid.
78. "Air Canada's Zip Shut Down," [Online] available at www.cbc.ca/story/business/national/2004/09/08/zip_040908.html, 03 October 2005; Canadian Press, "Air Canada to Emerge from Creditor Protection," [Online] available at www.ctv.ca/servlet/ArticleNews/story/CTVNews/20040926/air_canada_040926/20040926/, 3 October 2005; Keith McArthur, "Air Canada Aims to Cut 7,000 Jobs," *Globe and Mail*, 22 May, 2003, A1; Keith McArthur, "Air Canada Cuts Routes, Grounds 40 Planes," *Globe and Mail*, 14 May 2003, A1. Sheila McGovern, "Skies Friendly for Air Canada," *CanWest News*, 5 August 2005, 1; C.C. Miller, "Strategic Planning and Firm Performance: A Synthesis of More than Two Decades of Research," *Academy of Management Review* 37 (1994): 1649–1665; Kevin Restivo, "Air Canada Unions Won't Acquiesce to Pay Cuts: Want Books Opened First," *National Post*, 5 May 2003, FP 1; Peter Verburg, "Emergency Exit," *Canadian Business* 75, no. 19 (14 October 2002), 16; Konrad Yakabuski, "Catch Me If You Can," *Report on Business Magazine* 22, no. 5 (December 2005), 46.
79. M. Miller, "Should Email Be Private? UC, Employees Tangle over Rights of University to Access Computers of Staff on Leave," *Los Angeles Times*, 12 November 1995; D.H. Seifman & C.W. Trepanier, "Email and Voicemail

Systems," *Employee Relations Law Journal*, 1 December 1995; D. Young, "Office Email: There's No Right of Privacy," *Chicago Tribune*, 8 April 1996.

80. S. Shellenbarger, "Should Employers Set Limits on Cellphone Use in Vehicles?" *The Wall Street Journal*, 18 July 2001, B1; "Survey Shows About 3 Percent of Drivers Are Using Cellphones at Any Time," *The Wall Street Journal*, B1, 24 July 2001, www.wsj.com, www.ctv.ca/servlet/ArticleNews/story/CTVNews/1049066881078_88//, accessed 20 May, 2003.
81. "20 Hot Job Tracks," *U.S. News & World Report*, 30 October 1995, 98–104. C. Boivie, "Planning for the Future ... Your Future," *Journal of Systems Management* 44 (1993): 25–27; J. Connelly, "How to Choose Your Next Career," *Fortune*, 6 February 1995, 145–146; P. Sherrid, "A 12-Hour Test of My Personality," *U.S. News & World Report*, 31 October 1994, 109.

Chapter 5

1. "IT Will Drive the Future," *Computer Weekly*, 1 July 2003, 23; "The Road Tolls for Thee," *Economist*, 12 June 2004. "Xerox Mobile Engineers Twenty Years Ahead of Mayor Livingstone," *PR Newswire Europe*, 24 February 2003; S. Bayley, "Traffic Is a Sign of Enterprise, Life and Freedom. No, Really ...," *Independent*, 20 February 2005, 5; C. Blackhurst, "Don't Turn Us into a Ghost Town," *Evening Standard*, 7 December 2004; R. Hustwayte, "Congestion Payment Scheme Turned Down," *Newsquest Media Group Newspapers*, 29 June 2005; M. Knights, "TfL Says Congestion Charge IT a Success," *Computing*, 3 March 2005, 20; S. Mathieson, "A Beacon Method for Charging," *Guardian*, 9 June 2005, 19; M. Mills, "Congestion Charge Faces Late Payment Jams—London and Londoners Unprepared for Driving Fees with Just ...," *Guardian*, 18 January 2003, 11; S. Sanghera, "£5 Please," *Financial Times*, 31 May 2003, 20. D. Williams, "Traffic Growth Has Stalled, but You'll Still Pay £8 From Monday," *Evening Standard*, 29 June 2005.
2. R. Lenzner, "The Reluctant Entrepreneur," *Forbes*, 11 September 1995, 162–166.
3. M. Rich, "Dear CEO: Are You Tracking Your Cubicles?" *The Wall Street Journal*, 19 April 2001, B8.
4. Ibid.
5. "Cable Modem Market Stats & Projections," *Cable Datacom News*, Kinetics Strategies Inc. [Online] available at www.cabledatanews.com, 9 September 2002.
6. These findings come from two studies conducted by Solutions Research Group, among more than 2800 randomly selected Canadians and Americans in May/June 2005.
7. R.D. Buzzell & B.T. Gale, *The PIMS Principles: Linking Strategy to Performance* (New York: Free Press, 1987); M. Lambkin, "Order of Entry and Performance in New Markets," *Strategic Management Journal* 9 (1988): 127–40.
8. N. Deogun, "Banks Introduce New ATMs That Deliver Host of Services," *The Wall Street Journal Interactive Edition*, 5 June 1996.
9. G.L. Urban, T. Carter, S. Gaskin, & Z. Mucha, "Market Share Rewards to Pioneering Brands: An Empirical Analysis and Strategic Implications," *Management Science* 32 (1986): 645–659.
10. G. Hamel, "Smart Mover, Dumb Mover: Think the First Mover Advantage Is a Myth? You're Wrong: Most Pioneering Dot Coms Failed Not Because They Were First but Because They Were Dumb," *Fortune*, 3 September 2001, 191.
11. E. Nelson, "Retailing: Why Wal-Mart Sings, 'Yes, We Have Bananas!'" *The Wall Street Journal*, 6 October 1998, B1.
12. U. Tosi, "Commercial Aircraft Are Fast Becoming Flying Computer Systems: Their Downlinked Bitstreams Can Be Critical to High Profits and Happy Landings," *Forbes ASAP*, 4 December 1995, 100–102.
13. Ibid.
14. Ibid.
15. Ibid.
16. J. Novack, "The Data Miners," *Forbes*, 12 February 1996.
17. M. Halper, "Setting Up Is Hard to Do: Data Warehouses Do Not Grow on Trees," *Forbes ASAP*, 8 April 1996, 50–51.
18. J. Novack, "The Data Miners," *Forbes*, 12 February 1996.
19. M. Santosus, "Technology Recycling: Rising Costs of High-Tech Garbage," *CIO*, 15 April 2003, 36; Californians Against Waste, "Book Review of 'Made to Break: Technology Obsolescence in North America,'" *Recycling News*, 20 May 2006, www.cawrecycles.org/taxonomy/term/12?from=12.
20. N. Hutheesing, "Get the Bugs Out," *Forbes*, 8 April 1996.
21. T. Mack & T. Ewing, "In the Real World, Meanwhile ... ," *Forbes*, 18 December 1995, 284.
22. Steven D. Lubar, *Infoculture* (Boston: Houghton Mifflin, 1993).
23. Finnegan, "WinWedge 32 May Be Too Good; Easy-To-Use Software Collects Data So Well It's Overloading Federal Systems," *Government Computer News* 15 (15 April 1996): 35.
24. Steven D. Lubar, *Infoculture* (Boston: Houghton Mifflin, 1993).
25. N. Rubenking, "Hidden Messages," *PC Magazine*, 22 May 2001, 86.
26. "Data Mining: Advanced Scout," *IBM Research Website*, [Online] available at www.research.ibm.com/xw-scout, 31 December 1995.
27. "Data Mining: Advanced Scout," *IBM Research Website*, [Online] available at www.research.ibm.com/xw-scout, 31 December 1995.
28. N. Rubenking, "Hidden Messages," *PC Magazine*, 22 May 2001, 86.
29. F.J. Derfler, Jr., "Secure Your Network," *PC Magazine*, 27 June 2000, 183–200.
30. N. Winfield, "A Stolen Laptop Spells Trouble for Qualcomm Chief Jacobs," The *Wall Street Journal Interactive Edition*, 19 September 2000.
31. "Nortel Sets Cable-Free Example in Motion: Wireless LAN: In-Office Mobility Is Key to Greater Productivity at Giant Telecom Firm," *National Post*, 17 June 2005.
32. A. Laplante, "Invitation to Customers: Come into Our Database," *Forbes ASAP*, 28 August 1995, 124–130.
33. C. Ey, "E-Mail Saves Companies Time, Money and Effort," *Dallas Business Journal*, 17 November 1995, C13–14.
34. M.A. Verespej, "The E-Mail Monster: Can One Manager Handle 250 E-Mail Messages a Day, Plus 15 Voicemails an Hour?" *Industry Week*, 19 June 1995, 52–53.
35. M. Campanelli & N. Friedman, "Welcome to Voice Mail Hell: The New Technology Has Become a Barrier Between Salespeople and Customers. Here's How Smart Sellers Are Breaking Through," *Sales & Marketing Management* 147 (May 1995): 98–101.
36. T. Andrews, "E-Mail Empowers, Voice-Mail Enslaves," *PC Week*, 10 April 1995, E11.
37. P. Hise, "Life after Voice-Mail Hell. Winguth, Donahue and Co., Los Altos, CA Executive Search Firm, Brings Back Human Receptionist Due to Customer Dissatisfaction with Voice Mail Service," *Inc.*, August 1994, 101.

38. C.O'Malley, "Document Conferencing," *Computer Shopper Online*, [Online] available at www.zdnet.com/ cshopper/content/ 9604/feature3/sub1 .html, 23 June 1996. Originally published in the April 1996 issue of *Computer Shopper*.
39. J. Young, "The Transcontinental Blackboard," *Forbes*, 23 October 1995, 322–323.
40. J. van den Hoven, "Executive Support Systems & Decision Making," *Journal of Systems Management* 47, no. 8 (March-April 1996): 48.
41. "Intranet," Webopoedia [Online] available at www.webopedia.com/ TERM/i/ intranet.html, 26 August 2001.
42. "Market Statistics—Intranet Usage" Numotion.com, Retrieved 29 September 2006, www.numotion.net/ news/blog/market-statistics-intranet -usage.
43. J. Barlow, "Intranet Replaces Office Grapevine," *Houston Chronicle*, 7 May 2000, Business 1.
44. V.S. Pasher, "Employee Benefits Info within a Few Clicks," *National Underwriter Life & Health—Financial Services Edition*, 14 April 1997, S4.
45. R. Ayre, "Intranet How-To: Setting Up Shop," *PC Magazine*, 23 April 1996, 151–158.
46. F.J. Derfler, "The Intranet Platform: A Universal Client?" *PC Magazine*, 23 April 1996, 105–113.
47. R.C. Kennedy, "Intranets in Action," *PC/Computing*, June 1996, 150.
48. D. Zimmerman, "Report on EDI Tracks Labor Savings," *Supermarket News*, 16 January 1995, S2.
49. D. Tobey, "Paperless Purchasing," *Hotel & Motel Management* 2, no. 3 (6 November 1995): 104.
50. "Extranet," Webopoedia, [Online] available at www.webopedia.com/ TERM/ E/extranet.html, 26 August 2001.
51. S. Hamm, D. Welch, W. Zellner, F. Keenan, & P. Engardio, "Down but Hardly Out: Downturn Be Damned. Companies Are Still Anxious to Expand Online Because the Net Is a Way to Boost Sales and Shrink Costs," *Business Week*, 26 March 2001, 126.
52. M. McDonald, "SWA: Ticket Less Travel Saved Us Millions in Agent Pay," *Travel Weekly* 2 (20 November 1995): 1.
53. S. Hamm, D. Welch, W. Zellner, F. Keenan, & P. Engardio, "Down but Hardly out Downturn Be Damned. Companies Are Still Anxious to Expand Online Because the Net Is a Way to Boost Sales and Shrink |Costs," *Business Week*, 26 March 2001, 126.
54. K.C. Laudon & J.P. Laudon, *Management Information Systems: Organization and Technology* (Upper Saddle River, NJ: Prentice Hall, 1996).
55. T. Chea, "Apache Shareholders Approve Sale of Assets," *Washington Post*, 14 June 2001, E5.
56. S. Oliver, "What Are My Chances, Doc?" *Forbes*, 31 July 1995, 136–137.
57. M. France, "Smart Contracts," *Forbes ASAP* 2 (29 August 1994): 117.
58. "IT Will Drive the Future," *Computer Weekly*, 1 July 2003, 23. "The Road Tolls For Thee," *Economist*, 12 June 2004; "Xerox Mobile Engineers Twenty Years Ahead of Mayor Livingstone," *PR Newswire Europe*, 24 February 2003; S. Bayley, "Traffic Is a Sign of Enterprise, Life and Freedom. No, Really ...," *Independent*, 20 February 2005, 5. C. Blackhurst, "Don't Turn Us into a Ghost Town," *Evening Standard*, 7 December 2004. R. Hustwayte, "Congestion Payment Scheme Turned Down," *Newsquest Media Group Newspapers*, 29 June 2005; M. Knights, "TfL Says Congestion Charge IT a Success," *Computing*, 3 March 2005, 20. S. Mathieson, "A Beacon Method For Charging," *Guardian*, 9 June 2005, 19. M. Mills, "Congestion Charge Faces Late Payment Jams—London and Londoners Unprepared for Driving Fees with Just ...," *Guardian*, 18 January 2003, 11; S. Sanghera, "£5 Please," *Financial Times*, 31 May 2003, 20. D. Williams, "Traffic Growth Has Stalled, but You'll Still Pay £8 from Monday," *Evening Standard*, 29 June 2005.
59. M. Hicks, "Telling Customers the Bad News—When and How to Get the Word Out That Your Security's Been Breached," *eWeek*, 19 February 2001.
60. "Web Form Can Be Used by Consumers to Protect Privacy," *The Wall Street Journal*, 25 May 2001; P. Davidson, "Capitol Hill Support Brews for Internet Privacy Laws," *USA Today*, 12 July 2001; H. Green, "Your Right to Privacy: Going ... Going ...," *Business* Week, 23 April 2001.

Chapter 6

1. Anonymous, "Cashing in on Voisey's Bay," *Canadian Mining Journal*, February 1996, 11–12; Thomas Brockelbank, "Falkonbridge Makes Bid for Diamond Fields Resources," *The Northern Miner*, 19 February 1996, 1; John Gray, "Decision May Delay Mine," *Globe and Mail*, 27 January 1997, A1; Mark Heinzl, "Inco to Acquire Holding of 30% in Nickel Site," *Wall Street Journal*, 9 June 1995, B2; Mark Heinzl, "Mineral Finds Spur Mad Scramble ...," *Wall Street Journal*, 18 March 1995, C2; Sharon Reier, "The Treasure of Voisey Bay," *Financial World*, 18 July 1995, 16; Marilyn Scales, "Cross-country Hook-up," *Canadian Mining Journal*, February 1995, 6–9.
2. L.A. Hill, *Becoming a Manager: Mastery of a New Identity* (Boston: Harvard Business School Press, 1992).
3. K.R. MacCrimmon, R.N. Taylor, & E.A. Locke, "Decision Making and Problem Solving" in *Handbook of Industrial and Organizational Psychology*, ed. M.D. Dunnette (Chicago: Rand McNally, 1976), 1397–1453.
4. Patrick Brethour, "How to Grind the Oil Sands into a 'Sausage Factory'," *Globe and Mail*, 21 May 2005, B3.
5. K.R. MacCrimmon, R.N. Taylor, & E.A. Locke, "Decision Making and Problem Solving" in *Handbook of Industrial and Organizational Psychology*, ed. M.D. Dunnette (Chicago: Rand McNally, 1976), 1397–1453.
6. G. Kress, "The Role of Interpretation in the Decision Process," *Industrial Management* 37 (1995): 10–14.
7. S. Hansell, "Listen Up! It's Time for a Profit," *New York Times*, 20 May 2001, 1.
8. Nick Wingfield, "Leading the News: Amazon Boosts Forecasts as Sales Soar," *The Wall Street Journal*, 24 January 2003, A3.
9. J. Delaney, "Small Business Desktops: The Essential Buying Guide," *PC Magazine*, [Online] available at www.pcmag.com/article2/0,1759,1634891,00.asp, 7 September 2004.
10. J. Koblenz, "How a Car Earns a Best Buy," *Consumers Digest*, 1 January 1993, 54.
11. P. Djang, "Selecting Personal Computers," *Journal of Research on Computing in Education*, 25 (1993): 327.
12. "PLUS—A Process for Ethical Decision Making," Ethics Resource Center, [Online] available at www.ethics.org/ plus_decisionmaking.html, 19 February 2005.
13. J.G. March, *A Primer on Decision Making: How Decisions Happen* (New York: Free Press, 1994).
14. R. Johnson, "Surviving a Slowdown—Strategies for the Storm: How Some Managers Are Hoping to Weather the

Economic Slump," *The Wall Street Journal*, 14 May 2001, R6.
15. J. Orbell, "Hamlet and the Psychology of Rational Choice under Uncertainty," *Rationality and Society* 5 (1993): 127–140.
16. J. Nocera, "Bill Gross Blew Through $800 Million in 8 Months (and He's Got Nothing to Show for It). Why Is He Still Smiling?" *Fortune*, 5 March 2001, 70.
17. M.H. Bazerman, *Judgment in Managerial Decision Making* (New York: John Wiley & Sons, 1994).
18. Harvey Schachter, "Gulp1", *Profit*, June 2005, 70–74.
19. John R. Patton, "Intuition in Decisions", *Management Decisions* 41 (2003): 986–989.
20. P.J. Hoffman, P. Slovic, & L.G. Rorer, "An Analysis-of-Variance Model for Assessment of Configural Cue Utilization in Clinical Judgment," *Psychological Bulletin* 69 (1968): 338–349.
21. Statistics Canada, CANSIM Series V1540423, Table 2530001.
22. Louie Rosella, "Safest City Not So Safe, Survey Finds," *Mississauga News*, 30 March 2005, A1.
23. K.C. Cole, "Brain's Use of Shortcuts Can Be a Route to Bias," *Los Angeles Times*, 1 May 1995, A1.
24. P.J. Schoemaker & J.E. Russo, "A Pyramid of Decision Approaches," *California Management Review*, Fall 1993, 9–33.
25. I. Graham, I. Stiell, A. Laupacis, L. McAuley, M. Howell, M. Clancy, P. Durieux, N. Simon, J. Emparanza, J. Aginaga, Jr., A. O'Connor, & G. Wells, "Awareness and Use of the Ottawa Ankle and Knee Rules in 5 Countries: Can Publication Alone Be Enough to Change Practice?" *Annals of Emergency Medicine* 37, no. 3 (2001): 259–66.
26. G. Bell, "'I Want My MVT' Drive Marketing Results with Multivariable Testing Techniques," *Direct Marketing* 60, no. 8 (December 1997): 346.
27. R. Koselka, "The New Mantra: MVT," *Forbes*, 11 March 1996, 114–118.
28. G. Bell, "'I Want My MVT' Drive Marketing Results with Multivariable Testing Techniques," *Direct Marketing* 60, no. 8 (December 1997): 346.
29. Ibid.
30. W. Mossberg, "In Time for Elections: Software to Help You Make Up Your Mind," *The Wall Street Journal*, 8 February 1996.
31. K. Yakai, "To Do or Not to Do: Two Business-Oriented Decision Makers," *PC Magazine*, 23 January 1996.
32. B.M. Staw, "Knee-Deep in the Big Muddy: A Study of Escalating Commitment to a Chosen Course of Action," *Organizational Behavior and Human Performance* 16 (1976): 27–44.
33. A. Curry, "The First Couldn't Last," *U.S. News & World Report*, 8 January 2001, 37; J. McCormick, "You Snooze, You Lose," *Newsweek*, 21 July 1997, 50.
34. Paul Kedrosky, "BC's Fast Ferry Fiasco a Voyage into Dark Sea of Government Bungling," *Financial Post*, 30 January 1999, D5.
35. Daphne Bramham, "Fast Ferries—They'll Stick Around to Make Taxpayers Seasick," *The Vancouver Sun*, 29 March 2003, B1; "A Chronology of BC Ferries' Problem-Plagued Fast Ferry Project," *Canadian Press Newswire*, 13 March 2000; John Schreiner, "A Really Fast Boat to Nowhere," *Financial Post*, 26 February 1999, C9.
36. J. McCormick, "You Snooze, You Lose," *Newsweek*, 21 July 1997, 50.
37. D. Ghosh, "De-Escalation Strategies: Some Experimental Evidence," *Behavioral Research in Accounting* 9 (1997): 88–112.
38. Ibid.
39. Derek DeCloet, "Scuttle the Fleet! Why Cancelling the Second and Third Fast Ferries Might Be the Only True Course," *British Columbia Report*, 22 March 1999, 22.
40. J. Ross & B.M. Staw, "Organizational Escalation and Exit: Lessons from the Shoreham Nuclear Power Plant," *Academy of Management Journal* 36 (1993): 701–732.
41. J. Angwin, "Can These Dot-Coms Be Saved?—Profit Eludes Priceline as Expansion Takes Its Toll," *The Wall Street Journal*, 25 January 2001, B1.
42. Press Releases, "WebHouse Club Announces 90-Day Wind-Down of Name-Your-Price Grocery and Gasoline Internet Service," Priceline.com [Online] available at www.corporate-ir.net/ireye/ir_site.zhtml?ticker=pcln&script=410&layout=-6&item_id=121342, October 5, 2000.
43. Ray Dyck & Norman Halpern, "Team-Based Organizations Redesign at Celestica," *The Journal for Quality and Participation*, 22, no. 5 (Sept./Oct. 1999): 36–40.
44. L. Pelled, K. Eisenhardt, & K. Xin, "Exploring the Black Box: An Analysis of Work Group Diversity, Conflict, and Performance," *Administrative Science Quarterly* 44, no. 1 (March 1, 1999): 1.
45. T. Gutner, "Do Top Women Execs = Stronger IPOs? A Study Finds That the More of Them a Startup Has, The Better It Does," *Business Week*, 5 February 2001, 122.
46. "How to Form Hiring Teams," *Personnel Journal* 73, no. 3 (August 1994): S14.
47. I.L. Janis, *Groupthink* (Boston: Houghton Mifflin, 1983).
48. C.P. Neck & C.C. Manz, "From Groupthink to Teamthink: Toward the Creation of Constructive Thought Patterns in Self-Managing Work Teams," *Human Relations* 47 (1994): 929–952.
49. G. Moorhead, R. Ference, & C.P. Neck, "Group Decision Fiascoes Continue: Space Shuttle Challenger and a Revised Framework," *Human Relations* 44 (1991): 539–550.
50. A. Mason, W.A. Hochwarter, & K.R. Thompson, "Conflict: An Important Dimension in Successful Management Teams," *Organizational Dynamics* 24 (1995): 20.
51. C. Olofson, "So Many Decisions, So Little Time: What's Your Problem?" *Fast Company*, 1 October 1999, 62.
52. Ibid.
53. R. Cosier & C.R. Schwenk, "Agreement and Thinking Alike: Ingredients for Poor Decisions," *Academy of Management Executive* 4 (1990): 69–74.
54. Ibid.
55. K. Jenn & E. Mannix, "The Dynamic Nature of Conflict: A Longitudinal Study of Intragroup Conflict and Group Performance," *Academy of Management Journal* 44, no. 2 (2001): 238–251; R.L. Priem, D.A. Harrison, & N.K. Muir, "Structured Conflict and Consensus Outcomes in Group Decision Making," *Journal of Management* 21 (1995): 691–710.
56. C.R. Schwenk, "Effects of Devil's Advocacy and Dialectical Inquiry on Decision Making: A Meta-Analysis," *Organizational Behavior and Human Decision Performance* 47 (1990): 161–176.
57. A. Van De Ven & A.L. Delbecq, "Nominal Versus Interacting Group Processes for Committee Decision Making Effectiveness," *Academy of Management Journal* 14 (1971): 203–212.
58. A.R. Dennis & J.S. Valicich, "Group, Sub-Group, and Nominal Group Idea Generation: New Rules for a New

Media?" *Journal of Management* 20 (1994): 723–736.
59. S.G. Robelberg, J.L. Barnes-Farrell, & C.A. Lowe, "The Stepladder Technique: An Alternative Group Structure Facilitating Effective Group Decision Making," *Journal of Applied Psychology* 77 (1992): 730–737; S.G. Rogelberg & M.S. O'Connor, "Extending the Stepladder Technique: An Examination of the Self-Paced Stepladder Groups," *Group Dynamics: Theory, Research, and Practice* 2 (1998): 82–91.
60. R.B. Gallupe, W.H. Cooper, M.L. Grise, & L.M. Bastianutti, "Blocking Electronic Brainstorms," *Journal of Applied Psychology* 79 (1994): 77–86.
61. Greg Crone, "Electrifying Brainstorms: Strategic-Planning Sessions Can Easily Collapse under the Weight of Rancorous Debate and Filibustering. But a High-Tech Approach Developed at Queen's University Lets Everyone Have Their Say, Without Recrimination," *National Post*, 3 July 1999, D11.
62. R.B. Gallupe & W.H. Cooper, "Brainstorming Electronically," *Sloan Management Review*, Fall 1993, 27–36.
63. Ibid.
64. G. Kay, "Effective Meetings through Electronic Brainstorming," *Management Quarterly* 35 (1995): 15.
65. A. LaPlante, "90s Style Brainstorming," *Forbes ASAP*, 25 October 1993, 44.
66. Donald Coxe, "The Buzz from Below," *Maclean's*, 21 March 2005, 48–49; Charles Finaly, "Give Me a V...!" *Canadian Business*, 8–22 July 2002, 14; John Gray, "Decision May Delay Mine," *Globe and Mail*, 27 January 1997, A1; Mark Heinzl, "Inco's Newfoundland Mining Dream Still Unfulfilled," *Wall Street Journal*, 15 October 1995, 1; Mark Heinzl, "Inco Vows Nickel Growth Plan Isn't Just Small Change," *Wall Street Journal*, 1 July 1997, B4; Mark Heinzl, "Inco's Nickel Mine in Newfoundland Opens Its Doors After Long Battle," *Wall Street Journal*, 22 September 2005, 1; John Schofield, "Tension on the Tundra," *Maclean's*, 8 September 1997, 44–45; Paul Simao, "Inco Wants to Resume Talks on Labrador Nickel Project," *Journal of Commerce*, 12 August 1998, 9; Jane Werniuk, "Made in Canada," *Canadian Mining Journal*, April 2004, 8–16.
67. M. Schrage, "I'll Have the Pasta Primavera, With a Side of Strategy," *Fortune*, 8 January 2001.
68. G. Klein & K. Weick, "Decisions: Making the Right Ones. Learning from the Wrong Ones," *Across the Board*, June 2000.

Chapter 7

1. Interview with Karyn Brooks, 2004, Acadia Management Interview Series Video Database.
2. R. Leifer & P.K. Mills, "An Information Processing Approach for Deciding upon Control Strategies and Reducing Control Loss in Emerging Organizations," *Journal of Management* 22 (1996): 113–137.
3. "Say Baa-Baa to Bad Driving," *London Times*, 28 July 1996.
4. W. Mossberg & K. Swisher, "Using a Computer to Clean Up Spilled Milk," *Wall Street Journal*, 24 May 2005, D5.
5. Neil Sutton "Certicom Aims to Speed Digital Signature Verification," *Computing Canada*, 9 September 2005, 8.
6. P. Scott, "Selling Civility: Secret Shoppers," *The Wall Street Journal,* 29 June 2001, W17.
7. "Service Intelligence, Inc.—Press Room," [Online] available at www.serviceintelligence.com/intheNews.html, 21 August 2003.
8. Laura Bobomolny, "Toned and Ready," *Canadian Business*, 24 April–7 May, 2006, 59–63.
9. R. Guth, "The To-Do List: Make Software More Reliable," *Wall Street Journal*, 17 November 2003, R4.
10. R. Simons, "Control in an Age of Empowerment," *Harvard Business Review*, March-April 1995, 80–98.
11. H. Koontz & R.W. Bradspies, "Managing Through Feedforward Control: A Future-Directed View," *Business Horizons*, June 1972, 25–36.
12. B. Canton, "Acrobatic Squirrels Give New Meaning to Term 'Brownout'—Pole Guards, Noise, Fake Owls—Nothing Utilities Try Thwarts High-Wire Act," *The Wall Street Journal,* 4 February 2002, A1.
13. P. Seidenman, "Safety & Regulatory News: Maintaining Airliners under Pressure Communication Issues Also Highlighted during Aviation Safety Alliance Seminar," *Overhaul & Maintenance,* 1 March 2003, 19.
14. R. Guth, "The To-Do List: Make Software More Reliable," *Wall Street Journal*, 17 November 2003, R4.
15. R. Leifer & P. K. Mills, "An Information Processing Approach for Deciding upon Control Strategies and Reducing Control Loss in Emerging Organizations," *Journal of Management* 22 (1996): 113–137.
16. B. Warner, "Deluged Telecoms Boss Bans Staff E-Mails," *Yahoo News (Reuters)*, [Online] available at http://story.news.yahoo.com/news?tmpl=story&cid=582&ncid=582&e=4&u=/nm/20030919/wr_nm/technology_britain_email_dc, 19 September 2003.
17. B. Warner, "Deluged Telecoms Boss Bans Staff E-Mails," *Yahoo News (Reuters)*, [Online] available at http://story.news.yahoo.com/news?tmpl=story&cid=582&ncid=582&e=4&u=/nm/20030919/wr_nm/technology_britain_email_dc , 19 September 2003.
18. B. Wysocki, Jr., "The Lack of Vaccines Goes Beyond Flu Inoculations—Eight Shortages Since 2000," *Wall Street Journal*, 8 December 2003, A1.
19. Senator Bill Frist, "Letters to the Editor: Alarming Shortage of Eight Vaccines," *The Wall Street Journal,* 30 August 2002, A9; Editorial, "A Needless Vaccine Shortage," *The Wall Street Journal,* 21 May 2002, A18.
20. N. Watson, "What's Wrong with This Printer? Believe It or Not, It's Too Solid," *Fortune,* 17 February 2003, 120.
21. Simon Avery, "Smart Cards to Make Credit, Debit Dealings Easier—and Safer," *Globe and Mail*, 11 October 2005, B9.
22. S. Greenhouse, "Workers Assail Night Lock-Ins by Wal-Mart," *New York Times*, 18 January 2004, 1.
23. Ibid.
24. Ibid.
25. Ibid.
26. S. Shellenbarger, "Is the Awful Behavior of Some Bad Bosses Rooted in Their Past?" *The Wall Street Journal,* 17 May 2000, B1.
27. Ibid.
28. M. Weber, *The Protestant Ethic and the Spirit of Capitalism* (New York: Scribner's, 1958).
29. M. Boyle, "Expensing It: Guilty as Charged When Times Are Tough, Employees Become Even More Devoted to Mastering the Art of Self-Perking," *Fortune,* 9 July 2001, 179; R. Grugal, "Be Honest and Dependable Integrity—The Must-Have," *Investor's Business Daily,* 11 April 2003.
30. C. Forelle, "On the Road Again, but Now the Boss Is Sitting Beside You," *Wall Street Journal*, 14 May 2004, A1.
31. P. Jonsson, "That a Spreadsheet on Your Screen, or Solitaire?" *Seattle Times*, 12 June 2005, F3.

32. Mark Jaffe, "No Bonus for CEO at Precision Drilling: 'Pretty Fair' Formula," *National Post*, 11 April 2003, FP 8.
33. Ken MacQueen, "The Anti-Retailer: Vancouver's Mountain Equipment Co-op Succeeds in Spite of Itself," *Maclean's*, 29 April 2002, 30.
34. J.R. Barker, "Tightening the Iron Cage: Concertive Control in Self-Managing Teams," *Administrative Science Quarterly* 38 (1993): 408–437.
35. Ibid.
36. Ibid.
37. C. Manz & H. Sims, "Leading Workers to Lead Themselves: The External Leadership of Self-Managed Work Teams," *Administrative Science Quarterly* 32 (1987): 106–128.
38. J. Slocum & H.A. Sims, "Typology for Integrating Technology, Organization and Job Design," *Human Relations* 33 (1980): 193–212.
39. C.C. Manz & H.P. Sims, Jr., "Self-Management as a Substitute for Leadership: A Social Learning Perspective," *Academy of Management Review* 5 (1980): 361–367.
40. S. Levy, "Strip Mining the Corporate Life," *Newsweek*, 12 August 1996, 54–55.
41. J. Lublin, "More Big Companies End Perks; Critics Say Cutbacks Sap Morale," *The Wall Street Journal*, 4 January 2001, B1.
42. R.S. Kaplan & D.P. Norton, "Using the Balanced Scorecard as a Strategic Management System," *Harvard Business Review*, January–February 1996, 75–85; R.S. Kaplan & D.P. Norton, "The Balanced Scorecard: Measures That Drive Performance," *Harvard Business Review*, January–February 1992, 71–79.
43. S.L. Fawcett, "Fear of Accounts: Improving Managers' Competence and Confidence Through Simulation Exercises," *Journal of European Industrial Training*, February 1996, 17.
44. M.H. Stocks & A. Harrell, "The Impact of an Increase in Accounting Information Level on the Judgment Quality of Individuals and Groups," *Accounting, Organizations and Society*, October–November 1995, 685–700.
45. B. Morris, "Roberto Goizueta and Jack Welch: The Wealth Builders," *Fortune*, 11 December 1995, 80–94.
46. Ibid.
47. Kevin Lawrence, "How to Profit from Customer Complaints," *The Canadian Manager*, Fall 2000, 25, 29.
48. M. Hepworth, "Connecting Customer Loyalty to the Bottom Line," *Canadian Business Review*, 1 January 1994, 40.
49. C.B. Furlong, "12 Rules for Customer Retention," *Bank Marketing* 5 (January 1993): 14.
50. M. Hepworth, "Connecting Customer Loyalty to the Bottom Line," *Canadian Business Review*, 1 January 1994, 40.
51. T.K. Gilliam, "Closing the Customer Retention Gap," *Bank Marketing* 3 (December 1994): 51.
52. C.A. Reeves & D.A. Bednar, "Defining Quality: Alternatives and Implications," *Academy of Management Review* 19 (1994): 419–445.
53. "Readers' Choice Poll 1997: International Airline Rankings," *Conde Nast Traveler*, [Online] available at http://travel. epicurious.com/travel/g_cnt/05_poll97/air/inter_intro.html, 26 June 1998.
54. "Airline Way Above Rest in Rankings," *South China Morning Post*, 9 August 1996.
55. D.R. May & B.L. Flannery, "Cutting Waste with Employee Involvement Teams," *Business Horizons*, September–October 1995, 28–38.
56. F. Etherington, "Leak in City's Water Valve Angers Kitchener Man," *Kitchener-Waterloo Record*, 1 August 2002, B4.
57. "Pollution Prevention Pays (3P)," *3M*, [Online] available at http://solutions.3m.com, 20 June 2005.
58. O. Kharif, "Earth's Best Friend: Corporate America?" *Business Week Online*, [Online] available at http://yahoo.businessweek.com/technology/content/may2003/tc2003051_4006_te108.htm, 6 May 2003.
59. A. Gynn, "Sears, WMI Continue Recycling Program," *Waste News*, 5 March 2001, 2.
60. M. Conlin & P. Raeburn, "Industrial Evolution: Bill McDonough Has the Wild Idea He Can Eliminate Waste. Surprise! Business Is Listening," *Business Week*, 8 April 2002, 70.
61. Ibid.
62. J. Sprovieri, "Environmental Management Affects Manufacturing Bottom Line," *Assembly*, 1 July 2001, 24.
63. B. Byrne, "EU Says Makers Must Destroy Their Own Brand End-of-Life Cars," *Irish Times*, 23 April 2003, 52.
64. J. Sabatini, "The Color of Money," *Automotive Manufacturing & Production*, 1 June 2000, 74.
65. J. Szekely & G. Trapaga, "From Villain to Hero (Materials Industry's Waste Recovery Efforts)," *Technology Review*, 1 January 1995.
66. M. Keller, "Many in Dark about Disposal of Fluorescents," *Minneapolis-St. Paul City Business*, 14 January 1994, 11.
67. C.A. Reeves & D.A. Bednar, "Defining Quality: Alternatives and Implications," *Academy of Management Review* 19 (1994): 419–445.
68. Interview with Karyn Brooks, 2004, Acadia Management Interview Series Video Database.
69. John W. Gainsford, Annie Lam, & Ana Fradkin, "Costs of Obesity for Employers and Employees: A Canadian Analysis," *Canadian Healthcare Manager* 6, no. 5 (August–September, 1999): Insert 3; Larry Jackson & Cyprian McFarlane, "Trending Upwards: Why Major Canadian Group Insurers Are Projecting Increases in Employer-Sponsored Health Plan Costs," *Canadian Healthcare Manager* 8, no. 4 (August 2001): 41; L. Litvan, "Preventive Medicine," *Nation's Business*, 1 September 1995, 32; Celia Milne, "Controlling Drug Costs," *Medical Post* 39, no. 17 (29 April 2003): 30; M. Parent, "How to Launch a Corporate Fitness Program," *Boston Business Journal*, 28 June 1996, 39; L. Postman, "Employers Banking on Worker Wellness," *Indianapolis Business Journal*, 10 June 1996, 25; M.A. Robbins, "Giving Workers Healthy Incentives," *Trustee*, 1 February 1996, 30; D. Stokols, K.R. Pelletier, & J.E. Fielding, "Integration of Medical Care and Worksite Health Promotion," *The Journal of the American Medical Association*, 12 April 1995; "Wellness Programs Pay Dividends," *Business & Health*, 1 March 1995, 23.
70. R. Buckman, "Microsoft Offers Prizes to Identify Orders of PCs Without Windows," *The Wall Street Journal*, 2 May 2001; B. Kruger, "High-Tech Firms Get Piracy Alert," *Electronic News*, 7 February 2000; J. Stevenson, "Piracy Plague," *Business Mexico*, November 2000; Z. Thomas, "High Tech's Dirty Little Software Piracy Secret," *Electronic Business*, November 2000; F. Gallegos, "Software Piracy: Some Facts, Figures, and Issues," *Information System Security*, Winter 2000; Andrew Whal, "Rumors of War," *Canadian Business* 75, no. 17 (16 September 2002): 67.
71. S. Caulkin, "If You Want to Stay a Winner, Learn from Your Mistakes," *The Observer*, 3 March 1996, 7; J. Hyatt, "Failure 101," *Inc.*, January

1989, 18; B. McMenamin, "The Virtue of Making Mistakes," *Forbes*, 9 May 1994, 192–194; P. Sellers, "So You Fail," *Fortune*, 1 May 1995, 48–66; P. Sellers, "Where Failures Get Fixed," *Fortune*, 1 May 1995, 64; B. Weiner, I. Freize, A. Kukla, L. Reed, S. Rest, & R.M. Rosenbaum, "Perceiving the Causes of Success and Failure," in *Attribution: Perceiving the Causes of Behavior*, eds. E. Jones, D. Kanouse, H. Kelley, R. Nesbitt, S. Valins, and B. Weiner (Morristown, N.J.: General Learning Press, 1971): 45–61.

Chapter 8

1. K. Capell, C. Belton, T. Lowry, M. Kripalani, B. Bremner, & D. Roberts, "MTV's World Mando-Pop. Mexican Hip Hop. Russian Rap. It's All Fueling The Biggest Global Channel," *Business Week*, 18 February 2002, 40; B. Carter, "He's Cool. He Keeps MTV Sizzling. And, Oh Yes, He's 56," *New York Times*, 16 June 2002, 1; J. Davis, "The Beat Goes On," *The Independent*, 22 February 2005, 2, 3; C. Goldsmith, "Music Channel Tries Shows That Can Cross Cultures; Jennifer Lopez Flees a Fire," *Wall Street Journal*, 21 July 2003, B1; R. Grover, T. Lowry, C. Yang, K. Capell, & M. Kripalini, "With DirecTV, Murdoch Finally Has a Global Satellite Empire. Get Ready for a Fierce New Media War," *Business Week*, 19 January 2004, 52; S. Hares, "Interview-MTV Intn'l Targets Strong '04 Ads, Asia Profits," *Reuters News*, 13 February 2004, 36; N. Hopkins, "MTV Grows into Far More than Just Music Television," *The Times*, 15 April 2005, 58.
2. Micro-Economic Policy Analysis Branch of Industry Canada, "Trends in Canada's Inward FDI," [Online] available at http://strategis.ic.gc.ca. Retrieved 10 April 2003.
3. Micro-Economic Policy Analysis Branch of Industry Canada, "Trends in Canada's Inward FDI," [Online] available at http://strategis.ic.gc.ca. Retrieved 10 April 2003.
4. Science and Engineering Indicators, National Science Foundation, [Online] available at www.nsf.gov/statistics/seind06/c0/c0s1.htm#c0s1l2, Retrieved, 3 October 2006.
5. PPI Trade Fact of Week, 27 April, Progressive Policy Institute, [Online] available at www.ppionline.org.
6. "Japan: Annual Fresh Deciduous Fruit Report," *U.S. Department of Agriculture Reports*, 17 September 1997.
7. "At Loggerheads: The Canada–U.S. Softwood Lumber Dispute," [Online] available at www.archives.CBC.ca. Accessed 8 March 2003.
8. M. du Bois, "EC Car Sales Plunged 11% in September," *The Wall Street Journal*, 8 October 1993, B4B.
9. World Trade Organization, "The Agreements: Anti-Dumping, Subsidies, Safeguards, Contingencies, etc.," [Online] available at www.wto.orgabout/agmnts7.htm#subsidies, 24 January 1999.
10. Associated Press, "U.S. Takes Aim at Chinese Beetle in Trade Battle," *The Plain Dealer*, 12 September 1998, 2c.
11. C. Goldsmith, "After Trailing Boeing for Years, Airbus Aims for 50% of the Market," *The Wall Street Journal*, 16 March 1998, A1.
12. A. Tanzer, "Here's One Asian Industry That Isn't Declining: Software Piracy. It Is Costing American Companies Billions of Dollars in Lost Revenues," *Forbes*, 7 September 1998, 162.
13. Links to National Parliaments' Web sites, www.europarl.eu.int/natparl/en/Linkspem.htm.
14. Wikipedia, "European Union," http://en.wikipedia.org/wiki/European_Union#Member_states_and_enlargement, 4 October 2006.
15. G. Smith & E. Malkin, "Mexico's Makeover," *Business Week*, 21 December 1998, 28; D. Blount, "Canada Favors Life after NAFTA," *Denver Post*, 22 November 1998, A10.
16. P. Behr, "NAFTAmath: A Texas-Sized Surge in Trade; Six Months after Treaty's Enactment, Booming Sales to Mexico Overshadow U.S. Job Losses," *Washington Post*, 21 August 1994, H1.
17. Declaration of Principles, Summit of the Americas, "Free Trade Area of the Americas," [Online] available at www.ftaa-alca.org/EnglishVersion/miami_e.htm, 27 January 1999.
18. P. Dwyler, P. Engardio, Z. Schiller, & S. Reed, "Tearing Up Today's Organization Chart," *Business Week*, 18 November 1994, 80–83.
19. "Canada's Tilano Fresco Cracks U.S. Market," *CanadExport* 21, no. 6 (1 April 2003): 1–2.
20. "Workplace Code of Conduct," Fair Labor Association, [Online] available at www.fairlabor.org/all/code/index.html, 12 May 2003; A. Bernstein, M. Shari, & E. Malkin, "A World of Sweatshops," *Business Week*, 6 November 2000, 84.
21. A. Sundaram & J.S. Black, "The Environment and Internal-Organization of Multinational Enterprises," *Academy of Management Review* 17 (1992): 729–757.
22. H.S. James, Jr., & M. Weidenbaum, *When Businesses Cross International Borders: Strategic Alliances and Their Alternatives* (Westport, CT: Praeger Publishers, 1993).
23. "Canadian Wine in Sweden, Finland and Norway," *CanadExport* 21, no. 6 (1 April 2003): 1–6.
24. "China's Hot Economy to Benefit Canada," *The Ottawa Citizen*, 28 March 2004, D1.
25. L. Luxner, "Getting a Slice of the Onion Market," *The Atlanta Journal Constitution*, 30 December 1994, C1.
26. McDonald's Corporation, "McDonald's Reports Global Results (Part 2 of 2)," [Online] available at www.mcdonalds.com/whatsnew/pressrelease/Press_Release15880642.html, 17 April 1998; Pizza Hut, Wikipedia [Online] available at http://en.wikipedia.org/wiki/Pizza_Hut. Retrieved, 4 October 2006.
27. "Nortel, IBM Create Strategic Alliance," *Calgary Herald*, 21 May 2005, E12.
28. A. Choi, "International: GM Seeds Grow Nicely in Eastern Europe, Strategy of Starting Small and Expanding Pays Off," *The Wall Street Journal*, 3 May 1995, A11.
29. B.R. Schlender, "How Toshiba Makes Alliances Work," *Fortune*, 4 October 1993, 116–120.
30. B.A. Walters, S. Peters, & G.G. Dess, "Strategic Alliances and Joint Ventures: Making Them Work," *Business Horizons*, July–August 1994, 5–10.
31. W. Beaver, "Volkswagen's American Assembly Plant: Fahrvernugen Was Not Enough," *Business Horizons*, 11 November 1992, 19.
32. M.W. Hordes, J.A. Clancy, & J. Baddaley, "A Primer for Global Start-Ups," *Academy of Management Executive*, May 1995, 7–11.
33. B.M. Oviatt & P. P. McDougall, "Toward a Theory of International New Ventures," *Journal of International Business Studies*, Spring 1994, 45–64.
34. L. Brokaw, "Foreign Affairs: Start-Ups Such as National Gyp-Chipper Are Proving That, When You Move from Doing Business Next Door to Doing Business Around the World, the Same Basic Rules Still Apply," *Inc.*, 1 November 1990, 92.
35. *Local Authority*. Beverage World, 15 October 2000, 58–60.
36. B. Ortega, "Foreign Forays: Penney Pushes Abroad in Unusually Big Way

as It Pursues Growth," *The Wall Street Journal,* 1 February 1994, A1.

37. R. Martin, & C. Ketels, "How Four Seasons Weathered Global Competition," *Calgary Herald,* 14 May 2002, D9.
38. K.D. Miller, "A Framework for Integrated Risk Management in International Business," *Journal of International Business Studies,* 2nd Quarter 1992, 311.
39. M. Farley, "Foreign Investors in China Feel Cold Slap of Reality," *Los Angeles Times,* 27 December 1994, A-1.
40. G. Anping, "Old Contract Laws Need Repair to Fit into New Reality," *China Daily,* 7 May 1994, 4-1.
41. F. Bleakley, "High School Seniors Mind Their Business and Even Profit by It: Teens Learn by Their Goofs in Import-Export World; Racy Towels Go Too Far," *The Wall Street Journal,* 20 June 1995, A1.
42. G. Hofstede, "The Cultural Relativity of the Quality of Life Concept," *Academy of Management Review* 9 (1984): 389–398; G. Hofstede, "The Cultural Relativity of Organizational Practices and Theories," *Journal of International Business Studies,* Fall 1983, 75–89; G. Hofstede, "The Interaction Between National and Organizational Value Systems," *Journal of Management Studies,* July 1985, 347–357.
43. R. Hodgetts, "A Conversation with Geert Hofstede," *Organizational Dynamics, Spring* 1993, 53–61.
44. M. Janssens, J.M. Brett, F.J. Smith, "Confirmatory Cross-Cultural Research: Testing the Viability of a Corporation-Wide Safety Policy," *Academy of Management Journal* 38 (1995): 364–382.
45. R.G. Linowes, "The Japanese Manager's Traumatic Entry into the United States: Understanding the American-Japanese Cultural Divide," *Academy of Management Executive* 7 (1993): 21–40.
46. J.S. Black, M. Mendenhall, & G. Oddou, "Toward a Comprehensive Model of International Adjustment: An Integration of Multiple Theoretical Perspectives," *Academy of Management Journal* 16 (1991): 291–317; R.L. Tung, "American Expatriates Abroad: From Neophytes to Cosmopolitans," *Columbia Journal of World Business,* 22 June 1998, 125.
47. L. Copeland & L. Griggs, *Going International* (New York: Random House, 1985).
48. R.A. Swaak, "Expatriate Failures: Too Many, Too Much Cost, Too Little Planning," *Compensation and Benefits Review* 27, no. 6 (21 November 1995): 47.
49. J.S. Black & M. Mendenhall, "Cross-Cultural Training Effectiveness: A Review and Theoretical Framework for Future Research," *Academy of Management Review* 15 (1990): 113–136.
50. S.P. Deshpande & C. Viswesvaran, "Is Cross-Cultural Training of Expatriate Managers Effective: A Meta-Analysis," *International Journal of Intercultural Relations* 16, no. 3 (1992): 295–310.
51. W. Arthur, Jr., & W. Bennett, Jr., "The International Assignee: The Relative Importance of Factors Perceived to Contribute to Success," *Personnel Psychology* 48 (1995): 99–114.
52. R. Donkin, "Recruitment: Overseas Gravy Train May Be Running Out of Steam—Preparing Expatriate Packages Is Challenging the Expertise of Human Resource Management," *The Financial Times,* 30 November 1994, 10.
53. K. Capell, C. Belton, T. Lowry, M. Kripalani, B. Bremner, & D. Roberts, "MTV's World Mando-Pop. Mexican Hip Hop. Russian Rap. It's All Fueling The Biggest Global Channel," *Business Week*, 18 February 2002, 40; B. Carter, "He's Cool. He Keeps MTV Sizzling. And, Oh Yes, He's 56," *New York Times*, 16 June 2002, 1; J. Davis, "The Beat Goes On," *The Independent*, 22 February 2005, 2, 3; C. Goldsmith, "Music Channel Tries Shows That Can Cross Cultures; Jennifer Lopez Flees a Fire," *Wall Street Journal*, 21 July 2003, B1; R. Grover, T. Lowry, C. Yang, K. Capell, & M. Kripalini, "With DirecTV, Murdoch Finally Has a Global Satellite Empire. Get Ready for a Fierce New Media War," *Business Week*, 19 January 2004, 52; S. Hares, "Interview-MTV Intn'l Targets Strong '04 Ads, Asia Profits," *Reuters News*, 13 February 2004, 36; N. Hopkins, "MTV Grows into Far More than Just Music Television," *The Times*, 15 April 2005, 58.
54. S. Lubman, "Round and Round: To Survive Your Business Negotiations, You'll Need Patience, Skill—and Perhaps an Extra Coat," *The Wall Street Journal*, 10 December 1993, R3; I. Matthee, "Accountant Opens Trade Doors: Firm Helps Businesses Gain Access to China," *Seattle Post-Intelligencer*, 3 October 1997, E1; M.A. Sabo & S. Leith, "What West Michigan Wants: A Payoff on the Business Gamble and the Costly Foothold," *The Grand Rapids Press*, 21 June 1998, D1; S.E. Weiss, "Negotiating with 'Romans'—Part 1," *Sloan Management Review*, Winter 1994, 51–61; T. Yeung & L.L. Yeung, "Negotiations in the People's Republic of China: Results of a Survey of Small Businesses in Hong Kong," *Journal of Small Business Management*, 1 January 1995, 70.
55. J.S. Black, "Serving Two Masters: Managing the Dual Allegiance of Expatriate Employees," *Sloan Management Review*, Summer 1992, 61–71; H.B. Gregersen, "Commitments to a Parent Company and a Local Work Unit during Repatriation," *Personnel Psychology* 45 (1992): 29–54; J. Kaufman, "In China, John Aliberti Gets VIP Treatment; At Home, Grass Grows in the Patio," *The Wall Street Journal*, 19 November 1996, A1.

Chapter 9

1. Interview with Hanspeter Stutz, 2005; Acadia Management Interview Series Video Database, Nova Scotia Wines—The New Contender; The Canadian Wine Industry, Agriculture and Agrifood Canada, Food Value Chain Bureau, www.agr.gc.ca/misb/fb-ba/index_e.php?s1=proc-trans&s2=prof&page=wine-vin, Retrieved, January 26, 2006; J.C. Lewis, A. Jamieson, R. Gordon, & G. Lewis, *2005: Opportunities and Challenges for Wine Grape Production in Nova Scotia*; C. Dobson, "Fruit of the Vine," *Atlantic Business Magazine,* 16, no. 5 September–October 2005; www.tasteofnovascotia.com/, Retrieved January 26, 2006; Domaine de Grand Pre—The Estate, www.grandprewines.ns.ca/ModifiedWebSite/estate/history.html, Retrieved, January 26, 2006; 2005 Vision 1st Award Winner, Hanspeter Stutz, Grand Pre Wines, Nova Scotia Vision for Tourism, www.nstourismvision.com/vision/visionaward/, Retrieved, January 26, 2006.
2. J. Barney, "Firm Resources and Sustained Competitive Advantage," *Journal of Management* 17 (1991): 99–120; J. Barney, "Looking Inside for Competitive Advantage," *Academy of Management Executive* 9 (1995): 49–61.
3. S. Hart & C. Banbury, "How Strategy-Making Processes Can Make a Difference," *Strategic Management Journal* 15 (1994): 251–269.
4. S. Hart & C. Banbury, "How Strategy-Making Processes Can

Make a Difference," *Strategic Management Journal* 15 (1994): 251–269; C.C. Miller & L.B. Cardinal, "Strategic Planning and Firm Performance: A Synthesis of More than Two Decades of Research," *Academy of Management Journal* 37 (1994): 1649–1665; C.R. Schwenk, "Effects of Formal Strategic Planning on Financial Performance in Small Firms: A Meta-Analysis," *Entrepreneurship Theory and Practice*, Spring 1993, 53–64.

5. R.A. Burgelman, "Fading Memories: A Process Theory of Strategic Business Exit in Dynamic Environments," *Administrative Science Quarterly,* 39 (1994): 24–56; R.A. Burgelman & A.S. Grove, "Strategic Dissonance," *California Management Review* 38 (1996): 8–28.
6. M. Robichaux, "The Pizza-Pan-Size Dishes Fly Off the Shelves; Prices Plunge," *The Wall Street Journal Interactive Edition*, 7 November 1996.
7. A. Fiegenbaum, S. Hart, & D. Schendel, "Strategic Reference Point Theory," *Strategic Management Journal* 17 (1996): 219–235.
8. S. Alsop, "Apple's Next Move Misses the Mark," *Fortune,* 3 February 1997.
9. P. Buller & G. McEvoy, "Creating and Sustaining Ethical Capability in the Multi-National Corporation," *Journal of World Business* 34 (1999): 326–343.
10. D.J. Collis, "Research Note: How Valuable Are Organizational Capabilities?" *Strategic Management Journal* 15 (1994): 143–152.
11. A. Fiegenbaum & H. Thomas, "Strategic Groups as Reference Groups: Theory, Modeling and Empirical Examination of Industry and Competitive Strategy," *Strategic Management Journal* 16 (1995): 461–476.
12. R.K. Reger & A.S. Huff, "Strategic Groups: A Cognitive Perspective," *Strategic Management Journal* 14 (1993): 103–124.
13. W.B. Werther, Jr. & J.L. Kerr, "The Shifting Sands of Competitive Advantage," *Business Horizons,* May-June 1995, 11–17.
14. Ibid.
15. M. Lubatkin, "Value-Creating Mergers: Fact or Folklore?" *Academy of Management Executive,* 2 (1988): 295–302; M. Lubatkin & S. Chatterjee, "Extending Modern Portfolio Theory into the Domain of Corporate Diversification: Does It Apply?" *Academy of Management Journal,* 37 (1994): 109–136; M.H. Lubatkin & P.J. Lane, "Psst ... The Merger Mavens Still Have It Wrong!" *Academy of Management Executive* 10 (1996): 21–39.
16. M. Maremont, J. Hechinger, J. Markon, & G. Zuckerman, "Tainted Chief: Kozlowski Quits under a Cloud, Worsening Worries about Tyco," *The Wall Street Journal,* 4 June 2002, A1; R. Charan & J. Useem, "Why Companies Fail," *Fortune,* 27 May 2002, 50.
17. E. Reguly. "Get Outta Town; If BCE Wants to Be a Phone Company with a Growth Story, It Has but One Choice: Look Abroad," *Globe and Mail Report on Business Magazine*, 29 April 2005, 33.
18. J.A. Pearce, II, "Selecting Among Alternative Grand Strategies," *California Management Review,* Spring 1982, 23–31.
19. J. Hayes, "Acquisition Is Fine, but Organic Growth Is Better," *Forbes,* 30 December 1996, 52–55.
20. P. Damas, "Danzas Refines 'Core Carriers' Policy," *American Shipper,* August 1996, 39–40.
21. J.A. Pearce, II, "Retrenchment Remains the Foundation of Business Turnaround," *Strategic Management Journal* 15 (1994): 407–417.
22. S. Silcoff, "Moore CEO's Exit 'Shocks' Market: Shares Fall 11%: Robert Burton Says 'Objectives Have Been Realized,' *Financial Post*, 10 December 2002, FP5.
23. "Business Forms Maker Moore Corp. Reports Big Q2 Earning Turnaround," *Financial Post*, 24 July 2002; "Moore Swings Back to Profit in Third Quarter," *Financial Post*, 24 October 2002, FP2.
24. Autobytel Web site, "Customer Endorsements," [Online] available at www.autobytel.com, 8 March 1997.
25. S. Kichen, "Cruising the Internet (Car-Shopping on the Internet)," *Forbes,* 24 March 1997, 198.
26. E. Tanouye & R. Langreth, "Top Firms Must Prepare for Onslaught of Generics," *The Wall Street Journal Interactive Edition,* 12 August 1997.
27. R.E. Miles & C.C. Snow, *Organizational Strategy, Structure, and Process* (New York: McGraw-Hill, 1978); S. Zahra & J.A. Pearce, "Research Evidence on the Miles-Snow Typology," *Journal of Management* 16 (1990): 751–768; W.L. James & K.J. Hatten, "Further Evidence on the Validity of the Self Typing Paragraph Approach: Miles and Snow Strategic Archetypes in Banking," *Strategic Management Journal* 16 (1995): 161–168.
28. L. Zehr, "Biovail Sales Pitch Falls on Deaf Ears; Lineup of New Drugs to Replace Cash Cow Wellbutrin XL Fails to Impress the Street," *Globe and Mail,* 8 July 2005, B10.
29. E. Ramstad, "Using a Personal Approach, Many Tiny PC Firms Thrive," *The Wall Street Journal Interactive Edition,* 8 January 1997.
30. R. Gibson & C.Y. Coleman, "How Burger King Emerged as a Threat to McDonald's," *The Wall Street Journal Interactive Edition,* 27 February 1997.
31. Ibid.
32. M. Chen, "Competitor Analysis and Interfirm Rivalry: Toward a Theoretical Integration," *Academy of Management Review* 21 (1996): 100–134; J.C. Baum & H.J. Korn, "Competitive Dynamics of Interfirm Rivalry," *Academy of Management Journal* 39 (1996): 255–291.
33. M. Chen, "Competitor Analysis and Interfirm Rivalry: Toward a Theoretical Integration," *Academy of Management Review* 21 (1996): 100–134.
34. M. Stopa, "Wendy's New Fashioned Growth: Buy Hardee's," *Crain's Detroit Business*, 21 October 1996.
35. N. Shirouzu, "Though Japan Nears Saturation, Burger King Turns Up the Heat," *The Wall Street Journal Interactive Edition,* 31 January 1997.
36. R. Narisetti, "P&G Diaper-Patent Trial Expected to Begin Monday," *The Wall Street Journal Interactive Edition,* 3 February 1997.
37. R. Narisetti, "P&G Diaper-Patent Trial Expected to Begin Monday," *The Wall Street Journal Interactive Edition,* 3 February 1997.
38. J.C. Baum & H.J. Korn, "Competitive Dynamics of Interfirm Rivalry," *Academy of Management Journal* 39 (1996): 255–291.
39. G.T. Lumpkin & G.G. Dess, "Clarifying the Entrepreneurial Orientation Construct and Linking It to Performance," *Academy of Management Review* 21 (1996): 135–172.
40. R.B. Lieber, "Beating the Odds," *Fortune,* 31 March 1997, 82–90.
41. D. Miller & P. Friesen, "Archetypes of Strategy Formulation," *Management Science* 24 (1978): 921–933.
42. N. Venkatraman, "Strategic Orientation of Business Enterprises: The Construct, Dimensionality, and Measurement," *Management Science,* 35 (1989): 942–962.
43. Z. Moukheiber, "Cybercops," *Forbes,* 10 March 1997, 170–172.

44. Interview with Hanspeter Stutz, 2005; Acadia Management Interview Series Video Database, Nova Scotia Wines—The New Contender; C. Moreira, "Bye-Bye Chowder—Foodies Are Flocking to the East Coast Town of Wolfville for Venison and a Glass of L'Acadie Blanc," *Globe and Mail*, 23 November 2005, R8; C. Dobson, "Fruit of the Vine," *Atlantic Business Magazine* 16, no. 5, September/October 2005; "The Canadian Wine Industry," Agriculture and Agrifood Canada, Food Value Chain Bureau, www.agr.gc.ca/misb/fb-ba/index_e.php?s1=proc-trans&s2=prof&page=wine-vin, Retrieved 26 January 2006; J.C. Lewis, A. Jamieson, R. Gordon & G. Lewis, "Opportunities and Challenges for Wine Grape Production in Nova Scotia," www.tasteofnovascotia.com/, Retrieved 26 January 2006; Domaine de Grand Pre—The Estate, www.grandprewines.ns.ca/ModifiedWebSite/estate/history.html, Retrieved, 26 January 2006; 2005 Vision 1st Award Winner, Hanspeter Stutz, Grand Pre Wines, Nova Scotia Vision for Tourism, www.nstourismvision.com/vision/visionaward/, Retrieved, 26 January 2006.
45. E. Beck, "New 3-D Tea Bag Rattles Some Tea Cups in the U.K," *The Wall Street Journal Interactive Edition*, 24 March 1997; L. Bray, "Boiling Points: Life Is Not an Easy Ride for Tea and Coffee Manufacturers These Days, with Innovation in Other Beverage Categories Increasing All the Time," *Grocer*, 16 November 1996, 45–46; N. Clayton, "Workforce Is Showing Bags of Innovation," *The Times of London*, 2 October 1994; R. Mulholland, "Storm Brewing in Britain's Teacups," *Agence France-Presse*, 24 February 1996; R. Turcsik, "A Bounty of Teas," Supermarket News, 13 November 1995, 42–43.
46. D.A. Blackmon, "FedEx Plans to Establish a Marketplace in Cyber Space–Shipper Aims to Deliver the Goods as it Moves into Internet Commerce," *The Wall Street Journal*, 9 October 1996; D.A. Blackmon, "Federal Express Sees Strong 4Q, Backs Yr View above $3/Shr," *Dow Jones News Service*, 31 March 1997; D.A. Blackmon, "Federal Express Plans 3-Day Service to Challenge UPS," *The Wall Street Journal*, 2 April 1997; "Dietzgen's New Same-Day Satellite Document Delivery Service for Architectural and Engineering Blueprints Takes Direct Aim at Overnight Courier Business," *Business Wire*, 21 March 1997; T. Lappin, "FedEx: The Airline of the Internet," *Wired Magazine*, December 1996.
47. K.R. Brousseau, M.J. Driver, K. Eneroth, & R. Larsson, "Career Pandemonium: Realigning Organizations and Individuals," *Academy of Management Executive*, November 1996, 52–66; D.T. Hall, "Protean Careers of the 21st Century," *Academy of Management Executive*, November 1996, 8–16; D. Seligman, "Does Money Buy Happiness?" *Forbes*, 21 April 1997, 394–396.

Chapter 10

1. Interview with Pierre Lafontaine, 2006; Acadia Management Interview Series Video Database; William Houston, "The Globe and Mail's List of the Top 25 Most Influential People in Sports," *Globe and Mail*, 14 December 2005; Josh Brown, "Laurier Out as National Swim Centre; Swimming Canada Expected to Operate in Montreal, Victoria," *Kitchener-Waterloo Record*, 25 August 2005; Dave Stubbs, "Lafontaine's Mission Is Paying Off," *Montreal Gazette*, 22 August 2005; Dave Stubbs, "Swim Boss Waters the Grassroots: Lafontaine Has Renewed Hope in Canada's Pools," *National Post*, 22 August 2005. Randy Starkman, "Ontario's Pool of Top-Class Swimmers Running Dry; Sports Program Here 'in Shambles'; Number of Factors Cited for Decline," *The Toronto Star*, 2 August 2005, D08; Dave Stubbs, "How about a Slice of Humble Pie? Canada's Swimmers Bounce Back after Athens Debacle," *National Post*, 2 August 2005, S10.
2. H. Fraser, "Getting From 'Design Thinking' to 'Design Doing'; Three Important Forces Have to Converge: Deep User Understanding, Multiple Prototyping and Strategic Business Design," *Globe and Mail Report on Business*, 9 May 2006, B11.
3. B. Richards, "Ad Business for Blimps Rises Because of One Bright Idea," *The Wall Street Journal Interactive*, 14 October 1997.
4. T.M. Amabile, R. Conti, H. Coon, J. Lazenby, & M. Herron, "Assessing the Work Environment for Creativity," *Academy of Management Journal* 39 (1996): 1154–1184.
5. Canada's Innovation Strategy, National Summit on Innovation and Learning. Government of Canada, [Online] available at www.innovationstrategy.gc.ca, Retrieved 9 April 2003.
6. P. Anderson & M.L. Tushman, "Managing Through Cycles of Technological Change," *Research/Technology Management*, May/June 1991, 26–31.
7. R.N. Foster, *Innovation: The Attacker's Advantage* (New York: Summit, 1986).
8. iComp Index 2.0, Intel Corporation Web site, [Online] available at www.intel.com/procs/performance/icomp/index.htm, 5 December 1997.
9. J. Burke, *The Day the Universe Changed* (Boston: Little, Brown, and Company, 1985).
10. W. Gibson, "The Thin Web Line," *Canadian Business* 75, no. 19 (2003): 85–86.
11. M.L. Tushman, P.C. Anderson, & C. O'Reilly, "Technology Cycles, Innovation Streams, and Ambidextrous Organizations: Organization Renewal Through Innovation Streams and Strategic Change," in *Managing Strategic Innovation and Change*, eds. M.L. Tushman & P. Anderson (1997), 3–23.
12. "Pony Express," Encyclopedia Britannica Online. [Online] available at www.eb.com:180/bol/topic?eu=62367&sctn=1, 6 March 1999.
13. J.R. Aldern, "The Victorian Internet: The Remarkable Story of the Telegraph and the Nineteenth Century's On-Line Pioneers (Review)," *Smithsonian*, 1 January 1999.
14. E. Schlossberg, *Interactive Excellence: Defining and Developing New Standards for the Twenty-First Century* (New York: Ballantine, 1998).
15. D. Murphy, "Ways That Managers Can Help Workers—Or Hinder Them," *San Francisco Chronicle*, 26 November 2000, J1; M. Schrage, "Your Idea Is Brilliant; Glad I Thought of It," *Fortune*, 16 October 2000, 412.
16. W. Abernathy & J. Utterback, "Patterns of Industrial Innovation," *Technology Review*, 2 (1978): 40–47.
17. K.M. Eisenhardt, "Accelerating Adaptive Processes: Product Innovation in the Global Computer Industry," *Administrative Science Quarterly* 40 (1995): 84–110.
18. Ibid.
19. R. Gibson, "Starbucks Plans to Test a Paper Cup that Insulates Hands from Hot Coffee," *The Interactive Wall Street Journal*, 22 February 1999; S. Kravetz,

"These People Search for a Cup that Suits the Coffee It Holds," *The Wall Street Journal*, 24 March 1998, A1.
20. F. Yanor, "No Friend of Mines," *Canadian Business* 75, no. 19 (14 October 2003): 89–90.
21. R. Winslow, "Atomic Speed: Utility Cuts Red Tape, Builds Nuclear Plant Almost on Schedule," *The Wall Street Journal*, 22 February 1984.
22. L. Kraar, "25 Who Help the U.S. Win: Innovators Everywhere Are Generating Ideas to Make America a Stronger Competitor. They Range from a Boss Who Demands the Impossible to a Mathematician with a Mop," *Fortune*, 22 March 1991.
23. M.W. Lawless & P.C. Anderson, "Generational Technological Change: Effects of Innovation and Local Rivalry on Performance," *Academy of Management Journal* 39 (1996): 1185–1217.
24. S. Anderson & M. Uzumeri, "Managing Product Families: The Case of the Sony Walkman," *Research Policy* 24 (1995): 761–782.
25. P. Ponticel, "Integrated Product Process Development," *Automotive Engineering*, 1 October 1996.
26. T. Parker, "Avon's Retooling to Include Fewer Products, Retail Stores," *The Wall Street Journal*, 27 October 1997.
27. P. Strebel, "Choosing the Right Change Path," *California Management Review*, Winter 1994, 29–51.
28. K. Lewin, *Field Theory in Social Science: Selected Theoretical Papers* (New York: Harper & Brothers, 1951).
29. W. Weitzel & E. Jonsson, "Reversing the Downward Spiral: Lessons from W.T. Grant and Sears Roebuck," *Academy of Management Executive* 5 (1991): 7–22.
30. Ibid.
31. Tom McFeat & John McHutchion, "The Nortel Headache (or the Pain of Watching $397 Billion Disappear)," CBC News Online [Online] available at www.cbc.ca, accessed 27 September 2002.
32. Tom McFeat, "Nortel—The Rise and Fall of Canada's Most Watched Stock," CBC News In-Depth Backgrounder, [Online] available at www.cbc.ca, accessed 16 September 2002.
33. Douglas Hunter, "Nortel's Slide Toward Penny-Stock Status," *The Financial Post*, 15 October 2002, FP1, FP6.
34. K. Lewin, *Field Theory in Social Science: Selected Theoretical Papers* (New York: Harper & Brothers, 1951).
35. G.S. Cotton, "Where People Want to Come to Work," *Calgary Herald*, 30 October 2003, D1.
36. J. Bolt, "The Acadia Advantage," in *Ubiquitous Computing*, ed. D.G. Brown (Bolton, MA: Anker Publishing Company, 2003), 117–127.
37. S. Cramm, "A Change of Hearts," *CIO*, 1 April 2003, [Online] available at www.cio.com/archive/040103/hs_leadership.html, 20 May 2003.
38. R.H. Schaffer & H.A. Thomson, J.D., "Successful Change Programs Begin with Results," *Harvard Business Review on Change* (Boston: Harvard Business School Publishing, 1998), 189–213.
39. H.A. Thomson, personal phone conversation, 9 April 2003.
40. R.N. Ashkenas & T.D. Jick, "From Dialogue to Action in GE Work-Out: Developmental Learning in a Change Process," in *Research in Organizational Change and Development*, Vol. 6, eds. W.A. Pasmore & R.W. Woodman (Greenwhich, CT: JAI Press, 1992), 267–287.
41. J.D. Duck, "Managing Change: The Art of Balancing," *Harvard Business Review on Change* (Boston: Harvard Business School Publishing, 1998), 55–81.
42. L. Landro, "Viacom Names Team to Consolidate Assets of Paramount and Blockbuster," *The Wall Street Journal*, 16 March 1994, B4.
43. W.J. Rothwell, R. Sullivan, & G.M. McLean, *Practicing Organizational Development: A Guide for Consultants* (San Diego, CA: Pfeiffer & Company, 1995).
44. W.J. Rothwell, R. Sullivan, & G.M. McLean, *Practicing Organizational Development: A Guide for Consultants* (San Diego, CA: Pfeiffer & Company, 1995).
45. P.J. Robertson, D.R. Roberts, & J.I. Porras, "Dynamics of Planned Organizational Change: Assessing Empirical Support for a Theoretical Model," *Academy of Management Journal* 36 (1993): 619–634.
46. R.N. Ashkenas & T.D. Jick, "From Dialogue to Action in GE Work-Out: Developmental Learning in a Change Process," in *Research in Organizational Change and Development*, Vol. 6, eds. W.A. Pasmore & R.W. Woodman (Greenwich, CT: JAI Press, 1992), 267–287.
47. J.P. Kotter, "Leading Change: Why Transformation Efforts Fail," *Harvard Business Review* 73, no. 2 (March–April 1995): 59.
48. Interview with Pierre Lafontaine, 2006, Acadia Management Interview Series Video Database; William Houston, "The Globe and Mail's List of the Top 25 Most Influential People in Sports," *Globe and Mail*, 14 December 2005; Josh Brown, "Laurier Out as National Swim Centre; Swimming Canada Expected to Operate in Montreal, Victoria," *Kitchener-Waterloo Record*, 25 August 2005. Dave Stubbs, "Lafontaine's Mission Is Paying Off," *Montreal Gazette*, 22 August 2005; Dave Stubbs, "Swim Boss Waters the Grassroots: Lafontaine Has Renewed Hope in Canada's Pools," *National Post*, 22 August 2005; Randy Starkman, "Ontario's Pool of Top-Class Swimmers Running Dry; Sports Program Here 'in Shambles'; Number of Factors Cited for Decline, *The Toronto Star*, 2 August 2005, D08; Dave Stubbs, "How about a Slice of Humble Pie? Canada's Swimmers Bounce Back after Athens Debacle, *National Post*, 2 August 2005, S10.
49. S. Ascarelli, "European Telecom R&D Labs Adjusting: Scientists Must Think in Terms of Profit and Loss," *The Wall Street Journal*, 15 March 1996; L. Hooper, "Technology (A Special Report): Genius: The Creative Edge: Nurturing High-Tech Talent Requires a Delicate Balancing Act; But the Payoff Can Be Huge," *The Wall Street Journal*, 24 May 1993; J. Keller, "Technology (A Special Report): Finding and Feeding: Ignoring the Bottom Line: NEC's U.S. Research Lab Has a Theory: The Freedom Not to Worry about Products May Lead to the Best Products of All," *The Wall Street Journal*, 24 May 1993; G. Naik, "Corporate Research: How Much Is It Worth? Top Labs Shift Research Goals to Fast Payoffs," *The Wall Street Journal*, 22 May 1995; B. Ziegler & G. Naik, "Bell Labs Faces Mundane Future under Breakup Plan," *The Wall Street Journal*, 22 September 1995.

Chapter 11

1. Interview with Alex MacBeath, Acadia Management Interview Series Video Database, accessed, 1 February 2006; "An Interview with Alex MacBeath (CA, MBA), CEO of Grant Thornton Canada," *Canadian Journal of Administrative Sciences*, December 2004.
2. "Reynolds Metals Announces Organizational and Management Changes," Reynolds Metals Press Release, [Online] available at

www.rmc.com/pressrel/reorg0397.html, 27 March 1997.

3. J.G. March & H.A. Simon, *Organizations* (New York: John Wiley & Sons, 1958).
4. "Outline of Principal Operations," Sony Corporation, [Online] available at www.sony.com/SCA/outline.html, 4 November 2001.
5. "Business Segments," Bayer Group, [Online] available at www.bayer.com/en/unternehmen/arbeitsgebiete/index.html, 4 November 2001.
6. H. Mintzberg, *Structure in Fives: Designing Effective Organizations* (New York: Prentice Hall, 1992).
7. General Electric's Annual Report, [Online] available at www.ge.com/annual00/financial/images/GEannual00_financials.pdf , November 3, 2001.
8. L.R. Burns, "Adoption and Abandonment of Matrix Management Programs: Effects of Organizational Characteristics and Interorganizational Networks," *Academy of Management Journal* 36 (1993): 106–138.
9. H. Fayol, *General and Industrial Management, translated by Constance Storrs* (London: Pitman Publishing, 1949).
10. M. Weber, *The Theory of Social and Economic Organization,* translated and edited by A.M. Henderson & T. Parsons (New York: The Free Press, 1947).
11. H. Fayol, *General and Industrial Management,* translated by Constance Storrs (London: Pitman Publishing, 1949).
12. G. Teel, "Admin Professionals Gain Recognition," *Winnipeg Free Press,* 4 June 2005.
13. E.E. Lawler, S.A. Mohrman, & G.E. Ledford, *Creating High Performance Organizations: Practices and Results of Employee Involvement and Quality Management in Fortune 1000 Companies* (San Francisco: Jossey-Bass, 1995).
14. C. Quintanilla, "Food: Come and Get It! Drive-Throughs Upgrade Services," *The Wall Street Journal,* 5 May 1994.
15. "Changing the Image: Government Has to Make Public Service Attractive Place to Work," *Calgary Herald,* 17 March 2001, WS.01.
16. "Carpal Tunnel Syndrome," National Institute for Occupational Safety and Health, [Online] available at www.cdc.gov/niosh/ctsfs.html, 23 May 2003; "Carpal Tunnel Syndrome Fact Sheet," National Institute of Neurological Disorders and Stroke, [Online] available at www.ninds.nih.gov/health_and_medical/ pubs/carpal_tunnel.htm, 23 May 2003; "Table 9. Percent Distribution of Nonfatal Occupational Injuries and Illnesses Involving Days Away from Work by Selected Injury or Illness Characteristics and Number of Days Away from Work, 2001," *News: Bureau of Labor Statistics, U.S. Department of Labor,* [Online] available at www.bls.gov/news.release/osh2.t09.htm, 23 May 2003.
17. R.W. Griffin, *Task Design* (Glenview, IL: Scott, Foresman, 1982).
18. F. Herzberg, *Work and the Nature of Man* (Cleveland, OH: World Press, 1966).
19. T. Burns & G.M. Stalker, *The Management of Innovation* (London: Tavistock, 1961).
20. M. Hammer & J. Champy, *Reengineering the Corporation: A Manifesto for Business Revolution* (New York: HarperBusiness, 1993).
21. M. Hammer & J. Champy, *Reengineering the Corporation: A Manifesto for Business Revolution* (New York: HarperBusiness, 1993).
22. J.D. Thompson, *Organizations in Action* (New York: McGraw-Hill, 1967).
23. J.B. White, "'Next Big Thing': Re-Engineering Gurus Take Steps to Remodel Their Stalling Vehicles," *The Wall Street Journal Interactive Edition,* 26 November 1996.
24. G.M. Spreitzer, "Individual Empowerment in the Workplace: Dimensions, Measurement, and Validation," *Academy of Management Journal* 38 (1995): 1442–1465.
25. D.A. Morand, "The Role of Behavioral Formality and Informality in the Enactment of Bureaucratic Versus Organic Organizations," *Academy of Management Journal,* 20 (1995): 831–872.
26. S. Hwang, "Cubicle Culture: Office Vultures Circle Still-Warm Desks Left Empty by Layoffs," *The Wall Street Journal,* 14 August 2002, B1.
27. K.A. Edelman, "Take Down the Walls!" *Across the Board* 34 (1 March 1997).
28. "Designing the Ever-Changing Workplace," *Architectural Record,* September 1995, 32–37.
29. R. Nilson, "Virtual Corporations: From the Rolling Stones to IBM to Start-ups, 'Outsourcing' Is the Way to Go," *Sunday Telegram,* 30 July 1995.
30. G.G. Dess, A.M.A. Rasheed, K.J. McLaughlin, & R.L. Priem, "The New Corporate Architecture," *Academy of Management Executive* 9 (1995): 7–18.
31. "Building the CEO: Robert Eaton Has Parlayed Teamwork and Technology to Turn a Troubled Auto," *Industry Week,* 16 September 1996, 10–14.
32. H. Voss, "Virtual Organizations: The Future Is Now," *Strategy & Leadership,* 17 July 1996.
33. C.C. Snow, R.E. Miles, & H.J. Coleman, Jr., "Managing 21st Century Network Organizations," *Organizational Dynamics,* Winter 1992, 5–20.
34. J.H. Sheridan, "The Agile Web: A Model for the Future?" *Industry Week,* 4 March 1996.
35. D. Ulrich & S. Kerr, "Creating the Boundaryless Organization: The Radical Reconstruction of Organization Capabilities," *Planning Review,* September–October 1995, 41–45.
36. R. Ashkenas, D. Ulrich, T. Jick, & S. Kerr, *The Boundaryless Organization: Breaking the Chains of Organizational Structure* (San Francisco: Jossey-Bass, 1995).
37. G.G. Dess, A.M.A. Rasheed, K.J. McLaughlin, & R.L. Priem, "The New Corporate Architecture," *Academy of Management Executive* 9 (1995): 7–18.
38. Interview with Alex MacBeath, Acadia Management Interview Series Video Database, accessed 1 February 2006; "An Interview with Alex MacBeath (CA, MBA), CEO of Grant Thornton Canada," *Canadian Journal of Administrative Sciences,* December 2004.
39. S. Bothe, "Outsourcing for Small and Mid-Sized Businesses," *The CPA Journal,* May 2001; J. Bowles, "Build or Outsource?" *Customer Interface,* June 2001; E. Garaventa & T. Tellefsen, "Outsourcing: The Hidden Costs," *Review of Business,* Spring 2001.
40. M. Budman, "The Persistence of Perks," *Across the Board,* 1 February 1994; L. Fleeson, "In Today's Efficient, Egalitarian Offices, Plush Perks Are Passe," *The News Tribune,* 10 July 1994; S. Lohr, "Cubicle or Cavern? Egalitarian Work Space Duels with Need for Privacy Among Brainy Folks in High-Tech Firms," *Rocky Mountain News,* 7 September 1997; T. Schellhardt, "Executive Pay (A Special Report)—Passing of Perks: Company Cars, Country Club Memberships, Executive Dining Rooms; Where Have All the Goodies Gone?" *The Wall Street Journal,* 13 April 1994.
41. K. Freiberg & J. Freiberg, *Nuts! Southwest Airlines' Crazy Recipe for Business and Personal Success* (Austin, TX: Bard Press, 1996).

Chapter 12

1. "Cessna Skyhawk," Learn to Fly.com, [Online] available at http://learntofly.com/howto/skyhawk.chtml, 29 May 2003; T. Greenwood, M. Bradford, & B. Greene, "Becoming a Lean Enterprise: A Tale of Two Firms," *Strategic Finance*, 1 November 2002, 32; B. Milligan, "Cessna Uses Baldrige Process to Identify Best Suppliers," *Purchasing*, 6 April 2000, 75; J. Morgan, "Cessna Charts a Supply Chain Flight Strategy," *Purchasing*, 7 September 2000, 42. J. Morgan, "Cross-Functional Buying: Why Teams Are Hot," *Purchasing*, 5 April 2001, 27; J. Morgan, "Cessna Aims to Drive SCM to Its Very Core: Here Are 21 Steps and Tools It's Using to Make This Happen," *Purchasing*, 6 June 2002, 31; P. Siekman, "Cessna Tackles Lean Manufacturing," *Fortune*, 1 May 2000, I222 B+; P. Siekman, "The Snap-Together Business Jet; Bombardier's New Recipe: A Dozen Big Pieces, Four Days to Assemble Them, and It's Ready to Fly," *Fortune*, 21 January 2002, 104A.
2. J.R. Katzenback & D.K. Smith, *The Wisdom of Teams* (Boston: Harvard Business School Press, 1993).
3. "Born-Again Basket Case," *Canadian Business* 66, no. 5 (May 1993): 38–44.
4. S.E. Gross, *Compensation for Teams* (New York: American Management Association, 1995); B.L. Kirkman & B. Rosen, "Beyond Self-Management: Antecedents and Consequences of Team Empowerment," *Academy of Management Journal* 42 (1999): 58–74; G. Stock & T.M. Hout, *Competing Against Time* (New York: Free Press, 1990); S.C. Wheelwright & K.B. Clark, *Revolutionizing New Product Development* (New York: Free Press, 1992).
5. R.S. Wellins, W.C. Byham, & G.R. Dixon, *Inside Teams* (San Francisco: Jossey-Bass, 1994).
6. R.D. Banker, J.M. Field, R.G. Schroeder, & K.K. Sinha, "Impact of Work Teams on Manufacturing Performance: A Longitudinal Field Study," *Academy of Management Journal* 39 (1996): 867–890.
7. R.S. Wellins, W.C. Byham, & G.R. Dixon, *Inside Teams* (San Francisco: Jossey-Bass Publishers, 1994).
8. C. Fishman, "Whole Foods Is All Teams," *Fast Company,* April 1996, 103.
9. "Beating the Joneses (Learning What the Competition Is Doing)," *Industry Week* 1 (7 December 1998): 27.
10. G. Stalk & T.M. Hout, *Competing Against Time: How Time-Based Competition Is Reshaping Global Markets* (New York: The Free Press, 1990).
11. H.K. Bowen, K.B. Clark, C.A. Holloway, & S.C. Wheelwright, *The Perpetual Enterprise Machine* (New York: Oxford Press, 1994).
12. J.L. Cordery, W.S. Mueller, & L.M. Smith, "Attitudinal and Behavioral Effects of Autonomous Group Working: A Longitudinal Field Study," *Academy of Management Journal* 34 (1991): 464–476; T.D. Wall, N.J. Kemp, P.R. Jackson, & C.W. Clegg, "Outcomes of Autonomous Workgroups: A Long-term Field Experiment," *Academy of Management Journal* 29 (1986): 280–304.
13. J. Cooper, "The Friendly Factor," *Canadian Grocer* 111, no. 7 (September 1997): 14–17.
14. "Declaration of Interdependence," Whole Foods Market, [Online] available at www.wholefoodsmarket.com/company/declaration.html, 15 January 2002.
15. C. Fishman, "The Anarchist's Cookbook: John Mackey's Approach to Management Is Equal Parts Star Trek and 1970s Flashback," *Fast Company*, 1 July 2004, 70.
16. R.S. Wellins, W.C. Byham, & G.R. Dixon, *Inside Teams* (San Francisco: Jossey-Bass Publishers, 1994).
17. J. Hoerr, "The Payoff from Teamwork—The Gains in Quality Are Substantial—So Why Isn't It Spreading Faster?" *Business Week,* 10 July 1989, 56.
18. J. George, "Extrinsic and Intrinsic Origins of Perceived Social Loafing in Organizations," *Academy of Management Journal* 35 (1992): 191–202.
19. T.T. Baldwin, M.D. Bedell, & J.L. Johnson, "The Social Fabric of a Team-Based M.B.A. Program: Network Effects on Student Satisfaction and Performance," *Academy of Management Journal* 40 (1997): 1369–1397.
20. J. Hoerr, "The Payoff from Teamwork—The Gains in Quality Are Substantial—So Why Isn't It Spreading Faster?" *Business Week,* 10 July 1989, 56.
21. C. Joinson, "Teams at Work," *HRMagazine,* 1 May 1999, 30.
22. R. Wageman, "Critical Success Factors for Creating Superb Self-Managing Teams," *Organizational Dynamics* 26, no. 1 (1997): 49–61.
23. M.A. Cusumano, "How Microsoft Makes Large Teams Work Like Small Teams," *Sloan Management Review* 39, no. 1 (Fall 1997): 9–20.
24. R.T. King, Jr., "Jeans Therapy: Levi's Factory Workers Are Assigned to Teams, and Morale Takes a Hit—Infighting Rises, Productivity Falls as Employees Miss the Piecework System— 'It's Not the Same Company,'" *The Wall Street Journal,* 20 May 1998, A1.
25. R.T. King, Jr., "Jeans Therapy: Levi's Factory Workers Are Assigned to Teams, and Morale Takes a Hit—Infighting Rises, Productivity Falls as Employees Miss the Piecework System— 'It's Not the Same Company,'" *The Wall Street Journal,* 20 May 1998, A1.
26. M. Fischetti, "'Team Doctors, Report to ER': Is Your Team Headed for Intensive Care? Our Specialists Offer Prescriptions for the Five Illnesses That Can Afflict Even the Best Teams," *Fast Company,* 1 February 1998, 170; S. Sherman, "Stretch Goals: The Dark Side of Asking for Miracles," *Fortune,* 13 November 1995.
27. M. Curtius, "There Is No 'I' in 'Team'—And Maybe No Point, Either: The Trend Continues but Doesn't Always Succeed. Finding the Proper Structure, Motivating Employees and Getting Managers Out of the Way Can Sometimes Help," *Los Angeles Times,* 24 February 1997, D25.
28. R.T. King, Jr., "Jeans Therapy: Levi's Factory Workers Are Assigned to Teams, and Morale Takes a Hit—Infighting Rises, Productivity Falls as Employees Miss the Piecework System— 'It's Not the Same Company,'" *The Wall Street Journal,* 20 May 1998, A1.
29. B.L. Kirkman & B. Rosen, "Beyond Self-Management: Antecedents and Consequences of Team Empowerment," *Academy of Management Journal* 42 (1999): 58–74.
30. M. Curtius, "There Is No 'I' in 'Team'—And Maybe No Point, Either: The Trend Continues but Doesn't Always Succeed. Finding the Proper Structure, Motivating Employees and Getting Managers Out of the Way Can Sometimes Help," *Los Angeles Times,* 24 February 1997, D25.
31. "Now Everyone Can Be a Boss," *Canadian Business* 65, no. 5 (May 1994): 48–50; J. Terrett, "Honeywell Wins NQI's Quality Trophy," *Plant* 59, no. 17 (27 November 2000).
32. B.L. Kirkman & B. Rosen, "Beyond Self-Management: Antecedents and Consequences of Team Empowerment,"

Academy of Management Journal 42 (1999): 58–74.
33. K. Kelly, "Managing Workers Is Tough Enough in Theory. When Human Nature Enters the Picture, It's Worse," *Business Week,* 21 October 1996, 32.
34. S. Easton & G. Porter, "Selecting the Right Team Structure to Work in Your Organization," in *Handbook of Best Practices for Teams,* Volume 1, ed. Glenn M. Parker (Amherst, MA: Irwin, 1996).
35. D. Stafford, "Hotel Lets Its Workers 'Own' Their Duties: Ritz-Carlton, Kansas City, Tries a Program That Emphasizes Teamwork, Self-Direction," *The Kansas City Star,* 6 February 1996, D1.
36. Susan Hirshorn, "Team-Work-Team," *OH&S Canada*, January–February 2005, 32–37.
37. C. Fishman, "Engines of Democracy: The General Electric Plant in Durham, North Carolina Builds Some of the World's Most Powerful Jet Engines. But the Plant's Real Power Lies in the Lessons That It Teaches about the Future of Work and about Workplace Democracy," *Fast Company,* 1 October 1999, 174.
38. R.J. Recardo, D. Wade, C.A. Mention, & J. Jolly, *Teams* (Houston: Gulf Publishing Company, 1996).
39. D.R. Denison, S.L. Hart, & J.A. Kahn, "From Chimneys to Cross-Functional Teams: Developing and Validating a Diagnostic Model," *Academy of Management Journal* 39, no. 4 (1996): 1005–1023.
40. A.M. Townsend, S.M. DeMarie, & A.R. Hendrickson, "Virtual Teams: Technology and the Workplace of the Future," *Academy of Management Executive* 13, no. 3 (1998): 17–29.
41. A.M. Townsend, S.M. DeMarie, & A.R. Hendrickson, "Are You Ready for Virtual Teams?" *HRMagazine* 41, no. 9 (1996): 122–126.
42. Charlene Marmer Solomon, "Managing Virtual Teams," *Workforce,* June 2001, 60–64.
43. R.S. Wellins, W.C. Byham, & G.R. Dixon, *Inside Teams* (San Francisco: Jossey-Bass Publishers, 1994).
44. A.M. Townsend, S.M. DeMarie, & A.R. Hendrickson, "Virtual Teams: Technology and the Workplace of the Future," *Academy of Management Executive* 13, no. 3 (1998): 17–29.
45. R. Katz, "The Effects of Group Longevity on Project Communication and Performance," *Administrative Science Quarterly* 27 (1982): 245–282.
46. D. Mankin, S.G. Cohen, & T.K. Bikson, *Teams and Technology: Fulfilling the Promise of the New Organization* (Boston: Harvard Business School Press, 1996).
47. Ron Richardson, "Toronto Airport People Mover Gets Ready to Roll," *Design Engineering,* June 2005, 16–17.
48. L. Holpp & H.P. Phillips, "When Is a Team Its Own Worst Enemy?" *Training,* 1 September 1995, 71.
49. S. Asche, "Opinions and Social Pressure," *Scientific America* 193 (1995): 31–35.
50. S.G. Cohen, G.E. Ledford, & G.M. Spreitzer, "A Predictive Model of Self-Managing Work Team Effectiveness," *Human Relations* 49, no. 5 (1996): 643–676.
51. L. Clarke, "Changing Work Systems, Changing Social Relations," *Relations Industrielles* 52, no. 4 (1997): 839–862.
52. K. Bettenhausen & J.K. Murnighan, "The Emergence of Norms in Competitive Decision-Making Groups," *Administrative Science Quarterly* 30 (1985): 350–372.
53. M.E. Shaw, *Group Dynamics* (New York: McGraw-Hill, 1981).
54. J.R. Katzenback & D.K. Smith, *The Wisdom of Teams* (Boston: Harvard Business School Press, 1993).
55. S.E. Jackson, "The Consequences of Diversity in Multidisciplinary Work Teams," in *Handbook of Work Group Psychology,* ed. Michael A. West (Chichester, England: Wiley, 1996).
56. A.M. Isen & R.A. Baron, "Positive Affect as a Factor in Organizational Behavior," in *Research in Organizational Behavior* 13, eds. L.L. Cummings & B.M. Staw (Greenwich, CT: JAI Press, 1991), 1–53.
57. C.R. Evans & K.L. Dion, "Group Cohesion and Performance: A Meta-Analysis," *Small Group Research* 22, no. 2 (1991): 175–186.
58. R. Stankiewicsz, "The Effectiveness of Research Groups in Six Countries," in *Scientific Productivity,* ed. F.M. Andrews (Cambridge: Cambridge University Press, 1979), 191–221.
59. F. Rees, *Teamwork from Start to Finish* (San Francisco: Jossey-Bass, 1997).
60. S.M. Gully, D.S. Devine, & D.J. Whitney, "A Meta-Analysis of Cohesion and Performance: Effects of Level of Analysis and Task Interdependence," *Small Group Research* 26, no. 4 (1995): 497–520.
61. S.M. Gully, D.S. Devine, & D.J. Whitney, "A Meta-analysis of Cohesion and Performance: Effects of Level of Analysis and Task Interdependence," *Small Group Research* 26, no. 4 (1995): 497–520.
62. F. Tschan & M.V. Cranach, "Group Task Structure, Processes and Outcomes," in *Handbook of Work Group Psychology,* ed. Michael A. West (Chichester, England: Wiley, 1996).
63. D.E. Yeatts & C. Hyten, *High Performance Self-Managed Teams* (Thousand Oaks, CA: Sage Publications, 1998).
64. Ibid.
65. D.S. Kezsbom, "Re-Opening Pandora's Box: Sources of Project Team Conflict in the '90s," *Industrial Engineering* 24, no. 5 (1992): 54–59.
66. A.C. Amason, W.A. Hochwarter, & K.R. Thompson, "Conflict: An Important Dimension in Successful Management Teams," *Organizational Dynamics* 24 (1995): 20.
67. A.C. Amason, "Distinguishing the Effects of Functional and Dysfunctional Conflict on Strategic Decision Making: Resolving a Paradox for Top Management Teams," *Academy of Management Journal* 39, no. 1 (1996): 123–148.
68. K.M. Eisenhardt, J.L. Kahwajy, & L.J. Bourgeois, "How Management Teams Can Have a Good Fight," *Harvard Business Review,* July–August 1997, 77–85.
69. Ibid.
70. C. Nemeth & P. Owens, "Making Work Groups More Effective: The Value of Minority Dissent," in *Handbook of Work Group Psychology*, ed. Michael A. West (Chichester, England: Wiley, 1996).
71. J.M. Levin & R.L. Moreland, "Progress in Small Group Research," *Annual Review of Psychology* 9 (1990): 72–78; S.E. Jackson, "Team Composition in Organizational Settings: Issues in Managing a Diverse Work Force," in *Group Processes and Productivity*, eds. S. Worchel, W. Wood, & J. Simpson (Beverly Hills, CA: Sage, 1992).
72. K.M. Eisenhardt, J.L. Kahwajy, & L. Bourgeois, III, "How Management Teams Can Have a Good Fight," *Harvard Business Review* 75, no. 4 (July–August 1997): 77–87.
73. B.W. Tuckman, "Development Sequence in Small Groups," *Psychological Bulletin* 63, no. 6 (1965): 384–399.
74. S.E. Gross, *Compensation for Teams* (New York: American Management Association, 1995).

75. J.F. McGrew, J.G. Bilotta, & J.M. Deeney, "Software Team Formation and Decay: Extending the Standard Model for Small Groups," *Small Group Research* 30, no. 2 (1999): 209–234.
76. J.F. McGrew, J.G. Bilotta, & J.M. Deeney, "Software Team Formation and Decay: Extending the Standard Model for Small Groups," *Small Group Research* 30, no. 2 (1999): 209–234.
77. J. Case, "What the Experts Forgot to Mention: Management Teams Create New Difficulties, but Succeed for XEL Communication," *Inc.*, 1 September 1993, 66.
78. J.R. Hackman, "The Psychology of Self-Management in Organizations," in *Psychology and Work: Productivity, Change, and Employment,* eds. M.S. Pallak, & R. Perloff (Washington DC: American Psychological Association, 85–136).
79. O. Leary-Kelly, J.J. Martocchio, & D.D. Frink, "A Review of the Influence of Group Goals on Group Performance," *Academy of Management Journal* 37, no. 5 (1994): 1285–1301.
80. Nucor Homepage, "The Nucor Story," [Online] available at www.nucor.com/story.htm, 10 May 1999.
81. A. Zander, "The Origins and Consequences of Group Goals," in *Retrospections on Social Psychology,* ed. L. Festinger (New York: Oxford University Press, 1980), 205–235.
82. M. Erez & A. Somech, "Is Group Productivity Loss the Rule or the Exception? Effects of Culture and Group-Based Motivation," *Academy of Management Journal* 39, no. 6 (1996): 1513–1537.
83. S. Sherman, "Stretch Goals: The Dark Side of Asking for Miracles," *Fortune,* 13 November 1995.
84. B. Nardelli, P. Sellers, & J. Schlosser, "It's His Home Depot Now After Nearly Four Years at the Helm, Ex-GE Guy Bob Nardelli Tells Us How He's Finally Getting Results," *Fortune*, 20 September 2004, 115.
85. K.R. Thompson, W.A. Hochwarter, & N.J. Mathys, "Stretch Targets: What Makes Them Effective?" *Academy of Management Executive* 11, no. 3 (1997): 48–60.
86. S. Sherman, "Stretch Goals: The Dark Side of Asking for Miracles," *Fortune,* 13 November 1995.
87. S. Shellenbarger, "Are Saner Workloads the Unexpected Key to More Productivity?" *The Wall Street Journal,* 10 March 1999, B1.
88. C. Ashton, "KI Pembroke Succeeds Through Teamwork, Empowerment and Rewards," *Human Resource Management International Digest* 8, no. 7.
89. B. Dumaine, "The Trouble with Teams," *Fortune,* 5 September 1994, 86–92.
90. G.A. Neuman, S.H. Wagner, & N.D. Christiansen, "The Relationship Between Work-Team Personality Composition and the Job Performance of Teams," *Group & Organization Management* 24, no. 1 (1999): 28–45.
91. M.A. Campion, G.J. Medsker, & A.C. Higgs, "Relations Between Work Group Characteristics and Effectiveness: Implications for Designing Effective Work Groups," *Personnel Psychology* 46, no. 4 (1993): 823–850.
92. B.L. Kirkman & D.L. Shapiro, "The Impact of Cultural Values on Employee Resistance to Teams: Toward a Model of Globalized Self-Managing Work Team Effectiveness," *Academy of Management Review* 22, no. 3 (1997): 730–757.
93. C. Fishman, "Engines of Democracy: The General Electric Plant in Durham, North Carolina Builds Some of the World's Most Powerful Jet Engines. But the Plant's Real Power Lies in the Lessons That It Teaches about the Future of Work and about Workplace Democracy," *Fast Company,* 1 October 1999, 174.
94. Carol Stephenson, "Leveraging Diversity to Maximum Advantage" *Ivey Business Journal Online*, September–October 2004, A1.
95. L. Clarke, "Changing Work Systems, Changing Social Relations," *Relations Industrielles* 52, no. 4 (1997): 839–862.
96. M.A. Verespej, "Super Sack," *Industry Week,* 16 October 1995, 53.
97. R.S. Wellins, W.C. Byham, & G.R. Dixon, *Inside Teams* (San Francisco: Jossey-Bass Publishers, 1994).
98. C. Joinson, "Teams at Work," *HRMagazine,* 1 May 1999, 30.
99. K. Mollica, "Stay Above the Fray: Protect Your Time—and Your Sanity—by Coaching Employees to Deal with Interpersonal Conflicts on Their Own," *HR Magazine*, April 2005, 111.
100. R.S. Wellins, W.C. Byham, & G.R. Dixon, *Inside Teams* (San Francisco: Jossey-Bass Publishers, 1994).
101. S. Caudron, "Tie Individual Pay to Team Success," *Personnel Journal* 73, no. 10 (October 1994): 40.
102. Ibid.
103. S.E. Gross, *Compensation for Teams* (New York: American Management Association, 1995).
104. R.S. Wellins, W.C. Byham, & G.R. Dixon, *Inside Teams* (San Francisco: Jossey-Bass Publishers, 1994).
105. J.R. Schuster & P.K. Zingheim, *The New Pay: Linking Employee and Organizational Performance* (New York: Lexington Books, 1992).
106. R.E. Yates, "Molding a New Future for Manufacturer, Keys Are Planning, People—and Plastics," *Chicago Tribune,* 2 January 1994.
107. S.G. Cohen & D.E. Bailey, "What Makes Teams Work: Group Effectiveness Research from the Shop Floor to the Executive Suite," *Journal of Management* 23, no. 3 (1997): 239–290.
108. "How NCR Uses Compensation to Support Teams," *ACA Journal* 5, no. 4 (Winter 1996): 74–75.
109. J.H. Sheridan, "'Yes' to Team Incentives," *Industry Week,* 4 March 1996, 63.
110. "Cessna Skyhawk," Learn to Fly.com [online] available http://learntofly.com/howto/skyhawk.chtml, 29 May 2003; T. Greenwood, M. Bradford, & B. Greene, "Becoming a Lean Enterprise: A Tale of Two Firms," *Strategic Finance*, 1 November 2002, 32; B. Milligan, "Cessna Uses Baldrige Process to Identify Best Suppliers," *Purchasing*, 6 April 2000, 75; J. Morgan, "Cessna Charts a Supply Chain Flight Strategy," *Purchasing*, 7 September 2000, 42; J. Morgan, "Cross-Functional Buying: Why Teams Are Hot," *Purchasing*, 5 April 2001, 27; J. Morgan, "Cessna Aims to Drive SCM to Its Very Core: Here Are 21 Steps and Tools It's Using to Make This Happen," *Purchasing*, 6 June 2002, 31; P. Siekman, "Cessna Tackles Lean Manufacturing," *Fortune*, 1 May 2000, I222 B+; P. Siekman, "The Snap-Together Business Jet; Bombardier's New Recipe: A Dozen Big Pieces, Four Days to Assemble Them, And It's Ready to Fly," *Fortune*, 21 January 2002, 104A.
111. J. George, "Extrinsic and Intrinsic Origins of Perceived Social Loafing in Organizations," *Academy of Management Journal* 35 (1992): 191–202; R.E. Kidwell, Jr. & N. Bennett, "Employee Propensity to Withhold Effort: A Conceptual Model to Intersect Three Avenues Research," *Academy of Management Review* 18, no. 3 (1993): 429–456; P.W. Mulvey, J.F. Veiga, & P.M. Elsass, "When Teammates Raise a

White Flag," *Academy of Management Executive* 10, no. 1 (1996): 40–49.
112. "AT&T Universal Card Services," *Business America* 113, no. 22 (1992): 12–13; S.E. Gross, *Compensation for Teams* (New York: American Management Association, 1995); P.A. Murphy, "It's No Longer Just Teleservices," *Credit Card Management* 11, no. 1 (1998): 115–119.
113. Michael A. West, ed., *Handbook of Work Group Psychology* (Chichester, England: Wiley, 1996).

Chapter 13

1. "BHP Billiton Diamonds Inc.—EKATI Diamond Mine," [Online] available at www.ainc-inac.gc.ca/ps/nap/diamin/ekat/eka_e.html, 23 January 2006; "Discovery," [Online] available at http://ekati.bhpbilliton.com/docs/Discovery.pdf, 23 January 2006; "Diamond Exploration Picks Up Steam in 1997," *The Northern Miner*, 5–11 January 1998, 6; Alison Campbell and Kurtis Kitagawa, "Building Essential Skills in the Workplace: Shaping Performance at BHP Billiton Diamonds Inc.," case study, Conference Board of Canada, 2005; Benjamin Fulford, "Northern Ice," *Forbes*, 14 December, 1998, 104.
2. M. Barrier, "Hiring the Right People," *Nation's Business* 84, no. 6 (June 1996): 18.
3. Jill Vardy, "High-Tech Friend Worth $3,000 to Employees: Firm's Incentive," *Financial Post*, 13 January 2001, D1, D7.
4. G.A. Poole, "Silicon Valley Serves Up Worker Perks: Fine Dining, Fitness Rooms, Concerts Are Used to Keep Top Talent," *Houston Chronicle*, 14 February 1999, 8.
5. Geoffrey Downey, "Skills Shortage, Part Two, Imminent," *Computing Canada* 28, no. 11 (24 May 2002): 19.
6. Andrew Nikiforuk, "The Downside of Boom," *Canadian Business*, 22 May–4 June 2006, 25–26.
7. B. Schneider & N. Schmitt, *Staffing Organizations*, 2nd ed. (Glenview, IL: Scott, Foresman and Company, 1986).
8. M. Jones, "Four Trends to Reckon With," *HR Focus* 73 (1996): 22–24.
9. C. Joinson, "Moving at the Speed of Dell," *HRMagazine* 44, no. 4 (1 April 1999): 50.
10. D.M. Atwater, "Workforce Forecasting," *Human Resource Planning* 18, no. 4 (1995): 50.
11. Mark Evans, "Telus Offers Departure Packages to 11,000 Staff: Part of $300 Million in Cuts," *Financial Post*, 8 June 2002, FP1, FP8.
12. Mark Evans, "3,500 Jobs Go as Nortel Lowers Bar on Sales," *Financial Post*, 30 May 2002, FP1, FP10.
13. D.M. Atwater, "Workforce Forecasting," *Human Resource Planning* 18, no. 4 (1995): 50; D. Ward, "Workforce Demand Forecasting Techniques," *Human Resource Planning* 19, no. 1 (1996): 54.
14. C. Joinson, "Moving at the Speed of Dell," *HRMagazine* 44, no. 4 (1 April 1999): 50.
15. A.J. Walker, "The Analytical Element Is Important to an HRIS," *Personnel Administrator* 28 (1983): 33–35, 85.
16. L. Asinof, "Click & Shift: Workers Control Their Benefits On-Line," *The Wall Street Journal*, 21 November 1997, C1.
17. Robert Colman, "Flip the Switch," *CMA Management* 76, no. 6 (September 2002): 34–37.
18. L. Asinof, "Click & Shift: Workers Control Their Benefits On-Line," *The Wall Street Journal*, 21 November 1997, C1.
19. T. Jolls, "Technology Continues to Redefine HR's Role," *Personnel Journal* 76, no. 7 (July 1997): 46.
20. Ibid.
21. Ibid.
22. Vanessa Mariga, "Caretaker's Death Lands School Board Fine," *OH & S Canada*, April/May 2005, 13.
23. Alex Kondra & Richard Sparkman, "Modeling U.S. and Canadian Equality Programs," *Journal of Individual Employment Rights* 10, no. 2 (2003): 133–149.
24. Ibid.
25. E. Peirce, C.A. Smolinski, & B. Rosen, "Why Sexual Harassment Complaints Fall on Deaf Ears," *Academy of Management Executive* 12, no. 3 (1998): 41–54.
26. A. Levin, "Prudential Hit with 10 Discrimination Suits," *National Underwriter* 103, no. 4 (1999): 2.
27. W. Peirce, C.A. Smolinski, & B. Rosen, "Why Sexual Harassment Complaints Fall on Deaf Ears," *Academy of Management Executive* 12, no. 3 (1998): 41–54.
28. U.S. Equal Employment Opportunity Commission, "Facts about Sexual Harassment," [Online] available at www.eeoc.gov/facts/fs-sex.html, 23 May 1999.
29. Cheryl Cornacchia, "Female Boss Accused," *The Montreal Gazette*, 14 September 1998, F1; Howard Levitt, "Sexual Harassment Is Not Just Between Men and Women," *National Post*, 12 July 1999, D9.
30. Rick Ouston, "Customer's Conduct Ruled as Harassment," *Vancouver Sun*, 4 November 1996, B2.
31. W. Peirce, C.A. Smolinski, & B. Rosen, "Why Sexual Harassment Complaints Fall on Deaf Ears," *Academy of Management Executive* 12, no. 3 (1998): 41–54.
32. John Geddes & Stephanie Nolen, "Answering the Call," *Maclean's*, 8 June 1998, 28–31.
33. Scott Haggett, "Shell's Oilsands Bill Rockets to $7.3 Billion," *CanWest News*, 10 August 2005, 1; James Stevenson, "Shell Canada Warns of Higher Costs for Oilsands Project in Northern Alberta," *Canadian Press Newswire*, 24 October 2001.
34. "In Oil-Rich Fort McMurray, Service Industry Jobs Go Begging," *Financial Post*, 1 June 2000, C6.
35. Andrew Nikiforuk, "The Downside of Boom'" *Canadian Business*, 22 May–4 June 2006, 25–26.
36. Virginia Galt, "Keeping Key Workers a Tougher Task," *Globe and Mail*, 25 October 2005.
37. P. Nakache, "Cisco's Recruiting Edge Find 'Em, Lure 'Em, Keep 'Em Happy: Devising New Ways to Steal Top Talent from Competitors Has Given This Silicon Valley Standout an Important Advantage," *Fortune*, 29 September 1997, 275.
38. R.D. Gatewood & H.S. Field, *Human Resource Selection* (Fort Worth, TX: Dryden Press, 1998).
39. Ibid.
40. *The Worklife Report* 14, no. 2 (2002): 13.
41. J.A. Breaugh, *Recruitment: Science and Practice* (Boston: PWS-Kent, 1992).
42. A. Campbell, "Baxter Healthcare Gets to the Root of the Issue," *HR Focus* 75, no. 8 (1998): S9.
43. Andrew Allentuck, "Room at the Top," *Canadian Grocer*, November 2003, 26.
44. P.R. Chowdhury, "Human Resources: Beyond Downsizing, Growing the TCM Manager," *Business Today*, 7 January 1999, 172.
45. P. Nakache, "Cisco's Recruiting Edge Find 'Em, Lure 'Em, Keep 'Em Happy: Devising New Ways to Steal Top Talent from Competitors Has Given This

Silicon Valley Standout an Important Advantage," *Fortune*, 29 September 1997, 275.

46. "Life on the Web for Matters of Life, Liberty, and the Pursuit of a Nicer Job, There's Help on the Internet," *Fortune*, Special Issue, Technology Buyer's Guide (Winter 1999).
47. L.J.S. Vohra, "Online Recruiting Fills Positions," *Denver Business Journal*, 9 August 1996, 27A.
48. J. King, "Who's in the Online Pool?" *Computerworld*, 10 February 1997, 24; L.J.S. Vohra, "Online Recruiting Fills Positions," *Denver Business Journal*, 9 August 1996, 27A.
49. "Research Demonstrates the Success of Internet Recruiting," *HR Focus*, April 2003, 7.
50. "New .jobs Suffix Approved for Worldwide Recruiting/Hiring," *Human Resource Department Management Report*, May 2005, 9.
51. D. Fenn, "Hiring: Searching for the Chosen Few," *Inc.*, March 1996, 96.
52. J.S. Pouliot, "Topics to Avoid with Applicants," *Nation's Business* 80, no. 7 (1992): 57.
53. K. Maher, "Career Journal: The Jungle," *The Wall Street Journal*, 6 May 2003, B8.
54. J. Tamen, "Job Applicants' Résumés Are Often Riddled with Misinformation," *South Floridan Sun-Sentinel*, 24 February 2003.
55. S. Adler, "Verifying a Job Candidate's Background: The State of Practice in a Vital Human Resources Activity," *Review of Business* 15, no. 2 (1993/1994): 3–8.
56. Jonathan Finer, "A Résumé Full of Lies," *Far Eastern Economic Review* 165, no. 20 (23 May 2002): 55; Robin Raizel, "He Likes to Watch: Applying for a Job?" *Canadian Business* 74, no. 16 (3 September 2002): 38–41.
57. Kyle Mamoch, "Simulating Business," *Profit*, November 2003, 83–84.
58. J. Hunter, "Cognitive Ability, Cognitive Aptitudes, Job Knowledge, and Job Performance," *Journal of Vocational Behavior* 29 (1986): 340–362.
59. "Canada's Spy Agency Steps Up Recruitment," *Expositor*, 28 October 2002, A6; G. Dean, "The Bottom Line: Effect Size," in *The Write Stuff: Evaluations of Graphology—The Study of Handwriting Analysis*, ed. B. Beyerstein & D. Beyerstein (Buffalo, NY: Prometheus Books, 1992); K. Dunham, "Career Journal: The Jungle, Seeing the Future," *The Wall Street Journal*, 15 May 2001, B12; J. Kurtz, & W. Wells, "The Employee Polygraph Protection Act: The End of Lie Detector Use in Employment Decisions?" *Journal of Small Business Management* 27, no. 4 (1989): 76–80; B. Leonard, "Reading Employees," *HR Magazine*, April 1999, 67; S. Lilienfeld, J. Wood, & H. Garb, "The Scientific Status of Projective Techniques," *Psychological Science in the Public Interest* 1 (2000): 27–66; E. Neter & G. Ben-Shakhar, "The Predictive Validity of Graphological Inferences: A Meta-Analytic Approach," *Personality and Individual Differences* 10 (1989): 737–745.
60. Victor M. Catano, Steven F. Cronshaw, Willi H. Wiesner, Rick D. Hackett, & Laura L. Methot, *Recruitment and Selection in Canada* (Toronto: ITP Nelson, 1997).
61. J.R. Glennon, L.E. Albright, & W.A. Owens, *A Catalog of Life History Items* (Greensboro, NC: The Richardson Foundation, 1966).
62. Victor M. Catano, Steven F. Cronshaw, Willi H. Wiesner, Rick D. Hackett, & Laura L. Methot, *Recruitment and Selection in Canada* (Toronto: ITP Nelson, 1997); R.D. Gatewood & H.S. Field, *Human Resource Selection* (Fort Worth, TX: Dryden Press, 1998).
63. J.M. Digman, "Personality Structure: Emergence of the Five-Factor Model," *Annual Review of Psychology* 41 (1990): 417–440; M.R. Barrick & M.K. Mount, "The Big Five Personality Dimensions and Job Performance: A Meta-Analysis," *Personnel Psychology* 44 (1991): 1–26.
64. F.L. Schmidt & J.E. Hunter, "The Validity and Utility of Selection Methods in Personnel Psychology: Practical and Theoretical Implications of 85 Years of Research Findings," *Psychological Bulletin* 124, no. 2 (1998): 262–274.
65. M.S. Taylor & J.A. Sniezek, "The College Recruitment Interview: Topical Content and Applicant Reactions," *Journal of Occupational Psychology* 57 (1984): 157–168.
66. M.A. Campion, D.K. Palmer, & J.E. Campion, "A Review of Structure in the Selection Interview," *Personnel Psychology* 50, no. 3 (1997): 655–702.
67. D. Stafford, "Workers Train, Companies Gain: Harmon Industries, Sprint, Others Make a Big Commitment," *Kansas City Star*, 16 February 1999, D1.
68. K. Ellis, "Individual Development Plans," *Training*, December 2004, 20–24; D. Stafford, "Workers Train, Companies Gain: Harmon Industries, Sprint, Others Make a Big Commitment," *Kansas City Star*, 16 February 1999, D1.
69. S. Livingston, T.W. Gerdel, M. Hill, B. Yerak, C. Melvin, & B. Lubinger, "Ohio's Strongest Companies All Agree That Training Is Vital to Their Success," *Plain Dealer*, 21 May 1997, 30S; Harvey Schachter, "Leading-Edge Learning," *Canadian Banker* 107, no. 2 (Second Quarter 2002): 16–27.
70. G. Kesler, "Why the Leadership Bench Never Gets Deeper: Ten Insights about Executive Talent Development," *Human Resource Planning*, 1 January 2002, 32.
71. "Canadian Training Investments Lags Competitors," *CMA Management*, August/September 2005, 9.
72. J.D. Moore & R.L. Gehrig, "Rehearsing for a Robbery," *Security Management* 35, no. 8 (1991): 51.
73. Susanne Baillie-Ruder, "Sweet Devotion," *Profit*, December 2004, 44–48.
74. D.L. Kirkpatrick, "Four Steps to Measuring Training Effectiveness," *Personnel Administrator* 28 (1983): 19–25.
75. J. Stack, "The Curse of the Annual Performance Review," *Inc.*, 1 March 1997, 39.
76. Terry H. Wagar and Lynn Langrock, "Performance Appraisal and Compensation in Small Firms," *Canadian HR Reporter*, 12 July 2004, 10.
77. T.D. Schellhardt, "Annual Agony: It's Time to Evaluate Your Work, and All Involved Are Groaning—Employees Dislike Reviews, Even If Favorable; Bosses Wonder How to Do Them, Some Prefer Frequent Talks," *The Wall Street Journal*, 19 November 1996, A1.
78. Ian Gray, "Fear and Loathing Behind Closed Doors," *Financial Post* 91, no. 15 (12/14 April 1997): 26.
79. J. Yankovic, "Are the Reviews In?" *Pittsburgh Business Times* 16 (28 October 1996): 7.
80. T.D. Schellhardt, "Annual Agony: It's Time to Evaluate Your Work, and All Involved Are Groaning—Employees Dislike Reviews, Even If Favorable; Bosses Wonder How to Do Them, Some Prefer Frequent Talks," *The Wall Street Journal*, 19 November 1996, A1.
81. U.J. Wiersma & G.P. Latham, "The Practicality of Behavioral Observation Scales, Behavioral Expectation Scales, and Trait Scales," *Personnel Psychology* 39 (1986): 619–628; U.J. Wiersma, P.T. Van Den Berg, & G.P. Latham, "Dutch Reactions to Behavioral Observation,

Behavioral Expectation, and Trait Scales," *Group & Organization Management* 20 (1995): 297–309.
82. Terry H. Wagar and Lynn Langrock, "Performance Appraisal and Compensation in Small Firms," *Canadian HR Reporter*, 12 July 2004, 10.
83. D.J. Woehr & A.I. Huffcutt, "Rater Training for Performance Appraisal: A Quantitative Review," *Journal of Occupational and Organizational Psychology* 67, no. 3 (1994): 189–205.
84. J. Stack, "The Curse of the Annual Performance Review," *Inc.*, 1 March 1997, 39.
85. B.O'Reilly, "360-Degree Feedback Can Change Your Life," *Fortune*, 17 October 1994, 93.
86. Paddy Kamen, "The Way That You Use It," *CMA Management*, April 2003, 10–12.
87. D.A. Waldman, L.E. Atwater, & D. Antonioni, "Has 360 Feedback Gone Amok?" *Academy of Management Executive* 12, no. 2 (1998): 86–94.
88. Stephane Brutus & Mehrdad Derayeh, "Multisource Assessment Programs in Organizations: An Insider's Perspective," *Human Resource Development Quarterly* 13, no. 2 (Summer 2002): 187–202.
89. H.H. Meyer, "A Solution to the Performance Appraisal Feedback Enigma," *Academy of Management Executive* 5, no. 1 (1991): 68–76.
90. T.D. Schellhardt, "Annual Agony: It's Time to Evaluate Your Work, and All Involved Are Groaning—Employees Dislike Reviews, Even If Favorable; Bosses Wonder How to Do Them, Some Prefer Frequent Talks," *The Wall Street Journal*, 19 November 1996, A1.
91. G.C. Thornton, "Psychometric Properties of Self-Appraisals of Job Performance," *Personnel Psychology* 33 (1980): 263–271.
92. H.H. Meyer, "A Solution to the Performance Appraisal Feedback Enigma," *Academy of Management Executive* 5, no. 1 (1991): 68–76.
93. Deborah Tetley, "Fort McMurray Desperate for Housing, Workers," *National Post*, 26 October 2005, WK3.
94. G.T. Milkovich & J.M. Newman, *Compensation*, 4th ed. (Homewood, IL: Irwin, 1993).
95. M.L. Williams & G.F. Dreher, "Compensation System Attributes and Applicant Pool Characteristics," *Academy of Management Journal* 35, no. 3 (1992): 571–595.
96. Kathryn May, "Federal Auditors Vow to Make Businesses Pay unless Wage Fight Settled: Government Salaries Far below Those in the Private Sector," *Ottawa Citizen*, 30 April 1998, C4.
97. "Sun, Hangovers Keep Teenagers from Summer Jobs," *Daily Commercial News*, 28 September 1998, B8.
98. PRT Frontier Resource Management, "Recruiting Information" [Online] available at www.prtgroup.com/locations/ft/planting.html, 3 December 2005.
99. James Ott, "Trauma in the Down Cycle," *Aviation Week and Space Technology*, 28 February 2005, 46.
100. Perry Phillips, "ESOPs Offer IT Staff a Piece of the Ownership Pie," *Computing Canada* 24, no. 6 (16 March 1998): 34.
101. James Ott, "Trauma in the Down Cycle," *Aviation Week and Space Technology*, 28 February 2005, 46.
102. M. Bloom, "The Performance Effects of Pay Dispersion on Individuals and Organizations," *Academy of Management Journal* 42, no. 1 (1999): 25–40.
103. W. Grossman & R.E. Hoskisson, "CEO Pay at the Crossroads of Wall Street and Main: Toward the Strategic Design of Executive Compensation," *Academy of Management Executive* 12, no. 1 (1998): 43–57.
104. M. Bloom, "The Performance Effects of Pay Dispersion on Individuals and Organizations," *Academy of Management Journal* 42, no. 1 (1999): 25–40.
105. J.S. Rosenbloom, "The Environment of Employee Benefit Plans," in *The Handbook of Employee Benefits*, ed. J.S. Rosenbloom (Chicago: Irwin, 1996), 3–13.
106. KPMG Competitive Alternatives G7-2004 Edition, [online] 5 December 2005, www.investincanada.gc.ca/en/882/Facts_and_Figures.html.
107. A.E. Barber, R.B. Dunham, & R.A. Formisano, "The Impact of Flexible Benefits on Employee Satisfaction: A Field Study," *Personnel Psychology* 45 (1992): 55–75; B. Heshizer, "The Impact of Flexible Benefits on Job Satisfaction and Turnover Intentions," *Benefits Quarterly* 4 (1994): 84–90; D.M. Cable & T.A. Judge, "Pay Preferences and Job Search Decisions: A Person-Organization Fit Perspective," *Personnel Psychology* 47 (1994): 317–348.
108. B.T. Beam & J.J. McFadden, *Employee Benefits* (Chicago: Dearborn Financial Publishing, 1996).
109. Gloria Gonzalez, "Flexible Benefit Plans Grow Popular Among Canadian Employers," *Business Insurance*, 15 August 2005, 11–14.
110. K. Labich & E.M. Davies, "How to Fire People and Still Sleep at Night," *Fortune*, 10 June 1996, 64.
111. Ibid.
112. P. Michal-Johnson, *Saying Good-Bye: A Manager's Guide to Employee Dismissal* (Glenview, IL: Scott, Foresman and Company, 1985).
113. M. Bordwin, "Employment Law: Beware of Time Bombs and Shark-Infested Waters," *HR Focus*, 1 April 1995, 19.
114. S. Gruner, "Hot Tip," *Inc.*, December 1996, 121.
115. J.R. Morris, W.F. Cascio, & C.E. Young, "Downsizing after All These Years: Questions and Answers about Who Did It, How Many Did It, and Who Benefited from It," *Organizational Dynamics* 27, no. 3 (1999): 78–87.
116. "Los Angeles Times. Layoffs Rise as Firms Find It's Profitable; 523,000 Are Fired as of Oct., 200,000 More than in 1997; Pink Slips in Golden Times; Study Shows Strategy May Ultimately Lower Earnings, Stock Prices," *Baltimore Sun*, 30 November 1998, 5C.
117. J.R. Morris, W.F. Cascio, & C.E. Young, "Down-sizing after All These Years: Questions and Answers about Who Did It, How Many Did It, and Who Benefited from It," *Organizational Dynamics* 27, no. 3 (1999): 78–87.
118. Rick Maurer, "Stop! Downsizing Doesn't Work," *The Canadian Manager* 24, no. 1 (Spring 1999): 11–13.
119. K.E. Mishra, G.M. Spreitzer, & A.K. Mishra, "Preserving Employee Morale during Downsizing," *Sloan Management Review* 39, no. 2 (1998): 83–95.
120. David Brown, "Take My Workers Please," *Canadian HR Reporter* 15, no. 3 (11 February 2002): 3.
121. R. Mullins, "Early Retirement Programs Can End Up Being Costly," *Business Journal-Milwaukee*, 20 January 1996, Section 1, p. 25.
122. D.R. Dalton, W.D. Todor, & D.M. Krackhardt, "Turnover Overstated: The Functional Taxonomy," *Academy of Management Review* 7 (1982): 117–123.
123. J.R. Hollenbeck & C.R. Williams, "Turnover Functionality versus Turnover Frequency: A Note on Work Attitudes

and Organizational Effectiveness," *Journal of Applied Psychology* 71 (1986): 606–611.

124. C.R. Williams, "Reward Contingency, Unemployment, and Functional Turnover," *Human Resource Management Review* 9, no. 4 (Winter 1999): 549–576.
125. "O'Leary Community Hospital Nursing Staff List Concerns," *Journal Pioneer*, 3 November 2003, 3.
126. "BHP Billiton Diamonds Inc.—EKATI Diamond Mine," [Online] available at www.ainc-inac.gc.ca/ps/nap/PDF/ekat/ekadia_e.pdf, 23 January 2006; "BHP Billiton Diamonds Inc.—EKATI Diamond Mine," [Online] available at www.ainc-inac.gc.ca/ps/nap/diamin/ekat/eka_e.html, 23 January 2006; Alison Campbell and Kurtis Kitagawa, "Building Essential Skills in the Workplace: Shaping Performance at BHP Billiton Diamonds Inc.," case study, Conference Board of Canada, 2005; Benjamin Fulford, "Northern Ice," *Forbes*, 14 December 1998, 104; Lisa Gregoire, "Diamond Miners Polish Skills at Company's Expense," *Edmonton Journal*, 18 September 2002; Uyen Vu, "Northern Mine Develops Essential Skills in its Workforce," *Canadian HR Reporter*, 18 July 2005, 8–9.

Chapter 14

1. S. Carter, "Toyota Comes Out on Top Again in Quality Study," *USA Today*, 19 May 2005, B3; E. Eldridge, "Costly Doesn't Mean Reliable; 'Consumer Reports' Hits Some Pricey Rides," *USA Today*, 9 November 2004, B4; E. Eldridge, "Buyers Rate Hyundai as High-Quality; Value, Reliability Put It Second Only to Lexus," *USA Today*, 4 October 2004, B1; J. Fahey, "Speed Kills; The Carmaker Wants to Scale Up—and Go Upscale," *Forbes*, 31 March 2003, 68; B. Fulford & T. Jones, "Up from Lemons: An Enlarged Hyundai Motor Is Readying for a Comeback—If It Can Overcome Its Image. Easier Said Than Done," *Forbes*, 14 June 1999, 122; M. Ihlwan, "Hyundai: Crowding into the Fast Lane," *Business Week*, 20 June 2005, 26; M. Ihlwan, L. Armstrong, & M. Eidam, "Hyundai: Kissing Clunkers Goodbye; A Five-Year Focus on Quality Has Sent Customer Satisfaction Soaring," *Business Week*, 17 May 2004, 45; M. Ihlwan, L. Armstrong, & K. Kerwin, "Hyundai Gets Hot: Chairman Chung Has Boosted Quality and Design While Keeping Prices Low. And as Sales Soar, the Big Leagues Beckon," *Business Week*, 17 December 2001, 16; M. Ihlwan & C. Dawson, "Building a 'Camry Fighter': Can Hyundai Transform Itself into One of the World's Top Auto Makers?" *Business Week*, 6 September 2004, 62; D. Kiley, "Hyundai Pulls Off a Head-Spinning U-Turn; Its Once-Dismal Quality Rank Could Beat Toyota," *USA Today*, 28 April 2004, B01; D. Kirk, "Contract at Hyundai Raises Sights of Korean Workers," *New York Times*, 19 August 2003, 1; J. Muller & R. Meredith, "Last Laugh; How Hyundai's Carmaking Prowess Went from Punchline to Powerhouse—And Is Shaking Up the World's Auto Industry," *Forbes*, 18 April 2005, 98; J. Sapsford, S. Park, & N. Shirouzu, "Hyundai Steers for the Top—As Sales Surge, Quality Improves, Auto Maker Targets the Titans," *Wall Street Journal*, 29 April 2005, B2; N. Shirouzu & R. Brooks, "South Korea's Hyundai Motor Chooses Alabama Site for Firm's First U.S. Plant," *Wall Street Journal*, 2 April 2002, A8; E. Thornton, "Car Deal—Or Car Crash? Hyundai's Takeover of Kia Won't Cure Korea's Auto Industry," *Business Week*, 9 November 1998, 536; D. Welch, "Sorry, Detroit. The Garage Is Full; Demand May Slow as Rates Rise and Incentives Fall," *Business Week*, 6 December 2004, 40; C. Woddyard, "Hyundai, Kia Shift Gears to Overtake Competition," *USA Today*, 23 March 2005, B1.
2. T. Petzinger, Jr., "How a Ski Maker Recovered from a Potential Fatal Spill," *The Wall Street Journal Interactive Edition*, 3 October 1997.
3. W.M. Cox & R. Alm, *The Myths of Rich & Poor* (New York: Basic Books, 1999); R.L. Bartley, "The Seven Fat Years," *The Wall Street Journal*, 30 April 1992; S. Nasar & L. Smith, "Do We Live as Well as We Used To?" *Fortune*, 14 September 1987.
4. O. Suris, "Chrysler Leads Big Three in Efficiency of Car Factories, But All Trail Japanese," *The Wall Street Journal*, 30 May 1996.
5. J.B. White, "Wide Gap Exists Between GM, Rivals in Labor Productivity," *The Wall Street Journal*, 16 July 1998, A4.
6. Bureau of Labor Statistics, "Multifactor Productivity: Frequently Asked Questions," [Online] available at http://stats.bls.gov/mprfaq.htm, 7 March 1998.
7. "Multifactor Productivity," *The Daily*, Statistics Canada, 10 July 2003, [Online] available at www.statcan.ca/daily/english/030710/.
8. E. Peters, "Dawn of the Trouble-Free Automobile?" *Consumers' Research Magazine*, 1 January 1998.
9. American Society for Quality, "ASQ Glossary of Terms Search," [Online] available at www.asq.org/abtquality/glossary.cgi, 24 March 1998.
10. R.E. Markland, S.K. Vickery, & R.A. Davis, "Managing Quality" (Chapter 7), *Operations Management: Concepts in Manufacturing and Services* (Cincinnati, OH: South-Western College Publishing, 1998).
11. B. Weber, "Quicker Fixes: Big 3 Innovations Make 1997 Cars Easier to Repair," *Chicago Tribune*, 3 November 1996.
12. Lightsource.com, [Online] available at www.light-source.com/incandescent.html, 28 March 1998.
13. L.L. Berry & A. Parasuraman, *Marketing Services* (New York: Free Press, 1991).
14. S. McCartney, "A Service-Minded Manager Is Improving Newark Airport," *The Wall Street Journal Interactive Edition*, 9 June 1997.
15. Ibid.
16. American Society for Quality, "ANSI ASC Z-1 Committee on Quality Assurance Answers the Most Frequently Asked Questions about the ISO 9000 (ANSI/ASQ Q9000) Series," [Online] available at www.asq.org/standcert/iso.html, 29 March 1998.
17. R. Henkoff, "The Not New Seal of Quality (ISO 9000 Standard of Quality Management)," *Fortune*, 28 June 1993.
18. Ibid.
19. National Quality Institute, *Canada Awards for Excellence*, [Online] available at www.nqi.ca.
20. J.W. Dean, Jr. & D.E. Bowen, "Management Theory and Total Quality: Improving Research and Practice through Theory Development," *Academy of Management Review* 19 (1994): 392–418.
21. G. Baum, "The Dynamic 100 Cisco's CEO John Chambers: If You Can't Beat 'Em, Buy 'Em," *Forbes ASAP*, 23 February 1998.
22. R.L. Rose, "Kentucky Plant Workers Are Cranking Out Good Ideas," *The Wall Street Journal*, 13 August 1996.
23. R. Hallowell, L.A. Schlesinger, & J. Zornitsky, "Internal Service Quality, Customer and Job Satisfaction: Linkages

and Implications for Management," *Human Resource Planning* 19 (1996): 20–31; J.L. Heskett, T.O. Jones, G.W. Loveman, W.E. Sasser, Jr., & L.A. Schlesinger, "Putting the Service-Profit Chain to Work," *Harvard Business Review,* March–April 1994, 164–174.

24. G. Brewer, "The Ultimate Guide to Winning Customers: The Customer Stops Here," *Sales & Marketing Management* 150 (March 1998): 30.
25. S. Hale, "The Customer Is Always Right—Usually—Some Are Just Annoying, but Others Deserve the Boot," *Orlando Sentinel,* 15 April 2002, 54.
26. T. Levitt, "Production-Line Approach to Service," *Harvard Business Review,* September–October 1972, 41–52; T. Levitt, "Industrialization of Service," *Harvard Business Review,* September–October 1976, 63–74.
27. L.L. Berry & A. Parasuraman, "Listening to the Customer—The Concept of a Service-Quality Information System," *Sloan Management Review* 38, no. 3 (Spring 1997): 65; C.W.L. Hart, J.L. Heskett, & W.E. Sasser, Jr., "The Profitable Art of Service Recovery," *Harvard Business Review*, July–August 1990, 148–156.
28. B. Gladstone, "Trusting in the Power of People," *Globe and Mail,* 21 October 1997.
29. D.E. Bowen & E.E. Lawler, III, "The Empowerment of Service Workers: What, Why, How, and When," *Sloan Management Review* 33 (Spring 1992): 31–39; D.E. Bowen & E.E. Lawler, III, "Empowering Service Employees," *Sloan Management Review* 36 (Summer 1995): 73–84.
30. D.E. Bowen & E.E. Lawler, III, "The Empowerment of Service Workers: What, Why, How, and When," *Sloan Management Review* 33 (Spring 1992): 31–39.
31. R. Henkoff, "Finding Training and Keeping the Best Service Workers," *Fortune,* 3 October 1994.
32. A. Serwer, L. Smith, & P. de Llosa, "Michael Dell Rocks," *Fortune,* 11 May 1998, 58.
33. J. Leib, "Wilkerson's Breath of Fresh Air: Pneumatics Firm Re-Engineers Its Production Ways," *Denver Post,* 9 June 1997, E1.
34. G.V. Frazier & M.T. Spiggs, "Achieving Competitive Advantage through Group Technology," *Business Horizons* 39 (1996): 83–88.
35. "Bottling Line Catapults Beermaker Beyond Microbrewing," *Packaging Digest,* 1 September 1995, 8.
36. J. Kunerth, "Manufacturing Finds Foothold: Companies Praise the Area's Diverse Labor Pool, But Some Smaller Firms Say Finding Financing Can Be Difficult," *Orlando Sentinel,* 23 September 1996, 14.
37. "Ford to Close Plant for 2 Weeks, Adjust Levels of Its Inventory," *The Wall Street Journal Interactive Edition,* 20 February 1998.
38. C. Marshall, "Linerboard: Market Recovery Will Continue; Price Hikes Predicted for 1998," *Pulp & Paper,* 1 January 1998, 13.
39. B. Alpert, "3Com Says Inventory Glut, Asian Slump Depress Profits," *Barrons,* 8 December 1997, 5.
40. G. Taninecz, "Best Practices & Performances, Part 2," *Industry Week,* 1 December 1997, 28.
41. F. Zappa, "The End of Paperwork? Electronic Commerce Promises to Save Billions of Dollars and Millions of Hours," *Nation's Restaurant News,* 3 November 1997, S10.
42. J.R. Henry, "Minimized Setup Will Make Your Packaging Line S.M.I.L.E.," *Packaging Technology & Engineering,* 1 February 1998, 24.
43. F. Brookman, "Managing Inventory (EDI)," *Women's Wear,* 19 September 1997, 20.
44. T. Minahan, "JIT: A Process with Many Faces," *Purchasing,* 4 September 1997, 42.
45. "Fully Automated System Achieves True JIT," *Modern Materials Handling,* 1 April 1998, DPI22.
46. T. Minahan, "JIT: A Process with Many Faces," *Purchasing,* 4 September 1997, 42.
47. Ibid.
48. C. Crowell, "Seeing the Big Picture through Software (Manufacturing Resource Planning Computer Programs)," *American Metal Market,* 22 July 1997, 12.
49. "Criteria for Performance Excellence," *Baldrige National Quality Program 2005*, [Online] available at www.quality.nist.gov/PDF_files/2003_Business_Criteria.pdf, 2 July 2005; S. Carter, "Toyota Comes Out on Top Again in Quality Study," *USA Today*, 19 May 2005, B3; E. Eldridge, "Costly Doesn't Mean Reliable; 'Consumer Reports' Hits Some Pricey Rides," *USA Today*, 9 November 2004, B4; E. Eldridge, "Buyers Rate Hyundai as High-Quality; Value, Reliability Put It Second Only to Lexus," *USA Today*, 4 October 2004, B1; J. Fahey, "Speed Kills; The Carmaker Wants to Scale Up—And Go Upscale," *Forbes*, 31 March 2003, 68; B. Fulford & T. Jones, "Up from Lemons: An Enlarged Hyundai Motor Is Readying for a Comeback—If It Can Overcome Its Image. Easier Said than Done," *Forbes*, 14 June 1999, 122; M. Ihlwan, "Hyundai: Crowding Into the Fast Lane," *Business Week*, 20 June 2005, 26; M. Ihlwan, L. Armstrong, & M. Eidam, "Hyundai: Kissing Clunkers Goodbye: A Five-Year Focus on Quality Has Sent Customer Satisfaction Soaring," *Business Week*, 17 May 2004, 45; M. Ihlwan, L. Armstrong, & K. Kerwin, "Hyundai Gets Hot: Chairman Chung Has Boosted Quality and Design While Keeping Prices Low. And as Sales Soar, the Big Leagues Beckon," *Business Week*, 17 December 2001, 16; M. Ihlwan & C. Dawson, "Building a 'Camry Fighter'; Can Hyundai Transform Itself into One of the World's Top Auto Makers?" *Business Week*, 6 September 2004, 62; D. Kiley, "Hyundai Pulls Off a Head-Spinning U-Turn; Its Once-Dismal Quality Rank Could Beat Toyota," *USA Today*, 28 April 2004, B01; D. Kirk, "Contract at Hyundai Raises Sights of Korean Workers," *New York Times*, 19 August 2003, 1; J. Muller & R. Meredith, "Last Laugh; How Hyundai's Carmaking Prowess Went from Punchline to Powerhouse—And Is Shaking Up the World's Auto Industry," *Forbes*, 18 April 2005, 98; J. Sapsford, S. Park, & N. Shirouzu, "Hyundai Steers for the Top—As Sales Surge, Quality Improves, Auto Maker Targets the Titans," *Wall Street Journal*, 29 April 2005, B2; N. Shirouzu & R. Brooks, "South Korea's Hyundai Motor Chooses Alabama Site for Firm's First U.S. Plant," *Wall Street Journal*, 2 April 2002, A8; E. Thornton, "Car Deal—Or Car Crash? Hyundai's Takeover of Kia Won't Cure Korea's Auto Industry," *Business Week*, 9 November 1998, 536; D. Welch, "Sorry, Detroit. The Garage Is Full; Demand May Slow as Rates Rise and Incentives Fall," *Business Week*, 6 December 2004, 40; C. Woddyard, "Hyundai, Kia Shift Gears to Overtake Competition," *USA Today*, 23 March 2005, B1.

50. M. Jordan, "Penney Blends Two Business Cultures," *The Wall Street Journal*, 5 April 2001, www.wsj.com.
51. E. Gehrman, "Factory Facts Show Heart, Soul of America," *Boston Herald*, 29 January 1998; E. Perkins, "Factory Tour Can Be Fun, Not to Mention Real Cheap," *Orlando Sentinel*, 1 February, 1998, L6; L. Singhania (Associated Press), "Breakfast for Battle Creek's New Cereal City," *Grand Rapids Press*, 24 May 1998, F2; C. Quintanilla, "Planning a Vacation? Give Some Thought to Spamtown USA," *The Wall Street Journal*, 30 April 1998, A1.

Chapter 15

1. "The Ups and Downs of Reform at Nortel," 12 January 2005, A14; Dave Ebner, "TSE Star Nortel Battered," *Globe and Mail*, 25 October 2000; Stephen Foerster, "After the Bubble Bursts," *Report on Business Magazine,* May 2001, 111; Charlie Gillis, "The Nortel Shipwreck," *Maclean's*, 10 May 2004, 28–29; Mark Heinzel, "Nortel to Restate Results Going Back to 2000," *Wall Street Journal*, 24 October 2003, B4; Ross Laver, "Nortel's Driving Force," *Maclean's,* 2 August 1999, 12–18; Jared Mitchell, "Top 1000," *Report on Business Magazine,* July 2000, 152–154; Anna Sharratt, "Plan Sponsors Join Nortel Class Action in U.S.," *Benefits Canada*, September 2002, 57.
2. J.P. Campbell & R.D. Pritchard, "Motivation Theory in Industrial and Organizational Psychology," *Handbook of Industrial and Organizational Psychology*, ed. M.D. Dunnette (Chicago: Rand McNally, 1976).
3. P. Thomas, "Waitress Makes the Difference in Bringing Deaf to Pittsburgh," *The Wall Street Journal Interactive Edition*, 2 March 1999.
4. J. Spencer, "Shirk Ethic: How to Fake a Hard Day at the Office—White-Collar Slackers Get Help from New Gadgets; The Faux 4 A.M. E-Mail," *The Wall Street Journal*, 15 May 2003, D1.
5. Katherine Macklem, "Canada's Top 100 Employers," *Maclean's*, 28 October 2002, 26–34.
6. K.A. Dolan, "When Money Isn't Enough," *Forbes*, 18 November 1996, 164–170.
7. E.A. Locke, "The Nature and Causes of Job Satisfaction," *Handbook of Industrial and Organizational Psychology*, ed. M.D. Dunnette (Chicago: Rand McNally, 1976).
8. A.H. Maslow, "A Theory of Human Motivation," *Psychological Review* 50 (1943): 370–396.
9. C.P. Alderfer, *Existence, Relatedness, and Growth: Human Needs in Organizational Settings* (New York: Free Press, 1972).
10. D.C. McClelland, "Toward a Theory of Motive Acquisition," *American Psychologist* 20 (1965): 321–333; D.C. McClelland & D.H. Burnham, "Power Is the Great Motivator," *Harvard Business Review* 54, no. 2 (1976): 100–110.
11. F. Herzberg, B. Mausner & B.B. Snyderman, *The Motivation to Work* (New York: Wiley, 1959); H.M. Weiss & R. Cropanzano, "Affective Events Theory: A Theoretical Discussion of the Structure, Causes and Consequences of Affective Experiences at Work," *Research in Organizational Behavior* 18 (1996): 1–74.
12. J.H. Turner, "Entrepreneurial Environments and the Emergence of Achievement Motivation in Adolescent Males," *Sociometry* 33 (1970): 147–165.
13. L.W. Porter, E.E. Lawler, III, & J.R. Hackman, *Behavior in Organizations* (New York: McGraw-Hill, 1975).
14. E.E. Lawler, III & L.W. Porter, "The Effect of Performance on Job Satisfaction," *Industrial Relations* 7 (1967): 20–28.
15. L.W. Porter, E.E. Lawler, III, & J.R. Hackman, *Behavior in Organizations* (New York: McGraw-Hill, 1975).
16. P. Kuitenbrouywer, "Daddy, I'm Almost a Millionaire," *Financial Post*, 21 April 2000, C1, C3.
17. L.W. Porter, E.E. Lawler, III, & J.R. Hackman, *Behavior in Organizations* (New York: McGraw-Hill, 1975).
18. D. Whitford, "A Human Place to Work," *Fortune,* 8 January 2001, 108.
19. C. Caggiano, "What Do Workers Want?" *Inc.,* November 1992, 101–104; "National Study of the Changing Workforce," Families and Work Institute, [Online] available at www.familiesandwork .org/summary/nscw.pdf, 31 May 2005.
20. L. Buchanan, "Managing One-to-One," *Inc.,* 1 October 2001, 82.
21. Ibid.
22. John Tompkins & Sarah Beech, "Do Benefits Attract and Retain Talent?" *Benefits Canada* 26, no. 10 (October 2002): 49–54.
23. Aon Consulting, "America@ Work: A Focus on Benefits and Compensation," [Online] available at www.aon.com/pdf/america/awork2.pdf, 12 June 1999.
24. D. Woodruff, "Salary Spread in Euroland May Force Firms to Compete More for Top Workers," *The Wall Street Journal*, 20 January 1999, B9B.
25. "Europe Company: How the Euro Is Affecting Executive Pay," *Country ViewsWire*, 8 April 2003.
26. C.T. Kulik & M.L. Ambrose, "Personal and Situational Determinants of Referent Choice," *Academy of Management Review* 17 (1992): 212–237.
27. J.S. Adams, "Toward an Understanding of Inequity," *Journal of Abnormal Social Psychology* 67 (1963): 422–436.
28. Zena Olijnyk, "Workers Steal Less When Paid More," *Financial Post Daily*, 15 April 1997, 25.
29. J. Greenberg, "Employee Theft as a Reaction to Underpayment Inequity: The Hidden Costs of Pay Cuts," *Journal of Applied Psychology* 75 (1990): 561–568.
30. R.A. Cosier & D.R. Dalton, "Equity Theory and Time: A Reformulation," *Academy of Management Review* 8 (1983): 311–319; M.R. Carrell & J.E. Dittrich, "Equity Theory: The Recent Literature, Methodological Considerations, and New Directions," *Academy of Management Review* 3 (1978): 202–209.
31. Drew Hasselback, "BC Chapters Employees Await Word on Union Request," *Financial Post*, 7 July 1999, C4.
32. Jack Keating, "Unhappy Kids Ripe for Union Cards," *The Province*, 21 August 1998, A2.
33. K. Aquino, R.W. Griffeth, D.G. Allen, & P.W. Hom, "Integrating Justice Constructs into the Turnover Process: A Test of a Referent Cognitions Model," *Academy of Management Journal* 40, no. 5 (1997): 1208–1227.
34. B. Orwall & K. Swisher, "Of Mouse and Men: As Web Riches Beckon, Disney Ranks Become a Poacher's Paradise—Media Giant Can't Compete in Giving Stock Options, and Isn't 'Freewheeling'—Eisner Flames the Techies," *The Wall Street Journal*, 9 June 1999, A1.
35. D. Gullapalli, "Take This Job and ... File It—Burdened by Extra Work Created by the Sarbanes-Oxley Act, CPAs Leave the Big Four for Better Life," *Wall Street Journal*, 4 May 2005, C1.
36. Virginia Galt, "Falling in Love (with Work) All Over Again," *Globe and Mail,* 23 November 2005, C1, C8.
37. R. Folger & M.A. Konovsky, "Effects of Procedural and Distributive Justice on Reactions to Pay Raise Decisions," *Academy of Management Journal* 32 (1989): 115–130.

38. E. Barret-Howard & T.R. Tyler, "Procedural Justice as a Criterion in Allocation Decisions," *Journal of Personality and Social Psychology* 50 (1986): 296–305; R. Folger & M.A. Konovsky, "Effect of Procedural and Distributive Justice on Reactions to Pay Raise Decisions," *Academy of Management Journal* 32 (1989): 115–130.
39. R. Folger & J. Greenberg, "Procedural Justice: An Interpretive Analysis of Personnel Systems," in *Research in Personnel and Human Resources Management*, Volume 3, eds. K. Rowland & G. Ferris (Greenwich, CT: JAI Press, 1985); R. Folger, D. Rosenfield, J. Grove, & L. Corkran, "Effects of 'Voice' and Peer Opinions on Responses to Inequity," *Journal of Personality and Social Psychology* 37 (1979): 2253–2261; E.A. Lind & T.R. Tyler, *The Social Psychology of Procedural Justice* (New York: Plenum Press, 1988).
40. K.A. Dolan, "When Money Isn't Enough," *Forbes*, 18 November 1996, 164–170.
41. V.H. Vroom, *Work and Motivation* (New York: John Wiley & Sons, 1964); L.W. Porter & E.E. Lawler, III, *Managerial Attitudes and Performance* (Homewood, IL: Dorsey Press & Richard D. Irwin, 1968).
42. L. Buchanan, "Managing One-to-One," *Inc.*, 1 October 2001, 82.
43. Ibid.
44. Owen Parker & Liz Wright, "The Missing Link: Pay and Employee Commitment," *Ivey Business Journal* 65, no. 3 (January/February 2001): 70–73.
45. S. Scholl, "Allstate Pay for Performance Methodology Rewards Excellence," *ACANEWS* 41, no. 8 (1998): 24.
46. K.W. Thomas & B.A. Velthouse, "Cognitive Elements of Empowerment," *Academy of Management Review* 15 (1990): 666–681.
47. C. Hymowitz, "In the Lead: How Cynthia Danaher Learned to Stop Sharing and Start Leading," *The Wall Street Journal*, 16 March 1999, B1.
48. G. Colvin, "The Changing Art of Becoming Unbeatable," *Fortune*, 24 November 1997, 299–300; Katherine Macklem, "Then There Were Three," *Maclean's*, 21 May 2001, 72–73.
49. W. Bennis, "Why Leaders Can't Lead," *Training & Development Journal* 43, no. 4 (1989).
50. "CEOs Talk," *Canadian HR Reporter* 15, no. 17 (7 October 2002): 18, 20.
51. C. Hymowitz, "In the Lead: Some Managers Are More than Bosses—They're Leaders, Too," *The Wall Street Journal*, 8 December 1998, B1.
52. A. Zaleznik, "Managers and Leaders: Are They Different?" *Harvard Business Review* 55 (1977): 76–78; A. Zaleznik, "The Leadership Gap," *The Washington Quarterly* 6 (1983): 32–39.
53. W. Bennis, "Why Leaders Can't Lead," *Training & Development Journal* 43, no. 4 (1989): 35–39.
54. K. Voigt, "Enron, Andersen Scandals Offer Ethical Lessons—Businesspeople Can Strive to Avoid Common Pitfalls through the 'Three Ms,'" *The Wall Street Journal Europe*, 3 September 2002, A12.
55. J.P. Howell, D.E. Bowen, P.W. Dorfman, S. Kerr, & P.M. Podsakoff, "Substitutes for Leadership: Effective Alternatives to Ineffective Leadership," *Organizational Dynamics*, 22 June 1990, 20; S. Kerr & J.M. Jermier, "Substitutes for Leadership: Their Meaning and Measurement," *Organizational Behavior and Human Performance* 22 (1978): 375–403.
56. T.A. Stewart, A. Harrington, & M.G. Solovar, "America's Most Admired Companies: Why Leadership Matters," *Fortune*, 2 March 1998, 70.
57. S.A. Kirkpatrick & E.A. Locke, "Leadership: Do Traits Matter?" *Academy of Management Executive* 5, no. 2 (1991): 48–60.
58. Ibid.
59. Jim Doak, "Frank Stronach," *Report on Business*, April 2005, 47.
60. Michael Posner," The Invisible Man," *Report on Business,* June 2005, 26–36.
61. T.A. Stewart, A. Harrington, & M.G. Solovar, "America's Most Admired Companies: Why Leadership Matters," *Fortune*, 2 March 1998, 70.
62. J.J. Gabarro, *The Dynamics of Taking Charge* (Boston: Harvard Business School Press, 1987).
63. J.B. Fuller, C.E.P. Patterson, K. Hester, & D. Stringer, "A Quantitative Review of Research on Charismatic Leadership," *Psychological Reports* 78 (1996): 271–287; R.G. Lord, C.L. De Vader, & G.M. Alliger, "A Meta-Analysis of the Relation Between Personality Traits and Leadership Perceptions: An Application of Validity Generalization Procedures," *Journal of Applied Psychology* 71, no. 3 (1986): 402–410.
64. B. Morris, "The Accidental CEO," *Fortune*, 28 June 2003, 58.
65. Ibid.
66. S.A. Kirkpatrick & E.A. Locke, "Leadership: Do Traits Matter?" *Academy of Management Executive* 5, no. 2 (1991): 48–60.
67. E.A. Fleishman, "The Description of Supervisory Behavior," *Personnel Psychology* 37 (1953): 1–6; L.R. Katz, *New Patterns of Management* (New York: McGraw-Hill, 1961).
68. B. Morris, "The Accidental CEO," *Fortune*, 28 June 2003, 58.
69. Gerald H. Seijts, "Walking on Water or Sinking Without a Trace? Six Behaviours that Describe Strong Crisis Leaders," *Ivey Business Journal*, November/December 2004, C1.
70. P. Weissenberg & M.H. Kavanagh, "The Independence of Initiating Structure and Consideration: A Review of the Evidence," *Personnel Psychology* 25 (1972): 119–130.
71. R.J. House & T.R. Mitchell, "Path Goal Theory of Leadership," *Journal of Contemporary Business* 3 (1974): 81–97; F.E. Fiedler, "A Contingency Model of Leadership Effectiveness," in ed. L. Berkowitz, *Advances in Experimental Social Psychology* (New York: Academic Press, 1964); V.H. Vroom & P.W. Yetton, *Leadership and Decision Making* (Pittsburgh: University of Pittsburgh Press, 1973); P. Hersey & K.H. Blanchard, *The Management of Organizational Behavior,* 4th ed. (Englewood Cliffs, NJ: Prentice-Hall, 1984); S. Kerr & J.M. Jermier, "Substitutes for Leadership: Their Meaning and Measurement," *Organizational Behavior and Human Performance* 22 (1978): 375–403.
72. F.E. Fiedler & M.M. Chemers, *Leadership and Effective Management* (Glenview, IL: Scott, Foresman, 1974).
73. F.E. Fiedler, "The Effects of Leadership Training and Experience: A Contingency Model Interpretation," *Administrative Science Quarterly* 17, no. 4 (1972): 455; F.E. Fiedler, *A Theory of Leadership Effectiveness* (New York: McGraw-Hill, 1967).
74. Augsuta Dwyer et al., "Tim Fowler, 37," *Globe and Mail*, 3 May 2005, T2.
75. L.S. Csoka & F.E. Fiedler, "The Effect of Military Leadership Training: A Test of the Contingency Model," *Organizational Behavior and Human Performance* 8 (1972): 395–407.
76. P. Hersey & K. Blanchard, *Management of Organizational Behavior: Utilizing Human Resources,* 4th ed. (Englewood Cliffs, NJ: Prentice Hall, 1982).
77. W. Blank, J.R. Weitzel, & S.G. Green, "A Test of the Situational Leadership

Theory," *Personnel Psychology* 43, no. 3 (1990): 579–597; W.R. Norris & R.P. Vecchio, "Situational Leadership Theory: A Replication," *Group & Organization Management* 17, no. 3 (1992): 331–342.

78. W. Blank, J.R. Weitzel, & S.G. Green, "A Test of the Situational Leadership Theory," *Personnel Psychology* 43, no. 3 (1990): 579–597; W.R. Norris & R.P. Vecchio, "Situational Leadership Theory: A Replication," *Group & Organization Management* 17, no. 3 (1992): 331–342.
79. R.D. Ireland & M.A. Hitt, "Achieving and Maintaining Strategic Competitiveness in the 21st Century: The Role of Strategic Leadership," *Academy of Management Executive* 13, no. 1 (1999): 43–57.
80. J.A. Byrne, "A Close-up Look at How America's #1 Manager Runs GE," *Business Week*, 8 June 1998, 90.
81. P. Thoms & D.B. Greenberger, "Training Business Leaders to Create Positive Organizational Visions of the Future: Is It Successful?" *Academy of Management Journal* [Best Papers & Proceedings], 1995, 212–216.
82. M. Weber, *The Theory of Social and Economic Organizations*, translated by R.A. Henderson & T. Parsons (New York: Free Press, 1947).
83. D.A. Waldman & F.J. Yammarino, "CEO Charismatic Leadership: Levels-of-Management and Levels-of-Analysis Effects," *Academy of Management Review* 24, no. 2 (1999): 266–285.
84. P. Sellers, "What Exactly Is Charisma?" *Fortune*, 15 January 1996, 68.
85. K.B. Lowe, K.G. Kroeck, & N. Sivasubramaniam, "Effectiveness Correlates of Transformational and Transactional Leadership: A Meta-analytic Review of the MLQ Literature," *Leadership Quarterly* 7 (1996): 385–425.
86. J.M. Howell & B.J. Avolio, "The Ethics of Charismatic Leadership: Submission or Liberation?" *Academy of Management Executive* 6, no. 2 (1992): 43–54.
87. J. Sonnenfeld, "Three Cheers for Charisma," *Wall Street Journal*, 12 November 2002.
88. S. Ellison, "New Task for Colgate CEO: Grooming His Replacement," *Wall Street Journal*, 12 July 2004, B1.
89. P. Sellers, "What Exactly Is Charisma?" *Fortune*, 15 January 1996, 68.
90. J.M. Howell & B.J. Avolio, "The Ethics of Charismatic Leadership: Submission or Liberation?" *Academy of Management Executive* 6, no. 2 (1992): 43–54.
91. Ibid.
92. J.M. Burns, *Leadership* (New York: Harper & Row, 1978). B.M. Bass, "From Transactional to Transformational Leadership: Learning to Share the Vision," *Organizational Dynamics* 18 (1990): 19–36.
93. B.M. Bass, "From Transactional to Transformational Leadership: Learning to Share the Vision," *Organizational Dynamics* 18 (1990): 19–36.
94. B.M. Bass, *A New Paradigm of Leadership: An Inquiry into Transformational Leadership* (Alexandra, VA: U.S. Army Research Institute for the Behavioral and Social Sciences, 1996).
95. P. Sellers, "The New Breed: The Latest Crop of CEOs Is Disciplined, Deferential, Even a Bit Dull. What a Relief," *Fortune*, 18 November 2002, 66.
96. Ibid.
97. B. Morris, "The Accidental CEO," *Fortune*, 23 June 2003, 58.
98. J. Byrne, "How to Lead Now: Getting Extraordinary Performance When You Can't Pay for It," *Fast Company*, 1 August 2003, 62.
99. B.M. Bass, "From Transactional to Transformational Leadership: Learning to Share the Vision," *Organizational Dynamics* 18 (1990): 19–36.
100. B.M. Bass, "From Transactional to Transformational Leadership: Learning to Share the Vision," *Organizational Dynamics* 18 (1990): 19–36; F.E. Fiedler, "A Contingency Model of Leadership Effectiveness," in ed. L. Berkowitz, *Advances in Experimental Social Psychology* (New York: Academic Press, 1964); J.J. Gabarro, *The Dynamics of Taking Charge* (Boston: Harvard Business School Press, 1987); P. Hersey & K.H. Blanchard, *The Management of Organizational Behavior*, 4th ed. (Englewood Cliffs, NJ: Prentice-Hall, 1984); R.J. House & T.R. Mitchell, "Path-Goal Theory of Leadership," *Journal of Contemporary Business* 3 (1974): 81–97; S. Kerr & J.M. Jermier, "Substitutes for Leadership: Their Meaning and Measurement," *Organizational Behavior and Human Performance* 22 (1978): 375–403; S.A. Kirkpatrick & E.A. Locke, "Leadership: Do Traits Matter?" *Academy of Management Executive* 5, no. 2 (1991): 48–60; Steve Maich, "Selling Ethics at Nortel," *Maclean's*, 24 January 2005, 32; Catherine McLean, "New Boss at Nortel Mines GE for New Executives," *Globe and Mail*, 6 February 2006, B1, B11; V.H. Vroom & P.W. Yetton, *Leadership and Decision Making* (Pittsburgh: University of Pittsburgh Press, 1973); Andrew Wahl & John Gray, "Nortel's Secret Weapon," *Canadian Business*, 14–27 February 2005, 47–56.

Chapter 16

1. K. Brooker & J. Schlosser, "The Un-CEO; A. G. Lafley Doesn't Over-promise. He Doesn't Believe in the Vision Thing. All He's Done Is Turn Around P&G in 27 Months," *Fortune*, 16 September 2002, 88; B. Belton, "CEO Q&A: Procter & Gamble's Renovator-in-Chief," *Business Week Online*, 11 December 2002, [Online] available at www.businessweek.com/bwdaily/dnflash/dec2002/nf20021211_7599.htm, 16 June 2003; D. Eisenberg & D. Fonda, "A Healthy Gamble; How Did A.G. Lafley Turn Procter & Gamble's Old Brands into Hot Items? Here's the Beauty of It," *Time*, 16 September 2002, 46; S. Ellison, "P&G Lays Out Wella Strategy—After $5.75 Billion Deal, CEO Vows to Tread Lightly in Salons," *The Wall Street Journal*, 19 March 2003, B3; G. Farrell, "Impatient P&G Ousts Jager—Board Loses Confidence in CEO after 18 Months," *USA Today*, 9 June 2000, 01B; J. Neff, "P&G Inks Deal with PlanetFeed—Back for Pampers and Tide," *Advertising Age*, 15 July 2002, 11; E. Nelson, "Rallying the Troops at P&G—New CEO Lafley Aims to End Upheaval by Revamping Program of Globalization," *The Wall Street Journal*, 31 August 2000, B1; E. Nelson & N. Deogun, "Course Correction: Reformer Jager Was Too Much for P&G; So What Will Work?—Under New Boss Lafley, Firm Still Has a Need to Get Its Sales Growth Moving—Another Earnings Warning," *The Wall Street Journal*, 9 June 2000, A1.
2. E.E. Lawler, III, L.W. Porter, & A. Tannenbaum, "Manager's Attitudes toward Interaction Episodes," *Journal of Applied Psychology* 52 (1968): 423–439; H. Mintzberg, *The Nature of Managerial Work* (New York: Harper & Row, Publishers, 1973).
3. Ralph Beslin and Chitra Reddin, "How Leaders Can Communicate to Build Trust," *Ivey Business Journal*, November/December 2004, G1.

4. J.D. Maes, T.G. Weldy, & M.L. Icenogle, "A Managerial Perspective: Oral Communication Competency Is Most Important for Business Students in the Workplace," *Journal of Business Communication* 34 (1997): 67–80.
5. R. Lepsinger & A.D. Lucia, *The Art and Science of 360 Degree Feedback* (San Francisco: Pfeiffer, 1997).
6. "We Need to Talk: CFO Survey Reveals Poor Communication Is Most Common Management Mistake," *Canadian Manager* 25, no. 1 (Spring 2000): 1.
7. J. Sandberg, "Bosses Often Sugarcoat Their Worst News, but Staffers Don't Bite," *Wall Street Journal*, 21 April 2004, B1.
8. E.E. Jones & K.E. Davis, "From Acts to Dispositions: The Attribution Process in Person Perception," in *Advances in Experimental and Social Psychology*, Volume 2, ed. L. Berkowitz (New York: Academic Press, 1965), 219–266; R.G. Lord & J.E. Smith, "Theoretical, Information-Processing, and Situational Factors Affecting Attribution Theory Models of Organizational Behavior," *Academy of Management Review* 8 (1983): 50–60.
9. E.E. Jones & K.E. Davis, "From Acts to Dispositions: The Attribution Process in Person Perception," in *Advances in Experimental and Social Psychology*, Volume 2, ed. L. Berkowitz (New York: Academic Press, 1965), 219–266; R.G. Lord & J.E. Smith, "Theoretical, Information-Processing, and Situational Factors Affecting Attribution Theory Models of Organizational Behavior," *Academy of Management Review* 8 (1983): 50–60.
10. H.H. Kelly, *Attribution in Social Interaction* (Morristown, NJ: General Learning Press, 1971).
11. J.M. Burger, "Motivational Biases in the Attribution of Responsibility for an Accident: A Meta-Analysis of the Defensive-Attribution Hypothesis," *Psychological Bulletin* 90 (1981): 496–512.
12. D.A. Hofmann & A. Stetzer, "The Role of Safety Climate and Communication in Accident Interpretation: Implications for Learning from Negative Events," *Academy of Management Journal* 41, no. 6 (1998): 644–657.
13. C. Perrow, *Normal Accidents: Living with High-Risk Technologies* (New York: Basic Books, 1984).
14. A.G. Miller & T. Lawson, "The Effect of an Informational Opinion on the Fundamental Attribution Error," *Journal of Personality and Social Psychology* 47 (1989): 873–896; J.M. Burger, "Changes in Attribution Errors over Time: The Ephemeral Fundamental Attribution Error," *Social Cognition* 9 (1991): 182–193.
15. E. Bernstein, "The Stagnant, Uncriticized Employee—But Those Open to Feedback Seen as Approachable, Primed for Success," *San Antonio Express-News*, 20 February 1997, 1F.
16. F. Heider, *The Psychology of Interpersonal Relations* (New York: Wiley, 1958); D.T. Miller & M. Ross, "Self-Serving Biases in Attribution of Causality: Fact or Fiction?" *Psychological Bulletin* 82 (1975): 213–225.
17. J.R. Larson, Jr., "The Dynamic Interplay between Employees' Feedback-Seeking Strategies and Supervisors' Delivery of Performance Feedback," *Academy of Management Review* 14, no. 3 (1989): 408–422.
18. "Crisis in Communications: Are You Prepared to Communicate Clearly and Effectively During an Emergency?" *Occupational Health and Safety* 1, no. 2 (April/May 1996): 48–50.
19. "What Is Zee True International Language?" *Canadian Press Newswire*, May 12, 1995.
20. David A. Ricks, *Big Business Blunders* (Homewood, IL: Dow Irwin Jones, 1983).
21. M. Reddy, "The Conduit Metaphor—A Case of Frame Conflict in Our Language about Our Language," in *Metaphor and Thought*, ed. A. Ortony (Cambridge, England: Cambridge University Press, 1979), 284–324.
22. G.L. Kreps, *Organizational Communication: Theory and Practice* (New York: Longman, 1990).
23. Ibid.
24. D. Roth, "How to Cut Pay, Lay Off 8,000 People, And Still Have Workers Who Love You," *Fortune*, 4 February 2002, 62.
25. David M. Saunders & Joanne D. Leck, "Formal Upward Communication Procedures: Organizational and Employee Perspectives," *Canadian Journal of Administrative Sciences* 10, no. 3 (September 1993): 255–268.
26. "A Rising Star in the West: With Sales of $13.5m and Growing, Sundog Printing Has Staked Its Claim as One of Calgary's Top Printers," *Canadian Printer* 101, no. 9 (November 1993): 20–21; Ian McKinnon, "DBF Acquires Sundog Printing," *Financial Post*, 2 April 1999, C6.
27. A. Sinickas, "Communicating Is Not Optional," *Harvard Management Communication Letter* 4, issue 6 (June 2001): 1.
28. G.L. Kreps, *Organizational Communication: Theory and Practice* (New York: Longman, 1990).
29. J. Sandberg, "Ruthless Rumors and the Managers Who Enable Them," Wall Street Journal, 29 October 2003, B1.
30. K. Moran, "Web Used to Answer Rumors: UT Medical Staff Gets Truth Quickly," *Houston Chronicle*, 18 April 1999, 35.
31. W. Davis & J.R. O'Connor, "Serial Transmission of Information: A Study of the Grapevine," *Journal of Applied Communication Research* 5 (1977): 61–72.
32. J. Sandberg, "Ruthless Rumors and the Managers Who Enable Them," *Wall Street Journal*, 29 October 2003, B1.
33. "CEOs Talk," *Canadian HR Reporter* 15, no. 5 (11 March 2002): 17–19.
34. C. Hymowitz, "Managing: Spread the Word, Gossip Is Good," *The Wall Street Journal*, 4 October 1988.
35. W. Davis & J.R. O'Connor, "Serial Transmission of Information: A Study of the Grapevine," *Journal of Applied Communication Research* 5 (1977): 61–72; C. Hymowitz, "Managing: Spread the Word, Gossip Is Good," *The Wall Street Journal*, 4 October 1988.
36. K. McDonald, "Out of Site, Still in Mind—Website Protests Morgan Stanley Ban," *New York Post*, 12 May 1999, 46.
37. D. Kirkpatrick, "Why There's No Escaping the Blog," *Fortune (Europe)*, 24 January 2005, 64.
38. W.C. Redding, *Communication within the Organization: An Interpretive View of Theory and Research* (New York: Industrial Communication Council, 1972).
39. Uyen Vu, "Answering Call Centre Turnover," *Canadian HR Reporter*, 15 August 2005, 13.
40. D.T. Hall, K.L. Otazo, & G.P. Hollenbeck, "Behind Closed Doors: What Really Happens in Executive Coaching," *Organizational Dynamics* 27, no. 3 (1999): 39–53.
41. "Surviving a Work-Life Crisis: Troubles at Home Can Make It Hard for Workers to Do Their Best Job," *Buffalo News*, 24 August 1999, D1.
42. Gloria Gonzalez, "Canadian EAPs Making a Comeback," *Business Insurance*, 20 June 2005, 26.

43. M. McWhorter, "Energen CEO Believes Open Communication Is the Key to Successful Management," *Business First—Birmingham*, Volume 6, Section 1 (1992): 8.
44. A. Joyce, "Confidentiality as a Valued Benefit; Loose Lips Can Defeat the Purpose of an Employee Assistance Program," *Washington Post*, 11 May 2003, F05.
45. A. Mehrabian, "Communication without Words," *Psychology Today* 3 (1968): 53; A. Mehrabian, *Silent Messages* (Belmont, CA: Wadsworth, 1971); R. Harrison, *Beyond Words: An Introduction to Nonverbal Communication* (1974); A. Mehrabian, Non-Verbal Communication (Chicago, IL: Aldine, 1972).
46. M.L. Knapp, *Nonverbal Communication in Human Interaction*, 2nd ed. (New York: Holt, Reinhart & Winston, 1978).
47. H.M. Rosenfeld, "Instrumental Affiliative Functions of Facial and Gestural Expressions," *Journal of Personality and Social Psychology* 24 (1966): 65–72; P. Ekman, "Differential Communication of Affect by Head and Body Cues," *Journal of Personality and Social Psychology* 2 (1965): 726–735; A. Mehrabian, "Significance of Posture and Position in the Communication of Attitude and Status Relationships," *Psychological Bulletin* 71 (1969): 359–372.
48. R.B. Schmitt, "Judges Try Curbing Lawyers' Body-Language Antics," *The Wall Street Journal*, 9 September 1997, B1.
49. Ibid.
50. C.A. Bartlett & S. Ghoshal, "Changing the Role of Top Management: Beyond Systems to People," *Harvard Business Review*, May–June 1995, 132–142.
51. P. Roberts, "Homestyle Talkshows," *Fast Company*, October 1999, 162.
52. Ibid.
53. R.G. Nichols, "Do We Know How to Listen? Practical Helps in a Modern Age," in *Communication Concepts and Processes*, ed. J. DeVitor (Englewood Cliffs, NJ: Prentice Hall, 1971); P.V. Lewis, *Organizational Communication: The Essence of Effective Management* (Columbus, OH: Grid Publishing Company, 1975).
54. E. Atwater, *I Hear You*, revised ed. (New York: Walker, 1992).
55. R. Adler & N. Towne, *Looking Out/ Looking In* (San Francisco: Rinehart Press, 1975).
56. K. Brooker & J. Schlosser, "The Un-CEO; A.G. Lafley Doesn't Overpromise. He Doesn't Believe in the Vision Thing. All He's Done Is Turn Around P&G in 27 Months," *Fortune*, 16 September 2002, 88.
57. B.D. Seyber, R.N. Bostrom, & J.H. Seibert, "Listening, Communication Abilities, and Success at Work," *Journal of Business Communication* 26 (1989): 293–303.
58. E. Atwater, *I Hear You*, revised ed. (New York: Walker, 1992).
59. N. Grammer, "The Art—and Importance—of Listening," *Globe and Mail*, 25 June 1999, B11.
60. H.H. Meyer, "A Solution to the Performance Appraisal Feedback Enigma," *Academy of Management Executive* 5, no. 1 (1991): 68–76.
61. T.D. Schellhardt, "Annual Agony: It's Time to Evaluate Your Work, and All Involved Are Groaning—Employees Dislike Reviews, Even If Favorable; Bosses Wonder How to Do Them—Some Prefer Frequent Talks," *The Wall Street Journal*, 19 November 1996, A1.
62. "Make Your Next Performance Review Count," *Financial Post*, 11 April 1998, R14.
63. L. Reibstein, "What to Do When an Employee Is Talented and a Pain in the Neck," *The Wall Street Journal*, 8 August 1986.
64. R. Mead, *Cross-Cultural Management* (New York: Wiley, 1990).
65. J.S. Black & M. Mendenhall, "Cross-Cultural Training Effectiveness: A Review and Theoretical Framework for Future Research," *Academy of Management Review* 15 (1990): 113–136.
66. R. Mead, *Cross-Cultural Management* (New York: Wiley, 1990).
67. E.T. Hall & W.F. Whyte, "Intercultural Communication: A Guide to Men of Action," *Human Organization* 19, no. 1 (1961): 5–12.
68. Nicholas Benedict, "Sojourn in the Gulf," *Maclean's*, 18 November 2002, 96.
69. N. Libman, "French Tip: Just Walk the Walk and Talk the Talk, but Not Too Loud," *Chicago Tribune*, 17 March 1996.
70. H. Lancaster, "Global Managers Need Boundless Sensitivity, Rugged Constitutions," *The Wall Street Journal*, 13 October 1998, B1.
71. R. Miller, "Going Inside with the Internet," *IABC Communication World*, November 1995.
72. Jonathan Kay, "Someone Will Watch over Me," *National Post Business*, January 2001, 59–64.
73. H. Lancaster, "Contributors to Pools of Company Know-How Are Valued Employees," *The Wall Street Journal*, 9 December 1997, B1.
74. T.A. Stewart, "Telling Tales at BP Amoco: Knowledge Management at Work," *Fortune*, 7 June 1999, 220.
75. R. Beslin & C. Reddin, "How Leaders Can Communicate to Build Trust," *Ivey Business Journal Online*, November/December 2004, G1.
76. M. Campanelli & N. Friedman, "Welcome to Voice Mail Hell: The New Technology Has Become a Barrier Between Salespeople and Customers. Here's How Smart Sellers Are Breaking Through," *Sales & Marketing Management* 147 (May 1995): 98–101.
77. E.W. Morrison, "Organizational Silence: A Barrier to Change and Development in a Pluralistic World," *Academy of Management Review* 25 (2000): 706–725.
78. "The Accident's Organizational Causes," *Report of Columbia Accident Investigation Board, Volume I*, [Online] available at http://anon.nasa-global.speedera.net/anon.nasa-global/CAIB/CAIB_lowres_chapter7.pdf, 14 June 2005.
79. Toyota Motor Manufacturing, USA, *Team Member Handbook*, February 1988, 52–53; G. Dessler, "How to Earn Your Employees' Commitment," *Academy of Management Review* 13, no. 2 (1999): 58–67.
80. Uyen Vu, "Top Firms See Advantage in Employee Satisfaction," *Canadian HR Reporter*, 27 January 2003, 1–2.
81. B. O'Reilly, "Forget Hertz and Avis: Enterprise's Quiet Invasion of Small-Town America—Along with Quirky Hiring Practices and a Generous Supply of Doughnuts—Has Made It the Nation's Biggest Rental Car," *Fortune*, 28 October 1996, 125.
82. D. Kirkpatrick & D. Roth, "Why There's No Escaping the Blog," *Fortune (Europe)*, 24 January 2005, 64.
83. K. Brooker & J. Schlosser, "The Un-CEO; A.G. Lafley Doesn't Overpromise. He Doesn't Believe in the Vision Thing. All He's Done Is Turn Around P&G in 27 Months," *Fortune*, 16 September 2002, 88; B. Belton, "CEO Q&A: Procter & Gamble's Renovator-in-Chief," *Business Week Online*, 11 December 2002, [Online] available at www.businessweek.com/bwdaily/dnflash/dec2002/nf20021211

_7599.htm, 16 June 2003; D. Eisenberg & D. Fonda, "A Healthy Gamble; How Did A. G. Lafley Turn Procter & Gamble's Old Brands into Hot Items? Here's the Beauty of It," *Time*, 16 September 2002, 46; S. Ellison, "P&G Lays Out Wella Strategy—After $5.75 Billion Deal, CEO Vows to Tread Lightly in Salons," *The Wall Street Journal*, 19 March 2003, B3; G. Farrell, "Impatient P&G Ousts Jager—Board Loses Confidence in CEO after 18 Months," *USA Today*, 9 June 2000, 01B; J. Neff, "P&G Inks Deal with PlanetFeed—Back for Pampers and Tide," *Advertising Age*, 15 July 2002, 11; E. Nelson, "Rallying the Troops at P&G—New CEO Lafley Aims to End Upheaval by Revamping Program of Globalization," *The Wall Street Journal*, 31 August 2000, B1; E. Nelson & N. Deogun, "Course Correction: Reformer Jager Was Too Much for P&G; So What Will Work?—Under New Boss Lafley, Firm Still Has a Need to Get Its Sales Growth Moving—Another Earnings Warning," *The Wall Street Journal*, 9 June 2000, A1.

84. D. Benton, *Applied Human Relations*, 5th Edition (Prentice Hall, 1995), 533–544; G. Hofstede, "Organizational Dynamic," *AMACOM*, Summer 1980, 375–394.

Self-Assessment Appendix

1. P.L. Hunsaker, *Management: A Skills Approach* (Upper Saddle River, NJ: Pearson Prentice Hall, 2005) 24–25.
2. D.L. McCain, "The MSTAT-I: A New Measure of an Individual's Tolerance for Ambiguity," *Educational and Psychological Measurement*, 53 (1993): 183–190.
3. J.E. Wanek, P.R. Sackett, & D.S. Ones, "Towards an Understanding of Integrity Test Similarities and Differences: An Item-Level Analysis of Seven Tests," *Personnel Psychology* 56 (2003): 873–894.
4. R.J Aldag & L.W. Kuzuhara, Mastering Management Skills: A Manager's Toolkit (Mason, OH: Thomson South-Western, 2005) 172–173.
5. M.D. Miller & R.K. Rainer, Jr., "Assessing and Improving the Dimensionality or the Computer Anxiety Rating Scale," *Educational and Psychological Measurement*, August 1995, 652–657.
6. M. Tuckey, N. Brewer, & P. Williamson, "The Influence of Motives and Goal Orientation on Feedback Seeking," *Journal of Occupational and Organizational Psychology* 75, no. 2 (2002): 195.
7. R.W. Boader, "Study Abroad: Impact on Student Worldmindedness," *Journal of Teaching in International Business* 2, no. 2 (1990): 13–17; R.W. Boader, "Worldminded Attitude Change in a Study Abroad Program: Contact and Content Issues," *Journal of Teaching in International Business* 3, no. 4 (1992): 59–68; H. Lancaster, "Learning to Manage in a Global Workplace (You're on Your Own)," *The Wall Street Journal*, 2 June 1998, B1; D. L. Sampson & H.P. Smith, "A Scale to Measure Worldminded Attitudes," *Journal of Social Psychology* 45 (1957): 99–106.
8. J.M. Houston & R.D. Smither, "The Nature of Competitiveness: The Development and Validation of the Competitiveness Index," *Educational and Psychological Measurement* 52 (1992): 407–418.
9. J.E. Etdie & R.D. O'Keefe, "Innovative Attitudes, Values, and Intentions in Organizations," *Journal of Management Studies* 19 (1982): 163–182.
10. G.C. Bruner, P.J. James, & K.E. Hensel, *Marketing Scales Handbook*, (Chicago, IL: American Marketing Association) 931–934.
11. J.A. Wagner, "Studies of Individualism-Collectivism: Effects on Cooperation in Groups," *Academy of Management Journal* 38, no. 1 (1995): 152–172.
12. J. McCarthy and R. Goffin, "Measuring Job Interview Anxiety: Beyond Weak Knees and Sweaty Palms," *Personnel Psychology* 54, no. 3 (2004): 31.
13. J.A. Perriat, S. LeMay, S. Chakrabarty, "The Selling Orientation–Customer Orientation (SOCO) Scale: Cross-Validation of the Revised Version," *Journal of Personal Selling & Sales Management* 24, no. 1 (2004): 49–54.
14. C.A. Arnolds and C. Boshoff, "Compensation, Esteem Valence, and Job Performance: An Empirical Assessment of Alderfer's ERG Theory," *International Journal of Human Resource Management* 13, no. 4 (2002): 697–719.
15. C.G. Pearce, I.W. Johnson, & R.T. Barker, "Assessment of the Listening Styles Inventory: Progress in Establishing Reliability and Validity," *Journal of Business and Technical Communication* 17, no. 1 (2003): 84–113.

name/organization index

subject index

What Would You Do?

What Really Works

Doing the Right Thing

Self-Assessment

Management Decisions